MW01232626

Modern Family Law

EDITORIAL ADVISORS

ASPEN CASEBOOK SERIES

Modern Family Law

Cases and Materials

Eighth Edition

D. Kelly Weisberg

Hon. Raymond L. Sullivan Professor of Law
University of California College of the Law, San Francisco

Courtney G. Joslin

Martin Luther King, Jr. Professor of Law
University of California, Davis School of Law

ASPEN PUBLISHING

To contact Customer Service, e-mail customer.service@aspenpublishing.com, call 1-800-950-5259, or mail correspondence to:

Aspen Publishing
Attn: Order Department
1 Wall Street
Burlington, MA 01803

Printed in the United States of America.

1 2 3 4 5 6 7 8 9 0

ISBN: 979-8-8890-6287-5

Library of Congress Cataloging-in-Publication Data

Names: Weisberg, D Kelly, author. | Joslin, Courtney G, author.
Title: Modern family law : cases and materials / D Kelly Weisberg, Courtney G Joslin.
Description: Eighth edition. | Burlington : Aspen Publishing, 2024. | Includes bibliographical references and index. | Summary: "Cases and materials on family law for law students taking a family law course"—Provided by publisher.
Identifiers: LCCN 2023059786 | ISBN 9798889062875 (hardcover) | ISBN 9798889062882 (ebook)
Subjects: LCSH: Domestic relations—United States—Cases.
Classification: LCC KF505 .W453 2024 | DDC 346.7301/5—dc23
LC record available at https://lccn.loc.gov/2023059786

SUSTAINABLE FORESTRY INITIATIVE

Certified Chain of Custody
Promoting Sustainable Forestry

www.forests.org
SFI-01681

SFI label applies to the text stock

About Aspen Publishing

Aspen Publishing is a leading provider of educational content and digital learning solutions to law schools in the U.S. and around the world. Aspen provides best-in-class solutions for legal education through authoritative textbooks, written by renowned authors, and breakthrough products such as Connected eBooks, Connected Quizzing, and PracticePerfect.

The Aspen Casebook Series (famously known among law faculty and students as the "red and black" casebooks) encompasses hundreds of highly regarded textbooks in more than eighty disciplines, from large enrollment courses, such as Torts and Contracts to emerging electives such as Sustainability and the Law of Policing. Study aids such as the *Examples & Explanations* and the *Emanuel Law Outlines* series, both highly popular collections, help law students master complex subject matter.

Major products, programs, and initiatives include:

- **Connected eBooks** are enhanced digital textbooks and study aids that come with a suite of online content and learning tools designed to maximize student success. Designed in collaboration with hundreds of faculty and students, the Connected eBook is a significant leap forward in the legal education learning tools available to students.

- **Connected Quizzing** is an easy-to-use formative assessment tool that tests law students' understanding and provides timely feedback to improve learning outcomes. Delivered through CasebookConnect.com, the learning platform already used by students to access their Aspen casebooks, Connected Quizzing is simple to implement and integrates seamlessly with law school course curricula.

- **PracticePerfect** is a visually engaging, interactive study aid to explain commonly encountered legal doctrines through easy-to-understand animated videos, illustrative examples, and numerous practice questions. Developed by a team of experts, PracticePerfect is the ideal study companion for today's law students.

- The **Aspen Learning Library** enables law schools to provide their students with access to the most popular study aids on the market across all of their courses. Available through an annual subscription, the online library consists of study aids in e-book, audio, and video formats with full text search, note-taking, and highlighting capabilities.

- Aspen's **Digital Bookshelf** is an institutional-level online education bookshelf, consolidating everything students and professors need to ensure success. This program ensures that every student has access to affordable course materials from day one.

- **Leading Edge** is a community centered on thinking differently about legal education and putting those thoughts into actionable strategies. At the core of the program is the Leading Edge Conference, an annual gathering of legal education thought leaders looking to pool ideas and identify promising directions of exploration.

Dedicated to families everywhere

■ SUMMARY OF CONTENTS

■ CONTENTS

II. Getting Married 85

III. Being Married: Regulation of the Intact Marriage   209

V. Nonmarital Relationships   367

VI. Divorce   435

VII. Financial Consequences of Dissolution   523

IX. Parentage: Establishment and Disestablishment   723

■ PREFACE

The theme of this book—the conflict between respect for privacy and deference to state authority—offers a lens for examining family law today. Each chapter of this book uses this lens to explore the actual and appropriate role of the state in family decisionmaking. Chapter I considers the constitutional underpinnings of a right to privacy for the family and its members. Chapters II and III address the state's regulation of marriage before and after celebration. Intimate partner violence provides the focus of Chapter IV. Chapter V explores the legal treatment of nonmarital relationships, during the intact relationship as well as after its termination through dissolution or death. Chapters VI and VII cover state regulation of divorce, including financial consequences, and Chapter VIII examines the state's role in child custody matters. Chapter IX explores the establishment and the disestablishment or termination of the parent-child relationship.

Modern Family Law provides valuable interdisciplinary perspectives on family law. The field of family law has been heavily influenced by work in history, psychology, sociology, social work, medicine, anthropology, and philosophy. A comparative law perspective also helps students understand developments in the field. Many of the excerpts, as well as the Notes and Questions, incorporate all these different perspectives to shed new light on the nature of legal regulation of the family.

In addition, this book reflects an awareness of the impact that legal rules have on persons' lives. Family law affects individuals in profound ways that legal abstractions cannot capture. The book attempts to reveal (through presentation of current sociological and psychological research as well as narratives) the subjective experiences of family members as they interact with the legal system. The narratives are a distinctive feature of the book that highlight the problems, concerns, and achievements of the parties and their lawyers in a way that evokes human interest and empathy. The book emphasizes throughout that family law is not just analyzed and applied—it is experienced.

Changes in the Eighth Edition

This edition reflects important updates. Substantively, this edition incorporates legal developments on many topics included in the book. It reflects, for example, the significant impact of the Supreme Court's decision in Dobbs v. Jackson's Women's Health Organization on both the law and the lives of people and their families.

In addition to the inclusion of the Supreme Court's recent *Dobbs* opinion on abortion, this Eighth Edition includes riveting new principal cases or updates that explore issues of discrimination based on sexual orientation and gender identity and the First Amendment (303 Creative v. Elenis); fault-based grounds for divorce (i.e., cruelty); spousal support; child support jurisdiction; child custody cases involving transgender children (Smith v. Smith); the validity of the Indian Child Welfare Act (Haaland v. Brackeen); the application of the Hague Convention on the Civil Aspects of International Child Abduction (Golan v. Saada); and victim protection in the context of domestic violence (U.S. v. Rahimi and Counterman v. Colorado). Many of these newly added cases are landmark decisions that transform the law.

The book continues to include materials that bring life to the law. New epilogues and background accounts have been added to many principal cases, including Roe v. Wade; California Federal Savings & Loan Association v. Guerra; Shahar v. Bowers; Marvin v. Marvin; Brewer v. Blumenthal; Beckwith v. Dahl; Feltmeier v. Feltmeier; and Haaland v. Brackeen.

The Eighth Edition highlights new state and federal legislation, as well as pending and recently promulgated uniform and model laws, including provisions of the pending American Law Institute's Restatement of the Law: Children and the Law; Uniform Cohabitants' Economic Remedies Act (2021); Uniform Unregulated Child Custody Transfer Act (2021); Uniform Nonparent Custody and Visitation Act (2018); Uniform Parentage Act (2017); and the American Bar Association's Model Act Governing Assisted Reproduction (2019).

This updated version also includes additional background information on abortion (implications of abortion denial on the lives of pregnant people and their children; differential impact on abortion restrictions based on race and class; abortion restrictions targeting minors); the practice of online dating; First Amendment exceptions to nondiscrimination mandates and the impact of these exceptions on the lives of LGBTQ people; risks of child marriages; Pregnant Workers' Fairness Act of 2023; impact of COVID on various aspects of family law; demographic information on the decline of marriage and the rise in cohabitation; socioeconomic differences in marriage and cohabitation rates; economic inequalities among families; multigenerational households; fluidity among family types (dubbed "relational migration"); consideration of sex, sexual orientation, and gender identity in child custody proceedings; parentage of children born through assisted reproduction; multi-parent families; embryo disposition disputes; regulation of the fertility industry; the child welfare or family regulation system and its effect on children and families, particularly children and families of color; and background on the Indian Child Welfare Act and the history that led to its enactment. Throughout the book, the cases and materials seek to identify and highlight the ways in which race, ethnicity, class, sex, sexual orientation, gender identity, religion, and immigration status impact the legal and social experiences of families and their members.

Like earlier editions, this revision gives instructors considerable flexibility in designing family law courses of varying lengths and emphases. The book can be adapted easily for shorter or longer courses from two to four units. For the problem-oriented instructor and student, the book includes many questions and problems, often derived from actual cases and current events. The Teacher's Manual accompanying the book provides further pedagogical suggestions and sample syllabi. Video clips and PowerPoint slides are also available to instructors to enhance learning and stimulate class discussion.

Editorial Matters

Cases and excerpts have all been edited, often quite extensively. Most deletions are indicated by ellipses, with some exceptions. Some concurring and dissenting opinions have been eliminated; citations have been modified or eliminated; some footnotes and references have been omitted; and paragraphs have been modified, and sometimes combined, to save space and to make the selections more coherent. Brackets are used at times to indicate substantial deletions. Original footnotes in cases and excerpts are reprinted nonconsecutively throughout the book. The author's textual footnotes are numbered consecutively and appear in brackets to differentiate them from original footnotes in the cases and excerpts. The book follows *A Uniform System of Citation* except when that style conflicts with the publisher's style.

D. Kelly Weisberg
Courtney G. Joslin
March 2024

■ INTRODUCTION

Family law explores the legal regulation of the family and its members. These members include spouses, nonmarital partners, parents, and children, as well as others who have close relationships with these family members.

Family law today reflects a fundamental tension between respect for family privacy and deference to state authority. This conflict forms the overarching theme of this book. Specifically, the book explores the issue: How does the law allocate responsibility for decisionmaking about family matters? A respect for privacy gives consideration to families' and individual family members' decisional autonomy on matters that intimately affect them.

Conversely, deference to state authority recognizes that the state has important interests (such as protection of vulnerable family members, financial support for dependent individuals, and dispute resolution) that may precipitate intervention in the family. Such concerns necessarily raise questions about the actual, as well as the appropriate, relationship of the state to the family. The book also highlights how this balance between family privacy and state interference differs for different families.

Because the state accords legal protection to the family and family members, even basic definitions—what constitutes a "family" and who is a "family member"—are contested. Thus, a central issue explored throughout the book is: Which personal relationships qualify for legal protection and for what purposes?

Family law is a field in transition. Change is apparent in the evolving roles and responsibilities of family members, the definitions of a family, and the nature of legal regulation of the family and its members.

Historically, the dynamic nature of the field of family law results, in part, from societal influences on family law. Over the past several decades, many different social developments have prompted significant changes in the field, including:

(1) the women's movement and the resulting changes in gender roles and public policy;
(2) the children's rights movement leading to children's increased role in decisionmaking;
(3) the role of religion and morality in issues affecting the family;
(4) the decline in marriage rates with its concomitant increase in nonmarital families and the increased fluidity between different family forms;
(5) the advent of marriage equality and the increasing visibility of LGBTQ people and families;
(6) dissatisfaction with traditional dispute resolution processes and the growth of alternative forms of dispute resolution;
(7) developments in reproductive technology that have expanded methods of family formation;

(8) the widening income gap between upper- and middle- and lower-income households; and

(9) the "culture wars" in the political arena, where matters of family law continue to be a key battleground.

All of these developments are challenging the rules governing the family and parenthood.

Family law also reflects several important legal trends:

(1) the federalization of family law (that is, the increasing congressional role in family policy);

(2) the constitutionalization of family law (that is, the recognition of the constitutional dimensions of the regulation of intimate relationships); and

(3) the push and pull toward and away from uniformity of state law.

These factors partly explain the changing role of the state in the contemporary regulation of the family.

States historically have played important roles in developing and implementing rules governing the family. That said, the federal government has also participated in the regulation of the family, through, among other things, statutes and other rules governing the distribution of benefits to specified family members. In more recent decades, Congress has also enacted statutes regarding a range of other family law issues, including child support, child custody, child abuse and neglect, foster care, adoption, parental leaves, and violence against women, to name a few. In addition, beginning in the 1960s, the Supreme Court handed down a number of constitutional decisions that placed limits on state regulation of the family. These decisions include ones regarding access to contraception and abortion, but also decisions placing limits on state definitions of families and their members.

Because many family law rules are set by the states, legal regulations applicable to the family often vary across the country. In an effort to bring uniformity to the field, the Uniform Law Commission (formerly the National Conference of Commissioners on Uniform State Laws) has promulgated important model statutes (addressing marriage and divorce, premarital agreements, marital property, parentage establishment, child custody, spousal and child support, adoption, and the rights of nonmarital cohabitants). Another unifying influence has been the American Law Institute (ALI), which has proposed a reconceptualization of many aspects of family dissolution, clarifying the underlying principles and making policy recommendations to guide the states.

In the midst of so many societal changes and legal developments, family law has become an active theoretical site, generating fresh thinking about the field and its purposes. Some scholars understand family law as a system designed to privatize dependency, while others argue that it should be a system through which the state seeks to support families and help them flourish. Some critics challenge family law's conventional boundaries by urging consideration of previously excluded relationships, such as nonmarital relationships, friendships, and other care networks. Others seek to decenter marriage (or sex), and still others seek to incorporate welfare law in family law and to make more salient the consequences of economic and racial inequalities among families. Substantive equality (as distinguished from formal equality) remains important unfinished business on many theorists' agendas. Although this book uses the lens of privacy versus state intervention to examine family law, these alternative perspectives offer illuminating contrasts, and the book refers to them when relevant.

Today's family law classes offer the challenge and excitement of exploring this rapidly changing legal and theoretical landscape.

■ ACKNOWLEDGMENTS

The authors extend gratitude to the many individuals who contributed to this project. Tony Pelczynski of the UC College of the Law, San Francisco, Law Library (formerly Hastings College of the Law) provided valuable reference assistance. The research assistance of Nikki Viavant of UC Law SF and Alyssa Morris and Carmel Wright of UC Davis School of Law was invaluable. Finally, the authors express appreciation to Aspen Publishers staff, especially Jordan Jepsen (managing editor), Suzanne Rapcavage (production director at The Froebe Group), Troy Froebe (CEO at The Froebe Group), Kathy Langone (development editor at The Froebe Group), as well as to the anonymous reviewers who offered such useful suggestions.

The authors would like to thank the following copyright holders for permission to excerpt their materials:

Text

Advancing New Standards in Reproductive Health. *The Harms of Denying a Woman a Wanted Abortion: Findings from the Turnaway Study*. University of California, San Francisco, 2020. Reprinted with permission.

Anderson, Jack. "Adventures Among the Polygamists." *Investigative Reporter Magazine* (Jan. 1982). Reprinted with permission from the author.

Arendell, Terry. *Mothers and Divorce: Legal, Economic, and Social Dilemmas*. Oxford University Press, 1986.

Artiga, Samantha, et al. "What Are the Implications of the Overturning of Roe v. Wade for Racial Disparities?" KFF.org (July 15, 2022). Copyright © KFF. Licensed under CC BY-NC-ND 4.0 DEED, https://creativecommons.org/licenses/by-nc-nd/4.0/

Bailey, Beth L. *From Front Porch to Back Seat: Courtship in Twentieth-Century America*. Copyright © 1988, 1989 The Johns Hopkins University Press.

Balsam, Kimberly F. et al. "Predictors of Relationship Dissolution Among Same-Sex and Heterosexual Couples," Williams Institute, Mar. 1, 2018. Press release.

Barroso, Amanda and Juliana Menasce Horowitz. "The Pandemic Has Highlighted Many Challenges for Mothers, but They Aren't Necessarily New." Pew Research Center, Mar. 17, 2021, www.pewresearch.org/short-reads/2021/03/17/the-pandemic-has-highlighted-many-challenges-for-mothers-but-they-arent-necessarily-new/.

Barroso, Amanda and Richard Fry. "On Some Demographic Measures, People in Same-Sex Marriages Differ from Those in Opposite-Sex Marriages." Pew Research Center, July 7, 2021, www.pewresearch.org/fact-tank/2021/07/07/on-some-demographic-measures-people-in-same-sex-marriages-differ-from-those-in-opposite-sex-marriages/.

Bernard, Jessie. "The Good-Provider Role: Its Rise and Fall." American Psychologist, Vol. 36, No. 1 (1981). American Psychological Association.

Bohannon, Paul. "The Six Stations of Divorce." *Divorce and After*, edited by Paul Bohannan. Copyright © 1968, 1970 by Paul Bohannan. Used by permission of Doubleday, an imprint of the Knopf Doubleday Publishing Group, a division of Penguin Random House LLC. All rights reserved.

Brito, Tonya L. et al. "Chronicle of a Debt Foretold: Zablocki v. Red Hail, 434 U.S. 374." *The Poverty Law Canon: Exploring the Major Cases*, edited by Ezra Rosser and Marie A. Failinger. University of Michigan Press, 2016. Reprinted with permission.

Brown, Gretchen Livingston and Anna Brown. "Intermarriage in the U.S. 50 Years after Loving v. Virginia." Pew Research Center's Social & Demographic Trends Project, May 18, 2017, www.pewsocialtrends.org/2017/05/18/intermarriage-in-the-u-s-50-years-after-loving-v-virginia.

Cahn, Naomi. "Family Law, Federalism, and the Federal Courts," Iowa Law Review, Vol. 79, 1995.

Cain, Stephanie. "Just a Wedding" (Aug. 16, 2018). From The New York Times. Copyright © 2018 The New York Times Company. All rights reserved. Used under license.

Callahan, Sidney. "Abortion and the Sexual Agenda." Commonweal, vol. 113, 1986. Reprinted with permission from the Commonweal Foundation.

Chamie, Joseph. "The end of marriage in America?" The Hill (Aug. 10, 2021), https://thehill.com/opinion/finance/567107-the-end-of-marriage-in-america/.

Chesser, Mary E. "Comment, Joint Representation in a Friendly Divorce: Inherently Unethical?" Journal of the Legal Profession, Vol. 27, 2002-2003. Reprinted with permission.

Cohn, D'Vera et al. "The Demographics of Multigenerational Households." Pew Research Center's Social & Demographic Trends Project, Mar. 24, 2022, www.pewresearch.org/social-trends/2022/03/24/the-demographics-of-multigenerational-households/.

Cohn, D'Vera. "Research from 2018 Demographers' Conference: Migration, Self-Identity, Marriage and Other Key Findings." Pew Research Center, May 24, 2018, www.pewresearch.org/short-reads/2018/05/24/research-from-2018-demographers-conference-migration-self-identity-marriage-and-other-key-findings/.

Cole, Harriette. *Jumping the Broom: The African-American Wedding Planner*. Henry Holt, 1993.

Compton, Julie. "Meet the Couple behind the Masterpiece Cakeshop Supreme Court Case." NBC News, Dec. 6, 2017, www.nbcnews.com/feature/nbc-out/meet-couple-behind-masterpiece-cakeshop-supreme-court-case-n826976.

Cooper Davis, Peggy. "Moore v. East Cleveland: Constructing the Suburban Family." Family Law Stories, edited by Carol Sanger. Foundation Press, 2008.

Crusco, Kysa. "Ross v. Ross: Celibacy Pending Adultery Claim." New Hampshire Family Law Blog, Feb. 10, 2017, www.nhfamilylawblog.com/2017/02/articles/divorce/ross-v-ross-celibacy-pending-adultery-claim/.

Dailey, Anne C. "Federalism and Families," University of Pennsylvania Law Review, Vol. 143, 1995.

Demos, John. *A Little Commonwealth: Family Life in Plymouth Colony*. Oxford University Press, 2000.

Duddy, Roy A. "The Background Story of Graves v. Estabrook." Personal communication from Dec. 5, 2012. Reprinted with permission.

Ellman, Ira Mark. "The Theory of Alimony," California Law Review, Vol. 77, No. 1, 1989.

Farr, Rachel H., and Abbie E. Goldberg. "Same-Sex Relationship Dissolution and Divorce: How Will Children Be Affected in LGBTQ Divorce and Relationship Dissolution." *LGBTQ Divorce and Relationship Dissolution*, edited by Abbie E. Goldberg and Adam P. Romero, Oxford University Press, 2019.

"Fathers Need Paid Family and Medical Leave." National Partnership for Women & Families, June 2018.

Friedman, Lawrence M. *A History of American Law*. Touchstone Books, 2005. Reprinted with permission.

Garrison, Marsha. "Nonmarital Cohabitation: Social Revolution and Legal Regulation," Family Law Quarterly, Vol. 42, No. 3, Fall 2008. American Bar Association.

Garrow, David J. "Toward a More Perfect Union." The New York Times Magazine, May 9, 2004. Reprinted with permission from the author.

Gelles, Richard J. and Murray A. Straus. Intimate Violence. Simon and Schuster, 1988.

"Global Family Structure." The Sustainable Demographic Dividend, 2011, sustaindemographicdividend.org/articles/international-family-indicators/global-family-structure.

Goodman, David J. "How Medical Care for Transgender Youth Became 'Child Abuse' in Texas," Mar. 11, 2022. From The New York Times. Copyright © 2022 The New York Times Company. All rights reserved. Used under license.

Gordon, Linda. *The Moral Property of Women: A History of Birth Control Politics in America*. University of Illinois Press, 2002.

Greenberg, Judith G. "Domestic Violence and the Danger of Joint Custody Presumptions." Northern Illinois University Law Review, Vol. 25, 2005. Reprinted with permission.

Grossberg, Michael. *Governing the Hearth: Law and the Family in Nineteenth-Century America*. The University of North Carolina Press, 1985. Reprinted with permission.

Halem, Lynne Carol. *Divorce Reform: Changing Legal and Social Perspectives*. Reprinted and edited with the permission of The Free Press, a Division of Simon & Schuster. Copyright © 1980 by The Free Press. All rights reserved.

Hall, Julie H., and Frank D. Fincham. "Relationship Dissolution Following Infidelity." *Handbook of Divorce and Relationship Dissolution*, edited by Mark A. Fine and John H. Harvey, Taylor & Francis, 2006.

Hamilton, Vivian. "Mistaking Marriage for Social Policy." Virginia Journal of Social Policy and the Law, 2004, Vol. 11. Reprinted with permission.

Harvey, Morris Lane. "The Legacy of Feltmeier v. Feltmeier: Twenty-Year Retrospective." Commentary. Reprinted with permission.

Hochschild, Arlie and Anne Machung. *The Second Shift*. Copyright © 1989, 2003, 2012 by Arlie Hochschild. Used by permission of Viking Books, an imprint of Penguin Publishing Group, a division of Penguin Random House LLC. All rights reserved.

Horowitz, Juliana Menasce, et al. "The State of Marriage and Cohabitation in the U.S." Pew Research Center's Social & Demographic Trends Project, Nov. 6, 2019, www.pewresearch.org/social-trends/2019/11/06/the-landscape-of-marriage-and-cohabitation-in-the-u-s/.

Isenberg, Sheila. *Women Who Love Men Who Kill*. AuthorHouse, 2000.

Joseph, Elizabeth. "My Husband's Nine Wives," The New York Times, May 23, 1991.

Jurow, Judge George L. "Reflections on the Legacy of In re Rebecca B." Personal communication from May 12, 2015. Reprinted with permission.

Kelson, Stephen D. "Threats and Violence against Family Law Practitioners." Domestic Violence Report, Vol. 24, 2019. Reprinted with permission from the Civics Research Institute.

Kershaw, Sarah. "In Some Adoptions, Love Doesn't Conquer All," Apr. 18, 2010. From The New York Times. Copyright © 2010 The New York Times Company. All rights reserved. Used under license.

"Key Facts: The Family and Medical Leave Act." National Partnership for Women & Families, Feb. 2023. "Social Indicators of Marital Health & Well-Being: Trends of the Past Five Decades: Unmarried Cohabitation."

Kressel, Kenneth, et al. "Professional Intervention in Divorce: The Views of Lawyers, Psychotherapists, and Clergy." *Divorce and Separation*, edited by George Levinger & Oliver C. Moles. Taylor & Francis, 1979.

LaFleur, Jo Carol. "Go Home and Have Your Baby." *The Courage of Their Convictions*, edited by Peter Irons. Copyright © 1988 Simon & Schuster.

LaRosa, John. "Top 6 Things to Know about the U.S. Fertility Clinics Industry." Marketresearch.com, 2018, blog.marketresearch.com/top-6-things-to-know -about-the-u.s.-fertility-clinics-industry.

Luker, Kristin. *Abortion and the Politics of Motherhood*. Copyright © 1984 University of California Press.

Mahoney, Martha. "Legal Images of Battered Women: Redefining the Issue of Separation." Michigan Law Review, Vol. 90, 1991.

Masci, David, et al. "5 Facts about Same-Sex Marriage." Pew Research Center, Pew Research Center, Jun. 24, 2019, www.pewresearch.org/fact-tank/2019/06/24/ same-sex-marriage/.

Masters, Jeffrey. "Jim Obergefell: We Still Don't Enjoy True Marriage Equality." www.advocate.com, Mar. 16, 2021, www.advocate.com/politics/2021/3/12/ jim-obergefell-dont-enjoy-true-marriage-equality-hodges-supreme-court.

Mauro, Tony. "A 'Cultural Milestone' at the High Court: Lawrence Gay Attorneys Turned Out in Force to Witness Lawrence Arguments," The Texas Lawbook, Mar. 31, 2004.

Meier, Joan S. "Domestic Violence, Child Custody, and Child Protection: Understanding Judicial Resistance and Imagining the Solutions," American University Journal of Gender, Social Policy & the Law, Vol. 11, 2003. Reprinted with permission.

Mnookin, Robert H. "Child-Custody Adjudication: Judicial Functions in the Face of Indeterminacy," Law & Contemporary Problems, Vol. 39. Duke University School of Law, 1975. Reprinted with permission.

NeJaime, Douglas. "The Nature of Parenthood." Yale Law Journal, Vol. 126, No. 8, June 2017.

Newbeck, Phyl. *Virginia Hasn't Always Been for Lovers: Interracial Marriage Bans and the Case of Richard and Mildred Loving*. Southern Illinois University Press, 2008.

Obergefell, Jim. "The Legacy of Obergefell v. Hodges." Personal communication from July 28, 2015. Reprinted with permission.

Okin, Susan Moller. *Justice, Gender, and the Family*. Basic Books, 1989.

Olsen, Frances. "Comment: Unraveling Compromise," Harvard Law Review, Vol. 103, 1989.

Papke, David Ray. "State v. Oakley, Deadbeat Dads, and American Poverty." Western New England Law Review, Vol. 26, No. 1, Jan. 2009. Reprinted with permission from the author.

Parkman, Allen M. *Good Intentions Gone Awry: No-Fault Divorce and the American Family*. Copyright © 2000 Rowman and Littlefield Publishing Group Inc.

Parker, Kim and Renee Stepler. "As U.S. Marriage Rate Hovers at 50%, Education Gap in Marital Status Widens." Pew Research Center, Pew Research Center, Sept. 14, 2017, www.pewresearch.org/fact-tank/2017/09/14/as-u-s-marriage-rate-hovers-at-50-education-gap-in-marital-status-widens/.

Pearson, Jessica and Nancy Thoennes. "The Denial of Visitation Rights," Law and Policy, Vol. 10. Wiley-Blackwell, 1988. Reprinted with permission.

Portions of the Uniform Cohabitants' Economic Remedies Act, the Uniform Premarital Agreement Act, the Uniform Marriage and Divorce Act, the Uniform Nonparent Custody and Visitation Act, the Uniform Child Custody Jurisdiction and Enforcement Act, and the Uniform Parentage Act. Copyright © Uniform Law Commission. Reprinted with permission. All rights reserved.

Pratt, Robert A. "Crossing the Color Line: A Historical Assessment and Personal Narrative of Loving v. Virginia," Howard Law Journal, Vol. 41, 1998. Reprinted with permission.

Presser, Stephen B. "The Historical Background of the American Law of Adoption." Journal of Family Law, Vol. 11, 1971. Reprinted with permission.

Principles of the Law of Family Dissolution: Analysis and Recommendations. Copyright © 2002 by The American Law Institute. Reproduced with permission. All rights reserved.

Reinert, Patty. "Pair Proud They Could Get Sodomy Law Thrown Out," The Houston Chronicle, Apr. 25, 2004. Copyright © 2004 The Houston Chronicle.

Rhode, Deborah L. and Martha Minow. "Reforming the Questions, Questioning the Reforms: Feminist Perspectives on Divorce Law." Divorce Reform at the Crossroads, edited by Stephen D. Sugarman & Herma Hill Kay. Copyright © 1990 Yale University Press.

Riessman, Catherine K. *Divorce Talk: Women and Men Make Sense of Personal Relationships*. Copyright © 1990 Rutgers University Press.

Roraback, Catherine G. "Griswold v. Connecticut: A Brief Case History," Ohio Northern University Law Review, Vol. 16, 1989. Reprinted with permission.

Rosenwald, Michael S. "How Jim Obergefell Became the Face of the Supreme Court Gay Marriage Case," Apr. 6, 2015. Copyright © The Washington Post.

Scott, Elizabeth S. & Robert Emery. "Child Custody Dispute Resolution: The Adversarial System and Divorce Mediation," Psychology and Child Custody Determinations: Knowledge, Roles and Expertise, edited by Lois A. Weithorn. University of Nebraska Press, 1987. Reprinted with permission.

Sections from the Restatement of Conflict of Laws, Second (1971). American Law Institute.

Sepper, Elizabeth. "'Expressing' Inferiority: 303 Creative and the (Re)Creation of a Discriminatory Marketplace," American Constitution Society, Mar. 1, 2023, www.acslaw.org/expertforum/expressing-inferiority-303-creative-and-the-recreation-of-a-discriminatory-marketplace/.

Shahar, Robin. "Postscript." Personal communication from July 8, 2015. Reprinted with permission.

"Social Indicators of Marital Health & Well-Being: Trends of the Past Five Decades: Unmarried Cohabitation." *The State of Our Unions: Marriage in America*, edited by William Bradford Wilcox and Elizabeth Marquardt. National Marriage Project, University of Virginia, 2012.

Sugarman, Stephen D. "Dividing Financial Interests on Divorce." *Divorce Reform at the Crossroads*, edited by Stephen D. Sugarman & Herma Hill Kay. Copyright © 1990 Yale University Press.

Taub, Nadine and Elizabeth M. Schneider. "Women's Subordination and the Role of Law." The Politics of Law: A Progressive Critique, edited by David Kairys. Basic Books, 1998.

Thomson, Judith Jarvis. "A Defense of Abortion," Philosophy & Public Affairs, Vol. 1. Copyright © 1971 Springer Nature.

Vogels, Emily A. "10 Facts about Americans and Online Dating." Pew Research Center, Pew Research Center, Feb. 6, 2020, www.pewresearch.org/fact-tank/2020/02/06/10-facts-about-americans-and-online-dating/.

Walker, Lenore E. *Terrifying Love: Why Battered Women Kill and How Society Responds*. Copyright © 1989. Used by permission of HarperCollins Publishers.

Ward, David. "Postscript: In Re Marriage of Black." Personal correspondence dated Aug. 2, 2019. Reprinted with permission.

Websdale, Neil. "Assessing Risk in Domestic Violence Cases." *Encyclopedia of Domestic Violence*, edited by Nicky Ali Jackson. Taylor & Francis, 2007.

Weddington, Sarah. *A Question of Choice: Roe v Wade*, 40th Anniversary Edition. Copyright © 1992, 2013 by Sarah Weddington. Reprinted with the permission of The Permissions Company, LLC on behalf of The Feminist Press at the City University of New York, www.feministpress.org.

Weisberg, D. Kelly. "Collateral Damage: Discrimination in Failure-To-Protect Laws for Children's Wellbeing." *Child Rights and International Discrimination Law: Implementing Article 2 of the UN Convention on the Rights of the Child*, edited by Marit Skivenes and Karl Harald Søvig, Routledge, 2019.

Wilcox, W. Bradford. "Marriage in Decline: No Big Deal? 3 Reasons Yglesias Is Wrong." Institute for Family Studies, Apr. 1, 2015, ifstudies.org/blog/marriage-in-decline-yglesias/.

Williams, Joan. "Is Coverture Dead: Beyond a New Theory of Alimony," Georgetown Law Journal, Vol. 82, 1994. Reprinted with permission.

Williams, Wendy W. "Equality's Riddle: Pregnancy and the Equal Treatment/Special Treatment Debate." New York University Review of Law & Social Change, Vol. 13, 1984-1985. Reprinted with permission.

Wolfer, Judith A. "Top Ten Myths About Domestic Violence," Maryland Bar Journal, Vol. 42. Maryland State Bar Association, 2009. Reprinted with permission.

Zuccardy, Jill M. "Nicholson v. Williams: The Case," Denver University Law Review, Vol. 82, 2005. Reprinted with permission.

Images

ALI Principles of the Law of Family Dissolution, book cover. Photograph. Reprinted by permission from the American Law Institute.

Baird, William, photograph. Reproduced by permission of Peter Simon.

Bonauto, Mary, attorney, photograph. Reproduced by permission of the Gay & Lesbian Advocates & Defenders (GLAD).

Bradwell, Myra, in 1870, photograph. Courtesy Wikimedia Commons.

Brown, Edmund "Pat," California governor, photograph. Wikimedia Commons.

Child Marriage Poses Serious Risks to Children. Infographic. Tahirih Justice Center. Reprinted with permission.

Clair, Bernard E., who represented Renee B., photograph. Reproduced with permission from Bernard E. Clair.

Coin toss. Photograph. ICMA Photos via Wikimedia Commons. Licensed under CC BY-SA 2.0 DEED, https://creativecommons.org/licenses/by-sa/2.0/deed.en.

Collier, Nathan, and his wives, photograph. Courtesy of Nathan Collier's Facebook page.

Comstock, Anthony, photograph. Courtesy of the New York Public Library.

Elonis, Anthony, photograph. Courtesy of Facebook.

France, Megan, and Brian, photograph. Courtesy of The Daytona Beach News-Journal.

Garland, Lillian, and her daughter, photograph. Copyright © Alan Levenson. Reprinted with permission.

Garner, Tyrone, and John Lawrence, photograph. Copyright © Associated Press / Michael Stravato.

Griswold, Estelle, photograph. Copyright © Bettmann/Getty Images.

Haaland, Deb, photograph. Doi.gov.

Hand over woman's mouth, photograph. Copyright © iStock.

Hansen, Justin, photograph. Associated Press.

Harvey, Morris Lane, photograph. Reprinted with permission.

Hudson, Rock, photograph. Copyright © Allstar Picture Library Ltd / Alamy Stock Photo.

Jackson Women's Health Organization, now a second-hand consignment shop, photograph. Copyright © Rogelio V. Solis / Associated Press.

Jennings, Sandra, and William Hurt, photograph. Copyright © Ron Galella / Getty Images.

Ketubah, photograph. Reproduced by permission of Yale University.

LaFleur, Jo Carol (now Jo Carol Nesset-Sale), photograph. Courtesy of Jo Carol Nesset-Sale.

Lenahan, Jessica Gonzales, and her children, photograph. Courtesy of Adequate Images.

Loving, Mildred, and Richard, photograph. Copyright © Bettmann / Getty Images.

MacGinnis, Marc Christian, photograph. Copyright © Lennox McLendon / Associated Press.

Marvin, Lee, and Michelle, photograph. Copyright © Hulton Deutsch/Getty Images.

McCorvey, Norma. Reproduced by permission of Lorie Shaull and Creative Commons.

Millville Rescue Squad, photograph. Reproduced by permission of Daily Journal / USA Today / IMAGN Content Service.

Minter, Shannon, photograph. Reprinted with permission.

Mullins, David, and Charlie Craig, photograph. Copyright © Associated Press.

Nicholson, Sharwline, photograph. Reprinted with permission.

Obergefell, Jim, and John Arthur, photograph. Reproduced with permission from Jim Obergefell.

Public Remains Supportive of Same-Sex Marriage; Wide Partisan Gap Persists, graph. Pew Research Center, www.pewresearch.org/short-reads/2019/06/24/same-sex -marriage/ft_19-06-24_samesexmarriagefacts_public-remains-supportive-same -sex-marriage-partisan-gap-persists-3/.

Shahar, Robin, photograph. Reprinted with permission.

Shanks, Randall J., attorney, photograph. Reprinted with permission.

Stern, Elizabeth, and William, photograph. Copyright © Mike Derer / Associated Press.

Troxel, Gary, and Jennifer, photograph. Copyright © Richard Bowman / Associated Press.

Wallerstein, Dr. Judith, photograph. Courtesy of Dr. Judith Wallerstein.

Weddington, Sarah, photograph. Reprinted with permission.

Whitehead, Mary Beth, photograph. Copyright © Dennis Cook / Associated Press.

Younger, Jeffrey, photograph. Emil Lippe for The Texas Tribune. Copyright © The Texas Tribune.

Modern Family Law

Private Family Choices: Constitutional Protection for the Family and Its Members

The Supreme Court has held that certain deeply personal decisions related to family form and family formation are interests protected from undue state interference under the U.S. Constitution. Indeed, the Supreme Court has written often about "the private realm of family life which the state cannot enter." What is the constitutional source of this "privacy" protection, whom does it protect, and what family-related decisions fall within it? What room does it leave for states to regulate the family?

This chapter explores these questions. It begins with the development of the Supreme Court's privacy doctrine, returns to consider its roots, and then traces its evolution. Throughout, the cases, narratives, and other excerpts center on some of today's most divisive legal issues: contraception, abortion, and sexual freedom. This chapter also provides a lens through which to examine the outer limits of the government's power to regulate personal and family decisionmaking.

A. Evolution of Privacy

1. Birth of Privacy

GRISWOLD v. CONNECTICUT
381 U.S. 479 (1965)

Justice Douglas delivered the opinion of the Court.

Appellant Griswold is Executive Director of the Planned Parenthood League of Connecticut. Appellant Buxton is a licensed physician and a professor at the Yale Medical School who served as Medical Director for the League at its Center in New

Haven. [Appellants were arrested and charged with giving information, instruction, and medical advice to married persons on means of preventing conception.]

The [statute] whose constitutionality is involved . . . provides:

> Any person who uses any drug, medicinal article, or instrument for the purpose of preventing conception shall be fined not less than fifty dollars or imprisoned not less than sixty days nor more than one year or be both fined and imprisoned. . . .

The appellants were found guilty as accessories and fined $100 each, against the claim that the accessory statute as so applied violated the Fourteenth Amendment. . . . We think that appellants have standing to raise the constitutional rights of the married people with whom they had a professional relationship. . . .

Coming to the merits, we are met with a wide range of questions that implicate the Due Process Clause of the Fourteenth Amendment. Overtones of some arguments suggest that Lochner v. New York, 198 U.S. 45 [(1905)], should be our guide. But we decline that invitation. We do not sit as a super-legislature to determine the wisdom, need, and propriety of laws that touch economic problems, business affairs, or social conditions. This law, however, operates directly on an intimate relation of husband and wife and their physician's role in one aspect of that relation.

The association of people is not mentioned in the Constitution nor in the Bill of Rights. The right to educate a child in a school of the parents' choice — whether public or private or parochial — is also not mentioned. Nor is the right to study any particular subject or any foreign language. Yet the First Amendment has been construed to include certain of those rights.

By Pierce v. Society of Sisters, [268 U.S. 510 (1925)] the right to educate one's children as one chooses is made applicable to the States by the force of the First and Fourteenth Amendments. By Meyer v. Nebraska, [262 U.S. 390 (1923)] the same dignity is given the right to study the German language in a private school. . . . In NAACP v. Alabama, 357 U.S. 449, 462 [(1958)] we protected the "freedom to associate and privacy in one's associations," noting that freedom of association was a peripheral First Amendment right. . . . In other words, the First Amendment has a penumbra where privacy is protected from governmental intrusion. [Association] is a form of expression of opinion; and while it is not expressly included in the First Amendment, its existence is necessary in making the express guarantees fully meaningful.

The foregoing cases suggest that specific guarantees in the Bill of Rights have penumbras, formed by emanations from those guarantees that help give them life and substance. See Poe v. Ullman, 367 U.S. 497, 516-522 [(1961)] (dissenting opinion). Various guarantees create zones of privacy. The right of association contained in the penumbra of the First Amendment is one, as we have seen. The Third Amendment in its prohibition against the quartering of soldiers "in any house" in time of peace without the consent of the owner is another facet of that privacy. The Fourth Amendment explicitly affirms the "right of the people to be secure in their persons, houses, papers, and effects, against unreasonable searches and seizures." The Fifth Amendment in its Self-Incrimination Clause enables the citizen to create a zone of privacy which government may not force him to surrender to his detriment. The Ninth Amendment provides: "The enumeration in the Constitution, of certain rights, shall not be construed to deny or disparage others retained by the people." . . . We have had many controversies over these penumbral rights of "privacy and repose." See, e.g., Skinner v. Oklahoma, 316 U.S. 535, 541 [(1942)]. . . .

The present case, then, concerns a relationship lying within the zone of privacy created by several fundamental constitutional guarantees. And it concerns a law which, in forbidding the use of contraceptives rather than regulating their manufacture or sale, seeks to achieve its goals by means having a maximum destructive impact upon that relationship. Such a law cannot stand in light of the familiar principle, so often applied by this Court, that a "governmental purpose to control or prevent activities constitutionally subject to state regulation may not be achieved by means which sweep unnecessarily broadly and thereby invade the area of protected freedoms." NAACP v. Alabama, 377 U.S. 288, 307 [(1964)]. Would we allow the police to search the sacred precincts of marital bedrooms for telltale signs of the use of contraceptives? The very idea is repulsive to the notions of privacy surrounding the marriage relationship.

We deal with a right of privacy older than the Bill of Rights — older than our political parties, older than our school system. Marriage is a coming together for better or for worse, hopefully enduring, and intimate to the degree of being sacred. It is an association that promotes a way of life, not causes; a harmony in living, not political faiths; a bilateral loyalty, not commercial or social projects. Yet it is an association for as noble a purpose as any involved in our prior decisions. Reversed.

Justice GOLDBERG, whom THE CHIEF JUSTICE and Justice BRENNAN join, concurring.

I agree with the Court that Connecticut's birth-control law unconstitutionally intrudes upon the right of marital privacy. . . . I add these words to emphasize the relevance of [the Ninth] Amendment to the Court's holding. . . . The Amendment is almost entirely the work of James Madison. . . . It was proffered to quiet expressed fears that a bill of specifically enumerated rights could not be sufficiently broad to cover all essential rights and that the specific mention of certain rights would be interpreted as a denial that others were protected. . . .

To hold that a right so basic and fundamental and so deep-rooted in our society as the right of privacy in marriage may be infringed because that right is not guaranteed in so many words by the first eight amendments to the Constitution is to ignore the Ninth Amendment and to give it no effect whatsoever. [T]he Ninth Amendment simply lends strong support to the view that the "liberty" protected by the Fifth and Fourteenth Amendments from infringement by the Federal Government or the States is not restricted to rights specifically mentioned in the first eight amendments. . . .

Justice HARLAN, concurring in the judgment. . . .

In my view, the proper constitutional inquiry in this case is whether this Connecticut statute infringes the Due Process Clause of the Fourteenth Amendment because the enactment violates basic values "implicit in the concept of ordered liberty," Palko v. Connecticut, 302 U.S. 319, 325 [(1937)]. For reasons stated at length in my dissenting opinion in Poe v. Ullman, [367 U.S. 497, 522 (1961)], I believe that it does. . . .

Judicial self-restraint will . . . be achieved in this area, as in other constitutional areas, only by continual insistence upon respect for the teachings of history, solid recognition of the basic values that underlie our society, and wise appreciation of the great roles that the doctrines of federalism and separation of powers have played in establishing and preserving American freedoms. . . .

[In a separate concurring opinion, Justice White agrees that the statute violates the liberty protected by the Due Process Clause, questioning how the statutory ban serves the state's asserted interest in deterring illicit sexual relationships.]

Justice BLACK, with whom Justice STEWART joins, dissenting. . . .

The Court talks about a constitutional "right of privacy" as though there is some constitutional provision or provisions forbidding any law ever to be passed which might abridge the "privacy" of individuals. But there is not. . . . I like my privacy as well as the next one, but I am nevertheless compelled to admit that government has a right to invade it unless prohibited by some specific constitutional provision. . . .

My Brother Goldberg has adopted the recent discovery[12] that the Ninth Amendment as well as the Due Process Clause can be used by this Court as authority to strike down all state legislation which this Court thinks violates "fundamental principles of liberty and justice," or is contrary to the "traditions and [collective] conscience of our people." He also states, without proof satisfactory to me, that in making decisions on this basis, judges will not consider "their personal and private notions." One may ask how they can avoid considering them. Our Court certainly has no machinery with which to take a Gallup Poll. And the scientific miracles of this age have not yet produced a gadget which the Court can use to determine what traditions are rooted in the "[collective] conscience of our people." . . .

Justice STEWART, whom Justice BLACK joins, dissenting.

. . . I think this is an uncommonly silly law. As a practical matter, the law is obviously unenforceable, except in the oblique context of the present case. As a philosophical matter, I believe the use of contraceptives in the relationship of marriage should be left to personal and private choice, based upon each individual's moral, ethical, and religious beliefs. As a matter of social policy, I think professional counsel about methods of birth control should be available to all, so that each individual's choice can be meaningfully made. But we are not asked in this case to say whether we think this law is unwise, or even asinine. We are asked to hold that it violates the United States Constitution. And that I cannot do. . . . With all

---

12. See Patterson, The Forgotten Ninth Amendment (1955). . . . In Redlich, Are There "Certain Rights . . . Retained by the People"?, 37 N.Y.U. L. Rev. 787 [(1962)], Professor Redlich, in advocating reliance on the Ninth and Tenth Amendments to invalidate the Connecticut law before us, frankly states:

> But for one who feels that the marriage relationship should be beyond the reach of a state law forbidding the use of contraceptives, the birth control case poses a troublesome and challenging problem of constitutional interpretation. He may find himself saying, "The law is unconstitutional — but why?" There are two possible paths to travel in finding the answer. One is to revert to a frankly flexible due process concept even on matters that do not involve specific constitutional prohibitions. The other is to attempt to evolve a new constitutional framework within which to meet this and similar problems which are likely to arise.

Id., at 798.

deference, I can find no such general right of privacy in the Bill of Rights, in any other part of the Constitution, or in any case ever before decided by this Court.

At the oral argument in this case, we were told that the Connecticut law does not "conform to current community standards." But it is not the function of this Court to decide cases on the basis of community standards. . . . If, as I should surely hope, the law before us does not reflect the standards of the people of Connecticut, the people of Connecticut can freely exercise their true Ninth and Tenth Amendment rights to persuade their elected representatives to repeal it. That is the constitutional way to take this law off the books.

Michael Grossberg, Governing the Hearth: Law and the Family in Nineteenth-Century America
156-157, 175-177, 189-193 (1985)

At the heart of the nineteenth-century controversy over family limitation lay the quiet determination of American mothers and fathers to reduce the number of children they reared. They initiated what historical demographers now designate the "demographic transition": a reduction in family size that character-ized most Western nations. In America, white female fertility, the critical measure of family size, declined in each decade of the century, falling from 7.04 in 1800 to 3.56 a hundred years later. . . .

Although the exact sources [of this transition] remain uncertain, some characteristics of the republican household offer clues. . . . These include the child-centered nature of the republican home in which numerous offspring seemed to inhibit proper child care; the rise of what historian Daniel Scott Smith terms "domestic

ANTHONY COMSTOCK
SECRETARY
NEW YORK SOCIETY FOR THE SUPPRESSION OF VICE

Anthony Comstock, the purity crusader who led the state and federal campaigns against contraception

feminism," or the determination of women to assert their individuality and household authority by regulating pregnancy and marital sexuality; the economic incentives of market capitalism in which large families seemed a burden and in which moderation and self-control became prized virtues; the companionate nature of republican matrimony, which fostered the separation of sexual pleasure from protection; and the emerging American insistence on overcoming what had previously been considered natural forces beyond human control. . . .

Though it is difficult to pierce the privacy surrounding family limitation, at the beginning of the nineteenth century, husbands and wives apparently still relied on age-old methods of birth control such as delayed marriage, breast feeding, and abstinence (as well as *coitus interruptus* and other active contraceptive practices). . . .

Although statutes prohibiting various forms of abortion had been on the books since the 1820s, there were few explicit restrictions on contraception until the 1870s. But federal and state acts labeling both abortion and contraception as obscene capped the growing determination of family savers to ban all forms of family limitation. [For example, although] he sympathized with women's fears about childbirth and rearing large families, [Augustus] Gardner confidently insisted that efforts made "to avoid propagation, are ten thousand-fold more disastrous to the health and constitution, to say nothing of the demoralization of mind and heart. . . ." Gardner [and his followers] looked to the criminal law for relief.

Self-appointed purity campaigners led the drive against contraception. New Yorkers created the first purity society in 1872, the New York Society for the Suppression of Vice. [T]he society's point man for purity reform was a little known ex-dry goods salesman, Anthony Comstock. The son of devout Connecticut parents, he tried unsuccessfully to make his fortune as a businessman in New York City. The flagrant vices he encountered in the city shocked him into a highly publicized vigilante campaign. It culminated in his appointment as the antivice society's chief agent, thus launching his career as late nineteenth-century America's self-avowed savior of public morals.

Comstock regarded the feeble statutes then on the books as the weakest link in his war on vice. . . . In 1872 he convinced the antivice society to send him to Washington to press for a rigorous national statute. [There] the vice crusader succeeded beyond his wildest expectations. Armed with a display case of vice paraphernalia and vivid tales of his fights with the panderers of obscenity, Comstock enlisted the aid of Vice President Henry Wilson and Supreme Court Justice William Strong to draft a new obscenity law. The bill passed with little debate and became law on 1 March 1873. [It became known as the "Comstock law."]

The act's primary purpose was to ban the circulation and importation of obscene materials through the national mails. Specifically included on the list of banned goods was every article designed, adapted, or intended "for preventing conception or producing abortion, or for indecent or immoral use; and every article, instrument, substance, drug, medicine, or thing which is advertised or described in a manner calculated to lead another to use or apply it for preventing conception or producing abortion, or for any indecent or immoral purpose. . . ." The act set punishment at a $5,000 fine, one to ten years at hard labor, or both.

[P]urity crusaders also prodded state legislators into action. Antivice societies, and after 1885 the Social Purity Alliance, succeeded in persuading twenty-two legislatures to enact general obscenity laws and another twenty-four to specifically ban birth control and abortion. [Courts upheld convictions under these laws.] Let loose by Congress, state legislatures, and the courts, vice hunters prowled the nation sniffing out their prey. Posing as customers or using decoy letters, federal agents and local societies purchased proscribed items and then arrested sellers. . . . Comstock in fact caught his most famous victim with a birth-control ploy. Having been warned not to tangle with the infamous Madame Restell, he took her capture as a personal challenge. In the guise of an impoverished father, Comstock pleaded for contraceptive information because his meager finances could support no more children. When she obliged, he arrested her. Faced with the almost certain prospect of jail at the age of 67, Restell slit her throat with a carving knife. Comstock experienced no remorse: "a bloody end to a bloody life."

. . . Congress strengthened the federal ban in 1908. By the 1930s eight states specifically prohibited the flow of contraceptive information while the rest acted through broadened obscenity laws. Contraception remained a taboo subject, even though, much like prohibition, the statutes expressed a moral standard clearly at odds with actual practices. . . . Birth control, no matter how essential family limitation had become to the republican family, still violated the nation's code of proper domestic behavior. Fears aroused by the immigration of seemingly fecund non-Protestant women, charges of race suicide leveled against non-immigrant mothers who regulated their child bearing, and the ever-present concern over changes in gender responsibilities reinvigorated the stigma attached to the practice.

The constitutionality of the ban was also impenetrable. [Judicial cases] demonstrated the formidable opposition facing birth-control advocates. . . . Birth control continued to be an obscene subject banished from polite society. . . .

NOTE: WHO WAS ESTELLE GRISWOLD?

Catherine G. Roraback, Griswold v. Connecticut: A Brief Case History
16 Ohio N.U. L. Rev. 395, 395-401 (1989)

The [Connecticut] ban on the use of contraceptives had been on the statute books of this state for some *eighty-six* years. Many other jurisdictions had similar laws, but by the late 1950's these laws had been either repealed or their impact minimized by judicial interpretation. In 1958 only Connecticut had an absolute ban on contraceptive devices, one without an exception even for situations where the life of the mother might be endangered by

Estelle Griswold (left) and a Planned Parenthood colleague celebrate the Supreme Court victory.

a pregnancy. [T]here were regular attempts to obtain legislative repeal of the statute. In each biennial session of the General Assembly a repealer bill was introduced, vociferous and vituperative hearings were held, and the bill was eventually voted down. . . .

[I]t is hard to remember the attitudes toward birth control in the 1950's. The statutory prohibition on the use of contraceptives even by married persons was accepted by many as a legitimate exercise of the police powers of the state. That is not to say that private doctors did not provide such advice and services to their private patients, nor that patients able to afford private medical care did not obtain contraceptive advice. However, even that private care was often circumspect and clandestine, and some private physicians refused to provide these services at all. Certainly these services were not available to unmarried persons.

Although contraceptives were available for purchase in drugstores throughout the state, that availability was usually "under-the-counter." Druggists also sold such items on prescription of a private physician. The activities of the state Planned Parenthood League were limited to educational and legislative programs and a referral service to clinics in neighboring New York and Rhode Island, with transportation furnished by volunteers to enable the women to take advantage of the out-of-state services.

But no medical source of contraceptive advice or services was available in this state to those dependent on publicly provided health care. It was the physicians and medical personnel operating in public clinics who were subjected to public scrutiny and threat of prosecution. And because it was here that these statutes impacted, it was the poor people of this state who were deprived of medically supervised contraceptive advice and services. [After 1940, when nine Planned Parenthood clinics were closed, no public or private facility provided free birth control.]

In 1957, Estelle Griswold, a dynamic, vivacious woman, had only recently become the executive director of the Planned Parenthood League of Connecticut. She found herself frustrated by the legal situation in Connecticut and her inability to organize Planned Parenthood clinics in the state.

In the course of preparations that year for the biennial legislative hearing on repeal of the anti-birth-control statute, she arranged for C. Lee Buxton to testify. Buxton had only recently come to New Haven as professor and chairman of the Department of Obstetrics and Gynecology at the Yale University School of Medicine. . . . He felt deeply that the statute banning the use of contraceptive devices and the accessory statute preventing him from giving what he felt to be the advice and care his patients deserved were gross invasions of his patients' rights, and highly improper impediments on his ability to practice his profession.

It was at this point, as legend has it, that Estelle invited both Lee Buxton and Fowler Harper to her home one day in the fall of 1957 and introduced them over cocktails. Fowler, then a professor at the Yale Law School, taught — among other subjects — family law. He was a social activist, involved in the community, always ready to take on a cause and to use his full energies and legal skills to cure an inequity. . . . He most certainly reacted with verve and gusto as Lee spoke of his frustrations about the Connecticut law banning the use of contraceptives and his inability to properly serve his patients. And, the legend holds, it was from this conversation that the litigation which culminated in *Griswold* originated. . . .

[The chosen strategy was for Dr. Buxton and some of his married patients to seek in state court a declaratory judgment that the statute was unconstitutional or should not apply when pregnancy threatened a woman's life or health.] One of the patients bringing suit was Jane Doe, a young twenty-five-year-old housewife. . . . While hospitalized [for pregnancy complications] she had suffered a stroke, her pregnancy could not be aborted, and she had had to continue the pregnancy until at term she had a stillbirth. As a result she was permanently paralyzed on her right side, her speech was impaired and she had residual kidney damage. It was Dr. Buxton's opinion that she would not survive another pregnancy.

The other plaintiff-patients were two married couples. One, the Poes, had had three abnormal children, none of whom had survived more than ten weeks. They sought contraceptive advice because they did not feel they could emotionally survive the birth of another such child. The other couple, the Hoes, had conflicting blood groupings and were considered unlikely to have a normal child born to them.

When these suits were begun in May of 1958, there was . . . no discussion of rights of privacy. . . . The due process arguments in the briefs filed in the Connecticut courts stressed rights to life and liberty, to health, to happy marital relationships, free of governmental intrusion. But the obverse of that phrase — privacy — was not used. . . . It was in the due process arguments presented on the appeal [by the law's challengers] to the United States Supreme Court in this case that the first specific mention of "privacy" occurred in this litigation. However, the Supreme Court never reached this or any of the other substantive arguments raised on this appeal. Rather, it held [in Poe v. Ullman, 367 U.S. 497 (1961),] that there was no controversy before the Court, that there had been an absence of any prosecutions under the statutes, and that therefore Dr. Buxton and his patients faced no realistic threat of prosecution.

In Connecticut the implications of this disconcerting outcome were pondered. . . . After much consultation and discussion, it was finally decided that the Planned Parenthood League of Connecticut would open one facility in New Haven, and that if no prosecution ensued, it would expand such services to other cities. Thus on November 1, 1961, the Planned Parenthood League of Connecticut opened the first birth control clinic in [Connecticut] since 1940, with Estelle T. Griswold as its director and C. Lee Buxton as its medical director. [Ten days later, they were arrested and charged with aiding and abetting] certain married women to "use a drug, medicinal article and instrument, for the purpose of preventing conception." The clinic closed its doors. . . .

From the beginning of this prosecution, the defense attacked the statutory contraceptive ban, repeating in depth all of the prior arguments as to the unconstitutionality of the statute but adding now, specifically the infringement which it imposed on the patient's right to privacy. . . .

Notes and Questions

1. Sources. What are the constitutional sources of the right to privacy, according to *Griswold*? According to the concurring opinions? Explain the majority's difficulty in identifying the source of this right. On what basis do the dissenters disagree?

2. State intrusion. What aspect of the statute disturbs the majority? If Connecticut had sought to prevent the use of contraceptives by, say, banning the manufacture or sale of such materials, what result? How significant is the fact that Connecticut prohibited couples' behavior with regard to contraceptive use, as distinguished from some other sex-related activity (e.g., possession of pornography or access to sex toys)?

3. Role of marriage. How critical is the marital status of the contraceptive users? To whom does the right to privacy belong, according to *Griswold*? Each spouse? The marital unit? Suppose the spouses disagree. May the state resolve the disagreement?

4. State interests. Why did Connecticut enact this legislation? What do the excerpts by historian Michael Grossberg and attorney Catherine Roraback (counsel to Planned Parenthood League of Connecticut during *Griswold*) suggest? What role do the state's reasons play in *Griswold*?

5. Privacy's origins. In an omitted footnote, Justice Black's dissent claims that the concept of a "right to privacy" originated in an 1890 article by Samuel Warren and his then-law partner Louis Brandeis. Reportedly written in response to considerable press coverage of the wedding of Warren's socialite daughter, the article sought a basis in tort law for the protection of privacy from threats posed by the technologies of photography and broadcasting. As a Supreme Court Justice, Brandeis later cited the Constitution in support of "the right to be let alone."[1] Justice Goldberg's concurrence in *Griswold* invokes Brandeis's understanding. How closely does the *Griswold* majority's concept of privacy resemble that of Warren and Brandeis? Does *Griswold*'s notion of privacy protect the right not to have information made public? The right to be let alone? The right to self-determination?

Professor Cary Franklin suggests that using the privacy frame in a case in which the parties are seeking access to birth control from public clinics may not be as "ironic" as it might first appear: "Privacy has never entailed merely the right to be left alone," she writes. "In order to make autonomous decisions about sexuality and reproduction," Franklin continues, "women need access to birth control. As *Griswold* recognized, some women gain this access through private doctors; others require public clinics."[2]

---

[1]. See Samuel D. Warren & Louis B. Brandeis, The Right to Privacy, 4 Harv. L. Rev. 193 (1890). The subsequent popularization of the telephone and the invention of wiretapping reportedly revived Brandeis's interest in recognition of a constitutional right to privacy in his dissenting opinion in Olmstead v. United States, 277 U.S. 438, 478 (1928) (recognizing Fourth Amendment protection against governmental wiretapping).

[2]. Cary Franklin, *Griswold* and the Public Dimensions of the Right to Privacy, 124 Yale L.J. Forum 332, 338 (2015).

6. Resurrection of the Comstock Act. A recent Fifth Circuit Court of Appeals ruling seems to resurrect the Comstock Act, thereby potentially threatening access to any drugs (or other medical devices) used in abortion, including one of the two drugs used today in medication abortions—mifepristone. Alliance for Hippocratic Med. v. Food & Drug Admin., 2023 WL 2913725, at *21 (5th Cir. 2023). In the case, anti-abortion doctors and medical organizations invoked the Comstock Act in their challenge to the 23-year-old approval of mifepristone by the Food and Drug Administration (FDA). Among other things, the parties argued that the FDA's approval of the drug was impermissible because it failed to take the Comstock criminal prohibitions into account. At the trial court level, district judge Matthew Kacsmaryk issued a nationwide preliminary injunction blocking the FDA's approval of mifepristone altogether. Alliance for Hippocratic Med. v. FDA, 2023 WL 2825871 (N.D. Tex. 2023). The Fifth Circuit affirmed on narrower grounds, declining to stay the original approval of mifepristone but enjoining a number of rules expanding access.

Shortly thereafter, the Supreme Court stayed the decision of the district court until resolution of the case by the Supreme Court. Another case grappling with the FDA's approval of mifepristone is pending in a federal district court in Washington State. Washington v. FDA, 2023 WL 2941567 (E.D. Wash. 2023). The issue will likely make its way back to the Supreme Court.

7. Birth control movement. The radical birth control movement in the United States emerged as part of the Socialist Party's agenda in the early 1900s. Activist Margaret Sanger's role in the movement grew out of her encounter as a visiting nurse with a poor woman who died because she could not avoid another pregnancy. Sanger also appreciated the broader implications of birth control:

> Most American socialists at this time, primarily oriented to class relations, saw birth control . . . in terms of economics. They were concerned to help raise the standard of living of workers and thus increase their freedom to take political control over their own lives. Measured against this goal, birth control was at most an ameliorative reform. Seen in terms of sexual politics, however, birth control was revolutionary because it could free women entirely from the major burden that differentiated them from men and made them dependent on men. Sanger gained this perspective in Europe from the sexual liberation theorists such as Havelock Ellis. . . . His idealism about the potential beauty and expressiveness of human sexuality and his rage at the damage caused by sexual repression fired Sanger with a sense of the overwhelming importance, urgency, and profundity of the issue of birth control. . . .[3]

Sanger founded the American Birth Control League, which later became Planned Parenthood. Her legacy, however, has been tarnished by the recognition of her belief in eugenics—the now-discredited theory of improving the genetic quality of the human population by "selective breeding."

---

[3]. Linda Gordon, The Moral Property of Women: A History of Birth Control Politics in America 145 (2002). See also Serena Mayeri, Intersectionality and the Constitution of Family Status, 32 Const. Comment. 377 (2017) (exploring the ways in which laws regulating the family have always been "deeply intertwined with inequalities of race, class, gender, and region").

8. Birth control and race. In the above excerpt, Grossberg recounts how fears of "race suicide" (that is, a declining birth rate among whites at a time of growing immigration) supported birth control restrictions. In contrast to their white counterparts' focus on access to birth control, women of color embraced a larger agenda. Black women's understanding of reproductive rights was shaped by the history of sexual exploitation during slavery, sterilization abuse, and societal inattention to high maternal and infant mortality rates. Many supported birth control and abortion rights, despite Black Nationalist organizations' condemnation in the 1970s of such measures as tools for genocide. Puerto Rican activists' advocacy for women's autonomy and state-supported health care stemmed from U.S.-sponsored sterilization there and harm suffered by some Puerto Rican participants in clinical trials for the birth control pill.[4]

9. Privacy vs. economic justice. As Catherine Roraback makes clear in the above excerpt, although Connecticut's statute did not facially discriminate on the basis of socioeconomic status, it did not impact all people equally. As a practical matter, more affluent people in Connecticut could find ways to access contraceptives. By contrast, Roraback continues, "no medical source of contraceptive advice or services was available in this state to those dependent on publicly provided health care." And, indeed, Professor Franklin (mentioned above) argues that this is how *Griswold* was initially understood—as a case about economic injustice.[5] Would this have been a better theory of the case?

EISENSTADT v. BAIRD
405 U.S. 438 (1972)

Activist William Baird speaks to the press after his birth control lecture at Boston University.

Justice BRENNAN delivered the opinion of the Court.

Appellee William Baird was convicted at a bench trial in the Massachusetts Superior Court under Massachusetts General Laws Ann., c. 272, §21, first, for exhibiting contraceptive articles in the course of delivering a lecture on contraception to a group of students at Boston University and, second, for giving a young woman a package of Emko vaginal foam at the close of his address. The

---

[4]. See Jennifer Nelson, Women of Color and the Reproductive Rights Movement 19, 186 (2003); Dorothy Roberts, Killing the Black Body: Race, Reproduction, and the Meaning of Liberty 22-55 (2d ed. 2017). See also Melissa Murray, Race-ing *Roe*: Reproductive Justice, Racial Justice, and the Battle for Roe v. Wade, 134 Harv. L. Rev. 2025, 2033 (2021).

[5]. Franklin, supra note [2], at 333 ("Before *Griswold* became part of the line of modern reproductive rights cases, it was part of a series of Warren Court decisions that suggested the Constitution, properly understood, was concerned with certain forms of material deprivation and economic injustice.").

Massachusetts Supreme Judicial Court unanimously set aside the conviction for exhibiting contraceptives on the ground that it violated Baird's First Amendment rights, but by a four-to-three vote sustained the conviction for giving away the foam. Commonwealth v. Baird, 355 Mass. 746, 247 N.E.2d 574 (1969). . . .

Massachusetts General Laws Ann., c. 272, §21 [provides] a maximum five-year term of imprisonment for "whoever . . . gives away . . . any drug, medicine, instrument, or article whatever for the prevention of conception," except as authorized in §21A. . . . As interpreted by the State Supreme Judicial Court, these provisions make it a felony for anyone, other than a registered physician or pharmacist acting in accordance with the terms of §21A, to dispense any article with the intention that it be used for the prevention of conception. [M]arried persons may obtain contraceptives to prevent pregnancy, but only from doctors or druggists on prescription; . . . single persons may not obtain contraceptives from anyone to prevent pregnancy. . . .

The question for our determination in this case is whether there is some ground of difference that rationally explains the different treatment accorded married and unmarried persons under Massachusetts General Laws Ann., c. 272, §§21 and 21A.7 . . .

First. [W]e cannot agree that the deterrence of premarital sex may reasonably be regarded as the purpose of the Massachusetts law.

It would be plainly unreasonable to assume that Massachusetts has prescribed pregnancy and the birth of an unwanted child as punishment for fornication, which is a misdemeanor under Massachusetts General Laws Ann., c. 272, §18. Aside from the scheme of values that assumption would attribute to the State, it is abundantly clear that the effect of the ban on distribution of contraceptives to unmarried persons has at best a marginal relation to the proffered objective. . . . Like Connecticut's laws [in *Griswold*], §§21 and 21A do not at all regulate the distribution of contraceptives when they are to be used to prevent, not pregnancy, but the spread of disease. Nor, in making contraceptives available to married persons without regard to their intended use, does Massachusetts attempt to deter married persons from engaging in illicit sexual relations with unmarried persons. Even on the assumption that the fear of pregnancy operates as a deterrent to fornication, the Massachusetts statute is thus so riddled with exceptions that deterrence of premarital sex cannot reasonably be regarded as its aim. . . .

Second. . . . If health were the rationale of §21A, the statute would be both discriminatory and overbroad. . . . The Court of Appeals [stated]: "If the prohibition [on distribution to unmarried persons] . . . is to be taken to mean that the same physician who can prescribe for married patients does not have sufficient skill to protect the health of patients who lack a marriage certificate, or who may be currently divorced, it is illogical to the point of irrationality." 429 F.2d, at 1401. Furthermore, we must join the Court of Appeals in noting that not all contraceptives are potentially dangerous. . . . "If [health] was the Legislature's goal, §21 is not required" in view of the federal and state laws *already* regulating the distribution of harmful drugs. . . .

Third. If the Massachusetts statute cannot be upheld as a deterrent to fornication or as a health measure, may it, nevertheless, be sustained simply as a prohibition on contraception? . . . We need not and do not, however, decide that important question in this case because, whatever the rights of the individual to access to contraceptives may be, the rights must be the same for the unmarried and the married alike.

If under *Griswold* the distribution of contraceptives to married persons cannot be prohibited, a ban on distribution to unmarried persons would be equally impermissible. It is true that in *Griswold* the right of privacy in question inhered in the marital relationship. Yet the marital couple is not an independent entity with a mind and heart of its own, but an association of two individuals, each with a separate intellectual and emotional makeup. If the right of privacy means anything, it is the right of the *individual*, married or single, to be free from unwarranted governmental intrusion into matters so fundamentally affecting a person as the decision whether to bear or beget a child. See Stanley v. Georgia, 394 U.S. 557 (1969). See also Skinner v. Oklahoma ex rel. Williamson, 316 U.S. 535 (1942); Jacobson v. Massachusetts, 197 U.S. 11, 29 (1905).

On the other hand, if *Griswold* is no bar to a prohibition on the distribution of contraceptives, the State could not, consistently with the Equal Protection Clause, outlaw distribution to unmarried but not married persons. In each case the evil, as perceived by the State, would be identical, and the underinclusion would be invidious.

. . . We hold that by providing dissimilar treatment for married and unmarried persons who are similarly situated, Massachusetts General Laws Ann., c. 272, §§21 and 21A, violate the Equal Protection Clause. The judgment of the Court of Appeals is affirmed.

Notes and Questions

1. **Beyond *Griswold*.** How does *Eisenstadt* resolve the issues left open in *Griswold*: the *distribution* of contraceptives to *unmarried* individuals?

2. **Privacy's meaning.** How does *Eisenstadt* define "privacy"? How does the meaning of "privacy" articulated in *Eisenstadt* differ from that in *Griswold*? How does *Eisenstadt* answer the question whether the right to privacy belongs to the family unit or each member of the family? Does it indicate how to resolve conflicts between family members over "private" matters? What would a relational understanding of privacy and autonomy entail?

3. **The equal protection basis.** Why does the Court rely on the Equal Protection Clause instead of the constitutional provisions relied upon in *Griswold*? Does *Eisenstadt*'s approach provide a firmer basis for the protection? To what extent does *Eisenstadt* implicitly reflect concerns about gender equality?

4. **State interests: privacy versus privatization.** Why did Massachusetts enact the challenged law? How does the Court address the state's interests? What does the Massachusetts law contribute to the understanding of family law as part of a systematic effort to channel sexual activity into marriage? Consistent with this view, several commentators see family law as regulation aimed at keeping

dependency private (the "privatization of dependency").[6] Does this theory help explain the state intrusion experienced by the poor, who critics say often must bargain away their family privacy for state assistance?

5. Scope of protection. States routinely create legal distinctions based on marriage, awarding family benefits only to married couples. The Supreme Court emphasized the unique material and psychic advantages of marriage when holding in Obergefell v. Hodges, 576 U.S. 644 (2015) (reprinted in Chapter II), that the Constitution requires equal access for same-sex couples. How do you reconcile the Court's assumptions in *Obergefell* with *Eisenstadt's* rejection of discrimination based on marital status?[7]

6. Distribution. The Court subsequently addressed the substantive issue avoided in *Eisenstadt*. Carey v. Population Services International, 431 U.S. 678 (1977), struck down a statute barring distribution of all contraceptives except by licensed pharmacists. The majority explained that such limitations on access impose burdens similar to limitations on use; hence, both must satisfy the compelling state interest test.

7. The pill. Why did contraception become a constitutional issue at this time in history? The birth control pill, approved by the FDA in 1960, quickly came to symbolize the sexual revolution and women's liberation. Subsequently, critics dubbed legislative and political efforts to restrict access to contraception as a "war on women" and a revival of attitudes from the Comstock era.

It is still the case today, more than 50 years after attempts to develop a male birth control pill, that the only medication contraception is for women. However, a safe and effective *male* birth control pill is now one step closer to reality, according to recent research.[8] If it becomes available, how will the advent of the male birth control pill redefine privacy for the family, its members, and family law?

8. Birth control and class. Roraback, in the above excerpt, notes that criminal prohibitions disproportionately affected clients of public family planning clinics. Contemporary studies document a class divide in contraceptive use and marriage,

---

[6]. See, e.g., Martha Albertson Fineman, The Autonomy Myth: A Theory of Dependency (2004); Anne L. Alstott, Private Tragedies? Family Law as Social Insurance, 4 Harv. L. & Pol'y Rev. 3 (2010). On the privacy right as a function of class, see Khiara M. Bridges, Pregnancy, Poverty, and the State: The Poverty of Privacy Rights (2017).

[7]. See generally Clare Huntington, Postmarital Family Law: A Legal Structure for Nonmarital Families, 67 Stan. L. Rev. 167 (2015); Melissa Murray, Obergefell v. Hodges and Nonmarriage Inequality, 104 Calif. L. Rev. 1207 (2016) (noting how family law both prioritizes marriage and discounts nonmarital families). But see Courtney G. Joslin, The Gay Rights Canon and the Right to Nonmarriage, 97 B.U. L. Rev. 425 (2017) (rereading the gay rights canon to support the "extension of constitutional protection to those living outside marriage").

[8]. See NIH Research Matters, Male Contraceptive Disables Sperm, Feb. 28, 2023, https://www.nih.gov/news-events/nih-research-matters/male-contraceptive-disables-sperm. On the history of the pill, see generally Elaine Tyler May, America and the Pill: A History of Promise, Peril, and Liberation (2010). On the "missing science of men's reproductive health," see Rene Almeling, GUYnecology: The Missing Science of Men's Reproductive Health (2020).

with lower rates for both among the economically vulnerable.[9] How might *Griswold* and *Eisenstadt* operate to reduce poverty?[10]

Since its original approval in 1960, birth control pills have been available only through a prescription. Starting in 2024, the birth control pill will become available over the counter.[11] What impact do you think that will have on the lives of women? Families?

9. Contraception and governmental regulation. How is *Eisenstadt*'s legacy influenced by such contemporary developments as the Patient Protection and Affordable Care Act (ACA)'s contraceptive mandate that requires large employers to provide free coverage for contraception and recent federal restrictions on reproductive health services (explored further below)? Even before *Eisenstadt*, Congress enacted the Family Planning and Population Research Act of 1970 (Title X), Pub. L. No. 91-572, to provide federal funding to support family planning services and other preventive health care for low-income and uninsured individuals. What is the appropriate role of government in the individual's and family's decision regarding such private matters as contraception?

NOTE: THE CONTRACEPTIVE MANDATE, *HOBBY LOBBY*, AND SUBSEQUENT FEDERAL DEVELOPMENTS

The ACA, enacted by Congress in 2010, requires large employers that provide their employees with health insurance to cover some contraceptive costs in their health insurance plans. Pursuant to federal regulations, coverage must include free preventive care and screenings, including a broad range of contraceptive methods. This "contraceptive mandate" recognizes that women pay more for preventive care, that cost barriers thwart their access to contraception, and that access problems result in unintended pregnancies, with personal and economic effects.

Federal regulations offered exemptions to religious employers (such as churches) and accommodations for nonprofit employers with religious objections, but not to *for-profit corporations*. In Burwell v. Hobby Lobby Stores, Inc., 573 U.S. 682 (2014), for-profit corporations, owned by devout fundamentalist Christians, raised religious objections to covering four specific contraceptive methods that the business owners deemed "life-terminating." The owners argued that the ACA contraceptive mandate substantially burdened their religious beliefs in violation of the federal Religious Freedom Restoration Act (RFRA).

A closely divided Supreme Court sided with the challengers. The majority reasoned that the contraceptive mandate, as applied to for-profit closely-held corporations (private corporations with relatively few owners), substantially burdened the exercise of religion for purposes of RFRA; and that less restrictive means

---

[9]. See generally June Carbone & Naomi Cahn, Marriage Markets: How Inequality Is Remaking the American Family (2014); Isabel V. Sawhill, Generation Unbound: Drifting into Sex and Parenthood without Marriage (2014).

[10]. See Susan Frelich Appleton, The Forgotten Family Law of Eisenstadt v. Baird, 28 Yale J.L. & Feminism 1 (2016).

[11]. Pam Belluck, F.D.A. Approves First U.S. Over-the-Counter Birth Control Pill, N.Y. Times, July 13, 2023, https://www.nytimes.com/2023/07/13/health/otc-birth-control-pill.html.

were available to meet the governmental interest in public health and gender equality.[12] The majority based its ruling on the assumption that the female employees in question would have coverage for all approved, essential medical care without cost from some other source, and disclaimed any implications for religion-based objections to other types of health care or employee benefits (such as those triggered by same-sex marriage).

The Trump Administration announced final rules under the ACA that set forth broader exemptions, making it even easier for some employers to exclude contraceptive coverage from their employer-provided health plans. 83 Fed. Reg. 57,592 (Nov. 15, 2018). Regulations allow employers (both nonprofit and for-profit) to exclude some or all contraceptive methods and services from their health plans if employers have religious objections and also extend the same right to some employers with nonreligious moral objections. The Supreme Court upheld these regulations in Little Sisters of the Poor Saints Peter & Paul Home v. Pennsylvania, 140 S. Ct. 2367 (2020).

In early 2023, the Biden Administration proposed rules that would rescind the morals-based exception and provide a means for employees to receive contraception coverage where their employer has claimed protection under the religious exception. 88 Fed. Regis. 7236 (Feb. 2, 2023). Several members of the House of Representatives are challenging the proposed contraceptive-coverage rules, claiming that they violate the First Amendment and RFRA.

Problem

Suppose that a "grandfathered" employer (exempt from the ACA mandate because of a preexisting plan) provides employees with comprehensive prescription drug coverage that includes Viagra, a prescription drug used by some men to facilitate or enable them to engage in sexual intimacy, but not prescription contraceptives, which are available only for women and which accomplish a similar objective for some women. Would such action violate laws that prohibit sex-based discrimination in the workplace (Title VII and the Pregnancy Discrimination Act)? See Standridge v. Union Pac. R.R. Co., 479 F.3d 936 (8th Cir. 2007). Would excluding both Viagra and contraceptives from the plan eliminate any discrimination? See Erickson v. Bartell Drug Co., 141 F. Supp. 2d 1266 (W.D. Wash. 2001); Sylvia A. Law, Sex Discrimination and Insurance for Contraception, 73 Wash. L. Rev. 363 (1998).

2. Roots of Privacy

The earliest decisions extending constitutional protection to family autonomy and family decisions established the principle that parents have constitutionally

---

[12]. For an exploration of these types of "complicity-based conscience claims" and the ways in which they "amplify the material and dignitary harms that accommodation of the claims can inflict on other citizens," see Douglas NeJaime & Reva B. Siegel, Conscience Wars: Complicity-Based Conscience Claims in Religion and Politics, 124 Yale L.J. 2516 (2015). For an argument that the contraception mandate discriminates on the basis of sex, see Greer Donley, Contraceptive Equity: Curing the Sex Discrimination in the ACA's Mandate, 71 Ala. L. Rev. 499, 500 (2019).

protected interests with respect to important decisions about their children, as the cases below reveal.

MEYER v. NEBRASKA
262 U.S. 390 (1923)

Schoolchildren in the 1920s

Justice MCREYNOLDS delivered the opinion of the Court.

Plaintiff in error was tried and convicted . . . under an information which charged that on May 25, 1920, while an instructor in Zion Parochial School he unlawfully taught the subject of reading in the German language to Raymond Parpart, a child of 10 years, who had not attained and successfully passed the eighth grade. [A Nebraska statute prohibited any person from teaching languages other than English, except to pupils who had successfully completed the eighth grade, and classified a violation as a misdemeanor, punishable by a fine and/or imprisonment. The state supreme court affirmed the conviction.]

The problem for our determination is whether the statute as construed and applied unreasonably infringes the liberty guaranteed to the plaintiff in error by the Fourteenth Amendment: "No state . . . shall deprive any person of life, liberty or property without due process of law."

While this court has not attempted to define with exactness the liberty thus guaranteed, [w]ithout doubt, it denotes not merely freedom from bodily restraint but also the right of the individual to contract, to engage in any of the common occupations of life, to acquire useful knowledge, to marry, establish a home and bring up children, to worship God according to the dictates of his own conscience, and generally to enjoy those privileges long recognized at common law as essential to the orderly pursuit of happiness by free men. The established doctrine is that this liberty may not be interfered with, under the guise of protecting the public interest, by legislative action which is arbitrary or without reasonable relation to some purpose within the competency of the state to effect. Determination by the Legislature of what constitutes proper exercise of police power is not final or conclusive but is subject to supervision by the courts.

The American people have always regarded education and acquisition of knowledge as matters of supreme importance which should be diligently promoted. . . . Corresponding to the right of control, it is the natural duty of the parent to give his children education suitable to their station in life; and nearly all the states, including Nebraska, enforce this obligation by compulsory laws.

Practically, education of the young is only possible in schools conducted by especially qualified persons who devote themselves thereto. The calling always has been regarded as useful and honorable, essential, indeed, to the public welfare. Mere knowledge of the German language cannot reasonably be regarded as harmful. . . . Plaintiff in error taught this language in school as part of his occupation. His right thus to teach and the right of parents to engage him so to instruct their children, we think, are within the liberty of the Amendment. . . . Evidently the Legislature has attempted materially to interfere with the calling of modern language teachers, with the opportunities of pupils to acquire knowledge, and with the power of parents to control the education of their own.

It is said the purpose of the legislation was to promote civic development by inhibiting training and education of the immature in foreign tongues and ideals before they could learn English and acquire American ideals, and "that the English language should be and become the mother tongue of all children reared in this state." It is also affirmed that the foreign born population is very large, that certain communities commonly use foreign words, follow foreign leaders, move in a foreign atmosphere, and that the children are thereby hindered from becoming citizens of the most useful type and the public safety is imperiled.

That the state may do much, go very far, indeed, in order to improve the quality of its citizens, physically, mentally and morally, is clear; but the individual has certain fundamental rights which must be respected. The protection of the Constitution extends to all, to those who speak other languages as well as to those born with English on the tongue. Perhaps it would be highly advantageous if all had ready understanding of our ordinary speech, but this cannot be coerced by methods which conflict with the Constitution — a desirable end cannot be promoted by prohibited means. . . . No emergency has arisen which renders knowledge by a child of some language other than English so clearly harmful as to justify its inhibition with the consequent infringement of rights long freely enjoyed. We are constrained to conclude that the statute as applied is arbitrary and without reasonable relation to any end within the competency of the state.

As the statute undertakes to interfere only with teaching which involves a modern language, leaving complete freedom as to other matters, there seems no adequate foundation for the suggestion that the purpose was to protect the child's health by limiting his mental activities. It is well known that proficiency in a foreign language seldom comes to one not instructed at an early age, and experience shows that this is not injurious to the health, morals or understanding of the ordinary child. [Reversed.]

PIERCE v. SOCIETY OF SISTERS
268 U.S. 510 (1925)

Justice McReynolds delivered the opinion of the Court. . . .

[The Compulsory Education Act, effective September 1, 1926,] requires every parent, guardian, or other person having control or charge or custody of a child between 8 and 16 years to send him "to a public school for the period of time a public school shall be held during the current year" in the district where the child resides; and failure so to do is declared a misdemeanor. . . . The manifest purpose is to compel general attendance at public schools by normal children, between 8 and 16, who have not completed the eighth grade. And without doubt enforcement of the statute would seriously impair, perhaps destroy, the profitable features of appellees' business and greatly diminish the value of their property.

Appellee, the Society of Sisters, is an Oregon corporation, organized in 1880, with power to care for orphans, educate and instruct the youth, establish and maintain academies or schools, and acquire necessary real and personal property. . . . The Compulsory Education Act of 1922 has already caused the withdrawal from its schools of children who would otherwise continue, and their income has steadily declined. The appellants, public officers, have proclaimed their purpose strictly to enforce the statute.

[T]he Society's bill alleges that the enactment conflicts with the right of parents to choose schools where their children will receive appropriate mental and religious training, the right of the child to influence the parents' choice of a school, the right of schools and teachers therein to engage in a useful business or profession, and is accordingly repugnant to the Constitution and void. And, further, that unless enforcement of the measure is enjoined the corporation's business and property will suffer irreparable injury. [Similarly, appellee Hill Military Academy, an elementary, college preparatory, and military training school for boys, alleges a violation of its Fourteenth Amendment rights and seeks an injunction.]

[The court below ruled for appellees, based on the Fourteenth Amendment's guarantee against the deprivation of property without due process of law and the liberty of parents and guardians to direct the education of children by selecting reputable teachers and places; it determined that appellees' schools were not unfit or harmful to the public.]

No question is raised concerning the power of the state reasonably to regulate all schools, to inspect, supervise, and examine them, their teachers, and pupils; to require that all children of proper age attend some school, that teachers shall be of good moral character and patriotic disposition, that certain studies plainly essential to good citizenship must be taught, and that nothing be taught which is manifestly inimical to the public welfare.

The inevitable practical result of enforcing the act under consideration would be destruction of appellees' primary schools, and perhaps all other private primary schools for normal children within the state of Oregon. Appellees are engaged in a kind of undertaking not inherently harmful, but long regarded as useful and meritorious. [T]here are no peculiar circumstances or present emergencies which demand extraordinary measures relative to primary education.

Under the doctrine of Meyer v. Nebraska, 262 U.S. 390 [(1923)], we think it entirely plain that the Act of 1922 unreasonably interferes with the liberty of parents and guardians to direct the upbringing and education of children under their control. As often heretofore pointed out, rights guaranteed by the Constitution may not be abridged by legislation which has no reasonable relation to some purpose within the competency of the state. The fundamental theory of liberty upon which all governments in this Union repose excludes any general power of the state to standardize its children by forcing them to accept instruction from public teachers only. The child is not the mere creature of the state; those who nurture him and direct his destiny have the right, coupled with the high duty, to recognize and prepare him for additional obligations. . . .

The decrees below [restraining enforcement of the Act] are affirmed.

Notes and Questions on *Meyer* and *Pierce*

1. Substantive due process.

a. Foundational principles. Meyer and *Pierce* establish the foundation for constitutional protection for the family, rooted in principles of privacy and liberty. Why does the Court recognize this protection? Whose interests does each case vindicate? What is the connection between parents' privacy or liberty interests and the professional and proprietary interests of teachers and schools protected by the Court? These cases were decided during the *Lochner* era, a period in which the Court was using substantive due process to protect economic interests. Although many of the other substantive due process decisions from this period—including, most notably, *Lochner*—have been overruled, these cases remain good law. Although neither *Meyer* nor *Pierce* mentions "privacy," *Griswold*—the first case to articulate a constitutional right to privacy—relies on both precedents.

b. Parental autonomy. Despite holdings addressing the economic claims raised by a schoolteacher and private schools, respectively, *Meyer* and *Pierce* include dicta establishing *parental autonomy*—the right of parents to control the upbringing of their children. Through these dicta, these cases extend substantive due process found in the constitutional protection of personal "liberty" to limit the authority of government to interfere in certain family matters. On what basis do the Justices decide what "liberty" encompasses?

As noted, the broad liberal principles of family autonomy found in *Meyer* and *Pierce* survived the Court's subsequent repudiation of economic substantive due process. And indeed, these cases form the foundation of subsequent decisions establishing important protections for the family and other decisions related to the family, including decisions about access to and use of contraception (Griswold v. Connecticut (1965) and Eisenstadt v. Baird (1972)) and abortion (Roe v. Wade (1973) and Planned Parenthood v. Casey (1992)).

2. Whose privacy? Does the nascent interest in privacy recognized in *Meyer* and *Pierce* belong to the family unit or to individual family members? Why? The attorney challenging the state law in *Meyer* argued that state authority over children was really about "to whom the child belongs" in the 1920s climate, with its rampant fears about the implications of state-controlled education for the family and society.[13] Does this background help assess why the Court extended protection for the parent-child relationship?

3. Slavery, families, and pluralism. Professor Peggy Cooper Davis emphasizes how *Meyer* and *Pierce*, rooted in antislavery traditions that originally produced the Fourteenth Amendment, promote pluralism. Slavery denied recognition and protection to ignored family relationships involving enslaved people. In so doing, it

---

[13]. Jeffery Shulman, *Meyer, Pierce*, and the History of the Entire Human Race: Barbarism, Social Progress, and (the Fall and Rise of) Parental Rights, 32 Hastings Const. L.Q. 337 (2016) (citing worries in the 1920s that the "state as educator would soon be able to take children from their parents and bring them up for its own ends and purposes").

compromised individual autonomy. The enactment of the Fourteenth Amendment, Davis continues, sought to repudiate this history and to confer protection for these important decisions, prohibiting slave parents from teaching chosen moral values to their children. By contrast, she continues, the autonomy recognized by *Meyer* and *Pierce* allows families room to make their own choices and embrace their own values.[14]

4. State interests. What reasons prompted enactment of the laws struck down in *Meyer* and *Pierce*? What standard of review does the Court use to evaluate the constitutionality of these laws? Why does the Court find the absence of an emergency in either case?

5. History. Professor Barbara Woodhouse explains that the Nebraska law in *Meyer* stemmed from post-World War I anti-German bias. At the time, 16 states had similar English-only laws. By contrast, the Oregon law at issue in *Pierce*, reflecting the movement for universal free public education, was influenced by egalitarian Populist notions, as well as anti-Catholic and anti-immigrant sentiments, common in the 1890s.[15]

6. Additional sources for procreative freedom. Roots of privacy and family autonomy can be found in Skinner v. Oklahoma, 316 U.S. 535 (1942), which invalidated as a denial of equal protection a statute punishing some incarcerated individuals with sterilization. The Court applied strict scrutiny because the statute "involves one of the basic civil rights of man" and inflicts permanent deprivation of "a basic liberty." This respect for procreative freedom contrasts with the Court's earlier approach in Buck v. Bell, 274 U.S. 200 (1927), upholding compulsory sterilization for an inmate of the State Colony for Epileptics and Feeble Minded, citing protection of the public welfare, and saying "[t]hree generations of imbeciles are enough." *Buck*, which generated considerable criticism, reflected the culmination of popular attraction to the eugenics movement that sought to improve the human race by curbing reproduction. Does state interference with the ability to procreate evoke the same analysis as interference with the ability to *avoid* procreation?

7. Modern applications. The U.S. Supreme Court subsequently reaffirmed the importance of *Meyer* and *Pierce* when it struck down the application of a broad third-party visitation statute in Troxel v. Granville, 530 U.S. 57 (2000) (reprinted in Chapter VIII). Although the latter case sharply divided the Court, several Justices took the opportunity both to reaffirm parents' fundamental liberty interest in childrearing and to note the changing nature of the American family. Are the assumptions that underpin parents' fundamental interest in childrearing still appropriate today? What is a "family" for purposes of understanding the rights articulated in *Meyer* and *Pierce*?

8. Contemporary controversies. In recent years, "parental rights" rhetoric has been invoked in the context of a number of high-profile controversies. During the early years of the COVID pandemic, for example, some parents claimed that laws

---

[14]. Peggy Cooper Davis, Contested Images of Family Values: The Role of the State, 107 Harv. L. Rev. 1348, 1361 (1994).

[15]. Barbara Bennett Woodhouse, "Who Owns the Child?": *Meyer* and *Pierce* and the Child as Property, 33 Wm. & Mary L. Rev. 995, 1004, 1017-1018 (1992).

or rules requiring children to be vaccinated and/or to mask violated their rights to make decisions about their children. Do requirements of this type impermissibly interfere with a parent's right to control the care and upbringing of their children? Are there state interests that are furthered by such policies and, if so, are those state interests sufficiently strong and furthered to justify any interference with parental rights? Another context reflecting this rhetoric involves transgender youth. See Problem 2 below. Compare Mirabelle v. Olson, 2023 WL 5976992 (S.D. Cal. 2023) (holding school that follows state policy that generally defers to students regarding whether the school should disclose to parents that the student identifies as transgender violates parents' constitutional rights), with Konen v. Caldeira, 2023 WL 4955143 (N.D. Cal. 2023) (contra).

Problems

1. Members of Congress proposed an amendment to the Constitution regarding parental rights. The Parental Rights Amendment (PRA) provides (in part) as follows:

- **Section 1.** The liberty of parents to direct the upbringing, education, and care of their children is a fundamental right.
- **Section 2.** The parental right to direct education includes the right to choose, as an alternative to public education, private, religious, or home schools, and the right to make reasonable choices within public schools for one's child.
- **Section 3.** Neither the United States nor any State shall infringe these rights without demonstrating that its governmental interest as applied to the person is of the highest order and not otherwise served. . . .

In introducing the amendment, Representative Jim Banks (R.-Ind.) noted: "Without fundamentally guaranteeing parental rights with a constitutional amendment, these natural rights of parents are left to the discretion and interpretation of government bureaucrats and elected officials. As the father of three young girls, I find the continual erosion of parental oversight and care in their children's lives unacceptable, and I urge my colleagues to join me in solidifying parental rights as a fundamental right protected by the U.S. Constitution."[16]

Although Congress previously considered versions of the PRA, the current proposal has generated considerably more support in today's political climate, especially regarding the debate surrounding vaccinations and teaching about race and racism, as well as LGBTQ issues in the schools. Religious groups and conservative parents' groups support the PRA.

You are a legislative aide given the task of drafting a memo on the issue of whether parental rights should be expressly enumerated in the Constitution. In your memo, consider the benefits and shortcomings of this amendment, as well as the appropriate role of government in assuring parental rights.

[16]. Press Release, Rep. Jim Banks Introduces Parental Rights Amendment to the U.S. Constitution, Jan. 20, 2019, https://banks.house.gov/news/documentsingle.aspx?DocumentID=451. See also Parental Rights Amendment, H.J. Res. 36, 116th Cong. (2019-2020).

2. Parents generally are entitled to make medical decisions for their children. This right is encompassed within parents' constitutionally protected right to control the care of their children. However, parental rights are not absolute. Where the parent's conduct places a child's health at risk, the state may intervene. In some cases, the state's attempt to override a parent's decision is prompted by a parent's *objection* to the provision of care where the state has reason to believe denial will place the child at risk. In other cases, state intervention is prompted by allegations that the parent is subjecting the child to *unnecessary* medical care.

Recently, the latter type of claim has been asserted in the context of health care for transgender children. In February 2022, Texas Attorney General Ken Paxton released an opinion in which he stated that any parent who "facilitate[d]" the provision of gender-affirming health care for their child "could be engaged in child abuse." Tex. Attorney General Op. No. KP-0401, 1, 12 (Feb. 18, 2022). This was followed by a directive from Texas Governor Greg Abbott directing state officials to investigate any allegations of such conduct. If a parent is found to have engaged in child abuse, the state may be authorized to remove the child from the home. In some cases, such abuse can lead to termination of parental rights.

Suppose the state removed a child based on evidence that the parent facilitated the provision of gender-affirming care for their child. Does that action impermissibly infringe parental rights? Does/should it matter that "[a] solid body of reliable research has shown that the potential next steps in gender-affirming care for adolescents with gender dysphoria—puberty-blocking medications and hormone therapy—have major mental-health benefits, including higher levels of general well-being and significantly decreased levels of suicidality."[17] See generally Maxine Eichner, Bad Medicine: Parents, the State, and the Charge of "Medical Child Abuse," 50 U.C. Davis L. Rev. 205 (2016).

3. Expansion of Privacy to Abortion

a. Abortion as a Protected Choice

ROE v. WADE
410 U.S. 113 (1973)

Justice BLACKMUN delivered the opinion of the Court. . . .

The Texas statutes that concern us here . . . make it a crime to "procure an abortion," as therein defined, or to attempt one, except with respect to "an

---

[17]. Yale School of Medicine, Dean's Advisory Council on LGBTQI+ Affairs, Biased Science: The Texas and Alabama Measures Criminalizing Medical Treatment for Transgender Children and Adolescents Rely on Inaccurate and Misleading Scientific Claims (Apr. 28, 2022), https://medicine .yale.edu/lgbtqi/research/gender-affirming-care/report%20on%20the%20science%20of%20 gender-affirming%20care%20final%20april%2028%202022_442952_55174_v1.pdf.

abortion procured or attempted by medical advice for the purpose of saving the life of the mother." Similar statutes are in existence in a majority of the States. . . .

[Jane Roe sued for a declaratory judgment that the Texas criminal abortion statutes were unconstitutional on their face and an injunction restraining their enforcement.] Roe alleged that she was unmarried and pregnant; that she wished to terminate her pregnancy by an abortion "performed by a competent, licensed physician, under safe, clinical conditions"; that she was unable to get a "legal" abortion in Texas because her life did not appear to be threatened by the continuation of her pregnancy; and that she could not afford to travel to another jurisdiction in order to secure a legal abortion under safe conditions. She claimed that the Texas statutes were unconstitutionally vague and that they abridged her right of personal privacy, protected by the First, Fourth, Fifth, Ninth, and Fourteenth Amendments. By an amendment to her complaint Roe purported to sue "on behalf of herself and all other women" similarly situated. [The district court held that the Ninth and Fourteenth Amendments protected the fundamental right to choose to have children and that the Texas statutes were unconstitutionally vague.]

The principal thrust of appellant's attack on the Texas statutes is that they improperly invade a right, said to be possessed by the pregnant woman, to choose to terminate her pregnancy. Appellant would discover this right in the concept of personal "liberty" embodied in the Fourteenth Amendment's Due Process Clause; or in personal marital, familial, and sexual privacy said to be protected by the Bill of Rights or its penumbras, see Griswold v. Connecticut, 381 U.S. 479 (1965); Eisenstadt v. Baird, 405 U.S. 438 (1972); id., at 460 (White, J., concurring in result); or among those rights reserved to the people by the Ninth Amendment, Griswold v. Connecticut, 381 U.S., at 486 (Goldberg J., concurring). Before addressing this claim, we feel it desirable briefly to survey, in several aspects, the history of abortion, for such insight as that history may afford us, and then to examine the state purposes and interests behind the criminal abortion laws.

VI

It perhaps is not generally appreciated that the restrictive criminal abortion laws in effect in a majority of States today are of relatively recent vintage. Those laws, generally proscribing abortion or its attempt at any time during pregnancy except when necessary to preserve the pregnant woman's life, are not of ancient or even of common-law origin. Instead, they derive from statutory changes effected, for the most part, in the latter half of the 19th century. . . .

[A]t common law, abortion performed before "quickening" — the first recognizable movement of the fetus in utero, appearing usually from the 16th to the 18th week of pregnancy — was not an indictable offense. The absence of a common-law crime for prequickening abortion appears to have developed from a confluence of earlier philosophical, theological, and civil and canon law concepts of when life begins.

[I]n a frequently cited passage, [seventeenth-century British jurist Sir Edward Coke] took the position that abortion of a woman "quick with childe" is "a great misprision, and no murder." . . . A recent review of the common-law precedents argues, however, that those precedents contradict Coke and that even postquickening abortion was never established as a common-law crime. This is of some importance because while most American courts ruled, in holding or dictum, that abortion of an unquickened fetus was not criminal under their received common law, others followed Coke in stating that abortion of a quick fetus was a "misprision," a term they translated to mean "misdemeanor." That their reliance on Coke on this aspect of the law was uncritical and, apparently in all the reported cases, dictum (due probably to the paucity of common-law prosecutions for postquickening abortion), makes it now appear doubtful that abortion was ever firmly established as a common-law crime even with respect to the destruction of a quick fetus.

. . . England's first criminal abortion statute, Lord Ellenborough's Act, 43 Geo. 3, c. 58, came in 1803. It made abortion of a quick fetus, §1, a capital crime, but in §2 it provided lesser penalties for the felony of abortion before quickening, and thus preserved the "quickening" distinction. . . .

In this country, the law in effect in all but a few States until mid-19th century was the preexisting English common law. Connecticut, the first State to enact abortion legislation, adopted in 1821 that part of Lord Ellenborough's Act that related to a woman "quick with child." The death penalty was not imposed. Abortion before quickening was made a crime in that State only in 1860. In 1828, New York enacted legislation that, in two respects, was to serve as a model for early anti-abortion statutes. First, while barring destruction of an unquickened fetus as well as a quick fetus, it made the former only a misdemeanor, but the latter second-degree manslaughter. Second, it incorporated a concept of therapeutic abortion [necessary to save the life of the woman]. By 1840, when Texas had received the common law, only eight American States had statutes dealing with abortion. . . .

Gradually, in the middle and late 19th century the quickening distinction disappeared from the statutory law of most States and the degree of the offense and the penalties were increased. By the end of the 1950's, a large majority of the jurisdictions banned abortion, however and whenever performed, unless done to save or preserve the life of the mother. The exceptions, Alabama and the District of Columbia, permitted abortion to preserve the mother's health. . . . In the past several years, however, a trend toward liberalization of abortion statutes has resulted in adoption, by about one-third of the States, of less stringent laws, most of them patterned after the ALI Model Penal Code, §230.3. . . .

It is thus apparent that at common law, at the time of the adoption of our Constitution, and throughout the major portion of the 19th century, abortion was viewed with less disfavor than under most American statutes currently in effect. Phrasing it another way, a woman enjoyed a substantially broader right to terminate a pregnancy than she does in most States today. [The opinion then noted that the American Medical Association, American Public Health Association, and American Bar Association all supported liberalizing abortion laws.]

VII

Three reasons have been advanced to explain historically the enactment of criminal abortion laws in the 19th century and to justify their continued existence.

It has been argued occasionally that these laws were the product of a Victorian social concern to discourage illicit sexual conduct. Texas, however, does not advance this justification in the present case, and it appears that no court or commentator has taken the argument seriously. . . .

A second reason is concerned with abortion as a medical procedure. When most criminal abortion laws were first enacted, the procedure was a hazardous one for the woman. . . . Thus, it has been argued that a State's real concern in enacting a criminal abortion law was to protect the pregnant woman, that is, to restrain her from submitting to a procedure that placed her life in serious jeopardy.

Modern medical techniques have altered this situation. Appellants and various amici refer to medical data indicating that abortion in early pregnancy, that is, prior to the end of the first trimester, although not without its risk, is now relatively safe. Mortality rates for women undergoing early abortions, where the procedure is legal, appear to be as low as or lower than the rates for normal childbirth. Consequently, any interest of the State in protecting the woman from an inherently hazardous procedure, except when it would be equally dangerous for her to forgo it, has largely disappeared. Of course, important state interests in the areas of health and medical standards do remain. The State has a legitimate interest in seeing to it that abortion, like any other medical procedure, is performed under circumstances that insure maximum safety for the patient. . . . The prevalence of high mortality rates at illegal "abortion mills" strengthens, rather than weakens, the State's interest in regulating the conditions under which abortions are performed. Moreover, the risk to the woman increases as her pregnancy continues. Thus, the State retains a definite interest in protecting the woman's own health and safety when an abortion is proposed at a late stage of pregnancy.

The third reason is the State's interest — some phrase it in terms of duty — in protecting prenatal life. Some of the argument for this justification rests on the theory that a new human life is present from the moment of conception. The State's interest and general obligation to protect life then extends, it is argued, to prenatal life. Only when the life of the pregnant mother herself is at stake, balanced against the life she carries within her, should the interest of the embryo or fetus not prevail. . . . In assessing the State's interest, recognition may be given to the . . . claim that as long as at least *potential* life is involved, the State may assert interests beyond the protection of the pregnant woman alone.

Parties challenging state abortion laws have sharply disputed in some courts the contention that a purpose of these laws, when enacted, was to protect prenatal life. Pointing to the absence of legislative history to support the contention, they claim that most state laws were designed solely to protect the woman. Proponents of this view point out that in many States, including Texas, by statute or judicial interpretation, the pregnant woman herself could not be prosecuted for self-abortion or for cooperating in an abortion performed upon her by another. They claim that adoption of the "quickening" distinction through received common law and state statutes tacitly recognizes the greater health hazards inherent in late abortion and impliedly repudiates the theory that life begins at conception.

It is with these interests, and the weight to be attached to them, that this case is concerned.

VIII

The Constitution does not explicitly mention any right of privacy. In a line of decisions, however, going back perhaps as far as Union Pacific R. Co. v. Botsford, 141 U.S. 250, 251 (1891), the Court has recognized that a right of personal privacy, or a guarantee of certain areas or zones of privacy, does exist under the Constitution. In varying contexts, the Court or individual Justices have, indeed, found at least the roots of that right in the First Amendment, Stanley v. Georgia,

394 U.S. 557, 564 (1969); in the Fourth and Fifth Amendments; in the penumbras of the Bill of Rights, Griswold v. Connecticut, 381 U.S., at 484-485; in the Ninth Amendment, id., at 486 (Goldberg, J., concurring); or in the concept of liberty guaranteed by the first section of the Fourteenth Amendment, see Meyer v. Nebraska, 262 U.S. 390, 399 (1923). These decisions make it clear that only personal rights that can be deemed "fundamental" or "implicit in the concept of ordered liberty," are included in this guarantee of personal privacy. They also make it clear that the right has some extension to activities relating to marriage, procreation, contraception, family relationships, and child rearing and education [citing *Meyer, Pierce, Eisenstadt, Skinner,* and Loving v. Virginia, 388 U.S. 1 (1967)].

This right of privacy, whether it be founded in the Fourteenth Amendment's concept of personal liberty and restrictions upon state action, as we feel it is, or, as the District Court determined, in the Ninth Amendment's reservation of rights to the people, is broad enough to encompass a woman's decision whether or not to terminate her pregnancy. The detriment that the State would impose upon the pregnant woman by denying this choice altogether is apparent. Specific and direct harm medically diagnosable even in early pregnancy may be involved. Maternity, or additional offspring, may force upon the woman a distressful life and future. Psychological harm may be imminent. Mental and physical health may be taxed by child care. There is also the distress, for all concerned, associated with the unwanted child, and there is the problem of bringing a child into a family already unable, psychologically and otherwise, to care for it. In other cases, as in this one, the additional difficulties and continuing stigma of unwed motherhood may be involved. All these are factors the woman and her responsible physician necessarily will consider in consultation.

On the basis of elements such as these, appellant and some amici argue that the woman's right is absolute and that she is entitled to terminate her pregnancy at whatever time, in whatever way, and for whatever reason she alone chooses. With this we do not agree. Appellant's arguments that Texas either has no valid interest at all in regulating the abortion decision, or no interest strong enough to support any limitation upon the woman's sole determination, are unpersuasive. The Court's decisions recognizing a right of privacy also acknowledge that some state regulation in areas protected by that right is appropriate. As noted above, a State may properly assert important interests in safeguarding health, in maintaining medical standards, and in protecting potential life. At some point in pregnancy, these respective interests become sufficiently compelling to sustain regulation of the factors that govern the abortion decision. The privacy right involved, therefore, cannot be said to be absolute. In fact, it is not clear to us that the claim asserted by some amici that one has an unlimited right to do with one's body as one pleases bears a close relationship to the right of privacy previously articulated in the Court's decisions. The Court has refused to recognize an unlimited right of this kind in the past. Jacobson v. Massachusetts, 197 U.S. 11 (1905) (vaccination); Buck v. Bell, 274 U.S. 200 (1927) (sterilization).

We therefore conclude that the right of personal privacy includes the abortion decision, but that this right is not unqualified and must be considered against important state interests in regulation. . . . Where certain "fundamental rights" are involved, the Court has held that regulation limiting these rights may be justified only by a "compelling state interest," and that legislative enactments must be narrowly drawn to express only the legitimate state interests at stake. . . .

IX . . .

The appellee and certain amici argue that the fetus is a "person" within the language and meaning of the Fourteenth Amendment. In support of this, they outline at length and in detail the well-known facts of fetal development. If this suggestion of personhood is established, the appellant's case, of course, collapses, for the fetus' right to life would then be guaranteed specifically by the Amendment. . . .

The Constitution does not define "person" in so many words. Section 1 of the Fourteenth Amendment contains three references to "person." The first, in defining "citizens," speaks of "persons born or naturalized in the United States." The word also appears both in the Due Process Clause and in the Equal Protection Clause. "Person" is used in other places in the Constitution. . . . But in nearly all these instances, the use of the word is such that it has application only postnatally. None indicates, with any assurance, that it has any possible prenatal application.[54] All this, together with our observation, supra, that throughout the major portion of the 19th century prevailing legal abortion practices were far freer than they are today, persuades us that the word "person," as used in the Fourteenth Amendment, does not include the unborn. . . .

The pregnant woman cannot be isolated in her privacy. She carries an embryo and, later, a fetus. . . . The situation therefore is inherently different from marital intimacy, or bedroom possession of obscene material, or marriage, or procreation, or education, with which *Eisenstadt* and *Griswold, Stanley, Loving, Skinner* and *Pierce* and *Meyer* were respectively concerned. As we have intimated above, it is reasonable and appropriate for a State to decide that at some point in time another interest, that of health of the mother or that of potential human life, becomes significantly involved. The woman's privacy is no longer sole and any right of privacy she possesses must be measured accordingly.

Texas urges that, apart from the Fourteenth Amendment, life begins at conception and is present throughout pregnancy, and that, therefore, the State has a compelling interest in protecting that life from and after conception. We need not resolve the difficult question of when life begins. When those trained in the respective disciplines of medicine, philosophy, and theology are unable to arrive at any consensus, the judiciary, at this point in the development of man's knowledge, is not in a position to speculate as to the answer.

It should be sufficient to note briefly the wide divergence of thinking on this most sensitive and difficult question. There has always been strong support for the view that life does not begin until live birth [citing the Stoics and the Jewish and Protestant communities]. As we have noted, the common law found greater significance in quickening. Physicians and their scientific colleagues have

---

54. When Texas urges that a fetus is entitled to Fourteenth Amendment protection as a person, it faces a dilemma. Neither in Texas nor in any other State are all abortions prohibited. Despite broad proscription, [a therapeutic] exception always exists. . . . But if the fetus is a person who is not to be deprived of life without due process of law, and if the mother's condition is the sole determinant, does not the Texas exception appear to be out of line with the Amendment's command? There are other inconsistencies between Fourteenth Amendment status and the typical abortion statute. It has already been pointed out that in Texas the woman is not a principal or an accomplice with respect to an abortion upon her. If the fetus is a person, why is the woman not a principal or an accomplice? Further, the penalty for criminal abortion . . . is significantly less than the maximum penalty for murder. . . . If the fetus is a person, may the penalties be different?

regarded that event with less interest and have tended to focus either upon conception, upon live birth, or upon the interim point at which the fetus becomes "viable," that is, potentially able to live outside the mother's womb, albeit with artificial aid. Viability is usually placed at about seven months (28 weeks) but may occur earlier, even at 24 weeks. [T]he existence of life from the moment of conception [is] the official belief of the Catholic Church. [T]his is a view strongly held by many non-Catholics as well, and by many physicians. Substantial problems for precise definition of this view are posed, however, by new embryological data that purport to indicate that conception is a "process" over time, rather than an event, and by new medical techniques such as menstrual extraction, the "morning-after" pill, implantation of embryos, artificial insemination, and even artificial wombs.

In areas other than criminal abortion, the law has been reluctant to endorse any theory that life, as we recognize it, begins before live birth or to accord legal rights to the unborn except in narrowly defined situations and except when the rights are contingent upon live birth [citing tort and property law]. In short, the unborn have never been recognized in the law as persons in the whole sense.

X

In view of all this, we do not agree that, by adopting one theory of life, Texas may override the rights of the pregnant woman that are at stake. We repeat, however, that the State does have an important and legitimate interest in preserving and protecting the health of the pregnant woman, whether she be a resident of the State or a non-resident who seeks medical consultation and treatment there, and that it has still another important and legitimate interest in protecting the potentiality of human life. These interests are separate and distinct. Each grows in substantiality as the woman approaches term and, at a point during pregnancy, each becomes "compelling."

With respect to the State's important and legitimate interest in the health of the mother, the "compelling" point, in the light of present medical knowledge, is at approximately the end of the first trimester. This is so because of the now-established medical fact . . . that until the end of the first trimester mortality in abortion may be less than mortality in normal childbirth. It follows that, from and after this point, a State may regulate the abortion procedure to the extent that the regulation reasonably relates to the preservation and protection of maternal health [for example, by requiring licensure of abortion providers or certain facilities].

This means, on the other hand, that, for the period of pregnancy prior to this "compelling" point, the attending physician, in consultation with his patient, is free to determine, without regulation by the State, that, in his medical judgment, the patient's pregnancy should be terminated. If that decision is reached, the judgment may be effectuated by an abortion free of interference by the State.

With respect to the State's important and legitimate interest in potential life, the "compelling" point is at viability. This is so because the fetus then presumably has the capability of meaningful life outside the mother's womb. State regulation protective of fetal life after viability thus has both logical and biological justifications. If the State is interested in protecting fetal life after viability, it may go so far as to proscribe abortion during that period, except when it is necessary to preserve the life or health of the mother. . . .

XI

To summarize and to repeat:

1. A state criminal abortion statute of the current Texas type, that excepts from criminality only a *life-saving* procedure on behalf of the mother, without regard to pregnancy stage and without recognition of the other interests involved, is violative of the Due Process Clause of the Fourteenth Amendment.

(a) For the stage prior to approximately the end of the first trimester, the abortion decision and its effectuation must be left to the medical judgment of the pregnant woman's attending physician.

(b) For the stage subsequent to approximately the end of the first trimester, the State, in promoting its interest in the health of the mother, may, if it chooses, regulate the abortion procedure in ways that are reasonably related to maternal health.

(c) For the stage subsequent to viability, the State in promoting its interest in the potentiality of human life may, if it chooses, regulate, and even proscribe, abortion except where it is necessary, in appropriate medical judgment, for the preservation of the life or health of the mother. . . .

This holding, we feel, is consistent with the relative weights of the respective interests involved, with the lessons and examples of medical and legal history, with the lenity of the common law, and with the demands of the profound problems of the present day. The decision leaves the State free to place increasing restrictions on abortion as the period of pregnancy lengthens, so long as those restrictions are tailored to the recognized state interests. The decision vindicates the right of the physician to administer medical treatment according to his professional judgment up to the points where important state interests provide compelling justifications for intervention. Up to those points, the abortion decision in all its aspects is inherently, and primarily, a medical decision, and basic responsibility for it must rest with the physician. . . .

Justice Rehnquist, dissenting. . . .

I have difficulty in concluding, as the Court does, that the right of "privacy" is involved in this case. Texas, by the statute here challenged, bars the performance of a medical abortion by a licensed physician on a plaintiff such as Roe. A transaction resulting in an operation such as this is not "private" in the ordinary usage of that word. Nor is the "privacy" that the Court finds here even a distant relative of the freedom from searches and seizures protected by the Fourth Amendment to the Constitution, which the Court has referred to as embodying a right to privacy. Katz v. United States, 389 U.S. 347 (1967).

The fact that a majority of the States reflecting, after all, the majority sentiment in those States, have had restrictions on abortions for at least a century is a strong indication, it seems to me, that the asserted right to an abortion is not "so rooted in the traditions and conscience of our people as to be ranked as fundamental," Snyder v. Massachusetts, 291 U.S. 97, 105 (1934). . . . To reach its result, the Court necessarily has had to find within the scope of the Fourteenth Amendment a right that was apparently completely unknown to the drafters of the Amendment. [T]he drafters did not intend to have the Fourteenth Amendment withdraw from the States the power to legislate with respect to this matter. . . .

NOTE: WHO WERE JANE ROE AND HENRY WADE?

Norma McCorvey, also known as "Jane Roe"

The name "Jane Roe," from Roe v. Wade, was a pseudonym. Her real name was Norma McCorvey. McCorvey died in 2017 at the age of 69. Her story and her own views on abortion are complex. As McCorvey herself put it in her autobiography, "I wasn't the wrong person to become Jane Roe . . . I wasn't the right person to become Jane Roe. I was just the person who became Jane Roe, of Roe v. Wade. . . .And my life story, warts and all, was a little piece of history."[18]

McCorvey had a difficult life. "By her own account, she was the unwanted child of a broken home, a ninth-grade dropout who was raped repeatedly by a relative, and a homeless runaway[.]"[19] After becoming pregnant for the third time in 1969 at the age of 22, McCorvey unsuccessfully sought an abortion. Eventually, she was put in contact with Sarah Weddington and Linda Coffee, the young attorneys who litigated the case on behalf of "Roe." Although her lawyers won her case, by the time it was decided, McCorvey had long since given birth and placed the child for adoption.

For about a decade after the decision, McCorvey remained largely unknown. But in the 1980s, McCorvey publicly identified herself as Jane Roe and began speaking to the media. About a decade later, however, McCorvey's life shifted dramatically; she became a born-again Christian and an abortion rights opponent. Indeed, in 2005, 30 years after Roe, McCorvey asked the Supreme Court to overrule the famous decision bearing her name. According to writer David Garrow, author of Liberty and Sexuality: The Right to Privacy and the Making of Roe v. Wade, McCorvey's transformation from abortion rights supporter to abortion rights opponent "had to do with her feelings of being treated like poor, working-class, white trash,"[20] including by abortion rights supporters. McCorvey later reported in the movie AKA Jane Roe, however, that her shift to abortion rights opponent was not genuine; it was an act. She said that she was paid a total of almost $500,000 by Operation Rescue, an anti-abortion organization, "to pretend that the most famous name in the pro-choice movement had seen the error of her ways."[21]

---

[18]. Norma McCorvey, with Andy Meisler, I Am Roe: My Life, Roe v. Wade, and Freedom of Choice (1994).

[19]. Robert D. McFadden, Norma McCorvey, "Roe" in Roe v. Wade, Is Dead at 69, N.Y. Times, Feb. 18, 2017, https://www.nytimes.com/2017/02/18/obituaries/norma-mccorvey-dead-roe-v-wade.html.

[20]. Cited in Mary Rourke & Emily Alpert Reyes, Norma McCorvey, Once-Anonymous Plaintiff in Landmark Roe vs. Wade Abortion Case, Dies at 69, L.A. Times, Feb. 18, 2017, https://www.latimes.com/local/obituaries/la-me-norma-mccorvey-snap-story.html.

[21]. Michelle Ruiz, Who Was Jane Roe? A New Documentary Tries to Answer That Question, Vogue Mag., May 22, 2020, https://www.vogue.com/article/who-was-the-real-jane-roe-documentary-fx.

"I think it was a mutual thing," McCorvey said, "I took their money, and they put me out in front of the cameras and told me what to say, and that's what I'd say."[22]

Henry Wade was the district attorney of Dallas County, Texas, from 1951 to 1987. In addition to *Roe*, his office handled some other high-profile cases, including the prosecution of Jack Ruby, the man who shot and killed Lee Harvey Oswald (who was the person who shot and killed President John F. Kennedy). By some measures, Wade was very successful in his role. He "never lost a case he personally tried."[23] Others, however, view this record differently. Ronald Huff, the director of the Criminal Justice Research Center at the Ohio State University, said that Dallas County seemed "to convict an unusual number of innocent people."[24] It has been suggested that this may have been due in part to Wade's practice of tying "employees' promotions to the number of people they put behind bars and the length of their sentences."[25]

In terms of the Roe v. Wade case itself, while it was Wade's responsibility to enforce the Texas abortion ban within the county, Wade was not an anti-abortion crusader. According to Marian Faux, author of Roe v. Wade: The Untold Story of the Landmark Supreme Court Decision that Made Abortion Legal, Wade's office "had instigated virtually no abortion prosecutions."[26] According to writer David J. Garrow, Wade later acknowledged that "in some cases abortion is justified."[27]

NOTE: WHO WAS SARAH WEDDINGTON?

Sarah Weddington, A Question of Choice: Roe v. Wade 40th Anniversary Edition Revised and Updated[28]
14-16, 39-43, 49-62 (2013)

My mouth goes dry as I put myself back in those days in Austin [Texas, in 1967] when my period was late. I was in my third year of law school, going to school full-time and supporting myself by working several jobs. I was seriously dating Ron Weddington, who was finishing his undergraduate degree after returning from the army; he was planning to start law school the following summer. . . .

[Once my pregnancy was confirmed, we] began to go over the possibilities. Abortion was one, but we were worried about the risks of an illegal procedure. . . .

---

[22]. Id.
[23]. Michael S. Rosenwald, The Remarkable Story of Henry Wade, Abortion Case's Namesake, Wash. Post, June 25, 2022, https://www.washingtonpost.com/history/2022/06/25/henry-wade-roe-texas-prosecutor/.
[24]. Michelle Mittelstadt, Dallas County Justice Blind – and Fallible, Denver Rocky Mountain News, July 21, 1990.
[25]. Id.
[26]. Rosenwald, supra note [23].
[27]. Id.
[28]. Sarah Weddington died on December 26, 2021.

Sarah Weddington, the attorney who argued
Roe v. Wade before the Supreme Court

If we decided on abortion, the next problem was: Where to go? There were no ads in the phone books or newspapers; this was all undercover. You had to find someone who knew a name, a place — and I refused to tell anyone my situation. . . . Ron [heard] about a doctor in Piedras Negras, across [the Mexican border]. The doctor had some medical experience in the United States, spoke excellent English, and performed abortions. Abortion was illegal in Mexico, but the woman Ron spoke to told him [that] several women she knew had been to this doctor, and everything had turned out fine. He charged $400 — cash only. [Ron made the necessary arrangements, obtained a powerful painkiller, and got the name of someone who might help in case of medical trouble.]

I was grateful that at least the inside of the building was clean. I could not read what appeared to be a medical diploma on the wall, but it made me feel better. . . . I was one of the lucky ones. [W]hen I felt the anesthesia taking effect, my last thoughts were: I hope I don't die, and I pray that no one ever finds out about this. . . .

Roe v. Wade started at a garage sale, amid paltry castoffs. [Weddington and her friends were raising money for an abortion referral project.] The referral project volunteers were worried about being involved in covert activity. . . . While we sorted our prized junk at the garage sale, Judy [Smith] posed the primary questions that the volunteers wanted answered: Could they be prosecuted and/or convicted as accomplices to the crime of abortion simply for referring women? Would it make any legal difference if they sent women only to places where abortion was legal? . . . The [Texas] statute made it a crime to "furnish the means for procuring an abortion," but I didn't know whether that applied only to drugs and instruments, not information. I knew Texas also had a general accomplice statute that applied to a variety of crimes.

[I began spending time in the University of Texas] law library, meeting with project volunteers, spending more time in the library, and talking to law professors, law students, and other lawyers. [One day] Judy announced that she wanted a lawsuit filed to challenge the constitutionality of the Texas anti-abortion statute.

[I] had not focused on the possibility of *our* filing a lawsuit. After all, my total legal experience consisted of a few uncontested divorces for friends, ten or twelve uncomplicated wills for people with little property, one adoption for relatives, and a few miscellaneous matters. . . . The idea of challenging the Texas abortion law in federal court was overwhelming [but] I was the best free legal help available [and I wanted to help others avoid what we had gone through]. [P]erhaps my inexperience was a plus. I did not fully appreciate that the odds were stacked against our endeavor.

[Weddington asked former classmate Linda Coffee, who was familiar with federal litigation, to help.] [O]ur constant worry was about the right plaintiffs. . . . Then a woman went to Dallas lawyer Henry McCluskey, a friend of Linda's who knew of the proposed lawsuit. . . . She had had a rough life: She already had one child and did not want another. Her mother had taken her daughter away from her and she seldom got to see her. She had never finished the tenth grade, was working as a waitress, and knew she would lose her job if the pregnancy continued. She could barely support herself, much less a child. . . .

She had found an illegal place in Dallas, she admitted, but she didn't like the looks of it. She had no money to travel to another state. As the conversation continued [in our meeting at a Dallas pizza parlor, this woman] asked if it would help if she had been raped. We said no; the Texas law had no exception for rape. It was just as illegal for a doctor to do an abortion for someone who had been raped as it was in any other situation. I did ask, "Were there any witnesses? Was there a police report? Is there any way that we could prove a rape occurred?" Her answer in each instance was no.

Neither Linda nor I questioned her further about how she had gotten pregnant. I was not going to allege something in the complaint that I could not back up with proof. Also, we did not want the Texas law changed only to allow abortion in cases of rape. We wanted a decision that abortion was covered by the right of privacy. After all, the women coming to the referral project were there as a result of a wide variety of circumstances. . . .

We still had to name our plaintiffs [who would use pseudonyms to protect their privacy]. We picked names that rhymed. I liked "Jane Roe." To me the name represented all women, not just one. . . . We filed . . . against Henry Wade, the elected district attorney of Dallas County, the official responsible for law enforcement in that county. We wanted the court to tell Wade's office to leave doctors alone. [The case] became known as *Roe v. Wade.* . . .

Brief for the Amici Curiae Women Who Have Had Abortions and Friends of Amici Curiae in Support of Appellees, Webster v. Reproductive Health Services
492 U.S. 490 (1989) (No. 88-605)

Friends Letter — 172, At C29-30

When I was six years old, I was forced to endure a 40-mile trip to what was referred to as "Feather Annie's." I stayed in the car with my father and two brothers while my 41-year-old mother went inside the private residence. My father's serious attitude instilled fear and insecurity in my older brother and I. When my mother returned to the car she was crying. She repeated the words "I'm afraid I'll die — I'm afraid someone will find out I came here and I'll get her (referring to the woman who performed the abortion) in trouble with the law. I'm glad it's over, but I'm afraid — if I die, what will happen to the children?" It was an awful experience for a child who was too young to understand. All the way home she cried and repeated over and over her fear of dying. I do not remember . . . her expressing any regret, she expressed her relief that it was over. Her fears became contagious and needless to say it was traumatic for me and my older brother (one brother was less than 2 years old). Many years later when my brother and I recalled that day, we agreed that the only crime committed was by a society that forced a woman to have to submit herself to fear and agony of that magnitude. Our mother survived and imbued in us forever was our sympathy for her on that day. After all, she had already born six children, she was in poor health, and my father was unemployed in that year of 1936.

My mother told me that it was a terrible tragedy that the little 2 year old neighbor girl's mother died suddenly. When I became old enough to understand I found out that it was no secret, in the small town we lived in, that the young mother had died from a self-managed abortion. As a very young child I was terribly disturbed over the fact that this dear cute little girl had no mother for the reason that her mother had died because she didn't want to have another baby. I felt sad that such a thing could happen, it was hard for me to accept that "Jane's" pretty young mother had to die. I saw sadness in Jane's face and unhappiness was apparent in her father's behavior. I cannot justify a law that allowed such unfortunate circumstances to happen.

In the 1950's my sister lost a good friend who had an illegal abortion. The 28 year old woman who died had five small children. Her unplanned and unwanted pregnancy was more than she was able to handle and her untimely death was the result of not having a choice of a safe and legal abortion. A law with the potential effect of depriving a loving husband and five small children of the presence of a young wife and mother is a disgrace in a compassionate society.

Notes and Questions

1. *Roe*'s right. What is the nature of the right recognized by Roe v. Wade? Its parameters? Where in the Constitution does *Roe* situate this right? How does this approach compare with that of *Griswold*? Why is the right to terminate a pregnancy not absolute? Why is it "fundamental" (thereby evoking the compelling state interest test)? Over the years, *Roe*'s recognition of an abortion right has become a prominent basis of criticism for its so-called judicial activism. What are the costs of constitutionalizing abortion, instead of achieving abortion rights through legislative and political change?[29]

[29]. See Robin West, From Choice to Reproductive Justice: De-constitutionalizing Abortion Rights, 118 Yale L.J. 1394, 1409 (2009).

2. *Roe*'s precedents. Does the protection of childrearing and education in *Meyer* and *Pierce* support *Roe*'s holding? Does the right to abortion in *Roe* flow directly from *Griswold*? Does the right to privacy identified in *Eisenstadt* necessarily include abortion? Historical accounts attribute Justice Brennan's choice of the "*bear* or beget" language in *Eisenstadt* to his anticipation of the abortion cases.[30]

3. From privacy to liberty. In *Roe*, the Court at least tentatively grounds the right in the "liberty" protections extended by the Fourteenth Amendment's Due Process Clause. In subsequent cases, including Lawrence v. Texas (2003) and Obergefell v. Hodges (2015), the Court abandoned the privacy language altogether. Is "liberty" a better home or frame for the range of "fundamental" rights recognized by the Supreme Court, including the right to marry, protections for the parent-child relationship, and the right to access and use contraception?

4. Abortion restrictions. Two types of statutory restrictions were common in the *Roe* era. One type, like the Texas statute, prohibited abortion except to save the life of the pregnant person. A subsequent type, modeled on the American Law Institute's (ALI) Model Penal Code, permitted abortion if pregnancy would seriously and permanently injure the pregnant person's health; if the fetus suffered from a grave, permanent, and irremediable mental or physical defect; or if the pregnancy resulted from rape. In a companion case to *Roe*, Doe v. Bolton, 410 U.S. 179 (1973), the Court invalidated Georgia's ALI-inspired statute, including its procedural requirements of hospitalization, accreditation, committee approval, two-doctor concurrence, and residency.

5. Viability. Many early abortion restrictions disallowed abortions only after quickening (the first perception of fetal movement, usually between 16 and 18 weeks of gestation). Although quickening had no biological significance, it became important, in the absence of pregnancy tests, as the first indication of pregnancy. Without such evidence, prosecutors could not establish the elements of criminal abortion. *Roe* emphasizes viability rather than quickening. Why? Does the Court satisfactorily explain why the state's interest in protecting "potential life" becomes compelling only after viability?

In 1973, *Roe* placed viability at approximately 28 weeks. More recent studies suggest that prematurely born babies can survive outside the womb as early as 22 weeks of gestation.[31] In a post-*Roe* Supreme Court case, Justice Sandra Day O'Connor suggested, in a dissenting opinion, that this prospect put *Roe* on a "collision course" with itself. City of Akron v. Akron Ctr. for Reprod. Health, 462 U.S. 416, 458 (1983). What does her criticism mean?

---

[30]. David J. Garrow, Liberty and Sexuality: The Right to Privacy and the Making of Roe v. Wade 541-544 (updated ed. 1998).

[31]. Ruthann Richter, Premature Babies' Survival Rate Is Climbing, Study Says, Stanford Med. Blog, Feb. 10, 2022, https://healthier.stanfordchildrens.org/en/premature-babies-survival-rate-is-climbing/.

6. Physician's role. According to *Roe*, to whom does the privacy right belong — the pregnant person or the physician? What role *should* a physician play in the decision to terminate a pregnancy?

7. Gender equality. What alternative theoretical approaches might the Supreme Court have used? Some feminist commentators prefer an equal protection rather than a due process privacy/liberty-based approach on the theory that abortion freedom is essential for gender equality. For example, Professor Sylvia Law argues:

> Nothing the Supreme Court has ever done has been more concretely important for women [than Roe v. Wade]. Laws denying access to abortion have a sex-specific impact. Although both men and women seek to control reproduction, only women become pregnant. Only women have abortions. Laws restricting access to abortion have a devastating sex-specific impact. Despite the decision's overwhelming importance to women, it was not grounded on the principle of sex equality.[32]

Professor Reva Siegel takes this argument one step further. She contends that early proponents *intended* abortion restrictions to reinforce sex-based and sex-stereotyped roles for women:

> Those who advocated restricting women's access to abortion in the nineteenth century were interested in enforcing women's roles, an objective they justified with arguments concerning women's bodies. Analyzing the historical record reveals how social discourses concerning women's roles have converged with physiological discourses concerning women's bodies, as two distinct but compatible ways of reasoning about women's obligations as mothers. . . . Considered from this perspective, abortion-restrictive regulation presents many of the concerns that have traditionally triggered heightened equal protection scrutiny.[33]

What are the advantages and disadvantages of an equal protection rationale for the right to abortion? Proponents of this approach include Justice Ruth Bader Ginsburg, who as a litigator persuaded the Supreme Court to apply the Equal Protection Clause to gender discrimination.

8. State interest in potential life. How far should the state go in protecting *potential* life? Professor Frances Olsen ponders this question:

> How would men react to a law that forbad them to ejaculate outside a fertile woman's vagina? While most heterosexual men would probably prefer to ejaculate into a vagina, the idea that they could not ejaculate anywhere else would probably come to seem oppressive and absurd to them. Yet such a law would seem to promote a state interest in *potential life*, as well as a state interest in the life of sperm. To avoid overbreadth, the law could provide that if a man does ejaculate where he is not allowed to, he could avoid criminal liability by collecting as many of the sperm as possible and rushing them to a sperm bank. . . .

---

[32]. Sylvia A. Law, Rethinking Sex and the Constitution, 132 U. Pa. L. Rev. 955, 980-981, 1007 (1984).

[33]. Reva Siegel, Reasoning from the Body: A Historical Perspective on Abortion Regulation and Questions of Equal Protection, 44 Stan. L. Rev. 261, 265 (1992).

Of course, the burden such a law would place upon men is nothing like the burden that antiabortion laws place upon women. Many men would not be affected at all; other men would simply have to make periodic trips to sperm banks [that] would disrupt no one's life. . . . Many people would consider this example silly, but this putative silliness reflects the value that society places upon men's lives and their freedom. Only convenience prevents us from valuing sperm.[34]

9. Abortion and motherhood. Sociologist Kristin Luker attributes the sharp differences concerning abortion to a war over opposing visions of motherhood. Generally, the pro-choice position embraces feminist and progressive objectives, including equal opportunities in education and employment, freedom from gender-based assumptions, and the elimination of paternalism. By contrast, abortion opponents do not regard equality as a primary value because "they believe that men and women are intrinsically different [with] different roles in life" and that "motherhood — the raising of children and families — is the most fulfilling role that women can have."[35] What insights does this analysis provide in evaluating *Roe*? In understanding the controversy that persists today? Can one argue that abortion freedom advances respect for motherhood? Does the protection of childrearing in *Meyer* and *Pierce*, supra, support this argument?

10. Abortion and crime. Two economists cite empirical evidence to claim that legalizing abortion explains large decreases in crime.[36] The authors theorize that abortion prevented the birth of unwanted children who would have grown up to commit crimes. What relevance, if any, do such findings have for the legal and constitutional questions posed by *Roe*?

11. Abortion funding. Following Roe v. Wade, federal and state lawmakers found ways to make abortion more difficult to access by restricting public funding for the procedure. The most important restriction was the Hyde Amendment, implemented in 1977, which banned the use of federal funds for abortion through the Medicaid program (with exceptions for rape, incest, and endangerment of the life of the pregnant person). The Hyde Amendment left millions of women, especially low-income women and women of color, without coverage for abortion. Challenges to this restriction came swiftly.

In 1977, the Supreme Court decided three cases permitting states to refuse Medicaid coverage for nontherapeutic abortions: Beal v. Doe, 432 U.S. 438 (1977); Maher v. Roe, 432 U.S. 464 (1977); and Poelker v. Doe, 432 U.S. 519 (1977). Although the government subsidized medical services for pregnancy and childbirth, but not abortion, for the indigent, the majority in *Maher* found no "unduly burdensome interference" with the abortion decision, distinguishing the "obstacle" invalidated in *Roe*. Treating the refusal to fund abortion as state inaction calling for the rational basis test (rather than *Roe*'s strict scrutiny standard),

---

[34]. Frances Olsen, Comment: Unraveling Compromise, 103 Harv. L. Rev. 105, 129-130 (1989).

[35]. Kristin Luker, Abortion and the Politics of Motherhood 118, 159-160 (1984). See also Gordon, supra note [3], at 304-305; Siegel, supra note [33], at 308-314; Mary Ziegler, Beyond Abortion: Roe v. Wade and the Battle for Privacy 188-190 (2018).

[36]. John J. Donahue III & Steven D. Levitt, The Impact of Legalized Abortion on Crime, 116 Q.J. Econ. 379 (2001).

the Court held that state encouragement of childbirth over abortion was a "value judgment" that satisfied this less demanding standard of review. The Court used a similar analysis to reject challenges to governmental refusals to fund abortions necessary to preserve the woman's health. In Harris v. McRae, 448 U.S. 297 (1980), the Court held that *Roe's* protection of the right to abortion does not confer an entitlement to funds to realize that right.

Further, in Webster v. Reproductive Health Services, 492 U.S. 490 (1989), the U.S. Supreme Court upheld the constitutionality of state prohibitions on the use of public funds, facilities, and employees in performing, assisting with, or counseling on abortions. *Webster* established an important precedent upholding state restrictions on abortion funding. And in Rust v. Sullivan, 500 U.S. 173 (1991), issues of abortion funding coalesced with informed consent laws in upholding regulations disallowing physicians in federally funded clinics from discussing abortion, despite the patient's request for information, the physician's judgment that the patient should consider abortion, the health risks of pregnancy, and state malpractice laws requiring disclosure.

Under current law, funds from Title X (the federal family planning program providing birth control and reproductive services to low-income women) may not be used to fund abortions. How meaningful is the right to abortion (where it still exists) for individuals who lack the financial means to effectuate this choice? Currently, only about 16 states cover abortion under Medicaid using state dollars.[37]

12. Comparative perspective. Wide variations in abortion policy exist worldwide. Most European countries lie at the permissive end of the spectrum, allowing abortion without restriction (but most of these countries limit unrestricted abortion to the first trimester). At the other end of the spectrum are countries (mostly in Latin America, the Caribbean, and Africa) that *prohibit* abortion. Countries midway along the spectrum (other countries mostly in Latin America, the Caribbean, and Africa) allow abortion but only to save the life of the pregnant person or to avert a threat to their physical or mental health. The global trend is toward liberalization.[38]

b. Abortion Laws: Historical and Philosophical Perspectives

Kristin Luker, Abortion and the Politics of Motherhood
20-29 (1984)

In the second half of the nineteenth century, abortion began to emerge as a social problem: newspapers began to run accounts of women who had died

---

[37]. Guttmacher Inst., State Funding of Abortion under Medicaid (as of Feb. 1, 2023), https://www.guttmacher.org/state-policy/explore/state-funding-abortion-under-medicaid.

[38]. For an updated map of abortion access worldwide, see Ctr. for Reprod. Rights, The World's Abortion Laws, https://reproductiverights.org/maps/worlds-abortion-laws/.

from "criminal abortions," although whether this fact reflects more abortions, more lethal abortions, or simply more awareness is not clear. Most prominently, physicians became involved, arguing that abortion was both morally wrong and medically dangerous. [In 1859, the American Medical Association (AMA), founded in 1847 to protect the interests of the medical profession, passed a resolution condemning abortion and urging state legislatures to pass laws forbidding it.] Slowly, physicians responded to the AMA's call and began to lobby in state legislatures for laws forbidding abortion. . . .

Why should nineteenth-century physicians have become so involved with the question of abortion? . . . First, [the physicians themselves] argued, they were compelled to address the abortion question because American women were committing a moral crime based on ignorance about the proper value of embryonic life. According to these physicians, women sought abortions because the doctrine of quickening led them to believe that the embryo was not alive, and therefore aborting it was perfectly proper. Second, they argued, they were obliged to act in order to save women from their own ignorance because only physicians were in possession of new scientific evidence which demonstrated beyond a shadow of a doubt that the embryo was a child from conception onward. . . .

This stand had an important advantage for physicians. It meant that the American women who practiced abortion (and who were generally thought to be members of the "better classes") could be defined as *inadvertent* murderesses. . . . Thus, a physician could condemn the "sin" without the necessity of condemning the "sinner." . . .

[N]either part of the physicians' claim was, strictly speaking, true. Women (and the general public) knew that pregnancy was a *biologically* continuous process from beginning to end, and physicians were not in possession of remarkable new scientific discoveries to use to prove the case. . . . What the anti-abortion physicians achieved, therefore, was a subtle transformation of the grounds of the debate. . . .

[W]hy in the middle of the nineteenth century, did some physicians become anti-abortionists? James Mohr, in a pioneering work on this topic, argues that the proliferation of healers in the nineteenth century created a competition for status and clients. The "regular" physicians, who tended to be both wealthier and better educated than members of other medical sects, therefore sought to distinguish themselves both scientifically and socially from competing practitioners. . . . Mohr suggests that . . . outlawing abortion would remove a lucrative source of income from competitors [whom the "regulars"] called "quacks" and perhaps remove that temptation from the path of the "regulars" as well. In addition, the "regulars" were predominantly white, upper-income, and native-born; as such, they belonged to precisely the same group that was thought to harbor the primary users of abortion. As a result, they were likely to be concerned about the depopulation of their group in the face of mounting immigration (and the higher fertility of immigrants. . . .

[R]egular physicians succeeded in their campaign. . . . More than almost any other profession, medicine now rigorously exercises the right to control who shall enter the profession, how they shall practice, and how competitors will be treated; its nineteenth-century stand against abortion contributed substantially to this ultimate success. It is in the context of this drive of professionalization that the political activity of American physicians against abortion must be understood. When examined closely in this context, their actual behavior raises serious doubts about whether they had . . . an unparalleled commitment to the "sanctity of life" of the embryo. . . .

Sidney Callahan, Abortion and the Sexual Agenda
113 Commonweal 232, 232-236 (1986)

. . . Pro-life feminists, like myself, argue on good feminist principles that women can never achieve the fulfillment of feminist goals in a society permissive toward abortion. . . . The moral right to control one's own body does apply to cases of organ transplants, mastectomies, contraception, and sterilization; but it is not a conceptualization adequate for abortion. The abortion dilemma is caused by the fact that 266 days following a conception in one body, another body will emerge. One's own body no longer exists as a single unit but is engendering another organism's life. . . . Strained philosophical analogies fail to apply: having a baby is not like rescuing a drowning person, being hooked up to a famous violinist's artificial life-support system, donating organs for transplant — or anything else. . . . It does not matter (*The Silent Scream* notwithstanding) whether the fetus being killed is fully conscious or feels pain. . . . Pro-life feminists who defend the fetus empathetically identify with an immature state of growth passed through by themselves, their children, and everyone now alive.

It also seems a travesty of just procedures that a pregnant woman now, in effect, acts as sole judge of her own case, under the most stressful conditions. Yes, one can acknowledge that the pregnant woman will be subject to the potential burdens arising from a pregnancy, but it has never been thought right to have an interested party, especially the more powerful party, decide his or her own case when there may be a conflict of interest. If one considers the matter as a case of a powerful versus a powerless, silenced claimant, the pro-choice feminist argument can rightly be inverted; since hers is the body, hers the risk, and hers the greater burden, then how in fairness can a woman be the sole judge of the fetal right to life? . . .

As the most recent immigrants from non-personhood, feminists have traditionally fought for justice. . . . A woman, involuntarily pregnant, has a moral obligation to the now-existing dependent fetus whether she explicitly consented to its existence or not. . . . The woman's moral obligation arises both from her status as a human being embedded in the interdependent human community and her unique lifegiving female reproductive power. . . .

Pitting women against their own offspring is not only morally offensive, it is psychologically and politically destructive. Women will never climb to equality and social empowerment over mounds of dead fetuses. [Women] stand to gain from the same constellation of attitudes and institutions that will also protect the fetus in the woman's womb — and they stand to lose from the cultural assumptions that support permissive abortion. . . . By pro-choice reasoning, a man who does not want to have a child, or whose contraceptive fails, can be exempted from the responsibilities of fatherhood and child support. . . .

For that matter, why should the state provide a system of day care or child support, or require workplaces to accommodate women's maternity and the needs of childrearing? Permissive abortion, granted in the name of women's privacy and reproductive freedom, ratifies the view that pregnancies and children are a woman's private individual responsibility.

Judith Jarvis Thomson, a moral philosopher, makes a provocative argument below contending that the fetus's right to life does not trump the pregnant woman's right to control her own body and, therefore, abortion is morally permissible. Her imaginative essay is one of the most famous works in contemporary philosophy.

Judith Jarvis Thomson, A Defense of Abortion
1 Phil. & Pub. Aff. 47-63 (1971)

[Assuming the personhood of the fetus, the anti-abortionist argument goes like this: every person has a right to life. Therefore the fetus has a right to life. A woman has a right to decide what shall happen in and to her body. But surely a person's right to life is stronger and more stringent than the mother's right to decide what happens in and to her body. So the fetus may not be killed; an abortion may not be performed. But let me respond with a thought experiment.]

[L]et me ask you to imagine this. You wake up in the morning and find yourself back to back in bed with an unconscious violinist. A famous unconscious violinist. He has been found to have a fatal kidney ailment, and the Society of Music Lovers has canvassed all the available medical records and found that you alone have the right blood type to help. They have therefore kidnapped you, and last night the violinist's circulatory system was plugged into yours, so that your kidneys can be used to extract poisons from his blood as well as your own. The director of the hospital now tells you, "Look, we're sorry the Society of Music Lovers did this to you — we would never have permitted it if we had known. But still, they did it and the violinist now is plugged into you. To unplug you would be to kill him. But never mind, it's only for nine months. By then he will have recovered from his ailment, and can safely be unplugged from you." Is it morally incumbent on you to accede to this situation? No doubt it would be very nice of you if you did, a great kindness. But do you *have* to accede to it? . . .

In this case, of course, you were kidnapped; you didn't volunteer for the operation that plugged the violinist into your kidneys. Can those who oppose abortion on the ground I mentioned make an exception for a pregnancy due to rape? Certainly. . . . [Moreover] it cannot seriously be thought to be murder if the mother performs an abortion on herself to save her life. It cannot seriously be said that she *must* refrain, that she *must* sit passively by and wait for her death. . . . If anything in the world is true, it is that you do not commit murder, you do not do what is impermissible, if you reach around to your back and unplug yourself from that violinist to save your life. . . .

. . . Where the mother's life is not at stake, the argument [based on the fetus's right to life] seems to have a much stronger pull[:] "Everyone has a right to life, so the unborn person has a right to life." And isn't the child's right to life weightier than anything other than the mother's own right to life, which she might put forward as ground for an abortion?

This argument treats the right to life as if it were unproblematic. It is not, and this seems to me to be precisely the source of the mistake. [T]o return to the story I told earlier, the fact that for continued life that violinist needs the continued use of your kidneys does not establish that he has a right to be given the continued use of your kidneys. He certainly has no right against you that *you* should give him continued use of your kidneys. For nobody has any right to use your kidneys unless you give him such a right; and nobody has the right against you that you shall give him this right — if you do allow him to go on using your kidneys, this is a kindness on your part, and not something he can claim from you as his due. . . . Certainly he had no right against the Society of Music Lovers that they should plug him into you in the first place. And if you now start to unplug yourself, having learned that you will otherwise have to spend nine [months] [sic] in bed with him, there is nobody in the world who must try to prevent you, in order to see to it that he is given something he has a right to be given. . . .

But it might be argued that there are other ways one can have acquired a right to the use of another person's body than by having been invited to use it by that person. Suppose a woman voluntarily indulges in intercourse, knowing of the chance it will issue in pregnancy, and then she does become pregnant; is she not in part responsible for the presence, in fact the very existence, of the unborn person inside her?

[D]etails make a difference. If the room is stuffy, and I therefore open a window to air it, and a burglar climbs in, it would be absurd to say, "Ah, now he can stay, she's given him a right to the use of her house — for she is partially responsible for his presence there, having voluntarily done what enabled him to get in, in full knowledge that there are such things as burglars, and that burglars burgle." It would be still more absurd to say this if I had had bars installed outside my windows, precisely to prevent burglars from getting in, and a burglar got in only because of a defect in the bars. It remains equally absurd if we imagine it is not a burglar who climbs in, but an innocent person who blunders or falls in. Again, suppose it were like this: people-seeds drift about in the air like pollen, and if you open your windows, one may drift in and take root in your carpets or upholstery. You don't want children, so you fix up your windows with fine mesh screens, the very best you can buy. As can happen, however, and on very, very rare occasions does happen, one of the screens is defective. . . . Someone may argue that you are responsible for its rooting, that it does have a right to your house, because after all you *could* have lived out your life with bare floors and furniture, or with sealed windows and doors. But this won't do — for by the same token anyone can avoid a pregnancy due to rape by having a hysterectomy, or anyway by never leaving home without a (reliable!) army. . . .

[I]t is worth drawing attention to the fact that in no state in this country is any man compelled by law to be even a Minimally Decent Samaritan to any person. . . . By contrast, in most states in this country women are compelled by law to be not merely Minimally Decent Samaritans, but Good Samaritans to unborn persons inside them. This [at least shows] that there is a gross injustice in the existing state of the law.

4. The Evolution of Privacy and Its Contraction

PLANNED PARENTHOOD OF SOUTHEASTERN PENNSYLVANIA v. CASEY

505 U.S. 833 (1992)

Justice O'CONNOR, Justice KENNEDY, and Justice SOUTER delivered the opinion of the Court.

[The case involved a constitutional challenge to a Pennsylvania law imposing a number of restrictions on access to abortion, including: (1) a requirement that a person seeking an abortion give informed consent prior to the abortion procedure after having been provided certain information; (2) a 24-hour waiting period; (3) for minors, a requirement of the informed consent of one parent, but providing for a judicial bypass option if the minor does not wish to or cannot obtain a parent's consent; (4) for married women, a requirement that she sign a statement indicating that she has notified her husband of her intended abortion; and (5) certain reporting requirements on facilities that provide abortion services.]

After considering the fundamental constitutional questions resolved by *Roe*, principles of institutional integrity, and the rule of stare decisis, we are led to conclude this: the essential holding of Roe v. Wade should be retained and once again reaffirmed. . . .

Neither the Bill of Rights nor the specific practices of States at the time of the adoption of the Fourteenth Amendment marks the outer limits of the substantive sphere of liberty which the Fourteenth Amendment protects. . . . Its boundaries are not susceptible of expression as a simple rule. . . .

Our law affords constitutional protection to personal decisions relating to marriage, procreation, contraception, family relationships, child rearing, and education. . . . These matters, involving the most intimate and personal choices a person may make in a lifetime, choices central to personal dignity and autonomy, are central to the liberty protected by the Fourteenth Amendment. At the heart of liberty is the right to define one's own concept of existence, of meaning, of the universe, and of the mystery of human life. Beliefs about these matters could not define the attributes of personhood were they formed under compulsion of the State.

These considerations begin our analysis of the woman's interest in terminating her pregnancy but cannot end it, for this reason: though the abortion decision may originate within the zone of conscience and belief, it is more than a philosophic exercise. Abortion is a unique act. It is an act fraught with consequences for others: for the woman who must live with the implications of her decision; for the persons who perform and assist in the procedure; for the spouse, family, and society which must confront the knowledge that these procedures exist, procedures some deem nothing short of an act of violence against innocent human life; and, depending on one's beliefs, for the life or potential life that is aborted. Though abortion is conduct, it does not follow that the State is entitled to proscribe it in all instances. That is because the liberty of the woman is at stake in a sense unique to the human condition and so unique to the law. The mother who carries a child to full term is subject to anxieties, to physical constraints, to pain that only she must bear. That these sacrifices have from the beginning of the human race been endured by woman with a pride that ennobles her in the eyes of others and gives to the infant a bond of love cannot alone be grounds for the State to insist she make the sacrifice. Her suffering is too intimate and personal for the State to insist, without more, upon its own vision of the woman's role, however dominant that vision has been in the course of our history and our culture. The destiny of the woman must be shaped to a large extent on her own conception of her spiritual imperatives and her place in society. . . .

While we appreciate the weight of the arguments made on behalf of the State in the cases before us, arguments which in their ultimate formulation conclude that *Roe* should be overruled, the reservations any of us may have in reaffirming the central holding of *Roe* are outweighed by the explication of individual liberty we have given combined with the force of stare decisis. [Under that doctrine,] when this Court reexamines a prior holding, its judgment is customarily informed by a series of prudential and pragmatic considerations designed to test the consistency of overruling a prior decision with the ideal of the rule of law, and to gauge the respective costs of reaffirming and overruling a prior case. . . . So in this case we may enquire whether *Roe*'s central rule has been found unworkable; whether the rule's limitation on state power could be removed without serious inequity to those who have relied upon it or significant damage to the stability of the society governed by it; whether the law's growth in the intervening years has left *Roe*'s central rule a doctrinal anachronism discounted by society; and whether *Roe*'s premises of fact have so far changed in the ensuing two decades as to render its central holding somehow irrelevant or unjustifiable in dealing with the issue it addressed.

Although *Roe* has engendered opposition, it has in no sense proven "unworkable." While *Roe* has, of course, required judicial assessment of state laws affecting the exercise of the choice guaranteed against government infringement, and although the need for such review will remain as a consequence of today's decision, the required determinations fall within judicial competence.

The inquiry into reliance counts the cost of a rule's repudiation as it would fall on those who have relied reasonably on the rule's continued application. Since the classic case for weighing reliance heavily in favor of following the earlier rule occurs in the commercial context, where advance planning of great precision is most obviously a necessity, it is no cause for surprise that some would find no reliance worthy of consideration in support of *Roe*.

[O]ne can readily imagine an argument stressing the dissimilarity of this case to one involving property or contract. Abortion is customarily chosen as an unplanned response to the consequence of unplanned activity or to the failure of conventional birth control. . . . To eliminate the issue of reliance that easily, however, . . . would be simply to refuse to face the fact that for two decades of economic and social developments, people have organized intimate relationships and made choices that define their views of themselves and their places in society, in reliance on the availability of abortion in the event that contraception should fail. The ability of women to participate equally in the economic and social life of the Nation has been facilitated by their ability to control their reproductive lives. [W]hile the effect of reliance on *Roe* cannot be exactly measured, neither can the certain cost of overruling *Roe* for people who have ordered their thinking and living around that case be dismissed.

No evolution of legal principle has left *Roe*'s doctrinal footings weaker than they were in 1973. [S]ubsequent constitutional developments have neither disturbed, nor do they threaten to diminish, the scope of recognized protection accorded to the liberty relating to intimate relationships, the family, and decisions about whether or not to beget or bear a child. [O]ur cases since *Roe* accord with *Roe*'s view that a State's interest in the protection of life falls short of justifying any plenary override of individual liberty claims. . . .

We have seen how time has overtaken some of *Roe*'s factual assumptions: advances in maternal health care allow for abortions safe to the mother later in pregnancy than was true in 1973, and advances in neonatal care have advanced viability to a point somewhat earlier. But these facts go only to the scheme of time limits on the realization of competing interests, and . . . have no bearing on the validity of *Roe*'s central holding, that viability marks the earliest point at which the State's interest in fetal life is constitutionally adequate to justify a legislative ban on nontherapeutic abortions. . . .

A decision to overrule *Roe*'s essential holding under the existing circumstances would address error, if error there was, at the cost of both profound and unnecessary damage to the Court's legitimacy, and to the Nation's commitment to the rule of law. It is therefore imperative to adhere to the essence of *Roe*'s original decision, and we do so today.

From what we have said so far it follows that it is a constitutional liberty of the woman to have some freedom to terminate her pregnancy. . . . The woman's liberty is not so unlimited, however, that from the outset the State cannot show its concern for the life of the unborn, and at a later point in fetal development the State's interest in life has sufficient force so that the right of the woman to terminate the pregnancy can be restricted.

That brings us, of course, to the point where much criticism has been directed at *Roe,* a criticism that always inheres when the Court draws a specific rule from what in the Constitution is but a general standard. We conclude, however, that the urgent claims of the woman to retain the ultimate control over her destiny and her body, claims implicit in the meaning of liberty, require us to perform that function. Liberty must not be extinguished for want of a line that is clear. And it falls to us to give some real substance to the woman's liberty to determine whether to carry her pregnancy to full term.

We conclude the line should be drawn at viability, so that before that time the woman has a right to choose to terminate her pregnancy. We adhere to this principle for two reasons. First, as we have said, is the doctrine of stare decisis. . . . The second reason is that . . . there is no line other than viability which is more workable. . . . The viability line also has, as a practical matter, an element of fairness. In some broad sense it might be said that a woman who fails to act before viability has consented to the State's intervention on behalf of the developing child. The woman's right to terminate her pregnancy before viability is the most central principle of Roe v. Wade. It is a rule of law and a component of liberty we cannot renounce. . . .

Roe established a trimester framework to govern abortion regulations. . . . The trimester framework no doubt was erected to ensure that the woman's right to choose not become so subordinate to the State's interest in promoting fetal life that her choice exists in theory but not in fact. We do not agree, however, that the trimester approach is necessary to accomplish this objective. . . .

Though the woman has a right to choose to terminate or continue her pregnancy before viability, it does not at all follow that the State is prohibited from taking steps to ensure that this choice is thoughtful and informed. Even in the earliest stages of pregnancy, the State may enact rules and regulations designed to encourage her to know that there are philosophic and social arguments of great weight that can be brought to bear in favor of continuing the pregnancy to full term and that there are procedures and institutions to allow adoption of unwanted children as well as a certain degree of state assistance if the mother chooses to raise the child herself. . . .

We reject the trimester framework, which we do not consider to be part of the essential holding of *Roe*. . . . The trimester framework suffers from these basic flaws: in its formulation it misconceives the nature of the pregnant woman's interest; and in practice it undervalues the State's interest in potential life, as recognized in *Roe*.

As our jurisprudence relating to all liberties save perhaps abortion has recognized, not every law which makes a right more difficult to exercise is, *ipso facto*, an infringement of that right. . . . Only where state regulation imposes an undue burden on a woman's ability to make this decision does the power of the State reach into the heart of the liberty protected by the Due Process Clause. [T]he other basic flaw in the trimester framework [is that] it undervalues the State's interest in the potential life within the woman. . . .

In our view, the undue burden standard is the appropriate means of reconciling the State's interest with the woman's constitutionally protected liberty. . . . A finding of an undue burden is a shorthand for the conclusion that a state regulation has the purpose or effect of placing a substantial obstacle in the path of a woman seeking an abortion of a nonviable fetus. A statute with this purpose is invalid because the means chosen by the State to further the interest in potential life must be calculated to inform the woman's free choice, not hinder it. And a statute which, while furthering the interest in potential life or some other valid state interest, has the effect of placing a substantial obstacle in the path of a woman's choice cannot be considered a permissible means of serving its legitimate ends. . . .

Some guiding principles should emerge. What is at stake is the woman's right to make the ultimate decision, not a right to be insulated from all others in doing so. Regulations which do no more than create a structural mechanism by which the State, or the parent or guardian of a minor, may express profound respect for the life of the unborn are permitted, if they are not a substantial obstacle to the woman's exercise of the right to choose. Unless it has that effect on her right of choice, a state measure designed to persuade her to choose childbirth over abortion will be upheld if reasonably related to that goal. Regulations designed to foster the health of a woman seeking an abortion are valid if they do not constitute an undue burden.

[The Court applied the newly announced undue burden standard to the five challenged provisions of the Pennsylvania statute. Under application of the undue burden standard, the Court upheld all of the provisions except the provision requiring a married woman, in almost all cases, to provide a signed statement that she notified her husband that she planned to obtain an abortion. The Court held that for the subset of women who do not inform their husbands—many of whom are the victims of domestic violence—this requirement would operate as a substantial obstacle to their choice to undergo an abortion and was therefore invalid.]

Justice BLACKMUN, concurring in part, concurring in the judgment in part, and dissenting in part.

. . . The Court today reaffirms the long recognized rights of privacy and bodily integrity. . . . Throughout this century, this Court also has held that the fundamental right of privacy protects citizens against governmental intrusion in such intimate family matters as procreation, childrearing, marriage, and contraceptive choice. These cases embody the principle that personal decisions that profoundly affect bodily integrity, identity, and destiny should be largely beyond the reach of government. In *Roe v. Wade,* this Court correctly applied these principles to a woman's right to choose abortion.

State restrictions on abortion violate a woman's right of privacy in two ways. First, compelled continuation of a pregnancy infringes upon a woman's right to bodily integrity by imposing substantial physical intrusions and significant risks of physical harm. During pregnancy, women experience dramatic physical changes and a wide range of health consequences. Labor and delivery pose additional health risks and physical demands. In short, restrictive abortion laws force women to endure physical invasions far more substantial than those this Court has held to violate the constitutional principle of bodily integrity in other contexts.

Further, when the State restricts a woman's right to terminate her pregnancy, it deprives a woman of the right to make her own decision about reproduction and family planning—critical life choices that this Court long has deemed central to the right to privacy. The decision to terminate or continue a pregnancy has no less an impact on a woman's life than decisions about contraception or marriage. Because motherhood has a dramatic impact on a woman's educational prospects, employment opportunities, and self-determination, restrictive abortion laws deprive her of basic control over her life. For these reasons, "the decision whether or not to beget or bear a child" lies at "the very heart of this cluster of constitutionally protected choices."

A State's restrictions on a woman's right to terminate her pregnancy also implicate constitutional guarantees of gender equality. State restrictions on abortion compel women to continue pregnancies they otherwise might terminate. By restricting the right to terminate pregnancies, the State conscripts women's bodies into its service, forcing women to continue their pregnancies, suffer the pains of childbirth, and in most instances, provide years of maternal care. The State does not compensate women for their services; instead, it assumes that they owe this duty as a matter of course. This assumption—that women can simply be forced to accept the "natural" status and incidents of motherhood—appears to rest upon a conception of women's role that has triggered the protection of the Equal Protection Clause. The joint opinion recognizes that these assumptions about women's place in society "are no longer consistent with our understanding of the family, the individual, or the Constitution."

[In my view,] *Roe's* requirement of strict scrutiny as implemented through a trimester framework should not be disturbed. No other approach has gained a majority, and no other is more protective of the woman's fundamental right. Lastly, no other approach properly accommodates the woman's constitutional right with the State's legitimate interests. . . .

The Chief Justice and those who have joined him admit it . . . for all to see . . . : "We believe that *Roe* was wrongly decided, and that it can and should be overruled consistently with our traditional approach to stare decisis in constitutional cases." . . . But, we are reassured, there is always the protection of the democratic process. While there is much to be praised about our democracy, our country since its founding has recognized that there are certain fundamental liberties that are not to be left to the whims of an election. A woman's right to reproductive choice is one of those fundamental liberties. . . .

In one sense, the Court's approach is worlds apart from that of The Chief Justice and Justice Scalia. And yet, in another sense, the distance between the two approaches is short—the distance is but a single vote. I am 83 years old. I cannot remain on this Court forever, and when I do step down, the confirmation process for my successor well may focus on the issue before us today. That, I regret, may be exactly where the choice between the two worlds will be made.

Chief Justice REHNQUIST, with whom Justice WHITE, Justice SCALIA, and Justice THOMAS join, concurring in the judgment in part and dissenting in part.

. . . We believe that *Roe* was wrongly decided, and that it can and should be overruled consistently with our traditional approach to stare decisis in constitutional cases. . . .

Justice SCALIA, with whom Chief Justice REHNQUIST, Justice WHITE, and Justice THOMAS join, concurring in the judgment in part and dissenting in part.

. . . The issue is whether ["the power of a woman to abort her unborn child"] is a liberty protected by the Constitution of the United States. I am sure it is not. I reach that conclusion not because of anything so exalted as my views concerning the "concept of existence, of meaning, of the universe, and of the mystery of human life." Rather, I reach it for the same reason I reach the conclusion that bigamy is not constitutionally protected—because of two simple facts: (1) the Constitution says absolutely nothing about it, and (2) the longstanding traditions of American society have permitted it to be legally proscribed.

. . . [B]y foreclosing all democratic outlet for the deep passions this issue arouses, by banishing the issue from the political forum that gives all participants, even the losers, the satisfaction of a fair hearing and an honest fight, by continuing the imposition of a rigid national rule instead of allowing for regional differences, the Court merely prolongs and intensifies the anguish. We should get out of this area, where we have no right to be, and where we do neither ourselves nor the country any good by remaining.

Notes and Questions

1. **Basis of decision.** *Casey* affirms *Roe*'s central holding that the right to abortion is a protected liberty under the Due Process Clause. How does the controlling joint opinion reach that conclusion? Do you agree with the controlling opinion? Is it consistent with the approach used by the Court in other privacy/substantive due process cases?

2. Stare decisis. *Casey* was not the first Supreme Court case to consider the constitutionality of abortion restrictions. The Court held in *Roe,* and many times thereafter, that abortion was constitutionally protected. Under stare decisis, *Casey* concludes that those precedents should be retained. According to the joint opinion, why does stare decisis exist? What factors are relevant to determining whether precedent should be adhered to? How do those factors apply to the right to abortion? Did the controlling opinion reach the correct conclusion?

3. Impact on women. According to the controlling joint opinion, how do abortion restrictions affect the lives of people during their pregnancy and thereafter? Are those impacts significant? How should these impacts be taken into account or weighed when considering the permissibility of abortion restrictions?

4. Rule for evaluating abortion restrictions. What rule does the *Casey* Court adopt for evaluating the permissibility of abortion restrictions? Abortion bans? How does this compare to the rules established in *Roe*? Is one standard preferable? If so, which? What approach does concurring Justice Blackmun favor?

5. Restrictions that seek to influence the decision. In describing the new undue burden standard, the controlling joint opinion in *Casey* specifically declares that rules that "create a structural mechanism by which the State . . . may express profound respect for the life of the unborn are permitted, if they are not a substantial obstacle to the woman's exercise of the right to choose." What kinds of rules would pass muster under the undue burden standard? Which would fail?

6. Aftermath of *Casey* on state abortion laws. While the *Casey* decision preserved the "core" holding of *Roe*, it ushered in a new era of restrictions on access to abortion. Some restrictions enacted in the wake of *Casey* include:

a. Parental consent requirements. The majority of states passed laws limiting the ability of minors to obtain abortions. *Casey* itself upheld a law requiring minors either to get parental consent or approval by a court. Where a state scheme provided a judicial bypass option, it was typically held to be permissible under *Casey*'s undue burden standard. Some schemes, however, failed even under this standard. See, e.g., Reprod. Health Servs. v. Strange, 3 F.4th 1240 (11th Cir. 2021) (holding unconstitutional a judicial bypass provision that allowed parents to participate in the judicial proceeding and did not adequately ensure anonymity and confidentiality), *reh'g en banc granted, vacated sub nom.,* Repro. Health Servs. ex rel. Ayers v. Strange, 22 F.4th 1346 (11th Cir. 2022).

b. Informed consent requirements. Many states impose detailed and onerous requirements regarding disclosures and depictions to patients prior to obtaining abortion care. For example, many states required doctors not only to perform an ultrasound, but also to show it to the patient prior to performing the abortion. See, e.g., EMW Women's Surgical Ctr. v. Beshear, 920 F.3d 421 (6th Cir. 2019) (upholding a law that required ultrasounds and disclosure of the results). Other states required doctors to provide certain information, including information that was medically questionable. For example, some state laws require that the informed consent materials include statements regarding the ability of the fetus to feel pain, even though "researchers have not been able to conclusively determine at what point in development, if at all, a fetus perceives pain."[39]

   c. *Restrictions on abortion providers.* Some states passed laws imposing onerous requirements on abortion providers. These laws are sometimes referred to as Targeted Regulations of Abortion Providers (TRAP) laws. For example, some states required all abortion clinics to comply with state standards for ambulatory surgical centers. Some laws required abortion care providers to have admitting privileges at a nearby hospital. Some laws imposed both requirements. In Whole Woman's Health v. Hellerstedt, 579 U.S. 583 (2016) and in June Medical Services, LLC v. Russo, 591 U.S. 1101 (2020), decided four years later, the Court struck down these kinds of requirements under *Casey*'s undue burden standard. As the Court wrote in *Whole Woman's Health*, a review of the evidence demonstrated that "neither of these provisions confers medical benefits sufficient to justify the burdens upon access that each impose." Other kinds of TRAP laws, however, were upheld. See EMW Women's Surgical Ctr. v. Friedlander, 978 F.3d 418 (6th Cir. 2020) (upholding a Kentucky law that required agreements between abortion care providers and local ambulance services).

   d. *Novel enforcement mechanisms.* Texas enacted a particularly draconian law. The law—often referred to by its bill number, SB 8—not only bans almost all abortions, but also includes a novel civil enforcement mechanism. Private citizens are authorized to file civil lawsuits against health care providers, their staff, and even the patient's family or friends who "aid and abet" such procedures. The law authorizes a minimum award of $10,000 per illegal abortion if the lawsuit is successful. This law was immediately challenged. In a harbinger of the Court's later decision in *Dobbs*, the Court denied a request to block the law before it went into effect. Whole Woman's Health v. Jackson, 595 U.S. 30 (2021).

   e. *Religious refusal clauses.* As of July 2023, 46 states permitted some health care providers to refuse to provide abortion services, 12 states allowed them to refuse to provide contraception services, and 18 states permitted them to refuse to provide sterilization services.[40] On the federal level, the Trump Administration's expanded conscience rule established guidelines for punishing health care institutions with the loss of federal funds if they failed to respect the rights of these workers. 84 Fed. Reg. 23,170 (May 21, 2019). The Biden Administration has proposed rules that would rescind part of those guidelines. 88 Fed. Reg. 820 (proposed Jan. 5, 2023) (to be codified at 45 C.F.R. pt. 88).

   7. "Crisis pregnancy centers." So-called crisis pregnancy centers, often religiously based, purport to offer family planning medical services and advice but instead seek to dissuade people from obtaining an abortion. In National Institute

---

[39]. Chinué Turner Richardson & Elizabeth Nash, Misinformed Consent: The Medical Accuracy of State-Developed Abortion Counseling Materials, Guttmacher Inst., Oct. 23, 2006, https://www.guttmacher.org/gpr/2006/10/misinformed-consent-medical-accuracy-state-develo ped-abortion-counseling-materials.
[40]. Guttmacher Inst., Refusing to Provide Health Services, https://www.guttmacher.org/ state-policy/explore/refusing-provide-health-services, Aug. 21, 2023.

of Family and Life Advocates (NIFLA) v. Becerra, 138 S. Ct. 2361 (2018), the U.S. Supreme Court considered the constitutionality of a California law that required these facilities to post information about other alternatives (such as abortion), and, if unlicensed, to disclose their lack of medical certification. In a challenge based on the centers' right to free speech, the Supreme Court held (5-4, in an opinion by Justice Thomas) that both notices violate the First Amendment.

In September 2023, California Attorney General Rob Bonta instituted law-suits against two major anti-abortion groups that operate crisis pregnancy cen-ters, alleging that they are using fraudulent and misleading claims to promote the safety and efficacy of an experimental hormone therapy to stop a medication abortion from proceeding.[41]

8. Clinic violence. Violence creates access problems by dissuading patients as well as abortion providers. A federal statute, the Freedom of Access to Clinic Entrances Act (FACE) (18 U.S.C. §248), enacted in 1994, bars force, threats of force, or physical obstruction aimed at injuring, intimidating, or interfering with any patient or provider of reproductive health services. In McCullen v. Coakley, 573 U.S. 464 (2014), the Supreme Court held that a 35-foot buffer zone (imposed to keep protestors a specific distance from clinic entrances) was excessive and vio-lated the First Amendment. According to the Court, such protective measures sur-vive First Amendment challenges only if sufficiently tailored to burden no more speech than necessary and achieve the government's interest in protecting safety through narrowly focused means.

Despite the enactment of FACE, violence and threats against clinics, physicians, and staff continue. The National Abortion Federation (NAF), which has been com-piling statistics for 45 years, disclosed a staggering increase in violence and disrup-tion against abortion providers in 2021 compared to the previous year: a 600 percent increase in stalking, 450 percent increase in blockades, 163 percent increase in hoax devices/suspicious packages, and 128 percent increase in assault and battery.[42]

9. Abortion rates. Despite the enactment of increasingly onerous state restric-tions on access, abortions are common. According to data from 2017 by the Guttmacher Institute, "[n]early one in four women in the United States (23.7 per-cent) will have an abortion by age 45."[43] The report points out that abortion rates vary by age, race, ethnicity, and class. Black women have the highest abor-tion rates. Factors contributing to these higher rates of abortions by Black women likely include a long history of racism and discrimination, as well as their lack of access to high-quality, affordable health care and health insurance.

---

[41]. Kristen Hwang, California Sues Crisis Pregnancy Centers over "Abortion Pill Reversal" Claims, Cal Matters, Sept. 21, 2023, https://calmatters.org/health/2023/09/california-sues-crisis -pregnancy-centers-abortion-reversal/.

[42]. Nat'l Abortion Fed. Releases 2021 Violence & Disruption Rep., May 19, 2022, https://procho ice.org/national-abortion-federation-releases-2021-violence-disruption-report/. See also Dept. of Justice, Recent Cases on Violence Against Reproductive Health Care Providers, Oct. 18, 2022, https://www.justice.gov/crt/recent-cases-violence-against-reproductive-health-care-providers.

[43]. Guttmacher Inst., Abortion Is a Common Experience for U.S. Women, Despite Dramatic Declines in Rates, Oct. 17, 2017, https://www.guttmacher.org/news-release/2017/abortion-common -experience-us-women-despite-dramatic-declines-rates.

10. Public opinion. A strong majority of U.S. adults support access to abortion. According to a June 2022 Pew Research Center Report, 61 percent of "U.S. adults say abortion should be legal in all or most cases, while 37 percent think abortion should be *illegal* in all or most cases."[44] Support for abortion is higher among people who identify as Democrats and among women. Is or should public support for abortion access be relevant to assessing whether the Constitution protects the right to abortion?

DOBBS v. JACKSON WOMEN'S HEALTH ORGANIZATION

142 S. Ct. 2228 (2022)

Jackson Women's Health Organization is one of the more than 50 abortion clinics nationwide that has closed its doors in the wake of *Dobbs*. It is now a secondhand consignment shop.

Justice ALITO delivered the opinion of the Court.

Abortion presents a profound moral issue on which Americans hold sharply conflicting views. . . .

For the first 185 years after the adoption of the Constitution, each State was permitted to address this issue in accordance with the views of its citizens. Then, in 1973, this Court decided Roe v. Wade. Even though the Constitution makes no mention of abortion, the Court held that it confers a broad right to obtain one.

[44]. Hannah Hartig, About Six-in-Ten Americans Say Abortion Should Be Legal in All or Most Cases, Pew Research Ctr., June 13, 2022, https://www.pewresearch.org/fact-tank/2022/06/13/about-six-in-ten-americans-say-abortion-should-be-legal-in-all-or-most-cases-2/.

[I]n Planned Parenthood of Southeastern Pa. v. Casey (1992), [the controlling joint opinion] concluded that stare decisis . . . required adherence to what it called *Roe*'s "central holding"—that a State may not constitutionally protect fetal life before "viability" . . . .

We hold that *Roe* and *Casey* must be overruled. The Constitution makes no reference to abortion, and no such right is implicitly protected by any constitutional provision, including . . . the Due Process Clause of the Fourteenth Amendment. That provision has been held to guarantee some rights that are not mentioned in the Constitution, but any such right must be "deeply rooted in this Nation's history and tradition" and "implicit in the concept of ordered liberty." The right to abortion does not fall within this category.

[The doctrine of stare decisis] does not compel unending adherence to *Roe*'s abuse of judicial authority. *Roe* was egregiously wrong from the start. Its reasoning was exceptionally weak, and the decision has had damaging consequences. And far from bringing about a national settlement of the abortion issue, *Roe* and *Casey* have enflamed debate and deepened division.

It is time to heed the Constitution and return the issue of abortion to the people's elected representatives. . . .

I

The law at issue in this case, Mississippi's Gestational Age Act [bans almost all abortions after fifteen (15) weeks of pregnancy.] We granted certiorari to resolve the question whether "all pre-viability prohibitions on elective abortions are unconstitutional[.]" We begin by considering the critical question whether the Constitution, properly understood, confers a right to obtain an abortion. [*Casey*] grounded its decision solely on the theory that the right to obtain an abortion is part of the "liberty" protected by the Fourteenth Amendment's Due Process Clause.

We discuss this theory in depth below, but before doing so, we briefly address one additional constitutional provision that some of respondents' *amici* have now offered as yet another potential home for the abortion right: the Fourteenth Amendment's Equal Protection Clause. Neither *Roe* nor *Casey* saw fit to invoke this theory, and it is squarely foreclosed by our precedents, which establish that a State's regulation of abortion is not a sex-based classification and is thus not subject to the "heightened scrutiny" that applies to such classifications. The regulation of a medical procedure that only one sex can undergo does not trigger heightened constitutional scrutiny unless the regulation is a "mere pretex[t] designed to effect an invidious discrimination against members of one sex or the other." Geduldig v. Aiello (1974) [(holding that a state disability insurance program that excluded protection for disability did not discriminate on the basis of sex, stating: "The California insurance program does not exclude anyone from benefit eligibility because of gender but merely removes one physical condition—pregnancy—from the list of compensable disabilities. While it is true that only women can become pregnant it does not follow that every legislative classification concerning pregnancy is a sex-based classification[.]")]. And as the Court has stated, the "goal of preventing abortion" does not constitute "invidiously discriminatory animus" against women. . . .

With this new theory addressed, we turn to *Casey*'s bold assertion that the abortion right is an aspect of the "liberty" protected by the Due Process Clause of the Fourteenth Amendment. [O]ur decisions have held that the Due Process Clause protects . . . a select list of fundamental rights that are not mentioned anywhere in the Constitution.

In deciding whether a right falls into [this list of rights], the Court has long asked whether the right is "deeply rooted in [our] history and tradition" and whether it is essential to our Nation's "scheme of ordered liberty." And in conducting this inquiry, we have engaged in a careful analysis of the history of the right at issue. . . . "Liberty" is a capacious term. . . . On occasion, when the Court has ignored the "[a]ppropriate limits" imposed by "'respect for the teachings of history,'" it has fallen into the freewheeling judicial policymaking that characterized discredited decisions such as Lochner v. New York (1905). The Court must not fall prey to such an unprincipled approach. . . .

Until the latter part of the 20th century, there was no support in American law for a constitutional right to obtain an abortion. No state constitutional provision had recognized such a right. Until a few years before *Roe* was handed down, no federal or state court had recognized such a right. . . . Not only was there no support for such a constitutional right until shortly before *Roe*, but abortion had long been a *crime* in every single State. At common law, abortion was criminal in at least some stages of pregnancy and was regarded as unlawful and could have very serious consequences at all stages. American law followed the common law until a wave of statutory restrictions in the 1800s expanded criminal liability for abortions. By the time of the adoption of the Fourteenth Amendment, three-quarters of the States had made abortion a crime at any stage of pregnancy, and the remaining States would soon follow.

Roe either ignored or misstated this history, and *Casey* declined to reconsider *Roe*'s faulty historical analysis. It is therefore important to set the record straight. We begin with the common law, under which abortion was a crime at least after "quickening"—*i.e.*, the first felt movement of the fetus in the womb, which usually occurs between the 16th and 18th week of pregnancy.

The "eminent common-law authorities (Blackstone, Coke, Hale, and the like)," *all* describe abortion after quickening as criminal. . . . In sum, [no] common-law authorities . . . endorsed the practice. Moreover, we are aware of no common-law case or authority . . . that remotely suggests a positive *right* to procure an abortion at any stage of pregnancy. . . .

The original ground for drawing a distinction between pre- and post-quickening abortions is not entirely clear, but [a]t any rate, . . . the rule was abandoned in the 19th century. . . . In this country during the 19th century, the vast majority of the States enacted statutes criminalizing abortion at all stages of pregnancy. By 1868, the year when the Fourteenth Amendment was ratified, three-quarters of the States, 28 out of 37, had enacted statutes making abortion a crime even if it was performed before quickening. Of the nine States that had not yet criminalized abortion at all stages, all but one did so by 1910. . . .

This overwhelming consensus endured until the day *Roe* was decided. At that time, also by the *Roe* Court's own count, a substantial majority—30 States—still prohibited abortion at all stages except to save the life of the mother. And though *Roe* discerned a "trend toward liberalization" in about "one-third of the States," those States still criminalized some abortions and regulated them more stringently than *Roe* would allow. In short, [t]he inescapable conclusion is that a right to abortion is not deeply rooted in the Nation's history and traditions. . . . Instead of seriously pressing the argument that the abortion right itself has deep roots, supporters of *Roe* and *Casey* contend that the abortion right is an integral part of a broader entrenched right. . . . These attempts to justify abortion through appeals to a broader right to autonomy and to define one's "concept of existence" prove too much. Those criteria, at a high level of generality, could license fundamental rights to illicit drug use, prostitution, and the like.

[Moreover, what] sharply distinguishes the abortion right from the rights recognized in the cases on which *Roe* and *Casey* rely is something that both those decisions acknowledged: Abortion destroys what those decisions call "potential life" and what the law at issue in this case regards as the life of an "unborn human being." None of the other decisions cited by *Roe* and *Casey* [including *Griswold*, *Meyer*, and *Pierce*] involved the critical moral question posed by abortion. They are therefore inapposite. They do not support the right to obtain an abortion, and by the same token, our conclusion that the Constitution does not confer such a right does not undermine them in any way. . . .

III

We next consider whether the doctrine of stare decisis counsels continued acceptance of *Roe* and *Casey*. Stare decisis . . . serves many valuable ends. . . . We have long recognized, however, that stare decisis is "not an inexorable command," and it "is at its weakest when we interpret the Constitution" [because] we place a high value on having the matter "settled right." In addition, when one of our constitutional decisions goes astray, the country is usually stuck with the bad decision unless we correct our own mistake. . . .

Some of our most important constitutional decisions have overruled prior precedents [including Brown v. Board of Education (1954), overruling Plessy v. Ferguson (1896) (upholding the separate-but-equal doctrine), and West Coast Hotel Co. v. Parrish (1937), overruling Lochner v. New York (1905) (holding invalid a law setting maximum working hours).]

Our cases . . . have identified factors that should be considered in making such a decision. . . . In this case, five factors weigh strongly in favor of overruling *Roe* and *Casey*: the nature of their error, the quality of their reasoning, the "workability" of the rules they imposed on the country, their disruptive effect on other areas of the law, and the absence of concrete reliance.

The nature of the Court's error. An erroneous interpretation of the Constitution is always important, but some are more damaging than others. The infamous decision in Plessy v. Ferguson, was one such decision. . . . It was "egregiously wrong" on the day it was decided . . . . *Roe* was also egregiously wrong and deeply damaging. [W]ielding nothing but "raw judicial power," the Court usurped the power to address a question of profound moral and social importance that the Constitution unequivocally leaves for the people. . . . Together, *Roe* and *Casey* represent an error that cannot be allowed to stand. . . .

The quality of the reasoning. Under our precedents, the quality of the reasoning in a prior case has an important bearing on whether it should be reconsidered. [*Roe*] stood on exceptionally weak grounds. *Roe* found that the Constitution implicitly conferred a right to obtain an abortion, but it failed to ground its decision in text, history, or precedent. . . . *Roe*'s reasoning quickly drew scathing scholarly criticism, even from supporters of broad access to abortion. The *Casey* plurality, while reaffirming *Roe*'s central holding, pointedly refrained from endorsing most of its reasoning. It revised the textual basis for the abortion right, silently abandoned *Roe*'s erroneous historical narrative, and jettisoned the trimester framework. But it replaced that scheme with an arbitrary "undue burden" test . . . .

Workability. Our precedents counsel that another important consideration in deciding whether a precedent should be overruled is whether the rule it imposes is workable—that is, whether it can be understood and applied in a consistent and predictable manner. *Casey*'s "undue burden" test has scored poorly on the workability scale. . . .

Effect on other areas of law. Roe and *Casey* have led to the distortion of many important but unrelated legal doctrines [including the standard for facial constitutional challenges, third-party standing doctrine, res judicata principles, and severability], and that effect provides further support for overruling those decisions. . . .

Reliance interests. We last consider whether overruling *Roe* and *Casey* will upend substantial reliance interests. Traditional reliance interests arise "where advance planning of great precision is most obviously a necessity." In *Casey*, the controlling opinion conceded that those traditional reliance interests were not implicated. . . . Unable to find reliance in the conventional sense, the controlling opinion in *Casey* perceived a more intangible form of reliance. It wrote that "people [had] organized intimate relationships and made choices that define their views of themselves and their places in society . . . in reliance on the availability of abortion in the event that contraception should fail" and that "[t]he ability of women to participate equally in the economic and social life of the Nation has been facilitated by their ability to control their reproductive lives." But this Court is ill-equipped to assess "generalized assertions about the national psyche." *Casey*'s notion of reliance thus finds little support in our cases, which instead emphasize very concrete reliance interests, like those that develop in "cases involving property and contract rights." [Moreover, that form] of reliance depends on an empirical question that is hard for anyone—and in particular, for a court—to assess, namely, the effect of the abortion right on society and in particular on the lives of women. . . .

Having shown that traditional stare decisis factors do not weigh in favor of retaining *Roe* or *Casey*, we must address one final argument that featured prominently in the *Casey* plurality opinion. [This argument] was essentially [that there] is a special danger that the public will perceive a decision as having been made for unprincipled reasons when the Court overrules a controversial "watershed" decision, such as *Roe*. . . . The *Casey* plurality[] misjudged the practical limits of this Court's influence. . . . Whatever influence the Court may have on public attitudes must stem from the strength of our opinions, not an attempt to exercise "raw judicial power." . . . We can only do our job, which is to interpret the law, apply longstanding principles of stare decisis, and decide this case accordingly.

We therefore hold that the Constitution does not confer a right to abortion. *Roe* and *Casey* must be overruled, and the authority to regulate abortion must be returned to the people and their elected representatives. . . .

Under our precedents, rational-basis review is the appropriate standard for such challenges. . . . It follows that the States may regulate abortion for legitimate reasons, and when such regulations are challenged under the Constitution, courts cannot "substitute their social and economic beliefs for the judgment of legislative bodies." That respect for a legislature's judgment applies even when the laws at issue concern matters of great social significance and moral substance. A law regulating abortion, like other health and welfare laws, is entitled to a "strong presumption of validity." It must be sustained if there is a rational basis on which the legislature could have thought that it would serve legitimate state interests. These legitimate interests include respect for and preservation of prenatal life at all stages of development; the protection of maternal health and safety; the elimination of particularly gruesome or barbaric medical procedures; the preservation of the integrity of the medical profession; the mitigation of fetal pain; and the prevention of discrimination on the basis of race, sex, or disability. These legitimate interests justify Mississippi's Gestational Age Act. . . .

We end this opinion where we began. Abortion presents a profound moral question. The Constitution does not prohibit the citizens of each State from regulating or prohibiting abortion. *Roe* and *Casey* arrogated that authority. We now overrule those decisions and return that authority to the people and their elected representatives. . . .

Justice THOMAS, concurring.

I join the opinion of the Court because it correctly holds that there is no constitutional right to abortion. . . . I write separately to emphasize a . . . more fundamental reason why there is no abortion guarantee lurking in the Due Process Clause. . . . Because the Due Process Clause does not secure *any* substantive rights, it does not secure a right to abortion. . . . For that reason, in future cases, we should reconsider all of this Court's substantive due process precedents, including *Griswold, Lawrence,* and *Obergefell.* Because any substantive due process decision is "demonstrably erroneous," we have a duty to "correct the error" established in those precedents. . . . Accordingly, we should eliminate it from our jurisprudence at the earliest opportunity.

Justice KAVANAUGH, concurring.

. . . The *Roe* Court took sides on a consequential moral and policy issue that this Court had no constitutional authority to decide. By taking sides, the *Roe* Court distorted the Nation's understanding of this Court's proper role in the American constitutional system and thereby damaged the Court as an institution. . . .

In my judgment, on the issue of abortion, the Constitution is neither pro-life nor pro-choice. The Constitution is neutral, and this Court likewise must be scrupulously neutral. The Court today properly heeds the constitutional principle of judicial neutrality and returns the issue of abortion to the people and their elected representatives in the democratic process.

Chief Justice ROBERTS, concurring in the judgment.

We granted certiorari to decide one question: "Whether all pre-viability prohibitions on elective abortions are unconstitutional." . . . I agree with the Court that the viability line established by *Roe* and *Casey* should be discarded under a straightforward stare decisis analysis. . . . Our abortion precedents describe the right at issue as a woman's right to choose to terminate her pregnancy. That right should therefore extend far enough to ensure a reasonable opportunity to choose, but need not extend any further—certainly not all the way to viability. . . . The law at issue allows abortions up through fifteen weeks, providing an adequate opportunity to exercise the right *Roe* protects. [But that is all I would say, out of adherence to a simple yet fundamental principle of judicial restraint.] I therefore concur only in the judgment.

Justice BREYER, Justice SOTOMAYOR, and Justice KAGAN, dissenting.

For half a century, Roe v. Wade and Planned Parenthood v. Casey have protected the liberty and equality of women. . . . Respecting a woman as an autonomous being, and granting her full equality, meant giving her substantial choice over this most personal and most consequential of all life decisions.

Roe and *Casey* [recognized] that "the State has legitimate interests from the outset of the pregnancy in protecting" the "life of the fetus that may become a child." So the Court struck a balance, as it often does when values and goals compete. It held that the State could prohibit abortions after fetal viability, so long as the ban contained exceptions to safeguard a woman's life or health. It held that even before viability, the State could regulate the abortion procedure in multiple and meaningful ways. But until the viability line was crossed, the Court held, a State could not impose a "substantial obstacle" on a woman's "right to elect the procedure" as she (not the government) thought proper, in light of all the circumstances and complexities of her own life.

Today, the Court discards that balance. It says that from the very moment of fertilization, a woman has no rights to speak of. A State can force her to bring a pregnancy to term, even at the steepest personal and familial costs. An abortion restriction, the majority holds, is permissible whenever rational, the lowest level of scrutiny known to the law. And because, as the Court has often stated, protecting fetal life is rational, States will feel free to enact all manner of restrictions. [A]fter today's ruling, some States may compel women to carry to term a fetus with severe physical anomalies—for example, one afflicted with Tay-Sachs disease, sure to die within a few years of birth. States may even argue that a prohibition on abortion need make no provision for protecting a woman from risk of death or physical harm. Across a vast array of circumstances, a State will be able to impose its moral choice on a woman and coerce her to give birth to a child.

Enforcement of all these draconian restrictions will also be left largely to the States' devices. . . . Perhaps, in the wake of today's decision, a state law will criminalize the woman's conduct too, incarcerating or fining her for daring to seek or obtain an abortion. And as Texas has recently shown, a State can turn neighbor against neighbor, enlisting fellow citizens in the effort to root out anyone who tries to get an abortion, or to assist another in doing so.

The majority tries to hide the geographically expansive effects of its holding. Today's decision, the majority says, permits "each State" to address abortion as it pleases. That is cold comfort, of course, for the poor woman who cannot get the money to fly to a distant State for a procedure. Above all others, women lacking financial resources will suffer from today's decision. . . .

Whatever the exact scope of the coming laws, one result of today's decision is certain: the curtailment of women's rights, and of their status as free and equal citizens. Yesterday, the Constitution guaranteed that a woman confronted with an unplanned pregnancy could (within reasonable limits) make her own decision about whether to bear a child, with all the life-transforming consequences that act involves. And in thus safeguarding each woman's reproductive freedom, the Constitution also protected "[t]he ability of women to participate equally in [this Nation's] economic and social life." But no longer. As of today, this Court holds, a State can always force a woman to give birth, prohibiting even the earliest abortions. . . . Some women, especially women of means, will find ways around the State's assertion of power. Others—those without money or childcare or the ability to take time off from work—will not be so fortunate. Maybe they will try an unsafe method of abortion, and come to physical harm, or even die. Maybe they will undergo pregnancy and have a child, but at significant personal or familial cost. At the least, they will incur the cost of losing control of their lives. The Constitution will, today's majority holds, provide no shield, despite its guarantees of liberty and equality for all.

And no one should be confident that this majority is done with its work. The right *Roe* and *Casey* recognized does not stand alone. To the contrary, the Court has linked it for decades to other settled freedoms involving bodily integrity, familial relationships, and procreation. Most obviously, the right to terminate a pregnancy arose straight out of the right to purchase and use contraception. In turn, those rights led, more recently, to rights of same-sex intimacy and marriage. They are all part of the same constitutional fabric, protecting autonomous decisionmaking over the most personal of life decisions. The majority (or to be more accurate, most of it) is eager to tell us today that nothing it does "cast[s] doubt on precedents that do not concern abortion." But how could that be? The lone rationale for what the majority does today is that the right to elect an abortion is not "deeply rooted in history". . . . The same could be said, though, of most of the rights the majority claims it is not tampering with.

. . .The majority makes this change based on a single question: Did the reproductive right recognized in *Casey* exist in "1868, the year when the Fourteenth Amendment was ratified"? . . . The majority's core legal postulate, then, is that we in the 21st century must read the Fourteenth Amendment just as its ratifiers did. . . . But, of course, "people" did not ratify the Fourteenth Amendment. Men did. So it is perhaps not so surprising that the ratifiers were not perfectly attuned to the importance of reproductive rights for women's liberty, or for their capacity to participate as equal members of our Nation. . . . When the majority says that we must read our foundational charter as viewed at the time of ratification (except that we may also check it against the Dark Ages), it consigns women to second-class citizenship. . . .

[T]his Court has rejected the majority's pinched view of how to read our Constitution. [I]n the words of the great Chief Justice John Marshall, our Constitution is "intended to endure for ages to come," and must adapt itself to a future "seen dimly," if at all. That is indeed why . . . the Framers defined rights in general terms, to permit future evolution in their scope and meaning. And over the course of our history, this Court has taken up the Framers' invitation. It has kept true to the Framers' principles by applying them in new ways, responsive to new societal understandings and conditions.

Nowhere has that approach been more prevalent than in construing the majestic but open-ended words of the Fourteenth Amendment—the guarantees of "liberty" and "equality" for all. And nowhere has that approach produced prouder moments, for this country and the Court. Consider [what] the proposed, historically circumscribed approach would have meant for interracial marriage. The Fourteenth Amendment's ratifiers did not think it gave black and white people a right to marry each other. To the contrary, contemporaneous practice deemed that act quite as unprotected as abortion. Yet the Court in Loving v. Virginia read the Fourteenth Amendment to embrace the Lovings' union. . . . The Constitution does not freeze for all time the original view of what those rights guarantee, or how they apply. . . .

When the Court decimates a right women have held for 50 years, the Court is not being "scrupulously neutral." It is instead taking sides. . . .

By overruling *Roe*, *Casey*, and more than 20 cases reaffirming or applying the constitutional right to abortion, the majority abandons stare decisis, a principle central to the rule of law. . . . Stare decisis "contributes to the integrity of our constitutional system of government" by ensuring that decisions "are founded in the law rather than in the proclivities of individuals." [U]nder traditional stare decisis principles, the majority has no special justification for the harm it causes. . . . The majority has overruled *Roe* and *Casey* for one and only one reason: because it has always despised them, and now it has the votes to discard them. The majority thereby substitutes a rule by judges for the rule of law. . . .

Contrary to the majority's view, there is nothing unworkable about *Casey*'s "undue burden" standard. [I]t has given rise to no more conflict in application than many standards this Court and others unhesitatingly apply every day. . . . Anyone concerned about workability should consider the majority's substitute standard. . . . This Court will surely face critical questions about how that test applies. . . . How much risk to a woman's life can a State force her to incur, before the Fourteenth Amendment's protection of life kicks in? [T]he majority's ruling today [also] invites a host of questions about interstate conflicts. [The majority] discards a known, workable, and predictable standard in favor of something novel and probably far more complicated.

[N]o subsequent factual developments have undermined *Roe* and *Casey*. . . . The only notable change we can see since *Roe* and *Casey* cuts in favor of adhering to precedent: It is that American abortion law has become more and more aligned with other nations. . . .

The reasons for retaining *Roe* and *Casey* gain further strength from the overwhelming reliance interests those decisions have created. . . . "The most striking feature of the [majority opinion] is the absence of any serious discussion" of how its ruling will affect women. . . . For half a century now, in *Casey*'s words, "[t]he ability of women to participate equally in the economic and social life of the Nation has been facilitated by their ability to control their reproductive lives." Indeed, all women now of childbearing age have grown up expecting that they would be able to avail themselves of *Roe*'s and *Casey*'s protections. The disruption of overturning *Roe* and *Casey* will therefore be profound. Abortion is a common medical procedure and a familiar experience in women's lives. About 18 percent of pregnancies in this country end in abortion, and about one quarter of American women will have an abortion before the age of 45. [P]eople today rely on their ability to control and time pregnancies when making countless life decisions: where to live, whether and how to invest in education or careers, how to allocate financial resources, and how to approach intimate and family relationships. . . . Taking away the right to abortion, as the majority does today, destroys all those individual plans and expectations. . . .

It is [poor] women . . . who will suffer most. These are the women most likely to seek abortion care in the first place. Women living below the federal poverty line experience unintended pregnancies at rates five times higher than higher income women do, and nearly half of women who seek abortion care live in households below the poverty line. . . . Many will endure the costs and risks of pregnancy and giving birth against their wishes. Others will turn in desperation to illegal and unsafe abortions. They may lose not just their freedom, but their lives. . . .

With sorrow—for this Court, but more, for the many millions of American women who have today lost a fundamental constitutional protection—we dissent.

Notes and Questions

1. Holding and new standard of review. *Dobbs* clearly and definitively overrules *Roe* and *Casey*. In the questions below, consider how the Court reached this conclusion. Also consider whether this shift is the result of intervening legal developments or whether, as the dissent argues, the decision is best understood as a reflection of changes in the Supreme Court's composition. After *Dobbs*, what is the new constitutional standard for review of abortion restrictions? How does it differ from the standard(s) set forth in *Roe* and *Casey* for evaluating these restrictions? Are there any kinds of abortion restrictions that may fail this test? How did *Roe* and *Casey* characterize the state interests implicated by abortion? How does the *Dobbs* Court characterize these interests? How does the dissent respond?

2. Substantive due process/liberty analysis.

a. Demise of privacy rhetoric. In *Roe*, the Court held that the "right to privacy" included the right to terminate a pregnancy. More recently, the Court abandoned the privacy rhetoric and grounded the right to abortion in the "liberty" protected by the Fourteenth Amendment's Due Process Clause. According to the *Dobbs* majority, how does a court determine whether a particular interest is a "liberty" entitled to heightened protection under the Due Process Clause? What is the joint dissent's critique of this approach? According to the dissent, how *should* a court answer that question?

b. Originalism rationale. Part of the majority's argument is that at the time of the ratification of the Fourteenth Amendment, there was no history and tradition of state protection for reproductive autonomy regarding abortion. Is that an accurate description of the history? Some commentators vehemently disagree and argue that a key purpose of the Fourteenth Amendment was to do just that—to end a practice of denying reproductive and family autonomy to enslaved persons and to establish constitutional protection for those choices going forward.[45]

c. Precedents. Does the majority's approach accord with that applied in the Court's prior substantive due process decisions, such as *Griswold*? How *should* a court determine whether an interest is a protected due process liberty interest?

[45]. See, e.g., Peggy Cooper Davis, The Reconstruction Amendments Matter When Considering Abortion Rights, Wash. Post, May 3, 2022 (contending that "For more than 200 years, America lived with slavery and felt the brutality of its disregard of enslaved people's family ties and of their reproductive autonomy and choice. As a consequence, the United States amended its Constitution to strengthen its commitment to human liberty in the formation and families and the conduct of family life."), https://www.washingtonpost.com/outlook/2022/05/03/reconstruction-amendments-matter-when-considering-abortion-rights/.

What does Justice Thomas say about the future of "substantive due process" in his concurring opinion? After *Dobbs*, what is the status of the "right to privacy" established in *Griswold* and expanded in *Roe* and *Casey*? Or, to put it a different way, are those other substantive due process decisions now vulnerable after *Dobbs*?

3. Stare decisis and reliance. The *Dobbs* Court considers whether stare decisis applies. What factors are relevant in determining whether a prior precedent should be overruled, according to the majority? How do these factors compare to the ones identified in *Casey*? Does the majority prioritize any of these factors? Traditionally, the "workability" of prior precedents—that is, whether the precedents establish rules that can be "understood and applied in a consistent and predictable manner"—is a factor that the Court considers when deciding whether to adhere to that precedent. How do the majority and dissent differ in their characterization of the "workability" of the *Roe-Casey* standards? Reliance is another factor that the Court traditionally has considered under the doctrine of stare decisis. What does the majority say about the relevance of reliance and which kinds of reliance are relevant? What is the joint dissent's response? Which view is more persuasive?

4. Alternative theory: sex discrimination. What alternative approaches or theories might *Roe* have used rather than a right-to-privacy/substantive due process liberty rationale? Many feminist commentators (e.g., Sylvia Law, Reva Siegel, and Justice Ruth Bader Ginsburg) have long argued that abortion restrictions violate principles of equal protection. While a majority of the Court never invalidated an abortion restriction on this ground, recall that Justice Blackmun relied on this argument in his *Casey* concurrence. How does the *Dobbs* majority respond to the argument that abortion restrictions constitute impermissible sex discrimination? How does the dissent? Which response is more persuasive? What are the advantages and disadvantages of an equal protection rationale compared to the due process/right-to-privacy rationale? Does *Dobbs* foreclose the former approach for future challenges to abortion restrictions?

5. Impact of the *Dobbs* decision. A study released in 2020 by Advancing New Standards in Reproductive Health (ANSIRH), conducted by a team of researchers based at the University of California San Francisco Medical Center (UCSF), called the Turnaway Study, found "that when people are denied abortion care, they and their families experience harms for years to come, in the form of economic insecurity, poorer physical health, reduced ambitions, and negative effects on their relationships and their children."[46] Among other things, the Turnaway Study found that "[y]ears after an abortion denial, women were more likely to not have enough money to cover basic living expenses like food, housing and transportation."[47] The study also examined the impacts of abortion bans on children and found that

---

[46]. ANSIRH Statement on the Dobbs v. Jackson Decision, June 24, 2022, https://www.ansirh.org/research/research/ansirh-statement-dobbs-v-jackson-decision.

[47]. The Turnaway Study, https://www.ansirh.org/sites/default/files/publications/files/the_harms_of_denying_a_woman_a_wanted_abortion_4-16-2020.pdf. For more information, see Diane Greene Foster, The Turnaway Study: Ten Years, A Thousand Women, and the Consequences of Having—or Being Denied—an Abortion (2020). See also https://www.ansirh.org/research/ongoing/turnaway-study.

children are more likely to live below the poverty line if they are born as a result of abortion denial.

People may also experience physical health consequences as a result of abortion restrictions. Pregnancy can result in health complications for some people. When a person is experiencing health complications while pregnant, abortion bans may affect the care that they receive. In March 2023, a lawsuit was filed by several women who allege that they experienced harm due to delays in medical care during their pregnancies as a result of abortion bans.[48]

For some people, the inability to access abortion care will result in death. The evidence indicates that low-income women and women of color disproportionately experience this adverse health outcome. For example, Black women are three times more likely than white women to die from pregnancy-related causes.[49]

6. Legal penalties for participants.

a. Health care providers. All abortion bans and restrictions apply to abortion clinics that perform surgical abortions. Some laws also extend to physicians' offices or sites where only medication abortion is administered.[50] In addition, some states have enacted "SB 8 copycat laws," modeled after Texas SB 8, the Texas law that bans abortion at an early gestational age and is enforced through private actions.

b. Pregnant women. In the past, states rarely imposed penalties for accessing abortion care on pregnant women themselves. This reluctance seems to be changing, according to advocates who warn that criminal charges even for miscarriages and other pregnancy losses will become more common after *Dobbs*.[51] What are the arguments for and against the imposition of criminal penalties on the pregnant person?

c. Helpers. The criminalization movement extends not only to people for self-managing their own abortions, but also to people helping them do so. A recent empirical study of 61 cases of people "investigated or arrested for allegedly ending their own pregnancy or for helping someone else do so" reveals that 74 percent involved the imposition of the criminal process on people who self-manage their abortion care; 26 percent of cases involved people who helped others self-manage

---

[48]. See, e.g., Kate Zernike, Five Women Sue Texas over the State's Abortion Ban, N.Y. Times, Mar. 6, 2023.

[49]. See, e.g., Ctrs. for Disease Control & Prevention, Working Together to Reduce Black Maternal Mortality, Apr. 3, 2023, https://www.cdc.gov/healthequity/features/maternal-mortality/index.html.

[50]. Guttmacher Inst., Targeted Regulations of Abortion Providers, Apr. 24, 2023, https://www.guttmacher.org/state-policy/explore/targeted-regulation-abortion-providers.

[51]. See, e.g., Devin Dwyer & Patty See, ABC News, Prosecuting Pregnancy Loss: Why Advocates Fear a Post-*Roe* Surge of Charges, Sept. 23, 2022, https://abcnews.go.com/Politics/prosecuting-pregnancy-loss-advocates-fear-post-roe-surge/story?id=89812204; Melissa Jeltsen, The Coming Rise of Abortion as a Crime, Atlantic Mag., July 1, 2022, https://www.theatlantic.com/family/archive/2022/07/roe-illegal-abortions-pregnancy-termination-state-crime/661420/2. As part of a recent trend, several states (Arkansas, Georgia, Kentucky, South Carolina, and Oklahoma) are considering bills that impose felony liability on people who have had an abortion. Rose Mackenzie, ACLU, News & Commentary, No One Should Face the Death Penalty for Accessing Health Care, Mar. 14, 2023, https://www.aclu.org/news/reproductive-freedom/no-one-should-face-the-death-penalty-for-accessing-health-care. See also Idaho Code §18-606(2) ("A woman who knowingly submits to or solicits an illegal abortion for herself is guilty of a felony and (i) shall be fined up to $5,000, and (ii) imprisoned from one (1) to five (5) years").

their care. The vast majority of cases (87 percent) that involved law enforcement led to an arrest; most of these latter cases (92 percent) proceeded through the criminal court process. Although most cases came to the attention of law enforcement by health care professionals and social workers, a quarter of the cases were disclosed by friends, parents, or intimate partners.[52] In one well-publicized case, a man filed a wrongful death lawsuit against his wife's three friends who helped the man's wife obtain medication for her abortion. Two of the women then countersued him for invasion of privacy.[53] What is the purpose of these lawsuits against third parties?

7. Interstate implications.   An important question is whether states with restrictive laws can regulate access to abortion outside their borders. To what extent can anti-abortion lawmakers target conduct that happens outside their state lines? For example, can lawmakers ban their citizens from leaving the state to obtain abortions elsewhere, or impose criminal penalties when the person returns to the state after having obtained abortion care? Suppose that a person obtains medication abortion pills from an out-of-state provider but takes the pill(s) in a state that bans abortion. Can civil or criminal liability attach to the patient or the provider, even if the pills were legal in the state where they were dispensed? Can states impose penalties on state residents who help pregnant people obtain abortions in another state?[54]

8. Legal developments in the wake of *Dobbs*.

a. State efforts to ban and restrict access to abortion. Access to abortion throughout the country changed rapidly following *Dobbs*. As of August 2023, 15 states ban abortion.[55] Many of these laws do not include exceptions for rape and incest; and exceptions for situations when the life of the pregnant person is at risk are typically vague, leaving health care providers in doubt about the legality of their provision of abortion care.

b. State efforts to protect access to abortion. On the other hand, as of July 2023, abortion is protected under state law in 21 states and the District of Columbia.[56] Most of these states are on the West Coast and the Eastern Seaboard. In addition to protecting access to abortion, in the wake of *Dobbs*, some of these state laws expand the types of medical professionals who can provide abortion services to include nurse practitioners, midwives, and physician assistants—thereby expanding access as clinics prepare for a possible surge of patients traveling from restrictive states to obtain abortion care and expanding financial support for

---

[52]. Laura Huss et al., Lawyering for Reproductive Justice, Self-Care, Criminalized: August 2022 Preliminary Findings, file:///C:/Users/Kelly/Downloads/22_08_SMA-Criminalization-Research-Preliminary-Release-Findings-Brief_FINAL.pdf.

[53]. Emily Bazelon, Husband Sued over His Ex-Wife's Abortion; Now Her Friends Are Suing Him, N.Y. Times, May 4, 2023, https://www.nytimes.com/2023/05/04/us/texas-man-suing-ex-wife-abortion.html. See also Michelle Goldberg, Abortion Opponents Want to Make Women Afraid to Get Help from Their Friends, N.Y. Times, Mar. 13, 2023, https://www.nytimes.com/2023/03/13/opinion/abortion-lawsuit-texas.html.

[54]. See David S. Cohen, Greer Donley & Rachel Rebouché, The New Abortion Battleground, 123 Colum. L. Rev. 1 (2023) (posing these questions).

[55]. Tracking Abortion Bans Across the Country, N.Y. Times, https://www.nytimes.com/interactive/2022/us/abortion-laws-roe-v-wade.html (as of Aug. 1, 2023).

[56]. Ctr. for Reprod. Rights, After *Roe* Fell: Abortion Laws by State, https://reproductiverights.org/maps/abortion-laws-by-state/ (last viewed Sept. 19, 2023).

abortion access. In addition, some states (including California, Connecticut, and New York) have enacted so-called interstate shield laws that seek to provide some protection for abortion providers from civil and/or criminal penalties imposed under the laws of other states.

In light of the elimination of protection for abortion under the U.S. Constitution, abortion rights advocates are increasingly turning to state constitutions as potential sources of protection. This effort piggybacks on a previous reform approach that extended greater protection for the right to abortion under state constitutions.[57]

c. Federal proposals. Congress recently considered a bill that would have prohibited a range of restrictions on abortion access, including prohibitions on telemedicine abortion care, as well as certain state bans or restrictions on medication abortion. Women's Health Protection Act, S. 4132, 117th Cong. (2021-2022). The House of Representatives previously passed the bill (H.R. 3755) in a 218-211 vote, but the bill failed in the Senate, falling far short of the 60 votes needed to overcome the filibuster.

9. Abortion pills. Medication abortion, also known as "abortion with pills," is medical protocol for terminating a pregnancy. In the United States, this protocol generally involves taking two different drugs, mifepristone and misoprostol. The FDA approved the use of mifepristone in 2000. Today, medication abortions, which can be used through 10 weeks of pregnancy, account for more than half of all abortion procedures in the United States.

In January 2023, the FDA finalized a rule permitting mifepristone to be dispensed by retail pharmacies. It was speculated that this effort might increase access and availability of abortion pills in those jurisdictions in which they remain legal. As noted above, there is pending litigation challenging the FDA's approval of mifepristone. The issue is expected to be decided by the U.S. Supreme Court.[58]

10. Ending the abortion battle? In his majority opinion in *Dobbs*, Justice Alito argues that one reason for overruling *Roe* and *Casey* is that those decisions failed to bring an end to the abortion battle. Is *Dobbs* likely to defuse the issue?

11. Assisted reproduction. In vitro fertilization (IVF) is a form of assisted reproduction that involves creating embryos outside the body. See Chapter IX. Typically, many more embryos are created than are needed. Some people destroy unused embryos. Others have them stored, often indefinitely. Still others donate them to other recipients. What are the implications of *Dobbs* for these forms of assisted reproduction? Could a state ban IVF? Could a state ban the destruction of embryos created through IVF? On what grounds might someone challenge such a statute? If challenged on those grounds, how should a court rule?

12. Comparative perspective. Wide variations in abortion policy exist worldwide. How does the dissent address the evolution of abortion policy worldwide?

---

[57]. State Constitutions and Abortion Rights, Ctr. for Reprod. Rights, July 2022, https://reproductiverights.org/wp-content/uploads/2022/07/State-Constitutions-Report-July-2022.pdf.

[58]. See generally David S. Cohen, Greer Donley & Rachel Rebouché, Abortion Pills, 76 Stan. L. Rev. (forthcoming 2024).

How do *Roe* and *Casey* fit into that trend, according to the dissent? Note that our nearest neighbors, Canada and Mexico, both have more liberal abortion policies than the United States currently does. Last year, Mexico's Supreme Court unanimously ruled that penalizing abortion is unconstitutional. Canada allows abortion at any point during pregnancy. According to the Council on Foreign Relations, "[a]lthough the legal status of abortion varies considerably by region, a large majority of countries permit abortion under at least some circumstances. . . . Most industrialized countries allow the procedure without restriction."[59]

NOTE: IMPACTS OF *DOBBS* ON THE LIVES OF WOMEN AND THEIR CHILDREN

ANSIRH, University of California, San Francisco, *The Harms of Denying a Woman a Wanted Abortion: Findings from The Turnaway Study*[60]

https://www.ansirh.org/sites/default/files/publications/files/the_harms_of _denying_a_woman_a_wanted_abortion_4-16-2020.pdf

The Turnaway Study conducted at the University of California, San Francisco, shows that women experience harm from being denied a wanted abortion. These findings have far-reaching implications for lawmakers, judges, health agencies and others as they consider policies that restrict abortion access.

Denying a woman an abortion creates economic hardship and insecurity which lasts for years.

- Women who were turned away and went on to give birth experienced an increase in household poverty lasting at least four years relative to those who received an abortion.
- Years after an abortion denial, women were more likely to not have enough money to cover basic living expenses like food, housing and transportation.
- Being denied an abortion lowered a woman's credit score, increased a woman's amount of debt and increased the number of their negative public financial records, such as bankruptcies and evictions.

Women turned away from getting an abortion are more likely to stay in contact with a violent partner. They are also more likely to raise the resulting child alone.

---

[59]. Abortion Law: Global Comparisons, Council on Foreign Relations (June 24, 2022), https://www.cfr.org/article/abortion-law-global-comparisons.

[60]. The Turnaway Study is the first study to examine the long-term effects of receiving versus being denied a wanted abortion on women and their children. The sample included nearly 1,000 women seeking abortion from 30 facilities nationwide who were followed over a five-year period. Researchers compared the trajectories of those who received abortions to those who were turned away because they were past the facility's gestational age limit. More information about The Turnaway Study is available at https://www.ansirh.org/research/ongoing/turnaway-study.

- Physical violence from the man involved in the pregnancy decreased for women who received abortions but not for the women who were denied abortions and gave birth.
- By five years, women denied abortions were more likely to be raising children alone – without family members or male partners – compared to women who received an abortion.

The financial wellbeing and development of children is negatively impacted when their mothers are denied abortion.

- The children women already have at the time they seek abortions show worse child development when their mother is denied an abortion compared to the children of women who receive one.
- Children born as a result of abortion denial are more likely to live below the federal poverty level than children born from a subsequent pregnancy to women who received the abortion.
- Carrying an unwanted pregnancy to term is associated with poorer maternal bonding, such as feeling trapped or resenting the baby, with the child born after abortion denial, compared to the next child born to a woman who received an abortion.

Giving birth is connected to more serious health problems than having an abortion.

- Women who were denied an abortion and gave birth reported more life-threatening complications like eclampsia and postpartum hemorrhage compared to those who received wanted abortions.
- Women who were denied an abortion and gave birth instead reported more chronic headaches or migraines, joint pain, and gestational hypertension compared to those who had an abortion.
- The higher risks of childbirth were tragically demonstrated by two women who were denied an abortion and died following delivery. No women died from an abortion.

Women who receive a wanted abortion are more financially stable, set more ambitious goals, raise children under more stable conditions, and are more likely to have a wanted child later.

Samantha Artiga et al., What Are the Implications of the Overturning of Roe v. Wade for Racial Disparities?

KFF, July 15, 2022

*https://www.kff.org/racial-equity-and-health-policy/issue-brief
/what-are-the-implications-of-the-overturning-of-roe-v-wade-for-racial-disparities/*

[D]ata on abortions by race/ethnicity [shows] how overturning Roe v. Wade disproportionately impacts women of color [as explained below].

More than half of abortions are among women of color based on available data. In 2019, almost four in ten of abortions were among Black women (38%), one-third were among White women (33%), one in five among

Hispanic women (21%), and 7% among women of other racial and ethnic groups . . . .

There are a variety of potential reasons why abortion rates are higher among some women of color. [O]verall, Black, Hispanic, American Indian and Alaska Native (AIAN), and Native Hawaiian and Other Pacific Islander (NHOPI) women have more limited access to health care, which affects women's access to contraception and other sexual health services that are important for pregnancy planning. . . . Some women of color live in areas with more limited access to comprehensive contraceptive options. . . . Many women of color also report discrimination by individual providers, with reports of dismissive treatment, assumption of stereotypes, and inattention to conditions that take a disproportionate toll on women of color. . . . These factors have contributed to medical mistrust, which some women cite as a reason that they may not access contraception. In addition, inequities across broader social and economic factors—such as income, housing, and safety and education—that drive health, often referred to as social determinants of health, also affect decisions related to family planning and reproductive health. . . .

Over four in ten (43%) of women between ages 18-49 living in states where abortion has become or will likely become illegal are women of color. As of May 2022, 17 states had laws in place intended to immediately ban abortion, including four that had a law banning abortion in place predating Roe v. Wade. Overall, 18.1 million or 28% of women ages 18-49 live in these 17 states. Among women ages 18-49 living in these states, 22% are Hispanic, 14% are Black, and 4% are Asian . . . .

Variation in the availability of abortions by state due to the overturning of Roe v. Wade will likely result in women of color facing disproportionate barriers to accessing abortions. Women of color face more barriers to accessing health care in general and have more limited access to coverage of abortions. Moreover, due to underlying structural inequities, women of color have more limited financial resources and may face other increased barriers to accessing abortions if they need to travel out of state for one. . . .

Women of color between ages 18-49 face greater barriers to accessing health care overall compared to their White counterparts. Among women in this age group, roughly a quarter of Hispanic (24%) and AIAN (24%) women are uninsured as are 16% of NHOPI women and 13% of Black women. In contrast, less than one in ten (9%) of White women lack insurance. . . . Moreover, prior to the *Dobbs* decision, even among those who were insured, women of color had more limited access to abortion coverage since they are more likely to be covered by Medicaid, which has limited coverage for abortions. . . .

Women of color have more limited financial resources and transportation options than White women, which would make it more difficult for them to travel out of state for an abortion. The median self-pay cost of obtaining an abortion exceeds $500. Traveling out of state will raise the cost of abortion due to added costs for transportation, accommodations, and childcare. Moreover, it may result in more missed work, meaning greater loss of pay. . . .

Some women of color may also have immigration-related fears about traveling out of state for an abortion. Among women ages 18-49, over a third of Asian women (35%), over a quarter (27%) of Hispanic women, and one in five (20%) NHOPI women are noncitizens, who includes lawfully present and undocumented immigrants . . . . Noncitizen women and those living in mixed immigration status families may fear that traveling out of state could put them or a family member at risk for negative impacts on their immigration status or detention or deportation, especially if states move to criminalize abortion. . . .

NOTE: IMPLICATIONS OF *DOBBS* FOR PREGNANT MINORS

The teen pregnancy rate has been declining for decades.[61] Nonetheless, hundreds of thousands of minors in the United States become pregnant every year. These young people have always faced unique challenges to accessing abortion care. As noted above, prior to *Dobbs*, many states required minors to obtain permission either from their parents/guardians or from a court. Now, many states ban abortions for all people, including minors. Moreover, even where abortion is legally available, minors face many practical hurdles to access. These barriers—both legal and practical—have only grown in the wake of *Dobbs*.

Minors "face greater barriers to preventing pregnancy in the first place, including barriers to accessing contraception and limited access to comprehensive sexual health education."[62] As a result, they are more likely to have unplanned pregnancies. Teens may have a lack of awareness of their pregnancy, which can delay attempts to obtain abortion care. Moreover, in a post-*Dobbs* world, many people are hundreds of miles from access to abortion care.[63] Minors often do not have the financial resources to travel these distances,[64] and even if they have the financial resources, they may not be permitted to purchase plane or other tickets necessary to make the journey. (Moreover, as described below, people who help minors obtain abortion care may face legal risks.) The people who are "least likely to have resources and social networks to support them as they navigate barriers to abortion access," are those who have higher rates of teen pregnancies, "youth who are poor, people of color, LGBTQ+, and those who are in foster care or in the criminal justice system."[65]

---

[61]. Ctr. for Disease Control & Prevention, About Teen Pregnancy, https://www.cdc.gov/teenpregnancy/about/index.htm.

[62]. Tracey Wilkinson et al., A Major Problem for Minors: Post-*Roe* Access to Abortion, STAT News, June 26, 2022, https://www.statnews.com/2022/06/26/a-major-problem-for-minors-post-roe-access-to-abortion/.

[63]. For a visual map showing how this has changed post-*Dobbs*, see https://www.npr.org/sections/health-shots/2023/06/21/1183248911/abortion-access-distance-to-care-travel-miles.

[64]. Wilkinson et al., supra note [62].

[65]. Id.

NOTE: NEW IDAHO LAW TARGETS PEOPLE WHO HELP PREGNANT MINORS OBTAIN ABORTIONS

Idaho Governor Brad Little signed a law in April 2023 that makes abortion even more difficult for pregnant teens to access. The so-called abortion trafficking law is the first of its kind in the nation; the law makes it a crime to provide abortion pills to minors or to help them leave the state for abortion care. Idaho Code §18-623.

Under this law, adults are subject to felony liability and punishments from two to five years in prison for aiding a minor to procure an abortion. Procurement includes obtaining an abortion-inducing drug for the pregnant minor or recruiting, harboring, or transporting the pregnant minor within the state. The crime is committed if an adult drives a minor across state lines for an abortion or helps them find an abortion provider out of state.

The criminal ban provides an affirmative defense for adults who help pregnant minors access abortions with the consent of parents/legal guardians. However, this defense does not extend to out-of-state abortion providers or providers of abortion-inducing drugs. In other words, if a pregnant Idaho minor obtains an abortion from an out-of-state physician, that procedure is illegal (even if it is legal in the state where the abortion was obtained).

The criminal law strengthens the state's near-total abortion ban, which prohibits abortions unless the pregnancy is the result of rape or incest (which must be reported to law enforcement and filed with the doctor) or is intended to save the life of the patient.

Another Idaho state law imposes civil liability on the pregnant teen's helpers by allowing certain family members to file civil lawsuits against doctors (whether in state or out of state) who perform an abortion, subject to a fine of $20,000 per violation. Idaho Code §18-8807. The relevant statute of limitations is four years following the abortion.

Together, the new criminal and civil provisions make abortion care virtually impossible to access for pregnant Idahoan teens.

B. Sexual Intimacy

LAWRENCE v. TEXAS
539 U.S. 558 (2003)

Justice KENNEDY delivered the opinion of the Court.

Liberty protects the person from unwarranted government intrusions into a dwelling or other private places. In our tradition the State is not omnipresent in the home. And there are other spheres of our lives and existence, outside the home, where the State should not be a dominant presence. Freedom extends beyond spatial bounds. Liberty presumes an autonomy of self that includes freedom of thought, belief, expression, and certain intimate conduct. The instant case involves liberty of the person both in its spatial and more transcendent dimensions.

The question before the Court is the validity of a Texas statute making it a crime for two persons of the same sex to engage in certain intimate sexual conduct. In Houston, Texas, officers of the Harris County Police Department were dispatched to a private residence in response to a reported weapons disturbance. They entered an apartment where one of the petitioners, John Geddes Lawrence, resided. . . . The officers observed Lawrence and another man, Tyron Garner, engaging in a sexual act. The two petitioners were arrested, held in custody overnight, and charged and convicted before a Justice of the Peace. . . .

. . . The applicable state law is Tex. Penal Code Ann. §21.06(a) (2003). It provides: "A person commits an offense if he engages in deviate sexual intercourse with another individual of the same sex." The statute defines "deviate sexual intercourse" as follows: "(A) any contact between any part of the genitals of one person and the mouth or anus of another person"; or "(B) the penetration of the genitals or the anus of another person with an object." §21.01(1). [Petitioners entered pleas of *nolo contendere* and were fined $200 each. On appeal, the court rejected petitioners' equal protection and due process arguments.]

We conclude the case should be resolved by determining whether the petitioners were free as adults to engage in the private conduct in the exercise of their liberty under the Due Process Clause of the Fourteenth Amendment to the Constitution. For this inquiry we deem it necessary to reconsider the Court's holding in [Bowers v. Hardwick, 478 U.S. 186 (1986)].

There are broad statements of the substantive reach of liberty under the Due Process Clause in earlier cases [citing *Pierce* and *Meyer*]; but the most pertinent beginning point is our decision in Griswold v. Connecticut, 381 U.S. 479 (1965). [The Court then reviews *Griswold, Eisenstadt, Roe,* and Carey v. Population Services International, 431 U.S. 678 (1977) (invalidating restrictions on minors' contraceptive choices).] [These subsequent cases] confirmed that the reasoning of *Griswold* could not be confined to the protection of rights of married adults. . . .

The Court began its substantive discussion in *Bowers* as follows: "The issue presented is whether the Federal Constitution confers a fundamental right upon homosexuals to engage in sodomy and hence invalidates the laws of the many States that still make such conduct illegal and have done so for a very long time." That statement, we now conclude, discloses the Court's own failure to appreciate the extent of the liberty at stake. To say that the issue in *Bowers* was simply the right to engage in certain sexual conduct demeans the claim the individual put forward, just as it would demean a married couple were it to be said marriage is simply about the right to have sexual intercourse. The laws involved in *Bowers* and here are, to be sure, statutes that purport to do no more than prohibit a particular sexual act. Their penalties and purposes, though, have more far-reaching consequences, touching upon the most private human conduct, sexual behavior, and in the most private of places, the home. The statutes do seek to control a personal relationship that, whether or not entitled to formal recognition in the law, is within the liberty of persons to choose without being punished as criminals.

This, as a general rule, should counsel against attempts by the State, or a court, to define the meaning of the relationship or to set its boundaries absent injury to a person or abuse of an institution the law protects. It suffices for us to acknowledge that adults may choose to enter upon this relationship in the confines of their homes and their own private lives and still retain their dignity as free persons. When sexuality finds overt expression in intimate conduct with another person, the conduct can be but one element in a personal bond that is more enduring. The liberty protected by the Constitution allows homosexual persons the right to make this choice.

Having misapprehended the claim of liberty there presented to it, and thus stating the claim to be whether there is a fundamental right to engage in consensual sodomy, the *Bowers* Court said: "Proscriptions against that conduct have ancient roots." [However, laws] prohibiting sodomy do not seem to have been enforced against consenting adults acting in private. . . . It was not until the 1970's that any State singled out same-sex relations for criminal prosecution, and only nine States have done so. Post-*Bowers* even some of these States did not adhere to the policy of suppressing homosexual conduct. Over the course of the last decades, States with same-sex prohibitions have moved toward abolishing them. . . .

It must be acknowledged, of course, that the Court in *Bowers* was making the broader point that for centuries there have been powerful voices to condemn homosexual conduct as immoral. The condemnation has been shaped by religious beliefs, conceptions of right and acceptable behavior, and respect for the traditional family. For many persons these are not trivial concerns, but profound and deep convictions accepted as ethical and moral principles to which they aspire and which thus determine the course of their lives. These considerations do not answer the question before us, however. The issue is whether the majority may use the power of the State to enforce these views on the whole society through operation of the criminal law. "Our obligation is to define the liberty of all, not to mandate our own moral code." Planned Parenthood of Southeastern Pa. v. Casey, 505 U.S. 833, 850 (1992).

[O]ur laws and traditions in the past half century are of most relevance here. These references show an emerging awareness that liberty gives substantial protection to adult persons in deciding how to conduct their private lives in matters pertaining to sex. . . . This emerging recognition should have been apparent when *Bowers* was decided. In 1955 the American Law Institute promulgated the Model Penal Code and made clear that it did not recommend or provide for "criminal penalties for consensual sexual relations conducted in private." ALI, Model Penal Code §213.2, Comment 2, p 372 (1980). It justified its decision on three grounds: (1) The prohibitions undermined respect for the law by penalizing conduct many people engaged in; (2) the statutes regulated private conduct not harmful to others; and (3) the laws were arbitrarily enforced and thus invited the danger of blackmail. ALI, Model Penal Code, Commentary 277-280 (Tent. Draft No. 4, 1955). [Other states changed their laws accordingly.]

The sweeping references by Chief Justice Burger [concurring in *Bowers*] to the history of Western civilization and to Judeo-Christian moral and ethical standards did not take account of other authorities pointing in an opposite direction. A committee advising the British Parliament recommended in 1957 repeal of laws punishing homosexual conduct. The Wolfenden Report: Report of the Committee on Homosexual Offenses and Prostitution (1963). Parliament enacted the substance of those recommendations 10 years later. Sexual Offences Act 1967, §1. Of even more importance, almost five years before *Bowers* was decided the European Court of Human Rights considered a case with parallels to *Bowers* and to today's case. . . . The court held that the laws proscribing the conduct were invalid under the European Convention on Human Rights. Dudgeon v. United Kingdom, 45 Eur. Ct. H.R. (1981) P 52. Authoritative in all countries that are members of the

Council of Europe (21 nations then, 45 nations now), the decision is at odds with the premise in *Bowers* that the claim put forward was insubstantial in our Western civilization.

In our own constitutional system the deficiencies in *Bowers* became even more apparent in the years following its announcement. The 25 States with laws prohibiting the relevant conduct referenced in the *Bowers* decision are reduced now to 13, of which 4 enforce their laws only against homosexual conduct. In those States where sodomy is still proscribed, whether for same-sex or heterosexual conduct, there is a pattern of nonenforcement with respect to consenting adults acting in private. . . .

Two principal cases decided after *Bowers* cast its holding into even more doubt. In Planned Parenthood of Southeastern Pa. v. Casey, 505 U.S. 833 (1992), the Court reaffirmed the substantive force of the liberty protected by the Due Process Clause. The *Casey* decision again confirmed that our laws and tradition afford constitutional protection to personal decisions relating to marriage, procreation, contraception, family relationships, child rearing, and education. In explaining the respect the Constitution demands for the autonomy of the person in making these choices, we stated as follows:

> "These matters, involving the most intimate and personal choices a person may make in a lifetime, choices central to personal dignity and autonomy, are central to the liberty protected by the Fourteenth Amendment. At the heart of liberty is the right to define one's own concept of existence, of meaning, of the universe, and of the mystery of human life. Beliefs about these matters could not define the attributes of personhood were they formed under compulsion of the State."

[505 U.S. at 851.] Persons in a homosexual relationship may seek autonomy for these purposes, just as heterosexual persons do. The decision in *Bowers* would deny them this right.

The second post-*Bowers* case of principal relevance is Romer v. Evans, 517 U.S. 620 (1996). There the Court struck down class-based legislation directed at homosexuals as a violation of the Equal Protection Clause. *Romer* invalidated an amendment to Colorado's constitution which named as a solitary class persons who were homosexuals, lesbians, or bisexual either by "orientation, conduct, practices or relationships," and deprived them of protection under state antidiscrimination laws. We concluded that the provision was "born of animosity toward the class of persons affected" and further that it had no rational relation to a legitimate governmental purpose.

[Although petitioners have a tenable equal protection argument under *Romer,* we must] address whether *Bowers* itself has continuing validity. Were we to hold the statute invalid under the Equal Protection Clause, some might question whether a prohibition would be valid if drawn differently, say, to prohibit the conduct both between same-sex and different-sex participants.

Equality of treatment and the due process right to demand respect for conduct protected by the substantive guarantee of liberty are linked in important respects, and a decision on the latter point advances both interests. . . . When homosexual conduct is made criminal by the law of the State, that declaration in and of itself is an invitation to subject homosexual persons to discrimination both in the public and in the private spheres. The central holding of *Bowers* has been brought in question by this case, and it should be addressed. Its continuance as precedent demeans the lives of homosexual persons. . . .

The foundations of *Bowers* have sustained serious erosion from our recent decisions in *Casey* and *Romer*. When our precedent has been thus weakened, criticism from other sources is of greater significance [citing commentators, state constitutional decisions, and authorities from other countries that rejected *Bowers's* reasoning]. The doctrine of stare decisis is essential to the respect accorded to the judgments of the Court and to the stability of the law. It is not, however, an inexorable command. . . . *Bowers* was not correct when it was decided, and it is not correct today. It ought not to remain binding precedent. Bowers v. Hardwick should be and now is overruled.

The present case does not involve minors. It does not involve persons who might be injured or coerced or who are situated in relationships where consent might not easily be refused. It does not involve public conduct or prostitution. It does not involve whether the government must give formal recognition to any relationship that homosexual persons seek to enter. The case does involve two adults who, with full and mutual consent from each other, engaged in sexual practices common to a homosexual lifestyle. The petitioners are entitled to respect for their private lives. The State cannot demean their existence or control their destiny by making their private sexual conduct a crime. Their right to liberty under the Due Process Clause gives them the full right to engage in their conduct without intervention of the government. "It is a promise of the Constitution that there is a realm of personal liberty which the government may not enter." *Casey,* supra, at 847. The Texas statute furthers no legitimate state interest which can justify its intrusion into the personal and private life of the individual. [Reversed.]

Justice O'CONNOR, concurring in the judgment. . . .

This case raises a different issue than *Bowers*: whether, under the Equal Protection Clause, moral disapproval is a legitimate state interest to justify by itself a statute that bans homosexual sodomy, but not heterosexual sodomy. It is not. Moral disapproval of this group [homosexuals], like a bare desire to harm the group, is an interest that is insufficient to satisfy rational basis review under the Equal Protection Clause.

. . . While it is true that the law applies only to conduct, the conduct targeted by this law is conduct that is closely correlated with being homosexual. Under such circumstances, Texas' sodomy law is targeted at more than conduct. It is instead directed toward gay persons as a class. [T]he State cannot single out one identifiable class of citizens for punishment that does not apply to everyone else, with moral disapproval as the only asserted state interest for the law. . . . A law branding one class of persons as criminal solely based on the State's moral disapproval of that class and the conduct associated with that class runs contrary to the values of the Constitution and the Equal Protection Clause, under any standard of review. . . .

Justice SCALIA, with whom THE CHIEF JUSTICE and Justice THOMAS join, dissenting. . . .

I begin with the Court's surprising readiness to reconsider a decision rendered a mere 17 years ago in Bowers v. Hardwick. . . . Today's approach to stare decisis invites us to overrule an erroneously decided precedent (including an "intensely divisive" decision) *if*: (1) its foundations have been "eroded" by subsequent decisions; (2) it has been subject to "substantial and continuing" criticism; and (3) it has not induced "individual or societal reliance" that counsels against overturning. The problem is that [Roe v. Wade] itself — which today's majority surely has no disposition to overrule — satisfies these conditions to at least the same degree as *Bowers*.

[To] distinguish the rock-solid, unamendable disposition of *Roe* from the readily overrulable *Bowers* [we need to examine] the third factor. . . . It seems to me that the "societal reliance" on the principles confirmed in *Bowers* and discarded today has been overwhelming. Countless judicial decisions and legislative enactments have relied on the ancient proposition that a governing majority's belief that certain sexual behavior is "immoral and unacceptable" constitutes a rational basis for regulation [citing cases relying on *Bowers*]. State laws against bigamy, same-sex marriage, adult incest, prostitution, masturbation, adultery, fornication, bestiality, and obscenity are likewise sustainable only in light of *Bowers'* validation of laws based on moral choices. Every single one of these laws is called into question by today's decision. . . .

What a massive disruption of the current social order, therefore, the overruling of *Bowers* entails. Not so the overruling of *Roe*, which would simply have restored the regime that existed for centuries before 1973, in which the permissibility of and restrictions upon abortion were determined legislatively State-by-State.

[To establish that *Bowers* was wrongly decided, the majority relies on an] "emerging awareness that liberty gives substantial protection to adult persons in deciding how to conduct their private lives *in matters pertaining to sex*" (emphasis added). Apart from the fact that such an "emerging awareness" does not establish a "fundamental right," the statement is factually false. States continue to prosecute all sorts of crimes by adults "in matters pertaining to sex": prostitution, adult incest, adultery, obscenity, and child pornography. Sodomy laws, too, have been enforced "in the past half century," in which there have been 134 reported cases involving prosecutions for consensual, adult, homosexual sodomy. [W. Eskridge, Gaylaw: Challenging the Apartheid of the Closet 375 (1999).]

In any event, an "emerging awareness" is by definition not "deeply rooted in this Nation's history and traditions," as we have said "fundamental right" status requires. Constitutional entitlements do not spring into existence because some States choose to lessen or eliminate criminal sanctions on certain behavior. Much less do they spring into existence, as the Court seems to believe, because *foreign nations* decriminalize conduct. . . .

I turn now to the ground on which the Court squarely rests its holding: the contention that there is no rational basis for the law here under attack. This proposition is so out of accord with our jurisprudence — indeed, with the jurisprudence of any society we know — that it requires little discussion.

The Texas statute undeniably seeks to further the belief of its citizens that certain forms of sexual behavior are "immoral and unacceptable," *Bowers*, supra, at 196 — the same interest furthered by criminal laws against fornication, bigamy, adultery, adult incest, bestiality, and obscenity. *Bowers* held that this *was* a legitimate state interest. The Court today reaches the opposite conclusion. . . . This effectively decrees the end of all morals legislation. If, as the Court asserts, the promotion of majoritarian sexual morality is not even a *legitimate* state interest, none of the above-mentioned laws can survive rational-basis review. . . .

Finally, I turn to petitioners' equal-protection challenge. . . . To be sure, §21.06 does distinguish between the sexes insofar as concerns the partner with whom the sexual acts are performed: men can violate the law only with other men, and women only with other women. But this cannot itself be a denial of equal protection, since it is precisely the same distinction regarding partner that is drawn in state laws prohibiting marriage with someone of the same sex while permitting marriage with someone of the opposite sex.

[Justice O'Connor's] reasoning leaves on pretty shaky grounds state laws limiting marriage to opposite-sex couples. [Her] "preserving the traditional institution of marriage" is just a kinder way of describing the State's *moral disapproval* of same-sex couples. . . .

Today's opinion is the product of a Court, which is the product of a law-profession culture, that has largely signed on to the so-called homosexual agenda, by which I mean the agenda promoted by some homosexual activists directed at eliminating the moral opprobrium that has traditionally attached to homosexual conduct. . . . It is clear from this that the Court has taken sides in the culture war, departing from its role of assuring, as neutral observer, that the democratic rules of engagement are observed. Many Americans do not want persons who openly engage in homosexual conduct as partners in their business, as scoutmasters for their children, as teachers in their children's schools, or as boarders in their home. They view this as protecting themselves and their families from a lifestyle that they believe to be immoral and destructive. . . . So imbued is the Court with the law profession's anti-anti-homosexual culture, that it is seemingly unaware that the attitudes of that culture are not obviously "mainstream"; that in most States what the Court calls "discrimination" against those who engage in homosexual acts is perfectly legal; that proposals to ban such "discrimination" under Title VII have repeatedly been rejected by Congress; and that in some cases such "discrimination" is a constitutional right, see Boy Scouts of America v. Dale, 530 U.S. 640 (2000).

Let me be clear that I have nothing against homosexuals, or any other group, promoting their agenda through normal democratic means. Social perceptions of sexual and other morality change over time, and every group has the right to persuade its fellow citizens that its view of such matters is the best. . . . But persuading one's fellow citizens is one thing, and imposing one's views in absence of democratic majority will is something else. I would no more *require* a State to criminalize homosexual acts — or, for that matter, display *any* moral disapprobation of them — than I would *forbid* it to do so. . . .

NOTE: WHO WAS JOHN LAWRENCE?

Patty Reinert, Pair Proud They Could Get Sodomy Law Thrown Out

Hous. Chron., Apr. 25, 2004, at A1

Almost six years after police stormed his apartment and arrested him for having sex with another man, this is what John Lawrence remembers: Harris

County Sheriff's Department officers shoving him to the couch, shattering the porcelain birds that were a gift from his mother. The humiliating ride to the station, wearing only handcuffs and underwear. The fingerprinting and mugshot, the bologna sandwich he ate in jail, the jeans another inmate gave him for the ride home, the cabbie who took him, though he had no wallet to pay. And the call to his elderly father to tell him what had happened. . . .

Tyrone Garner (left) and John Lawrence celebrate the Supreme Court victory.

In [their first interview] since the case began, Lawrence and Garner said they are proud to have helped defeat an unjust law, overwhelmed by the support they've received and so glad it's over. "I got a sense of justice for being wronged by the state of Texas," Lawrence said as he sat with Garner in lawyer Mitchell Katine's office. "I feel I've been vindicated." . . . "Would I have done the same thing again? Yes," he said. "When somebody is wronged and they don't stand up for themselves, they're going to get wronged again. I wasn't going to stand for it."

Garner, 36, who sells barbecue from a street stand, agreed. "It was worth it," he said. On Sept. 17, 1998, Garner and his boyfriend, Robert Royce Eubanks, were drinking margaritas and eating dinner at a Mexican restaurant with their friend, Lawrence. . . . Back at [Lawrence's] apartment after dinner, though, Eubanks and Garner argued. Eubanks left angry, saying he was going to buy a soda. Instead, he went to a pay telephone and called the police, reporting that there was a man with a gun in Lawrence's apartment. "I think he was jealous," Garner said.

When two Harris County deputies arrived, the door to the apartment was unlocked. They walked in with Eubanks following and discovered Lawrence and Garner having sex. Lawrence and Garner said they had no idea why they were being arrested. They spent the night in jail.

The charges stemmed from the 1973 Texas Homosexual Conduct Law. . . . At the time, Kansas, Oklahoma and Missouri had similar laws, and nine other states — Louisiana, Mississippi, Alabama, Florida, South Carolina, North Carolina, Virginia, Idaho and Utah — made sodomy a crime for heterosexuals as well as homosexuals. . . . Eubanks was convicted and sentenced to 30 days in jail for filing a false report to a peace officer. Garner forgave him and continued their relationship; Lawrence couldn't. . . .

[After their arrest], Lawrence and Garner returned to their lives. But Lawrence was stewing. When Katine, a partner at Houston's Williams, Birnberg & Andersen, and the New York-based Lambda Legal Defense and Education Fund offered their services for free, Lawrence decided to fight. Garner was reluctant, but he agreed. "I didn't think we'd win," Garner said. And though his friends and family knew he was gay, he said, "I didn't enjoy being outed with my mugshot on TV. It was degrading to me." . . .

[The day that the decision was expected, Lawrence flipped on the television and heard the announcement.] "I bolted out of bed and shouted, 'Thank you, God!'" he said. . . . "I called my brother, and we celebrated with a couple of bottles of champagne," Garner said. By nightfall, hundreds had gathered for a rally at City Hall. Katine, who had spent years shielding his clients from the media, introduced them to the crowd. People stood in line to meet them. . . . Neither were activists before their case, and they still aren't. . . . Both support the right of gay people to marry but aren't interested themselves. "I'm single and love it," Lawrence said.

Garner is touched by people who recognize him at the grocery store or on the street, and Lawrence loves to tell the story of two burly cops, working security outside a gay nightclub, approaching to give them a hug. Both laugh at the idea of cashing in with a book or a TV movie deal, and they shun comparisons some have made to Jane Roe of abortion rights fame or Rosa Parks, a civil rights icon. "I don't really want to be a hero," Garner said. "But I want to tell other gay people, 'Be who you are, and don't be afraid.' " . . .

[Both men died a few years later: John Lawrence in 2011, and Tyron Garner in 2006.]

Tony Mauro, A "Cultural Milestone" at the High Court: Lawrence *Gay Attorneys Turned Out in Force to Witness* Lawrence *Arguments*

Tex. Law., Mar. 31, 2004, at 11

Paul Smith brought energy, agility and a full command of the case to the podium when he argued on behalf of the Lambda Legal Defense and Education Fund . . . in the landmark gay rights case Lawrence v. Texas. He also brought personal experience. Smith, managing partner in Jenner & Block's Washington, D.C., office, is gay, a fact that was not widely talked about. . . .

"I think it gave me a greater comfort level answering questions . . .," says Smith, 48, a veteran of eight [previous] U.S. Supreme Court arguments . . . . "And I think there is a symbolic importance to the community that I was up there. . . ." The symbolism was palpable in the courtroom. Dozens of prominent gay lawyers filled the lawyers' section of the gallery. "The most remarkable thing about the argument was the audience," said Walter Dellinger of O'Melveny & Myers, who wrote an amicus curiae brief for several gay and civil rights groups. The presence of so many [gay] prominent lawyers . . . was a "cultural milestone," Dellinger said. . . .

Smith's advocacy also marked a milestone for Jenner & Block, which has become well-known as a firm that welcomes gay and lesbian lawyers. . . . He joined the firm 10 years ago "when I was not very 'out' in general, but it has been a very supportive place." . . .

Smith's sexual orientation is notable for another reason: He clerked for the late Justice Lewis Powell in 1981. Five years later, historians have noted that as Powell deliberated in Bowers v. Hardwick, he mused to a law clerk that "I don't believe I've ever met a homosexual." Powell was apparently unaware not only that the clerk he was speaking to was gay, but also that several of his previous clerks were gay.

... Smith holds no animosity toward Powell, who was the deciding vote in favor of upholding Georgia's anti-sodomy law. Smith notes that after Powell left the court in 1987, he said he regretted his vote in *Bowers*. "Obviously it was very troubling to him, and he came to believe he had made a mistake," Smith says, "Justice Powell was very much on my mind as I argued."

Notes and Questions

1. Constitutional basis. What is the constitutional right protected by *Lawrence*? The majority's opinion begins with the word "liberty" and ends with the word "freedom." Does the Court's opinion reflect a broad libertarian approach under which substantive due process presumptively protects all personal interests?

What is the scope of the liberty protected in *Lawrence*? Does the majority hew to *Griswold*'s focus on the spatial privacy of the bedroom and the home? What do the "more transcendent dimensions" of "liberty of the person" encompass? *Lawrence* quotes language from *Casey* that critics, including Justice Scalia (in an omitted portion of his dissent), call the "sweet-mystery-of-life passage." 539 U.S. at 588 (Scalia, J., dissenting). Does this language help define the interest at stake?

What role do equality principles play in the majority opinion? How does the majority respond to Justice O'Connor's reliance on the Equal Protection Clause? Why do you suppose the majority did not use the Equal Protection Clause to decide *Lawrence*? What role does the type of "animosity" found in Romer v. Evans play in *Lawrence*?

Despite the *Lawrence* majority's primary reliance on due process principles, commentators say the opinion synthesizes autonomy and equality principles by rejecting criminal statutes that subordinate a particular group of citizens.[66] This synergy between liberty and equality as a foundation for gay rights culminated later in Obergefell v. Hodges, 576 U.S. 644 (2015), guaranteeing access to marriage for same-sex couples (reprinted in Chapter II).

2. Bowers. In Bowers v. Hardwick, the Supreme Court held that enforcement of a state sodomy statute did not violate the Constitution. Citing the "ancient roots" of sodomy proscriptions, the majority opinion in *Bowers* found no fundamental right to privacy at stake and saw no connection between "family, marriage, or procreation on the one hand and homosexual activity on the other." Why did the Supreme Court overturn *Bowers*? How does *Lawrence* explain its overruling of *Bowers*, consistent with the doctrine of stare decisis?

---

[66]. See, e.g., Joslin, supra note [7], at 449 (exploring the "fusion between principles of equality and liberty" in the Court's LGBTQ rights cases); Pamela S. Karlan, Foreword: Loving *Lawrence*, 102 Mich. L. Rev. 1447, 1449 (2004) ("*Lawrence* is a case about liberty that has important implications for the jurisprudence of equality."); Kenji Yoshino, The New Equal Protection, 124 Harv. L. Rev. 747, 749 (2011) (naming "such hybrid equality/liberty claims as 'dignity' claims").

3. Standard of review. *Bowers*, which saw no fundamental right at stake, used the rational basis test. What standard of review does *Lawrence* use? Does *Lawrence* shed any light on the level of scrutiny that should apply to discrimination based on sexual orientation? Commentators continue to debate that question.[67]

4. Morality and religion. The appropriate role of morality as well as religion are pervasive issues in family law. In *Bowers*, the Supreme Court concluded that Georgia satisfied the rational basis test because its electorate regarded sodomy as immoral and unacceptable. In *Lawrence*, why do majoritarian moral values fail to justify the Texas statute? Evaluate Justice Scalia's prediction that the *Lawrence* majority's approach dooms "all morals legislation." In Gonzales v. Carhart, decided by the Court shortly after *Lawrence*, Justice Kennedy invoked morality to uphold the constitutionality of an abortion procedure. His reasoning there contrasts with his rejection of morality as a justification for prohibitions on same-sex sodomy in *Lawrence*. What might explain the difference?

In *Lawrence*, Justice Scalia's use of the term "culture war" invites a discourse about a number of contested family law (and family values) issues, including reproductive rights, gender equality, gay rights, end-of-life decisions, and the legislatures' and courts' roles in such matters. What role should morality and religious beliefs play in official resolutions of such disputes?

5. Foreign law. What is the appropriate role for foreign legal authorities, such as those cited by the *Lawrence* majority, when battles in the culture wars reach American courts? Note that the Supreme Court previously relied on foreign and international law to invalidate certain punishments. See, e.g., Graham v. Florida, 560 U.S. 48 (2010) (juvenile life sentences).

6. Anti-subordination. In an omitted sentence, Justice O'Connor states that the Texas statute violates equal protection because it "threatens the creation of an underclass." The majority, rejecting Texas's argument that the statute simply punishes conduct, condemns the statute for targeting "gay persons as a class." Such language suggests an anti-subordination approach (which requires invalidation of laws and legal structures that perpetuate the subordination of disadvantaged groups). What groups count for purposes of this anti-subordination analysis?

Note that some supporters of gay rights find fault with *Lawrence*. According to Professor Catharine MacKinnon, *Lawrence* reinforces the pervasive problem of gender inequality, "securing for homosexuals heterosexuality's substantive privileges, including its male gendered dominance, by extending rather than dismantling them."[68] Professor Marc Spindelman agrees, identifying as the source of the problem *Lawrence*'s "'like-straight' logic," which protects gays and

---

[67]. See, e.g., Matthew Coles, Lawrence v. Texas and the Refinement of Substantive Due Process, 16 Stan. L. & Pol'y Rev. 23, 30-31, 37 (2005) (finding the Court used a balancing test); Laurence H. Tribe, Essay, Lawrence v. Texas: The "Fundamental Right" That Dare Not Speak Its Name, 117 Harv. L. Rev. 1893, 1917 (2004) (finding the Court used strict scrutiny review).

[68]. Catharine A. MacKinnon, The Road Not Taken: Sex Equality in Lawrence v. Texas, 65 Ohio St. L.J. 1081, 1094 (2004).

lesbians on the theory that their lives and relationships mirror those of het-erosexuals.[69] This assimilationist approach also has a confining rather than a liberating effect, according to Professor Katherine Franke, who writes:

> I fear that *Lawrence* and the gay rights organizing that has taken place in and around it have created a path dependency that privileges privatized and domesti-cated rights and legal liabilities, while rendering less viable projects that advance nonnormative notions of kinship, intimacy, and sexuality.[70]

7. A relationship test? Does *Lawrence* protect the right to engage in fleeting sexual relationships as well as more committed relationships? Is *Lawrence* simply a "sex positive" case, embracing a jurisprudence of sexual pleasure, regardless of the nature of the underlying relationships? The majority envisions sexual inti-macy as one part of a more encompassing relationship, criticizing *Bowers* for its assumption that the case concerned "simply the right to engage in certain sexual conduct . . ., just as it would demean a married couple were it to be said marriage is simply about the right to have sexual intercourse." Lawrence and Garner had no ongoing relationship. Does that matter? Does *Lawrence* assume that, for consti-tutional protection, sex must be part of an intimate relationship like marriage in *Griswold*? Alternatively, do all consensual sexual encounters, however brief, evoke the protection that *Lawrence* requires?

8. Race, class, and power. To what extent should the Court's analysis have paid more attention to race, class, and age — and power disparities? Consider the fol-lowing facts: Lawrence, age 59 and white, was a medical technician; Garner, some 20 years younger, an unemployed Black man, had a white roommate-boyfriend (Eubanks), who summoned police to Lawrence's residence with a false report of "a black male going crazy with a gun." In his book, Professor Dale Carpenter explores these background facts, including reports of the arresting officers, whose own racial backgrounds might have shaped their understanding of what they saw at Lawrence's residence.[71] What should be the legal relevance of such details?

Problem

The *Lawrence* decision relied upon and expanded the Court's line of substantive due process cases involving protected liberty interests, cases including *Griswold*, *Roe*, and *Casey*. In his concurring opinion in *Dobbs*, Justice Thomas expressly urged the Court to "reconsider all of this Court's substantive due process prec-edents, including *Griswold*, *Lawrence*, and *Obergefell*." *Dobbs*, 142 S. Ct. at 2301 (Thomas, J., concurring). In response, Justice Alito declared that nothing in the

---

[69]. Marc Spindelman, Surviving Lawrence v. Texas, 102 Mich. L. Rev. 1615, 1619-1632 (2004).

[70]. Katherine M. Franke, The Domesticated Liberty of Lawrence v. Texas, 104 Colum. L. Rev. 1399, 1414 (2004).

[71]. Dale Carpenter, Flagrant Conduct: The Story of Lawrence v. Texas (2012).

Dobbs opinion "should be understood to cast doubt on precedents that do not concern abortion." Id. at 2277-2278. The joint dissent was not assuaged by Justice Alito's assurance: "Should the audience for these too-much-repeated protestations be duly satisfied? We think not." Id. at 2331 (joint dissent).

With reference to the *Dobbs* and *Lawrence* opinions, articulate the arguments as to why *Lawrence* remains good law today. What are arguments that *Lawrence* must be overruled in the wake of *Dobbs*? Which side has the stronger *legal* position?

II

Getting Married

A. Introduction: Public Versus Private Dimensions of Courtship and Marriage

---

The decision to marry is one of life's most important choices. This chapter explores the law that governs the individual's decision to marry, emphasizing both the private nature of the decision and the state's regulatory authority. What are the personal interests at stake? The state interests? What are the constitutional limits on state regulation?

The chapter opens with a focus on the premarital relationship, including courtship, engagement, and premarital agreements. Next, the chapter examines a broad range of substantive and procedural restrictions on entry into marriage. Rapid changes in this regulatory regime in recent years challenge some of family law's basic foundations, including the role of tradition, the importance of gender, and the understanding of marriage itself.

1. Courtship Patterns

The premarital relationship has become increasingly private. The excerpts below explore the public and private dimensions of courtship over time.

John Demos, A Little Commonwealth: Family Life in Plymouth Colony
152, 154-155, 157-162 (2000)

[W]hen a courtship had developed to a certain point of intensity, the parents became directly involved. [If a man proposed marriage without first securing parental consent, the law provided fines or corporal punishment but placed limits on the power of parents to refuse their consent. Following parental approval, a series of steps remained.]

[T]he "betrothal" or "contract" [was] a simple ceremony which bears comparison to our own custom of "engagement." [This] was a very serious undertaking [as] failure to fulfill such a contract would create the likelihood of legal action. [S]exual intimacies between the contracted parties fell into a category all their own. [Although they were not officially condoned, the usual penalty was relatively light.]

[A]nother formal step became necessary: the "publishing" of the banns [that is, posting notice of the parties' intent to marry for 14 days or making an announcement to this effect three times in a public meeting]. [Still another important matter] was a set of transactions designed to underwrite the economic welfare of the contracted couple. [A] young man would receive the bulk of his portion in the form of land and housing, a woman would be given a variety of domestic furnishings, cattle, and/or money. . . .

[F]ourteen days was the minimum interval allowable between the betrothal ceremony and the wedding itself—between "contract and covenant," in the language of the time. [M]ost couples waited considerably longer: two or three months seems to have been quite customary. [T]radition has it that this was an occasion for sober reflection, and if need be, for reconsideration—before the final step was taken. . . .

Beth L. Bailey, From Front Porch to Back Seat: Courtship in Twentieth-Century America
19-22 (1988)

Between 1890 and 1925, dating . . . had gradually, almost imperceptibly, become a universal custom in America. By the 1930s it had transcended its origins. [Dating had its origins in the urban lower classes, who lacked the family space (such as the parlor) in which to conduct courtship activities and who took advantage of the excitement and opportunities presented by the urban environment.] The rise of dating was usually explained, quite simply, by the invention of the automobile [but the automobile simply accelerated] a process already well under way. . . .

Dating not only transformed the outward modes and conventions of American courtship, it also changed the distribution of control and power in courtship. One change was generational: the dating system lessened parental control and gave young men and women more freedom. The dating system also shifted power from women to men. [The older courtship practice of "calling" on a woman] gave women a large portion of control. First of all, courtship took place within the girl's home—in women's "sphere," as it was called in the nineteenth century—or at entertainments largely devised and presided over by women. Dating moved courtship out of the home and into man's sphere—the world outside the home. . . .

Second, in the calling system, the woman took the initiative. . . . Contrast these strictures with advice on dating etiquette from the 1940s and 1950s: An advice book for men and women warns that "girls who [try] to usurp the right of boys to choose their own dates" will "ruin a good dating career. . . ." An invitation to go out on a date . . . was an invitation into man's world—not simply because dating took place in the public sphere (commonly defined as belonging to men) [but also] because dating moved courtship into the world of the economy. Money—men's money—was at the center of the dating system. [M]oney shift[ed] control and initiative to men by making them the "hosts," [and] led contemporaries to see dating as a system of exchange. . . .

Emily A. Vogels, Ten Facts About Americans and Online Dating

Pew Research Ctr., Feb. 5, 2020
*https://www.pewresearch.org/fact-tank/2020/02/06/10-facts-about
-americans-and-online-dating/*

In the more than two decades since the launch of commercial dating sites, online dating has evolved into a multibillion-dollar industry serving customers around the world. A recent Pew Research Center study explores how dating sites and apps have transformed the way Americans meet and develop relationships, and how the users of these services feel about online dating. Here are 10 facts from the study [based on a survey of 4,860 U.S. adults]:

Online dating is a key source of potential partners.

1. Three-in-ten U.S. adults say they have ever used a dating site or app, but this varies significantly by age and sexual orientation. While 48 percent of 18- to 29-year-olds say they have ever used a dating site or app, the share is 38 percent among those ages 30 to 49 and even lower for those 50 and older (16 percent). . . . Lesbian, gay or bisexual (LGB) adults are roughly twice as likely as those who are straight to say they ever used a dating platform (55 percent vs. 28 percent).

2. A small share of Americans say they have been in a committed relationship with or married someone they met through a dating site or app. About one-in-ten U.S. adults say this, although these shares are higher among LGB adults, as well as those ages 18 to 49.

3. **Roughly six-in-ten online daters say they have had an overall positive experience with these platforms,** including 14 percent who describe their experience as very positive. . . .

4. **While online daters generally say their overall experience was positive, they also point out some of the downsides of online** dating [discussed below].

5. **Majorities of online daters say it was at least somewhat easy to find potentially compatible partners.** . . .

6. **Women are more likely than men to categorize certain information as essential to see in other users' profiles.** . . .[such as] religious beliefs (32 percent vs. 18 percent), occupation (27 percent vs. 8 percent) or height (22 percent vs. 8 percent). . . .

7. **There are stark gender differences in the amount of attention online daters say they received on these sites or apps.** [W]omen who have online dated [in the past 5 years] are five times as likely as men to think they were sent too many messages.

8. **Younger women are especially likely to report having troublesome interactions on online dating platforms.** About three-in-ten or more online dating users say someone continued to contact them on a dating site or app after they said they were not interested (37 percent), sent them a sexually explicit message or image they didn't ask for (35 percent) or called them an offensive name (28 percent). About one-in-ten (9 percent) say another user has threatened to physically harm them. These rates are even higher among younger women. . . .

9. **Americans have varying views about the safety of online dating.** Roughly half of Americans overall (53 percent) say dating sites and apps are a very or somewhat safe way to meet people, while 46 percent believe they are not. [W]omen are far more likely than men to say dating sites and apps are not a safe way to meet people (53 percent vs. 39 percent). . . .

10. **More than half of Americans (54 percent) say relationships that begin on a dating site or app are just as successful as those that begin in person.**

2. The Marriage Contract

A classic question asks: Is marriage a contract (a private agreement between two parties) or a status (a public institution regulated by the state)? Or does marriage retain features of both? In the following classic case affirming the state's right to regulate marriage and divorce, the Supreme Court addressed these questions.

MAYNARD v. HILL
125 U.S. 190 (1887)

Justice FIELD.

[While] marriage is often termed by text writers and in decisions of courts as a civil contract—generally to indicate that it must be founded upon the agreement of the parties, and does not require any religious ceremony for its solemnization—it is something more than a mere contract. The consent of the parties is of course essential to its existence, but when the contract to marry is executed by the marriage, a relation between the parties is created which they cannot change. Other contracts may be modified, restricted, or enlarged, or entirely released upon the consent of the parties. Not so with marriage. The relation once formed, the law steps in and holds the parties to various obligations and liabilities. It is an institution, in the maintenance of which in its purity the public is deeply interested, for it is the foundation of the family and of society, without which there would be neither civilization nor progress.

[The Supreme Court then cited approvingly a state supreme court's description of marriage as]

a social relation like that of parent and child, the obligations of which arise not from the consent of concurrent minds, but are the creation of the law itself, a relation the most important, as affecting the happiness of individuals, the first step from barbarism to incipient civilization, the purest tie of social life, and the true basis of human progress. [Adams v. Palmer, 51 Me. 481, 484-485 (Me. 1863)] . . . .

Henry Maine, Ancient Law
163-165 (1963)

The movement of the progressive societies has been uniform in one respect. [I]t has been distinguished by the gradual dissolution of family dependency and the growth of individual obligation in its place. The Individual is steadily substituted for the Family, as the unit of which civil laws take account. The advance has been accomplished at varying rates of celerity, and there are societies not absolutely stationary in which the collapse of the ancient organization can only be perceived by careful study. . . . But, whatever its pace, the change has not been subject to reaction or recoil, and apparent retardations will be found to have been occasioned through the absorption of archaic ideas and customs from some entirely foreign source. Nor is it difficult to see what is the tie between man and man which replaces by degrees those forms of reciprocity in rights and duties which have their origin in the Family. It is Contract. Starting, as from one terminus of history, from a condition of society in which all the relations of Persons are summed up in the relations of Family, we seem to have steadily moved towards a phase of social order in which all these relations arise from the free agreement of individuals. In Western Europe the progress achieved in this direction has been considerable. Thus the status of the Slave has disappeared—it has been superseded by the contractual relation of the servant to his master. The status of the Female under Tutelage, if the tutelage be understood of persons other than her husband, has also ceased to exist; from her coming of age to her marriage all the relations she may form are relations of contract. [W]e may say that the movement of the progressive societies has hitherto been a movement *from Status to Contract.*

Susan Moller Okin, Justice, Gender, and the Family
122-123 (1989)

[M]arriage itself has long been regarded as a contract, though it is a very peculiar one: it is a contract that does not conform with the *principles* (let alone the counter principles) of liberal contract doctrine. It is a preformed status contract, which restricts the parties' freedom to choose their partners (for example, there must be only one partner, and [traditionally] of the opposite sex) and of which they are not free to choose the terms.

The courts' refusal to enforce explicit contracts between husband and wife has been by no means completely attributable to reluctance to intrude into a private community supposedly built upon trust. It has been due at least as much to the fact that the courts have regarded the terms of marriage as already established. When, for example, they have refused to enforce intramarital agreements in which wives have agreed to forgo support for other consideration, and in which husbands have agreed to pay their wives for work done in a family business, they have done so on the grounds that the wife's right to support, in the former case, and her obligation to provide services for her husband, in the latter, are fixed by the marriage contract itself. Likewise, when courts have showed a reluctance to enforce the terms of the preformed contracted itself—for example, refusing to establish a level of adequate support that a wife must receive—it has been on the grounds that, so long as husband and wife cohabit, it is up to him as the family head to determine such matters. Another respect in which marriage is an anomalous contract is that the parties to it are not required to be familiar with the terms of the relationship into which they are entering. . . .

B. Preparing to Marry: Premarital Controversies

1. Breach of Promise to Marry

RIVKIN v. POSTAL

2001 WL 1077952 (Tenn. Ct. App. 2001)

KOCH, J.

. . . David Rivkin and Lori Postal met in April 1994 at a music convention in Memphis. Mr. Rivkin was a successful, award-winning producer [who was married with three children]. Ms. Postal was a 28-year-old divorcée [who] sold bathing suits at wholesale and had also started a record label. Ms. Postal was attending the Memphis convention to obtain a record contract for a singer and a band that she represented. . . . Within a short period of time, they began living together.

In early 1995, Ms. Postal discovered she was pregnant. . . . Mr. Rivkin suggested an abortion, but Ms. Postal did not agree. Their child was born in September 1995. Shortly after their child was born, Mr. Rivkin sold the house in Memphis, [and they moved to the Nashville area where they believed that he would have greater success as a producer.] Mr. Rivkin was the parties' sole source of support, and he was able to provide an exceptionally affluent lifestyle for Ms. Postal and their child despite his continuing obligations to his wife and children. He purchased a $420,000 home in Williamson County and horses for Ms. Postal. He also hired a nanny for the child. Not surprisingly, Ms. Postal took to this lifestyle. She did not work outside the home but rather spent her time raising the parties' child, training her horses, and entertaining her personal friends and Mr. Rivkin's business associates.

But all was not well with the parties. They entered counseling in an effort to save their relationship. One of their problems stemmed from Ms. Postal's concern that her family knew that she was living with a married man and had given birth to his child. She insisted that Mr. Rivkin buy her an engagement ring to enable her to save face with her family. When Mr. Rivkin did not purchase a ring for her, Ms. Postal ordered a ring herself. [She] told her parents that she and Mr. Rivkin were planning to wed after he was divorced, and Mr. Rivkin did not contradict her. However, the parties themselves never discussed specific wedding plans. . . .

Mr. Rivkin was finally divorced from his wife in March 1997. [Three months later, he ended his relationship with Ms. Postal.] [N]either party followed Emily Post's sage advice "to take the high road—and move on." In September 1997, Mr. Rivkin filed suit [seeking] partition of the parties' jointly-owned property and the return of his personal property that was still in Ms. Postal's possession. Ms. Postal responded with a counterclaim seeking damages for breach of promise to marry. . . .

In England, before the founding of this country, questions touching on marriage and breach of a promise of marriage were chiefly the province of the ecclesiastical courts. . . . Eventually, as marriage began to be viewed as "largely a property transaction, entered into as much for material advantages as for reasons of sentiment," actions for breach of promise to marry found their way into the King's Courts [where the parties obtained damages].

The common-law action for breach of promise to marry made its way to the American colonies along with most of the common law of England. Here, it started out as "popular means of soothing the sufferings of rejected love." In time, however, it became subject to abuse. Borrowing ideas from tort law, the courts began permitting juries to award punitive damages. Most breach of promise to marry actions were brought by women against men, and men's fears of excessive verdicts and their distaste for the scandal surrounding such suits gave women the power to wield the cause of action almost as blackmail.

By the 1930s, newspapers were publishing accounts of "spectacular 'extortion and blackmail rackets'" based on these claims. The publicity of the "unfounded suits, perjury, and excessive verdicts at the hands of . . . seemingly ever gullible [juries] armed with unrestrained discretion" eventually prompted a movement to reform these claims. Beginning with Indiana in 1935, the states began enacting statutes aimed at ending the perceived abuses associated with breach of promise claims.

Many states abolished the cause of action altogether, prompting courts to jump on a bandwagon of sorts that some thought went too far. It became increasingly evident that the pendulum was swinging too far in the other direction. The barriers erected to correct one evil gave legal protection to another. The courts, perhaps overzealous in their interpretation of legislative intent, construed these statutes as prohibiting tort actions between formerly betrothed parties for fraud and deceit.

Tennessee chose a middle course. Rather than abolish the common-law cause of action for breach of promise to marry, this state chose to rein it in a bit. In 1949, the Tennessee General Assembly passed [Tenn. Code Ann. §§36-3-401 to -405] which, according to its caption, was designed "to prevent certain injustices in suits for damages for the breach of promise or contract of marriage." This act circumscribes breach of promise claims in four significant ways [by providing that these claims could not be joined with other damage claims; requiring that promises or contracts of marriage could only be established using either signed, written evidence of the promise or contract or the testimony of at least two disinterested witnesses; requiring juries to consider the parties' age and experience in calculating damages; and, prohibiting punitive damages in cases where the alleged breaching party was over 60 years old].

. . . To meet [Ms. Postal's] burden of proof in this case, Tenn. Code Ann. §36-3-401 requires her to present either "written evidence of such contract, signed by the party against whom the action is brought" or with the testimony of "at least two disinterested witnesses." . . . We turn first to the "written evidence." [O]ne month after he purchased the Williamson County house, Mr. Rivkin executed a quitclaim deed conveying the property to himself and Ms. Postal as joint tenants with right of survivorship. . . .

"It is obvious," as one treatise puts it, "that not only are most engagements to marry arrived at informally and without witnesses or written record, but in many instances there is no explicit exchange of promises at all." [1 Homer H. Clark, Law of Domestic Relations §1.2 (1968).] Accordingly, proof of an engagement would be impossible if the plaintiff were required to produce evidence that at some specific moment the parties formally exchanged promises and reduced these promises to writing. Tenn. Code Ann. §36-3-401 is not intended to go that far. Rather, it calls for signed, written evidence that the parties were, by mutual agreement, on the way to becoming husband and wife. Many kinds of writings would suffice.[10]

Mr. Rivkin testified that he gave Ms. Postal a joint tenant's interest in the Williamson County house as a way of making sure that their child would be provided for should something happen to him. [He] never explained to her why he quitclaimed an interest in the Williamson County property to her.

Thus, the only evidence we have regarding the significance of the deed is the deed itself. Nothing within the four corners of the deed alludes to any promise or contract of marriage or to the parties' betrothed status. Executing quitclaim deeds is not only within the province of persons who have agreed or contracted to marry the grantee named in the deed. Quitclaim deeds are commonly used for business transactions between partners, conveyances between family members, cleaning up a title for title insurance purposes, or gifts. Thus, in light of the ubiquitous nature of quitclaim deeds, we decline to hold that an unexplained quitclaim deed between an unmarried man and an unmarried woman, without much, much more, suffices as signed, written evidence of a promise of marriage. . . .

Without a writing signed by Mr. Rivkin, Ms. Postal's only remaining avenue for proving that Mr. Rivkin promised to marry her consisted of presenting at least two disinterested witnesses who could substantiate Mr. Rivkin's promise. [T]he only witnesses she called regarding this issue were her parents. . . . While it is doubtful that a claimant's parent can ever be a disinterested witness in cases of this sort, Ms. Postal's parents are clearly not disinterested witnesses because at the time of trial they were also Ms. Postal's creditors. [W]e have concluded that Ms. Postal failed to carry the statutory burden of proof placed on persons seeking money damages for a breach of promise or contract of marriage. . . .

Notes and Questions

1. **Current state of the law.** A minority of jurisdictions still recognize the claim for breach of promise to marry.[1] Some of these states allow the tort but impose limitations. See, e.g., Md. Code Ann., Fam. Law §3-102 (permitting action only if plaintiff is pregnant); Tex. Civ. Prac. & Rem. Code Ann. §16.002 (setting a one-year statute of limitations). Do these limitations, as well as the limitation in *Rivkin*, appropriately "rein in" the cause of action?

2. **Historical background.** The modern action of breach of promise reflects Roman, Germanic, and canon law influences. In early Roman law, the consequences

10. While not intended to be an exhaustive list, the following signed writings might fit the bill: an application for a marriage license, an attested petition to waive the age or waiting requirements for marriage, correspondence between the parties, writing dealing with wedding arrangements, or prenuptial agreements.
[1]. On the history of the tort, see Jill Elaine Hasday, Intimate Lies and the Law 99-116 (2019).

of a broken promise to marry were mild, reflecting a belief in contractual freedom. In contrast, Germanic custom (adopting a moral stance) awarded damages to "punish" the breach. In both traditions, the consequences were more severe if the woman broke the engagement. The Germanic view of marriage influenced English ecclesiastical courts.

Criticisms of the action first emerged in the nineteenth century. In the United States, the controversy culminated in a movement in the 1930s when many states enacted statutes (termed "heartbalm" or "anti-heartbalm" legislation) to eliminate the action. Parliament abolished the action in 1970.

3. Damages. Breach of promise to marry is a hybrid action, reflecting roots in both contract and tort law. Traditionally, a plaintiff could recover the monetary and social value of the marriage (expectation damages), as well as expenses incurred in preparation for the marriage (reliance damages). Damages for mental anguish and humiliation, not normally compensable in contract, could also be recovered. Punitive damages are sometimes permitted.

In light of contemporary social norms and values, should states abolish such actions? If not, what damages should they allow? Loss of anticipated social position? Expectation damages? Reliance damages? Damages for emotional distress, or only economic loss?

How significant are reliance damages for a broken engagement? Consider that the average cost of a wedding (including ceremony and reception) is about $30,000.[2] As the wedding approaches, few costs are recoverable in the event of cancellation:

> Engagement rings can usually be returned for a full refund for 60 to 100 days after purchase. But some cities, including New York, allow caterers and hotels to charge for services and rooms that cannot be rebooked when canceled with less than six months' notice. Wedding gown makers typically require an initial nonrefundable deposit of half the price of the dress, with the balance on delivery. The week before the wedding, the cake and flowers are delivered. When an engagement is broken the day of the wedding, almost none of the cost can be recovered.[3]

The high cost of weddings has given rise to a specialized industry of online lenders who specialize in wedding loans. The popularity of these loans is attributable, in part, to the decreased expectation that the bride's parents will pick up the tab and the increasing amount of personal debt for the engaged parties who often lack the funds to pay for the wedding.[4] Given the high cost of weddings, should couples have premarital agreements that specify responsibility for expenses if the wedding is canceled?

---

[2]. Lane Gillespie & Karen Bennett, Average Wedding Cost: Wedding Planning Tips for 2023, Mar. 8, 2023, https://www.bankrate.com/personal-finance/average-wedding-cost/.

[3]. Keith Bradsher, Ditching Your Betrothed May Cost You: Wedding Rings, Gowns, Cakes, and Deposits Add Up, S.F. Chron., Mar. 20, 1990, at B5.

[4]. Bailey Schulz, From DoorDash to Egg Donations: Couples Putting in Extra Work to Pay Off 2022 Wedding Costs, USA Today, Mar. 31, 2022, https://www.usatoday.com/story/money/2022/03/31/wedding-cost-average-2022/7154269001/?gnt-cfr=1.

4. Defenses. Traditional defenses to breach-of-promise claims include physical and mental defects, plaintiff's lack of chastity or love for the defendant, and mutuality of the decision to end the engagement. Should a plaintiff's obsessive-compulsive disorder excuse a defendant's performance? See Wildey v. Springs, 840 F. Supp. 1259 (N.D. Ill. 1994), *rev'd*, 47 F.3d 1475 (7th Cir. 1995). (The Illinois legislature subsequently abolished the cause of action in 2016.) Should public policy preclude enforcement if unmarried parties are living together at the time of the promise? See Kelley v. Cooper, 751 S.E.2d 889 (Ga. Ct. App. 2013).

5. Class and gender. Historically, most breach-of-promise plaintiffs were women (often working class). Historically, the decline of such claims reflected the perceived decline in the value of middle-class female chastity.[5]

6. Conflict of laws. May a plaintiff recover for breach of promise to marry if the "promise" occurs in a jurisdiction that recognizes the cause of action, but the "breach" occurs in a jurisdiction that does not? See Callahan v. Parker, 824 N.Y.S.2d 768 (Sup. Ct. 2006) (dismissing claim based on statute banning such suits whether arising "within or without the state").

7. Online dating fraud and crimes. Fraudulent representations regarding marital status, height, wealth, age, and weight are common in online dating. Only a few states regulate online services for purposes of consumer safety. Should state law require online services to conduct mandatory background checks? How effective is such screening? New Jersey was the first state in 2008 to require dating sites to *disclose* whether they perform criminal background checks (although without requiring actual screening). N.J. Stat. Ann. §56:8-171. A few other states (Illinois, New York, and Texas) similarly require dating apps merely to have safety notifications. Proposed federal legislation (i.e., Online Dating Safety Act, H.R. 8946, 117th Cong. (2021-2022)) would require online dating services to provide safety awareness and ban notifications to inform users about those who defraud, mislead, or deceive and also to provide resources for reporting.

Research reveals increasing numbers of victims, especially college students, who report sexual assault after using dating apps.[6] In response, critics recommend improved safety standards. But few states require that dating apps screen for sexual predators against sex offender registries or require sex offenders to disclose their use of dating apps. What explains this reluctance? Are such safety concerns unique to *online* dating? Should online service providers face liability for these risks of online dating?

As remedies for "intimate deception," Professor Jill Hasday, supra, makes the following proposals: (1) courts impose a rebuttable presumption imposing the same legal rules and remedies for intimate-partner plaintiffs and non-intimates

---

[5]. Lawrence M. Friedman, Guarding Life's Dark Secrets: Legal and Social Controls over Reputation, Propriety, and Privacy 205-212 (2007).

[6]. Julie L. Valentine et al., Dating App Facilitated Sexual Assault: A Retrospective Review of Sexual Assault Medical Forensic Examination Charts, J. Interpersonal Violence, Oct. 29, 2022, https://journals.sagepub.com/doi/full/10.1177/08862605221130390.

and (2) laws increase accessibility to public records. What do you think of the likely effectiveness of these proposals?

Problem

Marilyn is dating Donald, a married man, when she discovers that she is pregnant. He promises her that if she has the abortion, he will pay her $75,000 plus medical and legal expenses. He also tells her that he will marry her when his divorce is final, and that they can later have a baby together. Marilyn accepts payment and has the abortion. When they break up, she sues for intentional and negligent infliction of emotional distress, battery, fraud, and misrepresentation. She alleges that the settlement agreement is unconscionable, violates public policy, and was subject to duress. Donald moves for summary judgment on the ground that the jurisdiction bans a claim for breach of promise to marry. What result? See M.N. v. D.S., 616 N.W.2d 284 (Minn. Ct. App. 2000).

2. Gifts in Contemplation of Marriage

CAMPBELL v. ROBINSON
726 S.E.2d 221 (S.C. Ct. App. 2012)

THOMAS, J.

These cross appeals arise out of a broken engagement between Matthew Campbell and Ashley Robinson. . . . Campbell proposed and presented a ring to Robinson in December 2005. In a spring 2006 phone conversation, they agreed to postpone the wedding. The engagement was later cancelled, and a dispute ensued over ownership of the ring.

. . . At trial, Robinson testified the engagement ended simply because Campbell cancelled it. She also testified that after the engagement was cancelled, she asked Campbell twice whether she should return the ring. She maintained that Campbell, in response to her inquiries, said she should keep the ring. Campbell testified that he gave Robinson the ring believing they would get married. He denied ending the engagement by himself and contended the cancellation was mutual. He also denied telling Robinson that she should keep the ring. He contended Robinson refused to give him the ring after he asked for its return. [He brought an action against Robinson to seek return of the engagement ring.]

An engagement ring by its very nature is a symbol of the donor's continuing devotion to the donee. Once an engagement is cancelled, the ring no longer holds that significance. Thus, if a party presents evidence a ring was given in contemplation of marriage, the ring is an engagement ring. As an engagement ring, the gift is impliedly conditioned upon the marriage taking place. Until the condition underlying the gift is fulfilled, the attempted gift is unenforceable and must be returned to the donor upon the donor's request.

The person challenging the assertions that the ring is an engagement ring and therefore impliedly conditioned upon marriage has the burden of presenting evidence to overcome those assertions. This burden may be satisfied by presenting evidence showing that the ring was not given in contemplation of marriage—it was not an engagement ring—or was not conditioned upon the marriage. If the parties do not dispute that the ring was originally an engagement ring conditioned upon the marriage, the burden may also be satisfied by presenting evidence establishing the ring subsequently became the challenger's property.

Jurisdictions differ on whether ownership of an engagement ring may be based upon fault in the breakup. Courts that do consider fault generally reason that it is unfair for a person to retain the fruit of a broken promise. In contrast, courts with a "no-fault" approach often base their decision upon the abolishment of heart balm actions, adoption of no-fault divorce, desire to limit courtroom dramatics, and reduction of the difficulty in determining the issue of what constitutes fault in the decline of a relationship.

We hold that the consideration of fault has no place in determining ownership of an engagement ring. . . . In other contexts, the culpability of one's conduct is determined by legal standards such as the reasonable person. In contrast, no legal standard exists by which a fact finder can adjudge culpability or fault in a prenuptial breakup. See, e.g., Aronow v. Silver, 538 A.2d 851, 853-854 (N.J. Super. Ct. Ch. Div. 1987) ("What fact justifies the breaking of an engagement? The absence of a sense of humor? Differing musical tastes? Differing political views? . . . They must be approached with intelligent care and should not happen without a decent assurance of success. When either party lacks that assurance, for whatever reason, the engagement should be broken. No justification is needed. Either party may act. Fault, impossible to fix, does not count."). . . .

[T]he adoption of the fault approach could cause ironic results. Two of the main purposes of an engagement are to prepare the couple for marriage and test the permanency of their compatibility. In some circumstances, the fault approach may penalize a party who innocently recognizes the couple's incompatibility. On the other hand, adoption of the no-fault approach would not diminish our state's intent to protect the marital relationship. . . .

Here, Campbell gave Robinson the ring during his proposal. Thus, he presented evidence that the ring was given in contemplation of marriage and therefore was an engagement ring conditioned upon the marriage occurring. Although Robinson kept the ring in a safe deposit box after the engagement was cancelled, without further evidence the ring would remain a conditional gift and Campbell would be entitled to recover it as a matter of law.

Robinson explicitly characterizes the ring as an engagement ring. However, she has presented evidence that the ring was converted into an absolute gift by testifying Campbell told her to keep the ring after the engagement was cancelled. Because Campbell disputes this contention, the evidence conflicts as to whether the ring was conditioned upon marriage. Accordingly, ownership of the ring was a jury issue, and a directed verdict on Campbell's claims for declaratory judgment and claim and delivery were not warranted. . . .

Here, the trial court provided an erroneous jury charge. . . . While the charge instructed the jury that the gift was conditional, it did not explain that the gift could become absolute. Moreover, the jury charge and verdict form hinged ownership of the ring upon fault in the breakup [which we hold has no place in determining ownership of an engagement ring]. [Campbell] is entitled to a new trial on those claims. . . .

Notes and Questions

1. Historical background. Legal disputes about the return of an engagement ring are far more common than actions for breach of promise to marry. The gift of a diamond engagement ring is a relatively recent custom. Before the Great Depression, etiquette did not dictate the gift of a diamond engagement ring. By 1945, however, the diamond engagement ring had evolved into an American tradition (based in large part on an extensive advertising campaign by the diamond industry).

2. Theories of recovery. At common law, actions for recovery of gifts given in contemplation of marriage were distinct from breach-of-promise actions. As a result, anti-heartbalm laws do not bar the former action. Courts generally hold that recovery of such gifts rests on *conditional gift* theory: the gift is conditioned on performance of the marriage. If the condition fails, the donor may recover the gift. The central question, as *Campbell* reveals, is whether the gift is conditional or absolute. Courts consider the nature of the gift, circumstances, and cause of the broken engagement.

3. Fault. Traditionally, fault barred recovery or retention of the engagement ring. Thus, the man could recover the ring if the woman unjustifiably ended the engagement or if the couple mutually dissolved it, but not if he unjustifiably terminated the engagement. The modernization of divorce law revealed the shortcomings of a fault-based analysis of personal relationships and their dissolution. Hence, the modern trend, as *Campbell* indicates, makes fault irrelevant. Do you find *Campbell*'s reasons persuasive for adopting this approach?

4. Other gifts. Sometimes plaintiffs seek recovery of *other* gifts given during an engagement. Should such gifts receive different treatment from engagement rings? See Northern Trust, NA v. Delley, 935 N.Y.S.2d 805 (App. Div. 2011) (real property). Suppose that the man gives the woman other jewelry. How does one determine which gifts are "in contemplation of marriage"? Can gifts to a *third party* qualify? See Cooper v. Smith, 800 N.E.2d 372 (Ohio Ct. App. 2003) (gifts to mother-in-law).

5. Married donee. Should it matter if the donor or donee is still married to someone else at the time of the engagement? See Cummins v. Goolsby, 255 So. 3d 1257 (Miss. 2018) (holding that gift of engagement and wedding rings while still married violated public policy and constituted unclean hands). If the donee knew that the donor was still married, does or should that knowledge preclude recovery? See Fontanarosa v. Connors, 2021 WL2878412 (Ohio Ct. App. 2021) (holding that if both parties are made aware of the situation, the doctrine of unclean hands does not apply). Should the donor or donee's marital status matter in states that follow the modern trend of making fault irrelevant?

6. Gender-based nature of the rule. The current doctrine "requires the return of engagements gifts [including engagement rings] while allowing no redress for pre-wedding expenses borne mainly by women."[7] Given that etiquette and custom dictate that in different-sex relationships, the bride pays for the wedding and the groom pays for the ring, do women bear a disproportionate financial burden for a broken engagement? Should courts hold that an engagement ring is an irrevocable gift to avoid gender bias? See Albinger v. Harris, 48 P.3d 711, 720 (Mont. 2002) (so holding). How should the gender basis of the rule be addressed? What do these gendered rules and customs mean for same-sex couples?

7. Policy. With the abolition movement for breach-of-promise suits, should the law also abolish actions for recovery of engagement rings? See McGrath v. Dockendorf, 793 S.E.2d 336 (Va. 2016). Are remedies of the marketplace appropriate for courtship controversies? Should courts refuse to intrude on this private matter and let the loss fall where it lies? See Liceaga v. Baez, 126 N.E.3d 682 (Ill. App. Ct. 2019). Or should the law facilitate the breaking of engagements? If so, what rule best achieves this goal?

Problems

1. Virginia, a nurse practitioner, and Stephen, an attorney, plan a lavish wedding and reception. He buys her a Tiffany engagement ring and gives it to her on Valentine's Day. They agree that, as professionals, Virginia will pay for wedding costs and, in return, Stephen will convey to her a half interest in his condo (which he does). When the engagement ends by mutual agreement, Stephen seeks return of the ring and restoration of full ownership of his condo. Virginia argues that Stephen referred to the ring as "a Valentine's Day present." He counters that the ring remained covered by his homeowner's policy. She seeks $16,000 for wedding expenses and the value of five engagement gifts that Stephen retained after the broken engagement. New York has anti-heartbalm legislation but permits actions for the return of gifts in contemplation of marriage. What result? DeFina v. Scott, 755 N.Y.S.2d 587 (Sup. Ct. 2003).

Suppose, instead, that Stephen experiences pressure from his family members who are opposed to the marriage because they do not like Virginia. Whose fault is it when Stephen decides to break off the engagement because Virginia is not the "right person" for him? How might this turn of events change the result? Clippard v. Pfefferkorn, 168 S.W.3d 616 (Mo. Ct. App. 2005).

2. Three months after Jody and Layne start dating, Layne gives Jody a ring. They make plans to marry once their finances improve. Jody loves to travel and, during their engagement, asks Layne to pay for trips to Alaska and France. She also asks him to purchase a car for her son and to have a vasectomy. Layne pays for a seven-day Alaskan cruise, a three-week trip to France, $2,400 toward Jody's son's car, and $3,500 for the vasectomy. Jody then breaks off the engagement, without

---

[7]. Rebecca Tushnet, Rules of Engagement, 107 Yale L.J. 2583, 2585 (1998).

any excuse, and returns the ring. Layne sells the ring for only half its purchase price. He then brings suit under theories of conditional gift and unjust enrichment, seeking reimbursement of $25,000 for the cost of the trips, the money he paid for the son's car, the cost of the vasectomy and a reversal procedure, and the difference between the ring's purchase price and sale price. What result? Hess v. Johnston, 163 P.3d 747 (Utah Ct. App. 2007).

Suppose that Layne also gives Jody an engagement present of a pedigree dog, which they register with the Kennel Club in their joint names. When they break up, Layne refuses to give Jody the dog, as he allegedly promised to do. She files suit under theories of conditional gift and breach of an oral agreement, seeking specific performance. What result? Houseman v. Dare, 966 A.2d 24 (N.J. Super. Ct. App. Div. 2009).

3. Dr. Christopher Cummins begins a romantic relationship with one of his employees, Leah Jordan. At the time, Christopher is separated, but not divorced, from his wife. Christopher and Leah have a child while they are living together. They become engaged, and Christopher gives Leah a valuable engagement ring. Eventually, the relationship sours. Leah realizes that Christopher has no plans to divorce his wife and decides to end the relationship. She then files a paternity suit and seeks child support for their child. Christopher counterclaims on a theory of conditional gift for the return of the ring. Alternatively, he argues that if the court awards Leah the value of the ring, the ring's value should be deducted from any child support obligation. What result? Cummins v. Goolsby, 255 So. 3d 1257 (Miss. 2018).

C. Premarital Contracts

1. Background

PRENUPTIAL AGREEMENTS ARE ON THE RISE

Prenuptial agreements are becoming more common. Of Americans who have been married or are currently engaged, 15 percent recently reported that they have signed a prenuptial agreement – an increase from 3 percent in 2010. Five reasons predominate to explain the rise in prenuptial agreements. First, millennials are marrying later. By the time they marry, they have had more time to build wealth in their careers in terms of investments, real property, and retirement accounts. Premarital agreements protect this property and any increase in value.

Second, marriages today are more likely to include at least one partner who has been previously married and who is more sophisticated about the need for prenuptial agreements. Moreover, many of these partners have children from prior relationships whom they want to protect in the event of death or divorce.

Third, couples are bringing more debt into the marriage. Today, younger Americans are facing historic levels of debt from student loans, business ventures, and medical bills. Prenuptial agreements can insulate one partner from the other's premarital debts.

Fourth, an increasing number of couples have issues that they want to work out in advance, such as assets that are difficult to value (like closely held business interests or stock options). Finally, more than one-third of millennials grew up with single or divorced parents. Therefore, they accept the fact that there is a larger probability that divorce one day may happen to them too, and they want to be financially prepared for that eventuality.[8]

2. State Approaches

SIMEONE v. SIMEONE
581 A.2d 162 (Pa. 1990)

FLAHERTY, Justice.

At issue in this appeal is the validity of a prenuptial agreement executed between the appellant, Catherine E. Walsh Simeone, and the appellee, Frederick A. Simeone. At the time of their marriage, in 1975, appellant was a twenty-three-year-old nurse and appellee was a thirty-nine-year-old neurosurgeon. Appellee had an income of approximately $90,000 per year, and appellant was unemployed. Appellee also had assets worth approximately $300,000. On the eve of the parties' wedding, appellee's attorney presented appellant with a prenuptial agreement to be signed. Appellant, without the benefit of counsel, signed the agreement. Appellee's attorney had not advised appellant regarding any legal rights that the agreement surrendered. The parties are in disagreement as to whether appellant knew in advance of that date that such an agreement would be presented for signature. . . .

The agreement limited appellant to support payments of $200 per week in the event of separation or divorce, subject to a maximum total payment of $25,000. The parties separated in 1982, and, in 1984, divorce proceedings were commenced. Between 1982 and 1984 appellee made payments which satisfied the $25,000 limit. In 1985, appellant filed a claim for alimony pendente lite [i.e., temporary support pending a divorce or separation].

We granted this appeal because uncertainty was expressed by the Superior Court regarding the meaning of our plurality decision in Estate of Geyer, 533 A.2d 423 (1987) [upholding a premarital agreement if it either made reasonable provision for the spouse or was entered into after full and fair disclosure]. Inasmuch as the courts below held that the provision made for appellant was a reasonable one, appellant's efforts to overturn the agreement here focused on an assertion that there was an adequate disclosure of statutory rights. Appellant continues to assert, however, that the payments provided in the agreement were less than reasonable.

The statutory rights in question are those relating to alimony pendente lite. . . . The present agreement [expressly stated] that alimony pendente lite was being relinquished. It also recited that appellant "has been informed and understands" that, were it not for the agreement, appellant's obligation to pay alimony pendente lite "might, as a matter of law, exceed the amount provided." Hence, appellant's claim is not that the agreement failed to disclose the particular right

---

[8]. See generally Jessica Dickler, How Millennials Are Getting Smarter About Marriage, CNBC, July 2, 2018, https://www.cnbc.com/2018/07/02/more-millennials-sign-prenups-before-marriage.html; Michael Waters, Prenups Aren't Just for Rich People Anymore, New Yorker (July 12, 2022), https://www.newyorker.com/news/us-journal/prenups-arent-just-for-rich-people-any-more; AJ Skiera, Harris Poll Brief: More Couples Are Signing Prenups Before Saying "I Do," July 12, 2022, https://theharrispoll.com/briefs/popularity-of-prenups-rising-2022/.

affected, but rather that she was not adequately informed with respect to the nature of alimony pendente lite. . . .

There is no longer validity in the implicit presumption that supplied the basis for *Geyer* and similar earlier decisions. Such decisions rested upon a belief that spouses are of unequal status and that women are not knowledgeable enough to understand the nature of contracts that they enter. Society has advanced, however, to the point where women are no longer regarded as the "weaker" party in marriage, or in society generally. Indeed, the stereotype that women serve as homemakers while men work as breadwinners is no longer viable. Quite often today both spouses are income earners. Nor is there viability in the presumption that women are uninformed, uneducated, and readily subjected to unfair advantage in marital agreements. Indeed, women nowadays quite often have substantial education, financial awareness, income, and assets.

Accordingly, the law has advanced to recognize the equal status of men and women in our society. Paternalistic presumptions and protections that arose to shelter women from the inferiorities and incapacities which they were perceived as having in earlier times have, appropriately, been discarded. It would be inconsistent, therefore, to perpetuate the standards governing prenuptial agreements that were described in *Geyer* and similar decisions, as these reflected a paternalistic approach that is now insupportable.

 Further, *Geyer* and its predecessors embodied substantial departures from traditional rules of contract law, to the extent that they allowed consideration of the knowledge of the contracting parties and reasonableness of their bargain as factors governing whether to uphold an agreement. Traditional principles of contract law provide perfectly adequate remedies where contracts are procured through fraud, misrepresentation, or duress. Consideration of other factors, such as the knowledge of the parties and the reasonableness of their bargain, is inappropriate. Prenuptial agreements are contracts, and, as such, should be evaluated under the same criteria as are applicable to other types of contracts. Absent fraud, misrepresentation, or duress, spouses should be bound by the terms of their agreements.

Contracting parties are normally bound by their agreements, without regard to whether the terms thereof were read and fully understood and irrespective of whether the agreements embodied reasonable or good bargains. Based upon these principles, the terms of the present prenuptial agreement must be regarded as binding, without regard to whether the terms were fully understood by appellant. *Ignorantia non excusat.*

Accordingly, we find no merit in a contention raised by appellant that the agreement should be declared void on the ground that she did not consult with independent legal counsel. To impose a per se requirement that parties entering a prenuptial agreement must obtain independent legal counsel would be contrary to traditional principles of contract law, and would constitute a paternalistic and unwarranted interference with the parties' freedom to enter contracts.

Further, the reasonableness of a prenuptial bargain is not a proper subject for judicial review. . . . By invoking inquiries into reasonableness, [the] functioning and reliability of prenuptial agreements is severely undermined. Parties would not have entered such agreements, and, indeed, might not have entered their marriages, if they did not expect their agreements to be strictly enforced. If parties viewed an agreement as reasonable at the time of its inception, as evidenced by their having signed the agreement, they should be foreclosed from later trying to evade its terms by asserting that it was not in fact reasonable. Pertinently, the present agreement contained a clause reciting that "each of the parties considers this agreement fair, just, and reasonable. . . ."

Further, everyone who enters a long-term agreement knows that circumstances can change during its term, so that what initially appeared desirable might prove to be an unfavorable bargain. Such are the risks that contracting parties routinely assume. Certainly, the possibilities of illness, birth of children, reliance upon a spouse, career change, financial gain or loss, and numerous other events that can occur in the course of a marriage cannot be regarded as unforeseeable. If parties choose not to address such matters in their prenuptial agreements, they must be regarded as having contracted to bear the risk of events that alter the value of their bargains.

We are reluctant to interfere with the power of persons contemplating marriage to agree upon, and to act in reliance upon, what they regard as an acceptable distribution scheme for their property. A court should not ignore the parties' expressed intent by proceeding to determine whether a prenuptial agreement was, in the court's view, reasonable at the time of its inception or the time of divorce. These are exactly the sorts of judicial determinations that such agreements are designed to avoid. Rare indeed is the agreement that is beyond possible challenge when reasonableness is placed at issue. Parties can routinely assert some lack of fairness relating to the inception of the agreement, thereby placing the validity of the agreement at risk. And if reasonableness at the time of divorce were to be taken into account an additional problem would arise. Virtually nonexistent is the marriage in which there has been absolutely no change in the circumstances of either spouse during the course of the marriage. Every change in circumstance, foreseeable or not, and substantial or not, might be asserted as a basis for finding that an agreement is no longer reasonable.

In discarding the approach of *Geyer* that permitted examination of the reasonableness of prenuptial agreements and allowed inquiries into whether parties had attained informed understandings of the rights they were surrendering, we do not depart from the longstanding principle that a full and fair disclosure of the financial positions of the parties is required. . . . Parties to these agreements do not quite deal at arm's length, but rather at the time the contract is entered into stand in a relation of mutual confidence and trust that calls for disclosure of their financial resources. It is well settled that this disclosure need not be exact, so long as it is "full and fair." In essence therefore, the duty of disclosure under these circumstances is consistent with traditional principles of contract law.

If an agreement provides that full disclosure has been made, a presumption of full disclosure arises. . . . The present agreement recited that full disclosure had been made, and included a list of appellee's assets totaling approximately $300,000. Appellant contends that this list understated by roughly $183,000, the value of a classic car collection which appellee had included at a value of $200,000. The master, reviewing the parties' conflicting testimony regarding the value of the car collection, found that appellant failed to prove by clear and convincing evidence that the value of the collection had been understated. . . .

Appellant's final contention is that the agreement was executed under conditions of duress in that it was presented to her at 5 p.m. on the eve of her wedding, a time when she could not seek counsel without the trauma, expense, and embarrassment of postponing the wedding. . . . Although appellant testified that she did not discover until the eve of her wedding that there was going to be a prenuptial agreement, testimony from a number of other witnesses was to the contrary. [T]he courts below properly held that the present agreement is valid and enforceable. Appellant is barred, therefore, from receiving alimony pendente lite. . . .

McDermott, Justice, dissenting. . . .

I am not willing to believe that our society views marriage as a mere contract for hire. . . . Our courts must seek to protect, and not to undermine, those institutions and interests which are vital to our society. [W]hile I acknowledge the longstanding rule of law that prenuptial agreements are presumptively valid and binding upon the parties, I am unwilling to go as far as the majority to protect the right to contract at the expense of the institution of marriage. Were a contract of marriage, the most intimate relationship between two people, not the surrender of freedom, an offering of self in love, sacrifice, hope for better or for worse, the begetting of children and the offer of effort, labor, precious time and care for the safety and prosperity of their union, then the majority would find me among them. . . .

At the time of dissolution of the marriage, a spouse should be able to avoid the operation of a prenuptial agreement upon clear and convincing proof that, despite the existence of full and fair disclosure at the time of the execution of the agreement, the agreement is nevertheless so inequitable and unfair that it should not be enforced in a court of this state. . . .

[T]he passage of time, accompanied by the intervening events of a marriage, may render the terms of the agreement completely unfair and inequitable. While parties to a prenuptial agreement may indeed foresee, generally, the events which may come to pass during their marriage, one spouse should not be made to suffer for failing to foresee all of the surrounding circumstances which may attend the dissolution of the marriage. Although it should not be the role of the courts to void prenuptial agreements merely because one spouse may receive a better result in an action under the Divorce Code to recover alimony or equitable distribution, it should be the role of the courts to guard against the enforcement of prenuptial agreements where such enforcement will bring about only inequity and hardship. It borders on cruelty to accept that after years of living together, yielding their separate opportunities in life to each other, that two individuals emerge the same as the day they began their marriage. . . .

IN RE MARRIAGE OF SHANKS

758 N.W.2d 506 (Iowa 2008)

Hecht, Justice.

. . . Randall Shanks is an attorney with a successful personal injury and workers' compensation practice in Council Bluffs. Teresa Shanks holds an associate degree in court reporting and a Bachelor of Science degree in marketing management. She has been employed in various roles, including a position in the marketing department of a casino, and employment as a bookkeeper, secretary, and office manager in Randall's law office.

Randall and Teresa were married in Jamaica on April 23, 1998. This was a second marriage for both parties. Randall had two children and Teresa had three children from prior marriages. While contemplating marriage, Randall and Teresa discussed Randall's goal of preserving his current and future assets for his children in the event their marriage were to end by his death or a divorce. Randall suggested they enter a premarital agreement, and Teresa agreed. . . .

[Randall drafted a premarital agreement and presented it to Teresa ten days before their wedding. After receiving the draft, Teresa asked Randall several questions. He answered her questions but insisted that she seek independent legal advice as to the meaning and effect of the agreement. She consulted a friend, who referred her to an out-of-state attorney, who in turn asked her associate to review the draft. The associate made several handwritten comments, including an exclamation that the proposed agreement would force Teresa to "waive all rights as spouse!" in Randall's pension assets. The associate also suggested that Teresa

Attorney Randall J. Shanks

should have an Iowa attorney review the document, but Teresa chose not to do so. In response to the associate's suggestions, Randall made some revisions and again told Teresa to review it with her lawyer.]

Despite Randall's urging that she have her lawyer review the revised draft, Teresa did not seek further counsel. . . . Randall attached to the revised agreement separate schedules listing the assets of each party. The parties signed the agreement [and] departed for Jamaica the next day. [Six years later, when the marriage ended Randall sought, and Teresa opposed, enforcement of the premarital agreement].

[P]remarital agreements [are] subject to the requirements of the Iowa Uniform Premarital Agreement Act (IUPAA), Iowa Code §596.12 [invalidating agreements if]: (1) The person did not execute the agreement voluntarily; (2) The agreement was unconscionable when it was executed; (3) Before the execution of the agreement the person was not provided a fair and reasonable disclosure of the property or financial obligations of the other spouse; and the person did not have, or reasonably could not have had, an adequate knowledge of the property or financial obligations of the other spouse. . . .

A. VOLUNTARINESS

The district court found the premarital agreement in this case was not executed voluntarily because Randall, as an attorney, had substantially greater power under the circumstances and Teresa did not receive the advice of independent Iowa counsel. . . . Neither the IUPAA nor the UPAA defines the term "voluntarily." [Prior case law explains that a voluntarily executed premarital agreement was one free from duress and undue influence.] There are two essential elements to a claim of duress in the execution of a contract: (1) one party issues a wrongful or unlawful threat and (2) the other party had no reasonable alternative to entering the contract. Here, Randall informed Teresa he would not get married again without a premarital agreement. We rejected [in prior case law] the argument that such an ultimatum was wrongful or unlawful. [Additionally] Teresa had the reasonable alternative of cancelling the wedding in the face of such a threat. These facts fall far short of a showing of duress sufficient to support a finding that Teresa involuntarily executed the agreement.

[W]e next consider whether the agreement is unconscionable and therefore unenforceable.

B. UNCONSCIONABILITY

While the IUPAA largely adopts the provisions of the Uniform Premarital Agreement Act (UPAA) verbatim, section 596.8(1) of the IUPAA differs from the UPAA in two important particulars. First, the UPAA (§6(a)(2)) allows a party to modify or eliminate spousal support in a premarital agreement, as long as the modification or elimination does not cause the other party to be eligible for public assistance at the time of enforcement. The IUPAA, on the other hand, prohibits premarital agreements from adversely affecting spousal support. Iowa Code §596.5(2). Thus, the district court correctly concluded the purported alimony waiver in this premarital agreement is invalid and unenforceable.

Second, under UPAA section 6(a)(2), a court may not consider the alleged unconscionability of the agreement unless it first finds there was no fair and reasonable financial disclosure, voluntary waiver of such disclosure, and the challenging party did not have, or reasonably could not have had an adequate knowledge of the other party's property and financial obligations. . . . Neither the IUPAA nor the UPAA attempts to define "unconscionability" in the context of premarital agreements. The comment to UPAA section 6 indicates the concept is patterned after section 306 of the Uniform Marriage and Divorce Act (UMDA), which states:

> The standard of unconscionability is used in commercial law, where its meaning includes protection against one-sidedness, oppression, or unfair surprise, and in contract law. . . . In the context of negotiations between spouses as to the financial incidents of their marriage, the standard includes protection against overreaching, concealment of assets, and sharp dealing not consistent with the obligations of marital partners to deal fairly with each other. . . .

The concept of unconscionability includes both procedural and substantive elements. . . .

1. Substantive Unconscionability

At the outset, we acknowledge premarital agreements are typically financially one-sided in order to protect the assets of one prospective spouse. Courts must resist the temptation to view disparity between the parties' financial circumstances as requiring a finding of substantive unconscionability. [T]he focus of the substantive unconscionability analysis is upon whether "the provisions of the contract are mutual or the division of property is consistent with the financial condition of the parties at the time of execution."

The district court found the agreement executed by Randall and Teresa was not substantively unconscionable. We agree. Most, but not all, of the provisions of the agreement are mutual in scope. The agreement basically sought to maintain the parties' premarital assets as separate property and to perpetuate their premarital financial conditions throughout the marriage. The parties agreed to maintain separate property during the marriage, with the exceptions of a marital home and a joint checking account. Any property acquired by either party in their sole name during the marriage was to remain separate property. The parties' earnings during the marriage were to remain separate, except to the extent they were deposited in the joint checking account.

The agreement specifically provides for the allocation of any jointly-owned property in the event of a dissolution. The accord dictates such property will be allocated between the parties in different percentages depending on the nature of the property and the length of the marriage. . . . While these provisions clearly contemplated the allocation of a greater portion of the marital assets to Randall than Teresa, we believe they were at least consistent with the parties' financial conditions at the time of the marriage, and were not so oppressive to Teresa as to justify a finding of unconscionability.

Additionally, although Teresa unilaterally waived any marital interest in certain assets (such as Randall's retirement assets), she also derived some potential benefits under the agreement [20 percent of any net proceeds in the marital home upon divorce, being named as a beneficiary of Randall's life insurance, and a percentage of the value of his law practice upon his death]. Because the agreement contemplated leaving both parties substantially in the same financial condition as they were before the marriage, included primarily mutual covenants and obligations, and provided for some potential financial benefits to Teresa, we conclude the agreement was not unduly harsh or oppressive, and therefore was not substantively unconscionable.

2. Procedural Unconscionability

[T]he primary focus of the procedural unconscionability inquiry is the advantaged party's exploitation of the disadvantaged party's lack of understanding or unequal bargaining power. Courts have found the following factors, among others, are relevant to procedural unconscionability: the disadvantaged party's opportunity to seek independent counsel; the relative sophistication of the parties in legal and financial matters; the temporal proximity between the introduction of the premarital agreement and the wedding date; the use of highly technical or confusing language or fine print; and the use of fraudulent or deceptive practices to procure the disadvantaged party's assent to the agreement.

In holding the agreement procedurally unconscionable, the district court stressed the fact that Randall is an attorney and therefore was in a vastly superior bargaining position to Teresa. It appears the district court believed there are no circumstances under which an attorney could enter into an enforceable premarital agreement with a spouse who is not represented by independent legal counsel. Although any doubt as to the conscionability of the agreement at issue in this case could have likely been avoided if both parties had been represented by competent Iowa-licensed counsel, we conclude such legal representation is not a condition of enforceability. While Randall certainly had greater inherent bargaining power as both the party whose assets were primarily protected by the agreement and as an attorney, he twice insisted Teresa should seek the advice of counsel in connection with the agreement. [Her out-of-state attorney] also urged Teresa to do so. The anti-paternalistic notions underlying the IUPAA lead us to conclude Teresa's decision to forgo her opportunity to seek further legal advice [was a choice] that emasculates her unconscionability claim. Equitable principles will not permit a party to eschew an opportunity to consult counsel as to the legal effect of a proposed contract, execute the contract, and then challenge the enforceability of the agreement on the ground she did not have adequate legal advice.

Temporal considerations can in some instances support a finding of unconscionability. Although Randall presented the agreement only ten days before the wedding date, Teresa had sufficient time to consider the implications of the agreement and an opportunity to seek advice of counsel. [Moreover, the trial court found Teresa was not an unsophisticated party because she was a college graduate, was previously divorced, and was a court reporter and paralegal.]

[In addition,] Randall communicated to Teresa his desire for a premarital agreement to protect his assets for his children. Teresa responded that she was not marrying Randall for his money, and acted accordingly by acquiescing, without thorough investigation or objection, to a premarital agreement that facilitated her marriage. Teresa's words and actions demonstrate she placed higher value on marriage and Randall's companionship than the opportunity for greater financial security. "Buyer's remorse" will not excuse Teresa's voluntary relinquishment of her marital property rights. . . .

[Finally, when the parties executed the agreement], schedules listing the parties' respective assets and their approximate value were attached. Teresa nonetheless contends the agreement is unenforceable under Iowa Code section 596.8(3) because Randall failed to provide her with fair and reasonable disclosure of his property and financial obligations. The trial court rejected this assertion, finding Teresa [who was Randall's paralegal and secretary] was sufficiently knowledgeable about Randall's financial circumstances to satisfy the IUPAA. We agree. . . .

Notes and Questions on *Simeone* and *Shanks*

1. Epilogue. After the events in the principal case, Randall Shanks became president of the Iowa Academy of Trial Attorneys and was invited to join the prestigious American College of Trial Lawyers. Teresa Shanks later became a financial adviser. Personal communication, Randall Shanks, Shanks Law Firm, July 27, 2015.

On remand in *Shanks*, the trial court divided the property according to the premarital agreement and awarded spousal support to Teresa. The appellate court reversed the award of $4,000/month rehabilitative alimony as "excessive," based on the short duration of the marriage and Teresa's ability to support herself. 805 N.W.2d 175 (Iowa Ct. App. 2011).

2. Background. Premarital (also "antenuptial" or "prenuptial") agreements generally limit property rights in the event of dissolution and death. Enforcement of these agreements combines traditional contract principles respecting private ordering with family law principles of equitable distribution. Prior to the 1970s, courts held that these agreements violated public policy as an inducement to divorce. In contrast, the modern view encourages such private ordering.

How do premarital agreements differ from ordinary contracts? First, the state has a greater interest in premarital agreements because it wishes to protect the welfare of the couple and their children, and also to preserve the privacy of the family, according to Professor Judith Younger. She continues:

> The second difference is the relationship of the parties to each other. It is a confidential relationship involving parties who are usually not evenly matched in bargaining power. The possibility, therefore, that one party may overreach the other is greater than in the case of ordinary contracts. The third difference is the fact that antenuptial agreements are to be performed in the future, in the context of a relationship which the parties have not yet begun and which may continue for many years after the agreement is executed and before it is enforced. The possibility that later events may make it unwise, unfair, or otherwise undesirable to enforce such agreements is also greater than in the case of ordinary contracts.[9]

3. Requirements. *Simeone* and *Shanks* reflect different approaches. *Simeone*, out of deference to private ordering, treats such agreements as ordinary contracts. *Shanks* underscores the need for special protection. Further, *Simeone* rejects an examination of substantive fairness (although still requiring voluntariness and adequate disclosure), whereas *Shanks* requires both substantive fairness and procedural fairness. Why does *Simeone* reject judicial review of reasonableness? Should a recitation of reasonableness in the agreement serve as a presumption of fairness? Or are premarital agreements "in the nature of contracts of adhesion" (as an omitted concurrence in *Simeone* states)? Why did the plaintiff in *Shanks* contend the prenuptial agreement was invalid? What was the court's response in that principal case?

a. UPAA: Unconscionability. The UPAA, although calling for review of both procedural and substantive fairness, sets a high standard for substantive unfairness, requiring "unconscionability." How does unconscionability differ from "fair and reasonable"? Is unconscionability (the standard for invalidating commercial contracts) an appropriate standard to apply to marital relationships?

UNIFORM PREMARITAL AGREEMENT ACT (UPAA)

§6.(a). A premarital agreement is not enforceable if the party against whom enforcement is sought proves that:

(1) that party did not execute the agreement voluntarily; or

(2) the agreement was unconscionable when it was executed and, before execution of the agreement, that party:

(i) was not provided a fair and reasonable disclosure of the property or financial obligations of the other party;

---

[9]. Judith T. Younger, Perspectives on Antenuptial Agreements: An Update, 8 J. Am. Acad. Matrim. Law. 1, 3 (1992).

(ii) did not voluntarily and expressly waive, in writing, any right to disclosure of the property or financial obligations of the other party beyond the disclosure provided; and

(iii) did not have, or reasonably could not have had, an adequate knowledge of the property or financial obligations of the other party.

What are some reasons that courts find premarital agreements to be unconscionable? See *Bevilacqua v. Bevilacqua*, 242 A.3d 542 (Conn. Ct. App. 2020) (finding that wife's injuries from car accident rendered agreement unconscionable); *Kelcourse v. Kelcourse*, 23 N.E.3d 124 (Mass. App. Ct. 2015) (agreement left wife with negative equity and required her to pay for major structural home repairs). Can a court find that a prospective spouse did not voluntarily sign a premarital agreement, but the agreement was not unconscionable? See *Matter of Estate of Eichstadt*, 983 N.W.2d 572 (S.D. 2022).

b. ALI Principles. Under rules approved by the American Law Institute (ALI), premarital agreements must meet standards of procedural fairness (i.e., informed consent and disclosure) and substantive fairness. A rebuttable presumption arises that the agreement satisfies the informed consent requirement if (1) it was executed at least 30 days prior to the marriage; (2) both parties had, or were advised to obtain, counsel and had the opportunity to do so; and (3) if one of the parties did not have counsel, the agreement contained understandable information about the parties' rights and the adverse nature of their interests. ALI, Principles of the Law of Family Dissolution: Analysis and Recommendations §7.04(3)(a), (b), and (c) (2002).

Finally, the court must undertake a review of substantive fairness at the time of enforcement, specifically regarding whether enforcement would work a "substantial injustice" based on the passage of time, the presence of children, or changed circumstances that were unanticipated and would have a significant impact on the parties or their children. ALI, Principles §7.05. Which approach do you favor—the UPAA or the ALI Principles? Why?

c. UPMAA. The UPAA has been adopted by 26 states and the District of Columbia. In 2012, the Uniform Law Commissioners (ULC) approved the Uniform Premarital and Marital Agreements Act (UPMAA) in an effort to treat premarital and marital agreements alike. To date, the UPMAA has been enacted only by Colorado and North Dakota. The UPMAA requires agreements to be in writing; provides a framework for determining validity; specifies that unconscionability and failure of disclosure are alternative grounds to deny enforcement; bars enforcement if an agreement is involuntary or results from duress; and affirms traditional principles of conflict of laws in determining an agreement's validity and meaning. The lack of state enactments of the UPMAA led to a recent ULC proposal to revise the Act to explore whether drafting new standards for postmarital agreements would result in greater enactability.

Should premarital and marital agreements be treated under the same set of principles? Or should the law recognize that different risks predominate in the two situations (such as changed circumstances for premarital agreements, and risks of duress/undue influence for marital agreements) that might militate against similar treatment? See ALI, Principles of the Law of Family Dissolution §7.01, cmt. e, at 953-954 (discussing different risks).

4. Waivers of spousal support. Waivers of spousal support are common in premarital agreements.[10] Many states impose restrictions on these provisions, while several other states prohibit them altogether. Still other states require consultation with independent counsel. Which approach is preferable? What does Iowa law require for waivers of spousal support? What rationale explains these rules?

5. Timing.

a. Timing of agreement. The plaintiffs in *Simeone* and *Shanks* claim duress based on the proximity of the execution of the agreement to the wedding. How do these courts resolve this issue? Should statutes require execution of premarital agreements a minimum amount of time before marriage? What do the ALI Principles require? Should the state enact a rebuttable presumption that all premarital contracts executed within a short period of marriage are void? Compare Penrod v. Penrod, 624 S.W.3d 905 (Mo. Ct. App. 2021) (rejecting wife's argument that the agreement was invalid because she did not know of premarital agreement until the day before wedding), with Potts v. Potts, 303 S.W.3d 177, 189 (Mo. Ct. App. 2010) (holding that one day's notice did not provide sufficient time for review of agreement). See also Cal. Fam. Code § 1615(c)(2)(B) (requiring seven days between first presentment of agreement and its execution). Empirical research (cited above) reveals that almost two-thirds of couples who execute premarital agreements sign their agreements within two weeks before the wedding. One-third of these couples sign within four days of the wedding.[11] What are the policy implications (if any) of these findings?

b. Timing of fairness determination. If substantive fairness is considered, should it be determined as of execution and/or enforcement? Compare the approaches in *Simeone* and *Shanks* with those of the UPAA and ALI Principles.

The dissent in *Simeone* suggests (in an omitted section) that the following circumstances at divorce might lead to invalidation of a premarital agreement: (1) a spouse's diminished employment prospects if that spouse remained home due to family responsibilities, such that the spouse would become a public charge or suffer a significantly reduced standard of living; (2) a dependent spouse in a long marriage who helped increase the value of the other's property; (3) an unanticipated serious illness rendering the spouse unable to provide self-support. Note that the UPAA provides that a premarital agreement will not be enforced at divorce if the enforcement of a provision that modifies or eliminates spousal support would cause one spouse to become a public charge (UPAA §6(b)).

6. Relative bargaining power. *Simeone* and *Shanks* assume that prospective spouses have equal bargaining power. On what basis might you question this assumption? What relevance should a court attach to such factors as age, financial

---

[10]. Elizabeth R. Carter, Are Premarital Agreements Really Unfair?: An Empirical Study, 48 Hofstra L. Rev. 387, 427 (2019) (finding that 38 percent of agreements from a parish in Louisiana waived permanent spousal support, and that waivers were most common in agreements by previously married husbands). See also Elizabeth R. Carter, Louisiana Family Law in Comparative Perspective 361-362 (2018).

[11]. Carter, Are Premarital Agreements Really Unfair?, supra note [10], at 28.

position, business acumen, obtaining (or rejecting) legal advice, the selection of counsel by the defendant, or a previous divorce?

One legal scholar, Professor Judith Younger, comments on the gendered aspects of premarital contracts as follows:

> By enforcing them, the courts are enabling the dominant party to acquire financial advantages and to shift the risk of a failed relationship from him, even though he can afford to bear it, to her, the weaker party who cannot easily bear such a burden. These judicial decisions work not only to her detriment but to the public's detriment as well.[12]

She recommends: (1) independent counsel for each party, with the requirement that each party have ample time and money for consultation; (2) a reasonable provision for postdivorce support if a party gives up income to become a homemaker; and (3) prior judicial approval of such agreements. What do you think of these suggestions?

Empirical research reveals that premarital agreements are more common in second marriages, and also that male parties to premarital agreements often marry women who are at least a decade younger.[13] What are the policy implications (if any) of these findings?

7. Disclosure. What do *Simeone* and *Shanks* require in terms of disclosure? Is this synonymous with "detailed" disclosure? Is a general approximation of income, assets, and liabilities sufficient? Can a party's conduct (such as failing to request financial information) constitute a waiver of the right to full disclosure? Does a prospective spouse have a legal duty to inquire into the other's financial status before executing the agreement? Are the parties' respective acknowledgments in the prenuptial agreement that they each made "a full and complete disclosure" conclusive on the issue of whether the disclosure was fair and reasonable? See In re Marriage of Woodrum, 115 N.E.3d 1021 (Ill. App. Ct. 2019). A majority of jurisdictions hold that prospective spouses share a confidential relationship. See Friezo v. Friezo, 914 A.2d 533, 549 (Conn. 2007) (survey). What does that term mean? How might that status affect the disclosure requirement for a valid premarital agreement?

8. Independent counsel. How does the court in *Shanks* respond to the plaintiff's claim that she did not have adequate legal advice in executing the agreement? Many states emphasize the importance of providing an *opportunity* to consult independent counsel. A California law reform suggests the following (for a premarital agreement to be voluntary): the presence of independent counsel for each party (or waiver after such advice), a seven-day waiting period following such advice between presentment and signature, and a finding of involuntariness absent that period, regardless of whether the party was represented (Cal. Fam. Code §1615). What do you think of such reforms? Should independent counsel for both parties be mandatory?

---

[12]. Judith T. Younger, Lovers' Contracts in the Courts: Forsaking the Minimum Decencies, 13 Wm. & Mary J. Women & L. 349, 427 (2007).

[13]. Carter, Are Premarital Agreements Really Unfair?, supra note [10], at 21-22 (age differential was extrapolated from data in Figure 7).

9. Specific couples. How should same-sex couples approach the possible termination of their marriages in their premarital agreements? How should senior citizens, so-called gray divorcées, handle such a situation?[14] What issues are of special importance to these couples?

10. Scope and limitation. UPAA supports a wide latitude regarding prospective spouses' contractual freedom. Among the permissible areas for premarital agreements, UPAA specifies "any other matter, including personal rights and obligations, not in violation of public policy or a statute imposing a criminal penalty." UPAA §3(a). The comment enumerates such examples as choice of abode, the freedom to pursue career opportunities, and the upbringing of children. Does this provision interfere with the doctrine of family privacy? Note that according to the general rule, premarital agreements may *not* restrict judicial discretion regarding either child custody or child support because of the state's concern with child welfare.

Problems

1. Suppose you are about to marry or begin a committed relationship. Discuss with your partner the pros and cons of having a prior agreement. What roles, responsibilities, and other decisions might you want to allocate during the relationship? Support? Property rights? Ownership of premarital assets and debts? Gifts from family members? Student loans? Spousal support or child support from a prior marriage? Choice of parties' respective surnames? Employment and its consequences? Domicile? Responsibilities for birth control? Number of children? Parenting responsibilities? Household division of labor? Career changes?

Draft an agreement to govern your relationship. What factors might evoke renegotiation or expiration of the agreement? Having children? Relationship duration of at least ten years? Reasons for ending the relationship? Any other factors?

2. Which of the following provisions are enforceable under the UPMAA? Which should the law enforce?
  a. A parent shall not interfere, in the presence of the children, in punishments by the other parent.
  b. Sexual intercourse shall be limited to once per week.
  c. One of the spouses shall reside in a certain locale.
  d. The husband's mother shall live with the parties, but not the children of the wife's prior marriage.
  e. Each spouse must undergo counseling before seeking a divorce and must not seek a divorce absent fault grounds or a two-year separation.
  f. If the husband obtains a no-fault divorce, he must pay the wife $15,000/month for five years, but if he divorces her on fault grounds, she pays him $5,000/month for two years.

---

[14]. See Linda J. Ravdin, Premarital Agreements and the Gray Divorce, 48 Est. Plan. 4 (Jan. 2021).

g. The wife will receive half of the husband's property upon divorce only if the parties remain married ten years or more; if the marriage ends sooner, she will receive only 25 percent.

3. Major League Baseball (MLB) player Barry Bonds meets Susann ("Sun") in Montreal after she emigrates from Sweden. Both are 23 years of age. Sun is working as a waitress and planning a career as a makeup artist for the rich and famous. The two take up residence in Phoenix, Arizona, and decide to marry. Barry is earning $106,000 at this time. The day before the wedding, the couple signs a premarital contract at Barry's lawyers' office, by which each waives any interest in the earnings and acquisitions of the other during the marriage. Sun declines the lawyers' advice that she retain her own counsel. The attorneys read the agreement to her and explain that it waives her community property rights. After a six-year marriage, Barry petitions for dissolution in California. At the time, he is earning $8 million annually. Sun, who has custody of the couple's two children, is awarded child support of $20,000 per month and spousal support of $10,000 per month for a four-year period.

Sun argues that the premarital agreement was not executed voluntarily. She claims that she did not understand the terms because of her limited English skills. She also asserts that she believed the agreement pertained only to property that was owned prior to the marriage. Barry's attorneys later testify that she understood the agreement and did not appear pressured or confused, but rather seemed confident and happy. What result? Is legal counsel essential to the enforceability of premarital contracts? How relevant is a party's waiver of legal counsel? See In re Marriage of Bonds, 5 P.3d 815 (Cal. 2000). Suppose Sun argues that the agreement is unconscionable because of drastically changed circumstances (i.e., Barry's increased wealth). What result? See Blue v. Blue, 60 S.W.3d 585 (Ky. Ct. App. 2001).

4. Dave, a successful entrepreneur, asks Tammy, a schoolteacher, to execute a premarital agreement before they marry. She agrees and signs the document after consultation with her lawyer. After their marriage, during a romantic moment, Dave takes all his copies of the premarital agreement and rips them up in front of Tammy. He tells her that he feels ashamed that he pressured her into signing the premarital agreement and informs her that the agreement is no longer valid.

After a 15-year marriage, Tammy files for divorce. When Dave countersues for divorce, he alleges that Tammy is not entitled to any spousal support or property based on their premarital agreement. In response, Tammy contends that the premarital agreement is unenforceable because it has been revoked. Has the premarital agreement been revoked? What constitutes an effective revocation? Why might a court hold that the revocation was ineffective? See UPA, Section 5 (requiring the same formalities for execution and revocation); UPMAA, Section 6, Cmt. (revocation must be in a signed writing, although states may apply "equitable doctrines" in "exceptional cases").

This problem is based on the divorce litigation surrounding the premarital agreement of Nicole Young and Dr. Dre (André Romelle Young), an American rapper and hip hop producer. See Kenzie Bryant, "It's Like the Dog Ate My Homework": Dr. Dre's Divorce Prenup Faces a Long-Shot Challenge, Vanity Fair, Aug. 7, 2020, https://www.vanityfair.com/style/2020/08/dr-dre-nicole-young-prenup-filing.

D. Getting Married: Substantive and Procedural Regulations

1. Constitutional Limits on State Regulation of Entry into Marriage

LOVING v. VIRGINIA
388 U.S. 1 (1967)

Chief Justice WARREN delivered the opinion of the Court.

This case presents a constitutional question never addressed by this Court: whether a statutory scheme adopted by the State of Virginia to prevent marriages between persons solely on the basis of racial classifications violates the Equal Protection and Due Process Clauses of the Fourteenth Amendment. . . .

In June 1958, two residents of Virginia, Mildred Jeter, a Negro woman, and Richard Loving, a white man, were married in the District of Columbia pursuant to its laws. Shortly after their marriage, the Lovings returned to Virginia and established their marital abode in Caroline County. [A] grand jury issued an indictment charging the Lovings with violating Virginia's ban on interracial marriages. [T]he Lovings pleaded guilty to the charge and were sentenced to one year in jail; however, the trial judge suspended the sentence for a period of 25 years on the condition that the Lovings leave the State and not return to Virginia together for 25 years. He stated in an opinion that:

> Almighty God created the races white, black, yellow, malay and red, and he placed them on separate continents. And but for the interference with his arrangement there would be no cause for such marriages. The fact that he separated the races shows that he did not intend for the races to mix. . . .

Virginia is now one of 16 States which prohibit and punish marriages on the basis of racial classifications. Penalties for miscegenation arose as an incident to slavery and have been common in Virginia since the colonial period. The present statutory scheme dates from the adoption of the Racial Integrity Act of 1924, passed during the period of extreme nativism which followed the end of the First World War. The central features of this Act, and current Virginia law, are the absolute prohibition of a "white person" marrying other than another "white person," a prohibition against issuing marriage licenses until the issuing official is satisfied that the applicants' statements as to their race are correct, certificates of "racial composition" to be kept by both local and state registrars [and a penalty of one to five years imprisonment].

In upholding the constitutionality of these provisions in the decision below, the Supreme Court of Appeals of Virginia referred to its 1955 decision in Naim v. Naim, 197 Va. 80, 87 S.E.2d 749, as stating the reasons supporting the validity of these laws. In *Naim*, the state court concluded that the State's legitimate purposes were "to preserve the racial integrity of its citizens," and to prevent "the corruption of blood," "a mongrel breed of citizens," and "the obliteration of racial pride," obviously an endorsement of the doctrine of White Supremacy. The court also reasoned that marriage has traditionally been subject to state regulation without federal intervention, and, consequently, the regulation of marriage should be left to exclusive state control by the Tenth Amendment.

[T]he State contends that, because its miscegenation statutes punish equally both the white and the Negro participants in an interracial marriage, these statutes, despite their reliance on racial classifications do not constitute an invidious discrimination based upon race. The second argument . . . is that, if the Equal Protection Clause does not outlaw miscegenation statutes because of their reliance on racial classifications, the question of constitutionality would thus become whether there was any rational basis for a State to treat interracial marriages differently from other marriages. On this question, the State argues, the scientific evidence is substantially in doubt and, consequently, this Court should defer to the wisdom of the state legislature in adopting its policy of discouraging interracial marriages.

Because we reject the notion that the mere "equal application" of a statute containing racial classifications is enough to remove the classifications from the Fourteenth Amendment's proscription of all invidious racial discriminations, we do not accept the State's contention that these statutes should be upheld if there is any possible basis for concluding that they serve a rational purpose. . . . The clear and central purpose of the Fourteenth Amendment was to eliminate all official state sources of invidious racial discrimination in the States.

There can be no question but that Virginia's miscegenation statutes rest solely upon distinctions drawn according to race. The statutes proscribe generally accepted conduct if engaged in by members of different races. Over the years, this Court has consistently repudiated "(d)istinctions between citizens solely because of their ancestry" as being "odious to a free people whose institutions are founded upon the doctrine of equality." At the very least, the Equal Protection Clause demands that racial classifications, especially suspect in criminal statutes, be subjected to the "most rigid scrutiny," and, if they are ever to be upheld, they must be shown to be necessary to the accomplishment of some permissible state objective, independent of the racial discrimination which it was the object of the Fourteenth Amendment to eliminate. . . .

There is patently no legitimate overriding purpose independent of invidious racial discrimination which justifies the classification. The fact that Virginia prohibits only interracial marriages involving white persons demonstrates that the racial classifications must stand on their own justification, as measures designed to maintain White Supremacy. We have consistently denied the constitutionality of measures which restrict the rights of citizens on account of race. There can be no doubt that restricting the freedom to marry solely because of racial classifications violates the central meaning of the Equal Protection Clause.

These statutes also deprive the Lovings of liberty without due process of law in violation of the Due Process Clause of the Fourteenth Amendment. The freedom to marry has long been recognized as one of the vital personal rights essential to the orderly pursuit of happiness by free men.

Marriage is one of the "basic civil rights of man," fundamental to our very existence and survival. Skinner v. State of Oklahoma, 316 U.S. 535, 541 (1942). See also Maynard v. Hill, 125 U.S. 190 (1888). To deny this fundamental freedom on so unsupportable a basis as the racial classifications embodied in these statutes, classifications so directly subversive of the principle of equality at the heart of the Fourteenth Amendment, is surely to deprive all the State's citizens of liberty without due process of law. The Fourteenth Amendment requires that the freedom of choice to marry not be restricted by invidious racial discriminations. Under our Constitution, the freedom to marry or not marry, a person of another race resides with the individual and cannot be infringed by the State. These convictions must be reversed. . . .

NOTE: WHO WERE MILDRED AND RICHARD LOVING?

Robert A. Pratt, Crossing the Color Line: A Historical Assessment and Personal Narrative of Loving v. Virginia
41 How. L.J. 229, 234-244 (1998)

. . . Richard Perry Loving and Mildred Delores Jeter had known each other practically all of their lives, as their families lived just up the road from each other in the rural community of Central Point, Virginia, located in Caroline County. . . . For twenty-three years, Richard's father had defied the racial mores of southern white society by working for Boyd Byrd, one of the wealthiest black farmers in the community. [T]he close-knit nature of their community [led] to an acceptance of personal relationships in a particular setting that

Mildred and Richard Loving who challenged Virginia's ban on interracial marriage

would have been anathema elsewhere. So when white Richard Loving, age seventeen, began courting "colored" Mildred Jeter, age eleven, their budding romance drew little attention from either the white or the black communities.

Mildred (part-black and part-Cherokee) had a pretty light-brown complexion accentuated by her slim figure, which was why practically everyone who knew her called her "Stringbean" or "Bean" for short. Richard (part-English and part-Irish) was a bricklayer by trade, but spent much of his spare time drag racing a car that he co-owned with two black friends, Raymond Green (a mechanic) and Percy Fortune (a local merchant). Despite their natural shyness, both Richard and Mildred were well-liked in the community, and the fact that they attended different churches and different schools did not hinder their courtship. When he was twenty-four and she was eighteen, Richard and Mildred decided to legalize their relationship by getting married.

Mildred did not know that interracial marriage was illegal in Virginia, but Richard did. This explains why, on June 2, 1958, he drove them across the Virginia state line to Washington, D.C., to be married. . . . Mr. and Mrs. Loving returned to Central Point to live with Mildred's parents; however, their marital bliss was short-lived. [Five weeks later], their quiet life was shattered when they were awakened early in the morning as three law officers "acting on an anonymous tip" opened the unlocked door of their home, walked into their bedroom, and shined a flashlight in their faces. Caroline County Sheriff R. Garnett Brooks demanded to know what the two of them were doing in bed together. Mildred answered, "I'm his wife," while Richard pointed to the District of Columbia marriage certificate that hung on their bedroom wall. "That's no good here," Sheriff Brooks replied. He charged the couple with unlawful cohabitation, and then he and his two deputies hauled the Lovings off to a nearby jail in Bowling Green.

[After their conviction and suspended sentences, the Lovings moved to Washington, D.C.] The years in Washington were not happy ones for the couple. Richard struggled to maintain permanent employment while Mildred busied herself tending to the needs of their three children. "I missed being with my family and friends, especially Garnet [her sister]. I wanted my children to grow up in the country, where they could run and play, and where I wouldn't worry about them so much. I never liked much about the city."

Virginia law would not allow Richard and Mildred Loving [to be] in the state at the same time; however, that did not stop them from trying or from succeeding on various occasions. Mildred and the children made frequent visits to Battery, Virginia, the rural black community where her sister and brother-in-law lived. When Mildred would arrive in Battery, some of the neighbors would begin to look at their watches to see how long it would be before Richard's car came cruising through the neighborhood. During those early years, Richard's visits [occurred] almost exclusively after dark. . . .

The Lovings had not really been that interested in the civil rights movement, nor had they ever given much thought to challenging Virginia's law. But with a major civil rights bill being debated in Congress in 1963, Mildred decided to write to Robert Kennedy, the Attorney General of the United States. The Department of Justice referred the letter to the American Civil Liberties Union [ACLU]. Bernard S. Cohen, a young lawyer doing pro bono work for the ACLU in Alexandria, Virginia, agreed to take the case. He would later be joined by another young attorney, Philip J. Hirschkop. . . .

[T]he U.S. Supreme Court agreed to hear the case. . . . In concluding his oral argument on April 10, 1967, Cohen relayed a message to the Justices from Richard Loving: "Tell the Court I love my wife, and it is just unfair that I can't live with her in Virginia." . . .

Mildred Loving [remained] the same intensely shy woman she has always been. [She saw] herself as an ordinary black woman who fell in love with an ordinary white man. [She] puts it this way:

> We weren't bothering anyone. And if we hurt some people's feelings, that was just too bad. All we ever wanted was to get married, because we loved each other. Some people will never change, but that's their problem, not mine. I married the only man I had ever loved, and I'm happy for the time we had together. For me, that was enough.

Gretchen Livingston & Anna Brown, Intermarriage in the U.S. 50 Years After Loving v. Virginia
Pew Research Ctr., May 18, 2017
*https://www.pewsocialtrends.org/2017/05/18/intermarriage-in
-the-u-s-50-years-after-loving-v-virginia/*

In 2015, 17% of all U.S. newlyweds had a spouse of a different race or ethnicity, marking more than a fivefold increase since 1967, when 3% of newlyweds were intermarried, according to a new Pew Research Center analysis of U.S. Census Bureau data. In that year, the U.S. Supreme Court in the Loving v. Virginia case ruled that marriage across racial lines was legal throughout the country. Until this ruling, interracial marriages were forbidden in many states.

More broadly, one-in-ten married people in 2015—not just those who recently married—had a spouse of a different race or ethnicity. This translates into 11 million people who were intermarried. The growth in intermarriage has coincided with shifting societal norms as Americans have become more accepting of marriages involving spouses of different races and ethnicities, even within their own families.

The most dramatic increases in intermarriage have occurred among black newlyweds. . . . Among blacks, intermarriage is twice as prevalent for male newlyweds as it is for their female counterparts. While about one-fourth of recently married black men (24%) have a spouse of a different race or ethnicity, this share is 12% among recently married black women.

[T]here are dramatic gender differences among Asian newlyweds as well, though they run in the opposite direction—Asian women are far more likely to intermarry than their male counterparts. . . . In contrast, among white and Hispanic newlyweds, the shares who intermarry are similar for men and women. Some 12% of recently married white men and 10% of white women have a spouse of a different race or ethnicity, and among Hispanics, 26% of newly married men and 28% of women do.

A more diverse population and shifting attitudes are contributing to the rise of intermarriage. [T]he growing share of the population that is Asian or Hispanic, combined with these groups' high rates of intermarriage, is further boosting U.S. intermarriage overall. . . .

Attitudes about intermarriage are changing as well. In just seven years, the share of adults saying that the growing number of people marrying someone of a different race is good for society has risen 15 points to 39%. . . .

Update: In 2019, 11 percent of all married U.S. adults had a partner who was a different race, according to the Pew Research Center. Among newlyweds that year, 19 percent entered interracial unions.[15]

---

[15]. Kim Parker & Amanda Barroso, In Vice President Kamala Harris, We Can See How America Has Changed, Pew Research Ctr., Feb. 25, 2021, https://www.pewresearch.org/fact-tank/2021/02/25/in-vice-president-kamala-harris-we-can-see-how-america-has-changed/.

ZABLOCKI v. REDHAIL

434 U.S. 374 (1978)

Justice MARSHALL delivered the opinion of the Court.

At issue in this case is the constitutionality of a Wisconsin statute, Wis. Stat. §245.10(1), (4), (5) (1973), which provides that members of a certain class of Wisconsin residents may not marry, within the State or elsewhere, without first obtaining a court order granting permission to marry. The class is defined by the statute to include any "Wisconsin resident having minor issue not in his custody and which he is under obligation to support by any court order or judgment." The statute specifies that court permission cannot be granted unless the marriage applicant submits proof of compliance with the support obligation and, in addition, demonstrates that the children covered by the support order "are not then and are not likely thereafter to become public charges." . . .

Appellee Redhail is a Wisconsin resident who, under the terms of §245.10, is unable to enter into a lawful marriage in Wisconsin or elsewhere so long as he maintains his Wisconsin residency. [W]hen appellee was a minor and a high school student, a paternity action was instituted against him in Milwaukee County Court, alleging that he was the father of a baby girl born out of wedlock on July 5, 1971. After he appeared and admitted that he was the child's father, the court [adjudged him] the father and ordered him to pay $109 per month as support for the child until she reached 18 years of age. From May 1972 until August 1974, appellee was unemployed and indigent, and consequently was unable to make any support payments.

On September 27, 1974, appellee filed an application for a marriage license with appellant Zablocki, the County Clerk of Milwaukee County, and a few days later the application was denied on the sole ground that appellee had not obtained a court order granting him permission to marry, as required by §245.10. [I]t is stipulated that he would not have been able to satisfy either of the statutory prerequisites for an order granting permission to marry. First, he had not satisfied his support obligations to his illegitimate child, and as of December 1974 there was an arrearage in excess of $3,700. Second, the child had been a public charge since her birth, receiving [welfare benefits]. [Appellee filed a class action, claiming violations of equal protection and due process. He prevailed in the District Court.] We agree with the District Court that the statute violates the Equal Protection Clause.

[The Court turns to the issue of the appropriate level of scrutiny.] Since our past decisions make clear that the right to marry is of fundamental importance, and since the classification at issue here significantly interferes with the exercise of that right, we believe that "critical examination" of the state interests advanced in support of the classification is required.

The leading case of this Court on the right to marry is Loving v. Virginia, 388 U.S. 1 (1967). [Loving] could have rested solely on the ground that the statutes discriminated on the basis of race in violation of the Equal Protection Clause. But the Court went on to hold that the laws arbitrarily deprived the couple of a fundamental liberty protected by the Due Process Clause, the freedom to marry. . . . Although Loving arose in the context of racial discrimination, prior and subsequent decisions of this Court confirm that the right to marry is of fundamental importance for all individuals. . . .

More recent decisions have established that the right to marry is part of the fundamental "right of privacy" implicit in the Fourteenth Amendment's Due Process Clause. . . . Cases subsequent to *Griswold* and *Loving* have routinely categorized the decision to marry as among the personal decisions protected by the right of privacy. . . . It is not surprising that the decision to marry has been placed on the same level of importance as decisions relating to procreation, childbirth, child rearing, and family relationships. [I]t would make little sense to recognize a right of privacy with respect to other matters of family life and not with respect to the decision to enter the relationship that is the foundation of the family in our society. . . .

By reaffirming the fundamental character of the right to marry, we do not mean to suggest that every state regulation which relates in any way to the incidents of or prerequisites for marriage must be subjected to rigorous scrutiny. To the contrary, reasonable regulations that do not significantly interfere with decisions to enter into the marital relationship may legitimately be imposed. See Califano v. Jobst, 434 U.S. 47 (1977). The statutory classification at issue here, however, clearly does interfere directly and substantially with the right to marry.

Under the challenged statute, no Wisconsin resident in the affected class may marry in Wisconsin or elsewhere without a court order, and marriages contracted in violation of the statute are both void and punishable as criminal offenses. Some of those in the affected class, like appellee, will never be able to obtain the necessary court order, because they either lack the financial means to meet their support obligations or cannot prove that their children will not become public charges. These persons are absolutely prevented from getting married. Many others, able in theory to satisfy the statute's requirements, will be sufficiently burdened by having to do so that they will in effect be coerced into forgoing their right to marry. And even those who can be persuaded to meet the statute's requirements suffer a serious intrusion into their freedom of choice in an area in which we have held such freedom to be fundamental.[12]

When a statutory classification significantly interferes with the exercise of a fundamental right, it cannot be upheld unless it is supported by sufficiently important state interests and is closely tailored to effectuate only those interests. Appellant asserts that two interests are served by the challenged statute: the permission-to-marry proceeding furnishes an opportunity to counsel the applicant as to the necessity of fulfilling his prior support obligations; and the welfare of the out-of-custody children is protected. We may accept for present purposes that these are legitimate and substantial interests, but, since the means selected by the State for achieving these interests unnecessarily impinge on the right to marry, the statute cannot be sustained.

---

12. The directness and substantiality of the interference with the freedom to marry distinguish the instant case from Califano v. Jobst, 434 U.S. 47 [(1977) (upholding the Social Security Act provision for termination of a dependent child's benefits upon marriage to a person not entitled to benefits under the Act)]. The Social Security provisions placed no direct legal obstacle in the path of persons desiring to get married, and . . . there was no evidence that the laws significantly discouraged, let alone made "practically impossible," any marriages. Indeed, the provisions had not deterred the individual who challenged the statute from getting married, even though he and his wife were both disabled (because of availability of other federal benefits, total payments to the Jobsts after marriage were only $20 per month less than they would have been had Mr. Jobst's child benefits not been terminated).

There is evidence that the challenged statute, as originally introduced in the Wisconsin Legislature, was intended merely to establish a mechanism whereby persons with support obligations to children from prior marriages could be counseled before they entered into new marital relationships and incurred further support obligations. Court permission to marry was to be required, but apparently permission was automatically to be granted after counseling was completed. The statute actually enacted, however, does not expressly require or provide for any counseling whatsoever, nor for any automatic granting of permission to marry by the court, and thus it can hardly be justified as a means for ensuring counseling of the persons within its coverage. Even assuming that counseling does take place—a fact as to which there is no evidence in the record—this interest obviously cannot support the withholding of court permission to marry once counseling is completed.

With regard to safeguarding the welfare of the out-of-custody children, appellant's brief does not make clear the connection between the State's interest and the statute's requirements. At argument, appellant's counsel suggested that, since permission to marry cannot be granted unless the applicant shows that he has satisfied his court-determined support obligations to the prior children and that those children will not become public charges, the statute provides incentive for the applicant to make support payments to his children. This "collection device" rationale cannot justify the statute's broad infringement on the right to marry.

First, with respect to individuals who are unable to meet the statutory requirements, the statute merely prevents the applicant from getting married, without delivering any money at all into the hands of the applicant's prior children. More importantly, regardless of the applicant's ability or willingness to meet the statutory requirements, the State already has numerous other means for exacting compliance with support obligations, means that are at least as effective as the instant statute's and yet do not impinge upon the right to marry. . . .

There is also some suggestion that §245.10 protects the ability of marriage applicants to meet support obligations to prior children by preventing the applicants from incurring new support obligations. But the challenged provisions of §245.10 are grossly underinclusive with respect to this purpose, since they do not limit in any way new financial commitments by the applicant other than those arising out of the contemplated marriage. The statutory classification is substantially overinclusive as well: given the possibility that the new spouse will actually better the applicant's financial situation, by contributing income from a job or otherwise, the statute in many cases may prevent affected individuals from improving their ability to satisfy their prior support obligations. And, although it is true that the applicant will incur support obligations to any children born during the contemplated marriage, preventing the marriage may only result in the children being born out of wedlock, as in fact occurred in appellee's case. Since the support obligation is the same whether the child is born in or out of wedlock, the net result of preventing the marriage is simply more illegitimate children.

The statutory classification created by §245.10(1), (4), (5) thus cannot be justified by the interests advanced in support of it. The judgment of the District Court is, accordingly, [a]ffirmed.

Justice STEWART, concurring in the judgment.

I cannot join the opinion of the Court. To hold, as the Court does, that the Wisconsin statute violates the Equal Protection Clause seems to me to misconceive the meaning of that constitutional guarantee. The Equal Protection Clause deals not with substantive rights or freedoms but with invidiously discriminatory classifications. . . . The problem in this case is not one of discriminatory classifications, but of unwarranted encroachment upon a constitutionally protected freedom. I think that the Wisconsin statute is unconstitutional because it exceeds the bounds of permissible state regulation of marriage, and invades the sphere of liberty protected by the Due Process Clause of the Fourteenth Amendment. . . .

The Constitution does not specifically mention freedom to marry, but it is settled that the "liberty" protected by the Due Process Clause of the Fourteenth Amendment embraces more than those freedoms expressly enumerated in the Bill of Rights. And the decisions of this Court have made clear that freedom of personal choice in matters of marriage and family life is one of the liberties so protected. . . . It is evident that the Wisconsin law now before us directly abridges that freedom. The question is whether the state interests that support the abridgement can overcome the substantive protections of the Constitution. . . .

As directed against either the indigent or the delinquent parent, the law is substantially more rational if viewed as a means of assuring the financial viability of future marriages. In this context, it reflects a plausible judgment that those who have not fulfilled their financial obligations and have not kept their children off the welfare rolls in the past are likely to encounter similar difficulties in the future. But the State's legitimate concern with the financial soundness of prospective marriages must stop short of telling people they may not marry because they are too poor or because they might persist in their financial irresponsibility. . . . A legislative judgment so alien to our traditions and so offensive to our shared notions of fairness offends the Due Process Clause of the Fourteenth Amendment. . . .

Justice STEVENS, concurring in the judgment. . . .

Under this statute, a person's economic status may determine his eligibility to enter into a lawful marriage. A noncustodial parent whose children are "public charges" may not marry even if he has met his court-ordered obligations. Thus, within the class of parents who have fulfilled their court-ordered obligations, the rich may marry and the poor may not. This type of statutory discrimination is, I believe, totally unprecedented, as well as inconsistent with our tradition of administering justice equally to the rich and to the poor. . . .

The statute prevents impoverished parents from marrying even though their intended spouses are economically independent. Presumably, the Wisconsin Legislature assumed (a) that only fathers would be affected by the legislation, and (b) that they would never marry employed women. The first assumption ignores the fact that fathers are sometimes awarded custody, and the second ignores the composition of today's work force. To the extent that the statute denies a hard-pressed parent any opportunity to prove that an intended marriage will ease rather than aggravate his financial straits, it not only rests on unreliable premises, but also defeats its own objectives.

These questionable assumptions also explain why this statutory blunderbuss is wide of the target in another respect. The prohibition on marriage applies to the noncustodial parent but allows the parent who has custody to marry without the State's leave. Yet the danger that new children will further strain an inadequate budget is equally great for custodial and non-custodial parents. . . .

. . . Even assuming that the right to marry may sometimes be denied on economic grounds, this clumsy and deliberate legislative discrimination between the rich and the poor is irrational in so many ways that it cannot withstand scrutiny under the Equal Protection Clause of the Fourteenth Amendment.

[Justice Rehnquist, dissenting, would have upheld the statute under the rational basis test as a permissible exercise of the state's power to regulate family life and to assure child support.]

NOTE: WHO IS ROGER REDHAIL?

Tonya L. Brito et al., Chronicles of a Debt Foretold: Zablocki v. Red Hail

in The Poverty Law Canon: Exploring the Major Cases 232, 233-234, 251-252 (Marie A. Failinger & Ezra Rosser eds., 2016)

The story behind Zablocki v. Red Hail spans the 1970s in Milwaukee, a period of great inequality and dynamic social change. . . . Roger Red Hail came from a very poor family and could not afford the $109 per month in child support he had been ordered to pay. The child support debt he owed had ballooned to nearly $4,000 by the time he sought a marriage license two years later. . . .

[Red Hail, now in his 50s, is a member of the Oneida Indian tribe.] Poverty was a stark reality of Red Hail's childhood, as it was for many of Milwaukee's Indians. Among American Indians, estimates for the time put 33.1 percent of the community under the poverty line. [The exorbitant size of Red Hail's child support order was especially problematic given his youth, poverty, and employment prospects.]

Although Zablocki v. Red Hail was a significant victory, the ruling did not secure justice for Roger Red Hail. . . . Red Hail is still paying on the child support debt that brought about the 1978 Supreme Court decision. The exorbitant $109 per month child support order that was entered in 1972 and prevented him from marrying in Wisconsin in 1974 is still pending *40 years later*. Roger Red Hail owes about $10,000 in child support for his daughter Angela, who is now 42 years old. Moreover, Red Hail owes child support in the tens of thousands of dollars for the three children—Dawn, Jennifer, and Roger—he and his wife Terry had together. They divorced after a seven-year marriage and Red Hail was faced with another child support order.

Red Hail's total child support debt now exceeds $63,000, and, pursuant to court order, he continues to pay the debt on a monthly basis. . . . The monthly payment, however, will never satisfy the staggering accumulated child support arrearage. [B]ecause the interest that accumulates on the debt annually—currently at 6 percent but previously as high as 18 percent—far exceeds Red Hail's annual court-ordered payments, the debt has grown and will continue to grow to unimaginable proportions.

[T]he large outstanding debt is an inhibiting and intimidating burden. [T]he debt prevents Roger [now age 60] and his fianceé Colleen from marrying.

[Roger and Colleen have been together for 19 years and would like to get married. But, just as it did 40 years ago, child support debt stands in the way.] [T]hey have been putting off marriage out of fear that the state's pursuit of Red Hail's child support arrears will [saddle Colleen with his debts]. Red Hail also worries that even though he pays his child support on a monthly basis as required, he will be imprisoned for the debt. . . .

Notes and Questions on *Loving* and *Zablocki*

1. *Loving* epilogue. Mildred Loving died of pneumonia in 2008 at age 68. Her husband, Richard, predeceased her in 1975, as explained below:

> Less than a month after the Lovings' fourteenth anniversary and slightly more than eight years after they had earned the right to live as husband and wife in Virginia, Richard was killed. The couple and Mildred's sister Garnet were returning from a visit with friends when their car was broadsided by a drunk driver who had run a stop sign on route 721 in Caroline County, just thirteen miles from their home. Richard, forty-two, died instantly. Mildred lost her right eye, and Garnet suffered minor injuries.
>
> There was a tremendous outpouring of sympathy from the community for this woman who, not so long before, had been an exile from the state. . . . Richard is buried in a mostly black graveyard just outside the local Baptist church. Even in death, he refused to be bound by the laws of segregation. . . .[16]

2. Historical background. The antimiscegenation statute under which the Lovings were convicted reflected a widespread policy stemming from beliefs about racial superiority. At one time, 38 states prohibited relationships between Blacks and whites. Even before Virginia enacted its prohibition in 1662, state officials whipped and publicly humiliated persons who entered into Black-white sexual relationships. Authorities claimed to be concerned, in large part, about the status of mulatto offspring in an economy based on slavery.

Anxieties over miscegenation increased after the Civil War, when the emancipation of slaves heightened racial tension. Bolstering this climate was the eugenics movement, which preached that most maladies were hereditary and that social engineering would improve the human race. This theory led to many state restrictions on marriage. From 1880 to 1920, 20 states and territories revised or added antimiscegenation laws.[17]

3. Empirical data. *Loving* marked the beginning of a steady increase in multiracial marriages. Currently, 19 percent of all U.S. newlyweds have a spouse of a different race or ethnicity, marking a more than fivefold increase since *Loving* (according to the Pew Research Center excerpt above). At the same time, the

---

[16]. Phyl Newbeck, Virginia Hasn't Always Been for Lovers: Interracial Marriage Bans and the Case of Richard and Mildred Loving 219-220 (2004). See also Peter Wallenstein, Race, Sex, and the Freedom to Marry: Loving v. Virginia (2015).

[17]. Michael Grossberg, Governing the Hearth: Law and the Family in Nineteenth-Century America 136, 138-139 (1985).

public has become more accepting of interracial marriages. In 2017, 39 percent of all adults said the growing number of people marrying someone of a different race is a "good thing for the country," representing an increase from 24 percent in 2010.[18]

4. Marrying in another state. Although Virginia's 1924 Racial Purity statute prohibited interracial marriage, the Lovings were convicted for violating a *different* statute (Va. Code §20-58, enacted in 1878), forbidding residents from leaving the state to marry, with intent to evade the state antimiscegenation law, and then returning to cohabit. This scenario raises questions of choice of law, full faith and credit, and marriage evasion acts – rules that historically have applied to invalidate or validate such marriages. Recent federal legislation (explained below) makes some of these approaches no longer necessary for some couples.

a. Choice of law. One state will ordinarily recognize a marriage validly celebrated in another state under the common law rule of *lex loci* (the "place of celebration" rule), which provides that a marriage that is valid where performed is valid everywhere. Why didn't this choice-of-law rule apply in *Loving*? States considered some marriages (e.g., interracial, polygamous, or incestuous unions) so offensive that they carved out exceptions to the rule based on public policy grounds, even without the existence of state bans on marriage evasion.

The Restatement (Second) of Conflict of Laws §283(1) (1971) addresses the issue as follows:

RESTATEMENT (SECOND) OF CONFLICT OF LAWS

§283. VALIDITY OF MARRIAGE

(1) The validity of a marriage will be determined by the local law of the state which, with respect to the particular issue, has the most significant relationship to the spouses and the marriage. . . .

(2) A marriage which satisfies the requirements of the state where the marriage was contracted will everywhere be recognized as valid unless it violates the strong public policy of another state which had the most significant relationship to the spouses and the marriage at the time of the marriage.

§284. INCIDENTS OF FOREIGN MARRIAGE

A state usually gives the same incidents to a foreign marriage, which is valid under the principles stated in §238, that it gives to a marriage contracted within its territory.

b. Full faith and credit. The Full Faith and Credit Clause (art. IV, §1) of the Constitution and federal statutes implementing it require that one state give full faith and credit to "the public acts, records, and judicial proceedings" of sister states. Courts have interpreted the language to require the most rigorous respect for "judicial proceedings," foreclosing choice-of-law analysis in a second state once a court in the first state rendered a final judgment or decree. Marriage is not

---

[18]. Parker & Barroso, supra note [15].

a judicial decree, so it does not evoke mandatory recognition and respect, even though a second state typically will choose to treat it as valid under lex loci or the Restatement. This approach leaves room for a state like Virginia to rely on its own public policy against interracial relationships to refuse to recognize the marriage that the Lovings validly celebrated in Washington, D.C.

c. Marriage evasion acts. The subject of marriage evasion was addressed by the Uniform Marriage Evasion Act (UMEA). Approved in 1912, UMEA did the following: (1) declared void all marriages of parties who married in another state for the purpose of evading home state restrictions; (2) allowed out-of-state residents to marry only if their marriage would be permissible in their home state; (3) required state officers to obtain proof that out-of-state applicants would be permitted to marry in their home state; and (4) provided misdemeanor liability for violations. Only five states (Illinois, Louisiana, Massachusetts, Vermont, and Wisconsin) adopted UMEA in whole or in part. The Uniform Marriage and Divorce Act (UMDA) superseded UMEA in 1970, with a requirement that states recognize marriages deemed valid either at the place of celebration or the parties' domicile (UMDA §210).

d. Federal protection for interracial marriages. Recently, Congress passed the Respect for Marriage Act (RFMA), Pub. L. No. 117-228, 136 Stat. 2305 (2022). The law marked an important turning point in the long process of providing legal protection for interracial marriages. The law requires the federal government to recognize the validity of interracial marriages (as well as lesbian, gay, bisexual, and transgender (LGBT) marriages) conducted in states where these marriages are legal. RFMA also repeals the Defense of Marriage Act (DOMA, 1996). DOMA specified a strict federal definition for marriage, specifying a union between one man and one woman; defined "spouse" as a "person of the opposite sex"; and permitted states to refuse to recognize same-sex marriages from other states. The RFMA bars any state from denying "full faith and credit" of any marriage "on the basis of the sex, race, ethnicity, or national origin of those individuals."

The impetus for RFMA stemmed from the concurring opinion of Justice Thomas in Dobbs v. Jackson Women's Health Organization (supra Chapter I, p. 54), where he called into question the legality of other constitutionally protected liberty interests, such as the rights to contraception, antisodomy laws, and same-sex marriage (although his opinion made no mention of *Loving*). What might explain his omission of *Loving*?

5. *Loving* and precedent. *Loving* cites precedents concerning divorce (Maynard v. Hill), compulsory sterilization (Skinner v. Oklahoma), and, in an omitted section, parental rights (Meyer v. Nebraska). Are the cases apt? Curiously, *Loving* does not cite *Griswold*, decided two years earlier. What explains this omission? What contribution might *Griswold* and subsequent privacy cases make to the analysis in *Loving*?

6. *Loving*'s constitutional basis. Is *Loving* a case about race or about freedom of choice in marriage? What standard of review does the Court apply? What triggers such review? *Loving* establishes that the right to marry is constitutionally protected. Why should the Constitution protect the right to marry? Where in the Constitution is this right? Does it rest on substantive due process or equal protection? What difference does that make? On the basis of which approach did the Court decide *Zablocki*? Why?

7. Relevance of *Loving* to marriage for same-sex couples. Before the advent of marriage equality, advocates of same-sex marriage often equated the ban on same-sex marriage with antimiscegenation laws. This analogy is explored later in this chapter.

8. Degrees of scrutiny. *Zablocki* establishes different degrees of scrutiny for classifications infringing the right to marry; that is, rigorous scrutiny for a significant interference but minimal scrutiny for "reasonable regulations that do not significantly interfere with decisions to enter into the marital relationship." Justice Powell (in an omitted concurrence) suggests that the Court does not present any means to distinguish between the two types of regulations. Do you agree? What distinguishes the regulation in *Zablocki* from that in Califano v. Jobst (cited in *Zablocki*)?

According to *Zablocki*, a significant interference calling for rigorous scrutiny must be "direct" and "substantial." Are these distinct requirements? What guidelines does *Zablocki* give for identifying a "direct" interference?

9. Regulation of the procreation-support link. The Wisconsin statute invalidated in *Zablocki* arose from legislative concern about the nonpayment of child support by "deadbeat dads." How does *Zablocki* inform our understanding of the normative link between marriage and procreation and/or support?[19] Brito et al.'s excerpt (above) and the Pew Research Center report (below) explore the relationship between income inequality and the readiness to marry. What light do they shed on the dilemmas faced by the defendant in Zablocki v. Redhail?

Problems

1. Virginia law (like the law in seven other states) requires couples to specify their race on their marriage license applications. Brandyn Churchill and his fiancée, Sophie Rogers, wish to apply for a marriage license, but they do not want to identify their race. They believe that the requirement is outdated and find it deeply offensive. Churchill and Rogers file a class action suit in federal district court, seeking a declaratory judgment that the law is unconstitutional and injunctive relief. Plaintiffs contend that the requirement violates constitutional protections of free speech, due process, and privacy. What result? See Rogers v. Virginia State Registrar, 507 F.Supp.3d 664 (E.D. Va. 2019).

2. Kaniska Berashk is a citizen of Afghanistan. Based on his marriage to Fauzia Din, a naturalized U.S. citizen, he applies to a consular officer in the U.S. embassy in Islamabad, Pakistan, for a visa to enter the United States. The

---

[19]. See Melissa Murray, Marriage as Punishment, 112 Colum. L. Rev. 1, 43-47 (2012).

official denies Kaniska's visa application. The officer gives no specific reason but merely relies on the immigration statute's broad definition of "terrorist activities." Kaniska presumes that the denial is based on his possible connection to the Taliban – that is, his job as a payroll clerk for the Afghan Ministry of Social Welfare, which was part of the national government that was controlled at one time by the Taliban. His wife, Fauzia, seeks judicial review of her husband's visa denial and his forced separation from her. She alleges that the visa denial violates her constitutional right to marry. What result? See Kerry v. Din, 576 U.S. 86 (2015).

NOTE: INCOME INEQUALITY AND READINESS TO MARRY

D'Vera Cohn, Research from 2018 Demographers' Conference: Migration, Self-Identity, Marriage and Other Key Findings

Pew Research Ctr., May 24, 2018
https://www.pewresearch.org/fact-tank/2018/05/24/research-from-2018-demographers-conference-migration-self-identity-marriage-and-other-key-findings/

MARRIAGE AND MONEY

Economic security plays a role in people's readiness to wed. A majority of Americans who have never married but may want to say one reason for not marrying is that they are not financially stable. This is especially true for young adults. And while in the past, marriage rates were linked to how well men were doing economically, a Census Bureau working paper suggests that for today's young adults, economic characteristics of both women and men might be related to marriage rates.

[Researchers studied four factors among adults ages 18-34 to explore their role in the readiness to marry]: labor force participation, wages, poverty and housing. Some indicators mattered more than others. Full-time work, median wages, women's poverty, housing costs, owning a home and living in a parent's home all were significantly linked with higher or lower marriage rates among young adults to some degree.

For today's young adults, economic characteristics of both women and men might be related to marriage rates.

Though past studies have found that men's financial stability is more important than women's to marriage rates, "the present study found little evidence to suggest that men's socioeconomic characteristics produced significant associations more often than those of women." . . .

Another paper by three Duke University researchers, which looked at marriage and cohabitation among low-income parents, had somewhat similar findings about economic security [in a study of 4,444 unmarried, low-income couples in eight cities who had newborns or were expecting babies, and believed they would later marry.]

When the couples were surveyed 15 months and/or 36 months after participating in an initial survey, most had broken up or were cohabiting, but not married. Those who did marry were more likely to have reached some threshold of economic security, measured by having at least four of seven achievements that included being employed, having health insurance and avoiding public assistance. Three years into the study, 17% of couples who met that threshold were married, modestly higher than the 13% of couples who had achieved less than that. The likelihood of marriage was highest for couples in which both partners met the bar. . . .

TURNER v. SAFLEY

482 U.S. 78 (1987)

Justice O'CONNOR delivered the opinion of the Court.

This case requires us to determine the constitutionality of regulations promulgated by the Missouri Division of Corrections relating to inmate marriages [that permit] an inmate to marry only with the permission of the superintendent of the prison, and provide that such approval should be given only "when there are compelling reasons to do so." The term "compelling" is not defined, but prison officials testified at trial that generally only a pregnancy or the birth of an illegitimate child would be considered a compelling reason. [Plaintiff inmates, who desire to marry, bring a class action for injunctive relief and damages.]

In support of the marriage regulation, petitioners first suggest that the rule does not deprive prisoners of a constitutionally protected right. They concede that the decision to marry is a fundamental right [under *Zablocki* and *Loving*], but they imply that a different rule should obtain "in . . . a prison forum." Petitioners then argue that even if the regulation burdens inmates' constitutional rights, the restriction should be tested under a reasonableness standard. They urge that the restriction is reasonably related to legitimate security and rehabilitation concerns.

We disagree with petitioners that *Zablocki* does not apply to prison inmates. It is settled that a prison inmate "retains those [constitutional] rights that are not inconsistent with his status as a prisoner or with the legitimate penological objectives of the corrections system." The right to marry, like many other rights, is subject to substantial restrictions as a result of incarceration.

Many important attributes of marriage remain, however, after taking into account the limitations imposed by prison life. First, inmate marriages, like others, are expressions of emotional support and public commitment. These elements are an important and significant aspect of the marital relationship. In addition, many religions recognize marriage as having spiritual significance; for some inmates and their spouses, therefore, the commitment of marriage may be an exercise of religious faith as well as an expression of personal dedication. Third, most inmates eventually will be released by parole or commutation, and therefore most inmate marriages are formed in the expectation that they ultimately will be fully consummated. Finally, marital status often is a precondition to the receipt of government benefits (e.g., Social Security benefits), property rights (e.g., tenancy by the entirety, inheritance rights), and other, less tangible benefits (e.g., legitimation of children born out of wedlock). These incidents of marriage, like the religious and personal aspects of the marriage commitment, are unaffected by the fact of confinement or the pursuit of legitimate corrections goals.

Taken together, we conclude that these remaining elements are sufficient to form a constitutionally protected marital relationship in the prison context. Our decision in Butler v. Wilson, 415 U.S. 953 (1974), is not to the contrary. That case involved a prohibition on marriage only for inmates sentenced to life imprisonment; and, importantly, denial of the right was part of the punishment for crime.

The Missouri marriage regulation prohibits inmates from marrying unless the prison superintendent has approved the marriage after finding that there are compelling reasons for doing so. . . . In determining whether this regulation impermissibly burdens the right to marry, we note initially that the regulation prohibits marriages between inmates and civilians, as well as marriages between inmates. Although not urged by respondents, this implication of the interests of nonprisoners . . . may entail a "consequential restriction on the [constitutional] rights of those who are not prisoners." We need not reach this question, however, because even under the reasonable relationship test, the marriage regulation does not withstand scrutiny.

Petitioners have identified both security and rehabilitation concerns in support of the marriage prohibition. The security concern emphasized by petitioners is that "love triangles" might lead to violent confrontations between inmates. With respect to rehabilitation, prison officials testified that female prisoners often were subject to abuse at home or were overly dependent on male figures, and that this dependence or abuse was connected to the crimes they had committed. The [prison] superintendent, petitioner William Turner, testified that in his view, these women prisoners needed to concentrate on developing skills of self-reliance, and that the prohibition on marriage furthered this rehabilitative goal. Petitioners emphasize that the prohibition on marriage should be understood in light of Superintendent Turner's experience with several ill-advised marriage requests from female inmates.

We conclude that on this record, the Missouri prison regulation, as written, is not reasonably related to these penological interests. No doubt legitimate security concerns may require placing reasonable restrictions upon an inmate's right to marry, and may justify requiring approval of the superintendent. The Missouri regulation, however, represents an exaggerated response to such security objectives. . . . Moreover, with respect to the security concern emphasized in petitioners' brief—the creation of "love triangles"—petitioners have pointed to nothing in the record suggesting that the marriage regulation was viewed as preventing such entanglements. Common sense likewise suggests that there is no logical connection between the marriage restriction and the formation of love triangles: surely in prisons housing both male and female prisoners, inmate rivalries are as likely to develop without a formal marriage ceremony as with one. Finally, this is not an instance where the "ripple effect" on the security of fellow inmates and prison staff justifies a broad restriction on inmates' rights. . . .

Nor, on this record, is the marriage restriction reasonably related to the articulated rehabilitation goal. First, in requiring refusal of permission absent a finding of a compelling reason to allow the marriage, the rule sweeps much more broadly than can be explained by petitioners' penological objectives. Missouri prison officials testified that generally they had experienced no problem with the marriage of male inmates, and the District Court found that such marriages had routinely been allowed as a matter of practice at Missouri correctional institutions prior to adoption of the rule. The proffered justification thus does not explain the adoption of a rule banning marriages by these inmates. Nor does it account for the prohibition on inmate marriages to civilians. Missouri prison officials testified that generally they had no objection to inmate-civilian marriages, and Superintendent Turner testified that he usually did not object to the marriage of either male or female prisoners to civilians. The rehabilitation concern appears from the record to have been centered almost exclusively on female inmates marrying other inmates or ex-felons. . . .

Moreover, although not necessary to the disposition of this case, we note that on this record the rehabilitative objective asserted to support the regulation itself is suspect. Of the several female inmates whose marriage requests were discussed by prison officials at trial, only one was refused on the basis of fostering excessive dependency. The District Court found that the Missouri prison system operated on the basis of excessive paternalism in that the proposed marriages of *all* female inmates were scrutinized carefully even before adoption of the current regulation . . . whereas the marriages of male inmates during the same period were routinely approved. That kind of lopsided rehabilitation concern cannot provide a justification for the broad Missouri marriage rule.

[On this record,] the almost complete ban on the decision to marry is not reasonably related to legitimate penological objectives. We conclude, therefore, that the Missouri marriage regulation is facially invalid.

The excerpt below presents a profile of women who love convicted murderers, based on interviews by a journalist with mental health professionals, law enforcement officials, and the couples themselves.

Sheila Isenberg, Women Who Love Men Who Kill
34-35, 223-236 (2000)

Unbelievable as it may seem, there is a population of women who are deeply drawn to men who have murdered. They meet the men while working in prison as nurses, teachers, social workers, or volunteers. Others become pen pals with murderers. Some, who are infatuated, write fan/love letters to celebrity killers [or] serial killers. . . . Women who love killers were often little girls lost, reared in dysfunctional families where they were victims of abuse at the hands of harsh, dictatorial fathers aided by passive mothers. A large percentage were raised as Catholics and were severely affected by oppressive church teachings, including sexism, subjugation of women, and repression of sexuality.

Fathers were missing: divorced, dead, always working, drunk, withdrawn. Occasionally, mothers took on fathers' role and behaved like demanding authoritarians. Women who love killers frequently found that their relationships with men mimicked the one they had with their fathers. . . .

As it was between medieval maidens and the courtly knights who protected them, sex and true intimacy between women and the killers they love is usually forbidden by prison systems. These women feel deeply, but what they feel is not mature love or adult sexual passion. It is *romantic* passion—a passion fueled by deprivation and suffering, enhanced by anguish. These women have found the key to never-ending romance: suffering and pain.

Because many women who love killers have real difficulties with intimacy because of the damage done to them in childhood, they have chosen to live a fantasy. The majority of these women don't love real men but an illusion that is based on denial. Each woman separates, or compartmentalizes, the murder from the man she loves. She denies his crime. For women who love serial killers, or other notorious murderers, there is the added thrill of fame. Each serial killer's status gives a woman with low self-esteem a sense of importance; her prestige rises in direct proportion with the heinousness of his crimes.

In our patriarchal culture, murderers are often viewed as more than male: the most macho, strong, violent, and brutal of all men. In a majority of movies and television shows, the violent mystique of the murderer—or the cop, spy, undercover agent, etc.—is the erotic centerpiece. . . . For some women, it *is* thrilling to dance with a master of death. If a woman is seeking excitement, passion, a meaning to life, loving a murderer can make her feel intensely alive. She becomes important, perhaps famous, because she loves a man who has killed. . . .

A murderer is often a con man who wins a woman by manipulation and lying. Some women, gullible, vulnerable, and needy, are ready to believe these charmers. Each woman hears a story that fits her needs: If she needs to believe that he's religious, he'll tell her that. If she wants sweet talk, he'll woo her. If she needs a brilliant existentialist hero, he'll sweep her off her feet with his verbiage. Some murderers are unbelievably charismatic. These men exude self-confidence. The narcissistic and antisocial personalities of these murderers cause them to act as though rules don't apply to them. They act tough and superior. They believe in themselves (or pretend they do) and easily convince susceptible women (literally little girls lost) to believe in them too. But, in truth, these are deeply disturbed men who, by murdering, have irrevocably broken one of our most basic laws. . . .

Notes and Questions

1. **Precedents.** Does *Turner*'s holding follow automatically from *Loving* and *Zablocki*?

2. **Rationale.** What rationale supports depriving life-sentence inmates of the right to marry, as the Supreme Court previously held (in Butler v. Wilson, cited in *Turner*)? Does this rationale dictate the automatic *dissolution* of marriages entered into by these inmates prior to incarceration? Cf. Langone v. Coughlin,

712 F. Supp. 1061 (N.D.N.Y. 1989) (invalidating a ban on marriages by "lifers" that exempted marriages of those "lifers" who were already married, as not reasonably related to legitimate penological objectives).

3. Gender. Why did the Department of Corrections policy in *Turner* focus on female inmates? Why did prison officials conclude that marriage could thwart the rehabilitation of females but not males? Are the problems of abuse and dependency in marriage gender specific? What additional "gendered" insights does Isenberg's excerpt (above) provide?

Problems

1. Alfie, an indigent prison inmate who is serving a life sentence, is denied a marriage license when he is unable to comply with state law by personally appearing at the county clerk's office. The prison offers two accommodations: transportation by the Sheriff's Office for a fee or application by video conferencing at the prison, subject to judicial approval. However, Alfie does not have the resources to pay transportation costs, and the court does not have equipment for video conferencing. Does a personal appearance requirement violate the fundamental right to marry? Does *Turner* require prison officials to facilitate and pay for benefits to enable prisoners to comply with procedural requirements to marry? See Jones v. Perry, 215 F. Supp. 3d 563 (E.D. Ky. 2016); In re Coats, 849 A.2d 254 (Pa. Super. Ct. 2004); Toms v. Taft, 338 F.3d 519 (6th Cir. 2003).

2. Suppose that Alfie prevails (in Problem 1), and the prison allows him to marry. Afterwards, he and his wife, who is 44 years old, wish to have a child. Alfie learns that the California Department of Corrections (CDC) prohibits conjugal visits for inmates serving life sentences. He requests that (1) a lab be permitted to mail him a semen collection container with a prepaid return mailer, (2) he be permitted to ejaculate into the container, and (3) the filled container be returned to the laboratory via overnight mail. Alternatively, he requests that his attorney be permitted to transport the specimen to the lab. He is willing to bear all costs.

When the CDC refuses his requests, he brings an action alleging a violation of his constitutional right to procreate pursuant to 42 U.S.C. §1983 and the Due Process Clause. What result? If the court were to agree that Alfie has a constitutional right to procreate noncoitally in this manner, does a female inmate have a right to be artificially inseminated? See Gerber v. Hickman, 291 F.3d 617 (9th Cir. 2002); Goodwin v. Turner, 908 F.2d 1395 (8th Cir. 1990). Suppose that Alfie also files a class action suit on behalf of all inmates at his prison challenging the ban on conjugal visitation. He argues that the policy violates: (1) prisoners' and spousal rights to marital privacy; (2) the right to procreate; (3) the constitutional prohibition on cruel and unusual punishment; and (4) the First Amendment right to religious freedom. What result? See Robertson v. Kansas, 2007 WL 4322781, at *2 (D. Kan. 2007). How meaningful is recognition of the right to marry without the provision of conjugal visits?

2. State Regulation of Entry into the Marital Relationship

a. Substantive Restrictions

(i) Eligibility to Marry

(1) Sex and Sexual Orientation

OBERGEFELL v. HODGES
576 U.S. 644 (2015)

Justice KENNEDY delivered the opinion of the Court.

The Constitution promises liberty to all within its reach, a liberty that includes certain specific rights that allow persons, within a lawful realm, to define and express their identity. The petitioners in these cases seek to find that liberty by marrying someone of the same sex and having their marriages deemed lawful on the same terms and conditions as marriages between persons of the opposite sex. . . . [The first question here] is whether the Fourteenth Amendment requires a State to license a marriage between two people of the same sex. The second is whether the Fourteenth Amendment requires a State to recognize a same-sex marriage licensed and performed in a State which does grant that right.

[T]he annals of human history reveal the transcendent importance of marriage. The lifelong union of a man and a woman always has promised nobility and dignity to all persons, without regard to their station in life. Marriage is sacred to those who live by their religions and offers unique fulfillment to those who find meaning in the secular realm. . . . Rising from the most basic human needs, marriage is essential to our most profound hopes and aspirations. The centrality of marriage to the human condition makes it unsurprising that the institution has existed for millennia and across civilizations. . . . There are untold references to the beauty of marriage in religious and philosophical texts spanning time, cultures, and faiths, as well as in art and literature in all their forms. It is fair and necessary to say these references were based on the understanding that marriage is a union between two persons of the opposite sex.

That history is the beginning of these cases. [For respondents], it would demean a timeless institution if the concept and lawful status of marriage were extended to two persons of the same sex. Marriage, in their view, is by its nature a gender-differentiated union of man and woman. . . . The petitioners acknowledge this history but contend that these cases cannot end there. Were their intent to demean the revered idea and reality of marriage, the petitioners' claims would be of a different order. . . . To the contrary, it is the enduring importance of marriage that underlies the petitioners' contentions. . . . Far from seeking to devalue marriage, the petitioners seek it for themselves because of their respect—and need—for its privileges and responsibilities. . . .

[T]hese cases illustrate the urgency of the petitioners' cause from their perspective. [James Obergefell and John Arthur established a committed relationship two decades ago. After Arthur was diagnosed with amyotrophic lateral sclerosis (ALS), which is progressive and incurable, they resolved to marry before he died. They arranged a medical transport jet to travel from Ohio to Maryland, which allowed same-sex marriage. Arthur died three months later.] Ohio law does not permit Obergefell to be listed as the surviving spouse on Arthur's death certificate. By statute, they must remain strangers even in death, a state-imposed separation Obergefell deems "hurtful for the rest of time." He brought suit to be shown as the surviving spouse on Arthur's death certificate.

[Plaintiffs April DeBoer and Jayne Rowse, both nurses, celebrated a commitment ceremony in 2007. They adopted infants with special needs, one of whom requires round-the-clock care.] Michigan, however, permits only opposite-sex married couples or single individuals to adopt, so each child can have only one woman as his or her legal parent. [The couple fears the problems the children would face in case of an emergency or if the legal parent died. . . . Plaintiffs Army Reserve Sergeant First Class Ijpe DeKoe and Thomas Kostura married in New York just after DeKoe received orders to deploy to Afghanistan. They now reside in Tennessee, where DeKoe works full time for the Army Reserve.] Their lawful marriage is stripped from them whenever they reside in Tennessee, returning and disappearing as they travel across state lines. DeKoe, who served this Nation to preserve the freedom the Constitution protects, must endure a substantial burden. . . .

The ancient origins of marriage confirm its centrality, but it has not stood in isolation from developments in law and society. The history of marriage is one of both continuity and change. That institution—even as confined to opposite-sex relations—has evolved over time. . . . This dynamic can be seen in the Nation's experiences with the rights of gays and lesbians. Until the mid-20th century, same-sex intimacy long had been condemned as immoral . . . a belief often embodied in the criminal law. For this reason, among others, many persons did not deem homosexuals to have dignity in their own distinct identity. A truthful declaration by same-sex couples of what was in their hearts had to remain unspoken. Even when a greater awareness of the humanity and integrity of homosexual persons came in the period after World War II, the argument that gays and lesbians had a just claim to dignity was in conflict with both law and widespread social conventions. Same-sex intimacy remained a crime in many States. Gays and lesbians were prohibited from most government employment, barred from military service, excluded under immigration laws, targeted by police, and burdened in their rights to associate.

For much of the 20th century, moreover, homosexuality was treated as an illness. When the American Psychiatric Association published the first Diagnostic and Statistical Manual of Mental Disorders in 1952, homosexuality was classified as a mental disorder, a position adhered to until 1973. Only in more recent years have psychiatrists and others recognized that sexual orientation is both a normal expression of human sexuality and immutable.

In the late 20th century, [same-sex couples] began to lead more open and public lives and to establish families. . . . After years of litigation, legislation, referenda, and the discussions that attended these public acts, the States are now divided on the issue of same-sex marriage.

. . . The fundamental liberties protected by [the Due Process Clause] extend to certain personal choices central to individual dignity and autonomy, including intimate choices that define personal identity and beliefs. The identification and protection of fundamental rights is an enduring part of the judicial duty to interpret the Constitution. . . . History and tradition guide and discipline this inquiry but do not set its outer boundaries. . . .

The nature of injustice is that we may not always see it in our own times. The generations that wrote and ratified the Bill of Rights and the Fourteenth Amendment did not presume to know the extent of freedom in all of its dimensions, and so they entrusted to future generations a charter protecting the right of all persons to enjoy liberty as we learn its meaning. When new insight reveals discord between the Constitution's central protections and a received legal stricture, a claim to liberty must be addressed.

[T]he Court has long held the right to marry is protected by the Constitution [citing *Loving*; *Zablocki*; and *Turner*]. Over time and in other contexts, the Court has reiterated that the right to marry is fundamental under the Due Process Clause. [F]our principles and traditions . . . demonstrate that the reasons marriage is fundamental under the Constitution apply with equal force to same-sex couples.

A first premise of the Court's relevant precedents is that the right to personal choice regarding marriage is inherent in the concept of individual autonomy. This abiding connection between marriage and liberty is why *Loving* invalidated interracial marriage bans under the Due Process Clause. Like choices concerning contraception, family relationships, procreation, and childrearing, all of which are protected by the Constitution, decisions concerning marriage are among the most intimate that an individual can make . . . .

The nature of marriage is that, through its enduring bond, two persons together can find other freedoms, such as expression, intimacy, and spirituality. This is true for all persons, whatever their sexual orientation. There is dignity in the bond between two men or two women who seek to marry and in their autonomy to make such profound choices.

A second principle in this Court's jurisprudence is that the right to marry is fundamental because it supports a two-person union unlike any other in its importance to the committed individuals. . . . The right to marry thus dignifies couples who "wish to define themselves by their commitment to each other." Marriage responds to the universal fear that a lonely person might call out only to find no one there. It offers the hope of companionship and understanding and assurance that while both still live there will be someone to care for the other.

As this Court held in *Lawrence*, same-sex couples have the same right as opposite-sex couples to enjoy intimate association. [*Lawrence*] acknowledged that "[w]hen sexuality finds overt expression in intimate conduct with another person, the conduct can be but one element in a personal bond that is more enduring." But while *Lawrence* confirmed a dimension of freedom that allows individuals to engage in intimate association without criminal liability, it does not follow that freedom stops there. Outlaw to outcast may be a step forward, but it does not achieve the full promise of liberty.

A third basis for protecting the right to marry is that it safeguards children and families and thus draws meaning from related rights of childrearing, procreation, and education [citing *Meyer* and *Pierce*]. "[T]he right to 'marry, establish a home and bring up children' is a central part of the liberty protected by the Due Process Clause." [M]arriage also confers more profound benefits. By giving recognition and legal structure to their parents' relationship, marriage allows children "to understand the integrity and closeness of their own family and its concord with other families in their community and in their daily lives." Marriage also affords the permanency and stability important to children's best interests.

[M]any same-sex couples provide loving and nurturing homes to their children, whether biological or adopted. . . . This provides powerful confirmation from the law itself that gays and lesbians can create loving, supportive families. . . . Without the recognition, stability, and predictability marriage offers, their children suffer the stigma of knowing their families are somehow lesser. They also suffer the significant material costs of being raised by unmarried parents, relegated through no fault of their own to a more difficult and uncertain family life. The marriage laws at issue here thus harm and humiliate the children of same-sex couples. . . .

Fourth and finally, this Court's cases and the Nation's traditions make clear that marriage is a keystone of our social order. . . . For that reason, just as a couple vows to support each other, so does society pledge to support the couple, offering symbolic recognition and material benefits to protect and nourish the union. Indeed, while the States are in general free to vary the benefits they confer on all married couples, they have throughout our history made marriage the basis for an expanding list of governmental rights, benefits, and responsibilities. . . .

There is no difference between same- and opposite-sex couples with respect to this principle. Yet by virtue of their exclusion from that institution, same-sex couples are denied the constellation of benefits that the States have linked to marriage. This harm results in more than just material burdens. Same-sex couples are consigned to an instability many opposite-sex couples would deem intolerable in their own lives. As the State itself makes marriage all the more precious by the significance it attaches to it, exclusion from that status has the effect of teaching that gays and lesbians are unequal in important respects. It demeans gays and lesbians for the State to lock them out of a central institution of the Nation's society. . . .

The limitation of marriage to opposite-sex couples may long have seemed natural and just, but its inconsistency with the central meaning of the fundamental right to marry is now manifest. With that knowledge must come the recognition that laws excluding same-sex couples from the marriage right impose stigma and injury of the kind prohibited by our basic charter.

[Respondents contend that petitioners seek a new "right to same-sex marriage." They argue that the Due Process Clause safeguards only those fundamental rights and forms of liberty that were specifically protected when the Constitution was ratified.] Yet [that approach] is inconsistent with the approach this Court has used in discussing other fundamental rights, including marriage and intimacy. *Loving* did not ask about a "right to interracial marriage"; *Turner* did not ask about a "right of inmates to marry"; and *Zablocki* did not ask about a "right of fathers with unpaid child support duties to marry." Rather, each case inquired about the right to marry in its comprehensive sense, asking if there was a sufficient justification for excluding the relevant class from the right. . . . If rights were defined by who exercised them in the past, then received practices could serve as their own continued justification and new groups could not invoke rights once denied. This Court has rejected that approach, both with respect to the right to marry and the rights of gays and lesbians [citing *Loving* and *Lawrence*].

Many who deem same-sex marriage to be wrong reach that conclusion based on decent and honorable religious or philosophical premises, and neither they nor their beliefs are disparaged here. But when that sincere, personal opposition becomes enacted law and public policy, the necessary consequence is to put the imprimatur of the State itself on an exclusion that soon demeans or stigmatizes those whose own liberty is then denied. Under the Constitution, same-sex couples seek in marriage the same legal treatment as opposite-sex couples, and it would disparage their choices and diminish their personhood to deny them this right.

The right of same-sex couples to marry that is part of the liberty promised by the Fourteenth Amendment is derived, too, from that Amendment's guarantee of the equal protection of the laws. The Due Process Clause and the Equal Protection Clause are connected in a profound way, though they set forth independent principles. Rights implicit in liberty and rights secured by equal protection may rest on different precepts and are not always co-extensive, yet in some instances each may be instructive as to the meaning and reach of the other. In any particular case, one Clause may be thought to capture the essence of the right in a more accurate and comprehensive way, even as the two Clauses may converge in the identification and definition of the right. This interrelation of the two principles furthers our understanding of what freedom is and must become.

The Court's cases touching upon the right to marry reflect this dynamic. In *Loving* the Court invalidated a prohibition on interracial marriage under both the Equal Protection Clause and the Due Process Clause. The Court first declared the prohibition invalid because of its unequal treatment of interracial couples. . . . With this link to equal protection, the Court proceeded to hold the prohibition offended central precepts of liberty. . . .

The synergy between the two protections is illustrated further in *Zablocki*. There the Court invoked the Equal Protection Clause as its basis for invalidating the challenged law, which, as already noted, barred fathers who were behind on child-support payments from marrying without judicial approval. The equal protection analysis depended in central part on the Court's holding that the law burdened a right "of fundamental importance." It was the essential nature of the marriage right, discussed at length in *Zablocki*, that made apparent the law's incompatibility with requirements of equality. Each concept—liberty and equal protection—leads to a stronger understanding of the other.

Indeed, in interpreting the Equal Protection Clause, the Court has recognized that new insights and societal understandings can reveal unjustified inequality within our most fundamental institutions that once passed unnoticed and unchallenged [citing the history of coverture as well as case law invalidating gender roles and stereotypes]. Like *Loving* and *Zablocki*, these precedents show the Equal Protection Clause can help to identify and correct inequalities in the institution of marriage, vindicating precepts of liberty and equality under the Constitution.

Other cases confirm this relation between liberty and equality. . . . In *Lawrence*, the Court acknowledged the interlocking nature of these constitutional safeguards in the context of the legal treatment of gays and lesbians. Although *Lawrence* elaborated its holding under the Due Process Clause, it acknowledged, and sought to remedy, the continuing inequality that resulted from laws making intimacy in the lives of gays and lesbians a crime against the State. *Lawrence* therefore drew upon principles of liberty and equality to define and protect the rights of gays and lesbians, holding the State "cannot demean their existence or control their destiny by making their private sexual conduct a crime."

This dynamic also applies to same-sex marriage. It is now clear that the challenged laws burden the liberty of same-sex couples, and it must be further acknowledged that they abridge central precepts of equality. Here the marriage laws enforced by the respondents are in essence unequal: same-sex couples are denied all the benefits afforded to opposite-sex couples and are barred from exercising a fundamental right. Especially against a long history of disapproval of their relationships, this denial to same-sex couples of the right to marry works a grave and continuing harm. The imposition of this disability on gays and lesbians serves to disrespect and subordinate them. And the Equal Protection Clause, like the Due Process Clause, prohibits this unjustified infringement of the fundamental right to marry.

These considerations lead to the conclusion that the right to marry is a fundamental right inherent in the liberty of the person, and under the Due Process and Equal Protection Clauses of the Fourteenth Amendment, couples of the same sex may not be deprived of that right and that liberty. The Court now holds that same-sex couples may exercise the fundamental right to marry. . . . [S]tate laws challenged by Petitioners in these cases are now held invalid to the extent they exclude same-sex couples from civil marriage on the same terms and conditions as opposite-sex couples.

There may be an initial inclination in these cases to proceed with caution—to await further legislation, litigation, and debate [before] deciding an issue so basic as the definition of marriage. [However,] petitioners' stories make clear the urgency of the issue they present to the Court. James Obergefell now asks whether Ohio can erase his marriage to John Arthur for all time. April DeBoer and Jayne Rowse now ask whether Michigan may continue to deny them the certainty and stability all mothers desire to protect their children, and for them and their children the childhood years will pass all too soon. Ijpe DeKoe and Thomas Kostura now ask whether Tennessee can deny to one who has served this Nation the basic dignity of recognizing his New York marriage. [T]he Court has a duty to address these claims and answer these questions. . . .

The respondents also argue allowing same-sex couples to wed will harm marriage as an institution by leading to fewer opposite-sex marriages. This may occur, the respondents contend, because licensing same-sex marriage severs the connection between natural procreation and marriage. That argument, however, rests on a counterintuitive view of opposite-sex couples' decisionmaking processes regarding marriage and parenthood. Decisions about whether to marry and raise children are based on many personal, romantic, and practical considerations; and it is unrealistic to conclude that an opposite-sex couple would choose not to marry simply because same-sex couples may do so. . . .

Finally, it must be emphasized that religions, and those who adhere to religious doctrines, may continue to advocate with utmost, sincere conviction that, by divine precepts, same-sex marriage should not be condoned. The First Amendment ensures that religious organizations and persons are given proper protection as they seek to teach the principles that are so fulfilling and so central to their lives and faiths, and to their own deep aspirations to continue the family structure they have long revered. . . .

[The Court also determined that the Constitution requires states to recognize same-sex marriages validly performed out of state.] [I]f States are required by the Constitution to issue marriage licenses to same-sex couples, the justifications for refusing to recognize those marriages performed elsewhere are undermined. The Court, in this decision, holds same-sex couples may exercise the fundamental right to marry in all States. It follows that the Court also must hold—and it now does hold—that there is no lawful basis for a State to refuse to recognize a lawful same-sex marriage performed in another State on the ground of its same-sex character.

No union is more profound than marriage, for it embodies the highest ideals of love, fidelity, devotion, sacrifice, and family. In forming a marital union, two people become something greater than once they were. As some of the petitioners in these cases demonstrate, marriage embodies a love that may endure even past death. It would misunderstand these men and women to say they disrespect the idea of marriage. Their plea is that they do respect it, respect it so deeply that they seek to find its fulfillment for themselves. Their hope is not to be condemned to live in loneliness, excluded from one of civilization's oldest institutions. They ask for equal dignity in the eyes of the law. The Constitution grants them that right. . . .

Chief Justice ROBERTS, with whom Justice SCALIA and Justice THOMAS join, dissenting.

Petitioners make strong arguments rooted in social policy and considerations of fairness. . . . But this Court is not a legislature. Whether same-sex marriage is a good idea should be of no concern to us. Under the Constitution, judges have power to say what the law is, not what it should be . . .

Although the policy arguments for extending marriage to same-sex couples may be compelling, the legal arguments for requiring such an extension are not. The fundamental right to marry does not include a right to make a State change its definition of marriage. And a State's decision to maintain the meaning of marriage that has persisted in every culture throughout human history can hardly be called irrational. In short, [t]he people of a State are free to expand marriage to include same-sex couples, or to retain the historic definition. . . .Stealing this issue from the people will for many cast a cloud over same-sex marriage, making a dramatic social change that much more difficult to accept.

The majority's decision is an act of will, not legal judgment. The right it announces has no basis in the Constitution or this Court's precedent. . . . This Court's precedents have repeatedly described marriage in ways that are consistent only with its traditional meaning. . . . As the majority notes, some aspects of marriage have changed over time [i.e., arranged marriages, coverture, or racial restrictions]. The majority observes that these developments "were not mere superficial changes" in marriage, but rather "worked deep transformations in its structure." They did not, however, work any transformation in the core structure of marriage as the union between a man and a woman. . . .

[The majority resolves these cases] almost entirely on the Due Process Clause. The majority purports to identify four "principles and traditions" in this Court's due process precedents that support a fundamental right for same-sex couples to marry. In reality, however, the majority's approach has no basis in principle or tradition, except for the unprincipled tradition of [judicial activism reflected in *Lochner* v. *New York*, 198 U.S. 45 (1905), which relied on substantive due process to invalidate laws on minimum wages, child labor, and other economic and social regulations]. Stripped of its shiny rhetorical gloss, the majority's argument is that the Due Process Clause gives same-sex couples a fundamental right to marry because it will be good for them and for society. If I were a legislator, I would certainly consider that view as a matter of social policy. But as a judge, I find the majority's position indefensible as a matter of constitutional law . . . .

Neither *Lawrence* nor any other precedent in the privacy line of cases supports the right that petitioners assert here. Unlike criminal laws banning contraceptives and sodomy, the marriage laws at issue here involve no government intrusion. They create no crime and impose no punishment. [T]he laws in no way interfere with the "right to be let alone." [T]he privacy cases provide no support for the majority's position, because petitioners do not seek privacy. Quite the opposite, they seek public recognition of their relationships, along with corresponding government benefits. [A]lthough the right to privacy recognized by our precedents certainly plays a role in protecting the intimate conduct of same-sex couples, it provides no affirmative right to redefine marriage and no basis for striking down the laws at issue here. . . .

One immediate question invited by the majority's position is whether States may retain the definition of marriage as a union of two people. [The majority] offers no reason at all why the two-person element of the core definition of marriage may be preserved while the man-woman element may not. Indeed, from the standpoint of history and tradition, a leap from opposite-sex marriage to same-sex marriage is much greater than one from a two-person union to plural unions, which have deep roots in some cultures around the world. If the majority is willing to take the big leap, it is hard to see how it can say no to the shorter one.

It is striking how much of the majority's reasoning would apply with equal force to the claim of a fundamental right to plural marriage. If "[t]here is dignity in the bond between two men or two women who seek to marry and in their autonomy to make such profound choices," why would there be any less dignity in the bond between three people who, in exercising their autonomy, seek to make the profound choice to marry? If a same-sex couple has the constitutional right to marry because their children would otherwise "suffer the stigma of knowing their families are somehow lesser," why wouldn't the same reasoning apply to a family of three or more persons raising children? If not having the opportunity to marry "serves to disrespect and subordinate" gay and lesbian couples, why wouldn't the same "imposition of this disability," serve to disrespect and subordinate people who find fulfillment in polyamorous relationships? . . .

Near the end of its opinion, the majority offers perhaps the clearest insight into its decision. Expanding marriage to include same-sex couples, the majority insists, would "pose no risk of harm to themselves or third parties." [T]his assertion of the "harm principle" sounds more in philosophy than law. . . . [A] Justice's commission does not confer any special moral, philosophical, or social insight sufficient to justify imposing those perceptions on fellow citizens under the pretense of "due process." . . .

In addition to their due process argument, petitioners contend that the Equal Protection Clause requires their States to license and recognize same-sex marriages. . . . The central point seems to be that there is a "synergy between" the Equal Protection Clause and the Due Process Clause, and that some precedents relying on one Clause have also relied on the other. Absent from this portion of the opinion, however, is anything resembling our usual [means-end] framework for deciding equal protection cases. . . . [T]he marriage laws at issue here do not violate the Equal Protection Clause, because distinguishing between opposite-sex and same-sex couples is rationally related to the States' "legitimate state interest" in "preserving the traditional institution of marriage." . . .

[Today's decision] creates serious questions about religious liberty. Many good and decent people oppose same-sex marriage as a tenet of faith, and their freedom to exercise religion is—unlike the right imagined by the majority—actually spelled out in the Constitution. Respect for sincere religious conviction has led voters and legislators in every State that has adopted same-sex marriage democratically to include accommodations for religious practice. . . . The majority graciously suggests that religious believers may continue to "advocate" and "teach" their views of marriage. The First Amendment guarantees, however, the freedom to "*exercise*" religion. Ominously, that is not a word the majority uses. . . . Unfortunately, people of faith can take no comfort in the treatment they receive from the majority today.

If you are among the many Americans—of whatever sexual orientation—who favor expanding same-sex marriage, by all means celebrate today's decision. Celebrate the achievement of a desired goal. Celebrate the opportunity for a new expression of commitment to a partner. Celebrate the availability of new benefits. But do not celebrate the Constitution. It had nothing to do with it. . . .

The following three excerpts provide additional background on Jim Obergefell (the lead plaintiff in Obergefell v. Hodges), the personal impact of his Supreme Court case, and his reflections about the significance of the case.

NOTE: WHO IS JIM OBERGEFELL?

Michael S. Rosenwald, How Jim Obergefell Became the Face of the Supreme Court Gay Marriage Case

Wash. Post, Apr. 6, 2015

http://www.washingtonpost.com/local/how-jim-obergefell-became-the-face-of-the -supreme-court-gay-marriage-case/2015/04/06/3740433c-d958-11e4-b3f2 -607bd612aeac_story.html

. . . It was not a long marriage, just three months and 11 days—the time it took his husband, John Arthur, to struggle to say, "I thee wed," and then die from [amyotrophic lateral sclerosis] [ALS]. [T]heir union, and the 20-year relationship that preceded it, is at the center of Obergefell v. Hodges. . . . For Jim Obergefell, the case is simply about that tricky-to-pronounce name [*Oh-ber-guh-fell*]: He wants it on Arthur's death certificate as the surviving spouse . . .

Plaintiff Jim Obergefell (left) and his spouse John Arthur (now deceased)

How Obergefell, a soft-spoken real estate broker with little previous interest in political activism, wound up in this spot is a story of judicial chance, but it's also about resolve, fate, and heartbreak. . . . Arthur was essentially on his deathbed when the couple decided to marry. . . .

In their two decades together, the couple talked about marriage but never considered it seriously . . . . But in 2013, the Supreme Court struck down a key portion of the Defense of Marriage Act, giving same-sex married couples federal benefits in the states where such unions were legal. Obergefell saw the news online. He leaned over, kissed Arthur on the head, and said, "Let's get married." "Okay," Arthur said.

Their wedding was a production. Obviously, they needed to travel to a different state, choosing Maryland on a friend's suggestion. But how to get there? A car trip was out. A medical flight was their only option, but how could they arrange one, much less come up with the $13,000 to pay for it? Obergefell sought advice on Facebook. Their friends and family offered more than guidance— [they] funded the entire trip.

And so on the morning of July 11, 2013, an ambulance transported them to the airport, where they boarded a medical jet with a nurse and Arthur's aunt, Paulette Roberts, who became ordained online to perform weddings. They flew to Baltimore-Washington International Marshall Airport. Roberts began the ceremony on the tarmac, in the plane, shortly after landing. The couple held hands, Obergefell's thumb rubbing Arthur's. They stared into each other's eyes. "With this ring," said Obergefell, slipping a ring on Arthur's hand, "I thee wed." Then he gently helped Arthur guide a ring onto his own hand. "With this ring," said Arthur, his speech distorted by ALS, "I thee wed." . . .

Today, Obergefell lives alone in the couple's condo. . . . In the TV room, a large painting of the couple hangs above the couch. They are young and in love and smiling at a beautiful old cemetery where they used to take long walks.

Jeffrey Masters, Jim Obergefell: We Still Don't Enjoy True Marriage Equality

The Advocate, Mar. 16, 2021
https://www.advocate.com/politics/2021/3/12/jim-obergefell-dont-enjoy-true
-marriage-equality-hodges-supreme-court

[Jim Obergefell met his husband, John Arthur, when he went to a campus bar near the University of Cincinnati with his friend Kevin.] We walked into this bar and sitting at the bar was this tall blonde man. Kevin said, "Oh, that's my friend, John." And he introduced us. John scared the daylights out of me because he was out. He was so comfortable in who he was, so comfortable in being an out gay man. . . .

I thought for certain he was going to call me. He didn't. [A couple of months later,] Kevin and I went back to that same bar and guess who was sitting at that bar again, drinking a gin and tonic? John. We met the second time. It was during that conversation, John said, "Well, Jim, you'd never go out with someone like me." [I answered:] "How do you know? You've never asked." And he still didn't. That was number two. [Over the holidays, John was having a New Year's Eve party.] Kevin invited me to that party. I went to the party, there was John. And I never left. John and I like to say it wasn't love at first sight. It was love at third sight. . . .

[I'll never forget] sitting in that courtroom [during Obergefell v. Hodges while listening to Justice Kennedy read his decision.] I burst into tears. People around the courtroom were crying. Al [Gerhardstein], our attorney, was there in the courtroom as well. He told me later, he has never seen so many attorneys crying in a courtroom. Of course, not surprisingly, my first thought was, "John, I wish you were here. I wish you could experience this. . . ."

[F]or the first time in my life, as an out gay man, I felt like an equal American. That was such a powerful realization, such a powerful feeling to have sitting in the highest court in our country. . . .

Jim Obergefell, *The Legacy of Obergefell v. Hodges*
Personal communication, July 28, 2015

I understand that this is a landmark decision that impacts our entire country, and also has an impact around the world. From an intellectual point of view, I know that my name and our case has become part of history. But I'm still coming to grips with that emotionally. I am hearing [that people are calling me] "hero" more and more [often].

While I understand why people say that, all I did was stand up for our marriage, and then fight to live up to the commitments I made to my husband.

This ruling means that all committed couples are able to make their relationship legal and public, and by doing so, enjoy the same rights and protections as any other couple. Because of this ruling, I—and other LGBT citizens—feel more like equal citizens. However, no matter how far we've come, there are still far too many individuals who are content to focus on how people differ instead of focusing on the fact that we're all humans who want the same basic things – the right to life, liberty, and the pursuit of happiness. Instead of embracing the ways we're the same and celebrating the beauty our differences bring to our country, too many people use those differences as reasons to hate. So the fight continues for all of us.

From the standpoint of the family, this ruling recognizes that families come in all shapes and sizes. Children need to be loved and brought up by two parents who nurture and support them as they journey from toddler to adolescence and beyond. Two dads, two moms, a mom and a dad—no matter the equation, the effect on the family overall is a positive one.

303 CREATIVE v. ELENIS
143 S. Ct. 2298 (2023)

Justice GORSUCH delivered the opinion of the Court.

Like many States, Colorado has a law forbidding businesses from engaging in discrimination when they sell goods and services to the public. Laws along these lines have done much to secure the civil rights of all Americans. But in this particular case, Colorado does not just seek to ensure the sale of goods or services on equal terms. It seeks to use its law to compel an individual to create speech she does not believe. The question we face is whether that course violates the Free Speech Clause of the First Amendment.

Through her business, 303 Creative LLC, Lorie Smith offers website and graphic design, marketing advice, and social media management services. Recently, she decided to expand her offerings to include services for couples seeking websites for their weddings. . . . While Ms. Smith has laid the groundwork for her new venture, she has yet to carry out her plans. She worries that, if she does so, Colorado will force her to express views with which she disagrees. . . . Specifically, she worries that, if she enters the wedding website business, the State will force her to convey messages inconsistent with her belief that marriage should be reserved to unions between one man and one woman.

[Ms. Smith worries that Colorado will use the state public accommodations law (Colorado Anti-Discrimination Act (CADA)) to compel her—in violation of the First Amendment—to create websites celebrating marriages that she does not endorse because of her faith as an evangelical Christian. CADA prohibits all "public accommodations" from denying "the full and equal enjoyment" of its goods and services to any customer based on his race, creed, disability, sexual orientation, or other statutorily enumerated trait. Colo. Rev. Stat. § 24–34–601(2)(a). The law defines "public accommodation" broadly to include almost every public-facing business in the State. Violators of the act incur penalties.

To clarify her rights, Ms. Smith filed this lawsuit seeking an injunction to prevent the state from forcing her to create websites celebrating marriages that defy her belief that marriage should be reserved to unions between one man and one woman. In the district court, both Ms. Smith and the state stipulated to the following facts: Ms. Smith is "willing to work with all people regardless of classifications such as race, creed, sexual orientation, and gender" and "will gladly create custom graphics and websites" for clients of any sexual orientation; she will not produce content that "contradicts biblical truth" regardless of who orders it; Ms. Smith's belief that marriage is a union between one man and one woman is a sincerely held conviction; Ms. Smith provides design services that are "expressive" and her "original, customized" creations "contribut[e] to the overall message" her business conveys "through the websites" it creates; the wedding websites she plans to create "will be expressive in nature," will be "customized and tailored" through close collaboration with individual couples, and will "express Ms. Smith's and 303 Creative's message celebrating and promoting" her view of marriage; viewers of Ms. Smith's websites will be told "[t]here are numerous companies in the State of Colorado and across the nation that offer custom website design services."

The district court ruled against Smith's request for an injunction and upheld the law's constitutionality. The Tenth Circuit Court of Appeals affirmed.

Acknowledging that her proposed wedding websites qualified as pure speech protected by the First Amendment, the appellate court reasoned that Colorado has a compelling interest in ensuring equal access to publicly available goods and services, and no option short of coercing speech from Ms. Smith can satisfy that interest because her "unique services" are unavailable elsewhere.]

We granted certiorari to review the Tenth Circuit's disposition.

[T]he First Amendment protects an individual's right to speak his mind regardless of whether the government considers his speech sensible and well intentioned or deeply "misguided." Equally, the First Amendment protects acts of expressive association. Generally, too, the government may not compel a person to speak its own preferred messages. Nor does it matter whether the government seeks to compel a person to speak its message when he would prefer to remain silent or to force an individual to include other ideas with his own speech that he would prefer not to include. All that offends the First Amendment just the same.

Applying these principles to this case, we align ourselves with much of the Tenth Circuit's analysis. The Tenth Circuit held that the wedding websites Ms. Smith seeks to create qualify as "pure speech" under this Court's precedents. We agree. It is a conclusion that flows directly from the parties' stipulations. They have stipulated that Ms. Smith's websites promise to contain "images, words, symbols, and other modes of expression." They have stipulated that every website will be her "original, customized" creation. And they have stipulated that Ms. Smith will create these websites to communicate ideas—namely, to "celebrate and promote the couple's wedding and unique love story" and to "celebrat[e] and promot[e]" what Ms. Smith understands to be a true marriage. . . .

A hundred years ago, Ms. Smith might have furnished her services using pen and paper. Those services are no less protected speech today because they are conveyed [over the Internet].

As surely as Ms. Smith seeks to engage in protected First Amendment speech, Colorado seeks to compel speech Ms. Smith does not wish to provide. As the Tenth Circuit observed, if Ms. Smith offers wedding websites celebrating marriages she endorses, the State intends to "forc[e her] to create custom websites" celebrating other marriages she does not. Colorado seeks to compel this speech in order to "excis[e] certain ideas or viewpoints from the public dialogue." Indeed, the Tenth Circuit recognized that the coercive "[e]liminati[on]" of dissenting "ideas" about marriage constitutes Colorado's "very purpose" in seeking to apply its law to Ms. Smith.

We part ways with the Tenth Circuit only when it comes to the legal conclusions that follow. While that court thought Colorado could compel speech from Ms. Smith consistent with the Constitution, our First Amendment precedents laid out above teach otherwise. . . . Here, Colorado seeks to put Ms. Smith to a similar choice: If she wishes to speak, she must either speak as the State demands or face sanctions for expressing her own beliefs. . . .

Under Colorado's logic, the government may compel anyone who speaks for pay on a given topic to accept all commissions on that same topic—no matter the underlying message—if the topic somehow implicates a customer's statutorily protected trait. Taken seriously, that principle would allow the government to force all manner of artists, speechwriters, and others whose services involve speech to speak what they do not believe on pain of penalty. The government could require "an unwilling Muslim movie director to make a film with a Zionist message," or "an atheist muralist to accept a commission celebrating Evangelical zeal," so long as they would make films or murals for other members of the public with different messages. Equally, the government could force a male website designer married to another man to design websites for an organization that advocates against same-sex marriage. Countless other creative professionals, too, could be forced to choose between remaining silent, producing speech that violates their beliefs, or speaking their minds and incurring sanctions for doing so. As our precedents recognize, the First Amendment tolerates none of that.

In saying this much, we do not question the vital role public accommodations laws play in realizing the civil rights of all Americans. This Court has recognized that governments in this country have a "compelling interest" in eliminating discrimination in places of public accommodation. This Court has recognized, too, that public accommodations laws "vindicate the deprivation of personal dignity that surely accompanies denials of equal access to public establishments." . . . At the same time, this Court has also recognized that no public accommodations law is immune from the demands of the Constitution. In particular, this Court has held, public accommodations statutes can sweep too broadly when deployed to compel speech. . . . When a state public accommodations law and the Constitution collide, there can be no question which must prevail. . . .

It is difficult to read the dissent and conclude we are looking at the same case. . . . The dissent claims that Colorado wishes to regulate Ms. Smith's "conduct," not her speech. Forget Colorado's stipulation that Ms. Smith's activities are "expressive," and the Tenth Circuit's conclusion that the State seeks to compel "pure speech." The dissent chides us for deciding a pre-enforcement challenge. But it ignores the Tenth Circuit's finding that Ms. Smith faces a credible threat of sanctions unless she conforms her views to the State's. The dissent suggests (over and over again) that any burden on speech here is "incidental." All despite the Tenth Circuit's finding that Colorado intends to force Ms. Smith to convey a message she does not believe with the "very purpose" of "[e]liminating . . . ideas" that differ from its own. . . .

Today, however, the dissent abandons what this Court's cases have recognized time and time again: A commitment to speech for only *some* messages and *some* persons is no commitment at all. By approving a government's effort to "[e]liminat[e]" disfavored "ideas," today's dissent is emblematic of an unfortunate tendency by some to defend First Amendment values only when they find the speaker's message sympathetic. But "[i]f liberty means anything at all, it means the right to tell people what they do not want to hear."

In this case, Colorado seeks to force an individual to speak in ways that align with its views but defy her conscience about a matter of major significance. . . . [A]s this Court has long held, the opportunity to think for ourselves and to express those thoughts freely is among our most cherished liberties and part of what keeps our Republic strong. Of course, abiding the Constitution's commitment to the freedom of speech means all of us will encounter ideas we consider "unattractive," "misguided, or even hurtful," But tolerance, not coercion, is our Nation's answer. The First Amendment envisions the United States as a rich and complex place where all persons are free to think and speak as they wish, not as the government demands. Because Colorado seeks to deny that promise, the judgment is reversed.

Justice SOTOMAYOR, with whom Justice KAGAN and Justice JACKSON join, dissenting.

Five years ago, this Court recognized the "general rule" that religious and philosophical objections to gay marriage "do not allow business owners and other actors in the economy and in society to deny protected persons equal access to goods and services under a neutral and generally applicable public accommodations law." Masterpiece Cakeshop, Ltd. v. Colorado Civil Rights Comm'n, 584 U. S. ___, ___ (2018) (slip op., at 9). The Court also recognized the "serious stigma" that would result if "purveyors of goods and services who object to gay marriages for moral and religious reasons" were "allowed to put up signs saying 'no goods or services will be sold if they will be used for gay marriages.'" . . .

"What a difference five years makes." And not just at the Court. Around the country, there has been a backlash to the movement for liberty and equality for gender and sexual minorities. New forms of inclusion have been met with reactionary exclusion. . . .

A business open to the public seeks to deny gay and lesbian customers the full and equal enjoyment of its services based on the owner's religious belief that same-sex marriages are "false." The business argues, and a majority of the Court agrees, that because the business offers services that are customized and expressive, the Free Speech Clause of the First Amendment shields the business from a generally applicable law that prohibits discrimination in the sale of publicly available goods and services. That is wrong. Profoundly wrong. [T]he law in question targets conduct, not speech, for regulation, and the *act* of discrimination has never constituted protected expression under the First Amendment. Our Constitution contains no right to refuse service to a disfavored group. . . .

A "public accommodations law" is a law that guarantees to every person the full and equal enjoyment of places of public accommodation without unjust discrimination. . . . A public accommodations law has two core purposes. First, the law ensures "*equal access* to publicly available goods and services." For social groups that face discrimination, such access is vital. . . . Second, a public accommodations law ensures *equal dignity* in the common market. Indeed, that is the law's "fundamental object": "to vindicate 'the deprivation of personal dignity that surely accompanies denials of equal access to public establishments.'" This purpose does not depend on whether goods or services are otherwise available. "'Discrimination is not simply dollars and cents, hamburgers and movies; it is the humiliation, frustration, and embarrassment that a person must surely feel when he is told that he is unacceptable as a member of the public because of his [social identity]. It is equally the inability to explain to a child that regardless of education, civility, courtesy, and morality he will be denied the right to enjoy equal treatment.'" When a young Jewish girl and her parents come across a business with a sign out front that says, "'No dogs or Jews allowed,'" the fact that another business might serve her family does not redress that "stigmatizing injury," Or, put another way, "the hardship Jackie Robinson suffered when on the road" with his baseball team "was not an inability to find *some hotel* that would have him; it was the indignity of not being allowed to stay in the *same hotel* as his white teammates.". . . This ostracism, this otherness, is among the most distressing feelings that can be felt by our social species.

Preventing the "unique evils" caused by "acts of invidious discrimination in the distribution of publicly available goods, services, and other advantages" is a compelling state interest "of the highest order." . . . The concept of a public accommodation thus embodies a simple, but powerful, social contact: A business that chooses to sell to the public assumes a duty to serve the public without unjust discrimination. [This duty] is deeply rooted in our history. . . . "At common law, innkeepers, smiths, and others who 'made profession of a public employment,' were prohibited from refusing, without good reason, to serve a customer." . . . Not only have public accommodations laws expanded to recognize more forms of unjust discrimination, such as discrimination based on race, sex, and disability, such laws have also expanded to include more goods and services as "public accommodations." . . . Today, laws like Colorado's cover "any place of business engaged in any sales to the public and any place offering services . . . to the public." Numerous other States extend such protections to businesses offering goods or services to "the general public."

This broader scope, though more inclusive than earlier state public accommodations laws, is in keeping with the fundamental principle—rooted in the common law, but alive and blossoming in statutory law—that the duty to serve without unjust discrimination is owed to everyone, and it extends to any business that holds itself out as ready to serve the public. . . .

Lesbian, gay, bisexual, and transgender (LGBT) people, no less than anyone else, deserve that dignity and freedom. [Throughout history,] others have sought to deny their existence, and to exclude them from public life. Those who would subordinate LGBT people have often done so with the backing of law. . . . State-sponsored discrimination was compounded by discrimination in public accommodations, though the two often went hand in hand. The police raided bars looking for gays and lesbians so often that some bars put up signs saying, "'We Do Not Serve Homosexuals.'" LGBT discrimination in public accommodations has continued well into the 21st century. . . .

[Today, the Court's decision], which conflates denial of service and protected expression, is a grave error. 303 Creative LLC is a limited liability company that sells graphic and website designs for profit. [However,] 303 Creative has never sold wedding websites. Smith now believes, however, that "God is calling her 'to explain His true story about marriage.'" For that reason, she says, she wants her for-profit company to enter the wedding website business. There is only one thing: Smith would like her company to sell wedding websites "to the public," but not to same-sex couples. She also wants to post a notice on the company's website announcing this intent to discriminate. . . . The breadth of petitioners' pre-enforcement challenge is astounding. [T]he company claims a categorical exemption from a public accommodations law simply because the company sells expressive services. The sweeping nature of this claim should have led this Court to reject it.

The First Amendment does not entitle petitioners to a special exemption from a state law that simply requires them to serve all members of the public on equal terms. Such a law does not directly regulate petitioners' speech at all. . . . Rather, "the focal point of its prohibition" is "on the *act* of discriminating against individuals in the provision of publicly available goods, privileges, and services." The State confirms this reading of CADA. The law applies only to status-based refusals to provide the full and equal enjoyment of whatever services petitioners choose to sell to the public. . . . Any effect on the company's speech is therefore "incidental" to the State's content-neutral regulation of conduct.

[P]etitioners' freedom of speech is not abridged in any meaningful sense, factual or legal. Petitioners remain free to advocate the idea that same-sex marriage betrays God's laws. Even if Smith believes God is calling her to do so through her for-profit company, the company need not hold out its goods or services to the public at large. . . . The company can put whatever "harmful" or "low-value" speech it wants on its websites. It can "tell people what they do not want to hear." All the company may not do is offer wedding websites to the public yet refuse those same websites to gay and lesbian couples. . . .

The Court reaches the wrong answer in this case because it asks the wrong questions. [T]he proper focus is on the character of state action and its relationship to expression. . . . [T]he majority insists that petitioners discriminate based on message, not status. The company, says the majority, will not sell same-sex wedding websites to anyone. It will sell only opposite-sex wedding websites; that is its service. Petitioners, however, "cannot define their service as 'opposite-sex wedding [websites]' any more than a hotel can recast its services as 'whites-only lodgings.' " To allow a business open to the public to define the expressive quality of its goods or services to exclude a protected group would nullify public accommodations laws. It would mean that a large retail store could sell "passport photos for white people."

The majority protests that Smith will gladly sell her goods and services to anyone, including same-sex *couples*. She just will not sell websites for same-sex *weddings*. Apparently, a gay or lesbian couple might buy a wedding website for their straight friends. This logic would be amusing if it were not so embarrassing. . . .

Today is a sad day in American constitutional law and in the lives of LGBT people. The Supreme Court of the United States declares that a particular kind of business, though open to the public, has a constitutional right to refuse to serve members of a protected class. The Court does so for the first time in its history. By issuing this new license to discriminate in a case brought by a company that seeks to deny same-sex couples the full and equal enjoyment of its services, the immediate, symbolic effect of the decision is to mark gays and lesbians for second-class status. In this way, the decision itself inflicts a kind of stigmatic harm, on top of any harm caused by denials of service. The opinion of the Court is, quite literally, a notice that reads: "Some services may be denied to same-sex couples."

"The truth is," these "affronts and denials" "are intensely human and personal." Sometimes they may "harm the physical body, but always they strike at the root of the human spirit, at the very core of human dignity." . . . What message does that send? . . . [I]t reminds LGBT people of a painful feeling that they know all too well: There are some public places where they can be themselves, and some where they cannot. Ask any LGBT person, and you will learn just how often they are forced to navigate life in this way. They must ask themselves: If I reveal my identity to this co-worker, or to this shopkeeper, will they treat me the same way? If I hold the hand of my partner in this setting, will someone stare at me, harass me, or even hurt me? It is an awful way to live. Freedom from this way of life is the very object of a law that declares: All members of the public are entitled to inhabit public spaces on equal terms.

This case cannot be understood outside of the context in which it arises. In that context, the outcome is even more distressing. . . . Wedding websites, birth announcements, family portraits, epitaphs. These are not just words and images. They are the most profound moments in a human's life. They are the moments that give that life personal and cultural meaning. . . .

The meaning of our Constitution is found not in any law volume, but in the spirit of the people who live under it. Every business owner in America has a choice whether to live out the values in the Constitution. Make no mistake: Invidious discrimination is not one of them. . . . The lesson of the history of public accommodations laws is altogether different. It is that in a free and democratic society, there can be no social castes. And for that to be true, it must be true in the public market. For the "promise of freedom" is an empty one if the Government is "powerless to assure that a dollar in the hands of [one person] will purchase the same thing as a dollar in the hands of a[nother]." Because the Court today retreats from that promise, I dissent.

Elizabeth Sepper, "Expressing" Inferiority: 303 Creative *and the (Re)Creation of a Discriminatory Marketplace*

ACS [American Constitution Society] Blog, Mar. 1, 2023
https://www.acslaw.org/expertforum/expressing-inferiority-303-creative-and-the
-recreation-of-a-discriminatory-marketplace/

In 303 Creative v. Elenis, the Supreme Court [gives] businesses open to the public a constitutional right to discriminate. The objecting business, a web design company, says state law requiring it to offer wedding services on equal terms to gay people compels it to speak in favor of same-sex marriage in violation of the First Amendment. It claims that its argument is limited to "expressive" or artistic businesses—whether website designing, cake baking, or flower arranging.

But *303 Creative* . . . gets it wrong. Service to customers communicates little, if anything. Because of our social expectations of first-come, first-served, a vendor signals no approval of its customers when it makes a sale. In requiring service on equal terms, the law compels no message. . . . As court after court held, such laws regulated wedding vendors' conduct—the sale of a wedding cake or website—not their speech.

What we have missed is that it is refusal of service that powerfully speaks. Refusal tells a would-be patron and the wider public that that person (or group) does not merit status as a consumer. . . . Denied flowers for his wedding to Robert Ingersoll, Curt Freed understood the message that "our business is no longer good business." Rejected by a bed and breakfast on their vacation, another same-sex couple heard that they were "inferior and unworthy of equal treatment in even a routine business transaction." When a business open to the public turns a person away, it powerfully expresses—as these couples understood—an ideology of a group's inferiority. [Refusal of service has been a longstanding feature of vendors' treatment of other marginalized groups, such as Jews and women.]

The line between speech and conduct may not always be clear. . . .What is clear is that a constitutional privilege to discriminate would destabilize longstanding conventions of full and equal access to commerce and leisure. . . . Exceptions—however the lines are drawn—would undermine an identity-neutral marketplace where dollars and people flow freely without the friction of information and search costs. They quite literally would reduce the space for individual dignity.

The following excerpt highlights the emotional impact on a gay male couple (David Mullins and Charlie Craig), after a Colorado cake baker (Jack Phillips) refused to make a cake for their wedding reception. The ensuing challenge to the denial of service culminated in the *Masterpiece Cakeshop* case (referenced in *303 Creative*).

Julie Compton, Meet the Couple Behind the Masterpiece Cakeshop *Supreme Court Case*

NBC News, Dec. 6, 2017
*https://www.nbcnews.com/feature/nbc-out/meet-couple-behind-masterpiece
-cakeshop-supreme-court-case-n826976*

Same-sex couple Charlie Craig and David Mullins met on the night of December 5, 2010, at a party near their home in Denver. "On that night we were doing a benefit for a friend, and I was the emcee, and [David] was a musician in a band playing for this benefit," Craig told NBC News. . . .

[P]recisely seven years to the day they met[,] the couple found themselves in a packed courtroom inside the Supreme Court. The men are ensnarled in a legal battle with a baker who refused to make them a wedding cake because they are gay.

Plaintiffs David Mullins (left) and Charlie Craig

Mullins, an office manager, and Craig, an interior designer, never thought they'd be at the center of a major civil rights case. "I have to admit, we were really surprised," Mullins said. "The idea of going to the Supreme Court—it's not something a lot of people consider in their lives."

The men, both in their 30s, got engaged in 2011. . . . Since the men couldn't legally marry in Colorado at the time, they made plans to marry in Provincetown, Massachusetts. They would travel back home for the reception after saying their vows. "We were really excited, and, like any couple getting married, we had a ton of details to finalize," Mullins said.

One of those details, the couple recalled, was a cake. Their reception planner recommended Masterpiece Cakeshop in Lakewood, Colorado. Craig's mother, Deb, who had traveled from Wyoming, accompanied them to the shop. The couple had a binder full of concepts they wanted to go over with the shop owner, Jack Phillips. "We never even got a chance to open it," Mullins said.

When the three sat down with Phillips, the baker immediately asked them who the cake was for, according to Mullins. "We told him it was for us, and he immediately said he would not make a cake for a same-sex wedding," he said. Mullins recalled a horrible silence. "We were just mortified and embarrassed," he said. The three quickly left.

For Craig, the interaction was devastating. He remembered how bullies had taunted him for being gay in the small Wyoming town where he grew up. He later attended the University of Wyoming, around the same time gay

student Matthew Shepard was murdered. He moved to Denver after he graduated, hoping to find sanctuary in the liberal city encircled by mountains and
high plains. "I really thought that would be a place where I could be myself and
express myself," he said. But the past followed him. . . .

Mullins and Craig married in 2012. They said the five-and-half-year legal
battle has, in a way, defined their marriage. "To this day, Dave and I still, when
we go into a business, really have to think, 'Can we show affection? Can we
talk about our relationship?'" Craig said. "It's the fear of getting lesser service
or denied service," he added. . . . The couple have heard countless stories of
other same-sex couples being denied service. For Craig, those stories "hit the
heart strings."

"Initially, we really wanted to stand up for ourselves," he said, "but
throughout this journey, I feel like we really want to recognize these other
people who have been discriminated against." . . . "We want to ensure that
people don't have to go through the same humiliation and helplessness that
we had to go through," Craig explained. "That's why we're here."

The following narrative provides background on the pioneering attorney who
argued *Obergefell* as well as other landmark marriage equality cases.

David J. Garrow, Toward a More Perfect Union
N.Y. Times, May 9, 2004, §6 (Mag.), at 52

**Attorney Mary Bonauto
who won landmark cases
on marriage equality**

Mary Bonauto vividly remembers her first day as a
lawyer at Gay and Lesbian Advocates and Defenders
(GLAD), the small public-interest law office that represents gays and lesbians in the six New England
states. "When I came here on March 19, 1990," she
recalled not long ago, "one of the things waiting for
me on my desk was a request from a lesbian couple
in western Massachusetts who wanted to get married."
At that time, though, she believed a lawsuit seeking a
right to gay marriage had no chance of success in any
American appellate court.

"It was absolutely the wrong time," she told
me, "and I said no." A generation or two from now,
March 19, 1990, may appear in history books the same
way that another date appears in accounts of Brown
v. Board of Education: Oct. 6, 1936, the day that Thurgood Marshall accepted a
full-time job at the N.A.A.C.P. Legal Defense Fund. Marshall, too, said no—for
more than a decade—to petitioners who asked him to challenge public-school
segregation in the South. Only in 1950, as the legal landscape began to shift,
did Marshall finally say yes. For Bonauto, the wait was shorter but the outcome
no less momentous. . . .

Bonauto grew up with her three brothers in what she describes as a "highly
Catholic" family. Her father worked as a pharmacist and her mother as a teacher.

[She attended Hamilton College and Northeastern University Law School.] When she joined a small law firm in Portland, Me., in 1987, Bonauto was one of only three openly gay lawyers in private practice in the state. In Portland, she also met her life partner, Jennifer Wriggins, now a professor at the University of Maine School of Law.

The late 1980s were an auspicious time for a young lawyer in New England with a commitment to gay equality. In 1989, Massachusetts became the second state, after Wisconsin, to provide anti-discrimination protection to gays in employment, housing, and public accommodations. . . .

[In 1997, Bonauto successfully challenged the constitutionality of Vermont's exclusion of same-sex couples from the right to marry. But the Vermont legislature ultimately enacted civil union legislation granting all the benefits of marriage to gay and lesbian couples, but not the label.] The distinction evoked a phrase that Thurgood Marshall knew all too well: "separate but equal," the pre-*Brown* label for the fictional fairness of segregation.

[Bonauto tried again in Goodridge v. Dept. of Public Health, 798 N.E.2d 941 (Mass. 2003), where] she insisted that "civil unions" would not satisfy the requirements of the Massachusetts Constitution. "The Vermont approach is not the best approach for this Court to take," she emphasized, for "when it comes to marriage, there really is no such thing as separating the word 'marriage' from the protections it provides. The reason for that is that one of the most important protections of marriage is the word, because the word is what conveys the status that everyone understands as the ultimate expression of love and commitment." To follow Vermont, she continued, by "creating a separate system, just for gay people, simply perpetuates the stigma of exclusion that we now face because it would essentially be branding gay people and our relationships as unworthy of this civil institution of marriage." . . .

While Bonauto waited for a decision, the legal climate improved [with the Supreme Court's decision in Lawrence v. Texas, invalidating anti-sodomy laws]. Five months later, the Massachusetts Supreme Judicial Court handed down the [*Goodridge*] ruling for which Bonauto had been waiting [legalizing same-sex marriage in Massachusetts]. . . . As Matt Coles, head of the American Civil Liberties Union's Lesbian and Gay Rights Project, observes, *Goodridge* "answered that question that *Lawrence* begged." And while "*Goodridge* is the earthquake," Coles says, *Goodridge* is the earthquake because of *Lawrence.* . . .

When asked to talk about herself, Bonauto insists that "it's totally not about me." [A colleague] emphasizes Bonauto's "modesty and humility," but insiders who fully appreciate how a very small network of gay lawyers has brought America to the threshold of another civil rights milestone know whom to credit. . . .

Epilogue. Mary Bonauto and her wife (law professor Jennifer Wriggins) faced a long uphill battle to marry, and then to have their marriage recognized in their home state. Although Bonauto brought marriage equality to Massachusetts in 2003, she was unable to marry there until 2008, when Massachusetts repealed its marriage evasion statute. Because the couple lived in Maine at the time, their marriage was not recognized until 2012, when Maine voters passed an initiative favoring marriage equality.

Amanda Barroso & Richard Fry, On Some Demographic Measures, People in Same-Sex Marriages Differ from Those in Opposite-Sex Marriages

Pew Research Ctr., July 7, 2021
https://www.pewresearch.org/fact-tank/2021/07/07/on-some-demographic-measures-people-in-same-sex-marriages-differ-from-those-in-opposite-sex-marriages/

[Census Bureau data] found that there were 568,000 same-sex married couples in the U.S. in 2019. A new Pew Research Center analysis of that data finds that adults – and particularly men – who are in same-sex marriages have a somewhat different demographic profile from adults in opposite-sex marriages. . . . Men in same-sex marriages have higher levels of education and higher annual incomes than men who are married to opposite-sex partners. Half of men in same-sex marriages have at least a bachelor's degree, compared with 38% of men in opposite-sex marriages . . . The median adjusted annual household income for men in same-sex marriages was roughly $132,300 in 2019, significantly higher than the median income for men in opposite-sex marriages ($90,700). . . .

When it comes to employment, men in opposite-sex marriages are more likely to be employed than those in same-sex marriages (89% vs. 80%) [whereas] [w]omen in same-sex marriages (76%) are more likely to be employed than their counterparts in opposite-sex marriages (72%).

The racial and ethnic profile of men in same-sex marriages is similar to that of men in opposite-sex marriages, but there are some differences among women. Women in same-sex marriages are more likely to be non-Hispanic White than women in opposite-sex marriages (69% vs. 63%), and they are less likely to be Asian or Hispanic.

Both men and women in same-sex marriages are more likely than their peers in opposite-sex marriages to be married to someone of a different race or ethnicity. Among men, 28% in same-sex marriages are intermarried, compared with 16% of men in opposite-sex marriages. The same is true among women: 20% of women in same-sex marriages are intermarried (vs. 16% of women in opposite-sex marriages). . . .

There are also some differences in family composition between adults in same-sex vs. opposite-sex marriages. Men and women in opposite-sex marriages are much more likely to be living with their own children younger than 18 than are their peers in same-sex marriages. Some 57% of men in opposite-sex marriages are living with their children, compared with only 9% of men in same-sex marriages. The gap closes for women: 57% of women in opposite-sex marriages live with their children in their household, which is about twice the share of women in same-sex marriages (28%).

Notes and Questions on *Obergefell* and *303 Creative*

1. Epilogue After becoming profoundly disillusioned by the Trump Administration's policies dismantling lesbian, gay, bisexual, transgender, and queer/questioning (LGBTQ) rights, Jim Obergefell sought, but lost, a bid to serve in the Ohio state legislature. He currently works for Family Equality, a nonprofit organization whose mission is to advance equality for LGBTQ families.

As for Lorie Smith (the plaintiff in *303 Creative*), after the Supreme Court decision in *303 Creative* was released, questions arose about the request from the prospective customer ("Stewart") who supposedly had requested that Smith create a website for his wedding to his partner, "Mike." Responding to questions by a reporter after the decision, "Stewart" maintained that although his correct contact information (name, phone number, and e-mail address) was on the inquiry form on Smith's website, he never submitted that form. Further, he explained that at the time of the website inquiry, he was married to a woman, and that he himself was a website developer.[20] Smith was represented by a faith-based legal organization called the Alliance Defending Freedom (ADF) in her suit against Colorado officials and Aubrey Elenis, the director of the Colorado Civil Rights Division.

2. Historical background.

a. Stonewall and early challenges. The gay liberation movement was triggered by a police raid of the Stonewall Inn, a popular Greenwich Village gay bar, in June 1969. The raid led to six days of demonstrations that served as the catalyst for the gay rights movement. Same-sex couples began challenging state bans on same-sex marriage during the 1970s. These early judicial decisions held that same-sex marriages were invalid based on either lack of capacity or the dictionary definition of marriage, thereby avoiding resolution of the constitutional issues. The 1990s witnessed a resurgence of state litigation that culminated in DOMA, discussed below. See, e.g., Baehr v. Lewin, 852 P.2d 44 (Haw. 1993); Brause v. Bureau of Vital Statistics, 1998 WL 88743 (Alaska Super. Ct. 1998).

b. Goodridge. As explained in the excerpt above about Mary Bonauto, Massachusetts became the first state to permit same-sex marriage. See Goodridge v. Department of Public Health, 798 N.E.2d 941 (Mass. 2003) (finding that under the state constitutional protections of liberty and equality, the ban did not survive a rational basis review). What explains the fact that *Goodridge* followed closely on the heels of *Lawrence*?

3. Background: DOMA and RFMA.

a. DOMA. Congress first addressed same-sex marriage in DOMA in 1996, which was enacted in response to a Hawaii Supreme Court ruling that was favorable to same-sex marriage (Baehr v. Lewin, 852 P.2d 44 (Haw. 1993)). The congressional concern was based on the possibility that if Hawaii legalized same-sex marriage, same-sex marriage would be valid everywhere because of the doctrine of lex loci. DOMA had two parts: Section 2 specified that states were *not* required to give effect to same-sex marriages that were validly celebrated in another state (28 U.S.C. §1738C); and Section 3 (1 U.S.C. §7) provided a heterosexual and gender-based definition for the terms "marriage" and "spouse" for purposes of federal benefits. Passage of DOMA prompted widespread bans on same-sex marriage on the state level. The Supreme Court invalidated DOMA's Section 3 definition of "marriage" and "spouse" for purposes of federal law in United States v. Windsor,

---

[20]. Victoria Bisset & Jaclyn Peiser, Man Cited in Supreme Court LGBTQ Rights Case Says He Was Never Involved, Wash. Post, July 1, 2023, https://www.washingtonpost.com/politics/2023/07/01/supreme-court-colorado-website/.

570 U.S. 744 (2013). Two years later, *Obergefell* invalidated all remaining same-sex marriage bans.

In response, officials in several states refused to issue marriage licenses to same-sex couples based on religious objections. See Davis v. Ermold, 141 S. Ct. 3 (2020) (denying appeal of county clerk's contempt conviction). Justice Thomas (joined by Justice Alito) used that occasion to issue a statement denouncing the harm that *Obergefell* purportedly caused to religious freedom.

b. RFMA. The Respect for Marriage Act (RFMA), Pub. L. No. 117-228, 136 Stat. 2305 (2022), repealed DOMA's Section 2 in 2022. RFMA bars any state from denying "full faith and credit" of any marriage "on the basis of the sex, race, ethnicity or national origin of those individuals." For additional discussion of RFMA, see p. 127 supra. Why did Congress enact RFMA? RFMA is a prophylactic measure that seeks to ensure that interracial and same-sex marriages will continue to be recognized nationwide, even if the Supreme Court overturns *Loving* or *Obergefell*, respectively. Note that most states still have statutory and constitutional same-sex marriage bans on the books that would go back into effect if *Obergefell* were overturned. While RFMA would not invalidate any such bans that related to access to marriage licenses within the state, it would require those states to recognize a marriage that had been entered into in another state.

4. *Obergefell*: **Holding and rationale.** On what constitutional provisions does *Obergefell* rest? Is marriage a "fundamental right" after *Obergefell*? How does the Court link the concepts of "liberty" and "equality"? Why does it do this? What were the questions before the Court, and how did the Court answer them? Did the Court create a new right or simply extend an existing right to same-sex couples? Does it matter? How does *Obergefell* respond to the argument that same-sex marriage cannot be a fundamental right because it is not deeply rooted in "history and tradition"?

a. Liberty. What is the understanding of liberty according to the majority in *Obergefell*? How does it resemble the freedoms recognized in the reproductive privacy cases and *Lawrence*? How does it differ? How would you answer Chief Justice Roberts's assertion that marriage differs from the interests at stake in those precedents?

b. Equality. The Supreme Court has adopted different standards of review to evaluate the constitutionality of discriminatory classifications under the Equal Protection Clause. To survive constitutional attack, the classification must be (1) necessary to a compelling state interest (strict scrutiny); or (2) substantially related to an important governmental objective (intermediate scrutiny); or (3) rationally related to a legitimate government purpose (lowest level of scrutiny). The Court evaluates racial classifications under the first test and sex-based classifications under the middle-tier test (although a few states, such as California, apply higher scrutiny to gender-based classifications). What level of scrutiny does the Court apply to sexual orientation-based classifications in *Obergefell*? Does the Court say anything about that issue in *303 Creative*? What level of scrutiny *should* the Court apply to sexual orientation-based classifications, and why?

c. Significance. Does *Obergefell* mean that same-sex married couples must be accorded all the marriage-based rights and benefits that are accorded to different-sex couples? See Pavan v. Smith (reprinted in Chapter III). Will the case have a broader impact on family law? For example, what is the likely impact of *Obergefell* on parentage issues? Does *Obergefell* obviate the need for same-sex partners to adopt each other? To adopt a partner's children? What is the likely impact of the case on other nontraditional families? Or is the significance of *Obergefell* limited to access to the *legal* status of marriage? Turning to *303 Creative*, how significant was the concept of marriage there?

d. Role of the judiciary and social change. How do the majority and dissent in *Obergefell* see the role of the judiciary in influencing or responding to social change? How do they see the role of the Constitution as society evolves? How do the majority and dissent in *303 Creative* differ in their views regarding the role of the courts and the Constitution in protecting the rights of marginalized citizens?

5. *Public opinion.* According to a recent Gallup poll, 10 percent of lesbian, gay, bisexual, or transgender (LGBT) adults in the United States are married to a same-sex spouse. Since *Obergefell*, the number of married same-sex households increased by almost 70 percent. Public opinion changed dramatically following *Obergefell*. A decade before *Obergefell*, approximately 60 percent of Americans *opposed* marriage equality; but currently, 71 percent of Americans say that they support legalized same-sex marriage.[21] What role should public opinion play in judicial opinions, in your view? What are the consequences of this evolution in public opinion for the LGBT community, the family, society, and family law?

6. Religious liberty accommodations.

a. Background. In Masterpiece Cakeshop v. Colorado Civil Rights Commission, 138 S. Ct. 1719 (2018), the Supreme Court was presented with an earlier challenge to Colorado's public accommodation law after a baker named Jack Phillips denied the request of a gay male couple to make their wedding cake, based on his religious objections to gay marriage. In response, the gay couple claimed discrimination under the Colorado Anti-Discrimination Act (CADA)'s ban on discrimination based on sexual orientation. Phillips raised two First Amendment defenses: (1) the act of requiring him to create a cake for a same-sex wedding pursuant to CADA would violate his First Amendment right to free speech by compelling him to exercise his artistic talents to express a message with which he disagrees, and (2) requiring him to create cakes for same-sex weddings would violate his right to the free exercise of religion. The Court narrowly ruled that the state civil rights commission had violated the baker's free exercise rights – not by refusing to exempt him from the requirements of the antidiscrimination law, but rather by failing to consider his claim in a neutral and respectful fashion (i.e., by disparaging his beliefs and treating his claims differently from those of other bakers). *Masterpiece Cakeshop* paved the way for *303 Creative*, as explained below.

---

[21]. Jeffrey M. Jones, LGBT Americans Married to Same-Sex Spouse Steady at 10%, Politics (Gallup News), Feb. 10, 2022, https://news.gallup.com/poll/389555/lgbt-americans-married-same-sex-spouse-steady.aspx; AP, Nearly 1 Million U.S. Households Composed of Same-Sex Couples, Sept. 17, 2020, https://www.nbcnews.com/feature/nbc-out/nearly-1-million-u-s-households-composed-same-sex-couples-n1240340; Justin McCarthy, Same-Sex Marriage Support Inches up to New High of 71%, Politics (Gallup News), June 1, 2022, https://news.gallup.com/poll/393197/same-sex-marriage-support-inches-new-high.aspx.

b. 303 Creative: Holding. Because of its narrow holding, the Supreme Court failed to reach the merits in *Masterpiece Cakeshop*: the resolution of the conflict between claims of free exercise and equality principles of antidiscrimination laws (i.e., whether businesses that provide public accommodations can refuse to furnish their services based on the First Amendment, and therefore be granted an exemption from laws ensuring nondiscrimination in public accommodations). How does *303 Creative* resolve that question?

In *303 Creative*, Justice Gorsuch phrases the question: whether applying a public-accommodation law to compel an artist to speak or stay silent violates the Free Speech Clause of the First Amendment. Why does the dissent respond that he is asking the "wrong question"? Why does the dissent in *303 Creative* believe that state public accommodations law should be able to compel merchants to serve customers in ways that violate the merchants' beliefs?

c. Exemptions and accommodations: **Obergefell** *and* **303 Creative.** It is generally understood that religious leaders have a constitutional right to refuse to solemnize a marriage that conflicts with their religious beliefs. Nonetheless, some states have enacted statutory exceptions clarifying that religious officials are exempt from having to solemnize such a marriage. And a few states have statutory provisions exempting vendors who provide wedding-related services contrary to their religious beliefs.[22] Although the Court in *303 Creative* did not rule on Free Exercise grounds (it ruled only on Free Speech grounds), does the majority opinion nonetheless give any indication about whether these kinds of exemptions are constitutionally required? If so, to whom must they be applied, and in what circumstances? To any vendor who is asked to provide any wedding-related goods and services to same-sex couples? Only vendors who supply *certain kinds* of wedding-related goods and services (so-called expressive goods and services), thereby allowing companies that provide customized, expressive products and services to pick and choose with whom they work? Does it extend beyond wedding-related goods and services?

d. 303 Creative: Expressive speech. In *303 Creative*, the majority held that Lorie Smith had a First Amendment right to refuse to provide her creative services to a same-sex couple who was planning to marry. Requiring her to make a creative wedding website for a same-sex couple, the Court held, would "represent an impermissible abridgement of the First Amendment's right to speak freely." How does the provision of web design services constitute expressive speech for First Amendment purposes? How important is the fact that the dispute involved designing a website rather than providing other wedding-related services, such as making videos, or floral arrangements? The dissent differentiates conduct from speech. What is that distinction, and why is it important?

e. Guiding principles. The majority opinion in *303 Creative* attempts to draw a distinction between turning away customers and making specific products. For example, according to the majority, the plaintiff would not be able to refuse to create a website for a business just because the owner of that business was gay. On the other hand, requiring a vendor to make a creative website site that conveys

---

[22]. Nelson Tebbe, Religion and Marriage Equality Statutes, 9 Harv. L. & Pol'y Rev. 25 (2015) (examining such statutes). See generally Robin Fretwell Wilson, The Contested Place of Religion in Family Law (2018).

a message she disagrees with would "compel speech," and as such, would violate the First Amendment. Does the majority give any guiding principles as to how to determine in which category a future case falls? Or how to determine which types of businesses or business transactions will qualify for First Amendment exemptions from nondiscrimination requirements?

f. Implications. In your opinion, will *303 Creative* have a broad or narrow impact on other situations in which individuals refuse to recognize or give effect to a same-sex marriage, or to same-sex relationships more broadly? Does it allow a wedding cake baker to refuse to make a wedding cake for a same-sex couple? A photographer to refuse to take photos for a same-sex wedding? Or family portraits for a family with same-sex parents? Does it allow a landlord who objects to same-sex marriage to refuse to rent an apartment to a same-sex married couple? Does it allow an employer to refuse to hire a person in a same-sex marriage? Or to provide spousal health insurance benefits to the same-sex spouse of an employee? What will be the potential impact of *303 Creative* on LGBTQ rights generally? On victims of discrimination based on sex, race, or disability? How meaningful is *Obergefell* in the wake of *303 Creative*?

7. Harm. Prior to *Obergefell*, what harm was caused to LGBTQ people by previously enforceable state bans on same-sex marriage? In the wake of *303 Creative*, what harm will be caused by vendors' refusal to provide LGBTQ people with goods and services? To what extent do the majority and dissenting opinions in *Obergefell* and *303 Creative*, respectively, address these harms? What do the excerpts in this section add to the understanding of these harms? Consider one commentator's view of the harms suffered by the parties in *Masterpiece Cakeshop*:

> [T]he refusal of any individual to serve another in a competitive marketplace means that the harm suffered by the couple is the well-nigh trivial cost of finding one of 67 nearby bakeries which advertised their willingness to design cakes for same-sex weddings. In contrast, the burden imposed on Phillips for the exercise of his rights of religion and speech includes the loss of his business license, heavy fines and mandatory participation in various re-education programs suitable only in totalitarian regimes.[23]

Are the harms inflicted by a vendor's refusal to provide services eliminated, or at least mitigated, by the existence of other vendors that are available and willing to provide the requested services? How does the dissent in *303 Creative* respond to that question? How might the refusal to provide goods and services to same-sex couples affect the welfare of their children?[24]

8. Bostock. In 2020, Justice Gorsuch authored an opinion holding that LGBTQ people cannot be discriminated against in employment. Bostock v. Clayton County,

---

[23]. Richard A. Epstein, Symposium: The Worst Form of Judicial Minimalism—*Masterpiece Cakeshop* Deserved a Full Vindication for Its Claims of Religious Liberty and Free Speech, SCOTUS Blog, June 4, 2018, https://www.scotusblog.com/2018/06/symposium-the-worst-form-of-judicial -minimalism-masterpiece-cakeshop-deserved-a-full-vindication-for-its-claims-of-religious-liberty -and-free-speech/.

[24]. See generally Jordan Blair Woods, Religious Exemptions and LGBTQ Child Welfare, 103 Minn. L. Rev. 2343 (2019).

140 S. Ct. 1731 (2020). The case addressed the plight of three LGBTQ plaintiffs, including Gerald Bostock, a gay child services coordinator who was terminated, despite numerous positive performance evaluations, when he mentioned that he had begun participating in a gay softball league. The Supreme Court ruled that Title VII of the Civil Rights Act of 1964 protects employees against discrimination based on sexual orientation or gender identity. How do you explain Justice Gorsuch's opinion in *303 Creative* in light of his opinion in *Bostock*?

9. Racial discrimination. Are antimiscegenation laws analogous to restrictions against same-sex marriage? If so, how? Should states treat sexual orientation similarly to, or differently from, race for purposes of exemptions from antidiscrimination law? That is, should courts adopt a two-tiered framework that grants religious exemptions from laws prohibiting sexual orientation discrimination but not from laws prohibiting racial discrimination—that is, thereby accommodating Lorie Smith's beliefs in *303 Creative* but not the beliefs of a racist baker?[25]

In *Masterpiece Cakeshop*, Justice Kennedy referred to Newman v. Piggie Park Enterprises, 390 U.S. 400 (1968), a civil rights era case in which the Supreme Court held that a barbecue vendor must serve Black customers even if the vendor perceives such service as a violation of their religious beliefs. How do the majority and dissent in *303 Creative* address the likely impact of that case on the rights of other marginalized groups?

10. Impact of marriage equality.

a. For recipients of federal benefits. Although *Obergefell* (and its predecessor, *Windsor*, supra) guaranteed access to federal benefits for same-sex married couples, the victory came too late for those partners who were denied Social Security survivor benefits because they were unable to satisfy the requisite nine-month durational eligibility period prior to marriage equality. Some plaintiffs prevailed in subsequent suits. See, e.g., Thornton v. Comm'r of Soc. Sec., 570 F. Supp. 3d 1010 (W.D. Wash. 2020).

b. For participants in civil unions. A few states currently allow civil unions and domestic partnerships—marriage alternatives authorized by some states prior to marriage equality. Partners in these unions enjoy fewer legal protections than married spouses; among other things, civil union partners and domestic partners are not entitled to most federal marriage-based rights and protections. After *Obergefell*, several states automatically converted civil unions into marriages.[26] Was this an appropriate state response to *Obergefell*, in your view?

c. For transgender people. Laws against same-sex marriage precluded recognition of marital rights and benefits for transgender people. What does *Obergefell*

---

[25]. See Douglas NeJaime & Reva Siegel, Religious Exemptions and Antidiscrimination Law in *Masterpiece Cakeshop*, 128 Yale L.J. F. 201, 205-210 (2018) (exploring this question).

[26]. Four states continue to allow couples to enter into civil unions: Colorado, Hawaii, Illinois, and New Jersey. Other states (California, District of Columbia, Maine, Nevada, Oregon, and Wisconsin) continue to allow domestic partnerships. Hawaii allows a similar relationship known as "reciprocal beneficiaries." Nat'l Conf. State Legislatures (NCSL), Civil Unions and Domestic Partnership Statutes, Mar. 10, 2020, https://www.ncsl.org/human-services/civil-unions-and-domestic-partnership-statutes.

mean for transgender people's right to marry? Or for other forms of discrimination that affect transgender people and their families? Some commentators predicted that *Obergefell* would have a salutary effect on transgender rights in general. However, the Trump Administration rolled back legal protections for transgender people in education, employment, health care, and immigration law; banned transgender people from military service; and allowed medical providers to deny treatment to transgender people on religious grounds. In 2022, the Biden Administration announced actions to support the mental health of transgender children, remove barriers that transgender people face while accessing critical government services, and improve the visibility of transgender people in national data.[27] Do such reforms go far enough?

Problem

Christine Geiger owns Studio 8 Hair Lab in Traverse City, Michigan. She recently wrote a Facebook post in which she said that she is exercising her free speech by refusing her services to specific customers. "If a human identifies as anything other than a man/woman, please seek services at a local pet groomer," the hair salon owner said. "You are not welcome at this salon. Period."

She said that she has no issue with serving lesbian, gay or bisexual customers, but that she will not support the "TQ+" community. "This stance was taken to ensure that clients have the best experience, and I am admitting that I am not willing to play the pronoun game or cater to requests outside of what I perceive as normal," Geiger said.

Michigan has a public accommodations statute that prohibits discrimination on the bases of sexual orientation and gender identity. Assuming that she did indeed refuse to serve a transgender person, would application of the statute to Christine Geiger's Studio 8 Hair Lab violate her First Amendment rights under *303 Creative*? Do her services qualify as "expressive speech"? Would the same analysis apply if Geiger's post had said that she refused to serve Black people and she then acted on that statement?

David Masci et al., *Five Facts About Same-Sex Marriage*
Pew Research Ctr., June 24, 2019
https://www.pewresearch.org/fact-tank/2019/06/24/same-sex-marriage/

[H]ere are five key facts about same-sex marriage:

1. The share of Americans who favor same sex-marriage grew steadily for most of the last decade, but public support has leveled off in the last few years. Around four-in-ten U.S. adults favored allowing gays and lesbians to wed in 2009, a share that rose to 62% in 2017. . . .

---

[27]. White House, Press Release, Fact Sheet: Biden-Harris Administration Advances Equality and Visibility for Transgender Americans, Mar. 31, 2022, https://www.whitehouse.gov/briefing-room/statements-releases/2022/03/31/fact-sheet-biden-harris-administration-advances-equality-and-visibility-for-transgender-americans/.

Public remains supportive of same-sex marriage; wide partisan gap persists

% who oppose allowing gays and lesbians to marry legally

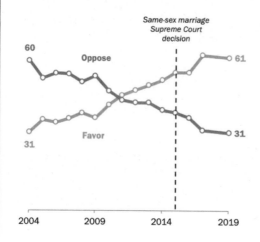

% who favor allowing gays and lesbians to marry legally

2. Although support in the U.S. for same-sex marriage has increased among nearly all demographic groups, there are still sizable demographic and partisan divides. For example, today, 79% of Americans who are religiously unaffiliated favor same-sex marriage, as do 66% of white mainline Protestants and 61% of Catholics. Among white evangelical Protestants, however, only 29% favor same-sex marriage. Still, this is roughly double the level (15%) in 2009.

While support for same-sex marriage has grown steadily across generational cohorts in the last 15 years, there are still sizable age gaps. For instance, 45% of adults in the Silent Generation (those born between 1928 and 1945) favor allowing gays and lesbians to wed, compared with 74% of Millennials (born between 1981 and 1996). There also is a sizable political divide: Republicans and Republican-leaning independents are much less likely to favor same-sex marriage than Democrats and Democratic leaners (44% vs. 75%).

3. Same-sex marriages are on the rise. Surveys conducted by Gallup in 2017 [and in 2019] find that about one-in-ten of LGBT Americans are married to a same-sex partner, up from the months before the high court decision (7.9%). As a result, a majority (61%) of same-sex cohabiting couples were married as of 2017, up from 38% before the ruling.

4. As with the general public, Americans who identify as lesbian, gay, bisexual or transgender (LGBT) are most likely to cite love as a very important reason for getting married. In a 2013 Pew Research Center survey, 84% of LGBT adults and 88% of the general public cited love as a very important reason for getting married, and at least seven-in-ten in both groups cited companionship (71% and 76%, respectively). But there were some differences, too. LGBT Americans, for instance, were twice as likely as those in the general public to cite legal rights and benefits as a very important reason for getting married (46% versus 23%), while those in the general public were nearly twice as likely as LGBT Americans to cite having children (49% versus 28%).

5. The U.S. is among 29 countries and jurisdictions [in 2023, 31 countries] that allow gay and lesbian couples to wed. The first nation to legalize gay marriage was the Netherlands in 2000. Since then, several other European countries—including England and Wales, France, Ireland, all of Scandinavia, Spain, and, most recently, Austria, Germany, and Malta—have legalized gay marriage. Outside of Europe, same-sex marriage is now legal in Argentina, Australia, Brazil, Canada, Colombia, Ecuador, New Zealand, South Africa, and Uruguay, as well as in parts of Mexico.

Update: In 2019, Taiwan and Ecuador legalized same-sex marriage; followed by Costa Rica in 2020; Chile and Switzerland in 2021; Cuba, Andorra, and Slovenia in 2022; and Estonia in 2023.

(2) Incest

IN RE ADOPTION OF M.

722 A.2d 615 (N.J. Super. Ct. Ch. Div. 1998)

BATTEN, J.S.C.

. . . The undisputed facts are troubling beyond description. [On] January 5, 1991, adoptive parents sought to adopt child M (hereinafter "petitioner"), born November 24, 1975, and voluntarily surrendered by her natural parents to the Division of Youth and Family Services, in May 1989. The adoption was uncontested. Final judgment of adoption entered January 25, 1991 [when] [p]etitioner was then fifteen years old. Two years and ten months later, on November 21, 1993, petitioner attained age eighteen.

At some point in time subsequent to the final judgment of adoption yet prior to September 8, 1997, the marital relationship between the adoptive parents failed. Adoptive mother, on this latter date, filed her complaint for divorce against adoptive father, alleging acts of extreme cruelty. [The adoptive parents actually separated several years prior to the time they filed for divorce.] On November 18, 1997, final judgment of divorce dissolved the marriage of the adoptive parents. On July 29, 1998, petitioner, then twenty-two years of age, gave birth to an infant son. The parties acknowledge that adoptive father is the natural father of the infant.

Poignant realities emerge. First, petitioner and the adoptive father conceived the infant child in or about October 1997, at which time petitioner was twenty-one years of age. Second, conception between petitioner and adoptive father therefore likely occurred *prior* to the November 18, 1997, dissolution of his marriage to adoptive mother. Third, *a fortiori*, adoptive father engaged in a carnal relationship with his adult adoptive daughter while he was yet married to her adoptive mother. Fourth, the foregoing circumstances suggest—and the record stipulated before the court specifically confirms—that the relationship between petitioner and adoptive father had transgressed the parameters of a parent-child relationship well prior to the act of conception. Now the natural parents of the minor child, they desire to marry. Their present legal relationship as adoptive father and adoptive daughter, however, clearly renders the former an "ancestor" of, and the latter a "descendant" to, the other, thereby precluding lawful marriage between them. N.J.S.A. 37:1-1 [invalidating marriage between persons and their siblings, nephews, nieces, ancestors, or descendants]. Hence, petitioner brings this application. [Although petitioner originally moved to vacate the adoption as to both her adoptive parents, she and her adoptive mother subsequently decided to leave their relationship undisturbed. Petitioner thus sought to vacate the adoption as to her adoptive father only.]

Final judgment of adoption marks a turning point in the status of the natural and adoptive parents. Entry of such a judgment terminates all relationships between the adopted child and his/her natural parents and all of the rights, duties, and obligations of any persons that are founded on such relationships. . . . Subsequent to judgment, the adoptive parents are, as a matter of law, the parents of that child as if the child had been born to the adoptive parents in lawful wedlock.

Under New Jersey law [a] final judgment of adoption "should not be set aside unless it is in the best interest of the child and adoptive parents," and upon the showing of "truly exceptional circumstances" as determined by the particular facts of each case. . . . Indeed, the Legislature has mandated that the Adoption Act of New Jersey "shall be liberally construed to the end that the *best interests of children* be promoted," and *"due regard shall be given to the rights of all persons affected by an adoption."* N.J.S.A. 9:3-37. [Emphasis added.] . . .

Certainly, the interests of "all persons affected" by this adoption have changed measurably. First, the adoptive child, in whose best interests the adoption occurred, is now, seven years later, (A) twenty-two years of age, (B) a natural mother of a two-month-old infant son, and (C) intent upon marriage to her son's natural father. The absence of any facts of record which might support a finding of abuse, neglect, domestic violence, or other unlawful act suggests a petitioner's conscious decision that her legal relationship with her adoptive father had achieved its purpose and, parent-child status notwithstanding, the complexities and realities of human emotions and relationships warrant transposition of that status from father-daughter co-parents to husband and wife. Through marriage, petitioner legitimizes not only her relationship with her son's father but the status of her infant son as well. . . .

Clearly, the facts here . . . constitute "truly exceptional circumstances" for several reasons. First, all reported cases contemplate an application to vacate a final judgment of adoption at a time during the minority of the adoptive child; here, the petitioner, as adopted child, moves post-emancipation to vacate the judgment of adoption. In this sense, the "best interests" standard of N.J.S.A. 9:2-4 no longer pertains to the adoptive child. Second, the stated purpose of the petition to vacate is eradication of a legal impediment to petitioner's marriage to her adoptive father, a relationship to which petitioner and adoptive father would be entitled absent their present legal status as father-daughter. Third, vacation of the final judgment of adoption would also shed adoptive father of his simultaneous status as natural father and legal grandfather of the minor infant, leaving him the natural father only. Fourth, vacation of the adoption judgment, through its cure of the statutory impediment to marriage, would further legitimize the infant, thereby advancing long-standing policy of this state to protect the status of children. More "truly exceptional circumstances" are difficult to imagine. . . . Petitioner's application to vacate the final judgment of adoption as pertains to her adoptive father is—as it must be—granted. . . .

NOTE: VOID AND VOIDABLE DISTINCTION

Statutes and the common law classify invalid marriages as either void or void-able. A void marriage is one that is invalid from inception (*void ab initio*)—that is, it never had legal existence. On the other hand, a voidable marriage is valid until subsequently declared invalid. The distinction becomes important in terms of who may assert the invalidity of a marriage and whether the validity of the marriage may be collaterally attacked.

If a marriage is void, then either party or a third party may challenge the validity of the marriage at any time and in any proceeding. On the other hand, the invalidity of a voidable marriage can be asserted only by one of the parties and only during the marriage (i.e., not after death of one of the parties). Further, voidable marriages cannot be collaterally attacked (i.e., in a related proceeding).

The consequences of a particular defect stem from history (ecclesiastical law), as well as public policy (the degree to which the defect offends public policy). Substantive defects (same-sex, bigamous, and incestuous unions) traditionally rendered the marriage void. Less serious substantive defects, such as age, may render the marriage voidable.

Notes and Questions

1. Historical background. Virtually all societies have some form of incest taboos. After William the Conqueror ascended the throne, incest became an ecclesiastical offense (similar to adultery and bigamy). Until the seventeenth century, prohibitions on incestuous marriages were extensive, but mitigated by dispensations to the wealthy. Incest became a crime in 1650, punishable by death. In 1908, the Punishment of Incest Act (8 Edw. 7, ch. 45) proscribed three to seven years' imprisonment.

2. Civil and criminal consequences. Every state specifies the degrees of consanguinity and affinity within which persons may marry. ("Consanguinity" refers to blood relations, while "affinity" refers to relations by marriage.) Marriage to one's parent, grandparent, brother, or sister is universally prohibited, as are marriages between aunts and uncles and nieces and nephews. Occasionally, states extend the prohibition to marriage to relatives by adoption and to step-relationships. Most jurisdictions regard incestuous marriages as void ab initio. Note that the degrees of relation for civil marriage restrictions and for the imposition of criminal liability may differ.

3. First-cousin marriages. Many states exempt first-cousin marriages from restrictions on marriage eligibility. See Hoffman v. Miller, 529 P.3d 101 (Ariz. Ct. App. 2023). Historically, first-cousin marriages enjoyed considerable popularity because marriage choice was limited by proximity. The practice waned because of changing social norms, increasing autonomy of women, and shrinking family sizes leading to a smaller pool of available first cousins. Today, 24 states ban such marriages, while 20 states allow them.[28] Some states allow first cousins to marry under limited circumstances, such as if both prospective spouses are over a certain age, if one or both are permanently infertile, and if the couple receives genetic counseling.

4. State interests. According to *Zablocki*, regulations that substantially and directly interfere with the freedom to marry must receive elevated scrutiny. Do incest laws qualify? What state interests are at stake? Several have been suggested, including the protection of the gene pool from harmful consequences of consanguineous sexual relationships, protection of persons from exploitation, protection of the family from the assumption of incompatible familial roles, and protection of societal concepts of decency. Are these state interests "sufficiently important" to justify the restrictions? Experts disagree about the consequences of inbreeding. If these state interests are sufficiently important, are the proscriptions sufficiently closely tailored to achieve these goals?

If the goal is prevention of the harmful consequences of procreation, should the state exempt those too old to reproduce? Require genetic testing for a marriage license? Prohibit marriages when one partner carries harmful genetic traits? Is the protection of the gene pool a justifiable function of government? Does the right to privacy dictate that the decision to perpetuate harmful genetic traits should be left to prospective parents?

5. Consensual relationships. In *Adoption of M.*, the father and daughter's sexual relationship was consensual. Incest laws are applicable to both nonconsensual and consensual acts of sexual intercourse or marriage between qualifying individuals. What is the impact of *Lawrence* on incest laws?

6. Relatives by adoption. *Adoption of M.* addresses prohibitions on marriage of persons related by adoption. What state interest supports such restrictions? How can that interest be served by prohibiting marriage by adoptive siblings who have grown up in separate households? May an adult who adopted a same-sex partner prior to marriage equality later annul that adoption so that the partners can marry? See In re Adoption of R.A.B., Jr., 153 A.3d 332 (Pa. Super. Ct. 2016) (holding that court had the authority to annul adult adoption so that same-sex partners could exercise their right to marry).

7. Criminal liability for parties and officials. Almost all states criminalize incest between consenting adults. Historically, the parties were subject to harsh penalties. See, e.g., Cal. Penal Code §285 (former incest statute authorized up to 50 years' imprisonment). Many statutes not only classify certain marriages as presumptively void but also subject to criminal liability those officials who knowingly issue marriage licenses to such couples. Are criminal sanctions appropriate to enforce civil limitations on marriage?

---

[28]. Eleanor Cummins, Go Ahead, Marry Your Cousin—It's Not That Bad for Your Future Kids, Popular Sci., July 2, 2021 (suggesting that the risk of genetic abnormalities from first-cousin marriages is small—that is, only 4 to 7 percent), https://www.popsci.com/marrying-cousins -genetics/.

8. Choice of law. Suppose that two first cousins marry in a jurisdiction permitting such marriages, but they move to a state with a prohibition. Which law applies? See Ghassemi v. Ghassemi, 998 So. 2d 731 (La. Ct. App. 2008) (holding that because Iranian citizens were married pursuant to Iranian law permitting first-cousin marriages, such a marriage is valid in Louisiana for purposes of issuance of a divorce). Does the result change if the parties chose the place of celebration for the purpose of evading their domicile's restrictions? See In re May's Estate, 114 N.E.2d 4 (N.Y. 1953).

Problem

The movie director Woody Allen, age 56, had an affair with Soon-Yi Previn, age 22, the adopted daughter of Allen's long-term lover, actress Mia Farrow. He later married Soon-Yi Previn and adopted two children with her. (Soon-Yi's adoptive father is Andre Previn, Farrow's former husband.) Although Allen and Farrow had had a biological child together and are the adoptive parents of two other young children, Allen and Farrow never married; in fact, they maintained separate residences. Should a state legislature criminalize sexual relationships such as Allen and Soon-Yi Previn's? Bar the issuance of marriage licenses to such couples? Declare any ensuing marriages void?

How does the incest taboo apply in the modern family, with the rise of divorce, remarriage, and cohabitation? Commentators suggest that the most significant damage from incest is psychological; that is, the disruption of the process of emotional separation from the family of origin.[29] How might this factor play a role in the Allen-Previn relationship? Does Lawrence v. Texas affect the analysis? See Lowe v. Swanson, 663 F.3d 258 (6th Cir. 2011); Muth v. Frank, 412 F.3d 808 (7th Cir. 2005).

(3) Bigamy

COLLIER v. FOX

2018 WL 1247411 (D. Mont. 2018)

TIMOTHY J. CAVAN, United States Magistrate Judge.

. . . Nathan and Vicki were legally married in Dillon, South Carolina, on April 26, 2000. They have been married continuously since that date. Nathan also is in a committed romantic relationship with Christine, and they desire to legally marry. Vicki and Christine are aware of Nathan's relationship with one another, and each consents to be married to Nathan simultaneously. The Colliers have "committed to raise, support, nurture, and care for one another's children,

---

[29]. See Anastasia Toufexis, What Is Incest?, Time Mag., Aug. 31, 1992, at 57 (quoting views of a child psychologist). See also Ramon Diaz, Incest and Its Impact on the Body, CPTSD Programs, Oct. 14, 2022, https://cptsdfoundation.org/2022/10/14/incest-and-its-impact-on-the-body/.

Nathan Collier (center) with wives Victoria (left) and Christine (right)

including [Christine's] children from a prior marriage." The Colliers have parented their eight children jointly for several years. There is no evidence to suggest that either of Nathan's romantic relationships—with Vicki or with Christine—involves dishonesty, coercion, fraud, abuse, or violence. [The Colliers were all formerly members of the Mormon Church but were excommunicated in 2010. *Eds.*]

On June 30, 2015, Nathan and Christine went to the Yellowstone County Clerk of District Court Marriage License Division to apply for a marriage license; the application was denied [because of a Montana law that criminalizes entering into multiple marriages and marrying a person knowing that the person is married to another. The Colliers challenged the constitutionality of Montana's anti-polygamy statutes.]

MONTANA'S CRIMINAL ANTI-POLYGAMY STATUTES

The bulk of the Colliers' claims are directed at Montana's criminal anti-bigamy statutes, and the Colliers' alleged fear of criminal prosecution under those statutes. Mont. Code Ann. §§45-5-611 criminalizes marrying while still being married to another, providing in relevant part: "[a] person commits the offense of bigamy if, while married, the person knowingly contracts or purports to contract to another marriage. . . . " Section 612 criminalizes marrying a bigamist, and states in part: "[a] person commits the offense of marrying a bigamist if the person contracts or purports to contract a marriage with another knowing that the other is committing bigamy. . . ."

It is undisputed that the Colliers have never faced prosecution for violation of either statute. Accordingly, the Colliers are raising a "pre-enforcement challenge" to these statutes. In asserting pre-enforcement challenges to a statute, plaintiffs may meet constitutional standing requirements by demonstrating "a realistic danger of sustaining a direct injury as a result of the statute's operation or enforcement." But when plaintiffs "do not claim that they have ever been threatened with prosecution, that a prosecution is likely, or even that a prosecution is remotely possible, they do not allege a dispute susceptible to resolution by a federal court." . . .

There is no dispute that Nathan and Christine are at least attempting to violate Mont. Code Ann. §§45-5-611 and 612. They claim to have entered into a marital contract, and evidence suggests that they generally refer to each other as husband and wife. They have also sought, albeit unsuccessfully, a state marriage license. It is less clear, however, whether Nathan and Christine have articulated anything that could be considered a "concrete plan to violate" Mont. Code Ann. §§45-5-611 or 612.

The State Defendants have taken the position that Nathan and Christine's declaration to be husband and wife, without the accompanying possession of a state-issued marriage license, is insufficient to violate the Montana bigamy statutes. Therefore, this case presents the unusual situation where the State of Montana has taken the position that the Colliers' conduct is not criminal, while the Colliers insist that it is. In light of the State Defendants' position as to the legality of the Colliers' present conduct, however, it is somewhat difficult to conclude that mere maintenance of the status quo constitutes a concrete plan to violate Mont. Code Ann. §§45-5-611 or 612.

[T]he Court will assume without deciding that Nathan and Christine can satisfy the first factor in determining the genuineness of a claimed threat of prosecution. Though the Colliers generally allege that they "fear that the State will imminently enforce anti-polygamy criminal statutes" against them, they do not allege that they have ever been prosecuted under Montana's criminal bigamy statutes, nor do they identify any specific threat of prosecution. The closest the Colliers come to identifying an actual threat of prosecution is their allegation that "Defendants enforced State anti-polygamy criminal statutes by using them to justify the State's denial of a State-issued marriage license to Christine and Nathan Collier." The Colliers are referring here to the Denial Letter, which specifically states that the Clerk's Office was correct to deny the license because "while both of you are lawfully married to each other, you seek to engage in yet another state licensed marriage. That act, by either or both of you, would be considered bigamy in Montana." This statement does not threaten prosecution. Instead, the Letter indicates a second marriage license could not be issued because, that would constitute a second state-sanctioned marriage, which would violate Montana's bigamy statutes. . . . Accordingly, this factor weighs strongly against finding a genuine threat of prosecution.

The Colliers also are unable to present a history of enforcement. Despite their avowed "fear" of prosecution, the Colliers have not identified a single instance of bigamy prosecution in Montana. This lack of past prosecution under these statutes weighs heavily against finding the Colliers face a genuine threat of prosecution. The mere existence of the challenged statutes is simply not enough to demonstrate the constitutionally required standing necessary to challenge these statutes.

Even after giving the Colliers the benefit of the substantial doubt that they have formulated a concrete plan to violate Mont. Code Ann. §§45-5-611 or 612, the Court finds that the Colliers have failed to demonstrate injury in fact because they have not shown a threat of prosecution or a history of enforcement, and therefore they do not have standing to challenge those criminal statutes. Accordingly, the Court recommends that summary judgment be granted in favor of Defendants with respect to the Colliers' challenge to Mont. Code Ann. §§45-5-611 and 612.

MONTANA'S CIVIL MARRIAGE LAWS

The standing analysis differs with respect to that claim [regarding the state's civil marriage laws]. The undisputed facts demonstrate that Nathan and Christine applied for a Montana marriage license [and] were denied due to Nathan's existing marriage to Vicki. That action is sufficient to confer standing upon them to challenge Montana's civil statute prohibiting plural marriage. It constitutes an alleged invasion of a legally protected interest (the right to marry) which is (a) concrete and particularized and (b) actual or imminent; (2) the injury would be fairly traceable to Defendants' refusal to grant the marriage license; and (3) a favorable decision from the Court could resolve their injury by ordering Defendants to provide a marriage license. Accordingly, the Court finds that the denial of Nathan's and Christine's marriage license application provides Nathan and Christine with standing to challenge Mont. Code Ann. §40-1-401(1)(a).

The question of whether state statutes prohibiting polygamy violate the United States Constitution was answered over a century ago in Reynolds v. U.S., 98 U.S. 145 (1878). *Reynolds* included a constitutional challenge to a federal statute that prohibited bigamy in a territory or other place within the exclusive jurisdiction of the United States. The Supreme Court upheld the validity of that statute, finding "there cannot be a doubt that, unless restricted by some form of constitution, it is within the legitimate scope of the power of every civil government to determine whether polygamy or monogamy shall be the law of social life under its dominion.". . . Although *Reynolds* is almost 140 years old, it is not antiquated and is still valid, binding authority. Several recent decisions have relied upon Reynolds to uphold the constitutionality of anti-polygamy statutes [citations omitted].

The Colliers point out Chief Justice Roberts' recent dissent in Obergefell v. Hodges, 135 S. Ct. 2584 (2015), in which the Court held that same-sex couples have a constitutionally protected right to marry. In his dissent, the Chief Justice commented that "[i]t is striking how much the majority's reasoning [in support of a fundamental right to same-sex marriage] would apply with equal force to the claim of a fundamental right to plural marriage." Chief Justice Roberts also added, however, that he did "not mean to equate marriage between same-sex couples with plural marriages in all respects. There may well be relevant differences that compel different legal analysis."

Regardless, Justice Roberts' dissent is not binding precedent, and it certainly cannot be said to have overruled *Reynolds*. Mindful of this Court's place in the federal judicial hierarchy, it is bound to follow *Reynolds* unless and until the Supreme Court decides to revisit the issue. Supreme Court "decisions remain binding precedent until [that Court sees] fit to reconsider them, regardless of whether subsequent cases have raised doubts about their continuing vitality."

To the extent that the Colliers allege Montana's anti-polygamy laws have infringed upon rights other than their claimed fundamental right to plural marriage—such as, inter alia, the rights to cohabitate, intermingle finances, raise children together, etc.—the Court does not find these challenges to be persuasive. First, the Colliers have not presented any evidence that Defendants have prevented them from exercising any of these alleged fundamental rights; on the contrary, the evidence suggests that the Colliers already are engaging in all of the conduct they discuss, with the sole exception being their desire to legally marry. Given Defendants' position that the Colliers are not violating any laws in spite of the fact that they otherwise live together as a family, with all that entails, the Court is not persuaded that Montana's anti-polygamy laws infringe upon any fundamental right incidental to marriage.

Rather, Mont. Code Ann. §40-1-401(1)(a) prohibits Nathan and Christine from procuring a legal marriage license because Nathan is already married to Vicki. Until the Supreme Court overrules *Reynolds*, that prohibition, in and of itself, is not unconstitutional. . . .

Epilogue. For three years, Nathan Collier and his wife, Vicki, sought to enter into a legal plural marriage with prospective second wife, Christine. (Nathan married Vicki in a legal marriage ceremony in 2000 and married Christine in a spiritual marriage ceremony in 2007.) During their lengthy legal challenge to Montana law, they were followed closely by fans of the pro-polygamy TV show *Sister Wives*. In 2022, Christine decided to end her relationship with Nathan and Vicki, citing irreconcilable differences. After leaving the Collier family, Christine began a relationship with a new intimate partner.

The following excerpt is the first investigative account of Jack Anderson, a Pulitzer Prize-winning journalist who was one of the founders of investigative reporting. He contributed to the exposure of Senator Joseph McCarthy's Communist witch hunts and the Nixon-era Watergate hearings.

Jack Anderson, Adventures Among the Polygamists
1 Investigative Rep. Mag. (Jan. 1982), at 4-42

. . . Growing up in a devout Mormon home, I was duly drilled in the subjugation of the flesh and shielded from the lustier chapters of my heritage. But now and again, I picked up a mournful whisper among the adults about some fallen soul who had sunk back into the old ways. I was 18 and a fledgling reporter for The Salt Lake Tribune when whispers of [my second cousin's] relapse made the family rounds. [M]y curiosity was reinforced by the reporter's license to snoop into the hidden and illegal. In due course, I located [an elderly man with a saintly visage, Joseph Musser].

[Musser] outlined a "fundamentalist" faith which stressed the traditional doctrines and the old-fashioned virtues. [H]is main theme [was] a review of the moral shambles of modern life, [which he traced to monogamy] with its inevitable spawn of divorces and mistresses, unmarried mothers and bachelor fathers, cast-off wives and abandoned children. Did not the rise of abortion and contraception clearly foreshadow its ultimate ends: the destruction of the family? Opposed to this theme of abominations, he said, was the sacred institution of plural marriage, practiced by the Old Testament prophets and rooted in God's great commandment to the human race:

"Be fruitful and multiply and replenish the earth." [He said that we] must restore the patriarchal order [and] aspire to stand at the head of a family as numerous as the sands on the seashore. . . . God would provide women in abundance who were prepared to do their duty; we bearers of the seed must extend ourselves to the utmost. . . .

Mormonism [is] a product of the frontier. [Thousands of converts followed founder Joseph Smith to Missouri in the 1830s.] Most of the converts to Mormonism came out of New England. They were a puritanical people, reserved in conduct and strict about sex—attitudes further stiffened by their new faith. [When Smith revealed to the Church leaders the religious basis for polygamy, they quickly divided over the issue.] Even Smith's great disciple, Brigham Young, teetered for a time on the brink of rejection, later saying of his initial reaction: "It was the first time in my life that I desired the grave."

ot only accepted polygamy but warmed to it and acquired 27 wives.

[T]he Mormons had settled a thousand miles from their nearest neighbors in a land so inhospitable they thought no one else would ever want it, in order to pursue their faith without friction. At last, they felt safe, far from vigilantes, in a territory they controlled. But they underestimated the righteous enmity of the fellow who hears that someone else is savoring a fruit forbidden to him. . . . In 1869, the geographic isolation of the Mormons was broken by the completion of the transcontinental railroad, and they found themselves invaded by miners, railroaders and entrepreneurs, a rowdy bunch not previously noted for their sexual scruples, who set up a great lamentation over Mormon heresies and inequities. It was aimed more at Washington than at heaven, however, for the enterprising Mormons controlled not only the women of Utah, but the land, the commerce, and the public offices. [In response to congressional efforts from 1862-1887 to make bigamy a federal crime and to limit the power of the Mormon Church, the Mormons provided that anyone practicing polygamy would be excommunicated.] So thorough going was the Mormon effort to obliterate all traces of plural marriage that by the time I came along in the third generation, only whispers remained of it. . . .

[The polygamous families that the author met] were generally hardworking and frugal. Although the upwardly mobile polygamist aspired for a separate home for each of his wives and broods, thus to perambulate from one to the other, most had to house their multiple families under one roof. . . . To neighbors, the proliferation of brassieres on clotheslines, or new female faces at the windows or a platoon of strange tots romping in the yard, were explained away as visiting aunts and cousins. . . .

The polygamists also appeared to be a sober people of earnest disposition, who would have been enraged to hear themselves called immoral. . . . Among the men, there was no locker-room hee-hawing and lip-smacking about things sexual. Procreation was seen as the central duty of their lives. . . . Such gratifications, as attended this duty, were to be accepted as the unmentioned rewards of a job well done. [But] I struck up conversations with wives who, once their hair was down, acknowledged it was a problem being forever a regimented and scheduled shareholder in love and home. . . .

[T]he most critical operation in a polygamous society is the selection process by which spouses are distributed. . . . I came quickly to suspect that the prophet Musser was making very liberal interpretations of the Lord's messages. Either that or the Lord had an unerring partiality for old codgers. The choicest girls were going to the leaders themselves or to the wealthier laymen who were the biggest contributors to the cause. . . .

Unknown to me, I was not the only investigator on the beat. [Church elders] hired trusted private investigators to keep an eye on the polygamists. [During meetings of polygamists,] the investigators would slip among the parked cars outside and copy the license numbers. [T]hus, it was that the license number of my father's old Plymouth, the only wheels available to me, kept appearing in the investigators' reports. In due course, my father was called in by his spiritual superiors for a confrontation that utterly confounded him. . . . [O]ne day I came home to find my father in a towering rage. The unspeakable had been spoken: He had been accused of an undercover flirtation with the polygamists. . . . I was a long time in the doghouse. [S]o ended my first adventures with the polygamists. . . .

Notes and Questions

1. Historical background. In medieval England, ecclesiastical law made bigamous marriages void. In 1603, Parliament made bigamy a felony. In the United States, polygamy has been associated primarily with the Mormon religion, even though the LDS Church formally repudiated the practice when Utah became a state. Law enforcement efforts took the form of raids of polygamist communities. In one famous raid on Short Creek, an isolated community straddling the Arizona-Utah border (now Colorado City), law enforcement officials took mothers and children into custody and prosecuted the men. See In re State ex rel. Black, 283 P.2d 887 (Utah 1955). Fifty years later, law enforcement officials again raided a polygamist compound in Eldorado, Texas, and took 468 children into custody. See In re Texas Dept. of Fam. & Protective Servs., 255 S.W.3d 613 (Tex. 2008).

2. Prevalence. Although mainstream members of the LDS Church reject polygamy, some fundamentalist Mormon sects do not. These sects are primarily located in the southwestern United States. However, prosecutions are rare. Polygamy—in which one man is married to multiple wives who do not have sexual relations with each other—is often religiously motivated.[30] Another type of multi-party relationship is polyamory, in which multiple people are in intimate relationships with each other. Polyamory is often not religiously motivated.

3. Civil and criminal consequences. Bigamy, like incest, has criminal and civil consequences. Civil restrictions limit the ability to contract a second marriage (while a valid first marriage exists) by making such marriages void. Such a marriage needs no decree to establish its invalidity. States also impose criminal penalties when a prior valid marriage exists. In the principal case, plaintiffs challenged the state's criminal as well as civil polygamy statutes. How did the court decide each of the plaintiffs' challenges?

In addition to civil restrictions and criminal sanctions, polygamy sometimes triggers other adverse legal consequences. See, e.g., Potter v. Murray City, 760 F.2d 1065 (10th Cir. 1985) (loss of employment); Shepp v. Shepp, 906 A.2d 1165 (Pa. 2006) (loss of child custody).

4. Constitutional challenges to polygamy laws.

a. First Amendment. Most challenges to polygamy laws are based on claims that such laws infringe on the free exercise of religion. What result does Reynolds v. United States dictate? What level of scrutiny should apply to a free exercise claim, and why?

b. Due process and precedent. Does Lawrence v. Texas mandate reconsideration of polygamy laws? Do polygamy bans violate the right to marry based on *Zablocki*? To what extent are such prohibitions "direct" and "substantial" interferences with

---

[30]. Andrew Solomon, How Polyamorists and Polygamists Are Challenging Family Norms, New Yorker Mag., Mar. 22, 2021 (estimating that 60,000 persons practice polygamy in the United States), https://www.newyorker.com/magazine/2021/03/22/how-polyamorists-and-polygamists -are-challenging-family-norms. See also Samantha Allen, Polygamy Is More Popular than Ever, June 2, 2015, https://www.thedailybeast.com/polygamy-is-more-popular-than-ever.

the right to marry? Or are such bans "reasonable regulations that do not significantly interfere with decisions to enter into the marital relationship"? What implications does *Obergefell* have regarding the legal status of polygamy, according to the Collier plaintiffs? According to the district court? Do *Lawrence* and *Obergefell* call into question all state "morals legislation" that implicates sexual privacy? What about adult incest? Adultery? Prostitution? Obscenity?

Utah had a unique criminal statute that extended its bigamy/polygamy prohibition to anyone who "purports to marry another person or cohabits with another person" while being married to another person. That latter provision was invalidated in a challenge by Kody Brown and his "sister wives" (who appeared in the reality TV show). Brown v. Buhman, 947 F. Supp. 2d 1170 (D. Utah 2013). The decision was vacated when the county attorney announced that it would not prosecute, thereby rendering the case moot. Brown v. Buhman, 822 F.3d 1151 (10th Cir. 2016).

In response to the Browns' lawsuit, the Utah legislature enacted Utah Code Ann. §76-7-101, clarifying the requirement that a party must cohabit with *and* (rather than "or") purport to marry the other spouse(s). At the same time, the legislature increased the penalty from 5 to 15 years if bigamy is accompanied by crimes of domestic abuse, child abuse, sexual abuse, human trafficking, or human smuggling, inducing marriage or bigamy under false pretenses, or fraud. In 2020, the Utah legislature reduced bigamy from a third-degree felony, punishable by up to five years in prison, to a mere infraction (subject to a $750 fine or community service). Utah Code Ann. §76-7-101. Does the law reform adequately address the constitutional issue posed by *Lawrence*?

c. State interests and harm. If the *Collier* plaintiffs had been threatened with prosecution, what possible state interests might have supported the imposition of criminal sanctions? What is the harm of polygamy—to the parties, the family, and the state? Does the state's interest in protecting vulnerable individuals from exploitation satisfy rational basis review? Note that Judge Waddoups in Brown v. Buhman (947 F. Supp. 2d at 1220) concurred with Chief Justice Durham (the dissenting judge in Utah v. Holm, 137 P.3d 726 (Utah 2006)) that evidence of a correlation between polygamy and other crimes exploiting women and children (e.g., incest, sexual assault, statutory rape, etc.) was "unconvincing." What light does the following account shed on the purported link between polygamy and crimes of sexual exploitation: Warren Jeffs, the famous leader of a fundamentalist Mormon sect in Colorado City, was sentenced to two consecutive life terms in 2011 for sexually assaulting two underage girls (one was 12 years old) when he took them as "brides" in "spiritual marriages." Of Jeffs's 79 wives, 24 were under the age of 17.

5. Same-sex marriage and plural marriages. Will the marriage equality movement lead to recognition of plural marriage? Why does Chief Justice Roberts in his dissent in *Obergefell* assert that the decision will lead to this result? Are there differences between same-sex marriage and polygamy that compel a different analysis? How expansive or limited is *Obergefell*'s rationale as applied to polygamy? What light does *Collier* shed on these issues?

6. Birth of a social movement. Pro-polygamy and polyamory activists seek the repeal of polygamy laws by minimizing the link between polygamy and abuse. They emphasize the consensual nature of the relationships and evoke the rhetoric of sexual liberation. Anti-polygamists also seek law reform (increased enforcement of the law) by highlighting the occurrence of abuse, as illustrated in accounts of women who fled polygamous relationships. Compare Jeffrey Michael Hayes, Polygamy Comes out of the Closet: The New Strategy of Polygamy Activists, 3 Stan. J. C.R.-C.L. 99, 105 (2007), with Kristyn Decker, Fifty Years in Polygamy: Big Secrets and Little White Lies (2013); and Susan Schmidt, Favorite Wife: Escape from Polygamy (2014). Which view do you find most persuasive?

7. Utah's child bigamy law. Among the state interests underlying polygamy prohibitions is the interest in preventing sexual exploitation. Should criminal liability attach only in cases involving teenage wives, not in cases involving consenting adults?

To address the problem of teen spiritual marriages, the Utah legislature enacted the Child Bigamy Amendment, which increases the penalties in cases involving teenage brides. Utah Code Ann. §76-7-101.5 (providing that marriage or cohabitation with a person under age 18, while the actor is validly married to another, constitutes a second-degree felony punishable by up to 15 years in prison). Is this provision constitutional? A different criminal provision provides that a parent who knowingly allows a minor to enter a marriage that is prohibited is guilty of a third-degree felony. Utah Code Ann. §30-1-9.1. In 2020, the Utah legislature decriminalized bigamy between consenting adults (as explained above). What are the possible implications of this law reform for teen brides?

8. Conflict of laws. Suppose that a man marries multiple wives in a country where this practice is permitted. The parties then move to a U.S. state that prohibits such marriages. Should the second jurisdiction recognize the marriages? Should it matter for what purpose the validity is at issue? Compare In re Dalip Singh Bir's Estate, 188 P.2d 499 (Cal. Ct. App. 1948) (inheritance law), with Al Sharabi v. Heinauer, 2011 WL 3955027 (N.D. Cal. 2011) (immigration).

9. Public opinion. Public opinion about the acceptability of polygamy seems to be changing. According to the 2022 Gallup Values and Beliefs poll, 23 percent of Americans believe that polygamy is "morally acceptable." That statistic has doubled from 11 percent in 2012.[31]

Problem

A Utah law amends the Child Welfare Code to protect runaway teens from parents who expose them to forced marriages. See Utah Code Ann. §§62A-4a-209, 62A-4a-501, 78A-6-105 (47), 78A-6-307. Former Utah law required persons who harbored runaways to inform the teens' parents within eight hours that the teens had taken refuge with them. The new law allows persons who harbor runaway teens to notify child welfare authorities only, thereby providing more time before parents are able to locate the teens.

---

[31]. See Gallup, Moral Issues (Polygamy) (2023), https://news.gallup.com/poll/1681/moral-issues.aspx.

The law also gives preference to a "friend" designated by the child in terms of emergency placement: "if (A) the child is of sufficient maturity to articulate the child's wishes and (B) the basis for removing the child is sexual abuse of the child." The law broadens the definition of sexual abuse to include "subjecting a child to participate in, or threatening to subject a child to participate in, a sexual relationship, regardless of whether that sexual relationship is part of a legal or cultural marriage." Formerly, the act of pressuring a child into marriage was not a legally cognizable reason for the child's removal from the home. Teenagers aged 16 and older who refuse to return home may petition for emancipation. But if emancipation is not possible or advisable, the judge takes into account the child's preference (for children of sufficient maturity) for placement with a relative or "friend."

The law originated in response to the plight of teenage girls who fled polygamous communities and sought shelter in homes of former plural wives who left the religious community. But the teens often were forced to return home immediately after they were located. Opponents of the law (representatives of a polygamous community on the Utah-Arizona state law) contend that the law (1) constitutes a significant interference with parental rights, (2) singles out a specific religious group, and (3) specifies a vague definition of abuse whereby any parent who suggests a future marriage could be defined as abusive.

You are a legislative aide whose employer in the state assembly solicits your opinion about the new law. Discuss the arguments of the various parties as well as the benefits and shortcomings of the law. What lessons can be gleaned from judicial bypass hearings regarding minors' abortion rights?

Elizabeth Joseph, My Husband's Nine Wives
N.Y. Times, May 23, 1991, at A15

I married a married man. In fact, he had six wives when I married him 17 years ago. Today, he has nine. . . .

. . . At first blush, [polygamy] sounds like the ideal situation for the man and an oppressive one for the women. For me, the opposite is true. [C]ompelling social reasons make the life style attractive to the modern career woman.

Pick up any women's magazine and you will find article after article about the problems of successfully juggling career, motherhood, and marriage. It is a complex act that many women struggle to manage daily. . . .

When I leave for the 60-mile commute to court at 7 A.M., my 2-year-old daughter, London, is happily asleep in the bed of my husband's wife, Diane. London adores Diane. When London awakes, about the time I'm arriving at the courthouse, she is surrounded by family members who are as familiar to her as the toys in her nursery. . . .

I share a home with Delinda, another wife, who works in town government. [Alex Joseph shares another house with seven other wives and their children.] Most nights, we agree we'll just have a simple dinner with our three kids. . . . Mondays, however, are different. That's the night Alex eats with us. . . . The same system with some variation governs our private time with him. While spontaneity is by no means ruled out, we basically use an appointment system. . . .

> Plural marriage is not for everyone. But it is the life style for me. It offers men the chance to escape from the traditional, confining roles that often isolate them from the surrounding world. More important, it enables women, who live in a society full of obstacles, to fully meet their career, mothering and marriage obligations. Polygamy provides a whole solution. I believe American women would have invented it if it didn't already exist.

(4) Age

KIRKPATRICK v. DISTRICT COURT
64 P.3d 1056 (Nev. 2003)

SHEARING, J. . . .

SierraDawn Kirkpatrick Crow is the daughter of Karen Karay and petitioner Bruce Kirkpatrick. . . . As part of the divorce decree, Karay and Kirkpatrick were awarded joint legal and physical custody of SierraDawn. In 1992, Karay and SierraDawn moved from California to New Mexico. In December 2000, when SierraDawn was fifteen years old, she informed her mother that she desired to marry her guitar teacher, 48-year-old Sauren Crow. SierraDawn's mother approved of the marriage.

However, under New Mexico law, SierraDawn was not permitted to marry. Therefore, SierraDawn, her mother, and Crow traveled to Las Vegas where SierraDawn and Crow could marry, if granted permission by the court. [New Mexico law (N.M. Stat. Ann. §§40-1-5, 40-1-6(B)) provides that a minor under age 16 shall not marry unless the marriage legitimizes a nonmarital child or the minor is pregnant, whereas Nevada law (Nev. Rev. Stat. §122.025) permits a minor under age 16 to marry based on one parent's consent and judicial authorization.]

Karay filed a petition [for] judicial authorization for SierraDawn's marriage. [In addition,] Karay filed an affidavit consenting to the marriage, in which she stated that she has "seen no other couple so right for each other," that they "have very real life plans at home, in the town in which we all reside," and that "[t]heir partnership and their talents will be most effectively utilized by this marriage." [The court found good cause under Nevada law for the marriage and ordered issuance of the license. The couple married in Las Vegas.]

When Kirkpatrick first learned of SierraDawn's marriage, he sought an ex parte temporary restraining order in the New Mexico district court. That court granted the temporary restraining order, and awarded Kirkpatrick immediate legal and physical custody of SierraDawn. Four days later, however, the court rescinded its order because it found that SierraDawn's marriage was valid under Nevada law, and that SierraDawn was emancipated as a result of the marriage.[3] . . . Thereafter,

---

3. At common law, marriage is generally sufficient to constitute emancipation. . . . It does not appear that judicial action is required for emancipation to occur. . . .

Kirkpatrick filed this petition seeking a writ of mandamus to compel the district court to vacate its order authorizing SierraDawn's marriage and to annul the marriage. . . .

It is well settled that states have the right and power to establish reasonable limitations on the right to marry. This power is justified as an exercise of the police power, which confers upon the states the ability to enact laws in order to protect the safety, health, morals, and general welfare of society. Pursuant to this power, the Nevada Legislature enacted Nev. Rev. Stat. §122.025 [requiring one-parent consent and judicial authorization for underage marriages].

Kirkpatrick argues that this statute violates his constitutional interest in the care, custody, and management of his daughter since it neither requires his consent nor gives him an opportunity to be heard on the issue of his daughter's marriage. The United States Supreme Court has held that parents have a fundamental liberty interest in the care, custody, and management of their children. However, the United States Supreme Court has also held that, although these rights are fundamental, they are not absolute. The state also has an interest in the welfare of children and may limit parental authority. The Supreme Court has even held, where justified, that parents can be totally deprived of their children forever. If the state can completely eliminate all parental rights, it can certainly limit some parental rights when the competing rights of the child are implicated.

The United States Supreme Court has held that the right to marry is a fundamental right [citing *Loving* and *Zablocki*]. . . . The Supreme Court has made it clear that constitutional rights apply to children as well as adults. . . . Marriage is the cornerstone of the family and our civilization. As marriage comprises the most sacred of relationships, the decision of whom and when to marry is highly personal, often involving reasons that are complex and vary from individual to individual. The decision to marry should rest primarily in the hands of the individual, with little government interference. As a society, we recognize that reasonable constraints on the right to marry are appropriate, especially when the marriage involves a minor.

There is no one set of criteria that can be set forth as a litmus test to determine if a marriage will be successful [or] whether a person is mature enough to enter a marriage. Age alone is an arbitrary factor. The Nevada Legislature recognized that although most fifteen-year-olds would not be mature enough to enter into a marriage, there are exceptions. Nevada provided for the exceptional case by allowing a fifteen-year-old to marry if one parent consents and the court approves. The statute provides a safeguard against an erroneous marriage decision by the minor and the consenting parent, by giving the district court the discretion to withhold authorization if it finds that there are no extraordinary circumstances and/or the proposed marriage is not in the minor's best interest, regardless of parental consent. The statute strikes a balance between an arbitrary rule of age for marriage and accommodation of individual differences and circumstances.

Consent of both parents is by no means a constitutional requirement for even the most important of decisions regarding minors [citing Hodgson v. Minnesota, 497 U.S. 417 (1990) (declaring a *two-parent* notification requirement for an abortion unconstitutional in the absence of a judicial bypass)]. The *Hodgson* Court went on to hold that two-parent notification "is an oddity among state and federal consent provisions governing the health, welfare, and education of children," such as enlisting in the armed services, obtaining a passport, participating in medical research, or submitting to any surgical or medical procedure. When the state requires the consent of only one parent for significant events in a minor's life, the state implicitly recognizes the common reality of modern families. A significant percentage of children under the age of eighteen live in single-parent households. . . .

Kirkpatrick asserts that he has been deprived of his fundamental right to the parent-child relationship, like the parents whose parental rights have been terminated. Contrary to what is apparently Kirkpatrick's view, the parental relationship does not end with the emancipation of a child. The only right that he has lost by his daughter's emancipation is his right to exercise legal control over his daughter during her minority. He still has all the other legal and social attributes of parenthood. Kirkpatrick retains the legal rights of inheritance, as well as all the bonds of love, care, companionship, and influence that any parents have after emancipation of their children. How he chooses to foster those bonds is up to him.

The Supreme Court has held that the usual standard for analyzing a substantive due process challenge to the constitutionality of a state statute that impinges on a fundamental constitutional right is whether the statute is narrowly tailored so as to serve a compelling interest. In family privacy cases involving competing interests within the family, however, the Court has deviated from the usual test. Various child rearing and custody cases demonstrate the Court's application of a more flexible "reasonableness" test, which "implicitly calibrat[es] the level of scrutiny in each case to match the particular degree of intrusion upon the parents' interests."

In this case, we have the interest of the daughter in marriage and the interest of the mother in her daughter's welfare and happiness balanced against the father's interest in the legal control of his daughter for the remainder of her minority. Nev. Rev. Stat. §122.025 strikes an appropriate balance between the various interests. . . .

Notes and Questions

1. Minimum age. Child marriage is defined as any marriage in which one or both of the parties are under 18 years old. Most states have exceptions to minimum age requirements that allow younger adolescents or pregnant minors to marry with parental and/or judicial consent. See, e.g., N.C. Gen. Stat. Ann. §51-2.1 (age 14 for pregnant minors, with judicial consent). Should the law include these requirements? If so, should it require *both* parental consent and judicial authorization? Compare UMDA §§203-204 (minor may marry with either parent's consent or after a finding that the minor is capable of assuming the responsibilities of marriage and that the marriage would be in his or her best interests), with Cal. Fam. Code §302 (requiring both parental consent and judicial authorization). Why did SierraDawn in *Kirkpatrick* decide to marry in Nevada rather than New Mexico? Are minors, such as SierraDawn, capable of informed consent on such "private" matters as marriage and abortion?

2. Historical background. The age of consent for marriage at early common law was 7 years old. Such marriages, however, were voidable if either party was too young to consummate the marriage. Betrothals of children occurred in order to ensure the passage of estates, settle disputes, and prevent the sovereign from selecting a youth's spouse. Parliament raised the age of consent in 1653 to 16 for boys and 14 for girls. Subsequent legislation declared a marriage void if either party was under 16.

3. Empirical data. Both men and women are marrying later, although men marry later than women. In 2018, the median age at first marriage was almost 30 for men and almost 28 for women (compared to age 26 for men and age 24 for women in 1990).[32] What factors contribute to this gender-based difference? What factors contribute to delayed marriage? What are the consequences for society of a later first-marriage age?

4. Inequality and instability. Underage marriage often leads to significant challenges for the parties in the form of lower educational attainment, reduced employment prospects, and a higher divorce rate. Children of these unions fare more poorly on health, behavioral, educational, and other measures.[33] Given these problems, should states require premarital counseling prior to teen marriages? See, e.g., Cal. Fam. Code §304; Mont. Code Ann §40-1-213(1). Should laws facilitate the marriage of pregnant teens to promote economic stability? If so, what might the state do to enhance the stability of underage marriages? Or should states follow the emergent restrictive trend (discussed below) and ban underage marriage?

5. Void-voidable distinction. State statutes reflect inconsistent treatment of the legal effect of nonage on marriage validity: Some states classify such marriages as void, while others regard them as voidable. Historically, nonage was classified as a civil rather than a canonical disability. Civil disabilities rendered marriages void; canonical disabilities made them voidable.

How do these rules apply in practice? Suppose Tom marries Jenny when he is 17. The marriage is rocky from its inception. Tom, discovering that the statutory minimum age is 18, decides to leave Jenny. Later, he meets and marries Polly, but without securing an annulment of his prior marriage. Tom is prosecuted for bigamy. May he raise the invalidity of his prior marriage in the criminal proceeding? If a statute makes the marriage void, then he may. But if the statute classifies the marriage as voidable, the marriage remains valid until annulled, thereby precluding collateral attack.

6. Minors' rights. Does a minor have a fundamental right to marry? How does *Kirkpatrick* respond? Do laws banning minor marriages impose a direct and substantial barrier to marriage, per *Zablocki*? What level of scrutiny should

---

[32]. U.S. Census Bureau, Median Age at First Marriage 1890–Present (table) (2018), https://www.census.gov/content/dam/Census/library/visualizations/time-series/demo/families-and-households/ms-2.pdf. See also Clare Huntington & Elizabeth S. Scott, The New Restatement of Children and the Law: Childhood in the Twenty-First Century, 54 Fam. L.Q. 91, 116 (2020).

[33]. Tahirih Justice Ctr., Child Marriage in the United States: A Serious Problem with a Simple First-Step Solution 1, 2, Dec. 12, 2018, https://www.tahirih.org/wp-content/uploads/2016/11/FINAL-12.12.18-Tahirih-Child-Marriage-Backgrounder_publisher-version-4.pdf. See also Vijayasri G. Aryama, Note, "I Don't": The Need for a Solution to the Child Marriage Problem in the United States, 39 Women's Rts. L. Rep. 386, 392-394 (2018) (negative impacts).

apply to restrictions on teen marriage? See Moe v. Dinkins, 669 F.2d 67 (2d Cir. 1982) (upholding state ban on underage marriage without parental permission based on rational basis review). Does an underage minor whose parents refuse consent have any recourse? Case law sometimes requires that the parents' refusal not be unreasonable. However, many statutes do not provide for override procedures. Should states institute judicial bypass proceedings to parental consent requirements that are similar to those in abortion decisionmaking?

7. Parental rights. Parental consent proves important if underage marriages are void and thus vulnerable to third-party attack. Requirements of parental consent lessen the likelihood of subsequent parental efforts to invalidate a marriage, such as in *Kirkpatrick*. Why did the court in *Kirkpatrick* refuse to permit SierraDawn's father to annul her marriage? How did *Kirkpatrick* balance the interests of the child, parents, and state? How *should* a court balance these interests when parents disagree, as in *Kirkpatrick*? Should the state ensure that parents exercise their consent wisely? Did SierraDawn's mother exercise her responsibility wisely? Suppose SierraDawn's father has sole (rather than joint) custody, and her mother has a history of mental illness and attempts to evade the father's role in decisionmaking. Should those factors change the result? See In re J.M.N., 2008 WL 2415490 (Tenn. Ct. App. 2008).

8. Legislative reform. A recent trend restricting teen marriages began in 2005 in response to a Nebraska case involving the marriage of a 14-year-old girl (see Problem 1, below), and later a Colorado case that allowed a 15-year-old girl to enter a common law marriage with a felon (In re Marriage of J.M.H. & Rouse, 143 P.3d 1116 (Colo. Ct. App. 2006)). In 2017, all 50 states allowed minors to marry in some cases. Today, 10 states (Connecticut, Delaware, Massachusetts, Michigan, Minnesota, New Jersey, New York, Pennsylvania, Rhode Island, and Vermont) ban all marriages before age 18. Other states raised age limits and limited exceptions. But most states continue to allow teens to marry at 16 or 17 with parental and judicial consent. A few states have no minimum marriage age.[34] Why have some states moved to ban child marriages? Specifically, what does the research reveal (see the excerpt "Child Marriage Poses Serious Risks to Children" infra) regarding the outcomes of such marriages, particularly for girls?

Congress previously considered the Status of Child Marriage Act in the United States, H.R. 8638, 116th Cong. (2019-2020). The bill would have required the U.S. Department of Health and Human Services to explore (1) child marriages that take place under force, fraud, or coercion and state laws that address these marriages; (2) the extent in which these marriages make individuals vulnerable to domestic violence, dating violence, sexual assault, or trafficking; (3) the impact of

[34]. Tahirih Justice Ctr., Child Marriage, supra note [33]; Erick Trickey, Why Is Child Marriage Still Legal?: A Young Lawmaker Tackles a Hidden Problem, Politico, Jan. 9, 2022 (citing study funded by the Gates Foundation), https://www.politico.com/news/magazine/2022/01/09/cassie-levesque-new-hampshire-child-marriage-524159; Unchained at Last, United States' Child Marriage Problem, Study Findings (Apr. 2021) (50 state survey), https://www.unchainedatlast.org/united-states-child-marriage-problem-study-findings-april-2021/; Tahirih Justice Ctr., New Report Compares Impact of Compromise Legislation to End Child Marriage in the U.S., Jan. 26, 2023, https://www.tahirih.org/news/new-report-compares-impact-of-compromise-legislation-to-end-child-marriage-in-the-u-s/.

state reforms on child marriages; and (4) the extent of interstate travel to enable underage minors to marry in states with weaker child marriage laws. The bill died in committee.

9. Choice of law. Conflict-of-laws issues sometimes arise with child marriages. Suppose a 15-year-old is married in State X, where marriage to a 15-year-old is legal, but then moves to State Y. Does State Y have to recognize the marriage if it would not be legal to enter into the marriage there? In other words, does lex loci compel State Y to recognize the marriage? See Broussard v. Arnel, 596 S.W.3d 911 (Tex. App. 2019).

10. International perspectives. Many countries allow child marriages. The reasons are primarily economic to relieve parents of financial burdens and the desire to control female sexuality. The practice is increasingly viewed as a form of child sexual abuse and a human rights violation. The international rate of child marriage soared during COVID because of school closures, economic hardship, service disruptions, parental death, and teen pregnancy. What, if anything, can be done globally to address the problem of child marriage? The United Nations announced an initiative to advance efforts to end child marriage by 2030 in the world. The initiative by the United Nations Children's Fund (UNICEF) and the United Nations Population Fund (UNFPA) is part of a global effort to prevent girls from marrying too young and to support underage girls already married in countries across Africa, Asia and the Middle East where child marriage rates are high.[35]

The Fact Sheet on the opposite page focuses on the implications of child marriage for children's well-being.

Problems

1. Crystal meets Matthew when he comes to play video games with her half-brother. When she is 12 and he is 20, they become a couple. A year later, Crystal's divorced mother petitions for a protective order restraining Matthew from seeing Crystal. Despite the court order, the two continue to see each other and eventually develop a sexual relationship. After Crystal becomes pregnant, her mother has a change of heart and, together with Matthew's parents, drives the couple to Kansas, where persons as young as 12 may marry with parental consent.

Nebraska, where the couple resides, prohibits marriages of persons under age 17 and also provides that sexual intercourse between a person who is 19 or older and another person who is younger than age 16 is statutory rape. Should the Kansas county clerk grant the marriage license? Should Matthew be charged

---

[35]. New UN Initiative Aims to Protect Millions of Girls from Child Marriage (2016), https://www.un.org/youthenvoy/2016/03/new-un-initiative-aims-to-protect-millions-of-girls-from-child-marriage/. See also Tahirih Justice Ctr., New Report, supra note [34] (suggesting that the federal government can take steps to address child marriage through the immigration system and incentivize states to strengthen their marriage age laws).

Child Marriage Poses Serious Risks to Children

PHYSICAL IMPACT

- Women who marry before age 19 have a 23% greater risk of developing a serious health condition (diabetes, cancer, heart attack, or stroke).[1]
- Teen girls who marry tend to have more children, earlier, and more closely spaced.[2] They are:
  - » Much more (130%) likely to get pregnant than unmarried teens who live with a partner[3]
  - » More likely to have their first child before age 18[4]
  - » 40% more likely to have a second birth within 24 months of their first[5]
  - » Nearly 3x more likely to have at least 5 children[6]
- Young women and girls aged 16-19 face intimate partner violence victimization rates almost 3x the national average.[7]
- Overall, women who marry as children are more likely to seek and access health services, compared to women who married in adulthood.[8]

ECONOMIC IMPACT

- Child brides tend to come from poverty and remain in poverty.[9]
  - » Girls who marry underage are up to 31 percentage points more likely to live in future poverty.[10]
  - » For teen mothers, getting married and later divorcing can more than double the likelihood of poverty.[11]
- Earning potential and work opportunities are limited by interrupted education and low education levels. Girls who marry under age 19 are:
  - » 50% more likely to drop out of high school
  - » 4x less likely to graduate college[12]

SOCIAL IMPACT

- Child brides tend to be isolated from support networks including school, friends, and family.
- The majority (70-80%) of marriages entered into when at least one person is under age 18 ultimately end in divorce.[13]
  - » According to one study based on census data, 23% of children who marry are already separated or divorced by the time they turn 18[14]
- These negative outcomes, combined with the economic impacts of child marriage which limit a woman's ability to become financially independent, increase vulnerability to multiple victimization and often result in consequences becoming cyclical and intergenerational.

MENTAL IMPACT

- Women who marry before age 18 are more likely to report stressful life events, and to present with significantly more psychiatric disorders, such as:
  - » mood and anxiety disorders including major depressive disorder
  - » antisocial personality disorder (prevalence nearly 3x higher)[15]
- Social isolation and feeling a lack of control over their lives can contribute to a child bride's poor mental health. In fact, agencies working with girls facing or trying to escape forced marriages report that nearly all have contemplated or attempted suicide.[16]

Forced Marriage Initiative | PreventForcedMarriage.org | tahirih.org | fmi@tahirih.org | 571-282-6161
Atlanta, GA | Baltimore, MD | Greater Washington, DC | Houston, TX | San Francisco Bay Area, CA

Child Marriage Poses Serious Risks to Children, Fact Sheet, Tahirih Justice Ctr., May 8, 2020

*https://www.tahirih.org/wp-content/uploads/2020/05/Child-Marriage-Impacts-One-Pager-updated-5.8
.-2020-REGULAR-PRINT.pdf*

with statutory rape in Nebraska? How should the state of Nebraska reconcile these laws? Should Nebraska take any action against Crystal's mother?

The Kosos later had another child. Does it affect your answers to the above questions to learn that the state child protective services temporarily removed the Koso children from their parents' custody due to neglect? Or that a court-appointed attorney filed a petition to terminate parental rights?

2. The state of Arkansas is considering banning child marriage. Under former state law, 16-year-old girls and 17-year-old boys could marry with the consent of both parents. In cases of pregnancy, a court could consent with no minimum age threshold. A state representative recently introduced legislation to raise the age of consent to marry to age 17 without exceptions. (In Arkansas, age 17 is the age of majority.) The legislator was influenced by data finding that from 2000 to 2015, nearly a quarter of a million adolescents under age 18 were legally married in the United States and that more than 80 percent of these cases involve a girl under 18 marrying an adult, often someone several years older.[36]

You are an aide to the state representative who solicits your opinion regarding the pros and cons of the proposed ban. Consider what factors should determine the minimum marital age. Should the ban be adopted? Are absolute bans constitutional? If so, should there be exceptions? On what basis? Are bans constitutional if they contain different minimum marital ages that are based on gender? See Moe v. Dinkins, supra. What support or opposition for an absolute ban might you expect from representatives of parental rights' groups? From children's rights groups?

(ii) State of Mind Restrictions: Fraud and Duress

BLAIR v. BLAIR

147 S.W.3d 882 (Mo. Ct. App. 2004)

ELLIS, Judge.

William Jerry Blair (Husband) appeals from a judgment entered in the Circuit Court of Platte County denying his petition for annulment of his marriage to Nancy Blair. For the following reasons, we affirm.

In July 1976, Husband and Wife had sexual intercourse on one occasion after having worked together for a couple of years. At that time, Wife was married to Jim Farra and was also involved in a long-standing sexual relationship with Sam Kelly. Subsequently, Wife gave birth to a son, Devin, on April 26, 1977. Husband visited Wife in the hospital shortly after Devin's birth, but did not discuss the paternity of the child with her and had no further contact with Wife until 1979.

In January 1979, Wife contacted Husband, told him that he was Devin's father, and asked whether he had any history of disease in his family that might affect Devin later in life. Husband met with Wife and Devin, and he resumed a sexual relationship with Wife a few days later. In March 1979, Wife separated from

---

[36]. See Trickey, supra note [34]. See also Unchained at Last, supra note [34]; Tahirih Justice Ctr., New Report, supra note [34].

Mr. Farra and filed a petition for dissolution of that marriage. Subsequently, Wife became pregnant with Husband's child, and on March 13, 1980, Wife gave birth to their daughter, Oralin.

Wife's marriage to Mr. Farra was dissolved in December 1980. Several days after her divorce from Mr. Farra became final, Husband and Wife were married on December 22, 1980. Husband later adopted both Devin and Oralin.

On November 20, 2001, Wife filed a petition for dissolution of her marriage to Husband. . . . Husband filed an amended answer and cross-petition requesting that the marriage be annulled. In support of his annulment claim, Husband averred that Wife had fraudulently represented to him before their marriage that he was Devin's father and had thereby induced him to marry her. Subsequent testing proved that Husband was indeed not Devin's father and that he [Devin] was the son of Sam Kelly. . . .

As grounds for granting an annulment, Husband asserted that Wife perpetrated a fraud upon him regarding Devin's paternity. In order to establish fraud, Husband was required to plead and prove the following elements: (1) a representation by Wife; (2) its falsity; (3) its materiality; (4) Wife's knowledge of its falsity or ignorance of its truth; (5) Wife's intent that the representation be acted upon by Husband; (6) Husband's ignorance of the falsity of the representation; (7) Husband's reliance on the truth of the representation; (8) Husband's right to rely on the representation; and (9) that Husband sustained consequent and proximate injury. . . .

Husband notes that he testified at trial that he would not have married Wife if he had known that he was not Devin's father. [T]he trial court was not required to accept Husband's own self-serving testimony that he would not have married Wife but for her representations related to Devin's paternity. Indeed, the overall gist of Husband's testimony appears to have been that he would never have seen Wife again after their one-night-stand if it had not been for her calling and telling him that he had a child and that the marriage was, therefore, the result of that representation. Such testimony does not establish that Husband relied upon the representations regarding Devin's paternity in deciding whether to marry Wife, only that it played a part in his decision to begin a relationship with her.

Sufficient evidence in the record supports the trial court's determination that Husband would have married Wife regardless of the representation as to Devin's paternity. Wife testified that Husband was crazy about her and that she was certain that he would have left his girlfriend and had a relationship with her regardless of Devin's paternity. Husband admitted on cross-examination that, during the two-year courtship the couple had between Wife's initial phone call and their marriage, he fell in love with Wife. In addition, nine months before their marriage, Oralin, who is undisputedly Husband's child, was born. The trial court could reasonably have inferred that Oralin's paternity would have been sufficient to cause Husband to marry Wife. Furthermore, testimony from both Husband and Wife reflects that Husband had questions about Devin's paternity prior to marriage, that he married her anyway, and that he subsequently adopted both children.

Based upon the foregoing testimony, the trial court could more than reasonably have found that Husband would have married Wife regardless of Wife's representations related to Devin's paternity. . . . Having determined that this ground for the trial court's denial of Husband's request for an annulment is not erroneous, we need not address Husband's remaining points. . . .

Notes and Questions

1. Consent requirement. A marriage may be set aside for lack of consent. Fraud (like duress) vitiates consent and serves as a ground for annulment. Because of the public policy in favor of marriage preservation, many courts apply a strict test for fraud, requiring that the misrepresentation go to the "essentials." "Essentials" generally includes the ability and willingness to engage in sexual relations and childbearing. Given the ease in obtaining a divorce, does this strict test make sense? Some states require only that the fraud be *material* (i.e., important or vital). Finally, courts in some states inquire whether the truth would have been a "deal-breaker," i.e., would the plaintiff-spouse have refused to marry the defendant had plaintiff known the truth. Which test does the court use in *Blair*?

What should be the standard of proof for fraud in the marriage context? Should it be the higher clear-and-convincing standard that applies in most civil fraud cases or the lower preponderance standard that applies in the consumer fraud context? Why? See, e.g., Wisniewski v. Dolecka, 489 P.3d 724 (Ariz. Ct. App. 2021) (discussing two tests).

2. Annulment versus divorce. An annulment declares that no marriage occurred because some impediment existed at the time of the ceremony. In contrast, divorce terminates a valid marriage, enabling the parties to remarry. Annulments were important when divorce was difficult to obtain, particularly in England before the Matrimonial Causes Act of 1857. Discontented marital partners could secure an annulment for fraud, duress, or nonage. Following modern divorce reform, the importance of annulments decreased.

3. Procedural differences and relation-back doctrine. Different procedural rules govern annulment and divorce. First, annulment jurisdiction exists at either party's domicile, the state of marriage celebration, or any state with personal jurisdiction over the spouses. In contrast, divorce jurisdiction rests on domicile. Second, an invalid marriage generally precluded spousal and child support and property division. Today, many states, by equitable remedies or statute, equate the financial consequences of annulment to those of divorce. Third, the "relation back" doctrine applies only to annulments. Because an annulment decree establishes that a marriage never existed, benefits lost by virtue of the marriage (such as employment benefits) may be reinstated. See, e.g., Haacke v. Glenn, 814 P.2d 1157 (Utah Ct. App. 1991) (annulment eliminates wife's employment-related conflict of interest stemming from husband's concealment of his felon status). Why might the plaintiff in *Blair* have sought an annulment rather than a divorce? Why did the court deny his request?

4. Consummation. When considering fraud to annul marriage, courts traditionally distinguished between consummated and unconsummated marriages, sometimes requiring a higher standard for the former. Why? Is there any place for consummation requirements in the wake of *Lawrence* and *Obergefell*? Note that when the United Kingdom legalized same-sex marriage, Parliament specifically excluded non-consummation as a ground for the annulment of a same-sex marriage.[37] Given current sexual mores, should consummation continue to influence the law of annulment?

5. Policy. What is the harm stemming from marriage fraud? How does marriage fraud harm the public? Does judicial examination of marriage for purposes of fraud constitute an invasion of privacy?

6. Duress. Agreements to marry that are procured by force, fear, or coercion are void. Although duress generally requires physical force or threat of force, lesser forms of duress may suffice if sufficient to overcome plaintiff's free will. English cases disagree about whether the test should be subjective or objective. What difference does it make?

7. Forced marriage. Forced marriages exist both in the United States and abroad. Approximately 3,000 cases of known or suspected forced marriages occurred in the United States over a recent two-year period.[38] Few states have laws regulating forced marriages or prevent/punish parents from forcing daughters into marriage.

Forced marriage is also practiced abroad, primarily in parts of the Middle East, Asia, and Africa. It occurs in Europe as well. An estimated 30,000 forced brides live in Germany and Austria, where support groups help these youth with securing annulments, housing, and new identities to avoid discovery.[39] Forced child marriage is correlated with high maternal and infant mortality rates, as well as a higher incidence of violence against women.

Some countries have laws that address this practice. Both Germany and the United Kingdom criminalize forced marriage (five years maximum imprisonment in Germany, and seven years maximum imprisonment in the United Kingdom). The United Kingdom's Forced Marriage Act of 2008 also authorizes restraining orders that prevent forced unions. France raised the minimum age for marriage in 2006 in an effort to discourage forced marriages.[40] Evaluate the effectiveness of these approaches.

---

[37]. Kathryn Mason, Annulment for Non-consummation, Mar. 1, 2016, https://vardags.com/family-law/annulment-for-non-consummation. See also Marriage (Same-Sex Couples) Act 2013, 2013 c. 30, http://www.legislation.gov.uk/ukpga/2013/30/contents/enacted.

[38]. See Tahirih Justice Ctr., Forced Marriage in Immigrant Communities in the United States (2011), 2011 National Survey Results, http://www.tahirih.org/pubs/forced-marriage-in-immigrant-communities-in-the-united-states/.

[39]. Eric Geiger, Muslim Girls in Austria Fighting Forced Marriages, S.F. Chron., Dec. 4, 2005, at A15.

[40]. Soeren Kern, Germans Stunned by Report on Forced Marriages, Gatestone Inst., Nov. 10, 2011, http://www.gatestoneinstitute.org/2575/german-forced-marriages; Laws in the UK: Forced Marriage Act, http://www.bbc.co.uk/ethics/forcedmarriage/crime_1.shtml (civil protection orders); The Anti-Social Behaviour, Crime and Policing Act 2014, 2014 c.12, Part 10, http://www.legislation.gov.uk/ukpga/2014/12/contents/enacted (criminal penalties); France: Marriage Age for Women Raised to 18, N.Y. Times, Mar. 24, 2006, at A9.

Problems

1. Mr. Patel, an Indian engineer who resides in New Jersey, travels to India to seek a wife of the same caste. A marriage broker arranges a match with Ms. Navitlal. They meet twice to discuss marriage and their respective backgrounds. Ms. Navitlal informs him that her parents are separated. She does not tell him that her mother is living with a person of a different caste. The couple is married in a civil ceremony, and the marriage is consummated. Mr. Patel returns to the United States but later returns to India, where he undergoes a religious ceremony with his wife. He later testifies that he underwent the Hindu ceremony only because of threats by his wife's brothers. Ms. Navitlal tires of waiting for her husband to send for her and travels to the United States. There, she discovers that her husband has no desire to live with her. He asserts that she married him for the sole purpose of gaining entry into the United States. He files for annulment. She counterclaims for divorce. What result? Patel v. Navitlal, 627 A.2d 683 (N.J. Super. Ct. Ch. Div. 1992).

2. Larry and Joy Farr have been married for 30 years. They divorce in 1999. They then remarry each other in 2004. According to Joy, she remarried Larry because he told her that he had a terminal illness (myelodysplastic syndrome) and that his death was imminent. In fact, at the time of their conversation, Larry showed Joy his medical records, but the records indicated that his disease had not progressed yet to a terminal form. Because Joy was unfamiliar with the medical terminology, though, she believed Larry's version of his prognosis. Three years later, Larry does not appear to be ill. His medical records confirm the state of his good health. Joy petitions for an annulment of their second marriage, alleging that Larry defrauded her into remarrying him by misrepresenting the seriousness of his illness. She testifies at trial (with confirmation by several of her friends) that she only agreed to remarry him because she believed that he was dying and she did not want him to die alone. Is this type of misrepresentation, if proven, grounds for annulment? What result based on the various tests for fraud? See In re Marriage of Farr, 228 P.3d 267 (Colo. 2010).

NOTE: MARRIAGE FRAUD IN IMMIGRATION

Marriage to a U.S. citizen exempts an alien from the quota restrictions of the Immigration and Nationality Act (INA), 8 U.S.C. §1151(a), (b), thereby avoiding lengthy delays in entering the country. According to the Act, a U.S. citizen can petition on behalf of designated "immediate relatives" (defined as a legal spouse, child, or parent) in order to adjust the relatives' legal permanent residence status (entitling them to "green cards"). This rule contributes to a strong incentive for aliens to marry U.S. citizens. Marriage fraud in immigration has been a long-standing problem—sometimes on a grand scale. In 2019, nearly 100 people were indicted in one massive marriage fraud scheme in Houston, Texas, that was aimed at securing green cards for Vietnamese nationals. The criminal activity led to the creation of over 500 sham marriages.[41]

Penalties for marriage fraud are strict. Individuals who knowingly enter into a marriage for the purpose of evading any provision of the immigration laws shall be imprisoned for not more than five years, or fined not more than $250,000, or both. Immigration and Nationality Act §275(c), 8 U.S.C. §1325(c). In addition, those charged with marriage fraud may be charged with immigration fraud, mail fraud, harboring an alien, conspiracy, or making false statements on federal documentation.

In the past several decades, an international marriage broker (IMB) industry has flourished. Congressional findings suggest that a substantial number of mail-order marriages are fraudulent. See Illegal Immigration Reform and Immigrant Responsibility Act (IIRIRA), (8 U.S.C. §1375a). The Internet contributed to the rapid growth of the mail-order industry. Until 1996, mail-order matchmaking was largely unregulated. In that year, Congress enacted §652 of the IIRIRA to obligate international marriage brokers to require American clients to submit to extensive background checks (about previous marriages and criminal histories) and then to disclose this information to mail-order brides. International marriage brokers must also disseminate information to foreign clients about the "battered spouse waiver" for conditional permanent residents, enacted as part of the Violence Against Women Act of 1994 (VAWA) (8 U.S.C. §1154(a)(1)(A)(iii)), which allows battered immigrant women to apply for permanent legal residence without their abusive citizen spouse's participation. (Before VAWA, immigration law mandated the cooperation of the citizen spouse in order for the alien spouse to obtain lawful status.)

To remedy shortcomings in the VAWA legislation, Congress enacted the Battered Immigrant Women Protection Act of 2000 as part of the Victims of Trafficking and Violence Protection Act, Pub. L. No. 106-386, 114 Stat. 1464, §§1501-1513. This law facilitates self-petitioning by abused spouses, expands the categories of eligible spouses, and establishes a special visa for those victims of domestic violence who are not eligible for self-petition or cancellation of deportation. In 2005, Congress enacted the International Marriage Broker Regulation Act (IMBRA) as part of the reauthorization of VAWA, Pub. L. No. 109-162, 119 Stat. 2960, to prohibit IMBs from providing contact information about minors, require IMBs to advise foreign clients of the rights and resources for victims of domestic violence, require sharing of criminal background checks with the foreign fiancée or spouse, and prohibit simultaneous petitions for visas for multiple fiancées.

With the reauthorization of VAWA in 2013, Congress improved oversight of the mail-order bride industry by authorizing the Attorney General to designate a specific office to bring criminal or civil charges against IMBs that violate IMBRA (S. 47, 113th Cong. Title VIII, §808(a)(2)(A)); mandating recordkeeping by IMBs

---

[41]. U.S. Immigration and Customs Enforcement, News Release, Mastermind Behind Massive Marriage Fraud Conspiracy Sentenced to 10 Years in Prison Following Investigation by HSI Houston, Federal Partners, Oct. 27, 2022, https://www.ice.gov/news/releases/mastermind -behind-massive-marriage-fraud-conspiracy-sentenced-10-years-prison.

showing their compliance with background checks and age requirements for foreign brides (§808(3)(A)(ii)); and providing penalties for clients who lie or fail to disclose a violent or criminal history (§808(4)(B)). For a famous case imposing liability on an IMB, see Fox v. Encounters Int'l, 2006 WL 952317 (4th Cir. 2006).

b. Procedural Requirements

(i) Licensure and Solemnization

CARABETTA v. CARABETTA

438 A.2d 109 (Conn. 1980)

PETERS, Associate Justice. . . .

The plaintiff and the defendant exchanged marital vows before a priest in the rectory of Our Lady of Mt. Carmel Church of Meriden, on August 25, 1955, according to the rite of the Roman Catholic Church, although they had failed to obtain a marriage license. Thereafter they lived together as husband and wife, raising a family of four children, all of whose birth certificates listed the defendant as their father. [After a 20-year marriage, the wife petitioned for divorce. The husband sought dismissal of her claim, arguing that the court lacked jurisdiction because the marriage was void.] Until the present action, the defendant had no memory or recollection of ever having denied that the plaintiff and the defendant were married.

The issue before us is whether, under Connecticut law, despite solemnization according to an appropriate religious ceremony, a marriage is void where there has been noncompliance with the statutory requirement of a marriage. This is a question of first impression in this state. The trial court held that failure to obtain a marriage license was a flaw fatal to the creation of a legally valid marriage and that the court therefore lacked subject matter jurisdiction over an action for dissolution. We disagree with the court's premise and hence with its conclusion.

. . . The governing statutes at the time of the purported marriage between these parties contained two kinds of regulations concerning the requirements for a legally valid marriage. One kind of regulation concerned substantive requirements determining those eligible to be married. Thus General Statutes (Rev. 1949) §7301 declared the statutorily defined degrees of consanguinity within which a "marriage shall be void." . . . For present purposes, it is enough to observe that, on this appeal, no such substantive defect has been alleged or proven.

The other kind of regulation concerns the formalities prescribed by the state for the effectuation of a legally valid marriage. These required formalities, in turn, are of two sorts: a marriage license and a solemnization. In Hames v. Hames, [316 A.2d 379 (1972)], we interpreted our statutes not to make void a marriage consummated after the issuance of a license but deficient for want of due solemnization.

Today we examine the statutes in the reverse case, a marriage duly solemnized but deficient for want of a marriage license.

As to licensing, the governing statute in 1955 was a section entitled "Marriage licenses." It provided, in subsection (a): "No persons shall be joined in marriage until both have joined in an application . . . for a license for such marriage." Its only provision for the consequence of noncompliance with the license requirement was contained in subsection (e): ". . . any person who shall join any persons in marriage without having received such (license) shall be fined not more than one hundred dollars." General Statutes (Rev. 1949) §7302, as amended by §1280b (1951 Supp.) and by §2250c (1953 Supp.). Neither this section, nor any other, described as void a marriage celebrated without license. . . .

In the absence of express language in the governing statute declaring a marriage void for failure to observe a statutory requirement, this court has held in an unbroken line of cases . . . that such a marriage, though imperfect, is dissoluble rather than void. . . . Then as now, the legislature had chosen to use the language of voidness selectively, applying it to some but not to all of the statutory requirements for the creation of a legal marriage. Now as then, the legislature has the competence to choose to sanction those who solemnize a marriage without a marriage license rather than those who marry without a marriage license. In sum, we conclude that the legislature's failure expressly to characterize as void a marriage properly celebrated without a license means that such a marriage is not invalid.

The plaintiff argues strenuously that our statutes, far from declaring void a marriage solemnized without a license, in fact validate such a marriage whenever it has been solemnized by a religious ceremony. The plaintiff calls our attention to the language of §7306, as amended, that "all marriages . . . solemnized according to the forms and usages of any religious denomination in this state shall be valid." To the extent that this language suggests greater validity for a marriage solemnized by a religious ceremony than for one solemnized by a civil ceremony, it is inconsistent with other provisions of the statutes with regard to solemnization and licensing. It has long been clear that, under our laws, all authority to join parties in matrimony is basically secular. . . . Whatever may be its antecedents, for present purposes it is sufficient to note that §7306 at the very least reenforces our conclusion that the marriage in the case before us is not void.

The conclusion that a ceremonial marriage contracted without a marriage license is not null and void finds support, furthermore, in the decisions in other jurisdictions. In the majority of states, unless the licensing statute plainly makes an unlicensed marriage invalid, "the cases find the policy favoring valid marriages sufficiently strong to justify upholding the unlicensed ceremony. This seems the correct result. Most such cases arise long after the parties have acted upon the assumption that they are married, and no useful purpose is served by avoiding the long-standing relationship." [Homer Clark, Law of Domestic Relations 41 (1968)].

Since the marriage that the trial court was asked to dissolve was not void, the trial court erred in granting the motion to dismiss. . . .

Wedding ceremonies vary significantly, as the excerpts below demonstrate.

Harriette Cole, Jumping the Broom: The African-American Wedding Planner
16-18 (1993)

When West Africans were brought forcibly to these shores some four hundred years ago, they were stripped of much of what was theirs. [A]fter the beginning of slavery, Africans were also denied the right to marry in the eyes of the law. Slaveholders apparently thought that their captives were not real people but were, instead, property to be bought and sold. As such, they had no rights. Further, if allowed formally to marry and live together, slaves might find strength in numbers that could lead to revolt. . . .

Yet the enslaved were spiritual people who had been taught rituals that began as early as childhood to prepare them for that big step into family life. . . . Out of their creativity came the tradition of jumping the broom. The broom itself held spiritual significance for many African peoples, representing the beginning of homemaking for a couple. For the Kgatla people of southern Africa, it was customary, for example, on the day after the wedding for the bride to help the other women in the family to sweep the courtyard clean, thereby symbolizing her willingness and obligation to assist in housework at her in-laws' residence until the couple moved to their own home. During slavery . . . a couple would literally jump over a broom into the seat of matrimony. Today, this tradition and many others are finding their way back into the wedding ceremony.

Stephanie Cain, A Gay Wedding Is a Wedding, Just a Wedding
N.Y. Times, Aug. 16, 2018
https://www.nytimes.com/2018/08/16/fashion/weddings/a-gay-wedding-is-a-wedding-just-a-wedding.html

When Jove Meyer, a wedding and event planner in Brooklyn, is working with a same-sex couple, he sometimes finds himself cringing when he hears a guest use the term "gay wedding." "But the couple is not getting 'gay' married. They are getting married. They're not having a 'gay wedding.' They're having a wedding. . . ."

. . . Mr. Meyer, who also advocates for the L.G.B.T.Q. community and identifies as a gay man, explained that labeling same-sex couples as different from any other wedding is the root of the cause. The qualifier to describe the wedding signals that it's unlike a wedding of a heterosexual couple. [He explains]: "The biggest mistake is when guests try to insert a same-sex couple into a heteronormative wedding story, so someone's got to be the man and someone's got to be the woman," Mr. Meyer said. For example, at a wedding for two brides, guests may wonder, even if jokingly, which woman will wear a pantsuit. To Mr.

Meyer, that's an oversimplification, since brides may both wear dresses, both don pants, or arrive in entirely untraditional attire altogether. The outfit may not even be white. . . .

"We also had several people ask us which one proposed to the other," Tanya Terry-Miller said [about her wedding to Emma Terry-Miller in Orem, Utah], noting that they both proposed to each other. "It creates an awkward moment with that question because it draws attention to the lack of a male getting down on one knee to propose to the woman—what is considered a 'normal' proposal." . . .

That extends to the walk down the aisle. Mr. Meyer noted that often same-sex couples invent ways to change what is thought of as a traditional ceremony. It's not necessarily one person at the altar and the other walking in with a bouquet. His couples have walked in together. Some have their parents join them on the walk. . . .

Families have drama no matter what the dynamic, but it's often more complex for same-sex couples. Not all loved ones are accepting when their child comes out, and that may result in the child being kicked out of the house or the relationship cut off entirely. Fast forward to the wedding, and the families may not want to attend the nuptials. . . .

Many same-sex couples also worry about how their public displays of affection are perceived during the celebration. [Wedding photographer Derek Chad Marsh], who notes that 90 percent of the weddings he shoots are with same-sex couples, explained that he has never seen a heterosexual couple worry about how they look while holding hands, kissing, or dancing. . . .

The best thing a guest can do is arrive at the wedding sans preconceived notions of how the day will go. . . . "Prepare by getting your dancing shoes ready, a cute outfit and retraining your brain to change your terminology," Mr. Meyer suggested. . . .

Notes and Questions

1. Licensure requirements. Statutes in almost all jurisdictions provide for the issuance of marriage licenses. Yet, the strong public policy favoring marriage validity gives rise to the rule announced in *Carabetta* that a violation of formality requirements, such as the failure to obtain a marriage license, will not invalidate a marriage. This rule operates unless the jurisdiction has a statute *expressly* making a marriage invalid without a license. See, e.g., N.B. v. F.W., 91 N.Y.S.3d 660 (N.Y. Sup. Ct. 2019) (upholding a marriage, performed without a license, because the relevant statute was only directory).

Three justifications exist for licensure statutes: (1) they aid in enforcing marriage laws by requiring persons not qualified to marry for reasons of age, health, or existing marital status to disclose such information; (2) they serve as public health measures by preventing marriages that would be damaging to the health of one spouse or would produce unhealthy children; and (3) licensure serves as proof that the marriage has occurred.

2. Solemnization. States mandate not only a marriage license but also solemnization by an authorized individual. Such persons include religious officials (for example, clergy) and some government officials. See, e.g., Ala. Code §30-1-9 (probate judges); Kan. Stat. Ann. §23-2505 (county clerks or judges). See also Universal Life Church v. Utah, 189 F. Supp. 2d 1302 (D. Utah 2002) (challenging statute prohibiting ordination of minister by mail and the Internet).

3. Formalities.

a. Where, how long, how much. Statutes in half the states require that licenses be procured in the county where one party resides or where the marriage is to be performed. The marriage license generally expires within a short time (typically 30 to 60 days).

Some states insist on the presence of both parties to apply for a license, while other states allow only one party to apply by affidavit. This dual-presence requirement sometimes poses a problem. For example, in *Obergefell* (discussed earlier in this chapter), one of the same-sex partner plaintiffs was too ill to cross state lines—which he needed to do twice: to apply for the license and also to get married. As a result, the couple chose to marry in Maryland, where only one party was required to apply for a marriage license.

Marriage license fees range from $24 (Rhode Island) to $80 (Arizona). Many states reduce the fee if the couple attends premarital counseling. In some states, fees fund domestic violence shelters. See, e.g., Cal. Welf. & Inst. Code §18305; Fla. Stat. Ann. §741.01. Does such a fee unconstitutionally interfere with the right to marry? See Jacobsen v. King, 971 N.E.2d 620 (Ill. App. Ct. 2012).

b. Waiting periods. The majority of jurisdictions require a waiting period (one to five days) between issuance of the license and the ceremony. What explains this requirement? Waiting periods can be waived for exigent circumstances.

4. Premarital blood tests. Many states have abolished the requirement of premarital blood tests. The enactment of these requirements in the early twentieth century stemmed from concerns about eugenics, urbanization, rising rates of immigration, and the pervasive sexual double standard that reflected fears of the consequences for innocent young women of men's "sowing their wild oats."

5. Effectiveness of procedural requirements. Do licensure statutes accomplish their purposes? For example, do they aid in the detection of marriages in which one partner already has a spouse? Does the possibility of sanctions, such as a penalty for perjury on a license application, deter violations? How can we enforce licensure statutes if a marriage is held to be valid in the absence of a license? Alternatively, are waiting periods effective? Do they represent unnecessary state paternalism? Are they constitutional? Do they meet the *Zablocki* standard? Finally, what purpose underlies the solemnization requirement by authorized persons?

6. Abolition of marriage licenses. The Alabama legislature enacted a law in 2019 (amending Ala. Code §§ 22-9A-17, 30-1-5, 30-1-12, & 30-1-16) that abolished marriage licenses in the state and replaced them with a system of marriage certificates and signed affidavits that are downloadable online. The measure was enacted because some probate judges responded to *Obergefell* by ceasing to issue marriage licenses to *anyone* (rather than issue marriage licenses to gay couples). Apparently, the change was made to ensure that no state official would be required to issue marriage licenses to same-sex couples. Thus, the new law changes the role of the probate judge from issuance of marriage licenses to mere recordation of affidavits.

Problems

1. Anna and Dickie are involved in a sexual relationship. Dickie tells Anna that his family believes that he will go to hell if they do not marry. He proposes a "fake" ceremony, and she agrees. They have a ceremony, solemnized by a minister, but fail to file the marriage license with the county clerk within 60 days of issuance as required by statute. Instead, Anna burns the license with Dickie's knowledge and consent. They live together for almost two months. Later, Dickie files for divorce and a division of property. Anna responds by denying the existence of the marriage or, in the alternative, for an order annulling the marriage on the basis of fraudulent inducement. What result? See Fryar v. Roberts, 57 S.W.3d 727 (Ark. 2001).

2. Deborah and Richard decide to marry during an extraordinarily busy time in their lives when they are in the midst of buying a new house and Richard is starting a new business. They set a wedding date, but neither of them obtains the necessary marriage license. When the rabbi arrives to perform the ceremony, he is surprised to learn about the absence of the license. Nonetheless, he and the couple decide to "deal with that problem later" because everyone is gathered for the wedding. Two weeks after the ceremony, the couple obtains the license and mails it to the rabbi who signs it, as of that date, and then submits it to the proper state authorities.

Ten years later, Richard wants to end the couple's relationship. He petitions for a declaration of marital status, contending that the parties were not lawfully married because they did not have a marriage license at the time of the ceremony. The applicable state law requires that "to contract a lawful marriage, the parties must obtain a license and afterward solemnize their union," along with a requirement that "a marriage occur within 60 days after obtaining a license," and a provision attaching a criminal penalty for the performance of a marriage ceremony without a license. What should the court rule? MacDougall v. Levick, 776 S.E.2d 456 (Va. Ct. App. 2015).

3. Traditionally, states require couples' presence within their boundaries for a valid marriage ceremony. In light of modern technology, two law professors propose a reform in marriage procedure (dubbed "E-marriage"). They suggest that states liberalize the rules about marriage procedure by offering marriages to persons outside state boundaries via such means as videoconference, the Internet, and telephone. Evaluate the advantages and disadvantages of this proposal. Do territorial restrictions continue to make sense today?[42]

---

[42]. See generally Adam Candeub & Mae Kuykendall, Modernizing Marriage, 44 U. Mich. J.L. Reform 735 (2011); Mae Kuykendall & Adam Candeub, Symposium Overview: Perspectives on Innovative Marriage Procedure, 2011 Mich. St. L. Rev. 1.

(ii) Note: Procedural Variations

(1) Proxy Marriages

A proxy marriage is one in which at least one party is represented at the ceremony by an agent. Marriage by proxy, once the exclusive practice of royalty, was valid in England until the mid-nineteenth century when legislation required the presence of both parties at the ceremony. Marriage by proxy has been most common in the modern era in time of war, frequently to legitimize children. The COVID pandemic also promoted proxy marriages for a limited time.

Another use of proxy marriage is to circumvent immigration laws. Prior to 1924 when Congress prohibited the practice, proxy marriages were valid for immigration purposes so long as the marriage was valid in the country where performed.[43] Proxy marriage has also been used to assist political refugees. See, e.g., Apt v. Apt, 1 All. E.R. 620 (1947) (permitting Jewish refugee from Nazi Germany to marry by proxy in Argentina, where husband resided). Yet another group resorting to proxy marriages is prisoners. Courts are suspect about the use of proxies in deathbed ceremonies. See, e.g., In re Estate of Crockett, 728 N.E.2d 765 (Ill. App. Ct. 2000).

States that allow proxy marriages generally require the presence of *either* the bride or groom. Until recently, Montana was the only state that permitted a "double-proxy" wedding, in which both parties were represented by proxies. The dramatic increase in such marriages there, stemming from Internet publicity, led the state legislature to enact an amendment (Mont. Code Ann. §40-1-301) requiring that at least one party be either a state resident or a member of the armed services on active duty.

Proxy marriages experienced a surge in popularity during the pandemic. In fact, Montana witnessed a sizable increase in the marriage rate in 2020, leading to the highest marriage rate recorded in the state in over 30 years – especially by military personnel who were not allowed to leave their bases during lockdown.[44]

Federal law reflects inconsistent treatment of proxy marriages by its recognition of such marriages for federal survivorship benefits but not for immigration purposes absent subsequent consummation. Thus, in a highly publicized case, a Marine died in combat in Iraq one month after he married his pregnant Japanese fiancée by proxy. Although his widow was able to collect social security survivor benefits, she was denied permission to emigrate to the United States to raise their child with her husband's family in Tennessee because the marriage was unconsummated *after* the ceremony due to the husband's deployment.[45]

---

[43]. 8 U.S.C. §224(m) (1924) (superseded by 8 U.S.C. §1101(a)(35) (2006)) (the terms "spouse," "wife," or "husband" do not include a spouse, wife, or husband by reason of any marriage ceremony where the contracting parties thereto are not physically present in the presence of each other, unless the marriage shall have been consummated).

[44]. See Sharon Lurye, States Where Marriage Rates Plummeted During the Pandemic. U.S. News & World Report, May 18, 2022, https://www.usnews.com/news/best-states/articles/2022-05 -18/states-with-the-biggest-drop-in-marriage-rates-in-2020.

[45]. Associated Press, Marine's Widow, Baby in Immigration Limbo, Sept. 17, 2009, http://www .nbcnews.com/id/32891829/ns/us_news-life/print/1/displaymode/1098/. See generally Kathryn Rae Edwards, Note, Kicking the INA out of Bed: Abolishing the Consummation Requirement for Proxy Marriages, 22 Hastings Women's L.J. 55 (2011).

(2) Other Variations

Some states provide for other variations that dispense with licensure or solemnization requirements. A few states permit marriage by declaration (e.g., Mont. Code Ann. §40-1-311; Tex. Fam. Code Ann. §§2.401-2.402). Others permit marriage by contracts acknowledged before a judge (e.g., N.Y. Dom. Rel. Law §11(4)). Unlike a marriage by declaration, however, the parties to a marriage by contract first must obtain a license. California permits "confidential marriages," which enable a couple to dispense with procuring a license, filing a health certificate, and filing a marriage certificate open to the public (but requiring a ceremony before an authorized official). The purpose is to encourage cohabitants to legalize their relationship and legitimize children. Cal. Fam. Code §§500-536. Finally, tribal marriages, contracted according to Native American laws or customs, are also recognized in some jurisdictions. See, e.g., Nev. Rev. Stat. Ann. §122.170.

c. Informal Marriages

(i) Common Law Marriage

JENNINGS v. HURT

N.Y. L.J., Oct. 4, 1989, at 24 (Sup. Ct. N.Y. Cty), *aff'd*, 554 N.Y.S.2d 220 (App. Div. 1990), *appeal denied*, 568 N.Y.S.2d 347 (N.Y. 1991)

Justice SILBERMANN.

[Plaintiff, Sandra Jennings, alleged the existence of a common-law marriage. Defendant, actor William Hurt, moved to dismiss.]

South Carolina is one of thirteen states (including the District of Columbia) that recognize common-law marriages. South Carolina became a common-law state early in the eighteenth century when it adopted the law of common-law marriage which was recognized in the Ecclesiastic Courts in England. . . .

Sandra Jennings (left) and Oscar-winning actor William Hurt, the parties in Jennings v. Hurt

South Carolina law is aptly stated in the case of Fryer v. Fryer, S.C. Eq. 85 (S.C. App. 1832):

Marriage, with us, so far as the law is concerned has ever been regarded as a mere civil contract. Our law prescribes no ceremony. It required nothing but the agreement of the parties, with an intention that the agreement shall, per se, constitute the marriage. They may express the agreement by parol, they may signify it by whatever ceremony their whim, or their taste, or their religious belief, may select: it is the agreement itself, and not the form in which it is couched, which constitutes the contract. The words used, or the ceremony performed, are mere evidence of a present intention and agreement of the parties. . . .

Although common-law marriages were abolished in New York as of April 29, 1933, New York does give effect to common-law marriages if they are recognized as valid under the law of the state in which it was supposedly contracted.

The sole question to be decided by this court is whether Sandra Jennings is the common-law wife of William Hurt. Since it is conceded that the parties never had a ceremonial marriage, the answer to that question rests upon certain events that allegedly transpired during the parties' stay in South Carolina and the law of South Carolina. . . .

Jennings and Hurt met in Saratoga, New York, in the summer of 1981 while each of them was working there. Shortly thereafter, upon their return to New York City, the parties began living together. [They ceased living together in 1984.] At the time their relationship began, Jennings knew Hurt was still married. The parties had many discussions in which Hurt explained to Jennings his disappointment at his own failure in marriage and his family's history in terms of failed marriages. Hurt frequently discussed his belief that marriage was a promise or a commitment to "God" and that he was experiencing "dismay about having broken that promise." Because of his feelings and pain relating to this subject, Hurt explained that marriage was "not in the cards" for him. This is corroborated by Hurt's conversation with Mary Beth Hurt when he asked for a divorce. Jennings herself stated "he wanted me to know that he did not necessarily mean a marital commitment. . . ."

In the Spring of 1982 Jennings became pregnant. Hurt's counsel began drafting an agreement governing the parties' financial arrangements of living together and for the support of the expected child. The earliest of these agreements is dated May 1982. The pregnancy prompted Hurt to commence divorce proceedings to terminate his marriage to Mary Beth Hurt. In September 1982, Hurt went to see his former wife to tell her he wanted to finalize the divorce since "Sandy is having a baby."

On October 31, 1982, Jennings joined Hurt in South Carolina where he was already engaged in the filming of "The Big Chill." During their stay in South Carolina from October 31, 1982, to January 10, 1983, the parties lived in the same house and shared a bed. Their social circle consisted of the cast and others connected with the film project. During this period as well as earlier and later times, their relationship was volatile and permeated by arguments.

On December 3, 1982, Hurt's divorce became final. He learned this sometime later from counsel. Jennings testified that she learned of his divorce on December 27, 1982 when he approached her with another version of the "prenuptial agreement" that had been the subject of negotiations between the parties and their counsel. That on that date he said they should sign the agreement, have blood tests and get married. Parenthetically, it is noted that South Carolina does not require blood tests in order to obtain a marriage license. She testified that they then went to a Notary Public to get the agreement signed and returned home. Hurt then spoke to his attorney and after that conversation a fight ensued in which he stated Jennings had tricked him, that the agreement was not valid because she did not have legal counsel. Jennings then allegedly went into the bedroom and started packing to go home to her mother, whereupon Hurt, according to Jennings, . . . "threw my suitcase on the ground and we had a huge fight and he ended up telling me that it didn't matter because as far as he was concerned we were married in the eyes of God and we had a spiritual marriage and this didn't matter. We were more married than married people." Jennings' claim to be Hurt's common-law wife is based inter alia, on these events. . . .

Documents admitted in evidence indicate [that] on December 27, 1982, Hurt's signature was notarized on the document entitled "Paternity Acknowledgment"; that on December 28, 1982, Jennings' signature was notarized on a sublease for her New York apartment, and that on December 28, 1982, Jennings spoke with someone at her attorneys' telephone number for 17 minutes. [T]he undisputed fact that Hurt signed a paternity acknowledgment on [December 27, 1982] is inconsistent with any immediate intention to marry, but is consistent with Hurt's testimony that though his commitment to his child was unequivocal, he had deep reservations about his relationship with Jennings.

The only evidence introduced of a holding forth as husband and wife while the parties were in South Carolina was a conversation with [lessors] in connection with the parties' renting of accommodations for their stay in South Carolina in which Hurt allegedly referred to Jennings as his wife and a telephone call by Hurt to Jennings' obstetrician, Dr. Credle's office, in which he asked about his "wife." The conversation with the [lessors] occurred on October 31, 1982 and thus is irrelevant because it predates the removal of the impediment to marriage. The date of the conversation with Dr. Credle is unknown but in any event is of little significance.

It is clear . . . that the community with whom the parties socialized knew Jennings and Hurt were not married. Nor is there a preponderance of credible evidence that the parties held themselves out as husband and wife after December 27, 1982. There is no evidence that Jennings filed tax returns or other forms as married. Significantly, the one document on which Jennings is alleged to have her name "Sandra Cronsberg Hurt" is clearly an altered xerox copy of the original with "Hurt" added afterwards and the document re-xeroxed. Indeed, documents signed by Hurt prior to the commencement of a lawsuit, i.e., will, pension, jury form—all indicated he considered himself single. Hurt's accountant testified that but for one tax return, where by error, the box "married" was checked, all taxes have been filed by Hurt as "single."

The testimony of persons who worked for Jennings for several months, years ago, and who each remember one isolated incident of Hurt referring to Jennings as his "wife" is unbelievable and even if true is barely relevant to prove a holding forth as husband and wife. Scheible, Hurt's employee's testimony is rejected as totally unworthy of belief. She appears as a disgruntled former employee attempting to get even as well as protect her own interests in a lawsuit. . . .

The courts of South Carolina [are] reluctant to declare a common-law marriage unless the proof of such marriage is shown by strong and competent testimony. . . . Jennings's claim that a common-law marriage existed stems, to a large extent, from her present recollection of Hurt's alleged utterance after an argument on December 27, 1982, about seven years ago, that as far as he was concerned they were married in the eyes of God and had a spiritual marriage. To which utterance Jennings says she agreed. Even were this court to find this testimony credible, the event described by Jennings and the words allegedly spoken do not evince an "intent" to solemnize a marriage but rather the kind of words used by one desiring to continue the parties' present state of living together, i.e., in a relationship short of marriage. . . .

Moreover, where as in this case, the relationship began while one of them was already married, a subsequent divorce does not per se transform this illicit relationship into a common-law marriage. Instead the prior relationship is presumed to continue and the party claiming a common-law marriage must show by a preponderance of the evidence that the relationship underwent some fundamental change following the removal of the impediment. . . . Accordingly, it would be incumbent on Jennings to show an agreement to enter a common-law marriage after the impediment was removed. . . . The evidence shows a paucity of any "declaration or acknowledgement of the parties" of a marital state. Not one friend of either of the parties testified that the parties held themselves out as married.

Indeed, [a cast member] testified that at his wedding Jennings "wished us luck and that we have a good marriage and expressed the hope that she would be next." This statement belies any change in the relationship of the parties having taken place on December 27 or 28, 1982. It indicates that the prior illicit relationship continued although a hope, at least by one of the parties, to one day marry existed. . . .

For all the foregoing reasons the court finds that Sandra Jennings is not the common-law wife of William Hurt.

Notes and Questions

1. **Epilogue.** Jennings sought equitable distribution of Hurt's assets of $5 to $7 million. Following their separation, Hurt began paying $60,000 annually in child support despite Jennings's request for $192,000. During the litigation, Hurt married someone else. Subsequently, an appellate court affirmed the judgment in Hurt's favor. 554 N.Y.S.2d 220, 221 (App. Div. 1990). Jennings and Hurt's son, Alex, completed a graduate degree in acting from New York University and acted alongside his father in a Harold Pinter play in Oregon. South Carolina (the setting of the principal case) abolished common law marriage prospectively in 2019. See Stone v. Thompson, 833 S.E.2d 266 (S.C. 2019). Hurt died of pancreatic cancer in 2022.

2. **Historical background.** American jurisdictions, which adopted common law marriage, followed English ecclesiastical law. Following the Norman Conquest, when ecclesiastical authorities regulated marriage in England, the Church recognized two types of informal marriage: (1) the exchange of promises to be husband and wife from the present moment; and (2) the exchange of promises to be husband and wife in the future, followed by sexual intercourse. Under the second form, the marriage became valid on subsequent consummation. Such marriages were recognized until the enactment of Lord Hardwicke's Act, 26 Geo. II, c. 33, in 1753, which required formalities of church ceremony, publication of banns, and a license. Subsequently, informal marriages continued to be valid only beyond the

statute's jurisdiction in Scotland (hence the importance of the first town across the border, Gretna Green) and Ireland.

Professor Lawrence Friedman explains that common law marriage in the United States stemmed from several social conditions:

> [T]here was a shortage of clergymen of every faith in some parts of the United States. Most of the population lived outside the cities; and parts of the country were thinly populated. [Couples] lived together after makeshift ceremonies, or no ceremony at all. . . . The doctrine of common-law marriage allowed the law to treat these "marriages" as holy and valid. . . .
>
> [T]he early settlers were inclined to make a virtue of necessity, or at least come to terms with it. Despite their "pure morals and stern habits," the settlers could not or would not go along with the strict English marriage laws or their American counterparts. . . . This was not just a matter of social stigma: It was a question of who got the farm, the house, the country acreage, the lot in town. . . .[46]

3. Requirements. Common law marriage has four elements: capacity to enter a marital contract, present agreement to be married, cohabitation, and holding out as husband and wife (or, today, as spouses). Fewer than a dozen states currently permit parties to enter into a common law marriage, and many of these states limit the application of the doctrine.[47] See, e.g., Tex. Fam. Code Ann. §2.401 (requiring suit within two years after separation, or else the proponent must overcome a rebuttable presumption that no agreement to marry existed). In some states, common law marriage is permitted only for specific purposes. See, e.g., N.H. Rev. Stat. Ann. §457:39 (recognizing common law marriage only for probate purposes).

Did Jennings and Hurt hold themselves out as married? What is the evidence for and against this position? The main reason for the requirement of a public reputation as man and wife is to prevent fraud. Although an agreement between the parties is necessary, the agreement may be inferred from cohabitation or other circumstantial evidence. How did Jennings attempt to prove their "agreement"? In terms of the standard of proof, most states require clear and convincing evidence.

Jennings also discusses the problem of an impediment: A valid common law marriage cannot come into existence while a prior marriage exists for one spouse. Why? Many jurisdictions require that the parties must renew their "agreement" and meet the other requirements following the removal of the impediment (in Hurt's case, following his divorce).

4. Dissolution or death. Many cases arise at dissolution of the relationship, as in *Jennings*, or at death when the survivor attempts to claim inheritance or health insurance benefits, workers' compensation, or Social Security survivor benefits. One problem in establishing a common law marriage after death is the Dead Man's Act, which prohibits parties from testifying about communications or transactions with the deceased. How is a surviving "spouse" to establish a common

---

[46]. Lawrence M. Friedman, A History of American Law 141-142 (2005).

[47]. Eight jurisdictions still permit common law marriage: Colorado, District of Columbia, Iowa, Kansas, Montana, New Hampshire, South Carolina, and Texas. World Population Rev., Common Law Marriage States, 2023, https://worldpopulationreview.com/state-rankings/common-law-marriage-states.

law marriage in the face of this statute? See Elk Mountain Ski Resort v. Workers' Compensation Appeal Bd., 114 A.3d 27 (Pa. Commw. Ct. 2015).

5. Choice of law. Can a couple who are domiciliaries in a non-common law jurisdiction obtain marital status by virtue of residing in another jurisdiction that does recognize common law marriage, and then returning to the non–common law marriage state? Why did the New York court look to South Carolina law to determine whether the two New Yorkers had entered a common law marriage, given New York's abolition of common law marriage?

A common misconception is that the parties must cohabit for a specified period of time. How long a stay in the non-domiciliary state is sufficient to confer common law marital status? A few days? Compare Kennedy v. Damron, 268 S.W.2d 22 (Ky. 1954) (mere visits are not enough), with Madewell v. United States, 84 F. Supp. 329 (E.D. Tenn. 1949) ("a number of days and nights" sufficient), and Metropolitan Life Ins. Co. v. Holding, 293 F. Supp. 854 (E.D. Va. 1968) (one year sufficient). The equities of the situation often influence courts.

6. Common law marriage and same-sex couples. *Obergefell* required that same-sex couples be permitted to enter marriage on the same terms as opposite-sex couples. In the wake of *Obergefell*, several states conferred common law marriage status *retroactively* as a means of providing rights and benefits to same-sex partners who were barred from entering ceremonial marriages by state laws that were subsequently declared unconstitutional. Retroactive application is especially important for determination of eligibility to some benefits (Social Security benefits, spousal support) that require a certain marriage duration. See Problem 3 below.

7. Policy. Would you support a revival of common law marriage? Commentators suggest that failure to recognize the doctrine has adverse consequences for women and minorities, especially for low-income individuals.[48] In contrast, critics of the doctrine point to modern social conditions (urbanization) that have eliminated the need for it, the need to prevent fraud in the transmission of property, confusion of public records, problems of proof, the desire to enforce health-related marital requirements through the licensing process, and administrative judicial efficiency. Which arguments are most convincing? In the face of this debate, UMDA includes alternative provisions of §211.

Problems

1. Sandra, a university student, begins dating the baseball player Dave Winfield. The couple spends frequent time in California, New Jersey, and Texas. After Sandra becomes pregnant, they discuss marriage. Dave, concerned about his

---

[48]. See Goran Lind, Common Law Marriage: A Legal Institution 955-1072 (2008); Cynthia Grant Bowman, A Feminist Proposal to Bring Back Common Law Marriage, 75 Or. L. Rev. 709, 769-770 (1996); Sarah Primrose, The Decline of Common Law Marriage and the Unrecognized Cultural Effect, 34 Whittier L. Rev. 187 (2013).

image as fathering a nonmarital child, tells Sandra he wants a private ceremony (just the two of them). He instructs Sandra to make a reservation at the Amfac Hotel under the name "Mr. and Mrs. David Winfield." After a three-day stay in the honeymoon suite, Sandra tells her mother she and Dave are married. She rents a condo in Houston for them; the name "Winfield" is on the mailbox. Dave pays for rent, food, furniture, medical, and travel expenses. Pursuant to Dave's instructions, Sandra continues to use her surname and signs the baby's birth certificate with her name.

A neighbor, who gave a party in their honor, is prepared to testify that she thought they were married. Further, when the couple vacations in the Bahamas, a local newspaper describes them as "husband and wife," as does an announcer at a softball game. Dave does not contradict this or ask for retraction. Sandra files income tax returns and health insurance forms as single, per Dave's instructions. She does not wear a wedding ring. While living with Sandra, Dave is dating other women, one of whom he eventually marries. Sandra files for divorce, claiming she is his common law wife. Dave testifies that he never agreed to be married, bought the condo to provide for his child and, further, does not recall staying at the Amfac Hotel at all. Texas recognizes common law marriage, although California and New Jersey do not. What result? Winfield v. Renfro, 821 S.W.2d 640 (Tex. App. 1991).

2. Maurice and Anne meet at a restaurant where Anne works as a waitress. Soon thereafter, they move into a home purchased by Maurice and titled in his name. Maurice gives Anne an engagement ring and wedding band and asks her to marry him (although the wedding never takes place). Anne wears the engagement ring but not the wedding band because she does not believe that she has the right to do so without a formal ceremony. A sign outside their home reads "Hunsakers, Home of the Classics" (referring to the classic car business they operate together). The telephone answering message states "This is the Hunsaker residence." A grandfather clock, displayed in the living room, has the letters "A," "M," and "H" intertwined. Anne is listed as Maurice's spouse on his insurance policy. They own stock and a time-share condominium as joint tenants. They keep separate bank accounts because Maurice has poor credit; they file income tax returns that list themselves as single. Maurice is listed as Anne's "significant other" on two hospital consent forms that Anne signed.

Shortly before his death, Maurice tells his attorney that he wants to bequeath his entire estate to Anne, whom he refers to as his "common law wife." He says that if he does not have a will, his family will "eat [Anne] alive." However, before the will can be drafted, Maurice dies. His surviving siblings claim his estate. Anne claims she was his common law wife based on their ten years' cohabitation. The jurisdiction recognizes common law marriage. What result? In re Estate of Hunsaker, 968 P.2d 281 (Mont. 1998).

3. Sabrina Maurer and Kimberly Underwood, longstanding same-sex partners, celebrate a commitment ceremony in Pennsylvania in 2001. They live together in that state until Underwood's death in 2013. Although they wanted to marry, they were unable to do so because Underwood's death occurred six months before Pennsylvania legalized same-sex marriage. Since her partner's death, Maurer has been unsuccessful in her efforts to be recognized as Underwood's spouse and to collect either spousal survivorship rights under Underwood's employer benefits plan or federal Social Security survivor benefits. In addition, Maurer was required to pay inheritance taxes on Underwood's estate that she would not have had to pay if the couple had been legally married. Maurer files suit for a declaratory judgment, claiming that she and her deceased partner had a common law marriage dating from the date of their commitment ceremony in 2001. Pennsylvania law recognized common law marriages until 2004. In that year, the state legislature abolished common law marriage except for those marriages that "occurred prior to January 1, 2005."

Does *Obergefell* establish a constitutional right to common law marriage? After *Obergefell*, must states that allow common law marriage for different-sex couples also allow it for same-sex couples? Does Maurer have a right to retroactive application of the state common law marriage doctrine? What result? See Estate of Underwood, 2015 WL 5052382 (Pa. Com. Pl. Orph., July 29, 2015). See generally Curtis Cook, Note, Same-Sex Common Law Marriage: An Examination of the Constitutionality of State Processes in Determining a Valid Common Law Marriage Post-Obergefell v. Hodges, 55 Creighton L. Rev. 561 (2022).

(ii) The Putative Spouse Doctrine and Other Curative Devices

Courts and legislatures often strain to recognize marriages that fail to comply with the formal requirements. In so doing, they have developed a variety of doctrines that cure or mitigate the harsh consequences of invalidity. The most important of these devices is the putative spouse doctrine. This doctrine recognizes the marriage of an individual who participated in a marriage ceremony in good faith, in the belief that a valid marriage took place and in ignorance of an impediment making the marriage void or voidable (for example, a preexisting marriage). See, e.g., Jahed v. Abraham, 524 P.3d 83 (Nev. Ct. App. 2023) (denying putative spouse status because wife lacked good-faith belief due to her knowledge that couple lacked a marriage license at time of ceremony). Must the good-faith belief be reasonable? Is the standard subjective or objective? See, e.g., Ceja v. Rudolph & Sletten, Inc., 302 P.3d 211 (Cal. 2013) (holding that the proper standard is subjective good faith that does not require the belief to be objectively reasonable).

Section 209 of UMDA takes the following approach:

> Any person who has cohabited with another to whom he is not legally married in the good faith belief that he was married to that person is a putative spouse until knowledge of the fact that he is not legally married terminates his status and prevents acquisition of further rights. A putative spouse acquires the rights conferred upon a legal spouse, including the right to maintenance following termination of his status, whether or not the marriage is prohibited (Section 207) or declared invalid (Section 208). If there is a legal spouse or other putative spouses, rights acquired by a putative spouse do not supersede the rights of the legal spouse or those acquired by other putative spouses, but the court shall apportion property, maintenance, and support rights among the claimants as appropriate in the circumstances and in the interests of justice.

In addition, presumptions can sometimes function as curative devices. Some states attach a presumption of validity to the later of two (or the latest in a series of) marriages. This presumption rests on policies favoring validation of marriages and the need to fulfill parties' expectations. See generally Mark Strasser, Fairness and the Putative Spouse, 81 La. L. Rev. 1235 (2021) (explaining the various state approaches to the putative spouse doctrine and recommending reforms).

Problems

1. When Dr. Norman J. Lewiston, a renowned expert in cystic fibrosis at Stanford University, dies of a heart attack in 1991, three women claim to be his widow. Records reveal that he married Diana Lewiston in 1960 in Connecticut, naming her in a 1966 will as his sole heir. (He suffers his fatal heart attack in the home they share in Palo Alto, California.) They have three children, all now adults. Katy Mayer-Lewiston, who marries him in 1985, attends university events with him. His colleagues believe that she is his wife. The two own a house in a town ten miles away. Robin Phelps of San Diego marries Dr. Lewiston in 1989 during his sabbatical in that city. Believing that he plans to retire soon in San Diego, Robin remains there. See Katherine Bishop, Respected Doctor, Professor and Family Man — 3 Families, in Fact, N.Y. Times, Oct. 23, 1991, at A7. Assume that California's community property law would give half of Dr. Lewiston's property acquired during marriage to the surviving spouse. If all three purported widows seek a share of his estate, to what extent do any of the curative and mitigative devices discussed above help resolve their claims? See also In re Estate of Vargas, 111 Cal. Rptr. 779 (Ct. App. 1974); In re Estate of Collier, 2011 WL 2420989 (Tex. App. 2011).

2. Several couples, noncitizens who reside in Alabama and desire to obtain a license to marry, challenge a policy that was implemented by a probate judge there, requiring non-U.S. citizens who are applicants for marriage licenses to present certain documentation. The policy states: "Non-citizens of the United States must provide proof of legal presence in the United States in the form of valid immigration documents or passport. Each applicant must provide one of the following: (1) an official picture ID; (2) an original certified copy of the state-issued birth certificate and original Social Security card; or (3) U.S. Government-issued Immigration Services Picture ID Card." Neither the Code of Alabama nor the Alabama Constitution requires applicants to provide proof of legal presence to secure a marriage license.

The plaintiffs, who are unable to provide the required documentation, seek declaratory and injunctive relief for violations of their rights to due process and equal protection. In response, the defendant-probate judge contends that the plaintiffs have not sustained any injury and thus lack standing because (1) they have not yet applied for a marriage license; and (2) Alabama recognizes common law marriage, and therefore the couples could simply enter into a common law marriage. What result? Does the availability of common law marriage solve the problem? See Loder v. McKinney, 896 F. Supp. 2d 1116 (M.D. Ala. 2012). See also Buck v. Stankovic, 485 F. Supp. 2d 576 (M.D. Pa. 2007); Ohio ex rel. Ten Residents of Franklin County v. Belskis, 755 N.E.2d 443 (Ohio Ct. App. 2001).

Being Married: Regulation of the Intact Marriage

A. Introduction: The Changing Nature of Marriage

Marriage and the family have evolved over time. Marriage has become more companionate. The family has lost some of its functions, and others have altered. Most of the gendered rules that were once inherent in the institution have been repealed or struck down. Same-sex couples can now marry in all 50 states. Significantly, these and other changes have contributed to an increase in family privacy in some respects—but not always with positive consequences. Despite the increase in family privacy, the state continues to exercise significant control over marriage.

The cases and materials that follow focus on the changing nature of marital rights, roles, and responsibilities. They explore the duty of support during marriage, the regulation of naming, employment, the work-family conflict, the application of tort law to spouses, and evidentiary privileges arising from the marital relationship. This exploration raises important questions: As a matter of law, what are the consequences of being married? How does the law regulate the relationship between the spouses? The relationship between spouses and third parties? To what extent does marriage as a legal institution diverge from marriage as practiced within families? In what ways has the increase in family privacy over time represented a positive versus negative development? Going forward, should state regulation in this realm grow or diminish?

The introductory section of the chapter examines the contemporary nature of marriage, focusing on the significant decline in the marriage rate and its implications for family members, the family, and society.

Joseph Chamie, The End of Marriage in America?

The Hill, Aug. 10, 2021
https://thehill.com/opinion/finance/567107-the-end-of-marriage-in-america/

While it may not have ended, marriage in America has unquestionably declined over the recent past and is now at historic low levels for the country. . . . Since the start of the 21st century, the U.S. marriage rate has declined from more than eight marriages per 1,000 down to six marriages per 1,000 population in 2019. That marriage rate is the lowest level since the U.S. government began keeping marriage records for the country in 1867.

Also, 70 years ago a large majority of U.S. households, approximately 80 percent, were made up of married couples. In 2020, the proportion of households consisting of married couples fell to 49 percent.

Some of the major factors behind the long-term decline in the marriage rate have been female education and labor force participation, women's economic independence and gender equality. America is also experiencing growing numbers of women and men living alone as well as increasing unmarried cohabitation. In addition to the 15 percent of U.S. adults living alone, no less than one-quarter of those aged 25 to 34 years are living with an unmarried partner.

American attitudes about childbearing and marriage have also changed markedly. For example, whereas in 2006 about half of U.S. adults said it was very important for couples having children together to legally marry, by 2020 that proportion had fallen to 29 percent. Today, the proportion of U.S. births to unmarried mothers is about 40 percent, double the percentage in 1980. Other factors that have contributed to lower marriage rates are declining religious adherence to marriage, public disenchantment with marriage, and more recently, unstable jobs and strained finances, particularly among low-income earners and those with only a high school education.

Delaying marriage has also played a role in lower marriage rates. The median ages at first marriage are now 30 years for men and 28 years for women, about eight years higher than the ages in the 1950s. . . . Some suspect that the COVID-19 pandemic may have driven the U.S. marriage rate below the historic low level of 2019. The pandemic's resulting economic insecurity limited socializing, home confinements and anxieties about the future are believed to have contributed to fewer marriages. . . .

The decline in marriage rates is not unique to America. [T]he trends of delayed marriage, increasing cohabitation and remaining single have taken place across the major regions of the world during the past several decades. . . .

The following excerpt reflects the ongoing debate among scholars and researchers about whether the decline in marriage rates is harmful for families and/or for society.

W. Bradford Wilcox, Marriage in Decline: No Big Deal?

Institute of Family Studies, Apr. 1, 2015
http://family-studies.org/marriage-in-decline-yglesias/

[M]arriage is declining and it's no big deal, right? Wrong. . . .

[O]ne of marriage's core social functions [is] attaching men to the children they help to bring into this world. [T]he rituals, customs, and norms associated with marriage have generally increased the odds that men will invest financially, practically, and emotionally in the lives of their children. . . . But because of the decline of marriage, fewer and fewer men have the opportunity to be this kind of father in America, and that matters for them, their kids, and the families that they failed to form or sustain. . . . That's because families formed outside of marriage (or split by divorce) typically end with the kids living with mom, while dad's day-to-day involvement declines.

What's more: because the decline of marriage is concentrated in working-class and poor communities, [these] disconnected dads are most likely to be found in the very communities that can least afford to support lots of single-mother-headed households. . . . The decline of marriage thus ends up being a major contributor to economic inequality, gender inequality, and social inequality. How does that work?

When a man is not married to the mother of his children, both the mother and those children are much less likely to see his money, and to enjoy the economies of scale that come from two parents sharing a household. [This gives rise to] broader economic implications of the growing class divide in marriage and family instability: namely, rising levels of single parenthood in poor and working-class communities, coupled with high levels of marital stability among more educated and affluent communities, necessarily translate into greater economic inequality between these two groups. . . .

The retreat from marriage also fuels two kinds of gender inequality. . . . First, working-class and poor mothers end up carrying a much bigger share of the load associated with raising children than do (absent) fathers: The parent who lives with the children, in most cases the mother, is predictably going to do most of the day-to-day household and child care chores. Second, boys from working-class and poor communities struggle more than their female peers to navigate life without the steady involvement of their fathers. [L]acking a father seems to hurt boys' performance and behavior at school more than girls', and boys may also be less likely to imagine a future tied to work and family life because their own father is not in the picture. . . .

[Finally], marital happiness has *declined* since the divorce revolution. . . . Well-educated Americans who have the financial means and the social skills to navigate today's "more optional and more brittle" soul-mate marriage model [continue to enjoy] high-quality marriages, but less-educated Americans are markedly less happy than they used to be. . . .

These are but a few of the reasons why the nation's retreat from marriage is a big deal. . . . But the bottom line is this: the decline of marriage is a problem because it is one of the primary reasons that the richer and poorer classes in our country are increasingly separate and unequal.[1]

B. Roles and Responsibilities in Marriage

1. The Common Law View

1 William Blackstone, Commentaries
**442-445*

Husband beating his wife, from a 19th-century illustration

By marriage, the husband and wife are one person in law: that is, the very being or legal existence of the woman is suspended during the marriage, or at least is incorporated and consolidated into that of the husband: under whose wing, protection, and *cover,* she performs everything; and is therefore called in our law-French a *feme-covert*; is said to be *covert-baron,* or under the protection and influence of her husband, her baron, or lord; and her condition during her marriage is called her *coverture.* Upon this principle, of a union of person in husband and wife, depend almost all the legal rights, duties, and disabilities, that either of them acquire by the marriage. . . .

For this reason, a man cannot grant anything to his wife, or enter into covenant with her: for the grant would be to suppose her separate existence; and to covenant with her, would be only to covenant with himself. . . . The husband is bound to provide his wife with necessities by law, [and] if she contracts debts for them, he is obliged to pay them: but for anything besides necessaries, he is not chargeable. . . . If the wife be injured in her person or her property, she can bring no action for redress without her

---

[1]. For other studies of the social transformation wrought by the decline of marriage on low-income families, see Paul R. Amato et al., Families in an Era of Increasing Inequality: Diverging Destinies (2014); Naomi Cahn et al., Unequal Family Lives: Causes and Consequences in Europe and the Americas (2018); June Carbone & Naomi Cahn, Marriage Markets: How Inequality Is Remaking the American Family (2014); Andrew J. Cherlin, Labor's Love Lost: The Rise and Fall of the Working-Class Family in America (2014).

husband's concurrence, and in his name, as well as her own: neither can she sue or be sued, without making the husband a defendant. . . . In criminal prosecutions, it is true, the wife may be indicted and punished separately; for the union is only a civil union. But, in trials of any sort, they are not allowed to be evidence for, or against, each other: partly because it is impossible their testimony should be indifferent; but principally because of the union of person.

But, though our law in general considers man and wife as one person, yet there are some instances in which she is separately considered; as inferior to him, and acting by his compulsion. And therefore all deeds executed, and acts done, by her, during her coverture, are void, or at least voidable; [except in a proceeding to avoid her dower rights] in which case she must be solely and secretly examined, to learn if her act be voluntary. She cannot by will devise lands to her husband, [because] she is supposed to be under his coercion. And in some felonies, and other inferior crimes, committed by her, through constraint of her husband, the law excuses her: but this extends not to treason or murder.

The husband also (by the old law) might give his wife moderate correction. For, as he is to answer for her misbehavior, the law thought it reasonable to entrust him with this power of restraining her, by domestic chastisement, in the same moderation that a man is allowed to correct his servants or children; for whom the master or parent is also liable in some cases to answer. But this power of correction was confined within reasonable bounds; and the husband was prohibited to use any violence to his wife [other than what is reasonably necessary to the discipline and correction of the wife].

These are the chief legal effects of marriage during the coverture; upon which we may observe that even the disabilities, which the wife lies under, are for the most part intended for her protection and benefit. So great a favorite is the female sex of the laws of England.

2. Marital Property Regimes

a. Introduction

The state, through its treatment of property acquired during marriage, regulates certain rights of spouses upon marriage. According to the historian Sir William Holdsworth:

No legal system which deals merely with human rules of conduct desires to pry too closely into the relationship of husband and wife. Dealings between husband and wife are for the most part privileged. But some rules it must have to regulate the proprietary relationships of the parties. . . . [2]

---

[2]. 3 W.S. Holdsworth, A History of English Law 404 (2d ed. 1909). See also 2 Frederick Pollock & Frederic William Maitland, The History of English Law Before the Time of Edward I 406 (S.F.C. Milsom ed., 1968) (1898).

Two marital property regimes exist in the United States: (1) the common law approach and (2) the community property approach. Each reflects a different philosophy. In the common law system, followed by most jurisdictions, the husband and wife own all property separately. During marriage, property belongs to the spouse who acquired it (traditionally, the wage-earning husband) unless he chooses another form of ownership.

On the other hand, in the community property system, the husband and wife own some property jointly. Equality of treatment of the spouses is the cardinal rule of the community property system. The community property system is characterized by the concept of a community of ownership under which the spouses are partners. Each spouse has a present, undivided, one-half interest in all property acquired by the efforts of either spouse during marriage. Unlike the common law system, community property recognizes the contributions, for example, of the homemaker spouse. Moreover, the community property system respects each spouse's separate property, such as the property that each brought to the marriage. Separate property also includes property acquired by a spouse during the marriage by means of gift or inheritance.[3] The community property system is in effect in nine states (Arizona, California, Idaho, Louisiana, Nevada, New Mexico, Texas, Washington, and Wisconsin).

b. Common Law Disabilities

The common law and community property systems reflect fundamental differences concerning the position of married women. Until the mid-nineteenth century, Blackstone's famous quotation on coverture, quoted above, described the status of married women at common law. The common law imposed on a married woman many disabilities, summarized below:

(1) *Wife's real property.* The husband acquired an estate in the wife's real property for the duration of the marriage. His interest, termed *jure uxoris,* entitled him to sole possession and control of any real property that the wife owned in fee—whether acquired by her before or after the marriage. If a child was born, the husband's rights became a life estate. Further, the husband could alienate the wife's real property without her consent.

(2) *Dower.* During marriage, the wife's primary protection from her husband's conveyances consisted of her right of dower—her life estate of one-third of any land of which the husband was seised in fee at any time during the marriage. The husband could not bar her dower right without her consent. She came into enjoyment of her dower right if she survived her husband.

(3) *Wife's personal property.* The wife, similarly, had no right to possess personal property. Whatever personal property she owned before marriage, or might

---

[3]. Note, however, that some states' equitable distribution schemes take separate property into account in awarding marital property.

acquire after, became her husband's. She also lacked a right of testamentary disposition.

(4) *Wife's lack of rights to husband's personal property.* During the marriage, the husband had the power of disposition (inter vivos or by will) over his personal property. Similarly, all his personal property (including what we might think of as the wife's property) was subject to his creditors. The only exception was the wife's necessary clothes. However, the husband could sell or give away his wife's jewels, trinkets, or ornaments (termed her "paraphernalia") during his lifetime.

(5) *Husband's liability.* The husband was liable for the wife's premarital debts, as well as for torts she committed before or during the marriage.

(6) *Wife's contracts.* A wife could not execute contracts except as her husband's agent.

The legal status of married women changed little until the nineteenth century when many states enacted Married Women's Property Acts that enabled women to own property that they brought to the marriage or acquired thereafter by gift or inheritance. The movement began in 1839 when Mississippi enacted a statute specifying that the wife could continue to possess slaves she owned prior to marriage or thereafter acquired (although the husband continued to manage them and reap the profits of their labor). New York legislation, the most progressive, enabled married women to sue and to retain their own earnings. By 1865, 29 states had Married Women's Property Acts.[4] These acts significantly liberalized the rules to which married women had been subject for centuries.

c. Managerial Rules

The husband as master of the household was an entrenched common law principle. Paradoxically, the community property system also reflected this rule because statutes placed management of community property in husbands' hands. Limited exceptions to male management and control existed. For example, in many community property states, the wife retained management and control of her earnings. The Supreme Court marked the end of such gender-based rules in Kirchberg v. Feenstra, 450 U.S. 455 (1981), which invalidated, on equal protection grounds, a Louisiana statute designating the husband "head and master" of the community.

Three different, facially gender-neutral rules emerged in response to the unconstitutionality of male managerial rules: (1) extension of the separate property philosophy to link management to the source of earnings; (2) joint control (requiring consent of both spouses for community property transactions); and (3) equal control (either may manage community property regardless of the source of earnings or without the other's consent). Most community property jurisdictions follow the last approach.

---

[4]. See Norma Basch, In the Eyes of the Law: Women, Marriage, and Property in Nineteenth-Century New York 27-28 (1982).

Reforms narrowed the gap between the common law and community property systems. Although title theory determines ownership and management in common law states during an intact marriage, many common law states permit spouses to opt for a tenancy by the entireties in which spouses share the right of control (i.e., neither can alienate or encumber property without the other's consent). At divorce, common law states now follow an equitable distribution approach. Equitable distribution, which attempts to divide marital property in a fair or equitable manner based on a number of factors, purports to achieve more equal treatment of women.

Another significant development, the Uniform Marital Property Act (UMPA), imposes a sharing rule from the beginning of the marriage. Under UMPA §5, absent an agreement, a spouse acting alone can manage and control marital property held in that spouse's name alone, that not held in the name of either spouse, and that held in the name of both spouses in the alternative ("A or B" form). Spouses must act together with respect to marital property held in the name of both. The UMPA also allows spouses to enter into agreements with each other regarding the management and control of property. Id. at §10(c)(2).

3. Duty of Support

McGUIRE v. McGUIRE

59 N.W.2d 336 (Neb. 1953)

MESSMORE, Justice.

The plaintiff, Lydia McGuire, brought this action . . . against Charles W. McGuire, her husband . . . to recover suitable maintenance and support money. . . .

The record shows that the plaintiff and defendant were married in Wayne, Nebraska, on August 11, 1919. At the time of the marriage the defendant was a bachelor 46 or 47 years of age and had a reputation for more than ordinary frugality, of which the plaintiff was aware. She had visited in his home and had known him for about 3 years prior to the marriage. [P]laintiff had been previously married. Her first husband . . . died intestate, leaving 80 acres of land in Dixon County. The plaintiff and each of [their two] daughters inherited a one-third interest therein. At the time of the marriage of the plaintiff and defendant, the plaintiff's daughters were 9 and 11 years of age. By working and receiving financial assistance from the parties to this action, the daughters received a high school education in Pender. One daughter attended Wayne State Teachers College for 2 years and the other daughter attended a business college in Sioux City, Iowa, for 1 year. [Both] are married and have families of their own. [At trial] plaintiff was 66 years of age and the defendant nearly 80 years of age. No children were born to these parties. . . .

The plaintiff testified that she was a dutiful and obedient wife, worked and saved, and cohabited with the defendant until the last 2 or 3 years. She worked in the fields, did outside chores, cooked, and attended to her household duties such as cleaning the house and doing the washing. For a number of years, she raised as high as 300 chickens, sold poultry and eggs, and used the money to buy clothing, things she wanted, and for groceries. She further testified that the defendant was the boss of the house and his word was law; that he would not tolerate any charge accounts and would not inform her as to his finances or business; and that he was a poor companion. . . . On several occasions the plaintiff asked the defendant for money. He would give her very small amounts, and for the last 3 or 4 years he had not given her any money nor provided her with clothing, except a coat about 4 years previous. . . . The defendant had not taken her to a motion picture show during the past 12 years. . . .

For the past 4 years or more, the defendant had not given the plaintiff money to purchase furniture or other household necessities. Three years ago he did purchase an electric, wood-and-cob combination stove which was installed in the kitchen, also linoleum floor covering for the kitchen. [T]he house is not equipped with a bathroom, bathing facilities, or inside toilet [or kitchen sink]. Hard and soft water is obtained from a well and cistern. She has a mechanical Servel refrigerator, and the house is equipped with electricity. . . . She had requested a new furnace but the defendant believed the one they had to be satisfactory. She related that the furniture was old and she would like to replenish it, [that] one of her daughters was good about furnishing her clothing, at least a dress a year, or sometimes two; that the defendant owns a 1929 Ford coupe equipped with a heater which is not efficient, and on the average of every 2 weeks he drives the plaintiff to Wayne to visit her mother; and that he also owns a 1927 Chevrolet pickup which is used for different purposes on the farm. The plaintiff was privileged to use all of the rent money she wanted to from the 80-acre farm, and when she goes to see her daughters, which is not frequent, she uses part of the rent money for that purpose, the defendant providing no funds for such use. . . . At the present time the plaintiff is not able to raise chickens and sell eggs. [P]laintiff has had three abdominal operations for which the defendant has paid. [P]laintiff further testified that [the] telephone was restricted [because] defendant did not desire that she make long distance calls. . . .

It appears that the defendant owns 398 acres of land with 2 acres deeded to a church, the land being of the value of $83,960; that he has bank deposits in the sum of $12,786.81 and government bonds in the amount of $104,500; and that his income, including interest on the bonds and rental for his real estate, is $8,000 or $9,000 a year. . . .

While there is an allegation in the plaintiff's petition to the effect that the defendant was guilty of extreme cruelty towards the plaintiff, and also an allegation requesting a restraining order be entered against the defendant for fear he might molest plaintiff or take other action detrimental to her rights, the plaintiff made no attempt to prove these allegations and the fact that she continued to live with the defendant is quite incompatible with the same.

The plaintiff relies upon Earle v. Earle, 43 N.W. 118 (Neb. 1889), [in which the defendant sent his wife away and] ceased to provide for her support and the support of his child. The wife instituted a suit in equity against her husband for maintenance and support. . . .The question presented was whether or not the wife should be compelled to resort to a proceeding for a divorce, which she did not desire to do. . . . [A]t the present time there is no statute governing this matter. The court stated that it was a well-established rule of law that it is the duty of the husband to provide his family with support and means of living—the style of support, requisite lodging, food, clothing, etc., to be such as fit his means, position, and station in life—and for this purpose the wife has generally the right to use his credit for the purchase of necessaries. The court held that if a wife is abandoned by her husband, without means of support, a bill in equity will lie to compel the husband to support the wife without asking for a decree of divorce. . . .

In the case of Brewer v. Brewer, 113 N.W. 161 (Neb. 1907), the plaintiff lived with her husband and his mother. The mother dominated the household. The plaintiff went to her mother. . . . The court held that a wife may bring a suit in equity to secure support and alimony without reference to whether the action is for divorce or not; that every wife is entitled to a home corresponding to the circumstances and condition of her husband over which she may be permitted to preside as mistress; and that she does not forfeit her right to maintenance by refusing to live under the control of the husband's mother. . . .

In the instant case the marital relation has continued for more than 33 years, and the wife has been supported in the same manner during this time without complaint on her part. The parties have not been separated or living apart from each other at any time. In the light of the cited cases it is clear, especially so in this jurisdiction, that to maintain an action such as the one at bar, the parties must be separated or living apart from each other.

The living standards of a family are a matter of concern to the household, and not for the courts to determine, even though the husband's attitude toward his wife, according to his wealth and circumstances, leaves little to be said in his behalf. As long as the home is maintained and the parties are living as husband and wife, it may be said that the husband is legally supporting his wife and the purpose of the marriage relation is being carried out. Public policy requires such a holding. It appears that the plaintiff is not devoid of money in her own right. She has a fair sized bank account and is entitled to use the rent from the 80 acres of land left by her first husband, if she so chooses. . . .

One source of marital difficulty in *McGuire* was the husband's neglect of his role of "good provider." The excerpt below explores the evolution of this gender-based role.

Jessie Bernard, The Good-Provider Role: Its Rise and Fall

36 Am. Psychol. 2-10 (1981)

. . . Webster's second edition defines the good provider as "one who provides, especially, colloq., one who provides food, clothing, etc. for his family; as, he is a good or an adequate provider." More simply, he could be defined as a man whose wife did not have to enter the labor force. . . .

The good provider as a specialized male role seems to have arisen in the transition from subsistence to market—especially money—economies that accelerated with the industrial revolution. The good-provider role for males emerged in this country roughly, say, from the 1830s, when de Tocqueville was observing it, to the late 1970s, when the 1980 census declared that a male was not automatically to be assumed to be head of household. This gives the role a life span of about a century and a half. Although relatively short-lived, while it lasted the role was a seemingly rock-like feature of the national landscape.

As a psychological and sociological phenomenon, the good-provider role had wide ramifications for all of our thinking about families. . . . It did not have good effects on women: The role deprived them of many chips by placing them in a peculiarly vulnerable position. Because she was not reimbursed for her contribution to the family in either products or services, a wife was stripped to a considerable extent of her access to cash-mediated markets. By discouraging labor force participation, it deprived many women, especially affluent ones, of opportunities to achieve strength and competence. It deterred young women from acquiring productive skills. They dedicated themselves instead to winning a good provider who would "take care" of them. . . .

The good-provider role, as it came to be shaped [was] restricted in what it was called upon to provide. Emotional expressivity was not included in that role. One of the things a parent might say about a man to persuade a daughter to marry him, or a daughter might say to explain to her parents why she wanted to, was not that he was a gentle, loving, or tender man but that he was a good provider. He might have many other qualities, good or bad, but if a man was a good provider, everything else was either gravy or the price one had to pay for a good provider. . . . Loving attention and emotional involvement in the family were not part of a woman's implicit bargain with the good provider. . . .

To be a man one had to be not only a provider but a *good* provider. Success in the good-provider role came in time to define masculinity itself. The good provider had to achieve, to win, to succeed, to dominate. He was a bread *winner*. . . . The good provider became a player in the male competitive macho game. What one man provided for his family in the way of luxury and display had to be equaled or topped by what another could provide. . . . The psychic costs could be high. . . .

[I]n an increasing number of cases, the wife has begun to share this role. [T]he role-sharing wife now feels justified in making demands on [her husband]. [Two such demands are (1) greater intimacy, expressivity, and nurturance; and (2) more sharing of housework and childcare.] The good-provider role with all its prerogatives and perquisites has undergone profound changes. It will never be the same again. . . .

Postscript. Since publication of the above excerpt, fathers have been adopting a more active role in family life, especially during the COVID-19 pandemic. As a result, they face increasing social pressure to act as engaged parents, as well as equal partners in the division of labor. This new masculine ideal means that men currently face many of the same work-family conflict issues as women. The demise of the male good-provider role, however, continues to take a toll on women because it has *not* resulted in a major reallocation of the household division of labor, as subsequent materials in this chapter on the work-family conflict reveal.

Notes and Questions

1. Doctrines of support and nonintervention. *McGuire* illustrates two doctrines. First, the case reflects the common law duty of support. At common law, a husband had a duty to provide support to his wife; the wife had a correlative duty to render domestic services. Second, the common law doctrine of nonintervention specifies that the state rarely will adjudicate spousal responsibilities in an ongoing marriage. Thus, marital support obligations are enforceable only after separation or divorce. This principle of family privacy stems from judicial reluctance to disrupt marital harmony or to interfere with the husband's authority.

Was there any marital harmony in the McGuires' marriage to disrupt? Should stereotypical rationale trump spousal welfare? Why do you think Mrs. McGuire did not seek a divorce instead of filing this lawsuit?

2. Necessaries doctrine. The common law doctrine of necessaries was the basis of the lower court opinion in Mrs. McGuire's favor. This doctrine imposed liability on a husband to a merchant who supplied necessaries to a wife. "Necessaries" generally include food, clothing, shelter, and medical care. Case law sometimes extends the term's meaning to other items, such as funeral expenses and legal fees.

Many American jurisdictions codified the common law duty of support of dependents via so-called family expense statutes, which render both spouses liable for the support of family members. Such statutes are broader than the common law doctrine (that is, applying to "family expenses" rather than merely "necessaries").

3. Third-party interests. Why should the state permit a creditor, but not a spouse, a remedy for support? Professor Marjorie Shultz argues that "the presence of third-party interests, even though minimal compared to the spouses' duties to one another, has been viewed as sufficient to allow disruption of the domestic harmony that could not be disturbed for the sake of resolving the spouses' own problems."[5] Further, Shultz points out, the necessaries doctrine encourages dealings with a creditor behind the back of the other spouse. Does this approach promote marital harmony?

4. Criticisms. Feminist commentators have been especially critical of the doctrine of nonintervention. Professors Nadine Taub and Elizabeth Schneider note:

> The state's failure to regulate the domestic sphere is now often justified on the ground that the law should not interfere with emotional relationships involved in the family realm because it is too heavy-handed. Indeed, the recognition of a familial privacy right in the early twentieth century [Meyer v. Nebraska, 262 U.S. 390 (1923); Pierce v. Society of Sisters, 268 U.S. 510 (1925)] has given this rationale a constitutional dimension. . . .
> Isolating women in a sphere divorced from the legal order contributes directly to their inferior status by denying them the legal relief that they seek to improve their situations and by sanctioning conduct of the men who control their lives. . . . But beyond its direct, instrumental impact, the insulation of women's

[5]. Marjorie Maguire Shultz, Contractual Ordering of Marriage: A New Model for State Policy, 70 Cal. L. Rev. 204, 238 (1982).

world from the legal order also conveys an important ideological message to the rest of society. Although this need not be the case in all societies, in our society the law's absence devalues women and their functions. . . . [6]

5. Equal protection problems. The gender-based common law necessaries doctrine poses equal protection problems. The issue arises when health care providers attempt to impose liability on a wife for services rendered to the husband prior to death or divorce. See, e.g., St. Catherine Hosp. v. Alvarez, 383 P.3d 184 (Kan. 2016). Most jurisdictions today, by statute or case law, impose a gender-neutral rule for interspousal liability for debts.

6. Civil and criminal remedies for nonsupport. What additional remedies might Mrs. McGuire have had? Civil remedies include suits for separate maintenance based either on statute or equity jurisdiction if the couple is living apart. Criminal remedies also exist in many states for nonsupport of a child and spouses. What purposes do criminal remedies serve? Would you have advised Mrs. McGuire to pursue these?

Problem

During the course of their marriage, Wife pays for most household expenses, although Husband occasionally contributes to the utility and grocery bills. After 12 years of marriage, Wife informs Husband that she wants a divorce and asks him to leave. She informs him that she is removing him from her health insurance policy. Husband refuses to leave and makes no effort to secure his own coverage. Two years later, Wife files for divorce. They sign an agreement whereby each takes responsibility for his or her own debts. Two days later, Husband is admitted to the hospital with a terminal condition. He submits an outdated insurance card from Wife's policy. Finding it unnecessary to pursue the divorce, Wife instructs her attorney to dismiss the proceedings. Husband dies, leaving a hospital debt of $150,000. The hospital seeks to recover payment from Wife. The jurisdiction has a spousal liability statute providing that both spouses shall be liable "for all debts contracted for necessaries for themselves, one another, or their family during the marriage." What result? Queen's Medical Ctr. v. Kagawa, 967 P.2d 686 (Haw. Ct. App. 1998). See also Lawrence v. Gude, 285 A.3d 1198 (Conn. Ct. App. 2022) (spousal liability for unpaid rent in a state with a family expense doctrine).

NOTE: CONSTITUTIONAL LIMITS ON SEX-STEREOTYPED ROLE ASSIGNMENTS

Marriage has been described as "the vehicle through which the apparatus of the state can shape the gender order."[7] Constitutional law once reflected the

[6]. Nadine Taub & Elizabeth M. Schneider, Women's Subordination and the Role of Law, in The Politics of Law: A Progressive Critique 328, 333 (David Kairys ed., 1998).
[7]. Nancy F. Cott, Public Vows: A History of Marriage and the Nation 3 (2000).

common law's prescription of appropriate gender roles for husbands and wives. In the late nineteenth and early twentieth century, the Supreme Court upheld discrimination against women in employment based on the "separate spheres doctrine" (that is, women occupy the private sphere of home and family while men occupy the public arena of work and politics). Thus, for example, the Court upheld rules barring married women from the practice of law (Bradwell v. Illinois, 83 U.S. (16 Wall.) 130 (1873)) and laws giving working women special legislation to protect them in their childbearing capacity (Muller v. Oregon, 208 U.S. 412 (1908)).

The women's movement in the 1960s triggered major reform in constitutional doctrine. In 1971, the Supreme Court first held that sex discrimination violated the Fourteenth Amendment's Equal Protection Clause. In Reed v. Reed, 404 U.S. 71 (1971), the Court invalidated an Idaho law that gave preference to men over women as administrators of intestate estates. The Court reasoned that the statute, which was based on stereotypical gender roles, lacked a rational basis. *Reed* heralded the beginning of an era of equal protection challenges to sex-based legislation.

The Court announced the applicable level of constitutional scrutiny for gender-based distinctions in Craig v. Boren, 429 U.S. 190 (1976), a challenge to the constitutionality of an Oklahoma statute proscribing different ages for men and women to drink beer. The Court applied an intermediate standard of review, maintaining that the classification must serve *important* governmental objectives and must be *substantially* related to achievement of those objectives. This standard, although lower than the strict scrutiny applied to race discrimination ("necessary to a compelling state interest"), was higher than the rational basis test ("rationally related to a legitimate governmental objective") applied to most social legislation. The Supreme Court later elevated the standard of review slightly and now requires an "exceedingly persuasive justification" for gender classifications. United States v. Virginia, 518 U.S. 515 (1996). Note that some *states* go further, applying strict scrutiny to gender-based classifications under their state constitutions (e.g., Sail'er Inn v. Kirby, 485 P.2d 529 (Cal. 1971)).

The Supreme Court has also embraced measures designed to dismantle traditional gender *stereotypes*. For example, in Price Waterhouse v. Hopkins, 490 U.S. 228 (1989), the Court recognized that employment discrimination based on gender-based assumptions (about how persons of a certain sex should dress and behave) constitutes unlawful sex discrimination under Title VII. And, in reading the family care provisions of the Family and Medical Leave Act (FMLA) (discussed later in this chapter) as an antidiscrimination measure, the Court approved this legislative effort to combat "[s]tereotypes about women's domestic roles [and] parallel stereotypes presuming a lack of domestic responsibilities for men." Nevada Dept. of Human Res. v. Hibbs, 538 U.S. 721, 736 (2003). And, in Sessions v. Morales-Santana, 582 U.S. 47 (2017), the Court held that different physical-presence requirements in the Immigration and Nationality Act for citizen-fathers and citizen-mothers (to pass their citizenship by descent to their children) were based on outdated gender-based stereotypes and violated equal protection.

However, the Court has had far more difficulty applying equal protection when confronted with classifications that it interpreted to reflect "real" (biological) differences. See Michael M. v. Superior Court, 450 U.S. 464, 469 (1981) (stating that the Court has upheld gender classifications that "realistically reflect[] the fact that the sexes are not similarly situated in certain circumstances"). Our abstract standard of equality, based on the Aristotelian notion, guarantees that likes (that is, "those similarly situated") will be treated alike. But how does one treat women like men in the face of biological differences? And should men provide the norm? Difficulties arose particularly in the Court's treatment of pregnancy. Further, the Court's preference for analyzing cases about reproduction under the Fourteenth Amendment's Due Process Clause ("privacy") left this strand of equal protection doctrine incomplete. In other cases, the Court treated socially imposed differences (e.g., the male as aggressor) as biological differences to justify differential treatment. Thus, despite disclaimers, the Court relied on gender-based stereotypes to exclude women from combat (Rostker v. Goldberg, 453 U.S. 57 (1981)) and certain employment (for example, prison guards) (Dothard v. Rawlinson, 433 U.S. 321 (1977)), and to uphold criminal laws applicable to only one sex (e.g., statutory rape laws) (*Michael M.*, supra). The marriage equality movement has prompted renewed examination of the Supreme Court's jurisprudence on gender equality, as we will continue to explore throughout the rest of this book.

4. Names in the Family

MELBOURNE v. NEAL
147 A.3d 1151 (D.C. Ct. App. 2016)

Ruiz, Senior Judge:

. . . Ms. Melbourne and Mr. Taylor were married and living together in the District of Columbia when their daughter was born on May 11, 2012. A month later, the couple separated, and Mr. Taylor moved to Florida to live with his parents but, in an attempt at reconciliation, Ms. Melbourne and the child soon moved to Florida to live with Mr. Taylor. The attempt at reconciliation failed, and Ms. Melbourne and the child moved back to the District of Columbia in September of 2012. . . .

Following the divorce, Ms. Melbourne filed the name change application [for the daughter]. At trial, Ms. Melbourne testified that she wished to change her daughter's name due to having "difficulties [] establishing that [she is] the mother [of her] daughter." Ms. Melbourne recounted an instance when she had taken her daughter to temporary childcare for the day because her primary daycare provider was closed. Ms. Melbourne testified that a childcare worker must have assumed that Ms. Melbourne and her child shared a last name, and recorded Ms. Melbourne's name incorrectly, as "Taylor," on the pickup sheet. When Ms. Melbourne came to collect her daughter later that day, her identification showed a different name than that on the pickup sheet, and did not match the child's last name. She was initially prevented from leaving with her child. Eventually, after a director was called, "it all got straightened out," but it was a "process" that Ms. Melbourne wished to avoid in the future.

Ms. Melbourne also testified about another incident. While in the waiting room at the hospital where her daughter was having ear surgery, a hospital staff person called out to have "Ms. Taylor" come back to see the child, and another woman (presumably, named Ms. Taylor) was taken to see Ms. Melbourne's daughter. In a nutshell, Ms. Melbourne testified that she wished to change the child's last name to hers in order to avoid what had been a recurring problem where someone assumed, incorrectly, that she and the child had the same last name and she was temporarily hindered as the custodial parent. Ms. Melbourne explained that her motive in wanting to have the child's last name changed was to end those problems, not to cause an estrangement between the child and her father. She commented, however, that Mr. Taylor had not manifested a continuing interest in the child, stating that Mr. Taylor had not called, emailed, or contacted her in any other way in order to facilitate the father-child relationship over the preceding twelve months. She further testified that after she had applied for the name change, she received an email from Mr. Taylor in March 2014 in which he threatened to kill the child. Ms. Melbourne did not contact the police after receiving the threat because she thought he was only trying to scare her into dropping the name-change application and, in any event, he was in Florida and did not know where she and the child lived. He did, however, have her email address and telephone number.

Mr. Taylor testified that he opposed the name change because he and Ms. Melbourne agreed when the child was born that she would pick the child's first and middle names and the child would bear his last name. Mr. Taylor denied that he had sent the threatening email. . . . He testified that he had made an effort to stay in the child's life, but that his efforts had been thwarted by Ms. Melbourne. Mr. Taylor testified that he had made "four or five" attempts during the preceding year to exercise his visitation rights but that Ms. Melbourne always said that the dates did not work for her or the child's schedules. . . . Mr. Taylor said that if the child's name were changed, he would not treat his daughter any differently. However, because he was being prevented from seeing the child, he thought their relationship would be diminished as he believed the only reason the child "knows who [he is] is because she [has his] last name."

After hearing testimony from both parties, the trial court issued a written order denying Ms. Melbourne's name-change application "in consideration of the best interest of the child pursuant to D.C. Code §16-831 et seq." In order to determine the best interests of the child the court set out four factors . . . and addressed each factor in turn:

> (1) [c]hildren ought not to have another name foisted upon them until they reach an age when they are capable of making an intelligent choice in the matter of a name;
> (2) [t]he bond between a divorced father and his children is tenuous at best and if their name is changed the bond may be weakened if not destroyed; and the name under which a child is registered in school goes far to effect a name change;
> (3) [w]hen a father supports a child, manifests a continuing interest in him, is guilty of no serious misconduct and without unreasonable delay, objects to an attempted change of name, the Court should decide the issue by determining what is for the child's best interest; and
> (4) [a] change of name may not be in the child's best interest if the effect of such change is to contribute to a further estrangement of the child from a father who exhibits a desire to preserve the parental relationship.

Applying these factors, the trial court found that: (1) as the child was then only two years old, her name should not be changed because she is unable to make an intelligent choice on the matter; (2) the father's physical absence from the child's life for more than a year—whatever the reason—meant that a name change "would weaken—and likely destroy—the bond" between the child and Mr. Taylor; (3) the father is current in his child support obligations, has demonstrated a continuing interest in the child, has not engaged in any misconduct, and filed a timely objection to the name-change application; and (4) the father has a desire to preserve a parental relationship with the child, but in light of the acrimony between the parents, a name change would "further estrange the relationship."

Ms. Melbourne argues that the judgment of the trial court must be reversed because the standard applied was erroneous. [We agree.] First, application of the factors which the court cited . . . was legal error. [These factors] contain doubtful premises that this court should not accept or perpetuate. For example, the notion that "the bond between a divorced father and his children is tenuous at best and if their name is changed the bond may be weakened if not destroyed" is itself tenuous at best. As a general proposition, divorced fathers, as well as mothers, may have primary physical custody, or even exclusive legal custody of their children. Some parents never marry, so divorce is not an issue with respect to their ability to maintain strong connections with their children. Some parents are same-sex couples and the gender distinction is inapt. Some children are born into families where the custom is for children's surnames to incorporate both the father's and the mother's last names, as is often the case for persons of Latin American or Spanish heritage. In other words, there is no one-size-fits-all resolution.

Moreover, the notion that the father's bond with his daughter would be weakened if she did not have his last name finds no support in the evidence in this case. Here, even though Mr. Taylor is not the parent with primary custody, he testified that his love for and treatment of his daughter would "definitely not" be altered if her last name were to be changed. His concern that the child would not know he is her father if she used her mother's name may be sincere, but there was no evidence to support that concern. More compelling factors in ensuring his parental relationship with a young child would be his continuing presence in her life through visits and other communications that express his interest and affection, as well as compliance with child support obligations.

In addition to their doubtful factual premises, the [above] factors perpetuate gender-based distinctions that have come under increasing judicial scrutiny since [precedent] was decided over half a century ago. These distinctions are based on stereotypes about the relationship between fathers and their children and do not take into account (or even mention) how a name change might affect the bond between mother and child. As they are based largely on gender stereotypes, and not grounded on the best interests of the child, these distinctions raise significant constitutional issues and are contrary to the law of the District of Columbia. . . .

[Second], it is clear that factors applied by the trial court included gender-based stereotypes that could not serve as a substitute for a determination of the best interests of a child. Third, the error affected substantial rights. [A]s the trial court based its ruling solely on the erroneous factors, there is no doubt that they affected the outcome. . . .

[We reverse and remand.] On remand the party requesting the name change has the burden of proof to show by a preponderance of the evidence, that the touchstone standard—the best interests of the minor child—is met. The court's determination whether a name change is in the best interests of the child should not be based on general presumptions or stereotypes but on individualized determinations that are gender-neutral, family-specific and, above all, child-centered. [P]roper factors to be considered include but are not limited to: how long and how widely the child has been known by her current name, the extent to which the child's name has become embedded in the child's own mind and identity, and the view of the child (depending on the age of the child). Another factor critical to the child's best interest is how the proposed name change would affect the safety and well-being of the child, which may include consideration of parental misconduct (especially involving an intrafamily offense) or reputation but only to the extent that it might affect the child's safety or sense of self and well-being. . . .

PAVAN v. SMITH

582 U.S. 563 (2017)

Per Curiam.

As this Court explained in Obergefell v. Hodges, 135 S. Ct. 2584 (2015), the Constitution entitles same-sex couples to civil marriage "on the same terms and conditions as opposite-sex couples." Id., at 2605. In the decision below, the Arkansas Supreme Court considered the effect of that holding on the State's rules governing the issuance of birth certificates. When a married woman gives birth in Arkansas, state law generally requires the name of the mother's male spouse to appear on the child's birth certificate—regardless of his biological relationship to the child. According to the court below, however, Arkansas need not extend that rule to similarly situated same-sex couples: The State need not, in other words, issue birth certificates including the female spouses of women who give birth in the State. Because that differential treatment infringes *Obergefell*'s commitment to provide same-sex couples "the constellation of benefits that the States have linked to marriage," id. at 2601, we reverse the state court's judgment.

The petitioners here are two married same-sex couples who conceived children through anonymous sperm donation. Leigh and Jana Jacobs were married in Iowa in 2010, and Terrah and Marisa Pavan were married in New Hampshire in 2011. Leigh and Terrah each gave birth to a child in Arkansas in 2015. When it came time to secure birth certificates for the newborns, each couple filled out paperwork listing both spouses as parents—Leigh and Jana in one case, Terrah and Marisa in the other. Both times, however, the Arkansas Department of Health issued certificates bearing only the birth mother's name.

The department's decision rested on a provision of Arkansas law, Ark. Code §20-18-401, that specifies which individuals will appear as parents on a child's state-issued birth certificate. "For the purposes of birth registration," that statute says, "the mother is deemed to be the woman who gives birth to the child." And "[i]f the mother was married at the time of either conception or birth," the statute instructs that "the name of [her] husband shall be entered on the certificate as the father of the child." There are some limited exceptions to the latter rule—for example, another man may appear on the birth certificate if the "mother" and "husband" and "putative father" all file affidavits vouching for the putative father's paternity. But as all parties agree, the requirement that a married woman's husband appear on her child's birth certificate applies in cases where the couple conceived by means of artificial insemination with the help of an anonymous sperm donor. See Ark. Code §9-10-201(a) ("Any child born to a married woman by means of artificial insemination shall be deemed the legitimate natural child of the woman and the woman's husband if the husband consents in writing to the artificial insemination").

The Jacobses and Pavans brought this suit in Arkansas state court against the director of the Arkansas Department of Health—seeking, among other things, a declaration that the State's birth-certificate law violates the Constitution. The trial court agreed, holding that the relevant portions of §20-18-401 are inconsistent with *Obergefell* because they "categorically prohibi[t] every same-sex married couple . . . from enjoying the same spousal benefits which are available to every opposite-sex married couple." But a divided Arkansas Supreme Court reversed that judgment, concluding that the statute "pass[es] constitutional muster." 505 S.W.3d 169, 177. In that court's view, "the statute centers on the relationship of the biological mother and the biological father to the child, not on the marital relationship of husband and wife," and so it "does not run afoul of *Obergefell*." Two justices dissented from that view, maintaining that under *Obergefell* "a same-sex married couple is entitled to a birth certificate on the same basis as an opposite-sex married couple."

The Arkansas Supreme Court's decision, we conclude, denied married same-sex couples access to the "constellation of benefits that the State has linked to marriage." *Obergefell*, 135 S. Ct., at 2601. As already explained, when a married woman in Arkansas conceives a child by means of artificial insemination, the State will—indeed, must—list the name of her male spouse on the child's birth certificate. And yet state law, as interpreted by the court below, allows Arkansas officials in those very same circumstances to omit a married woman's female spouse from her child's birth certificate. As a result, same-sex parents in Arkansas lack the same right as opposite-sex parents to be listed on a child's birth certificate, a document often used for important transactions like making medical decisions for a child or enrolling a child in school.

Obergefell proscribes such disparate treatment. As we explained there, a State may not "exclude same-sex couples from civil marriage on the same terms and conditions as opposite-sex couples." 135 S. Ct., at 2605. Indeed, in listing those terms and conditions—the "rights, benefits, and responsibilities" to which same-sex couples, no less than opposite-sex couples, must have access—we expressly identified "birth and death certificates." That was no accident: Several of the plaintiffs in *Obergefell* challenged a State's refusal to recognize their same-sex spouses on their children's birth certificates. In considering those challenges, we held the relevant state laws unconstitutional to the extent they treated same-sex couples differently from opposite-sex couples. That holding applies with equal force to §20-18-401.

Echoing the court below, the State defends its birth-certificate law on the ground that being named on a child's birth certificate is not a benefit that attends marriage. Instead, the State insists, a birth certificate is simply a device for recording biological parentage—regardless of whether the child's parents are married. But Arkansas law makes birth certificates about more than just genetics.

As already discussed, when an opposite-sex couple conceives a child by way of anonymous sperm donation—just as the petitioners did here—state law requires the placement of the birth mother's husband on the child's birth certificate. And that is so even though (as the State concedes) the husband "is definitively not the biological father" in those circumstances. Arkansas has thus chosen to make its birth certificates more than a mere marker of biological relationships: The State uses those certificates to give married parents a form of legal recognition that is not available to unmarried parents. Having made that choice, Arkansas may not, consistent with *Obergefell*, deny married same-sex couples that recognition. . . .

Justice Gorsuch, with whom Justice Thomas and Justice Alito join, dissenting.

[T]o be sure, *Obergefell* addressed the question whether a State must recognize same-sex marriages. But nothing in *Obergefell* spoke (let alone clearly) to the question whether §20-18-401 of the Arkansas Code, or a state supreme court decision upholding it, must go. The statute in question establishes a set of rules designed to ensure that the biological parents of a child are listed on the child's birth certificate. Before the state supreme court, the State argued that rational reasons exist for a biology-based birth registration regime, reasons that in no way offend *Obergefell*—like ensuring government officials can identify public health trends and helping individuals determine their biological lineage, citizenship, or susceptibility to genetic disorders.

In an opinion that did not in any way seek to defy but rather earnestly engage *Obergefell*, the state supreme court agreed. And it is very hard to see what is wrong with this conclusion for, just as the state court recognized, nothing in *Obergefell* indicates that a birth registration regime based on biology, one no doubt with many analogues across the country and throughout history, offends the Constitution. . . . Neither does anything in today's opinion purport to identify any constitutional problem with a biology-based birth registration regime. So whatever else we might do with this case, summary reversal would not exactly seem the obvious course. . . .

Notes and Questions

1. Married women's surname change. The feminist movement highlighted the impact of marital surname changes on a woman's identity. At common law, adoption of the husband's surname was a custom rather than a legal requirement. Early litigation focused on married women's right to have their birth name (formerly "maiden name") entered on voting records, automobile registration, and driver's licenses. Currently, all states recognize a woman's right to retain her birth name upon marriage.

Two methods of surname change exist: the common law method of consistent nonfraudulent use and a statutorily prescribed judicial procedure. Most women change their name upon marriage by the first method. Married women who elect to change their names must alter their driver's licenses, vehicle titles, voter registrations, passports, bank records, credit cards, medical records, insurance forms, wills, contracts, Social Security card, and Internal Revenue Service (IRS) forms.

Given the complications of name change, would a requirement of name retention be less confusing, be less onerous, and pose less risk of fraud to creditors?

2. Surname choices. Spouses who want to change their surname based on marriage are limited by state law in their choice of surname. Although all states provide for married women to retain their birth surname, fewer states explicitly provide for hyphenating surnames. And, fewer still allow blended surnames (i.e., a combination of parts of both current surnames to create an entirely *new* surname). Only four states explicitly allow blended surnames on a marriage license. Three additional states allow couples to blend surnames by virtue of permitting spouses to adopt any surname.[8]

3. Cultural norms. In the United States, most women married to men adopt their husband's family name when they marry. The practice of taking the husband's surname remains an entrenched cultural norm. What factors influence decisionmaking about surname change? Are gender-based stereotypes associated with women's surname change versus name retention? For example, does a spouse's surname choice influence how people perceive the distribution of power in a marriage?[9]

4. Postdivorce name resumption. Statutes often provide for a married woman to resume her birth name upon divorce. Early cases wrestled with whether the wife needed her husband's consent and whether denial of the wife's request could rest on potential detriment to children from having a different last name. Should courts take these factors into account? Cf. Cal. Fam. Code §2081 (court shall not deny restoration of petitioner's surname based on her custody of a child with a different surname).

5. Men's surnames upon marriage. Men married to women occasionally adopt hyphenated or blended surnames. However, husbands' adoption of wives' surnames is rare. Why don't more men adopt this practice? Few states explicitly provide for men's right to change their names upon marriage. Even fewer states provide for men's surname resumption at divorce. Does denial of a man's right to adopt his wife's surname raise an equal protection problem?

6. Name change: Contemporary contexts.

a. Same-sex couples. Today, even after marriage equality, many states have failed to update their laws by deleting sex-specific statutory language about

---

[8]. Hannah Haksgaard, Blending Surnames at Marriage, 30 Stan. L. & Pol'y Rev. 307, 310 (2019).
[9]. Rachael D. Robnett et al., Does a Woman's Marital Surname Choice Influence Perceptions of Her Husband? An Analysis Focusing on Gender-Typed Traits and Relationship Power Dynamics, 79 Sex Roles 59 (July 2018) (so suggesting), https://link.springer.com/article/10.1007%2Fs11 199-017-0856-6. See also Maddy Savage, Why Do Women Still Change Their Names?, BBC News, Sept. 23, 2020 (explaining that more than 70 percent of married women in the U.S. adopt their husband's surname whereas almost 90 percent of British women do so), https://www.bbc.com /worklife/article/20200921-why-do-women-still-change-their-names.

marital name change. Available data suggest that most same-sex spouses retain their respective surnames following marriage.[10]

b. Transgender people. Accuracy in identity documents (birth certificates, driver's licenses) is extremely important for transgender people. In the past, completion of gender confirmation surgery was necessary before states would alter these documents. Because surgery is not accessible for many people, and because it is not medically necessary for some transgender people, some states changed the required standard of adherence to transitioning guidelines (proof of "clinically appropriate treatment"). See, e.g., Cal. Health & Safety Code §§103425, 103.430 (requiring only self-attestation). However, five states (Kansas, Montana, North Dakota, Oklahoma, and Tennessee) refuse to allow transgender people to change gender markers on their birth certificates.[11]

c. Victims of domestic violence. Victims of domestic violence sometimes change their names to hide from abusers. Statutes that require the publication of name-change requests pose the risk of disclosure of the new identity. Some state laws address this problem by sealing records of a name change and providing that publication may be waived in cases of threats to safety. See, e.g., N.M. Stat. Ann. §40-8-2(B); Wash. Rev. Code §4.24.130(5).

7. Children's surnames.

a. Standards. Traditionally, marital children take their father's surname. In response to the women's movement, many state laws give married parents the right to choose the father's surname, the mother's birth surname, or a hyphenated surname for a child. Nonmarital children, historically, took the mother's surname absent the father's consent or a judicial determination of paternity. (Parentage issues for nonmarital children are explored further in Chapter IX.)

In name disputes between parents, courts resort to one of three standards: a custodial parent presumption, a presumption favoring the status quo, or a test to determine the best interests of the child. The majority approach is the best interests standard. What standard does *Melbourne* use?

b. Factors. What factors are relevant in the best interests determination for a child's surname change, according to *Melbourne*? Which factors perpetuate gender-based distinctions, according to the court? How? How relevant should the following factors be: the child's preference, effect of the name change on parent-child relationship, length of time the child used the surname, identification of the child as part of a family unit, social difficulties the child might encounter, the presence of parental misconduct or neglect (such as failure to maintain contact or provide support), and the mother's surname postdivorce? Should these factors apply regardless of the child's age? Parents' marital status? Should it matter if the

---

[10]. Suzanne A. Kim & Katherine A. Thurman, Social Rites of Marriage, 17 Geo. J. Gender & L. 745, 759-760 (2016) (citing research). See also Suzanne A. Kim, Marital Naming/Naming Marriage: Language and Status in Family Law, 85 Ind. L.J. 893, 922 (2010).

[11]. Movement Advancement Project, Identity Documents Laws and Policies (July 17, 2023), https://www.lgbtmap.org/equality-maps/identity_documents. See also Tenn. Code Ann. § 68-3-203(d) ("The sex of an individual will not be changed on the original certificate of birth as a result of sex change surgery.").

father's attempts at visitation were "thwarted" by the mother, as Mr. Taylor alleged in *Melbourne*? Should third parties have standing to object to the proposed surname change? If so, which third parties?

8. Same-sex parents and birth certificates.

a. Marital presumption. At common law, a marital presumption provided that a husband was automatically presumed to be the legal parent of his wife's child. This rule, known as "Lord Mansfield's presumption," was a rule of evidence that disqualified a husband from testifying to lack of access to his wife. The rule derives from an opinion of the British jurist Lord Mansfield, in Goodright *ex dim.* Stevens v. Moss, 98 Eng. Rep. 1257 (K.B. 1777), intended to preserve marital privacy and prevent bastardization of children. Today, all 50 states retain some variation of the marital presumption. (See Chapter IX.) Consistent with this parentage doctrine, state laws generally provide that a husband's name can (or in some states must) be listed on the birth certificate of a marital child, even if he is not the genetic parent.

b. Challenges for same-sex couples. Same-sex partners have faced challenges (both pre- and post-*Obergefell*) in state recognition of their relationship on such documents as birth certificates, children's hospital records, and death certificates What is the importance of a birth certificate in terms of recognition of parental rights? Did the state's refusal to grant birth certificates on equal terms to married same-sex parents in *Pavan* inflict harm on these parents? Their children? Their families? Was that harm relevant to the outcome?

What is the harm if a woman (specifically, an ex-spouse who was not the child's biological parent) is designated as "parent" rather than "mother" on a child's birth certificate? See In re Marriage of McLaughlin v. Swanson, 476 P.3d 336 (Ariz. Ct. App. 2020).

c. Influence of **Obergefell**. Did *Obergefell* mention the importance of birth certificates for same-sex parents? For what purposes? Contrast the majority and dissent's view in *Pavan* on whether Arkansas law ran afoul of *Obergefell*. Are birth certificates important records of purely *biological* parentage (rather than legal parentage)? The Arkansas Supreme Court, in a view shared by Justice Gorsuch in his dissent in *Pavan*, based its decision on the rationale that the state must capture biological information on its birth certificates. How was that view rebutted by Arkansas's own statutory scheme?

d. International development. In reflection of a backlash against LGBTQ families, the Italian government recently ordered local authorities to stop registering the children of same-sex parents with both parents' names pursuant to legislation passed by the "traditional family-first" government of Prime Minister Giorgia Meloni. As of July 2023, the city of Padua had removed the names of 27 non-biological lesbian mothers from their children's birth certificates.[12]

---

[12]. Barbie Latza Nadeau & Jack Guy, Italy Starts Removing Lesbian Mothers' Names from Children's Birth Certificates, CNN, July 21, 2023, https://localnews8.com/news/national-world/cnn-world/2023/07/21/italy-starts-removing-lesbian-mothers-names-from-childrens-birth-certificates-2/.empirical.

9. Constitutional issues. Is the right to choose a child's surname "fundamental"? See Henne v. Wright, 904 F.2d 1208 (8th Cir. 1990) (finding no fundamental right). Do you agree that this parental decision "possesses little, if any, inherent resemblance to the parental rights of training and education recognized by *Meyer* and *Pierce*"? Id. at 1214. In *Henne*, the U.S. Court of Appeals for the Eighth Circuit held that the statute restricting children's surnames (by requiring a legally established parental connection) bore a rational relationship to legitimate state interests. What are the state interests underlying restrictions on children's surnames? Should the state regulate name changes or defer to personal autonomy?

10. International perspectives. Some countries have very different customs and regulations about children's names. For example, Latin American and Spanish customs use a two-part surname representing both parents' lineages. Some countries require governmental approval of a child's name. Germany has an approved list of names and limits the number of first names and hyphenated surnames. The European Union (EU) also regulates surnames. In China, authorities draw lots to decide when parents disagree. Japan is the only industrialized country that makes it illegal for married couples to bear different surnames. What do you think of these various rules?

Problems

1. When Lisa and Robb Stratton divorced, the court awarded custody of their daughters (Lana, age 13, and Cara, age 16) to Lisa and visitation to Robb. Robb has not participated in the girls' lives for the past six years because he chooses to avoid family conflicts and to not jeopardize his tenuous bonds with his daughters. He pays child support and health insurance premiums. When Lisa remarried, she and the girls began using her new husband's surname, Kelley. To enable Cara to obtain a driver's license with her stepfather's surname, Lisa filed a petition to change the children's surname from Stratton to Kelley. Robb objected, arguing that his surname is the girls' last link to his family and that it should not be severed merely on the grounds of convenience. What result? In re Stratton ex rel. Kelley, 90 P.3d 566 (Okla. Civ. App. 2003).

Suppose, instead, that when Lisa remarried, she wanted Lana and Cara to bear a hyphenated name that includes the surnames of both fathers. However, Robb wants the girls to retain his surname, contending that it is in their best interests for traditional reasons and to promote their self-identification. What result? In re Eberhardt, 920 N.Y.S.2d 216 (App. Div. 2011).

2. A married couple, Barbara and John Smith, who are each the fifth child in their respective families, decide to call their newborn son by the name of "5 + 5." They agree to call him "5" for short. When Barbara attempts to enter that name on the birth certificate, hospital personnel (on instructions from the Department of Health) inform Barbara that she cannot do so based on a state statute that limits the choice of a child's surname to that of the mother's birth name, father's surname, or a combination of the two. What arguments would you make on Barbara's and John's behalf? Suppose, instead, that Barbara and John want to give their son the name "Adolf Hitler." Can (should) hospital personnel and/or state authorities reject the name? See In re Ritchie III, 206 Cal. Rptr. 239 (Ct. App. 1984); In re Change of Name of Ravitch, 754 A.2d 1287 (Pa. Super. Ct. 2000). See also Lisa W. Foderaro, Naming Children for Nazis Puts Spotlight on the Father, N.Y. Times, Jan. 19, 2009, at A28.

5. Employment

BRADWELL v. ILLINOIS
83 U.S. (16 Wall.) 130 (1873)

[Mrs. Myra Bradwell, a resident of Illinois, applied to the Illinois State Supreme Court for a license to practice law. Accompanying her petition was the requisite certificate attesting to her good character and qualifications. The Supreme Court of Illinois denied her application. The United States Supreme Court affirmed. Justice Bradley's concurring opinion below is a classic statement of separate spheres ideology.]

Justice BRADLEY [joined by Justices SWAYNE and FIELD], concurring: . . .

. . . The Supreme Court of Illinois denied the application on the ground that [the legislature] had simply provided that no person should be admitted to practice as attorney or counsellor without having previously obtained a license for that purpose from two justices of the Supreme Court, and that no person should receive a license without first obtaining a certificate from the court of some county of his good moral

Myra Bradwell (in 1870), one of the first women lawyers

character. In other respects it was left to the discretion of the court to establish the rules by which admission to the profession should be determined. The court, however, regarded itself as bound by at least two limitations. One was that it should establish such terms of admission as would promote the proper administration of justice, and the other that it should not admit any persons, or class of persons, not intended by the legislature to be admitted, even though not expressly excluded by statute. In view of this latter limitation the court felt compelled to deny the application of females to be admitted as members of the bar. Being contrary to the rules of the common law and the usages of Westminster Hall from time immemorial, it could not be supposed that the legislature had intended to adopt any different rule.

The claim . . . under the Fourteenth Amendment of the Constitution, which declares that no State shall make or enforce any law which shall abridge the privileges and immunities of citizens of the United States . . . assumes that it is one of the privileges and immunities of women as citizens to engage in any and every profession, occupation, or employment in civil life.

It certainly cannot be affirmed, as an historical fact, that this has ever been established as one of the fundamental privileges and immunities of the sex. On the contrary, the civil law, as well as nature herself, has always recognized a wide difference in the respective spheres and destinies of man and woman. Man is, or should be, woman's protector and defender. The natural and proper timidity and delicacy which belongs to the female sex evidently unfits it for many of the occupations of civil life. The constitution of the family organization, which is founded in the divine ordinance, as well as in the nature of things, indicates the domestic sphere as that which properly belongs to the domain and functions of womanhood. The harmony, not to say identity, of interest and views which belong, or should belong, to the family institution is repugnant to the idea of a woman adopting a distinct and independent career from that of her husband. So firmly fixed was this sentiment in the founders of the common law that it became a maxim of that system of jurisprudence that a woman had no legal existence separate from her husband, who was regarded as her head and representative in the social state; and, notwithstanding some recent modifications of this civil status, many of the special rules of law flowing from and dependent upon this cardinal principle still exist in full force in most States. One of these is that a married woman is incapable, without her husband's consent, of making contracts which shall be binding on her or him. This very incapacity was one circumstance which the Supreme Court of Illinois deemed important in rendering a married woman incompetent fully to perform the duties and trusts that belong to the office of an attorney and counsellor.

It is true that many women are unmarried and not affected by any of the duties, complications, and incapacities arising out of the married state, but these are exceptions to the general rule. The paramount destiny and mission of woman are to fulfill the noble and benign offices of wife and mother. This is the law of the Creator. And the rules of civil society must be adapted to the general constitution of things, and cannot be based upon exceptional cases. . . .

Notes and Questions

1. Holding. The Illinois Supreme Court denied Mrs. Bradwell's application to the bar, in part, based on married women's inability to contract. Why, then, could *unmarried* women not practice law?

2. Equal protection. In *Bradwell*, the Supreme Court failed to consider the applicability of the Equal Protection Clause. When the Fourteenth Amendment was ratified in 1868, it engrafted the word "male" in the Constitution for the first time, causing considerable concern to nineteenth-century feminists. The Equal Protection Clause was not applied to invalidate gender-based discrimination until Reed v. Reed, 404 U.S. 71 (1971) (holding that an Idaho law preferring men to women as administrators of estates constituted sex-based discrimination).

3. Separate spheres ideology. What authority does Justice Bradley cite in his concurrence to support his recognition of women's separate spheres? What is the danger of relying on history when considering the expansion of constitutional rights? See Aviam Soifer, Complacency and Constitutional Law, 42 Ohio St. L.J. 383, 409 (1981) ("To settle for the constitutionalization of the status quo is to bequeath a petrified forest."). Nineteenth-century cases denying women admission to the bar rested on legal and social rationales that were directed at married women, in particular.

NOTE: MARRIED WOMAN'S DOMICILE

Domicile is, essentially, a person's legal home. The law of the state of domicile is relevant to determination of marriage validity, the award of a divorce, custody, adoption, tax liability, probate and guardianship, as well as the right to vote, to hold and run for public office, to receive state benefits, or to qualify for tuition benefits at state colleges and universities.

Domicile requires two elements: presence plus intent to remain. A "domicile of choice" is acquired by persons who have legal capacity. A "domicile by operation of law" is assigned to those without legal capacity—traditionally, a category that included married women. At common law, the fiction of marital unity led to the assignment to a married woman of her husband's legal domicile. The first Restatement of Conflict of Laws §§26, 27, 30, 40 (1934) reflected this rule.

The common law rule caused married women hardship and inconvenience. The rule began to change in the 1970s after the harshness of the common law rule became apparent in the field of divorce. Constitutional challenges contributed to the rule's demise. See, e.g., Samuel v. University of Pittsburgh, 375 F. Supp. 1119 (W.D. Pa. 1974). Finally, in 1988, the Restatement (Second) of Conflict of Laws §21 conferred upon married women the ability to acquire a domicile of choice Case law now recognizes that neither spouse has a paramount right to select the marital domicile.

VAUGHN v. LAWRENCEBURG POWER SYSTEM
269 F.3d 703 (6th Cir. 2001)

BOGGS, Circuit Judge.

Plaintiffs Keith Vaughn and Jennifer Vaughn, former employees of defendant Lawrenceburg Power System (LPS), filed an action in Tennessee state court alleging that their terminations [violated their rights] pursuant to 42 U.S.C. §1983, and under the Tennessee Human Rights Act (THRA), Tenn. Code Ann. §4-21-101 et seq. Specifically, the Vaughns objected to LPS's "anti-nepotism" policy, which requires the resignation of one spouse in the event two employees marry. . . .

Keith Vaughn began work for LPS in 1987 and has worked there in several capacities [including maintaining grounds and buildings] over a ten-year period. [Jennifer Vaughn] started a full-time job as a cashier [in 1996]. [I]n September

1997, they became engaged. Unfortunately for the Vaughns, their marriage was against power system policy. The "employment of relatives" or "anti-nepotism" portion of the LPS manual, which it is undisputed that both Vaughns received, reads as follows:

> It is the policy of the System to employ only one member of a family. No immediate relatives of employees, officers, members of the city governing body, by blood, marriage or adoption, shall be employed for permanent positions. . . . For purposes of this policy, said relatives are as follows: Spouse, parent, child, brother, sister, grandparent, grandchild, son-in-law, daughter-in-law, father-in-law, mother-in-law, brother-in-law, and sister-in-law. *When two employees working for the Lawrenceburg Power system are subsequently married, one must terminate employment.* (Emphasis added.)

The Vaughns ran afoul of the second part of this section forbidding marriages within the system, which may be termed LPS's rule of "exogamy."

It soon became common knowledge that the Vaughns were to be married. . . . [LPS Superintendent Ronald Cato] met with the Vaughns several times to inform them of the policy and to request that they decide which one of them was going to leave LPS. Cato told them he would need a decision before the marriage took place; he also told them that if they remained unmarried and merely lived together, there would be no problem with the exogamy rule. The Vaughns were reluctant to pursue this option, in large part because Jennifer had become pregnant that fall with Keith's son, who was born the following July.

The Vaughns disagreed with the policy's applicability to their situation. Mr. Vaughn knew of three other groups of relatives working at LPS, two brother-in-law/sister-in-law dyads, and a father-in-law/son-in-law pair. Keith Vaughn interpreted the overall anti-nepotism policy as being contravened by the presence of these related co-workers. He states that he so informed Michael Meek, the Administrative Services Manager, who Vaughn claims told him that the other employees were "grandfathered in." . . . Despite urging from Cato, neither of the Vaughns indicated they would resign. Instead, they took their case to a meeting of the Power Board in mid-December 1998, where Keith argued he should be "treated like everybody else." The Power Board was not convinced by the Vaughns' interpretation, apparently distinguishing between the first part of the employment of relatives' policy, which does not mandate termination, and the second part, the exogamy rule dealing specifically with employee intermarriage, which does. The Board also refused to change the rule or make an exception. . . .

Jennifer and Keith's wedding day was January 16, 1998. Keith had met with Cato the previous day and said "okay" in response to Cato's request for a decision. But Keith did not then tell Cato whether he or Jennifer would leave LPS. When the couple arrived back from their honeymoon, they found a letter suspending both of them for a minimum of two weeks, until February 9, 1998 (or until they reached a decision). . . . On February 6, 1998, Keith Vaughn met with Ron Cato and told him the couple planned to have Keith, who was paid more than Jennifer, continue working at LPS while Jennifer resigned. . . . The following Monday, February 9, Keith Vaughn, but not Jennifer Vaughn, arrived at LPS at 8 a.m. to begin work. Cato called Vaughn [into his office]. Fifteen to thirty minutes later, when Vaughn left Cato's office, he had been fired [presumably because the couple did not provide their employer with the requested letter of resignation from Jennifer]. . . . [In response,] the Vaughns filed a lawsuit [alleging] violations of 42 U.S.C. §1983 based on "the fundamental right of marriage and freedom of association." . . .

We must first decide at what "level of scrutiny" to evaluate the challenged provision in the LPS manual. In order to trigger heightened constitutional scrutiny, the challenged portion of the anti-nepotism policy, the exogamy rule requiring termination of employment, must be shown to place "a 'direct and substantial' burden on the right of marriage." Our analysis of the case law . . . indicated that we would find direct and substantial burdens only where a large portion of those affected by the rule are absolutely or largely prevented from marrying, or where those affected by the rule are absolutely or largely prevented from marrying a large portion of the otherwise eligible population of spouses.

[T]he essential fact [is] that the policy did not bar Jennifer or Keith from getting married, nor did it prevent them marrying a large portion of population even in Lawrence County. It only made it economically burdensome to marry a small number of those eligible individuals, their fellow employees at LPS. Once Jennifer and Keith decided to marry one another, LPS's policy became onerous for them, but ex ante, it did not greatly restrict their freedom to marry or whom to marry. As a consequence, the exogamy rule in itself must be considered a non-oppressive burden on the right to marry, and so subject only to rational basis review. . . .

LPS asserts that its rule exists to (1) prevent one employee from assuming the role of "spokesperson" for both, (2) to avoid involving or angering a second employee when an employee is reprimanded, (3) and to avoid marital strife or fraternization in the workplace. [A] government employer may have a legitimate concern about the inherent loyalty that one spouse will show to another, making discipline more difficult. Therefore, we conclude LPS has demonstrated its exogamy rule advances a legitimate governmental interest.

The Vaughns claim that the rule, even if advancing a legitimate interest, is an unreasonable means of doing so. They point out that the rule does not affect those willing merely to cohabitate (which in their case would have also involved the bearing of an out-of-wedlock child); the Vaughns note that cohabitating couples may well show a similar degree of loyalty and create the same problems the rule seeks to avoid. . . . There is, no doubt, wide variation in the nature and intensity of the relationships one finds among both married and unmarried couples. Yet there is good reason to believe that the level of commitment signified by marriage—and its attendant legal, moral, and financial obligations—marks those relationships in which, on average, there is likely to be intense loyalty. Whatever the situation may be, de facto, married and unmarried couples are not the same de jure; the law treats them differently, and LPS may do so as well.

The Vaughns raise a better argument by noting again that the consequences to them are inherently more severe than those affecting the couple in [Montgomery v. Carr, 101 F.3d 1117 (6th Cir. 1996) where the antinepotism policy required one spouse to transfer]. Here, both the Vaughns were terminated, and the policy mandated this for, at least, one of them. . . . In response, LPS points out that they simply do not have the option of having a transfer policy, because LPS is an operation of only 50 to 70 employees. . . .

Keith Vaughn claimed [also] to have been terminated in violation [of the Tennessee Human Rights Act]. An employee-at-will generally may not be discharged for attempting to exercise a statutory or constitutional right or for other reasons that violate a clear public policy evidenced by an unambiguous constitutional, statutory or regulatory provision. [The THRA] "makes it a discriminatory practice to retaliate against a person because such person has opposed a practice declared discriminatory by" the Act. It is this latter "opposition" provision that has been asserted by the Vaughns. As the defendant points out, however, this provision is integrally connected to the types of discrimination the THRA has specifically forbidden. Tennessee has not included marital status in its list of forbidden employment classifications, and without an unambiguous provision, it is unlikely that a Tennessee court would abrogate its employment-at-will doctrine. . . . Keith Vaughn's claim under THRA was properly dismissed. . . .

Notes and Questions

1. **Historical background.** Derived from the Latin word for "nephew," the word *nepotism* was coined during the Middle Ages to describe Pope Calixtus III's appointment of his unqualified nephews as cardinals. Some of these "nephews" may have been illegitimate sons.

2. **"No-spouse rules."** Antinepotism laws and policies differ based on the qualifying relationships (i.e., "spouses" or "close relatives"). Policies generally apply to hiring, employment in the same department, and supervision. The rules create severe hardship in small communities and narrow specialties where the lack of alternatives may make one spouse unemployable. Do female employees disproportionately bear the burden of the no-spouse rule? If so, why?

3. **Business rationale.** Antinepotism policies attempt to ensure that unqualified relatives are not hired. Yet, paradoxically, they ban qualified relatives from being hired as well. The following arguments support antinepotism policies: Spouses bring quarrels to work; they advance their own interests, leading to complaints of favoritism; and their employment promotes dual absenteeism because both partners want the same vacation or shifts. Opposing arguments include: The best candidate should not be passed over (or fired) simply because of being married to an employee; the willingness to hire couples enables employers to hire a "star"; personnel benefits for employee-spouses are less costly; no-spouse restrictions violate public policy by encouraging cohabitation; and no-spouse policies discriminate against female employees. What do you think of these rationales—both in general and as applied to the plaintiffs in the principal case?

4. **Causes of action.** Federal and state grounds exist to challenge antinepotism rules.

a. Constitutional challenges—marriage is a fundamental right. This cause of action is available only to public employees because constitutional limitations do not apply to private employers. To date, challenges on this ground (such as *Vaughn*) have not been successful. When might a no-spouse rule "directly and substantially" interfere with the right to marry?

b. Title VII. Title VII of the Civil Rights Act of 1964, 42 U.S.C. §2000e-2(a)(1), provides another avenue of attack. Title VII prohibits discrimination in the workplace based on race, color, religion, sex, or national origin (but *not* marital status). Claims may be based on either disparate treatment (that is, intentional discrimination) or disparate impact. Most antinepotism litigation under Title VII is based on the latter, challenging policies that do not facially distinguish between employees but, in practice, adversely affect a particular class of employees. For example, note that in *Vaughn*, Jennifer planned to resign because Keith earned more money. Given that women on average earn less than men, no-spouse rules might result in the loss of a wife's job more often than her husband's. However, an employer in a disparate impact action may successfully defend by showing that the policy was justified (for example, by business necessity).

c. State civil rights statutes. In contrast to Title VII, some state civil rights statutes prohibit discrimination based on marital status. Why weren't the Vaughns successful under their state statute? Cases often turn on the interpretation of the term "marital status." Some jurisdictions apply the term broadly to include the identity of the spouse. Compare Miller v. C.A. Muer Corp., 362 N.W.2d 650 (Mich. 1985) (legislature did not intend term "marital status" to include the identity, occupation, and place of employment of one's spouse), with Minn. Stat. §363A.03 (defining marital status to include "identity, situation, actions, or beliefs of a spouse or former spouse"). Other jurisdictions limit it to the status of being married or single (and sometimes expand it to divorced and widowed spouses).

5. Empirical data. How common is romance in the workplace? The number of workplace romances has been rising. One-third of employees are currently romantically involved or have been involved with a co-worker (up from 27 percent before 2020).[13] In response, should more companies adopt formal antifraternization prohibitions? See Problem 2 below.

6. Policy. Business have adopted different approaches to fraternization rules. Some businesses ban all employee dating; others ban boss/subordinate relationships; still others ban relationships between employees who work in the same department. Some businesses require couples to disclose their relationships to Human Resources. Other companies discourage fraternization without actually banning it, or allow fraternization but intervene if it harms others in the workplace. Do no-dating policies in the workplace constitute employment discrimination? Violate privacy laws? Should employers impose their code of morality outside the office? Are antinepotism policies out of sync with the modern workplace? Or, should workplace romances be regulated because they create a hostile work environment for *other* employees? Should employers review their no-dating policies in light of the #MeToo anti–sexual harassment movement?

---

[13]. Susan Milligan, Workplace Romance Is on the Rise, SHRM HR Mag., June 7, 2022, https://www.shrm.org/hr-today/news/hr-magazine/summer2022/pages/workplace-romance-is-on-the-rise.aspx.

Problems

1. Jim and Coleen are state troopers in the same squad in a small Illinois town. Their district is patrolled by three one-person squads (each person patrols in a separate car). The squads rotate every eight hours. Jim and Coleen decide to marry. When they notify their supervisor, he informs them of an unwritten policy that prohibits spouses from working on the same shift in the patrol area. Jim and Coleen could remain in the same patrol area on different shifts, or one could transfer to a different patrol area and work the same shift. Jim chooses the latter. After their marriage, they challenge the no-spouse policy under state law, which prohibits workplace discrimination based on marital status (defined as "the legal status of being married, single, separated, divorced, or widowed"). What result? See Boaden v. Department of Law Enforcement, 664 N.E.2d 61 (Ill. 1996).

2. Some employers are addressing workplace romances by means of "love contracts"—a required document signed by employees who are currently in a dating relationship that declares the consensual nature of their relationship and their agreement to adhere to appropriate workplace behavior. As general counsel for a corporation, you have been asked to explore the potential risks for the corporation and to draft a "love contract" policy. Draft an opinion as to the potential liability of the corporation and the scope of a workplace policy (such as the prohibition on physical contact during work hours, etc.), likely effectiveness, and advantages/disadvantages in comparison to an antinepotism policy. How should the contracts be modified in the #MeToo era? For example, should relationships between supervisors and subordinates be barred? Result in transfers to other departments? See generally Romance in the Workplace: Risks and Solutions, Thomson Reuters Blog, Feb. 11, 2022, https://legal.thomsonreuters.com/blog/romance-in-the-workplace-risks-and-solutions/.

6. Parenting

a. Pregnancy Leave

CLEVELAND BOARD OF EDUCATION v. LaFLEUR
414 U.S. 632 (1974)

Justice STEWART delivered the opinion of the Court. . . .

Jo Carol LaFleur and Ann Elizabeth Nelson . . . are junior high school teachers employed by the Board of Education of Cleveland, Ohio. Pursuant to a rule first adopted in 1952, the school board requires every pregnant school teacher to take maternity leave without pay, beginning five months before the expected birth of her child. . . . The teacher on maternity leave is not promised re-employment after the birth of the child; she is merely given priority in reassignment to a position for which she is qualified. Failure to comply with the mandatory maternity leave provisions is ground for dismissal.

Neither Mrs. LaFleur nor Mrs. Nelson wished to take an unpaid maternity leave; each wanted to continue teaching until the end of the school year.[2] Because of the mandatory maternity leave rule, however, each was required to leave her job in March 1971. The two women then filed separate suits. . . .

[Another petitioner,] Susan Cohen, was employed by the School Board of Chesterfield County, Virginia. That school board's maternity leave regulation requires that a pregnant teacher leave work at least four months prior to the expected birth of her child. [The teacher is] re-eligible for employment when she submits written notice from a physician that she is physically fit for re-employment, and when she can give assurance that care of the child will cause only minimal interference with her job responsibilities. The teacher is guaranteed re-employment no later than the first day of the school year following the date upon which she is declared re-eligible.

[Mrs. Cohen, who expected her baby around April 28, 1971] initially requested that she be permitted to continue teaching until April 1, 1971. The school board rejected the request, as it did Mrs. Cohen's subsequent suggestion that she be allowed to teach until January 21, 1971, the end of the first school semester. Instead, she was required to leave her teaching job on December 18, 1970. She subsequently filed this suit under 42 U.S.C. §1983. . . . We granted certiorari in both cases, in order to resolve the conflict between the Courts of Appeals regarding the constitutionality of such mandatory maternity leave rules for public school teachers.[8]

This Court has long recognized that freedom of personal choice in matters of marriage and family life is one of the liberties protected by the Due Process Clause of the Fourteenth Amendment. As we noted in Eisenstadt v. Baird, 405 U.S. 438, 453 [1972], there is a right "to be free from unwarranted governmental intrusion into matters so fundamentally affecting a person as the decision whether to bear or beget a child."

By acting to penalize the pregnant teacher for deciding to bear a child, overly restrictive maternity leave regulations can constitute a heavy burden on the exercise of these protected freedoms. Because public school maternity leave rules directly affect "one of the basic civil rights of man," the Due Process Clause of the Fourteenth Amendment requires that such rules must not needlessly, arbitrarily, or capriciously impinge upon this vital area of a teacher's constitutional liberty. The question before us in these cases is whether the interests advanced in support of the rules of the Cleveland and Chesterfield County School Boards can justify the particular procedures they have adopted.

The school boards in these cases have offered two essentially overlapping explanations for their mandatory maternity leave rules. First, they contend that

---

2. Mrs. LaFleur's child was born on July 28, 1971; Mrs. Nelson's child was born during August of that year.

8. . . . The practical impact of our decision in the present cases may have been somewhat lessened by several recent developments. At the time that the teachers in these cases were placed on maternity leave, Title VII . . . did not apply to state agencies and educational institutions. [However, Title VII was later amended to withdraw those exemptions.] Shortly thereafter, the Equal Employment Opportunity Commission promulgated guidelines providing that a mandatory leave or termination policy for pregnant women presumptively violates Title VII. While the statutory amendments and the administrative regulations are, of course, inapplicable to the cases now before us, they will affect like suits in the future. . . .

the firm cutoff dates are necessary to maintain continuity of classroom instruction, since advance knowledge of when a pregnant teacher must leave facilitates the finding and hiring of a qualified substitute. Secondly, the school boards seek to justify their maternity rules by arguing that at least some teachers become physically incapable of adequately performing certain of their duties during the latter part of pregnancy. By keeping the pregnant teacher out of the classroom during these final months, the maternity leave rules are said to protect the health of the teacher and her unborn child, while at the same time assuring that students have a physically capable instructor in the classroom at all times.[9]

It cannot be denied that continuity of instruction is a significant and legitimate educational goal. [W]hile the advance-notice provisions in the Cleveland and Chesterfield County rules are wholly rational and may well be necessary to serve the objective of continuity of instruction, the absolute requirements of termination at the end of the fourth or fifth month of pregnancy are not. Were continuity the only goal, cutoff dates much later during pregnancy would serve as well as or better than the challenged rules, providing that ample advance notice requirements were retained. Indeed, continuity would seem just as well attained if the teacher herself were allowed to choose the date upon which to commence her leave, at least so long as the decision were required to be made and notice given of it well in advance of the date selected.

In fact, since the fifth or sixth month of pregnancy will obviously begin at different times in the school year for different teachers, the present Cleveland and Chesterfield County rules may serve to hinder attainment of the very continuity objectives that they are purportedly designed to promote. For example, the beginning of the fifth month of pregnancy for both Mrs. LaFleur and Mrs. Nelson occurred during March of 1971. Both were thus required to leave work with only a few months left in the school year, even though both were fully willing to serve through the end of the term. Similarly, if continuity were the only goal, it seems ironic that the Chesterfield County rule forced Mrs. Cohen to leave work in mid-December 1970 rather than at the end of the semester in January, as she requested.

We thus conclude that the arbitrary cutoff dates embodied in the mandatory leave rules before us have no rational relationship to the valid state interest of preserving continuity of instruction. As long as the teachers are required to give substantial advance notice of their condition, the choice of firm dates later in pregnancy would serve the boards' objectives just as well, while imposing a far lesser burden on the women's exercise of constitutionally protected freedom.

The question remains as to whether the cutoff dates at the beginning of the fifth and sixth months can be justified on the other ground advanced by the school boards—the necessity of keeping physically unfit teachers out of the classroom.

---

9. The records in these cases suggest that the maternity leave regulations may have originally been inspired by other, less weighty, considerations. For example, Dr. Mark C. Schinnerer, who served as Superintendent of Schools in Cleveland at the time the leave rule was adopted, testified in the District Court that the rule had been adopted in part to save pregnant teachers from embarrassment at the hands of giggling schoolchildren; the cutoff date at the end of the fourth month was chosen because this was when the teacher "began to show." Similarly, at least several members of the Chesterfield County School Board thought a mandatory leave rule was justified in order to insulate schoolchildren from the sight of conspicuously pregnant women. . . . The school boards have not contended in this Court that these considerations can serve as a legitimate basis for a rule requiring pregnant women to leave work; we thus note the comments only to illustrate the possible role of outmoded taboos in the adoption of the rules.

There can be no doubt that such an objective is perfectly legitimate, both on educational and safety grounds. . . .

The mandatory termination provisions of the Cleveland and Chesterfield County rules surely operate to insulate the classroom from the presence of potentially incapacitated pregnant teachers. But the question is whether the rules sweep too broadly. That question must be answered in the affirmative, for the provisions amount to a conclusive presumption that every pregnant teacher who reaches the fifth or sixth month of pregnancy is physically incapable of continuing. There is no individualized determination by the teacher's doctor—or the school board's—as to any particular teacher's ability to continue at her job. [T]he Due Process Clause requires a more individualized determination.

. . . While the medical experts in these cases differed on many points, they unanimously agreed on one—the ability of any particular pregnant woman to continue at work past any fixed time in her pregnancy is very much an individual matter. Even assuming, arguendo, that there are some women who would be physically unable to work past the particular cut-off dates embodied in the challenged rules, it is evident that there are large numbers of teachers who are fully capable of continuing work for longer than the Cleveland and Chesterfield County regulations will allow. Thus, the conclusive presumption embodied in these rules . . . is neither "necessarily (nor) universally true," and is violative of the Due Process Clause.

The school boards have argued that the mandatory termination dates serve the interest of administrative convenience, since there are many instances of teacher pregnancy, and the rules obviate the necessity for case-by-case determinations. Certainly, the boards have an interest in devising prompt and efficient procedures to achieve their legitimate objectives in this area. . . . While it might be easier for the school boards to conclusively presume that all pregnant women are unfit to teach past the fourth or fifth month or even the first month, of pregnancy, administrative convenience alone is insufficient to make valid what otherwise is a violation of due process of law. The Fourteenth Amendment requires the school boards to employ alternative administrative means, which do not so broadly infringe upon basic constitutional liberty, in support of their legitimate goals. . . .

In addition to the mandatory termination provisions, both the Cleveland and Chesterfield County rules contain limitations upon a teacher's eligibility to return to work after giving birth. Again, the school boards offer two justifications for the return rules—continuity of instruction and the desire to be certain that the teacher is physically competent when she returns to work. As is the case with the leave provisions, the question is not whether the school board's goals are legitimate, but rather whether the particular means chosen to achieve those objectives unduly infringe upon the teacher's constitutional liberty. . . .

The respondents . . . do not seriously challenge either the medical requirements of the Cleveland rule or the policy of limiting eligibility to return to the next semester following birth. The provisions concerning a medical certificate or supplemental physical examination are narrowly drawn methods of protecting the school board's interest in teacher fitness; these requirements allow an individualized decision as to the teacher's condition, and thus avoid the pitfalls of the presumptions inherent in the leave rules. Similarly, the provision limiting eligibility to return to the semester following delivery is a precisely drawn means of serving the school board's interest in avoiding unnecessary changes in classroom personnel during any one school term.

The Cleveland rule, however, [requires] the mother to wait until her child reaches the age of three months before the return rules begin to operate. The school board has offered no reasonable justification for this supplemental limitation, and we can perceive none. To the extent that the three-month provision reflects the school board's thinking that no mother is fit to return until that point in time, it suffers from the same constitutional deficiencies that plague the irrebuttable presumption in the termination rules. The presumption, moreover, is patently unnecessary, since the requirement of a physician's certificate or a medical examination fully protects the school's interests in this regard. And finally, the three-month provision simply has nothing to do with continuity of instruction, since the precise point at which the child will reach the relevant age will obviously occur at a different point throughout the school year for each teacher.

Thus, we conclude that the Cleveland return rule, insofar as it embodies the three-month age provision, is wholly arbitrary and irrational, and hence violates the Due Process Clause of the Fourteenth Amendment. The age limitation serves no legitimate state interest, and unnecessarily penalizes the female teacher for asserting her right to bear children. . . .

We perceive no such constitutional infirmities in the Chesterfield County rule. In that school system, the teacher becomes eligible for re-employment upon submission of a medical certificate from her physician; return to work is guaranteed no later than the beginning of the next school year following the eligibility determination. The medical certificate is both a reasonable and narrow method of protecting the school board's interest in teacher fitness, while the possible deferring of return until the next school year serves the goal of preserving continuity of instruction. . . .

NOTE: WHO IS JO CAROL LaFLEUR?

Jo Carol LaFleur, "Go Home and Have Your Baby"
in The Courage of Their Convictions 320-328 (Peter Irons ed., 1988)

Jo Carol Nesset-Sale (formerly LaFleur), the former high school teacher who challenged maternity leave laws

I learned around January of 1971 that I was pregnant, with the child due to be born around the end of July. Teaching out the school year made perfect sense to me. . . . I thought I was actually contributing, partly by being a good role model [being] a married woman, having a baby, going to a doctor, getting good care. . . . Little did I know that you could not teach in the Cleveland schools past the fourth month of pregnancy.

[The principal, Mr. Wilkins, called Ms. LaFleur to his office about March 1.] Mr.

Wilkins said, "I understand you're having a baby in August. . . . You've got to go on maternity leave; you've got to fill out your papers." I said, "I don't have to do that, because I'm not leaving. I'm just going to teach until the end of the year." He said, "You can't do that; we have rules." I said, "My baby isn't scheduled to be born until the summer. I just want to teach school. This class that you just put me in has already lost one teacher. And I teach students who are pregnant." . . . He said, "You're a good teacher. I'm not going to fire you, but you've got to take this leave." Mr. Wilkins filled out the maternity leave papers for me, because I wouldn't fill them out. . . . I couldn't believe that anybody would yank from an inner-city school a person who was specially trained to teach there and who *wanted* to teach. . . .

[Ms. LaFleur then asked the teachers' union for help.] The union leader, who was a man, said, "Oh, Mrs. LaFleur, just go home and have your baby." . . . It was clear the union had no interest or sympathy whatever. [Later, she called the Women's Equity Action League, who referred her to a constitutional law professor, Jane Picker.]

Mr. Wilkins had given me a deadline to leave—near the end of March. . . . Jane tried to get an injunction in the federal court against the schools, to prevent them from barring me from my class. This district court judge, whose name was Connell—elderly, in his seventies—said at the injunction hearing, "Mrs. LaFleur will get exactly what she deserves, and she doesn't deserve an injunction." Since we knew he was the trial judge, Jane said, "This doesn't bode well. . . ."

. . . The school board put on a doctor, a male obstetrician, whose testimony I found really annoying. He was talking about all of the horrible complications that were possible with pregnancy, like placenta previa. There was absolutely *no* data that showed that the act of teaching made it more likely that you would have one of these conditions. . . . It was almost hilarious, in a very pathetic sense, listening to testimony about all of the possible complications of pregnancy. It's a wonder women *ever* have babies, if all of these horrible things happen. . . . The week before my son was born, I played nine holes of golf and I played a set of tennis. The only thing I didn't do was jump the net. . . .

[After losing, she appealed to the Sixth Circuit Court of Appeals and prevailed. The Supreme Court granted certiorari.] I remember Justice Blackmun asking the question of Jane Picker [at oral argument] whether she really saw any difference between a man losing his job because he refuses to shave his beard, and a woman losing her job because she's pregnant. And she stood up there, and she put her hands on both hips and she said, "Your Honor, that analogy is ludicrous. Simply *ludicrous*. What's the remedy for a man? You shave! For a woman it's abortion, to get rid of the problem. It's a little different, Your Honor." And I could see her husband at counsel table, with his head in his hands—"Jane, you shouldn't *say* such things." But Blackmun voted for us. . . .

I remember the day the decision came down. I was teaching a social studies class [with a guest speaker], and we were discussing death and dying. . . . I got called out of the class for a telephone call from a radio station that wanted my opinion on the decision. . . . I called Jane's office. They said, "The only thing we know is that you won." . . .

I went running back to my class, doing these *jetés*, these giant leaps down the hall. I went into my class and I calmed down, and I said, "Mr. Smith, could

> I have just one moment? I need to tell the class something." They knew I had been waiting every day. "*We won!* Thank you, please resume." He doesn't know what's going on. The kids are screaming, "*All right!*" . . .
>
>   Looking back, I'm not quite sure why I started my case. . . . When I got pregnant, I knew I wasn't sick. I knew I wasn't ill. How could a male-dominated school system say to me, Even though you're not ill, and pregnancy is a perfectly normal condition, you are unfit to teach. The fundamental unfairness of it seemed morally wrong, not just stupid but wrong. . . .

Postscript. Following the principal case, Jo Carol LaFleur (now Jo Carol Nesset-Sale) attended the University of Utah Law School. Subsequently, she practiced criminal defense work, medical malpractice, and mediation. She served as the assistant director of the Legal Aid Clinic at the University of Georgia Law School, and later taught trial techniques at Emory University School of Law and the John Marshall Law School. Currently, she has her own practice (Mediation and Law Office of Jo Carol Nesset-Sale) in Athens, Georgia.

PREGNANCY DISCRIMINATION ACT OF 1978

Title VII of the Civil Rights Act of 1964 prohibits discrimination with respect to an employee's "compensation, terms, conditions, or privileges of employment because of such individual's race, color, religion, sex, or national origin." 42 U.S.C. §2000e-2(a). The Pregnancy Discrimination Act of 1978 (PDA) amends, as follows, the definitional section that prohibits *sex discrimination* in employment:

> The terms "because of sex" or "on the basis of sex" include, but are not limited to, because of or on the basis of pregnancy, childbirth, or related medical conditions; and women affected by pregnancy, childbirth, or related medical conditions shall be treated the same for all employment-related purposes, including receipt of benefits under fringe benefit programs, as other persons not so affected but similar in their ability or inability to work. . . . 42 U.S.C. §2000e(k).

CALIFORNIA FEDERAL SAVINGS & LOAN ASSOCIATION v. GUERRA
479 U.S. 272 (1987)

Justice MARSHALL delivered the opinion of the Court.

The question presented is whether Title VII of the Civil Rights Act of 1964, as amended by the Pregnancy Discrimination Act of 1978, preempts a state statute that requires employers to provide leave and reinstatement to employees disabled by pregnancy.

California's Fair Employment and Housing Act (FEHA), Cal. Gov't Code Ann. §12900 et seq., is a comprehensive statute that prohibits discrimination in employment and housing. In September 1978, California amended the FEHA to proscribe certain forms of employment discrimination on the basis of pregnancy. Subdivision (b)(2)—the provision at issue here—is the only portion of the statute that applies to employers subject to Title VII. It requires these employers to provide female employees an unpaid pregnancy disability leave of up to four months. Respondent Fair Employment and Housing Commission, the state agency authorized to interpret the FEHA, has construed §12945(b)(2) to require California employers to reinstate an employee returning from such pregnancy leave to the job she previously held, unless it is no longer available due to business necessity. In the latter case, the employer must make a reasonable, good faith effort to place the employee in a substantially similar job. The statute does not compel employers to provide paid leave to pregnant employees. Accordingly, the only benefit pregnant workers actually derive from §12945(b)(2) is a qualified right to reinstatement.

Title VII of the Civil Rights Act of 1964 also prohibits various forms of employment discrimination, including discrimination on the basis of sex. However, in General Electric Co. v. Gilbert, 429 U.S. 125 (1976), this Court ruled that discrimination on the basis of pregnancy was not sex discrimination under Title VII. In response to the *Gilbert* decision, Congress passed the Pregnancy Discrimination Act of 1978 (PDA) [specifying] that sex discrimination includes discrimination on the basis of pregnancy.

Petitioner California Federal Savings and Loan Association (Cal. Fed.) [is] covered by both Title VII and §12945(b)(2). Cal. Fed. has a facially neutral leave policy that permits employees who have completed three months of service to take unpaid leaves of absence for a variety of reasons, including disability and pregnancy. Although it is Cal. Fed.'s policy to try to provide an employee taking unpaid leave with a similar position upon returning, Cal. Fed. expressly reserves the right to terminate an employee who has taken a leave of absence if a similar position is not available.

Lillian Garland was employed by Cal. Fed. as a receptionist for several years. In January 1982, she took a pregnancy disability leave. When she was able to return to work in April of that year, Garland notified Cal. Fed., but was informed that her job had been filled and that there were no receptionists or similar positions available. Garland filed a complaint with respondent Department of Fair Employment and Housing. . . . [Prior to the hearing before the Fair Housing and Employment Commission, Cal. Fed. brought this action seeking a declaration that §12945(b)(2) is inconsistent with, and preempted by, Title VII, as well as an injunction against enforcement of the section.]

In order to decide whether the California statute requires or permits employers to violate Title VII, as amended by the PDA, or is inconsistent with the purposes of the statute, we must determine whether the PDA prohibits the States from requiring employers to provide reinstatement to pregnant workers, regardless of their policy for disabled workers generally.

Petitioners argue that the language of the federal statute itself unambiguously rejects California's "special treatment" approach to pregnancy discrimination, thus rendering any resort to the legislative history unnecessary. They contend that the second clause of the PDA forbids an employer to treat pregnant employees any differently than other disabled employees. Because "[t]he purpose of Congress is the ultimate touchstone" of the preemption inquiry, however, we must examine the PDA's language against the background of its legislative history and historical context. . . .

By adding pregnancy to the definition of sex discrimination prohibited by Title VII, the first clause of the PDA reflects Congress' disapproval of the reasoning in *Gilbert* [holding that pregnancy discrimination was not sex discrimination].

Rather than imposing a limitation on the remedial purpose of the PDA, we believe that the second clause was intended to overrule the holding in *Gilbert* and to illustrate how discrimination against pregnancy is to be remedied. Accordingly, subject to certain limitations, we agree with the Court of Appeals' conclusion that Congress intended the PDA to be "a floor beneath which pregnancy disability benefits may not drop—not a ceiling above which they may not rise."

The context in which Congress considered the issue of pregnancy discrimination supports this view of the PDA. Congress had before it extensive evidence of discrimination against pregnancy, particularly in disability and health insurance like those challenged. . . . The reports, debates, and hearings make abundantly clear that Congress intended the PDA to provide relief for working women and to end discrimination against pregnant workers. In contrast to the thorough account of discrimination against pregnant workers, the legislative history is devoid of any discussion of preferential treatment of pregnancy, beyond acknowledgments of the existence of state statutes providing for such preferential treatment. Opposition to the PDA came from those concerned with the cost of including pregnancy in health and disability benefit plans and the application of the bill to abortion, not from those who favored special accommodation of pregnancy.

In support of their argument that the PDA prohibits employment practices that favor pregnant women, petitioners and several amici cite statements in the legislative history to the effect that the PDA does not *require* employers to extend any benefits to pregnant women that they do not already provide to other disabled employees. . . . On the contrary, if Congress had intended to *prohibit* preferential treatment, it would have been the height of understatement to say only that the legislation would not *require* such conduct. It is hardly conceivable that Congress would have extensively discussed only its intent not to require preferential treatment if in fact it had intended to prohibit such treatment.

We also find it significant that Congress was aware of state laws similar to California's but apparently did not consider them inconsistent with the PDA. . . . Title VII, as amended by the PDA, and California's pregnancy disability leave statute share a common goal. The purpose of Title VII is "to achieve equality of employment opportunities and remove barriers that have operated in the past to favor an identifiable group of . . . employees over other employees." Rather than limiting existing Title VII principles and objectives, the PDA extends them to cover pregnancy. As Senator Williams, a sponsor of the Act, stated: "The entire thrust . . . behind this legislation is to guarantee women the basic right to participate fully and equally in the workforce, without denying them the fundamental right to full participation in family life." 123 Cong. Rec. 29658 (1977).

Section 12945(b)(2) also promotes equal employment opportunity. By requiring employers to reinstate women after a reasonable pregnancy disability leave, §12945(b)(2) ensures that they will not lose their jobs on account of pregnancy disability. . . . California's pregnancy disability leave statute allows women, as well as men, to have families without losing their jobs. Thus, petitioners' facial challenge to §12945(b)(2) fails. The statute is not preempted by Title VII, as amended by the PDA, because it is not inconsistent with the purposes of the federal statute. . . .

Justice WHITE, with whom THE CHIEF JUSTICE and Justice POWELL join, dissenting. . . .

The second clause [of the PDA] could not be clearer: it mandates that pregnant employees "shall be treated the same for all employment-related purposes" as nonpregnant employees similarly situated with respect to their ability or inability to work. This language leaves no room for preferential treatment of pregnant workers. . . . In sum, preferential treatment of pregnant workers is prohibited by Title VII, as amended by the PDA. Section 12945(b)(2) of the California Gov't Code, which extends preferential benefits for pregnancy, is therefore preempted. . . .

NOTE: WHO IS LILLIAN GARLAND?

Lillian Garland was a receptionist with California Federal Savings and Loan Association (Cal Fed). After she became pregnant, she took a four-month pregnancy disability leave from January to April 1982. She gave birth to her daughter on February 12, 1982. After she recovered from the Caesarean section delivery, her doctor certified that she would be medically able to return to work on April 21. But when she informed the bank that she was ready to resume work, the bank told her that her position had been filled—and there were no openings for her.

Lillian Garland (the fired employee in California Federal Savings & Loan v. Guerra) and her daughter

Her situation became dire while she was unemployed. Without an income, she was evicted from her apartment and had to sleep on a woman friend's couch. Lacking financial resources, she lost custody of her daughter to her ex-husband because she could not afford rent or legal representation or funds to care for her baby.

At that point, she called California's Department of Fair Employment and Housing, who told her that Cal Fed's actions were illegal. Under the 1979 California Fair Employment Law, every woman is entitled to up to four months' unpaid leave, without losing her job, for medical disability caused by pregnancy or childbirth.

During the ensuing litigation, she returned to school and became a real estate agent and insurance broker. She purchased a franchise for a real estate agency that serves veterans. She later married her childhood sweetheart, a Black Hawk helicopter mechanic who served four tours of duty in Vietnam. They currently live in Virginia, where she serves on the board of a nonprofit agency that offers home repairs to low-income seniors, the disabled, and veterans.

She is proud of her role in combating pregnancy discrimination. Her fondest memory stems from a conversation at a White House ceremony where she was honored. She found herself seated next to Rosa Parks, the Black seamstress who sparked the civil rights movement by refusing to give up her seat on a Montgomery, Alabama, bus to a white man in 1955. "Little sister," Rosa Parks told her, "I've been following your career for years—and I am so proud of you!" "Imagine that," Ms. Garland remarks with wonder. "Rosa Parks was proud of *me*!"[14]

---

[14]. Phone conversation with Lillian Garland, Dec. 31, 2012. See also Stephanie M. Wildman, Pregnant and Working: The Story of California Federal Savings & Loan Ass'n v. Guerra, in Women and the Law Stories 253 (Elizabeth M. Schneider & Stephanie M. Wildman eds., 2011); Lillian Garland, YouTube, Speaking Out: Family and Medical Leave Act Advocate Describes Experience (2018), https://www.youtube.com/watch?v=c6xdg_8PW44.

Wendy W. Williams, Equality's Riddle: Pregnancy and the Equal Treatment/Special Treatment Debate

13 N.Y.U. Rev. L. & Soc. Change 325, 333-349 (1984-1985)

The treatment of pregnancy and maternity under the law developed in stages. . . .

A. STAGE ONE: 1870 TO 1970

[W]omen's "maternal functions" formed the basis of a dual system of law. The system treated women differently than men under the claim that it sought to accommodate to and provide for women's special needs. . . .

[T]here were, beginning in the 1940s, a very few provisions dealing specifically with pregnancy. [T]he U.S. Department of Labor recommended that pregnant women not work for six weeks before and two months after delivery. Some states adopted laws prohibiting employers from employing women for a period of time before and after childbirth to protect the health of women and their offspring during that vulnerable time. Where leaves were not accompanied by a guarantee of job security or wage replacement, they "protected" pregnant women right out of their jobs. . . . At the same time, the unemployment insurance laws of many states rendered otherwise eligible women [pregnant workers] ineligible for unemployment insurance if they were pregnant or had recently given birth. Women unemployed because of state laws or employer policies or mandatory unpaid leave thus were precluded from the resources available to other unemployed workers. Four states, including California, created disability insurance programs to provide partial wage replacement to temporarily disabled workers, but those programs either excluded pregnancy-related disabilities altogether or provided restricted benefits. . . . The absence of legislation concerning pregnancy and employment meant that the issue was left to employers (and, where there were unions, to collective bargaining).

By 1960, the dawn of a new decade that would usher in Title VII, many employers simply fired women who became pregnant. Others provided unpaid maternity leaves of absence, frequently accompanied by loss of seniority and accrued benefits. Few provided job security, much less allowed paid sick leave and vacation time to be used for maternity leave. Payment of disability benefits for childbirth was, at best, restricted, and employer sponsored medical insurance provided, at most, limited coverage of pregnancy-related medical treatment and hospitalization. Pervasively, pregnancy was treated less favorably than other physical conditions that affected workplace performance. The pattern of rules telegraphed the underlying assumption: a woman's pregnancy signaled her disengagement from the workplace. [These rules reflected a normative judgment]: when wage-earning women became pregnant they did, and should, go home.

B. STAGE TWO: 1970-1976

By 1970, women were in the workforce in unprecedented numbers. Moreover, an increasing number of them were staying after the birth of children. . . . Suits were filed under Title VII and the Equal Protection Clause on the theory that treating pregnancy disabilities differently and less favorably than other disabilities discriminates on the basis of sex. . . .

In 1974, however, the United States Supreme Court eliminated the Equal Protection Clause as a vehicle for an "equal treatment" attack on legislation singling out pregnancy for special treatment. The state statute challenged in Geduldig v. Aiello [417 U.S. 484 (1974)] created a state disability fund, providing temporary, partial wage replacement to private sector workers who became physically unable to work. The statute was liberally interpreted to cover every conceivable work disability, including, according to the record in the case, disability arising from cosmetic surgery, hair transplants, skiing accidents and prostatectomies. It excluded only one type of work disability from coverage—those "arising out of or in connection with" pregnancy. . . .

Justice Stewart, on behalf of a majority of the court, [stated] that the case did not involve discrimination based on gender as such: "The California insurance program does not exclude anyone from benefit eligibility because of gender but merely removes one physical condition—pregnancy—from the list of compensable disabilities." Translated, this means that the statute bases the exclusion on pregnancy, not on sex itself. . . .

The conclusion that discrimination on the basis of pregnancy was not sex discrimination freed the Court from the obligation to engage in the more activist review it reserves for sex discrimination cases. Indulging the strong presumption of constitutionality appropriate to rational basis review, it concluded that a legislature legitimately could exclude a costly disability. . . . The Court's explanation that exclusion was rational because the "additional" cost of covering pregnancy would upset the preestablished contribution rate or benefit level would apply to any frequent or prolonged disability that had been excluded from the program, however arbitrarily. . . .

Justice Brennan, joined in dissent by Justices Marshall and Douglas, adopted the plaintiffs' position in its entirety. Women disabled by pregnancy-related causes were comparable to other disabled workers for purposes of the California program. . . . Moreover, the exclusion of pregnancy-related disabilities constituted sex discrimination. . . .

[Yet], when the Court struck down the pregnancy policies in [Cleveland Board of Education v. LaFleur, 414 U.S. 632 (1974)], it invoked not the sex discrimination cases decided under the equal protection clause, but rather, the reproductive choice cases, such as [Eisenstadt v. Baird, 405 U.S. 438 (1972) and Roe v. Wade, 410 U.S. 113 (1973)]. . . . The doctrinal distinction between due process and equal protection analysis of pregnancy issues represented by LaFleur and Geduldig is in a sense a reiteration of the special treatment/equal treatment dichotomy. To oversimplify, the due process approach is not troubled by and, indeed, invokes a form of special treatment analysis. The liberty interest at stake, defined as the right to choose whether to bear or beget a child without undue state interference, is recognized as "fundamental" precisely because of the central and unique importance to the individual of reproductive choice. The characterization of pregnancy discrimination as sex discrimination, by contrast, requires the comparative analysis of the equal protection mode. Its emphasis is on what is not unique about the reproductive process of women. . . .

C. STAGE THREE: 1976-1978

In General Electric Company v. Gilbert, [429 U.S. 125 (1976)], the Supreme Court dropped the other shoe. Relying heavily on Geduldig v. Aiello, it interpreted Title VII as it had the equal protection clause: it held that discrimination on the basis of pregnancy was not sex discrimination. *Gilbert*, on its facts, was very similar to *Geduldig*. It involved a private employer's disability insurance plan almost identical to the California state plan both in its general scope and in its exclusion of pregnancy-related disabilities. . . .

Under Title VII, rules that are "neutral" but have a disproportionate sex-based effect may also violate the Act. However, the particular "neutral" General Electric pregnancy disability rule, said Justice Rehnquist [writing for the majority], could not even be viewed as having a discriminatory *effect* on women. Men and women, he said, are both covered by the disability program. Moreover, they are covered for the disabilities common to both sexes. Pregnancy disabilities are therefore an *"additional* risk, unique to women." Failure to compensate women for them does not upset the basic sex equality of the program. In a footnote, he drove home the point: Title VII does not require "that 'greater economic benefit[s]' . . . be paid to one sex or the other because of their differing roles in the 'scheme of human existence.'" This conclusion makes breathtakingly explicit the underlying philosophy of the majority of the justices in *Geduldig* and *Gilbert*. Pregnancy, for Rehnquist, is an "extra," an add-on to the basic male model for humanity. Equality does not contemplate handing out benefits for extras—indeed, to do so would be to grant special benefits to women, possibly discriminating against men. The fact that men were compensated under the program for disabilities unique to their sex troubled his analysis not at all.

Justice Brennan, in his dissent in *Geduldig,* almost grasped the essence of the problem when he observed that "the State has created a double standard for disability compensation; a limitation is imposed upon the disabilities for which women workers may recover, while men receive full compensation for all disabilities suffered, including those that affect only or primarily their sex. . . . " What eluded even Justice Brennan was that the statute did not create a "double" standard. Rather, it made man the standard (whatever disabilities men suffer will be compensated) and measured women against that standard (as long as she is compensated for anything he is compensated for, she is treated equally).

For Rehnquist, as long as women are treated in the same way as men in the areas where they are like men—in the disability program, this would mean coverage for things like heart attacks, broken bones, appendicitis—that's equality. To the extent the Court will consider the equities with respect to childbearing capacity, it will consider them only in the category where they belong—extra, separate, different. A family, marital, or reproductive right—yes, in appropriate circumstances. A public matter of equality and equal protection of women—no. . . .

[In response to the above Supreme Court decisions, Congress passed the PDA in 1978, thereby transforming employers' treatment of pregnancy and adopting the equal treatment model.]

Notes and Questions

1. **Rationale.** *LaFleur,* decided before the PDA, was based on due process. Why did the Supreme Court base its decision on due process rather than equal protection?

2. **Antidiscrimination rule.** The PDA does not mandate pregnancy leave. Rather, it is an antidiscrimination rule that requires employers to treat pregnancy the same as other physical conditions in terms of leave and other employment benefits. How does an employer treat pregnant women *the same as* "other persons not so affected but similar in their ability or inability to work"? And what should be the comparison group of disabled employees—employees with *occupational* injuries who are unable to work? Employees who are injured off the job (such as in recreational activities)? Or both?

3. **Pregnancy discrimination after the PDA.** The PDA will soon celebrate its 50th anniversary. Yet workers continue to experience cases of pregnancy discrimination. One in five mothers say that they have experienced pregnancy discrimination in the workplace.[15] Pregnancy discrimination affects women of all races and ethnicities. However, women of color and immigrants are at particular risk because they are more likely to hold physically demanding and low-wage jobs that present specific challenges for pregnant workers.

4. **Criticisms of PDA.** Criticisms of the PDA include its failure to protect women who are fired not *during* pregnancy, but *after* their return from leave because of employers' fears that the women may become pregnant again, or because of gender-based stereotypes about pregnant women's lack of competence. In addition, employers may offer nonpregnancy reasons (i.e., pretexts) for discharge or demotion. See, e.g., Groves v. Cost Planning & Mgmt. Int'l, Inc., 372 F.3d 1008

---

[15]. Ben Gitis et al., BPC – Morning Consult: 1 in 5 Moms Experience Pregnancy Discrimination in the Workplace, BiPartisanPolicy Blog, Feb. 11, 2022, https://bipartisanpolicy.org/blog/bpc-morning-consult-pregnancy-discrimination/. Nearly 31,000 pregnancy discrimination charges were filed with the Equal Opportunity Employment Commission (EEOC) (the agency charged with administering the PDA) and state-level fair employment practice agencies between October 2010 and September 2015. Nat'l P'ship for Women & Families, Pregnant Workers Fairness Act 1, 2 (Mar. 2021), https://nationalpartnership.org/report/pregnant-workers-fairness-act/.

(8th Cir. 2004) (holding that economic downturn was justifiable reason for termination despite prima facie case of discrimination). How can fired employees combat these rationales?

5. Pregnancy accommodations. Pregnant employees sometimes need workplace *accommodations* (such as sitting instead of standing) that would enable them to continue working while pregnant. After passage of the PDA, many courts interpreted the PDA narrowly, allowing employers to refuse to accommodate pregnant employees with medical needs despite accommodating workers with other disabilities.

The Supreme Court addressed the application of the PDA to pregnancy accommodations in Young v. United Parcel Service (UPS), 575 U.S. 206 (2015). A pregnant delivery driver requested workplace accommodations after her physician restricted her from lifting more than 20 pounds. Because UPS policy required lifting 70 pounds, her employer denied her request, even though UPS provided accommodations to other non-pregnant employees. In response to her claim of pregnancy discrimination, the Supreme Court held that failure to accommodate pregnant workers with medical needs, when an employer similarly accommodates non-pregnant employees, violates the PDA when the employer's policies impose a "significant burden" on pregnant workers and the employer has not raised a "sufficiently strong" justification. UPS later changed its policy to offer temporary light duty to pregnant workers. Currently, 30 states have laws exceeding federal mandates on accommodating pregnant workers, largely in response to court challenges under the PDA.[16]

a. ADAAA amendments. The Pregnancy Discrimination Act (PDA) is not the only law that requires employers to provide accommodations to pregnant women. In 2008, Congress extended the Americans with Disabilities Act with the Americans with Disabilities Act Amendment Act (ADAAA), Pub. L. No. 110–325, requiring employers to provide accommodations for pregnancy-related conditions that meet the definition of "disability." Note, however, that courts do not consider *normal pregnancy* as a disability under the ADAAA, although pregnancy-related impairments may qualify. 29 C.F.R. pt. 1630 App. §1630.2(h).

b. Pregnant Workers Fairness Act. On December 29, 2022, President Biden signed the Fiscal Year 2023 Omnibus Spending Bill, which included the Pregnant Workers Fairness Act (PWFA), H.R. 2617, 117th Cong. (2021-2022), effective June 27, 2023. The act strengthens the treatment of pregnancy accommodations by declaring that it is an unlawful employment practice to (1) fail to make reasonable accommodations to known limitations of covered job applicants or employees, unless the accommodation would impose an undue hardship on an entity's business operation; (2) deny employment opportunities based on the need of the entity to make such reasonable accommodations; (3) require such job applicants or employees to accept an accommodation without a prior discussion with the employer about the accommodation; (4) require such employees to take paid or

---

[16]. Stephen Joyce, State Laws Protecting Pregnant Workers Fill Gaps in Federal Law, Bloomberg Law News, Oct. 26, 2022, https://news.bloomberglaw.com/daily-labor-report/state-laws-protecting-pregnant-workers-fill-gaps-in-federal-law.

unpaid leave if another reasonable accommodation can be provided to accommodate their known limitations; or (5) take adverse action in terms, conditions, or privileges of employment against an employee requesting or using such reasonable accommodations. The PWFA does not replace federal, state, or local laws that are *more* protective of workers affected by pregnancy, childbirth, or related medical conditions. The act applies to private- and public-sector employers with at least 15 employees.

6. Equal versus special treatment. Is the provision of pregnancy benefits "special treatment" or "equal treatment"? To what extent does the provision of benefits for pregnant workers compromise women's employment opportunities? Might it revitalize early twentieth-century attitudes that women needed protective labor legislation (limiting the hours that women could work because of women's childbearing potential)? See Muller v. Oregon, 208 U.S. 412 (1908). On the other hand, without this form of "special treatment," what will happen to female employees who are likely to require time off from work because of pregnancy?

7. Nonmarital families. Although JoCarol LaFleur and Lillian Garland were both married at the time of their employment controversies, the issues that they faced are not based on marriage or limited to married couples. See, e.g., Crisitello v. St. Theresa School, 299 A.3d 781 (N.J. 2023) (upholding termination of unmarried pregnant teacher by religious employer). Indeed, the legal protections discussed above are especially important for nonmarital families and parents. For additional discussions of legal protections applicable to these families and parents, see Chapters V and IX.

Problems

1. Hunter Tylo is a soap opera star on prime-time television. On *Melrose Place,* she plays a happily married woman who suddenly begins an affair. Shortly after she accepts the job, Hunter becomes pregnant. She informs her employer, Spelling Entertainment Group. One month later, she is fired. Spelling informs her that they have a contractual right to terminate her if there was a "material change in [her] appearance." Further, Spelling argues that her pregnancy does not conform to the character she portrays. Tylo alleges a violation of the PDA. What result? See Tylo v. Superior Court, 64 Cal. Rptr. 2d 731 (Ct. App. 1997). Recall that the Supreme Court later decided Young v. UPS. How would *Young* influence the result?

2. When a public high school honors student becomes pregnant during her senior year, the principal informs her that she can no longer attend class "due to safety concerns," and that she is not permitted to attend commencement or to have her name printed in the graduation program. However, the school permits the baby's father to continue to participate in commencement exercises. The student comes to you for advice. Does she have a claim for pregnancy discrimination? Sex discrimination?

b. Balancing Work and Family

CALDWELL v. HOLLAND OF TEXAS, INC.
208 F.3d 671 (8th Cir. 2000)

Bright, Circuit Judge.

[Juanita Caldwell, mother of three-year-old Kejuan, had an excellent record working for three years for Holland, Inc., the owner of several Kentucky Fried Chicken restaurants in Texarkana, Arkansas, before she was fired based on the following events.]

On Saturday, June 7, 1997, Kejuan awoke with a high fever, pain in his ears, and congestion. Caldwell promptly notified Assistant Manager Loyce, prior to the start of her morning shift, that she would be absent because Kejuan required immediate medical attention. Loyce gave Caldwell permission to miss her shift. That morning, a doctor at an emergency clinic diagnosed Kejuan as having an acute ear infection. During this visit, the doctor prescribed a ten-day course of antibiotics and a two-day decongestant for Kejuan. At the same time, the treating physician informed Caldwell that her son's condition probably would require surgery if her son was to avoid permanent hearing loss, and he recommended that Caldwell schedule a follow-up examination with her son's regular pediatrician, Dr. Mark Wright.

Later that Saturday night, upon the request of an assistant manager, Caldwell worked an evening shift at one of Holland's other restaurant locations. While Caldwell was working, her elderly mother cared for her son and administered his medications. Caldwell did not have any shifts on Sunday. When Caldwell returned to her regular work on Monday morning, June 9, 1997, Mark Monholland, a manager at the Hickory Street restaurant, abruptly fired Caldwell without discussing her absence of June 7, 1997. [She filed suit, alleging that her termination violated the FMLA.]

The FMLA allows eligible employees to take up to a total of twelve workweeks of leave per year for, among other things, "serious health conditions" that afflict their immediate family members [such as a "spouse, son, daughter, or parent"]. See 29 U.S.C. §2612(a)(1)(C). The employee must show that her family member suffered a serious health condition and that her absence was attributable to the family member's serious health condition.

A "serious health condition" occurs, under the regulations, when the family member suffers an "illness, injury, impairment, or physical or mental condition" that requires "inpatient care" or "continuing treatment" by a health care provider. See 29 C.F.R. §825.114(a). Here, the parties agree that Kejuan never received inpatient care. The pertinent issue is whether Kejuan received continuing treatment. A family member receives continuing treatment if the person experiences "[a] period of *incapacity* . . . of more than three consecutive calendar days" and then receives subsequent treatment, or experiences further incapacity relating to, the same condition. The subsequent treatment must include, either "[t]reatment two or more times by a health care provider . . . ," or "[t]reatment by a health care provider on at least one occasion which results in a regimen of continuing treatment under the supervision of the health care provider." . . .

The applicability of the FMLA, here, turns on whether Caldwell can prove a two-pronged inquiry: first, she must show that Kejuan suffered "a period of incapacity of more than three consecutive calendar days"; second, she must show that Kejuan subsequently received continued, supervised treatment relating to the same condition. . . .

In assessing the first prong of Caldwell's case, we note at the outset that the question of what constitutes incapacity of a three-year-old raises an issue not directly addressed by the regulations. The regulations state that incapacity may be determined based on an individual's "inability to work, attend school, or perform other regular daily activities due to the serious health condition, treatment therefor, or recovery therefrom." Because most three-year-old children do not work or attend school, the standard offered by the regulations is an insufficient guide. The fact finder must determine whether the child's illness demonstrably affected his normal activity. In making this determination, the fact finder may consider a variety of factors, including but not limited to: whether the child participated in his daily routines or was particularly difficult to care for during that period, and whether a daycare facility would have allowed a child with Kejuan's illness to attend its sessions.

Caldwell avers that Kejuan's ear infection, which was severe enough to warrant emergency treatment, required constant care for a period of more than three days. She states in her supplemental affidavit that Kejuan was incapacitated beginning Saturday, June 7, 1997, for more than three consecutive days. She further states:

> He [Kejuan] remained inside the house and was kept in bed as much as possible. He did not participate in any of his normal activities. He was under the constant care of me (his mother) and his grandmother, and both the prescribed medications and a fever reducer were administered to him during this entire time.

In addition to Caldwell's affidavit, the medical records show that Kejuan's ear infection was a continuing, persistent condition that could only be treated by surgery. Kejuan's period of incapacity, therefore, may be measured over the entire time during which he was suffering from this illness and being treated for it. We note that Kejuan was treated for his condition for ten days following his first visit to the emergency clinic. The medical records state that the condition did not improve, and as a result, Dr. Wright, his regular physician, prescribed another ten-day course of antibiotics. Despite the two medical treatments, Kejuan's condition continued to persist until Dr. Trone, a surgical specialist, performed surgery to remove his tonsils and adenoids on July 17, 1997. This entire period, from June 7-July 17, 1997, may constitute Kejuan's period of incapacity if his illness and these various treatments disrupted his basic daily routines, and if, as the record suggests, his ongoing treatment was not successfully alleviating his condition of disability. . . .

Alternatively, the ten-day period beginning on June 7, 1997 could constitute Kejuan's period of incapacity. As we have noted, his mother's supplemental affidavit refers to constant care and administration of prescribed medications during "this entire time." . . . Even if Kejuan did not sustain "incapacity" under the regulations *prior* to his surgery, the record clearly shows that the inflammation and infection in his ears resulted in a period of incapacity that lasted more than three days once he had the tonsillectomy and adenoidectomy. . . .

FMLA's purpose is to help working men and women balance the conflicting demands of work and personal life. The law requires courts to consider the seriousness of the afflicted individual's condition because the law was designed to prevent individuals like Juanita Caldwell from having to choose between their livelihood and treatment for their own or their family members' serious health conditions. Upon examining the seriousness of Kejuan's ear infection, which required surgery to prevent deafness, we hold that there is at least a question of fact as to whether Kejuan's condition was "serious" under the regulations. . . .

On the second prong of the threshold inquiry, we believe that Caldwell has generated a genuine issue of fact regarding whether Kejuan received "subsequent treatment." Here, after the first ten-day antibiotic treatment, Kejuan was treated by Dr. Wright and later by Dr. Trone in surgery. . . . Furthermore, the record shows at least two postoperative medical visits to monitor Kejuan's condition. [T]he district court erred in granting a summary judgment of dismissal. . . .

FAMILY AND MEDICAL LEAVE ACT
29 U.S.C. §§2601, 2611, 2612, 2614

§2601. FINDINGS AND PURPOSES

(a) *Findings.* The Congress finds that

(1) the number of single-parent households and two-parent households in which the single parent or both parents work is increasing significantly; . . .

(3) the lack of employment policies to accommodate working parents can force individuals to choose between job security and parenting; . . .

(5) due to the nature of the roles of men and women in our society, the primary responsibility for family caretaking often falls on women, and such responsibility affects their working lives more than it affects the working lives of men; and

(6) employment standards that apply to one gender only have serious potential for encouraging employers to discriminate against employees and applicants for employment who are of that gender.

(b) *Purposes.* It is the purpose of this Act

(1) to balance the demands of the workplace with the needs of families, to promote stability and economic security of families, and to promote national interests in preserving family integrity;

(2) to entitle employees to take reasonable leave for medical reasons, for the birth or adoption of a child, and for the care of a child, spouse, or parent who has a serious health condition;

(3) to accomplish such purposes . . . in a manner that accommodates the legitimate interests of employers;

(4) to accomplish [such] purposes . . . in a manner that, consistent with the Equal Protection Clause of the Fourteenth Amendment, minimizes the potential for employment discrimination on the basis of sex by ensuring generally that leave is available for eligible medical reasons (including

maternity-related disability) and for compelling family reasons, on a gender-neutral basis; and

(5) to promote the goal of equal employment opportunity for women and men, pursuant to such clause.

§2611. DEFINITIONS . . .

(2)(A) "[E]ligible employee" means an employee who has been employed

(i) for at least 12 months by the employer with respect to whom leave is requested under section 2612; and

(ii) for at least 1,250 hours of service with such employer during the previous 12-month period. . . .

(4)(A) "[E]mployer"

(i) means any person engaged in commerce or in any industry or activity affecting commerce who employs 50 or more employees [for each workday, for 20 or more weeks in the current or proceeding year]. . . .

(5) "[E]mployment benefits" means all benefits provided or made available to employees by an employer, including group life insurance, health insurance, disability insurance, sick leave, annual leave, educational benefits, and pensions. . . .

(7) "[P]arent" means the biological parent of an employee or an individual who stood in loco parentis to an employee when the employee was a son or daughter. . . .

(11) "[S]erious health condition" means an illness, injury, impairment, or physical or mental condition that involves—

(A) inpatient care in a hospital, hospice, or residential medical care facility; or

(B) continuing treatment by a health care provider.

(12) "[S]on or daughter" means a biological, adopted, or foster child, a stepchild, a legal ward, or a child of a person standing in loco parentis, who is [under 18, or 18 years or older if mentally or physically disabled].

(13) "[S]pouse" means a husband or wife, as the case may be.

§2612. LEAVE REQUIREMENT

(a) In General.

(1) Entitlement to leave. [A]n eligible employee shall be entitled to a total of 12 workweeks of leave during any 12-month period for one or more of the following:

(A) Because of the birth of a son or daughter of the employee and in order to care for such son or daughter.

(B) Because of the placement of a son or daughter with the employee for adoption or foster care.

(C) In order to care for the spouse, or a son, daughter, or parent, of the employee, if such spouse, son, daughter, or parent has a serious health condition.

(D) Because of a serious health condition that makes the employee unable to perform the functions of the position of such employee.

(E) Because of any qualifying exigency (as the Secretary shall, by regulation, determine) arising out of the fact that the spouse, or a son, daughter, or parent of the employee is on covered active duty (or has been notified of an impending call or order to covered active duty) in the Armed Forces. . . .

(b) [Leave generally shall not be taken intermittently unless the employer and employee agree otherwise.]

(c) Unpaid Leave Permitted. [L]eave granted under subsection (a) may consist of unpaid leave. [However, the employee may choose to substitute, or the employer may require, accrued paid vacation leave, personal leave, or medical or sick leave be substituted for the unpaid 12-week leave.]

. . .

(e) Foreseeable leave.

(1) Requirement of notice.

[For a foreseeable leave based on a birth or child placement], the employee shall provide the employer with not less than 30 days' notice [except if] the date of the birth or placement requires leave to begin in less than 30 days, the employee shall provide such notice as is practicable. . . . [For a foreseeable leave based on planned medical treatment, the employee shall make a reasonable effort to schedule treatment so as not to disrupt unduly the operations of the employer and provide at least 30 days' notice or such notice as is practicable under the circumstances.]

(f) Spouses Employed by the Same Employer. [If husband and wife] are employed by the same employer, the aggregate number of workweeks of leave to which both may be entitled may be limited to 12 workweeks during any 12-month period. . . .

§2614. EMPLOYMENT AND BENEFITS PROTECTION

(a) Restoration to Position.

(1) In general. Except as provided in subsection (b), any eligible employee who takes leave under section 2612 for the intended purpose of the leave shall be entitled, on return from such leave—

(A) to be restored by the employer to the position of employment held by the employee when the leave commenced; or

(B) to be restored to an equivalent position with equivalent employment benefits, pay, and other terms and conditions of employment.

[The taking of leave shall not result in the loss of any employment benefit accrued prior to the date on which the leave commenced, but the restored employee has no right to the accrual of any seniority benefits during any period of leave.]

(b) Exemption Concerning Certain Highly Compensated Employees.

(1) Denial of restoration. An employer may deny restoration under subsection (a) to any eligible employee [if]—

(A) such denial is necessary to prevent substantial and grievous economic injury to the operations of the employer; . . .

(2) Affected employees. An eligible employee described in paragraph (1) is a salaried eligible employee who is among the highest paid 10 percent of the employees employed by the employer within 75 miles of the facility at which the employee is employed.

(c) [Employer is required to maintain health benefits for the duration of the leave.]

§2615. PROHIBITED ACTS

(a) Interference with rights. . . .

It shall be unlawful for any employer to interfere with, restrain, or deny the exercise of or the attempt to exercise, any right provided under this title. . . .

It shall be unlawful for any employer to discharge or in any other manner discriminate against any individual for opposing any practice made unlawful by this title. . . .

Notes and Questions

1. Background. The FMLA recently celebrated its 30th birthday. The act became law in 1993 after a lengthy battle. Opponents originally charged that the legislation would have a negative impact on industry. In 2022, nearly 15 million workers were supported by the FMLA—one-fifth to care for family members (such as a spouse or parent), and another one-fifth to care for a newborn, adopted, or foster child.[17]

2. Purposes. How does the FMLA redress the PDA's shortcomings? What is the purpose of the FMLA? To what extent does the FMLA accomplish the purposes enumerated in the statute?

3. Criticisms. The FMLA mandates *unpaid* leave. Are most employees able to take unpaid leave? Many employees, especially workers of color, are not protected by FMLA leave. See the article (*Key Facts*) below. For many low-wage workers, taking unpaid medical or family care leave leads to job loss.

Is the duration of unpaid leave (12 weeks) sufficient for most employees? Given that the period applies both to pregnancy and infant care, might a mother with pregnancy complications use all her leave before birth? Does the FMLA address the needs of *single* parents? Of fathers? Does it achieve its vision of caretaking leaves for men and women on equal terms? Professor Joanna Grossman responds:

> If only mothers take leave, then the FMLA only accommodates women's caretaking, protection that gives them a measure of job security but at the same time preserves employers' incentives to prefer male employees. It also does nothing to equalize the burdens of caretaking themselves.[18]

Will the FMLA achieve the antidiscrimination goal of "degendering" responsibilities for care work? See Nevada Dept. of Human Res. v. Hibbs, 538 U.S. 721 (2003).

---

[17]. Nat'l P'ship for Women & Families, U.S. Dept. of Labor, Key Facts: The Family and Medical Leave Act (Feb. 2023), https://nationalpartnership.org/report/fmla-key-facts/#:~:text=The%20National%20Partnership%20estimates%20that%20in%202022%20about%2010.9%20million,eligible%20and%20FMLA%2Dineligible%20workers.

[18]. Joanna L. Grossman, Job Security Without Equality: The Family and Medical Leave Act of 1993, 15 Wash. U. J.L. & Pol'y 17, 18 (2004).

Does the FMLA provide leave by *nontraditional* caregivers? Does it provide for the *full* range of childcare responsibilities, such as the need to attend school appointments or provide childcare during school closures? A proposed amendment providing FMLA leave to cover some important, but nonmedical, parenting responsibilities died in committee. See Family and Medical Leave Enhancement Act of 2016, H.R. 5518, 114th Cong. (2015-2016).

4. FMLA and nonmarital partners. How well does the FMLA address the needs of nonmarital partners? The FMLA requires leave to care only for spouses, children, and other enumerated family members. It does not require an employer to allow an employee to take leave to care for a sick nonmarital partner, regardless of how long the couple was together and regardless of whether they have children in common. Why do you think this line was drawn? Is this the right line to draw?

5. Paid leave.

a. State laws. Paid leave is especially important for low-wage workers. Currently, only 13 states and the District of Columbia provide paid family and medical leave.[19] Among states that offer paid family and medical leave, some states fund their programs through an employee payroll tax, while other states impose payroll taxes on both employees and employers. Wage replacement rates among these states range from 50 to 90 percent, while the length of family leave varies from 4 to 12 weeks (with longer periods for medical disability).

Some states are more generous than others in providing paid family leave to fathers. See, e.g., Cal. Fam. Rts. Act (CFRA), Cal. Gov't Code § 12945.2 (requiring private employers with more than 5 employees to provide 12 weeks of job-protected leave to new mothers, fathers, domestic partners, and their children, spouses, adult children, grandparents, grandchildren, or siblings).

b. Federal proposals. The United States is among a handful of nations without any national *paid* family or medical leave law. Congress recently considered several paid leave proposals. The Family and Medical Insurance Leave Act (known as the FAMILY Act), H.R. 804/S. 248, 117th Cong. (2021-2022), would provide employees with a portion of their wages for up to 12 weeks per year to care for their own serious health condition, the serious medical condition of a close family member, the birth or adoption of a child, or to provide military caregiving assistance. The benefits would be funded by employer and employee contributions to a federal national insurance program. The program would cover all workers, regardless of employer size, including those who are self-employed.

The Workflex in the 21st Century Act (known as the Workflex Act), H.R. 4248, 117th Cong. (2021-2022), would provide paid leave and workplace flexibility options. Employers would fund and administer their own programs. Important caveats are that the Act would not require employers to provide *any* paid leave or workplace flexibility options (unlike the FAMILY Act, which would mandate leave); the employer could count holidays as paid leave; and the Workflex Act, by amending the Employee Retirement Income Security Act (ERISA) and preempting

[19]. State Paid Family Leave Laws Across the U.S., BiPartisan Policy Ctr. Blog, Jan. 13, 2022, https://bipartisanpolicy.org/explainer/state-paid-family-leave-laws-across-the-u-s/.

state law, enables employers to ignore existing *state* employment leave/scheduling requirements.

The third proposal, the Economic Security for New Parents Act, S. 3345, 115th Cong. (2017-2018), is aimed solely at new parents. This bill would amend the Social Security Act to create an option for new parents to use a portion of their Social Security benefits as paid parental leave after the birth or adoption of a child. All three proposals died in committee. What are the pros and cons of each of the above proposals?

6. Serious health condition. *Caldwell* is an important case that interprets the FMLA requirement of a "serious health condition." How does the FMLA define the term? Did the toddler's ear infection in *Caldwell* qualify? What is a "serious health condition" for an infant or toddler? Does the definition differ for an adult? What qualifies as "subsequent treatment"? FMLA regulations in 2013 imposed a timetable within which visits to a health care provider must occur in order for a "serious health condition" to qualify. The incapacity must last more than three consecutive days and must involve one or more treatments by a health care provider within 30 days of the first day of incapacity. 29 C.F.R. §825.115. Chronic conditions are treated differently.

7. Domestic violence leave.

a. Federal proposal. Congress unsuccessfully considered expanding the FMLA (§§2601-2653) to provide leave to employees (1) who are addressing domestic violence, sexual assault, or stalking and their effects, if the employee is unable to perform any of the functions of the job; and (2) to care for a family member who is addressing domestic violence, sexual assault, or stalking and their effects. Specifically, leave would have been available for those seeking medical attention to recover from injuries; legal assistance; obtaining psychological counseling; participating in safety planning (including relocation); and participating in any other activity necessitated by domestic violence, which must be undertaken during the hours of employment. Domestic Violence Leave Act, H.R. 3151, 112th Cong. (2011-2013).

b. State laws. In contrast to the lack of federal protection for the full range of victims' needs, more than a dozen states require leave for victims to attend to not only medical needs, but also psychological counseling, social services, relocating, legal assistance, and participation in legal proceedings.[20]

c. Domestic violence leave: Comparative perspective. Some countries currently mandate *paid* leave for victims of domestic violence. For example, New Zealand and the Philippines offer 10 days of paid leave to victims.

8. Parental leave: International perspective. Most industrialized countries provide significant paid parental leave, ranging from three months to one year. In these countries, paid leave policies apply to *all* parents, whereas the FMLA covers only about 60 percent of employees (as the excerpt below reveals).

---

[20]. Legal Match, Domestic Violence Leave Laws, May 24, 2018 (15 states), https://www.legalmatch.com/law-library/article/domestic-violence-leave-laws.html.

Sweden is renowned for its generous parental leave policy. Currently, both parents share 16 months of paid parental leave at about 80 percent of their salary. They can decide how to allocate the time between themselves and whether to take the leave concurrently or consecutively. But 3 of the 16 months *must* be taken by fathers. Parents can take leave at any time before a child's eighth birthday. As a result of this liberal policy, 90 percent of Swedish fathers take parental leave.[21] Why is U.S. government support for parental leave so limited compared to that of other industrialized nations? What are some effects of generous governmental paid leave policies—for mothers, fathers, children, and society?

Key Facts: The Family and Medical Leave Act

National Partnership for Women & Families, Feb. 2023
https://nationalpartnership.org/report/fmla-key-facts/#:~:text=The%20National%20 Partnership%20estimates%20that%20in%202022%20about%2010.9%20million, eligible%20and%20FMLA%2Dineligible%20workers

The FMLA has helped to transform workplaces, but too many people – especially workers of color – are still left behind.

- About 44 percent of workers are not eligible for FMLA-supported leave because they work for small employers (15 percent), do not work enough hours or have not worked for their employer for long enough (21 percent), or both (7 percent).
- Workers of color are less likely to be eligible for FMLA-supported leave: 55 percent of workers who identify as Native American, Pacific Islander, or multiracial, 48 percent of Latinx, 47 percent of Asian American and 43 percent of Black workers are ineligible, compared to 42 percent of white workers.
- [I]n 2022, among workers who were not protected by FMLA, nearly 2.7 million needed leave but did not take it because they feared losing their job.
- Millions of workers cannot afford to take unpaid leave. [In 2022 about 10.9 million workers needed leave but did not take it, and two-thirds—more than 7.2 million—say it is because they could not afford unpaid leave.]
- The FMLA's limited definition of family—a spouse, parent or child under 18 or incapable of self-care—does not reflect the caregiving needs of many people. [I]n 2022, 8.4 million people (5.3 percent of all workers) took leave for a non-FMLA covered individual—meaning their jobs were not protected during leave. Among workers who did not take leave when they needed it, 14 percent said the person they needed to care for was not covered.

---

[21]. Why Swedish Men Take So Much Paternity Leave, The Economist, July 22, 2014, http:// www.economist.com/blogs/economist-explains/2014/07/economist-explains-15. See also Noele Illien, Switzerland Votes to Approve Paternity Leave, N.Y. Times, Sept. 28, 2020, https://www.nytimes .com/2020/09/27/world/europe/switzerland-paternity-leave.html.

Problems

1. Martha, a lawyer for a large corporation, and Michael, a computer engineer, are expecting quadruplets. During the fifth month of Martha's pregnancy, her physician advises complete bed rest. Martha can use her medical leave for this purpose. However, she will need someone to take care of her (fix her meals, run errands, and so forth). Michael, as well as Martha's sister, Miriam (who works for a brokerage firm), consider taking leave under the FMLA to care for Martha for the remainder of her pregnancy. What advice would you give them about the likelihood that their requests will be granted? Suppose that after the quadruplets' birth, Martha claims that she should be entitled to family leave to care for them. What result? See Navarro v. Pfizer Corp., 261 F.3d 90 (1st Cir. 2001).

2. Catherine Marzano is hired by Computer Science Co. (CSC) as a "junior technical recruiter." She is promoted several times. Shortly after her assignment to Mr. Marzi's unit, she learns that she is pregnant. She is reluctant to tell her boss because seven employees previously were terminated after their maternity leaves. After she does tell him, she notices that Mr. Marzi speaks "as if she wasn't coming back." During her leave, her unit begins experiencing losses (despite the stellar financial performance of CSC). Mr. Marzi eliminates Catherine's position and nine others. He notifies Catherine by saying that she "would be better off if [she] stays home with the baby and collects unemployment." Catherine alleges pregnancy discrimination and unlawful interference with her rights under the FMLA. What result? Marzano v. Computer Sci. Corp., 91 F.3d 497 (3d Cir. 1996).

How do employers accommodate fathers' need for parental leave? The next excerpt addresses this issue.

Fathers Need Paid Family and Medical Leave

National Partnership for Women & Families, June 2018
*http://www.nationalpartnership.org/our-work/resources/workplace/paid-leave
/fathers-need-paid-family-and-medical-leave.pdf*

Since 1965, fathers in the United States have nearly tripled the time they spend caring for children, and working fathers are now just as likely as working mothers to say they find it difficult to manage work and family responsibilities. Despite these changes, most men do not have access to leave that would allow them to take time away from work after the birth or adoption of a child.

Only 20 percent of private sector workers are employed at worksites that offer paid paternity leave to most or all male employees, and only 9 percent of private sector workers are employed at worksites that offer paid paternity leave to all male employees.

One study found that only one in 20 fathers in professional jobs took more than two weeks off after their most recent child was born—and a staggering three out of four took one week or less. Low-income fathers face even higher barriers: one study found that nearly 60 percent of low-income fathers reported taking zero weeks of paid time away from work after the birth or adoption of a child. . . .

Many fathers want to be more involved with their families, play a larger caregiving role, and support their partners' careers. But taking time away from work for family caregiving can bring harassment, discrimination or mistreatment that result in fathers being less likely to take the leave that is available to them. It is also a disincentive to take leave if doing so negatively affects their careers and their families' economic opportunities due to lower pay or being passed over for promotions.

A growing body of evidence makes clear that paid family leave has a positive impact on children and parents, families' economic security, employers and taxpayers:

Parental access to paid leave promotes children's development and family well-being. In two-parent, opposite-sex households, fathers who take two or more weeks off after the birth of a child are more involved in that child's direct care nine months after birth than fathers who take no leave. Involved fathers promote children's educational attainment and emotional stability and reduce maternal stress. . . .

Households are more equal when fathers have paid leave. When new dads in households with a mother and father take paid leave, their families experience a more equitable division of parental responsibilities, including household chores and direct caregiving. Fathers who take paid family leave also say they are more comfortable as active, responsible co-parents.

Paid leave for men supports working mothers. In more than 48 million U.S. households with children (69 percent), all parents are employed, and women are key breadwinners in nearly two-thirds of families with children. Yet women are still more likely than men to stop working or to work part time after the birth of a child. Paid paternity leave may increase women's labor force participation by promoting men's involvement at home and making it easier for women to return to the workforce. Access to paid leave also affects women's wages and, thus, their families' economic security. . . .

HICKS v. CITY OF TUSCALOOSA

870 F.3d 1253 (11th Cir. 2017)

WILSON, Circuit Judge:

[Stephanie] Hicks worked for the Tuscaloosa Police Department, first as a patrol officer and then as an investigator on the narcotics task force. She was working on the narcotics task force when she became pregnant in January 2012. Hicks's captain at the time, Jeff Synder, allowed her to work on pharmaceutical fraud cases so she could avoid working nights and weekends. Lieutenant Teena Richardson, Hicks's supervisor, admitted that it bothered her that Captain Synder allowed Hicks to avoid "on call" duty. Despite Richardson telling Hicks more than once that she should take only six weeks of FMLA leave, Hicks took twelve weeks of FMLA leave. Meanwhile, Captain Synder was . . . replaced with Captain Wayne Robertson.

Prior to her FMLA leave, Hicks received a performance review from her supervisor Richardson that said Hicks "exceeded expectations." But on Hicks's first day back from leave, she was written up [for minor infractions]. She was also told she should start working with five to seven confidential informants. Hicks overheard Richardson talking to Captain Robertson saying "that b* * * *" [which Richardson admitted at trial] and claiming she would find a way to write Hicks up and get her out of here. And another officer overheard Richardson talking loudly about Hicks saying "that stupid c* * * thinks she gets 12 weeks. I know for a fact she only gets six."

The City argued that Hicks only met with one informant and never even spoke to the others. The City also claimed that Hicks did not want to work nights, declined to meet with an informant after hours because she had to pick up her child from daycare, and chose not to attend a drug bust on a Saturday. Captain Robertson said he met with Hicks to determine why she was not working with the informants and helped her get started by arranging a ride-along with another agent and his informant. When Hicks did not follow up from the ride-along, Captain Robertson requested that Chief Steve Anderson reassign Hicks from the narcotics task force to the patrol division. Hicks countered that she worked several of the informants, and she was not introduced to the rest by their current agent. Hicks was also warned by another agent that Richardson had it out for her.

Following Captain Robertson's recommendation, Chief Anderson met with Hicks in December, only eight days after she returned from FMLA leave [and transferred her to the patrol division]. Captain Robertson testified that when he made his recommendation to Chief Anderson, he did not want it to look like Hicks was transferred because of her pregnancy, given that she had only been back eight days. As a result of the reassignment, Hicks lost her vehicle and weekends off, and she was going to receive a pay cut and different job duties. Additionally, officers in the narcotics task force are not required to wear ballistic vests all day, whereas patrol officers are.

After the reassignment, Richardson wrote a letter outlining the reasons for the demotion. The letter critiques Hicks because when officers went to Hicks's home to pick up her vehicle, Hicks did not come to the door. Yet the letter also admits that Hicks's husband came to the door and said Hicks was breastfeeding.

Before she started back in the patrol division, Hicks took time off when a physician diagnosed her with postpartum depression. Richardson admitted that she asked Hicks if she was suffering from postpartum depression because "something was different about [her] . . . [she] was a new mom and . . . new moms go through depressed states." During this leave for postpartum depression, Hicks's doctor wrote a letter to Chief Anderson recommending that she be considered for alternative duties because the ballistic vest she was now required to wear on patrol duty was restrictive and could cause breast infections that lead to an inability to breastfeed. But Chief Anderson did not believe that Hicks had any limitations because other breastfeeding officers had worn ballistic vests without any problems.

When she returned from leave, Chief Anderson met with Hicks again. In accordance with her doctor's suggestion, Hicks requested a desk job where she would not be required to wear a vest and assurances that she would be allowed to take breaks to breastfeed. But because Chief Anderson did not consider breastfeeding a condition that warranted alternative duty, he replied that Hicks's only options for accommodations were (1) not wearing a vest or (2) wearing a vest that could be "specially fitted" for her. . . . But to Hicks, not wearing a vest was no accommodation at all because it was so dangerous. Furthermore, the larger or "specially fitted" vests were also ineffective because they left gaping, dangerous holes. Hicks resigned that day. Hicks then filed this suit against the City of Tuscaloosa [alleging] (1) pregnancy discrimination, (2) constructive discharge, (3) FMLA interference, and (4) FMLA retaliation. [In response, the defendants argued that Hicks was demoted for her unsatisfactory job performance.]

REASSIGNMENT

The PDA amended Title VII to include discrimination "on the basis of pregnancy, childbirth, or related medical conditions." 42 U.S.C. §2000e(k). [T]he issue is whether there is a "convincing mosaic of circumstantial evidence that would allow a jury to infer intentional discrimination." To prove her claim [of retaliation] under the FMLA, Hicks must show that: "(1) [s]he availed [her]self of a protected right under the FMLA; (2) [s]he suffered an adverse employment decision; and (3) there is a causal connection between the protected activity and the adverse employment decision."

The evidence taken in the light most favorable to Hicks provides ample evidence that Hicks was both discriminated against on the basis of her pregnancy and that she was retaliated against for taking her FMLA leave. Multiple overheard conversations using defamatory language plus the temporal proximity of only eight days from when she returned to when she was reassigned support the inference that there was intentional discrimination. . . .

CONSTRUCTIVE DISCHARGE

Hicks argued that Chief Anderson's proffered options—patrolling without a vest or patrolling with an ineffective larger vest—made work conditions so intolerable that any reasonable person would have been compelled to resign. The City argued that Hicks failed to show that Chief Anderson harbored any discriminatory animus towards Hicks or that he deliberately made her working conditions intolerable. . . . However, the jury found that the conditions offered by Chief Anderson were so intolerable that a reasonable person would be forced to resign.

Constructive discharge claims are appropriate when "an employer discriminates against an employee to the point such that his working conditions become so intolerable that a reasonable person in the employee's position would have felt compelled to resign." "When the employee resigns in the face of such circumstances, Title VII treats that resignation as tantamount to an actual discharge."

. . . The PDA amended Title VII to add that discrimination "because of sex" or "on the basis of sex," includes discrimination "on the basis of pregnancy, childbirth, or related medical conditions." 42 U.S.C. §2000e(k). The issue here is whether breastfeeding is a "related medical condition." The Fifth Circuit Court of Appeals has held that lactation is a related medical condition to pregnancy and thus terminations based on a woman's need to breastfeed violate the PDA. When a woman was fired after telling her employer that she was lactating and asking whether she would be permitted to use a back room to pump milk, the Fifth Circuit looked at dictionary definitions of "medical condition" and found that it includes any physiological condition, which encompasses lactation. See E.E.O.C. v. Houston Funding II, Ltd., 717 F.3d 425, 428 (5th Cir. 2013). We agree with the Fifth Circuit's determination that lactation is a related medical condition and therefore covered under the PDA.

A plain reading of the PDA supports the finding that breastfeeding likewise is covered under the PDA. The explicit language of the PDA says that it covers discrimination "because of" or "on the basis of sex" and is "not limited to [discrimination] because of or on the basis of pregnancy, childbirth, or related medical conditions." The frequently used statutory interpretation canon *ejusdem generis* states that, "when a drafter has tacked on a catchall phrase" [like "other related conditions"] to an "enumeration of specifics," additional inclusions would be appropriate if they are sufficiently similar. Given that Congress included pregnancy and childbirth and explicitly used the words "not limited to," it is a common-sense conclusion that breastfeeding is a sufficiently similar gender-specific condition covered by the broad catchall phrase included in the PDA. Breastfeeding is a gender-specific condition because it "clearly imposes upon women a burden that male employees need not—indeed, could not—suffer."

Furthermore, reading the language of the PDA to cover breastfeeding is consistent with the purpose of the PDA. The PDA was meant to clarify that the protections of Title VII "extend[] to the whole range of matters concerning the childbearing process," and "to include the[] physiological occurrences peculiar to women." Indeed, the Supreme Court has recognized that the "entire thrust" behind the PDA was "to guarantee women the basic right to participate fully and equally in the workforce, without denying them the fundamental right to full participation in family life." We have little trouble concluding that Congress intended the PDA to include physiological conditions post-pregnancy. The PDA would be rendered a nullity if women were protected during a pregnancy but then could be readily terminated for breastfeeding—an important pregnancy-related "physiological process."

Our conclusion is not meant to displace the abundance of case law ruling that employers do not have to provide special accommodations to breastfeeding workers. The Fifth Circuit and many district courts have held that employers are not required to provide special accommodations for breastfeeding employees. The line between discrimination and accommodation is a fine one. Taking adverse actions based on woman's breastfeeding is prohibited by the PDA but employers are not required to give special accommodations to breastfeeding mothers. Hicks's case presents a scenario that appears to straddle that line. While the City may not have been required to provide Hicks with special accommodations for breastfeeding, the jury found that the City's action in refusing an accommodation afforded to other employees compelled Hicks to resign. In the eyes of a jury, this constituted a constructive discharge, which is effectively an adverse action. Phrasing Hicks's claim as merely a request for special accommodation is misleading. Hicks was not asking for a special accommodation, or more than equal treatment—she was asking to be treated the same as "other persons not so affected but similar in their ability or inability to work" as required by the PDA. Hicks showed that other employees with temporary injuries were given "alternative duty," and she merely requested to be granted the same alternative duty. . . .

A jury decided that Stephanie Hicks suffered discrimination in violation of the PDA, and retaliation, in violation of FMLA, when she was reassigned only eight days after returning from FMLA leave following childbirth. . . . We find that a plain reading of the PDA covers discrimination against breastfeeding mothers. This holding is consistent with the purpose of PDA and will help guarantee women the right to be free from discrimination in the workplace based on gender-specific physiological occurrences.

NOTE: WHO IS STEPHANIE HICKS?

Plaintiff Stephanie Hicks, former Narcotics Investigator

Stephanie Hicks worked her way up the ranks in the Tuscaloosa, Alabama, Police Department from patrol office to undercover agent in the Narcotics Division. Her job focused on prescription drug abuse, investigating the sale of drugs like Oxycontin and Adderall on the black market. She also trained new recruits on patrol. Although narcotics work was dangerous, she loved it. In her job, she sometimes posed undercover as a prostitute, other times as a drug dealer. She was proud of her prestigious position. Fewer than 10 percent of officers work undercover and train recruits.

And, she was very good at her job. In her performance review, her supervisor wrote that she "exceeded expectations." When she became pregnant, she worked until the week that she gave birth. After 12 weeks' parental leave, she returned to work. But she was still nursing her baby.

From the moment she returned, her supervisors treated her differently than before. On her first day back at work, she was written up for not changing the oil in her department-issued car. At trial, her employer failed to provide a single other instance in which any other officer had been sanctioned for that infraction. She also received a write-up for obtaining too many warrants. Her supervisors refused to accommodate her need for pumping breaks—requiring her to pump milk in a common locker room, in view of others, where co-workers mocked her. "Pumping in the locker room was awful," she later said. "Sitting there by the shower stall, where the dispatchers and the public could walk in. Somebody was always asking what I was doing." When she headed to the locker room to start her break to pump milk, she would hear taunting on her police radio from co-workers telling her to "wrap those boobs up" and get back to work.

In addition, her supervisors started to make disparaging comments about her. They criticized her for a lack of motivation, saying that she seemed "changed" and suggesting that it was because she had the "baby blues." Warned by a colleague that her supervisors were irritated about the length of time she had taken for FMLA leave, she began secretly taping her conversations with her supervisors.

Soon she was demoted to patrol duty, which required her to work weekends and night shifts, take a salary cut, and lose her service vehicle. She was also required to wear a bulletproof vest. Her doctor advised her that the heavy restrictive vest impeded lactation and caused infections. She requested a desk job but her request was denied even though other officers were routinely provided the same accommodation for other reasons. Given the choice of not wearing protective clothing on patrol or wearing an ill-fitting vest, she quit two months after her return from pregnancy leave. Then she filed suit against the police department for discrimination. During the trial, her husband, who was also an officer with the same police department, quit his job after he said his work environment became too hostile. At trial, Hicks was awarded $374,000 in damages and won a landmark victory for breastfeeding women nationwide.

Notes and Questions

1. Background. A significant number of mothers choose to breastfeed their babies. However, as *Hicks* illustrates, many new mothers face a choice between breastfeeding and keeping their jobs. Low-income wage earners have the least supportive work environments. Discrimination against breastfeeding mothers in the workplace is widespread and leads to serious consequences for employees. Almost two-thirds of breastfeeding discrimination cases end in nursing mothers losing their jobs. Claims are highest in male-dominated workplaces (like that of Stephanie Hicks), accounting for nearly half of breastfeeding discrimination cases.[22]

2. *Hicks*: holding. Hicks files suit against the Tuscaloosa Police Department based on the PDA and the FMLA. According to the court, did the employer violate the PDA and/or the FMLA?

a. PDA claim. Did Hicks's employer engage in intentional discrimination because of pregnancy? If so, how? How do lactation discrimination and breastfeeding discrimination constitute pregnancy discrimination? According to *Hicks*, are these forms of discrimination treated differently under the PDA? Why?

Prior to *Hicks*, some federal district courts held that lactation and breastfeeding are not "medical condition[s]" that are "related" to pregnancy or childbirth based on somewhat strained reasoning. See, e.g., Ames v. Nationwide Mutual Ins. Co., 2012 WL 12861597 (S.D. Iowa 2012) (reasoning that lactation can be induced even in people who have not experienced birth or pregnancy, and also that even men have milk ducts and hormones responsible for milk production); E.E.O.C. v. Houston Funding, 2012 WL 739494 (S.D. Tex. 2012) (reasoning that pregnancy "ends" by the time breastfeeding begins), *vacated*, 717 F.3d 425 (5th Cir. 2013). How does the Eleventh Circuit opinion resolve this issue?

The PDA prohibits such acts of pregnancy discrimination as demotion and firing. Did Hicks's "constructive discharge" qualify as pregnancy discrimination? Why? What were the defendant's reasons for making adverse employment decision(s) against Hicks? Did the court find those reasons persuasive?

Is breastfeeding accommodation considered "special treatment" for purposes of the PDA, according to *Hicks*? How does one equate breastfeeding women to a "similarly situated" class of men? After *Hicks*, do employers have an obligation to provide special accommodations to all breastfeeding employees? If not, why does Hicks prevail?

b. FMLA claim. What benefits was Hicks entitled to under the FMLA? Was her supervisor correct that Hicks was entitled to six weeks of FMLA leave? Hicks alleges the employer violated her FMLA rights by "interference" and "retaliation." How does the text of the FMLA protect against these acts (see supra p. 261)? How did the employer violate those rights, according to the plaintiff? Did the court agree?

---

[22]. Ctr. for WorkLife Law, Exposed: Discrimination Against Breastfeeding Workers 1, 4 (Jan. 2019), https://www.pregnantatwork.org/wp-content/uploads/WLL-Breastfeeding-Discrimination-Report.pdf.

3. Significance. Until recently, federal protection for breastfeeding was quite limited. The PDA did not explicitly protect the right to breastfeed or require accommodations for lactation or breastfeeding. *Hicks* and a Fifth Circuit Court of Appeals case (E.E.O.C. v. Houston Funding, supra) were groundbreaking decisions that expanded the law applicable to both lactation and breastfeeding. *Houston Funding* involved an employee who was fired the same day that she inquired whether she would be able to pump breast milk when she returned to work. *Houston Funding* was the first federal appellate case to determine that firing an employee because she is lactating or expressing breast milk constitutes sex discrimination and that lactation is a "medical condition" related to pregnancy for purposes of the PDA.

Hicks went further than *Houston Funding* by ruling that the PDA requires employers to treat requests for breastfeeding accommodations the same as other requests from non-pregnant workers, and that the failure to provide these accommodations may constitute constructive discharge if an employee feels compelled to resign as a result. *Hicks* follows from the Supreme Court's decision in Young v. U.P.S. (discussed supra p. 254), holding that an employer's refusal to provide workplace accommodations for pregnant employees violates the PDA if the employer provides accommodations to non-pregnant employees and does not have a strong justification for treating pregnant women differently.

4. Other federal protection. Congress enacted the Consolidated Appropriations Act in 2022, including the PUMP for Nursing Mothers Act (PUMP Act), H.R. 3110, 117th Cong. (2021-2022)), which expands the numbers of nursing mothers who are eligible to receive break time to pump and a private place to pump at work. Specifically, it broadens the requirement that employers provide certain accommodations to cover salaried employees and other types of workers not covered under existing law. Further, a mother's time expressing breast milk must be considered "hours worked" if she is also working. The law also extends from one year to two years the available time period for such accommodations.

Prior law, the Affordable Care Act (ACA), amended the Fair Labor Standards Act (FLSA) (the law establishing basic employment protections like minimum wage and overtime pay) by providing the first federal protections for lactation. The enactment of the ACA in 2010 amended the FLSA to require employers to provide a reasonable amount of break time for nursing mothers to express breast milk as frequently as needed for up to one year following the birth of a child. It also required that nursing mothers must be provided with a place (other than a bathroom) to express milk, and the space must be shielded from view and free from intrusion. Smaller employers (those with fewer than 50 employees) are exempt if these requirements impose undue hardship. Do "hardship" exemptions reflect the view that workplace lactation laws are an imposition on the rights of employers rather than an affirmative right of employees?

5. Breastfeeding and the Constitution. An early case, decided before the PDA and the FMLA, explored whether breastfeeding is protected by the Constitution. In Dike v. School Board, 650 F.2d 783 (5th Cir. 1981), Janice Dike, a kindergarten teacher, breastfed her infant at work until her employer directed her to stop because of a school board directive against bringing employees' children to work. The school board denied her request to nurse the baby off school grounds. Dike was compelled to take an unpaid leave of absence and sued the school board, alleging a violation of her constitutional rights. The Fifth Circuit Court of Appeals ruled that breastfeeding is a constitutional right based on the right of privacy. How is breastfeeding similar to the procreative liberties and the right to marry? How is it different? The holding in *Dike* was narrowed by subsequent case law. See Shahar v. Bowers (discussed in Chapter V) (overruling *Dike* insofar as it applied strict scrutiny instead of a balancing test). Would FMLA leave, had it been available, have helped Janice Dike?

6. State approaches. State protections for breastfeeding include: (a) exemptions of breastfeeding from public nudity and other criminal statutes, (b) protection of breastfeeding mothers in any public or private location, (c) protection of breastfeeding via civil rights remedies, (d) encouraging or mandating employer accommodation of breastfeeding, and (e) exemptions of breastfeeding women from jury duty. In addition, some states currently have parallel provisions to the federal Pregnant Workers Fairness Acts, defining pregnancy discrimination to include failure to accommodate lactation needs. Do such protections, applicable to women only, violate equal protection? What level of scrutiny should apply? Would they pass constitutional scrutiny? See State v. Lilley, 204 A.3d 198 (N.H. 2019) (evaluating constitutionality of a city ordinance, on First Amendment and Fourteenth Amendment grounds, that prohibited public nudity, including the exposure of the female breast).

7. Covering up while breastfeeding. Is it legal to ask a breastfeeding mother to "cover up"? Currently, all 50 states and the District of Columbia, allow women to breastfeed in any public or private location. Some of these laws allow breastfeeding in locations "where the mother is otherwise authorized to be." In such states, can a breastfeeding mother be arrested for trespassing if she is asked to leave the premises and refuses? Other state laws exempt breastfeeding from public indecency laws. Do the latter laws condition legal protection on the adherence to traditional feminine and maternal gender norms by permitting public breastfeeding only when done with "discretion" or "modesty"?

8. Breastfeeding in courthouses: American Bar Association (ABA) policy. Nursing lawyers, as well as courtroom personnel and jurors, face challenges because courthouses rarely have breastfeeding facilities. Only a few state laws require courtrooms to have breastfeeding facilities. See, e.g., 55 Ill. Comp. Stat. 5/5-1106 (requiring every facility that houses a circuit courtroom to include at least one lactation room or area for members of the public to express breast milk in private). In terms of federal law, Congress passed the Fairness for Breastfeeding Mothers Act, Pub. L. No. 116-20 (2019), which requires federal courthouses to provide a lactation room for all women who are breastfeeding. Finally, an ABA policy encourages legislatures to establish lactation areas in courthouses.[23]

---

[23]. ABA Resolution and Report to the ABA House of Delegates, ABA Midyear Meeting (Jan. 2019), https://www.americanbar.org/content/dam/aba/images/news/2019mymhodres/101a.pdf; Kelly Blount, Breastfeeding Rooms in Courthouses, Sept. 21, 2020, https://mothersesquire.org /mothersesquire-blog/2020/9/21/breastfeeding-rooms-in-courthouses.

Problem

Arleta Ramirez has been breastfeeding her daughter since she was born six months ago. After Arleta and her ex-husband, Mike, separated recently, Mike (the father) complains that breastfeeding is "interfering" with his parenting time. He accuses Arleta of "weaponizing" breastfeeding against him and contends that breastfeeding after six months is not medically necessary. The mother argues that the baby rejects the bottle and that breastfeeding is in the child's best interests. During the couple's marriage, Arleta breastfed their older child until he was two years old. Currently, the parents are engaged in a bitter custody battle. The trial court judge has ordered Arleta to bottle-feed the baby to accommodate the father's visitation schedule (four days per week and overnight visitation). What arguments would you present on appeal? How should the case be decided?

See Chelsea Ritschel, Outrage as Court Orders Breastfeeding Woman to Bottle Feed Baby to Suit Father's Custody Schedule, The Independent (UK), Feb. 28, 2023, https://www.independent.co.uk/life-style/health-and-families/breastfeeding-custody-dispute-judge-ruling-child-b2274776.html; Yaron Steinbuch, Breastfeeding Mom Ordered to Use Bottles in Custody Dispute with Dad, N.Y. Post, Feb. 8, 2023, https://nypost.com/2023/02/08/breastfeeding-mom-ordered-to-use-bottles-in-custody-dispute-with-dad/.

Breastfeeding concerns in custody disputes are surprisingly common, according to Stephanie Bodak Nicholson, president of La Leche League's USA Council (cited in Ritschel's article above). How should courts resolve these disputes? What factors should courts consider? Or should judges be prohibited from considering how babies are fed?

c. Work-Family Conflict

Arlie Hochschild & Ann Machung, The Second Shift: Working Families and the Revolution at Home
4, 7-10 (rev. ed. 2012)

[How well do couples work two full-time jobs and raise young children? The author interviewed 50 couples to answer this question by determining their allocation of household tasks.]

[I] discovered that women worked roughly fifteen hours longer [at home] each week than men. Over a year, they worked an *extra month of twenty-four-hour days a year.* . . . Just as there is a wage gap between men and women in the workplace, there is a "leisure gap" between them at home. Most women work one shift at the office or factory and a "second shift" at home. . . .

Men who share the load at home seemed just as pressed for time as their wives, and as torn between the demands of career and small children. . . . But the majority of men did not share the load at home. Some refused outright.

Others refused more passively, often offering a loving shoulder to lean on, an understanding ear as their working wife faced the conflict they both saw as hers. . . . But I came to realize that those husbands who helped very little at home were often indirectly just as deeply affected as their wives by the need to do that work, through the resentment their wives feel toward them. . . .

[E]ven when husbands happily shared the hours of work, their wives felt more *responsible* for home and children. More women kept track of doctors' appointments and arranged for playmates to come over. More mothers than fathers worried about the tail on a child's Halloween costume or a birthday present for a school friend. They were more likely to think about their children while at work and to check in by phone with the baby-sitter. . . .

Partly because of this, more women felt torn between one sense of urgency and another, between the need to soothe a child's fear of being left at day care and the need to show the boss she's "serious" at work. More women than men questioned how good they were as parents. . . .

Twenty percent of the men in my study shared housework equally. Seventy percent of men did a substantial amount (less than half but more than a third), and 10 percent did less than a third. Even when couples share more equitably in the work at home, women do two-thirds of the *daily* jobs at home, like cooking and cleaning up—jobs that fix them into a rigid routine. Most women cook dinner and most men change the oil in the family car. But, as one mother pointed out, dinner needs to be prepared every evening around six o'clock, whereas the car oil needs to be changed every six months. . . . A child needs to be tended daily, while the repair of household appliances can often wait. . . .

Another reason women may feel more strained than men is that women more often do two things at once—for example, write checks and return phone calls, vacuum and keep an eye on a three-year-old, fold laundry and think out the shopping list. . . . Beyond doing more at home, women also devote *proportionately more* of their time at home to housework and proportionately less of it to child care. Of all the time men spend working at home, more of it goes to child care. . . . Since most parents prefer to tend to their children rather than clean house, men do more of what they'd rather do. . . . Men also do fewer of the "undesirable" household chores: fewer men than women wash toilets and scrub the bathroom. . . .

All, in all, if in this period of American history, the two-job family is suffering from a speed-up of work and family life, working mothers are its primary victims. It is ironic, then, that often it falls to women to be the "time and motion expert" of family life. Watching inside homes, I noticed it was often the mother who rushed children, saying "Hurry up! It's time to go." . . . Sadly enough, women are more often the lightning rod for family aggressions aroused by the speed-up of work and family life. They are the "villains" in a process by which they are the primary victims. More than the longer hours, the sleeplessness, and feeling torn, this is the saddest cost to women of the extra month a year.

IMPACT OF COVID ON WORK-FAMILY CONFLICT

Amanda Barroso & Juliana Menasce Horowitz, The Pandemic Has Highlighted Many Challenges for Mothers But They Aren't Necessarily New

Pew Research Ctr. Rep., Mar. 17, 2021

https://www.pewresearch.org/short-reads/2021/03/17/the-pandemic-has-highlighted -many-challenges-for-mothers-but-they-arent-necessarily-new/

The COVID-19 pandemic has presented challenges and obstacles for many Americans, but one group has been getting a lot of attention lately: moms. [Some suggest] the disruptions caused by the pandemic might have long-lasting consequences for gender equality in the workplace. . . . Pew Research Center surveys have highlighted some of the unique challenges facing moms during the pandemic. For example, . . . among employed parents who were working from home all or most of the time, mothers were more likely than fathers to say they had a lot of child care responsibilities while working (36% vs. 16%). . . . But these dynamics aren't new. [Before the pandemic], women were already more likely than their spouses or partners to say they carried more of the load when it comes to both parenting and household responsibilities. In addition, working moms were more likely than working dads to say they faced certain challenges at work because they were balancing work and family responsibilities.

WORK AND FAMILY

[Before the pandemic], employed moms (50%) were more likely than employed dads (39%) to say being a working parent made it harder for them to advance in their career. Working moms were also more likely than dads to say there had been times where they needed to reduce their work hours (54% vs. 44%). . . . Around one-in-five working moms (19%) said they'd been passed over for an important assignment or a promotion because they have children, compared with smaller shares of dads. Similar patterns and gender differences were evident [during the pandemic]. . . .

DIVISION OF LABOR

The challenges of the pandemic have raised to the surface questions about the division of household chores and responsibilities among couples, particularly as many schools and day care centers remain closed. But even before the pandemic, about six-in-ten women in opposite-sex relationships (59%) said they did more than their spouse or partner when it came to handling these responsibilities. . . . In the same survey, roughly eight-in-ten moms (78%) said they did more than their spouse or partner when it came to managing their children's schedules and activities. . . .

Again, these patterns emerged when married and cohabiting adults in opposite-sex relationships were asked the same questions in October 2020, several months into the pandemic. . . .

Postscript. Hochschild's cited gender disparity existed before, and persisted during, the COVID pandemic. Before COVID, data revealed that, for different-sex couples with both parents working full time, the wife performed significantly more housework and childcare (14 hours/week on childcare and 18 hours/week on housework compared to fathers' 8 hours/week on childcare and 10 hours/week on housework). Fathers spent considerably more time than mothers on leisure activities.[24]

As the above excerpt reveals, the pandemic had a devastating effect on mothers' employment. According to U.S. Census data, the share of mothers who were actively working during the pandemic decreased more than fathers' share. Specifically, mothers' share declined 21.1 percentage points whereas fathers dropped 14.7 percentage points by April 2020. (Lockdowns started in March 2020.) As the pandemic wore on, approximately 3.5 million mothers living with school-age children left active work by taking leave (paid or unpaid), losing their job, or leaving the labor market entirely. The two most cited reasons for COVID's differential impact on mothers were (1) mothers' jobs were more heavily affected by pandemic closures; and (2) mothers are more likely to carry a heavier burden of household chores and childcare, which disrupted their ability to work for pay outside the home. The experience of mothers also varied by race and ethnicity, with nonwhite single mothers being hit hardest.[25] Some commentators optimistically predicted that the pandemic might level the playing field for men and women. In fact, working remotely turns out to be more advantageous for men than women.[26]

NOTE: WORK-FAMILY CONFLICT ISSUES

1. Mothers' dilemmas. Most women with young children are employed. Many of these women, especially Black and Latina mothers, serve as their family's sole or primary breadwinner. Single mothers have an especially hard time balancing work and family responsibilities.

Despite women's gains in the workplace, their largest career obstacle is the work-family conflict (i.e., the need to raise children at the same time as they are progressing in their careers). When women leave their careers to raise children, they find themselves at a huge career disadvantage. Children impact women's professional advancement more than men's. Women's time out of the workplace has a significant impact on their salaries (called the "motherhood penalty"). A larger share of mothers (four in ten full- and part-time workers) compared to fathers (two in ten) report that being a working parent has made it harder to advance in

---

[24]. Kim Parker & Gretchen Livingston, 7 Facts About Dads, Pew Research Ctr., June 13, 2018, https://www.pewresearch.org/fact-tank/2018/06/13/fathers-day-facts/; Bureau of Labor Statistics, American Time Use Survey Summary—2017 Results 2, 3 (2018), https://www.bls.gov /news.release/pdf/atus.pdf.

[25]. Misty L. Heggeness et al., Tracking Job Losses for Mothers of School-Age Children During a Health Crisis, U.S. Census Bureau Rep., Mar. 3, 2021, https://www.census.gov/library /stories/2021/03/moms-work-and-the-pandemic.html.

[26]. Tristan Bove, Remote Work Turns Out to Be a Much Better Deal for Men than for Women, New Study on "Gendered Differences" Finds, Fortune Mag., Jan. 5, 2023, https://fortune.com /2023/01/05/remote-work-for-women-leads-to-more-household-family-tasks-than-men/; Megan Leonhardt, Remote Work May Level the Playing Field and Ensure Women Aren't Forced to "Walk on Eggshells"; Fortune Mag., Nov. 3, 2022, https://fortune.com/2022/11/03/remote-work-may -level-the-playing-field-for-working-moms/.

their careers.[27] Although highly skilled mothers who work outside the home are hit the hardest, the income of lower-skilled mothers also drops significantly. The extent of mothers' economic loss depends on the length of their absence from the workplace.

2. Fathers' dilemmas. Men's role in the family has undergone dramatic changes. Currently, more men are stay-at-home dads and single fathers than ever before. Other key findings of the aforementioned Pew Research Center Report include: (1) fathers are as likely as mothers to view parenting as central to their identity and to appreciate the benefits of parenthood; (2) fathers are more involved in childcare (investing triple the amount of time) than they were 50 years ago; (3) fewer fathers (half as many) are their family's sole breadwinner compared to 50 years ago; and (4) more fathers face dilemmas negotiating the work-family conflict (half of working fathers agree that juggling work and family demands is "very or somewhat difficult to do").

Increasingly, fathers are asserting legal challenges to discriminatory parental leave policies. For example, in 2019, a father filed a class action lawsuit against JPMorgan Chase, alleging that the company's parental leave policy violated Title VII's prohibition on sex discrimination when it denied him the 16-week paid leave that it routinely granted to mothers. (The company offered him only 2 weeks' leave, on the ground that he was not the primary caregiver.) In a million-dollar settlement, the company agreed to administer its policy on a gender-neutral basis and to create a $5 million fund to compensate 5,000 fathers who had been short-changed. Similar lawsuits against Estée Lauder and CNN also resulted in favorable settlements for plaintiff-fathers.

3. Restructuring the workplace. Professor Joan Williams, a prominent feminist legal scholar, argues that the modern workplace is structured around the "ideal worker," a norm that is based on a stereotypical male model—that is, people who have *no* childcare responsibilities, who are able to work 40 hours per week, and who can work overtime on short notice. This view leads to significant difficulties for mothers in the workplace as they attempt to juggle work and family responsibilities. In response to this issue, Williams emphasizes the need to redesign the workplace. Other scholars concur that the state must take responsibility for structuring societal institutions to address the work-family conflict and support families' caretaking functions.[28]

4. Part-time employment and childcare. One solution to the work-family conflict is for employers to offer more *part-time employment*. Many parents prefer to work part time when their children are young. Yet part-time employees face arbitrary and irregular shift schedules; proportionately lower compensation in

[27]. Eileen Patten, How American Parents Balance Work and Family Life When Both Work, Nov. 4, 2015, https://www.pewresearch.org/fact-tank/2015/11/04/how-american-parents-balance-work-and-family-life-when-both-work/.
[28]. Joan Williams, Unbending Gender: Why Family and Work Conflict and What to Do About It 2-3 (2010). See also Maxine Eichner, The Supportive State (2010); Martha Albertson Fineman, The Autonomy Myth (2004); Clare Huntington, Failure to Flourish: How Law Undermines Family Relationships (2014).

terms of salary, benefits, and bonuses; and lack of eligibility for health benefits, pension plans, and retirement plans. Female part-time employees are less likely to have access to parental leave with reemployment rights, and they are typically excluded from the benefits of the FMLA. Employers offer part-time workers fewer opportunities for advancement. In addition, mothers who work part time are seriously affected by the motherhood penalty over their lifetimes.

5. Affordable childcare. Another solution is affordable childcare. Mothers are 40 percent more likely than fathers to report feeling the negative impact of childcare issues on their careers.[29] These problems are exacerbated because over the past few decades, the cost of childcare has more than doubled whereas wages have remained stagnant. Two federal programs provide free or subsidized childcare (the Child Care and Development Block Grant and Head Start). Both are targeted toward low-income families with young children. However, few eligible families benefit from these programs. One solution is increasing federal funding of childcare and early childhood education. Specific solutions for governments and employers to make childcare more accessible and affordable include (1) more government-provided childcare, (2) government funding of private childcare, (3) more loans and subsidies for childcare costs, and (4) mandates for employers and/or landlords to provide childcare.

Early in his term, President Biden announced an ambitious legislative agenda that included initiatives to make high-quality childcare accessible and affordable. Build Back Better Act of 2021, H.R. 5376, 117th Cong. (2021-2022).The initiatives would have been achieved in part by subsidizing families' out-of-pocket childcare costs while increasing care providers' wages to address staffing shortages. Although some of the President's legislative agenda (i.e., infrastructure, clean energy, etc.) won congressional support, his childcare proposals did not.

6. The "mommy track" and its effects on the family. Given the disproportionate impact of the work-family conflict on mothers, one reform might be separate employment tracks for different categories of women. In a classic article, Felice Schwartz (founder of the nonprofit consulting firm Catalyst) proposed that corporations distinguish between "career-primary" and "career-and-family" women. She suggested that corporations recognize the need to retain the latter by providing parental leave, support during relocation, flexible benefits, and quality, affordable childcare.[30] The media dubbed the proposal "the mommy track." Many critics worried about the impact of the mommy track. Some concerns have materialized. An increasing number of working mothers are charging that their employers engage in "mommy track discrimination." In one class action lawsuit, three female associates at Morrison Foerster accused the law firm of discriminating against mothers and pregnant women by denying them career advancement and

---

[29]. Ctr. for Am. Progress, The Child Care Crisis Is Keeping Women Out of the Workforce 1, Mar. 28, 2019, https://www.americanprogress.org/issues/early-childhood/reports/2019/03/28/467488/child-care-crisis-keeping-women-workforce/. See generally Joy Borkholder, Why Child Care in the U.S. Lags Behind Much of the World, Crosscut News, Jan. 5, 2022, https://crosscut.com/news/2022/01/why-child-care-us-lags-behind-much-world.

[30]. Felice N. Schwartz, Management Women and the New Facts of Life, 67 Harv. Bus. Rev. 65 (Jan.-Feb. 1989).

paying them less than their male colleagues. In stark contrast, some law firms are adopting generous parental leave policies.[31]

As discussed above, COVID had a profound impact on working mothers' employment. Some critics contended that COVID relegated more women to the second-class mommy track when the pandemic shuttered schools and childcare facilities – with the result that women found it increasingly difficult to juggle family responsibilities and work. Many women responded by exiting the workforce permanently. As the pandemic waned, some feared that the return to the office would penalize mothers in particular because remote and flexible work arrangements would become associated with them, creating a lower tier of workers.[32]

7. Stereotypes and family responsibilities discrimination. Mothers in the workplace may face gender stereotypes about their lack of competence and commitment. Such stereotypes are illustrations, according to Professor Joan Williams, of the "maternal wall"—barriers in the form of the perception that devotion to one's family renders one less capable of performing a job. The maternal wall may arise upon pregnancy, motherhood, or working part time. According to Williams, the maternal wall impedes mothers' ability to get anywhere near the glass ceiling.

Williams also identifies another form of employment discrimination based on stereotyping that she terms "family responsibilities discrimination" (FRD) that affects both men and women. FRD stems from stereotyping employees who take on caregiving responsibilities for children, elderly parents, spouses, or partners. Common forms of this type of caregiver discrimination include treatment based on assumptions about employees' additional family responsibilities when a second child arrives; treatment based on assumptions about commitment when employees care for elder relatives; assigning parents schedules that interfere with childcare while letting nonparents choose their schedules; harassing employees who take time off to care for their aging parents or sick spouses; and fabricating work infractions to justify dismissal of employees because of family responsibilities.[33]

8. Class and the work-family conflict. The work-family conflict affects all women—the poor as well as professionals and the middle class. Joan Williams

[31]. See Vivia Chen, Shock. The Mommy Track Is a Dead End, Am. Law., May 8, 2018, https://www.law.com/americanlawyer/2018/05/08/shock-shock-the-mommy-track-is-a-dead-end/; Ross Todd, In "Mommy Track" Lawsuit, MoFo Points to Its Track Record for Defense, Feb. 12, 2019, https://www.law.com/therecorder/2019/02/12/in-mommy-track-lawsuit-mofo-points-to-its-track-record-for-defense/. Several of the plaintiffs eventually settled. Houston-based Susman Godrey appears to offer an especially generous policy with its unlimited, paid, gender-neutral leave policy. See Don Packel, No Joke: Susman Godfrey's Unlimited Paid Parental Leave Bears Dividends, Law.com, July 2, 2019, https://www.law.com/americanlawyer/2019/07/02/no-joke-susman-godfreys-unlimited-paid-parental-leave-bears-dividends/.
[32]. Jessica Grose, Remote Work Doesn't Have to Be the 'Mommy Track', N.Y. Times, Mar. 2, 2022, https://www.nytimes.com/2022/03/02/opinion/remote-work.html.
[33]. Joan C. Williams et al., eds., The Maternal Wall: Research and Policy Perspectives on Discrimination Against Mothers (2004); Cynthia Thomas Calvert, Ctr. for WorkLife Law, Family Responsibilities Discrimination: Litigation Update, 2010, at 2-3 (2010); Fact Sheet: Family Responsibilities Discrimination (2019), https://worklifelaw.org/publication/family-responsibilities-discrimination-fact-sheet/.

contends that strategies to address the work-family conflict require an examination of class-based as well as gender-based assumptions. She identifies the many ways that the work-family conflict affects low-income families. For example, their jobs often involve unpredictable schedules that make it difficult to schedule childcare. Government policies to aid their families, such as low-cost childcare, are often unavailable or underfunded. One-quarter of poor single mothers do not participate in the labor force, partly because of the high cost of childcare. Moreover, low-income mothers are more likely to be providing direct care for elders because they cannot afford to pay others to do so.[34]

Many low-wage workers are at the mercy of "just-in-time scheduling," in which employers give employees very little advance notice of their schedules, call upon workers at the last minute, during non-scheduled times, to meet unforeseen consumer demand, and send workers home before the scheduled end of their shifts if business slows. These problems exacerbate employees' difficulties in juggling the work-family balancing act.

The fundamental problem is that today's workplace is still "perfectly designed for the workplace of 1960," when only 20 percent of mothers worked. Professor Williams urges the government to take a more active role in addressing work-family issues that cut across class-based lines through such reforms as (1) workplace flexibility; (2) short-term and extended time off; (3) childcare, adult care, and after-school care; and (4) the elimination of FRD. In short, the government must send the message that the "work-family conflict is not just a personal problem."[35]

Problem

Diane McCourtney's employer, Seagate Technology, dismisses the accounts clerk for excessive absenteeism. McCourtney's absences stem from her inability to find affordable day care for her infant, who suffers from frequent respiratory ailments. Following her dismissal, she files a claim for unemployment benefits, which is contested by Seagate and denied by the state Jobs and Training Department. She appeals. Minnesota, like many states, requires claimants to show that they are "available" for work, although such availability may be restricted for "good cause." To what extent is McCourtney available for work? Do the restrictions on her availability reflect "good cause"? Should the result depend on the availability for childcare of McCourtney's husband? See McCourtney v. Imprimis Tech., 465 N.W.2d 721 (Minn. Ct. App. 1991). Cf. Phillips v. Martin Marietta Corp., 400 U.S. 542 (1971).

---

[34]. Joan C. Williams & Heather Boushey, The Three Faces of Work-Family Conflict: The Poor, Professionals, and the Missing Middle, Ctr. for Am. Progress & WorkLife Law (Jan. 2010). See also Joan Williams, Reshaping the Work-Family Debate: Why Men and Class Matter (2010).

[35]. Williams & Boushey, Three Faces of Work-Family Conflict, supra note [34], at 3, 60-62.

C. Tort Law

1. Tort Actions Against Third Parties: Alienation of Affection and Criminal Conversation

AMMARELL v. FRANCE

2018 WL 2843441 (W.D.N.C. 2018)

Megan France with her former husband, NASCAR CEO Brian France

ROBERT J. CONRAD, JR., United States District Judge.

. . . On February 25, 2012, Plaintiff married Ryan Ammarell in Alabama. As she tells it, Plaintiff's marriage was one of genuine love and affection. The couple had a child and Mr. Ammarell owned a business in Mecklenburg, North Carolina, where he frequently traveled to from his home in Alabama. It was in North Carolina in December 2015, however, that Mr. Ammarell met Megan France ("Defendant") and began to forge a second life, resulting in an affair. Mr. Ammarell and Defendant were intimate when together and exchanged explicit photographs and texts when apart.

The affair eventually came to light in May of 2016 when Defendant called Plaintiff and described the sexual relationship she had established with Mr. Ammarell. She apparently sent Plaintiff the texts and photographs to prove it.

Defendant had planned a future with Mr. Ammarell. She scheduled an appointment to remove her birth control device in the hopes of bearing Mr. Ammarell's child. She purchased a residence and car for Mr. Ammarell to use when in North Carolina. She offered a total of $1,000,000 to Mr. Ammarell to leave his wife; and contemplated offering another $100,000 to Plaintiff if she was willing to walk away from her marriage.

Plaintiff's happy marriage began to crumble as a result. Mr. Ammarell suffered a mental breakdown of sorts, fueling episodes of domestic violence and triggering proceedings in which Plaintiff sought primary custody of their child in Alabama. Plaintiff now seeks redress for the damage she alleges Defendant caused [and asserts] North Carolina common law causes of action for alienation of affection and criminal conversation. . . . The State provides these causes of action to allow spouses injured by their partners' unfaithfulness to bring actions against third party interlopers. Under criminal conversation, Plaintiff must show "[an] actual marriage between the spouses and sexual intercourse between defendant and the plaintiff's spouse during the coverture." Under alienation of affection, Plaintiff must prove:

(1) that [she and her husband] were happily married, and that a genuine love and affection existed between them; (2) that the love and affection so existing was alienated and destroyed; [and] (3) that the wrongful and malicious acts of the

defendant[] produced and brought about the loss and alienation of such love and affection.

In her Motion to Dismiss, Defendant argues that criminal conversation and alienation of affection are unconstitutional because: (1) these claims violate the Due Process Clause; and (2) the alienation of affection claim impermissibly infringes on Defendant's First Amendment rights. . . .

Fundamental to Defendant's attack on the constitutionality of alienation of affection and criminal conversation is the interpretation of the United States Supreme Court case Lawrence v. Texas [539 U.S. 558 (2003)]. In that case, the Supreme Court recognized a substantive due process right to intimate same-sex conduct in a private place pursuant to liberty interests grounded in the Fourteenth Amendment. In doing so, the Court struck down a Texas law criminalizing same-sex conduct, concluding that it furthered no legitimate state interest.

Defendant argues that the right to private intimate conduct in *Lawrence* protects her intimate conduct with Mr. Ammarell. The Magistrate Judge disagreed. First, the Magistrate Judge found that the Supreme Court used the rational basis test in *Lawrence* to strike down the Texas law. Then, the Magistrate Judge used the same test to analyze Defendant's conduct. Strict scrutiny was found to be inapplicable because such a test is reserved for fundamental rights. The Magistrate Judge concluded that an extra-marital relationship is not a liberty interest deeply rooted in our nation's history, implicit in our concept of order[ed] liberty, nor would justice cease to exist if that conduct is regulated. Applying rational basis review, the Magistrate Judge concluded that the State furthered a legitimate interest in protecting the institution of marriage. Therefore, the Magistrate Judge found no violation to Defendant's due process liberty interests. . . .

This Court will not apply a higher standard than the Supreme Court did in *Lawrence*. Instead, the outcome determinative focus is on the two caveats that the Supreme Court raised in *Lawrence*. The liberty interests extend only to those cases where private, intimate conduct is regulated without: (1) injury to a person; or (2) "abuse of an institution the law protects." Therefore, States may regulate the intimate conduct between two people if that conduct injures another person or abuses an institution the law protects. The Court finds precisely this—the causes of action for criminal conversation and alienation of affection further a legitimate state interest and fall comfortably within *Lawrence*'s caveats.

To begin with, the sexual conduct alleged in this case clearly implicates injury to a person: Plaintiff. The Supreme Court of North Carolina has previously recognized that criminal conversation addressed the emotional injury felt by one spouse after the other engaged in sexual conduct with a third party. . . . Equally important, the sexual conduct alleged in this case abuses an institution which the law protects: marriage. In 1888, the Supreme Court stated that marriage had long been "a great public institution, giving character to our whole civil polity." Maynard v. Hill, 125 U.S. 190, 213 (1888). And it remains so today. As Justice Kennedy wrote in Obergefell v. Hodges:

> From their beginning to their most recent page, the annals of human history reveal the transcendent importance of marriage . . . . The centrality of marriage to the human condition makes it unsurprising that the institution has existed for millennia and across civilizations. Since the dawn of history, marriage has transformed strangers into relatives, binding families and societies together. Confucius taught that marriage lies at the foundation of government. This wisdom was

echoed centuries later and half a world away by Cicero, who wrote, "The first bond of society is marriage; next, children; and then the family." There are untold references to the beauty of marriage in religious and philosophical texts spanning time, cultures, and faiths, as well as in art and literature in all their forms.

135 S. Ct. 2584, 2595 (2015).

In terms of how our Nation has treated marriage, "[t]he States have contributed to the fundamental character of marriage by placing it at the center of many facets of the legal and social order." Id. at 2590. North Carolina is no exception. Here, the law has long respected a policy that "within reason favors maintenance of the marriage." . . . The fundamental place held by the institution of marriage justifies the protection afforded here.

Defendant presents several arguments to show that North Carolina's causes of action for criminal conversation and alienation of affection are neither narrowly tailored nor rationally related to the protection of marriage. Defendant's arguments, however, cut against the conclusion she advocates. First, Defendant points out that North Carolina's divorce rate ranked fifth in the United States. This statistic justifies North Carolina's retention of causes of action for alienation of affection and criminal conversation. The divorce rate is high and the State may combat that crisis by exercising its power to reduce it, such as penalizing adultery.

Second, Defendant cites N.C. Gen. Stat. §50-6, which allows couples in North Carolina to dissolve a marriage after one year of separation. Defendant states that this "no-fault divorce" statute shows that North Carolina has "legislated the amount of protection for marriages," neither encouraging nor discouraging extramarital affairs. This argument is unpersuasive. As the term itself implies, there is a level of consent present in no-fault divorces. Alienation of affection and criminal conversation, on the other hand, target fault and the lack of consent that harm a happy marriage. These causes of action aim to protect marriages where partners were together. It is rational for a State to penalize conduct that alienates affection within a happy marriage while at the same time providing remedies where parties separate and head for divorce. . . .

The bottom line is this: *Lawrence* does not protect all "private consensual sexual conduct" from state regulation—especially when that conduct knowingly and maliciously destroys the happy marriage of another or injures a party. . . .

The people of the state of North Carolina, through their elected representatives, have enacted legislative protections surrounding the institution of marriage and injury to a victim spouse in the form of alienation of affection and criminal conversation torts. The wisdom of those laws is challenged by the Defendant. But this is the wrong forum. Changes if they are to come should come through the voice of the people not a bang of the gavel.

Notes and Questions

1. Background. Megan France, the paramour in Ammarell v. France, was the second wife of Nascar CEO Brian France. The couple married in 2001, divorced in 2004, and then remarried and divorced again in 2008. Their twins were born in

2006. Divorce papers by Brian charged that his former wife spent a "staggering" amount of his fortune (estimated at $550 million) on her family and friends. She met Ryan Ammarell (the plaintiff's husband) in 2015, several years after her second divorce from Brian France.[36]

How did Ryan Ammarell's wife discover his affair? On what grounds did the plaintiff sue her husband's paramour? How did the plaintiff establish the requisite elements of her claim(s)?

2. Elements. At common law, interference with the marital relationship was remediable by tort actions for *alienation of affections* and *criminal conversation*. Alienation of affections requires (1) a valid marriage, (2) wrongful conduct by the defendant with the plaintiff's spouse, (3) the loss of affection or consortium, and (4) a causal connection between the defendant's conduct and the deprivation of affection. (Loss of consortium encompasses not merely loss of the sexual relationship, but also loss of comfort, affection, and companionship.)

Unlike alienation of affections, criminal conversation requires sexual intercourse. Criminal conversation has been called a strict liability tort because the only defenses are the plaintiff's (i.e., the injured spouse's) consent and the statute of limitations. The participating spouse's consent is not a defense. Should a couple's decision to have an "open marriage" constitute a defense?

3. Abolition movement. After its initial recognition by New York in 1866, the tort of alienation of affections was adopted by virtually every state. Currently, only six states (Hawaii, Mississippi, New Mexico, North Carolina, South Dakota, and Utah) recognize the claim for alienation of affections.[37] With the widespread abolition movement, should recovery be based on alternative theories, such as intentional or negligent infliction of emotional distress? Are such torts distinguishable from alienation of affections?

4. Rationales. What are the rationales for retaining tort liability for alienation of affections and criminal conversation, according to *Ammarell*? Would abolition of these torts "send the message that we are devaluing the marriage relationship"? Gorman v. McMahon, 792 So. 2d 307 (Miss. Ct. App. 2001). On the other hand, is recognition of these torts out of sync with current sexual mores and the changing role of women? See Beavers v. McMican, 877 S.E.2d 412, 422-425 (N.C. Ct. App. 2022) (Jackson, dissenting). Should divorce provide the sole remedy for marriages beset by adultery?

5. Constitutionality. What was the basis of defendant's argument that the torts of alienation of affections and criminal conversation are unconstitutional? How is Lawrence v. Texas relevant? Why did *Ammarell* find the laws passed constitutional

[36]. See FoxSports, France: Ex-wife Spent Tons of Money, May 8, 2013, https://www.foxsports.com/nascar/story/brian-france-divorce-documents-unsealed-says-former-wife-spent-staggering-amount-of-money-050813.

[37]. Meghann Mollerus, Yes, You Can Sue Your Marriage Homewrecker, But New Bills Aim to Get Rid of Alienation of Affection, WFMY News, Apr. 30, 2021, https://www.wfmynews2.com/article/news/local/alienation-of-affection-lawsuits-homewrecker-legislation-north-carolina-marriage-divorce-affair-wfmy/83-52f2e3f3-fec4-4f59-9fe2-7f85577a2229.

muster? Does *Lawrence* hold that there is a constitutional right to commit adultery, according to *Ammarell*? Why or why not?

6. Damages. Damages for the torts of alienation of affections and criminal conversation are often high. For example, a North Carolina judge gave a record award for alienation of affection to a former wife in 2011 when he ordered her ex-husband's lover to pay her $30 million. And in 2018, a different judge ordered a defendant to pay $8.8 million in damages, taking into account the plaintiff's loss of a valued employee (his wife!).[38] Is the harm caused by adultery alleviated by money damages? Do huge damage awards argue for or against retention of tort liability?

7. Choice of law. May a plaintiff recover for alienation of affections if the plaintiff is domiciled in a state that recognizes the tort, but all of the sexual conduct occurred outside the state? See Hayes v. Waltz, 784 S.E.2d 607 (N.C. Ct. App. 2016) (ruling that choice of law is based on where injury to marital relationship occurred and finding that text messages and telephone calls sufficed). But cf. Nordness v. Faucheaux, 170 So. 3d 454 (Miss. 2015) (paramour lacked sufficient minimum contacts with forum state).

8. Delayed discovery. Some extramarital affairs remain secret for a considerable time. If a spouse discovers the affair long after it ends, does/should the statute of limitations bar the suit? Compare Hancock v. Watson, 962 So. 2d 627 (Miss. Ct. App. 2007) (relevant time is when wife's and not plaintiff-husband's affections were alienated), with Misenheimer v. Burris, 637 S.E.2d 173 (N.C. 2006) (statute begins to run upon discovery of affair, not its commission).

Problems

1. Nicole and Vinnie have been married for five years. They have two children, ages two and four. Nicole consults Dr. Charles Brent for neck pain. Thereafter, Nicole and Dr. Brent begin talking on the phone and exchanging text messages, and eventually, they engage in consensual sexual relations on two occasions. Nicole's husband, Vinnie, discovers the text messages on Nicole's phone and immediately files for divorce. He then sues Dr. Brent, individually and on behalf of his two children, alleging the torts of alienation of affections and negligent infliction of emotional distress. Dr. Brent moves for summary judgment on the children's claims. Do children have standing to sue a parent's paramour who caused their parents to divorce? See Brent v. Mathis, 154 So. 3d 842 (Miss. 2014). See also In re Noland-Vance, 321 S.W.3d 398 (Mo. Ct. App. 2010); Sandi S. Varnado,

---

[38]. N.C. One of Seven States that Makes Cheaters Pay, WRAL News, Apr. 29, 2014, https://www.wral.com/nc-one-of-seven-states-that-makes-cheaters-pay/13599861/. Jilted spouses file about 200 amatory tort lawsuits annually in North Carolina, although most suits are used merely as leverage in divorce. Id. See also Isaac Stanley-Becker, $8.8 Million "Alienation of Affection" Penalty: Another Reason Not to Have an Affair in North Carolina, Wash. Post, July 31, 2018, https://www.washingtonpost.com/news/morning-mix/wp/2018/07/31/8-8-million-alienation-of-affection-award-another-reason-not-to-have-an-affair-in-north-carolina/.

Inappropriate Parental Influence: A New App for Tort Law and Upgraded Relief for Alienated Parents, 61 DePaul L. Rev. 113 (2011).

2. Marc and Amber Malecek are a married couple. Amber, a nurse, begins a sexual relationship with Derek Williams, a physician at the hospital where she works. After her husband discovers the affair, he sues Williams for alienation of affections and criminal conversation. Williams moves to dismiss the claims, alleging that the common law causes of action for alienation of affections and criminal conversation are facially unconstitutional under the Fourteenth Amendment by restraining one's liberty to have intimate sexual relations with another consenting adult. In support of this argument, Williams relies on the U.S. Supreme Court decision in Lawrence v. Texas. He also argues that the torts of alienation of affections and criminal conversation violate his rights to free speech, expression, and association guaranteed by the First and Fourteenth Amendments. What result? Does the tort of alienation of affection target a defendant's expression? In your opinion, are the state interests sufficiently important to justify private tort actions that restrict the right to engage in intimate sexual conduct with other consenting adults? See Malacek v. Williams, 804 S.E.2d 592 (N.C. Ct. App. 2017).

2. Tort Actions Between Spouses

EPSTEIN v. EPSTEIN
843 F.3d 1147 (7th Cir. 2016)

SYKES, Circuit Judge.
Barry Epstein sued his estranged wife, Paula, alleging that she violated the federal Wiretapping and Electronic Surveillance Act by intercepting his emails. The action arises from the couple's acrimonious divorce. . . . Paula and Barry Epstein married in 1970. In 2011 Paula filed for divorce in Cook County Circuit Court, accusing her husband of infidelity. The divorce case has dragged on since then and remains unresolved. During discovery Barry's lawyer sent Paula's lawyer a document request asking for production of "[a]ny and all communications, documents, e-mails, text messages, photographs, notes, credit card slips, bank statements, or other document whatsoever, which allegedly relate[] to [Paula's allegation of] infidelity."

Jay Frank was Paula's lawyer. In response to this document request, he produced (among other things) copies of email correspondence between Barry and several women. On the face of it, the messages seem to have been forwarded from Barry's email accounts to Paula's. This came as a shock to Barry; he inferred from this discovery response that Paula must have secretly placed a "rule" on his email accounts automatically forwarding his messages to her.

With the divorce action still ongoing, Barry filed this federal suit against Paula and Frank pursuant to 18 U.S.C. §2520, which authorizes civil actions against persons who violate the Wiretap Act. The complaint alleges that Paula unlawfully intercepted, disclosed, and used Barry's emails in violation of the Act, and that Frank violated the Act by unlawfully disclosing and using the emails in the divorce proceeding. . . . The Wiretap Act makes it unlawful to "intentionally intercept[] [or]

endeavor[] to intercept . . . any wire, oral, or electronic communication." 18 U.S.C. §2511(1)(a). The Act also prohibits the intentional "disclos[ure]" or "use[]" of the contents of an unlawfully intercepted electronic communication. "[I]ntercept" is defined as "the aural or other acquisition of the contents of any wire, electronic, or oral communication." . . . The parties' briefs are largely devoted to a debate about whether the Wiretap Act requires a "contemporaneous" interception of an electronic communication—that is, an interception that occurs during transmission. . . . We do not need to take a position today. Even if the Wiretap Act covers only contemporaneous interceptions, Barry has stated a Wiretap Act claim against Paula, and dismissal of the claim against her was error. . . .

The emails appear to come from one of Paula's email clients [an "email client" is a computer program to access email, such as Gmail]. Those that were sent from Barry's account to the other women show the time his email client sent the message; the emails he received from the other women show the time his email client received the message. Each email also shows the time Paula's email client received the forwarded message from Barry's account. The district judge read these "sent" and "received" markings in the defendants' favor, noting that there are gaps between the time Barry sent or received an email and the time Paula received the forwarded email. . . . Although this reasoning seems sensible on its face, there are three independently sufficient reasons why the time markings on the emails do not establish an "impenetrable defense" to the Wiretap Act claims.

First, the judge misunderstood when an interception occurs. He assumed that the time Paula's email client received the forwarded emails was the moment of interception. Although this interpretation of "interception" is understandable, . . . the interception of an email need not occur at the time the wrongdoer receives the email. Because Barry's case was dismissed on the pleadings, we do not know how Paula's auto-forwarding rule worked. For example, we cannot tell if a server immediately copied Barry's emails—at which point the interception would be complete—even though Paula's email client may not have received them until later.

Second, the judge mistakenly conflated the emails Barry received and those he sent. If we assume that the Wiretap Act prohibits only contemporaneous interceptions, the Act would apply to the acquisition of emails before they "cross[] the finish line of transmission," which happens when their intended recipient actually receives them. . . . The time markings on [the emails that Barry sent] tell us nothing about when transmission of the emails was complete. To know that we would need to know when the intended recipients—the women Barry was corresponding with—actually received the emails. The exhibit attached to the complaint includes a few email chains that do give this information, but for many of the emails Barry sent, it is impossible to know when the intended recipients received them. Because these emails don't conclusively establish when the transmissions were completed, it's possible that they were intercepted contemporaneously.

Finally, it is highly unlikely that the exhibit attached to the complaint contains all the emails that were forwarded to Paula's email addresses. . . . Barry alleges that Paula's auto-forward rule was in place for as long as five years; it is more likely that these few dozen emails are only a small fraction of a much larger volume. Because the emails attached to the complaint do not conclusively establish that there was no contemporaneous interception, [the judge] was wrong to dismiss the case against Paula on this ground.

[T]he claim against Frank (Paula's lawyer) fails for an independent reason. The complaint alleges that Frank "disclosed and used" the contents of the intercepted communications in violation of §2511(1)(c) and (d). More specifically, Barry advanced two alternative theories of liability against the lawyer: (1) Frank "disclosed" the contents of the emails when he produced them in response to the discovery request and (2) Frank "used" them in connection with the divorce litigation to embarrass Barry. The judge rejected both of these arguments and was right to do so.

The disclosure theory fails because Barry already knew the contents of the intercepted emails and indeed invited their disclosure by requesting them in discovery in the divorce action. The Wiretap Act doesn't prohibit the interception of electronic communications with consent. . . . The use theory fails for a more prosaic reason: The complaint doesn't identify any use Frank actually made of the emails. Rather, it alleges that Frank intended to use the emails to embarrass Barry during the divorce litigation—in cahoots with Paula and with the aim of extracting a favorable financial settlement. But the Wiretap Act does not prohibit inchoate intent. Accordingly, we affirm the judgment to the extent that it dismissed the case against Frank. The amended complaint states a Wiretap Act claim against Paula; to that extent the judgment is reversed. . . .

POSNER, Circuit Judge, concurring.

I agree with Judge Sykes that under the existing understanding of the Federal Wiretap Act, Paula Epstein violated it if she searched her husband's computer for evidence of adultery by him that she could use against him in divorce proceedings, without having obtained his consent to her accessing his computer. I write separately to raise a question that neither party addresses and is therefore not before us on this appeal—whether the Act should be thought applicable to such an invasion of privacy; for if not the husband's suit should be dismissed.

Obviously not all claims of privacy are or should be protected by law. Virtually every adult in a society such as ours values his or her privacy, but it doesn't follow that privacy is always, or even primarily, a social good, which is to say a good that promotes social welfare. "Privacy" means concealment of facts about a person. [I]f the concealment is of genuine misconduct, I am unclear why it should be protected by the law. I don't understand why law should promote dishonesty and deception by protecting an undeserved, a rightly tarnished, reputation.

Among the facts routinely attempted to be concealed for disreputable reasons is of course marital infidelity. Mr. Epstein wanted to conceal his infidelity from his wife primarily it seems because the revelation of it would give her added leverage in a divorce proceeding. I don't understand why federal, or for that matter state, law should protect an interest so lacking in any social benefit, especially when one considers that adultery remains a crime in 20 of the nation's 50 states—including Illinois where the parties reside—though it is a crime that is very rarely prosecuted. We might compare Mrs. Epstein to a bounty hunter—a private person who promotes a governmental interest. She has uncovered criminal conduct hurtful to herself, and deserves compensation, such as a more generous settlement in her divorce proceeding.

Her husband's suit under the Federal Wiretap Act is more than a pure waste of judicial resources: it is a suit seeking a reward for concealing criminal activity. Had the issue been raised in the litigation, I would vote to interpret the Act as being inapplicable to—and therefore failing to create a remedy for—wiretaps intended, and reasonably likely, to obtain evidence of crime, as in this case, in which the plaintiff invoked the Act in an effort to hide evidence of his adultery from his wife.

Notes and Questions

1. Interspousal immunity. At common law, the doctrine of interspousal immunity precluded interspousal tort suits. The doctrine was premised on the legal fiction of marital unity (i.e., because husband and wife shared a legal identity, interspousal tort suits were impossible), and later premised on concerns that litigation would undermine marital harmony and marital privacy. Abrogation occurred first for intentional acts, and subsequently for negligent acts. Almost all states have abrogated the doctrine either fully or partially.

2. Tort liability for transmission of STDs. Since the nineteenth century, courts have recognized spousal tort liability for negligent transmission of venereal disease. Historical concern about the impact of venereal disease on the family stemmed from the influence of the eugenics movement (i.e., the belief that social ills are transmitted through heredity); concerns about immigration (i.e., the myth that immigrants had high rates of infection); worries about industrialization (i.e., a preoccupation with the immorality engendered by city living); and concerns about the sexual double standard (i.e., fear that dissolute husbands transmitted venereal disease to chaste young women).[39] Many states recognize civil and sometimes criminal liability for transmission of a sexually transmitted disease (STD), regardless of marital status.

3. Spousal spying. Spouses sometimes spy on each other, as revealed in *Epstein*, to discover evidence of extramarital affairs. Before the Internet era, spousal spying consisted of tapping telephones. In 1968, Congress enacted the Wiretap Act (or Title III) to impose liability for nonconsensual intentional interception of wire or oral communications. In 1986, Congress added liability for interception of electronic communications. The Act imposes civil and criminal liability and also provides for steep damages (a minimum fine of $100 per day or $10,000, whichever is greater, plus punitive damages). 18 U.S.C. §2520(c)(2)(B). Some states also have wiretap statutes.

4. Interspousal immunity for spousal spying. Should the interspousal immunity doctrine apply to the Wiretap Act because of privacy concerns? What is the reasoning of Judge Posner, in his concurring opinion in *Epstein*, regarding the application of the Wiretap Act to interspousal spying for infidelity? Do you find his reasoning persuasive? A majority of federal courts, like *Epstein*, hold that spouses are not subject to immunity under the Wiretap Act. Should tort liability extend to

---

[39]. See generally Allan M. Brandt, No Magic Bullet: A Social History of Venereal Disease in the United States Since 1880 (1987); Sex, Sin, and Suffering: Venereal Disease and European Society Since 1870 (Roger Davidson & Lesley A. Hall eds., 2001).

spousal *installation* of spyware? See LaRocca v. LaRocca, 86 F. Supp. 3d 540 (E.D. La. 2015)? To global positioning satellite (GPS) electronic tracking devices?

5. Attorney's liability. The husband in *Epstein* sued not only his former wife but also her lawyer pursuant to the Wiretap Act. What was the extent of the lawyer's liability? When is an attorney subject to discipline for helping a client gather electronic evidence to support a client's case? Traditional ethical standards dictate that attorneys may not violate the law or assist their clients in violating the law in the gathering of evidence. Model Rule of Professional Conduct 4.4(a) (2016) prohibits using methods of gathering evidence that violate the legal rights of a third party. However, the rules are less clear on the obligation to *monitor* a client's efforts to gather evidence. How can a lawyer limit his or her risks surrounding the client's acquisition of such evidence?

Problem

Actor Alec Baldwin and his ex-wife, actress Kim Basinger, share joint custody of their 11-year-old daughter, Ireland. One day, Ireland fails to answer a prearranged phone call from her father. He then leaves the following message on her cell phone: "You have insulted me for the last time. I don't give a damn that you're 12 years old or 11 years old, or a child, or that your mother is a thoughtless pain in the ass who doesn't care about what you do." He calls her a "rude, thoughtless little pig." "You don't have the brains or the decency as a human being." He threatens: "I am going to get on a plane [and] straighten your ass out when I see you!" He screams, "This crap you pull on me . . . you would never dream of doing to your mother, and you do it to me constantly." The press prints the story. Baldwin believes that Basinger released the message to the press. Does Baldwin have a cause of action against Basinger for violation of wiretapping laws?[40]

D. Evidentiary Privileges Arising from the Marital Relationship

STATE v. GUTIERREZ
482 P.3d 700 (N.M. 2019)

NAKAMURA, Chief Justice.

[On April 8, 2002, Jose Valverde was found dead in a boxcar he used as his home in Clovis, New Mexico. He had been shot in the head with a shotgun.

---

[40]. See Sean Hannity & Alan Colmes, Alec Baldwin Leaves Abusive Message for His Daughter, FDCH Ent. Transcripts, Apr. 23, 2007, 2007 WLNR 7651405.

[M]ore than 13 years later, a grand jury indicted David Gutierrez for the murder. Gutierrez disclosed the fact that he killed Valverde to his first wife and later to his second wife. At his trial, he invoked the spousal communication privilege to preclude both women from testifying about his role in the killing.] Gutierrez's invocation of the spousal communication privilege prompts us to question its continued viability in New Mexico. . . .

Gutierrez's ex-wife Nicole Cordova offered the following testimony at trial. She married Gutierrez in 2002, and the marriage lasted only two years. The victim, her uncle, had raped her several times when she was thirteen or fourteen years old. She told Gutierrez about the rapes some months before the victim was killed, and Gutierrez told her "not to worry about anything anymore." . . . On the day of the murder, Gutierrez left home for about a half hour and was visibly upset when he returned. Gutierrez told her that he "took care of it," and although he did not explain further, she knew what had happened: Gutierrez had killed the victim. Gutierrez told her that he needed help to find a shotgun shell and then they drove to the victim's boxcar. When she entered the boxcar, she saw that it was in disarray and that the victim's body was face down on the floor. She sifted through some beer cans [and] found a shotgun shell. . . . Gutierrez later threatened that she would suffer the same fate as the victim if she ever told anyone about what happened. . . .

Gutierrez's second wife, Evelyn Franco, also testified at Gutierrez's trial. . . . At the time of trial, they were still legally married but had not spoken in years. In early 2006, she and Gutierrez lived with his parents. There was frequent fighting and arguing in the household. During these fights, Gutierrez's parents would threaten to "send him away for the rest of his life." When she asked Gutierrez what his parents were talking about, he informed her that he had committed a murder. He elaborated that his ex-wife's uncle had molested her, so he went to his house, walked up to where he was laying on the couch, and fired a shotgun into his face killing him.

[The jury found Gutierrez guilty of murder. He was sentenced to life imprisonment. On appeal, Gutierrez contends that the admission of the testimony of his former wives violates the spousal communication privilege.]

New Mexico's spousal communication privilege, provides that "[a] person has a privilege to refuse to disclose, or to prevent another from disclosing, a confidential communication by the person to that person's spouse while they were married." . . . [T]he United States Supreme Court described the policy concerns giving rise to the spousal communication privilege in the following manner:

> This rule is founded upon the deepest and soundest principles of our nature. Principles which have grown out of those domestic relations, that constitute the basis of civil society; and which are essential to the enjoyment of that confidence which should subsist between those who are connected by the nearest and dearest relations of life. To break down or impair the great principles which protect the sanctities of husband and wife, would be to destroy the best solace of human existence.

Stein v. Bowman, 38 U.S. 209, 223 (1839). [Thus the privilege] "is needed to encourage marital confidences, which confidences in turn promote harmony between husband and wife." The traditional justification for the privilege is considered to be an instrumental or utilitarian rationale because it views the privilege as a way to promote "the public good" by protecting the marital relationship.

In addition to the traditional justification, a variety of humanistic and privacy arguments have been offered to support the spousal communication privilege. [T]he privacy and humanistic "theories focus on the value of protecting individual rights."

One such justification offered for the spousal communication privilege is that it eliminates the " 'natural repugnance' " that would necessarily flow from forcing a person to testify against a spouse. The protection of informational privacy and avoidance of unwarranted governmental intrusion are offered as alternative justifications for the privilege. This "rationale recognizes that it is morally repugnant to require the disclosure of certain private information or to force an otherwise honest and decent person to choose among betraying his or her spouse, lying, or going to jail." . . .

The United States Supreme Court has recognized that married people have a constitutional right to privacy in their intimate relationships [citing Griswold v. Connecticut]. [C]ommentators have relied on this right to privacy to conclude that "the abolition of the [spousal communication] privilege would offend the spirit of the constitutional guarantees." . . .

When scrutinized, the traditional justification for the spousal communication privilege is not as forceful as it may initially seem. One of its principal weaknesses is that it rests on two untested assumptions: that (1) married people know the privilege exists, and (2) they rely on it when deciding how much information to share. Critics argue "that there is no empirical evidence to support [these] factual assumptions."

As to the first of these assumptions, it is likely that most people are entirely unaware of the privilege. . . . Even if married people are aware of the spousal communication privilege, it is unclear whether the availability of the privilege has any effect on the extent to which spouses communicate. [I]n a relationship involving a layperson and a professional, the absence of a privilege protecting confidentiality could chill beneficial communication because the layperson might refuse to communicate with the professional. . . . Unlike communication between a professional and a layperson, communication between spouses does not depend on a legal guarantee of confidentiality and does not come into existence because of that guarantee. . . . Because neither assumption underlying the traditional justification survives scrutiny, the traditional justification for the privilege seems entirely unfounded.

As with the traditional justification, questions have been raised as to whether the privacy and humanistic rationales are sufficient to justify recognition of the spousal communication privilege. For example, [John Henry Wigmore, a treatise writer on the law of evidence] argued that the natural repugnance people feel about compelling one spouse to testify against the other is nothing "more than a sentiment" and that sentimental feelings do not justify interference with courts' truth-seeking function. Others have "argued that married couples no longer care about privacy as it was supposed they did in an agrarian society." The increasing frequency with which modern Americans share their marital and familial problems with a public audience provides "contemporary confirmation for the claim that marital privacy is no longer an esteemed value." . . .

Critics have also looked to the ancient origins of the spousal communication privilege and its disparate gender impact to argue that the privilege has outlived its purpose. Blackstone described the legal principles—which by contemporary values can only be deemed misogynistic—that coincided with the creation of the privilege as follows: "By marriage the husband and wife are one person in law; that is, the very being or legal existence of the woman is suspended during the marriage or at least is incorporated or consolidated into that of the husband." These words make obvious why some commentators suggest that "the most serious concern about the privilege is its disparate gender impact[.]"

Despite drastic changes in law and society since Blackstone's day, "the spousal communication privilege perpetuates the role of male domination in the marriage because a husband usually invokes the privilege to prevent his wife's disclosure of confidential communications, thereby benefitting men more often than women." . . . Feminist scholars have vigorously attacked the privilege. [T]hey contend that "privacy is frequently used as an excuse to isolate the family from interference by the state, perpetuating traditional gender hierarchies and power imbalances." The rhetoric of "privacy," these theorists contend, simply ignores the fact that women are all too frequently the victims of a pernicious form of unseen and "private" violence and that appeals to privacy have rhetorical value in the abstract but are nothing short of repressive when applied to the actual social circumstances confronting women in our society. . . .

The traditional justification for the spousal communication privilege is premised on assumptions that do not withstand scrutiny. The privacy and humanistic justifications, when closely examined, seem little more than soaring rhetoric and legally irrelevant sentimentality. The misogynistic history of the privilege is obvious and odious. And it appears that the existence of the privilege perpetuates gender imbalances and, most critically, may even be partly responsible for sheltering and occluding marital violence that disproportionately affects women in entirely unacceptable ways.

Our review of the justifications for and criticisms of the privilege leaves us in agreement with Wigmore: "the occasional compulsory disclosure in court of even the most intimate marital communications would not in fact affect to any perceptible degree the extent to which spouses share confidences." Gutierrez's invocation of the privilege illustrates this point vividly and assures us that we have correctly weighed the competing interests and our decision to abandon the privilege is correct.

Gutierrez's decision to talk about the murder with his wives was not premised on any legal guarantee of confidentiality; to the contrary, he not only told his wives about the killing but also bragged about the murder to third parties who were not covered by the privilege. Gutierrez's case also illustrates that abolishment of the privilege is unlikely to chill candor between spouses, one of the putative reasons for recognizing the privilege.

Gutierrez told Nicole about the murder not because he required a confidant he knew could not divulge information shared; rather, he told Nicole about the murder because, it seems, he surmised that she would be pleased by what he had done. . . . Similarly, Evelyn learned of Gutierrez's role in the murder not because Gutierrez perceived her as a person legally obligated to maintain confidences, but because Gutierrez's parents [threatened] to expose him to the criminal consequences of the act. It is clear the spousal communication privilege, and the principles the privilege was intended to advance, played no role whatsoever in Gutierrez's decision to disclose to Nicole and Evelyn the fact that he killed the victim.

While the purported benefits of the spousal communication privilege are questionable, the resulting loss of evidence is nearly certain. . . . Permitting Gutierrez to use the spousal communication privilege to block the testimony of Nicole and Evelyn would have deprived the court of probative evidence without advancing spousal communication or marital harmony in any way. . . .

Having carefully examined the spousal communication privilege, we cannot accept that it meaningfully encourages marital confidences, promotes marital harmony, or produces any substantial public benefit that justifies its continued recognition. Rather, we believe that the privilege is a vestige of a vastly different society than the one we live in today and has been retained in New Mexico simply through inertia. [A]ccordingly, we prospectively abolish it. . . . Because abolishment is prospective, we must nonetheless assess its applicability in Gutierrez's case.

[W]e must decide what consequence flows from the erroneous admission of any confidential, spousal communications. [T]he State argues that even if the district court erred by permitting Nicole to testify about these statements, the spousal communication privilege did not preclude Nicole from testifying about her own observations and experiences. We agree. . . . "Generally, the defendant cannot invoke the marital communications privilege to prevent the spouse from testifying to what the witness-spouse saw." For these reasons, Nicole's first-hand testimony [regarding her observation of the victim's corpse and collection of shotgun-shell castings] was not privileged, and this conclusion is significant. Her admissible testimony renders the district court's erroneous admission of the privileged testimony harmless. . . .

The spousal communication privilege applied to Evelyn's testimony only if Gutierrez told her about the murder during the marriage. [T]o make this determination, Gutierrez had to prove by a preponderance of the evidence that he married Evelyn before the communication was made. Based on the evidence Gutierrez introduced at the hearing, the district court was unable to determine whether he and Evelyn were married when the statements were made. . . Accordingly, Gutierrez's statements to Evelyn were not privileged communications [and, therefore, we affirm] the district court's admission of Evelyn's testimony. . . . Gutierrez's first-degree murder conviction is affirmed.

VIGIL, Justice (concurring in part, dissenting in part).

I concur in the judgment affirming Defendant's conviction. . . . I respectfully dissent from the Majority's decision to abolish the spousal communications privilege [because] it plays a significant role in protecting the privacy rights of married couples. . . .

The spousal communications privilege serves to protect the private conversations that occur within a marriage. Marriage bridges several facets of the human experience. It is both a legal contract and a sentimental, and for some, religious, promise of fidelity and love. As a legal status, marriage grants a couple myriad benefits and protections offered by the state and federal government. As a solemn vow of unity, marriage creates for many a sacred space to share oneself with a chosen other. That space should remain free from state intrusion and compulsion that would demand one spouse to reveal the intimate secrets of the other.

While the Majority argues that the spousal communications privilege "has outlived its justifications," I contend that the privilege retains value in guarding the privacy of the marriage. I am not alone in my belief that the spousal communications privilege should remain a rule of evidence. With the Majority's decision in this case, New Mexico will be the only state in the nation that does not recognize any form of marital privilege. This gives me pause. . . .

"No union is more profound than marriage, for it embodies the highest ideals of love, fidelity, devotion, sacrifice, and family." [citing *Obergefell*]. Marriage "fulfils yearnings for security, safe haven, and connection that express our common humanity." Time and again, the United States Supreme Court has expressed its view of marriage as an institution to be held in the highest regard. . . . A strong marital relationship supports children and binds families together. Families, in turn, connect with numerous other esteemed societal institutions, such as schools, churches, work places, and ethnic groups. Our communities are strengthened by steadfast marriages, and marriages are strengthened when spouses are free to communicate with each other without fear of government intrusion into their confidential conversations. . . .

I am convinced that the durability of the spousal communications privilege is tied to our society's view that marriage is sacrosanct and should be guarded from excessive state intrusion. "In a liberal democracy, the spousal relationship is deemed one of the most sacred. In a democratic society, it is particularly abhorrent and repugnant for government to intrude upon the privacy of that relationship." . . . Eliminating the spousal communications privilege spells "nearly complete destruction of the privacy of marriage, in the interest of the conduct of ordinary litigation." . . . In weighing the equities of the judicial pursuit of truth and the freedom of married couples to share confidences absent government interference, I must conclude that marital privacy is more valuable than the collection of evidence in a given case. . . .

Notes and Questions

1. Epilogue. Following the principal case above, the New Mexico Supreme Court retracted the ruling abolishing the spousal communications privilege and reinstated the privilege pending a study of the matter by the state Rules of Evidence Committee. The court asked the committee to make a recommendation regarding abolition of the spousal communications evidentiary privilege, taking into account the various views expressed in the opinion. After reading the following notes and questions, what do you think the committee should decide, and why?

2. Spousal privileges. The common law recognized two different marital evidentiary privileges. The marital communications privilege prevents the admission of evidence of private communications between the spouses that were made during the marriage. This privilege lasts even after divorce. The adverse spousal testimonial privilege enables spouses to decline to testify adversely against each other in a criminal trial. This privilege allows the defendant-spouse to exclude evidence by the witness-spouse of criminal acts and of communications in the presence of third parties. The adverse spousal testimonial privilege terminates upon divorce.

Which privilege is at issue in *Gutierrez*? Why does the New Mexico Supreme Court hold that the admission of the first wife's testimony (regarding her observation of the victim's body) was not privileged? Why were the defendant's statements to his second wife also not privileged communications?

3. Rationale. What are the justifications for the marital communications privilege, according to *Gutierrez*? The court asserts that the privilege should be abolished because these justifications are "premised on assumptions that do not withstand scrutiny." What justifications and assumptions support abolition of the privilege? Do you agree that the privilege has "outlived its purpose"? Evaluate the respective views of the majority and dissent regarding the role of the privilege in protecting the privacy rights of married couples. Which view do you find more persuasive?[41]

4. *Trammel*. The U.S. Supreme Court addressed the adverse spousal testimony privilege in Trammel v. United States, 445 U.S. 40 (1980). The defendant, Otis Trammel, was indicted for importing, and conspiracy to import, heroin into the United States. His wife, a co-conspirator, agreed to testify against him in return for a grant of immunity. The husband unsuccessfully attempted to invoke the privilege against adverse spousal testimony to prevent her testimony.

The Supreme Court unanimously held that the witness-spouse alone (here, the wife) has a privilege to refuse to testify adversely. The Court reasoned that the promulgation of the Federal Rules of Evidence and recent state law trends had contributed to erosion of the privilege; courts should strictly construe the privilege based on the governmental interest in combatting crime; and the justification of preservation of marital harmony did not exist if one spouse was willing to testify against the other (as here). *Trammel* influenced many states to limit significantly the adverse spousal testimonial privilege. Note that *Trammel* left the marital communications privilege untouched in the federal courts.

5. Exceptions.

a. Joint participation. Should the law recognize an exception for either or both marital privileges when spouses have jointly participated in a crime or conspired to commit a crime? Compare United States v. Pineda-Mateo, 905 F.3d 13 (1st Cir. 2018) (barring government from compelling spouse's testimony), with United States v. Clark, 712 F.2d 299 (7th Cir. 1983) (contra).

b. Separated spouses. Some courts have held that the marital communications privilege is inapplicable if the spouses were permanently separated at the time of the communication. See, e.g., United States v. Singleton, 260 F.3d 1295, 1299 (11th Cir. 2001). Why?

c. Familial offenses. An exception exists to the adverse spousal testimonial privilege for offenses committed by one spouse against the other spouse or offenses against a child of a spouse. See, e.g., United States v. Seminole, 865 F.3d 1150 (9th

---

[41]. See generally Alexandra Aparicio, Her Alone: Feminist Perspectives on the Future of Spousal Privileges, U. Chi. L. Rev. Online, July 6, 2020, https://lawreviewblog.uchicago.edu/2020/07/06/spousal-privileges/.

Cir. 2017) (holding spousal privilege inapplicable when spouse is victim); State v. Sewell, 205 A.3d 966 (Md. Ct. App. 2019) (same for child victim). Should the exception apply to a violation of a protection order against the other spouse? See La. Code Evid. Ann. art. 505. What is the rationale for this exception? See also Problem 1 below.

d. Other exceptions. Should there be a "fraudulent marriage exception" to the marital privileges? See, e.g., Commonwealth v. Lewis, 39 A. 3d 341 (Pa. Super. Ct. 2012) (statute did not authorize an exception to the spousal testimonial privilege, even in the case of collusive marriages). See also Problem 3 below.

6. Voluntariness. In vesting the adverse spousal testimony privilege in the witness-spouse, *Trammel* emphasizes that Mrs. Trammel gave her testimony voluntarily. Therefore, the Supreme Court reasoned, there was little marital harmony to preserve. Was her testimony truly voluntary? Is one spouse's willingness to testify against the other an indication that the marriage is past saving? Do *Gutierrez* and *Trammel* put the government in the position of "forc[ing] or encourag[ing] testimony which might alienate husband and wife, or further inflame existing domestic differences," Hawkins v. United States, 358 U.S. 77, 79 (cited in *Trammel*)? If so, is this an appropriate governmental role vis à vis the family?[42]

7. Policy reform. As fewer people marry and as society grows more accepting of cohabitation, how should courts and legislatures treat the spousal evidentiary privileges? Should application of the privileges extend to intimate partners and members of nonmarital families? Why?

Problems

1. Kenneth Taylor, a police officer, is charged with aggravated battery of his girlfriend, Glenda Richard. The battery consisted of a severe beating with his fists, police flashlight, and service revolver. After Glenda's hospitalization, she agrees to testify against Kenneth and provides a typed statement, an affidavit expressing her desire to prosecute, and a videotape affirming that desire. Ten days before the trial, Glenda marries Kenneth. At trial, when the prosecutor calls Glenda as a victim-witness of the assault, she refuses to testify, invoking the spousal privilege for adverse testimony. The state has no spousal crime exception to the privilege. What arguments would you advance on behalf of Glenda? On behalf of the prosecution? See Louisiana v. Taylor, 642 So. 2d 160 (La. 1994) (abrogated by La. Code Evid. Ann. art. 505).

2. Former President Bill Clinton was accused of having an extramarital affair with a former White House intern, Monica Lewinsky, and of having committed perjury by denying it before a grand jury investigating his liaison with another woman, Paula Jones. To help build a case against Clinton, independent counsel

[42]. See Richard O. Lempert, A Right to Every Woman's Evidence, 66 Iowa L. Rev. 725 (1981) (arguing *Trammel* encourages the government to turn spouses against each other).

Kenneth Starr called Marcia Lewis, the mother of Lewinsky, to testify before a federal grand jury regarding her discussions about Lewinsky's relationship with Clinton. The resultant controversy (regarding the wisdom of compelling a mother to testify against her daughter) evoked a demand for an adverse testimonial privilege for parents and children. Do the rationales employed by *Trammel* with respect to the adverse spousal testimonial privilege apply with equal force to parents and children? To unmarried cohabitants? To siblings?

3. Dimitry, a Russian citizen, meets and marries Svetlana, a U.S. citizen, while he is studying on a student visa in the U.S. After their marriage, Svetlana applies for an alien resident visa for him, attaching copies of the couple's jointly filed tax returns. While Dimitry's immigration status is being processed, the IRS approaches Svetlana to inform her of their suspicion that the couple lied about their marital status on their tax returns. Svetlana agrees to assist their investigation by recording several telephone calls with Dimitry. In these recorded conversations, he expresses concern regarding his immigration status, saying, among other things, "do not set us up, me and you, in regard to the immigration as no one knows, . . . no one can prove anything." Soon thereafter, the couple divorces after six years of marriage.

The government then charges Dimitry with making false statements in immigration documents and tax documents based on the sham marriage. Dimitry moves to suppress the recordings of his conversations with Svetlana. He contends that the evidence is protected pursuant to the marital communications privilege because the statements were made while the couple was married. The government argues that Dimitry is not entitled to invoke the marital communications privilege because he married for fraudulent purposes. In support of this argument, the government cites cases recognizing a sham marriage exception to the spousal testimonial privilege and asks the court to extend that exception to the marital communications privilege.

What result? What are the policy interests behind the marital communications privilege? Would they be advanced by exclusion of the evidence in this case? Is there a competing societal interest that outweighs those policy interests? See United States v. Fomichev, 899 F.3d 766 (9th Cir. 2018).

IV

Intimate Partner Violence

A. Introduction

This chapter explores the legal response to intimate partner violence (IPV). The occurrence of IPV pits the need for state intervention against respect for family privacy, raising questions again about the appropriate relationship of the state to the family and its members.

The chapter begins by presenting background about the nature and scope of IPV. Introductory materials focus on the dynamics of abuse and the role of influential factors in domestic violence (such as age, gender, sexual orientation, disability, race, ethnicity, immigration status, and social class). The chapter then turns to the civil law response in the form of civil protection orders and later to the criminal justice response. Criminal topics include self-defense, mandatory arrest, no-drop policies, the duties of law enforcement, and high-lethality crimes (sexual assault, threats to kill, and stalking).

Next, the chapter explains the provisions of the landmark Violence Against Women Act (VAWA), including the Violence Against Women Reauthorization Act of 2022 (VAWA 2022). The chapter concludes by examining the problem of children's exposure to IPV, highlighting the contrast between the criminal justice response and that of the child protection system.

Richard J. Gelles & Murray A. Straus, Intimate Violence
84, 88-96 (1988)

[T]he range of homes where wife beating occurs seems to defy categorization. . . . The profile of those who engage in violence with their partners is quite similar to the profile of the parents who are abusive toward their children. The greater the stress, the lower the income, the more violence. Also, there is a direct relationship between violence in childhood and the likelihood of becoming a violent adult. . . .

One of the more interesting aspects of the relationship between childhood and adult violence is that *observing* your parents hit one another is a more powerful contributor to the probability of becoming a violent adult than being a victim of violence. The learning experience of seeing your mother and father strike one another is more significant than being hit yourself. Experiencing, and more importantly observing, violence as a child teaches three lessons:

1. Those who love you are also those who hit you, and those you love are people you can hit.
2. Seeing and experiencing violence in your home establishes the moral rightness of hitting those you love.
3. If other means of getting your way, dealing with stress, or expressing yourself do not work, violence is permissible. . . .

Lurking beneath the surface of all intimate violence are confrontations and controversies over power. [T]he risk of intimate violence is the greatest when all the decisionmaking in a home is concentrated in the hands of one of the partners. . . .

It goes without saying that intimate violence is most likely to occur in intimate settings. . . . [T]he bedroom is the most lethal room in the house. . . . The kitchen and dining room are the other frequent scenes of lethal violence between family members.

After 8:00 P.M., the risk for family violence increases. This is almost self-evident, since this is also the time when family members are most likely to be together in the home. . . . The temporal and spatial patterns of intimate violence support our notion that privacy is a key underlying factor. . . .

Centers for Disease Control & Prevention (CDC), National Intimate Partner and Sexual Violence Survey (NISVS)
2015 Data Brief—Updated Release 1, 9, Nov. 2018

VIOLENCE BY AN INTIMATE PARTNER

[The National Intimate Partner and Sexual Violence Survey (NISVS) surveyed approximately 16,000 adults about their experiences of sexual assault and IPV.]

- In the U.S., over 1 in 3 (36.4% or 43.6 million) women experienced contact sexual violence, physical violence, and/or stalking by an intimate partner during their lifetime.
- About 1 in 4 women (25.1% or 30.0 million) in the U.S. experienced contact sexual violence, physical violence, and/or stalking by an intimate partner during their lifetime and reported some form of IPV-related impact.
- Regarding specific subtypes of intimate partner violence, about 18.3% of women experienced contact sexual violence, 30.6% experienced physical violence (21.4% experienced severe physical violence), and 10.4% experienced stalking during their lifetime.
- An estimated 1 in 18 (5.5% or 6.6 million) women in the U.S. experienced contact sexual violence, physical violence, and/or stalking by an intimate partner during the 12 months preceding the survey.
- Over one-third of women (36.4% or 43.5 million) experienced psychological aggression by an intimate partner during their lifetime.

Shannan Catalano et al., Bureau of Criminal Statistics, Female Victims of Violence
2-3 (2009)

FATAL INTIMATE PARTNER VIOLENCE

- [I]ntimate partners committed 14% of all homicides in the U.S. . . . Females made up 70% of victims killed by an intimate partner. . . . Females were killed by intimate partners at twice the rate of males. . . .
- 24% of female homicide victims were killed by a spouse or ex-spouse; 21% were killed by a boyfriend or girlfriend; and 19% by another family member. . . .
- [B]lack female victims of intimate partner homicide were twice as likely as white female homicide victims to be killed by a spouse. . . . Black females were four times more likely than white females to be murdered by a boyfriend or girlfriend. . . .
- Among male homicide victims in 2007, 16% were murdered by a family member or intimate partner. Of male homicide victims, 2% were killed by a spouse or ex-spouse and 3% were killed by a girlfriend or boyfriend. . . .

Judith A. Wolfer, Top Ten Myths About Domestic Violence
42 Md. Bar J. 38, 38-41 (2009)

[This list of ten myths refutes common assumptions about domestic violence.]

MYTH #1: *Domestic violence happens when a batterer loses control of himself.*

Many of us hold the view that individuals who batter their partners simply lose control of themselves and their emotions; that, in an excess of anger or passion, batterers lose their reason and lash out at their partners. These outbursts are seen as unpredictable and, therefore, almost impossible to prevent. [However] domestic violence researchers and advocates have roundly rejected this explanation for domestic violence. We now know that domestic violence arises from a batterer's desire to control and dominate his (usually) female partner because he feels entitled to do so, not because he is suddenly angry.

Batterers utilize a wide array of coercive tactics to cement their control of their partners, such as isolating them from sources of help; humiliating them privately and in public; controlling their access to money, food, community and transportation; and micro-regulating their personal lives and those of their children. Physical violence only punctuates these coercive tactics—not the other way around. . . .

MYTH #2: *Men and women beat one another in equal numbers.*

The rates of domestic violence for both men and women have been studied regularly over the past 20 years with remarkably consistent results. Domestic violence continues to be the number one health and safety issue affecting women, but not men, in the United States. . . . Not only are women beaten more by male partners, but they are injured more. . . .

Women die at the hands of their intimate partners more often than men do. Of all the women killed annually in the United States, 40 to 50 percent of them are killed by an intimate partner. Only 3 percent of all men who are killed die at the hands of female intimate partners. . . .

MYTH #3: *If a woman does not leave her abuser, she must not really be afraid of him.*

Research demonstrates that a woman is most at risk of serious injury or death when she leaves her abuser than if she stays with him, so a battered woman's fear that leaving might be worse for her safety is an objectively reasonable fear. . . . In a Department of Justice study, 75 percent of the domestic assaults reported to law enforcement agencies were perpetrated on victims who were either divorced or separated from their assailants. . . .

Despite this grim reality, studies have also found that battered women often make multiple attempts to leave their abusers before they are finally successful in leaving their abusers permanently. A battered woman is often forced to weigh a staggering number of conflicting needs and realities against her fear of being abused again: she may have no other place to live, she may depend upon her partner's financial support to make ends meet, she may still care for him or feel responsible for him, she may stay with him for the sake of minor children, she may be too embarrassed to ask for help or too afraid to go out on her own, she may be isolated from family and friends and have no other source of help, or she may be simply too tired to move. These reasons are all highly rational and do not negate her fear of her abuser.

MYTH #4: *Getting a protective order does no good—it is just a sheet of paper.*

In fact, a protective order is much more than a mere piece of paper. It is quite clear now from the research that protective orders make a significant positive difference in victims' long-term experiences of safety and security. In a large study, researchers discovered that victims who had obtained protective orders experienced an 80 percent reduction in police-reported physical violence 12 months following the first reported incident. . . . This same effect did not occur, however, for victims who only obtained temporary orders . . . .

MYTH #5: *When a man threatens to kill his spouse or girlfriend, he does not really mean it—he's just blowing off steam.*

Statistically, it is more likely that he does mean it. In a large study involving 12 different cities across the country, researchers found that battered women who had been threatened with being killed were 15 times more likely to be killed than battered women who had never been threatened by their partners. . . .

MYTH #6: *There is no way to predict if a particular man will kill or seriously injure his partner.*

Actually, there is. Over the last few years, a group of public health researchers have disseminated the results of carefully designed, rigorous studies that looked for factors that were predictive of death from domestic violence. . . . The most predictive factor was the use or threatened use of a weapon.

The second most predictive factor was the batterer's threat to kill his partner. Other factors include the batterer's abuse of alcohol or drugs, an increase in the frequency or severity of battering, a report of choking or strangulation, forced sex, the presence of a child in the home from a previous relationship, abuse while pregnant, his unemployment, previous separations by the victim, stalking behavior, the existence of a new intimate partner for the victim, and the victim's subjective belief that the batterer could kill her. . . .

MYTH #7: *Just because a father abuses the mother of his children does not mean that he is not a good parent.*

Many members of the legal profession try to draw this distinction between how an abusive partner treats his intimate partner and what kind of parent he is. This distinction may be a false one in a majority of families. One study analyzed 36 separate studies that all looked at the risk of abuse of children where the mother reported being abused by the father. These studies revealed that 30 to 60 percent of those children whose mothers had been abused were themselves likely to be abused.

Even if children are not themselves physically abused, it is well settled in the field that living in a domestically violent home creates four distinct types of physical and emotional harms: the risk of exposure to traumatic events, the risk of neglect, the risk of being directly abused, and the risk of losing one or both of their parents. . . .

MYTH #8: *Women apply for protective orders to get a leg up on a custody case.*

[V]ictims apply for protective orders simply to get the abuse to stop. But they need a custody order to insure that there is no child snatching back and forth between the victim and abuser, and that exchanges can be safe and regulated. . . .

MYTH #9: *[Most state laws do not address domestic violence.]*

[In fact, most states have a variety of civil and criminal laws that address domestic violence. Protective orders and state criminal laws are explored later in this chapter.]

MYTH #10: *Rape or sexual assault really does not happen in a marriage.*

No act communicates domination and control better than rape or sexual assault. Rape and sexual assault occur in approximately 40 to 45 percent of all battering relationships, whether the parties are married or not. . . . [Sexual assault in intimate partner relationships is also a high-lethality indicator.]

B. The Role of Age: Teen Dating Violence

Teen dating violence is society's first indication of IPV. Today's teen victims of dating violence often become tomorrow's adult victims. This section focuses on the role of age in the law's response to IPV and explores the unique problems that teenagers face in seeking and obtaining legal relief.

EMILY K. v. LUIS J.

997 N.Y.S.2d 510 (N.Y. App. Div. 2014)

Garry, J.

[P]etitioner commenced this [protection order] proceeding on behalf of her daughter. . . . Respondent and the daughter were each 13 years old when the petition was filed, and they had been in an on-and-off dating relationship for several years. Following a fact-finding hearing, Family Court granted the petition, finding that the daughter and respondent were in an intimate relationship within the meaning of Family Ct. Act §812(1)(e) and that respondent had committed the family offenses of forcible touching and sexual misconduct. After a dispositional hearing, the court issued a two-year order of protection in the daughter's favor. Respondent appeals from both orders.

Respondent contends that petitioner lacks standing to bring this family offense proceeding. [I]t is well established that a parent has standing to commence a family offense proceeding on behalf of his or her child. However, the substance of respondent's argument is not truly addressed to standing, but instead challenges Family Court's subject matter jurisdiction. . . .

Respondent contends that his relationship with the daughter did not fall within the parameters of Family Ct. Act §812(1). This provision [provides] that Family Court has jurisdiction over family offense proceedings arising from certain acts committed by a respondent against a "member [] of the same family or household." Before 2008, the statutory definition of this phrase embraced only persons who were related by consanguinity or affinity, who were or had been married to one another, or who shared a common child. In 2008, the Legislature expanded the scope of the statute's protection by amending the definition to include "persons who are not related by consanguinity or affinity and who are or have been in an intimate relationship regardless of whether such persons have lived together at any time" (Family Ct. Act §812[1][e]).

The amended statute does not define the phrase "intimate relationship," but instead provides a nonexhaustive list of factors for consideration in determining whether such a relationship exists, including "the nature or type of relationship, regardless of whether the relationship is sexual in nature; the frequency of interaction between the persons; and the duration of the relationship" . . .

The daughter testified that she and respondent had been classmates since kindergarten and began a "boyfriend-girlfriend" relationship in fifth grade that continued, on and off, through eighth grade. At first, the relationship consisted of holding hands, kissing, and exchanging texts and phone calls. By sixth grade, according to the daughter, respondent was texting or calling her 5 or 10 times daily and becoming jealous, "controlling," and "isolat[ing]." The daughter testified that she and respondent had some sexual contact in sixth grade, including an incident in which he allegedly caused her to touch his erect penis at school in the presence of other students, and another in which he put his hand down her shirt to touch her breasts without her permission.

According to the daughter, she and respondent did not date for most of seventh grade. However, late in that year they began talking again, and in eighth grade they met twice, each time at respondent's request. The daughter testified that during the first encounter, she reluctantly acceded to respondent's request for oral sex, believing that he would "leave [her] alone" if she did so. When they met the second time, they had sexual intercourse; the daughter testified that she asked respondent to stop and that he complied at first, but then continued. The daughter distanced herself from respondent after these events, and reported them to petitioner after she began having suicidal thoughts.

Respondent did not dispute the factual accuracy of this testimony. Contrary to his claim, the youth of the participants does not preclude a determination that their relationship was intimate within the meaning of the statute; Family Ct. Act §812(1) expressly extends its jurisdiction to include respondents who are too young to be held criminally responsible, and nothing in the statutory language excludes young victims as participants in intimate relationships. Further, as the legislation expressly directs that such a relationship may exist between persons who have never lived together, the fact that the participants lived in their parents' separate households does not exclude them from the ambit of the statute. The record supports Family Court's determination that the intermittent dating relationship between respondent and the daughter qualified as an intimate relationship within the expanded reach of the revised statute. Accordingly, the Family Court had subject matter jurisdiction to entertain the proceeding . . . .

Notes and Questions

1. Background. IPV affects teenagers as well as adults. Dating violence starts as early as age 11. Violence in teen dating relationships may be quite severe, sometimes results in homicides, and may escalate into adult partner violence.[1] Teen dating violence has been called a "hidden epidemic." Why do you think that label applies?

Teen dating violence, like adult IPV, consists of physical, sexual, and psychological abuse. Both forms manifest similar signs: excessive jealousy; controlling

---

[1]. Michele C. Black et al., Ctrs. for Disease Control & Prevention, National Intimate Partner and Sexual Violence Survey (NISVS): 2010 Summary Report 49 (2011) (abuse starts between ages of 11 and 17) [hereinafter NISVS]; Laura Kann et al., Ctrs. for Disease Control & Prevention, Youth Risk Behavior Surveillance—United States, 2017, 67 Morbidity & Mortality Wkly. Rep. 1, 22 (2018). See also Callie Marie Rennison, Bureau of Justice Statistics, Special Report, Intimate Partner Violence and Age of Victim, 1993-1998 (Table 3) (2001) (adolescent girls, age 16-19, make up more than one-fifth of intimate partner homicides; 10 percent are age 12 to 15). For a recent study, see Nat'l Inst. Justice, Five Things About Teen Dating Violence, May 1, 2023, https://nij.ojp.gov/topics/articles/five-things-about-teen-dating-violence?utm_source=govdelivery&utm_medium=email&utm_campaign=publications.

behavior; rapid involvement in the relationship; unpredictable mood swings; explosive anger; threats of violence; verbal abuse; use of force during arguments; attempts at isolation from friends and family; hypersensitivity; belief in rigid sex roles; blame of others for problems or feelings; cruelty to animals; and mistreatment of other people. Electronic harassment is especially common among teen victims. However, teen victims differ from adult victims because the former are not typically financially dependent on their partners, lack experience in negotiating romantic relationships, and are subject to the influence of peers.

2. Order of protection. An order of protection is a legal document sought by victim (petitioner) against an alleged perpetrator (respondent) that is intended to prevent the recurrence of abuse. It can be temporary or permanent. A temporary ex parte order is issued without prior notice. After a hearing at which both parties may present evidence, the court can issue a permanent protection order. Protection orders are explored in more detail later in this chapter.

a. Grounds. What are the alleged acts of abuse triggering the order of protection in *Emily K.*? Did the boyfriend commit any criminal offenses? If so, which? Were criminal charges brought? If not, speculate on why not. How does a restraining order proceeding differ from a criminal proceeding? How does a restraining order differ from a harassment prevention order? Which of Emily's claims involved abuse versus harassment?

b. Standard. According to the principal case, what is the standard for issuance of a protection order – that the abuse occurred *and* is likely to recur? Or only that the abuse occurred? See Nguyen v. Bui, 536 P.3d 482 (N.M. 2023) (holding that only the former is necessary).

c. Eligible parties. Did Emily petition on her own behalf? Could she have? Fewer than a dozen states explicitly permit minors to petition on their own. In other states, application of the law to minors remains unclear. What problems are posed by statutes that require parents to petition on a minor's behalf?

d. Conditions. What was the nature of the order of protection sought by Emily's mother? What restrictions on the respondent should the judge impose?

e. Barriers for teens. What barriers do teens face in terms of their access to protection orders? How are these obstacles similar to, and different from, those facing adult victims?

3. Statutory application. How does the New York statute define the phrase "intimate relationship"? How did the statutory amendment change the definition? Would Emily have prevailed under prior law?

a. Age of victim. In some states, including New York, the law does not specify the age at which a juvenile is eligible to petition for a protection order. Should laws specify an age limit? If so, what age? See, e.g., Neilson ex rel. Crump v. Blanchette, 201 P.3d 1089 (Wash. Ct. App. 2009) (denying petition of 14-year-old girl who fell below eligible age of 16, based on former statute, later revised to apply to persons in dating relationships where both are at least 13 years of age).

b. "Same household." Some statutes apply to victims who are members of the offender's "family or household." What explains this limitation? How did the New York legislature expand the statutory definition? Why?

c. Definition of a "dating" or "intimate" relationship. Many statutes refer to "dating" relationships rather than "intimate" relationships. For example, the Washington statute provides:

> "Dating relationship" means a social relationship of a romantic nature. Factors that the court may consider in making this determination include: (a) The length of time the relationship has existed; (b) the nature of the relationship; and (c) the frequency of interaction between the parties. Wash. Rev. Code §26.50.010(2).

What issues arise in applying the term "dating relationship" to teen relationships?

"Dating relationships" are not covered in all state statutes or federal statutes. Recently, Congress voted to narrow significantly the so-called boyfriend loophole, which addresses dating relationships. The loophole refers to the fact that, although federal law barred firearm purchases by those convicted of domestic violence by certain persons (spouses, cohabitants, or co-parents), federal law omitted "dating partners" from the list of designated persons. This oversight is significant because a large proportion of violence and even murders is committed by dating partners. The Bipartisan Safer Communities Act of 2022 (Pub. Law No. 117-159, 136 Stat. 1322 (2022)) now extends the reach of the firearm ban for a period of five years to those in dating relationships, thereby partially closing the boyfriend loophole. 18 U.S.C.A. §921(32) & (33)(A)(ii). This legislation is discussed further below.

4. School-based responses. How do middle and high schools address teen dating violence? Currently, about half of the states have laws that confer a proactive role upon middle and high schools for TDV prevention education. What components should be included in such programs?[2] The Violence Against Women Reauthorization Act of 2013 provided funds for school programs to change attitudes, provide teacher training, and formulate prevention-based policies. Saving Money and Reducing Tragedies Through Prevention (SMART Prevention) Act, 42 U.S.C. §14043d-2. The Violence Against Women Reauthorization Act of 2022 reauthorized the SMART Prevention program.

5. Campus sexual assault. Most sexual assaults on college campuses are committed by acquaintances.[3]

a. Morrison case. The issue of acquaintance rape came before the U.S. Supreme Court in United States v. Morrison, 529 U.S. 598 (2000). A female college student at Virginia Polytechnic Institute was allegedly raped by two football players.

---

[2]. See generally D. Kelly Weisberg, Lindsay's Legacy: The Tragedy That Triggered Law Reform to Prevent Teen Dating Violence, 24 Hastings Women's L.J. 27 (2013).

[3]. DV as Prevalent as Sexual Assault on College Campuses, 21 Nat'l Bull. Domestic Violence Prevention 1 (Feb. 2015) (with one in five women reporting sexual assault).

When the school failed to punish the alleged perpetrators, the freshman filed a lawsuit alleging a violation of the Violence Against Women Act, 42 U.S.C. §13981 (providing a federal tort remedy for gender-motivated crimes). The Supreme Court held that Congress exceeded its power under the Commerce Clause in enacting the provision, reasoning that crime is an inherently local concern and that any aggregate effect of crime on the economy is insufficient to invoke federal regulation. Although a federal remedy no longer exists for gender-motivated violence, some states enacted similar laws.

b. Clery Act. Federal law addresses dating abuse on campus by means of the Jeanne Clery Disclosure of Campus Security Policy and Campus Crime Statistics Act or Clery Act, 20 U.S.C. §1092(f), requiring all colleges and universities participating in federal financial aid programs to compile and disclose information about campus crimes. (The law is named after a 19-year-old student at Lehigh University who was raped and murdered in her campus residence hall in 1986.)

A number of regulations (34 C.F.R. §668.46) were enacted in 2014 to implement Clery Act amendments. The rules strengthened victims' rights by (1) requiring notice of students' rights to seek protective orders as well as to seek assistance from law enforcement and campus authorities; (2) providing both victims and alleged perpetrators with the right to have others present in campus disciplinary proceedings and also to receive written notification of the outcome; (3) establishing a preponderance-of-the-evidence standard of proof; and (4) requiring training for campus personnel, assurances of confidentiality for the parties, and written specification of possible sanctions for perpetrators.

c. Recent developments. The policy was rescinded by Department of Education Secretary Betsy DeVos in 2017 and replaced with regulations that significantly strengthened protections for *suspects*. The policy required schools to allow direct cross-examination of student victims, raised the standard of proof to clear and convincing evidence; rescinded requirements allowing complainants to appeal not-guilty findings; allowed mediation between the parties; permitted schools to rely on law enforcement investigations to resolve Title IX complaints; and eliminated the 60-day time limit for completion of investigations. Critics argued that the revised policy treated sexual assault as a "disagreement," weakened protections for victims, and discouraged students from reporting sexual assaults.

More recently, President Biden signed an executive order directing his Secretary of Education to evaluate and rewrite the Title IX regulation to institute greater protections for student victims of sexual assault and to demand greater accountability and transparency by universities. Some states have also recently strengthened protections for student victims. See, e.g., Boermeester v. Carry, 532 P.3d 1084 (Cal. 2023) (holding that private colleges are not required to hold a hearing in which alleged abusers can cross-examine their accusers); Cal. Educ. Code §§66262.5, 66281.8 (enhancing rights of student victims and requiring greater transparency by educational institutions).

VAWA 2022 called for the creation of a joint-interagency Task Force on Sexual Violence in Education to provide recommendations to educational institutions for establishing sexual assault prevention and response teams that are culturally responsive; inclusive; and consider race, ethnicity, national origin, and immigrant status, among other factors, when assisting survivors. 20 U.S.C.A. §1689.

Problem

Karen Muscato and Mary Moore, who are both 14-year-old eighth graders, live in the state of Blackacre. They are best friends who are also "going out together." Karen's mother, Mrs. Muscato, finds sexually explicit text messages between the two girls on her daughter's cell phone. The text messages allegedly contain information intimating that Mary is sexually active and that Mary's mother had purchased a sex toy (namely, a vibrator) for her daughter. After that discovery, Mrs. Muscato tells her daughter that she does not want her spending time with Mary any longer. Mrs. Muscato repeats that message to Mary's mother and warns both Mary's mother and Mary from contacting her daughter again. Karen is unhappy about her mother's actions because she wants to continue her relationship with Mary, despite her mother's objections.

Mary's mother (Mrs. Moore) decides to ignore Mrs. Muscato's request. Mrs. Moore continues to text Karen and to encourage contact between the girls. In fact, Mrs. Moore sends Karen a text message urging her to hide all communications from her mother. The next Sunday, Mrs. Moore appears at Karen's church, when she knows that Karen will be volunteering in the religious school class, in an attempt to contact Karen and reunite the two friends. Karen sees Mrs. Moore coming into the church and unsuccessfully tries to evade her. The ensuing conversation with Mrs. Moore makes Karen so uncomfortable that she opts to spend the rest of her class in the ladies' room.

When Mrs. Muscato learns of these incidents, she files a police report and petitions for a protection order on behalf of her daughter, Karen. (In Blackacre, adult family or household members must file on behalf of teens under age 16.) Mrs. Muscato alleges that Mrs. Moore and her daughter Mary are guilty of stalking. The Blackacre Protection from Abuse Act contains the following definitions of stalking:

> **Section 61a.** "Stalking" consists of: the willful, malicious, and repeated following or harassment of a person by an adult, emancipated minor, or minor thirteen years of age or older, in a manner that would cause a reasonable person to feel frightened, intimidated, threatened, harassed, or molested and actually causes the person being followed or harassed to feel terrorized, frightened, intimidated, threatened, harassed or molested.
>
> **Section 61b.** "Stalking" also means a course of conduct composed of a series of two or more separate acts over a period of time, however short, evidencing a continuity of purpose or unconsented contact with a person that is initiated or continued without the consent of the individual or in disregard of the expressed desire of the individual that the contact be avoided or discontinued.

Should the court grant the protection order against Mrs. Moore? Against Mary? Should the issue of consent be considered from the perspective of Karen or Karen's parent? Should it matter if Mrs. Muscato's goal is to prevent the girls' sexual conduct rather than physical violence? Should it matter if the sexual conduct is a crime in Blackacre? Suppose that there is no hint of any sexual relationship between the two girls, but Mrs. Muscato merely objects to the girls' friendship on religious, racial, or ethnic grounds? Would you suggest statutory reforms to prevent parental "meddling" and judicial entanglement in similar private family disputes? This problem is a modified version of *Muscato ex rel. Butler v. Moore*, 338 P.3d 643 (Okla. Civ. App. 2014).

NOTE: THE ROLE OF OTHER INFLUENTIAL FACTORS

Various factors play an important role in the law's response to IPV, such as: age, gender, sexual orientation, disability, race and ethnicity, and immigration status. Consider how each of these factors plays a role in a victim's experience of IPV as well as the law's response.

1. Elder abuse. All states have laws addressing elder abuse. Perpetrators are most likely to be adult children or spouses.[4] Elder abuse includes physical abuse, abandonment, psychological abuse, financial abuse, and neglect. Victims are often reluctant to report abuse because of fear of retaliation, abandonment, or lack of ability to report. Federal law consists of the Elder Justice Act, enacted as part of the Affordable Care Act (ACA), Pub. L. No. 111-148, Title VI, §6703(d)(1), to "prevent, detect, treat, understand, intervene in and, where appropriate, prosecute elder abuse, neglect and exploitation." In addition, the Elder Abuse Prevention and Prosecution Act of 2017, Pub. L. No. 115-70, 131 Stat. 1207, authorizes the Department of Justice to combat elder abuse by creating an elder justice coordinator position, implementing comprehensive training on elder abuse for agents of the Federal Bureau of Investigation (FBI), and operating a resource group to assist prosecutors in pursuing elder abuse cases. The law also targets e-mail fraud of the elderly.

2. Gender. Women are significantly more likely than men to be victims of IPV—regardless of the type of abuse. Women are also more likely than men to suffer severe injuries and to be killed.[5] Despite overwhelming evidence to the contrary, advocates of the "gender symmetry" argument claim that women and men commit IPV at equal rates. Opponents refute that assertion by claiming that advocates simply count the number of incidents (without regard to their seriousness), omit measures of context (such as self-defense), and rely on narrow definitions of violence (without accounting for multiple forms of victimization).

3. Sexual orientation. IPV among same-sex couples occurs with the same or greater frequency as among different-sex couples.[6] Same-sex partner violence bears many similarities to that of different-sex couples, but important differences exist. For example, same-sex partners have an additional weapon, that is, the threat to "out"

---

[4]. Lucia Silecchia, Who Are the Victims of Elder Abuse? The Disabled, Cognitively Impaired and Poor, Wash. Post, June 15, 2017 (citing research), https://www.washingtonpost.com/news/post everything/wp/2017/06/15/who-are-the-victims-of-elder-abuse-the-disabled-cognitively-impaired -and-poor/.

[5]. NISVS, supra note [1], at iv, 1-2; Rennison, supra note [1], at 1 (three times as many female victims).

[6]. Luca Rolle et al., When Intimate Partner Violence Meets Same Sex Couples: A Review of Same Sex Intimate Partner Violence, 9 Frontiers Psychol. 1506 (2018), doi: 10.3389/ fpsyg.2018.01506.

their partners. In addition, lesbian, gay, bisexual, transgender, and queer/questioning (LGBTQ) victims are often reluctant to seek help because they fear legal consequences, such as loss of custody or housing due to homophobic attitudes. In 2017, the South Carolina Supreme Court ruled that the state's domestic violence laws violated equal protection because of the heterosexual definition of victims. Doe v. State, 808 S.E.2d 807 (S.C. 2017). But cf. N.C. Gen. Stat. §50B-1(b) (dating partners and cohabitants must be of different sexes to file for a protective order; still in effect in 2023).

Congress expanded federal protection for LGBTQ victims in the VAWA Reauthorization Act of 2013 (VAWA 2013) based on the recognition that LGBTQ victims face obstacles in accessing services (such as shelter services) by providers who lack "cultural competency" (i.e., an understanding of diversity). As a result, VAWA 2013 lists both "sexual orientation" and "gender identity" in the revised definition of "underserved populations" in order to expand eligibility of LGBTQ victims for various grant programs (42 U.S.C.A. §13925(a)(39)), and also prohibits discrimination on the basis of sexual orientation or gender identity in all VAWA-funded programs (42 U.S.C.A. §13925(b)(13)(A)).

The VAWA Reauthorization Act of 2022, S.3.623, 117th Cong. (2021-2022), established a new grant program aimed at addressing the needs of LGBTQ survivors of domestic violence, dating violence, sexual assault, and stalking. The program authorizes grants to fund community-specific, culturally sensitive, and survivor-focused services for LGBTQ survivors. VAWA and its reauthorizations are discussed later in this chapter.

4. Disability. Disabled women face a higher risk of IPV than nondisabled victims. They also suffer abuse by multiple partners, more severe abuse, more types of abuse, and abuse for longer duration.[7] The original VAWA omitted to provide services for disabled victims. VAWA 2000 remedied this omission. 42 U.S.C. §§3796gg, 3796hh. VAWA 2022, S. 3623, 117th Cong. (2021-2022) provides additional funding to support survivors who are 50 years of age or older, as well as survivors with disabilities. Note that the Americans with Disabilities Act of 1990 (ADA) (codified in relevant part at 42 U.S.C. §12182(a)) does not address domestic violence.

5. Race and ethnicity. Domestic violence affects members of all race and ethnic groups. However, Native American women and Black women are at particularly high risk. In fact, Native American women experience higher rates of IPV than any other demographic group—most commonly at the hands of non-Native men.[8]

[7]. Douglas A. Brownridge, Violence Against Women: Vulnerable Populations 236 (2009); Nat'l Coalition Against Domestic Violence (NCADV), Fact Sheet, Domestic Violence and Disabilities, http://www.hope-eci.org/_documents/disabilities.pdf (both discussing risk); Dena Hassouneh-Phillips & Elizabeth McNeff, "I Thought I Was Less Worthy": Low Sexual and Body Esteem and Increased Vulnerability to Intimate Partner Abuse in Women with Physical Disabilities, 23 Sexuality & Disability 227, 229 (2005) (discussing nature and duration of abuse).

[8]. NISVS, supra note [1], at 39 (reporting that approximately 40 percent of Black women and 40 percent of Native American women have been victims of rape, physical violence, and/or stalking by an intimate partner in their lifetime). See also Nat'l Cong. of American Indians Policy Research Ctr., Research Policy Update: Violence Against American Indian and Alaska Native Women (Feb. 2018), http://www.ncai.org/policy-research-center/research-data/prc-publications/VAWA_Data_Brief__FINAL_2_1_2018.pdf.

Black women face unique problems in obtaining legal relief. They often hesitate to report the abuse because of their fear of discrimination by law enforcement. They worry that they will be labeled or blamed for the violence. They feel protective of abusers (i.e., reluctant to subject them to a possibly racist or violent response from the police). They also refrain from reporting out of a desire to combat stereotypes about Black men and Black families.[9]

6. Immigration status. Immigrant women also suffer high rates of domestic violence. Their vulnerability is enhanced because of their limited host-language skills, social isolation from friends and family, lack of access to skilled employment, uncertain legal status, and negative previous encounters with authorities in their countries of origin. Moreover, abusers frequently use their partners' immigration status as a tool to force victims to remain in the relationship.[10]

Congressional concern about domestic violence in marriages between foreign women and U.S. citizens led to the creation in VAWA of a "self-petitioning" option to allow an abused foreign wife to submit a special petition to immigration authorities for legalization of her residency status. A battered foreign wife no longer must remain married and living with her abusive husband for two years prior to requesting an adjustment to lawful permanent residency status. VAWA also provides for "suspension of deportation" or "cancellation of removal" for victims without the need for the assistance of their citizen-spouses. 8 U.S.C. §1229b(b)(2). Requirements for self-petitioning include proof that the foreign spouse entered into the marriage in good faith and that she, or her children, has been battered or subjected to "extreme cruelty." 8 U.S.C. 1154(a)(1)(A)(iii)(I)(aa), (bb).

VAWA 2000, 8 U.S.C. §1101, created a nonimmigrant U-visa to enable a victim of crime, who cooperates with law enforcement, to petition for a temporary visa (even if her presence in the United States is unlawful). Victims must have suffered "substantial physical or mental abuse" as the result of a designated crime (e.g., rape, trafficking, domestic violence, sexual assault, or felonious assault).

7. Asylum. Victims of domestic violence face difficulties in applying for asylum. To obtain asylum, a person must prove that she is a "refugee," defined as a person who cannot return to her country of origin based on a well-founded fear of persecution by a government or group that the government is unable or unwilling to control on account of race, religion, nationality, membership in a "particular social group," or political opinion. 8 U.S.C. §1101(a)(42); 8 U.S.C. §1158. In 2014, the U.S. Board of Immigration Appeals acknowledged that women fleeing domestic violence could meet the definition of "refugee" and qualify for asylum. Matter of A-R-C-G- et al., 26 I&N Dec. 388 (BIA 2014) (concerning a Guatemalan victim of spousal abuse who encountered extreme indifference from Guatemalan police).

---

[9]. Lisa M. Martinson, Comment, An Analysis of Racism and Resources for African-American Female Victims of Domestic Violence in Wisconsin, 16 Wis. Women's L.J. 259, 264-273 (2001).
[10]. Futures Without Violence, Fact Sheet, The Facts on Immigrant Women and Domestic Violence, https://www.futureswithoutviolence.org/userfiles/file/Children_and_Families/Immigrant.pdf.

However, in 2018, former U.S. Attorney General Jeff Sessions issued a legal decision that overturned that legal precedent. He concluded that the Board of Immigrant Appeals had incorrectly applied the law because, according to Justice Department reasoning, domestic violence victims do not fit into a "particular social group" for the reason that they are defined by their "vulnerability to private criminal activity." Matter of A-B-, 27 I&N Dec. 316 (A.G. 2018). U.S. Attorney General Merrick Garland later rescinded this decision. U.S. Dept. of Justice, Memorandum for the Civil Division re Impact of Att'y Gen. decisions (June 16, 2021), https://www.justice.gov/asg/page/file/1404826/download.

C. Civil Protection Orders: Nature and Scope

All states currently provide civil protection orders for victims of domestic violence. Historically, courts issued injunctions against interspousal violence only in conjunction with divorce proceedings. However, in 1976, Pennsylvania became the first state to authorize restraining orders regardless of whether the victim was seeking a divorce. Within two decades, all states had similar laws. This section explores the nature of these orders.

What are they?

A protection order is a *civil* order that is issued by a court to a petitioner (the victim) against a respondent (the offender). A protection order directs a person to do or refrain from doing certain acts. States use different terms for this order, such as a "restraining order," "protection order," "domestic violence protection order," "personal protection order," "civil protection order," and "protection from abuse" order. Victims seek protection orders to prevent the recurrence of abuse rather than to punish the abuser. However, petitioning for a protection order does not preclude imposition of criminal charges.

Who can obtain an order of protection?

State statutes specify who may petition. Eligible parties include spouses and former spouses, "family and household members," cohabitants and former cohabitants, boyfriends/girlfriends and former boyfriends/girlfriends, co-parents, and, in some states, "dating partners" and former "dating partners."

What acts do protection orders cover?

The specific restrictions in a protection order depend on the circumstances and state law. A protection order can prohibit a person from threatening or harming the petitioner; entering the petitioner's home ("kick-out order"); coming within a certain distance of the petitioner and/or her children or coming to the petitioner's home, work, school, or the children's home or school ("stay-away" order); contacting the petitioner directly or indirectly, in person, by phone, e-mail, texting, mail, or through a third party; purchasing or owning firearms; and prohibiting the transfer or disposal of property. The order can also grant temporary child custody and award temporary child or spousal support; prevent the removal of children from a jurisdiction; require payment of rent, mortgage costs, medical costs, or property damage; order police to help the victim remove possessions from the home; and protect a family pet.

What acts are beyond the scope of protection orders?

A protection order *cannot* make a final child custody determination or determine title to property.

What are the types of protection orders?

An order of protection may be temporary or permanent. States have different forms of temporary orders: (1) an *emergency protection order* (EPO), issued upon exigent circumstances when a responding police officer requests the order from a judge (by phone, at any hour of day or night); (2) a *temporary restraining order* (TRO), issued by a family court upon the victim's petition and affidavit that demonstrate reasonable proof of past acts of domestic violence pursuant to statute; and (3) a *permanent protection order,* issued after an adversarial hearing on the merits, at which time both parties have the opportunity to present evidence.

Proceedings for restraining orders are subject to a preponderance-of-the-evidence standard. Both emergency and temporary protective orders are issued ex parte. In each case, the order must be served on the restrained party to be effective.

How long does a protection order last?

The court specifies the duration of the order. The maximum period is designated by statute. Orders of protection generally may be renewed at the petitioner's request. Note that so-called permanent protection orders are rarely actually permanent.

What is the consequence of the violation of a protection order?

Traditionally, civil protection orders were enforced by contempt proceedings. Today, most states make the violation of a protection order a crime. Although violations of protection orders generally are misdemeanors, some states treat repeat violations, or those involving a weapon, as felonies.

How do civil and criminal protective orders differ?

Civil protection orders can be supplemented by criminal protection orders. Criminal protective orders can be issued during arraignment, bail, pretrial release, and as a postconviction condition of probation. Criminal protection orders provide *less* relief than civil protection orders for several reasons. Criminal orders do not address issues of visitation or child support. Nor do they mandate treatment or enable eviction of the abuser. Moreover, criminal no-contact orders last only so long as criminal charges are pending.

D. Criminal Justice Response

1. Self-Defense

HAWTHORNE v. STATE
408 So. 2d 801 (Fla. Dist. Ct. App. 1982)

PER CURIAM. . . .

[Defendant's husband was shot to death in the home in the early morning hours of January 28, 1977, by bullets fired from a number of weapons belonging to the deceased. This was appellant's second trial for the murder of her husband after her first conviction for first-degree murder was reversed.]

The [first] argument by appellant that warrants discussion is that the trial court erred in disallowing the testimony of Dr. Lenore Walker, a clinical psychologist who would have testified as an expert with regard to the battered-woman syndrome. The purpose of such testimony would have been to give the jury a basis for considering whether appellant suffered from the battered-woman syndrome, not in order to establish a novel defense, but as it related to her claim of self-defense. We are aware of the conflicting decisions of various jurisdictions as to the admissibility of this type of expert testimony. The courts that have considered the admissibility of this type of expert testimony have generally analyzed it to see whether it meets three basic criteria: (1) the expert is qualified to give an opinion on the subject matter; (2) the state of the art or scientific knowledge permits a reasonable opinion to be given by the expert; and (3) the subject matter of the expert opinion is so related to some science, profession, business, or occupation as to be beyond the understanding of the average layman. . . .

The few case authorities which have considered the admissibility of this type of expert testimony disagree primarily with regard to (1) whether the study of the battered-woman syndrome is an area sufficiently developed to permit an expert to assert a reasonable opinion, and (2) whether the battered-woman syndrome is beyond the knowledge and experience of most laymen.

In [Ibn-Tamas v. United States, 407 A.2d 626 (D.C. 1979)] and [Smith v. State, 277 S.E.2d 678 (Ga. 1981),] the courts concluded that the expert testimony should have been allowed, inasmuch as the subject matter was "beyond the ken of the average layman." "[T]he expert's testimony explaining why a person suffering from battered woman's syndrome would not leave her mate, would not inform police or friends, and would fear increased aggression against herself, would be such conclusions that jurors could not ordinarily draw for themselves." . . . The *Ibn-Tamas* court determined, however, that the trial court had not ruled on whether the expert, Dr. Lenore Walker, was sufficiently qualified to give an opinion on whether "the state of the pertinent art or scientific knowledge" would permit an expert opinion. The court said that this third criterion depended on "whether

Dr. Walker's methodology for identifying and studying battered women" was generally accepted. The question whether the [criteria] were satisfied was remanded to the trial court. . . .

[Similarly, in the instant case,] there has been no determination below as to the adequacy of Dr. Walker's qualifications or the extent to which her methodology is generally accepted, indicating that the subject matter can support a reasonable expert opinion. Our determination that this expert testimony would provide the jury with an interpretation of the facts not ordinarily available to them is subject to the trial court determining that Dr. Walker is qualified and that the subject is sufficiently developed and can support an expert opinion.

Appellee argues that to admit this type of expert testimony would violate the rule [that] "testimony regarding the mental state of a defendant in a criminal case is inadmissible in the absence of a plea of not guilty by reason of insanity." In this case, a defective mental state on the part of the accused is not offered as a defense [to show that she was not responsible for her actions]. Rather, the specific defense is self-defense, which requires a showing that the accused reasonably believed it was necessary to use deadly force to prevent imminent death or great bodily harm to herself or her children. The expert testimony would have been offered in order to aid the jury in interpreting the surrounding circumstances as they affected the reasonableness of her belief. . . . It is precisely because a jury would not understand why appellant would remain in the environment that the expert testimony would have aided them in evaluating the case. [Reversed and remanded.]

NOTE: WHO IS JOYCE HAWTHORNE?

Dr. Lenore Walker, Terrifying Love: Why Battered Women Kill and How Society Responds
23-41 (1989)

I first met Joyce Hawthorne three years after [her husband] Aubrey's death. An ordinary-looking woman of forty, about 5'3" tall, weighing about 150 lbs., she didn't attract much attention. Her smile was rare but sweet; her eyes sparkled when she laughed. She looked just like the church-going mother of five that she was. Judging by her appearance alone, no one would have known that she'd killed a man much larger than herself, firing five guns in the process, even if sometimes her facial expression, at rest, revealed her fear and unhappiness. . . . Joyce never denied that she'd fired the fatal shots; rather, although she had no memory of it, she claimed that she had been justified in firing them because she had wanted to protect herself and her family from assault, rape, and death. . . . Although she did not remember shooting her husband, she had initially confessed to doing it in order to get the police to release her five children, who were being held for questioning at the time.

In reversing the judge's previous decision, an appellate court had ruled that evidence about the extensive family abuse in this case could be introduced in the upcoming trial; but nothing had been specifically stated about the permissibility of allowing an expert witness to explain what Joyce's behavior had meant. . . .

Battered Woman Syndrome had not previously been used in the state of Florida to support a self-defense argument (although several other states had, by that time, permitted such testimony in courts of law). Before, it would have been much more common for a woman like Joyce to plead insanity, arguing that her husband's terrible abuse had rendered her temporarily insane. . . . Shortly after Aubrey's death, Joyce Hawthorne had been examined by a psychiatrist, who had found that she knew right from wrong, the legal standard for Florida's insanity plea. I, too, would find that Joyce Hawthorne was legally sane—but terrified that she and her family would be slaughtered, just as Aubrey had threatened. In my opinion, her belief that she and her children were in danger that night had been reasonable, and reasonable perception of imminent physical danger is the legal standard for acting in self-defense.

. . . I agreed with [defense attorney] Leo Thomas that . . . without understanding the long history of marital abuse Joyce had endured, the average person sitting on a jury could not be expected to comprehend why she had believed her husband would kill her when she refused his sexual advances. . . . But Battered Woman Syndrome would provide the appropriate explanation; it would delineate the perception of imminence, and show how that perception was affected by the woman's state of mind. It would make her state of mind comprehensible, because battered women are always afraid of being hurt; any crisis situation may be perceived as a matter of life or death. . . .

Leo Thomas realized that he would have to [help the jury] understand why Joyce hadn't divorced Aubrey despite the daily horror of their marriage; he would have to corroborate Joyce's reports of domestic violence, even if no one else had seen Aubrey beat her; he would have to introduce convincing evidence to demonstrate that Joyce's fear had been reasonable on the night she finally killed him. All this would mean persuading the jury that Aubrey Hawthorne's repeated abuse of his wife had so affected her state of mind that she'd believed she needed to shoot him, to stop him from hurting her—as she perceived him coming toward her, even before he'd actually touched her—on that night in January 1977. Leo would have to help Joyce persuade the jury that her acute state of terror had induced her to use no less than five guns that night, firing at least nine bullets into her husband's body; that, in fact, her behavior had been a demonstration not of anger but of fear. . . .

. . . Most women are at a serious disadvantage when facing an attack from a man who is not only physically stronger but more ready and willing to fight. And battered women who kill are really like battered women who don't kill—they endure the same harassment, the same psychological torture; they experience the same terror—except that they have partners who are ready, able, and willing to kill them. When a battered woman kills her abuser, she has reached the end of the line. She is absolutely desperate, in real despair. She believes, with good reason, that if she does not kill, she will be killed. . . .

Epilogue. Joyce Hawthorne's initial conviction was reversed because of her illegally obtained confession and the exclusion of testimony about her husband's violent acts. 377 So. 2d 780 (Fla. Dist. Ct. App. 1979). Her second conviction was reversed when the appellate court remanded for a determination of the admissibility of "battered woman syndrome" (BWS) evidence (the principal case here). Upon rehearing, the trial court rejected the evidence, reasoning that its scientific basis was not sufficiently accepted. The appellate court affirmed. 470 So. 2d 770 (Fla. Dist. Ct. App. 1985). At Hawthorne's next trial, her attorney successfully argued that a retrial would constitute cruel and unusual punishment. All charges against her were dismissed.

Notes and Questions

1. Significance. *Hawthorne* was one of the first cases in which defense attorneys sought to introduce evidence about the dynamics of domestic violence for the purpose of helping a decisionmaker determine whether a defendant acted reasonably in exercising self-defense. All states now admit such evidence.

2. Common law. English common law recognized the right of husbands to discipline their wives by the use of physical force (the "privilege of chastisement"). Recall Blackstone (supra Chapter III, pp. 212–213). Divorce, rather than criminal sanctions, was considered the appropriate remedy.[11] Further, interspousal immunity precluded tort recovery. During the late nineteenth century, most courts declared wife beating illegal. Currently, all jurisdictions offer a range of remedies such as civil protection orders, tort suits, and criminal sanctions.

3. Battered woman syndrome (BWS). Battered women who kill their partners often rely on evidence of BWS as part of their self-defense claim. BWS is a theory of behavior that derives from the research of psychologist Lenore Walker in the 1970s with 400 battered women. BWS has two components: a three-stage cycle of violence and "learned helplessness." The cycle of violence consists of (1) a tension-building phase—a gradual escalation of tension during which the batterer displays hostility and the woman attempts to placate him; (2) an acute battering incident, in which the batterer explodes into uncontrollable disproportionate rage; and (3) the contrition phase, in which the batterer shows remorse and promises to end the abuse. "Learned helplessness" purports to explain why women stay in a battering relationship. Relying on the research of psychologist Martin Seligman involving shocks to laboratory animals, Walker posits that a battered woman becomes so depressed from repeated battering that she loses the motivation to respond.[12] According to Walker, BWS is not a mental disorder, but rather the psychological reaction of a normal person when exposed to traumatic events. Walker has since recharacterized BWS as a component of posttraumatic stress disorder (PTSD).

---

[11]. On the history of domestic violence legislation, see Linda Gordon, Heroes of Their Own Lives: The Politics and History of Family Violence, Boston, 1880-1960 (2002); Elizabeth Pleck, Domestic Tyranny: The Making of Social Policy Against Family Violence from Colonial Times to the Present (1989); Elizabeth Schneider, Battered Women and Feminist Lawmaking (2002).
[12]. Lenore Walker, The Battered Woman Syndrome 71 (3d ed. 2009).

4. Criticisms. BWS has prompted many criticisms: (1) it stereotypes victims as helpless, (2) it portrays them as mentally ill and hysterical, (3) it fails to explain that victims respond in different ways, (4) it disadvantages minorities, (5) it provides special treatment in violation of equal protection, and (6) it is subject to sexist applications by judges and juries. What do you think of these criticisms?

5. Defenses. Traditionally, the battered woman who kills her intimate partner faces difficulties in using self-defense because of the traditional elements: (1) a person must use only proportional force against unlawful armed force; (2) the defendant must reasonably fear that she is in imminent danger of bodily harm (and definitions of "reasonableness" and "imminence" were developed for paradigms such as "the barroom brawl," not IPV); (3) the defendant cannot have been the aggressor; and (4) in some jurisdictions, she must seek to retreat before the use of deadly force.

Several facts suggest the need for BWS testimony. First, the woman may use lethal force against a man who attacked with his hands. Second, the victim may not pose an immediate threat because he may be incapacitated (for example, asleep or drunk). Third, the woman appears to be the aggressor. BWS evidence overcomes these problems by addressing misconceptions that jurors hold about battered women, as well as their views about the reasonableness of the women's perception of the imminence and seriousness of the danger.

Applying Walker's theory, the victim experiences the growing tension of phase one and the acute incident in phase two. In response, she develops a constant fear of serious bodily harm that she perceives as imminent partially because of the unpredictability of her spouse's rage. The cycle theory of violence also addresses the element of the reasonableness of the amount of force necessary to repel the attack by suggesting that the woman perceives herself trapped in a cycle of potentially deadly violence and feels compelled to use deadly force to preempt the attack of the more powerful (even though perhaps unarmed) aggressor. Does this theory explain why Joyce Hawthorne used *five* weapons to kill her husband?

6. Admissibility of evidence: *Frye* and *Daubert*. All states and the District of Columbia now admit BWS evidence, at least to some degree, either by statute or case law. BWS has achieved such widespread acceptance that cases hold that an attorney's failure to present expert testimony on BWS constitutes ineffective assistance of counsel. See, e.g., Smith v. State, 144 P.3d 159 (Okla. Crim. App. 2006).

To determine the admissibility of novel scientific evidence, federal courts traditionally relied on the standard in Frye v. United States, 293 F. 1013 (D.C. Cir. 1923): Evidence is admissible if it has become generally accepted by scientists in the particular field of study. This classic formulation was superseded by Daubert v. Merrell Dow Pharmaceuticals, Inc., 509 U.S. 579 (1993), which adopted Federal Rule of Evidence 702, and provides that evidence may be admitted if it is helpful to the trier of fact and also if the methodology is scientifically valid. Many state courts also adhere to these standards. Which test did *Hawthorne* follow? In addition, some courts admit BWS testimony for other purposes, such as to bolster the woman's credibility if she recants her testimony. See, e.g., Minnesota v. Vance, 685 N.W.2d 713 (Minn. Ct. App. 2004).

7. Exit from abusive relationships.

a. Why didn't she leave? One of the most difficult issues for jurors to understand, as *Hawthorne* explains, is why the battered woman killed rather than left her abuser. Professor Martha Mahoney sheds light on this issue:

> The "shopworn question" [Why didn't she leave?] reveals several assumptions about separation: that the right solution is separation, that it is the woman's responsibility to achieve separation, and that she could have separated. . . . When we ask the woman, "Exactly what did you do in your search for help?" the answer often turns out to be that she left—at least temporarily. In [one] study, more than seventy percent of the women had left home at some time in response to violence. . . .
>
> [T]he assumption that the woman's first separation should be permanent ignores the real dangers that the man will seek actively—and sometimes violently— to end the separation. [W]e need to reckon with the dangers she faces. . . . The story of the violent pursuit of the separating woman must become part of the way we understand domestic violence to help eliminate the question "Why didn't she leave?" from our common vocabulary.[13]

b. Separation assault. Professor Mahoney explains the primary reason that abused women are reluctant to leave: They fear that their abusers will kill them if they do. Mahoney points out that, contrary to common belief, separation does not end the violence. In fact, victims' attempts to leave actually increase the violence because the abuser retaliates against them to force them to stay. Mahoney coined the term "separation assault" to signify the violence that erupts when a victim attempts to leave. She was influential in debunking the idea (derived from learned helplessness theory) that battered women are passive victims of circumstances. She refutes the question "Why didn't the woman leave?" by contending that women repeatedly *try* to leave, but abusers sabotage their efforts. What are the implications of "separation assault" for legal policy?

c. Stages of change. The Transtheoretical Model of Behavioral Change (or "stages-of-change" model) brings a new understanding to IPV by explaining that the exit from abusive relationships is a process with five stages: precontemplation, contemplation, preparation, action, and maintenance. Progression through the stages is not linear. That is, the individual may revisit earlier stages before she reaches the final stage when she successfully exits the relationship. Interventions in the early stages, when the individual has not yet decided to leave the relationship, are unlikely to have a positive impact.

8. Policy. As the epilogue explains, all charges against Joyce Hawthorne were eventually dismissed. Was that an appropriate response by the criminal justice system? Some scholars suggest that the current approach to abusers (imprisonment) has been ineffective. Instead, they advocate decriminalizing domestic violence by deemphasizing the criminal justice system's role and replacing it with economic, public health, community, and human rights policies. Discuss

---

[13]. Martha Mahoney, Legal Images of Battered Women: Redefining the Issue of Separation, 90 Mich. L. Rev. 1, 61-62 (1991).

the pros and cons of this controversial theory. See generally Leigh Goodmark, Decriminalizing Domestic Violence: A Balanced Policy Approach to Intimate Partner Violence (2018) and Leigh Goodmark, Imperfect Victims: Criminalized Survivors and the Promise of Abolition Feminism (2022).

Problem

Ann and her husband, Jeff, are at a bar. When Jeff goes to the bathroom, Greg begins talking to Ann. Jeff returns and becomes jealous. He retrieves two hand-guns and shoots Greg when he exits. However, the grand jury indicts both Ann and Jeff after Ann lies to police that she fired the fatal shot accidentally during a struggle between the men. Ann and Jeff are convicted of first-degree murder and sentenced to life imprisonment. Ann files an application for postconviction relief, alleging that, as a victim of BWS, her husband forced her to relate the false account. She claims that he beat her over an 18-month period whenever she failed to relate the story to his satisfaction. What result? McMaugh v. State, 612 A.2d 725 (R.I. 1992). See also Dixon v. United States, 548 U.S. 1 (2006).[14]

2. Law Reform: Mandatory Arrest and No-Drop Policies

Police traditionally responded to domestic violence with indifference. Throughout the 1970s and early 1980s, police officers ignored domestic vio-lence calls; intentionally delayed responding; attempted to mediate cases with the parties; dealt with the violence by telling the abuser to take a "time out" by walking around the block; and admonished the victim to be a better wife.[15] Police rationalized their refusal to intervene on the ground that domestic vio-lence was a private matter.

The battered women's movement in the 1970s sought to improve the police response. The first step required changing the *common law warrant rule*. This rule prohibited arrests of misdemeanants without a warrant. The common law had different rules for arrest of felons and misdemeanants. A police officer could make a warrantless arrest for a misdemeanor *only* in cases in which the suspect com-mitted the criminal act in the officer's presence. In contrast, when a police officer believed a person has committed a felony, the officer does not actually have to witness the act. Rather, the officer can arrest the suspect without a warrant based on probable cause that the suspect had committed the felony.

Of course, abusers do not commit acts of domestic violence in a police offi-cer's presence. Because the warrant requirement derived from the common law, battered women's advocates pressured state legislatures to change that rule. By the 1980s, reformers had convinced many state legislatures to enact warrantless arrest

[14]. For a debate on the duress doctrine in the context of domestic violence, compare Joshua Dressler, Battered Women and Sleeping Abusers: Some Reflections, 3 Ohio St. J. Crim. L. 457 (2006), with Joan H. Krause, Distorted Reflections of Battered Women Who Kill: A Response to Professor Dressler, 4 Ohio St. J. Crim. L. 555 (2007).

[15]. Joan Zorza, The Criminal Law of Misdemeanor Domestic Violence, 1970-1990, 83 J. Crim. L. & Criminology 46, 47-48 (1992).

statutes permitting police to arrest an alleged misdemeanant, provided that the officer has probable cause to believe that domestic violence has occurred and that the suspect was the perpetrator. All 50 states now provide for warrantless misdemeanor arrests in domestic violence cases.

The enactment of warrantless arrest laws, however, failed to alter the policy of nonintervention. As a result, reformers called for an even stronger policy to limit police discretion. They advocated "mandatory arrest" laws that would require police to arrest an offender whenever police have probable cause to believe the offender has committed the crime.

Considerable support for mandatory arrest laws stemmed from: (1) a landmark study of police responses to misdemeanor domestic assaults that concluded that arrest was the most effective approach;[16] (2) class-action lawsuits against the police for failure to respond (discussed later in this chapter); and (3) the Violence Against Women Act, 42 U.S.C. §3796hh(c)(1)(a), requiring state and local governments to follow either a mandatory or preferred arrest policy if they wished to receive federal funding (discussed later in this chapter).

Many states subsequently enacted mandatory arrest statutes (although some states enacted pro-arrest statutes). However, the benefits and detriments of mandatory arrest remain contested. Advocates argue that the policy (1) communicates to offenders that society will not tolerate their behavior; (2) protects victims more effectively; (3) empowers victims; (4) equalizes the position of women; (5) clarifies the role of police by providing guidelines; (6) decreases police injuries during domestic disturbances; and (7) ensures that all perpetrators are treated similarly. On the other hand, opponents contend that mandatory arrest contributes to the escalation of violence, increases arrests of women who fight back and minority victims, deters women from contacting police, and reinforces the idea that a woman cannot make her own life decisions.[17]

The role of the prosecutor also has evolved since the early battered women's movement. In the 1970s and 1980s, prosecutors often failed to initiate charges, citing victim noncooperation and recantation as reasons. Domestic violence advocates pushed for reforms. Many prosecutors now follow "no-drop" policies that limit prosecutorial discretion. Some states follow "hard" no-drop policies, in which prosecutors proceed regardless of the victim's wishes, whereas other states follow "soft" no-drop policies, in which prosecutors merely encourage victims to proceed and provide support services.

The traditional reluctance of law enforcement personnel to interfere in domestic disputes also precipitated another response in the form of civil lawsuits, such as the famous case that follows below.

---

[16]. Lawrence W. Sherman & Richard A. Berk, The Specific Deterrent Effects of Arrest for Domestic Assault, 49 Am. Soc. Rev. 261 (1984).

[17]. For a summary of the debate, see Cheryl Hanna, No Right to Choose: Mandated Victim Participation in Domestic Violence Prosecutions, 109 Harv. L. Rev. 1849, 1860 n.37 (1996).

3. Duties of Law Enforcement

TOWN OF CASTLE ROCK v. GONZALES
545 U.S. 748 (2005)

Justice SCALIA delivered the opinion of the Court.

. . . The horrible facts of this case are contained in the complaint that respondent Jessica Gonzales filed in Federal District Court. [At] about 5 or 5:30 P.M. on Tuesday, June 22, 1999, respondent's [ex-]husband took [their] three daughters [ages 10, 9, and 7] while they were playing outside the family home. No advance arrangements had been made for him to see the daughters that evening. When respondent noticed the children were missing, she suspected her husband had taken them. At about 7:30 P.M., she called the Castle Rock Police Department, which dispatched two officers. The complaint continues: "When [the officers] arrived . . ., she showed them a copy of the TRO [that had been issued to her in conjunction with her divorce proceedings that ordered her ex-husband not to "molest or disturb the peace of [respondent] or of any child," and to remain at least 100 yards from the family home at all times.] [She] requested that it be enforced and the three children be returned to her immediately. [The officers] stated that there was nothing they could do about the TRO and suggested that [respondent] call the Police Department again if the three children did not return home by 10:00 P.M."

At approximately 8:30 P.M., respondent talked to her husband on his cellular telephone. He told her "he had the three children [at an] amusement park in Denver." She called the police again and asked them to "have someone check for" her husband or his vehicle at the amusement park and "put out an [all-points bulletin]" for her husband, but the officer with whom she spoke "refused to do so," again telling her to "wait until 10:00 P.M., and see if" her husband returned the girls.

At approximately 10:10 P.M., respondent called the police and said her children were still missing, but she was now told to wait until midnight. She called at midnight and told the dispatcher her children were still missing. She went to her husband's apartment and, finding nobody there, called the police at 12:10 A.M.; she was told to wait for an officer to arrive. When none came, she went to the police station at 12:50 A.M. and submitted an incident report. The officer who took the report "made no reasonable effort to enforce the TRO or locate the three children. Instead, he went to dinner."

At approximately 3:20 A.M., respondent's husband arrived at the police station and opened fire with a semiautomatic handgun he had purchased earlier that evening. Police shot back, killing him. Inside the cab of his pickup truck, they found the bodies of all three daughters, whom he had already murdered.

[Gonzales brought a civil rights action against the municipality and police officers under 42 U.S.C. §1983, claiming that she had a property interest in enforcement of the restraining order; and that the town deprived her of this property interest without due process by having a policy that tolerated nonenforcement of restraining orders.]

[W]e left a similar question [whether a statute conferred an entitlement to due process protection] unanswered in DeShaney v. Winnebago County Dept. of Social Servs., 489 U.S. 189 (1989), another case with "undeniably tragic" facts: Local child-protection officials had failed to protect a young boy from beatings by his father that left him severely brain damaged. We held that the so-called "substantive" component of the Due Process Clause does not "requir[e] the State to protect the life, liberty, and property of its citizens against invasion by private actors." We noted, however, that the petitioner had not properly preserved the argument that—and we thus "decline[d] to consider" whether—state "child protection statutes gave [him] an 'entitlement' to receive protective services in accordance with the terms of the statute, an entitlement which would enjoy due process protection."

The procedural component of the Due Process Clause does not protect everything that might be described as a "benefit." . . . Our cases recognize that a benefit is not a protected entitlement if government officials may grant or deny it in their discretion. . . .

. . . The Court of Appeals in this case determined that Colorado law created an entitlement to enforcement of the restraining order because the "court-issued restraining order . . . specifically dictated that its terms must be enforced" and a "state statute command[ed]" enforcement of the order when certain objective conditions were met (probable cause to believe that the order had been violated and that the object of the order had received notice of its existence). . . .

[The Tenth Circuit based its reasoning primarily on] language from the restraining order, the statutory text, and a state-legislative-hearing transcript. . . . The critical language in the restraining order [came from] the preprinted notice to law-enforcement personnel that appeared on the back of the order [describing] "peace officers' duties" related to the crime of violation of a restraining order [*A peace officer shall use every reasonable means to enforce a restraining order. . . . A peace officer shall arrest, or, if an arrest would be impractical under the circumstances, seek a warrant for the arrest of a restrained person. . . . A peace officer shall enforce a valid restraining order whether or not there is a record of the restraining order in the registry.* Colo. Rev. Stat. §18-6-803.5(3) (emphasis added).]

The Court of Appeals concluded that this statutory provision [about police officers' duties regarding enforcement of TROs]—especially taken in conjunction with a statement from its legislative history, and with another statute restricting criminal and civil liability for officers making arrests—established the Colorado Legislature's clear intent "to alter the fact that the police were not enforcing domestic abuse retraining orders," and thus its intent "that the recipient of a domestic abuse restraining order have an entitlement to its enforcement." Any other result, it said, "would render domestic abuse restraining orders utterly valueless."

This last statement is sheer hyperbole. Whether or not respondent had a right to enforce the restraining order, it rendered certain otherwise lawful conduct by her husband both criminal and in contempt of court. The creation of grounds on which he could be arrested, criminally prosecuted, and held in contempt was hardly "valueless"—even if the prospect of those sanctions ultimately failed to prevent him from committing three murders and a suicide.

We do not believe that these provisions of Colorado law truly made enforcement of restraining orders *mandatory*. A well-established tradition of police discretion has long coexisted with apparently mandatory arrest statutes [in the criminal law generally]. [A] true mandate of police action would require some stronger indication from the Colorado Legislature than "shall use every reasonable means to enforce a restraining order" (or even "shall arrest . . . or . . . seek a warrant"), §§18-6-803.5(3)(a), (b). That language is not perceptibly more mandatory than the Colorado statute which has long told municipal chiefs of police that they "shall pursue and arrest any person fleeing from justice in any part of the state" and that they "shall apprehend any person in the act of committing any offense . . . and, forthwith and without any warrant, bring such person before a . . . competent authority for examination and trial." Colo. Rev. Stat. §31-4-112.

It is hard to imagine that a Colorado peace officer would not have some discretion to determine that—despite probable cause to believe a restraining order has been violated—the circumstances of the violation or the competing duties of that officer or his agency counsel decisively against enforcement in a particular instance. The practical necessity for discretion is particularly apparent in a case such as this one, where the suspected violator is not actually present and his whereabouts are unknown.

The dissent correctly points out that, in the specific context of domestic violence, mandatory-arrest statutes have been found in some States to be more mandatory than traditional mandatory-arrest statutes. . . . Even in the domestic-violence context, however, it is unclear how the mandatory-arrest paradigm applies to cases in which the offender is not present to be arrested. As the dissent explains, much of the impetus for mandatory-arrest statutes and policies derived from the idea that it is better for police officers to arrest the aggressor in a domestic-violence incident than to attempt to mediate the dispute or merely to ask the offender to leave the scene. Those other options are only available, of course, when the offender is present at the scene. . . .

Respondent does not specify the precise means of enforcement that the Colorado restraining-order statute assertedly mandated—whether her interest lay in having police arrest her husband, having them seek a warrant for his arrest, or having them "use every reasonable means, up to and including arrest, to enforce the order's terms," Brief for Respondent 29-30. Such indeterminacy is not the hallmark of a duty that is mandatory. . . . The dissent, after suggesting various formulations of the entitlement in question, ultimately contends that the obligations under the statute were quite precise: either make an arrest or (if that is impractical) seek an arrest warrant. The problem with this is that the seeking of an arrest warrant would be an entitlement to nothing but procedure—which we have held inadequate even to support standing; much less can it be the basis for a property interest. . . .

Even if the statute could be said to have made enforcement of restraining orders "mandatory" because of the domestic-violence context of the underlying statute, that would not necessarily mean that state law gave *respondent* an entitlement to *enforcement* of the mandate. . . . Respondent's alleged interest stems only from a State's *statutory* scheme. . . . She does not assert that she has any common-law or contractual entitlement to enforcement. If she was given a statutory entitlement, we would expect to see some indication of that in the statute itself. . . .

Even if we were to think otherwise concerning the creation of an entitlement by Colorado, it is by no means clear that an individual entitlement to enforcement of a restraining order could constitute a "property" interest for purposes of the Due Process Clause. Such a right would not, of course, resemble any traditional conception of property. Although that alone does not disqualify it from due process protection . . ., the right to have a restraining order enforced does not "have some ascertainable monetary value." . . . Perhaps most radically, the alleged property interest here arises *incidentally,* not out of some new species of government benefit or service, but out of a function that government actors have always performed—to wit, arresting people who they have probable cause to believe have committed a criminal offense. . . . We conclude, therefore, that respondent did not, for purposes of the Due Process Clause, have a property interest in police enforcement of the restraining order against her husband. . . .

Epilogue. Jessica Gonzales later filed a petition with the Inter-American Commission on Human Rights (IACHR), alleging that the actions of police violated her human rights. Below is her testimony before the commission.

NOTE: WHO IS JESSICA GONZALES?

Testimony of Jessica Gonzales Lenahan Before the Inter-American Commission on Human Rights
Washington, D.C., Mar. 2, 2007

Jessica Gonzales Lenahan with her three daughters, who were murdered by their father, and her oldest son Simon (top left)

. . . I met my previous husband, Simon Gonzales, while still in high school. I married Simon in 1990 and we moved to Castle Rock, Colorado, in 1998. We lived together with our three children—Rebecca, Katheryn, and Leslie—and my son Jessie, from a previous relationship.

Throughout our relationship, Simon was erratic and abusive toward me and our children. By 1994, he was [becoming] more and more controlling, unpredictable, and violent. He would break the children's toys and other belongings, harshly discipline the children, threaten to kidnap them, drive recklessly, exhibit suicidal behavior, and verbally, physically, and sexually abuse me. He was heavily involved with drugs. Simon's frightening and destructive behavior got worse and worse as the years went by. One time I walked into the garage, and he was hanging there with a noose around his neck, with the children watching. I had to hold the rope away from his neck while my daughter Leslie called the police. Simon and I separated in 1999 when my daughters were 9, 8, and 6. But he continued scaring us. He would stalk me inside and outside my house, at my job, and on the phone at all hours of the day and night.

On May 21, 1999, a Colorado court granted me a temporary restraining order that required Simon to stay at least 100 yards away from me, my home, and the children. The judge told me to keep the order with me at all times, and that the order and Colorado law required the police to arrest Simon if he violated the order. Having this court order relieved some of my anxiety. But Simon continued to terrorize me and the children even after I got the restraining order. He broke into my house, stole my jewelry, changed the locks on my doors, and loosened my house's water valves, flooding the entire street. I called the Castle Rock Police Department to report these and other violations of the restraining order. The police ignored most of my calls. . . .

On June 4, Simon and I appeared in court, and the judge made the restraining order permanent. The new order granted me full custody of Rebecca, Katheryn, and Leslie, and said that Simon could only be with our daughters on alternate weekends and one prearranged dinner visit during the week. Less than 3 weeks later, Simon violated the restraining order by kidnapping my three daughters from our yard on a day that he wasn't supposed to see the girls. When I discovered they were missing, I immediately called the police, told them that the girls were missing and that I thought Simon had abducted them in violation of a restraining order, and asked them to find my daughters. . . .

[T]wo officers came to my house. I showed them the restraining order and explained that it was not Simon's night to see the girls, but that I suspected he had taken them. The officers said, "Well, he's their father; it's okay for them to be with him." And I said, "No, it's not okay. There was no prearranged visit for him to have the children tonight." The officers said there was nothing they could do, and told me to call back at 10 P.M. if the children were still not home. . . .

Soon afterwards, Simon's girlfriend called me and told me that Simon called her and was threatening to drive off a cliff. She asked me if he had a gun and whether or not he would hurt the children. I began to panic. I finally reached Simon on his cell phone around 8:30 P.M. He told me he was with the girls at an amusement park in Denver, 40 minutes from Castle Rock. I immediately communicated this information to the police. I was shocked when they responded that there was nothing they could do, because Denver was outside of their jurisdiction. . . . The officer told me I needed to take this matter to divorce court, and told me to call back if the children were not home in a few hours. The officer said to me, "At least you know that the children are with their father." . . .

I called the police again and again that night. When I called at 10 P.M., the dispatcher said to me that I was being "a little ridiculous making us freak out and thinking the kids are gone." Even at that late hour, the police were still scolding me and not acknowledging that three children were missing. [After midnight] I drove to the police station and told yet another officer about the restraining order and that the girls had been gone for seven hours. After I left, that officer went to a two-hour dinner and never contacted me again. I asked the police for help nine separate times that night—two times in person and seven times on the phone. . . .

I later learned that Simon had driven up to the Castle Rock Police station at 3:20 A.M. and opened fire with a semiautomatic handgun he had purchased earlier that evening, after he had abducted the children. The police returned fire, spraying the truck with bullets. After Simon was killed, they searched his truck and found the bodies of my three little girls inside. I was told that Simon had killed them earlier that evening. . . .

I never received an explanation for why Simon was approved in the FBI's background check system when he went to purchase the gun that night. Under federal law, gun dealers can't sell guns to people subject to domestic violence restraining orders. . . . So why did the police ignore my calls for help? Was it because I was a woman? A victim of domestic violence? A Latina? Because the police were just plain lazy? . . .

. . . I brought [a] petition to the Inter-American Commission on Human Rights because I have been denied justice in the United States. It's too late for Rebecca, Katheryn, and Leslie, but it's not too late to create good law and policies for others. Police have to be required to enforce restraining orders or else these orders are meaningless. . . .

Epilogue. In a landmark decision, the IACHR ruled that the American Declaration of the Rights and Duties of Man (the source of legal obligation for the commission's member-states) imposes an affirmative duty to protect citizens from private acts of domestic violence.[18] The commission recommended a full investigation into the "systemic failures" in the enforcement of Lenahan's restraining order. It also recommended the enactment of legislation to strengthen protection orders, protect children in cases of domestic violence, eliminate "socio-cultural patterns" that impede victims' protection, and the development of protocols for investigating reports of missing children in the context of restraining order violations. A documentary, "Home Truth," was recently released that tells the story of Jessica Lenahan's pursuit of justice.

Notes and Questions

1. No-duty rule. *Castle Rock* is one of several cases instituted by battered women, beginning in the 1970s, to force local police departments to treat their complaints seriously. Many suits, like *Castle Rock,* were brought pursuant to the Civil Rights Act of 1964, 42 U.S.C. §1983, which requires a plaintiff to show a deprivation under color of law of a constitutional right. Generally, no right to police protection exists for private acts of violence.

2. Exceptions. Two possible exceptions exist to the no-duty rule: (1) the special relationship doctrine; and (2) the state-created danger doctrine.

a. Special relationship doctrine. The special relationship doctrine was first applied to battered spouses in Balistreri v. Pacifica Police Department, 855 F.2d

---

[18]. Jessica Lenahan (Gonzales) v. United States of America, Inter-American Commission on Human Rights Report No. 80/11, Para. 170, www.oas.org › iachr › decisions.

1421 (9th Cir. 1988), upholding application of the doctrine to impose a duty of protection by law enforcement based on their repeated notice of the husband's assaults in violation of the wife's restraining order. However, after the Supreme Court severely limited the doctrine in DeShaney v. Winnebago County Department of Social Services, 489 U.S. 189 (1989), the Ninth Circuit reheard *Balistreri* and found no substantive due process violation for the police's failure to protect. 901 F.2d 696 (9th Cir. 1990).

DeShaney had significant implications for battered women despite its child abuse context. In *DeShaney,* the Court found that, absent a special relationship, state social workers did not violate a child's *substantive* due process rights by their failure to protect him from his father's abuse.

Post-*DeShaney,* plaintiffs were restricted to other theories, such as claiming (1) an exception to *DeShaney* (i.e., such as invocation of the "custodial relationship doctrine" conferring on police an affirmative duty to protect a victim who is in state custody); (2) a violation of procedural, rather than substantive, due process (i.e., the claim of an entitlement to procedural safeguards); (3) a violation of equal protection; and (4) liability under state tort theories. Because *DeShaney* failed to raise the procedural due process claim in a timely manner (the issue raised in *Castle Rock*), the Supreme Court had refused to consider it.

b. State-created danger doctrine. The state-created danger doctrine (another exception to *DeShaney*) allows victims to seek redress from state actors who increase the harm. In a landmark case, the Second Circuit Court of Appeals made it easier for victims to prove their §1983 claims in the domestic violence context by liberalizing the requirement that police must *explicitly* enhance the danger. The Second Circuit permitted an affirmative act to qualify if it merely communicated an *implicit* sanction of the violence and also allowed repeated *inaction* to suffice to condone the violence. Okin v. Village of Cornwall-on-Hudson Police Dept., 577 F.3d 415 (2d Cir. 2009). Some courts limit the state-created danger doctrine to egregious cases. See, e.g., Waldron v. Spicher, 349 F. Supp. 3d 1202 (M.D. Fla. 2018). If *Okin* had been decided after *Castle Rock*, would *Okin* have helped Jessica Gonzales?

3. *Castle Rock*: Dissent. In a sharp dissent in *Castle Rock,* Justice Stevens (joined by Justice Ginsburg) charged that the majority failed to take seriously (1) the purpose and nature of restraining orders and (2) other state laws recognizing that mandatory arrest statutes and restraining orders create a private right to police action. The dissent criticized the majority's lack of regard for legislative intent in the passage of state mandatory arrest statutes as part of the law reform movement to redress police reluctance to enforce restraining orders. According to the dissent, mandatory arrest statutes "undeniably create an entitlement to police enforcement of restraining orders" because, under the state statute, the police "were *required* to provide enforcement; they *lacked the discretion to do nothing.*" 545 U.S. at 784-785 (emphasis in the original). Finally, the dissent added that cases have found "property interests" in other state benefits and services (such as welfare benefits, disability benefits) and, therefore, reasoned that police enforcement of a restraining order is a government service that is "no less concrete." Id. at 791 (Stevens, J., dissenting).

4. Police nonintervention. What factors explain the refusal of the police to intervene in *Castle Rock*? Gonzales herself speculates about various possibilities in her testimony above. What other reasons might exist?

5. Victim cooperation. Police are sometimes reluctant to intervene because of the difficulty of securing the victim's cooperation to testify. Prosecutors have known for years that victims frequently recant or refuse to testify. Perhaps as many as 80 percent of domestic violence cases that reach the court system involve victim recantation or refusal to testify.[19] What explains the victim's response? What role should her decision play in prosecution of the abuser? Are there sound policy reasons to compel her to testify? Or should the criminal justice system honor her wishes? What other strategies might the prosecutor adopt to encourage the victim to testify?

6. Restraining orders: Effectiveness. How effective are restraining orders before and after *Castle Rock*? Are they "valueless," or is that "sheer hyperbole"? A significant percentage of battered women seek and obtain restraining orders. Victims resort to restraining orders not as a form of early intervention, but rather as a last resort. Further, temporary restraining orders are violated frequently. Problems of enforcement abound: Many state courts fail to issue restraining orders regularly; many restraining orders are never served; and lax enforcement exists regarding restrictions on firearm possession.[20] What legal reforms might make restraining orders more effective?

7. Mandatory arrest. As we have seen, many states provide mandatory arrest for misdemeanor domestic violence offenses. Do mandatory arrest laws give rise to a private cause of action for failure to protect victims, according to *Castle Rock*? Why or why not?

8. Other remedies.

a. Contempt. Justice Scalia claims that the restraining order was not "valueless" because Jessica Gonzales had an alternative—an action for contempt. Is his reasoning persuasive?

b. State tort theories. Courts are reluctant to recognize claims that police were negligent in the performance of their duties. Law enforcement agencies have protection from suit by virtue of state tort immunity laws. Such laws require plaintiffs to file a written notice of claim, subject them to short statutes of limitations, and provide immunity from certain types of lawsuits and claims for punitive damages.

c. Human rights violation. An innovative remedy treats domestic violence as a violation of human rights (recall Jessica Gonzales's victory before the IACHR).

---

[19]. Amy E. Bonomi et al., New Insights on the Process of Victim Recantation, 18 Domestic Violence Rep. 49 (April/May 2013).

[20]. See Nat'l Inst. of Justice, Practical Implications of Current Domestic Violence Research: For Law Enforcement, Prosecutors and Judges, Section 9, June 2009 (victims petition for protection orders after failing to stop the abuse through other means; almost 50 percent of protection orders are violated within two years), https://www.ncjrs.gov/pdffiles1/nij/225722.pdf. See also Office of Attorney General, Attorney General Lockyer Report on Domestic Violence Finds Criminal Justice System Is Failing to Protect Victims, Families, AG's Task Force Makes 44 Recommendations to Reduce Domestic Violence, July 26, 2005 (discussing problems of enforcement), https://oag.ca.gov/news/press-releases/attorney-general-lockyer-report-domestic-violence-finds-criminal-justice-system.

Following *Castle Rock*, several municipalities passed domestic violence-related human rights resolutions recognizing freedom from domestic violence as a fundamental human right. In 2014, President Barack Obama issued two proclamations concerning violence against women, affirming the right to be free from violence and abuse as a basic human right. Evaluate the effectiveness of this human rights remedy.

9. Reform after Castle Rock. One suggested reform is to make mandatory arrest statutes "more" mandatory. How could this be accomplished? Professor Kristian Miccio responds with cynicism:

> After *Castle Rock*, advocates believed that if we did what Scalia told us to do, specifically go back to the legislative drawing board and make our laws "more mandatory," the promise of the Fourteenth Amendment Due Process Clause would be attainable in our lifetime. Remember, Scalia told us that "shall," meant "maybe or maybe not," dismissing out of hand the legislative history of thirty-two states and the plain statutory meaning of the word. I guess to the good Justice, the Ten Commandments are merely the ten suggestions. From a policy standpoint, I cannot envision how one makes "a peace officer shall arrest, or . . . seek a warrant," more mandatory.[21]

Should mandatory arrest laws be amended to include unambiguous mandatory language that "police will arrest without discretion" if a protective order is violated? Should reformers pressure legislators to craft exceptions to governmental immunity for police failure to protect victims? What is the likelihood of success of these approaches?

Problem

Shala wants to leave her abusive husband, Dwayne. One Sunday, she tells Dwayne that she wants to attend church. He threatens to kill her two children if she fails to return. Instead of attending church, Shala informs police that Dwayne has violated an order of protection. She explains that she fears him because he has beaten her and threatened to kill her, and that he possesses a handgun. She begs them to help her remove her personal belongings and remove her children. Two officers accompany her home. When they see Dwayne, they do not separate him or search him. While Shala is retrieving her personal belongings, Dwayne draws a revolver from a pocket, kills Shala, and then kills himself. The personal representative of Shala's estate brings a §1983 claim, claiming that the city violated her due process rights. What result? See Simmons v. City of Inkster, 323 F. Supp. 2d 812 (E.D. Mich. 2004).

---

[21]. G. Kristian Miccio, The Death of the Fourteenth Amendment: *Castle Rock* and Its Progeny, 17 Wm. & Mary J. Women & L. 277, 293 (2011).

E. High-Lethality Crimes: Marital Rape, Threats to Kill, and Stalking

1. Lethality Assessment

Lethality assessment is the evaluation of various risk factors to predict cases in which IPV is likely to be fatal. Below, criminologist Neil Websdale explains the markers that identify the risk of death based on his work with fatality review teams.

Neil Websdale, Assessing Risk in Domestic Violence Cases
in Encyclopedia of Domestic Violence 38, 38-40 (Nicky Ali Jackson ed., 2007)

Red flags, such as threats to kill, forced sex, and non-fatal strangulation, loom large as predictive factors in the murder of intimate partners.

Risk assessment procedures seek to identify the most dangerous perpetrators. [I]dentifying cases that will escalate to the occurrence of the abuse victim's death is an inexact science at best. Nevertheless, risk assessment and management are integral and important aspects of the delivery of all kinds of services to victims. . . .

RED FLAGS OR RISK MARKERS

. . . Certain red flags loom large in both the research literature and in risk assessment instruments. These red flags are outlined below.

A PRIOR HISTORY OF INTIMATE PARTNER VIOLENCE

The first and most important red flag is a prior history of intimate partner violence. Under this broad umbrella of "prior history," some researchers note the predictive significance of particular forms of violence such as "choking" and "forced sex." Using data from the Danger Assessment Instrument, Campbell et al., found that compared with the control group of abused women, murdered women were forced to have sex 7.6 more times and were 9.9 times more likely to be choked.

"Stalking" appears as a prominent correlate in a number of works. According to the research of McFarlane et al., "Stalking is revealed to be a correlate of lethal and near lethal violence against women and, coupled with physical assault, is significantly associated with murder and attempted murder."

A prior history of intimate partner violence may include the use of a weapon. According to Campbell et al.'s Danger Assessment study, abused women who were threatened or assaulted with a gun or other weapon were 20 times more likely than other women to be murdered. The mere presence of a gun in the home meant that an abused woman "was six times more likely than other abused women to be killed." . . .

PENDING OR ACTUAL SEPARATION OR ESTRANGEMENT

The extant research literature contends that women experience an increased risk of lethal violence when they leave intimate relationships with men. More recent research from Campbell et al.'s eleven-city case control study found, "Women who separated from their abusive partners after cohabitation experienced increased risk of femicide, particularly when the abuser was highly controlling."

OBSESSIVE POSSESSIVENESS OR MORBID JEALOUSY

The research literature consistently identifies obsessive or morbid jealousy as central to intimate partner homicides. For example, [some researchers point to the role of male sexual proprietariness in homicides cross-culturally, particularly obsessive or pathological jealousy in terms of the perpetrator seeing his partner as part of his own identity]. Consequently, any threat of the female's leaving threatens the man's identity. The emphasis with this red flag is firmly on "extreme" or "morbid" forms of jealousy.

MAKING THREATS TO KILL

Threats to kill constitute one of the most consistent correlates of intimate partner homicide when compared with abused women in general. "Women whose partners threatened them with murder were 15 times more likely than other women to be killed." Batterers' threats to take their own lives, perhaps as a means of gaining some control in the relationship, also appear as risk indicators for homicide. [B]atterers' suicidal threats, ideation, and plans [are] very significant risk markers. . . .

Note that several of the above risk factors reflect *high* lethality, including non-fatal strangulation, forced sex, stalking, threats to kill, possession of a firearm, and recent separation.

An important lethality assessment tool for measuring a victim's risk of homicide or severe physical violence is the Danger Assessment Instrument. The tool was developed by Professor Jacquelyn Campbell of Johns Hopkins University School of Nursing after consultation with victims and professionals. Her assessment device measures the severity and frequency of IPV by means of the use of a calendar to increase a victim's recall, raise the consciousness of the victim, and reduce the victim's denial or minimization of the abuse. A fascinating finding of

Campbell's research is the inaccuracy of women's own perceptions of their risk. That is, fewer than half of the women who are eventually killed by their partners accurately perceived their risk of death.[22]

The Danger Assessment Instrument is one of the few evidence-based measures of lethality that have been scientifically validated in multicity studies. The tool is widely accepted as a "best practice" that many states now require or encourage by police, prosecutors, court personnel, and service providers. The Violence Against Women Reauthorization Act of 2013 gave its imprimatur to lethality assessment in its emphasis on the need to integrate "evidence-based indicators to assess the risk of domestic and dating violence homicide" in VAWA-funded programs. §101(2)(K)(i).

2. Marital Rape

PEOPLE v. HARRIS
2012 WL 1651015 (Cal. Ct. App. 2012)

O'ROURKE, J.

A jury convicted Shawn Michael Harris of forcible oral copulation [pursuant to California Penal Code §288a, subd. (c)(2)]. It deadlocked on charges of sodomy by force and forcible spousal rape, and the court dismissed those charges. . . . Harris contends the court erred in admitting an "excessive" number of prior acts evidence under Evidence Code sections 1108 [permitting the admission of evidence of a prior sexual assault by defendant] and 1109 [permitting evidence of defendant's other acts of domestic violence] . . . .

Harris's wife, C.H., testified that the day before Easter in 2008, which was one week before the forcible oral copulation incident, Harris was driving a car with her and their son in it through their church parking lot, when someone drove towards them. Harris made a rude gesture to the other driver, and C.H. criticized him for it. Harris responded by striking a snow cone out of C.H.'s hand, pressed her neck hard, and said, "Don't push my buttons." . . .

The relationship between C.H. and Harris reached a critical point on March 28, 2008, when the oral copulation incident occurred. As soon as C.H. got home from work that afternoon, Harris, a stay-at-home father, asked her, "Do you want to leave or do you want me to because I can't stand to be around you." C.H. went to the master bedroom to nap. Shortly afterwards, Harris asked her if she wanted to have sex. She said no, because they needed to discuss events of the past week. Harris asked C.H. if she had called a woman friend of his, whom he had met at a "mommy and me class." Based on her answer, he accused her of lying to him and said she needed

[22]. See Jacquelyn C. Campbell et al., The Danger Assessment: Validation of a Lethality Risk Assessment Instrument for Intimate Partner Femicide, 24 J. Interpersonal Violence 653, 669 (2009). On the history of lethality assessment, see D. Kelly Weisberg, Lethality Assessment: An Impressive Development in Domestic Violence Law in the Past 30 Years, 30 Hastings Women's L.J. 211 (2019).

to be punished. C.H. excused herself to the bathroom, and used a tape recorder to secretly record the entire ensuing interaction with Harris. A copy of the recording was played for the jury.

On the audiotape, Harris gave C.H. this ultimatum: "You suck or get butt fucked." She interpreted that as a demand to perform oral sex on him or he would force her to have anal sex. While he was choking her, she protested that he was hurting her neck, and said, "Okay, okay, okay! I'll suck it!" She testified that she relented out of fear, and to avoid the hurt from forced anal sex. [During the oral copulation incident,] C.H. protested, "I can't breathe. I can't breathe. I'm sorry, I'm sorry, I can't breathe. I'm sorry, I can't . . ." [She repeatedly] tried to talk her way out of orally copulating him. She pleaded, "I don't want to be raped. Nobody deserves to be raped." Harris responded, "I'll go get a knife downstairs if I fucking have to." He added that she was not dumb or confused, and he would "be sure to carve that on [her] fuckin' head when [he dumped her] body." . . . [At one point] Harris asked C.H. if she was going to call the police. . . . She retorted, "If I could survive the phone call, I would have called." C.H. testified that her retort referred to her fear of calling the police because Harris had threatened that if she did call, he would kill her before the police arrived. She was certain he would carry out the threat. . . .

Before trial, the People moved *in limine* to admit testimony regarding Harris's prior acts under Evidence Code sections 1108 and 1109. [O]ver Harris's objections, the court admitted C.H.'s testimony regarding [several] prior incidents of sexual or domestic abuse during their marriage [as follows]. . . .

C.H. testified that in 1998, approximately two years after they were married, she and Harris got into an argument, he called her a "bitch," and hit her as they were driving to work. She got a restraining order against him, and he was convicted of misdemeanor battery. In November 2003, Harris and C.H. got into an argument and he threatened to throw a four-foot tall play structure for cats at her. Police were called, but she filed no charges against Harris. In April 2004, Harris poured water on their bed, and C.H. went to sleep on a couch. He followed her, pushed her head into the ground. . . . She called police, initially sought a restraining order, but withdrew the request because she hoped Harris would change.

In an August 2007 incident, C.H. sought to discuss their outstanding problems, but Harris did not want to; therefore, C.H. hid his keys to stop him from leaving the house. He pressed her head to the floor as hard as he could, and kicked her. She said she would divorce him, and he threatened to kill her, telling her no one would protect her, not even the police. She called 911, and the recording of the call was played for the jury. In November or December 2007, while they were discussing their marriage, Harris pretended to fall asleep; therefore, C.H. lied about having an affair, in order to get a reaction out of him. Harris immediately straddled her and started choking her. She did not report the incident to police because she was afraid of Harris's death threats. . . .

[At trial] Harris testified that both before and throughout their marriage, he and C.H. had engaged in sexual role playing, and the March 28, 2008 incident was a scenario they had acted out several times before. While acknowledging C.H. had orally copulated him, Harris denied it was forcible and dismissed the notion he was choking her. He insisted, "It's all verbal. It's just acting. I'm not punching her, holding her, tying her down, none of that." . . . He testified C.H. enjoyed the role play. . . . He denied threatening to kill C.H. that night, saying, "I have no desire to kill my ex-wife. It's [*sic*] the mother of my children. I've got no interest in that." . . .

On Harris's cross-examination, this exchange took place:

> "[Prosecutor:] On the recording that we heard here in court during your—your role play with [C.H.] on March 28th, 2008, do you know approximately how many times she expresses to you 'No' or 'Stop' or 'I don't want to do this'?
>
> "[Harris:] No. But I'm sure you're going to tell me.
>
> "[Prosecutor:] She tells you that approximately 50 times. Does that sound about right?
>
> "[Harris:] Whatever is in the scene is in the scene."

Harris generally denied C.H.'s testimony regarding each prior act, and denied ever threatening to kill C.H., choking her, or forbidding her from calling the police. . . . Harris contends the court erred in admitting evidence of his prior acts under Evidence Code sections 1108 and 1109 because "the sheer number of the other incidents resulted in a clear portrayal of [himself] in an extremely negative light, one that would necessarily influence the jury. . . ."

Under Evidence Code section 352, the trial court has discretion to exclude evidence "if its probative value is substantially outweighed by the probability that its admission will . . . create substantial danger of undue prejudice, of confusing the issues, or of misleading the jury." . . . In other words, in cases involving the proffer of evidence of prior acts of domestic violence under Evidence Code section 1109, the question is whether there is a likelihood the evidence will inflame the jury members so that they will base their verdict not on the evidence presented as to the charged offenses, but rather on an emotional response to the defendant's commission of other acts or crimes. . . . We review for abuse of discretion a court's ruling on relevance and admission or exclusion of evidence. . . .

As a preliminary matter, the approximately eight prior acts that were admitted into evidence were not excessive. Also, they were not cumulative, in that they showed different ways Harris exerted control over C.H. at different times during their marriage. Next, we conclude it was not reasonably likely the prior acts evidence so inflamed the jury that it based its verdict on those incidents. It was not likely the jury was confused regarding the specific charged offense of a forcible oral copulation incident, which was more egregious than the prior act incidents because of its sustained duration, and the sexual aggression it entailed. Further, that incident was unique in that the audiotape documented it from start to finish. . . .

Harris's belief that he was prejudiced amounts to speculation. The jury was specifically instructed [that] it may consider [prior acts of domestic violence] in assessing guilt. "Jurors are presumed able to understand and correlate instructions and are further presumed to have followed the court's instructions." Moreover, the jury acquitted Harris of two charges, showing the jurors limited their consideration of the Evidence Code section 1109 evidence as instructed.

Finally, we note that Harris denied C.H.'s versions of each of the prior incidents. Therefore, the jury was afforded an opportunity to evaluate the conflicting versions and make credibility determinations. Based on the above, we conclude that the trial court did not err in admitting evidence of Harris's prior domestic violence and sexual assault. . . .

Notes and Questions

1. Epilogue. Harris was sentenced to six years in prison. In a remarkable outcome, the judge in the parallel divorce proceedings awarded spousal support to Harris (a stay-at-home father), in the amount of $1,000 per month (upon his release from prison), as well as $47,000 in legal fees (payable by the victim). In response to public outrage, the state legislature enacted California Family Code §4324.5, precluding spousal support in cases in which a spouse is convicted of a sexual felony against the other spouse, prohibiting awards of attorneys' fees from the injured spouse's separate property, and awarding the injured spouse 100 percent of the community property interest in her retirement and pension benefits.

2. Forced sex: Characteristics. Sexual assaults are a common feature of IPV. About 10 percent of women are sexually assaulted by an intimate partner. Physical abuse often accompanies the sexual assault.[23] Did C.H. in the principal case experience both types of violence?

Sexual assault of an intimate partner spans a spectrum, including coercion to engage in sex or particular sexual acts; degrading and/or humiliating tactics before, during, or after sex; forced sex on a partner who is sleeping, physically ill, or who recently gave birth; being hit, kicked, or burned during sex; coerced substance abuse during sex; use of sex as punishment; nonconsensual insertion of objects; holding a partner captive during sex; forcing the partner to have sex in public (e.g., in a parked car); and coercing the partner to involve others in sexual acts. Sexual assaults can be an alternative form of physical abuse, a form of punishment, or a misguided reconciliation tactic. Such assaults reflect the abuser's sense of entitlement to the partner's sexual and reproductive services. What evidence suggests any of these motivations for the defendant in *Harris*?

Lethality assessment, as the above excerpt by Neil Websdale reveals, seeks to identify the most dangerous cases of abuse. Forced sex is a high-lethality factor. What other lethality indicators do you discern in *Harris*?

3. Victims' voluntary "consent." Many victims "consent" to sexual activity with an abusive partner because they fear retaliation or hope to deescalate a conflict. Given these motivations, how can a fact finder determine whether the sexual activity was truly consensual? What factors militated against a jury finding in *Harris* that the sexual activity was consensual? Why do you think the jury deadlocked on the charges of sodomy by force and forcible spousal rape? Should a victim's engaging in consensual sex *following* an incident of physical assault preclude her eligibility for a protection order? See Durham v. Metzger, 2012 WL 1556490 (Ky. App. Ct. 2012).

4. Use of evidence. What is the inference that follows from admission of prior acts of evidence ("propensity evidence")? Why did the court in *Harris* overrule the

---

[23]. NISVS, supra note [1], at 39 (percentage of victims who are sexually assaulted). See also Jennifer A. Bennice & Patricia A. Resick, Marital Rape: History, Research, & Practice, Trauma, Violence, & Abuse 4, 228, 234, 238 (2003) (reporting that from one-third to one-half of battered women are also sexually assaulted); Raquel Kennedy Bergen, The Intersection of Sexual and Physical Violence: Understanding Women's Experiences of Sexual Violence by Their Male Intimate Partners, 28 Domestic Violence Rep. 93 (Aug./Sept. 2023) (citing research).

defendant's objection to the prosecutor's motion to admit the evidence? Suppose that the defendant wanted to admit "propensity evidence" on the part of the victim? Did the defendant's claim that the couple was "role-playing" a sexual fantasy carry any weight with the jury? Should it have? What other problems do victims face in convincing fact finders of the occurrence of marital rape?

5. Severity. A commonly held belief is that intimate partner rape is less serious than stranger rape. What is the basis for this belief? In fact, research reveals that intimate relationships accompanied by physical violence and rape are marked by *more* severe violence and *repeated* sexual victimizations.[24]

6. Marital rape exemption. At common law, a husband was exempt from prosecution for raping his wife. American law reflected the "marital rape exemption" based on the British jurist Sir Matthew Hale's assertion that marriage signified a wife's presumed and irrevocable consent to her husband's sexual demands.

In People v. Liberta, 474 N.E.2d 567 (N.Y. 1984), the New York Court of Appeals held that the marital exemption to the rape and sodomy statutes violated equal protection. The court reasoned that the underlying rationales (wives' irrevocable consent to sex and wives-as-property) were archaic notions that did not withstand rational basis review. The court also rejected the justification of marital privacy, reasoning that the marital rape exemption fails to accomplish that objective because the privacy right protects only consensual acts. Should the right to marital privacy ever supersede the individual right to privacy?

Following *Liberta*, courts and legislatures gradually abrogated the marital rape exception. Despite widespread reform, however, some states still maintain some form of marital rape exemption for spouses who rape partners when the latter are drugged or otherwise incapacitated. Efforts to repeal these laws began in 2019.[25]

7. Strangulation. C.H. was choked by the defendant in the course of the assault. Nonfatal strangulation (commonly referred to as "choking") is a frequent occurrence in IPV. Such incidents are also highly predictive of homicide. The occurrence of prior strangulation attempts has been identified in 30-60 percent of women killed by an intimate partner.[26]

Strangulation is difficult to discover because it often leaves no visible marks. As a result, police need to be trained to look for subtle signs, such as visual changes, dizziness, changes in the victim's voice, petechiae (small red spots created by increased venous pressure), loss of consciousness, or the victim's urination or defecation during an assault (indicators of lack of oxygen). If bruises do occur,

---

[24]. Bennice & Resick, supra note [23], at 238-239; T.K. Logan et al., A Mixed-Methods Examination of Sexual Coercion and Degradation Among Women in Violent Relationships Who Do and Do Not Report Forced Sex, 22 Violence & Victims 71, 87, 89 (2007).

[25]. Julie Carr Smyth & Steve Karnowski, Some States Seek to Close Loopholes in Marital Rape Laws, AP News, May 4, 2019, https://www.apnews.com/3a11fee6d0e449ce81f6c8a50601c 687. See also New Law Makes Condom Stealthing Illegal in California, Corrigan Welbourne Stokke Blog, Jan. 31, 2022 (highlighting a new California law that treats rape of a spouse the same as that of a non-spouse), https://www.cwsdefense.com/blog/2022/january/new-law-makes -condom-stealthing-illegal-in-calif/.

[26]. Gael B. Strack et al., Investigation and Prosecution of Strangulation Cases, 19 Domestic Violence Rep. 83 (Aug./Sept. 2014).

they may not appear until several days after the incident. In fact, some victims, without visible symptoms, may die 36 or more hours after the incident due to internal swelling and undetected internal injuries. Nonfatal strangulation assaults may result in long-term neurological consequences.

A common belief is that abusers choke their victims with the intent to kill them. However, research reveals that abusers choke their victims to show that they *can* kill them any time they wish.[27] What message was Harris attempting to convey to his ex-wife by choking her? Should Harris have been criminally charged for strangling C.H.?

8. State and federal law reform. Traditionally, nonfatal strangulation was not charged, prosecuted as a misdemeanor, reduced to lesser charges, or simply dismissed. Today all states have criminalized the offense as a felony.[28] In addition, federal law applies. The VAWA Reauthorization Act of 2013 amends the federal assault statute (18 USCA §113(8)) by punishing "assault of a spouse, intimate partner, or dating partner by strangling, suffocating, or attempting to strangle or suffocate, by a fine under this title, imprisonment for not more than 10 years, or both."

Problems

1. Henry met Donna in their church choir when both were almost 70 years old and had suffered the death of their respective spouses. Henry was a member of the Iowa House of Representatives. Two years later, they married. By all accounts, they were quite affectionate with each other and held hands wherever they went. Four years into the marriage, Donna was diagnosed with early-onset Alzheimer's. She suffered frequent bouts of forgetfulness, drove on the wrong side of the road, and once put a single sock into the dryer instead of a full load of laundry. When her daughter once took her out for lunch, Donna wore a coat over pajamas that left her breasts exposed and she tried to wash her hands in the restaurant toilet. Soon thereafter, Donna's two adult daughters by a prior marriage moved Donna into a nursing home—a move that Henry resisted. Her daughters drew up a care plan for her with the nursing home staff that concluded that Donna was no longer able to make decisions about her well-being, including consent to sex. They informed Henry of that fact.

But one week later, a surveillance video showed Henry spending a half hour in his wife's room. When he left, he was holding Donna's underwear, which he dropped into a laundry bag in the hallway. Donna's roommate told nursing home staff that Henry had entered the room and closed the privacy curtain around his wife's bed. The roommate then heard noises indicating that the couple was having sex. A rape test kit and analysis of her underwear and bedding confirmed

---

[27]. Casey Gwinn et al., Law Reform Targets the Crime of Strangulation, 19 Domestic Violence Rep. 81, 81 (Aug./Sept. 2014).

[28]. Sarah Buduson, Law that Makes Strangulation a Felony Takes Effect Tuesday in Ohio, News5Cleveland, Apr. 4, 2023 (Ohio joins rest of country in making crime a felony), https://www.news5cleveland.com/news/local-news/investigations/law-that-makes-strangulation-a-felony-takes-effect-tuesday-in-ohio.

that account. Shortly thereafter, a state investigator interviewed Henry about the incident. Henry admitted having "sexual contact" with his wife on the relevant date. However, he argued that it was consensual and that Donna still enjoyed his expressions of affection. Henry was arrested and charged with marital rape. What result?[29]

How would the following additional information (introduced as expert testimony) affect your answer? Some experts in geriatric health care have begun to emphasize the value of touch, intimacy, and sex among older adults, especially those in care facilities. For example, the Hebrew Home in Riverdale, N.Y., has pioneered a "sexual rights policy" for its residents. As one expert explains: "Touch is one of the last pleasures we lose . . . . So much of aging and so much of being in a long-term care facility is about loss, loss of independence, loss of friends, loss of ability to use your body. Why would we want to diminish that?" Others have analogized sexual relations to eating and drinking—a basic instinct that should be satisfied even among the elderly with impaired cognitive functioning. See Pam Belluck, Sex, Dementia, and a Husband on Trial at Age 78, N.Y. Times, Apr. 14, 2015, at A1.

2. Sara files a domestic violence petition against her husband, Jeffrey. She alleges that his violent, controlling, and unstable behavior makes her fear for her own safety. She is particularly afraid because they had recently separated and she was seeking a divorce. Sara recounts numerous examples of Jeffrey's controlling behavior, including setting up surveillance cameras inside their home, locking her out of bank accounts, not allowing her to drive her own car, accessing her private e-mail/social media accounts, and breaking her cell phone. She relates how Jeffrey became angry and abused the family pet in front of their daughter. Furthermore, she explains that Jeffrey has become mentally unstable and boasted about keeping a firearm in their home even though he is a convicted felon. He threatened the life of his former wife and claimed to be an ex-Central Intelligence Agency (CIA) agent. Based on an analysis of the lethality factors, the court issues the emergency protective order, finding by a preponderance of the evidence that "an act or acts of domestic violence and abuse has occurred and may again occur" (the statutory requirement). Jeffrey appeals, arguing that the family court erred when it relied on the lethality factors as the standard for issuing the restraining order rather than the statute. What result? Which lethality factors were present? Did the family court judge erroneously rely on the lethality factors, as the respondent alleged? See Pettingill v. Pettingill, 480 S.W.3d 920 (Ky. 2015).

3. Craig Hutchinson has been involved in an intimate relationship with Jane Smith for the past six months. Jane insists that he wear condoms whenever they have sex because, as she repeatedly explains, she does not want to become pregnant. After Jane expresses some doubt about continuing with their relationship, Craig decides to sabotage the condoms. Over a period of several weeks, he pokes

---

[29]. For discussion of the case, see Sarah Kaplan, In an Iowa Courtroom, an Astonishing Case of Sex and Alzheimer's, Wash. Post, Apr. 7, 2015, http://www.washingtonpost.com/news/morning-mix/wp/2015/04/07/in-an-iowa-courtroom-an-astonishing-case-of-sex-and-alzheimers/.

holes in the condoms in an effort to impregnate Jane and thus encourage her to stay with him. After Jane becomes pregnant, she questions Craig about his use of birth control. He admits his deceit in a series of text messages to her.

Jane promptly obtains an abortion and then reports Craig's conduct to the police. Craig is charged with aggravated sexual assault. A defense to the jurisdiction's Criminal Code governing sexual assault is the "voluntary agreement of the complainant to engage in the sexual activity in question." At trial, Craig contends that he cannot be convicted of sexual assault because Jane consented to sex, and his deceit about the condition of the condoms did not invalidate her consent to have sex. What result? Does Jane have any civil remedies against Craig? Should rape law be revised to take this form of intimate partner abuse into account? See R. v. Hutchinson, [2014] 1 SCR 346.

California became the first state in 2021 to make nonconsensual condom removal (known as "stealthing") a civil offense. See Cal. Civ. Code. §1708.5 (amending definition of "sexual battery" to include removal of a condom during intercourse, or rendering it ineffective without the partner's verbal consent). The United Kingdom punishes stealthing as rape. See generally Claire Wolters, Why We Need to Talk About "Stealthing" Now, Very Well Health News, Oct. 26, 2021, https://www.verywellhealth.com/stealthing-non-consensual-condom-remo val-5207150.

3. Threats to Kill and Stalking

ELONIS v. UNITED STATES
575 U.S. 723 (2015)

Chief Justice ROBERTS delivered the opinion of the Court.

Federal law makes it a crime to transmit in interstate commerce "any communication containing any threat . . . to injure the person of another." 18 U.S.C. §875(c). Petitioner was convicted of violating this provision under instructions that required the jury to find that he communicated what a reasonable person would regard as a threat. The question is whether the statute also requires that the defendant be aware of the threatening nature of the communication, and—if not—whether the First Amendment requires such a showing.

Anthony Elonis, who asserted a First Amendment defense after he posted threats to kill his wife on Facebook

Anthony Douglas Elonis was an active user of the social networking Web site Facebook. Users of that Web site may post items on their Facebook page that are accessible to other users, including Facebook "friends" who are notified when new content is posted. In May 2010, Elonis's wife of nearly seven years left him, taking with her their two young children. Elonis began "listening to more violent music" and posting self-styled "rap" lyrics inspired by the music. Eventually, Elonis changed the user name on his Facebook page from his actual name to a rap-style nom de plume, "Tone Dougie," to distinguish himself from his "on-line persona." The lyrics Elonis posted as "Tone Dougie" included graphically violent language and imagery. This material was often interspersed with disclaimers that the lyrics were "fictitious," with no intentional "resemblance to real persons." Elonis posted an explanation to another Facebook user that "I'm doing this for me. My writing is therapeutic."

Elonis's co-workers and friends viewed the posts in a different light. Around Halloween of 2010, Elonis posted a photograph of himself and a co-worker at a "Halloween Haunt" event at the amusement park where they worked. In the photograph, Elonis was holding a toy knife against his co-worker's neck, and in the caption Elonis wrote, "I wish." . . . [T]he chief of park security was a Facebook "friend" of Elonis, saw the photograph, and fired him. In response, Elonis posted a new entry on his Facebook page [that included his claim that he still had the keys to the park, and also included his threat to break into the park at night during the Halloween Haunt.] This post became the basis for Count One of Elonis's subsequent indictment, threatening park patrons and employees.

Elonis's posts frequently included crude, degrading, and violent material about his soon-to-be ex-wife. [In one example, he wrote: "I'm not going to rest until your body is a mess, soaked in blood and dying from all the little cuts."] Shortly after he was fired, Elonis posted an adaptation of a satirical sketch that he and his wife had watched together. In the actual sketch, called "It's Illegal to Say . . .," a comedian explains that it is illegal for a person to say he wishes to kill the President, but not illegal to explain that it is illegal for him to say that. When Elonis posted the script of the sketch, however, he substituted his wife for the President. The posting was part of the basis for Count Two of the indictment, threatening his wife:

"Hi, I'm Tone Elonis.

Did you know that it's illegal for me to say I want to kill my wife? . . .

It's one of the only sentences that I'm not allowed to say . . . .

Now it was okay for me to say it right then because I was just telling you that it's illegal for me to say I want to kill my wife . . . .

Um, but what's interesting is that it's very illegal to say I really, really think someone out there should kill my wife . . . .

But not illegal to say with a mortar launcher.

Because that's its own sentence . . . .

I also found out that it's incredibly illegal, extremely illegal to go on Facebook and say something like the best place to fire a mortar launcher at her house would be from the cornfield behind it because of easy access to a getaway road and you'd have a clear line of sight through the sun room . . . .

Yet even more illegal to show an illustrated diagram [revealing a diagram of his ex-wife's house]."

At the bottom of the post, Elonis included a link to the video of the original skit, and wrote, "Art is about pushing limits. I'm willing to go to jail for my Constitutional rights. Are you?"

After viewing some of Elonis's posts, his wife felt "extremely afraid for [her] life." A state court granted her a three-year protection-from-abuse order. . . . [Elonis questioned whether the protection order was "thick enough to stop a bullet," and maintained that he had "enough explosives to take care of the State Police and the Sheriff's Department."] At the bottom of this post was a link to the Wikipedia article on "Freedom of speech." Elonis's reference to the police was the basis for Count Three of his indictment, threatening law enforcement officers.

. . . Elonis [later] posted an entry that gave rise to Count Four of his indictment [by threatening to "make a name for himself" and "initiat[ing] the most heinous school shooting ever imagined" and "hell hath no fury like a crazy man in a Kindergarten class"]. [After this post, FBI Agent Denise Stevens and her partner visited Elonis at his house.] Following their visit, during which Elonis was polite but uncooperative, Elonis posted another entry on his Facebook page, called "Little Agent Lady," which led to Count Five. [He threatened that it took all his strength, when she knocked, not to "Pull my knife, flick my wrist, and slit her throat/Leave her bleedin' from her jugular in the arms of her partner" . . . and suggested that he was a "crazy sociopath" who was "strapped with a bomb" and warned that if law enforcement returned to his home, they better bring a SWAT team.]

A jury convicted Elonis on four of the five counts against him [threatening his estranged wife, police officers, a kindergarten class, and an FBI agent], acquitting only on the charge of threatening park patrons and employees. Elonis was sentenced to three years, eight months' imprisonment and three years' supervised release. Elonis renewed his challenge to the jury instructions [contending] that the jury should have been required to find that he intended his posts to be threats.

. . . This statute requires that a communication be transmitted and that the communication contain a threat. It does not specify that the defendant must have any mental state with respect to these elements. In particular, it does not indicate whether the defendant must intend that his communication contain a threat. . . .

[Elonis's conviction] was premised solely on how his posts would be understood by a reasonable person. Such a "reasonable person" standard is a familiar feature of civil liability in tort law, but is inconsistent with "the conventional requirement for criminal conduct—*awareness* of some wrongdoing." Having liability turn on whether a "reasonable person" regards the communication as a threat—regardless of what the defendant thinks—"reduces culpability on the all-important element of the crime to negligence," and we "have long been reluctant to infer that a negligence standard was intended in criminal statutes". . . .

In light of the foregoing, Elonis's conviction cannot stand. The jury was instructed that the Government need prove only that a reasonable person would regard Elonis's communications as threats, and that was error. Federal criminal liability generally does not turn solely on the results of an act without considering the defendant's mental state. . . . [The Court declined to address the issue of whether a finding of recklessness would be a sufficient mental state because neither party argued the point.] [T]he case is remanded for further proceedings consistent with this opinion.

Justice ALITO, concurring in part and dissenting in part.

. . . It is settled that the Constitution does not protect true threats. And there are good reasons for that rule: True threats inflict great harm and have little if any social value. A threat may cause serious emotional stress for the person threatened and those who care about that person, and a threat may lead to a violent confrontation. It is true that a communication containing a threat may include other statements that have value and are entitled to protection. But that does not justify constitutional protection for the threat itself.

Elonis argues that the First Amendment protects a threat if the person making the statement does not actually intend to cause harm. In his view, if a threat is made for a "'therapeutic' purpose," to "'deal with the pain' . . . of a wrenching event," or for "cathartic" reasons, the threat is protected. But whether or not the person making a threat intends to cause harm, the damage is the same. And the fact that making a threat may have a therapeutic or cathartic effect for the speaker is not sufficient to justify constitutional protection. Some people may experience a therapeutic or cathartic benefit only if they know that their words will cause harm or only if they actually plan to carry out the threat, but surely the First Amendment does not protect them.

Elonis also claims his threats were constitutionally protected works of art. Words like his, he contends, are shielded by the First Amendment because they are similar to words uttered by rappers and singers in public performances and recordings. To make this point, his brief includes a lengthy excerpt from the lyrics of a rap song in which a very well compensated rapper imagines killing his ex-wife and dumping her body in a lake. If this celebrity can utter such words, Elonis pleads, amateurs like him should be able to post similar things on social media. But context matters. "Taken in context," lyrics in songs that are performed for an audience or sold in recorded form are unlikely to be interpreted as a real threat to a real person. Statements on social media that are pointedly directed at their victims, by contrast, are much more likely to be taken seriously. To hold otherwise would grant a license to anyone who is clever enough to dress up a real threat in the guise of rap lyrics, a parody, or something similar. . . .

There was evidence that Elonis made sure his wife saw his posts. And she testified that they made her feel "'extremely afraid'" and "'like [she] was being stalked.'" Considering the context, who could blame her? Threats of violence and intimidation are among the most favored weapons of domestic abusers, and the rise of social media has only made those tactics more commonplace. A fig leaf of artistic expression cannot convert such hurtful, valueless threats into protected speech.

It can be argued that §875(c), if not limited to threats made with the intent to harm, will chill statements that do not qualify as true threats, e.g., statements that may be literally threatening but are plainly not meant to be taken seriously. We have sometimes cautioned that it is necessary to "exten[d] a measure of strategic protection" to otherwise unprotected false statements of fact in order to ensure enough "'breathing space'" for protected speech. A similar argument might be made with respect to threats. But we have also held that the law provides adequate breathing space when it requires proof that false statements were made with reckless disregard of their falsity. . . . I would vacate the judgment below and remand for the Court of Appeals to decide in the first instance whether Elonis's conviction could be upheld under a recklessness standard. . . .

Notes and Questions

1. Epilogue. On remand, the Third Circuit Court of Appeals upheld defendant's convictions. After his release, he was convicted of another domestic violence-related assault for hitting his new girlfriend's mother in the head with a metal pot during an argument. And, in 2022, he was convicted in federal court on three counts of cyberstalking based on e-mails that he sent in 2020 to the prosecutor in his 2010 case—including threatening to burn a cross on the attorney's lawn—as well as phone calls, text messages, and e-mails targeting both the defendant's ex-wife and a former girlfriend in violation of protection orders.

2. Holding. In the principal case, Elonis is charged with violating the Interstate Communications Act, 18 U.S.C. §875(c), which makes it a federal crime to transmit in interstate commerce "any communication containing any threat . . . to injure the person of another." Congress enacted the statute in 1939 to regulate threatening speech as one of a series of laws directed at extortion in kidnapping cases, stemming from the Lindbergh baby kidnapping in 1932. Under the federal statute, what elements does the prosecutor have to prove? What mental state is required?

3. Standard. The Supreme Court regulates the content of speech reluctantly, although exceptions exist. One such exception is the "true threats" doctrine that prohibits statements that communicate an expression of an intent to commit an act of violence to an individual or group. *Elonis* raised the issue of the standard for determining whether speech constitutes a "true threat." The trial court adopted a negligence standard. What standard did the defendant advocate? What standard did the appellate court adopt? What did the Supreme Court hold?

4. Recklessness Standard: Counterman v. Colorado. The Supreme Court subsequently considered issues that *Elonis* left open: whether the First Amendment requires proof of a subjective mindset in true-threats cases, and if so, what *mens rea* standard is sufficient. In Counterman v. Colorado, 143 S. Ct. 2106 (2023), Billy Raymond Counterman, who had been previously convicted of sending threatening messages to others, was charged with stalking a female musician (C.W.) after sending her threatening Facebook messages. The defendant argued that Colorado law was unconstitutional because its objective standard (requiring that a reasonable person would understand the messages as threats) was too low. Further, he denied that he had intended to cause injury or harm and therefore contended that his messages were protected by the First Amendment. Rejecting his arguments, the state court of appeals found that (based on the totality of the circumstances) his statements constituted true threats.

Reversing and vacating the conviction, Justice Kagan concluded that the First Amendment requires a subjective understanding of the threat, based on a recklessness standard (i.e., a speaker is aware of the threatening nature of his communications but delivers them anyway). Such a test, she reasoned, strikes the proper balance between avoiding the risk of suppressing non-threatening speech versus allowing states to effectively protect "against the profound harms" that can flow from true threats. Dissenting, Justices Barrett and Thomas would have upheld the state court decision and Counterman's conviction. Justice Barrett highlighted the difficulties with determining a speaker's intent, saying "A delusional speaker may lack awareness of the threatening nature of her speech; a devious speaker may strategically disclaim such awareness; and a lucky speaker may leave behind no evidence of mental state for the government to use against her." Id. at 2141. The Supreme Court remanded the case based on the new recklessness standard. What are the implications of the ruling for domestic violence victims that specific intent to harm is required for a communication to constitute a "true threat"?

5. First Amendment. What was the defendant's argument that the federal law violated his First Amendment rights? The amicus brief of the American Civil Liberties Union (ACLU) expressed concern that "criminalizing threats that may be considered merely offensive or crude statements" might impinge upon "core political, artistic, and ideological speech."[30] On the other hand, the amicus brief of the Domestic Violence Legal Empowerment and Appeals Project (DVLEAP) emphasized that "threats are the essence of domestic violence and most protection order cases."[31] Which argument do you find more convincing?

6. Stalking: Elements. Stalking is a pattern of repeated and unwanted attention, harassment, contact, or other course of conduct that is directed at a specific person that would cause a reasonable person to feel fear. Stalking, an indicator of high lethality in the domestic violence context, may take the form of contact via phone calls, letters, e-mails, and sometimes even presents or flowers. Victims are followed, spied upon, and subject to rumors. Stalking frequently leads to murder.[32]

Could the defendant have been charged with stalking under the state law below? Pennsylvania law provides that a person commits stalking when he or she either:

> (1) engages in a course of conduct or repeatedly commits acts toward another person, including following the person without proper authority, under circumstances which demonstrate either an intent to place such other person in reasonable fear of bodily injury or to cause substantial emotional distress to such other person; or
> (2) engages in a course of conduct or repeatedly communicates to another person under circumstances which demonstrate or communicate either an intent to place such other person in reasonable fear of bodily injury or to cause substantial emotional distress to such other person. 18 Pa. C.S.A. §2709.1.

What elements does the statute require? Some states enhance the penalties for stalking if the stalker is subject to a restraining order. See, e.g., Fla. Stat. §784.048(4). Stalking is an indicator of high lethality. Assess the lethality of the risk that Elonis posed to his ex-wife.

---

[30]. Brief for American Civil Liberties Union et al. as Amici Curiae Supporting Petitioner, Elonis v. United States of America, 2014 WL 4215752 (Aug. 22, 2014) (No. 13-983), at 5.

[31]. Brief for Domestic Violence Legal Empowerment and Appeals Project (DVLEAP) & Prof. Margaret Drew as Amici Curiae Supporting Respondent, Elonis v. United States of America, 2014 WL 5035111 (Oct. 6, 2014) (No. 13-983), at 23.

[32]. Katrina Baum et al., Bureau of Justice Statistics, Dept. of Justice, Stalking Victimization in the United States (2009).

7. Stalking: Characteristics. Most stalking victims tend to be *former* intimate partners. Stalkers' intention often is to coerce the victim to remain in the relationship or to punish the victim for leaving. What do you think was Elonis's motivation for his conduct?

The DVLEAP amicus brief (mentioned above) referred to research suggesting that "threats of violence by former partners who are stalking are an even better predictor of future violence than the prior violence used by these ex-partners," and another study finding that approximately half of women who are murdered by their abusers previously had been threatened with death.[33] Does the Supreme Court's decision take into account this reality?

8. State and federal stalking laws. Both state and federal laws address stalking.

a. State laws. Prior to the enactment of stalking laws, victims had limited recourse absent physical injury or conduct involving enumerated offenses (i.e., annoying or obscene phone calls). California was the first state to enact a stalking law (Cal. Penal Code §646.9) in 1990 after an obsessed fan stalked and killed television actress Rebecca Schaeffer, following his acquisition of her address from the Department of Motor Vehicles. Schaeffer's murder also led to enactment of the Driver's Privacy Protection Act, 18 U.S.C. §§2721-2725.

In most states, stalking is a misdemeanor. States enhance the penalty if the defendant is a repeat offender; violates a protection order or conditions of probation, pretrial release, or bond; commits stalking with a deadly weapon; or physically harms the victim. Stalking statutes underwent several stages of revision, including expansion of categories of victims; increases in penalties; expansion of types of threats; revision of the intent and fear requirements (from narrow definitions of "death or great bodily harm" to threats intended to place the victim in reasonable fear for his/her safety or that "of a family member"); notification of victims prior to stalkers' release; provisions enabling prosecution of stalkers who threaten victims from prison; and requirements that stalkers register as sex offenders.

b. Federal law. Federal law also covers stalking. VAWA's crime of interstate stalking (18 U.S.C §2261A) prohibits interstate travel with the intent to "kill, injure, harass, or place under surveillance with intent to kill, injure, harass, or intimidate" a person. The statute (reprinted pp. 351-352) requires that the victim experience "reasonable fear" of death or serious bodily injury. The crime also covers use of the "mail, any interactive computer service, or any facility of interstate or foreign commerce" with the above intent in order to place a victim in reasonable fear of death or serious bodily injury. Did Elonis commit the crime of interstate stalking? VAWA's other federal criminal provisions are discussed later in this chapter.

9. Cyberstalking. Modern forms of communication, such as cell phones and the Internet, facilitate stalking.[34] Formerly, abusers who wanted to track a partner

---

[33]. DVLEAP Amicus Brief, supra note [31], at 25.
[34]. Rahul Chatterjee et al., The Spyware Used in Intimate Partner Violence, 2018 IEEE Symposium on Security and Privacy, https://pages.cs.wisc.edu/~chatterjee/ppts/IPV_spyware.pdf.

were limited to the use of car odometers for measuring a partner's mileage. Most current spyware tools are dual-use apps that have a legitimate purpose (child safety or anti-theft) that can be easily repurposed for spying on an intimate partner. Stalkers install monitoring software and/or hardware in computers to locate and harass victims. Some abusers also use surveillance techniques, such as GPS devices. Virtually all state legislatures have expanded stalking laws to address cyber harassment and/or cyberstalking. Admissibility of evidence from spyware in the context of divorce is discussed in Chapters III and VI.

Several federal laws also address cyberstalking and/or cyber harassment. In addition to the Interstate Communications Act at issue in *Elonis*, the Telephone Harassment Act, 47 U.S.C. §223 & 223(a)(1)(C), makes it a crime to use a telephone or an interactive computer service to transmit in interstate or foreign commerce any message "to annoy, abuse, harass, or threaten a person." In 2019, Congress enacted the Combat Online Predators Act, H.R. 570, S. 134, 116th Cong. (2019-2021), which enhanced criminal penalties for stalkers by up to five years if the victim is a minor.

F. Violence Against Women Act (VAWA)

In 1994, Congress enacted the Violence Against Women Act (VAWA), Pub. L. No. 103-322, 108 Stat. 1796, as part of major anti-crime legislation. VAWA's primary goals are to improve law enforcement as well as community-based responses to domestic violence. To accomplish these ends, the act provided grants for investigation and prosecution, created a federal tort remedy for gender-motivated violence (later ruled unconstitutional), authorized interstate enforcement of protection orders, established new federal crimes, and created firearm restrictions (explored below).

1. Grants. VAWA's grant programs address domestic violence, dating violence, sexual assault, and stalking by strengthening victim services. The most important program, the STOP Violence Against Women Formula Grant Program, provides funding for law enforcement and prosecution.

2. VAWA's civil rights remedy. VAWA also created a federal civil rights remedy (Title III) for victims of gender-motivated violent crimes. The Supreme Court invalidated this remedy in United States v. Morrison, 529 U.S. 598 (2000) (holding that the VAWA provision for gender-motivated violent crimes permitting victims to sue their attackers in federal court was unconstitutional because it exceeded the powers granted to Congress under the Commerce Clause).

3. Interstate enforcement of restraining orders. The effectiveness of restraining orders is especially problematic if the victim relocates from the issuing state to a different state. To address this problem, VAWA specifies that protection orders are entitled to full faith and credit, so long as the issuing state had personal and subject matter jurisdiction and also that the defendant had reasonable notice and an opportunity to be heard. 18 U.S.C. §2265(a). Subsequently, in 2000, the Uniform Law Commission promulgated the Uniform Interstate Enforcement of Domestic-Violence Protection Orders Act (UIEDVPOA) to improve interstate enforcement of protection orders. The Act establishes uniform procedures that enable courts to enforce valid domestic protection orders issued in other jurisdictions. It supplements VAWA's full faith and credit provisions for protection orders.

4. VAWA's federal criminal provisions. The original VAWA created several federal criminal provisions: (1) interstate crimes of domestic violence, and (2) firearm restrictions. Prior to VAWA, crimes of domestic violence were traditionally subject to state jurisdiction. Jurisdictional gaps led to interstate offenses going unpunished because of the difficulty of determining the state in which a given offense began and/or ended—a prerequisite for establishing jurisdiction over offenders who committed crimes in two or more states. VAWA also enables federal prosecutors to devote superior resources to prosecution of interstate offenses and provides for harsher sentences for offenders.

a. Interstate crimes of domestic violence. VAWA created three new federal crimes: interstate travel to commit domestic violence, interstate stalking, and interstate travel to violate an order of protection (explored below).

Interstate Travel to Commit Domestic Violence, 18 U.S.C. §2261

It is a federal crime to travel across state lines to commit domestic violence or to cause a victim to cross state lines in the commission of an act of domestic violence. Specifically, this law provides:

> A person who travels in interstate or foreign commerce . . . with the intent to kill, injure, harass, or intimidate a spouse, intimate partner, or dating partner, and who, in the course of or as a result of such travel, commits or attempts to commit a crime of violence against that spouse, intimate partner, or dating partner, shall be punished. . . .

The law also prohibits causing an intimate partner (by "force, coercion, duress, or fraud") to travel in interstate commerce and, in the course of such travel, committing or attempting to commit a crime of violence against that intimate partner.

Interstate Stalking, 18 U.S.C §2261A

This law criminalizes interstate travel for the purpose of stalking. Specifically, it prohibits:

> (1) travel in interstate or foreign commerce . . . with the intent to kill, injure, harass, intimidate, or place under surveillance with intent to kill, injure, harass, or intimidate another person, and in the course of, or as a result of, such travel or presence engages in conduct that—
> (A) places that person in reasonable fear of the death of, or serious bodily injury . . . or
> (B) causes, attempts to cause, or would be reasonably expected to cause substantial emotional distress to a person described [above]; or
> (2) with the intent to kill, injure, harass, intimidate, or place under surveillance with intent to kill, injure, harass, or intimidate another person, uses the

mail, any interactive computer service or electronic communication service or electronic communication system of interstate commerce, or any other facility of interstate or foreign commerce to engage in a course of conduct that [causes the above response in the victim]. . . .

Interstate Travel to Violate an Order of Protection, 18 U.S.C. §2262(a)

This offense prohibits interstate travel with the intent to violate an order of protection. Specifically, the law provides:

A person who travels in interstate or foreign commerce . . . with the intent to engage in conduct that violates the portion of a protection order that prohibits or provides protection against violence, threats, or harassment against, contact or communication with, or physical proximity to, another person, or that would violate such a portion of a protection order in the jurisdiction in which the order was issued, and subsequently engages in such conduct, shall be punished. . . .

b. VAWA's firearm offenses and other federal firearm laws. Firearms pose special threats to victims because they are abusers' weapon of choice to threaten, harm, or kill their victims. Nearly two-thirds of intimate partner homicides in the United States are committed with a gun.[35] The original VAWA amended the Gun Control Act of 1968 (18 U.S.C. §921 et seq.) to prevent individuals who are subject to restraining orders from owning firearms. In 1996, Congress enacted the Lautenberg Amendment to criminalize firearm possession for those who commit misdemeanor crimes of domestic violence (MCDV) under state law (18 U.S.C. §921(a)(33)(A), §922(d)(8)-(9), §922(g)(8)-(9)). The U.S. Supreme Court expanded the definition of MCDV for purposes of the federal firearm ban in United States v. Castleman, 572 U.S. 157 (2014), in which the Court ruled that the degree of physical force required for an MCDV is the same as that for common law battery (rejecting a stricter requirement of violent force).

c. Recent developments. As mentioned earlier, Congress enacted the Bipartisan Safer Communities Act in 2022 to implement changes in firearm safety laws. The specific changes include partial closure of the boyfriend loophole by expanding the restriction on firearm purchases to disqualify anyone found guilty of a domestic violence charge in a dating relationship, for a five-year period (after which the right to own a firearm is restored if the purchaser commits no additional violent crimes). Congress is considering further strengthening firearm protections for victims of stalking and dating violence by preventing convicted stalkers and all former dating partners convicted of a domestic violence offense from buying or owning firearms, regardless of when the relationship occurred. See Strengthening Protections for Domestic Violence and Stalking Survivors Act of 2023, H.R. 905, S.321, 118th Cong. (2023-2024) (introduced in response to the case of United States v. Rahimi, described below).

d. Background checks. In addition to the above federal firearm regulations, the Brady Handgun Violence Prevention Act of 1993, 18 U.S.C. §922(s), requires federally licensed firearm dealers to conduct a background check of certain prohibited

---

[35]. Everytown, Report: Guns and Violence Against Women, Apr. 10, 2023, https:// everytownresearch.org/report/guns-and-violence-against-women-americas-uniquely-lethal -intimate-partner-violence-problem/.

persons (listed in the federal Gun Control Act). Congress expanded background checks, pursuant to the Bipartisan Safer Communities Act to apply to gun purchasers under the age of 21 and to prohibit the purchase of a firearm if the purchaser committed a disqualifying crime while under age 18 (Sec. 12001). Proposed legislation would establish new background check requirements for firearm transfers between private parties (i.e., unlicensed individuals) by prohibiting a firearm transfer between private parties unless a licensed gun dealer, manufacturer, or importer first takes possession of the firearm to conduct a background check. Bipartisan Background Checks Act of 2023, H.R.715, 118th Cong. (2023-2024).

In addition, in March 2023, President Biden announced an Executive Order to increase the number of background checks by ensuring that all background checks required by law are conducted before firearm purchases, moving the country closer to universal background checks without the need for additional legislation. Further, in August 2023, the Department of Justice proposed a rule seeking to implement provisions of the Bipartisan Safer Communities Act that would require additional firearms dealers, specifically people who sell firearms online or at gun shows (persons who are not registered as federal firearms dealers), to run background checks.[36]

5. Second Amendment: *Rahimi* case. A three-judge panel of the Fifth Circuit Court of Appeals recently decided U.S. v. Rahimi, 61 F.4th 443 (5th Cir. 2023), declaring unconstitutional the federal prohibition on firearm possession by abusers subject to a qualifying civil protective domestic violence order (18 U.S.C. §922(g)(8)). In invalidating the prohibition, the court referred to the U.S. Supreme Court decision in N.Y. State Rifle & Pistol Association, Inc. v. Bruen, 142 S. Ct. 2111 (2022), where the Court set out a new test for firearm regulations that requires courts to determine whether the government demonstrated that the prohibition at issue is consistent with the history of firearm regulation under the Second Amendment.

In holding the ban unconstitutional in *Rahimi*, the Fifth Circuit panel reasoned that at the time of the nation's founding, no laws existed to bar firearm ownership by someone who had not yet been convicted of a crime but had only been found in a civil proceeding to have committed an act of domestic violence. (Legislatures began enacting domestic violence restraining orders only in the 1970s.) Rahimi, a drug dealer in Texas with a history of armed violence, was charged under the federal ban after he assaulted his intimate partner and was found with firearms in his possession when police searched his home because he was a suspect in a series of shootings. The Supreme Court granted certiorari to consider the constitutionality of the federal ban on the possession of guns by individuals who are subject to qualifying domestic violence restraining orders. U.S. v. Rahimi, 143 S. Ct. 2688 (2023).

[36]. White House, Fact Sheet: President Biden Announces New Actions to Reduce Gun Violence and Make Our Communities Safer, Mar. 14, 2023, https://www.whitehouse.gov/briefing-room/statements-releases/2023/03/14/fact-sheet-president-biden-announces-new-actions-to-reduce-gun-violence-and-make-our-communities-safer/; Dept. of Justice, Justice Department Proposes New Regulation to Update Definition of "Engaged in the Business" as a Firearms Dealer, Aug. 31, 2023, https://www.atf.gov/news/pr/justice-department-proposes-new-regulation-update-definition-engaged-business-firearms.

NOTE: VAWA REAUTHORIZATIONS

VAWA has been reauthorized four times (in 2000, 2005, 2013, and 2022). The first reauthorization in 2000 increased funding for law enforcement and shelters; expanded services to the elderly, the disabled, and Native Americans; incorporated the crimes of dating violence and stalking; improved legal services; expanded transitional housing; promoted supervised visitation; and strengthened protections for immigrant victims by creating U- and T-visas. VAWA 2005 added protections against housing discrimination, provided funding for rape centers, developed culturally and linguistically specific services, and enhanced services for disabled victims and children.

VAWA 2013 improved services to LGBTQ victims and prohibited discrimination in services based on sexual orientation or gender identity; integrated lethality assessments in VAWA-funded programs; expanded tribal court jurisdiction over non-Indian perpetrators; expanded housing protections for victims; provided funds for teen dating violence prevention education; and improved services on college campuses for victims of domestic violence, dating violence, sexual assault, and stalking.

Congress enacted the Violence Against Women Reauthorization Act in 2022 as part of the Consolidated Appropriations Act (Pub. L. 117-103, 136 Stat. 49), reauthorizing all current VAWA grant programs until 2027. VAWA 2022 accomplishes the following (among other provisions): (1) it expands the special criminal jurisdiction of tribal courts to cover non-Native American perpetrators of sexual assault, child abuse, and stalking on tribal lands; (2) increases support for survivors from underserved and marginalized communities, including LGBTQ survivors of domestic violence, dating violence, sexual assault, and stalking; (3) establishes a federal civil cause of action for individuals whose intimate visual images are disclosed without their consent; (4) strengthens the application of evidence-based practices by law enforcement in responding to gender-based violence, including by promoting the use of trauma-informed, victim-centered training and improving homicide reduction initiatives; (5) updates programs to reduce dating violence and help children who have been exposed to domestic violence; and (6) enacts the National Instant Criminal Background Check System (NICS) Denial Notification Act to help state law enforcement investigate and prosecute cases against those individuals prohibited from purchasing firearms.

Problem

Alex is in a three-year intimate relationship with Tim in the state of Blackacre. One night, in the middle of a drunken brawl concerning overdue rent, Tim beats Alex with a baseball bat, breaks his arm, chokes him, and threatens to kill him. Alex moves out and files for a restraining order. A judge grants Alex a three-year protection order that requires Tim to refrain from "abusing, harassing, or molesting" Alex and prohibits Tim from having any contact with Alex, including requiring him to "stay away" from Alex, his home, place of employment, business, or school.

Shortly thereafter, Tim's employer transfers him to the state of Greenacre. Alex is relieved that Tim has left Blackacre. He is looking forward to moving on with his life. Tim, however, is still angry with Alex. One weekend, Tim drives from Greenacre to Blackacre with the intent to kill Alex. A drunken Tim appears, without warning, at Alex's apartment. Tim bangs on the door, yells and screams at Alex, and threatens to kill him. Alex immediately calls the police. Is Tim subject to any federal charges under the criminal provisions of VAWA?[37] Does the parties' sexual orientation matter? Would Tim be subject to any federal charges if he had made the same threat via the Internet?

G. Children's Exposure to IPV

The past few decades have witnessed increasing awareness of the overlap between domestic violence and child maltreatment. Approximately 10 to 20 percent of children are exposed to IPV each year.[38] State law increasingly recognizes that these children also suffer harm by the occurrence of violence in the home. How does the law respond to the problem?

NICHOLSON v. SCOPPETTA

820 N.E.2d 840 (N.Y. 2004)

KAYE, Chief Judge.

. . . Sharwline Nicholson, on behalf of herself and her two children [and similarly situated mothers and children], brought an action pursuant to 42 U.S.C. §1983 against the New York City Administration for Children's Services (ACS). . . . Plaintiffs alleged that ACS, as a matter of policy, removed children from mothers who were victims of domestic violence [solely on the ground that the mothers had failed to prevent their children from witnessing acts of domestic violence against the mothers] without probable cause and without due process of law. That policy, and its implementation—according to plaintiff mothers—constituted, among other wrongs, an unlawful interference with their liberty interest in the care and custody of their children in violation of the United States Constitution. . . .

[The District Court granted a preliminary injunction. In re Nicholson, 181 F. Supp. 2d 182 (E.D.N.Y. 2002). The Second Circuit Court of Appeals affirms the finding that ACS's practice of removing children from the home based on parents' failure to prevent their children from witnessing domestic violence amounted to a policy or custom of ACS and that, in some circumstances, the removals raised serious questions of federal constitutional law. However, the court certified questions regarding the scope of the state statutes under which the city had acted, in particular the question of whether New York law authorized such a policy and

---

[37]. This problem is a revised version of a hypothetical problem in YWCA, Criminal Provisions of the Violence Against Women Act—Who's Covered?, www.ywcahbg.org/sites/default/files/legal%20news%20winter.pdf.

[38]. Resource Ctr. on Domestic Violence, Rates of Child Abuse and Child Exposure to Domestic Violence (2017) (reviewing literature), https://www.rcdvcpc.org/rates-of-child-abuse-and-child-exposure-to-domestic-violence.html.

whether the definition of child neglect included a parent's exposure of the child to domestic violence.]

CERTIFIED QUESTION: NEGLECT

"Does the definition of a 'neglected child' under N.Y. Family Ct. Act §1012(f), (h) include instances in which the sole allegation of neglect is that the parent or other person legally responsible for the child's care allows the child to witness domestic abuse against the caretaker?" . . .

Family Court Act §1012(f) is explicit in identifying the elements that must be shown to support a finding of neglect. . . . [A] party seeking to establish neglect must show, by a preponderance of the evidence, first, that a child's physical, mental or emotional condition has been impaired or is in imminent danger of becoming impaired and second, that the actual or threatened harm to the child is a consequence of the failure of the parent or caretaker to exercise a minimum degree of care in providing the child with proper supervision or guardianship. The drafters of article 10 were "deeply concerned" that an imprecise definition of child neglect might result in "unwarranted state intervention into private family life."

The first statutory element requires proof of actual (or imminent danger of) physical, emotional or mental impairment to the child. This prerequisite to a finding of neglect ensures that the Family Court, in deciding whether to authorize state intervention, will focus on serious harm or potential harm to the child, not just on what might be deemed undesirable parental behavior. "Imminent danger" reflects the Legislature's judgment that a finding of neglect may be appropriate even when a child has not actually been harmed; "imminent danger of impairment to a child is an independent and separate ground on which a neglect finding may be based." Imminent danger, however, must be near or impending, not merely possible.

In each case, additionally, there must be a link or causal connection between the basis for the neglect petition and the circumstances that allegedly produce the child's impairment or imminent danger of impairment. [In Matter of Nassau County Dept. of Social Servs. (Dante M.) v. Denise J., 637 N.Y.S.2d 666 (N.Y. 1995)], for example, we held that the Family Court erred in concluding that a newborn's positive toxicology for a controlled substance alone was sufficient to support a finding of neglect because the report, in and of itself, did not prove that the child was impaired or in imminent danger of becoming impaired. We reasoned, "[r]elying solely on a positive toxicology result for a neglect determination fails to make the necessary causative connection to all the surrounding circumstances that may or may not produce impairment or imminent risk of impairment in the newborn child" [id. at 669]. . . .

The cases at bar concern, in particular, alleged threats to the child's emotional, or mental, health. The statute specifically defines "[i]mpairment of emotional health" and "impairment of mental or emotional condition" to include:

> a state of substantially diminished psychological or intellectual functioning in relation to, but not limited to, such factors as failure to thrive, control of aggressive or self-destructive impulses, ability to think and reason, or acting out or misbehavior, including incorrigibility, ungovernability or habitual truancy.

Family Ct. Act §1012[h]. Under New York law, "such impairment must be clearly attributable to the unwillingness or inability of the respondent to exercise a minimum degree of care toward the child." Here, the Legislature recognized that the source of emotional or mental impairment—unlike physical injury—may be murky, and that it is unjust to fault a parent too readily. The Legislature therefore specified that such impairment be "clearly attributable" to the parent's failure to exercise the requisite degree of care.

Assuming that actual or imminent danger to the child has been shown, "neglect" also requires proof of the parent's failure to exercise a minimum degree of care. As the Second Circuit observed, "a fundamental interpretive question is what conduct satisfies the broad, tort-like phrase, 'a minimum degree of care.' [*Nicholson*, 344 F.3d at 169]. The Court of Appeals has not yet addressed that question, which would be critical to defining appropriate parental behavior."

"[M]inimum degree of care" is a "baseline of proper care for children that all parents, regardless of lifestyle or social or economic position, must meet." Notably, the statutory test is "minimum degree of care"—not maximum, not best, not ideal—and the failure must be actual, not threatened.

Courts must evaluate parental behavior objectively: would a reasonable and prudent parent have so acted, or failed to act, under the circumstances then and there existing? The standard takes into account the special vulnerabilities of the child, even where general physical health is not implicated. Thus, when the inquiry is whether a mother—and domestic violence victim—failed to exercise a minimum degree of care, the focus must be on whether she has met the standard of the reasonable and prudent person in similar circumstances.

[F]or a battered mother—and ultimately for a court—what course of action constitutes a parent's exercise of a "minimum degree of care" may include such considerations as: risks attendant to leaving, if the batterer has threatened to kill her if she does; risks attendant to staying and suffering continued abuse; risks attendant to seeking assistance through government channels, potentially increasing the danger to herself and her children; risks attendant to criminal prosecution against the abuser; and risks attendant to relocation. Whether a particular mother in these circumstances has actually failed to exercise a minimum degree of care is necessarily dependent on facts such as the severity and frequency of the violence, and the resources and options available to her.

Only when a petitioner demonstrates, by a preponderance of evidence, that both elements of section 1012(f) are satisfied may a child be deemed neglected under the statute. When "the sole allegation" is that the mother has been abused and the child has witnessed the abuse, such a showing has not been made. This does not mean, however, that a child can never be "neglected" when living in a household plagued by domestic violence. Conceivably, neglect might be found where a record establishes that, for example, the mother acknowledged that the children knew of repeated domestic violence by her paramour and had reason to be afraid of him, yet nonetheless allowed him several times to return to her home, and lacked awareness of any impact of the violence on the children; or where the children were exposed to regular and continuous extremely violent conduct between their parents, several times requiring official intervention, and where caseworkers testified to the fear and distress the children were experiencing as a result of their long exposure to the violence.

In such circumstances, the battered mother is charged with neglect not because she is a victim of domestic violence or because her children witnessed the abuse, but rather because a preponderance of the evidence establishes that the children were actually or imminently harmed by reason of her failure to exercise even minimal care in providing them with proper oversight. . . .

In the excerpt below, lawyer Jill Zuccardy, who was co-counsel in Nicholson v. Williams, 203 F. Supp. 2d 153 (E.D.N.Y. 2002), relates the background of the case.

NOTE: WHO IS SHARWLINE NICHOLSON?

Sharwline Nicholson, the plaintiff in the principal case

Jill M. Zuccardy, Nicholson v. Williams: The Case

82 Denv. U. L. Rev. 655, 657-660, 663-665, 667, 669 (2005)

[I]n 1999, I met Sharwline Nicholson. Sharwline had been separated from her child's father for some time. He lived in South Carolina. Although he had not been a model partner during the relationship, he was never physically abusive toward her or threatened physical abuse during the relationship.

From time to time [however] after Sharwline and her child's father separated, he came to New York to visit his infant daughter. During one visit, he got into an argument with Sharwline and became enraged. He beat her very badly. She managed to call 911, and he took off. Her son was at school and her infant daughter was asleep in the other room.

Sharwline was very seriously injured. She had a broken arm; she had a concussion; she was bleeding from numerous wounds. Yet, even before the police arrived, her first thought was of her children. She called her neighbor, who was her regular child care provider, and had the neighbor come over, get the baby, and pick up the son from school. Sharwline was removed by ambulance, thinking that her children were safely with the babysitter. . . .

While Sharwline was in the hospital, the police—and to this day we don't know why—went to the neighbor's home with their guns drawn and took custody of the children. This all sounds incredible, but it's true. They called Sharwline at the hospital and said, "We have your children here at the precinct. We can't allow them to be in the custody of a stranger," which is not an accurate statement of New York law by any means. A fit parent has the right to make child care arrangements for his or her child. In any event, they said, "You have to call a relative to take care of the children."

So, Sharwline called her cousin in New Jersey. By now, it was ten or eleven o'clock at night. Sharwline's cousin went to the hospital, told Sharwline that she would go to the precinct and get the children and everything would be okay. However, when Sharwline's cousin went to the precinct, the police refused to release the children, saying the children could not be taken out of state to New Jersey. Again, this was not a proper statement of the law.

Sharwline received a telephone call early the next morning—and the person on the other end of the line said, "This is ACS. We have your children. If you want to see them, you'll need to go to court. We'll call you back and tell you the date." . . . When Sharwline finally had an opportunity to appear in court, she learned that she had been charged with child neglect for "engaging in domestic violence." Make no mistake. Sharwline was not accused of perpetrating any violence. She was accused of being a victim and she was accused of being a neglectful mother because she was a victim. . . .

When I got Sharwline's case, I was blown away. . . . I thought the case was some sort of aberration, some sort of a mistake. . . . In the class action which ultimately came to pass . . . the theory in all of [the] cases was that the children were suffering, or in danger of suffering, emotional harm from exposure to domestic violence against their mothers and, therefore, should be removed from their mothers. These were not cases in which the City alleged that the children were in danger of physical harm, or that the mother had failed to protect the child from physical harm. Rather, they all focused on the presumption that exposure to domestic violence, per se, constituted impairment rising to the level of imminent harm and neglect under our child welfare statutes. . . .

[T]he city put forth one defense only, "We don't do this. We don't remove children solely or primarily because of domestic violence, period." The city said, "We employ best practices. Look at our written policies." And, in fact, except for [their] mission statement . . ., the ACS domestic violence policies and guiding principles looked really good on paper. Thus, it made the case simpler for us that ACS actually agreed with us as to what constituted best practices in child welfare cases involving domestic violence. They claimed they already employed them; we claimed that they didn't. . . .

The city [] waved its written policies like a banner throughout the case. And, as I mentioned, their written policies were actually pretty good. The problem was the disconnection between the written policies and the actual policies and practices. We illustrated this disconnection. . . . The child protective managers' description of the agency's practices with regard to domestic violence supported our contentions. . . .

I think *Nicholson* was a unique case for systemic reform: we believed that due to the nature of the lawsuit, because the safety of children was involved, the case could not just be about proving that the city's practices were unconstitutional or that they violated the civil rights of battered mothers and their children. We firmly believed that in order to prevail, we must educate, and challenge head-on some of society's most deeply held biases and judgments regarding domestic violence and child welfare. And we had to show that what the city was doing was hurting children. . . .

We also felt that we had to challenge the notion that removing children from their parents is erring on the side of safety. You hear that a lot. There is a notion that foster care provides safety for children. This is simply not true. . . . Many of our clients' children suffered in foster care, ranging from the physical abuse of Sharwline's son, to various incidents of medical neglect and emotional harm. The mothers' testimony about their children's experience in foster care was very powerful. But we did not only use the mothers, the literature and the experts to help us establish the trauma and danger of foster care.

We called the older children as witnesses. Listening to one fourteen-year-old describe her experience, Judge Weinstein and everyone in the courtroom, including the city's attorneys, became teary-eyed and Judge Weinstein had to call a ten-minute recess. Listening to her describe her trauma of being taken from her mother and being placed in foster care was one of the most wrenching moments in the trial. . . .

The *Nicholson* decision had a domino effect locally and nationwide. ACS stopped removing children from battered mothers, and the case spurred them to make vast improvements in their child welfare practice . . . .

NOTE: THE GREEN BOOK INITIATIVE

Traditionally, domestic violence advocates and child welfare professionals manifested a troubled relationship. Child welfare agencies often removed children from homes because of mothers' "failure to protect" their children from exposure to domestic violence. Domestic violence advocates criticized this approach for placing responsibility for the violence on the abused mother rather than holding the batterer accountable. In addition, child welfare professionals, who tend to view domestic violence as a symptom of dysfunctional families, traditionally strive to reestablish the family unit. Conversely, domestic violence advocates view separation from the perpetrator as the best option to provide safety for the victim and her children.

Amid this atmosphere, a collaboration of family court judges and experts in the fields of domestic violence and child welfare produced an influential report in 1999 that contained recommendations for the improvement of child welfare proceedings involving families that experience domestic violence.[39] The recommendations advocated culturally competent practice, batterer accountability, improved services for battered immigrant women, and the use of supervised visitation. The project criticized the removal of a child from a nonabusive parent, and also prioritized the protection of the victim and child by all relevant agencies. The group recognized the need to improve collaboration between service providers to achieve these goals. The recommendations suggested the creation of multiple points of entry into the system for families needing services; the provision of services without the need to routinely open a child protection case; and continuous screening and assessment of the family by courts and welfare agencies. The report also advocated improved training for service providers and courts about the dynamics of domestic violence. In addition, it encouraged juvenile courts to remain in close contact with criminal courts to ensure batterer accountability.

The Green Book had a significant influence on legal policy when the trial court in In re Nicholson, 181 F. Supp. 2d 182 (E.D.N.Y. 2000), relied heavily on its findings. Together, the Green Book and the *Nicholson* decision changed the approach of child protective services to cases involving domestic violence. They influenced child welfare agencies to revise their routine practice of removing children from abused mothers and also improved coordination between child welfare agencies and domestic violence advocates.

Notes and Questions

1. Juvenile court jurisdiction. The law generally takes three approaches to children's exposure to domestic violence: (1) imposition of tort liability for intentional infliction of emotional distress (IIED); (2) imposition of criminal liability on caretakers; and (3) defining exposure to domestic violence as a form of maltreatment. New York, in *Nicholson*, followed the third approach.

Every state has a jurisdictional statute that authorizes courts to assume jurisdiction over children who are endangered because of parental abuse or neglect. Most states refer to this authority as "dependency jurisdiction" because the child victims become "dependents" of the state based on the doctrine of "parens patriae" (the idea of the state being the "parent of the country" with the power to intervene in the family for those children in need of protection). Typically, these statutory standards are broad and vague.

2. Constitutional right to family integrity. The right to family integrity is protected by substantive due process. The U.S. Supreme Court cases of Meyer v. Nebraska, 262 U.S. 390 (1923), and Pierce v. Society of Sisters, 268 U.S. 510 (1925) (reprinted in Chapter I), established broad liberal principles of family autonomy in the face of government intervention. These foundational cases affirm that parents have a constitutional right to the care, custody, and control of their children.

---

[39]. See Nat'l Council of Juv. & Fam. Ct. Judges, Effective Intervention in Domestic Violence and Child Maltreatment Cases: Guidelines for Policy and Practice (1999) (popularly known as the "Green Book" because of the color of its cover).

However, this parental right is not absolute. In Prince v. Massachusetts, 321 U.S. 158 (1944), the Supreme Court established that the state has the right to intervene to remove children from the home in cases of child endangerment. What role does constitutional protection of the parent-child relationship play in the analysis in *Nicholson*? How did the New York child welfare procedures violate the mothers' constitutional rights?

3. Stages of intervention. State intervention in cases of child abuse and neglect takes two forms: summary seizure or the assertion of temporary custody. If the court determines that an emergency exists, the court may order (in an ex parte hearing) that the child be immediately removed from the home. Soon thereafter, an adversarial proceeding (a "jurisdictional hearing") occurs to determine whether the child falls within the statutory definition of an abused or neglected child. The next stage of juvenile court intervention occurs when the court conducts a "dispositional hearing" to choose among various dispositions (for example, conditions on custody, foster care, termination of parental rights). What were the various forms of state intervention in Sharwline Nicholson's case?

4. *Nicholson*: holding. Was *Nicholson* a challenge to the constitutionality of New York's child welfare law or practice? What does the New York statute require for a finding of child neglect? How were the children in *Nicholson* allegedly neglected by their mothers? What actions did the state social service workers take in response to their beliefs that the children were neglected? How did the state agencies' written policies differ from their actual practices? How did these practices violate plaintiffs' rights?

5. Exposure to domestic violence. Children's exposure to domestic violence can take several forms: being involved in an event as an eyewitness, intervenor, or shield; experiencing the aftermath of a violent event; being forced to watch or participate in the abuse of the parent; comforting a parent who is a victim; being used as a spy to interrogate the parent; or being used as a pawn to coerce the victim into returning to the violent relationship. Children sometimes suffer accidental physical harm, such as when the abused parent is holding the child or when children intervene in violent episodes. How were Sharwline Nicholson's children exposed to domestic violence?

6. New research on children's exposure. The term "exposure" may be inaccurate, according to recent groundbreaking empirical research of children and their abused mothers. Professor Emma Katz contends that the traditional concept of exposure is based on the idea that children are harmed by *witnessing* physical violence. Yet Professor Katz contends that children are harmed by a more common type of psychological abuse – coercive control – directed at them and/ or their mothers. She identifies three ways that children are harmed by this form of abuse: (1) as a by-product of fathers' restricting, undermining, and controlling the mother's everyday life and resources (e.g., restricting the mother's activities leads to the children's activities being restricted); (2) as tools to abuse the mother; and (3) as co-victims of the father's tactics of coercive control (e.g., he stalks both children and mother or locks up both).[40] Katz advocates for greater recognition of this form of abuse and more supportive interventions for children.

7. Blanket presumptions. In *Nicholson*, the New York Court of Appeals ruled that exposure to domestic violence does not presumptively establish neglect and that removal requires additional particularized evidence. Other blanket presumptions exist in the context of domestic violence. For example, one presumption prohibits court-ordered visitation of a child to a parent who murdered the other parent (absent the child's consent). Does this last presumption have the same constitutional infirmities as the presumption in *Nicholson*?

8. Harm from exposure versus harm from removal. Children who are exposed to domestic violence face behavioral, social, and emotional problems (aggression, anger, hostility, fear, anxiety, withdrawal, depression, poor social relationships, low self-esteem); cognitive and attitudinal problems (lower cognitive functioning, poor academic performance, acceptance of violent behaviors and attitudes, belief in rigid gender stereotypes); and long-term consequences (depression, trauma symptoms, and tolerance for and use of violence in adult relationships). Studies have found that the cumulative effect of repeated exposures to multiple forms of violence is especially harmful.[41] Yet, as noted in *Nicholson*, sometimes the harm of removing a child from the home outweighs the harm experienced in the home where domestic violence occurs. *Nicholson*, 820 N.E.2d at 849. What explains this seeming paradox?[42]

A national initiative addressed the nature of children's exposure to domestic violence from 2010-2012 with the creation of a task force to study the problem and identify promising practices to address it. The task force's recommendations emphasized the importance of early identification and the provision of services. A subsequent task force focused on children's exposure in tribal communities in light of data revealing especially high rates of tribal children's victimization. This latter task force recommended increased funding for tribal child protection systems and the recognition of tribal authority to prosecute non–tribal members who commit crimes against children in Indian country.[43]

---

[40]. Emma Katz, Coercive Control in Children's and Mothers' Lives 99-107 (2022) (based on in-depth interviews with 15 mothers and 15 children over 13 months, both during and after the relationship ended). See also Evan Stark, The Coercive Control of Children (2023).

[41]. For the classic study of the impact of polyvictimization on children, see Ctrs. for Disease Control & Prevention, Adverse Childhood Experiences (ACEs), https://www.cdc.gov/violencepre vention/aces/index.html. See also Nat'l Governors' Assoc., Resource Guide on State Actions to Prevent and Mitigate Adverse Childhood Experiences and Trauma (June 28, 2023) (report highlighting best practices to mitigate effects of ACES and trauma), https://www.nga.org/publicati ons/resource-guide-on-state-actions-to-prevent-and-mitigate-adverse-childhood-experiences-and -trauma/. The foundational ACES study was conducted from 1995-1997.

[42]. See Sharwline Nicholson, Balancing the Harms (Trailer), Jan. 15, 2007, http://www.yout ube.com/watch?v=P5ne2rapK9M&feature=player_embedded#at=45.

[43]. See Report of the Attorney General's National Task Force on Children Exposed to Violence (Dec. 12, 2012), https://www.justice.gov/defendingchildhood/cev-rpt-full.pdf; Attorney General's Advisory Committee on American Indian/Alaska Native Children Exposed to Violence: Ending Violence So Children Can Thrive (Nov. 2014), https://www.justice.gov/sites/default/files/defendi ngchildhood/pages/attachments/2014/11/24/aian_executive_summary.pdf.

NOTE: THE TROUBLED LEGACY OF NICHOLSON v. SCOPPETTA

D. Kelly Weisberg, Collateral Damage: Discrimination in Failure-to-Protect Laws for Children's Wellbeing
117, 124-129 (2019)[44]

. . . *Nicholson*'s mandate has not been fulfilled either by the child welfare department or the family courts in New York City. [N]umerous post-*Nicholson* cases reveal that New York child welfare authorities persist in charging mothers' victimization as the basis for neglect and removing children from the custody of non-abusive mothers. Often these children are placed in foster care. Sometimes, the children are returned to the abusive father's custody. Child welfare workers still condition the return of the children on the mothers' entering a shelter, attending domestic violence counseling, enforcing an order of protection against the father, and cooperating with child welfare supervision by allowing unannounced home visits. In other cases, the court finds the mother neglectful solely based on her refusal to leave the abusive relationship. . . . [These findings are based on research reviewing post-*Nicholson* studies of reported cases, a meta-analysis of the child welfare literature focusing on case outcomes in families experiencing domestic violence, and an ethnographic study of the New York City child welfare system and family courts.]

Nicholson specified the importance of strict guidelines governing removals, such as adopting a standard of imminent risk for removal of children from the custody of the non-abusive parent. Nonetheless, family courts continue to hold neglect hearings involving battered mothers where child welfare authorities fail to meet the requisite "imminent risk" standard. In some cases, child welfare authorities inappropriately presume that the child is at risk based on the mother's *possible* actions. Sometimes, child welfare authorities remove children based on mere speculation that the mother *might* return to her abuser. Child protection agencies base removal decisions on other inappropriate criteria. Sometimes they assume that the mother is unfit based on the *father's* actions. Some child welfare authorities remove children from non-abusive mothers based on the fact that the father had violated an order of protection. . . .

Even more serious ramifications occur. Following *Nicholson*, many states criminalized battered mothers' failure to protect their children from abuse. Currently, at least 29 states have such criminal laws. The offense goes by different names, such as "permitting child abuse," "enabling child abuse," or "injury to a child by omission." . . . Battered women, who are non-abusive parents, have been sentenced to lengthy prison sentences (in some cases, 10 years or more) for failing to protect their children who died from injuries inflicted by an abusive intimate partner.

---

[44]. The above excerpt appeared as Chapter 8 in Child Rights and International Discrimination Law: Implementing Article 2 of the UN Convention on the Rights of the Child (Marit Skivenes & Karl Harald Søvig eds., 2019).

[W]hy do discriminatory child welfare practices, such as those enshrined in Nicholson v. Scoppetta, persist? The answer lies in a combination of institutional constraints and the phenomenon of mother blaming. First, structural constraints impose various pressures on the child welfare system. These consist of the need for institutional accountability, limited financial resources, and political pressures. . . .

[Second, the phenomenon of mother blaming persists.] [S]ocial workers have unbridled discretion to make decisions about children's welfare. *Nicholson* is an example of a social welfare practice that permitted the exercise of vast discretion in the removal process. The exercise of that discretion enables the perpetuation of decision making based on stereotypes about mothers, especially poor women of color, that contribute to the persistence of removing children from the homes of battered women.

The theme of mother-blaming runs through the law's response to battered mothers and child welfare practices. [T]he battered woman's role as mother overshadows her role as victim of domestic violence. The law holds mothers to an unrealistic high standard: "We expect mothers to transcend their victimization, to act on behalf of their children regardless of their own situations." Mothers are expected to overcome all obstacles to protect their children—even in the face of their own victimization. Gender bias operates as a double standard. "In legal proceedings, this bias operates as an unspoken and unconscious double standard for mothers and fathers, such that mothers are expected to be much better and more powerful parents than fathers, always putting their children's needs above their own and protecting their children from all harm." These beliefs are premised on the myths that the battered mother has the power to attain safety from her abuser and that she, alone, has the responsibility to end the abuse. . . .

Nicholson suggested a number of theoretical and practical improvements in welfare practices for children exposed to domestic violence. Yet, the experience of the child welfare system in the post-*Nicholson* era emphasizes the troubled legacy of the case. The child protection system continues to hold battered mothers accountable for their victimization and for the impact of domestic violence on children. In this way, the child protection system continues to serve as another source of victimization for the adult victims of domestic violence and their children.

V

Nonmarital Relationships

The form of the American family has experienced dramatic changes. Families consisting of a married husband and wife with their resident children have been on the decline for some time. Currently, fewer than one in five families conforms to this model.[1] Before turning to the question of how the law treats nonmarital relationships, it is helpful to have a sense of who these families are and how family structures in the United States have changed over time.

The transformations in family structure reflect a number of trends. Overall, fewer Americans are getting married. Instead of marrying, more people are turning to *cohabitation*. Those who do marry tend to marry later in life. Not only has the diversity of family forms increased, but so has their fluidity, leading to family structures that are often evolving (e.g., nonmarital cohabitation, marriage, divorce, remarriage, single parenthood) across the life span. Many unmarried individuals are having children. On the flip side, increasing numbers of adults are not having children at all. Moreover, these changes are not consistent across all racial, ethic, and socioeconomic groups. For those without a college degree, marriage rates are low, and those who do marry are more likely to divorce.[2]

This chapter explores the law's response to nonmarital families. After setting forth some demographic context, the materials then turn to the changing legal meaning of "family." It considers whether and to what extent the constitutional protection for the family extends beyond the marital family. Next, it examines how these relationships are treated under law for a range of purposes. Throughout, the chapter also considers a normative question: How should the law treat these families?

---

[1]. Alexandre Tanzi, U.S. Married Couple Households with Children Fall to Record Low, Bloomberg News, Dec. 3, 2021, https://www.bloomberg.com/news/articles/2021-12-03/u-s-married-couple-households-with-children-fall-to-record-low#xj4y7vzkg.

[2]. June Carbone & Naomi Cahn, Marriage Markets: How Inequality Is Remaking the American Family 19-20 (2014).

A. Changing Family Forms: Context

Juliana Menasce Horowitz et al., The Landscape of Marriage and Cohabitation in the U.S.

Pew Research Ctr., Nov. 6. 2019
https://www.pewresearch.org/social-trends/2019/11/06/the-landscape
-of-marriage-and-cohabitation-in-the-u-s/

. . . Today, 53% of U.S. adults ages 18 and older are married, down from 58% in 1995. Over the same period, the share of Americans who are cohabiting has risen from 3% to 7%. . . . Taken together, six-in-ten Americans are either married or living with a partner, a share that has remained largely unchanged since 1995.

Over the past few decades, marriage rates have declined, particularly among younger Americans. Today, 18% of adults younger than 30 are married, compared with 31% in 1995. Among adults ages 30 to 49 and those 50 and older, 62% are married—down somewhat from 1995, when marriage rates for these age groups were 68% and 65%, respectively.

At the same time, cohabitation rates have increased across all age groups since 1995, though this growth has slowed in the past decade. Among adults younger than 30, 12% are now living with an unmarried partner, compared with 5% in 1995. By comparison, 9% of adults ages 30 to 49 and 4% of adults 50 and older are cohabiting (up from 3% and 1%, respectively, in 1995).

There is substantial variation in marriage rates by race and ethnicity. While 57% of white adults and 63% of Asian adults are married, fewer than half of Hispanic (48%) and black adults (33%) are. Since 1995, marriage rates have declined among white, black and Hispanic adults, but for Asian adults they have stayed roughly constant. Cohabitation rates are more consistent across racial and ethnic groups – 8% of whites and Hispanics and 7% of blacks are cohabiting, as are 3% of Asians. Cohabitation has risen more among white, black and Hispanic adults in recent decades than it has for Asian adults.

Marriage rates also vary by education. Among people ages 25 and older, those with a bachelor's degree or higher (66%) are more likely than those with some college experience (56%) or with a high school diploma or less education (54%) to be married. These differences were less pronounced in 1995, when 70% of college graduates were married, compared with 66% of those with some college and 62% of those with a high school education or less. This education gap is evident among black and white adults, while educational differences in marriage rates are smaller among Hispanic and Asian adults.

The share of adults in cohabiting relationships has risen across all educational levels. Among those ages 25 and older with a bachelor's degree or more, this increase in cohabitation offset the decline in marriage, and as a result the share of college graduates who are either married or living with a partner is unchanged since 1995. Among those with less education, however, the increase in cohabitation only partially counteracts the decline in marriage. Consequently, adults without a bachelor's degree are somewhat less likely to be either married or living with a partner today than in 1995.

Kim Parker & Renee Stepler, As U.S. Marriage Rate Hovers at 50%, Education Gap in Marital Status Widens

Pew Research Ctr., Sept. 14, 2017
*https://www.pewresearch.org/fact-tank/2017/09/14/as-u-s-marriage-rate
-hovers-at-50-education-gap-in-marital-status-widens/*

Among adults who have never been married but say they are open to marrying in the future, about six-in-ten (59%) say that a major reason they are not married is that they haven't found the right person. An additional 13% say this is a minor reason they are not married today. Majorities across a range of demographic groups cite this as a major reason why they are not married.

About four-in-ten never-married adults (41%) who say they may want to marry in the future say that not being financially stable is a major reason they are not currently married, and 28% point to this as a minor reason. Fewer – but still a substantial share – say that a major (24%) or minor (30%) reason they are not married is that they aren't ready to settle down.

Never-married adults with family incomes under $75,000 are more likely than those with higher incomes to say that not being financially secure is a major reason they are not married: 47% of those with incomes less than $30,000 and 40% of those with incomes of $30,000 to $74,999 say this is the case, compared with 21% of those with incomes of $75,000 or higher.

Nonwhite adults who have never been married are also more likely than whites to say a major reason they aren't married is that they are not financially stable (48% vs. 33%).

For young adults who have never been married, not being financially stable and not being ready to settle down loom large as reasons why they are not married. Roughly half of never-married adults ages 18 to 29 (51%) say not being financially stable is a major reason they are not married, compared with 27% of those ages 30 to 49 and 29% of those 50 and older.

Young adults are also more likely than their older counterparts to cite not being ready to settle down as a major reason why they aren't currently married: 31% of never-married adults ages 18 to 29 say this, compared with 14% of those ages 30 to 49 and 18% of those 50 and older. . . .

B. Constitutional Limits on Definitions of "Family"

1. The Constitution and the Nonmarital Family

U.S. DEPARTMENT OF AGRICULTURE v. MORENO
413 U.S. 528 (1973)

Justice BRENNAN delivered the opinion of the Court.

This case requires us to consider the constitutionality of §3(e) of the Food Stamp Act of 1964, 7 U.S.C. §2012(e), [established] in 1964 in an effort to alleviate hunger and malnutrition among the more needy segments of our society. Eligibility for participation in the program is determined on a household rather than an individual basis. An eligible household purchases sufficient food stamps to provide that household with a nutritionally adequate diet. The household pays for the stamps at a reduced rate based upon its size and cumulative income. The food stamps are then used to purchase food at retail stores, and the Government redeems the stamps at face value, thereby paying the difference between the actual cost of the food and the amount paid by the household for the stamps.

As initially enacted, §3(e) defined a "household" as "a group of related or non-related individuals, who are not residents of an institution or boarding house, but are living as one economic unit sharing common cooking facilities and for whom food is customarily purchased in common." In January 1971, however, Congress redefined the term "household" so as to include only groups of related individuals. Pursuant to this amendment, the Secretary of Agriculture promulgated regulations rendering ineligible for participation in the program any "household" whose members are not "all related to each other."

Appellees in this case consist of several groups of individuals who allege that, although they satisfy the income eligibility requirements for federal food assistance, they have nevertheless been excluded from the program solely because the persons in each group are not "all related to each other." Appellee Jacinta Moreno, for example, is a 56-year-old diabetic who lives with Ermina Sanchez and the latter's three children. They share common living expenses, and Mrs. Sanchez helps to care for appellee. Appellee's monthly income, derived from public assistance, is $75; Mrs. Sanchez receives $133 per month from public assistance. The household pays $135 per month for rent, gas and electricity, of which appellee pays $50. Appellee spends $10 per month for transportation to a hospital for regular visits, and $5 per month for laundry. That leaves her $10 per month for food and other necessities. Despite her poverty, appellee has been denied federal food assistance solely because she is unrelated to the other members of her household. Moreover, although Mrs. Sanchez and her three children were permitted to purchase $108 worth of food stamps per month for $18, their participation in the program will be terminated if appellee Moreno continues to live with them.

Appellee Sheilah Hejny is married and has three children. Although the Hejnys are indigent, they took in a 20-year-old girl, who is unrelated to them because "we felt she had emotional problems." The Hejnys receive $144 worth of food stamps each month for $14. If they allow the 20-year-old girl to continue to live with them, they will be denied food stamps by reason of §3(e).

Appellee Victoria Keppler has a daughter with an acute hearing deficiency. The daughter requires special instruction in a school for the deaf. The school is located in an area in which appellee could not ordinarily afford to live. Thus, in order to make the most of her limited resources, appellee agreed to share an apartment near the school with a woman who, like appellee, is on public assistance. Since appellee is not related to the woman, appellee's food stamps have been, and will continue to be, cut off if they continue to live together.

These and two other groups of appellees instituted a class action . . . seeking declaratory and injunctive relief against the enforcement of the 1971 amendment of §3(e) and its implementing regulations. In essence, appellees contend, and the District Court held, that the "unrelated person" provision of §3(e) creates an irrational classification in violation of the equal protection component of the Due Process Clause of the Fifth Amendment. We agree. . . .

The challenged statutory classification (households of related persons versus households containing one or more unrelated persons) is clearly irrelevant to the stated purposes of the Act. As the District Court recognized, "(t)he relationships among persons constituting one economic unit and sharing cooking facilities have nothing to do with their abilities to stimulate the agricultural economy by purchasing farm surpluses, or with their personal nutritional requirements." 345 F. Supp., at 313.

Thus, if it is to be sustained, the challenged classification must rationally further some legitimate governmental interest. . . . Regrettably, there is little legislative history to illuminate the purposes of the 1971 amendment of §3(e). The legislative history that does exist, however, indicates that that amendment was intended to prevent so-called "hippies" and "hippie communes" from participating in the food stamp program. The challenged classification clearly cannot be sustained by reference to this congressional purpose. For if the constitutional conception of "equal protection of the laws" means anything, it must at the very least mean that a bare congressional desire to harm a politically unpopular group cannot constitute a legitimate governmental interest. . . .

Although apparently conceding this point, the Government maintains that the challenged classification should nevertheless be upheld as rationally related to the clearly legitimate governmental interest in minimizing fraud in the administration of the food stamp program.[7] In essence, the Government contends that, in adopting the 1971 amendment, Congress might rationally have thought (1) that households with one or more unrelated members are more likely than "fully related" households to contain individuals who abuse the program

---

7. The Government initially argued to the District Court that the challenged classification might be justified as a means to foster "morality." In rejecting that contention, the District Court noted that "interpreting the amendment as an attempt to regulate morality would raise serious constitutional questions." 345 F. Supp. 310, 314. Indeed, citing this Court's decisions [in Griswold v. Connecticut, Stanley v. Georgia, and Eisenstadt v. Baird], the District Court observed that it was doubtful at best, whether Congress, "in the name of morality," could "infringe the rights to privacy and freedom of association *in the home*." 345 F. Supp., at 314. (Emphasis in original.) Moreover, the court also pointed out that the classification established in §3(e) was not rationally related "to prevailing notions of morality, since it in terms disqualifies all households of unrelated individuals, without reference to whether a particular group contains both sexes." 345 F. Supp., at 315. The Government itself has now abandoned the "morality" argument.

by fraudulently failing to report sources of income or by voluntarily remaining poor; and (2) that such households are "relatively unstable," thereby increasing the difficulty of detecting such abuses. But even if we were to accept as rational the Government's wholly unsubstantiated assumptions concerning the differences between "related" and "unrelated" households we still could not agree with the Government's conclusion that the denial of essential federal food assistance to all otherwise eligible households containing unrelated members constitutes a rational effort to deal with these concerns.

At the outset, it is important to note that the Food Stamp Act itself contains provisions, wholly independent of §3(e), aimed specifically at the problems of fraud. . . . The existence of these provisions necessarily casts considerable doubt upon the proposition that the 1971 amendment could rationally have been intended to prevent those very same abuses.

[I]n practical operation, the 1971 amendment excludes from participation in the food stamp program, not those persons who are "likely to abuse the program," but, rather, only those persons who are so desperately in need of aid that they cannot even afford to alter their living arrangements so as to retain their eligibility. Traditional equal protection analysis does not require that every classification be drawn with precise "mathematical nicety." But the classification here in issue is not only "imprecise," it is wholly without any rational basis. The judgment of the District Court holding the "unrelated person" provision invalid under the Due Process Clause of the Fifth Amendment is therefore affirmed. . . .

Justice DOUGLAS, concurring. . . .

. . . As the facts of this case show, the poor are congregating in households where they can better meet the adversities of poverty. This banding together is an expression of the right of freedom of association that is very deep in our traditions.

Other like rights have been recognized that are only peripheral First Amendment rights—the right to send one's child to a religious school, the right to study the German language in a private school, the protection of the entire spectrum of learning, teaching, and communicating ideas, the marital right of privacy. As the examples indicate, these peripheral constitutional rights are exercised not necessarily in assemblies that congregate in halls or auditoriums but in discrete individual actions such as parents placing a child in the school of their choice. Taking a person into one's home because he is poor or needs help or brings happiness to the household is of the same dignity.

Congress might choose to deal only with members of a family of one or two or three generations, treating it all as a unit. Congress, however, has not done that here. Concededly an individual living alone is not disqualified from the receipt of food stamp aid, even though there are other members of the family with whom he might theoretically live. Nor are common-law couples disqualified: they, like individuals living alone, may qualify under the Act if they are poor—whether they have abandoned their wives and children and however antifamily their attitudes may be. In other words, the "unrelated" person provision was not aimed at the maintenance of normal family ties. It penalizes persons or families who have brought under their roof an "unrelated" needy person. It penalizes the poorest of the poor for doubling up against the adversities of poverty.

But for the constitutional aspects of the problem, the "unrelated" person provision of the Act might well be sustained as a means to prevent fraud. . . . I could not say that this "unrelated" person provision has no "rational" relation to control of fraud. We deal here, however, with the right of association, protected by the First Amendment. People who are desperately poor but unrelated come together and join hands with the aim better to combat the crises of poverty. The need of those living together better to meet those crises is denied, while the need of households made up of relatives that is no more acute is serviced. Problems of the fisc . . . are legitimate concerns of government. But government "may not accomplish such a purpose by invidious distinctions between classes of its citizens." . . . The right of association, the right to invite the stranger into one's home is too basic in our constitutional regime to deal with roughshod. If there are abuses inherent in that pattern of living against which the food stamp program should be protected, the Act must be "narrowly drawn," to meet the precise end. The method adopted and applied to these cases makes §3(e) of the Act unconstitutional by reason of the invidious discrimination between the two classes of needy persons. . . .

[Dissenting Justice Rehnquist would have upheld the provision under rational basis review, reasoning that Congress could have rationally concluded that a family of related persons exists for some valid purpose other than to collect food stamps.]

Notes and Questions

1. **Definition of family.** *Moreno* highlights different definitions of "family." Formal definitions tend to define the concept according to blood ties (consanguinity) or legal ceremony (such as marriage or adoption). In contrast, functional approaches define family by virtue of its functions (support, affection, caregiving, etc.). What are the implications of the respective approaches?

2. **"Family" or "household"?** In *Moreno*, the Supreme Court was willing to include unrelated persons in a definition of "household" for food stamp purposes. Would the Court have reached the same result if the legislation determined eligibility on a "family" basis, instead of a "household" basis? How do the terms differ? If "family" were defined in terms of "a single housekeeping unit," how would that change the analysis?

In contrast to *Moreno*, consider Village of Belle Terre v. Boraas, 416 U.S. 1, 2 (1974), in which the U.S. Supreme Court upheld a zoning ordinance that restricted land use to "one-family dwellings" and defined a "family" as follows:

> (o)ne or more persons related by blood, adoption, or marriage, living and cooking together as a single housekeeping unit, exclusive of household servants. A number of persons but not exceeding (2) living and cooking together as a single housekeeping unit though not related by blood, adoption, or marriage shall be deemed to constitute a family.

In this challenge to a zoning ordinance by a landlord who rented a house to six college students, Justice Douglas found no violation of the freedom of association (because a "family" may entertain whomever it pleases) or any other fundamental right. In upholding the ordinance, the Court analogized the group of students to other "urban problems" such as "boarding houses, fraternity houses, and the like . . ." in which "[m]ore people occupy a given space; more cars rather continuously pass by; more cars are parked; noise travels with crowds." Applying the rational basis test to the ordinance, the Court saw nothing impermissible in the village's goal of "lay[ing] out zones where family values, youth values, and the blessings of quiet seclusion and clean air make the area a sanctuary for people." Most states have upheld similar restrictions on the number of unrelated persons who live together.

3. Views of family. How do the Court's views of the "families" in *Moreno* and *Belle Terre* differ? For example, *Belle Terre* reveals concerns about transiency, overcrowding, and congestion. Yet *Moreno* is skeptical about the government's "unsubstantiated assumptions" about the instability of households of unrelated persons. What factors explain the different results? Why might the Court have shown greater deference to the government's interest in *Belle Terre* than in *Moreno*? Why does Justice Douglas concur in *Moreno*, given his majority opinion in *Belle Terre*? Was the outcome different, perhaps, because the *Moreno* plaintiffs conformed more to our concept of the traditional family?

What family values do the groups in *Moreno* and *Belle Terre* reflect? Did the group sharing a home in *Belle Terre* pose a greater risk to the "family value" of permanency than the groups excluded by the food stamp restriction that was invalidated in *Moreno*?

4. Federal constitutional rights. Courts have tended to apply rational basis review to zoning provisions that limit the number of unrelated individuals residing in single-family dwellings. How would the Supreme Court respond to an ordinance that limited or excluded unmarried couples after Lawrence v. Texas? Should courts apply a heightened standard of review to such provisions because they implicate fundamental rights, such as the right to privacy and the right of association? See Schwartz v. Lisitsa, 2014 WL 7639147 (Pa. Com. Pl. 2014). Commentators have long criticized *Moreno* for its unwillingness to address the degree to which the Constitution protects the right to choose with whom to share a home.[3] Are *Moreno* and *Belle Terre* incompatible with the Supreme Court's modern jurisprudence on privacy and the right of intimate association? If so, what explains their continued vitality?

5. Protection from state interference. It is often said that the family is protected from undue state interference. But is this true for all families? Or, maybe more specifically, to which families does this constitutional protection attach? And why these families but not others? What interests does this protection vindicate? To the extent that this constitutional protection attaches to nonmarital families, what rights and protections are afforded to these families? Does the Constitution extend only negative rights, protecting the individuals from undue interference from the state? Or does it give rise to some positive rights, such as the right to access certain benefits and protections accorded by the state?

---

[3]. See, e.g., J. Harvie Wilkinson III & G. Edward White, Constitutional Protection for Personal Lifestyles, 62 Cornell L. Rev. 563, 584 (1977).

6. Other group living arrangements.

a. Student groups. In a post-*Belle Terre* case, ten college students challenged an ordinance of a New Jersey town that limited occupancy by defining a "family" as

> one or more persons occupying a dwelling unit as a single non-profit house-keeping unit, who are living together as a stable and permanent living unit, being a traditional family unit or the functional equivalency thereof.

Borough of Glassboro v. Vallorosi, 568 A.2d 888, 889 (N.J. 1990). The *Vallorosi* ordinance, similar to that in *Belle Terre,* aimed to preserve stable, permanent housing. Influenced by state precedents equating "single family" with "single housekeeping unit," the New Jersey Supreme Court adopted a functional standard and held that the group complied because they planned to live together for three years, ate together, and shared household tasks and expenses. Is *Vallorosi*'s functional standard superior to *Belle Terre*'s focus on associational ties?

b. Group homes. Belle Terre (and *Vallorosi*) illustrate the elasticity of the definition of "family" in the use of zoning as an agent of social control. The Supreme Court later examined the issue in City of Cleburne v. Cleburne Living Center, 473 U.S. 432 (1985), in which the city denied an exemption from the local ordinance to a home for the cognitively impaired. In response to the group's claim that the ordinance violated equal protection, the Court held the ordinance invalid as applied, reasoning that the city's denial rested on irrational prejudice. Did the *Belle Terre* ordinance, as applied, rest on "irrational prejudice" against students? Is resort to the police power to enforce zoning ordinances appropriate to exclude "undesirables" from the community?

Two of the three named family groups in *Moreno* consist of households of single mothers who were caring for dependent adults. The number of single-mother families has risen dramatically over the past four decades. Black single mothers constitute a significant proportion of these families. The article below criticizes American family policy that prioritizes the marital family over other family forms such as the single-parent family.

Vivian Hamilton, Mistaking Marriage for Social Policy
11 Va. J. Soc. Pol'y & L. 307, 355-360, 368-370 (2004)

IN SICKNESS AND IN HEALTH: THE CARETAKING FUNCTION OF MARRIAGE

Society currently designates the nuclear, preferably marital, family as the social structure that supports child caretaking. . . . The rhetorical importance placed on child caretaking in the U.S. stands in stark contrast to family support policies that are the stingiest in the industrial world. [O]ther countries consistently do more to assist caretakers. France and the Scandinavian countries are among those that have implemented family support policies that directly support caretaking. These policies include subsidized day care, paid parental leave, universal health care, and income supplements to low-earning caretakers. . . .

Married couples [in the United States] receive more protections and benefits than do nonmarital couples—Social Security, pension, and health insurance benefits are among the measures that assist marital families. [U]nmarried men and women who live together are almost as likely to be raising children as are married couples. But because they have chosen not to formalize their relationships, they must manage caretaking without many of the benefits accorded marital families. Also, social support for single-parent families, the vast majority of which are headed by women, can vary dramatically. . . . Divorced and never-married mothers [are dependent] on the vicissitudes of the uncertain child support and welfare systems. Not only are these families affected materially, but they also suffer from a social stigma that is reinforced by the existing legal structure.

Some commentators retort that two-parent marital families are best for children, so it is therefore appropriate for the state to subsidize or privilege this family form over others. There are several problems with this argument. [S]ociologist Sara McLanahan has found that data does not support the conclusion that what harms children is the absence of one parent. Instead, McLanahan says, single parenting currently leads to certain types of instability that can harm children. Much of the link between single parenting and negative child outcomes can thus be attributed to low income, less-stable adult presence, and residential mobility after divorce. . . .

Rather than emphasizing the importance of marriage, government should instead enact more carefully targeted policies to support caretaking and the economic well-being of its citizenry. . . . What would this look like in practice? First, the state would deemphasize family form. It would eliminate government-sanctioned privileges that currently accompany heterosexual monogamous marriage and that devalue and stigmatize other family structures. It would also introduce programs that directly bolster dependent caretaking and the economic supports that make such caretaking possible. . . . Possible programs could include subsidized or public day care, longer school days and school years, more affordable health care, and workplace protections (including paid family leave policies and flexible schedules). To further ensure the economic security of dependents, the state should also make modifications to the welfare, social security, and tax systems. . . .

Some might suggest that it is incongruous to demand privacy from government intervention in certain aspects of family life but seek its intervention in other aspects. But incongruity appears only if the marital family is viewed as an indivisible unit. Dissecting that unit into its functional parts brings into sharp relief and permits examination of its different components. Once family life has been dissected, the question becomes not how one can justify treating certain aspects of the family differently, but instead how one can justify treating such radically different aspects of the family the same. Why should government privilege . . . one form of companionate relationship over others that may serve the same societal functions?

2. The Extended Family

MOORE v. CITY OF EAST CLEVELAND
431 U.S. 494 (1977)

Justice POWELL announced the judgment of the Court, and delivered an opinion in which Justice BRENNAN, Justice MARSHALL, and Justice BLACKMUN joined.

East Cleveland's housing ordinance, like many throughout the country, limits occupancy of a dwelling unit to members of a single family. But the ordinance contains an unusual and complicated definitional section that recognizes as a "family" only a few categories of related individuals, §1341.08.[2] Because her family, living together in her home, fits none of those categories, appellant stands convicted of a criminal offense. The question in this case is whether the ordinance violates the Due Process Clause of the Fourteenth Amendment.

Appellant, Mrs. Inez Moore, lives in her East Cleveland home together with her son, Dale Moore Sr., and her two grandsons, Dale, Jr., and John Moore, Jr. The two boys are first cousins rather than brothers; we are told that John came to live with his grandmother and with the elder and younger Dale Moores after his mother's death.

In early 1973, Mrs. Moore received a notice of violation from the city, stating that John was an "illegal occupant" and directing her to comply with the ordinance. When she failed to remove him from her home, the city filed a criminal charge. [She was convicted and sentenced to five days in jail and a $25 fine. She claims that the ordinance is facially unconstitutional.]

The city argues that our decision in Village of Belle Terre v. Boraas, 416 U.S. 1 (1974), requires us to sustain the ordinance attacked here. . . . But one overriding factor sets this case apart from *Belle Terre*. The ordinance there affected only *unrelated* individuals. It expressly allowed all who were related by "blood, adoption, or marriage" to live together, and in sustaining the ordinance we were careful to note that it promoted "family needs" and "family values." East Cleveland, in contrast, has chosen to regulate the occupancy of its housing by slicing deeply into the family itself. This is no mere incidental result of the ordinance. On its face it selects certain categories of relatives who may live together and declares that others may not. In particular, it makes a crime of a grandmother's choice to live with her grandson in circumstances like those presented here.

When a city undertakes such intrusive regulation of the family, neither *Belle Terre* nor *Euclid* governs; the usual judicial deference to the legislature is

---

2. Section 1341.08 (1966) provides:

"Family" means a number of individuals related to the nominal head of the household or to the spouse of the nominal head of the household living as a single housekeeping unit in a single dwelling unit, [including spouse, parent, or unmarried children, provided the unmarried children have no co-resident children, but] a family may include not more than one dependent married or unmarried child of the nominal head of the household or of the spouse of the nominal head of the household and the spouse and dependent children of such dependent child. . . .

inappropriate. "This Court has long recognized that freedom of personal choice in matters of marriage and family life is one of the liberties protected by the Due Process Clause of the Fourteenth Amendment." A host of cases, tracing their lineage to Meyer v. Nebraska, 262 U.S. 390, 399-401 (1923), and Pierce v. Society of Sisters, 268 U.S. 510, 534-535 (1925), have consistently acknowledged a "private realm of family life which the state cannot enter." Of course, the family is not beyond regulation. But when the government intrudes on choices concerning family living arrangements, this Court must examine carefully the importance of the governmental interests advanced and the extent to which they are served by the challenged regulation.

When thus examined, this ordinance cannot survive. The city seeks to justify it as a means of preventing overcrowding, minimizing traffic and parking congestion, and avoiding an undue financial burden on East Cleveland's school system. Although these are legitimate goals, the ordinance before us serves them marginally, at best. For example, the ordinance permits any family consisting only of husband, wife, and unmarried children to live together, even if the family contains a half dozen licensed drivers, each with his or her own car. At the same time it forbids an adult brother and sister to share a household, even if both faithfully use public transportation. The ordinance would permit a grandmother to live with a single dependent son and children, even if his school-age children number a dozen, yet it forces Mrs. Moore to find another dwelling for her grandson John, simply because of the presence of his uncle and cousin in the same household. . . .

The city would distinguish the cases based on Meyer and Pierce. It points out that none of them "gives grandmothers any fundamental rights with respect to grandsons," . . . and suggests that any constitutional right to live together as a family extends only to the nuclear family, essentially a couple and their dependent children.

To be sure, these cases did not expressly consider the family relationship presented here. They were immediately concerned with freedom of choice with respect to childbearing, or with the rights of parents to the custody and companionship of their own children, or with traditional parental authority in matters of child rearing and education. But unless we close our eyes to the basic reasons why certain rights associated with the family have been accorded shelter under the Fourteenth Amendment's Due Process Clause, we cannot avoid applying the force and rationale of these precedents to the family choice involved in this case. . . .

Substantive due process has at times been a treacherous field for this Court. There *are* risks when the judicial branch gives enhanced protection to certain substantive liberties without the guidance of the more specific provisions of the Bill of Rights. As the history of the *Lochner*-era demonstrates, there is reason for concern lest the only limits to such judicial intervention become the predilections of those who happen at the time to be Members of this Court. That history counsels caution and restraint. But it does not counsel abandonment, nor does it require what the city urges: cutting off any protection of family rights at the first convenient, if arbitrary boundary—the boundary of the nuclear family.

Appropriate limits on substantive due process come not from drawing arbitrary lines but rather from careful "respect for the teachings of history (and), solid recognition of the basic values that underlie our society." Griswold v. Connecticut, 381 U.S., at 501. Our decisions establish that the Constitution protects the sanctity of the family precisely because the institution of the family is deeply rooted in this Nation's history and tradition. It is through the family that we inculcate and pass down many of our most cherished values, moral and cultural.

Ours is by no means a tradition limited to respect for the bonds uniting the members of the nuclear family. The tradition of uncles, aunts, cousins, and especially grandparents sharing a household along with parents and children has roots equally venerable and equally deserving of constitutional recognition. Over the years millions of our citizens have grown up in just such an environment, and most, surely, have profited from it. Even if conditions of modern society have brought about a decline in extended family households, they have not erased the accumulated wisdom of civilization, gained over the centuries and honored throughout our history, that supports a larger conception of the family. Out of choice, necessity, or a sense of family responsibility, it has been common for close relatives to draw together and participate in the duties and the satisfactions of a common home. Decisions concerning child rearing, which . . . *Meyer, Pierce* and other cases have recognized as entitled to constitutional protection, long have been shared with grandparents or other relatives who occupy the same household, indeed who may take on major responsibility for the rearing of the children. Especially in times of adversity, such as the death of a spouse or economic need, the broader family has tended to come together for mutual sustenance and to maintain or rebuild a secure home life. This is apparently what happened here [when John Moore, Jr., came to live with his grandmother, as an infant, after his mother's death].

Whether or not such a household is established because of personal tragedy, the choice of relatives in this degree of kinship to live together may not lightly be denied by the State. [T]he Constitution prevents East Cleveland from standardizing its children and its adults by forcing all to live in certain narrowly defined family patterns. . . .

Justice BRENNAN, with whom Justice MARSHALL joins, concurring.

I join the plurality's opinion. . . . I write only to underscore the cultural myopia of the arbitrary boundary drawn by the East Cleveland ordinance in the light of the tradition of the American home that has been a feature of our society since our beginning as a Nation. . . .

. . . The "extended family" that provided generations of early Americans with social services and economic and emotional support in times of hardship, and was the beachhead for successive waves of immigrants who populated our cities, remains not merely still a pervasive living pattern, but under the goad of brutal economic necessity, a prominent pattern virtually a means of survival for large numbers of the poor and deprived minorities of our society. For them compelled pooling of scant resources requires compelled sharing of a household.

The "extended" form is especially familiar among black families. We may suppose that this reflects the truism that black citizens, like generations of white immigrants before them, have been victims of economic and other disadvantages that would worsen if they were compelled to abandon extended, for nuclear, living patterns. . . . In black households whose head is an elderly woman, as in this case, . . . 48% of such black households, compared with 10% of counterpart white households, include related minor children not offspring of the head of the household.

I do not wish to be understood as implying that East Cleveland's enforcement of its ordinance is motivated by a racially discriminatory purpose: The record of this case would not support that implication. But the prominence of other than nuclear families among ethnic and racial minority groups, including our black citizens, surely demonstrates that the "extended family" pattern remains a vital tenet of our society. It suffices that in prohibiting this pattern of family living as a means of achieving its objectives, appellee city has chosen a device that deeply intrudes into family associational rights that historically have been central, and today remain central, to a large proportion of our population. . . .

[The concurring opinion of Justice Stevens, emphasizing Mrs. Moore's right to use her property as she sees fit, has been omitted.]

Justice STEWART, with whom Justice REHNQUIST joins, dissenting. . . .

The *Belle Terre* decision . . . disposes of the appellant's contentions to the extent they focus not on her blood relationships with her sons and grandsons but on more general notions about the "privacy of the home." Her suggestion that every person has a constitutional right permanently to share his residence with whomever he pleases, and that such choices are "beyond the province of legitimate governmental intrusion," amounts to the same argument that was made and found unpersuasive in *Belle Terre.* . . .

The appellant is considerably closer to the constitutional mark in asserting that the East Cleveland ordinance intrudes upon "the private realm of family life which the state cannot enter." Several decisions of the Court have identified specific aspects of what might broadly be termed "private family life" that are constitutionally protected against state interference.

Although the appellant's desire to share a single-dwelling unit also involves "private family life" in a sense, that desire can hardly be equated with any of the interests [which we have previously protected]. The ordinance about which the appellant complains did not impede her choice to have or not to have children, and it did not dictate to her how her own children were to be nurtured and reared. The ordinance clearly does not prevent parents from living together or living with their unemancipated offspring.

But even though the Court's previous cases are not directly in point, the appellant contends that the importance of the "extended family" in American society requires us to hold that her decision to share her residence with her grandsons may not be interfered with by the State. This decision, like the decisions involved in bearing and raising children, is said to be an aspect of "family life" also entitled to substantive protection under the Constitution. Without pausing to inquire how far under this argument an "extended family" might extend, I cannot agree. . . . To equate [Moore's] interest with the fundamental decisions to marry and to bear and raise children is to extend the limited substantive contours of the Due Process Clause beyond recognition.

The appellant also challenges the single-family occupancy ordinance on equal protection grounds [an issue which the majority did not reach]. Her claim is that the city has drawn an arbitrary and irrational distinction between groups of people who may live together as a "family" and those who may not. . . . I do not think East Cleveland's definition of "family" offends the Constitution. The city has undisputed power to ordain single-family residential occupancy. And that power plainly carries with it the power to say what a "family" is. Here the city has defined "family" to include not only father, mother, and dependent children, but several other close relatives as well. The definition is rationally designed to carry out the legitimate governmental purposes identified in the *Belle Terre* opinion. . . .

Obviously, East Cleveland might have as easily and perhaps as effectively hit upon a different definition of "family." But a line could hardly be drawn that would not sooner or later become the target of a challenge like the appellant's. If "family" included all of the householder's grandchildren there would doubtless be the hard case of an orphaned niece or nephew. If, as the appellant suggests, a "family" must include all blood relatives, what of longtime friends? . . .

NOTE: WHO WAS INEZ MOORE?

Peggy Cooper Davis, Moore v. East Cleveland: Constructing the Suburban Family
Family Law Stories 77, 88-89 (Carol Sanger ed., 2008)

The trouble seems to have begun for Inez Moore and her family in 1973 when John Jr. started school. It was then that Raiford Williams, an East Cleveland Deputy Housing Inspector, began to visit the Moore house on Garfield Road and to record violations. The structural violations—leaking sinks and tubs, a defective light, walls that needed replastering—Mrs. Moore began to repair. But there was one violation she would not address: *"John Moore, 7, is an illegal occupant. . . . Correct within 15 days."* . . .

East Cleveland officials were proud of their zoning regulations. [T]he city had balanced its enforcement policies with a program of enlightened and socially responsible development. . . . The zoning regulations had been carefully considered and repeatedly refined: They were a key part of the city's strategy for attracting and maintaining a middle-class base and realizing the vision of East Cleveland as a "City of Achievement." Working from a vision of the prototypical middle-class suburban family, and undoubtedly having in mind both the problems of overcrowding and the pathologies thought to be associated with female-headed extended families, the regulations provided that a single-family dwelling could house spouses and their parents and children, but could house only one set of grandchildren. . . .

"On the surface, it looks like somebody's trying to be mean," said the city's Law Director, "but studies show a correlation between population density and trouble: more cars, crowded schools, more family fights that can lead to violence." . . . To Ms. Moore, the zoning regulations were not just mean, but also irrational. Speaking to a CBS News reporter, she said, "I could go out and bring in a foster child, and it would be legal. I could bring in a stepson or something, and it would probably be legal. But these are my grandchildren and it's not legal. I don't know why." The Law Director's statement to the same reporter was candid; he said that the zoning regulation "was written to avoid slums. It was written to avoid violence. It was written to avoid all the problems that the inner cities are experiencing throughout the country." But was it constitutionally permissible? . . .

D'Vera Cohn et al., Financial Issues Top the List of Reasons U.S. Adults Live in Multigenerational Homes

Pew Research Ctr., Mar. 24, 2022
https://www.pewresearch.org/social-trends/2022/03/24/the-demographics
-of-multigenerational-households/

. . . After declining in earlier decades, multigenerational living has grown steadily in the U.S. since the 1970s. From 1971 to 2021, the number of people living in multigenerational households quadrupled, while the number in other types of living situations is less than double what it was. The share of the U.S. population in multigenerational homes has more than doubled, from 7% in 1971 to 18% in 2021. . . .

Among major racial and ethnic groups, Americans who are Asian, Black or Hispanic are more likely than those who are White to live in a multigenerational family household. About a quarter of Asian (24%), Black (26%) and Hispanic (26%) Americans lived in multigenerational households in 2021, compared with 13% of those who are White. Immigrant status also is linked to the likelihood of multigenerational living. A higher share of foreign-born Americans (26%) than U.S.-born Americans (17%) live in a multigenerational family home. . . .

Americans in metropolitan areas (19%) are somewhat more likely than those in rural communities (16%) to live in multigenerational family homes. . . .

Both the share and number of Americans living in multigenerational households have risen steadily since 1971, when this group numbered 14.5 million compared with 2021's 59.7 million. Growth accelerated during the Great Recession of 2007-2009 and has continued at a slower pace since then, but there is no sign that the multigenerational household population total has peaked.

. . . Since 2000, the multigenerational household population has grown by 22.1 million people, but some groups played a larger role than others in driving that change. Americans younger than 40 accounted for almost half (49%) of the increase in the multigenerational household population but only 17% of overall population growth. In general, young adults are marrying later and staying in school longer than previous generations, which may contribute to their rising inclination to live with other family members under one roof. . . .

Multigenerational households can have financial advantages. Pooling financial resources means that family helps out in hard times. Some of these households have more earners than non-multigenerational arrangements, providing a safety net if one person loses a job. However, multigenerational households are larger than other types, so any money brought in may need to cover more people. . . . Groups that are more economically vulnerable had even more benefit from living in multigenerational households. . . .

. . . Four-in-ten adults in multigenerational households say financial issues are a major reason why they live with adult family members other than a spouse or partner; another 28% say this is a minor reason. Similar shares across racial, ethnic and income groups cite financial issues as a reason why they live in a multigenerational household. . . . While financial issues are widely cited as a reason for living in a multigenerational household, adults with lower incomes are particularly likely to say this type of living arrangement is helpful to them financially. . . .

Notes and Questions

1. Formal versus functional definition. Does the *Moore* family conform to a formal and/or functional definition of the family? Given the presence of Mrs. Moore's blood ties with her grandsons, why doesn't the Moore household qualify as a "family" under the East Cleveland zoning ordinance?

2. Erasure of race. East Cleveland, a suburb of Cleveland, is a predominantly Black community. Mrs. Moore was Black. Did the Court adequately take the role of race into account? Does Justice Powell's plurality opinion, with its general reference to the "tradition" of the extended family, erase the significance of the extended family in Black communities? How does Justice Brennan respond in his concurrence? Although demographic data support the *mythical* status of the extended family among whites, the extended family form has long been prevalent among Black families.[4]

Professor Robin Lenhardt charges that race was the backdrop against which *Moore* played out, despite the Court's reluctance or unwillingness to acknowledge the impact of racial bias or inequality.[5] She elaborates that the *Moore* opinion made no mention of the fact that the defendant was Black, she lived in a Black community, and the ordinance was passed within days of a race riot in a neighboring city. Lenhardt's research reveals that Justice Powell was vehemently opposed to viewing *Moore* as a race case. What are the implications of this race-blindness approach for Black families? For families generally, and for family law?

3. Return of the extended family. The extended family fell out of favor after World War II. From 1940 to 1980, the percentage of people living in such households dropped by half. Recently, the percentage has risen. As noted in the Cohn et al. excerpt above, almost 20 percent of the population now lives in multigenerational households. The resurgence of the extended family stems in part from the economy, the opioid epidemic, the COVID pandemic, and delayed first-marriage age.

Grandparents in racial and ethnic minority groups, like Mrs. Moore, are overrepresented in the population of caregivers. In addition to zoning problems, what legal issues do these grandparents face?

4. *Belle Terre* distinguished. In applying a stricter standard of constitutional scrutiny than it used in *Belle Terre*, the Court treats *Moore* as involving not zoning, but rather family privacy. Why does the Belle Terre ordinance serve "family needs" and "family values," but the East Cleveland ordinance "slic[es] deeply into the family itself"? Is the latter ordinance directed at the same ends (eliminating traffic congestion and overcrowding) or at other family values? Professor Robert Burt responds:

> The plurality did not consider that the purpose of the ordinance was quite straightforward: to exclude from a middle-class, predominantly black community, that saw itself as socially and economically upwardly mobile, other black families most characteristic of lower-class ghetto life.

---

[4]. See William J. Goode, World Revolution and Family Patterns 6 (1970) (referring to the extended family as the "family form of Western nostalgia"); Ronald L. Taylor, Diversity Within African American Families, in Family in Transition: Families in Society 432, 430 (Arlene S. Skolnick & Jerome H. Skolnick eds., 2011).

[5]. R.A. Lenhardt, The Color of Kinship, 102 Iowa L. Rev. 2071, 2093 (2017).

Perhaps the Court did not see this purpose or, if it did, considered this an "ille-gitimate goal," though in other cases the Court had been exceedingly solicitous of white middle-class communities' attempts to preserve a common social identity — "zones," as the Court had put the matter [in *Belle Terre*] — "where family values, youth values, and the blessings of the quiet seclusion and clean air make the area a sanctuary for people." . . . I find in [Justice Brennan's] characterization of the East Cleveland ordinance, as "senseless" and "eccentric," precisely what he alleges in it: "a depressing insensitivity toward the economic and emotional needs" of the current majority of residents of East Cleveland.[6]

In an omitted dissent, Justice White disputes the idea that Mrs. Moore's interest in living with her grandchildren is protected by the Due Process Clause. He reasons that the ordinance prevents her from living only in East Cleveland, but she is free to move elsewhere in Cleveland. What do you think of his suggestion? Does it respond to Professor Burt's criticism above?

5. Criteria for family. Are blood and legal ties conclusive evidence of a family? Suppose that John Moore, Jr. were an adult grandchild who was employed, finan-cially independent, and pays rent to his grandmother but seldom interacted with her. Or suppose that Inez Moore took into her home a neighbor's child when the friend became terminally ill. Does a blood relationship merit protection of John Jr.'s residential right, but not the child's? What factors, other than consanguinity and marriage, are suggestive of the existence of a family? A parent-child relation-ship? What problems does this approach perpetuate?

Problem

After their respective divorces, two friends, Alicia Wrob and Sheri Clark, rent a unit in a duplex in Eureka, Missouri. Wrob's two school-age children stay there every other week, and Clark's 21-year-old daughter has a room in the basement of the three-bedroom, two-bathroom dwelling. The city has cited them for illegal occupancy in an area zoned for "single families." Wrob and Clark claim they do constitute a family, sharing living expenses, dividing household labor, and relying on one another for emotional support. Eureka's zoning ordinance defines "family" as "[one] or more persons, related or unrelated, living together as a single inte-grated household unit." If the case goes to court, what arguments should Wrob and Clark make, and what result should they obtain? See Sarah Wilson, Eureka Lawsuit Questions Living Situation, Definition of Family, Newsmagazine Network, Aug. 28, 2015, http://www.newsmagazinenetwork.com/nn/2013012330275/eureka-lawsuit-questions-living-situation-definition-of-family/.

[6]. Robert A. Burt, The Constitution of the Family, 1979 Sup. Ct. Rev. 329, 389.

C. Cohabitation: Unmarried Couples

The first two excerpts below present background on cohabitation in the United States (its history as well as demographic characteristics). The third offers a comparative view of cohabitation from an international perspective.

1. Introduction

Marsha Garrison, Nonmarital Cohabitation: Social Revolution and Legal Regulation
42 Fam. L.Q. 309, 311-314 (2008)

[Before the 1960s] cohabitation outside of marriage was widely viewed as shameful. . . . What almost no one foresaw [was] the rapidity with which the stigma traditionally attached to nonmarital cohabitation would vanish. . . .

Among the remarkable cultural shifts of the 1960s was a new attitude toward premarital sex. To be more precise, the 1960s witnessed a profound shift in attitudes toward *female* premarital sex. Before the 1960s, a young man could "sow a few wild oats" without fear of serious social censure. Of course, he risked venereal disease if he patronized a prostitute. And he risked a shotgun wedding if he impregnated a girl from a respectable family. But if the young man got away with it . . . he typically suffered no reputational harm.

For young women, on the other hand, premarital sex posed extraordinary risks. The first and largest of these risks was pregnancy. The best outcome that pregnancy could produce was a shotgun wedding. A furtive stay at a home for unwed mothers or an illegal, and perhaps dangerous, abortion represented the only alternatives to that wedding. Even if pregnancy was averted, the young woman who engaged in premarital sex risked serious reputational loss. "Nice" girls did not; "fast" girls who did faced gossip, snickers, and damaged marriage prospects.

During the 1960s, technology and social change combined to change these traditional norms. The new birth control pill offered young women, for the first time, near certain protection from pregnancy. . . . The women's movement offered [these young women] the chance to imagine gaining what had always been male prerogatives, including the possibility of premarital sex without reputational loss. And the social upheaval that accompanied the civil rights movement and Vietnam War produced a new world in which the vision of sex without reputational harm became a reality. . . .

Nat'l Marriage Project, Social Indicators of Marital Health & Well-Being: Trends of the Past Five Decades: Unmarried Cohabitation

in The State of Our Unions: Marriage in America 76-77 (2012)

Between 1960 and 2009 . . . , the number of cohabiting couples in the United States increased more than fifteenfold. About a quarter of unmarried women age 25 to 39 are currently living with a partner, and an additional quarter has lived with a partner at some time in the past. More than 60 percent of first marriages are now preceded by living together, compared to virtually none 50 years ago. . . .

Cohabitation is more common among those of lower educational and income levels. Among women in the 25 to 44 age range, 75 percent of those who never completed high school have cohabited, compared to 50 percent of college graduates. Cohabitation is also more common among those who are less religious than their peers, those who have been divorced, and those who have experienced parental divorce, fatherlessness, or high levels of marital discord during childhood. A growing percentage of cohabiting-couple households, now over 40 percent, contain children.

The belief that living together before marriage is a useful way "to find out whether you really get along," and thus avoid a bad marriage and an eventual divorce, is now widespread among young people. But the available data on the effects of cohabitation fail to confirm this belief. In fact, a substantial body of evidence indicates that those who live together before marriage are more likely to break up after marriage.

This evidence is controversial, however, because it is difficult to distinguish the *selection effect* from the *experience of cohabitation effect*. The selection effect refers to the fact that people who cohabit before marriage have different characteristics from those who do not, and it may be these characteristics, and not the experience of cohabitation, that leads to marital instability. . . . What can be said for certain is that no research from the United States has yet been found that those who cohabit before marriage have stronger marriages than those who do not.

Social Trends Institute, Global Family Structure

http://sustaindemographicdividend.org/articles/international-family -indicators/global-family-structure

[N]ot surprisingly, cohabitation is more common in countries with comparatively low marriage rates, and uncommon where marriage is stronger. There are several countries where less than 2 percent of adults are living together but unmarried: China, Taiwan, South Korea, Japan, Indonesia, Malaysia, Egypt, Saudi Arabia, and Nigeria. This list primarily consists of the high marriage-rate countries of Asia and the Middle East. . . .

There is considerable variation in cohabitation levels across Africa. For example, [the decline in cohabitation in Nigeria from 7 percent in 1990 to

1 percent in 2008] may be linked to religious changes in the country, as Islamic and evangelical Protestant groups have tried to assert more control over young adult sexuality in recent years. . . . In contrast, cohabitation is 4 percent in Kenya and 11 percent in South Africa.

Among European countries, Poland, Spain, and Italy have relatively low cohabitation rates, while France and Sweden have some of the highest rates. Cohabitation is obviously common in the Americas, but Colombia is still an outlier at 31 percent, 13 percentage points higher than even Sweden, the leader in cohabitation in Europe at 18 percent. However, it is important to note that consensual unions have a long history in Latin America, where they often function much like legal marriages and are typically more stable than cohabiting unions in North America.

When these statistics are taken together, adults in Asian countries are more likely to marry and less likely to cohabit than their counterparts in other regions, but the stability of their marriages has declined over time. Middle Eastern countries have not witnessed this same rise in divorce, and for them cohabitation is essentially nonexistent; consequently, these countries appear to maintain a traditional attitude toward marriage. Countries in Latin America exhibited low divorce rates in the 1970s (divorce was illegal in some of our target countries in 1970), but since that time, rising rates of divorce and high rates of cohabitation in many South and Central American countries demonstrate that marriage is not as normative a part of the adult life course in this region as it is in Asia and the Middle East. African adults are also spending fewer of their adult years married than they did in the past. . . .

Canada more closely resembles a European country than its neighbor, the United States. Similarly, Australia and New Zealand have marriage, divorce, and cohabitation rates that look more like Europe than like their Southeast Asian neighbors. Overall, then, marriage continues to play a strong role in guiding the adult life course in Asia and the Middle East, while its hold is somewhat weaker on nations in Africa, the Americas, Europe, and Oceania.

Postscript. Some countries and some U.S. states have formal legal statuses other than marriage that couples can enter into. For example, France has a famous and frequently used alternative relationship status—*pacte civil de solidarité,* or PACS—created by the French Parliament in 1999. French PACS confer the right to file joint tax returns, exempt partners from inheritance taxes, permit partners to share insurance policies, ease access to residency permits for foreigners, and make partners responsible for each other's debts. PACS are available to both same-sex and different-sex couples.

In the United States, much of the impetus for the creation of these marriage-alternative statuses was the exclusion of same-sex couples from marriage.[7] After nationwide marriage equality was achieved, some states that previously had

---

[7]. See, e.g., William N. Eskridge Jr., Family Law Pluralism: A Guided-Choice Regime of Menus, and Override Rules, 100 Geo. L.J. 1881 (2012); Douglas NeJaime, Before Marriage: The Unexplored History of Nonmarital Recognition and Its Relationship to Marriage, 102 Cal. L. Rev. 87 (2014).

alternative statuses phrased them out.[8] Some jurisdictions continue to allow couples to enter into these statuses. Contrary to the experience of some other countries including France, however, here in the United States very few people have entered into these alternative statuses in the wake of the Supreme Court's decision in *Obergefell*.

2. Sanctions (Criminal/Noncriminal) Based on Nonmarital Status

Traditionally, nonmarital cohabitation and "fornication" (i.e., sex between people who are not married to each other) were subject to criminal sanctions. Criminalization was aimed at prohibiting the affront to public morals and also at encouraging marriage. Criminal sanctions also attempted to discourage the birth of nonmarital children.

Efforts to revise or repeal criminal statutes against cohabitation and fornication began in the 1950s. The Model Penal Code (MPC) proposed criminalizing cohabitation only if it was "open and notorious."[9] Subsequently, the ALI Council voted to delete the MPC section because the law was seldom enforced, inconsistent with the widespread policy of nonenforcement of moral standards, without deterrent value, and prone to discriminatory enforcement.[10] Many states followed suit by liberalizing the law. In the wake of Lawrence v. Texas, a number of courts held unconstitutional remaining laws criminalizing cohabitation and fornication. In addition to criminal penalties, some individuals in nonmarital relationships were (and still are) subjected to noncriminal sanctions. Consider the following case. As you read it, consider whether it would be permissible to subject people to these noncriminal sanctions today, in the wake of the *Lawrence* decision.

SHAHAR v. BOWERS
114 F.3d 1097 (11th Cir. 1997)

EDMONDSON, Circuit Judge:

[Plaintiff Robin Shahar, a law student, worked as a law clerk with Georgia Attorney General Michael J. Bowers. In September 1990, the Attorney General offered Shahar the position of staff attorney when she graduated from law school. Shahar accepted the offer and was scheduled to begin work in September 1991.]

In the summer of 1990, Shahar began making plans for her "wedding." [She] and her partner invited approximately 250 people, including two Department employees, to the "wedding." The written invitations characterized the ceremony as a "Jewish, lesbian-feminist, outdoor wedding." The ceremony took place in a public park in South Carolina in June 1991.

In November 1990, Shahar filled out the required application for a Staff Attorney position. In response to the question on "marital status," Shahar indicated that

---

[8]. See, e.g., Kaiponanea T. Matsumura, A Right Not to Marry, 84 Fordham L. Rev. 1509, 1518 (2016).

[9]. MPC §207.1 (Tent. Draft No. 4, 1955).

[10]. Id. at cmt.

she was "engaged." She altered "spouse's name" to read "future spouse's name" and filled in her partner's name: "Francine M. Greenfield." In response to the question "Do any of your relatives work for the State of Georgia?" she filled in the name of her partner as follows: "Francine Greenfield, future spouse."

Sometime in the spring of 1991, Shahar and her partner were working on their "wedding" invitations at an Atlanta restaurant. [While there, they met a paralegal and staff attorney, Susan Rutherford, from the Attorney General's office and mentioned to them the wedding preparations.] In June 1991, Shahar told Deputy Attorney General Robert Coleman that she was getting married at the end of July, changing her last name, taking a trip to Greece and, accordingly, would not be starting work with the Department until mid-to-late September. At this point, Shahar did not say that she was "marrying" another woman. [Eventually, word got out that] Shahar was planning on "marrying" another woman. This revelation caused a stir.

Senior aides to the Attorney General became concerned about what they viewed as potential problems in the office resulting from the Department's employment of a Staff Attorney who purported to be part of a same-sex "marriage." Upon the Attorney General's return to the office, he was informed of the situation [and withdrew Shahar's offer by stating that it has]:

> become necessary in light of information which has only recently come to my attention relating to a purported marriage between you and another woman. As chief legal officer of this state, inaction on my part would constitute tacit approval of this purported marriage and jeopardize the proper functioning of this office.

[Shahar instituted suit seeking damages, injunctive relief, and "reinstatement." She argued that revocation of the employment offer based on her purported "marriage" to another woman violated the rights to free exercise and association, equal protection, and substantive due process. The district court granted the Attorney General's motion for summary judgment.]

Even when we assume, for argument's sake, that either the right to intimate association or the right to expressive association or both are present, we know they are not absolute. Georgia and its elected Attorney General also have rights and duties which must be taken into account. . . . In reviewing Shahar's claim, we stress that this case is about the government acting as employer.

Shahar argues that we must review the withdrawal of her job offer under strict scrutiny. The only precedent to which Shahar refers us for the proposition that strict scrutiny is to be applied to the government as employer is Dike v. School Board, 650 F.2d 783 (5th Cir. 1981). In Dike, the Fifth Circuit—our predecessor—implied that a school district's refusal to allow a teacher to breast-feed her child on her lunch hour must withstand strict scrutiny. To the extent that Dike might be interpreted as requiring strict scrutiny review of a government employee's freedom of intimate association claim, it misstates the appropriate standard; and we overrule it now. . . . We conclude that the appropriate test for evaluating the constitutional implications of the State of Georgia's decision [is] the same test as the test for evaluating the constitutional implications of a government employer's decision based on an employee's exercise of her right to free speech, that is, the Pickering [Pickering v. Board of Educ., 391 U.S. 563 (1968)] balancing test. . . .

To decide this case, we are willing to accord Shahar's claimed associational rights (which we have assumed to exist) substantial weight. But, we know that the weight due intimate associational rights, such as those involved in even a state-authorized marriage, can be overcome by a government employer's interest in maintaining the effective functioning of his office.

In weighing her interest in her associational rights, Shahar asks us also to consider the "nonemployment related context" of her "wedding" and "marriage" and that "[s]he took no action to transform her intimate association into a public or political statement." In addition, Shahar says that we should take into account that she has affirmatively disavowed a right to benefits from the Department based on her "marriage."

To the extent that Shahar disclaims benefits bestowed by the State based on marriage, she is merely acknowledging what is undisputed, that Georgia law does not and has not recognized homosexual marriage. We fail to see how that technical acknowledgment counts for much in the balance.

If Shahar is arguing that she does not hold herself out as "married," the undisputed facts are to the contrary. Department employees, among many others, were invited to a "Jewish, lesbian-feminist, outdoor wedding" which included exchanging wedding rings: the wearing of a wedding ring is an outward sign of having entered into marriage. Shahar listed her "marital status" on her employment application as "engaged" and indicated that her future spouse was a woman. She and her partner have both legally changed their family name to Shahar by filing a name change petition with the Fulton County Superior Court. They sought and received the married rate on their insurance. And, they, together, own the house in which they cohabit. These things were not done secretly, but openly.

[T]he Attorney General's worry about his office being involved in litigation in which Shahar's special personal interest might appear to be in conflict with the State's position [is] not unreasonable. In addition, the Department, when the job offer was withdrawn, had already engaged in and won a recent battle [Bowers v. Hardwick, 478 U.S. 186 (1986)] about homosexual sodomy—highly visible litigation in which its lawyers worked to uphold the lawful prohibition of homosexual sodomy. This history makes it particularly reasonable for the Attorney General to worry about the internal consequences for his professional staff (for example, loss of morale, loss of cohesiveness and so forth) of allowing a lawyer, who openly—for instance, on her employment application and in statements to coworkers—represents herself to be "married" to a person of the same sex, to become part of his staff. . . .

Shahar also argues that, at the Department, she would have handled mostly death penalty appeals and that the *Pickering* test requires evidence of potential interference with these particular duties. Even assuming Shahar is correct about her likely assignment within the Department, a particularized showing of interference with the provision of public services is not required. [I]t is not for this court to tie the Department's hands by telling it which Staff Attorneys may be assigned to which cases or duties or to force upon the Attorney General a Staff Attorney of limited utility.

. . . Shahar argues that [the Attorney General] may not justify his decision by reference to perceived public hostility to her "marriage." We have held otherwise about the significance of public perception when law enforcement is involved. [A]ssessing what the public perceives about the Attorney General and the Law Department is a judgment for the Attorney General to make in the day-to-day course of filling his proper role as the elected head of the Department, not for the federal judiciary to make with hindsight or from a safe distance away from the distress and disturbance that might result if the decision was mistaken. . . .

Shahar says that by taking into account these concerns about public reaction, the Attorney General impermissibly discriminated against homosexuals; and she refers us to the Supreme Court's recent decision in Romer v. Evans, [517 U.S. 620 (1996)]. In *Romer*, the Supreme Court struck down an amendment to a state constitution as irrational because the amendment's sole purpose was to disadvantage a particular class of people (to "den[y] them protection across the board"), and because the government engaged in "classification of persons undertaken for its own sake, something the Equal Protection Clause does not permit."

Romer is about people's condition; this case is about a person's conduct. And, *Romer* is no employment case. Considering (in deciding to revoke a job offer) public reaction to a future Staff Attorney's conduct in taking part in a same-sex "wedding" and subsequent "marriage" is not the same kind of decision as an across-the-board denial of legal protection to a group because of their condition, that is, sexual orientation or preference.

This case is about the powers of government as an employer, powers which are far broader than government's powers as sovereign. In addition, the employment in this case is of a special kind: employment involving access to the employer's confidences, acting as the employer's spokesperson, and helping to make policy. This kind of employment is one in which the employer's interest has been given especially great weight in the past. Furthermore, the employment in this case is employment with responsibilities directly impacting on the enforcement of a state's laws: a kind of employment in which appearances and public perceptions and public confidence count a lot.

Particularly considering this Attorney General's many years of experience and Georgia's recent legal history, we cannot say that he was unreasonable to think that Shahar's acts were likely to cause the public to be confused and to question the Law Department's credibility; to interfere with the Law Department's ability to handle certain controversial matters, including enforcing the law against homosexual sodomy; and to endanger working relationships inside the Department. We also cannot say that the Attorney General was unreasonable to lose confidence in Shahar's ability to make good judgments as a lawyer for the Law Department.

[W]e hold that the Attorney General's interest—that is, the State of Georgia's interest—as an employer in promoting the efficiency of the Law Department's important public service does outweigh Shahar's personal associational interests. . . . Georgia's Attorney General has made a personnel decision which none of the asserted federal constitutional provisions prohibited him from making. . . .

NOTE: WHO IS ROBIN SHAHAR?

Postscript by Robin Shahar
Personal communication, Aug. 8, 2023

I worked in the City of Atlanta Law Department for 26 years, beginning in 1993. During my last six years, in addition to being an Atlanta Chief Counsel, I served as the Mayor's Advisor on LGBT Issues. My Advisor role allowed me to learn the challenges faced by the City's LGBTQ citizens and influence the City's

Robin Shahar, the plaintiff in Shahar v. Bowers

laws and policies accordingly. Over time, the position expanded to include human rights work more generally.

In 2019, I was deeply concerned that human rights advances in the United States were increasingly in jeopardy. I no longer wanted to divide my professional efforts between my Chief Counsel and LGBT Advisor duties; I retired from the City to work full time on human rights. I now have my own practice and focus primarily on criminal justice reform and voter protection (which is a pressing issue in Georgia).

As a former plaintiff in a lesbian/ gay employment discrimination case, I was moved by the Supreme Court's 2020 decision in Bostock v. Clayton County, Georgia which held that Title VII prohibits employers from discriminating based on sexual orientation and gender identity. When my attorneys filed the Shahar v. Bowers complaint in 1991, the claims were based solely on the United States Constitution. It was inconceivable that Title VII would protect lesbians and gay men – so inconceivable that Mr. Bowers stated his reason for termination in his dismissal letter to me. Twenty-nine years later, a solid majority of Supreme Court Justices afforded desperately needed protection to LGBT employees across the country.

Notes and Questions

1. Epilogue. One week after the ruling in *Shahar*, the former state Attorney General Michael Bowers confessed his 15-year adulterous affair with a former employee. Shahar promptly filed a motion for rehearing, arguing that Bowers's prohibited conduct under Georgia law undermined the court's reasoning. The Eleventh Circuit denied her petition, saying that she was terminated not because of her sexual conduct, but because of her public celebration of her relationship. Bowers subsequently changed his view on employment discrimination based on sexual orientation. Bowers has publicly and emphatically opined that firing people because of their sexual orientation is "dumb, plain dumb." With respect to his decision to fire Shahar in 1991, Mr. Bowers stated: "I wish it had never happened."[11]

2. State interests. Shahar argued that her constitutional rights were violated because she lost her offer of employment at the hands of a state actor. The appellate

---

[11]. Both direct quotes are cited in Robin McDonald & Kathleen Baydala Joyner, ExAG Bowers: Religious Freedom Bills are "Ill-Conceived" and "Mean-Spirited," Fulton Cty. Daily Rep., Feb. 24, 2015, http://www.dailyreportonline.com/id=1202718840481/ExAG-Bowers-Religious-Freedom-Bills-Are-IllConceived-and-MeanSpirited?slreturn=20150608114424.

court relied on the *Pickering* balancing test because of the state-employer's special interests. Do you believe that plaintiff's nonmarital same-sex relationship would have interfered with the performance of her daily duties? What role should public perception play in employment decisions involving state actors?

3. Impact of *Lawrence*. The *Shahar* court reached its decision six years before the Supreme Court decided Lawrence v. Texas (which overturned Bowers v. Hardwick). What effect, if any, might *Lawrence* have had on the result in *Shahar*?

4. Public versus private. Does the *Shahar* decision suggest that the plaintiff was fired because she made her relationship "public"? While cases like Shahar's are less common today than they were in the 1990s, lesbian, gay, bisexual, transgender, and queer/questioning (LGBTQ) workers continue to face discrimination in the workplace. A 2018 study, for example, found that 1 in 5 LGBTQ workers reported "having been told or had coworkers imply that they should dress in a more feminine or masculine manner" and "53% of LGBTQ+ workers report hearing jokes about lesbian or gay people at least once in a while."[12] Data also reveal that almost half of LGBTQ employees remain closeted at work, even in the wake of the *Obergefell* decision and nationwide marriage equality.

Some workers continue to experience workplace discrimination for being open about their sexual orientation or gender identity. For example, in a 2018 Texas case, a schoolteacher at Charlotte Anderson Elementary School in Arlington, Texas, filed suit against her school district for suspending her for making her sexual orientation public to her students. She was terminated after a parent complained that she had shown a picture of herself and her then-partner (later wife) to her students.[13]

5. Employment discrimination: Sexual orientation and gender identity. In June 2020, the U.S. Supreme Court ruled that the federal law prohibiting sex discrimination in employment—Title VII of the Civil Rights Act of 1964—covers discrimination based on sexual orientation and gender identity. Bostock v. Clayton Cty., 140 S. Ct. 1731 (2020). Writing for the Court, Justice Gorsuch explained that "it is impossible to discriminate against a person for being homosexual or transgender without discriminating against that individual based on sex." *Bostock*, 140 S. Ct. at 1741. Justice Alito dissented. Among other things, Alito highlighted the likely impact of the decision on many other federal statutes that also prohibit sex discrimination, including Title IX, the Affordable Care Act (ACA), and the Fair Housing Act.

Consistent with Justice Alito's prediction, in 2021, relying on the *Bostock* decision, the U.S. Departments of Housing and Urban Development, Justice Department, Department of Health and Human Services, and Department of Education issued guidance documents clarifying that various federal statutes

---

[12]. Human Rights Campaign, A Workplace Divided: Understanding the Climate for LGBTQ Workers Nationwide (2018), https://www.hrc.org/resources/a-workplace-divided-understanding-the-climate-for-lgbtq-workers-nationwide.

[13]. Christine Hauser, Texas Teacher Showed a Photo of Her Wife, and Was Barred from the Classroom, N.Y. Times, May 10, 2018, https://www.nytimes.com/2018/05/10/us/gay-teachers-wife-texas.html.

prohibiting sex discrimination prohibit discrimination against LGBTQ individuals.[14] At the state level, more than 20 states and the District of Columbia have laws prohibiting employment discrimination based on sexual orientation and gender identity (but not Georgia, the setting of the principal case).[15]

6. Military discharge: Sexual orientation and gender identity. In the past, LGB service members faced discharge if they revealed their sexual orientation. The military policy of "Don't Ask, Don't Tell" (DADT), 10 U.S.C. §654, required the discharge from the military of any person who disclosed that they were lesbian, gay, or bisexual or engaged in any "homosexual conduct." Following the enactment of the DADT policy in 1993, the military discharged more than 10,000 people under the policy.[16] Congress repealed DADT in 2012.

In addition, historically, service members could be discharged for being transgender. In 2016, transgender troops began serving openly after the Obama Administration lifted the ban for those service members already in military service. The military set July 1, 2017 as the date when transgender people would be allowed to enlist. However, before that date, the Trump Administration banned transgender people from serving or enlisting. Shortly after he took office, President Biden issued an executive order that restored and expanded Obama-era protections that opened the armed services to transgender service personnel.[17]

7. Employment discrimination and marital status. Unmarried couples—different-sex and same-sex—may also face adverse employment actions, especially if one or both partners work in the public sector. Does *Lawrence* preclude such actions? See Coker v. Whittington, 858 F.3d 304 (5th Cir. 2017) (holding that termination of police officers for nonmarital cohabitation with each other's wives did not violate the constitutional right to privacy based on the public interest in maintaining cohesive police force and upholding the reputation of the department). See generally Melissa Murray, Accommodating Nonmarriage, 88 S. Cal. L. Rev. 6611 (2015) (exploring cases in which individuals experienced discrimination by virtue of being in a nonmarital relationship).

8. Housing discrimination and marital status. Unmarried couples also sometimes face housing discrimination by landlords, real estate agents, and property owners who reject their applications or charge them higher rent. In terms of state protections, only about half the states ban housing discrimination based on "marital status." Even in some of these states, it is not clear that the statutory protection applies to *unmarried* couples rather than simply to those persons who are single, married, or divorced. In states without statutory protection against

[14]. Sharita Gruberg, Beyond *Bostock*: The Future of LGBTQ Civil Rights, Ctr. for Am. Progress News, Aug. 26, 2020, https://www.americanprogress.org/issues/lgbtq-rights/reports /2020/08/26/489772/beyond-bostock-future-lgbtq-civil-rights/.

[15]. Human Rights Campaign, State Maps of Laws and Policies, Employment, June 7, 2019, https://www.hrc.org/state-maps/employment.

[16]. Carolyn Lochhead, "Don't Ask" Repeal Losing Momentum, S.F. Chron., May 8, 2009, at A16.

[17]. See Helene Cooper, Biden Ends Trump Ban on Transgender Troops and Opens Path to Transition Care, N.Y. Times, Apr. 1, 2021, p. A12; Dan De Luce & Shannon Pettypiece, Biden Admin Scraps Trump's Restrictions on Transgender Troops, Mar. 31, 2021, https://www.nbcnews .com/news/military/biden-admin-scraps-trump-s-restrictions-transgender-troops-n1262646.

housing discrimination, landlords may not be legally barred from refusing to rent to unmarried couples. Courts in only a few states have ruled explicitly that the term "marital status" in state housing discrimination laws applies to unmarried couples.[18] Should states ban housing discrimination against people based on their status of being in a nonmarital relationship? Why or why not?

9. Religious and/or morality defense. Landlords' refusal to rent to people in nonmarital relationships and employer's actions against employees is sometimes based on religious or moral grounds. Is the First Amendment a valid defense to violations of federal and/or state housing antidiscrimination laws? See Smith v. Fair Emp. & Hous. Comm'n, 913 P.2d 909 (Cal. 1996); Swanner v. Anchorage Equal Rights Comm'n, 874 P.2d 274 (Alaska 1994). Does the Supreme Court's decision in *303 Creative* (excerpted in Chapter II) have any impact on the issue?[19]

3. Extension of Rights and Protections

After Lawrence v. Texas (2003), nonmarital relationships are no longer considered criminal. But are nonmarital relationships entitled to *protections,* either during the intact relationship or upon dissolution, based on the relationship, either with respect to each other, or as against third parties or the government?[20]

a. Unmarried Couples' Rights Inter Se

MARVIN v. MARVIN
557 P.2d 106 (Cal. 1976)

TOBRINER, Justice.

During the past 15 years, there has been a substantial increase in the number of couples living together without marrying. Such nonmarital relationships lead to

---

[18]. See, e.g., Courtney G. Joslin, Marital Status Discrimination 2.0, 95 B.U. L. Rev. 805 (2015) (exploring existing laws prohibiting marital status discrimination and how they have been interpreted and applied); Nicole Buonocore Porter, Marital Status Discrimination: A Proposal for Title VII Protection, 46 Wayne L. Rev. 1, 15 (2000).

[19]. For discussions of these questions, see, e.g., Andrew Koppelman, Gay Rights, Religious Accommodations, and the Purposes of Antidiscrimination Law, 88 S. Cal. L. Rev. 619 (2015); Douglas Laycock & Thomas C. Berg, Protecting Same-Sex Marriage and Religious Liberty, 99 Va. L. Rev. In Brief 1 (2013); Ira C. Lupu & Robert W. Tuttle, Same-Sex Family Equality and Religious Freedom, 5 Nw. J. L. & Soc. Pol'y 274, 276 (2010); Douglas NeJaime & Reva B. Siegel, Conscience Wars: Complicity-Based Complicity Claims in Religion and Politics, 124 Yale L.J. 2516 (2015); Douglas NeJaime, Marriage Inequality: Same-Sex Relationships, Religious Exemptions, and the Production of Sexual Orientation Discrimination, 100 Calif. L. Rev. 1169 (2012); Elizabeth Sepper, Free Speech and the "Unique Evils" of Public Accommodations Discrimination, 2020 U. Chi. Legal F. 273 (2020); Elizabeth Sepper, Doctoring Discrimination in the Same-Sex Marriage Debates, 89 Ind. L.J. 703 (2014).

[20]. Clare Huntington, Postmarital Family Law: A Legal Structure for Nonmarital Families, 67 Stan. L. Rev. 167, 178-179 (2015) ("In the case of certain rights and privileges, legislatures and courts believe marriage is a necessary condition for receipt of benefits.").

legal controversy when one partner dies or the couple separates. Courts of Appeal, faced with the task of determining property rights in such cases, have arrived at conflicting positions. . . . We take this opportunity to resolve that controversy and to declare the principles which should govern distribution of property acquired in a nonmarital relationship. . . .

. . . In the instant case plaintiff and defendant lived together for seven years without marrying; all property acquired during this period was taken in defendant's name. When plaintiff sued to enforce a contract under which she was entitled to half the property and to support payments, the trial court granted judgment on the pleadings for defendant, thus leaving him with all property accumulated by the couple. [Plaintiff appeals.]

Plaintiff avers that in October of 1964 she and defendant "entered into an oral agreement" that while "the parties lived together they would combine their efforts and earnings and would share equally any and all property accumulated as a result of their efforts whether individual or combined." Furthermore, they agreed to "hold themselves out to the general public as husband and wife" and that "plaintiff would further render her services as a companion, homemaker, housekeeper and cook to . . . defendant."

Shortly thereafter plaintiff agreed to "give up her lucrative career as an entertainer [and] singer" in order to "devote her full time to defendant . . . as a companion, homemaker, housekeeper and cook"; in return defendant agreed to "provide for all of plaintiff's financial support and needs for the rest of her life."

Plaintiff alleges that she lived with defendant from October of 1964 through May of 1970 and fulfilled her obligations under the agreement. During this period the parties as a result of their efforts and earnings acquired in defendant's name substantial real and personal property, including motion picture rights worth over $1 million. In May of 1970, however, defendant compelled plaintiff to leave his household. He continued to support plaintiff until November of 1971, but thereafter refused to provide further support. . . .

[D]efendant offers some four theories to sustain the ruling. . . . Defendant first and principally relies on the contention that the alleged contract is so closely related to the supposed "immoral" character of the relationship between plaintiff and himself that the enforcement of the contract would violate public policy. He points to cases asserting that a contract between nonmarital partners is unenforceable if it is "involved in" an illicit relationship. A review of the numerous California decisions concerning contracts between nonmarital partners, however, reveals that the courts have not employed such broad and uncertain standards to strike down contracts. The decisions instead disclose a narrower and more precise standard: a contract between nonmarital partners is unenforceable only *to the extent* that it *explicitly* rests upon the immoral and illicit consideration of meretricious sexual services. . . .

Although the past decisions hover over the issue in the somewhat wispy form of the figures of a Chagall painting, we can abstract from those decisions a clear and simple rule. The fact that a man and woman live together without marriage, and engage in a sexual relationship, does not in itself invalidate agreements between them relating to their earnings, property, or expenses. Neither is such an agreement invalid merely because the parties may have contemplated the creation or continuation of a nonmarital relationship when they entered into it. Agreements between nonmarital partners fail only to the extent that they rest upon a consideration of meretricious sexual services. Thus the rule asserted by defendant, that a contract fails if it is "involved in" or made "in contemplation" of a nonmarital relationship, cannot be reconciled with the decisions. . . .

The principle that a contract between nonmarital partners will be enforced unless expressly and inseparably based upon an illicit consideration of sexual services not only represents the distillation of the decisional law, but also offers a far more precise and workable standard than that advocated by defendant. [A] standard which inquires whether an agreement is "involved" in or "contemplates" a nonmarital relationship is vague and unworkable. Virtually all agreements between nonmarital partners can be said to be "involved" in some sense in the fact of their mutual sexual relationship, or to "contemplate" the existence of that relationship. Thus defendant's proposed standards, if taken literally, might invalidate all agreements between nonmarital partners, a result no one favors. Moreover, those standards offer no basis to distinguish between valid and invalid agreements. By looking not to such uncertain tests, but only to the consideration underlying the agreement, we provide the parties and the courts with a practical guide to determine when an agreement between nonmarital partners should be enforced.

Defendant secondly relies upon the ground suggested by the trial court: that the 1964 contract violated public policy because it impaired the community property rights of Betty Marvin, defendant's lawful wife. . . . In the present case Betty Marvin, the aggrieved spouse, had the opportunity to assert her community property rights in the divorce action. . . . Defendant's third contention is [that] that enforcement of the oral agreement between plaintiff and himself is barred by Civil Code section 5134, which provides that "All contracts for marriage settlements must be in writing. . . ." A marriage settlement, however, is an agreement in contemplation of marriage. . . . The contract at issue here does not conceivably fall within that definition. [The court also rejected "as a rather strained contention" the defendant's fourth argument that the plaintiff was asserting a claim for breach of promise to marry, barred by statute.]

In summary, we base our opinion on the principle that adults who voluntarily live together and engage in sexual relations are nonetheless as competent as any other persons to contract respecting their earnings and property rights. Of course, they cannot lawfully contract to pay for the performance of sexual services, for such a contract is, in essence, an agreement for prostitution and unlawful for that reason. . . . So long as the agreement does not rest upon illicit meretricious consideration, the parties may order their economic affairs as they choose, and no policy precludes the courts from enforcing such agreements.

In the present instance, plaintiff alleges that the parties agreed to pool their earnings, that they contracted to share equally in all property acquired, and that defendant agreed to support plaintiff. The terms of the contract as alleged do not rest upon any unlawful consideration. We therefore conclude that the complaint furnishes a suitable basis upon which the trial court can render declaratory relief. . . .

As we have noted, both causes of action in plaintiff's complaint allege an express contract; neither assert any basis for relief independent from the contract. In In re Marriage of Cary, [109 Cal. Rptr. 862 (1973),] however, the Court of Appeal held that, in view of the policy of the Family Law Act, property accumulated by nonmarital partners in an actual family relationship should be divided equally. . . . Although our conclusion that plaintiff's complaint states a cause of action based on an express contract alone compels us to reverse the judgment for defendant, resolution of the *Cary* issue will serve both to guide the parties upon retrial and to resolve a conflict presently manifest in published Court of Appeal decisions. . . .

[A]s of 1973, the time of the filing of In re Marriage of Cary, the cases apparently held that a nonmarital partner who rendered services in the absence of express contract could assert no right to property acquired during the relationship. The facts of *Cary* demonstrated the unfairness of that rule. Janet and Paul Cary had lived together, unmarried, for more than eight years. They held themselves out to friends and family as husband and wife, reared four children, purchased a home and other property, obtained credit, filed joint income tax returns, and otherwise conducted themselves as though they were married. Paul worked outside the home, and Janet generally cared for the house and children.

In 1971 Paul petitioned for "nullity of the marriage." [T]he trial court awarded Janet half the property acquired during the relationship, although all such property was traceable to Paul's earnings. The Court of Appeal affirmed the award [reasoning that prior cases that denied relief were based] upon a policy of punishing persons guilty of cohabitation without marriage. The Family Law Act, the court observed, aimed to eliminate fault or guilt as a basis for dividing marital property. But once fault or guilt is excluded, the court reasoned, nothing distinguishes the property rights of a nonmarital "spouse" from those of a putative spouse. Since the latter is entitled to half the "quasi marital property," the Court of Appeal concluded that, giving effect to the policy of the Family Law Act, a nonmarital cohabitator should also be entitled to half the property accumulated during an "actual family relationship."

Cary met with a mixed reception in other appellate districts. [W]e agree [with the view] that *Cary* distends the act. No language in the Family Law Act addresses the property rights of nonmarital partners, and nothing in the legislative history of the act suggests that the Legislature considered that subject. [A]lthough we reject the reasoning of *Cary* . . ., we share the perception [that] the application of former precedent in the factual setting of those cases would work an unfair distribution of the property accumulated by the couple. . . . The principal reason why the pre-*Cary* decisions result in an unfair distribution of property inheres in the court's refusal to permit a nonmarital partner to assert rights based upon accepted principles of implied contract or equity. We have examined the reasons advanced to justify this denial of relief, and find that none have merit.

First, we note that the cases denying relief do not rest their refusal upon any theory of "punishing" a "guilty" partner. Indeed, to the extent that denial of relief "punishes" one partner, it necessarily rewards the other by permitting him to retain a disproportionate amount of the property. Concepts of "guilt" thus cannot justify an unequal division of property between two equally "guilty" persons.

Other reasons advanced in the decisions fare no better. The principal argument seems to be that "[e]quitable considerations arising from the reasonable expectation of . . . benefits attending the status of marriage . . . are not present (in a nonmarital relationship)" [Vallera v. Vallera, 134 P.2d 761, 763 (Cal. 1943)]. But, although parties to a nonmarital relationship obviously cannot have based any expectations upon the belief that they were married, other expectations and equitable considerations remain. The parties may well expect that property will be divided in accord with the parties' own tacit understanding and that in the absence of such understanding the courts will fairly apportion property accumulated through mutual effort. We need not treat nonmarital partners as putatively married persons in order to apply principles of implied contract, or extend equitable remedies; we need to treat them only as we do any other unmarried persons.

The remaining arguments advanced from time to time to deny remedies to the nonmarital partners are of less moment. There is no more reason to presume that services are contributed as a gift than to presume that funds are contributed as a gift; in any event the better approach is to presume . . . "that the parties intend to deal fairly with each other."

The argument that granting remedies to the nonmarital partners would discourage marriage [also] must fail. . . . Although we recognize the well-established public policy to foster and promote the institution of marriage, perpetuation of judicial rules which result in an inequitable distribution of property accumulated during a nonmarital relationship is neither a just nor an effective way of carrying out that policy.

[W]e believe that the prevalence of nonmarital relationships in modern society and the social acceptance of them, marks this as a time when our courts should by no means apply the doctrine of the unlawfulness of the so-called meretricious relationship to the instant case. As we have explained, the nonenforceability of agreements expressly providing for meretricious conduct rested upon the fact that such conduct, as the word suggests, pertained to and encompassed prostitution. To equate the nonmarital relationship of today to such a subject matter is to do violence to an accepted and wholly different practice.

We are aware that many young couples live together without the solemnization of marriage, in order to make sure that they can successfully later undertake marriage. This trial period, preliminary to marriage, serves as some assurance that the marriage will not subsequently end in dissolution to the harm of both parties. We are aware, as we have stated, of the pervasiveness of nonmarital relationships in other situations.

The mores of the society have indeed changed so radically in regard to cohabitation that we cannot impose a standard based on alleged moral considerations that have apparently been so widely abandoned by so many. Lest we be misunderstood, however, we take this occasion to point out that the structure of society itself largely depends upon the institution of marriage, and nothing we have said in this opinion should be taken to derogate from that institution. The joining of the man and woman in marriage is at once the most socially productive and individually fulfilling relationship that one can enjoy in the course of a lifetime.

We conclude that the judicial barriers that may stand in the way of a policy based upon the fulfillment of the reasonable expectations of the parties to a nonmarital relationship should be removed. As we have explained, the courts now hold that express agreements will be enforced unless they rest on an unlawful meretricious consideration. We add that in the absence of an express agreement, the courts may look to a variety of other remedies in order to protect the parties' lawful expectations.[24]

---

24. We do not seek to resurrect the doctrine of common law marriage, which was abolished in California by statute in 1895. Thus we do not hold that plaintiff and defendant were "married," nor do we extend to plaintiff the rights which the Family Law Act grants valid or putative spouses; we hold only that she has the same rights to enforce contracts and to assert her equitable interest in property acquired through her effort as does any other unmarried person.

The courts may inquire into the conduct of the parties to determine whether that conduct demonstrates an implied contract or implied agreement of partnership or joint venture, or some other tacit understanding between the parties. The courts may, when appropriate, employ principles of constructive trust. Finally, a nonmarital partner may recover in quantum meruit for the reasonable value of household services rendered less the reasonable value of support received if he can show that he rendered services with the expectation of monetary reward.[25]

Since we have determined that plaintiff's complaint states a cause of action for breach of an express contract, and, as we have explained, can be amended to state a cause of action independent of allegations of express contract, we must conclude that the trial court erred. [Reversed and remanded.]

NOTE: WHO WERE LEE MARVIN AND MICHELLE TRIOLA MARVIN?

Lee Marvin (left) and Michelle Triola Marvin

Lee Marvin was an Oscar-winning actor who was known as the "consummate tough guy."[21] He served in the Marine Corps during World War II and was awarded a Purple Heart. After the war, he stumbled into acting while working as a plumber's assistant at a local theater.[22] He appeared in more than 50 movies and numerous TV shows. Lee Marvin won an Academy Award for his role in the 1965 movie *Cat Ballou*, in which he starred with Jane Fonda. Lee's first marriage in 1952 was to Betty Ebeling. They divorced in 1967 after living apart for a number of years. As the principal case indicates, during part of his marital separation, Lee Marvin lived with Michelle Triola Marvin. After his relationship with Michelle ended, Lee Marvin married again in 1970, this time to Pamela Feeley, his childhood sweetheart. They remained married until his death in 1987.

---

25. Our opinion does not preclude the evolution of additional equitable remedies to protect the expectations of the parties to a nonmarital relationship in cases in which existing remedies prove inadequate; the suitability of such remedies may be determined in later cases in light of the factual setting in which they arise.

[21]. AP Online, Funeral Private for Movie Tough-Guy, Public Memorial Planned in Hollywood, Aug. 31, 1987.

[22]. Sun-Sentinel Wire Services, Marvin Remembered as Tough-Guy Softie, Sept. 1, 1987, 1987 WLNR 1635075.

Michelle Marvin, born Michelle Triola, met Lee Marvin in 1964 while working as an extra with Lee in the movie *Ship of Fools*. Their nonmarital relationship lasted six years. Michelle made history by suing Lee Marvin, seeking a share of the assets he accumulated during their relationship and future support, even though the couple never married. Although Michelle and her attorney, Marvin Mitchelson, established an important precedent for former nonmarital male partners, the ruling was of no help to Michelle herself, as explained below in the Notes and Questions. According to her family spokesperson, Bob Palmer, Michelle "didn't dwell on the case and wasn't bitter."[23] Michelle began a relationship with actor Dick Van Dyke in the late 1970s. They lived together for over 30 years, until Michelle's death in 2009.

BLUMENTHAL v. BREWER
69 N.E.3d 834 (Ill. 2016)

Justice KARMEIER delivered the judgment of the court.

[W]e are called on to consider the continued viability and applicability of our decision in Hewitt v. Hewitt, 394 N.E.2d 1204 (Ill. 1979), which held that Illinois public policy, as set forth in this State's statutory prohibition against common-law marriage, precludes unmarried cohabitants from bringing claims against one another to enforce mutual property rights where the rights asserted are rooted in a marriage-like relationship between the parties.

The issue has arisen here in the context of an action brought by Dr. Jane E. Blumenthal for partition of the family home she shared and jointly owned with Judge Eileen M. Brewer [who had been her domestic partner since 1981]. The couple had maintained a long-term, domestic relationship and raised a family together but had never married. Blumenthal sought partition of the residence when the relationship ended and she moved out. . . .

The facts of the present case are almost indistinguishable from *Hewitt*, except, in this case, the parties were in a same-sex relationship. During the course of their long-term, domestic relationship, Brewer alleges that she and Blumenthal had a relationship that was "identical in every essential way to that of a married couple." Although the parties were not legally married, they acted like a married couple and held themselves out as such. For example, the former domestic partners exchanged rings as a symbol of their commitment to each other, executed wills and trusts, each naming the other as the sole beneficiary of her assets, and appointed each other as fiduciary for financial and medical decision making. Blumenthal and Brewer also began to commingle their personal and financial assets, which allowed them to purchase investment property as well as the Chicago home where they raised their three children.

Much like in *Hewitt*, Brewer alleges that she contributed to Blumenthal's purchase of an ownership interest in the medical group [Gynecologic Specialists of Northwestern S.C., or GSN], helping Blumenthal earn the majority of income for the parties and "thereby guaranteeing the family's financial security." Because

[23]. Daily Record, "Palimony" Figure Michelle Triola Marvin Dies, Oct. 31, 2009, 2009 WLNR 21757062.

Blumenthal was able to earn a high income, Brewer was able to devote more time to raising the couple's children and to attend to other domestic duties. Once Blumenthal's and Brewer's relationship ended, Brewer, like Victoria Hewitt, brought suit seeking various common-law remedies to equalize their assets and receive an interest in Blumenthal's business. . . .

Hewitt clearly declared the law on the very issue in this case. Yet, the appellate court in this case declined to follow our ruling, despite the facts being almost identical to *Hewitt*. This was improper [under the doctrine of stare decisis]. The appellate court was also ill-advised to adopt the reasoning in *Marvin*, given that in *Hewitt* we unquestionably rejected *Marvin*. Determining that the [Illinois] legislature deliberately declined to follow the reasoning in *Marvin*, this court noted that during the time *Marvin* was being decided, the Illinois legislature adopted the civil-law concept of the putative spouse, which involves a situation where a person goes through a marriage ceremony and cohabits with another in the good-faith belief that he or she is validly married. Once the putative spouse learns that the marriage is not valid, his status as a putative spouse terminates because "common law marriages are expressly excluded." This enactment was essential to *Hewitt*'s holding because it provided specific evidence of the General Assembly's intent to depart from *Marvin*'s pure contract theory. . . .

When considering the property rights of unmarried cohabitants, our view of *Hewitt*'s holding has not changed. As in *Hewitt*, the issue before this court cannot appropriately be characterized solely in terms of contract law, nor is it limited to considerations of equity or fairness as between the parties in such marriage-like relationships. These questions undoubtedly involve some of the most fundamental policy concerns in our society. Permitting such claims, as sought by Brewer, would not only impact the institution of marriage but also raise questions pertaining to other family-related issues. . . .

Because rejection of *Hewitt* is essential to her counterclaim, Brewer requests that we revisit the decision and overrule it. [W]e reject Brewer's invitation. . . . According to Brewer's counterclaim, one of the ways Blumenthal and Brewer's domestic relationship was identical to that of a married couple was, among other things, their decision to "commingle[] their personal property and their finances." . . . The decision between Blumenthal and Brewer to commingle their finances and use those joint funds to make property and financial investments demonstrates that the funds were economically dependent on the parties' marriage-like relationship. . . .

Brewer is correct in labeling Blumenthal's and her purchase of GSN as an investment. But it was an investment for the family, which included Blumenthal, Brewer, and their children. It was not an investment between business partners. Nor was it the kind of arm's-length bargain envisioned by traditional contract principles. Rather, the arrangement to use the parties' commingled funds was an arrangement of a fundamentally different kind, which [is] intimately related and dependent on Brewer's marriage-like relationship with Blumenthal. . . . Our decision in *Hewitt* bars such relief if the claim is not independent from the parties' living in a marriage-like relationship for the reason it contravenes the public policy, implicit in the statutory scheme of the Marriage and Dissolution Act, disfavoring the grant of mutually enforceable property rights to knowingly unmarried cohabitants.

Next, Brewer respectfully asks this court to affirm the appellate court's decision, which held in her favor that former cohabitants who live outside the bonds of marriage, but live in a marriage-like relationship, may bring common-law property claims. [According to Brewer,] the state's evolving public policy now contradicts *Hewitt*'s rule [citing state laws on no-fault divorce, the Uniform Parentage Act equalizing the status of nonmarital and marital children, and the rights of unmarried couples to adopt children]. We disagree.

These post-*Hewitt* amendments demonstrate that the legislature knows how to alter family-related statutes and does not hesitate to do so when and if it believes public policy so requires. Nothing in these post-*Hewitt* changes, however, can be interpreted as evincing an intention by the legislature to change the public policy concerning the situation presently before this court. [I]f this court were to recognize the legal status desired by Brewer, we would infringe on the duty of the legislature to set policy in the area of domestic relations. [W]e do not find a compelling reason to reverse course now and depart from our earlier legislative interpretation, especially in light of almost two score years of legislative inaction on the matter. . . .

We also reject Brewer's argument that changes in law since *Hewitt* demonstrate that the "legislature no longer considers withholding protection from nonmarital families to be a legitimate means of advancing the state's interest in marriage." To the contrary, this court finds that the current legislative and judicial trend is to uphold the institution of marriage. Most notably, within the past year, the United States Supreme Court in Obergefell v. Hodges, 135 S. Ct. 2584 (2015), held that same-sex couples cannot be denied the right to marry. In doing so, the Court found that "new insights [from the developments in the institution of marriage over the past centuries] have strengthened, not weakened, the institution of marriage." For the institution of marriage has been a keystone of our social order and "remains a building block of our national community." Accordingly, the Supreme Court invalidated any state legislation prohibiting same-sex marriage because excluding same-sex couples from marriage would be excluding them "from one of civilization's oldest institutions."

While the United States Supreme Court has made clear that "[t]he Constitution . . . does not permit the State to bar same-sex couples from marriage on the same terms as accorded to couples of the opposite sex," nothing in that holding can fairly be construed as requiring states to confer on non-married, same-sex couples common-law rights or remedies not shared by similarly situated non-married couples of the opposite sex. . . .

The determination that the trial court did not err in dismissing Brewer's counterclaim does not end this appeal, for Brewer argues that the continued application of *Hewitt*'s rule would violate the Illinois and federal constitutional guarantees of due process and equal protection. Brewer claims that *Hewitt*'s rule preventing unmarried domestic partners the ability to bring common-law claims available to all other persons, solely because they are in a marriage-like relationship, does not rationally advance a legitimate governmental purpose and that it deliberately seeks to penalize unmarried partners for exercising their constitutionally protected right to enter into an intimate relationship. . . .

We disagree with Brewer's claim that *Hewitt*'s holding denies unmarried domestic partners the ability to bring common-law claims solely because they are in an intimate relationship with another. This court's decision in *Hewitt* only disallows unmarried cohabitants who live in a marriage-like relationship from accessing, under the guise of an implied contract, the rights and protections specified in the Marriage and Dissolution Act. In other words, individuals can enter into an intimate relationship, but the relationship itself cannot form the basis to bring common-law claims. Thus, *Hewitt*'s holding does not prevent or penalize unmarried partners from entering into intimate relationships. Rather, it acknowledges the legislative intent to provide certain rights and benefits to those who participate in the institution of marriage. . . .

Since marriage is a legal relationship that all individuals may or may not enter into, Illinois does not act irrationally or discriminatorily in refusing to grant benefits and protections under the Marriage and Dissolution Act to those who do not participate in the institution of marriage. As noted in *Hewitt* and the line of cases that follow its holding, unmarried individuals may make express or implied contracts with one another, and such contracts will be enforceable if they are not based on a relationship indistinguishable from marriage. Indeed, *Hewitt* did nothing more than effectuate the policy established by the legislature to prevent knowingly unmarried cohabitants from evading the statutory abolition of common-law marriage [by] employing theories of implied contract to achieve the same result. [W]e, therefore, reject Brewer's claims. . . .

Justice THEIS, concurring in part and dissenting in part:

[*Hewitt* etched into Illinois law] the arcane view that domestic partners who choose to cohabit, but not marry, are engaged in "illicit" or "meretricious" behavior at odds with foundational values of "our family-based society." "Meretricious" means "of or relating to a prostitute" (Webster's Third New International Dictionary 1413 (1986)), so this court labeled such people as prostitutes. The majority's attempt to distance itself from *Hewitt*'s sweeping and near-defamatory statement is unconvincing. . . .

To state uncategorically that "our view of *Hewitt*'s holding has not changed" and insist that "it remains good law" is to reaffirm an oddly myopic and moralistic view of cohabitation. The majority assertion that *Hewitt*'s "core reasoning and ultimate holding . . . did not rely nor was dependent on the morality of cohabiting adults" is plainly incorrect because the court's discussion of the role of the legislature in setting public policy on domestic relations and the prohibition of common-law marriage comes as an even-if afterthought. Insulating the institution of marriage from the "changing mores of our society" was the clear impetus for our holding in that case.

To begin its analysis, the *Hewitt* court discussed at length the so-called rule of legality [under which "[a] bargain in whole or in part for or in consideration of illicit sexual intercourse or of a promise thereof is illegal," which was enshrined in the First Restatement of Contracts]. *Hewitt*'s support for the rule of illegality has disappeared. In 1979, Illinois still criminalized cohabitation. [T]he prohibition against cohabitation was repealed in 1990. . . . The Second Restatement of Contracts [1981] deleted the section of the First Restatement quoted in *Hewitt* and ceased to define all bargains between people in intimate relationships as illegal. [T]oday, the treatise recognizes that cohabiting adults are a family and notes, "The courts' treatment of contracts entered into by cohabiting parties evolved in the last part of the twentieth century and is clear evidence of how the courts' view of what might be against public policy varies with changes in society's views." According to the treatise, courts across the country no longer perceive a conflict between the public policies of protecting and encouraging marriage and discouraging any exchange of sexual activity for value and enforcing agreements between former cohabitants.

The treatise also refers to the landmark "palimony" case of Marvin v. Marvin, 557 P.1d 106 (1976), remarking:

> Whereas cases decided [prior to] *Marvin* may have presumed that the sexual relationship was the substance of the agreement, cases after *Marvin* seem to presume that the relationship is not the substance of the agreement. These cases are not concerned that the agreement exists in the context of a sexual relationship, but rather are concerned only if the contract's "primary" reason is sexual relations for value.

Brewer and the amici supporting her cite many of those cases, but the majority declines to follow them because they are not binding authority and "do not adequately consider the deeply rooted public policy in Illinois." [A]ccording to the majority, that policy is embodied in prohibition of common-law marriage that "has remained completely untouched and unqualified" in the nearly four decades since *Hewitt*.

Obviously, Illinois's common-law marriage ban is still in effect. Parallel statutes are in effect across the country, but only Georgia and Louisiana have rulings similar to *Hewitt*. Courts in a vast majority of the remaining states, as well as the District of Columbia, that have chosen not to recognize common-law marriages also have chosen to recognize claims between former domestic partners like Blumenthal and Brewer. The recognition of claims between domestic partners has not revived the doctrine of common-law marriage in jurisdictions that have abolished it. . . . We recognize that the state has a strong public policy interest in encouraging legal marriage. We do not, however, believe that policy is well served by allowing one participant in a meretricious relationship to abscond with the bulk of the couple's acquisitions. . . .

Justice THEIS, dissenting upon denial of rehearing.

I continue to believe that the majority was wrong to reaffirm Hewitt v. Hewitt. This court should grant rehearing because the majority . . . ignored a key aspect of [Brewer's] constitutional challenge. . . . [B]rewer asserted that applying *Hewitt* to bar her restitution claim would violate due process and equal protection because our holding in that case effectively penalizes unmarried domestic partners who cohabitate for exercising their right to an intimate relationship, as recognized by the United States Supreme Court in Lawrence v. Texas, 539 U.S. 558 (2003). Consequently, *Hewitt*'s holding is not rationally related to a legitimate governmental interest. Brewer added that it would be "particularly irrational" to expand *Hewitt* from its fact context of opposite-sex domestic partners who could have married, but chose not to do so, to the fact context here of same-sex domestic partners who could not have married. According to Brewer, she and Blumenthal "did not choose not to marry; they were barred from it" by a law, like those declared unconstitutional in Obergefell v. Hodges, that has since been repealed and replaced.

The majority overlooked that point, relying on a false version of history in which all Illinoisans could marry as the justification for its application of *Hewitt*. Of course, it is not irrational or discriminatory to deny the protections of the Act's dissolution provisions to persons who never used its marriage provisions. A question remains whether it is irrational and discriminatory to deny the protections of the common law to persons who never could have used the marriage provisions because of their sexual orientation. . . .

NOTE: WHO ARE JANE BLUMENTHAL AND EILEEN BREWER?[24]

Shannon Minter, counsel for Judge Eileen Brewer

Dr. Jane Blumenthal and the now-retired Judge Eileen Brewer began a relationship in 1981 while they were both studying at the University of Chicago. Brewer later obtained a law degree at Harvard Law School, and Blumenthal obtained a medical degree from the University of Michigan. Throughout their 26-year relationship, their home state of Illinois barred them from marriage. Nonetheless, they held themselves out as a committed couple, including by registering as domestic partners with Cook County in 2003 shortly after the registry became available.

The two women decided to expand their family to include children. Brewer gave birth to their two older children—one in 1990 and the second in 1992. Blumenthal gave birth to their youngest child in 1993. Together, Blumenthal and Brewer decided that Brewer would be the primary caregiver for the couple's three children and the one primarily responsible for other domestic and homemaking tasks. Accordingly, after taking some time off to provide full-time child care, Brewer pursued public-sector employment so that she would have more regular hours and no travel obligations. As a result of their allocation of domestic responsibilities, Blumenthal was able to focus on developing her medical career and practice. Blumenthal's annual earnings came to be about two to three times that of Brewer's. Blumenthal also accumulated more investments and savings compared to Brewer. In January 2008, Dr. Blumenthal "unilaterally" ended their relationship.

According to Shannon Minter, counsel for Judge Brewer, the decision was particularly harmful for same-sex couples who were placed in an "impossible

[24] The facts here are taken from Blumenthal v. Brewer, 24 N.E.3d 168, 170-172 (Ill. App. Ct. 2014), *rev'd in part, vacated in part,* 69 N.E.3d 834 (Ill. 2016).

double-bind," "penaliz[ed] for failing to marry even though Illinois law barred them from the right to marry during the entire span of their relationship."[25] With regard to unmarried couples more broadly, Minter said, "The decision is a huge step backward for Illinois, which is now dramatically out of step with the rest of the country and with basic principles of fairness and equal access to the courts."[26] Counsel for Dr. Blumenthal, Reuben Bernick, countered: "If they want to take advantage of the provisions available only in divorce, yes, they should get married. If they don't care about that, then nobody's making them get married."[27]

In terms of an update, in 2016, after 28 years in public service, including 14 years as an Illinois state court judge, Judge Eileen Brewer joined JAMS, the largest private provider of mediation and arbitration services. Dr. Jane Blumenthal continued to be a practicing board-certified obstetrician/gynecologist with more than 30 years of experience. Her medical practice has expanded to two locations and a staff of five physicians.

Notes and Questions

1. Epilogue to *Marvin*. On remand, the trial court found neither an express contract nor an implied contract based on the parties' conduct. Nonetheless, the trial judge awarded Michelle Marvin $104,000 in "rehabilitative alimony" based on several factors: the state supreme court's contemplation of broad equitable remedies (in footnote 25 of the case), the plaintiff's resort to unemployment benefits for support, and the defendant's net worth at separation exceeding $1 million. The judge arrived at the amount by calculating (for a two-year period) plaintiff's highest salary as a singer prior to the cohabitation.

The appellate court reversed, reasoning that the trial court had merely established plaintiff's need and defendant's ability to pay. The appellate court elaborated:

> . . . A court of equity admittedly has broad powers, but it may not create totally new substantive rights under the guise of doing equity. [I]n view of the already-mentioned findings of no damage (but benefit instead), no unjust enrichment and no wrongful act on the part of defendant with respect to either the relationship or its termination, it is clear that no basis whatsoever, either in equity or in law, exists for the challenged rehabilitative award.[28]

2. The *Blumenthal* rule. Why did the majority in *Blumenthal* conclude that Brewer's claim was not *independent* of the parties' intimate relationship? How would a plaintiff show the independence of the claim? Did the majority in *Blumenthal* offer guidelines?

Does the application of the rule established in *Hewitt* and reaffirmed in *Blumenthal* cause significant harm to members of nonmarital families and, in turn,

---

[25]. NCLR Press Release, NCLR Client Asks Illinois Supreme Court to Rehear Decision Barring Property Claims by Unmarried Partners, Targeted News Service, Sept. 8, 2016.

[26]. Id.

[27]. Carla K. Johnson, Gay Rights Setback Seen in Illinois Supreme Court Ruling, AP News, Aug. 19, 2016.

[28]. 5 Fam. L. Rep. (BNA) 3079, 3085 (Apr. 24, 1979).

"disrespect and subordinate them"? If so, are these the very same kinds of harms identified by Justice Kennedy in *Obergefell* (included in Chapter II)? If so, does the *Blumenthal* rule raise constitutional concerns? What does the dissent say about this? How does the majority respond?[29]

3. State approaches. Most states follow *Marvin*. Illinois falls into a small minority of states that purport to bar all claims between former cohabitants that arise out of the parties' "marriage-like" but nonmarital relationship. Other states fall somewhere in the middle; some states recognize only express and implied agreements, whereas other states recognize only express agreements.[30]

In practice, even in states that purport to allow nonmarital partners to pursue the full range of contract-based and equitable claims, most plaintiffs experience the same fate as Michelle Marvin—they are rarely successful. As Professor Elizabeth Scott explains, former nonmarital partners "have not had an impressive record of success in the post-*Marvin* period."[31]

4. Legal significance of *Marvin*. *Marvin* permits recovery based on express agreements, and in the absence thereof, implied-in-fact and implied-in-law agreements. Note that *Marvin*'s statements regarding implied agreements are dicta because the plaintiff pleaded an express agreement. Because most agreements between cohabitants are not express, *Marvin*'s importance rests on this dictum and on the suggestion (in footnote 25) of "additional equitable remedies." Implied-in-fact remedies are applicable when a court infers contractual intent from the parties' conduct. Implied-in-law remedies are impressed judicially to prevent unjust enrichment, regardless of the parties' intent. Thus, the latter, of course, are not really contracts.

What guidelines does *Marvin* give for determining the existence of implied agreements or the application of additional equitable remedies? Does the court assume that the parties have identical expectations? Is this assumption borne out in reality? The court also advocates adherence to a presumption that the parties intend to deal fairly with each other. What facts should rebut that presumption? Does this presumption interfere with freedom of contract and constitute impermissible state intervention? Does recognition of cohabitants' contract rights alleviate gender inequality? Is *Marvin* an advance or a setback for women?

5. Domestic services. In *Marvin*, the plaintiff asserts that she provided homemaking, among other services, in return for the defendant's promise of support. Although *Marvin* states that such services should not be excluded from protection, in practice, plaintiffs rarely receive recovery for them.[32] In rejecting such claims,

---

[29]. For consideration of this issue, see, e.g., Courtney G. Joslin, The Gay Rights Canon and the Right to Nonmarriage, 97 B.U. L. Rev. 425, 469-470 (2017).

[30]. See, e.g., Albertina Antognini, Against Nonmarital Exceptionalism, 51 U.C. Davis L. Rev. 1891, 1913 (2018) (surveying state approaches); Marsha Garrison, Nonmarital Cohabitation: Social Revolution and Legal Regulation, 42 Fam. L.Q. 309 (2008).

[31]. Elizabeth S. Scott, Domestic Partnerships, Implied Contracts, and Law Reform, in Reconceiving the Family: Critique on the American Law Institute's Principles of the Law of Family Dissolution 331, 349 (Robin Fretwell Wilson ed., 2006).

[32]. See, e.g., Albertina Antognini, Nonmarital Coverture, 99 B.U. L. Rev. 2139, 2173 (2019); Courtney G. Joslin, Nonmarriage: The Double Bind, 90 Geo. Wash. L. Rev. 571, 631 (2022); Developments in the Law—Unjust Enrichment (ch. 3), 133 Harv. L. Rev. 2124, 2127 (2020).

courts rely on a range of different theories—that the services presumptively were provided gratuitously; that the plaintiff already received the benefit of her bargain. Why do you think courts have been particularly reluctant to award compensation for domestic services? Professor Antognini attributes the explanation to coverture:

> [A] central—and disabling—consequence of coverture was that . . . [a]ny property she happened to own came under her husband's control and any work the wife expended on her family, either by raising children or maintaining the home, was considered her "wifely" duty, which she owed to her husband. In this way, the law kept the work the wife undertook separate from the market, and any value it may have had did not accrue to her, but to her husband. The nonmarital case law perpetuates this state of affairs: courts insulate the sphere of the home from that of the market, declare that the labor done within the former has no monetary value, and prevent the homemaker from accessing any property as a result.[33]

Should such services be eligible for compensation? If so, how do courts value them?

6. Relationship to marriage.

a. Undermining marriage. Does legal recognition of cohabitants' rights undermine marriage? Signify a return to common law marriage? Contrast the opinions of the majority and dissent on this point in *Blumenthal*. How do the legal consequences of applying the *Marvin* rule compare to the legal consequences flowing from a common law marriage? Would resurrection of common law marriage help cohabitants? Support or weaken marriage? *Blumenthal* suggests that the legislature is the appropriate body to address this issue. Do you think the court or legislature is more apt to reform the law on cohabitants' rights? What light does marriage equality litigation shed on this question?

b. Marriage as the standard. How did the partners' respective relationships in the principal cases approximate marital relationships? How did they differ? Which public policy considerations support extending some marriage-based rights to unmarried partners? Do these considerations support extending all marriage-based rights and obligations to nonmarital couples?[34] For example, on remand in *Marvin*, the trial court awarded "rehabilitative alimony," using the traditional factors for spousal support. Should cohabitants be entitled to post-dissolution support regardless of contractual intent? Should the law confer some or all marital rights on sufficiently committed or long-term unmarried couples? If so, what factors should be relevant?

7. Status-based approach. *Marvin* disapproved the status-based approach of In re Marriage of Cary, 109 Cal. Rptr. 862 (Ct. App. 1973), which treated unmarried cohabitants like spouses for purposes of distributing property accumulated during the relationship.

---

[33]. Antognini, Nonmarital Coverture, supra note [32], at 2144-2145.
[34]. See Lawrence W. Waggoner, Marriage Is on the Decline and Cohabitation Is on the Rise: At What Point, If Ever, Should Unmarried Partners Acquire Marital Rights?, 50 Fam. L.Q. 215 (2016) (so arguing).

a. Washington State approach. While California rejected this approach, a small number of states do follow a "status-based approach" to nonmarital cohabitation for purposes of property division upon dissolution. Most notably, Washington courts apply what is now called the "committed intimate relationship doctrine." If the couple is found to be in a committed intimate relationship, they are treated similarly to married spouses for purposes of property division at dissolution and at death. See Connell v. Francisco, 898 P.2d 831 (Wash. 1995). Washington courts consider the following factors in determining whether the parties were in a committed intimate relationship: (1) continuous cohabitation, (2) duration of the relationship, (3) purpose of the relationship, (4) pooling of resources and services for joint projects, and (5) the intent of the parties. See In re Kelly & Moesslang, 287 P.3d 12 (Wash. Ct. App. 2012).

b. The ALI Principles. The American Law Institute (ALI) Principles of the Law of Family Dissolution (discussed in more detail below) also adopt a status-based approach to property and support claims of unmarried cohabitants. According to the Principles, if the parties are in a "domestic partnership" (see below for a definition of that term), they are entitled to the same property division and spousal support rights as married spouses. ALI, Principles of the Law of Family Dissolution: Analysis and Recommendations §6.03. How would these approaches apply based on the facts in *Marvin* and *Blumenthal*? Which approach do you prefer?

8. Unmarried couples and autonomy. Some commentators argue in favor of the *Marvin* approach on autonomy grounds. For example, Professors June Carbone and Naomi Cahn posit that the parties' failure to transition to marriage is a deliberate decision based on "an unwillingness to make a financial commitment to a partner."[35] Accordingly, nonmarital partners should only have financial obligations to each other when they have entered into clear agreements to take on those financial obligations. Professor Marsha Garrison argues that "cohabitation is simply not . . . the functional or expressive equivalent of marriage." Treating these fundamentally different relationships like marriage, she continues, would therefore "diminish personal autonomy."[36]

Other commentators argue that *Marvin* does a poor job reflecting the choices that the parties have made about their relationships. For instance, Professor Courtney Joslin argues:

> The conventional doctrine only allows for consideration of a very limited array of decision points: the formal decision to marry (or its absence) and decision to enter into an agreement to share (or its absence). [R]ules that look only to a limited set of formal decisions render invisible an enormous range of quotidian decisions and actions. In many cases, other inquiries, including how the parties interacted with one another, how long these interactions lasted, whether the parties viewed themselves as family members, and the degree to which the parties relied on each other are more insightful and important questions to ask. If the goal is to offer meaningful choices with regard to family form, and to give effect to those decisions

---

[35]. June Carbone & Naomi Cahn, Nonmarriage, 76 Md. L. Rev. 55, 78 (2016).
[36]. Marsha Garrison, Marriage Matters: What's Wrong with the ALI's Domestic Partnership Proposal, in Reconceiving the Family, supra note [31], at 306.

once made, the law must allow for a more holistic consideration of the nature of these relationships.[37]

Which position do you find more persuasive?

9. Extending *Marvin* to same-sex couples. How were the legal issues in each of the principal cases similar? How were they different? What were the parties' various arguments? How does each court respond? Did the parties in *Blumenthal* have an express contract? Why wouldn't the court apply the implied contract doctrine? Why did the *Blumenthal* court refused to overturn Hewitt v. Hewitt? What was the impact, if any, of *Obergefell* on the Illinois Supreme Court's decision in *Blumenthal*?

Brewer and Blumenthal were together from 1981 until 2008. Why do you think they never married? How does the dissenting judge view that fact? For those same-sex couples in Illinois who married after *Obergefell*, how will *Blumenthal* apply to the assets acquired during their relationships, but before they could marry? If Illinois courts treat these premarital and marital assets differently, would that outcome raise constitutional concerns? What advice would you give to same-sex unmarried partners in Illinois who are concerned about protecting their property rights upon dissolution?[38]

10. Comparative perspective. Some countries, including Australia, Canada, Ireland, New Zealand, and Scotland, treat cohabiting partners whose relationships reveal a deep level of commitment as if they were married for purposes of conferring property rights on them.[39] Why do you think the United States lags so far behind?

Problems

1. Patricia files suit against her long-term paramour, noted criminal defense attorney Johnnie L. Cochran, Jr. (who successfully defended O.J. Simpson at his murder trial). The couple's 17-year relationship began in 1966, when Johnnie was still married to his first wife (whom he divorced in 1978). In 1973, Patricia and Johnnie have a son, and the next year, they purchase a house together. Many people believe that the couple is married, especially after Patricia changes her surname to Cochran. Johnnie manages Patricia's finances and, at various times, directs her to quit her jobs and forgo her career in order to take care of him and their child. During his first marriage and until 1985, when Johnnie informs Patricia that he is remarrying another woman, he lives with Patricia from two

---

[37]. Courtney G. Joslin, Autonomy in the Family, 66 UCLA L. Rev. 912, 965-966 (2019) (footnote omitted).

[38]. For a consideration of differences in the ways that courts apply these doctrines to different-sex and same-sex couples, see Antognini, Nonmarital Cohabitation, supra note [32].

[39]. Waggoner, supra note [34], at 216, 233-234.

to four nights per week. After his remarriage, they never again spend the night, although he frequently visits Patricia and takes meals there.

Patricia contends that, in 1983, Johnnie orally promised to support her for the rest of her life, and that he did so until 1995, when he became angry after she discussed their relationship on television. Johnnie, citing *Marvin*, argues that the support agreement is unenforceable because the couple was not living together full time when the promise was made, and he also contends that it violates public policy because he was married. He characterizes the relationship as little more than "dating." What result? See Cochran v. Cochran, 106 Cal. Rptr. 2d 899 (Ct. App. 2001).

2. Helen, age 23, works as a medical receptionist for an ophthalmologist, Frank, who is 51 years old and has been married for 20 years. They begin a romantic relationship. Frank continues living with his wife while providing Helen with expenses, a car, a home, and funds for her undergraduate and graduate education. They spend vacations together and dine together three or four times weekly, but rarely spend the night together. Helen contends that Frank told her repeatedly that he would divorce his wife and marry her. After a 20-year relationship, Frank ends the affair. After he discovers that Helen has started another relationship, Frank sues to eject her from the condo that he purchased for her. She counters with a complaint for palimony. Should a long-term intimate partner who has maintained a separate residence be entitled to enforce a support agreement? See Devaney v. L'Esperance, 949 A.2d 743 (N.J. 2008). Is this case distinguishable from *Cochran*, above? Cf. Bergen v. Wood, 18 Cal. Rptr. 2d 75 (Ct. App. 1993).

LAW REFORM DEVELOPMENTS

There are two uniform or model statutory schemes regarding the economic rights of nonmarital partners. In 2021, the Uniform Law Commission (ULC) promulgated the Uniform Cohabitants' Economic Remedies Act (UCERA). UCERA largely follows the *Marvin* approach.[40] The other scheme—the ALI Principles of the Law of Family Dissolution, promulgated in 2001—adopts a status-based approach, under which qualifying "domestic partners" are treated like marital spouses for purposes of property division and spousal support.

UNIFORM COHABITANTS' ECONOMIC REMEDIES ACT

§4. RIGHT OF COHABITANT TO BRING ACTION

(a) An individual who is or was a cohabitant may commence an action on a contractual or equitable claim that arises out of contributions to the relationship. The action is not:

---

[40]. As described by the Drafting Committee, "[t]he goal of the Act is not to create a new status for certain relationships but rather to enable two people who are cohabiting with one another to contract with, or to bring equitable claims against, one another, in the same manner and to the same extent that individuals who are not cohabiting, may under applicable state law." May 30, 2021 Memorandum from Turney Berry and Mary Devine, Co-Chairs; Naomi Cahn, Reporter, https://www.uniformlaws.org/HigherLogic/System/DownloadDocumentFile.ashx?Document FileKey=973d85be-6ba8-6edd-9e78-657a3936a4cd&forceDialog=0. For more information about UCERA see https://www.uniformlaws.org/committees/community-home?CommunityKey=5f044 999-b4b3-458a-b6d4-d984885d913b.

(1) barred because of a sexual relationship between cohabitants;

(2) subject to additional substantive or procedural requirements because the parties are or were cohabitants or because of a sexual relationship between the cohabitants; or

(3) extinguished by the marriage of cohabitants to each other. . . .

§6. COHABITANTS' AGREEMENTS

(a) A cohabitants' agreement may be oral or in a record, express or implied-in-fact.

(b) Contributions to the relationship are sufficient consideration for a cohabitants' agreement.

(c) A claim for breach of a cohabitants' agreement accrues on breach and may be commenced, subject to [cite to the applicable statute of limitations], during cohabitation or after termination of cohabitation. . . .

§7. EQUITABLE RELIEF

(a) Unless inconsistent with a valid provision of a cohabitants' agreement, and in addition to any remedies otherwise available, a cohabitant may maintain an equitable action concerning entitlement to property against the other cohabitant based on contributions to the relationship.

(b) An equitable claim that is based on contributions to the relationship accrues on termination of cohabitation and is subject to equitable defenses.

(c) In addition to other provisions of law governing an equitable claim, the court adjudicating a claim under this section shall consider:

(1) the nature and value of contributions to the relationship by each cohabitant, including the value to each cohabitant and the market value of the contributions;

(2) the duration and continuity of the cohabitation;

(3) the extent to which a cohabitant reasonably relied on representations or conduct of the other cohabitant;

(4) the extent to which a cohabitant demonstrated an intent to share, or not to share, property with the other cohabitant; and

(5) other factors the court considers relevant.

AMERICAN LAW INSTITUTE, PRINCIPLES OF THE LAW OF FAMILY DISSOLUTION §6.03 (2002)

(1) For the purpose of defining relationships to which this Chapter applies, domestic partners are two persons of the same or opposite sex, not married to one another, who for a significant period of time share a primary residence and a life together as a couple.

(2) Persons are domestic partners when they have maintained a common household, as defined in Paragraph (4), with their common child, as defined in Paragraph (5), for a continuous period that equals or exceeds a duration, called the *cohabitation parenting period,* set in a rule of statewide application.

(3) Persons not related by blood or adoption are presumed to be domestic partners when they have maintained a common household, as defined in Paragraph (4), for a continuous period that equals or exceeds a duration, called

the *cohabitation period,* set in a rule of statewide application. The presumption is rebuttable by evidence that the parties did not share life together as a couple, as defined by Paragraph (7).

(4) Persons *maintain a common household* when they share a primary residence only with each other and family members; or when, if they share a household with other unrelated persons, they act jointly, rather than as individuals, with respect to management of the household.

(5) Persons have a *common child* when each is either the child's legal parent or parent by estoppel, as defined by §2.03.

(6) When the requirements of Paragraph (2) or (3) are not satisfied, a person asserting a claim under this Chapter bears the burden of proving that for a significant period of time the parties shared a primary residence and a life together as a couple, as defined in Paragraph (7). Whether a period of time is significant is determined in light of all the Paragraph (7) circumstances of the parties' relationship and, particularly, the extent to which those circumstances wrought change in the life of one or both parties.

(7) Whether persons share a life together as a couple is determined by reference to all the circumstances, including:

(a) the oral or written statements or promises made to one another, or representations jointly made to third parties, regarding their relationship;

(b) the extent to which the parties intermingled their finances;

(c) the extent to which their relationship fostered the parties' economic interdependence, or the economic dependence of one party upon the other;

(d) the extent to which the parties engaged in conduct and assumed specialized or collaborative roles in furtherance of their life together;

(e) the extent to which the relationship wrought change in the life of either or both parties;

(f) the extent to which the parties acknowledged responsibilities to each other, as by naming the other the beneficiary of life insurance or of a testamentary instrument, or as eligible to receive benefits under an employee-benefit plan;

(g) the extent to which the parties' relationship was treated by the parties as qualitatively distinct from the relationship either party had with any other person;

(h) the emotional or physical intimacy of the parties' relationship;

(i) the parties' community reputation as a couple;

(j) the parties' participation in a commitment ceremony or registration as a domestic partnership;

(k) the parties' participation in a void or voidable marriage that, under applicable law, does not give rise to the economic incidents of marriage;

(l) the parties' procreation of, adoption of, or joint assumption of parental functions toward a child;

(m) the parties' maintenance of a common household, as defined by Paragraph (4).

Notes and Questions

1. UCERA. How does UCERA compare to the rule set forth under *Marvin*? Are there ways in which the rules under UCERA depart from the rules applicable under

Marvin? How? Do you think that plaintiffs will be more likely to recover under UCERA compared to *Marvin*? Why or why not? Of the two approaches—*Marvin* and UCERA—which do you think is better from a policy perspective, and why?

2. Standard for recognizing nonmarital couples.

a. Correct standard? Assuming arguendo that some nonmarital couples *should* be treated like married spouses for purposes of default inter se property and spousal support rights, do the ALI Principles set forth the correct standard for determining which couples qualify? If not, what changes would you make, and why?

b. Children in common. The ALI Principles take the position that if the parties have a child in common and have lived together in a common household for the required period of time—to be set forth by the state—that they *are* domestic partners. By contrast, if the parties do not have a child in common, they are *presumed* to be domestic partners if they have lived together in a common household for the required period of time—again to be set forth by the state. In such cases (that is, ones involving partners with no children in common), this presumption that they are domestic partners can be rebutted. (To be clear, as with married spouses, the Principles permit the parties to opt out of the default sharing rules that apply to people found to be domestic partners.) Why did the drafters treat these two situations differently? Is the presence of a child in common an important difference? Should the default sharing rules be *rebuttable* when the parties do not have a child in common? What time requirements should apply to these two groups of people—those with children in common and those without?

c. Other factors. Under the ALI Principles, even if the parties have not lived together for the required periods of time, a party can still establish that they were domestic partners by "proving that for a significant period of time the parties shared a primary residence and a life together as a couple," determined in light of the factors listed in Paragraph (7). Should couples who have been together for shorter periods of time still have the option of establishing that they are "domestic partners" within the meaning of the Principles?

3. Multi-party relationships.
How should the law apply to multi-party relationships, where all of the parties are in a relationship with each other, or where one person is in more than one relationship at the same time? Recall that in *Marvin* itself, Lee Marvin was still married to his wife during some of his period of cohabitation with Michelle Marvin. The *Marvin* Court seemed to pay little mind to this fact and did not bar the claim.

UCERA likewise takes the position that the claim is not barred simply because the cohabitant was married to someone else during some or all of the period of cohabitation. UCERA, §8, Cmt. The drafters recognized that many cohabitants are married to others, and if that fact barred the claim, it might result in unfair or inequitable results. UCERA, §8, Alternatives A–D (alternative provisions to apply in such cases). The ALI Principles do not expressly address the issue. How should the law treat situations where there are more than two claimants?

4. UCERA vs. ALI Principles.
As noted above, UCERA and the ALI Principles adopt fundamentally different approaches to inter se rights as between former

nonmarital partners. UCERA treats nonmarital partners like other legal strangers, without barring their contractual or equitable claims based on the existence of their sexual relationship or subjecting them to additional substantive or procedural hurdles. By contrast, the Principles take the position that if the relationship is sufficiently committed, the parties should be treated like married spouses for purposes of property division and future spousal support. Which approach is preferable from a public policy perspective? Which approach best furthers fairness between the parties? Are there any concerns with treating nonmarital partners like married spouses for these purposes?

Problem

In 2013, Andre purchased a two-bedroom house. The money used for the down payment was from Andre's savings. In 2014, Andre began a relationship with Bella. After dating for six months, Bella moved into Andre's house. At that time, the couple also opened joint checking and saving accounts in both their names, into which they each placed their earned income. This account was used to pay for household expenses. Although both parties were working full time, Andre earned significantly more than Bella. In 2015, the couple decided to sell the house and purchase a bigger home. Andre took title of the new house in his name alone. He explained to Bella that he had more equity and it would be easier for them to get a good mortgage rate that way. During conversations about the house and the title of the house, Andre assured Bella that he would take care of her. Bella did not contribute to the down payment for the new home. The subsequent mortgage payments were taken directly from the couple's joint checking account. After they purchased the house, both Andre and Bella spent many months working on improvements. For example, they repainted most of the rooms and refinished all the hardwood floors in the house.

In 2023, Andre and Bella end their (still nonmarital) relationship. Bella sues Andre, seeking some portion of the equity in the home and a portion of the funds in the checking and saving accounts. What result in a jurisdiction that follows: (1) *Marvin*; (2) *Hewitt/Blumenthal*; (3) UCERA; (4) the ALI Principles? How do these results compare to the outcome if the parties had been married? Which approach produces the most fair result? Why?

b. Claims Against Third Parties and the State

The last section considered how the law should treat claims by a person *against a former nonmarital partner* with respect to property accumulated during their relationship. This next section raises the issue of nonmarital partners' claims against third parties.

(i) Tort Claims for Death or Injuries to a Nonmarital Partner

GRAVES v. ESTABROOK
818 A.2d 1255 (N.H. 2003)

DUGGAN, J.

[Catrina] Graves was engaged to Brett A. Ennis and had lived with him for approximately seven years. On September 23, 2000, Ennis was riding his motorcycle while Graves followed immediately behind him in a car. At an intersection, Estabrook's vehicle failed to yield at a stop sign and collided with Ennis. As Graves looked on, Ennis flipped over the hood of Estabrook's car and landed on the pavement. Graves immediately stopped her car and ran to the aid of her fiancé. She saw blood coming from his mouth and significant trauma to his head. She followed the ambulance that transported her fiancé to the hospital, stayed by his side while he was being treated, and attempted to comfort his parents and son. Ennis died the next day. Graves alleges that as a result of witnessing the collision and death of her fiancé, she suffered shock, severe mental pain and emotional distress.

The issue before us is whether a plaintiff who lived with and was engaged to marry the decedent may recover for negligent infliction of emotional distress. . . .

Many of the first states to recognize bystander liability for negligent infliction of emotional distress limited its scope by applying the "physical impact test," without considering foreseeability. Under the physical impact test, the plaintiff must have sustained a physical impact, no matter how slight, in order to recover. New Hampshire never adopted the physical impact test but instead followed the zone of danger rule [permitting] recovery only when the bystander was within a physical zone of danger created by the defendant's negligence. [However, the court later rejected the zone of danger rule in favor of the traditional negligence analysis of foreseeability.] We adopted the test first enunciated in Dillon v. Legg, 441 P.2d 912, 920 (Cal. 1968), in which the California Supreme Court set forth three factors for determining whether a defendant should reasonably foresee injury to a bystander: (1) Whether plaintiff was located near the scene of the accident as contrasted with one who was a distance away from it. (2) Whether the shock resulted from a direct emotional impact upon plaintiff from the sensory and contemporaneous observance of the accident, as contrasted with learning of the accident from others after its occurrence. (3) Whether plaintiff and the victim were closely related, as contrasted with an absence of any relationship or the presence of only a distant relationship. . . .

This case requires us to examine the scope of *Dillon*'s third factor. The defendant argues that we should continue to follow the California Supreme Court and adopt its subsequent holding in Elden v. Sheldon, 758 P.2d 582 (Cal. 1988). There, the court held that unmarried cohabitants are not "closely related" and cannot recover for negligent infliction of emotional distress. Other courts have adopted the same rule [citing cases in Florida, New Mexico, and Texas].

As noted by the New Jersey Supreme Court in Dunphy v. Gregor, 642 A.2d 372, 375 (N.J. 1994), the [California Supreme Court] in *Elden* was reacting to the experience of the California courts with bystander liability under the *Dillon* standard. After *Dillon*, California courts had significantly expanded the scope of bystander liability [e.g., to eliminate the requirement of visual perception of the injury and to expand the "closely related" factor to include foster parent-child relationships]. Thus, one reason for the holding in *Elden* was a need to rein in the expansion of bystander liability in California. [U]nlike the California Supreme Court, we are not faced with a need to curb bystander liability.

Notwithstanding this difference, the defendant urges us to construe the third factor [literally]. He argues that we should limit the meaning of "closely related" to a dictionary definition: people "connected by consanguinity," or "persons connected by kinship, common origin or marriage." . . . The appropriate analysis is not to resort to a dictionary definition but rather to use our traditional analysis of foreseeability.

In *Elden*, the California Supreme Court rejected a traditional analysis of foreseeability for three policy reasons. . . . First is the State's strong interest in marriage. . . . *Elden* found no convincing reason to permit recovery to couples who bear no legal obligations to each other to the same extent as those who undertake such obligations. The court in *Elden* apparently relied upon the dubious assumption that the possibility of recovery in tort litigation is an incentive to marry. Rejecting this assumption, the New Jersey Supreme Court observed that "a person who would not otherwise choose to marry would not be persuaded to do so in order to assure his or her legal standing in a future personal injury action should that person have the misfortune of witnessing the serious injury of his or her spouse." *Dunphy*, 642 A.2d at 379. . . . We agree.

The second reason relied upon in *Elden* was the "difficult burden on the courts." *Elden* reasoned that "[a] determination whether a partner in an unmarried cohabitation relationship may recover damages for emotional distress based on such matters as the sexual fidelity of the parties and their emotional and economic ties would require a court to undertake a massive intrusion into the private life of the partners." Again, we agree with the New Jersey Supreme Court, which noted that "[o]ur courts have shown that the sound assessment of the quality of interpersonal relationships is not beyond a jury's ken and that courts are capable of dealing with the realities, not simply the legalities, of relationships to assure that resulting emotional injury is genuine and deserving of compensation." . . . Third, the court in *Elden* relied upon [the need to limit the class of plaintiffs by means of a bright line rule]. The court stated that the absence of a bright line rule "would result in the unreasonable extension of the scope of liability of a negligent actor." . . .

Rejecting the bright line rule in *Elden*, however, does not place an intolerable burden upon society or unfair burden upon a negligent defendant. Rather, it allows recovery for an eminently foreseeable class of plaintiffs. . . . *Elden* argued that "[t]he need to draw a bright line in this area of the law is essential" because there is no "principled distinction between an unmarried cohabitant who claims to have a de facto marriage relationship with his partner and de facto siblings, parents, grandparents or children." While this observation is accurate, it fails to consider that there is also no logical distinction between denying recovery to a fiancée who has lived with her betrothed for seven years and allowing recovery to a wife who met and married her husband a week before the accident. A bright line rule that includes only individuals related by blood or marriage is

> overinclusive because it permits recovery when the suffering accompanies a legal or biological link between bystander and victim, regardless of whether the relationship between the two is estranged, alienated, or in some other way removed. Conversely, the [rule] is underinclusive because it arbitrarily denies court access to persons with valid claims that they could prove if permitted to do so.

[Note, It's All Relative: A Graphical Reasoning Model for Liberalizing Recovery for Negligent Infliction of Emotional Distress Beyond the Immediate Family, 30 Val. U. L. Rev. 913, 917 (1996).]

More fundamentally, we decline to adopt a bright line rule when a "flexible approach, designed to account for factual nuances" is available. . . . We conclude that "to foreclose [an unmarried cohabitant] from making a claim based upon emotional harm because her relationship with the injured person does not carry a particular label is to work a potential injustice . . . where the emotional injury is genuine and substantial and is based upon a relationship of significant duration that . . . is deep, lasting and genuinely intimate." [*Dunphy*, 642 A.2d at 378.] A number of courts have reached a similar conclusion [citing cases in Hawaii, Nebraska, Ohio, Pennsylvania, Tennessee, West Virginia]. We thus recognize that unmarried cohabitants may have a close relationship, i.e., a "relationship that is stable, enduring, substantial, and mutually supportive . . . cemented by strong emotional bonds and provid[ing] a deep and pervasive emotional security." [Id. at 380.] In determining whether a relationship meets this standard, a court should

> take into account the duration of the relationship, the degree of mutual dependence, the extent of common contributions to a life together, the extent and quality of shared experience, and . . . whether the plaintiff and the injured person were members of the same household, their emotional reliance on each other, the particulars of their day to day relationship, and the manner in which they related to each other in attending to life's mundane requirements.

Id. at 378 (quotation omitted).

In this case, the plaintiff alleged in her complaint that she was engaged to the decedent and that they had lived together for seven years immediately preceding the accident. Construing all reasonable inferences in the light most favorable to the plaintiff, we conclude that it is reasonable to infer that in the course of their lengthy cohabitation the plaintiff and her fiancé enjoyed mutual dependence, common contributions to a life together, emotional reliance on each other and attended to life's mundane requirements together. . . .

NOTE: WHO IS CATRINA GRAVES?

Roy A. Duddy, The Background Story of Graves v. Estabrook[41]

Personal Communication, Dec. 5, 2012

One late Saturday afternoon, 32-year-old Brett Ennis was riding his motorcycle on Route 102 in Londonderry, New Hampshire, after spending the day at a friend's home cleaning and polishing their motorcycles in preparation for a fundraiser. Following immediately behind Brett in her vehicle was his long-term fiancée, Catrina Graves. They had just eaten lunch at a local restaurant. Route 102 is a two-lane roadway that handles a large volume of traffic at a relatively high speed limit of 50 mph. As Brett approached an uncontrolled intersection (controlled via a STOP sign that required any driver on a secondary road to stop prior to entering Route 102), a vehicle owned by Franklin Estabrook accelerated into the intersection immediately in front of Brett's motorcycle. Brett, who was operating at 45-50 mph, swerved to avoid the Estabrook vehicle, but Estabrook's vehicle struck Brett. Brett was thrown into the air, striking the vehicle on the hood. He cartwheeled through the air, landing on his back in the middle of the traffic lane.

Catrina screamed when she saw what was happening. She saw Brett flying through the air and saw his feet hit the pavement, then his head. She swerved to avoid the crash. She immediately stopped her car, jumped out, and ran to Brett's side where she observed blood coming from his mouth. She attempted to clear his mouth and to loosen his jacket and sweatshirt. Brett's eyes were open, and he wasn't moving. Catrina held his hand and attempted to comfort him, all the while she was crying.

Catrina followed the ambulance to the medical center where she stayed at Brett's side for almost 30 hours until he was removed from life support. Brett was kept on life support in order to harvest certain organs and in order to allow Brett's son from a former marriage to arrive from Arkansas in order to "say his good-byes." Catrina sought counseling almost immediately after the accident to deal with the tragedy and remained in counseling for a considerable period of time.

Approximately one month after the accident, Catrina and Brett's father came to see me. It was very clear to me that Catrina and Brett, along with Brett's family, had a real and genuine love for one another. Catrina saw Brett's parents and sisters on a weekly basis. Brett's parents treated Catrina as though she were their own daughter. She called them "Mom" and "Dad." Catrina also had a good relationship with Brett's son. In fact, Catrina expressed concern that Brett's son should receive any insurance that Brett's estate might obtain. She was more concerned about making certain that Brett's son was taken care of than she was about her own future.

---

[41]. Roy A. Duddy, of Duddy Law Offices, Hampton, New Hampshire, was the attorney for Catrina Graves. He died in 2018.

In my mind, this young woman had suffered more egregiously than almost anyone I had met in more than 20 years of practice. She was so selfless in her dealings with Brett's son and his family that I felt if ever there was a case to present the issue as to whether a bystander, not related by blood or marriage to the decedent—yet having the deep, intimate familial ties to the decedent—can recover on a claim for negligent infliction of emotional distress (NIED), this was the case.

As I expected, the superior court granted defense counsel's motion to dismiss on the ground that New Hampshire does not recognize the right of an unmarried cohabitant to maintain a cause of action for NIED. I filed a motion to reconsider—which was denied. I then appealed to the New Hampshire Supreme Court, which accepted the case.

I approached the New Hampshire Trial Lawyers to ask them to submit an amicus brief. The Amicus Committee voted not to recommend to the Board of Governors that the case be accepted or an amicus brief be filed. The majority of the committee felt that there was no likelihood of success and that the reputation of the Trial Lawyers would be tarnished by presenting a brief in support of my appeal. I was very disheartened by its position. Nonetheless, I presented my case to the entire Board of Governors, and a vote was taken to support filing the amicus brief.

Three months after oral argument, a divided New Hampshire Supreme Court (3 to 2) issued an opinion that held that Catrina Graves "may recover damages for emotional distress as the result of witnessing the collision." Subsequently, the parties reached a confidential settlement.

Notes and Questions

1. Negligent infliction claims. Unmarried cohabitants sometimes sue for relationship injuries (such as those resulting from personal injury or death of a partner) in tort actions based on negligent infliction of emotional distress (NIED), loss of consortium, and wrongful death. Unlike claims for NIED and loss of consortium, actions for wrongful death are purely statutory. Wrongful death statutes restrict tort recovery to legal spouses.

As *Graves* explains, under the traditional rule, recovery for NIED from witnessing the negligent injury to another was limited to those witnesses who either suffered a physical impact themselves or were in the zone of danger. Most jurisdictions follow Dillon v. Legg, 441 P.2d 912 (Cal. 1968), limiting recovery based on the foreseeability of the trauma to bystanders. The third prong of *Dillon* focuses on whether the plaintiff had a *sufficiently close relationship* with the victim. As *Graves* explains, courts are split regarding the availability of such claims for unmarried cohabitants, although the vast majority of courts disagree with *Graves* and hold that unmarried partners *cannot* bring NIED claims.

2. Rationale. According to *Graves*, what are the arguments pro and con recognizing cohabitants' claims for NIED? Justice Garibaldi, in a dissent in *Dunphy* (cited in *Graves*), protests that exclusion of cohabitants conforms to societal expectations regarding differential treatment of spouses and is less likely to lead to confusion because spouses are treated differently in many legal contexts (e.g., intestacy, alimony, etc.). She adds that exclusion is consistent with nonrecognition of common law marriage. How persuasive are these arguments? Does the extension of liability advance the objectives of the tort system?

3. Quality or status? According to *Graves*, how does a plaintiff prove the quality of the relationship? What evidence would minimize the quality of the relationship? How workable is the *Dunphy* standard (adopted by *Graves*) that focuses on the duration of the relationship, the degree of mutual dependence, the extent of common contributions to a life together, the extent and quality of shared experience, and co-residence?

4. Engaged couples. In *Graves*, the plaintiff and victim were cohabitants who were engaged to marry. Does this latter fact strengthen a plaintiff's claim? Should it? Which approach does a long engagement support? How does a plaintiff prove an engagement? What result if the accident occurs the day before the wedding? See, e.g., Smith v. Toney, 862 N.E.2d 656 (Ind. 2007); Eskin v. Bartee, 262 S.W.3d 727, 740 (Tenn. 2008).

In what ways are cohabitants' claims similar to, or different from, those of engaged partners? Professor Grace Blumberg advocates recovery for both, contending that it is "socially prudent" to encourage both to remain with injured victims of tortfeasors even though they are not bound to do so.[42] Do you find her reasoning persuasive? How serious is the worry that treating engaged couples as sufficiently "closely related" will lead to limitless liability? Compare Yovino v. Big Bubba's BBQ, 896 A.2d 161, 166-167 (Conn. Super. Ct. 2006), with Milberger v. KBHL, 486 F. Supp. 2d 1156, 1166-1167 (D. Haw. 2007).

5. Loss of consortium. Most states deny recovery for loss of consortium to unmarried cohabitants who never marry. Does the analysis change if the parties married after the accident? Suppose, for example, that Brett Ennis in *Graves* was injured rather than killed, and that the couple married after the accident. Should Catrina Graves be able to recover for the loss of companionship, affection, sex, economic contribution, and services that she *subsequently* experienced stemming from the premarital injury? Compare Leonard v. John Crane, Inc., 142 Cal. Rptr. 3d 700 (Ct. App. 2012) (permitting postmarital recovery), with Bransteter v. Moore, 579 F. Supp. 2d 982 (N.D. Ohio 2008) (contra).

6. Other types of cases. In what other contexts might people seek to have their nonmarital relationship recognized by third parties? Other contexts might include eligibility for insurance and survivor benefits, parental rights claims, domestic abuse, and the availability of testimonial privileges. Professor Kaiponanea Matsumura identifies and explores some of these other contexts in a recent study examining published cases over a two-year period involving disputes in which

---

[42]. Grace Ganz Blumberg, Cohabitation Without Marriage: A Different Perspective, 28 UCLA L. Rev. 1125, 1138-1139 n.80 (1981). Professor Blumberg was a Reporter for the ALI Principles, for which she authored the chapters on child support and nonmarital cohabitation.

one of the partners or a third party "sought the court's assistance in recognizing an informal relationship."[43]

7. Marvin **distinguished.** Has California adopted a paradoxical position toward unmarried couples? Does it make sense to allow recovery by unmarried cohabitants against each other in contract law and under equitable theories (*Marvin*) but to bar recovery under tort law against third parties (*Elden*)?

(ii) Housing Protection for Nonmarital Partners

BRASCHI v. STAHL ASSOCIATES CO.

543 N.E.2d 49 (N.Y. 1989)

TITONE, Judge. . . .

Appellant Miguel Braschi was living with Leslie Blanchard in a rent-controlled apartment located at 405 East 54th Street from the summer of 1975 until Blanchard's death in September of 1986. [R]espondent, Stahl Associates Company, the owner of the apartment building, served a notice to cure on appellant contending that he was a mere licensee with no right to occupy the apartment since only Blanchard was the tenant of record [and threatened eviction proceedings]. The present dispute arises because the term "family" is not defined in the rent-control code and the legislative history is devoid of any specific reference to the noneviction provision. All that is known is the legislative purpose underlying the enactment of the rent-control laws as a whole.

Rent control was enacted to address a "serious public emergency" created by "an acute shortage in dwellings," which resulted in "speculative, unwarranted, and abnormal increases in rents" (L. 1946 ch. 274, codified, as amended, at McKinney's Uncons. Laws of N.Y. §8581 et seq.). These measures were designed to regulate and control the housing market so as to "prevent exactions of unjust, unreasonable, and oppressive rents and rental agreements and to forestall profiteering, speculation and other disruptive practices tending to produce threats to the public health [and] to prevent uncertainty, hardship and dislocation" (id.). [The legislation was] initially designed as an emergency measure to alleviate the housing shortage attributable to the end of World War II. . . .

To accomplish its goals, the Legislature recognized that not only would rents have to be controlled, but that evictions would have to be regulated and controlled as well. Hence, [New York City Rent and Eviction Regulations provide for] noneviction protection to those occupants who are either the "surviving spouse of the deceased tenant or *some other member of the deceased tenant's family* who has been living with the tenant [of record]" (emphasis supplied).

[R]espondent argues that the term "family member" as used in 9 NYCRR 2204.6(d) should be construed, consistent with this State's intestacy laws, to mean

---

[43]. Kaiponanea T. Matsumura, Beyond Property: The Other Legal Consequences of Informal Relationships, 51 Ariz. St. L.J. 1325, 1335, 1337-1338 (2019).

relationships of blood, consanguinity and adoption in order to effectuate the overall goal of orderly succession to real property. Under this interpretation, only those entitled to inherit under the laws of intestacy would be afforded noneviction protection. [R]espondent relies on our decision in Matter of Robert Paul P., 471 N.E.2d 424 [(N.Y.1984)], arguing that since the relationship between appellant and Blanchard has not been accorded legal status by the Legislature, it is not entitled to the protections of section 2204.6(d). . . . Finally, respondent contends that our construction of the term "family member" should be guided by the recently enacted noneviction provision of the Rent Stabilization Code (9 NYCRR 2523.5[a], [b][1], [2]) [which includes a precise definition of family members based on the existence of marital or blood ties].

However, as we have continually noted, the rent-stabilization system is different from the rent-control system in that the former is a less onerous burden on the property owner, and thus the provisions of one cannot simply be imported into the other. Respondent's reliance on Matter of Robert Paul P. is also misplaced, since [that case] was based solely on the purposes of the adoption laws and has no bearing on the proper interpretation of a provision in the rent-control laws.

We also reject respondent's argument that the purpose of the noneviction provision of the rent-control laws is to control the orderly succession to real property in a manner similar to that which occurs under our State's intestacy laws. The noneviction provision does not concern succession to real property but rather is a means of protecting a certain class of occupants from the sudden loss of their homes. . . . Moreover, such a construction would be inconsistent with the purposes of the rent-control system as a whole, since it would afford protection to distant blood relatives who actually had but a superficial relationship with the deceased tenant while denying that protection to unmarried lifetime partners. . . .

Contrary to all of these arguments, we conclude that the term family, as used in 9 NYCRR 2204.6(d), should not be rigidly restricted to those people who have formalized their relationship by obtaining, for instance, a marriage certificate or an adoption order. The intended protection against sudden eviction should not rest on fictitious legal distinctions or genetic history, but instead should find its foundation in the reality of family life. In the context of eviction, a more realistic, and certainly equally valid, view of a family includes two adult lifetime partners whose relationship is long term and characterized by an emotional and financial commitment and interdependence.

This view comports both with our society's traditional concept of "family" and with the expectations of individuals who live in such nuclear units. In fact, Webster's Dictionary defines "family" first as "a group of people united by certain convictions or common affiliation" (Webster's Ninth New Collegiate Dictionary 448 [1984]). Hence, it is reasonable to conclude that, in using the term "family," the Legislature intended to extend protection to those who reside in households having all of the normal familial characteristics. Appellant Braschi should therefore be afforded the opportunity to prove that he and Blanchard had such a household. . . .

The determination as to whether an individual is entitled to noneviction protection should be based upon an objective examination of the relationship of the parties. In making this assessment, the lower courts of this State have looked to a number of factors, including the exclusivity and longevity of the relationship, the level of emotional and financial commitment, the manner in which the parties have conducted their everyday lives and held themselves out to society, and the reliance placed upon one another for daily family services. These factors are most helpful, although it should be emphasized that the presence or absence of one or more of them is not dispositive since it is the totality of the relationship as evidenced by the dedication, caring and self-sacrifice of the parties which should, in the final analysis, control. Appellant's situation provides an example of how the rule should be applied.

Appellant and Blanchard lived together as permanent life partners for more than 10 years. They regarded one another, and were regarded by friends and family, as spouses. The two men's families were aware of the nature of the relationship, and they regularly visited each other's families and attended family functions together, as a couple. Even today, appellant continues to maintain a relationship with Blanchard's niece, who considers him an uncle.

In addition to their interwoven social lives, appellant clearly considered the apartment his home. He lists the apartment as his address on his driver's license and passport, and receives all his mail at the apartment address. Moreover, appellant's tenancy was known to the building's superintendent and doormen, who viewed the two men as a couple.

Financially, the two men shared all obligations, including a household budget. The two were authorized signatories of three safe-deposit boxes, they maintained joint checking and savings accounts, and joint credit cards. In fact, rent was often paid with a check from their joint checking account. Additionally, Blanchard executed a power of attorney in appellant's favor so that appellant could make necessary decisions—financial, medical and personal—for him during his illness. Finally, appellant was the named beneficiary of Blanchard's life insurance policy, as well as the primary legatee and coexecutor of Blanchard's estate. Hence, a court examining these facts could reasonably conclude that these men were much more than mere roommates. [The court concludes that appellant has demonstrated a likelihood of success on the merits and remands the case.]

Notes and Questions

1. Functional definition. *Braschi* (like Graves v. Estabrook) adopts a functional definition of "family." At the time—a time when same-sex couples could not marry—the significance of this definition for LGBTQ people was monumental.

2. Familial characteristics. *Braschi* reasons that the legislature intended to protect those persons who reside in households "having all of the normal familial characteristics." Which "normal" familial characteristics did the Braschi household exhibit? Which did it not? Should the state define and impose a legal meaning of "family" on all persons without exception, or should the law honor private choices, so long as a given unit acts like a family and performs familial functions?

3. Criticisms. *Braschi* suggests factors to determine qualifications as a "family member" for noneviction protection. Do you agree with the dissent that these factors "produce[] an unworkable test that is subject to abuse" and could lead to extended litigation "focusing on such intangibles as the strength and duration of the relationship and the extent of the emotional and financial interdependency"? Does the need for proof of financial interdependence cause difficulty for partners who keep their finances separate, or for low-income cohabitants? Does *Braschi* sanction legal distinctions between those couples who do and those who do not fit the "traditional" family model (e.g., by requiring sexual fidelity, co-residence, and commingling finances)?

4. Expansive family definitions. Does the married couple serve as the model for expanded definitions of "family" in *Braschi*? Is there some other standard that could or should be used when deciding whether to recognize and extend rights and protections (and obligations) to nonmarital partners? Should the presence of children be a key factor? Most people in the United States hold an expansive view, believing that all the following family forms constitute a family: a single parent and child, an unmarried couple living together with a child, and a same-sex couple raising a child. However, if a cohabiting couple is childless, a majority of the public believes that they are *not* a family—although if the childless couple is married, the majority do consider them to be a family.[44] Why might the presence of a child or the existence of marriage convey the image that the parties constitute a "family"?

Assuming that nonmarital relationships are recognized by law, should they be recognized for all purposes? Some? If the latter, which ones? Should the standards or tests be the same across contexts?

5. Multi-party relationships. Should the *Braschi* rule be extended to relationships that include more than two people? In a recent case, a New York court replied affirmatively, reasoning: "Why does a person have to be committed to [only] one other person in only certain prescribed ways in order to enjoy stability in housing after the departure of a loved one? . . . The existence of a triad should not automatically dismiss respondent's claim to noneviction protections." W. 49th St., LLC v. O'Neill, 178 N.Y.S.3d 874 (N.Y. Civ. Ct. 2022). Do you agree? Are courts up for the task of determining which relationships qualify? See id. at 884 ("The court recognizes the difficulty . . . of not interpreting the *Braschi* Court's interpretation of the word 'family' as drawing a bright line [at the] traditional dyadic relationship. . . . But, . . . we should do what courts are in the business of doing—deciding cases as best they fallibly can." (citing *Braschi*, 74 N.Y.2d 201, 215-216 (Bellacosa, J., concurring)).

6. Multi-party relationships and other rights and protections. Recently, the cities of Somerville and Cambridge in Massachusetts enacted multi-party domestic partnership ordinances. However, the protections are fairly limited. See, e.g., Cambridge, Mass., Ordinances tit. 2, ch. 2.119, §2.119.060(A)(1) & §2.119.070(F) (2021) (hospital visitation rights for persons at city health care facilities and bereavement leave for city employees). Should other localities pass similar ordinances? If so, what protections should be included? Excluded? Should multiple

---

[44]. Pew Research Ctr., Social and Demographic Trends Report, The Decline of Marriage and Rise of New Families, Exec. Summary, Nov. 18, 2010, http://www.pewsocialtrends.org/2010/11/18/the-decline-of-marriage-and-rise-of-new-families/.

partners, for example, have a right to access spousal/domestic partner employer-provided health insurance benefits?[45]

7. Single people. Should people without partners or children be protected from discrimination? Should they be entitled to access benefits or protections on that basis? If so, which ones, and why? Should they, for example, get paid more in salary by their employer because they do not need health insurance benefits for a spouse or domestic partner?[46]

Problem

In the wake of the *Braschi* decision, the New York legislature amended the Rent Control and Stabilization Code to be consistent with that decision. NY Landlord & Tenant Rent Control & Stabilization §2204.6. Specifically, the law now defines "family member" for purposes of an eviction proceeding to include people "residing with the tenant in the housing accommodation as a primary residence who can prove emotional and financial commitment, and interdependence between such person and the tenant." The statute goes on to list a number of factors to be considered when assessing whether a person should qualify under the provision. These factors include, but are not limited to:

1. Longevity of the relationship
2. Sharing of or relying upon each other for payment of household or family expenses, and/or other common necessities of life
3. Intermingling of finances as evidenced by, among other things, joint ownership of bank accounts, personal and real property, credit cards, loan obligations, sharing a household budget for purposes of receiving government benefits, etc.
4. Engaging in family-type activities by jointly attending family functions, holidays and celebrations, social and recreational activities, etc.
5. Formalizing of legal obligations, intentions, and responsibilities to each other by such means as executing wills naming each other as executor and/or beneficiary, conferring upon each other a power of attorney and/or authority to make health care decisions each for the other, entering into a personal relationship contract, making a domestic partnership declaration, or serving as a representative payee for purposes of public benefits, etc.
6. Holding themselves out as family members to other family members, friends, members of the community or religious institutions, or society in general, through their words or actions
7. Regularly performing family functions, such as caring for each other or each other's extended family members, and/or relying upon each other for daily family services

---

[45]. See, e.g., Katharine K. Baker, The Polyamorous Threat to Nonmarriage, 61 Fam. Ct. Rev. 81 (2023); Kaiponanea T. Matsumura, Beyond Polygamy, 107 Iowa L. Rev. 1903 (2022).

[46]. See, e.g., Elizabeth F. Emens, Compulsory Sexuality, 66 Stan. L. Rev. 303 (2014); Trina Jones, Single and Childfree! Reassessing Parental and Marital Status Discrimination, 46 Ariz. St. L.J. 1253 (2014); Nancy Leong, Negative Identity, 88 S. Cal. L. Rev. 1357 (2015); Kaiponanea T. Matsumura, The Marital Habitus, 99 Wash. U.L. Rev. 2033, 2060 (2022).

8. Engaging in any other pattern of behavior, agreement, or other action which evidences the intention of creating a long-term, emotionally committed relationship

This section further states, "In no event would evidence of a sexual relationship between such persons be required or considered." Id. Consider how these provisions apply to the following fact pattern:

Scott Anderson was a tenant in an apartment. After Scott's death, the landlord brought an eviction proceeding against the other tenant, Markyus O'Neill. Markyus claimed protection under the above law as a family member of the decedent.

The landlord objected to this characterization and pointed to the following facts: Scott and Markyus "never comingled their finances or jointly owned real or personal property, held themselves out as a family unit, executed documents formalizing legal obligations, jointly celebrated most major holidays, or attended important events with each other's families." The landlord further argued that Scott had been in a 25-year relationship with another man—Robert Romano. According to Robert, although they had separate residences, Scott and Robert "considered each other family and incorporated one another into each other's immediate family." They shared cell phone and credit card accounts. Scott was the beneficiary of Robert's retirement fund, and vice versa.

To support his claim that he should be recognized as a family member for purposes of rent control protections, Markyus added the following: He met Scott in 2011. They quickly became "more than friends," even though Scott was in a relationship with another person (that person being Robert). When Scott moved into a new apartment in 2012, he "offered [Markyus] a room" in the apartment, "provided that [Markyus] agreed to keep [their] relationship quiet and discreet." Markyus stated that Scott spent "substantially more time" with him than Scott spent with Robert. Markyus further averred that he and Scott took a trip together to Boston. Markyus did concede that "he was never invited to visit [Scott's] family in Maine, where [Scott] traveled several times a year." Markyus further declared that when he contributed to household expenses, "he would make those contributions to [Scott] in cash from his tips as a bartender. [Markyus] often made deposits into what he later discovered to be a joint bank account that [Scott] held with [Robert]."

Assuming that Markyus's claim is not automatically barred by the fact that the decedent (Scott) was in a relationship with another person at the time of his death (but a person who was ineligible for the protection since he was not living in the apartment), should the court find that Markyus is a family member within the meaning of the rent control statute? Why or why not? This fact pattern is drawn from W. 49th St., supra.

(iii) Inheritance Protection for Nonmarital Partners

BECKWITH v. DAHL
141 Cal. Rptr. 3d 142 (Ct. App. 2012)

O'LEARY, P.J.

[Brent] Beckwith and his partner, Marc Christian MacGinnis, were in a long-term, committed relationship for almost 10 years. They leased an apartment together and were occasional business partners. MacGinnis had no children and his parents were deceased. His sister, Susan Dahl, with whom he had an estranged relationship, was his only other living family member. At some point during their relationship, MacGinnis showed Beckwith a will he had saved on his computer. The will stated that upon MacGinnis's death, his estate was to be divided equally between Beckwith and Dahl. MacGinnis never printed or signed the will.

In May 2009, MacGinnis's health began to decline. On May 25, 2009, MacGinnis was in the hospital awaiting surgery to repair holes in his lungs. He asked Beckwith to locate and print the will so he could sign it. Beckwith went to their home and looked for the will, but he could not find it. When Beckwith told MacGinnis that he could not locate the will, MacGinnis asked Beckwith to create a new will so he could sign it the next day. That night, Beckwith created a new will for MacGinnis using forms downloaded from the Internet [stating that the estate was to be equally divided between Beckwith and Dahl].

Before Beckwith presented the will to MacGinnis, he called Dahl to tell her about the will and e-mailed her a copy. Later that night, Dahl responded to Beckwith's e-mail stating: "'I really think we should look into a Trust for [MacGinnis]. There are far less regulations and it does not go through probate. The house and all property would be in *our names* and if something should happen to [MacGinnis] *we* could make decisions without it going to probate and the taxes are less on a trust rather than the normal inheritance tax. I have [two] very good friends [who] are attorneys and I will call them tonight.' [Emphasis added.]" After receiving the e-mail, Beckwith called Dahl to discuss the details of the living trust. Dahl told Beckwith not to present the will to MacGinnis for signature because one of her friends would prepare the trust documents for MacGinnis to sign "in the next couple [of] days." Beckwith did not present the will to MacGinnis.

Two days later, on May 27, MacGinnis had surgery on his lungs. Although the doctors informed Dahl there was a chance MacGinnis would not survive the surgery, the doctors could not discuss the matter with Beckwith since he was not a family member under the law. . . . After the surgery, MacGinnis was placed on a ventilator and his prognosis worsened. Six days later, Dahl, following the doctors' recommendations, removed MacGinnis from the ventilator. On June 2, 2009, MacGinnis died intestate. He left an estate worth over $1 million.

. . . Two weeks [later], Dahl opened probate in Los Angeles Superior Court. . . . Beckwith e-mailed Dahl [several times], asking about the probate proceedings. [Eventually] Dahl responded by e-mail, stating: "'Because [MacGinnis] died without a will, and the estate went into probate. I was made executor of his estate. The court then declared that his assets would go to his only surviving family member which is me.'" [At the hearing on the petition for final distribution of the estate], the probate judge found that Beckwith had no standing because he was "not a creditor of the estate" and he had "no intestate rights".

[T]he threshold question before this court is whether California should recognize a tort remedy for [Intentional Interference with Expected Inheritance or IIEI]. [Although California has not yet recognized the tort, 25 of the 42 states that considered it have validated it.] In addition, IIEI is outlined in section 774B of the Restatement Second of Torts. . . . In general, most states recognizing the tort adopt it with the following elements: (1) an expectation of receiving an inheritance; (2) intentional interference with that expectancy by a third party; (3) the interference was independently wrongful or tortious; (4) there was a reasonable certainty that, but for the interference, the plaintiff would have received the inheritance; and (5) damages. . . .

In order to decide whether a new tort cause of action should be recognized, we must consider the relevant policy considerations and balance the benefits of such recognition against any potential burdens and costs that recognition of the tort would bring. . . . [One concern is] that an expectancy in an inheritance is too speculative to warrant a tort remedy because the testator may have changed his mind notwithstanding any interference from a third party. However, where there is a strong probability that an expected inheritance would have been received absent the alleged interference, whether or not the decedent changed his mind is a question of fact necessary to prove an element of the tort and is not a reason to refuse to recognize the existence of the tort altogether. . . .

[W]e conclude that a court should recognize the tort of IIEI if it is necessary to afford an injured plaintiff a remedy. The integrity of the probate system and the interest in avoiding tort liability for inherently speculative claims are very important considerations. However, a court should not take the "drastic consequence of an absolute rule which bars recovery in all . . . cases[]" when a new tort cause of action can be defined in such a way so as to minimize the costs and burdens associated with it. . . . California case law in analogous contexts shields defendants from tort liability when the expectancy is too speculative. In addition, case law from other jurisdictions bars IIEI claims when an adequate probate remedy exists. By recognizing similar restrictions in IIEI actions, we strike the appropriate balance between respecting the integrity of the probate system, guarding against tort liability for inherently speculative claims, and protecting society's interests in providing a remedy for injured parties.

[Next,] we turn to whether Beckwith sufficiently stated the cause of action [for IIEI] in his complaint. . . . Here, Beckwith alleged he had an expectancy in MacGinnis's estate that would have been realized but for Dahl's intentional interference. However, Beckwith did not allege Dahl directed any independently tortious conduct at MacGinnis. The only wrongful conduct alleged in Beckwith's complaint was Dahl's false promise to him. Accordingly, Beckwith's complaint failed to sufficiently allege the IIEI tort.

We must still decide "whether there is a reasonable possibility that the defect can be cured by amendment. . . ." Under the circumstances here, Beckwith did not have a fair opportunity to correct the deficiencies with regard to his IIEI cause of action. The trial court found Beckwith's IIEI cause of action insufficient on its face, based on its conclusion the tort was not legally recognized in California. Accordingly, the court did not inquire into the sufficiency of the factual allegations supporting the IIEI claim. In light of the subsequent guidance provided by this opinion, we think it is appropriate Beckwith be given an opportunity to amend his complaint to address, if possible, the defects we have pointed out.

[With regard to Beckwith's claim of promissory fraud, we conclude that] Beckwith's complaint sufficiently alleged each of the elements of fraud with the requisite specificity and particularity. [I]n a promissory fraud action, to sufficiently allege defendant made a misrepresentation, the complaint must allege (1) the defendant made a representation of intent to perform some future action, i.e., the defendant made a promise, and (2) the defendant did not really have that intent at the time that the promise was made, i.e., the promise was false. . . .

Beckwith's complaint alleged that on May 25, 2009, Dahl promised him, via e-mail and a telephone call, she would "promptly prepare and deliver trust documents to [MacGinnis] for him to sign, equally dividing [MacGinnis's] estate between [Dahl] and [Beckwith] in accordance with [MacGinnis's] wishes." The complaint also alleged, "[Dahl] did not intend to perform this promise when it was made." Thus, the complaint clearly and specifically alleged (1) who made the promise, (2) to whom the promise was made, (3) where and when the promise was made, (4) by what means the promise was made, and (5) that the promise was made with no intention of performance. Accordingly, Beckwith's complaint sufficiently alleged the first element of promissory fraud, a false promise.

[With regard to the requisite elements of intent, reliance, and damages,] Beckwith clearly alleged Dahl made specific promises to prepare and deliver trust documents to MacGinnis, but she did not intend to prepare them at all when she made that promise. . . . Further, Beckwith alleged that because of his "trust in [Dahl] to help effectuate [MacGinnis's] wishes, [Beckwith] reasonably relied on [Dahl's] representation that she would have trust documents prepared and that no will was necessary." Thus, Beckwith alleged he believed Dahl's promises to be true and in reliance on that belief, he did not present MacGinnis with the will. He sufficiently pled actual reliance. . . .

In addition to pleading actual reliance, the plaintiff must set "forth facts to show that his or her actual reliance on the representations was justifiable, so that the cause of the damage was the defendant's wrong and not the plaintiff's fault." . . . Here, the complaint alleged that "[g]iven the circumstances, [MacGinnis's] condition, [Beckwith's] emotionally vulnerable state, and [Beckwith's] trust in [Dahl] to help effectuate [MacGinnis's] wishes, [Beckwith] reasonably relied on [Dahl's] representations that she would have trust documents prepared and that no will was necessary." . . . Beckwith has sufficiently alleged all of the elements of promissory fraud with the required specificity to state a claim. Accordingly, we conclude the trial court erred in sustaining Dahl's demurrer. . . .

NOTE: WHO WAS MARC CHRISTIAN MacGINNIS?

Marc Christian MacGinnis was the former partner of actor Rock Hudson. MacGinnis met Hudson in 1982. They began a relationship several months later. After Hudson died of AIDS in 1985, MacGinnis sued Hudson's estate and Hudson's former secretary, Mark Miller, alleging that he suffered emotional distress by having been put at risk of contracting HIV. This was at a time when being HIV+ was essentially a death sentence and few treatments were available.

Marc Christian MacGinnis (left), former partner of actor Rock Hudson, with his attorney Marvin Mitchelson (right)

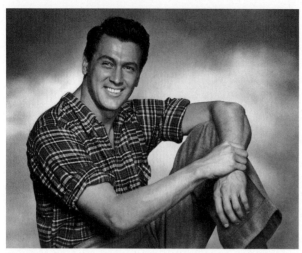

Rock Hudson, actor and former partner of Marc Christian MacGinnis

Hudson had concealed his HIV status from MacGinnis despite their ongoing sexual relationship. After learning that he was HIV+ and after becoming ill, Hudson told MacGinnis his weight loss was the result of dieting.[47] MacGinnis ultimately learned of Hudson's illness when it was publicly disclosed in 1985 on television after Hudson traveled to Paris to seek treatment. A jury initially awarded MacGinnis over $20 million, but this amount was later reduced to $5.5 million and the parties ultimately reached a settlement in the case.

At the time, MacGinnis was portrayed as a "gold-digging hustler."[48] MacGinnis challenged this characterization, explaining in a *People* magazine article that his goal was "not to sleaze Rock. It was to say that if you have AIDS, you ought to tell your partner, whether you're a movie star or a postman."[49] MacGinnis filed the lawsuit after his request to Hudson's managers to place funds in a trust to cover his medical expenses in the event that he tested positive for HIV was denied. In the litigation, MacGinnis was represented by Marvin Mitchelson, the attorney who represented Michelle Marvin in Marvin v. Marvin (supra p. 395).

For his part, Hudson was diagnosed in 1984 after the former first lady Nancy Reagan, a longtime friend, suggested that he get a mole checked.[50] In 1985, the day before he made his diagnosis public, Hudson sought help from the Reagans to get access to then-experimental treatments for HIV in Paris. According to the biography *Elizabeth Taylor: The Grit and Glamour of an Icon* by Kate Anderson Brower, the Reagans refused Hudson's request for help. Indeed, a Reagan staffer, Mark Weinberg, wrote a note saying: "I spoke with Mrs. Reagan about the attached telegram [regarding Hudson's request for help]. She did not feel this was something the White House should get into and agreed to my suggestion that we refer the writer to the US embassy, Paris."[51]

Ronald Reagan, who was U.S. President in 1981 when the first reports of HIV appeared, famously remained "largely silent and unresponsive to the health

---

[47]. Elaine Woo, Marc Christian MacGinnis Dies at 56; Rock Hudson's Ex-Lover, L.A. Times, Dec. 5, 2009.

[48]. Id.

[49]. Id. (quoting article).

[50]. Andrea Cavallier, Ronald and Nancy Reagan "Turned Their Backs" on Friend Rock Hudson When He Was Diagnosed with AIDS, Daily Mail, Dec. 7, 2022, https://www.dailymail.co.uk/news/article-11512997/Ronald-Nancy-Reagan-turned-backs-Rock-Hudson-AIDS.html

[51]. Alexandra Topping, Nancy Reagan Refused to Help Dying Rock Hudson Get AIDS Treatment, The Guardian, Feb. 3, 2015, https://www.theguardian.com/us-news/2015/feb/03/nancy-reagan-refused-help-dying-rock-hudson-get-aids-treatment.

emergency" in the early years of the crisis.[52] President Reagan did not publicly mention AIDS until four years later, in 1985, at which time the disease had already become an epidemic. This mention was made, coincidentally, on the same day that Rock Hudson died of AIDS. Hudson's death brought more public attention to the disease.

Notes and Questions

1. Inheritance law. In all 50 states, if a married person dies without a will (i.e., intestate), the surviving spouse is entitled to a share of the decedent's estate.[53] With the exception of Washington State (see Note 2), this protection does not apply to nonmarital partners. Nor do unmarried cohabitants have other "spousal" rights, such as the right to a family support allowance during estate administration, protection against disinheritance, or priority in administration of an intestate estate. This is true regardless of the duration of their cohabitation or the existence of children in common.

2. Washington State—the outlier. Washington State is the one exception to this general rule of no right to intestate recovery. In Washington, people in "committed intimate relationships" are entitled to a "just and equitable division" of all income and property acquired during the relationship. In re Estate of Langeland, 312 P.3d 657, 662 (Wash. Ct. App. 2013). See also Connell v. Francisco, 898 P.2d 831, 834 (Wash. 1995) (defining term as a "stable, marital-like relationship" in which both parties are aware of the lack of a marriage and identifying relevant factors as cohabitation, duration of the relationship, purpose of the relationship, pooling of resources and services, and intent). This doctrine applies both at dissolution and death.

3. Policy. Should states permit recovery by a nonmarital partner only where the decedent left a will providing for that result? Or should courts have the authority to award recovery in the absence of a will if the relationship was sufficiently committed and long-standing? If the "committed intimate relationship" doctrine in Washington had applied to the facts of Beckwith v. Dahl, do you think Beckwith would have been able to establish a right to recovery? If so, what property would Beckwith have been entitled to recover?

4. Holding. Because California does not extend intestate protection to nonmarital partners, Beckwith had to rely on alternative theories. What were these theories? What legal obstacles did he face? What was he hoping to gain? Would it have made a difference if Beckwith and MacGinnis had been a different-sex unmarried couple? Spouses? Why did the court recognize the tort? How likely are

---

[52]. Joseph Bennington-Castro, How AIDS Remained an Unspoken—But Deadly—Epidemic for Years, History.com, June 1, 2020, https://www.history.com/news/aids-epidemic-ronald -reagan.

[53]. Adam J. Hirsch, Inheritance on the Fringes of Marriage, 2018 U. Ill. L. Rev. 235 (2018); Laura A. Rosenbury, Two Ways to End A Marriage: Divorce or Death, 2005 Utah L. Rev. 1227 (2005).

surviving nonmarital partners to succeed under this tort theory? What is the larger significance of the recognition of the tort for nonmarital families and partners? See generally John C.P. Goldberg & Robert H. Sitkoff, Torts and Estates: Remedying Wrongful Interference with Inheritance, 65 Stanford L. Rev. 335 (2013).

5. Same-sex nonmarital partners premarriage equality. In one high-profile wrongful death lawsuit, a California court held that denying the claim by a non-marital same-sex partner on the ground that she was not married *at a time when she could not marry* was unconstitutional. Smith v. Knoller, 2001 WL 36128129 (Cal. Super. Ct. 2001) (holding that the absolute barrier to recovery by same-sex nonmarital partners at a time when they could not marry was "not reasonably related to any legitimate public purpose"). Does the availability of same-sex marriage change the legal analysis with regard to whether it is permissible to deny *unmarried* same-sex partners rights that are extended to *married* spouses?

6. Death benefits. In addition to the right to intestate succession, there are other important protections that apply in the event of the death of a spouse, including the right to various private and government benefits, such as Social Security survivors' benefits. Spouses also have an automatic right to make a range of important decisions after death, including decisions about disposition of remains and funeral arrangements. Nonmarital partners generally are not entitled to these default protections, and challenges to their exclusion have generally failed. For example, the partner of a deceased highway patrolman challenged a rule regarding access to retirement benefits that was limited to legal spouses in Glossip v. Missouri Department of Transportation and Highway Patrol Employees' Retirement System (MPERS), 411 S.W.3d 796 (Mo. 2013), after his long-term same-sex partner died in the line of duty. In rejecting his claim, the Missouri Supreme Court concluded that the spousal limitation bore a reasonable relation to the legitimate state interests of administrative efficiency and the policy goal of ensuring support to dependent spouses who were economically dependent on the deceased, whereas no such duty of financial support exists for unmarried couples.

Problem

You are an aide to a state legislator who is considering whether to propose a bill that would extend protections to nonmarital partners. The legislator asks you to draft a memo setting forth (1) the arguments for and against adopting a status-based rule for recognizing nonmarital relationships, (2) the best status-based standard for recognizing such relationships should one be adopted, and (3) the protections or rights that should be extended to nonmarital partners under this status-based rule, and why.

VI

Divorce

A. Introduction

For centuries, marriage was regarded as a lifelong commitment. Today, developments in family law make it considerably easier for spouses to dissolve their relationship. This chapter explores state regulation of the dissolution process. In particular, it contrasts the traditional fault-based system with the system of no-fault divorce that replaced it. It also addresses issues of access to divorce, divorce discrimination, the role of counsel, and divorce jurisdiction.

The evolution of divorce law and procedure raises important questions about individual autonomy and the interest of the state. How does divorce law change the parties' roles and responsibilities toward each other and the state? How have developments in divorce law altered the legal meaning of marriage?

1. Divorce as a Historical Phenomenon

Lawrence M. Friedman, A History of American Law
142-144, 378-381 (3d ed. 2005)

England had been a "divorceless society," and remained that way until 1857. Henry VIII had gotten a divorce; but ordinary Englishmen had no such privilege. The very wealthy might squeeze a rare private bill out of Parliament. Between 1800 and 1836 there were, on the average, three of these a year. For the rest, unhappy husbands and wives had to be satisfied with annulment (no easy matter), or divorce from bed and board (*a mensa et thoro*), a form of legal separation, which did not entitle either spouse to marry again. . . . No court before 1857 had authority to grant a divorce. The most common solutions, of course, when a marriage broke down, were adultery and desertion.

In the colonial period, the South was generally faithful to English tradition. . . . In New England, however, courts and legislatures occasionally granted divorce. In Pennsylvania, Penn's laws of 1682 gave spouses the right to a "Bill of Divorcement" if their marriage partner was convicted of adultery. . . . After Independence, the law and practice of divorce began to change, but regional differences remained quite strong. [In the South, legislatures passed private divorce laws.] North of the Mason-Dixon line, courtroom divorce became the normal mode rather than legislative divorce. Pennsylvania passed a general divorce law in 1785, Massachusetts one year later. Every New England state had a divorce law before 1800, along with New York, New Jersey, and Tennessee. Grounds for divorce varied somewhat from state to state. New York's law of 1787 permitted absolute divorce only for adultery. Vermont, on the other hand, in 1798 allowed divorce for impotence, adultery, intolerable severity, three years' willful desertion, and long absence with presumption of death.

[These] divorce laws surely represented a real increase in the demand for legal divorce. More marriages seemed to be cracking under the strains of nineteenth-century life. . . . To many devout and respectable people, [the rising divorce rate] was an alarming fire bell in the night, a symptom of moral dry rot and a cause in itself of further moral decay. [T]he family was changing. There was a slow but real revolution in the way men and women related to each other. William O'Neill put it this way: "when families are large and loose, arouse few expectations, and make few demands, there is no need for divorce." That need arises when "families become the center of social organization." At this point, "their intimacy can become suffocating, their demands unbearable, and their expectations too high to be easily realizable. Divorce then becomes the safety valve that makes the system workable." Moreover, a divorceless state is not a state without adultery, prostitution, fornication. It is certainly not a place where there are no drunken, abusive husbands. What it may be—or rather, what it became later in the century—was a place where the official law and the world of real life were sharply different.

[By 1880, legislative divorce was abolished. From 1850 to 1870, many states adopted highly liberal divorce laws. Divorce was easiest to obtain in western states especially, those least stratified by class.] After 1870, the tide began to turn. Influential moral leaders had never stopped attacking loose divorce laws. Horace Greeley thought that "easy divorce" had made the Roman Empire rot. America could suffer a similar fate. [In 1881, a New England Divorce Reform League was formed which later became the National Divorce Reform League. By 1882, the Connecticut law had been repealed.] Maine's law fell in 1883. A more rigorous divorce law replaced it, with tougher grounds, a six-month wait before divorce decrees became "absolute," and a two-year ban on remarriage of the plaintiff without court permission; the guilty defendant could *never* remarry without leave of the court.

[A dramatic increase occurred in the divorce rate between 1867 and 1881.] What accounts for the rising demand for divorce? [A] large number of people simply wanted *formal* acceptance of the fact that their marriages were dead. Just as more of the middle class wanted, and need, their deeds recorded, their wills made out, [and] their marriages solemnized, so they wanted the honesty and convenience of divorce, the right to remarry in bourgeois style, to have legitimate children with their second wife (or husband), and the right to decent, honest disposition of their worldly goods. . . .

"Divorce rings" operated practically in the open. Manufactured adultery was a New York specialty. Henry Zeimer and W. Waldo Mason, arrested in 1900, had lured young secretaries and other enterprising girls for this business. The girls would admit on the witness stand that they knew the plaintiff's husband, then blush, shed a few tears, and leave the rest to the judge. . . .

The migratory divorce, for people with money and the urge to travel, was another detour around strict enforcement of divorce law. To attract the "tourist trade," a state needed easy laws and a short residence period. [I]n the twentieth century, Nevada become *the* place. . . .

The last part of the nineteenth century was an era of national panic over morality, eugenics, the purity of the bloodline, and the future of old-fashioned white America. Whores and divorce had to be constrained. An irresistible force (the demand) met an immovable object (the resistance to divorce). The result was a stalemate. [M]oralists had their symbolic victory, a stringent law strutting proudly on the books. But nobody enforced these laws, least of all the judges. A cynical traffic in runaway and underground divorce flourished in the shadows. . . .

Postscript. Divorce rates started rising sharply in the 1960s and 1970s with the advent of no-fault divorce and reached a peak in 1981. Since then, the divorce rate has been declining. Whereas half of all marriages in the United States ended in divorce in the 1980s, today that rate is 39 percent.[1] Several factors explain the decline, including delays in first marriage age and the fact that marriage is increasingly sought by the wealthier and well-educated—factors that contribute to greater marital stability.

COVID-19 also affected the divorce rate. During the early stages of the pandemic, the strain of lockdowns led to a surge in couples ending troubled relationships. As the pandemic wore on, however, divorce filings plummeted due to spouses' fears of financial instability and the lack of access to divorce attorneys and courts due to the lockdowns.[2]

2. Divorce as a Social Phenomenon

Paul Bohannon, The Six Stations of Divorce
in Divorce and After 29-32 (Paul Bohannon ed., 1970)

The complexity of divorce arises because at least six things are happening at once. They may come in a different order and with varying intensities, but [they include]: (1) the emotional divorce, which centers around the problem of

---

[1]. Belinda Luscombe, The Divorce Rate Is Dropping. That May Not Actually Be Good News, Time Mag., Nov. 26, 2018, https://time.com/5434949/divorce-rate-children-marriage-benefits/.

[2]. Victoria Bekiempis, How Pandemics Affect Divorce Rates Now — and 100 Years Ago, The Guardian, Sept. 10, 2022 (citing demographic research noting a 12 percent decline in divorce in 2020), https://www.theguardian.com/lifeandstyle/2022/sep/10/pandemic-divorce-spanish-flu -influenza; Vincent M. Mallozzi, Divorce Rates Are Now Dropping. Here Are Some Reasons Why, N.Y. Times, Mar. 24, 2021, https://www.nytimes.com/2021/03/24/style/divorce-rates-dropping .html.

the deteriorating marriage; (2) the legal divorce, based on grounds [and now, on no-fault]; (3) the economic divorce, which deals with money and property; (4) the coparental divorce, which deals with custody, single-parent homes, and visitation; (5) the community divorce, surrounding the changes of friends and community that every divorcee experiences; and (6) the psychic divorce, with the problem of regaining individual autonomy.

The first visible stage of a deteriorating marriage is likely to be what psychiatrists call emotional divorce. This occurs when the spouses withhold emotion from their relationship because they dislike the intensity or ambivalence of their feelings. They may continue to work together as a social team, but their attraction and trust for one another have disappeared. [They become] mutually antagonistic and imprisoned, hating the vestiges of their dependence. Two people in emotional divorce grate on each other because each is disappointed. . . .

The economic divorce must occur because in Western countries husband and wife are an economic unit. [T]hey certainly have many of the characteristics of a legal corporation. [A]n economic settlement must be made, separating the assets of the "corporation" into two sets of assets, each belonging to one person. This is the property settlement. . . .

The coparental divorce is necessary if there are children. When the household breaks up, the children have to live somewhere. Taking care of the children requires complex arrangements for carrying out the obligations of parents.

All divorced persons suffer more or less because their community is altered. Friends necessarily take a different view of a person during and after divorce — he ceases to be a part of a couple. . . .

Finally comes the psychic divorce. It is almost always last, and always the most difficult. Indeed, I have not found a word strong or precise enough to describe the difficulty of the process. Each partner to the ex-marriage, either before or after the legal divorce — usually after, and sometimes years after — must turn himself or herself again into an autonomous social individual. People who have been long married tend to have become socially part of a couple or a family; they lose the habit of seeing themselves as individuals. . . .

Divorce is an institution that nobody enters without great trepidation. In the emotional divorce, people are likely to feel hurt and angry. In the legal divorce, people often feel bewildered — they have lost control, and events sweep them along. In the economic divorce, the reassignment of property and the division of money (there is *never* enough) may make them feel cheated. In the parental divorce, they worry about what is going to happen to the children; they feel guilty for what they have done. With the community divorce, they may get angry with their friends and perhaps suffer despair because there seems to be no fidelity in friendship. In the psychic divorce, in which they have become autonomous again, they are probably afraid and are certainly lonely.

However, the resolution of any or all of these various six divorces may provide an elation of victory that comes from having accomplished something that had to be done and having done it well. . . . I know a divorced man who took great comfort in the fact that one of his business associates asked him, when he learned of his divorce, "Do I feel sorry for you or do I congratulate you?" He thought for a moment and said — out of bravado as much as conviction — "Congratulate me." It was, for him, the beginning of the road back.

3. Divorce as a Gender-Based Phenomenon

Men and women experience divorce differently, as the excerpt below reveals.

Catherine K. Riessman, Divorce Talk: Women and Men Make Sense of Personal Relationships
65-72 (1990)

. . . For women, marriage flounders because husbands fail to be emotionally intimate in the ways wives expect them to be. This element of the companionate marriage is the centerpiece in women's accounts, working class and middle class alike. For men, the explanatory schema is very different: particularly for more economically advantaged men, the marriage failed because other relationships—with children, kin, and friends—were not subordinated to it; the marital relationship was not self-contained or was not primary enough to the wife. For both husbands and wives there was a failure in companionship; yet the particular activities women and men wanted to "do together" are strikingly different, especially in working-class marriages. And both women and men lament acts of sexual infidelity and incompatibility, though the interpretations they place on these events are not the same. For women, infidelity is an act of betrayal, living proof the marriage is over. Men have complex and differentiated views of infidelity, even as sex is central to their definition of what a good marriage should provide.

Some might argue that these different constructions arise out of the very different personality structures of women and men. Feminist psychological theory suggests that masculinity becomes defined through separation, whereas femininity becomes defined through relationships. Women and men, in bringing these different orientations into marriage, put severe strains on it. Women define the institution of marriage interpersonally. The relationship with the spouse is one of a series of interpersonal ties that coexist for them—not without conflict, of course. Yet at the same time women want marriage to be emotionally intimate through talking about feelings, problems, and daily experiences, and through understandings that go beyond words. Further, they expect talk to be reciprocal: their husbands will disclose to them at the same time as they share with their husbands. Divorced women's accounts describe men who could not or did not express love in these ways, or whose needs for separation, some might argue, precluded this kind of emotional intimacy.

Men want something very different from marriage. Especially prominent is their desire for the undivided attention of their wives. [Men] want the marital relationship to be exclusive and primary; women in contrast, add it to their other relational investments. Men value the autonomy of the marital pair rather than its interconnectedness. They expect to achieve emotional closeness with their wives through sex and a particular kind of companionship. It is these "doing" aspects of marriage that they emphasize. [T]he masculine style of love emphasizes practical help, shared physical activities, spending time together, and sex—manifestations of love that achieve connection through action rather than talk, just as providing for a family does. This style of love fits well with cultural expectations for men more generally, for achievement, responsibility, instrumentality. . . .

> Neither the women nor the men interviewed, whether working class or middle class, questioned the ideology of the companionate marriage. It was the failure of their particular partners to live up to the ideal that was defined as the problem, not the dream itself. . . .

Postscript. Subsequent research confirms the persistence of gender-based differences in divorce. Psychologist Mavis Hetherington reports that women are more likely to initiate divorce. She adds that the reasons for remaining in an unhappy marriage differ by gender. Women are concerned about finances and raising a male child alone. Other research on gender-based differences in divorce suggests that, for men, the stress of divorce is transient, whereas for women, the stress is chronic because women suffer from larger, more persistent losses in household income, as well as enhanced risk of poverty and single parenting.[3]

Kimberly F. Balsam et al., *Predictors of Relationship Dissolution Among Same-Sex and Heterosexual Couples*

Williams Institute, Mar. 1, 2018
https://williamsinstitute.law.ucla.edu/press/breakup-prediction-press-release/

A new study examining the predictors of relationship termination in same-sex and married heterosexual couples found that male-male couples were the least likely to break up. In addition, women in same-sex relationships were twice as likely as men in same-sex couples and 1.5 times as likely as heterosexual couples to have ended their relationships.

Researchers followed 515 couples in Vermont from 2002 to 2014 and found that, when considering all couple types together, longer relationship length, older age, and better relationship quality reduced the chances of a breakup. [T]here were no differences in break-up rates between same-sex couples who had legalized their relationship and those who had not.

[Key findings include the following:]

- For female-female couples,
    - Each added year of relationship length reduced the odds of a breakup by 13%;
    - Each year of age lowered the likelihood of a breakup by 4%;
    - Each year of increase in education reduced the odds by 16%;
    - Each unit of increase in relationship quality reduced the likelihood by 82%.
- When looking at all couple types together,
    - Each year of relationship length reduced the odds of a breakup by 9%.
    - Each additional year of age lowered the likelihood of a breakup by 2%.
    - Each unit of increase in relationship quality reduced the risk by 61%.

---

[3]. E. Mavis Hetherington & John Kelly, For Better or for Worse: Divorce Reconsidered 40-41 (2002); Thomas Leopold, Gender Differences in the Consequences of Divorce: A Study of Multiple Outcomes, 55 Demography 3, 769–797 (2018), doi: 10.1007/s13524-018-0667-6.

[F]or all groups, lower income and whether or not couples had children did not affect the odds of a relationship ending. . . .[4]

B. Fault-Based Grounds for Divorce

1. Adultery

BROWN v. BROWN

665 S.E.2d 174 (S.C. Ct. App. 2008)

PER CURIAM.

. . . Husband and Wife (collectively the Browns) married in Ohio on November 27, 1982. They had five children together during their [20-year] marriage. . . . In 1995, Husband and Wife built a new home on the property in Traveler's Rest where they resided throughout the remainder of the marriage.

Chris Craft sold and installed the windows in the Browns' new home. A few months later, Craft and his wife began socializing with the Browns. Around Christmas of 1996, Husband took the children to church while Wife remained at home with their baby. Husband returned home and unexpectedly discovered Craft there. In explaining Craft's presence, Wife told Husband Craft had stopped by to look at their Christmas lights.

Wife and Craft became close and began having lunch without either of their spouse's knowledge. On several occasions, Craft and Wife met in a remote part of a restaurant's parking lot and fondled each other in Wife's car. In 1998, Husband discovered Craft and Wife were having lunch together. After confronting Wife, she temporarily ceased contact with Craft but admitted to subsequently resuming their relationship. Additionally, Craft and Wife frequently talked on the phone. In late 2000, Husband discovered Wife had a cell phone for which she had the bill sent to her mother's address, and Husband testified Wife had called Craft several dozen times from Wife's cell phone. [Husband filed for divorce, alleging adultery. He contends that the family court erred in failing to find that Wife committed adultery.]

Proof of adultery as a ground for divorce must be "clear and positive and the infidelity must be established by a clear preponderance of the evidence." . . . Because of the "clandestine nature" of adultery, obtaining evidence of the commission of the act by the testimony of eyewitnesses is rarely possible, so direct evidence is not necessary to establish the charge. Accordingly, adultery may be proven by circumstantial evidence that establishes both a disposition to commit the offense

---

[4]. For the full study, see Kimberly F. Balsam et al., Longitudinal Predictors of Relationship Dissolution Among Same-Sex and Heterosexual Couples, 6 Couple & Fam. Psychol. Res. & Prac. 247 (2017).

and the opportunity to do so. Generally, "proof must be sufficiently definite to identify the time and place of the offense and the circumstances under which it was committed." Evidence placing a spouse and a third party together on several occasions, without more, does not warrant the conclusion the spouse committed adultery.

Our courts have not specifically stated what sexual acts constitute adultery. . . . South Carolina has rejected the argument equating adultery with intercourse. In [Nemeth v. Nemeth, 481 S.E.2d 181 (S.C. Ct. App. 1997),] the wife took a cruise and stayed in a cabin with a man other than her husband. The wife denied she committed adultery and introduced evidence she had chronic pain that made intercourse difficult for her. This Court found adultery, stating sexual intercourse is not required to establish adultery; sexual intimacy is enough. . . .

This Court [has asserted] that circumstantial evidence indicating opportunity and inclination is sufficient to sustain a finding of adultery. In [McLaurin v. McLaurin, 363 S.E.2d 110 (S.C. Ct. App. 1987),] we affirmed the family court's finding that the husband committed adultery when the only evidence of adultery was the wife's testimony that her husband admitted committing adultery and a process server's statement that the divorce pleadings were served on the husband at the alleged paramour's residence where the paramour answered the door "comfortably clothed". . . .

[Here] Husband has the burden of proving Wife committed adultery. While Husband is not required to show direct evidence of the actual act, he must demonstrate Wife's inclination and opportunity to commit adultery. The family court determined Wife and Craft may have had the opportunity to commit adultery at two locations: (1) in the Browns' home around Christmas when Husband was at church and (2) in the car in a parking lot at lunchtime. . . .

We agree that Craft and Wife's presence in the Browns' home, without more, is not sufficient to establish adultery. However, we disagree with the family court's finding that Wife and Craft's continued and secretive meetings in various parking lots did not provide sufficient evidence to establish an opportunity to commit adultery. The family court found Craft and Wife met approximately twenty-four times over a four-to-five-year period. While the admitted meetings were during the daytime in a car parked in public parking lots, Wife's and Craft's admissions to the conduct that occurred while in the car are circumstantial evidence that adultery was committed.

Furthermore, Wife's and Craft's own admissions establish they were inclined to commit adultery. Craft testified the activities he and Wife engaged in were sexual in nature. Wife and Craft admitted that when they would meet for lunch, they would often kiss in Wife's car. Craft also touched Wife's breast and removed her bra. Both Wife and Craft touched one another below the waist, outside of their clothing. Wife also admitted Craft touched Wife "under her panties" once or twice. Additionally, Wife stated she was in love with Craft and that she discussed marriage with him. Further, she admitted their relationship was sexual to a degree, and she desired to have sexual intercourse with Craft. . . .

The evidence here of opportunity and inclination is too compelling to be brushed aside on the basis of Wife's "strict moral upbringing" and her claims that the romantic rendezvous always stopped short of sexual intercourse. Therefore, based on the evidence Husband presented, we hold Husband met his burden in proving Wife committed adultery. . . .

Notes and Questions

1. Background. Historically, adultery was one of the most common fault-based grounds. Until the 1970s, adultery was a ground for divorce in all states. In New York, adultery was the *only* ground until 1967. A double standard once governed adultery. For purposes of divorce, a wife had to prove that a husband's adultery constituted a "course of conduct," although a husband merely had to prove that his wife committed a single act. Possible reasons for the gender bias are that wives were considered husbands' property (i.e., adultery was regarded as a form of theft), and adultery involving a married woman threatened the male lineage.

2. Elements. What are the requisite elements to establish adultery as a ground for divorce in South Carolina (the setting in *Brown*)? How did Mr. Brown establish those elements? What type of evidence is required, according to *Brown*? Why? What might have motivated Mr. Brown to file for divorce on a fault-based ground rather than a no-fault ground?

At common law, the crime of adultery could be committed only with a married woman. For divorce purposes, however, many states define adultery as the voluntary sexual intercourse of a married person with someone other than his or her spouse. How does South Carolina law define adultery? Under the traditional definition, are same-sex partners exempt from application of adultery law?

3. Influence of Lawrence v. Texas. At the time of *Lawrence* in 2003, adultery was a ground for divorce in 29 states, as well as a crime in 23 states and the District of Columbia.[5] Today, adultery is a ground for divorce in 30 states, and a crime in 16 states.[6] These criminal laws, however, are rarely enforced. Does *Lawrence* raise constitutional questions about such laws?

4. "Open" relationships. Contemporary adherents of polyamory engage in sexual relationships with multiple partners (often during marriage to one person). How does adultery law apply to persons who engage in such relationships? Does participation in these relationships imply consent/condonation?[7]

5. Adultery in the military. The military still subjects service personnel who commit adultery to disciplinary action pursuant to the Uniform Code of Military Justice Art. 234, and the Manual for Courts-Martial, MCM pt. IV ¶62. In 2019, Congress passed a new Military Justice Act (Article 134), changing the previous definition of adultery that required sexual intercourse between a man and a woman. The new definition ("extra-marital sexual conduct") broadens the definition to include

[5]. Nat'l Survey of State Laws 396-411 (Richard A. Leiter ed., 2003) (extrapolation from survey data).

[6]. Nat'l Survey of State Laws, 2022 (9th ed.), https://heinonline-org.uclawsf.idm.oclc.org/HOL/NSSL?collection=nssl&law=GROUNDS%20FOR%20DIVORCE&edition=Interim; Lauren Mattiuzzo, The Fine Print of Love: Uncovering the Not-So Unwritten Rules (crime), Feb. 14, 2023, https://home.heinonline.org/blog/2023/02/the-fine-print-of-love-uncovering-the-not-so-unwritten-rules/.

[7]. Jennifer R. Povey, Is Adultery Still a Crime in the United States?, Medium Blog, Sept. 12, 2022, https://jenniferrpovey.medium.com/is-adultery-still-a-crime-in-the-united-states-62ea8d4bf6bb.

oral and anal acts and same-sex affairs, and provides that legal separation is a defense. The maximum punishment for extramarital sexual conduct under this provision is a dishonorable discharge, forfeiture of all pay and allowances, and confinement for up to one year. What explains the military's continued concern with adultery?

The most famous case of adultery in the military involved the retired four-star general David Petraeus, who resigned abruptly in 2012 as director of the Central Intelligence Agency (CIA) after admitting an extramarital affair. Petraeus claimed that the affair began when he started work at the CIA (after his retirement from the military)—hence, military law was inapplicable. He later pleaded guilty—not to adultery, but rather to providing his lover with classified information, subjecting him to two years' probation and a $40,000 fine.

6. Law reform movement. Several states recently amended or repealed their adultery and fornication statutes—most for the first time since the statutes were enacted.[8] What might explain the recent legislative activity? Why do so many states continue to have adultery laws if these laws are rarely enforced, sexual mores have evolved, and fault-based divorce has given way to no-fault divorce?

7. Comparative perspective. Adultery continues to be strictly prohibited in some countries (e.g., Pakistan, Philippines, Saudi Arabia, and Somalia). Countries governed by Islamic law have the strictest prohibitions. Adultery laws in some Muslim countries are imposed on female victims of rape.

8. Adultery gender gap. Women are closing the adultery gender gap, although men are still more likely to engage in extramarital affairs. In the 1940s and 1950s, half of married men, compared to 26 percent of married women, reported extramarital affairs. Today, the percentage is 20 percent of men and 10 percent of women.[9] The gender gap is closing, in part because of the greater acceptability of divorce and because working women have less to lose economically from divorce.

9. Modern application. Some Internet users engage in online sex (i.e., the discussion of sexual fantasies, usually involving sexual self-stimulation). When one or both Internet users are married, their online sex constitutes "online infidelity." Does online infidelity qualify as adultery in jurisdictions that retain fault-based grounds?

———————————

The following study explores the role of adultery in the decision to divorce for different-sex couples.

———————————

[8]. Joanne Sweeney, Adultery and Fornication: Why Are States Rushing to Get These Outdated Laws Off the Books?, Salon.com, May 6, 2019, https://www.salon.com/2019/05/06/adultery-and-fornication-why-are-states-rushing-to-get-these-outdated-laws-off-the-books/.

[9]. Jeffery Dew, Predicting Infidelity: An Updated Look at Who Is Most Likely to Cheat in America, Inst. for Family Stud., Sept. 21, 2020, https://ifstudies.org/blog/predicting-infidelity-an-updated-look-at-who-is-most-likely-to-cheat-in-america; Alfred C. Kinsey et al., Sexual Behavior in the Human Male 585 (1948); Alfred C. Kinsey et al., Sexual Behavior in the Human Female 416 (1953).

Julie H. Hall & Frank D. Fincham, *Relationship Dissolution Following Infidelity*

in Handbook of Divorce and Relationship Dissolution 153, 154, 156, 157-158, 159-160 (Mark A. Fine & John H. Harvey eds., 2006)

Infidelity is the leading cause of divorce. . . . The impact of infidelity on a couple's decision to separate depends in large part on the nature of the infidelity and how it was discovered. . . . Catching one's partner red-handed [leads] to high rates of relationship dissolution (83.3 percent), whereas 68 percent of those who heard of their partner's infidelity from a third party then ended the relationship. Unsolicited disclosure by the unfaithful party was least likely to lead to relationship dissolution. This may be because individuals who voluntarily confess their infidelity to a partner are more committed to repairing the relationship and are willing to make amends. However, it may also be that these individuals provide more mitigating accounts of their infidelity. . . .

[Gender also has been shown to play a role in the relationship between infidelity and relationship dissolution.] [O]verall, women are more likely to report that their divorce was caused by infidelity, specifically their partners' infidelity, than are men. [I]t is evident that men and women react differently to infidelity. [W]omen tend to show a more negative overall emotional reaction to infidelity than do men. Women are more likely than men to feel nauseated or repulsed, depressed, undesirable or insecure, helpless or abandoned, or anxious in reaction to a partner's infidelity. . . .

The association between infidelity and relationship dissolution may also vary depending on the nature or quality of the relationship. [T]he risk of divorce following infidelity appears to decrease with the length of the marriage. Couples who experience infidelity in the early years of marriage are more likely to divorce than those who experience infidelity later in marriage.

[I]nfidelity-related divorces may be even greater stressors than other divorces, because the heavy emotional and psychological toll associated with adultery is compounded with the distress of divorce. Indeed, individuals who divorce following infidelity are more distressed after the dissolution than those who divorce without infidelity. They are also less well adjusted to the divorce and more attached to the former spouse than are those whose divorce was not related to infidelity. . . .

2. Cruelty

MOSS v. MOSS

361 So. 3d 140 (Miss. 2022)

BARNES, C.J., for the court:

Clay and Vicky Moss married on February 14, 1987, and separated on or about July 7, 2018. They had two children. On August 14, 2018, Vicky filed for divorce on the statutory ground of habitual cruel and inhuman treatment. . . .

[At] trial, Vicky stated that Clay habitually belittled and humiliated her throughout their thirty-year relationship. She testified that Clay controlled what she wore, called her a "tramp" or "slut" when he deemed her clothing immodest, and inspected her clothing daily. . . . Clay would tell her to bend over to test if he could see her bra or cleavage before she went to work, and he often told her to change clothes. When he disapproved of her clothing, he stated, "[N]o self-respecting Christian would ever wear that." [Clay] repeatedly accused her of adultery. In a 2017 note he wrote to Vicky threatening suicide, Clay questioned the paternity of their eldest daughter.

. . . Clay also habitually criticized Vicky's completion of basic household tasks, including how she did the laundry, scooped the kitty litter, and changed their daughters' diapers. Vicky testified that Clay regularly called her "small-minded" and "idiotic" and told her that she was not a good role model for her children. Additionally, Vicky testified that Clay forced her to quit a women's softball league and isolated her from her friends. . . .

In the years following, Vicky and Clay's relationship further deteriorated. Beginning in 2017, Clay and Vicky discussed separation. Clay sent Vicky a series of emails informing her that he would not agree to a divorce [unless she] "admitted [she] was never a true Christian." [He] called Vicky "a presumptuous sinner." Clay continued sending these emails after Vicky repeatedly asked him to stop. . . .

Between 2017 and 2018, Clay left Vicky three notes threatening suicide. . . . Clay wrote to Vicky, "Let [our children] know just before I pull the trigger, I will pray for your radical transformation to Christ." . . .

In July 2018, Vicky's lawyer referred her to a counselor [and] Vicky's doctor prescribed her medication for depression, which Vicky took for a short period before stopping due to side effects. . . . At trial, Vicky testified that Clay's conduct made her anxious, made her cry uncontrollably, and resulted in her feeling worthless. She also testified that her symptoms of stress led to picking at her eyelashes, as well as loss of sleep, chest pain, and headaches. . . .

Habitual cruel and unusual treatment must be proved by a preponderance of the evidence. . . . To prove habitual cruelty, a party must show conduct that either:

> (1) endangers life, limb, or health, or creates a reasonable apprehension of such danger, rendering the relationship unsafe for the party seeking relief, or (2) is so unnatural and infamous as to make the marriage revolting to the nonoffending spouse and render it impossible for that spouse to discharge the duties of marriage, thus destroying the basis for its continuance.

"[A] finding of physical violence is not a prerequisite to establishing habitual cruel and inhuman treatment." "Mere unkindness, rudeness, petty indignities, frivolous quarrels, incompatibility or lack of affection are not sufficient." "On the other hand, habitual ill-founded accusations, threats and malicious sarcasm, insults and verbal abuse may cause such mental suffering as to destroy health and endanger the life of an innocent spouse." A court may find that the habitually cruel standard is met when emotional abuse "falls 'along the lines of habitual ill-founded accusations, insults[,] and threats.'"

In determining whether the habitual cruel and inhuman treatment standard is met, "[t]here is a dual focus on the conduct of the offending spouse and the impact of that conduct on the offended spouse." "The effect of the conduct on the offended spouse is determined by a subjective standard, which is to say that an attempt is made to weigh the likely effects of the conduct on the offended spouse, as opposed to a normative standard." . . .

The offended spouse may show a negative impact through mental or physical symptoms. . . . In determining whether the habitual-cruel-and-inhuman-treatment standard is met, courts may take into consideration the totality of the offending spouse's conduct. "There are many kinds of acts such as wil[l]ful failure to support, verbal abuse, neglect, and the like which, if taken alone will not constitute cruelty, but when taken together will manifest a course of conduct as a whole which may amount to cruelty." "But if these combined acts manifest a course of revolting conduct, they may give rise to cruelty." . . .

"[F]alse accusations of infidelity, made habitually over a long period of time without reasonable cause . . . constitute cruel and inhuman treatment." Controlling behavior leading to social isolation may also contribute to a finding of habitual cruel and inhuman treatment. . . . The standard may be satisfied by "habitual or continuous behavior over a period of time, close in proximity to the separation, or continuing after a separation occurs." . . .

Here, the chancellor referred to Clay's "incessant, constant humiliation, shame, [and] correction" of Vicky over the course of the relationship. [T]he chancellor deemed Vicky's testimony credible and stated that Clay was "very self-advocating," had a "domineering-type persona," and engaged in "veiled threats of manipulation." . . . Additionally, as previously stated, Vicky received medical treatment for her symptoms of anxiety and depression, and her testimony was corroborated by her family. As in other cases where the court found habitually cruel treatment, Clay engaged in some type of cruel conduct on a daily basis. The chancellor stated that Clay's behaviors of cruelty and humiliation were continuous and "incessant." [W]e find that the chancellor did not err in holding that Clay's conduct, in totality, constituted habitual cruel and inhuman treatment. . . .

Notes and Questions

1. Elements. Cruelty (sometimes called "indignities" or "cruel and inhuman treatment") traditionally provided a ground for divorce in most states and still exists as a ground in some states. Courts generally require a *course of conduct* of cruel behavior and sometimes require an *adverse health effect*. What is a "course of conduct"? "Adverse health effect"? What did the Mississippi statute require in *Moss*? Did the court find that the evidence was sufficient to satisfy the statute? Why? How "adverse" does the effect on health have to be? See In re Guy, 969 A.2d 373 (N.H. 2009) (holding that wife's becoming "angry, upset, and distraught" upon discovery of husband's e-mails to other women was not sufficient). Further, several courts maintain that one incident will not satisfy the "course of conduct" requirement. However, a single incident may suffice if the act is particularly brutal.

2. Battered spouses. In the nineteenth century, divorce on grounds of cruelty was often the only remedy that was available to battered spouses. In *Moss*, was physical abuse required for a divorce based on the ground of cruelty? Why?

3. Mental cruelty. English ecclesiastical courts required actual or threatened bodily harm. Courts gradually expanded the definition to include mental cruelty. Many states require that the cruelty be extreme and/or sufficiently severe as to threaten safety or health or make continued cohabitation "unreasonable" or "insupportable." See, e.g., N.J. Stat. Ann. §2A:34-2. What did Mississippi law require in *Moss*? What acts established mental cruelty in the principal case?

Does/should the following conduct suffice? Exposing a spouse to a sexually transmissible disease? Engaging in an affair? Unreasonable demands regarding sex or birth control? See Jizmejian v. Jizmejian, 492 P.2d 1208 (Ariz. Ct. App. 1972). Transmission of an STD? See Farris v. Farris, 202 So. 3d 223 (Miss. Ct. App. 2016). Excessive gambling? See Rocconi v. Rocconi, 196 S.W.3d 499 (Ark. Ct. App. 2004). Permitting relatives to live with the couple? See Ferro v. Ferro, 871 So. 2d 753 (Miss. Ct. App. 2004). Sexual abuse of a child? See In re Henry, 37 A.3d 320 (N.H. 2012). Do any of these preceding acts raise constitutional problems?

4. Coercive control. Coercive control is a form of domestic violence consisting of emotional abuse that may or may not be accompanied by physical abuse. It consists of a pattern of acts of threats, humiliation, and intimidation that is used to harm, punish, or frighten a victim. The term derives from a landmark book by sociologist Evan Stark, Coercive Control: How Men Entrap Women in Personal Life (2007, 2d ed. 2023). No state currently includes it as a ground for divorce. Nonetheless, a recent small-scale study reveals that a majority of women cite coercive control as the main reason for seeking a separation or divorce.[10] What might explain the lack of legal recognition of the doctrine as a ground for divorce? For additional discussion of coercive control, see Chapter IV.

5. Higher level of proof for longer marriages. New York formerly required a higher degree of proof of cruelty for divorce involving a long-term marriage. See S.C. v. A.C., 798 N.Y.S.2d 348 (Sup. Ct. 2004). What purpose does this rule serve? Is it sound? New York's recent adoption of no-fault divorce is discussed later in this chapter.

6. Corroboration. In the fault-based era, corroboration was widely required to prove acts of marital misconduct for purposes of divorce. The corroboration requirement necessitated eyewitness testimony and contributed to the adversarial nature of divorce proceedings. Was corroboration necessary in *Moss*? What is the rationale for the corroboration requirement? Does adherence to the requirement make sense today?

---

[10]. Noel Baker, Majority of Women Cite Coercive Control as Reason for Their Divorce or Separation, Irish Examiner, Oct. 26, 2021 (citing study of 40 women by social work professors at two Irish universities), https://www.irishexaminer.com/news/arid-40729860.html.

3. Desertion

REID v. REID

375 S.E.2d 533 (Va. Ct. App. 1989)

KOONTZ, Chief Judge.

[Judith N. Reid sought a divorce on the ground of constructive desertion. Dr. Robert Reid responded, seeking a divorce on the ground of desertion. The commissioner recommended denial of the divorce on fault grounds but entry of a no-fault divorce decree. This appeal followed.]

The parties were married on June 26, 1965, in Denver, Colorado. Mrs. Reid had obtained a degree in medical technology and was employed at a local hospital. Dr. Reid was in medical school. In 1966, the first of their four children was born. In 1967 the parties moved to New York City where Dr. Reid completed his internship and residency. [Following Dr. Reid's stint in the Navy,] the parties moved to Charlottesville, Virginia, where Dr. Reid obtained a position at the University. He ultimately became tenured, head of his division, and director of the nurse practitioner program. [He subsequently left the university position to establish a medical corporation.]

During the first years of the marriage in which the parties' remaining children were born, Mrs. Reid was a homemaker. In 1980 she began part-time employment with [her husband's corporation] and ultimately became its controller. In 1985 Mrs. Reid and two other individuals, with the concurrence of Dr. Reid, formed King Travel, Inc., a travel agency, [and became president].

In his report, the commissioner reflected: "The testimony of Dr. Reid and Mrs. Reid rarely conflicts. They were talking about two different aspects [perceptions] of what were actually separate lives." The record amply supports the appropriateness of this statement. Mrs. Reid testified in detail as to the gradual breakdown in the marital relationship during this nineteen-year marriage. The commissioner concluded that in each specific instance Mrs. Reid identified a marital problem, Dr. Reid did not perceive a problem. In fact, almost to the very end of the marriage, as if they lived separate lives, Dr. Reid considered himself happily married, while Mrs. Reid considered her emotional health endangered.

[Mrs. Reid] does not challenge the chancellor's finding that Dr. Reid did not constructively desert her. [Rather, she asserts she was justified in leaving her husband when she moved out in 1984 because her emotional health was endangered by virtue of the following marital problems]: (1) sexual inactivity, (2) Dr. Reid's excessive work habits, (3) Dr. Reid's failure to assist in the disciplining and rearing of their children, and (4) a lack of "intimacy within the marriage." . . .

It is apparent from the record and particularly Mrs. Reid's testimony that, following the birth of their first child in 1966, the sexual pattern which developed between the couple can best be described as infrequent. While three additional children were conceived and born over the ensuing years, many months passed between acts of sexual intercourse. These periods of abstinence gradually increased until no intercourse occurred for approximately two to three years prior to the final separation. It is also apparent that Dr. Reid suffered periods of sexual impotency, and that the infrequency of intercourse was more a concern to Mrs. Reid than to Dr. Reid.

Compounding this difficult situation, Mrs. Reid described the work pattern of Dr. Reid which she considered excessive. From the beginning of the marriage, Dr. Reid held more than one job. During the Navy years, he worked at night conducting insurance physicals. After accepting the position at the University of Virginia, he worked at night at the emergency room of a nearby hospital, opened a nearby clinic with two other doctors, and ultimately formed Commonwealth Clinical. There is no dispute that these activities severely limited the time available for Dr. Reid to spend at home with his wife and children. . . . Mrs. Reid felt that Dr. Reid was not appropriately supportive of her efforts to discipline [one child in particular] and, rather, conveyed to her the sense that this problem was solely her responsibility.

Mrs. Reid's description of the lack of "intimacy within the marriage," while conceptually understandable, is nebulous at best. On brief, she partially summarizes it as Dr. Reid's refusal "to talk to her about their lives with its joys and its sorrows, about the family and where it was and where it was going, or any other matter not directly related to one of the family financial concerns." . . . It is fair to say that while Dr. Reid was financially supportive, Mrs. Reid bore the major responsibility for raising the children and maintaining the home. In the process she became unhappy and felt unfulfilled. We accept the commissioner's conclusion that this condition was due in major part to Dr. Reid's denial or lack of recognition of the needs and feelings of Mrs. Reid.

While not specifically asserted by Mrs. Reid as a justification for her leaving, it is clear from the evidence that the marital problems of this couple were compounded by the additional responsibilities assumed by Mrs. Reid when she undertook her duties at Commonwealth Systems and eventually King Travel. These activities were encouraged by Dr. Reid, but they did not produce the personal satisfaction or the lessening of Mrs. Reid's frustration as they both apparently had hoped. Finally, the purchase of a large sailing boat and Mrs. Reid's enthusiastic involvement in sailing without Dr. Reid, in turn, merely added more stress to the marriage.

. . . The issue remains, however, whether as a matter of law these circumstances provide a justification for leaving the marriage. In that regard, the additional facts surrounding her leaving become critical.

In April 1983, in what she describes as an effort to get Dr. Reid's attention, Mrs. Reid informed Dr. Reid that she could no longer endure the stress created by the problems in their marriage. As a result, the parties underwent counseling, which was unsuccessful. Mrs. Reid asserts that at that point she was totally committed to saving the marriage, but that Dr. Reid did not perceive the extent of their problems. The record supports this assertion. Subsequently, in October of that year, Mrs. Reid went on a month-long sailing cruise to the Virgin Islands. Upon returning she advised Dr. Reid that she wanted a separation. The separation was delayed because Mrs. Reid underwent a gallbladder operation and she did not want to upset the children at Christmas. . . . Mrs. Reid testified that she eventually made a deposit on an apartment and on a Friday night again discussed the marriage with Dr. Reid. There was no agreement for a mutual separation. She described this conversation as "not being intimate" but rather, "a superficial sort of thing."

On the following Monday, without Dr. Reid's knowledge, Mrs. Reid moved to this apartment. She testified that her intent in leaving the marital home was to make Dr. Reid realize that they had a problem, and that she "couldn't go on with it without doing something about it." This separation occurred on April 16, 1984. Mrs. Reid filed her suit for divorce on June 13, 1984. The chancellor sustained the commissioner's finding that as a matter of law Mrs. Reid did not intend to desert the marriage. We disagree. . . . "Proof of an actual breaking off of matrimonial cohabitation combined with the intent to desert . . . constitutes desertion as grounds for divorce. However, reasons for leaving the marriage other than an intent to desert may justify discontinuance of the relationship without giving rise to grounds for divorce." Under the law existing at the time of the present suit, fault, such as desertion, was a bar to spousal support. . . .

Mrs. Reid's description of her feelings and emotional condition are understandable in terms of human experience. The *cause* of her feelings and emotional condition, however, cannot be attributed factually or legally solely to the conduct of Dr. Reid. Rather, the evidence established that the pattern of conduct, indeed the entire marital relationship, established by both parties in this marriage resulted in her frustration and guided her decision to terminate the marriage. Mrs. Reid's complaints that Dr. Reid absented himself from the home and his proper share of the child discipline while working to provide financially for her and the family cannot serve as the justification for leaving him. Mrs. Reid would have us draw a fine line between where perhaps he excelled in one duty to the family at a sacrifice of another duty. This we cannot do. Her complaint of a "lack of intimacy in the marriage" is, in the final analysis, no more than a reflection of the different personalities of these marital partners and their method of relating to each other. It can be considered no more than a general complaint of unhappiness on the part of one spouse, which is the regrettable risk in all marriages. Finally, her complaint of the infrequency of sexual intercourse was a pattern developed uniquely between them almost from the beginning of the marriage. Moreover, Dr. Reid's periodic impotency was a mutual problem; the solution to which, obviously, was not within his sole control.

Under these circumstances, the most that can be concluded is that there was a gradual breakdown in the marriage relationship. As a result, Mrs. Reid understandably became unhappy and believed her emotional health was endangered. Her response to this problem was to terminate matrimonial cohabitation. The fact that she filed for divorce within two months thereafter belies an intent for a temporary separation. In so doing, she legally deserted the marriage and forfeited her right to spousal support. For these reasons, the commissioner erred in his conclusions of law. . . .

Notes and Questions

1. Background. Virginia permits divorce on the no-fault ground of a year's separation, as well as on fault-based grounds (adultery, conviction of a felony, cruelty, desertion or abandonment, or causing reasonable apprehension of bodily harm). Va. Code Ann. §20-91. If both fault-based and no-fault grounds exist, the judge may use discretion to select the most appropriate ground. What motivates a spouse to sue or defend on a fault-based ground or defense, given the existence of no-fault divorce?

When *Reid* was filed, fault barred spousal support. The current Virginia statute allows courts to consider "any ground for divorce" in determining awards of spousal support. Va. Code Ann. §20-107.1(E)(13). In reasoning highly reminiscent of Reid v. Reid, a Virginia court of appeals recently denied spousal support based on a finding of fault because the wife left the marital home. See Payne v. Payne, 886 S.E.2d 752 (Va. Ct. App. 2023).

2. Epilogue. Following the principal case, Dr. Reid petitioned for restitution of spousal support that he previously paid to Mrs. Reid. A panel of the court of appeals affirmed the trial court's denial of his motion. At a subsequent rehearing en banc, the court concluded that restitution could be ordered and remanded for a determination of the amount. The Virginia Supreme Court reversed, holding that the trial court lacked the authority to order restitution of support. Reid v. Reid, 429 S.E.2d 208 (Va. 1993). In 2001, Dr. Reid moved to Washington State, where he continued to practice internal medicine. He died in Seattle in 2014.

3. Elements. Desertion constitutes a ground for divorce in many jurisdictions. A spouse's mere departure is not sufficient. Desertion requires a cessation of cohabitation, without cause or consent, but with intent to abandon, continuing for a statutory period. Although intent (to desert, abandon, or terminate the relationship) is essential, the separation and intent need not occur contemporaneously. Separation without the requisite intent will not constitute desertion; subsequent intent formed after a separation will suffice, however. The desertion, then, dates from the time that the intention is formed. Did Mrs. Reid satisfy the requisite elements? Desertion must also occur without justification. Why did the court deem Mrs. Reid's reasons unjustified? See also *Payne*, supra (finding wife's leaving of marital home was not legally justified by her mental health).

Some statutes require that desertion be voluntary. Does desertion caused by imprisonment suffice? Can a spouse who was ordered out of the marital home claim desertion? Compare Knepp v. Niece, 2003 WL 175192 (Va. Ct. App. 2003) (husband deserted by breaking off marital cohabitation when he ordered wife to leave), with Royer v. Royer, 2004 WL 2093443 (Va. Cir. Ct. 2004) (finding that wife's departure after being told to leave was not desertion). Must abandonment be total? See Jeffries v. Jeffries, 138 N.W.2d 882, 884 (Iowa 1965) (some financial support by husband barred wife's claim). Does desertion constitute intentional infliction of emotional distress (IIED)? See Herbert v. Herbert, 2023 WL 3069523 (Miss. Ct. App. 2023).

Does refusal to engage in sexual relations constitute desertion? See, e.g., B.M. v. M.M., 880 N.Y.S.2d 850 (Sup. Ct. 2009) (finding constructive abandonment). Suppose that the refusal to engage in sex stems from health reasons? Religious beliefs? Objections to the other spouse's sexual practices?

4. Constructive desertion. Recall that Mrs. Reid filed for divorce on the ground of constructive desertion. Dr. Reid cross-complained for desertion. Constructive desertion constitutes intolerable conduct by one spouse toward an innocent spouse that causes the innocent spouse to leave the marital abode. Thus, if Dr. Reid's conduct gives the plaintiff justification for leaving the home, then Mrs. Reid is not guilty of desertion. Under this ground, a spouse (in this case, Dr. Reid) need not specifically intend that the plaintiff leave. Did Dr. Reid provide just cause for Mrs. Reid to leave, in the court's view? In your view?

5. Gender differences. To what extent does *Reid* exemplify the thesis of Catherine Riessman (in the above excerpt) about gender-based differences in divorce experiences? How does the judge in *Reid* interpret the facts? For example, compare the description of Dr. Reid's work, requiring absence from the home, as "excel[ling] in one duty," with its assessment of Mrs. Reid's work, which the court found "[compounded] the marital problems of this couple."

6. Statutory period. Many states require that the desertion continue for at least one year. Why require a statutory period of desertion for divorce? Proposed legislation in Virginia (the jurisdiction of the principal case) would eliminate the one-year waiting period for grounds of cruelty, reasonable apprehension of bodily harm, or willful desertion or abandonment by either party. 2022 Va. H.B. 1720, Va. 2023 Reg. Sess. What might have motivated the legislative reform?

7. Other fault-based grounds. Additional statutory fault-based grounds in some states include willful nonsupport, criminal conviction or imprisonment, drunkenness and drug addiction, impotence, and insanity.

C. Fault-Based Defenses

1. Recrimination

IN THE MATTER OF ROSS
146 A.3d 1232 (N.H. 2016)

HICKS, J.

The respondent, Christopher Ross, appeals an order of the Circuit Court dismissing his petition for a fault-based divorce and the final order of the court in his divorce from the petitioner, Danielle Ross. He argues that the trial court erred: (1) in granting the petitioner's motion to dismiss based upon the defense of recrimination. . . .

The trial court found, or the record supports, the following facts. The parties were married on July 27, 2002, and had two children prior to their separation in 2011. [Husband and wife met in dental school and later married. Husband, who had his own endodontist practice, helped the wife open and build her orthodontist practice. The couple separated the day that the husband discovered that the wife was having an affair with another dentist. The parties had been married for nine years at the time they filed for divorce.] The petitioner filed for divorce in December 2011, alleging both fault and irreconcilable differences as grounds for divorce. The respondent cross-petitioned for divorce on fault-based grounds, due to the petitioner's alleged adultery, and irreconcilable differences.

Approximately eleven months after the petitioner filed for divorce, the respondent began a sexual relationship with another woman [the ex-wife of the male dentist with whom his wife had had her affair]. The petitioner filed a motion to dismiss, alleging recrimination by the respondent. The trial court granted the motion over the respondent's objection. In 2015, the court entered a final decree of divorce citing irreconcilable differences as the cause of the marital breakdown. This appeal followed.

The respondent appeals the trial court's dismissal of the fault-based ground in his cross-petition for divorce. Specifically, he argues that his infidelity, which occurred eleven months after the parties' separation, could not be used as a basis for the defense of recrimination. The petitioner argues that the trial court did not err in granting the motion to dismiss because the respondent was not an "innocent party" within the meaning of the statute. . . .

Resolution of this issue requires us to engage in statutory interpretation. . . . RSA 458:7 states that "[a] divorce from the bonds of matrimony shall be decreed in favor of *the innocent party* for any of" the enumerated causes including "[a]dultery of either party." RSA 458:7 (emphasis added). "[I]nnocent" means "free from guilt," and "[o]ur court has stated flatly that a spouse who is guilty of an offense against the other spouse, which would be grounds for divorce, cannot himself obtain" a divorce under RSA 458:7. Rockwood v. Rockwood, 194 A.2d 771 (N.H. 1963)."In other words, recrimination is a defense against a spouse who is not innocent."

"Generally, although the misconduct of the plaintiff occurs after the commencement of his or her suit, it is as fully effective to bar the right to a [fault-based] divorce therein as if it had occurred previous to the commencement of the suit." This general proposition is reflected in the plain language of RSA 458:7, which states that a divorce "shall be decreed in favor of the innocent party." The statute necessarily requires that one be an "innocent party" at the time of the decree. The statute makes no exception for fault-based grounds that arise prior to the final decree, regardless of whether they arise before or after the filing of the divorce petition. Therefore, the trial court correctly considered the respondent's post-petition conduct when deciding the motion to dismiss.

Here, it is undisputed that the respondent was still married when he began a sexual relationship with a woman who was not his wife. See In the Matter of Blanchflower & Blanchflower, 834 A.2d 1010 (N.H. 2003) (defining adultery as "voluntary sexual intercourse between a married man and someone other than his wife" (quotation omitted)); see also In the Matter of Dube & Dube, 44 A.3d 556 (N.H. 2012) (holding that husband's infidelity precluded him from claiming status as an "innocent party" under RSA 458:7). Thus, we are not persuaded that the trial court erred by granting the petitioner's motion to dismiss.

The respondent argues that the defense of recrimination is unavailable to the petitioner because his adultery did not cause the breakdown of the marriage. However, recrimination does not turn upon which party's conduct caused the marital breakdown. Rather, the "right to set up one matrimonial offense in bar of another is an application of the equitable rule that one who invokes the aid of a court must come into it with a clear conscience and clean hands." Thus, it need only be shown that a spouse is not an "innocent party" because he or she "is guilty of an offense against the other spouse, which would be grounds for divorce." Causation is not an element of the defense of recrimination.

The respondent also asserts that "[i]t is not reasonable to suggest, in these times of protracted discovery and litigation, that a party to a divorce must remain celibate for the duration of the proceedings" to obtain a fault-based divorce. However, this argument is made in the wrong forum. "Matters of public policy are reserved for the legislature, and we therefore leave to it the task of addressing the [respondent's] concerns." [The court affirms the dismissal of the husband's cross petition for a fault-based divorce and grants the divorce based on irreconcilable differences.]

Notes and Questions

1. Elements. What is the nature of the recrimination defense? Is the defense limited to acts that cause the breakdown of the marriage? Is it applicable to conduct that occurs *after* one party files for divorce? Why or why not?

2. Policy. Does this defense prevent "the dissolution of those very marriages most appropriate for dissolution"?[11] Should divorce be granted only to "innocent" parties? What are the policies underlying the recrimination defense? One court suggests the following:

> (a) By rendering divorces more difficult to procure, recrimination promotes marital stability. (b) The rule tends to deter immorality, since a spouse is less likely to commit adultery (or any other marital offense) if he knows that his misdeed may bar him from obtaining a divorce at some future time. (c) The doctrine serves to protect the wife's economic status. (d) Recrimination prevents persons who are obviously poor marriage risks from being freed to contract—and probably ruin—another marriage.[12]

Do any of these policies justify the application of the recrimination doctrine in *Ross*? Traditionally, a successful recrimination defense barred divorce. In *Ross*, however, after the trial judge dismissed the petition and counterpetition based on fault, the judge granted the divorce on the no-fault ground of irreconcilable differences.

3. Motivation. What might motivate a spouse to sue or defend on a fault-based ground or defense? The defense of recrimination tends to be raised when one party is dissatisfied with the property arrangements. What considerations may have influenced the parties in *Ross*? One New Hampshire family law attorney speculates as follows:

> It appears in this case that there was some significant bad blood between the parties. Husband had helped wife open her orthodontic practice and contributed

---

[11]. Homer H. Clark, Jr., The Law of Domestic Relations in the United States 527 (2d ed. 1988).

[12]. Jenkins v. Jenkins, 519 So. 2d 1232, 1235-1236 (Miss. 1988).

financially and emotionally to that endeavor. In return, wife carried on an affair with a colleague for approximately five years. Wife changed the locks to the house two days after husband left. Husband may have been pursuing the emotional victory of a fault-based divorce for wife's cheating.

Husband may also have been pursuing the adultery grounds for the financial benefit. [New Hampshire law provides for an unequal division of property on fault-based grounds if fault caused the breakdown of the marriage and also (1) Caused substantial physical or mental pain and suffering; or (2) Resulted in substantial economic loss to the marital estate or the injured party. N.H. Rev. Stat. Ann. §458:16-a, II.] With the dental practices, marital home and savings and investments on the line, an uneven split makes a substantial difference in the outcome.[13]

If recrimination were abolished as a fault-based defense to divorce, should fault be retained, nonetheless, to determine alimony? That is, should fault trump financial need? Should it be retained to determine child custody?

4. Law reform. Does the recrimination defense make sense today, given the evolution of sexual mores and the pervasiveness of no-fault divorce? Do you agree with the husband in *Ross* that it is not reasonable to require a marital partner to remain celibate during the pendency of divorce proceedings? (In his case, his affair began 11 months after the wife filed for divorce; the divorce proceedings lasted 4 years.) Should states make the recrimination defense subject to the judge's discretion? See, e.g., Miss. Code Ann. §93-5-3 (if a party seeking a divorce "shall prove grounds entitling him to a divorce, it shall not be mandatory on any chancellor to deny such party a divorce, even though the evidence might establish recrimination").

5. Constitutional issues. Does application of the recrimination defense in cases of adultery evoke constitutional problems after Lawrence v. Texas?

2. Condonation

GERTY v. GERTY
265 So. 3d 121 (Miss. 2018)

RANDOLPH, Presiding Justice, for the Court.

In September 2013, the Gertys filed a joint complaint for an irreconcilable-differences divorce. [The parties then put the complaint on hold for almost two years, during which time they executed a Property Settlement Agreement (PSA)] that provided that Michael would have physical custody of the couple's minor child. Joesie had full knowledge that Michael was required to move to the Great Lakes area to fulfill a three-year military commitment when she agreed that their

---

[13]. Kysa Crusco, Ross v. Ross: Celibacy Pending Adultery Claim, NH Family Law Blog, Feb. 10, 2017, https://www.nhfamilylawblog.com/2017/02/articles/divorce/ross-v-ross-celibacy-pending-adultery-claim/.

son would move with Michael. Joesie made the decision not to move to the Great Lakes area with their son and Michael. By her own admission, her decision was due to Michael's lack of intimacy and her desire to live as a single woman. . . .

[W]ithout his knowing her connection, Joesie had Michael assist her in moving her belongings into the house of her paramour's mother, Robin Caldwell Fitzgerald. For nearly two years, Michael and their son lived apart from Joesie. She chose to spend Thanksgiving of 2013 and 2014 and Christmas of 2012 and 2013 with Kyle [her paramour] and his family, unknown to Michael. The sexual nature of her affair with Kyle ended in January 2014 or May 2014, depending upon what testimony from Joesie is to be accepted. . . .

In January of 2015, Michael informed Joesie that reconciliation was impossible and that he wanted her to sign and finalize the divorce papers. Joesie, upon the advice of her attorney, surreptitiously told Michael that she also was ready to complete the irreconcilable-differences divorce. Based on the advice of her counsel, Joesie waited until her summer visitation had begun pursuant to the PSA and until her son was physically in Mississippi before withdrawing her consent to an irreconcilable-differences divorce. Joesie and Michael then filed separate complaints for divorce on the ground of adultery, and alternatively sought an irreconcilable-differences divorce. [The details of Michael's alleged adultery are unspecified.]

After a temporary hearing on July 13, 2015, the chancellor granted physical custody to Joesie. The trial began in December 2015 and concluded May 2016. Six months later, in November 2016, the chancellor entered a final judgment and decreed that a divorce should be granted, but that neither party was entitled to a fault-based divorce. She found that Joesie had failed to establish adultery [on Michael's part]. She found that Michael had proved adultery because Joesie had admitted it, but that Michael had condoned Joesie's adulterous conduct. [Michael raises issues next regarding Joesie's condonation defense.]

"In Mississippi one seeking a divorce on the grounds of adulterous activity must show by clear and convincing evidence both an adulterous inclination and a reasonable opportunity to satisfy that inclination." "Adultery may be shown by evidence or admissions[,] and either [is] sufficient to support a decree of divorce." Furthermore, in cases concerning an allegation of adultery, the chancellor is required to make a finding of fact. Both parties charged the other with adultery. Their obligation of proof is well defined. However, the chancellor failed to make any findings of fact regarding Joesie's multiple adulterous acts, nor did she make any findings of fact about whether Michael knew about or condoned any adulterous acts outside the "fling."

No factual dispute exists about whether Joesie had an extended affair with Kyle while she still was married to Michael, but she admitted only a very limited time frame of her overall adulterous conduct to Michael in August 2013 when he confronted her. Michael testified that, once he confronted her, she produced approximately ten pictures depicting a beach trip with Kyle and others. Joesie admitted during the trial that the affair with Kyle had spanned portions of 2012, 2013, and 2014. Her witnesses testified that in addition to those years, the affair occurred also during portions of 2011 and 2015.

Ample evidence in the record supports a finding that Joesie failed to disclose the extent and time frame of her extramarital affairs with Kyle. . . . Joesie admitted that she never informed Michael that she continued to have a sexual relationship with Kyle through January 2014 or May 2014. She never admitted that she engaged in an extramarital affair in 2012 while Michael was deployed to Guam. While Joesie never admitted that the illicit affair with Kyle began before December 2012, she did testify that it continued for nearly a year without Michael's knowledge. No one produced evidence that Michael's knowledge exceeded what Joesie had told him about the 2013 summer "fling." There is no proof in the record that Michael condoned anything other than that summer "fling." Michael cannot condone extramarital conduct that he did not know about or that was ongoing after Joesie's admission. . . .

Condonation, an affirmative defense, was pleaded by Joesie, thus she had the burden of proving that Michael had condoned her infidelity. Joesie must establish, after Michael condoned her multiple acts of adultery beyond her self-confessed "fling" in the summer of 2013, that she did not resume her previous, adulterous inclinations. Failure to mend her prior conduct results in a revival of Michael's ground for divorce, i.e., adultery. By her own admission, Joesie continued her infidelity long after seeking Michael's condonation of the summer 2013 fling.

The defense of condonation is recognized in our law. Condonation is the forgiveness of a marital wrong on the part of the wronged party. Condonation may be expressed or implied. The mere resumption of residence does not constitute a condonation of past marital sins and does not act as a bar to a divorce being granted.

In practical effect, condonation places the offending spouse on a form of temporary probation. Any subsequent conduct within a reasonable time after resumption of cohabitation which evidences an intent not to perform the conditions of the condonation in good faith, may be sufficient to avoid the defense of condonation, even though the conduct so complained of in and of itself may not be grounds for divorce. An entire course of conduct rule applies. *A party's conduct both before and after the alleged condonation can be joined together to establish the cause for divorce.* Wood v. Wood, 495 So.2d 503, 505 (Miss. 1986) (citing Armstrong v. Armstrong, 32 Miss. 279, 283 (1856) (emphasis added)).

[Our detailed review of the record] reveals that Joesie lied about the beginning, timing, and duration of the affair and attempted to obscure the continuous adulterous relationship with Kyle after Michael had condoned a brief summer "fling," not [her] course of adulterous behavior spanning years. The chancellor found that Joesie's credibility was questionable about the extent of her relationship with Kyle. Joesie failed to mend her ways by texting Kyle, communicating with Kyle over Facebook, attending the same parties as Kyle, taking overnight trips with Kyle, spending holidays with Kyle and his family, and having sexual relations with Kyle, all after Joesie informed Michael that she had a summer "fling" and had ended it. Michael believed that both he and Joesie were working toward reconciling their marriage. However, Joesie never rid herself of the adulterous inclinations, and she continued to place herself in situations which allowed her a reasonable opportunity to satisfy her adulterous inclinations.

Joesie's continued secretive, evasive, and deceptive relationship with Kyle, after she informed Michael of her brief fling leading him to attempt to reconcile, "evidences an intent not to perform the conditions of the condonation in good faith." These facts preclude application of the affirmative defense of condonation and revive her previous adulterous offenses, entitling Michael to a divorce on the ground of adultery. . . .

Notes and Questions

1. Definition. With the advent of no-fault divorce (discussed in the next section), many jurisdictions abolished fault-based defenses. Nonetheless, as *Gerty* reveals, some jurisdictions continue to recognize some or all these defenses.

According to the condonation doctrine, a spouse who has condoned marital misconduct is barred from using that misconduct as grounds for divorce. Grounds that may be condoned include adultery, cruelty, habitual drunkenness, and desertion (also termed "abandonment"). Some courts limit the condonation defense to divorces based on adultery. See, e.g., P.K. v. R.K., 820 N.Y.S.2d 844 (Sup. Ct. 2006).

Did Michael Gerty condone Joesie's adultery? If so, why didn't condonation bar him from using her conduct as grounds for divorce?

2. Requirements. What does condonation require? Cases are not always clear. Forgiveness of marital misconduct *and* resumption of sexual relations? See In re Marriage of Hightower, 830 N.E.2d 862, 867 (Ill. App. Ct. 2005) (condonation is "a question of intent [involving] a combination of factors" and finding that wife condoned husband's infidelity by her ensuing cohabitation). Is resumption of cohabitation enough by itself to establish condonation? See Vinson v. Vinson, 880 So. 2d 469 (Ala. Civ. App. 2003) (holding that sexual intercourse may be presumed from cohabitation). For how long must cohabitation resume? See Srivastava v. Srivastava, 769 S.E.2d 442, 448 (S.C. Ct. App. 2015) (cohabitation for "any considerable period of time" shows an intention to forgive). Is it appropriate to assume that the resumption of sexual relations constitutes forgiveness? See Hoffman v. Hoffman, 762 A.2d 766 (Pa. Super. Ct. 2000) (holding that husband's resumption of sexual relations was evidence of condonation despite his refusal to withdraw a custody action).

3. Attorneys' role. Because of the possible application of the condonation defense, should divorce attorneys regularly counsel their clients at their first interview and at every opportunity, "Do not under any circumstances have sex with your spouse again"?

4. Policy. The rationale for the condonation defense, dating back to the ecclesiastical courts, is the idea that the law should encourage forgiveness of an errant spouse and reconciliation. Does the doctrine promote these policies? Does the condonation defense raise constitutional issues of family privacy? Should condonation continue to serve as a ground for denying divorce? For transforming a fault-based divorce into a no-fault divorce? Should it serve as a bar to alimony?

NOTE: OTHER FAULT-BASED DEFENSES

In the fault-based era, other common defenses to divorce were connivance and collusion. Connivance constitutes express or implied consent by the plaintiff to the misconduct alleged. Three justifications exist for the connivance defense: First, according to the Latin maxim *volenti non fit injuria*, "He who consents cannot receive an injury." Second, a petitioner with unclean hands is not entitled to equitable relief. Third, some states limited divorce to the innocent party, and a conniving spouse was not an innocent party.

Collusion is an agreement between husband and wife to (1) commit a marital offense in order to obtain a divorce, (2) introduce false evidence of a transgression not actually committed, or (3) suppress a valid defense. Before no-fault divorce, the collusive divorce appears to have been the norm. Insanity traditionally provided a ground for divorce as well as a defense.

Problems

1. Richard, an accountant, and Sandra, a schoolteacher, have been married for eight years. They have no children. Richard believes that a husband should be in charge of the family's finances. He puts Sandra on a strict allowance, insists that she account for every cent, forbids her from writing checks or using credit cards, and requires her to surrender all receipts of her purchases to him. He is highly critical of Sandra's spending habits, castigating her for the amount that she spends on groceries and gasoline, and at the beauty salon. In addition, he limits her to two showers per week to save money on hot water. He habitually belittles her, insults her in front of other people, refuses to allow her friends to visit, and makes baseless charges that she is unfaithful.

Sandra complains that she and Richard have little in common. She chides him that his only interests are football and other women. She yells at him for refusing to help around the house and leaving his dirty clothes everywhere for her to pick up. She subjects him to constant verbal abuse over their inability to conceive. Sandra is so upset by Richard's incessant harping at her about money that she suffers from insomnia and depression. She begins spending an increasing amount of time online. Sandra discovers an online game called "Second Life," which provides players with their own avatars and the opportunity to purchase services and goods. She soon begins playing "Second Life" six to eight hours daily. Richard, who declines to join Sandra in the virtual world, learns that Sandra has a "virtual husband," Oscar. Although Sandra never meets Oscar in real life, she begins skipping meals and outings to spend more time online with him. Richard feels angry and betrayed by Sandra's emotional withdrawal.

Richard, who has a drinking problem, attends Alcoholics Anonymous (AA) weekly. After a meeting, he invites an AA member, Lorraine, to have coffee with him. Richard starts coming home late from the meetings. Although Sandra has no evidence of Richard's infidelity, she gets so furious at his late hours that she confronts him with a handgun when he returns home one evening. Richard denies having an affair. The couple separates, and then reconciles briefly, but Richard eventually moves out. During the separation, Sandra observes his Mercedes parked in front of Lorraine's apartment at night.

Sandra and Richard decide to file for divorce. Their jurisdiction permits divorce based on either no-fault or fault-based grounds. Both Sandra and Richard consult attorneys to explore possible fault-based grounds and defenses. What should their respective attorneys advise them?[14]

2. Lois Hollis seeks a divorce from her husband, Rex, on the ground of adultery. During the divorce proceedings, Rex contends that Lois urged him to date

---

[14]. See Allie Volpe, What Actually Counts as Cheating in the Metaverse?, Bustle Blog, Feb. 18, 2022, https://www.bustle.com/wellness/what-counts-cheating-metaverse-infidelity.

other women during the marriage. He introduces into evidence her handwritten note to him, stating her hope that he would fall in love with another woman so that Lois could leave the marriage. After he began an affair, Lois again wrote to him that she hoped that he and his new love would live together for some time (prior to marriage). Further, Rex testifies that when he and his new woman friend first had sexual relations at a hotel, they received flowers and a card from Lois saying, "My very best wishes to you both today, to your new beginning." What result? See Hollis v. Hollis, 427 S.E.2d 233 (Va. Ct. App. 1993).

D. No-Fault Divorce

1. Divorce Reform

All states have some form of no-fault divorce. Considerable variation exists, however, as to that form. Two common models, the California Family Law Act and the Uniform Marriage and Divorce Act (UMDA), are discussed below.

Allen M. Parkman, Good Intentions Gone Awry: No-Fault Divorce and the American Family
72-75, 79-81 (2000)

The nation's unequivocal no-fault law became effective in California in 1970. [T]he California legislature took its first steps in that direction in 1963. . . . Four major themes emerged from the 1964 hearings in the California Assembly which set the agenda for the legislative proposals that followed. There were widespread concerns about:

1. the high divorce rate,
2. the adversary process creating hostility, acrimony, and trauma,
3. a need to recognize the inevitability of divorce for some couples and attempt to make the legal process less destructive for them and their children, and
4. charges made by divorced men that the divorce law and its practitioners worked with divorced women to acquire an unfair advantage over former husbands.

California Governor Edmund ("Pat") Brown, who launched the first law reform commission that recommended no-fault divorce

The hearings reached no conclusions, nor was any legislation proposed. . . . In 1966, Governor Edmund G. Brown, who was enthusiastic about divorce law reform, established a twenty-two member Commission on the Family [consisting of] one minister, four legislators, six lawyers, four judges, three psychiatrists, two law professors, one medical doctor, and one member of the State Social Welfare Board. . . .

The commission [made] recommendations in two areas: First, it suggested revisions in the substantive law of divorce. Second, it examined the feasibility of establishing a system of family courts. The commission proposed legislation in the form of a model Family Court Act that would have created a family court, eliminated fault as a ground for divorce, and revised the community property distribution rules. The family court proposal included both the creation of a family court system and the establishment of procedures to encourage the parties to use the court's conciliation and counseling services. The commission also recommended that dissolution should be granted whenever the court found that the legitimate objectives of the marriage had been destroyed and that there was no reasonable likelihood that the marriage could be saved.

[The major objection was the potentially high cost of the counseling.] James A. Hayes, a member of the Assembly Judiciary Committee, independently put together another proposal that eliminated the major cost-incurring features—a separate family court system and mandatory counseling structure—but kept the marriage-breakdown theory of divorce. [The subsequent bill, which incorporated this approach, was enacted as the Family Law Act of 1969.]

The new Family Law Act established two grounds for marital dissolution, "irreconcilable differences which have caused the irremediable breakdown of the marriage" and incurable insanity. [The new act had no provision for a family court system or counseling.] Other changes emphasized a new orientation in divorce proceedings. The term *divorce* was replaced by *dissolution of marriage*. A neutral petition form, *In re the Marriage of Mrs. Smith and Mr. Smith*, replaced the adversarial form *Smith v. Smith*. The parties were called "petitioner" and "respondent" rather than "plaintiff" and "defendant." . . .

Under the prior law, the property division was unequal when the grounds for divorce were adultery, extreme cruelty, or incurable insanity, with the innocent party allocated a disproportionately large share of the community property. Under the new act, community property usually was to be divided equally, with no regard for fault, unless the division would impair the value of the property, such as a business, or when community funds had been deliberately squandered or misused by one spouse to the extent that an equal division of the remaining assets would no longer be equitable. Alimony was redefined as "support" and was determined by fairness rather than fault. . . .

Often ignored in the histories of no-fault divorce in California was the special interest that Hayes brought to his advocacy of no-fault. James A. Hayes was involved in a bitter divorce action during the evolution of no-fault in the California legislature. [Hayes divorced his homemaker wife in 1969, after 25 years of marriage and four children. The final decree was generous to his wife. However, in 1973, after passage of the new law, Hayes successfully petitioned to reduce significantly his financial obligations to his wife because he had remarried and assumed new financial obligations.] Hayes was obviously not a casual observer. He was instrumental in enacting no-fault divorce in California [in an attempt] to reduce the financial arrangements to which he had agreed as a condition for his divorce. . . .

In most histories of the passage of the law, James Hayes's role is given only passing notice. If anything, he is pictured as a very active public servant. But the passage of no-fault in California bears witness to the process of legislative self-interest. . . . This is a law that was passed by a legislature dominated by men . . . reinforced by the lobbying efforts of men's interest groups and maneuvered through the California legislature by a man who personally had a great deal to gain from a reduction in the negotiating power of married women. . . .

Lynne Carol Halem, Divorce Reform: Changing Legal and Social Perspectives
269-277 (1980)

[THE UNIFORM MARRIAGE AND DIVORCE ACT: BACKGROUND]

The idea of a national marriage and divorce statute, either in the form of an amendment to the Constitution or a singular law to be adopted by each state, was first proposed in 1884 and continued to spark debates for many years. [T]he Uniform Marriage and Divorce Act [was] ratified by the National Conference of Commissioners on Uniform State Laws in 1970. [The original intent was to remove the concept of fault by substituting the term "irretrievable breakdown" for fault-based grounds and to reject the no-fault ground of separation because it might be construed as a form of punishment.]

The critical blow came from the members of the Family Law Section of the American Bar Association [(ABA)]. Whereas in the past, the ABA had been most supportive of the commissioners' bills, this statute proved to be the exception. Without discrediting the concept of no-fault, the Bar attacked the statute on three grounds: the ease and speed with which a divorce could be granted; the absence of conciliation provisions or other brakes on hasty divorce; and the lack of specificity in the regulations governing property division. . . . Using standard conservative arguments, the ABA charged that passage of the act would legalize "easy" or "quickie" divorces. It may be that this position reflected the fear of an insidious plot to minimize the role of legal counsel. . . .

[The commissioners drafted three versions of the statute before they received an endorsement from the ABA in 1974.] The new statute introduced a clause for the no-fault ground of separation even if the waiting period was abbreviated to 180 days; the term "marital discord" was implicitly linked to the ground of "cruel and inhuman treatment" even if "marital misconduct" was not mentioned; references to reconciliation were more obtrusive even if they were not clearly defined; and the ABA's denouncement of demand divorce received credence through the addition of new safeguards even if they were weak and inoperable.

In other ways, however, the Uniform Marriage and Divorce Act was more progressive than California's law. Issues of marital misconduct were considered irrelevant to custody. [Evidence of fault was relevant to custody in early versions of the California statute but not after 1993.] The effort to discourage spousal maintenance by basing awards on the needs and resources of the parties might eventually prove a more realistic and less acrimonious approach to the problem of postdivorce economics.

Further, incurable insanity and irreconcilable differences did not appear as grounds for dissolution. Whereas the former was largely superfluous in the California act, the latter troubled some purists who objected to the multiplicity of possible translations. Quite obviously [UMDA's] bill had other vagaries. The term "irretrievably broken" was not defined, nor were precise directives furnished to curtail the discretionary powers of the judiciary. Hence many of the indeterminacies in the California model were duplicated in this statute. But in California the reformers could predict fairly accurately the court's interpretation would be liberal. This was not the case with the Uniform Act. . . .

Many states follow either the California or the UMDA model. Other jurisdictions have taken different approaches (illustrated below).

CALIFORNIA FAMILY CODE

§2310. GROUNDS FOR DISSOLUTION OR LEGAL SEPARATION

Dissolution of the marriage or legal separation of the parties may be based on either of the following grounds, which shall be pleaded generally:
(a) Irreconcilable differences, which have caused the irremediable breakdown of the marriage.
(b) Permanent legal incapacity to make decisions.

§2311. IRRECONCILABLE DIFFERENCES DEFINED

Irreconcilable differences are those grounds which are determined by the court to be substantial reasons for not continuing the marriage and which make it appear that the marriage should be dissolved.

§2335. MISCONDUCT; ADMISSIBILITY OF SPECIFIC ACTS OF MISCONDUCT

Except as otherwise provided by statute, in a pleading or proceeding for dissolution of marriage or legal separation of the parties, including depositions and discovery proceedings, evidence of specific acts of misconduct is improper and inadmissible.

UNIFORM MARRIAGE AND DIVORCE ACT

§302. DISSOLUTION OF MARRIAGE; LEGAL SEPARATION

(a) The [_____] court shall enter a decree of dissolution of marriage if . . .
(2) the court finds that the marriage is irretrievably broken, if the finding is supported by evidence that (i) the parties have lived separate and apart for a period of more than 180 days next preceding the commencement of the proceeding, or (ii) there is serious marital discord adversely affecting the attitude of one or both of the parties toward the marriage. . . .

§305. IRRETRIEVABLE BREAKDOWN

(a) If both of the parties by petition or otherwise have stated under oath or affirmation that the marriage is irretrievably broken, or one of the parties has so stated and the other has not denied it, the court, after hearing, shall make a finding whether the marriage is irretrievably broken.

(b) If one of the parties has denied under oath or affirmation that the marriage is irretrievably broken, the court shall consider all relevant factors, including the circumstances that gave rise to filing the petition and the prospect of reconciliation, and shall:

(1) make a finding whether the marriage is irretrievably broken; or

(2) continue the matter for further hearing not fewer than 30 nor more than 60 days later, or as soon thereafter as the matter may be reached on the court's calendar, and may suggest to the parties that they seek counseling. The court, at the request of either party shall, or on its own motion may, order a conciliation conference. At the adjourned hearing the court shall make a finding whether the marriage is irretrievably broken.

(c) A finding of irretrievable breakdown is a determination that there is no reasonable prospect of reconciliation.

NEW YORK DOMESTIC RELATIONS LAW

§170. ACTION FOR DIVORCE

An action for divorce may be maintained by a husband or wife to procure a judgment divorcing the parties and dissolving the marriage on any of the following grounds:

(1) The cruel and inhuman treatment of the plaintiff by the defendant such that the conduct of the defendant so endangers the physical or mental well being of the plaintiff as renders it unsafe or improper for the plaintiff to cohabit with the defendant.

(2) The abandonment of the plaintiff by the defendant for a period of one or more years.

(3) The confinement of the defendant in prison for a period of three or more consecutive years after the marriage of plaintiff and defendant.

(4) The commission of an act of adultery [defined as] as the commission of an act of sexual intercourse, oral sexual conduct or anal sexual conduct, voluntarily performed by the defendant, with a person other than the plaintiff after the marriage of plaintiff and defendant. . . .

(5) The husband and wife have lived apart pursuant to a decree or judgment of separation for a period of one or more years after the granting of such decree or judgment, and satisfactory proof has been submitted by the plaintiff that he or she has substantially performed all the terms and conditions of such decree or judgment.

(6) The husband and wife have lived separate and apart pursuant to a written agreement of separation . . . for a period of one or more years after the execution of such agreement and satisfactory proof has been submitted by the plaintiff that he or she has substantially performed all the terms and conditions of such agreement. . . .

(7) The relationship between husband and wife has broken down irretrievably for a period of at least six months, provided that one party has so stated under oath. . . .

Postscript. New York had the strictest divorce law in the country until 2010, permitting divorce only on fault-based grounds or subject to both parties' agreement (e.g., if the spouses lived apart for at least one year pursuant to a written agreement or both sought a judicial separation). In 2010, the state legislature added a unilateral no-fault provision (N.Y. Dom. Rel. Law §170(7)).

2. Legal Problems Raised by No-Fault Divorce

a. Early Problems of No-Fault

The advent of no-fault divorce brought its share of legal problems. One problem focused on the method of proof to secure a no-fault divorce, stemming from a reluctance to make divorce too easy to obtain. Early case law sometimes required that petitioners make a personal appearance and attest to the existence of irreconcilable differences (rather than merely submitting an affidavit). Many states now dispense with the need for a personal appearance. Summary dissolution procedures also exist today that authorize divorce by affidavit in some circumstances (e.g., childless spouses, short marriages, lack of real property, few debts or assets, and a willingness to waive spousal support).

Another problem concerned discomfort with unilateral divorce (i.e., a divorce desired by only one spouse). Some courts resisted no-fault divorce over the objection of one party. Some states found other ways to make divorce more difficult when only one spouse wanted the divorce. See, e.g., Mo. Rev. Stat. §452.320 (requiring proof of fault or two-year separation in such cases). Finally, opponents of no-fault divorce unsuccessfully challenged early legislation on constitutional grounds of vagueness, impairment of contract, equal protection, and freedom of religion. For a rare constitutional challenge that occurred recently, see Dycus v. Dycus, 949 N.W.2d 357 (Neb. 2020).

Problems

1. The Whiteacre legislature recently proposed a simplified divorce procedure. A bill proposes electronic divorces, wherein petitioners could divorce without making a personal appearance if (1) the couple has no minor children and the wife is not pregnant, (2) neither party has real property, (3) neither party desires spousal support, (4) the couple's debts do not exceed $10,000, and (5) the marital property totals less than $15,000. Mary Jones, a Whiteacre legislator, is concerned that cutbacks in legal services following the pandemic resulted in vast numbers of persons whose needs for divorce are not being met. She would like to adopt the simplified procedure and perhaps extend it further. As her legislative intern, what do you advise?

2. A bill pending in the Greenacre legislature would require that, in marriages with children, both parties to a no-fault divorce must consent to terminate the marriage. The state's current law requires that, in the absence of adultery or cruelty, either spouse can petition to end the marriage without the other's consent. You are a legislative aide who has been asked to comment on the proposed reform. What do you advise? See Lynne Marie Kohm, On Mutual Consent to Divorce: A Debate with Two Sides to the Story, 8 Appalachian J.L. 35 (2008).

b. Living Separate and Apart

BENNINGTON v. BENNINGTON

381 N.E.2d 1355 (Ohio Ct. App. 1978)

McCormac, Judge.

Mary Bennington commenced an action for alimony only, claiming gross neglect of duty and abandonment without just cause as grounds therefor. Larry Bennington answered, denying grounds for alimony, and counterclaimed for divorce, alleging gross neglect of duty and extreme cruelty. His counterclaim was later amended, asserting the grounds for divorce of living separate and apart for at least two years without cohabitation. . . .

Plaintiff and defendant were married in 1946. No children have been born to the marriage. In 1963, plaintiff suffered a stroke rendering her permanently and totally disabled and causing her left side to become paralyzed. There have been no sexual relations between the parties since that time.

In 1974, Larry Bennington moved out of the house and into a travel van located adjacent to the house on the same premises. His primary reason for moving into the van was that his wife kept the heat in the house at about 85 to 90 degrees Fahrenheit. He was also irritated about the fact that his wife locked and bolted the door to the house and, when he arrived home from work, it frequently took her fifteen to twenty minutes to come to the door to let him into the house. Her reason for locking the door was apparently for security purposes.

There were also other areas of conflict between the parties. However, there was no intention on the part of Larry Bennington to abandon his marital responsibilities when he moved from the house to the van in 1974. On the contrary, he continued to help his disabled wife with household chores, pretty much the same as before moving into the travel van. There was a conflict as to whether he ever slept inside the house again after moving to the van, or whether he used the house otherwise for his comfort and enjoyment. It is clear, however, that he did enter the house regularly to assist his disabled wife.

On November 26, 1976, Larry Bennington finally became thoroughly disenchanted with the entire arrangement and decided to leave home. He went to Arizona for about one month. He then returned, regaining his job. After his return, he lived off of the premises in the van for about three months and then obtained an apartment elsewhere.

R.C. §3105.01(K) provides grounds for divorce "... [w]hen husband and wife have, without interruption for two years, lived separate and apart without cohabitation. . . ."

The trial court found that when the husband moved from the house to the van located on the same premises that he was living separate and apart without cohabitation. . . .

The trial court erroneously included the time that the husband lived in the van adjacent to the house as part of the two-year period, as the parties were not living "separate and apart" during that time. During that time there was no cessation of marital duties and relations between the wife and husband. Approximately the same duties were performed by the husband to the wife and by the wife to the husband as prior to the time that the husband moved outside of the house to the van. . . . While the parties were living apart in a limited sense, they were not living separately in a marital sense. . . . Judgment reversed.

Notes and Questions

1. **Mixed grounds.** With the movement toward no fault, many states merely added no-fault grounds (such as living separate and apart) to their traditional fault-based grounds. Thus, many states reflect a "mixed" fault/no-fault regime. This approach contrasts with "pure" no-fault laws in other jurisdictions, such as California. If both fault and no-fault grounds exist, trial judges can use their discretion to select the ground upon which to grant the divorce.

2. **Statutory variations.** Statutes reflect different types of "living separate and apart" provisions. Some states require that the parties live apart under a judicial decree or separation agreement for a prescribed period. Some states require that the spouses "mutually and voluntarily" live separate and apart, and sometimes specify a shorter duration for consensual compared to judicial separations. UMDA merely requires proof that the parties live apart for a statutorily designated period. UMDA §302(a)(2). Which does the statute in *Bennington* require?

3. **Duration.** Many states had living-apart statutes prior to California's adoption of no fault. However, such statutes were aimed at forestalling rather than facilitating divorce. In addition, the requisite statutory periods were so long (generally five to ten years) that the statutes were seldom utilized. Currently, durational periods for "living separate and apart" range from six months (e.g., UMDA §302(a)(2)) to five years (e.g., Idaho Code Ann. §32-610). In jurisdictions with lengthy separation requirements prior to filing for a no-fault divorce, an unhappy spouse must resort to traditional fault-based grounds. What purposes do lengthy separation requirements serve? Do they undermine the purpose of no fault?

4. **Elements.** Why does *Bennington* conclude the parties were not "living separate and apart"? Suppose that the van was not adjacent to the house? Down the street? Across town? Is the geographic location determinative? Suppose that Mr.

Bennington moved out and obtained an apartment, and yet still returned daily to assist his wife. Is he living separate and apart? May parties who separate and then reside in different bedrooms ever establish that they are "living separate and apart"? Compare In re Marriage of Davis, 189 Cal. Rptr. 3d 835 (Cal. 2015) (abrogated by Cal. Fam. Code §70), with In re Marriage of Tomlins, 983 N.E.2d 118 (Ill. App. Ct. 2013). Should a party wishing to separate be forced to vacate the marital home, even if not financially able to do so?

5. Outcome. Did Mrs. Bennington's acts constitute sufficient cruelty for divorce? How did her disability affect the outcome? Were Mr. Bennington's chores in the household, after moving to the van, "marital duties and relations" or caretaking of a disabled person? Should Mr. Bennington's altruistic behavior preclude his divorce?

6. Comparison. How is living separate and apart similar to, and different from, fault-based grounds generally? How is it similar to, and different from, desertion? Why is a statutory period required? What difference does it make when the period commences? What should toll the statutory period? Suppose that the Benningtons were intimate once during the statutory period. Recall the condonation defense. Should fault-based defenses be available?

7. Privacy. One rationale for living-apart statutes was that they spared parties the intrusion into their privacy that fault divorce proceedings mandated. Is this an apt characterization of the proceedings in *Bennington*?

8. Legal separation distinguished. Legal separations, constituting an alternative to divorce, were quite common during the fault-based era, when divorce was difficult to obtain. Such judicial separations were once called "divorce from bed and board" (from the Latin *divorce a mensa et thoro*) to be distinguished from absolute divorce (or *divorce a vinculo matrimonii* from the bonds of marriage). Decrees of legal separation do not free the parties to remarry but relieve them from cohabitation. Today, some states continue to require judicial decrees of separation to satisfy statutory requirements for "living separate and apart."

NOTE: ABOLITION OF FAULT-BASED DEFENSES

One important legal issue after the adoption of no fault was the status of fault-based defenses. Many states abolished them legislatively whereas other states abolished them judicially. Still other states that added no-fault divorce to their fault grounds continue to maintain the defenses. See, e.g., Me. Rev. Stat. Ann. tit. 19-A, §§902(3) (recrimination), 902(4) (condonation); N.Y. Dom. Rel. Law §171 (retaining connivance, condonation, recrimination, and statute of limitations defenses to adultery). Fault-based defenses are important in states with lengthy separation requirements (which force parties who want a speedier divorce to resort to traditional fault-based grounds) and/or in jurisdictions in which fault still plays a role in spousal support or property division.

c. What Role for Fault?

FELTMEIER v. FELTMEIER
798 N.E.2d 75 (Ill. 2003)

Justice RARICK delivered the opinion of the court:

Plaintiff, Lynn Feltmeier, and defendant, Robert Feltmeier, were married on October 11, 1986, and divorced on December 16, 1997. [O]n August 25, 1999, Lynn sued Robert for the intentional infliction of emotional distress. . . . The first matter before us for review is whether Lynn's complaint states a cause of action for intentional infliction of emotional distress. . . . According to the allegations contained in Lynn's complaint, since the parties' marriage in October 1986, and continuing for over a year after the December 1997 dissolution of their marriage: "[Robert] entered into a continuous and outrageous course of conduct with either the intent to cause emotional distress to [Lynn] or with reckless disregard as to whether such conduct would cause emotional distress to [Lynn] . . . including, but not limited to, the following:

> A. On repeated occasions, [Robert] has battered [Lynn] by striking, kicking, shoving, pulling hair, and bending and twisting her limbs and toes. . . .
> B. On repeated occasions, [Robert] has prevented [Lynn] from leaving the house to escape the abuse. . . .
> C. On repeated occasions, [Robert] has yelled insulting and demeaning epithets at [Lynn]. Further, [Robert] has engaged in verbal abuse which included threats and constant criticism of [Lynn] in such a way as to demean, humiliate, and degrade [Lynn]. . . .
> D. On repeated occasions, [Robert] threw items at [Lynn] with the intent to cause her harm. . . .
> E. On repeated occasions, [Robert] attempted to isolate [Lynn] from her family and friends and would get very upset if [Lynn] would show the marks and bruises resulting from [Robert's] abuse to others.
> F. On repeated occasions since the divorce, [Robert] has engaged in stalking behavior. . . .
> G. On at least one occasion, [Robert] has attempted to interfere with [Lynn's] employment by confiscating her computer. Additionally, [Robert] broke into [Lynn's] locked drug cabinet for work on or about March 23, 1997.

[The court then sets forth the elements for intentional infliction of emotional distress (IIED): extreme and outrageous conduct; the actor must either intend that his conduct inflict severe emotional distress, or know that there is at least a high probability that his conduct will cause severe emotional distress; and the conduct must in fact cause severe emotional distress.]

Robert first contends that the allegations of Lynn's complaint do not sufficiently set forth conduct which was extreme and outrageous when considered "[i]n the context of the subjective and fluctuating nature of the marital relationship." In support of this contention, Robert cites several cases from other jurisdictions that have addressed the policy ramifications of allowing a spouse to maintain an action for intentional infliction of emotional distress based upon acts occurring during the marriage. [W]hile we agree that special caution is required in dealing with actions for intentional infliction of emotional distress arising from conduct occurring within the marital setting, our examination of both the law of this state and the most commonly raised policy concerns leads us to conclude that no valid reason exists to restrict such actions or to require a heightened threshold for outrageousness in this context.

One policy concern that has been advanced is the need to recognize the "mutual concessions implicit in marriage," and the desire to preserve marital harmony. However, in this case, brought after the parties were divorced, "there is clearly no marital harmony remaining to be preserved." Moreover, we agree [that] "behavior that is 'utterly intolerable in a civilized society' and is intended to cause severe emotional distress is not behavior that should be protected in order to promote marital harmony and peace." Indeed, the Illinois legislature, in creating the Illinois Domestic Violence Act of 1986 (Act) (750 ILCS 60/101 *et seq.* (West 2002)), has recognized that domestic violence is "a serious crime against the individual and society." . . . Thus, it would seem that the public policy of this state would be furthered by recognition of the action at issue.

A second policy concern is the threat of excessive and frivolous litigation if the tort is extended to acts occurring in the marital setting. Admittedly, the likelihood of vindictive litigation is of particular concern following a dissolution of marriage, because "the events leading to most divorces involve some level of emotional distress." However, we believe that the showing required of a plaintiff in order to recover damages for intentional infliction of emotional distress provides a built-in safeguard against excessive and frivolous litigation. . . .

Another policy consideration which has been raised is that a tort action for compensation would be redundant. [However,] the laws of this state provide no compensatory relief for injuries sustained [here]. An action for dissolution of marriage also provides no compensatory relief for domestic abuse. In Illinois, as in most other states, courts are not allowed to consider marital misconduct in the distribution of property when dissolving a marriage. . . .

[W]e now examine the allegations set forth in Lynn's complaint to determine whether Robert's conduct satisfies the "outrageousness" requirement. . . . The issue of whether domestic abuse can be sufficiently outrageous to sustain a cause of action for intentional infliction of emotional distress is apparently one of first impression in Illinois. Other jurisdictions, however, have found similar allegations of recurring cycles of physical and verbal abuse, wherein the conduct went far beyond the "trials of everyday life between two cohabiting people," to be sufficiently outrageous to fall within the parameters of section 46 of the Restatement (Second) of Torts. In the instant case, we must agree with the appellate court that, when the above-summarized allegations of the complaint are viewed in their entirety, they show a type of domestic abuse that is extreme enough to be actionable. . . .

[The court then rejected Robert's contention that Lynn did not suffer sufficiently severe emotional distress, pointing to her claims of loss of self-esteem, difficulty in forming other relationships, Post-traumatic Stress Disorder (PTSD), depression, fear of men, and curtailed enjoyment of life. The ultimate question, however, is when the statute of limitations began to run in the instant case. Generally, a limitations period begins to run when facts exist that authorize one party to maintain an action against another. However, under the "continuing tort" or "continuing violation" rule, "where a tort involves a continuing or repeated injury, the limitations period does not begin to run until the date of the last injury or the date the tortious acts cease." A continuing tort, therefore, does not involve tolling the statute of limitations because of delayed or continuing injuries, but instead involves viewing the defendant's conduct as a continuous whole for pre-scriptive purposes. . . .

In the instant case, Robert . . . maintains that "each of the alleged acts of abuse inflicted by Robert upon Lynn over a 12-year period are separate and distinct incidents which give rise to separate and distinct causes of action [and therefore, if occurring prior to August 25, 1997, would be time barred], rather than one single, continuous, unbroken, violation or wrong which continued over the entire period of 12 years." We must disagree. While it is true that the conduct set forth in Lynn's complaint could be considered separate acts constituting separate offenses of, *inter alia*, assault, defamation and battery, Lynn has alleged, and we have found, that Robert's conduct *as a whole* states a cause of action for intentional infliction of emotional distress. . . .

We believe the appellate court herein properly applied this reasoning to the facts of this case where:

> "The alleged domestic violence and abuse endured by Lynn . . . spanned the entire 11-year marriage. No one disputes that the allegations set forth the existence of ongoing abusive behavior. Lynn's psychologist, Dr. Michael E. Althoff, found that Lynn suffered from the "battered wife syndrome." He described the psycholog-ical process as one that unfolds over time. The process by which a spouse exerts coercive control is based upon 'a systematic, repetitive infliction of psychological trauma' designed to 'instill terror and helplessness.' Dr. Althoff indicated that the posttraumatic stress disorder from which Lynn suffered was the result of the entire series of abusive acts, not just the result of one specific incident."

The purpose behind a statute of limitations is to prevent stale claims, not to preclude claims before they are ripe for adjudication, and certainly not to shield a wrongdoer. [Therefore,] we agree [with] the growing number of jurisdictions that have found that the continuing tort rule should be extended to apply in cases of intentional infliction of emotional distress. [Accordingly, Lynn's claims,] based on conduct prior to August 25, 1997, are not barred by the applicable statute of limitations. . . .

NOTE: WHO ARE LYNN AND ROBERT FELTMEIER?

Morris Lane Harvey, The Legacy of Feltmeier v. Feltmeier: Twenty-Year Retrospective
Personal Communication, Aug. 9, 2023

Twenty years have passed since the landmark *Feltmeier* decision. As the attorney for plaintiff Lynn Feltmeier, I have often reflected on the case. Lynn Feltmeier found her way to my office in 1999. Lynn initially retained me for fairly typical post-judgment matters. Her ex-husband, Robert, who owned Mt. Vernon Glass Company, was not paying child support as ordered, was abusing visitation, and had not complied with some property provisions in the divorce judgment. As I have a longstanding family law practice in this area, Lynn initially sought my assistance to enforce the dissolution judgment.

Morris Lane Harvey, attorney for plaintiff Lynn Feltmeier

The facts of her case were clearly egregious. When she came in to see me, she had a black eye. I asked her about it, and she told me her story. If there is anything that I hate in the world, it's a bully — and the defendant in *Feltmeier* certainly fits that description. His abusive acts are well documented in the reported case. The abuse continued throughout their eleven-year marriage and even for two years afterwards.

The *Feltmeier* appellate court ruled, and the state supreme court affirmed, that these acts were sufficiently extreme to be actionable as IIED. When the defendant appealed, first to the Illinois Appellate Court and later to the Illinois Supreme Court, I was ecstatic. I had litigated four IIED cases before, but it had taken me a decade to get this issue before an Illinois court that could chisel the result in stone. Arguing the case before the highest court in our state was undoubtedly one of the most satisfying professional experiences of my life. For me, the outcome was never in doubt.

Feltmeier's legacy stems from its deep understanding of the nature of domestic violence and its application of that knowledge to effectuate law reform. *Feltmeier* provides a route to monetary compensation that forces the wrongdoer to compensate the victim for the serious toll (monetary and emotional) of dealing with the long-term effects of his conduct. IIED holds abusers accountable for their actions. Too often abusers evade the criminal justice system. IIED also enables the legal system to expose the abuser's conduct to the public. Such a tort suit finally unmasks the abuser for what he really is. Finally, public exposure of the abusive conduct and the victim's financial compensation is not only just but also therapeutic. For the victim, it is the first step to restoring her dignity and reminding her that she is a person of worth. It certainly was for Lynn Feltmeier.

Notes and Questions

1. Background. Several factors contribute to the application of tort law to the divorce context, including the abolition of interspousal immunity, recognition and extension of tort liability for emotional injury, awareness of domestic violence, and the demise of fault-based divorce. *Feltmeier* reveals the split among jurisdictions over the recognition of interspousal suits for emotional distress in the divorce context. On what basis does *Feltmeier* decide to recognize such suits?

2. Higher threshold? Should courts adopt a higher threshold for extreme and outrageous behavior in the marital context? See McCulloh v. Drake, 24 P.3d 1162, 1169-1170 (Wyo. 2001) (setting high standard for recovery "so that the social good which comes from recognizing the tort in a marital setting will not be undermined by an invasive flood of meritless litigation" [and] "to protect defendants from the possibility of long and intrusive trials on frivolous claims").

Some commentators contend that determinations of "outrageousness" should be limited to cases in which a spouse's conduct is criminal.[15] What role does such a high threshold play in the context of domestic violence?

3. Policy. *Feltmeier* first explores whether courts should permit interspousal actions for IIED in divorce actions. Do you agree with *Feltmeier*'s resolution of this issue? Does recognition of emotional distress claims in the context of divorce undermine no-fault divorce law? Resurrect the fault-based ground of cruelty? Further or disserve the goals of tort law? Lead to recovery for domestic disputes that are trivial and/or widespread? Lead to double recovery in cases in which fault plays a role in property distribution? Do problems of causation militate against recovery (i.e., the difficulty of proving that the emotional distress was caused by the spouse's conduct and not by the marital difficulties)? Should notions of privacy militate against the recognition of IIED claims in the marital context?[16]

4. Special rules? If tort claims are permitted in the divorce context, should courts limit them to interspousal torts involving injury or physical violence? How does *Feltmeier* resolve the issue whether statutes of limitations should be tolled for victims of spousal abuse who endure years of abuse before filing for divorce? Why do battered spouses often wait to file tort suits, thereby incurring problems with the statute of limitations? Note that some states recognize a distinct tort of "domestic violence." See Cal. Civ. Code §1708.6 (creating this tort).

5. Joinder. Tort liability in the context of divorce also presents the issue of whether courts should *require* joinder of tort claims and divorce claims. Some courts that permit interspousal actions for IIED prohibit joinder, others mandate joinder, and still others adopt a permissive policy of joinder (permitting but not mandating joinder). Since *Feltmeier* was decided, most jurisdictions have adopted a permissive approach. Joinder fulfills the policies of conserving judicial resources by concentrating all claims, reducing private transaction costs, and achieving a swifter settlement of marital differences.

Do the different purposes of tort actions and divorce militate in favor of — or against — joinder? Do the different procedural characteristics? For example, if joinder is required, how should a court resolve access to jury trials (normally

---

[15]. See Ira Mark Ellman & Stephen D. Sugarman, Spousal Emotional Abuse as a Tort?, 55 Md. L. Rev. 1268, 1335 (1996).

[16]. On the policy arguments, compare Ira Mark Ellman, The Place of Fault in a Modern Divorce Law, 28 Ariz. St. L.J. 773 (1996) and Harry D. Krause, On the Danger of Allowing Marital Fault to Re-Emerge in the Guise of Torts, 73 Notre Dame L. Rev. 1355, 1363-1366 (1998), with Pamela Laufer-Ukeles, Reconstructing Fault: The Case for Spousal Torts, 79 U. Cin. L. Rev. 207 (2010).

permitted in tort actions)? If a jury trial is ordered, where shall the claim be litigated—in family court or civil court? How should a court resolve the problem of attorneys' fees (because contingent fees are not permitted in divorce actions)?

Problems

1. Jane and John Doe have been married for seven years and have a son and twin girls. Unbeknownst to John, his wife had a sexual affair with her art professor during the marriage. John discovers a letter that reveals to him that the children may have been fathered by the professor. DNA testing confirms that John is father of the son, but not the twins. The next day, John petitions for divorce, alleging adultery, and sues to recover damages for fraud and IIED. Should he be permitted to bring the tort claims in the divorce proceeding? Should his tort claims be barred by the interspousal immunity doctrine? Does the wife's conduct satisfy the requirements for IIED? See Doe v. Doe, 747 A.2d 617 (Md. 2000). See generally Linda L. Berger, Lies Between Mommy and Daddy: The Case for Recognizing Spousal Emotional Distress Claims Based on Domestic Deceit That Interferes with Parent-Child Relationships, 33 Loy. L. Rev. 449 (2000).

2. A state legislator in the State of Blackacre is considering adopting a bill that would prohibit all tort actions between spouses until after the spouses are divorced. The bill would not abrogate the interspousal immunity doctrine. Rather, once the spouses obtained a judgment of divorce or a judgment of legal separation, they would be placed in the same situation with respect to each other, as if no marriage had ever been contracted between them. The rationale is that such suits disrupt domestic tranquility; but once the couple is divorced, the policy reasons for such immunity become moot. You are a legislative aide to the legislator. Advise her as to the benefits and shortcomings of the proposed bill. See La. Stat. Ann. §9:291. See also Monica Hof Wallace, A Primer on Marriage in Louisiana, 64 Loy. L. Rev. 557, 566-567 (2018).

3. Assessment of the No-Fault "Revolution"

a. Divorce Reform in the United States

Deborah L. Rhode & Martha Minow, Reforming the Questions, Questioning the Reforms: Feminist Perspectives on Divorce Law

in Divorce Reform at the Crossroads 191-199, 209-210
(Stephen D. Sugarman & Herma Hill Kay eds., 1990)

The leading proponents of initial no-fault reform were lawyers, judges, and law professors. Their primary focus was on the legal grounds for divorce; their primary purposes were to reduce expense, acrimony, and fraud in resolving matters envisioned as essentially private concerns. What is, perhaps, most revealing about these original efforts are the issues that were not on the agenda. Early reform strategies neglected gender equality and public responsibilities.

Although no-fault initiatives coincided with the resurgence of a women's rights movement, proponents of these reforms generally were not seeking to remedy women's disadvantages under traditional family policies. Indeed, to the extent that gender equity appeared at all in discussions among decision makers, the focus involved equity for men. The dominant concern was beleaguered ex-husbands, crippled by excessive alimony burdens, and threats of blackmail. Although this problem was grossly exaggerated, the absence of systematic data allowed policymakers to rely on anecdotal experiences to formulate the problem they sought to reform.

In part, the absence of women's concerns from the debate reflected the absence of women. Those with greatest influence in policy-making—practicing attorneys, politicians, and family law experts—were overwhelmingly male. The newly emerging women's rights movement was not significantly involved with early divorce reforms, in part because it was understaffed and overextended during this period, but more important, because the implications of such reforms were not yet apparent. Only as the divorce rate escalated and scholars concerned with women's issues began to chronicle its impact did the focus of debate begin to change.

Even when reformers identified gender equality as an objective, they relied almost exclusively on gender-neutral formulations. For example, they succeeded in eliminating explicitly sex-linked provisions (such as those granting alimony only to wives) and in reformulating rules for marital property distribution to require "equal" or "equitable" division of assets. Yet . . . such provisions have secured equality in form, but not equality in fact.

The assumptions underlying early reforms also marginalized the public implications of divorce doctrine. No-fault initiatives began from the premise that decisions involving the termination of marriage should rest with private parties; the public's responsibility was simply to provide efficient legal rules for processing their agreement and resolving any disputes. Within this framework, a couple's allocation of financial and child-rearing obligations appeared to be primarily matters for private ordering. If parties failed to reach agreement, their differences would be resolved under broad discretionary standards mandating equality or equity between the spouses in financial matters and the best interest of the child in custody contests. Public norms about the kinds of resolutions society should endorse receded to the background. As a result, the state was given little responsibility for guiding, enforcing, or supplementing judicial awards.

Paradoxically, this move toward private ordering failed adequately to acknowledge the diversity of private family circumstances. Those who framed and interpreted legal doctrine often overlooked the fact that marriages of different durations, formed during different decades with different expectations, could leave divorcing parties in sharply divergent situations. One single, discretionary standard was thought adequate to deal with circumstances ranging from a couple married for one year while the parties finished college to a couple married for twenty-five years while the woman worked in the home and the husband held paid employment.

Early no-fault reforms gave no special attention to the concerns of particularly vulnerable groups such as displaced homemakers with limited savings, insurance, and employment options; families with inadequate income to support two households (a problem disproportionately experienced by racial minorities); or couples with no children, no significant property, and no need for a formal adjudicative procedure. Nor was child support central to the reform agenda; it appeared only as a side issue, buried within custody and other financial topics.

It bears emphasis what such a limited conception of public responsibility left out. The early reform agenda did not specify clear public norms concerning financial and child-care responsibilities to guide parties' decisionmaking or judicial review. Nor did it mandate effective, affordable enforcement procedures for spousal and child support awards, or state subsidies where private resources were inadequate. Reformers also neglected the impact of postdivorce property divisions—such as the forced sale of the family home—on dependent children. And what was most critical, no-fault initiatives omitted criteria for assessing the outcomes of divorce, outcomes affecting not only the parties and their children but subsequent marriages, stepfamilies, and public welfare responsibilities.

[Early] divorce reform tended to amplify rather than redress gender inequalities. . . . Norms governing termination of a marriage should be consistent with the ideal to which marriage aspires—that of equal partnerships between spouses who share resources, responsibilities, and risks. . . . Gender equality and child welfare should become priorities in practice, not just theory, under contemporary divorce law. . . .

b. Divorce Reform: The Comparative-Law Perspective

NOTE: DIVORCE AROUND THE WORLD

The Philippines and Vatican City are the last countries that ban divorce. Even the Philippines, however, is considering legalizing divorce. Several bills have been proposed there in past legislatures. Most recently, in March 2023, a panel of representatives in the House of Representatives approved a bill allowing for absolute divorce. But the bill faces stiff opposition in the full House, as well as the Senate, in this overwhelmingly Roman Catholic country.

Among countries that allow divorce, the Maldives, Kazakhstan, and Russia have the highest divorce rates. In contrast, Sri Lanka, Guatemala, and Vietnam have the lowest divorce rates. (The United States ranks ninth.) In 2022, the United Kingdom adopted no-fault divorce as part of the Divorce, Dissolution and Separation Act. See Divorce, Dissolution and Separation Act 2020 (Consequential Amendments) Regulations 2022 No. 237. Couples there no longer need to prove one of the existing five fault grounds (i.e., adultery, behavior, desertion, two years' separation with consent or five years' separation). Instead, they can point to the "irretrievable breakdown" of their relationship. A no-fault divorce takes approximately six months to obtain.[17]

---

[17]. See World Population Rev., Divorce Rates by Country 2023, https://worldpopulation review.com/country-rankings/divorce-rates-by-country. On the U.K. divorce reform, see A New Dawn for Divorce Law, Hill Dickinson Blog, Apr. 6, 2022, https://www.hilldickinson.com/insights /articles/new-dawn-divorce-law-6-april-2022.

c. Divorce Reform: The Return of Fault Movement

A movement began in the late 1990s to reintroduce fault in the dissolution process. Some states (Arkansas, Arizona, and Louisiana) offer "covenant marriage," which is designed to preserve the lifelong character of marriage. Covenant marriage is characterized by (1) mandatory premarital counseling that emphasizes the seriousness of marriage; (2) execution of a statement (the covenant) containing each party's promise to take reasonable steps to preserve the marriage if problems arise; and (3) limitation on the grounds for divorce (i.e., fault on the part of one spouse or, in the absence of fault, a designated period of living separately and apart).

Supporters of covenant marriage claim that covenant marriage reaffirms the meaning of marriage and—by making divorce more difficult to obtain—promotes children's well-being. Critics suggest that it raises constitutional concerns (placing an undue burden on the right to make decisions regarding family life); conflict-of-laws and choice-of-law issues (possibly forcing non–covenant marriage states to recognize covenant marriages and denying no-fault divorces to spouses who seek them outside their home state); and unauthorized practice of law problems (requiring clergy marriage counselors to counsel couples regarding the "nature and purpose" of marriage). The debate continues regarding the effect of covenant marriages on preserving the family, protecting women and children and lowering juvenile crime rates. Another concern is that covenant marriage makes it more difficult for victims of domestic violence to exit abusive marriages. Covenant marriages have not been as popular as supporters initially hoped.

E. Access to Divorce

BODDIE v. CONNECTICUT
401 U.S. 371 (1971)

Justice HARLAN delivered the opinion of the Court.

Appellants, welfare recipients residing in the State of Connecticut, brought this action in the Federal District Court for the District of Connecticut on behalf of themselves and others similarly situated, challenging, as applied to them, certain state procedures for the commencement of litigation, including requirements for payment of court fees and costs for service of process, that restrict their access to the courts in their effort to bring an action for divorce.

It appears from the briefs and oral argument that the average cost to a litigant for bringing an action for divorce is $60. Section 52-259 of the Connecticut General Statutes provides: "There shall be paid to the clerks of the supreme court or the superior court, for entering each civil cause, forty-five dollars. . . . " An additional $15 is usually required for the service of process by the sheriff, although as much as $40 or $50 may be necessary where notice must be accomplished by publication.

There is no dispute as to the inability of the named appellants in the present case to pay either the court fees required by statute or the cost incurred for the service of process. The affidavits in the record establish that appellants' welfare income in each instance barely suffices to meet the costs of the daily essentials of life and includes no allotment that could be budgeted for the expense to gain access to the courts in order to obtain a divorce. . . .

[Appellants challenged the constitutionality of the statute and sought an injunction to permit them to proceed without payment of fees and costs. A three-judge court found the statute constitutional.] We now reverse. Our conclusion is that, given the basic position of the marriage relationship in this society's hierarchy of values and the concomitant state monopolization of the means for legally dissolving this relationship, due process does prohibit a State from denying, solely because of inability to pay, access to its courts to individuals who seek judicial dissolution of their marriages. . . .

Without [the] guarantee [of the Fifth and Fourteenth Amendments] that one may not be deprived of his rights, neither liberty nor property, without due process of law, the State's monopoly over techniques for binding conflict resolution could hardly be said to be acceptable under our scheme of things. . . .

Such [due process] litigation has, however, typically involved rights of defendants—not, as here, persons seeking access to the judicial process in the first instance. This is because our society has been so structured that resort to the courts is not usually the only available, legitimate means of resolving private disputes. . . .

As this Court on more than one occasion has recognized, marriage involves interests of basic importance in our society [citing *Loving*, Skinner v. Oklahoma, 316 U.S. 535 (1942), and Meyer v. Nebraska]. It is not surprising, then, that the States have seen fit to oversee many aspects of that institution. Without a prior judicial imprimatur, individuals may freely enter into and rescind commercial contracts, for example, but we are unaware of any jurisdiction where private citizens may covenant for or dissolve marriages without state approval. Even where all substantive requirements are concededly met, we know of no instance where two consenting adults may divorce and mutually liberate themselves from the constraints of legal obligations that go with marriage, and more fundamentally the prohibition against remarriage, without invoking the State's judicial machinery.

Thus, although they assert here due process rights as would-be plaintiffs, we think appellants' plight, because resort to the state courts is the only avenue to dissolution of their marriages, is akin to that of defendants faced with exclusion from the only forum effectively empowered to settle their disputes. Resort to the judicial process by these plaintiffs is no more voluntary in a realistic sense than that of the defendant called upon to defend his interests in court. For both groups this process is not only the paramount dispute-settlement technique, but, in fact, the only available one. In this posture we think that this appeal is properly to be resolved in light of the principles enunciated in our due process decisions that delimit rights of defendants compelled to litigate their differences in the judicial forum.

[P]recedent has firmly embedded in our due process jurisprudence two important principles upon whose application we rest our decision in the case before us. [First,] due process requires, at a minimum, that absent a countervailing state interest of overriding significance, persons forced to settle their claims of right and duty through the judicial process must be given a meaningful opportunity to be heard. . . . Our cases further establish that a statute or a rule may be held constitutionally invalid as applied when it operates to deprive an individual of a protected right although its general validity as a measure enacted in the legitimate exercise of state power is beyond question. . . .

No less than these rights, the right to a meaningful opportunity to be heard within the limits of practicality, must be protected against denial by particular laws that operate to jeopardize it for particular individuals. . . . Just as a generally valid notice procedure may fail to satisfy due process because of the circumstances of the defendant, so too a cost requirement, valid on its face, may offend due process because it operates to foreclose a particular party's opportunity to be heard. The State's obligations under the Fourteenth Amendment are not simply generalized ones; rather, the State owes to each individual that process which, in light of the values of a free society, can be characterized as due.

Drawing upon the [these] principles . . . we conclude that the State's refusal to admit these appellants to its courts, the sole means in Connecticut for obtaining a divorce, must be regarded as the equivalent of denying them an opportunity to be heard upon their claimed right to a dissolution of their marriages, and, in the absence of a sufficient countervailing justification for the State's action, a denial of due process.

The arguments for this kind of fee and cost requirement are that the State's interest in the prevention of frivolous litigation is substantial, its use of court fees and process costs to allocate scarce resources is rational, and its balance between the defendant's right to notice and the plaintiff's right to access is reasonable.

In our opinion, none of these considerations is sufficient to override the interest of these plaintiff-appellants in having access to the only avenue open for dissolving their allegedly untenable marriages. Not only is there no necessary connection between a litigant's assets and the seriousness of his motives in bringing suit, but it is here beyond present dispute that appellants bring these actions in good faith. Moreover, other alternatives exist to fees and cost requirements as a means for conserving the time of courts and protecting parties from frivolous litigation, such as penalties for false pleadings or affidavits, and actions for malicious prosecution or abuse of process, to mention only a few. In the same vein we think that reliable alternatives exist to service of process by a state-paid sheriff if the State is unwilling to assume the cost of official service. This is perforce true of service by publication which is the method of notice least calculated to bring to a potential defendant's attention the pendency of judicial proceedings. We think in this case service at defendant's last known address by mail and posted notice is equally effective as publication in a newspaper. . . .

In concluding that the Due Process Clause of the Fourteenth Amendment requires that these appellants be afforded an opportunity to go into court to obtain a divorce, we wish to re-emphasize that we go no further than necessary to dispose of the case before us, a case where the bona fides of both appellants' indigency and desire for divorce are here beyond dispute. We do not decide that access for all individuals to the courts is a right that is, in all circumstances, guaranteed by the Due Process Clause of the Fourteenth Amendment so that its exercise may not be placed beyond the reach of any individual, for, as we have already noted, in the case before us this right is the exclusive precondition to the adjustment of a fundamental human relationship. The requirement that these appellants resort to the judicial process is entirely a state-created matter. Thus we hold only that a

State may not, consistent with the obligations imposed on it by the Due Process Clause of the Fourteenth Amendment, preempt the right to dissolve this legal relationship without affording all citizens access to the means it has prescribed for doing so. . . .

Justice DOUGLAS, concurring in the result. . . .

. . . The Court today puts "flesh" upon the Due Process Clause by concluding that marriage and its dissolution are so important that an unhappy couple who are indigent should have access to the divorce courts free of charge. [However,] invidious discrimination based on poverty is adequate for this case. While Connecticut has provided a procedure for severing the bonds of marriage, a person can meet every requirement save court fees or the cost of service of process and be denied a divorce. [U]nder Connecticut law, divorces may be denied or granted solely on the basis of wealth. . . . Affluence does not pass muster under the Equal Protection Clause for determining who must remain married and who shall be allowed to separate.

Notes and Questions

1. Background. On remand, the court ordered state officials to waive filing fees. Boddie v. Connecticut, 329 F. Supp. 844 (D. Conn. 1971). As *Boddie* reveals, all states impose filing fees and costs for divorce petitions. *Boddie* (in combination with subsequent U.S. Supreme Court cases in the contexts of bankruptcy and welfare) established the principle that courts may condition access based on the payment of mandatory filing fees, although the Due Process Clause requires an exception for indigents in cases when the only avenue of relief is resort to the courts. When *Boddie* was decided, approximately 32 states (excluding Connecticut) had statutes permitting indigents to avoid such fees by proceeding *in forma pauperis*.[18] Filing fees for divorce currently average $300 but can run as high as $500 in some states.

2. Importance of marriage. The majority rests its opinion on "the basic position of the marriage relationship in this society's hierarchy of values and the concomitant state monopolization of the means for legally dissolving this relationship." Are both aspects necessary to the result, or are they independent grounds? How does the language about the importance of marriage in *Obergefell* (discussed in Chapter II) reinforce the reasoning in *Boddie*?

3. Extension to other divorce-related costs? If *Boddie* rests on both premises (societal values and monopoly), does an indigency exemption for other divorce expenses (for example, attorneys' fees) follow? Should it matter if the fees are paid to the court or to third parties? How meaningful is a right of access without an

---

[18]. Charles Brooks, Note, Boddie v. Connecticut: The Rights of Indigents in a Divorce Action, 11 J. Fam. L. 121, 122 n.5 (1971).

attorney? At least one court has decided, based on state law rather than constitutional grounds, that an indigent has the right to appointed counsel in a divorce proceeding. Sholes v. Sholes, 760 N.E.2d 156 (Ind. 2001).

How far does *Boddie* protect indigents' rights to counsel in civil cases generally? If it rests on the monopoly rationale, then *Boddie* might guarantee such representation in many civil contexts. But cf. United States v. Kras, 409 U.S. 434 (1973) (no right to free bankruptcy discharge); Ortwein v. Schwab, 410 U.S. 656 (1973) (there is no right to waive filing fees for welfare appeals). How is divorce distinguishable from bankruptcy and welfare? Does *Boddie* mandate waiver of fees in other family law matters (e.g., annulment, paternity, custody, or adoption)? Marriage license fees? Does *Boddie* mandate a right to counsel in a dissolution action involving child custody? See King v. King, 174 P.3d 659 (Wash. 2007). In a civil contempt proceeding for failure to pay child support? See Turner v. Rogers, 564 U.S. 431 (2011) (discussed in Chapter VII).

4. Empirical data. The high cost of divorce is one of many factors that limit access. Other factors affecting cost include the contested versus uncontested nature of the divorce, the hourly rate of lawyers, the geographical location where the divorce is filed, local filing fees, the nature of the disputes (regarding custody, alimony. or property division), and mediation. For a divorce with representation, costs include attorneys' fees and the need to employ experts (e.g., tax advisers, child custody evaluators, and real estate appraisers). Without an attorney, many low-income people remain trapped in unhappy marriages.[19]

Problems

1. Blackacre has an explicit provision in its state constitution protecting the right to privacy. The Blackacre legislature has just repealed its no-fault laws and reintroduced fault. The Blackacre Family Code permits divorce only for adultery, cruelty, and desertion. John and Jane Doe, a married couple, challenge the statute, alleging that it violates their constitutional right of privacy by disallowing divorce by mutual consent. What result? Does *Boddie* guarantee a constitutional right to divorce, similar to the constitutional right to marry? See Ferrer v. Commonwealth, 4 Fam. L. Rep. (BNA) 2744 (Sept. 26, 1978) (deciding a somewhat similar issue based on Puerto Rican law). See generally Kenneth L. Karst, The Freedom of Intimate Association, 89 Yale L.J. 624, 671-672 (1980).

2. Public interest groups in Arkansas, Arizona, and Louisiana argue that "covenant marriage" laws are unconstitutional in light of *Boddie*. What arguments should they make? See generally David M. Wagner, The Constitution and

---

[19]. Ruth Lee Johnson, Divorce: The Constitutional Right Many Cannot Afford, Psychol. Today, June 14, 2021, https://www.psychologytoday.com/us/blog/so-sue-me/202106/divorce-the -constitutional-right-many-cannot-afford; Rachel Reed, Breaking up Is Hard to Do, Especially When You Don't Have a Lawyer, Harv. Law Today, Apr. 29, 2021 (reporting findings of study of 311 participants), https://today.law.harvard.edu/breaking-up-is-hard-to-do-especially-when-you -dont-have-a-lawyer/.

Covenant Marriage Legislation: Rumors of a Constitutional Right to Divorce Have Been Greatly Exaggerated, 12 Regent U. L. Rev. 53 (1999).

SMITH v. MILLVILLE RESCUE SQUAD
139 A.3d 1 (N.J. 2016)

Judge CUFF (temporarily assigned) delivered the opinion of the Court.

This appeal addresses the scope of the marital status protection afforded to employees by the Law Against Discrimination (LAD), N.J.S.A. 10:5-1 to -42. [Plaintiff Robert Smith was a certified emergency medical technician and paramedic for Millville Rescue Squad (MRS) for 17 years. Plaintiff's wife at the time, Mary, was also employed by MRS, as were her mother and

Millville Rescue Squad

two sisters.] In early 2005, plaintiff commenced an extramarital affair with an MRS volunteer [whom he supervised]. Mary learned of plaintiff's affair and reported it to [his supervisor John Redden]. Shortly thereafter, plaintiff informed Redden of the affair. During that conversation, plaintiff testified that Redden told him that he could not promise that the affair would not affect plaintiff's job. According to plaintiff, on the subject of plaintiff's continuing employment with MRS, Redden stated, "All depends on how it shakes down."

The MRS volunteer left MRS on June 27, 2005, but the affair continued, leading to irreconcilable discord between plaintiff and Mary. . . On January 2, 2006, plaintiff informed Redden that his marriage to Mary had collapsed. According to plaintiff's testimony, Redden thanked plaintiff for keeping him informed and asked to be notified of any developments regarding his marital status.

On February 16, 2006, plaintiff and Redden met again. According to plaintiff's testimony, Redden told plaintiff that he did not think there was any chance of reconciliation between plaintiff and Mary and that he believed there would be an "ugly divorce." Plaintiff testified that Redden informed him that if there had been even the slightest chance of reconciliation, Redden would not have to take the issue to the MRS Board of Directors (the Board). According to plaintiff, Redden stated, "You had eight months to make things right with your wife." . . .

Plaintiff asked Redden if he was being terminated because he was the one who had the affair. Redden replied that if he had to terminate plaintiff, it would be for one of four reasons. Two of those reasons were elimination of plaintiff's job because of restructuring and "poor work performance[.]" Plaintiff testified that he could not recall the other two reasons.

[The board terminated the plaintiff, and he filed suit.]

Plaintiff testified that the MRS Employee Information Manual (the Manual) provided that plaintiff was an "at will" employee who could resign or be terminated at any time with or without cause or notice. . . . Plaintiff testified that other employees had divorced while working at MRS, but he did not know of any other employee who had been terminated because of a divorce. Furthermore, in January 2001, he learned that Mary had an affair with an MRS mechanic. . . . Mary was not terminated or disciplined because of the affair.

Plaintiff also testified that, during the course of his employment, he was never subject to formal discipline. Plaintiff emphasized that he was promoted twice and received raises annually, even after Redden learned of the affair. The Manual called for regular performance evaluations, but plaintiff testified that he only received one informal performance evaluation, in October 2000, which was conducted by Redden and which plaintiff characterized as positive. . . .

In March 2006, plaintiff and Mary filed for divorce. Their divorce was finalized that September. Plaintiff testified that the divorce was "amicable," and not "messy," and that he continues to have a good relationship with Mary.

[Plaintiff's] complaint asserted two counts: wrongful discrimination on the basis of sex and marital status in violation of the LAD, N.J.S.A. 10:5-1 to -42, and the State Constitution (count one); and common law wrongful discharge (count two). . . . As to plaintiff's marital-status-discrimination claim, the trial court determined that plaintiff had failed to present any evidence "that he was terminated because he was either married or unmarried" or because he was having an affair, or "any evidence that employees were treated differently based on whether they were single, married, separated or divorced." Instead, the court found that plaintiff presented proof that he was terminated because management was concerned about the likelihood of an ugly or messy divorce, which the court held did not give rise to a marital-status-discrimination claim. . . .

The threshold issue before the Court is whether the LAD's prohibition against discrimination based on marital status extends to a person who has separated from their spouse and is in the process of obtaining a divorce. . . . The LAD identifies several actions taken by an employer against an employee or prospective employee as unlawful employment practices. Those actions include the failure to employ, the discharge of an employee, or the forced retirement of an employee based on factors such as race, sex, marital status, national origin, and age. Marital status is not a defined term. . . .

New Jersey does not stand alone in barring discrimination based on marital status. At least twenty states offer some form of protection from discrimination based on marital status. Many states have not defined the term. Other states define "marital status" in their anti-discrimination statutes but are divided on the scope of the marital-status protection. Compare . . . 775 Ill. Comp. Stat. 5/1-103(J) ("'Marital status' means the legal status of being married, single, separated, divorced or widowed."); [with] Minn. Stat. §363A.03 (Subd. 24) ("'Marital status' means whether a person is single, married, remarried, divorced, separated, or a surviving spouse and, in employment cases, includes protection against discrimination on the basis of the identity, situation, actions, or beliefs of a spouse or former spouse.").

To determine the scope and limits of the protection afforded by the LAD to an employee's marital status, we must identify and implement the legislative intent. . . . "[We] must recognize that "the LAD is remedial legislation intended to 'eradicate the cancer of discrimination' in our society[,]" and should therefore be liberally construed "in order to advance its beneficial purposes.". . . Despite the absence of a definition of "marital status" or legislative history demarcating the boundaries of this protection, the stated purpose and goals of the LAD strongly suggest that we should consider "marital status" as more than the state of being single or married. A broader interpretation is consistent with the remedial purpose of the statute, advances the goal of "eradication 'of the cancer of discrimination' in the workplace," and prevents employers from resorting to invidious stereotypes to justify termination of the employment of a never-married employee, an engaged employee, a separated employee, an employee involved in divorce litigation, or a recently widowed employee. . . .

We therefore conclude that marital status should be interpreted to include those who are single or married and those who are in transition from one state to another. This interpretation embraces basic decisions an employee makes during his or her lifetime. A person considering marriage or divorce or confronting the death of a spouse should not fear that a marriage ceremony, a divorce decree, or a funeral would trigger a loss of employment or a promised promotion.

Moreover, the interpretation of marital status that we adopt today does not interfere with an employer's legitimate business judgment and policies regarding its workforce. An employer is not prevented from disciplining or terminating an employee who is inattentive to his job responsibilities or whose actions disrupt the efficient performance of critical tasks. Rather, our interpretation prevents an employer from resorting to stereotypes in its assessment of a potential employee or an existing employee that bear no relation to the employee's actual performance in the workplace. Protecting those employees who are single, married, or transitioning between those marital states prevents an employer from engaging in commonplace stereotypes that a single employee is not committed to his career or that an engaged employee will be distracted by wedding preparations, or that a divorcing employee will be distracted from his job and even disruptive in the workplace, particularly if the estranged spouse or the spouse's friends and family are employed by the same employer. . . .

Here, the facts asserted by plaintiff, if assumed to be true, demonstrate that plaintiff was discharged "in significant part" based on his marital status. Plaintiff was not merely terminated because of the identity of his spouse, an MRS employee. Plaintiff was terminated based on his employer's stereotypes about the impact his divorce might have on the work performance of him and others. . . . Viewing that direct evidence in the light most favorable to plaintiff, the trial court should have denied defendants' motion and permitted the jury to render a verdict on plaintiff's marital-status-discrimination claim. . . .

Notes and Questions

1. Significance. *Millville Rescue Squad* is a landmark employment discrimination case that highlights how discrimination can be an obstacle to access to divorce. What legal protections exist against divorce discrimination? State statutes that include "marital status" among the protected categories for prohibitions on employment discrimination date from the 1970s. Such bans emerged when divorced and widowed women were denied credit because they were not married, and when married women were denied employment in certain jobs (such as flight attendants and teachers) because they were not single. The principal case questions whether such statutory protections apply to divorce discrimination. What is the scope of protection in cases of divorce discrimination, according to the court?

2. Rationale. Plaintiff sued initially not only based on marital status discrimination but also sex discrimination. But the trial court dismissed the latter claim. Was plaintiff fired because of his gender?

Despite the lack of legislative history to shed light on the meaning of the statutory term "marital status," the state supreme court reasoned that policy rationale dictated a broad interpretation of the term. Why? What was plaintiff's direct evidence of discrimination?

3. Stereotypes. Stigma about divorce sometimes plays a role in employment decisions, as *Millville Rescue Squad* reveals. What stereotypes about divorce and/or divorced persons led to plaintiff's firing? Why did the defendant believe that plaintiff's divorce might create harm in the workplace? Underlying this stigma are traditional beliefs that divorce is "a neurotic procedure of neurotic people," and that "divorce is not a chance occurrence but unconsciously self-provoked, even if only by the choice of a neurotic partner."[20] Do stereotypes about divorce persist?

In another recent divorce discrimination case, a male English professor at an evangelical Christian liberal arts college resigned, rather than face being fired because of his pending divorce. The college allowed faculty members to continue employment if their divorce was based only on adultery or abandonment.[21] What stereotypes are embedded in this employment policy? Is this case distinguishable from *Millville Rescue Squad*?

4. Different state approaches. Currently, 25 states (including New Jersey) and the District of Columbia prohibit marital status discrimination in employment.[22] How did the New Jersey state statute define the term "marital status"? How did the definition help or hurt plaintiff?

5. Federal law. Title VII of the Civil Rights Act of 1964 prohibits discrimination based only on color, national origin, race, religion, and sex (not marital status). Should Congress amend Title VII to add marital status as a protected classification in order to avoid the inconsistency of current state approaches? Would that solve the issue in *Millville Rescue Squad*?

---

[20]. Cited in Lynn Halem, Divorce Reform: Changing Legal and Social Perspectives 181-183 (1980).

[21]. Cited in Catrin Einhorn, At College, a High Standard on Divorce, N.Y. Times, May 4, 2008, at 27, https://www.nytimes.com/2008/05/04/education/04wheaton.html.

[22]. Marital Status Discrimination, Exec. Summary 152, Dec. 2022 Update (available on Westlaw).

NOTE: PRO SE DIVORCE

In the fault-based system, lawyers were essential to prove the existence of marital fault. The adoption of no-fault divorce eroded the role of lawyers and spurred the growth of pro se divorce. Self-help divorce kits and services proliferated. Less than a decade after the advent of no fault, a study on the effectiveness of pro se divorce found that most self-represented clients resolved property, support, and custody issues. The authors of the study expressed doubts about the need for counsel in terms of judicial efficiency or public welfare.[23] In contrast, an empirical study funded by the ABA reported various shortcomings of pro se divorce, including (1) pro se litigants become progressively less satisfied with the terms of their divorces as their cases become more complex, (2) they are less likely to receive tax advice or information about alternative dispute resolution, and (3) many petitioners and respondents encounter difficulties that are never resolved.[24]

In addition, a different empirical study of low-income divorce litigants emphasizes the importance of representation. Almost half of those who were represented by legal services attorneys succeeded in terminating their marriages, compared to 9 percent of the unrepresented control group.[25] Few low-income individuals were able to navigate the divorce system themselves because they faced such barriers as unfamiliar terminology, complicated instructions, mandatory wait times, limited hours at important facilities, and burdensome paperwork that sometimes required access to photocopiers, typewriters, or computers. The author of the study proposes simplifying the divorce process and providing more access to less expensive educational resources. In fact, many courts and legal service programs have simplified legal forms and instructions, created self-help centers, and developed Internet-based forms of assistance. And more companies, including some law firms, are providing consumers with do-it-yourself divorce apps, as well as instructional videos, templates, legal coaching, and paralegal help.

Despite the shortcomings of pro se representation, the number of litigants who represent themselves in family law cases is remarkably high. These litigants create difficulties for judges, who must determine how to ensure a fair trial to them without appearing to compromise their own neutrality, and also for court officials, who must distinguish between providing information and giving legal advice.

Some states have responded to the growth in pro se divorce by permitting limited representation services. Thus, a lawyer might represent a parent in a child support matter, but not a related custody dispute. However, limited-scope representation may jeopardize clients' interests.[26]

---

[23]. Ralph C. Cavanaugh & Deborah L. Rhode, Project, The Unauthorized Practice of Law and Pro Se Divorce: An Empirical Analysis, 86 Yale L.J. 104, 128-129 (1976).

[24]. Bruce D. Sales et al., Is Self-Representation a Reasonable Alternative to Attorney Representation in Divorce Cases?, 37 St. Louis U. L.J. 553 (1993).

[25]. Jim Greiner et al., Using Random Assignment to Measure Court Accessibility for Low-Income Divorce Seekers, Proceedings of the National Academy of Sciences (PNAS), Apr. 6, 2021, https://www.pnas.org/content/118/14/e2009086118.

[26]. See, e.g., Suzanne Valdez, Addressing the Pro Se Litigant Challenge in Kansas State Courts, 78 J. Kan. B. Ass'n 25, 26-28 (2009).

NOTE: RELIGIOUS OBSTACLES SURROUNDING DIVORCE

A traditional Jewish *Ketubah*, from Bombay, India, 1911

Religious issues sometimes present obstacles to divorce. Under traditional Jewish law, a religious divorce (known as a *get*) is necessary to end an Orthodox Jewish marriage, and only a husband may grant a *get*. A wife whose husband refuses to give her a *get* remains a "bound" woman (*agunah*), and unable to remarry in the faith. If she does remarry without the *get,* she is considered an adulteress, and any of her subsequent children are considered illegitimate. These consequences may motivate some husbands to use the threat of denying a *get* to extract concessions during the divorce.

Dilemmas arise when wives ask American secular courts to enforce either (1) the religious prenuptial agreement (called a *Ketubah*) that obligates the husband to provide the *get*, or (2) the decision of the religious tribunal (the *Beth Din*) that arranges religious divorces and orders husbands to grant the religious divorce. Constitutional issues implicate the Free Exercise and Establishment Clauses of the First Amendment.

In response to the problem of recalcitrant husbands, the New York legislature passed a *get* statute providing that no final judgment of divorce may be ordered unless the party who commences the proceeding alleges that he or she has taken or will take (prior to entry of judgment) "all steps" within his or her power to "remove any barrier" to the defendant's remarriage. N.Y. Dom. Rel. Law §253. Despite widespread doubts as to the statute's constitutionality, the state legislature subsequently extended the statute by amending the equitable distribution law to permit a judge to consider the effect of any "barrier to remarriage" (such as the husband's refusal to give the wife a *get*) in awards of property distribution and spousal support. N.Y. Dom. Rel. Law §236B(5)(h), §253(6). The New York State legislature unsuccessfully considered a bill (A.B. 392, 242th Leg. Sess. (N.Y. 2019)) that would have imposed sanctions on recalcitrant spouses of $2,500 per week until such barriers to remarriage are removed.

California has adopted a different approach. In a recent case, a state law reform in the definition of domestic violence (which includes "coercive control") facilitated one woman's receiving a Jewish divorce that her husband had long denied.

Prospectively, that determination may allow some courts to use the leverage of custody and visitation to protect a woman's access to religious divorce.[27]

The United Kingdom has adopted yet another approach. In 2021, Parliament enacted a law criminalizing Orthodox Jewish husbands' refusal to grant their wives a religious divorce. An amendment to the Domestic Abuse Bill and the Serious Crime Act (Section 76) amends the definition of "controlling or coercive behavior" to allow these wives to file charges for domestic abuse, which could result in fines or jail for their husbands.

Islamic marriage contracts also implicate constitutional concerns. Such contracts provide for a *mahr,* or a sum of money payable by the husband to the wife, part received upon marriage and part received upon divorce or death. Judicial enforcement of these agreements, similarly, may violate the Constitution by giving rise to impermissible governmental entanglement in religion. For a recent *mahr* enforcement case, see Parbeen v. Bari, 337 So. 3d 343 (Fla. Dist. Ct. App. 2022) (exploring whether a *mahr* agreement abrogates traditional notions of equitable distribution and spousal support).

F. The Role of Counsel

1. Emotional Aspects of Divorce

Kenneth Kressel et al., *Professional Intervention in Divorce: The Views of Lawyers, Psychotherapists, and Clergy*
in Divorce and Separation 246, 250-255 (George Levinger & Oliver C. Moles eds., 1979)

Much more frequently than either therapists or clergy, [the divorce lawyers in our sample] mentioned sources of stress inherent in the nature of their work. . . . Let us set forth the major sources of role strain reflected in the lawyer interviews.

The adversary nature of the legal proceedings. Despite many changes in recent years, divorce remains largely an adversary process in the eyes of the law. [T]he law's formal bias, the availability of legal threats and counter-threats, as well as the emotional agitation of clients, may push even the most cooperative of lawyers toward serious escalation of conflict. (No-fault divorce has not removed the problem; couples still file bitter suits and countersuits over who shall have custody, how much child support shall be paid, etc.)

The one-sidedness of the lawyer's view. The lawyer's objective appraisal of the marital situation is greatly limited by the professional injunction that lawyers deal with only one of the spouses. Our respondents referred frequently to the difficulty of ascertaining the true state of affairs from the perspective provided

---

[27]. Louis Keene, California Ruling Deemed Step Forward for Jewish Women Stuck in Abusive Marriages, Forward News, Apr. 21, 2022, https://jweekly.com/2022/04/21/california-ruling-deemed-step-forward-for-jewish-women-stuck-in-abusive-marriages/.

by their own clients. Hearing only one side, the lawyer is more easily led to over-identify with the client's point of view—and the client may have strong motives, conscious or unconscious, for wishing to use the adversary system as a vehicle for retribution.

The shortage of material resources. Since two households cannot be supported as cheaply as one, it is highly unlikely that both parties to a divorce will be happy with the terms of the economic settlement. The attorney, therefore, is often in the position of being the bearer of bad news. . . .

The economics of the law office. "There are some lawyers who want to litigate, litigate. They get better fees that way—the taxicab with the meter running." How widespread this phenomenon is nobody knows. It represents nonetheless a serious potential conflict of interest between lawyer and client.

Another potential source of conflict stems from the fact that it is generally the husband who pays the wife's legal costs. The lawyer who represents the wife, therefore, is in the anomalous position of having his fee paid by the opposing side. Unconscious pressures may thus be created for a less than totally effective representation of the wife's interests. The wife herself may have doubts about the degree of allegiance which she can expect from the arrangement.

The non-legal nature of many of the issues. In major areas of their activity, lawyers are operating largely outside the domain of law or legal training. Relatively few of the issues that arise are strictly "issues of law." Moreover, even many legal and financial issues engage psychological judgment and expertise, or personal values (e.g., custody or visitation arrangements that would best meet the emotional needs of both children and parents). Unfortunately, the training of lawyers poorly equips them to understand or handle the psychological and interpersonal issues in divorce, even though such issues may be crucial for creating equitable and workable agreements.

The difficulties in the lawyer-lawyer relationship. Almost universally the lawyers noted that a crucial determinant of divorce outcomes is the relationship between the two opposing attorneys. Indeed, for some respondents a constructive divorce was defined as one in which the two attorneys "come to operate within each other's framework." . . .

[The authors identify six roles that lawyers adopt in response to the problems of divorce practice:]

1. The Undertaker. This metaphor (supplied, incidentally, by one of our respondents) rests on two assumptions: that the job is essentially thankless and messy; and that the clients are in a state of emotional "derangement." This stance is also characterized by a general cynicism about human nature and the doubt that good or constructive divorces are ever possible. . . .

2. The Mechanic. This is a pragmatic, technically oriented stance. It assumes that clients are basically capable of knowing what they want. The lawyer's task primarily involves ascertaining the legal feasibility of doing what the client wants. . . . A good outcome lies in producing "results" for the client, "results" usually understood in financial terms. . . .

3. The Mediator. This stance is oriented toward negotiated compromise and rational problem solving, with an emphasis on cooperation with the other side and, in particular, the other attorney. . . . Unlike the Undertaker and

Mechanic, but like the following three stances, the Mediator tends to downplay the adversary aspect of his role. [A] good outcome is a "fair" negotiated settlement that both parties can "live with" (a frequently used phrase). . . .

4. The Social Worker. This stance centers around a concern for the client's postdivorce adjustment and overall social welfare. Regarding women clients in particular, there may be an emphasis on the client's "marketability."

The main thing is to fully explore [the client's] ability to contribute to her own support. I have had agreements where I have been able to get money for college or a business course. . . .

Even though the attorney represents only one of the parties, there may also be a tendency to consider the interests of the entire family [such as the children]. This stance is also frequently associated with the view that, contrary to many clients' expectations, divorce is not usually an easy solution to marital unhappiness. The involvement of therapists or clergy is welcome. [A] "good" outcome is perceived to be one in which the client achieves social reintegration.

5. The Therapist. This stance involves active acceptance of the fact that the client is in a state of emotional turmoil. There is a concomitant assumption that the legal aspects of a divorce situation can be adequately dealt with only if the emotional aspects are engaged by the lawyer. Correspondingly, there is an orientation toward trying to understand the client's motivations. . . . A "good" outcome is conceptualized more or less as it would be in a therapeutically oriented crisis-intervention situation: personal reintegration of the client after a trying, stressful period. Predictably enough, this is also a stance that welcomes involvement of psychotherapists and in which clients may be encouraged to seek such assistance.

6. The Moral Agent. In this final stance there is a more or less explicit rejection of neutrality; it is assumed that the lawyer should not hesitate to use his or her sense of "right" and "wrong." This stance appears to be particularly salient when the divorcing couple has children, with the lawyer attempting to serve as a kind of guardian and protector of the children's interests. . . . A constructive outcome is one in which the lawyer's sense of "what is right" is satisfied, not only in relation to the client, but to the other spouse and the children.

We have sought to explain this typology of lawyer stances largely as a product of the role strains characteristic of matrimonial practice. . . .

MOSES v. MOSES

1 Fam. L. Rep. (BNA) 2604 (July 22, 1975), *aff'd,* 344 A.2d 912 (Pa. Super. Ct. 1975)

CERCONE, J.

This appeal has been taken by the husband, Dr. Lawrence Moses, from the lower court's award of attorney's fees and expenses to his wife's counsel. . . .

From December 16, 1968 until February 4, 1969, Mrs. Moses consumed many of the hours for which Mr. Fox billed Dr. Moses in personal and telephonic conversations of staggering numbers. Although the content of those conversations is privileged, there are indications in the record that large parts of the discussions are based upon Mr. Fox's friendship with both Dr. and Mrs. Moses, as well as his professional relationship with Mrs. Moses. Her phone calls to Mr. Fox at all hours of the day and night eventually grew so burdensome that they were apparently the principal case of Mr. Fox's withdrawal from the case in favor of Mr. Robinson.

After his withdrawal, Mr. Fox tendered a bill for $4,842 in counsel fees (121 hours and 5 minutes at $40 per hour) and expenses of $112.10. Only fifty-six days elapsed from the time that Mr. Fox began consulting with Mrs. Moses until he withdrew on February 10, 1969, so that he averaged two hours every day, including weekends and holidays, working on Mrs. Moses' problems. The only tangible result of this labor was the support award for Mrs. Fox and the children of $275 weekly. Indeed, to this day the parties are not divorced. . . .

The difficulty in the instant case is that there can be little doubt that Mr. Moses is able to pay, and Mrs. Moses is unable to pay, the fees charged by Mr. Fox. We also do not dispute the finding by the lower court that Mr. Fox actually spent 121 hours on the case, and that $40 per hour is a fair hourly charge for those services. We do challenge, however, the propriety of Mr. Fox investing so much time in this case. We feel that there is an obligation upon counsel, if he expects his fee to be paid by the other spouse, to control excessive demands upon his time, energy and intellect by the dependent spouse. We find that Mr. Fox failed to exercise such control in the instant case. [C]ase law in other jurisdictions . . . supports our view herein. . . .

Finally, our decision is supported by the American Bar Association's Code of Professional Responsibility, Disciplinary Rule 2-106 (1970), [now Rule 1.5 of the ABA Model Rules of Professional Conduct], which sets forth the factors that counsel should consider in determining the reasonableness of his fee: "(1) The time and labor required, the novelty and difficulty of the questions involved, and the skill requisite to perform the legal service properly. (2) The likelihood, if apparent to the client, that the acceptance of the particular employment will preclude other employment by the lawyer. (3) The fee customarily charged in the locality for similar legal services. (4) The amount involved and the results obtained. (5) The time limitations imposed by the client or by the circumstances. (6) The nature and length of the professional relationship with the client. (7) The experience, reputation, and ability of the lawyer performing the services. (8) Whether the fee is fixed or contingent."

We find that the time and labor required, the results obtained, and the nature and length of Mr. Fox's professional relationship with Mrs. Moses, all militate against the allowance of fees and expenses of roughly $5,000 in the instant case. [T]he allowance for attorney's fees and expenses is reduced to $3,000. . . .

Notes and Questions

1. **Overlapping roles.** *Moses* reveals the overlap between the divorce attorney's role as advocate and psychological counselor. Given the court's advice, how would you recommend that an attorney "control [such] excessive demands upon his time, energy, and intellect"?

2. Marital counseling. If the divorce attorney believes that a client should consult a therapist, should the attorney so suggest? How can the attorney do so in a nonthreatening manner? How might such a suggestion backfire? If the client refuses to heed the advice, should the attorney withdraw? Some divorce law firms address this problem by hiring full-time mental health professionals (and sometimes financial advisors) to assist clients with emotional and financial issues that arise during the divorce process.

3. Empirical data. Many divorce lawyers provide far less emotional support than the attorney in *Moses*. A small-scale empirical study of 40 divorce cases characterizes representation as a conversational tug-of-war: Clients seek to include a "broader picture of their lives, experiences, and needs" (especially regarding the failure of their marriage), whereas lawyers resist these efforts. Lawyers tend to be interested "only in those portions of the client's life that have tactical significance for the prospective terms of the divorce settlement or the conduct of the case." Thus, lawyers do not usually provide psychological or emotional support, but rather emphasize communicating their legal knowledge in order "to move clients toward positions that [the lawyers] deem to be reasonable and appropriate."[28]

These findings confirm those of another small-scale empirical study (60 women) by sociologist Terry Arendell, who reports that almost all the clients had complaints about their lawyers:

> Most of the women said their attorneys had showed little interest in their present or future problems and had not tried to keep them informed about divorce legalities and the overall legal process. Although they had been sought out as counselors in a personal life crisis, these lawyers soon appeared to be bureaucratic technicians, more concerned with forms, figures, and procedures than with a client's history, fears, or future well-being. . . . Oversights by attorneys provoked a great deal of anger and frustration. Failure to return phone calls, the most frequent complaint, eroded the attorney-client relationship and increased the woman's sense of stress. . . .[29]

What advice for the family lawyer do you derive from the above studies?

2. Conflicts of Interest

FLORIDA BAR v. DUNAGAN
731 So. 2d 1237 (Fla. 1999)

PER CURIAM.

. . . In July 1992, [attorney Walter Dunagan] prepared a bill of sale purporting to transfer certain assets of a restaurant business, "Biscuits 'N' Gravy 'N' More"

[28]. Austin Sarat & William L. F. Felstiner, Divorce Lawyers and Their Clients: Power and Meaning in the Legal Process 144-145 (1995).
[29]. Terry Arendell, Mothers and Divorce: Legal, Economic, and Social Dilemmas 10-11 (1986). Of the seven women in Arendell's study who had no complaints about their lawyers, three of them prepared and filed their own divorce papers, three negotiated a spousal agreement before retaining an attorney, and the remaining woman was a law student!

("B & G"), to the joint ownership of William and Paula Leucht. Dunagan also prepared the fictitious name filing for this business but, according to a letter sent by him to the Leuchts, inadvertently omitted Paula Leucht's name on the registration form. Subsequently, a commercial lease dispute arose between B & G and Bay-Walsh Properties. . . . The suit filed by Bay-Walsh named B & G, William Leucht, and Paula Leucht as defendants. Dunagan represented B & G and the Leuchts in this action and specifically moved to dismiss Paula Leucht as an improper party to the suit.

Later in 1994, Dunagan was involved in negotiations between the Leuchts and a third party to open another B & G restaurant in Daytona Beach [and] also represented B & G and the Leuchts in an eminent domain suit against the Florida Department of Transportation.

On or about February 23, 1996, Dunagan sent a letter to the Port Orange Police Department and city attorney in which he stated that he represented William Leucht, that William Leucht was the sole owner of B & G, and that although there was a bill of sale which was "considered to put the business in the name of William and Paula Leucht," this "instrument and the legal consequences thereof were duly considered, and it was determined with deliberation that William Leucht would remain the sole owner." The letters further advised that Mr. Leucht intended to fire two employees, after which they would no longer be welcome on the premises of the restaurant, and that if they entered the premises, they would be ejected. The letters purported to notify the police "in order to prevent a breach of the peace from occurring."

Several days after sending these letters, Dunagan filed a petition for dissolution of marriage on behalf of William Leucht against Paula Leucht. A few days later, Paula Leucht called B & G Restaurant and was told by an employee that William Leucht was the sole owner and she could not come to the restaurant. Ms. Leucht went to the restaurant anyway and was arrested for disorderly conduct and forcibly removed from the premises. Prior to, during, and after her arrest, Ms. Leucht informed the police that she co-owned the restaurant.

Finally, on May 2, 1996, the judge in the divorce proceeding ordered that William and Paula Leucht were to share equally in the net proceeds from both B & G restaurants, and on October 31, 1996, Dunagan filed a motion to withdraw from representation of William Leucht in the divorce proceeding after Paula Leucht hired an attorney to file a malpractice lawsuit against him. . . .

Dunagan first argues that the referee erred in finding that his representation of William Leucht in the divorce proceeding after having jointly represented William and Paula Leucht in matters relating to their business presented a conflict of interest. Dunagan argues that the business matters in which he represented the Leuchts were completely unrelated to the dissolution of marriage and that ownership of the business was not a central issue in the divorce; therefore, he reasons, there was no conflict of interest. This argument is without merit.

Rule 4-1.9(a) of the Rules Regulating the Florida Bar prohibits a lawyer who has formerly represented a client from representing another person "in the same or a substantially related matter" where that person's interests are materially adverse to the former client's interests. Whether two legal matters are substantially related depends upon the specific facts of each particular situation or transaction. Further, the comment to rule 4-1.9 states that "[w]hen a lawyer has been directly involved in a specific transaction, subsequent representation of other clients with materially adverse interests clearly is prohibited." . . .

[H]ere, Dunagan represented William and Paula Leucht in the formation of their business and, specifically, prepared a bill of sale transferring assets of the business to their joint ownership. Because the business was begun during the marriage, it was a marital asset and as such was inherently an issue in the divorce. Additionally, the petition for dissolution of marriage filed by Dunagan on William Leucht's behalf specifically raised the issue of the ownership of the business and impliedly disputed the validity of the bill of sale prepared by Dunagan in that it alleged that William Leucht "is the sole owner of the restaurant known as 'Biscuits 'N' Gravy 'N' More'." While ownership of the business may not have been a hotly contested issue, it was still an issue involved in the divorce; therefore, at least one prior matter in which Dunagan jointly represented the Leuchts was substantially related to the divorce. . . .

Dunagan next argues that the referee erred in finding that Paula Leucht did not consent to Dunagan's representation of William Leucht in the dissolution of marriage action. Under certain circumstances, a lawyer may be permitted to represent a client despite a conflict of interest, but only if he or she obtains the consent of the appropriate party or parties after consultation. Here, the referee found that "no disclosure of the conflict or waiver of same took place, given the uncontested fact that no testimony was provided that the respondent ever consulted with Paula Leucht as to the circumstances which led him to represent William Leucht in the divorce, and to what her position was vis-a-vis his representing William Leucht." This finding is supported by the evidence.

Without consulting with or obtaining Paula Leucht's consent, Dunagan filed a petition for dissolution of marriage against her and on behalf of William Leucht. Shortly thereafter, Paula Leucht arrived home from a trip and discovered that the dissolution petition had been filed. Only then, after first calling Mr. Dunagan's office, did Paula Leucht seek and retain another attorney to represent her in the divorce. Only after she had retained an attorney of her own did Dunagan claim he sought her consent through her attorney.

Dunagan testified that he contacted Ms. Leucht's original and subsequent attorneys who gave their consent as attorneys for her. Ms. Leucht's original attorney, Mr. Beck, submitted an affidavit stating that "pursuant to a conference with my client, Paula K. Leucht, it was agreed that there would be no objection raised to the Respondent, Walter B. Dunagan, Esq., representing William Leucht." Paula Leucht acknowledged that she discussed Dunagan's representation of William Leucht with Beck and he advised her that there were better attorneys to be up against; so, she testified, "we never did say anything about him representing me." However, Ms. Leucht also testified that Beck never clearly advised her of her rights or the possible prejudice Dunagan's representation of her ex-husband presented. Accordingly, Ms. Leucht's and her attorney's failure to affirmatively object cannot be construed as "consent after consultation" as required by the rules. . . . The rules state that an attorney *shall not represent* conflicting interests unless the client consents. Especially where the conflict exists prior to the beginning of the representation, this can only mean that the necessary consent should be obtained before the attorney agrees to represent the conflicting interest. This was clearly not done in this case. . . .

Dunagan also argues that the referee erred in concluding that his letters to the Port Orange police and city attorney violated Rule 4-1.9(b) [that] prohibits a lawyer from using information relating to the representation of a former client to the former client's disadvantage. . . . Dunagan essentially argues that the information in the letter was not used to Paula Leucht's disadvantage because it only addressed who had the right to sole possession of the premises, and Paula Leucht was arrested for disorderly conduct, not trespassing. Therefore, he argues, the letters did not cause her to be arrested.

However, the evidence supports the referee's finding that the letters contributed, at least to some degree, to Ms. Leucht's being arrested and forcibly removed from the premises of the business. Although she was charged with disorderly conduct, the arrest report filled out by the police officer clearly shows that the police officers relied on the letter from Dunagan. [B]ecause Dunagan clearly used information relating to his representation of Paula Leucht to her disadvantage. . . . Finally, Dunagan argues that the recommended discipline, a ninety-one-day suspension, is too harsh. . . . We find that the recommended suspension is appropriate. . . .

Notes and Questions

1. Epilogue. After Dunagan's 91-day suspension, he filed a petition for reinstatement. The referee recommended that he not be reinstated for the following reasons: he had remained the attorney of record in several cases during his suspension; he failed to notify an employer (a company for which he lectured) of his suspension; he disagreed with the finding that his representation constituted a conflict of interest; he failed to correct deficiencies in his trust accounting procedures; and he presented no evidence of postsuspension community service. Nonetheless, the Florida Supreme Court found the referee's factual findings insufficient to justify denying Dunagan's petition for reinstatement. Florida Bar ex rel. Dunagan, 775 So. 2d 959 (Fla. 2000). Dunagan died in Edgewater, Florida, in 2004.

2. Rationale. The divorce lawyer may face several ethical problems, including conflicts of interest. In *Dunagan*, what was the nature of the conflict of interest? Why does the court reject Dunagan's arguments that no conflict of interest existed? For example, how were the couple's business matters and divorce related? How were Mr. Leucht's interests materially adverse to his ex-wife's interests?

3. Scope. Courts wrestle with the issue how broadly to interpret the term "conflict of interest" for disciplinary or disqualification purposes. Courts also continue to address whether conflicts of interest arise from two legal matters being sufficiently "substantially related" to result in the disqualification of, or sanctions on, an attorney. See, e.g., Hurley v. Hurley, 923 A.2d 908 (Me. 2007) (holding that an attorney who previously represented a wife in a personal injury action was properly disqualified from later representing her husband in their divorce action given the fact that the attorney had obtained confidential information from wife previously about her health, employment history, and response to contested litigation); In re Conduct of Balocca, 151 P.3d 154 (Or. 2007) (finding a bankruptcy case and paternity action brought by the bankrupt to be "substantially related").

4. Joint representation. Is joint representation permissible? If so, when? According to current ethical rules (Rule 1.7, Model Rules of Professional Conduct), joint representation is permitted if the attorney reasonably believes he or she can adequately represent both clients' interests and if both clients consent after full disclosure of the risks of such representation. The Restatement (Third) of the Law Governing Lawyers §128 reaffirms this rule.

On the other hand, some states condemn the practice of joint representation in their disciplinary rules, case law, or state bar opinions. The American Academy of Matrimonial Lawyers (a voluntary association of lawyers and judges that establishes ethical standards for family law practitioners that exceed those of the ABA and most state ethics codes) also admonishes against joint representation, even if clients consent. Which point of view is more persuasive?

5. Client consent. Did Mrs. Leucht consent to Mr. Dunagan's representation of her ex-husband in the dissolution? Why did the Florida Supreme Court hold that her "failure to affirmatively object" could not be construed as consent pursuant to the state bar rules?

Problems

1. Wife files a petition for a restraining order for protection against domestic violence from her husband. The court grants her petition, but before the hearing to determine whether the order should be made permanent, Wife files a motion seeking disqualification of Husband's attorney, Charles Esposito. She alleges that she previously consulted Esposito's partner (Davis Upchurch) to ask him to represent her in divorce proceedings; in the course of that one consultation, she claims that she divulged confidential information to Upchurch. Upchurch did not charge her for the consultation; he claims that he was not retained to represent Wife and does not remember anything she told him that might have been confidential. Should Wife's motion be granted?

Consider the following: (1) Can an attorney-client relationship be established based on one visit? (2) To fulfill the requirements for disqualification, must the client prove that confidential communications were actually disclosed? (3) Does the existence of the attorney-client privilege depend on whether the client actually hires the attorney? (4) Were the two proceedings (the restraining order and the dissolution) substantially related — that is, did the law firm subsequently represent an interest adverse to the former client in a matter that was the same or substantially related to the matter in which it represented the former client? See Metcalf v. Metcalf, 785 So. 2d 747 (Fla. Dist. Ct. App. 2001).

2. After Marie and Theodore have been married for more than 25 years, Marie files for divorce. She seeks division of the couple's property, permanent spousal support, and attorney fees and costs. Theodore decides to retain their adult son, Mark, as his attorney. Marie then files a motion to disqualify Mark. Does representation by an adult child of one of the parents in a divorce action constitute a disqualifying conflict of interest? What additional facts might you want to know to make this determination? See Liapis v. District Court, 282 P.3d 733 (Nev. 2012). What should be the appropriate standard for disqualification in this case: avoidance of the appearance of impropriety or actual prejudice? See State v. Eighth Jud. Dist. Ct. (Zogheib), 321 P.3d 882 (Nev. 2014).

Ethics Opinion 243. District of Columbia Bar

Joint Representation in Divorce Cases (Feb. 1, 2007)

A lawyer may not jointly represent a divorcing husband and wife who seek assistance in reaching agreement as to the terms of their divorce.

Ethics Committee, State Bar of Montana, Opinion 10

Law. Manual on Prof'l Conduct (ABA/BNA) 801:5401 (Dec. 1980)

A lawyer may represent both spouses in a joint petition for dissolution as a non-adversary procedure. A lawyer may represent both spouses if it is obvious that he can adequately represent the interest of each after each consents to the representation after full disclosure of the possible effect of such representation on the exercise of his independent professional judgment on behalf of each. DRs 5-104; Canon 5.

Mary E. Chesser, Comment, Joint Representation in a Friendly Divorce: Inherently Unethical?

27 J. Legal Prof. 155, 158-161 (2002-2003)

[W]hat are the major reasons that an uncontested divorce may be so problematic for an attorney wishing to represent both of the divorcing parties? First, there is an inherent conflict in a divorce, especially where the parties must divide property and/or the parties have children. When conflicts exist, an attorney is expected to diligently represent his or her client. However, when an attorney represents both parties to a divorce, he or she cannot exhibit the "level of partisanship" that is generally expected in a lawyer-client relationship. For instance, when an attorney represents both spouses, he or she is unable to diligently seek the best property distribution or child custody arrangement for one over the other. If, instead, a wife obtained separate counsel from her husband, her attorney would probably "seek to maximize the client's share of the marital property, reduce the tax consequences of the transfers, and protect custody, support, and visitation rights." Where the same attorney represents both parties, such diligence is impossible.

Second, confidentiality between client and attorney is compromised in joint representation, because an attorney must inform co-clients of all information relevant during the representation. This results in tension between Model Rules 1.4 and 1.6 because these rules mandate that the attorney must keep both clients adequately informed and maintain their confidentiality. Although the attorney-client privilege protects clients against discovery by outsiders, any confidences will be shared among co-clients. In other words, "as between commonly represented clients, the privilege does not attach." Furthermore, both clients should be aware that if the divorce proceedings eventually lead to litigation, their attorney-client privilege with their joint attorney would not protect any communications from either spouse.

Third, an attorney serving in a dual capacity must be certain that the property arrangement is fair and equitable. If an attorney, in the course of representing a couple during a divorce, discovers that a settlement is not fair to one of the parties, he or she has an obligation to point this unfairness out to that client. If the attorney chooses not to scrutinize the property arrangement, a defrauding party might be able to conceal assets that a separately represented spouse might have discovered. If the attorney scrutinizes the property settlement, however, and discovers fraud or a power imbalance between the parties, he or she will have to withdraw. This creates an obvious economic disincentive for an attorney to seek the truth.

Fourth, there is an appearance of impropriety when an attorney represents both parties in a divorce case. Although the drafters of the Model Rules excluded a prohibition against "even the appearance of impropriety," and replaced such a standard with Model Rules 1.7 through 1.12, the legal community, rather appropriately, still frowns on any appearance of impropriety.

Finally, even with consultation and full disclosure by the lawyer, clients may still believe that dual representation provides for true adversarial representation when it clearly does not. It is good practice for attorneys to put joint representation agreements in writing in order to alleviate some of the confusion. As previously mentioned, the Model Rules now require that both clients provide their consent in writing if there is a conflict under Rule 1.7(a). The purpose of the writing is to "impress upon clients the seriousness of the decision the client is being asked to make and to avoid disputes or ambiguities that might later occur in the absence of a writing." However, even a written agreement does not guarantee that the consultation and consent is sufficient; "the lawyer ... has an obligation to ensure that the parties fully understand the implications of dual representation." Part of this disclosure includes a detailed discussion of the potential conflicts that may arise and what impact that may have on intermediation, including the possibility that the attorney would then have to withdraw and both parties would need to find new, independent representation. . . .

Because of these and other considerations, the American Academy of Matrimonial Lawyers warns that a lawyer should not represent both husband and wife even if they request dual representation. . . .

3. Sexual Ethics

IOWA SUPREME COURT ATTORNEY DISCIPLINARY BOARD v. MORRISON

727 N.W.2d 115 (Iowa 2007)

STREIT, J.

. . . William Morrison was admitted to the Iowa bar in 1989. . . . In June 2005, Morrison reported to the Iowa Supreme Court Attorney Disciplinary Board ("Board") he "engaged in a sexual relationship with a female client while representing her in a dissolution proceeding." Morrison represented this client from October 2004 through February 2005. They had sex on several occasions from November 2004 through March 2005. Morrison did not have a personal relationship with this client prior to November 2004.

The Board filed a complaint against Morrison alleging he violated the Iowa Code of Professional Responsibility for Lawyers by engaging in a sexual relationship with a client. In lieu of an evidentiary hearing before the Grievance Commission, the Board and Morrison agreed to submit the matter upon stipulation. The parties stipulated to the facts above. Morrison acknowledged his conduct was unethical. The Board noted Morrison cooperated with its investigation. The parties also included with the stipulation a private admonition Morrison received from the Board in March 2004. Morrison was admonished for "solicitation of a dissolution client for a social relationship by reason of that dissolution client's 'attractiveness.'" The parties jointly recommend Morrison's conduct warrants suspension of his Iowa law license for sixty days. The Grievance Commission recommends Morrison's license to practice law be suspended for six months and that he enter and complete a counseling program to address his "boundary issues." Morrison reports he has already completed such a counseling program with a psychologist in addition to marriage counseling. . . .

. . . Morrison admits he had a sexual relationship with a client. This is a patent violation of Iowa Code of Professional Responsibility for Lawyers DR 5-101(B) (lawyer shall not engage in sexual relations with a client) and DR 1-102(A)(1) and (6) (lawyer shall not violate a disciplinary rule or engage in any other conduct that adversely reflects on the fitness to practice law). "Professional responsibility involves many gray areas, but sexual relationships between attorney and client is not one of these. Such conduct is clearly improper." Iowa Supreme Ct. Bd. of Prof'l Ethics & Conduct v. Furlong, 625 N.W.2d 711, 714 (Iowa 2001). Before determining the appropriate sanction, we review the sound reasons for prohibiting attorney-client sexual relationships.

First, "[t]he unequal balance of power in the attorney-client relationship, rooted in the attorney's special skill and knowledge on the one hand and the client's potential vulnerability on the other, may enable the lawyer to dominate and take unfair advantage." Iowa Code of Prof'l Responsibility EC 5-25. This is why the client's consent is irrelevant. We have previously stated, "the professional relationship renders it impossible for the vulnerable layperson to be considered 'consenting.'" Iowa Supreme Ct. Bd. of Prof'l Ethics & Conduct v. Hill, 540 N.W.2d 43, 44 (Iowa 1995) (*Hill II*).

Second, a sexual relationship between attorney and client may be harmful to the client's interest. This is true in any legal representation but "presents an even greater danger to the client seeking advice in times of personal crises such as divorce, death of a loved one, or when facing criminal charges." Iowa Code of Prof'l Responsibility EC 5-25.

Third, an attorney-client sexual relationship may prevent the attorney from competently representing the client. An attorney must be able to objectively evaluate the client's case. The American Bar Association stated, "[t]he roles of lover and lawyer are potentially conflicting ones as the emotional involvement that is fostered by a sexual relationship has the potential to undercut the objective detachment that is often demanded for adequate representation." ABA Comm. on Ethics and Prof'l Responsibility, Formal Op. 92-364 (1992).

Finally, an attorney initiating a sexual relationship with a client or attempting to do so may undercut the client's trust and faith in the lawyer. "Clients may rightfully expect that confidences vouchsafed to the lawyer will be solely used to advance the client's interest, and will not be used to advance the lawyer's interest, sexual or otherwise." Iowa Code of Prof'l Responsibility EC 5-25.

We now turn to the appropriate sanction. We consider:

> the nature and extent of the respondent's ethical infractions, his fitness to continue practicing law, our obligation to protect the public from further harm by the respondent, the need to deter other attorneys from engaging in similar misconduct, our desire to maintain the reputation of the bar as a whole, and any aggravating or mitigating circumstances.

Iowa Supreme Ct. Bd. of Prof'l Ethics & Conduct v. Kallsen, 670 N.W.2d 161, 164 (Iowa 2003). . . .

This court does not tolerate attorney-client sexual relationships. In the present case, the Grievance Commission recommends Morrison's license to practice law be suspended for six months and that he be required to complete a counseling program to address his "boundary issues." The Board on the other hand recommends a sixty-day suspension because "this case does not involve aggravating factors such as forced sexual advances or commercial exploitation."

Our review is hindered by a limited record. Based on the parties' stipulation, Morrison's conduct does not appear to be particularly egregious in comparison to our previous cases involving attorney-client sexual relationships. But even a purely consensual sexual relationship between attorney and client is clearly prohibited by DR 5-101(B) for the reasons we have already stated.

Like this case, *Hill I* involved an attorney representing a client in a dissolution action. There, we said:

> A lawyer undertaking a divorce action must recognize reconciliation is possible and may be in the best interest of his client. An attorney must be aware that the actions of the client and attorney may affect negotiations in the dissolution case, including determination of custody and visitation of minor children. Sexual intercourse between the lawyer and a client seeking a dissolution of marriage carries a great potential of prejudice both to the client and to the minor children of the marriage. *Hill I*, 436 N.W.2d at 59.

Morrison's client and her husband had at least one minor child. We do not know from the record if the relationship between Morrison and his client prejudiced her in the dissolution action. Nevertheless, at least the potential for harm existed and exists in any attorney-client representation. See Iowa Supreme Ct. Bd. of Prof'l Ethics & Conduct v. Steffes, 588 N.W.2d 121, 123 (Iowa 1999) (sexual harassment by attorney made client uncomfortable going to attorney's office so client did not seek attorney's advice regarding pending criminal charges).

Moreover, Morrison has previously been admonished for making a sexual advance toward another client. He became sexually involved with the client in this particular case just eight months after the admonishment. Clearly, Morrison has not learned his lesson. A suspension of Morrison's license to practice law is necessary and appropriate. We hereby suspend Morrison's license to practice law in Iowa for a minimum of three months. . . .

Notes and Questions

1. Majority. *Morrison* represents the majority approach (influenced by the ABA) of prohibiting sexual relationships between attorneys and clients. The ABA Model Rules of Professional Conduct currently provide that "a lawyer shall not have sexual relations with a client unless a consensual sexual relationship existed between them when the client-lawyer relationship commenced." Model Rules of Prof'l Conduct R. 1.8(j). The previous provision merely *recommended* a ban. See ABA Comm. on Ethics and Prof'l Responsibility, Formal Op. 92-364 (1992).

2. Background. California was the first state whose bar association approved a rule proscribing attorney-client sexual relationships. California Rules of Professional Conduct Rule 3-120(B) (effective 1992) prohibited an attorney from (1) requiring or demanding sexual relations as a condition of representation; (2) employing coercion, intimidation, or undue influence in entering into sexual relations; or (3) continuing to represent a client after having sexual relations with that client if the sexual relationship causes the attorney to perform legal services incompetently. The Rule exempts preexisting sexual relationships and spousal relationships. Originally, the state bar rejected an absolute ban based on concerns that it was not the least restrictive alternative and would infringe on freedom of association of the attorney and client. However, in May 2018, the California Supreme Court approved a new rule that brought California in line with the majority approach.[30]

3. Consensual nature of sexual relationship. Does the consensual nature of the relationship militate against the imposition of sanctions? Are even apparently

---

[30]. On the background of ABA Rule 1.8(j), see N. Gregory Smith, Sexual Misconduct by Louisiana Lawyers, 81 La. L. Rev. 767, 770-774 (2021). On the various state approaches, see id. at 848-859; Hannah Thompson Stilley, Comment, Attorney-Client Sexual Relationships: A Call for All States to Adopt Model Rule 1.8(j), 32 J. Am. Acad. Matrim. Law. 499, 512-525 (2020).

consensual attorney-client sexual relationships "dangerous and exploitative" such that regulation is necessary to protect clients and establish public trust in the legal profession?[31]

Should it matter if the client, rather than the attorney, initiates the sexual relationship? See Committee on Prof'l Ethics & Conduct v. Hill, 436 N.W.2d 57 (Iowa 1989) (suspending attorney even though client initiated the sexual relationship, reasoning that attorney should have recognized the potential adverse effects). Some commentators argue that attorney-client sex can never be voluntary because of the power imbalance and the client's emotional and financial status.[32] Do you agree?

Do you think that the sanction (a three-month suspension) was appropriate in *Morrison*? Note that courts take a particularly dim view of attorneys' misconduct when the sexual relationship is coerced. See, e.g., Iowa Supreme Court Attorney Disciplinary Bd. v. McGrath, 713 N. W.2d 682 (Iowa 2006) (three-year suspension for soliciting sexual favors in exchange for legal services).

4. Harm.   What is the harm of attorney-client sexual conduct? To the profession? To the client? See Brown v. Virginia State Bar ex rel. Sixth District Comm., 886 S.E.2d 492 (Va. 2023). How does *Morrison* respond to this issue? Does the attorney's withdrawal as counsel in the client's divorce case "cure" the ethical violation?

5. Exceptions. Should rules regulating sexual conduct between lawyers and clients have exceptions? Does an exemption for prior intimate relationships address the problems? Or is representation following preexisting intimate relationships just as problematic?[33]

6. Therapist-client rules. Although no empirical studies investigate the effects of lawyers' sexual misconduct with clients, the effects of sexual relations between therapists and clients are well known. For example, 90 percent of patients in one study suffered negative effects, including loss of motivation, impaired social adjustment, suicidal feelings or behavior, and increased substance abuse.[34] How is the attorney-client relationship similar to, and different from, the psychotherapist-client relationship? Are similar effects to attorneys' clients likely to occur?

Regulations currently prohibit sexual conduct between psychotherapists and clients. See, e.g., Cal. Bus. & Prof. Code §726. Although some statutes limit prohibitions to sexual conduct within two years of termination of therapy (e.g., Cal.

---

[31]. Malinda L. Seymore, Attorney-Client Sex: A Feminist Critique of the Absence of Regulation, 15 Yale J.L. & Feminism 175 (2003) (so arguing).

[32]. Jennifer Tuggle Crabtree, Does Consent Matter? Relationships Between Divorce Attorneys and Clients, 23 J. Legal Prof. 221, 229-232 (1998).

[33]. See Phillip R. Bower & Tanya E. Stern, Current Development 2002-2003, Conflict of Interest? The Absolute Ban on Lawyer-Client Sexual Relationships Is Not Absolutely Necessary, 16 Geo. J. Legal Ethics 535, 545 (2003) (so arguing).

[34]. Jacqueline Bouhoutsos et al., Sexual Intimacy Between Psychotherapists and Patients, 14 Prof. Psychol.: Res. & Prac. 185, 191 (1983) (study with a sample of 559 patients).

Civ. Code §43.93 (b)(2)), most statutes contain *absolute* prohibitions (e.g., Fla. Stat. Ann. §491.0112). Should lawyer-client relationships be treated similarly? If so, which approach is preferable?

7. Other sanctions. Different types of sanctions also apply to sexual misconduct, such as those for violations of state business and professions codes. Suspensions and disbarment are possible. Tort remedies, such as IIED or malpractice, might apply. Criminal statutes also might be relevant. What approach or approaches do you favor?

8. Privacy. Does an outright ban on attorney-client sexual relations constitute an unconstitutional intrusion on the attorney's and client's respective rights to privacy? In Committee on Professional Ethics & Conduct v. Hill, 436 N.W.2d 57 (Iowa 1989), an attorney was disciplined for engaging in sexual intercourse, purportedly in exchange for money, with a divorce client involved in child custody litigation. The attorney argued that the court's consideration of his conduct violated his right to privacy, protecting private acts between two consenting adults. How should the court rule? What is the impact of Lawrence v. Texas?

Problems

1. You receive a telephone call from a former law school friend. He asks for your advice, explaining that he is very attracted to a woman whom he is representing in a contentious divorce case. Although he is eager to become romantically involved, he would like to know more about potential ethical issues. He confesses that he is so smitten that he has lost his objectivity. Nonetheless, he believes that he can continue to represent her effectively, even if they begin to see each other romantically. What would you advise? This problem is posed in Ethics: Affairs of the Heart, A.B.A. J., June 1990, at 82.

2. Cheryl retains Sam Drucker to represent her in her divorce. During an initial consultation, she discusses her marriage and treatment for an anxiety disorder. On her second visit, she alleges that Drucker held her hand, embraced her, and told her about his marriage. When he apologized and offered to refer her to another lawyer, she declined. Drucker called her at home to tell her that he was attracted to her. Cheryl alleges that they engaged in sexual activity three times. She pinpoints two of the encounters based on surrounding events (i.e., Drucker's daughter was ill; another client was in the office). After Drucker ends the relationship, Cheryl's husband discovers her diary. He confronts her in the presence of their son, who is the subject of a custody dispute. Drucker denies the sexual relationship. The Committee on Professional Conduct seeks to suspend Drucker from practice. What result? Drucker's Case, 577 A.2d 1198 (N.H. 1990).

4. Risks of Practicing Family Law

Stephen D. Kelson, Another "Spillover Effect" of Domestic Violence: Threats and Violence Against Family Law Practitioners
24 Domestic Violence Rep. 53-64 (Apr./May 2018)

[The author is an attorney and mediator at the law firm of Christensen & Jensen, P.C., in Salt Lake City, Utah. For more than a decade, he has conducted statewide surveys regarding violence against lawyers and studied methods to prevent workplace violence.]

[B]ased on the infrequent publicized reports of threats and violence against the legal profession, one might think that such incidents are unique and extremely rare. However, threats and violence against the legal profession, including those against family law practitioners, is a real and serious issue, and may be increasing. Family law practitioners face a disproportionate amount of threats and violence compared to many other areas of practice, and the "spillover effect" of domestic violence increases the chance of threats and violence against the victim's attorney. . . .

While there is no national method for reporting threats and violence against the legal profession, the author, independently and through state bar associations, has conducted 28 statewide surveys, regarding threats and violence against the legal profession. These surveys, including responses from more than 28,000 attorneys, provide a rare insight into the nature and frequency of work-related threats and violence experienced by in-state/active members of the legal profession, the overwhelming majority of which have never been publicly reported. The results also show that contrary to public perception, members of the legal profession, especially family law practitioners, are not exempt from workplace violence, but in fact, many face danger from their own clients, opposing parties and interested parties, at any place and at any time.

Acts of violence reported by attorneys in these state surveys include numerous shootings, stabbings, assaults and batteries, as well as vandalism to businesses and personal property. The numerous threats of violence reported include stalking, phone calls, written letters, emails, texts, on-line posts, verbal threats of physical violence and death threats, and even attempts to hire hit men to kill attorneys and judges. . . .

[B]roken out by practice area, family lawyers consistently have one of the highest rates of threats and violence. Focusing solely on attorneys who identify their practice area as family law/divorce, the survey responses show that at least 47% of respondents have been the recipients of threats and/or violence. Moreover, many respondents who reported their principal practice area as "general litigation" reported a substantial number of threats and violence which occurred in family law cases. [The] spillover of domestic violence directed at family law attorneys is not always aimed at just the attorneys themselves, but many times also involves attorneys' families, office staff, [and their] personal property. . . .

What, if anything, can family law attorneys do to minimize this occupational hazard?

G. Divorce Jurisdiction

1. Over the Plaintiff and Defendant

IN RE MARRIAGE OF KIMURA
471 N.W.2d 869 (Iowa 1991)

LAVORATO, Justice. . . .

Ken and Fumi Kimura were married in Japan in 1965. Both are Japanese citizens. They have a daughter and a son [in their 20s]. Ken and Fumi have lived apart since September 1973. Ken graduated from Kobe University Medical School in Japan. Currently, he is a pediatric surgeon at the University of Iowa Hospitals and Clinics in Iowa City.

[In July 1986, Ken took a position at the Long Island Jewish Medical Center in New Hyde Park, New York. He had an H-1 temporary visa that is issued to persons with special talents or abilities. After receiving his permanent residency status in 1987, he was hired at the University of Iowa as an associate professor of medicine.]

In March 1988, Ken filed a divorce mediation proceeding with the family court in Japan [but] withdrew from the proceeding [because, apparently, he could not attend that court's reconciliation proceeding due to his work].

In December, Ken filed a petition for dissolution of marriage in Johnson County District Court. He alleged that he had resided in Iowa for more than one year. He further alleged that his residency was not just for the purpose of obtaining a dissolution. Finally, he alleged a breakdown of the marital relationship. Because personal service was not possible on Fumi in Iowa, a copy of the petition was mailed to her in Japan. In addition, notice of the petition was published in the *Iowa City Press Citizen.* . . .

In February 1989 Fumi [contested] the district court's subject matter and personal jurisdiction. [Her affidavit pointed out that Ken could not obtain a divorce under Japanese law because his conduct had caused the marital problems. At the final hearing, Fumi did not personally appear, but her attorney did. After testimony about Ken's employment, residence status, and the breakdown of the marriage, the court concluded that Ken satisfied the residency requirements and dissolved the marriage. Fumi appealed.]

II. THE DUE PROCESS CHALLENGE

Fumi poses the issue this way: "Iowa's assertion of jurisdiction over respondent (who has no contacts with Iowa) or her marriage based solely on petitioner's alleged residence in Iowa violates the due process clauses of the United States and Iowa Constitutions." . . .

Early on, due process required the personal presence of the defendant in the forum state as a condition for rendering a binding personal or in personam judgment against the defendant [citing Pennoyer v. Neff, 95 U.S. 714, 733 (1878); International Shoe Co. v. Washington, 326 U.S. 310 (1945)]. [Now] [d]ue process only requires that the defendant have certain minimum contacts with the forum state. However, those contacts must be such "that the maintenance of the suit does not offend traditional notions of fair play and substantial justice." *International Shoe*, 326 U.S. at 316. Simply put, there must be a connection among the forum, the litigation, and the defendant.

Fumi relies on [Shaffer v. Heitner, 433 U.S. 186 (1977)] in support of her contention that jurisdiction to grant the dissolution must be tested by the minimum contacts standard of *International Shoe*. A footnote in *Shaffer* suggests her reliance is misplaced. See *Shaffer*, 433 U.S. at 208 n.30. One commentator seems to agree:

> Although the *Shaffer* Court concluded that all assertions of state-court jurisdiction must conform to the standards of *International Shoe* and, thus, be based upon a nexus among the forum, the litigation, and the defendant, the nexus requirement is unlikely to apply to cases in which status provides the basis of the asserted jurisdiction. The power to dissolve the marriage status in an ex parte proceeding normally is thought to stem, at least in part, from the perception of the marriage status as a res, and thus, as a "thing" to which the court's jurisdiction can attach. . . . [T]he forum-litigation-plaintiff nexus [rather than the forum-litigation-defendant nexus] recognized as sufficient by the Court in Williams v. North Carolina seems to remain a valid basis of jurisdiction for ex parte divorces.

State-Court Jurisdiction, 63 Iowa L. Rev. at 1005-06 (citations omitted).

In Williams v. North Carolina, 317 U.S. 287, 298-299 (1942) [hereinafter *Williams I*], the question was whether full faith and credit had to be given to a foreign divorce decree where only one spouse was domiciled in the foreign state and the other spouse had never been there. The Supreme Court held that the foreign state's high interest in the marital status of its domiciliaries required that full faith and credit be given such a decree. The Court did require, however, that substituted service on the absent spouse meet due process standards, that is, reasonably calculated to give the absent spouse actual notice and an opportunity to be heard.

In *Williams I*, the Court had difficulty classifying dissolution proceedings. Though it did not view such proceedings as in rem actions, neither did it view them as mere in personam actions. According to the Court, domicile of one spouse within the forum state gave that state the power to dissolve the marriage regardless of where the marriage occurred. This court too has deemed domicile as essential to dissolution of marriage jurisdiction.

The cases generally adopt the following explanation of the components for a dissolution of marriage proceeding:

> It is commonly held that an essential element of the judicial power to grant a divorce, or jurisdiction, is domicile. A court must have jurisdiction of the res, or the marriage status, in order that it may grant a divorce. The res or status follows the domiciles of the spouses; and therefore, in order that the res may be found within the state so that the courts of the state may have jurisdiction of it, one of the spouses must have a domicile within the state.

24 Am. Jur. 2d Divorce & Separation §238, at 336 (1983).

Williams v. North Carolina reached the Supreme Court a second time. The Court held that while the finding of domicile by the state that granted the decree is entitled to prima facie weight, it is not conclusive in a sister state but might be relitigated there. Williams v. North Carolina, 325 U.S. 226, 238-39 (1945) [*Williams II*].

The divisible divorce doctrine emerged in Estin v. Estin, 334 U.S. 541, 549 (1948). In *Estin* the Court held that Nevada in an ex parte divorce proceeding could change the marital status of those domiciled within its boundaries. The power to do so stems from Nevada's "considerable interest in preventing bigamous marriages and in protecting the offspring of marriages from being [illegitimate]." *Estin*, 334 U.S. at 546. But Nevada could not wipe out the absent spouse's claim for alimony under a New York judgment in a prior separation proceeding because Nevada had no personal jurisdiction over the absent spouse. So New York did not have to give full faith and credit to that part of the Nevada decree which purported to eliminate the support obligation of its domiciliary. . . .

The divisible divorce doctrine simply recognizes the court's limited power where the court has no personal jurisdiction over the absent spouse. In these circumstances, the court has jurisdiction to grant a divorce to one domiciled in the state but no jurisdiction to adjudicate the incidents of the marriage, for example, alimony and property division. In short, the divisible divorce doctrine recognizes both the in rem and in personam nature of claims usually raised in dissolution of marriage proceedings.

[We conclude that] the courts of this state have the power to grant dissolution of marriage decrees provided the petitioner is domiciled in this state. Such power exists even though the petitioner's spouse is absent from this state, has never been here, and was constructively rather than personally served. [Here, the lower court adjudicated only marital status because the court did not have personal jurisdiction over Fumi.] [W]e are left with the question whether Ken established his domicile or residency in this state. . . .

III. CHALLENGE TO DOMICILE OR RESIDENCY

. . . Fumi contends that even if minimum contacts were not the standard, Ken still had to establish that he met the residency requirements of this state before the court could dissolve the marriage. She argues that Ken failed to establish those requirements and so the district court should not have dissolved the marriage. [W]e disagree. . . .

According to [Iowa Code §598.6] Ken had to establish the following: (1) he resided in Iowa for at least one year before the petition was filed; and (2) his residence here was in good faith and not just for the purpose of obtaining a marriage dissolution. Residence for the purpose of section 598.6 has the same meaning as domicile. To have a residence or domicile within the meaning of this section, "one must have a fixed habitation with no intention of" leaving it.

Once a domicile is established, it continues until a new one is established. A new domicile is established if all of the following things happen: (1) the former domicile is abandoned; (2) there is an actual removal to, and physical presence in the new domicile; and (3) there is a bona fide intention to change and to remain in the new domicile permanently or indefinitely. This intention must be a present and fixed intention and not dependent on some future or contingent event. . . .

We think Ken amply proved that he met the residency requirements of section 598.6. . . .[He] swore to a number of facts showing that he had abandoned his domicile in Japan in favor of the one here. For example, he swore that he had no other permanent residence other than his residence in Johnson County. In addition, he swore that since moving to Iowa, he had obtained an Iowa driver's license and had opened bank accounts at local banks. Finally, he swore that he intends to remain here for an indefinite period so long as his employment at the university is satisfactory to him and the university. . . .

We see nothing in the evidence to support Fumi's contention that Ken's residence here was in bad faith and only for the purpose of obtaining a dissolution of marriage. It may be that one reason Ken came here was—as Fumi suggests—because of our liberal dissolution marriage law as compared to Japan's. But that fact is not sufficient to preclude Ken from establishing a domicile or residence in Iowa, especially in light of his intention to remain here indefinitely. Nor does Ken's continued Japanese citizenship preclude such a domicile or residence. A foreign citizenship does not—standing alone—bar one from establishing a domicile or residence for dissolution of marriage purposes. . . .

IV. CHALLENGE TO COURT'S RULING REFUSING TO DECLINE JURISDICTION BASED ON FORUM NON CONVENIENS DOCTRINE

[Fumi next contends that the district court should have declined jurisdiction based on forum non conveniens, arguing] that Japan is the more convenient forum and is the nation with the most significant contacts to the marital status of the parties. [Under the forum non conveniens doctrine,] a court may decline to proceed with an action though venue and jurisdiction are proper. The doctrine is a self-imposed limit on jurisdictional power that can be used to avoid unfair, vexatious, oppressive actions in a forum away from the defendant's domicile. . . .

What the moving party must show is that the relative inconveniences are so unbalanced that jurisdiction should be declined on an equitable basis. Factors that bear on this determination include the following: the relative ease of access to sources of proof; the availability of compulsory process for attendance of unwilling, and the cost of obtaining attendance of willing, witnesses; the possibility of view of the premises, if view would be appropriate to the action; the enforceability of the judgment if one is obtained; and all other practical problems that make trial of a case easy, expeditious, and inexpensive. All of these factors pertain to the private interest of the litigant.

Factors of public interest are also considered. They include the administrative difficulties for courts, trial in the forum that is the home of the state law which governs the case, and the burden of jury duty imposed on citizens of a forum with no relation to the litigation. Residency of the plaintiff is also considered but only as one of the many factors in the balancing process.

Whether to apply the doctrine of forum non conveniens lies in the sound discretion of the district court. . . . In deciding whether the district court abused its discretion in this case, we think it would be helpful to look at the divorce process in Japan. Japan has a variety of ways to dissolve a marriage [in contested cases] . . .: divorce through mediation in the family court, divorce by judicial decree in the family court, and divorce by judicial decree in the district court. A person seeking a divorce by judicial decree in the district court must prove fault. . . .

The family court may grant a divorce without proof of such grounds. But a divorce by judicial decree in the family court is rare because if either party objects, the divorce becomes invalid. So a decree of divorce by judicial decision usually issues from the district court.

Before the parties may proceed to the district court they must attempt mediation in the family court. Divorce can be effected without resort to litigation if the parties can agree on terms. If the parties fail to reach agreement, a divorce petition may then be submitted to and processed by the district court. Mediators in family court have no power to arbitrate disputes and are likely to oppose the idea of divorce. As a practical matter, a failure to agree to terms in mediation may mean no divorce in district court.

A divorce in Japan means the severance of all ties between the parties—they virtually become strangers. Usually a lump sum property settlement occurs. Because of enforcement problems, a settlement involving installment payments is rare. Alimony and other postdivorce maintenance payments are not available under Japanese law. Indeed, there is no legal requirement that property be divided or that support be paid. . . .

It has been suggested that divorce in Japan is quick and easy if a party can bribe, coerce, threaten, or persuade the other party to a divorce by mutual consent. A nonconsensual divorce is difficult, if not impossible, to obtain. . . .

For several reasons, the district court here could have determined that Japan is the more convenient forum for the parties. First, Japan has complete jurisdiction over the marital status of the parties and over all the incidents of the marriage. Second, a Japanese court has a societal interest in the marital status of its citizens. Third, given the nature of the divorce proceedings in Japan, Fumi's bargaining power in a family court mediation may be reduced by permitting a dissolution of marriage here. Fourth, Fumi may be at a cultural disadvantage with regard to customs and language in an Iowa proceeding. Last, Iowa is an inconvenient forum in relation to her residence.

On the other hand we think the district court was well within its discretion to deny Fumi's request to decline jurisdiction. Iowa too has an interest in the marital status of its residents. Right or wrong, our legislature has opted for no-fault divorce. One reason, we suspect, was to eliminate the extortion leverage an "innocent" spouse had over a "guilty" spouse. Had the district court honored Fumi's request, Ken—an Iowa resident—would have been denied the protection of Iowa's dissolution law. In short, a ruling in Fumi's favor may have resulted in no dissolution at all for one of this State's residents.

In addition we are impressed with the vigorous representation Fumi enjoyed in the district court and here. We doubt there would be any less representation in a postdissolution action for alimony and property division. . . . Our liberal discovery rules should allow Fumi to discover all of Ken's assets and his income in such an action. This is in contrast to Japan where it is difficult to discover a party's assets in divorce proceedings. Given our liberal rules on alimony and property division, we suspect Fumi might even fare better here than in Japan. . . . The district court did not violate Fumi's rights under either the federal or state constitutions. . . .

Notes and Questions

1. Special rules. *Kimura* reveals that special jurisdictional rules, unlike those in other civil actions, apply to divorce. To terminate a marriage, the plaintiff must be domiciled in the forum state. *Personal jurisdiction over the defendant is not required.* (Although personal jurisdiction is not required merely to terminate the marriage, it is required to resolve the financial incidents of the marriage.) However, *notice* to the defendant that complies with due process is required to inform the defendant of the pendency of the action. A divorce without proper notice may be challenged for lack of jurisdiction.

2. Ex parte divorces. As *Kimura* indicates, some divorce decrees issued in one state may be collaterally attacked in another state for want of jurisdiction. Williams v. North Carolina, 317 U.S. 287 (1942), established that the domiciliary state of one spouse may grant an "ex parte" divorce, entitled to full faith and credit in all other states. (The term "ex parte" here means that the forum lacks jurisdiction over the respondent-spouse.) Because divorce courts routinely apply local substantive law, *Williams I* reinforced the practice of migratory divorce during the fault era, when an unhappy spouse often traveled to a new "domicile" to seek a divorce under the latter state's more permissive grounds.

The Supreme Court limited that holding in Williams v. North Carolina, 325 U.S. 226 (1945). *Williams II* held that, although the full faith and credit obligation assumes that the forum has valid jurisdiction as the domicile of the petitioner, a subsequent showing of *lack of domicile* will allow sister states to refuse to recognize the divorce. The holding thus allowed North Carolina to prosecute for bigamy two North Carolina residents who purported to establish a domicile in Nevada, where each got a divorce, married each other, and then immediately returned home to North Carolina.

What rationale underlies the judicial willingness to recognize ex parte divorces? Is the ex parte divorce fair to the "stay-at-home spouse"? To the state whose laws the migratory petitioning-spouse seeks to evade? On the history of migratory divorce, see Michael J. Higdon, If You Grant It, They Will Come: The History and Enduring Legal Legacy of Migratory Divorce, 2022 Utah L. Rev. 295 (2022).

3. Bilateral divorce. In another line of cases, the Supreme Court indicated that, when the forum has personal jurisdiction over *both* spouses in a migratory divorce, the principles of full faith and credit forbid collateral attack. If the petitioning spouse has not genuinely established a domicile in the divorce forum (a jurisdictional prerequisite for all divorces, ex parte and bilateral alike), why should personal jurisdiction over the respondent spouse prevent collateral attack, say, by way of a bigamy prosecution? What good is a state's restrictive divorce law if a resident spouse can simply cross state lines, purport to establish a new domicile, and—after the personal appearance of the other spouse—obtain a divorce immune from collateral attack?

4. Transitory presence. The Supreme Court elaborated on the standards for *in personam jurisdiction* over a defendant in Burnham v. Superior Court, 495 U.S. 604 (1990), which held that transitory presence can satisfy due process even when the defendant lacks a substantial connection to the forum. The Court upheld California's assertion of jurisdiction over a New Jersey resident who was personally served during a brief business trip and visit to his children in California (his wife's home). The plurality determined that due process was satisfied because (1) the minimum-contacts/fairness approach (initiated by *International Shoe*) addresses only absent (not present) defendants, and (2) the longstanding rule conferring jurisdiction on defendants personally served in the forum accords with "traditional notions of fair play and substantial justice." Note that, as a result of the Court's holding in *Burnham*, the divorce action in *Burnham* becomes a bilateral, rather than an ex parte, proceeding, allowing the forum to resolve the financial incidents of the dissolution.

5. Foreign-country divorces. In the fault era, disputes arose about foreign divorces that were obtained by U.S. residents seeking to evade restrictive laws. American courts do not owe full faith and credit to decrees from foreign countries, although they may recognize such divorces under principles of "comity." However, courts will refuse to apply comity if the foreign divorce procedure fails to comport with procedural due process protections. See DAB v. MAS, 180 N.Y.S.3d 815 (N.Y. Sup. Ct. 2022).

6. Marriage alternatives. Do courts have jurisdiction to dissolve a marriage alternative, such as a civil union or domestic partnership (family forms created before the advent of marriage equality), that was entered into in another state? See Neyman v. Buckley, 153 A.3d 1010 (Pa. Super. Ct. 2016) (holding that the principle of comity required recognizing an out-of-state civil union as the legal equivalent of marriage for purposes of dissolution).

7. Attorney's role. Has an attorney in a restrictive state violated ethical principles by facilitating a client's out-of-state or foreign-country divorce? See, e.g., In re Donnelly, 470 N.W.2d 305 (Wis. 1991) (suspending lawyer's license for two years for his national advertisements of his arrangement of Dominican Republic divorces, without cautioning clients about the questionable validity of such decrees).

Problem

According to Islamic law, a husband can end his marriage by telling his wife, "I divorce you" three times. A Muslim man sends his wife, who is residing in the American state of Greenacre, an e-mail message via the Internet, informing her that he is divorcing her. The husband relies on Internet notice because he is studying in a foreign country. Based on that notice, the wife subsequently remarries. After her first husband completes his studies, he returns to Greenacre. When he sees his ex-wife again, he changes his mind about the divorce. He threatens to sue the wife if she will not leave her new husband and return to him. The wife requests the court to rule on the sufficiency of the husband's e-mail notice. What result? If the court rules that the husband's notice is insufficient, can the wife be convicted of bigamy? Would the husband's notice comply with the requirements of due process?[35]

2. Durational Residency Requirements

SOSNA v. IOWA
419 U.S. 393 (1975)

Justice REHNQUIST delivered the opinion of the Court.

Appellant Carol Sosna married Michael Sosna on September 5, 1964, in Michigan. They lived together in New York between October 1967 and August 1971, after which date they separated but continued to live in New York. In August 1972, appellant moved to Iowa with her three children, and the following month she petitioned the District Court of Jackson County, Iowa, for a dissolution of her marriage. Michael Sosna, who had been personally served with notice of the action when he came to Iowa to visit his children, made a special appearance to contest the jurisdiction of the Iowa court. The Iowa court dismissed the petition for lack of jurisdiction, finding that Michael Sosna was not a resident of Iowa and appellant had not been a resident of the State of Iowa for one year preceding the filing of her petition. In so doing the Iowa court applied the provisions of Iowa Code §598.6 (1973) requiring that the petitioner in such an action be "for the last year a resident of the state." . . .

The durational residency requirement under attack in this case is a part of Iowa's comprehensive statutory regulation of domestic relations, an area that has long been regarded as a virtually exclusive province of the States. Cases decided by this Court over a period of more than a century bear witness to this historical fact. . . . In Pennoyer v. Neff, 95 U.S. 714, 734-735 (1878), the Court said: "The State . . . has absolute right to prescribe the conditions upon which the marriage relation between its own citizens shall be created, and the causes for which it may be dissolved." . . .

The imposition of a durational residency requirement for divorce is scarcely unique to Iowa, since 48 States impose such a requirement as a condition for maintaining an action for divorce. As might be expected, the periods vary among the States and range from six weeks to two years. The one-year period selected by Iowa is the most common length of time prescribed.

Appellant contends that the Iowa requirement of one year's residence is unconstitutional for two separate reasons: *first*, because it establishes two classes of persons and discriminates against those who have recently exercised their right to travel to Iowa, thereby contravening the Court's holdings in Shapiro v. Thompson, 394 U.S. 618 (1969); Dunn v. Blumstein, 405 U.S. 330 (1972); and Memorial Hospital v. Maricopa County, 415 U.S. 250 (1974); and, *second*, because

---

[35]. See Associated Press, Egypt Dismisses Net Divorce Case, June 2000, http://www.belief net.com/Entertainment/2000/06/Egypt-Dismisses-Net-Divorce-Case.aspx. See also Andy Soltis, Islamic Ruling Is Bad News for Divorcée, N.Y. Post, June 2, 2000, 2000 WLNR 8156388.

it denies a litigant the opportunity to make an individualized showing of bona fide residence and therefore denies such residents access to the only method of legally dissolving their marriage.

State statutes imposing durational residency requirements were, of course, invalidated when imposed by States as a qualification for welfare payments, *Shapiro*, supra; for voting, *Dunn*, supra; and for medical care, *Maricopa County*, supra. But none of those cases intimated that the States might never impose durational residency requirements. . . . What those cases had in common was that the durational residency requirements they struck down were justified on the basis of budgetary or recordkeeping considerations which were held insufficient to outweigh the constitutional claims of the individuals. But Iowa's divorce residency requirement is of a different stripe. Appellant was not irretrievably foreclosed from obtaining some part of what she sought, as was the case with the welfare recipients in *Shapiro*, the voters in *Dunn*, or the indigent patient in *Maricopa County*. She would eventually qualify for the same sort of adjudication which she demanded virtually upon her arrival in the State. Iowa's requirement delayed her access to the courts, but, by fulfilling it, she could ultimately have obtained the same opportunity for adjudication which she asserts ought to have been hers at an earlier point in time.

Iowa's residency requirement may reasonably be justified on grounds other than purely budgetary considerations or administrative convenience. A decree of divorce is not a matter in which the only interested parties are the State as a sort of "grantor," and a divorce petitioner such as appellant in the role of "grantee." Both spouses are obviously interested in the proceedings, since it will affect their marital status and very likely their property rights. Where a married couple has minor children, a decree of divorce would usually include provisions for their custody and support. With consequences of such moment riding on a divorce decree issued by its courts, Iowa may insist that one seeking to initiate such a proceeding have the modicum of attachment to the State required here.

Such a requirement additionally furthers the State's parallel interests both in avoiding officious intermeddling in matters in which another State has a paramount interest, and in minimizing the susceptibility of its own divorce decrees to collateral attack. [See Williams v. North Carolina, 325 U.S. 226 (1945).] A State such as Iowa may quite reasonably decide that it does not wish to become a divorce mill for unhappy spouses who have lived there as short a time as appellant had when she commenced her action in the state court after having long resided elsewhere. . . .

Nor are we of the view that the failure to provide an individualized determination of residency violates the Due Process Clause. . . . An individualized determination of physical presence plus the intent to remain, which appellant apparently seeks, would not entitle her to a divorce even if she could have made such a showing. For Iowa requires not merely "domicile" in that sense, but residence in the State for a year in order for its courts to exercise their divorce jurisdiction.

In Boddie v. Connecticut, [401 U.S. 371 (1971),] this Court held that Connecticut might not deny access to divorce courts to those persons who could not afford to pay the required fee. Because of the exclusive role played by the State in the termination of marriages, it was held that indigents could not be denied an opportunity to be heard "absent a countervailing state interest of overriding significance." 401 U.S., at 377. But the gravamen of appellant Sosna's claim is not total deprivation, as in *Boddie*, but only delay. . . . Affirmed.

Justice MARSHALL, with whom Justice BRENNAN joins, dissenting. . . .

The Court omits altogether what should be the first inquiry: whether the right to obtain a divorce is of sufficient importance that its denial to recent immigrants constitutes a penalty on interstate travel. In my view, it clearly meets that standard. The previous decisions of this Court make it plain that the right of marital association is one of the most basic rights conferred on the individual by the State. The interests associated with marriage and divorce have repeatedly been accorded particular deference [citing *Loving* and *Boddie*]. . . .

Having determined that the interest in obtaining a divorce is of substantial social importance, I would scrutinize Iowa's durational residency requirement to determine whether it constitutes a reasonable means of furthering important interests asserted by the State. . . .

Iowa's residency requirement, the Court says, merely forestalls access to the courts; applicants seeking welfare payments, medical aid, and the right to vote, on the other hand, suffer unrecoverable losses throughout the waiting period. This analysis, however, ignores the severity of the deprivation suffered by the divorce petitioner who is forced to wait a year for relief. The injury accompanying that delay is not directly measurable in money terms like the loss of welfare benefits, but it cannot reasonably be argued that when the year has elapsed, the petitioner is made whole. The year's wait prevents remarriage and locks both partners into what may be an intolerable, destructive relationship. . . . The Court cannot mean that Mrs. Sosna has not suffered any injury by being foreclosed from seeking a divorce in Iowa for a year. It must instead mean that it does not regard that deprivation as being very severe.

I find the majority's second argument no more persuasive. The Court forgoes reliance on the usual justifications for durational residency requirements—budgetary considerations and administrative convenience. . . . In their place, the majority invokes a more amorphous justification—the magnitude of the interests affected and resolved by a divorce proceeding. Certainly the stakes in a divorce are weighty both for the individuals directly involved in the adjudication and for others immediately affected by it. The critical importance of the divorce process, however, weakens the argument for a long residency requirement rather than strengthens it. . . .

The Court's third justification seems to me the only one that warrants close consideration. Iowa has a legitimate interest in protecting itself against invasion by those seeking quick divorces in a forum with relatively lax divorce laws, and it may have some interest in avoiding collateral attacks on its decrees in other States. These interests, however, would adequately be protected by a simple requirement of domicile—physical presence plus intent to remain—which would remove the rigid one-year barrier while permitting the State to restrict the availability of its divorce process to citizens who are genuinely its own. . . .

Notes and Questions

1. Residency requirements. As *Sosna* explains, many states require a divorce petitioner to reside in the forum state for a period of time. In some states, residence alone suffices for divorce jurisdiction. Other jurisdictions mandate both durational residence and domicile requirements.[36] Most states' durational residence requirements specify a six-month period.[37] Some states have special provisions for military service personnel to obtain divorce decrees.

2. Rationale. Justice Rehnquist distinguishes a one-year delay for permitting the dissolution of marriage from a delay for the purpose of allowing voting, welfare benefits, and medical aid. Is the distinction persuasive?

3. Significance of delay. In *Sosna*, Justices Rehnquist and Marshall disagree about the significance of delay in petitions for dissolution and the consequences of such delay. Whose argument is more persuasive? Further, Justice Rehnquist distinguishes *Boddie* by claiming the filing fee foreclosed access while the residency requirement in *Sosna* imposes "only delay." Do you agree that indigent plaintiffs have a stronger claim than recent immigrants do? Does the decision in *Sosna* neglect the interests of recent immigrants and present hardships for victims of domestic violence? Does the decision reflect discrimination against women who tend to predominate among custodial parents (i.e., moving for jobs, proximity to parents, or a new relationship)?

4. Divorce mills. Justice Marshall, dissenting, intimates that the state's real goal is to avoid becoming known as a "divorce mill." During the fault era, because residency requirements for divorce varied from state to state, some states with shorter durational requirements and more lenient grounds for divorce (such as Arkansas, Idaho, Florida, Nevada, and South Dakota) developed a reputation of being divorce mills. Why does such a reputation pose problems? How important are problems of migratory divorce and divorce mills in the no-fault era?

5. *Zablocki*'s impact. One commentator points out that *Sosna* was decided a decade before *Zablocki*. "The case is therefore not indicative either of how the Court would decide the right to divorce issue today nor how it should decide it." She elaborates: "[P]etitioners did not raise any challenges on substantive due process grounds or right to privacy grounds."[38] How would *Sosna* be decided today? Note Justice Marshall's view that the right to divorce is equivalent to the right to marry.

---

[36]. However, *Williams*, discussed in *Sosna*, makes clear that domicile is necessary for full faith and credit, regardless of the statutory language. In some instances, durational residency requirements may provide evidence of domicile.

[37]. FindLaw, Divorce Residency FAQs (2019), https://family.findlaw.com/divorce/divorce-residency-faq-s.html.

[38]. Laura Bradford, Note, The Counterrevolution: A Critique of Recent Proposals to Reform No-Fault Divorce Laws, 49 Stan. L. Rev. 607, 636 n.112 (1997).

6. Policy. In our increasingly mobile society, does it make sense to limit divorce jurisdiction to the state of the parties' domicile?[39]

7. States' rights. How much deference do the majority and dissent give to the state's exclusive control over family law matters? The parameters of federal versus state authority are reflected in the case below.

Problem

Jeffrey, who has been living with his wife, Andrea, and their two children in Ohio for ten years, accepts a new job in California with Andrea's acquiescence. Together, they visit California to look for a house, visit churches, and familiarize themselves with the community. Four months later, they sell their Ohio home and move to California. A month later, Jeffrey tells Andrea that he has been having an affair. Andrea returns to Ohio with the children and files for divorce. Jeffrey moves for dismissal of her action for lack of subject matter jurisdiction, alleging that she has not satisfied the statutory six-month residency requirement. Andrea counters that Jeffrey fraudulently induced her to abandon her Ohio residency in order that he might take advantage of California's more liberal divorce laws. Should the court grant Jeffrey's motion to dismiss on jurisdictional grounds? Should there be a fraud exception to the residency requirements for divorce? That is, should a court consider the motives of either spouse with regard to his or her establishment of residency? Barth v. Barth, 862 N.E.2d 496 (Ohio 2007).

3. Domestic Relations Exception to Diversity Jurisdiction

ANKENBRANDT v. RICHARDS
504 U.S. 689 (1992)

Justice WHITE delivered the opinion of the Court. . . .

Petitioner Carol Ankenbrandt, a citizen of Missouri, brought this lawsuit . . . on behalf of her daughters L.R. and S.R. against respondents Jon A. Richards and Debra Kesler, citizens of Louisiana, in the United States District Court for the Eastern District of Louisiana. Alleging federal jurisdiction based on the diversity-of-citizenship provision of §1332, Ankenbrandt's complaint sought monetary damages for alleged sexual and physical abuse of the children committed by Richards and Kesler. Richards is the divorced father of the children and Kesler his

[39]. For commentary advocating the abrogation of the domicile rule for divorce purposes, see Courtney Joslin, Modernizing Divorce Jurisdiction: Same-Sex Couples and Minimum Contacts, 91 B.U. L. Rev. 1669 (2011).

female companion. [T]he District Court granted respondents' motion to dismiss this lawsuit[, concluding] that this case fell within what has become known as the "domestic relations" exception to diversity jurisdiction, and that it lacked jurisdiction over the case. . . .

We granted certiorari limited to the following questions: "(1) Is there a domestic relations exception to federal jurisdiction? (2) If so, does it permit a district court to abstain from exercising diversity jurisdiction over a tort action for damages?" . . . We address each of these issues in turn.

The domestic relations exception upon which the courts below relied to decline jurisdiction has been invoked often by the lower federal courts. The seeming authority for doing so originally stemmed from the announcement in Barber v. Barber, 21 How. 582 (1859), that the federal courts have no jurisdiction over suits for divorce or the allowance of alimony. In that case, the Court heard a suit [by a wife, in federal district court pursuant to diversity jurisdiction, to enforce a New York State decision granting a divorce and awarding her alimony. After the divorce decree, the husband had moved to Wisconsin, whereupon he sued for divorce and, in response to the wife's enforcement action in Wisconsin federal district court, alleged that the New York federal district court lacked jurisdiction. The Wisconsin federal district court ruled for the wife.]

On appeal [in Barber], it was argued that the District Court lacked jurisdiction on two grounds: first, that there was no diversity of citizenship because although divorced, the wife's citizenship necessarily remained that of her former husband; and second, that the whole subject of divorce and alimony, including a suit to enforce an alimony decree, was exclusively ecclesiastical at the time of the adoption of the Constitution and that the Constitution therefore placed the whole subject of divorce and alimony beyond the jurisdiction of the United States courts. [T]he Court rejected both arguments. After an exhaustive survey of the authorities, the Court concluded that a divorced wife could acquire a citizenship separate from that of her former husband and that a suit to enforce an alimony decree rested within the federal courts' equity jurisdiction. The Court reached these conclusions after summarily dismissing the former husband's contention that the case involved a subject matter outside the federal courts' jurisdiction. In so stating, however, the Court also announced the following limitation on federal jurisdiction:

> Our first remark is—and we wish it to be remembered—that this is not a suit asking the court for the allowance of alimony. That has been done by a court of competent jurisdiction. The court in Wisconsin was asked to interfere to prevent that decree from being defeated by fraud.
>
> We disclaim altogether any jurisdiction in the courts of the United States upon the subject of divorce, or for the allowance of alimony, either as an original proceeding in chancery or as an incident to divorce a vinculo, or to one from bed and board.

Barber, supra, at 584. . . .

The statements disclaiming jurisdiction over divorce and alimony decree suits, though technically dicta, formed the basis for excluding "domestic relations" cases from the jurisdiction of the lower federal courts. . . . Because we are unwilling to cast aside an understood rule that has been recognized for nearly a century and a half, we feel compelled to explain why we will continue to recognize this limitation on federal jurisdiction.

Counsel argued in *Barber* that the Constitution prohibited federal courts from exercising jurisdiction over domestic relations cases. An examination of Article III, *Barber* itself, and our cases since *Barber* makes clear that [Article III, §2 of the Constitution] contains no limitation on subjects of a domestic relations nature. Nor did *Barber* purport to ground the domestic relations exception in these constitutional limits on federal jurisdiction. The Court's discussion of federal judicial power to hear suits of a domestic relations nature contains no mention of the Constitution, and it is logical to presume that the Court based its statement limiting such power on narrower statutory, rather than broader constitutional, grounds. Subsequent decisions confirm that *Barber* was not relying on constitutional limits in justifying the exception. . . .

The dissenters in *Barber* [suggested] that the federal courts had no power over certain domestic relations actions because the court of chancery lacked authority to issue divorce and alimony decrees. . . . We have no occasion here to join the historical debate. [We] are content to rest our conclusion that a domestic relations exception exists as a matter of statutory construction not on the accuracy of the historical justifications on which it was seemingly based, but rather on Congress' apparent acceptance of this construction of the diversity jurisdiction provisions in the years prior to 1948, when [Congress last amended the rules applicable to federal diversity jurisdiction]. . . .

The *Barber* Court thus did not intend to strip the federal courts of authority to hear cases arising from the domestic relations of persons unless they seek the granting or modification of a divorce or alimony decree. The holding of the case itself sanctioned the exercise of federal jurisdiction over the enforcement of an alimony decree that had been properly obtained in a state court of competent jurisdiction. . . .

Subsequently, this Court expanded the domestic relations exception to include decrees in child custody cases. In a child custody case brought pursuant to a writ of habeas corpus, for instance, the Court held void a writ issued by a Federal District Court to restore a child to the custody of the father. "As to the right to the control and possession of this child, as it is contested by its father and its grandfather, it is one in regard to which neither the Congress of the United States nor any authority of the United States has any special jurisdiction." In re Burrus, [136 U.S. 586, 594 (1890)].

. . . This application is consistent with *Barber*'s directive to limit federal courts' exercise of diversity jurisdiction over suits for divorce and alimony decrees. We conclude, therefore, that the domestic relations exception, as articulated by this Court since *Barber*, divests the federal courts of power to issue divorce, alimony, and child custody decrees. Given the long passage of time without any expression of congressional dissatisfaction, we have no trouble today reaffirming the validity of the exception as it pertains to divorce and alimony decrees and child custody orders.

Not only is our conclusion rooted in respect for this long-held understanding, it is also supported by sound policy considerations. Issuance of decrees of this type not infrequently involves retention of jurisdiction by the court and deployment of social workers to monitor compliance. As a matter of judicial economy, state courts are more eminently suited to work of this type than are federal courts, which lack the close association with state and local government organizations dedicated to handling issues that arise out of conflicts over divorce, alimony, and child custody decrees. Moreover, as a matter of judicial expertise, it makes far more sense to retain the rule that federal courts lack power to issue these types of decrees because of the special proficiency developed by state tribunals over the past century and a half in handling issues that arise in the granting of such decrees.

By concluding, as we do, that the domestic relations exception encompasses only cases involving the issuance of a divorce, alimony, or child custody decree, we necessarily find that the Court of Appeals erred by affirming the District Court's invocation of this exception. This lawsuit in no way seeks such a decree; rather, it alleges that respondents Richards and Kesler committed torts against L.R. and S.R., Ankenbrandt's children by Richards. Federal subject-matter jurisdiction pursuant to §1332 thus is proper in this case. . . .

Notes and Questions

1. Rule and rationale. Under the "domestic relations exception to federal jurisdiction," federal courts traditionally declined to exercise jurisdiction over matters of domestic relations, even in cases in which plaintiffs could establish the requisite diversity of citizenship and amount in controversy. The rationale was that domestic relations cases involve matters peculiarly of state, rather than federal, law. *Ankenbrandt* narrowed this exception, limiting the types of cases that federal courts could refuse to adjudicate. After *Ankenbrandt*, federal courts could decline jurisdiction only over those cases involving the issuance of divorce decrees and the issuance or modification of property division awards, child custody, or alimony, including any enforcement of court orders.

2. Abstention doctrine. *Ankenbrandt* left open an alternative means by which federal courts can still "slam shut" the federal courthouse door to some domestic relations matters that do not involve divorce, alimony, or custody. In an omitted portion of the opinion, the Court holds that neither the domestic relations exception nor the "abstention doctrine" bars *Ankenbrandt*'s tort claim. The abstention doctrine, delineated in Younger v. Harris, 401 U.S. 37 (1971), is founded on principles of federalism. It provides that federal courts may refuse to adjudicate civil proceedings that involve important state interests or substantial policy concerns. *Ankenbrandt* concluded, by way of dicta, that abstention might be proper

> when a case presents "difficult questions of state law bearing on policy problems of substantial public importance whose importance transcends the result in the case then at bar" (citation omitted). Such might well be the case if a federal suit were filed prior to effectuation of a divorce, alimony, or child custody decree, and the suit depended on a determination of the status of the parties. 504 U.S. 689, 705 (1992).

3. Advantages? Why did Carol Ankenbrandt prefer to litigate her tort claim alleging sexual abuse in a federal, rather than state, court? What are the benefits as well as detriments that will ensue from *Ankenbrandt* for litigants? For families? For society?

4. Federalism. Various considerations have led federal courts to decline jurisdiction over domestic relations issues, including recognition of special state expertise, federal docket congestion, and the ability of state courts to provide local support assuring compliance with decrees. However, critics point out that federal courts are less susceptible to influence and have better evidentiary and discovery processes; state courts have often been criticized for their handling of family law cases (state judges rotate out of family law courts after only one year); the confining authority of local control over family law often restricts the rights of traditionally subordinated groups; distinctions between marital property and marital status are blurry; and federal courts have been willing to intervene in family law cases when constitutional rights were at issue. For example, Professor Anne Dailey, writing in defense of state sovereignty, notes:

> [N]ational authority over family law raises a serious threat of governmental tyranny over the moral identities of developing citizens. To begin with, a politics of the good family life entails a degree of civic engagement and a sense of shared community identity unattainable at the national level. Although family law does not require the moral homogeneity characteristic of strong communitarian cultures, it does demand a political discourse built upon the normative commitments of a specific historical community. States . . . are far better situated than the national government to develop and sustain a normative political discourse on family. Moreover, regulatory diversity among the fifty states preserves some measure of individual and family choice in matters touching upon the formative conditions of human identity.[40]

Professor Naomi Cahn counters:

> Throughout the country, family law has traditionally reflected community norms, [and] the federal courts have attempted to protect the local character of domestic relations law. . . . The belief in local control over family law, however, beyond suggesting an inevitability to this means of family regulation, also overlooks the negative aspects of the community. While community can be a powerfully positive force, it can also be an extremely confining form of authority. The courts' examination of whether certain customs are based in community traditions, for instance, may enshrine majoritarian conventions. . . . The many and various state regulations held unconstitutional by the Supreme Court provide yet further examples of the danger of trusting family law to community mores.[41]

Which view do you find more persuasive?

---

[40]. Anne C. Dailey, Federalism and Families, 143 U. Pa. L. Rev. 1787, 1791-1792 (1995). See also Brian H. Bix, State of the Union: The States' Interest in the Marital Status of Their Citizens, 55 U. Miami L. Rev. 1, 18-19 (2000) (suggesting that local control of family law matters may also be favored because it allows states to be treated as laboratories, developing a variety of responses to questions of law instead of having a uniform federal response).

[41]. Naomi Cahn, Family Law, Federalism, and the Federal Courts, 79 Iowa L. Rev. 1073, 1123 (1994). See also Joseph A. Carroll, Family Law Is Not "Civil": The Faulty Foundation of the Domestic Relations Exception to Federal Jurisdiction, 52 Fam. L.Q. 125, 144 (2019) (warning that the domestic relations exception risks "foreclosing the invaluable federal forum to family law issues"); Meredith Johnson Harbach, Is the Family a Federal Question?, 66 Wash. & Lee L. Rev. 131 (2009) (emphasizing the important role of federal courts in supporting and protecting the family); Courtney G. Joslin, Federalism and Family Status, 90 Ind. L.J. 787, 828 (2015) (offering a framework "to maximize the benefits garnered from local control, [while] guard[ing] against the dangers of dogmatic family status localism").

Problems

1. Jeanne sues in state court, charging that Joseph (the man with whom she has been cohabiting) breached his agreement to provide financial support for the rest of her life. Joseph removes the case to federal court on the basis of diversity. The court raises, on its own motion, the issue whether this "palimony" case falls within the domestic relations exception to federal jurisdiction, requiring remand to state court. See Anastasi v. Anastasi, 544 F. Supp. 866 (D.N.J. 1982). How would this case be decided after *Ankenbrandt*? See also Carino v. O'Malley, 2007 WL 951953 (D.N.J. 2007).

2. Ariane Cometa and Gerard Dunn are a married couple living in Maine. While Ariane is pursuing a medical residency, Gerard suffers a catastrophic brain injury that leaves him severely disabled. Ariane puts him in a care facility. Three years later, Gerard's father is appointed his conservator and takes him to Georgia to live. Ariane subsequently enters a liaison with another man. One year later, her petition for divorce is granted. She is ordered to pay Gerard alimony for five years based on her ability to pay, employment potential, and Gerard's disability. One year later, Gerard's father, acting on behalf of himself and Gerard, brings an action against Ariane in federal district court in Maine, alleging her mismanagement of Gerard's care, private health insurance, and property; IIED and negligent infliction of emotional distress (NIED) by keeping him in care facilities rather than at home (allegedly so that she could conduct an affair); breaching a contract with Gerard's father as to payment for construction work on a Georgia house for Gerard; and unjust enrichment for the care provided to Gerard by his father. Ariane moves to dismiss the claims as within the domestic relations exception to federal court jurisdiction. What result? See Dunn v. Cometa, 238 F.3d 38 (1st Cir. 2001).

Financial Consequences of Dissolution

Approximately one in three adults in the United States has divorced.[1] Divorce often involves a division of property and an award of spousal support. In marriages with children, a divorce decree also provides for their support. This financial framework raises foundational questions, such as the place of fault, the value of domestic labor, and policies about remarriage and new relationships. Additional complications arise from spousal investments in pensions and careers, students' postmajority dependency, and rising bankruptcy and poverty rates.

This chapter emphasizes theory and practice, guided by the following inquiries: What are the distinct theoretical bases traditionally undergirding property division, spousal support, and child support? How has our understanding of each evolved in the era of no-fault divorce? What happens to these theoretical distinctions when, in practice, different financial issues typically get resolved together? Finally, what roles do the state and the parties themselves play in making and enforcing these financial decisions? Note that while the property division and spousal support rules discussed in this chapter apply only to marital spouses, the child support rules apply equally to marital and nonmarital parents.

A. Introduction: The Demise of Fault?

Although every state now has some form of no-fault divorce, differences persist in the role of fault in dividing property and determining spousal support (once called "alimony" and now often referred to as "maintenance").[2] California's

---

[1]. According to the most recent census data, 34 percent of women and 33 percent of men have divorced. U.S. Census Bureau, Number, Timing, and Duration of Marriages and Divorces: 2016 (Apr. 2021), https://www.census.gov/content/dam/Census/library/publications/2021/demo/p70-167.pdf.

[2]. Charts (A Review of the Year in Family Law), 54 Fam. L.Q. 345-355 (2020) (listing 26 jurisdictions that consider marital fault as an alimony factor). An earlier compendium lists 35 jurisdictions that consider *economic* misconduct in dividing property. Charts (A Review of the Year in Family Law), 48 Fam. L. Q. 654-655 (2015).

early adoption of no-fault divorce (disregarding marital misconduct in property division and spousal support) prompted a famous study by sociologist Lenore J. Weitzman.[3]

According to Weitzman, fault previously played a dual role in determining the economic consequences of divorce. First, marital misconduct provided a rationale for judicial awards and settlements, requiring a "guilty" husband to "pay for his transgressions with alimony" or with an additional portion of marital property. Second, fault offered valuable leverage to an "innocent" spouse, who could obtain financial concessions in exchange for cooperation from the other party in settling the case.

Weitzman found that California's transition to a no-fault regime unexpectedly impoverished women and children: Family homes, formerly awarded to "innocent wives," were now being sold (and children displaced) so that the proceeds could be divided equally between the spouses. Likewise, support awards were shrinking for women, primarily mothers and homemakers, who were now expected to be self-sufficient. And even a "guilty" spouse could now divorce unilaterally, eliminating the bargaining power of the resisting spouse, often the wife.

Weitzman's empirical study concluded that, just one year after divorce, men were experiencing a 42 percent improvement in their standard of living, and women a 73 percent decline.[4] These dramatic figures proved enormously influential, prompting not only a feminist critique of no-fault divorce, but also the passage of new divorce laws. Subsequent research substantiates Weitzman's general finding that men's standard of living continues to rise after divorce, while that of women and children declines.[5]

Since California initiated no-fault divorce, three questions about the economic consequences have emerged: First, what role should fault play? Second, what theories for dividing property and awarding spousal support might take the place of fault? Third, how should law ensure that one group (men, women, or children) does not bear an unfair economic burden? The next two sections of this chapter explore these questions, examining several modern rationales for property division and spousal support awards, respectively, while subsequent sections on child support and enforcement consider the economic impact of divorce on children.

---

[3]. Lenore J. Weitzman, The Divorce Revolution: The Unexpected Social and Economic Consequences for Women and Children in America (1985) (empirical study based on 2,500 court dockets over a ten-year period and interviews with 169 family law attorneys, 44 family law judges, and 228 divorced men and women approximately one year after divorce).

[4]. Id. at 339.

[5]. See Angela Guarin, Is the Gender Gap Universal? Economic Consequences of Divorce and Separation for Women in Colombia Compared to 6 OECD Countries, Paper Presented at the Annual Meeting of the Society for Social Work & Research (Jan. 18, 2019), https://sswr.con fex.com/sswr/2019/webprogram/Paper34572.html; Thomas Leopold, Gender Differences in the Consequences of Divorce: A Study of Multiple Outcomes, 55 Demography 769 (June 2018), https://link.springer.com/article/10.1007/s13524-018-0667-6. Studies reveal that divorce harms Black women economically even more than white women. Liana C. Sayer, Economic Aspects of Divorce and Relationship Dissolution, in Handbook of Divorce and Relationship Dissolution 394 (Mark A. Fine & John H. Harvey eds., 2006).

B. Property Distribution: From Title Theory to Contribution

What property can a court allocate between the spouses at dissolution? What theory determines how much to award to each?

FERGUSON v. FERGUSON
639 So. 2d 921 (Miss. 1994) (en banc)

PRATHER, Presiding Justice. . . .

[Linda Ferguson, age 44, and Billy Cleveland Ferguson, Sr., age 48, were married in 1967 and separated in 1991. They had two children. During their 24 years of marriage, Linda worked both as a homemaker and as a cosmetologist/beautician. Billy, employed by South Central Bell as a cable repair technician, installed and maintained local telephone service. Linda filed for divorce, which the chancellor awarded to her on the ground of Billy's adultery. The chancellor also awarded her custody of the 14-year-old son and $300 a month child support, as well as the marital home and its contents, four acres of land comprising the homestead, with title to the marital home to be divested from Billy and vested in Linda, debt free; one-half interest in Billy's pension plan, stock ownership plan, and savings and security plan; and periodic alimony in the amount of $400 per month and lump sum alimony in the sum of $30,000 to be paid at the rate of $10,000 annually beginning on January 1, 1992. Billy appeals.]

States have devised various methods to divide marital assets at divorce, and approaches have usually followed one of three systems [separate property, equitable distribution, and community property]. Mississippi [and some other states] previously followed the separate property system, which was a system that merely determined title to the assets and returned that property to the title-holding spouse.

Our separate property system at times resulted in unjust distributions, especially involving cases of a traditional family where most property was titled in the husband, leaving a traditional housewife and mother with nothing but a claim for alimony, which often proved unenforceable. In a family where both spouses worked, but the husband's resources were devoted to investments while the wife's earnings were devoted to paying the family expenses or vice versa, the same unfair results ensued. The flaw of the separate property system, however, is not merely that it will occasionally ignore the financial contributions of the non-titleholding spouse. The system . . . is also unable to take account of a spouse's non-financial contribution. In the case of many traditional housewives such non-financial contributions are often considerable. Thus, to allow a system of property division to ignore non-financial contributions is to create a likelihood of unjust division of property.

The non-monetary contributions of a traditional housewife have been acknowledged by this Court, and to some extent, case law has helped lessen the unfairness to a traditional housewife in the division of marital property. [T]his

Court has allowed lump sum alimony as an adjustment to property division to prevent unfair division. The lump sum award has been described as a method of dividing property under the guise of alimony. . . .

Courts have acknowledged that the power and authority of the chancery court to award alimony and child support have been historically derived from the legal duty of the husband to support the family. As to division of marital assets, it is the broad inherent equity powers of the chancery court that give it the authority to act. General equity principles of fairness undergird this authority. That duty was codified in Miss. Code. Ann. §93-5-23 (Supp. 1993). . . . This Court, therefore, holds that the chancery court is within its authority and power to equitably divide marital assets at divorce. . . .

[T]his Court recognizes the need for guidelines to aid chancellors in their adjudication of marital property division. Therefore, this Court directs the chancery courts to evaluate the division of marital assets by the following guidelines [including, inter alia, substantial contribution to the accumulation of the property, the market and emotional value of the assets, tax and other economic consequences of the distribution, the parties' needs, and any other factor relevant to an equitable outcome.]

[F]airness is the prevailing guideline in marital division. . . . All property division, lump sum or periodic alimony payment, and mutual obligations for child support should be considered together. "Alimony and equitable distribution are distinct concepts, but together they command the entire field of financial settlement of divorce. Therefore, where one expands, the other must recede." [LaRue v. LaRue, 304 S.E.2d 312, 334 (W. Va. 1983) (Neely, J., concurring).] Thus, the chancellor may divide marital assets, real and personal, as well as award periodic and/or lump sum alimony, as equity demands. [F]indings of fact by the chancellor, together with the legal conclusions drawn from those findings, are required. . . .

Billy contends that he owned all the interest in the pension plan, stock, and savings [obtained through his employer, Bell South], and that it was his separate property. On appeal [of the chancellor's allocation of one-half these assets to Linda], Billy claims Linda in no way contributed to the acquisition of this property, and nothing was ever issued in her name. . . .

When a couple has been married for twenty-four years, yet the only retirement benefits accumulated throughout the marriage are titled in the name of only one spouse, is it equitable to find only one spouse entitled to financial security upon retirement when both have benefitted from the employer funded plan along the way? When one spouse has contributed directly to the fund, by virtue of his/her labor, while the other has contributed indirectly, by virtue of domestic services and/or earned income which both parties have enjoyed rather than invested, the spouse without retirement funds in his/her own name could instead have been working outside the home and/or investing his/her wages in preparation for his/her own retirement. . . .

[In addition,] Billy contends the chancellor lacked the authority to order him to convey, free of all encumbrances, his one-half interest in the jointly owned four acres on which the marital home was situated. . . . "A spouse who has made a material contribution toward the acquisition of property which is titled in the name of the other may claim an equitable interest in such jointly accumulated property incident to a divorce proceeding." Jones v. Jones, 532 So. 2d 574, 580 (Miss. 1988). [W]e said that "[i]f 'contribution' toward the acquisition of assets is proven by a divorcing party, then the court has the authority to divide these 'jointly' accumulated assets." *Jones*, 532 So. 2d at 580. . . .

[There were two mortgages on the marital home.] This Court holds that under existing case law the chancellor was within his authority to order Billy to effect a transfer of title to Linda to the marital home and the surrounding four acres [free and clear of any liens] to accomplish an equitable division. . . . Nonetheless, this issue is remanded for consideration together with the other assets [for equitable] division to be guided by the factors promulgated today. . . .

The chancellor stated on the record that he tended to believe the testimony of [Billy's paramour that he] had withdrawn $30,000.00 from his Bell South Savings and Security Plan and put it where nobody could get to it or find it. He awarded this amount to Linda as lump sum alimony to be paid in three installments. . . . Linda worked and contributed to Billy's financial status, but had no assets of her own; her separate estate pales in comparison to Billy's. This award of lump sum alimony may have been made by the chancellor to give Linda financial security. An explanation of the basis of this award will help this Court determine whether the distribution represents an abuse of discretion or a division supported by the record. Therefore, a remand is warranted on this issue. . . .

UNIFORM MARRIAGE AND DIVORCE ACT

§307. [DISPOSITION OF PROPERTY][6]

(a) [The court in a dissolution or legal separation proceeding] shall assign each spouse's property to him. It also shall divide the marital property without regard to marital misconduct in just proportions considering all relevant factors including:

(1) contribution of each spouse to acquisition of the marital property, including contribution of a spouse as homemaker;

(2) value of the property set apart to each spouse;

(3) duration of the marriage; and

(4) economic circumstances of each spouse when the division of property is to become effective, including the desirability of awarding the family home or the right to live therein for reasonable periods to the spouse having custody of any children.

(b) For purposes of this Act, "marital property" means all property acquired by either spouse subsequent to the marriage except:

(1) property acquired by gift, bequest, devise, or descent;

(2) property acquired in exchange for property acquired before the marriage or in exchange for property acquired by gift, bequest, devise, or descent;

(3) property acquired by a spouse after a decree of legal separation;

(4) property excluded by valid agreement of the parties; and

[6]. This provision appears in the original 1970 version of the Uniform Marriage and Divorce Act (UMDA). The drafters later replaced it with two alternatives: Alternative A for states following the common law approach and Alternative B for community property states.

(5) the increase in value of property acquired before the marriage.

(c) All property acquired by either spouse after the marriage and before a decree of legal separation is presumed to be marital property, regardless of whether title is held individually or by the spouses in some form of co-ownership such as joint tenancy, tenancy in common, tenancy by the entirety, and community property. The presumption of marital property is overcome by a showing that the property was acquired by a method listed in subsection (b).

Stephen D. Sugarman, Dividing Financial Interests on Divorce

in Divorce Reform at the Crossroads 130, 136-141 (Stephen D. Sugarman & Herma Hill Kay eds., 1990)

[The author attempts to identify a theoretical framework or legal analogy for understanding the financial incidents of divorce. He rejects fault as a suitable principle, given the high social cost imposed. He also rejects the notion of "marriage as contract," in part because modern no-fault, unilateral divorce leaves no room for "the concept of breach and resultant damages." He then considers partnership law.]

Perhaps a better legal analogy to no-fault divorce can be found in partnership law. The idea is that through marriage the man and woman have joined together (50-50?) in an economic partnership, which, like partnerships generally, can be dissolved by either party. On the ending of the marriage partnership, like other partnerships, there is to be a winding up of the partnership's activities and a distribution of the partnership assets. . . .

Under the partnership analogy all earnings generated by the couple during the marriage would seem to belong to the partnership, as would any things bought with those earnings and any earnings left unspent and saved or invested. . . . In the marriage setting [unlike in traditional financial partnerships], it is as though, as a general rule, all the extra income and asset appreciation of the partnership is simply retained and reinvested in the partnership. . . .

[J]ust as financial partners contribute only some of their property to the typical partnership, certain items of property belonging to the husband and wife could be seen as outside the marital partnership and not subject to division on the marriage's termination. They might include assets the parties bring to the marriage and do not commingle with other marital property, and those gifts and inheritances separately received by either party during the marriage and maintained separately.

If marriage under no-fault is to be seen as a conventional partnership, no formal distinctions would be made between long- and short-duration marriages; to be sure, in long-duration marriages, there might be more assets to distribute. So, too, the family home would not be treated differently from any other asset. The implication of minor children would be ambiguous since there is no obvious counterpart in ordinary partnerships. Does gaining custody mean that you have obtained a partnership asset, or merely that you have assumed a partnership liability for which you should be compensated?

Most important, under the partnership analogy, there would be no spousal support. That is, in the traditional partnership, even though the partners agree to make their earning capacity available to the partnership during its lifetime, they ordinarily just walk away from the dissolved partnership with all their own human capital. This applies both to the human capital they brought to the partnership and to any enhanced human capital they gained during the operation of the partnership. . . .

Traditional financial partners, of course, may anticipate certain problems of partnership breakup and, if they wish, enter into alternative arrangements at the outset. . . . They [even] might agree to be other than 50-50 partners originally. Perhaps married couples could also be encouraged to make specific agreements in advance. . . .

Notes and Questions on the Theory of Property Division

1. Development of equitable distribution. Most states follow the common law approach to spousal ownership of property during marriage. Eight states use a community property approach derived from their French or Spanish heritage; Wisconsin's system is modeled on the Uniform Marital Property Act (UMPA).

The common law scheme reflects "title theory." Title to property (as evidenced in a deed, for example) determines ownership between the spouses. Property acquired or earned during marriage belongs to the acquiring or earning spouse unless that spouse acts affirmatively to create joint ownership (for example, buying a house titled jointly in the names of both spouses). Upon divorce, the court assigns property to the owner. After the advent of no-fault divorce, many states abandoned the title theory in favor of "equitable distribution." In *Ferguson*, Mississippi became the last state to abandon the title system in divorce cases.

One influential model was the original 1970 version of the Uniform Marriage and Divorce Act (UMDA) (as discussed above). Using definitions typical of community property systems, UMDA distinguished separate property from marital property and listed factors that courts should consider in making a just division of the latter. Laws following this model bring common law states much closer to community property states in the treatment of property at divorce. That is, equitable distribution laws in common law states create a *deferred* community property system, with the concept of marital property becoming effective upon divorce.

Although most states adopted equitable distribution by statute (often modeled on UMDA), Mississippi did so by judicial decision in *Ferguson*. What is the source of *Ferguson*'s authority to adopt a new property distribution system? Does the ruling deprive Billy Ferguson of his property without due process?

2. Homemaker services. Title theory, as *Ferguson* reveals, evokes criticism because of its treatment of the traditional homemaker upon divorce. The long-standing devaluation of homemakers' activities followed from the husband's rights, at common law, to the wife's property and earnings. During the era of divorce reform, feminist activists helped secure equitable distribution laws, designed to take into account homemaking contributions upon divorce. UMDA served as an influential catalyst for such reform. How do *Ferguson* and UMDA treat homemaker services?

3. Partnership. Does *Ferguson*'s contribution theory treat marriage as a partnership, the approach examined by Professor Sugarman? What is the difference? Does the partnership analogy, first developed in community property states, provide fair outcomes for homemakers?

4. What to divide and distribute?

a. Marital property versus "hotchpot." Note how UMDA identifies the property that is subject to division. Statutes in states following this model define "marital property" as that acquired by either spouse during the marriage, except when acquired by gift, inheritance, or in exchange for nonmarital or "separate" property. Such statutes often presume that all property acquired during the marriage is marital. What theory explains the distinct treatment of marital and separate property?

A later version of UMDA §307 proposed an alternative model for common law states (Alternative A) that gives the court authority to divide equitably the great "hotchpot" of assets owned by either spouse, whenever and however acquired. (Alternative B addressed property distribution for community property states.) Can theories of partnership or contribution explain judicial authority to divide

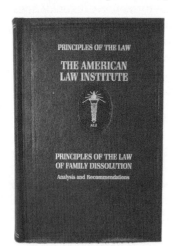

ALI Principles of the Law of Family Dissolution

property acquired before marriage or received by one spouse as a gift?

Under yet another approach, a "hybrid system," the court distributes nonmarital property only after the distribution of marital property, if equity requires. Which approach is more fair—marital property, hotchpot, or hybrid? Which approach does *Ferguson* follow?

b. The ALI's model: Recharacterizing separate property. The American Law Institute (ALI)'s Principles of the Law of Family Dissolution ("ALI Principles") addresses divorce-related property division by "recharacterizing" some of each spouse's separate property as marital property based on the length of the marriage. This approach claims to reflect the reasonable expectations of spouses, as the comment below explains:

> After many years of marriage, spouses typically do not think of their separate-property assets as separate, even if they would be so classified under the technical property rules. Both spouses are likely to believe, for example, that such assets will be available to provide for their joint retirement, for a medical crisis of either spouse, or for other personal emergencies. The longer the marriage the more likely it is that the spouses will have made decisions about their employment or the use of their marital assets that are premised in part on such expectations about the separate property of both spouses. ALI Principles §4.12 cmt. a.

c. Debts. Property division at divorce includes debts as well as assets. For example, *Ferguson* addresses responsibility for mortgages. Typically, the same considerations that apply to assets govern debts, including the distinction between separate and marital debts.

d. Dissipated assets. *Ferguson* acknowledges evidence that Billy withdrew and hid $30,000. Although the trial court awarded this sum to Linda as lump sum alimony, courts typically will include the value of such dissipated marital assets in determining the marital property available for division and then count that amount as part of the share of the dissipating spouse. What expenditures constitute dissipation? Frivolous household expenditures? Gifts to a paramour? What factors should a court consider in determining dissipation? Squandering any marital asset in a way in which the other spouse disapproves? Can a court following a strict no-fault approach take into account dissipated assets?

5. "Equitable" distribution. Once a court determines the property subject to division and its value, how does the court determine the amount each party should get? UMDA §307 directs an "equitable" apportionment according to a wide-ranging list of factors of unidentified weight. Other statutes direct the court to divide such property "in just proportions." Are these standards helpful?

6. Fault. Should marital misconduct play a role in the equitable or just division of property? Does Billy's adultery in *Ferguson* explain the court's departure from title theory? Was the court punishing him for his "fault"? Does consideration of fault in dividing property mitigate harsh effects of no-fault divorce? Even if dissolution should be available without regard to fault, does it follow that the law should impose economic punishment for behavior during marriage? What position does UMDA take on the role of fault in property division? Although fault considerations (other than financial misconduct) have receded in property division (as in spousal support awards), an increasing number of states have enacted statutes allowing consideration of the role of domestic violence in property division and spousal support (discussed later in the chapter).

Note that although the ALI Principles disregard fault in the distribution of property, they include an exception for financial misconduct with marital assets (§4.10). Why? (UMDA has a similar exception.)

7. Equal division. Community property principles, explicitly recognizing marriage as a partnership, give each spouse an undivided one-half interest in property acquired by spousal labor during the marriage. Most community property states apply a *presumption* of equal division for community property at dissolution. (Note that an equal division contemplates equality in value, not dividing each asset in half.) The ALI Principles also dictate a presumption of equal division of marital property (§4.09).

8. Need. Can need provide a theory for property division at dissolution? In *Ferguson*, on what basis did Linda "need" the marital home and the other property that was titled to her husband but awarded to her? How would a need-based approach affect the share awarded to the homemaker spouse? How would you reconcile need as a factor in property distribution with the egalitarian assumptions of the contribution and partnership rationales? Does consideration of need in property distribution help expose family law's persistent gender inequalities? Alternatively, does need make more sense as a basis for alimony than for property division? Consider the materials in the next section.

9. Role of premarital agreements. Prospective spouses sometimes execute premarital agreements that limit spouses' interest in each other's property at death or divorce. These agreements, which generally prevail over marital settlement agreements, are strictly construed. See Thompson v. Wolfram, 162 N.E.3d 498 (Ind. Ct. App. 2020) (holding that an increase in husband's retirement accounts was divisible because premarital agreement was silent about treatment of such increases).

Problem

Rolando and Julieta separated two years after marrying. During the separation, Rolando sent money to their children (all born before the marriage) and paid for Julieta's surgery. Eight years after separating, they reconciled for four years. In subsequent divorce proceedings, Rolando challenges the court's classification of assets that he acquired during the separation as marital, rather than separate, property. Assuming that the UMDA governs (the original version), what result, and why? See Rodriguez v. Rodriguez, 908 P.2d 1007 (Alaska 1995); In re Marriage of Perez, 7 N.E.3d 1009 (Ind. Ct. App. 2014); In re Marriage of English, 194 P.3d 887 (Or. Ct. App. 2009). If the court considers property acquired while spouses are "living separate and apart" as separate property (not marital or community), does this criterion require that they occupy separate residences? See In re Marriage of Davis, 352 P.3d 401 (Cal. 2015) (abrogated by Cal. Fam. Code §70).

C. Spousal Support: Theories of Need, Self-Sufficiency, and Beyond

The concept of divorce as the dissolution of a partnership leaves unexplained the duty to provide future support for a former spouse. The next cases and statutes explore the following questions: What is the rationale for spousal support? How should the amount be determined? How long should the duty continue?

ALIZZI v. ALIZZI

350 So. 3d 758 (Fla. Dist. Ct. App. 2022)

GERBER, J.

. . . The parties had a 23-year marriage. The parties separated when they were in their late sixties. Before the parties' separation, they had owned a successful restaurant and had lived in an expensive home. Upon the parties' separation, the wife moved into the three-bedroom home of her daughter from a previous marriage.

The parties had been separated for 16 months by the time the circuit court heard the wife's amended motion for temporary [alimony]. During that hearing, the wife testified as follows. When the parties separated, she retained an attorney and a forensic accountant for the ensuing dissolution action. At that time, her liquid assets consisted of $82,000 in two checking accounts and $215,000 in her IRA. [B]y the time of the temporary relief hearing, the wife had paid a total of $128,000 in attorney's fees and forensic accounting fees. The wife also had withdrawn $75,000 from her IRA to use towards her daughter's down payment on a larger four-bedroom house in which she, her daughter, and her daughter's two sons would live. Those and other expenses had reduced the wife's liquid assets to approximately $10,000 in her checking accounts and $72,000 in her IRA.

The wife also had incurred a $40,911 tax penalty for withdrawing funds from her IRA. The wife further owed another $17,000 in attorney's fees and $6,300 in forensic accounting fees. The wife's health insurance also cost $781 per month, and she paid $1,800 in monthly rent and utilities to her daughter. The wife's only income was from Social Security and a pension which combined to provide $3,424 per month. The wife testified she required the husband's support to enable her to live in the manner which she had enjoyed before the separation.

The wife's forensic accountant testified the wife's net worth was approximately $36,000. The accountant further determined the wife's financial needs, after offsetting income, was $10,174 per month, including $7,000 for monthly rent for her own furnished apartment. However, the accountant conceded those amounts were not the wife's actual expenses but were anticipated expenses based on her historical lifestyle and expenses before the parties' separation. The husband's forensic accountant testified that, pursuant to the wife's second amended financial affidavit, her actual expenses totaled $6,858 per month. The husband's accountant agreed with the wife's income calculation.

After the hearing, the circuit court entered a written order granting in part and denying in part the wife's amended motion for temporary relief. The circuit court began by finding "[t]here is no question that the Husband has the ability to pay temporary support." The circuit court then made findings regarding the wife's income which mirrored the amounts to which the wife and the accountants had testified. However, regarding the wife's needs, the circuit court concluded, in pertinent part:

> In determining whether and to what extent an award of temporary alimony is proper, the Court is to look at the Wife's actual need and the Husband's ability to pay, taking into account the parties' standard of living, the parties['] ages, the employment history and ability of the parties, as well as the other factors under Florida Statute Section 61.08.
>
> The Wife has included in her "needs" extras, gifts, expenses she is not actually incurring and other items not appropriate for purposes of Temporary Relief. . . .
>
> Although temporary awards of alimony are within the trial court's broad discretion, they must be supported by competent, substantial evidence that demonstrates the actual need for support and the paying spouse's ability to pay. The temporary alimony request in this case is not accompanied by any evidence concerning the Wife's actual need for this award of temporary support. . . . Applying the Wife's net income . . . pursuant to the Wife's Second Amended [] Financial

Affidavit . . . the Court finds the Wife actual needs to be $1,494.00 per month for purposes of temporary alimony.

[On appeal, the wife argues that the circuit court erred in: directing the husband to pay the wife only $1,494 in temporary monthly support.] On the temporary monthly support issue, we agree with the circuit court's finding that the wife's requested financial need of $10,174 per month, including $7,000 for monthly rent, was not supported by competent substantial evidence. As the wife's forensic account candidly acknowledged, those amounts were not based on the wife's actual expenses, but the wife's anticipated expenses. The wife has not resided in, nor did the evidence indicate she will reside in, a furnished rental apartment which would cost $7,000 per month. Instead, the wife chose to give her daughter $75,000 towards a down payment on a larger four-bedroom house in which both of them now reside, and the wife is paying her daughter $1,800 monthly for rent and utilities.

The wife's argument that she was entitled to additional temporary support solely based upon the standard of living during the marriage lacks merit. See Donoff v. Donoff, 940 So. 2d 1221, 1225 (Fla. 4th DCA 2006) ("The standard-of-living is not a super-factor in setting the amount of alimony—trumping all others. . . . When the living standard during marriage was significantly high and the payor has the ability to pay more than minimum wage (so to speak), its purpose is to avoid having alimony set at bare subsistence levels.").

Although we agree with the circuit court's finding that the wife's requested financial need of $10,174 per month was not supported by competent substantial evidence, we see no competent substantial evidence in the record to support the circuit court's ruling directing the husband to pay the wife only $1,494 in temporary monthly support. As the husband's forensic accountant testified, pursuant to the wife's second amended financial affidavit, her expenses totalled $6,858 per month. Also, the husband did not dispute that the wife's only income was from Social Security and a pension which combined to provide $3,424 per month. Thus, based on the circuit court's findings that the wife had a need for, and the husband had the ability to pay, temporary monthly support, the circuit court's ruling should have directed the husband to pay the wife at least $3,434 in temporary monthly support [to equal her total expenses of $6,858 per month, according to the husband's forensic accountant's calculation]. For this reason, we reverse the circuit court's temporary monthly support award of $1,494, and remand for the circuit court to enter a temporary monthly support award of $3,434. . . .

MANI v. MANI

869 A.2d 904 (N.J. 2005)

Justice LONG delivered the opinion of the Court. . . .

. . . Plaintiff, Brenda Mani and defendant, James Mani met in 1970 when she went to work for him in his seasonal amusement business on the Seaside Heights boardwalk. James, a college graduate, was at the time, a half-owner of the boardwalk business and a partner in a travel agency in Florida that later failed; Brenda was a college student. Brenda graduated in 1971 and taught preschool for two years while working with James at his business during the summer.

[The couple had no children. During summers, they worked together at the boardwalk business. During winters, they vacationed in Florida and Mexico. Brenda received valuable gifts from her father, including $10,000 annually during the early years of the marriage; tax-free bonds; and stock in a family business that later appreciated considerably. Using proceeds from Brenda's stock and the couple's first home, the parties built a lavish new home titled in Brenda's name.]

[W]hen they were in their 40's, the parties retired from the boardwalk business and lived, in the words of the trial judge, an "extravagant" lifestyle almost exclusively out of Brenda's investment income. Their monthly budgetary expenses ranged from $7,360 [Brenda's estimate] to $13,143 [James's estimate]. [Later, James] worked briefly for real estate brokers. Although he provided a few referrals, he never showed a property for the firms and earned only about $20,000 in income in all. The couple spent seven years together in retirement before Brenda discovered that her husband was having an affair. with a woman with whom the parties socialized. Brenda filed a complaint for divorce alleging adultery and extreme cruelty. . . .

[At trial,] James claimed entitlement to a permanent alimony award of $68,320 per year and Brenda sought to deny alimony altogether. [After allocating the property,] the judge awarded James [alimony of] $610 per week based "in substantial part on the defendant's economic dependency." In reaching that conclusion, the judge attributed to James the ability to earn a minimum of $25,000 annually and denominated the alimony award as necessary to maintain the marital standard of living. [Both parties appealed.] [In affirming, the Appellate Division] observed that "the Manis' standard of living was not the result of the parties' joint efforts, but rather solely due to gifts from plaintiff's father." [Also,] James' adultery was significant and "his marital indiscretions warrant consideration in the amount of that award." . . .

James asks us to establish, as a rule of law, that in modern matrimonial practice, fault should play no part in an alimony determination or in an award of counsel fees. . . . Brenda counters that N.J.S.A. 2A:34-23(b) gives courts discretion to "consider any other factors which the court may deem relevant" in arriving at an alimony decision, including marital fault. . . . Amicus Curiae [the New Jersey State Bar Association] urges us to rule that fault should not be a factor in the determination of alimony except in the most egregious circumstances and that the focus of alimony should remain, as is the present practice, on the parties' financial circumstances. . . .

The history of alimony is instructive. In early England, two forms of marital dissolution existed. The most common was an ecclesiastical divorce from bed and board (a mensa et thoro) [or legal separation]. The other form—a civil divorce (a vinculo matrimonii)—which literally means severing the chains of matrimony, although technically available, was extremely rare because it required an act of Parliament. Alimony was granted only in the former class of cases on the theory that the husband was obliged to continue to support his wife as long as they remained married. Somehow, with the passage of time, the distinction between true divorce and mere separation was obliterated and alimony began to be awarded in all cases. No rationale was advanced to explain why parties, who were no longer married, remained economically bound to one another.

. . . The concept of alimony also carried over [to the American colonies]. Again, as had been the case in England, the reason for alimony, outside the legal separation scenario, remained an enigma. . . . Indeed, many distinct explanations have been advanced for alimony. They include its characterization as damages for breach of the marriage contract; as a share of the benefits of the marriage partnership; as damages for economic dislocation (based on past contributions); as damages for personal dislocation (foregoing the chance to marry another); as compensation for certain specific losses at the time of the dissolution; as deterrence or punishment for marital indiscretion; and as avoidance of a drain on the public fisc. Obviously, some of those purposes favor consideration of fault and some disfavor it. . . .

New Jersey cases have long expressed the view that alimony is neither a punishment for the payor nor a reward for the payee. When ordering alimony, a "court shall consider" a non-exclusive list of enumerated factors [including the actual need and ability of the parties to pay; the duration of the marriage; the age, physical and emotional health of the parties; the standard of living established in the marriage and the likelihood that each party can maintain a reasonably comparable standard of living; the parties' earning capacities; the equitable distribution of property ordered; and any other factors which the court may deem relevant]. As is obvious, the words "marital fault" and "responsibility for the breakdown in the marriage" do not appear in the statute, although the so-called "catch all category" arguably permits a court to consider "any other factor" it may "deem relevant." . . .

[A]lthough our case law has consistently recognized that, under our statutory scheme, fault may be considered in calculating alimony, for over a quarter of a century, courts have declined to place their imprimatur on a wide-ranging use of fault in that context. . . . The thirteen alimony factors listed in N.J.S.A. 2A:34-23(b) clearly center on the economic status of the parties. That is the primary alimony focus. . . .

[O]ur task in this case is to search for a principled approach to the relationship between fault and alimony consistent with legislative intent. [Commentators' views] reflect the full spectrum of approaches. For example, one commentator argues that even in the era of no-fault divorce, there should be consideration of fault in determining alimony to morally coerce better marital conduct. Another contends that legal recognition of fault may "provide protection and compensation for victims of abuse [of] spousal trust." [Citations omitted.] Other scholars counter that "the potentially valid functions of a fault principle are better served by the tort and criminal law, and attempting to serve them through a fault rule risks serious distortions in the resolution of the dissolution action." Ira Mark Ellman, The Place of Fault in a Modern Divorce Law, 28 Ariz. St. L.J. 773, 808-09 (1996). That view aligns with the most recent report of the American Law Institute on Principles of the Law of Family Dissolution: Analysis and Recommendations. That report concluded that economic fault is a valid alimony factor, but that consideration of non-economic fault should be avoided because of its deleterious effect on the dissolution action. More particularly, the ALI report notes that, in a scheme such as ours, in which alimony has economic roots, it will be the unusual case in which the fairness of the result will be improved by a judicial inquiry into the relative virtue of the parties' intimate conduct. . . .

We agree [with this last view] and hold that in cases in which marital fault has negatively affected the economic status of the parties, it may be considered in the calculation of alimony. By way of example, if a spouse gambles away all savings and retirement funds, and the assets are inadequate to allow the other spouse to recoup her share, an appropriate savings and retirement component may be included in the alimony award.

[Although economic misconduct is relevant to alimony, the] same relevance notion does not apply to the ordinary fault grounds for divorce that lurk in the margins of nearly every case. . . . Moreover, without concomitant benefit, considering non-economic fault can only result in ramping up the emotional content of matrimonial litigation and encouraging the parties to continually replay the details of their failed relationship. Not only is non-economic fault nearly impossible to factor into an alimony computation, but any attempt to do so would have the effect of generating complex legal issues regarding the apportionment of mutual fault, which is present in nearly all cases. That, in turn, would result in the protraction of litigation and the undermining of the goals of no-fault divorce, again without a corresponding benefit. Thus we hold that to the extent that marital misconduct affects the economic status quo of the parties, it may be taken into consideration in the calculation of alimony. Where marital fault has no residual economic consequences, it may not be considered in an alimony award.

The only exception to that rule is the narrow band of cases involving [egregious fault]. [For example,] California has legislatively barred alimony payments to a dependent spouse who has attempted to murder the supporting spouse. Cal. Fam. Code §4324. [S]ome conduct, by its very nature, is so outrageous that it can be said to violate the social contract, such that society would not abide continuing the economic bonds between the parties. In the extremely narrow class of cases in which such conduct occurs, it may be considered by the court, not in calculating an alimony award, but in the initial determination of whether alimony should be allowed at all.

In this case, there was no allegation that James's marital fault had any economic consequences or that it was, in any way, egregious. [W]e do not know whether the court would have reached the same conclusion in the absence of the fault consideration. We therefore reverse and remand the case to the Appellate Division for reconsideration of alimony without regard to fault. . . .

One final note on the alimony-fault intersection. . . . By delimiting the kinds of fault that may be taken into account in an alimony calculus, we have not only created a template for uniformity and predictability in decision-making but have relieved matrimonial litigants and their counsel from the need to act upon the nearly universal and practically irresistible urge for retribution that follows on the heels of a broken marriage. . . .

Justice RIVERA-SOTO, concurring in part and dissenting in part. . . .

[T]he paradigm we adopt today undoubtedly will generate its own flood of litigation because it defies definition. As a result, it takes little imagination to foresee the unending number of claims the standard adopted today—that a party's fault "affected the parties' economic life"—will bring. . . . Similarly, determining what constitutes "fault [that] so violates societal norms that continuing the economic bonds between the parties would confound notions of simple justice" is too subjective a standard, converting the analysis into a simple question of whose personal value system will prevail. It is not a stretch to conclude that having your spouse engage in sexual relations with your friend and yet still demand that you support his lifestyle after divorce at the rate of over $150,000 per year "confounds notions of simple justice." If that is not what this standard means, then it is meaningless. If, on the other hand, that is precisely what this new standard means, then we have created a new and unproven process to achieve a result already reached by tried-and-true methods. . . .

UNIFORM MARRIAGE AND DIVORCE ACT

§308. [MAINTENANCE]

(a) [The court in a dissolution or legal separation proceeding] may grant a maintenance order for either spouse only if it finds that the spouse seeking maintenance:

(1) lacks sufficient property to provide for his reasonable needs; and

(2) is unable to support himself through appropriate employment or is the custodian of a child whose condition or circumstances make it appropriate that the custodian not be required to seek employment outside the home.

(b) The maintenance order shall be in amounts and for periods of time the court deems just, without regard to marital misconduct, and after considering all relevant factors including:

(1) the financial resources of the party seeking maintenance, including marital property apportioned to him, his ability to meet his needs independently, and the extent to which a provision for support of a child living with the party includes a sum for that party as custodian;

(2) the time necessary to acquire sufficient education or training to enable the party seeking maintenance to find appropriate employment;

(3) the standard of living established during the marriage;

(4) the duration of the marriage;

(5) the age and the physical and emotional condition of the spouse seeking maintenance; and

(6) the ability of the spouse from whom maintenance is sought to meet his needs while meeting those of the spouse seeking maintenance.

MASSACHUSETTS ALIMONY REFORM ACT
Mass. Gen. Laws, Ch. 208

§49. TERMINATION, SUSPENSION, OR MODIFICATION OF GENERAL TERM ALIMONY . . .

(b) Except upon a written finding by the court that deviation beyond the time limits of this section are required in the interests of justice, if the length of the marriage is 20 years or less, general term alimony shall terminate no later than a date certain under the following durational limits:

(1) [For marriages of 5 years or less, the maximum period of alimony is half the marriage duration];

(2) [For marriages of more than 5 to 10 years, the maximum period of alimony is 60 percent of the marriage duration];

(3) [For marriages of more than 10 to 15 years, the maximum period of alimony is 70 percent of the marriage duration];

(4) [For marriages of more than 15 to 20 years, the maximum period of alimony is 80 percent of the duration of the marriage].

(c) [For marriages longer than 20 years, the court may order indefinite alimony]. . . .

(d) General term alimony shall be suspended, reduced or terminated upon the cohabitation of the recipient spouse when the payor shows that the recipient spouse has maintained a common household, as defined in this subsection, with another person for a continuous period of at least 3 months. . . .

(e) Unless the payor and recipient agree otherwise, general term alimony may be modified in duration or amount upon a material change of circumstances warranting modification. Modification may be permanent, indefinite or for a finite duration, as may be appropriate. Nothing in this section shall be construed to permit alimony reinstatement after the recipient's remarriage, except by the parties' express written agreement.

(f) Once issued, general term alimony orders shall terminate upon the payor attaining the full retirement age. . . .

§53. DETERMINATION OF FORM, AMOUNT, AND DURATION; DEVIATIONS . . .

(a) [In determining the form, amount, and duration of alimony], a court shall consider: the length of the marriage; age of the parties; health of the parties; income, employment and employability of both parties, including employability through reasonable diligence and additional training, if necessary; economic and non-economic contribution of both parties to the marriage; marital lifestyle; ability of each party to maintain the marital lifestyle; lost economic opportunity as a result of the marriage; and such other factors as the court considers relevant and material.

(b) Except for reimbursement alimony or circumstances warranting deviation for other forms of alimony, the amount of alimony should generally not exceed the recipient's need or 30 to 35 per cent of the difference between the parties' gross incomes established at the time of the order being issued. . . .

(e) In setting an initial alimony order, or in modifying an existing order, the court may deviate from duration and amount limits for general term alimony and rehabilitative alimony upon written findings that deviation is necessary. Grounds for deviation may include:

(1) advanced age; chronic illness; or unusual health circumstances of either party;

(2) tax considerations applicable to the parties;

(3) whether the payor spouse is providing health insurance and the cost of health insurance for the recipient spouse;

(4) whether the payor spouse has been ordered to secure life insurance for the benefit of the recipient spouse and the cost of such insurance;

(5) sources and amounts of unearned income, including capital gains, interest and dividends, annuity and investment income from assets that were not allocated in the [parties'] divorce;

(6) significant premarital cohabitation that included economic partnership or marital separation of significant duration, each of which the court may consider in determining the length of the marriage;

(7) a party's inability to provide for that party's own support by reason of physical or mental abuse by the payor;

(8) a party's inability to provide for that party's own support by reason of that party's deficiency of property, maintenance or employment opportunity; and

(9) upon written findings, any other factor that the court deems relevant and material.

(f) In determining the incomes of parties with respect to the issue of alimony, the court may attribute income to a party who is unemployed or underemployed. . . .

Notes and Questions on the Rationales for Postdissolution Support

1. Standard. Alimony has its roots in a husband's duty under coverture to support his wife during the marriage. What is the standard in determining whether and to what extent an award of alimony is proper, according to the circuit court in *Alizzi*? How did the spouses arrive at their different estimates of the wife's needs? Did the appellate court consider the wife's actual or anticipated expenses? What was the role of the couple's pre-divorce standard of living in the court's determination? How did the appellate court arrive at its final determination of the wife's needs?

2. Gender-based nature of the award. The U.S. Supreme Court invalidated gender-specific alimony rules in Orr v. Orr, 440 U.S. 268 (1979), concluding that Alabama's statutory scheme of imposing alimony obligations only on husbands violates equal protection. Applying intermediate scrutiny, the Court rejected the use of gender as a proxy for need, whether based on the important governmental objectives of helping needy spouses or compensating women for past discrimination. The Court reasoned that individualized hearings to set alimony makes reliance on a proxy unnecessary and that a gender-neutral law would achieve the state's ends better while avoiding the risk of reinforcing gender-based stereotypes about women's proper place and their need for protection.

Although suggesting that "need" furnishes the underlying rationale for alimony, *Orr* rejects reliance on gender to determine need. Despite *Orr*, however, Professor Ira Ellman invokes gendered roles to identify alimony's theoretical basis. He writes:

> [Marriage] is a relationship in which the wife makes many initial investments of value only to her husband, investments a self-interested bargainer would make only in return for a long-term commitment. [T]he traditional wife makes her marital investment early in the expectation of a deferred return: sharing in the fruits of her husband's eventual market success. The traditional husband realizes his gains

from the marriage in its early years, in the form of increased earning capacity and the production of children; his contribution is deferred until the marriage's later years when he shares the fruits of his enhanced earning capacity with his wife. In any relationship in which the flow of payments and benefits to the parties is not symmetrical over time, [t]he party who has already received a benefit has an incentive to terminate the relationship before the balance of payments shifts. . . .

The function of alimony [is thus] to reallocate the postdivorce financial consequences of marriage in order to prevent distorting incentives. [B]y eliminating any financial incentives or penalties that might otherwise flow from different marital lifestyles, this theory maximizes the parties' freedom to shape their marriage in accordance with their nonfinancial preferences. They can allocate domestic duties according to these preferences without putting one spouse at risk of a much greater financial loss than the other if the marriage fails. . . .[7]

3. A continuing duty? *Mani* poses the unresolved question of "why parties, who [are] no longer married, remain[] economically bound to one another." Which of the explanations for alimony listed in *Mani* is most persuasive to answer this question? Even if an economically dependent spouse needs support after dissolution, why does a former spouse (rather than parents, children, or the state) bear this responsibility? Does Ellman's excerpt above successfully explain why the duty of spousal support continues after divorce?

4. Contract? Does the marriage contract explain why the duty of support continues after divorce? According to the classic rationale, alimony can be justified on the ground that it places the obligation to support a needy spouse upon the other party (rather than the state) by virtue of the compact of marriage. Does this explanation suggest that part of the marriage contract remains binding after divorce? Or that alimony serves as a remedy for breach of this contract? Does Ellman's theory also reflect a contractual rationale?

5. Residual role for fault? What role should fault play in the financial consequences of dissolution? Whose fault should the court consider—the recipient, the obligor, or both? See, e.g., Mick-Skaggs v. Skaggs, 766 S.E.2d 870 (S.C. Ct. App. 2014) (wife's adultery justifies denial of alimony); Riley v. Riley, 138 P.3d 84, 88-89 (Utah Ct. App. 2006) (justifying award to wife that exceeded her need, in part because of husband's fault).

Why does *Mani* limit consideration of fault in determining alimony? What explains *Mani*'s two exceptions to its no-fault approach: economic misconduct and egregious fault? Why should courts consider these exceptions "not in calculating an alimony award, but in the initial determination of whether alimony should be allowed at all"? Why would the New Jersey Bar Association urge a no-fault approach, with an exception for egregious circumstances? Evaluate the *Mani* dissent's critique of the two exceptions. Are tort damages a preferable way to address marital misconduct?

6. Standard of living. What does "need" mean for the purposes of computing spousal support? Does it refer only to necessities? The marital standard of living?

---

[7]. Ira Mark Ellman, The Theory of Alimony, 77 Cal. L. Rev. 1, 42-43, 50-51 (1989).

How does UMDA measure "reasonable needs"? Should the marital standard of living determine the level of support even after a *brief* marriage? Some alimony reform proposals seek to eliminate the marital "standard of living" as a criterion in determining alimony for the supported spouse based on the rationale that both parties will have a lower standard of living postdivorce. See S.B. 1596, H.B. 1325, 2019 Reg. Leg. Sess. (Fla. 2019) (died in committee). Evaluate this approach.

7. Types of alimony. States permit several types of alimony based on different objectives and rationales. *Temporary alimony* is a series of payments for a fixed period of time to a dependent spouse based either on a divorce decree or separation agreement. *Permanent* (sometimes called "lifetime") *alimony* was more commonly awarded during the fault-based era to homemaker spouses in long-term marriages. *Rehabilitative alimony* lasts only a limited period, as determined by the time necessary for the dependent spouse to obtain adequate training or employment to become self-supporting. *Reimbursement alimony* refers to spousal support that is awarded to recompense a spouse for making contributions to the payor-spouse for the latter's education and training during the marriage (discussed later in the chapter). *Alimony pendente lite* is temporary alimony while an action for separation or divorce is pending. See *Alizzi*, supra.

What criteria might justify awards of permanent alimony today? Should the length of the marriage alone be determinative? See Fla. Stat. Ann. §61.08(8)(b) (replacing permanent alimony with durational alimony based on length of marriage: 50 percent of the length of a short-term marriage (less than 10 years), 60 percent of the length of a moderate-term marriage (between 10 and 20 years), or 75 percent of the length of a long-term marriage (20 years or longer), but allowing for showing by clear-and-convincing evidence of additional factors).

8. Rehabilitation for self-sufficiency.

a. UMDA's influence. UMDA provided an early model for alimony statutes that were formerly based on fault and gender. According to UMDA §308, a court first makes a determination of need and, only if need exists, considers the factors relevant to setting the amount of duration. Which approach is more "progressive," UMDA's or *Mani*'s? How does UMDA frame the parameters of "need"? Note that UMDA makes maintenance a remedy of last resort, to be awarded only when a spouse's "reasonable needs" remain unmet because of the absence of sufficient property or income from appropriate employment. Why did UMDA's drafters make maintenance a disfavored remedy, to be awarded only when equitable distribution of property fails to achieve economic justice? Once this need threshold is satisfied, however, the court has discretion to order support in an amount and duration that is "just," based on all relevant factors.

Jurisdictions following UMDA view self-sufficiency as an important objective, making support a temporary, transitional measure that often contemplates postdivorce paid employment even for homemaker spouses. However, stark differences exist in state interpretations of self-sufficiency. See, e.g., Tex. Fam. Code Ann. §8.054 (limiting maintenance to shortest reasonable period that allows spouse seeking maintenance to earn sufficient income to provide for the spouse's minimum reasonable needs).

well-being of women and men post-divorce consistently shows larger decreases for women.[13]

Problems

1. Brian, a 48-year-old commercial pilot, and Ruth, a 47-year-old school-teacher, divorce after 27 years of marriage. They have two adult children for whom Ruth was the primary parent because of Brian's erratic schedule. Brian's annual salary is $150,000; Ruth's is $43,000. The trial court divides the marital property equally and awards Ruth half the difference in their incomes for two years to enable her to obtain additional university credits. Alimony will cease at the end of the two-year period. Ruth appeals, asking for a higher monthly award and alimony for at least ten years. She claims that even a doctorate degree would not significantly increase her income as a teacher, and Brian will continue to have much greater income than she can ever expect. Brian also appeals, arguing that Ruth does not need support and she never expressed interest in additional education before the divorce. See Gardner v. Gardner, 881 P.2d 645 (Nev. 1994). What result under UMDA? Under the Massachusetts statute? What result under an "income-sharing" approach in which the spouses' post-marital incomes are divided equally or, alternatively, a "buyout" approach, in which one spouse buys out the other's interest (as an "exit price") to reflect the partnership analogy and egalitarian views of marriage? See generally Cynthia Lee Starnes, The Marriage Buyout: The Troubled Trajectory of U.S. Alimony Law (2014). What are the advantages and disadvantages of these approaches over UMDA's approach and the Massachusetts statute? Do these approaches, although gender neutral, operate like other feminist arguments for alimony that further entrench gendered divisions of family labor?

2. Derek Young, president of Fidelity Investment's global asset allocation division, files for divorce from his wife, Joy, in 2013 after a 24-year marriage. The parties agreed early in their marriage that Joy would be a stay-at-home mom, and, as a result, she has never worked outside the home. Their children are currently in college. Derek receives an annual base salary of $350,000, with additional compensation through various stock plans. His gross income reflects a steadily upward trajectory—approximately $1.5 million in 2008, $2 million in 2009, $4 million in 2010, $7 million in 2011, and $7.76 million in 2012. The spouses enjoyed an affluent lifestyle, including a lavish eight-bedroom home and a summer home in Nantucket, luxury vehicles, dining out frequently, designer clothing, and expensive vacations. At the time Derek filed for divorce, Joy's living expenses total $450,000 per year. One year later, her expenses have increased to $650,000 per year. She requests that the court award her lifetime alimony. What result under UMDA? Under the Massachusetts statute? Under a "buyout" or "income-sharing" approach? What is Joy's "need" for alimony? How should a court determine

---

[13]. Thomas Leopold, Gender Differences in the Consequences of Divorce, 55 Demography 679-797 (June 2018) (summarizing research revealing that women suffer disproportionate declines in household income and standard of living post-divorce, as well as higher risks of losing home ownership), https://www.ncbi.nlm.nih.gov/pmc/articles/PMC5992251/.

her need relative to the marital standard of living? Should Joy's alimony award increase after the divorce based on increases in her ex-husband's income? When, if ever, should judges issue self-modifying alimony awards that increase annually as a percentage of the supporting spouse's income? See Young v. Young, 81 N.E.3d 1165 (Mass. 2017).

D. "Winding Up" a Marriage: Applying Theories of Property Division and Support

1. A Case Study

Despite different theoretical bases, courts typically confront property and support questions together, along with related questions such as attorneys' fees, tax liability, and pension rights. The following case presents one specific factual context in which to analyze the application of the theories explored above, while illustrating the interconnections among all the financial incidents of dissolution. Consider what result would be fair. Which approach of those canvassed above would most likely achieve it?

WOLFE v. WOLFE
273 P.3d 915 (Or. Ct. App. 2012)

HASELTON, P.J. . . .

[H]usband [age 63] and wife [age 60] met in 1974 while husband was completing his [ophthalmology] internship and wife, who was a nurse practitioner, was working at the same hospital. After the parties married in 1975, husband completed his residency and fellowships. [They later moved to Oregon, where they lived until they separated in 2006.]

[H]usband worked for a clinic in Corvallis, and wife worked as a nurse practitioner for the county health department. In 1980, the parties purchased a farm, and, in 1982, about the time that their daughter was born, they moved into the home that they had recently built there. Although wife planned to continue working in her profession, by the time that the parties' son was born in 1983, she chose to be a homemaker. [When husband opened his own ophthalmology practice in 1991, wife handled the bookkeeping, the training and supervision of employees, and served as a substitute when an employee missed work. She also volunteered at the children's school, carpooled, did volunteer work to promote her husband's medical practice, and oversaw various aspects of the 78-acre farm.]

Despite wife's significant contributions to the ophthalmology practice, for many years, she did not draw a salary in order to, as husband noted, "better [their] tax situation" . . . so that the parties would not have to pay Social Security and Medicare taxes related to her work in the practice. That arrangement, in turn, maximized the amount of husband's earnings that were ultimately deposited into joint accounts and used for family purposes. In other words, husband's earnings effectively included wife's compensation for her contributions to the ophthalmology practice. [After the parties separated, husband could not do all the work performed by wife, so he sold the practice to another physician, for whom he continued working part time,] earning approximately $11,000 per month, and wife was employed part time as a bookkeeper, earning approximately $2,300 per month. However, wife planned to retire in the near future, and husband planned to retire within a couple of years.

[T]he parties had a very comfortable, but not overly extravagant, standard of living during the marriage. [T]hrough their efforts, the parties acquired assets—including real property and retirement and investment accounts—worth approximately $5 million at the time of trial.

[In addition to the income generated by the medical practice and the parties' joint investments, husband had other assets (called here the "disputed property") that he would periodically use to supplement that income, flowing from a testamentary trust established by husband's grandfather and consisting of stocks, bonds, and real property, managed by husband's father as trustee, for the use and benefit of husband and his two siblings.] Husband's father managed the property held in the testamentary trust, and, at some point, placed husband's earnings in an investment account [at Smith Barney and UBS] in husband's name. . . .

The disputed property—that is, the . . . trust and the Smith Barney and UBS accounts—was essentially managed by third parties [including husband's father and financial advisors]. Earnings from the disputed property were reinvested. Significantly, none of the parties' earned income was ever invested in the disputed property. To the extent that the disputed property appreciated in value during the marriage, that appreciation was passive and did not result through the efforts—either direct or otherwise—of husband or wife.

During the marriage, husband periodically used funds from what he referred to as his "separate money"—which included the Smith Barney account—to supplement the parties' earned income. Most substantially, husband used that money to (1) help finance the acquisition of the parties' farm and the construction of their home; (2) annually make maximum contributions to both parties' individual retirement accounts; and (3) pay for some incidental vacation expenses. Husband's use of those funds within his control occurred in an overarching context in which the parties generally made financial decisions together based on what was in the best interests of their family. . . .

It was against that historic and financial backdrop that the parties framed their respective positions concerning the division of property and spousal support to the trial court. [W]ife contended that (1) husband's interest in the disputed property was a marital asset; (2) husband had not rebutted the presumption of equal contribution with regard to that property in light of wife's contributions to the ophthalmology practice and as a homemaker; and (3) in all events, a just and equitable division "dictates that the parties in this case leave the marriage on equal footing." Wife also requested spousal support—the amount of which would "depend on the court's determination of how the assets are to be divided."

Conversely, husband contended that the disputed property was a premarital asset because it originated from the devise from his grandfather in the 1950s. Alternatively, husband contended that, to the extent that a portion of the disputed property was a marital asset, he had rebutted the presumption of equal contribution by demonstrating that the disputed property was managed by third parties and that any appreciation was essentially passive. In all events, husband contended that it was just and equitable to award him the $10.3 million in disputed assets [and that a spousal support] award was unnecessary because the property division, without reference to the disputed property, would generate sufficient income to enable wife to be economically self-sufficient and to enjoy a standard of living not overly disproportionate to the one that the parties enjoyed during the marriage.

[T]he trial court awarded wife approximately $2.6 million in assets, and awarded husband approximately $2.4 million in assets [as a just and equitable division]. Further, the trial court awarded husband the disputed property valued at $10.3 million as his separate property. . . . With regard to spousal support, the trial court determined that wife was entitled to support until she reached full retirement age. For that reason, the court awarded wife maintenance support of $2,000 per month for two years, followed by $1,000 per month for three years thereafter. Finally, over wife's objection, the trial court determined that each party was responsible for his or her respective attorney fees and costs and disbursements. . . .

On appeal, wife [contends]: (1) The trial court erred in awarding the $10.3 million in disputed assets to husband. (2) The trial court erred in the amount and duration of its award of maintenance spousal support, which, wife contends, should be increased to $10,000 per month indefinitely. And (3) the trial court erred in denying her request for attorney fees before reviewing it.

. . . Our resolution of [the first] matter is guided and circumscribed by ORS 107.105(1)(f) (2007):

> "(f) For the division or other disposition between the parties of the real or personal property, or both, of either or both of the parties as may be just and proper in all the circumstances. . . . The court shall consider the contribution of a spouse as a homemaker as a contribution to the acquisition of marital assets. There is a rebuttable presumption that both spouses have contributed equally to the acquisition of property during the marriage, whether such property is jointly or separately held."

Under the statute, our initial inquiry is to determine . . . whether and to what extent husband's interest in the disputed property was acquired during the marriage—that is, whether and to what extent the disputed property is a "marital asset" to which the presumption of equal contribution applies. Although that inquiry is straightforward in many cases, it is not here. [A]fter the parties married, the configuration of property was continually evolving. . . . Nevertheless, at least, it is patent that wife did not contribute to the initial devise of property to husband from his grandfather decades before the parties' marriage. Moreover, and in all events, to the extent that some portion of the disputed property is, doubtless, a marital asset, husband rebutted the presumption of equal contribution [on two bases.]

First, the earnings from the disputed property were reinvested, and none of the parties' earned income was deposited into the Smith Barney or UBS accounts. Under those circumstances, husband's entire interest in the disputed property at the time of trial is traceable to his premarital interest in the property. . . . Second, to the extent that a portion of the disputed property is a marital asset—through either the acquisition of new property or appreciation—neither husband nor wife contributed to the acquisition of that property during the marriage. [T]he acquisition of new property and the appreciation during the marriage occurred passively and independent of any contribution of either husband or wife. . . .

Accordingly, husband has rebutted the presumption of equal contribution as to any portion of the disputed property that is a marital asset. [Next, the court considers "what is just and proper in all the circumstances."] [T]wo equitable considerations—neither of which appears to have been considered by the trial court—guide our review. . . . First, we consider the "social and financial objectives of the dissolution." Second, we consider the extent to which husband has integrated his interest in the disputed property "into the common financial affairs of the marital partnership through commingling."

With respect to the first consideration, we have previously explained that, "in a long-term marriage, . . . 'the parties should separate on as equal a basis as possible.'" In re Marriage of Boyd, 203 P.3d 312 [(Or. Ct. App. 2009)]:

> "[w]hen couples enter marriage, they ordinarily commit themselves to an indefinite shared future of which shared finances are a part. Acquisitions are made, forgone, or replaced for the good of the family unit rather than for the financial interests of either spouse. Property is bought, sold, enhanced, diminished, intermixed and used without regard to ease of division upon termination of the marriage."

In fact, this long-term marriage was marked by the dynamic contemplated in *Boyd*.

With respect to the second consideration, as previously indicated, the parties generally made financial decisions together based on what was in the best interest of their family as a whole. For example [wife did not draw a salary and husband did not buy life insurance]. On balance, . . . it is just and proper for wife to receive a portion of those assets. In reaching a contrary determination, the trial court appears to have focused only on the fact that wife would achieve economic self-sufficiency without sharing in the disputed property. However, in a case such as this, in which the parties have more than ample assets, economic self-sufficiency is not the dispositive factor in the equitable calculus. . . .

[I]t is just and proper for wife to receive an additional $2 million in property. In the end, wife will leave the marriage with approximately $4.6 million in assets, and husband will leave the marriage with $10.7 million in assets. In order to effectuate that award, we will not disturb any portion of the trial court's property division other than to award wife an equalizing judgment in the amount of $2 million.

. . . On appeal, wife contends that, if she is not awarded half of the disputed property, she is entitled to $10,000 per month in indefinite maintenance support in light of the substantial income that husband's investment property will generate. We disagree. . . . "[T]he primary goal of spousal support in a long-term marriage such as this is to provide a standard of living roughly comparable to the one enjoyed during the marriage." [W]ife will receive assets that will generate income sufficient to allow her to enjoy a standard of living that is not overly disproportionate to the one that the parties enjoyed during the marriage. Accordingly, we reject wife's contentions but otherwise affirm the trial court's spousal support award. . . .

Notes and Questions

1. Interwoven analysis. Questions of property division and spousal support typically arise together in divorce litigation, as *Wolfe* illustrates. The analysis generally addresses property first, considering the following questions: Is it in fact "property" (the identification question)? Is it marital or nonmarital/separate (the characterization question)? How much is it worth (the valuation question)? How much of it does each spouse get (the distribution question)?

2. Classifying property. On the characterization question, *Wolfe* presents the common situation of separate property that is brought into the marriage by one spouse (such as an inheritance) and that increases in value during the marriage. Why does *Wolfe* find ascertaining the specific "configuration" of the "disputed property" so difficult? In the face of this difficulty, how does the court classify the disputed property—as marital asset, separate property, or some of each? On what rationale? How does the court treat the portion of the disputed property that represents appreciation of the original assets? Consider the extent to which *Wolfe* implemented any of the following approaches—tracing, marital efforts, and recharacterization.

Note that Oregon (the setting for *Wolfe*) is a hotchpot state. Even in a hotchpot state, *Wolfe* reveals how the premarital/separate nature of an asset can be taken into account.

a. Tracing. Most community property jurisdictions classify appreciation and income from separate property as separate property. This approach traces existing assets to their source: Assets traceable to separate property are treated as separate property, while those traceable to marital funds are treated as marital. The minority approach treats as community property any income generated during marriage, even income from separate property.

b. Marital efforts. Equitable distribution states (like Oregon in *Wolfe*) often treat income or appreciation from separate property as marital based on "marital efforts" or the active role of either spouse. The classification of income or appreciation from separate property proves particularly important when a breadwinner spouse works in a family or other closely held business (as in *Wolfe*) and can decide what portion of the business earnings to take as salary (marital property) and what portion to retain or reinvest in the company.

c. Recharacterization. Recall the gradual recharacterization of separate property in the ALI Principles. To what extent does the couple's own treatment of the "disputed property" in *Wolfe* mirror the ALI's rationale for recharacterization (discussed earlier in the chapter)? How far does the court go in embracing this rationale? What role should the parties' intent play?

3. Equitable distribution. After valuing the assets (which often requires expert testimony), the court must distribute the property to be divided. Oregon has a presumption of equal contribution to marital assets. In *Wolfe*, how did husband rebut this presumption? How did the court decide that awarding wife an additional $2 million would be "just and proper"? What standards guide judicial discretion under standards like Oregon's or UMDA §307 above? What role did the wife's contributions play? The "two equitable considerations" emphasized by the court? On what rationale might the wife in *Wolfe* have merited *more* than roughly half the marital property? See, e.g., Cartee v. Cartee, 239 P.3d 707 (Alaska 2010) (affirming an award of 60 percent to a wife who shouldered childrearing and chose to forgo career opportunities).

4. Support.

a. Amount. Why does the support award in *Wolfe* depend on the allocation of property? How does the court arrive at a support award that is "just and equitable"? Which of the following purposes does the support award serve? "Spousal maintenance has multiple purposes, including 'to correct the . . . inequality of income resulting from the divorce,' 'to equalize the standard of living of the parties for an appropriate period of time,' 'to assist the recipient-spouse in becoming self-supporting,' and 'to compensate a homemaker for contributions to family well-being not otherwise recognized in the property distribution.'" Gravel v. Gravel, 980 A.2d 242, 250 (Vt. 2009).

b. Duration. On what basis does the court affirm the trial court's decision to end maintenance after five years? When should courts award indefinite support, as the wife in *Wolfe* requested? Scholars discern a greater willingness to award indefinite term alimony "when parties are divorcing after a marriage of long duration, the parties' incomes are quite different, and the recipients cannot realistically be retrained."[14] How would this aspect of *Wolfe* be decided under the Massachusetts statute above?

5. Attorneys' fees and costs.

Courts sometimes require one spouse to pay the other's attorneys' fees and litigation costs, the issue remanded in *Wolfe*. Today, many jurisdictions impose such fees and costs on the spouse in the superior financial position, treating the award as an additional distribution of property or a species of spousal support and reflecting a balance of the equities. Most jurisdictions disallow contingent fees in divorce litigation based on the rationale that lawyers should not have financial incentives to discourage reconciliation.

Problem

Deborah and Dennis divorce after 15 years of marriage with no children. During the marriage, the couple relocated to different parts of the country several times because of Deborah's employment with a large corporation, which frequently promoted her. For five years of the marriage, Dennis, who had a master's degree in journalism, found work in the various cities in which they lived. Thereafter, pursuant to the couple's agreement, he stayed home to write fiction and perform the domestic tasks. None of his writing was accepted for publication, however, and evidence shows that Dennis's domestic habits were "lax." Under a statute identical to UMDA §307 and §308 (both reprinted above), the trial court awards Deborah

---

[14]. J. Thomas Oldham, Changes in the Economic Consequences of Divorces, 1958-2008, 42 Fam. L.Q. 419, 432 (2008).

75 percent of the marital property and Dennis 25 percent; further, it denies the maintenance that Dennis requested to pursue additional training so that he can succeed as a journalist. Dennis appeals both the property division and support denial, seeking more property and rehabilitative maintenance. What result, and why? See Michael v. Michael, 791 S.W.2d 772 (Mo. Ct. App. 1990). Would your analysis change if the couple had a child? Suppose that in this scenario, Deborah argues that Dennis's care for their child did not impede his career because Dennis chose to stay home while the parties could have afforded childcare. See Cartee v. Cartee, 239 P.3d 707 (Alaska 2010).

2. Special Problems in Achieving a Fair Dissolution

With courts attempting to divide property "equitably" and to award "just" support, general considerations of fairness often overshadow theoretical distinctions between the two remedies. Given the practice of blurring these lines, what difference does it make whether a particular payment represents property or support? Will the purpose of the payment as property distribution or support always be clear? The following scenarios highlight such difficulties.

a. Changing Circumstances

MENNEN v. MENNEN
2019 WL 1468745 (N.J. Super. Ct. App. Div. 2019)

Per Curiam.

[T]he parties were divorced in January 2004 after a thirteen-year marriage. Their children [from previous respective marriages] are emancipated. As part of their settlement agreement incorporated into the judgment of divorce, defendant agreed to pay plaintiff $5500 monthly in permanent alimony [provided that alimony would terminate in the event of "Wife's cohabitation in the future with an unrelated person in a relationship tantamount to marriage"].

According to defendant, plaintiff has maintained a longstanding relationship with her significant other, J.K., in which the two of them allegedly interact and hold themselves out as the equivalent of spouses. In support of his contentions, defendant provided in his motion papers an unsigned and uncertified private investigator's report that stated J.K. was present 88 percent of the time during 32 of the investigator's visits spanning a 4-1/2 month period. The surveillance was conducted "early morning," "late evening," and during the "middle of the night"; during the week, weekends, and holidays; and on consecutive and alternating days. The investigator noted a pattern of visits, whereby J.K. would leave plaintiff's residence between 6:15 A.M. and 6:30 A.M. The report states that J.K. has a garage door opener to plaintiff's home, and that he does not own or rent property in New Jersey. He uses a post office box at a United Parcel Service in Chester as his address and on his driver's license, and he listed plaintiff's address as his residence on two occasions. Defendant claims that J.K. is "enmeshed" in the everyday life of plaintiff as supported by Facebook pictures, including his attendance at her daughter's wedding. The report stated [that plaintiff and J.K. shared two credit cards and he used the marital residence on two occasions for credit purposes].

In opposition to the motion, plaintiff certified that J.K. resides with his brother in Belvidere, a 45-minute drive from her home; they have been dating since 2009; and they have been photographed together at social events. In 31 pages of Facebook photographs, J.K. is only depicted in five of them, spanning a seven-year period, and there are no photographs of plaintiff on his Facebook page. J.K. lost his home in Chester to a short sale in 2015, sold his Andes, New York home, and filed for bankruptcy in January 2014. He has a garage door opener but no keys for plaintiff's residence. Plaintiff certified that J.K. stayed with her while performing contracting work at a Morris Township residence "to save nearly half the drive" to his brother's home in Belvidere. J.K. used plaintiff's vehicle once during the surveillance period. She denied having a cohabitation arrangement with him. In his bankruptcy petition, J.K. did not [name plaintiff as a co-debtor on his credit cards]. No evidence was provided to support the investigator's conclusion that J.K. listed the marital residence as his address on "official documents." . . .

As to the four trash pulls from her residence, plaintiff argues that "none of the pulls yielded any items addressed to or seemingly belonging to J.K.," and that "[t]he majority of the trash collected consisted of diapers, a significant amount of takeout food, credit card statements belonging to the [plaintiff's] daughter and feminine hygiene products." . . . The private investigator's report was "stale," being eight months old by the time the motion was filed according to plaintiff, and the so-called "findings" are "exaggerated" and unsupported by any documentation. . . .

We first consider the well-settled principles that guide our review. Alimony "may be revised and altered by the court from time to time as circumstances may require." To make such a modification, a showing of "changed circumstances" is required. A prima facie showing of cohabitation constitutes sufficient changed circumstances. [C]ohabitation has been defined as "an intimate relationship in which the couple has undertaken duties and privileges that are commonly associated with marriage." Where a supporting spouse seeks to decrease or terminate alimony because of the dependent spouse's cohabitation, "the test for modification of alimony is whether the relationship has reduced the financial needs of the dependent former spouse." Alimony may be modified "when (1) the third party contributes to the dependent spouse's support, or (2) the third party resides in the dependent spouse's home without contributing anything toward the household expenses."

"[A] showing of cohabitation creates a rebuttable presumption of changed circumstances shifting the burden to the dependent spouse to show that there is no actual economic benefit to the spouse or cohabitant." The court must focus on the cohabitant's economic relationship to discern "whether one . . . 'subsidizes the other.'" Whether this economic benefit exists requires a fact-intensive inquiry by the trial judge. . . .

Prior to the Legislature's adoption of the 2014 amendments, the legal criteria for cohabitation were not specified by statute but instead embodied in case law. [See, e.g., Konzelman v. Konzelman, 729 A.2d 7 (N.J. 1999).] Defendant relies on *Konzelman* arguing that he only needs to show plaintiff and her paramour are living together and he provides economic support.

As the Supreme Court explained in *Konzelman*, cohabitation is typified by the existence of a marriage-like relationship "shown to have stability, permanency[,] and mutual interdependence." Although "living together, intertwined finances such as joint bank accounts, shared living expenses and household chores, and recognition of the relationship in the couple's social and family circle" may support a finding of cohabitation, such illustrative examples must not be considered in a vacuum. "A mere romantic, casual, or social relationship is not sufficient to justify the enforcement of a settlement agreement provision terminating alimony," nor is simply sharing "a common residence, although that is an important factor." . . .

In 2014, the Legislature addressed cohabitation in subsection (n) of N.J.S.A. 2A:34-23. That provision sets forth the following considerations that bear upon cohabitation issues: . . .

> n. Alimony may be suspended or terminated if the payee cohabits with another person. Cohabitation involves a mutually supportive, intimate personal relationship in which a couple has undertaken duties and privileges that are commonly associated with marriage or civil union but does not necessarily maintain a single common household.
>
> (1)   Intertwined finances such as joint bank accounts and other joint holdings or liabilities;
> (2)   Sharing or joint responsibility for living expenses;
> (3)   Recognition of the relationship in the couple's social and family circle;
> (4)   Living together, the frequency of contact, the duration of the relationship, and other indicia of a mutually supportive intimate personal relationship;
> (5)   Sharing household chores;
> (6)   Whether the recipient of alimony has received an enforceable promise of support from another person . . .; and
> (7)   All other relevant evidence.

In evaluating whether cohabitation is occurring and whether alimony should be suspended or terminated, the court shall also consider the length of the relationship. A court may not find an absence of cohabitation solely on grounds that the couple does not live together on a full-time basis.

[W]e are mindful that the materials submitted to the motion judge—including the Facebook posting of J.K.—reflect that he and plaintiff take part with one another in a variety of social and family activities, and attended her daughter's wedding, family gatherings, and other such events together. Even so, the present record lacks any evidence that the couple's finances are intertwined or that plaintiff is financially dependent upon her significant other. Here, we agree with the judge that defendant failed to establish a prima facie case of cohabitation, and we find no abuse of discretion. [T]here is no proof of joint bank accounts or other joint asset holdings; no proof that the couple share living expenses; and no proof of any enforceable promise of support. There is no proof of shared household chores. [T]he record amassed by the defendant was reasonably deemed insufficient by the motion judge to rise to the level of a prima facie case. . . . Affirmed.

Notes and Questions

1. **Final or modifiable?** One important difference between spousal support and property distributions is that property distributions are final whereas awards of spousal support are modifiable. The prevailing standard for modification of spousal support is "a substantial change in circumstances." Courts have broad discretion in how they define that term, although certain circumstances lead to modification or termination of spousal support either by statute or agreement between the parties. What theories of property division and support awards best explain the finality of awards of property division and the modifiability of spousal support? What rationale supports this rule?

According to the general rule, spousal support is terminated upon the recipient's remarriage or the death of either party. Many states today also reduce or terminate spousal support upon the recipient's cohabitation. How did the issue of the ex-wife's cohabitation arise in *Mennen*?

2. **Automatic versus discretionary?** State laws vary in terms of their approach to reduction or termination of spousal support upon cohabitation. Some states reduce or terminate spousal support automatically regardless of a diminution in the recipient's need whereas other states require proof. Laws in the former jurisdictions incorporate an implicit assumption of a reduction in need if the spousal support recipient engages in cohabitation. The latter states require an explicit showing. Which approach does *Mennen* follow? Which approach do you prefer?

One factor in some states that triggers the cohabitation rule (or serves as a factor for consideration) is the length of time that the couple shares a residence. Durational requirements range from three months (Massachusetts) to one year (North Dakota, Virginia). Does living with a new romantic partner for a fixed period necessarily constitute a change in financial circumstances? How does New Jersey law, according to *Mennen*, address the duration of cohabitation?

3. **Factors.** The definition of "cohabitation" varies for purposes of modification or termination of spousal support. A common element is "holding out." Borrowed from definitions of common law marriage, the idea of holding out necessitates that the cohabiting parties have a marriage-like arrangement. What did the Mennens' marital settlement agreement require in terms of holding out? What did the state statute require? Did Mrs. Mennen and her new intimate partner (J.K.) have a marriage-like arrangement, according to the court? Which aspects of marriage were present? Which were absent? Based on New Jersey law, how relevant are such factors in holding out as financial interdependence, sexual relations, monogamy, full-time co-residence, intent to form a permanent relationship, shared children, or shared childcare tasks? How did these factors apply to Mrs. Mennen's relationship with J.K.? How relevant should such factors be? Should cohabitation be a factor in reduction or termination of *any* type of spousal support (i.e., reimbursement alimony, rehabilitative spousal support)?

4. **Evidence.** When the issue of cohabitation arises for purposes of spousal support modification, former spouses often argue about whether the new relationship rises to the requisite "cohabitation." The payor-spouse generally introduces evidence that the alimony recipient refutes. Sometimes children's statements about overnight visits are admissible. What evidence did the ex-husband in *Mennen* introduce? How

did the ex-wife refute that evidence? Based on the evidence, how did the court rule? Should there be limits on the admissibility of such evidence? How can a payor-spouse show that the recipient spouse is reporting a "phantom" residence while actually living with the new partner so that the recipient spouse can continue receiving alimony?

5. Rationales. What are the rationales for the cohabitation termination rule? Does the rule comport with contemporary understandings of alimony as an entitlement to compensation for reliance, restitution, or partnership interests in a past marriage? To what extent does the rule constitute a violation of privacy? Or, in other words, why is a spousal support recipient's sex life the business of her former spouse? Should the cohabitation rule be abandoned and changes in a recipient's economic circumstance be addressed by a general changed-circumstance modification rule without regard to the alimony recipient's intimate relationships?

6. Changed circumstances: Obligor. Traditionally, changes in either former spouse's circumstances may warrant reduction or termination of the spousal support obligation. What changes in the *obligor*'s circumstances should be relevant? See Delsing v. Delsing, 409 S.W.3d 574 (Mo. Ct. App. 2013) (medical injury to professional golfer). Should an increase in the obligor's income justify an upward modification? See Dan v. Dan, 105 A.3d 188 (Conn. 2014).

7. Forfeiture for acts of violence. Some states consider the role of domestic violence in awards of spousal support. California takes the strictest approach, disqualifying some abusers from receiving spousal support. See, e.g., Cal. Fam. Code §4324.5 (disqualifying felon convicted of sexual domestic violence from award of spousal support); Cal. Fam. Code §4234 (same for felon convicted of attempted murder of spouse). For domestic violence misdemeanants, California law creates a rebuttable presumption against an award of spousal support (Cal. Fam. Code §4325). Should a conviction be required to preclude spousal support? Why? Compare La. Civ. Code Ann. art. 112(B)(9) (court shall consider domestic abuse regardless of whether perpetrator was prosecuted).

In addition, some states mandate consideration of domestic violence in the distribution of property between divorcing spouses. See, e.g., N.Y. Dom. Rel. Law (DRL) §236B(5)(d)(14) (courts must consider "whether either party has committed an act or acts of domestic violence . . . and the nature, extent, duration and impact of such act or acts."). A recent California law extends such awards of property division to retirement benefits. See Cal. Fam. Code §4324.5(4). Do these statutes undermine no-fault divorce?

Neither UMDA nor the ALI Principles take domestic violence into account in determining awards of spousal support or property division. However, Professor Ira Ellman (Reporter for the ALI Principles) rejects a forfeiture rule for spousal support awards, even in cases of attempted murder, by reasoning that "the appropriate recourse is the same whether or not the perpetrator is the victim's spouse: the remedies provided by the tort law and the criminal justice system."[15] Do you find this view persuasive?

---

[15]. Ira Mark Ellman, The Place of Fault in a Modern Divorce Law, 28 Ariz. L.J. 773, 804 (1996). See generally Tiffany Sala, Comment, What Do You Get When You Abuse Your Spouse? Spousal Support, 50 U. Pac. L. Rev. 735 (2019).

Problems

1. An alimony reform bill has been introduced in the state of Blackacre. An objective of the proposed legislation, similar to that of the Massachusetts law above, is to terminate alimony upon the payor's retirement. In introducing the bill, the primary sponsor explained that when the payor's income decreases after retirement, payment of alimony at the same level as before retirement "creates a heavy burden and hardship."

The bill would provide retired payor-spouses with the right to request a hearing to determine whether retirement constitutes a substantial change in circumstances to warrant modification or termination of alimony. The bill provides the court with the following factors to consider when deciding whether to modify or terminate alimony:

(1) Whether retirement was contemplated when alimony was awarded
(2) The age of the supporting spouse
(3) The health of the supporting spouse
(4) Whether the retirement is mandatory or voluntary
(5) Whether retirement would result in a decrease in the supporting spouse's income
(6) Any other factors the court sees fit.

You serve as an aide to a law reform commission that is considering adoption of the above bill. How does the proposed bill compare to the Massachusetts Alimony Reform Act? How does it compare to UMDA §316 allowing termination or modification upon a showing of changed circumstances? Should retirement warrant termination of alimony or only a downward modification? Should retirement result in a rebuttable presumption that alimony shall terminate when the obligor spouse or partner attains retirement age? Can you prevent a payor-spouse from avoiding alimony obligations by taking early retirement? See N.J. Stat. Ann. §2A:34-23(j)(2). Which approach to reform do you favor—a presumption that alimony terminates upon retirement or a law that conditions modification or termination on fact-specific inquiries related to the parties' circumstances? Why? What other approaches should the commission consider? See S.C. Code Ann. §20-3-170.

2. Bill and Melissa divorce after almost 30 years of marriage. Their marital settlement agreement provides that Bill's alimony obligation ($2,250/monthly) shall terminate upon the death of either party or remarriage or cohabitation. Melissa, a retired school secretary, has a monthly pension of $1,000. She works part time in a clerical position but suffers from chronic fatigue syndrome stemming from thyroid cancer, which she manages with surgery and medication. Melissa took in a tenant for about a year, but the tenant paid no rent in return for doing yard work and maintenance. Melissa has an intimate partner (of 10+ years), with whom she spends weekends, vacations, entertains, and shares household chores. She and her partner hold themselves out as a couple. They have separate residences about 40 miles apart. They have keys to each other's house but enter each other's home only with permission. The partners do not contribute to each other's mortgage or utilities and do not leave personal items at each other's houses. Melissa lists her partner as her beneficiary on all her benefits policies.

Bill sold his funeral director business recently for $3 million and now earns $76,000 as a consultant. He has an investment portfolio exceeding $2 million. He has remarried and is the primary caretaker of his second wife, who is disabled due to cancer. He and his second wife recently purchased a beach house and, due to increased expenses from this purchase and his wife's disability, he files for termination of alimony to Melissa based on "substantial changed circumstances," as well as Melissa's cohabitation with her partner. What result? See Fletcher v. Feutz, 246 A.3d 540 (Del. 2021).

b. Bankruptcy

HOWARD v. HOWARD
336 S.W.3d 433 (Ky. 2011)

MINTON, C.J. . . .

[In dissolving the marriage of Roy Shane Howard and Sondra Howard, the trial court divided the parties' marital property and marital debts, assigning to Shane liability for a National City loan on the parties' Dodge Durango, which was repossessed by the time of the divorce decree. Shane was also ordered to pay child support. Shortly thereafter, in a separate proceeding, Shane successfully filed a bankruptcy petition in federal court for a Chapter 7 discharge of his debts; Sondra, who received notice of the bankruptcy proceeding, did nothing to challenge the discharge of his debts.

Shane then returned to state court, seeking to reduce his child support obligation, claiming health problems, inability to find correctional work (based on his prior job as a prison guard), and the bankruptcy discharge that he received after entry of the divorce decree. In this modification proceeding, Sondra successfully moved to have Shane held in contempt for failure to pay the debt on the repossessed Durango, for which she had been subjected to collection efforts by the creditor. Shane appealed, citing his bankruptcy discharge. The state Court of Appeals affirmed the contempt finding, reasoning that Shane had an obligation to pay the Durango debt under the divorce decree based on the Bankruptcy Abuse Prevention and Consumer Protection Act (BAPCPA).]

The Court of Appeals noted that this statute had been amended, effective in 2005, to provide that discharge under Chapter 7 does not discharge the debtor from any debt "to a spouse, former spouse, or child" for something other than a "domestic support obligation" (i.e., child support or maintenance) that "is incurred by the debtor in the course of a divorce or separation or in connection with a separation agreement, divorce decree, or other order of a court of record, or a determination made in accordance with State or territorial law by a governmental unit." [Shane appeals to this court.]

As the Court of Appeals states, obviously Shane had an obligation to pay the Durango debt under the divorce decree. But the tricky question is whether this was a debt to his former spouse that would not be subject to discharge under the post-BAPCPA version of 11 U.S.C. §523(a)(15). Obviously, Shane was not required to make a direct payment to Sondra under the relevant divorce decree provision, which simply stated that he was responsible for making payments to the creditor. . . .

Following the BAPCPA amendments, 11 U.S.C. §523(a)(5) recognized an exception to discharge for debts "for a domestic support obligation" without explicitly requiring that such debts be to a spouse, former spouse, or child.[25] On the other hand, 11 U.S.C. §523(a)(15) was amended to add language requiring that other divorce-related debts be "to a spouse, former spouse, or child of the debtor" to be excepted from discharge.[26] 11 U.S.C. §523(a)(15) was also amended to delete the former language that allowed for discharge if the debtor was not reasonably able to pay the debt and the benefits to the debtor outweighed the detriment to the other person(s) affected.

[Under BAPCPA, if] the obligation to make payments on the bank loan on the repossessed Durango meets the requirements of 11 U.S.C. §523(a)(15) as a debt to Sondra under the divorce decree, then Sondra is correct that she was not required to file anything in bankruptcy court in order later to obtain enforcement of Shane's obligation to her under the divorce decree in state court. We conclude that the obligation does meet the requirements of 11 U.S.C. §523(a)(15) and that Sondra was not required to file anything in bankruptcy court regarding Shane's Chapter 7 filing in order to preserve her right to enforcement in state court of Shane's obligation to her under the divorce decree. . . .

Actually, in the divorce decree provision incorporating the parties' agreement that Shane would make the payments on the bank loan on the repossessed Durango, "two distinct obligations" are at issue. Naturally, there is an underlying marital debt on the bank loan on the repossessed Durango. But the divorce decree also establishes a separate obligation to Sondra that Shane make payments on this loan as part of the division of marital property and debts even though there is no hold harmless provision. . . .

While the debtor's obligation on an underlying debt to a third-party creditor may be discharged because that underlying debt was not *to a spouse or former spouse or child*, the weight of authority holds that a separate, otherwise enforceable, obligation to one's present or former spouse under a separation agreement or a divorce decree to make payments on third-party debt is not dischargeable in Chapter 7 bankruptcy following the BAPCPA amendments. Our holding today is premised on the broad definition of debt encompassed within the bankruptcy statutes. This holding is especially clear in cases where the debtor-spouse has not only been ordered to, or agreed to, pay the debt, but has also been ordered to, or agreed to, hold the other spouse harmless or indemnify the other spouse.

When one spouse's obligation to make payments on third-party debt under a separation agreement or divorce decree is not accompanied by a hold harmless

---

25. 11 U.S.C. §523(a)(5) (2007) states that a Chapter 7 discharge does not discharge the debtor for a debt "for a domestic support obligation." 11 U.S.C. §101(14A)(B) (2007) defines a *domestic support obligation* as one "in the nature of alimony, maintenance or support. . . ."

26. 11 U.S.C. §523(a)(15) (2007) (stating that a Chapter 7 discharge does not discharge the debtor for a debt "to a spouse, former spouse, or child of the debtor and not of the kind described in paragraph 5 that is incurred by the debtor in the course of a divorce or separation or in connection with a separation agreement, divorce decree or other of a court of record, or a determination made in accordance with State or territorial law by a governmental unit.").

or indemnification clause [as here], the law is perhaps somewhat less settled. But some courts have still recognized that even in the absence of an indemnification or hold harmless provision, the debtor spouse's divorce-related obligation to make payments on third party debt is not dischargeable.. . . .

In view of the broad definition of debt under federal bankruptcy law and a Kentucky trial court's authority to use its contempt powers to enforce obligations under divorce decrees, we conclude that Shane's obligation to Sondra under the divorce decree for him to make payments on the bank loan debt on the repossessed Durango was not discharged in Chapter 7 bankruptcy. . . .

Notes and Questions

1. **Background.**   Bankruptcy and divorce often coincide. The three most common reasons for bankruptcies are job loss, dissolution, and health problems. Under the Bankruptcy Code, when an individual petitions for bankruptcy, the debtor's property becomes part of the bankrupt's "estate," distributed among creditors. 11 U.S.C. §541. To further the protective policy of bankruptcy, the debtor may claim exemption for certain property (e.g., a home or car). The Code also allows a debtor spouse to be discharged from certain obligations. The long-standing nondischargeability of spousal support obligations derives from judicial origin, but the rule was subsequently codified and extended to child support in 1903 amendments to the Bankruptcy Act of 1898.[16] By contrast, the debtor could discharge obligations based on a property division. What reasons explain the different treatment?

2. **Bankruptcy reform.**   As *Howard* explains, BAPCPA, which now applies to Chapter 7 bankruptcies, makes nondischargeable a "domestic support obligation," such as maintenance and child support obligations. 11 U.S.C. §523(a)(5). In addition, the statute makes nondischargeable other divorce- or separation-related obligations to a spouse, former spouse, or child—that is, those that are not "domestic support obligations" (see id. §523(a)(15))—thus eliminating the different treatment of support and property that had bedeviled judges. See, e.g., In re Taylor, 737 F.3d 670 (10th Cir. 2013) (statutory history and analysis). On the other hand, the support/property classification continues to control dischargeability in Chapter 13 bankruptcies. Id. at §1328(a)(2) (excepting from discharge §523(a)(5) obligations but not §523(a)(15) obligations).

Most bankruptcies are filed under either Chapter 7 or Chapter 13. A Chapter 13 bankruptcy is a reorganization bankruptcy for debtors with sufficient income to pay back all or a portion of their debts through a repayment plan (while allowing debtors to keep all or a substantial part of that property). In contrast, Chapter 7 is a liquidation bankruptcy (intended for people with more limited incomes) that eliminates most general unsecured debts (credit cards, medical bills) through

---

[16]. Jana B. Singer, Divorce Obligations and Bankruptcy Discharge: Rethinking the Support/ Property Distinction, 30 Harv. J. Legis. 43, 47, 53 (1993).

the sale of the debtor's assets (while allowing the debtor to keep limited exempt property).

3. Policy. State and federal courts have concurrent jurisdiction to construe a discharge and determine whether it includes a particular debt. What is the proper balance between bankruptcy law's objective of a "fresh start" for debtors and the fair resolution of the financial incidents of divorce? Why does BAPCPA continue to allow discharge of property division obligations in Chapter 13 bankruptcies? When categorizing obligations, how does a bankruptcy judge discern whether a particular divorce award constitutes spousal support or an allocation of property? Cases under both the new and old statutes reveal judicial efforts to enlarge the definition of "support" and "alimony" to thwart the debtor's attempted discharge. See, e.g., Quinn v. Quinn, 528 B.R. 203 (Bankr. D. Mass. 2015) (construing indemnification payments on second mortgage as nondischargeable "support," although parties waived alimony); Deichert v. Deichert, 587 A.2d 319 (Pa. Super. Ct. 1991) (classifying divorce award to wife of family home and car as nondischargeable support in shelter and transportation). To what extent does *Howard* illustrate this expansive approach?

4. Automatic stay. Bankruptcy law makes distinguishing support and property distribution obligations important for purposes of the automatic stay. When a person files for bankruptcy, a court order (called the "automatic stay") stops most civil lawsuits against the person and most collection actions against the person's property. The purpose of an automatic stay is to free debtors from the psychological toll of collection efforts. However, the automatic stay cannot prevent a lawsuit seeking to establish, modify, or collect child support or alimony. Note that the automatic stay only applies to those "domestic support obligations" that the debtor has specifically listed in his or her bankruptcy petition as part of the debtor's estate.

5. Debtor's bad faith. Under earlier versions of the bankruptcy law, obligors sometimes were able to manipulate settlement agreements to be in property terms rather than alimony terms, and thereby discharge their marital obligations in bankruptcy. How far does BAPCPA go in addressing this problem? Does the debtor's bad faith in filing for bankruptcy justify dismissing the bankruptcy petition altogether? 1 U.S.C.A. §707(b)(3)(A). Does bad faith require a dishonest motivation or simply a purpose inconsistent with bankruptcy law? See In re Bozard, 587 B.R. 656 (Bankr. D.S.C. 2018) (factors to assess bad faith may involve eve-of-bankruptcy purchases, filing incomplete or false schedules, or failure to cooperate with the bankruptcy trustee).

6. Indemnification. Marital settlements agreements can avert the problem experienced by the ex-wife in *Howard* by inclusion of a well-drafted indemnification and hold-harmless clause. Such a clause requires each spouse to "indemnify and hold harmless" the other spouse from debts assigned to one party, provided that the right to indemnification is specified as an element of support that one spouse owes to the other. Although such a clause may be included either in a marital settlement agreement or a divorce decree, neither apparently occurred here. What is the debtor-spouse's financial obligation to the other spouse in the absence of such a clause, according to *Howard*? Is that obligation dischargeable in a Chapter 7 bankruptcy in such a situation?

NOTE: THE FAMILY HOME

Frequently, the family home is the most significant asset of the divorcing couple. If the marital home is the separate property of one spouse, then the court awards the home to that spouse. This result follows unless the other spouse made contributions to the preservation and appreciation of the home, such that any increased equity during marriage becomes a divisible asset.

The situation becomes more complicated when the family home is marital property or community property. Rules requiring or favoring equal division of marital property often result in the sale of the family home. If the couple has no asset of comparable value to allocate to the spouse not to be awarded the home, the home must be sold so that the proceeds can be shared, to the disadvantage of children. To remedy this problem, some states allow courts to award the family home, at least temporarily, to the custodial parent, treating use of the residence as a form of child support and reflecting reluctance to uproot the children. See, e.g., Cal. Fam. Code §3802; ALI Principles §§3.11, 4.09(3). Commonly, a judge awards one spouse the marital home to live in until the youngest child turns 18, at which point the house must be sold. As part of this "deferred distribution" award, a court will usually require one or both spouses to cover maintenance fees, taxes, mortgage payments, and homeowner's insurance. If both parties remain on the mortgage, such a plan may make it difficult for the person who has moved out to obtain another mortgage to purchase a home elsewhere. Alternatively, if the family home represents a liability because of a large mortgage, the court can allocate responsibility for the debts in the distribution of property. The court generally assigns higher mortgage debt to the spouse who makes significantly more than the other spouse.

c. Pensions and Employee Benefits

BENDER v. BENDER

785 A.2d 197 (Conn. 2001)

Borden, J.

The principal issue in this certified appeal is whether, in a dissolution action, unvested pension benefits are property subject to equitable distribution. . . . The plaintiff and the defendant, who were married in 1976, have four children, two of whom were minors at the time of trial. . . . The principal cause for the breakdown of the marriage was the fact that nearly all of the defendant's free time was spent in pursuits that did not include the plaintiff or their children, [his] at least one adulterous relationship [and] some violence on the part of the defendant. Despite the defendant's fairly good income, . . . the parties had acquired virtually no assets and no savings. Furthermore, nearly all of the parties' discretionary income had been expended on the defendant's personal pursuits.

. . . At the time of trial, the defendant had been employed as a firefighter by the city of Meriden for approximately nineteen years. The defendant is entitled to a pension as a firefighter in the event that he reaches twenty-five years of service. His pension, therefore, is unvested, except for purposes of disability. If the defendant were to leave the fire department before twenty-five years of service, other than for a disability, he would receive only his contributions made to the pension, which, at the time of trial, were valued at approximately $27,741. . . .

[Defendant claims] that his unvested pension benefits are not property subject to equitable distribution under §46b-81. The plaintiff claims, to the contrary, that the defendant's interest in his unvested pension benefits is not a mere expectancy, but rather, a presently existing property interest, and, therefore, his unvested pension benefits constitute property subject to equitable distribution. We agree with the plaintiff.

The threshold question of whether unvested pension benefits constitute "property" pursuant to §46b-81 presents a question of statutory interpretation. . . . "Neither §46b-81 nor any other closely related statute defines property or identifies the types of property interests that are subject to equitable distribution in dissolution proceedings. . . . Black's Law Dictionary (6th Ed. 1990) defines property as the term commonly used to denote everything which is the subject of ownership, corporeal or incorporeal, tangible or intangible, visible or invisible, real or personal; everything that has an exchangeable value or which goes to make up wealth or estate. It extends to every species of valuable right and interest, and includes real and personal property, easements, franchises, and incorporeal hereditaments. . . ."

[Although this is a case of first impression, in past cases, we] repeatedly have stated, and several recent decisions from this court reflect, that trial courts are empowered "to deal broadly with property and its equitable division incident to dissolution proceedings." . . . In Thompson v. Thompson, 438 A.2d 839 [(Conn. 1981), we considered evidence of the pension benefits but did not treat them as property to be divided.] We reasoned that "[p]ension benefits represent a form of deferred compensation for services rendered. In re Marriage of Brown, 544 P.2d 561 [(Cal. 1976)]. As such they are conceptually similar to wages. . . ."

In Krafick v. Krafick, [663 A.2d 365 (Conn. 1995),] we concluded that *vested* pension benefits constitute property for the purposes of equitable distribution pursuant to §46b-81. In doing so, we emphasized that a broad construction of the term "property" is consistent with the purpose of §46b-81, namely, "to recognize that marriage is, among other things, a shared enterprise or joint undertaking in the nature of a partnership to which both spouses contribute—directly and indirectly, financially and nonfinancially—*the fruits of which* are distributable at divorce." We also recognized, however, that . . . "§46b-81 applies only to presently existing property interests, not mere expectancies." We thereafter engaged in an analysis whereby we determined that the contingencies to which the vested pension benefits were subject did not render them a mere expectancy because the holder of the benefits had a presently existing interest by way of an enforceable contract right. [Our] cases reflect a common theme, namely, that in determining whether a certain interest is property subject to equitable distribution under

§46b-81, we look to whether a party's expectation of a benefit attached to that interest was too speculative to constitute divisible marital property. . . .

In the present case, it is, of course, theoretically possible that the defendant's pension will not vest, whether because of the defendant's resignation, misconduct on his part that results in his dismissal, the defendant's death, or a decision on the part of the municipality to discontinue the pension plan. We conclude, however, that the defendant's expectation in his pension plan, as a practical matter, is sufficiently concrete, reasonable and justifiable as to constitute a presently existing property interest for equitable distribution purposes. Therefore, his unvested pension benefits are not too speculative to be considered property subject to equitable distribution under §46b-81. We believe that any uncertainty regarding vesting is more appropriately handled in the valuation and distribution stages, rather than in the classification stage.

Our conclusion that the defendant's unvested pension benefits are not a mere expectancy is consistent with the nature of retirement benefits, and the fact that employers and employees treat retirement benefits as property in the workplace. We previously have stated [in *Krafick*, supra] that "pension benefits represent a form of deferred compensation for services rendered" because an employee earning pension benefits presumably would receive higher current wages if he or she did not participate in the pension plan. . . .

Furthermore, the theme running through this area of our jurisprudence . . . pays mindful consideration to the equitable purpose of our statutory distribution scheme, rather than to mechanically applied rules of property law. . . . In view of that equitable purpose, the fact remains that nineteen of the twenty-five years necessary for the vesting of the defendant's pension benefits were years in which the parties were partners in marriage. We recognize that retirement benefits, whether vested or unvested, are significant marital assets, and may be, as in the present case, the only significant marital asset. To consider the pension benefits a nondivisible marital asset would be to blink our eyes at reality.

The defendant argues that the portion of his pension benefits that "would result from [his] future labors" is not subject to equitable distribution, and that the only portion subject to equitable distribution is the amount of the contributions in the fund at the time of dissolution. We disagree. The fact that a portion of the pension benefits, once vested, will represent the defendant's service to the fire department after the dissolution does not preclude us from classifying the entire unvested pension as marital property. . . .

ZARELLA, J., dissenting. . . .

[A]lthough unvested pension benefits should not be classified as property subject to equitable distribution, §46b-81(c) requires the trial court to *consider* them in fashioning property distribution orders at the time of dissolution. When a pension benefit becomes vested and is in payment status, the trial court may treat this situation as a changed circumstance warranting a modification of an award of periodic alimony under §46b-86. This approach remains faithful to the case law, the language of the relevant statutes and the legislative intent to expand the resources available for equitable distribution. . . .

Notes and Questions

1. Pensions at divorce. Pension benefits constitute a significant component of marital assets for many divorcing couples. In most states, retirement plan assets earned during a marriage are considered as marital property that can be divided.

2. Majority rule and rationale. Virtually all jurisdictions follow the approach in *Bender*: Nonvested, as well as vested, pensions are marital property subject to division upon dissolution. What arguments support recognition of vested pensions as marital assets? Nonvested pensions as marital assets? Do pension benefits constitute mere expectancies (like an anticipated inheritance), rather than property interests? How does the *Bender* majority answer this question? The dissent? Should a court consider such contingent interests in determining support rather than property distribution (say, on the theory of compensable loss under the ALI Principles §5.04, supra p. 554)?

3. Integrating federal and state law. The important role of pension plans in dissolution requires analysis under both federal and state law.

a. Federal regulation of private pension plans: ERISA and REA. The Employee Retirement Income Security Act of 1974, or ERISA, is a comprehensive federal law that protects employees' assets in retirement plans so that these assets will be available to them upon retirement. 29 U.S.C. §§1001 et seq. ERISA explicitly preempts state law. As originally enacted, ERISA failed to make adequate consideration for the division of pension benefits upon divorce. ERISA limited the right of the nonemployee spouse (e.g., the wife of a covered employee) to share in the employee's pension upon dissolution by an "anti-alienation rule" that barred assignment or alienation of pension plan benefits. This highly protective policy aimed to ensure that the employee-spouse could not consume retirement savings before retirement. Enacted in 1974 before no-fault divorce was widespread, ERISA made no exceptions for domestic relations claims against an employee's pension plan.

The Retirement Equity Act of 1984 (REA) remedied this problem (experienced primarily by divorced wives) by requiring that the anti-alienation rule must yield to certain state domestic relations decrees—thereby permitting a court to divide pension benefits in the same manner as other marital assets. In short, REA amended ERISA to provide for the enforcement of "qualified domestic relations orders" (QDROs) and removed such orders from ERISA's preemption scheme. See ERISA §§206(d)(3), 514(b)(7), 29 U.S.C. §§1056(d)(3), 1144(b)(7).

b. QDROs. Under REA, a QDRO means a domestic relations order "which creates or recognizes the existence of an alternate payee's right to, or assigns to an alternate payee the right to, receive all or a portion of the benefits payable with respect to a participant under a plan"; for purposes of this provision, a domestic relations order is a judgment, decree, or order "which relates to the provision of child support, alimony payments, or marital property rights to a spouse, former spouse, child, or other dependent of a participant," made "pursuant to a State domestic relations law (including a community property law)." ERISA §206(d)(3)(B), 29 U.S.C. §1056(d)(3)(B).

To qualify as a plan beneficiary under a QDRO, the nonemployee spouse must obtain a state court decree that specifies the extent to which the plan participant's liability shall be paid from pension assets. Note that pension assets can be distributed under a QDRO not only for property division, but also for spousal and child support obligations.

QDROs facilitate collection of divorce awards by directing retirement plan administrators to make payments *directly* to the "alternate payee." However, QDROs have some limitations. The extent of the nonemployee spouse's benefits is governed by those of the employee spouse—that is, the nonemployee former spouse may not obtain a lump sum distribution, for example, if this option is not available to the employee.

c. Federal pension benefits. Federal retirement benefit plans cover certain government employees. In response to U.S. Supreme Court cases holding that federal law prevented state divorce courts from dividing federal pension benefits, Congress enacted corrective legislation. For example, the federal Uniformed Services Former Spouses' Protection Act (USFSPA), 10 U.S.C. §1408, provides certain benefits to former spouses of military members and authorizes states to treat veterans' "disposable retired pay" as community property divisible upon divorce.

Suppose that after a state court divides the military pension, the military spouse converts the retirement pay to service-related disability pay. Can state courts treat the waived portion of military retirement pay as a divisible community asset? See Howell v. Howell, 581 U.S. 214 (2017) (holding that USFSPA preempted states from treating as divisible community property the military retirement pay that a veteran has waived in order to receive nontaxable service-related disability benefits, thereby preventing states from ordering reimbursement to the recipient-spouse to restore that portion of retirement pay lost due to the payor-spouse's post-divorce waiver).

4. Pension valuation and distribution. Various methods are utilized to value pensions. Three common methods include (1) the present value or immediate offset approach (after determining the present value of pension benefits and the portion to which the nonemployee spouse is entitled, a court awards other property to the nonemployee spouse as an offset to the latter's share of pension benefits); (2) the present division method (which determines at trial the percentage share of pension benefits to which the nonemployee spouse is entitled upon maturity); (3) the reserved jurisdiction method (reserves jurisdiction to distribute the pension until benefits have matured). Pension valuation and distribution often require the assistance of actuarial experts.

Problem

Karen and Robert divorce after 26 years of marriage. Karen, a part-time secretary for a church, is earning $645 per month; Robert, an employee of Miller Brewing Co., earns $2,900 per month. In the division of marital property, Robert receives his pension, valued at $11,355, and Karen receives property of roughly the same value (but no interest in Robert's pension). The court orders Robert to pay Karen $600 per month for maintenance. After taking voluntary retirement at age 55,

Robert now seeks to terminate maintenance payments, arguing that he has no income available. Karen seeks to continue maintenance, arguing that the $2,700 per month that Robert gets from his pension is income available for maintenance. What result, and why? Is it unfair "double counting" to consider Robert's pension plan both as an asset in the property division and as income for maintenance payments? See In re Marriage of Olski, 540 N.W.2d 412 (Wis. 1995). See also, e.g., N.J. Stat. Ann. §2A:34-23(b); Kazakis v. Kazakis, 2013 WL 5476330 (Ohio Ct. App. 2013); Donald J. DeGrazia & Stacy Preston Collins, The Double-Dipping Arguments, 31 Fam. Advoc. 16 (Spring 2009).

NOTE: MEDICAL COVERAGE FOLLOWING DISSOLUTION

Many women risk losing their health care coverage after divorce if they were previously on their husbands' health care plan. Concern about the high cost of medical insurance and its unavailability for dependent ex-spouses resulted in the 1985 enactment of the Consolidated Omnibus Budget Reconciliation Act (COBRA). 29 U.S.C. §§1161-1168. COBRA requires employers with group health plans to offer continued coverage at group rates to "qualified beneficiaries" who otherwise would lose benefits upon the occurrence of a "qualifying event." Qualifying events include divorce and legal separation (as well as job loss and the employee's death, among other events). A nonemployee spouse is entitled to continued coverage for 36 months following the date of divorce or legal separation. Coverage may not be conditioned on evidence of insurability. The qualified beneficiary must pay the required premiums after the COBRA election. Several states supplement COBRA by providing for continuation coverage for a limited period of time past the federal cut-off date. E.g., Cal. Ins. Code §10116.5; N.Y. Ins. Law §4305(e).

The Affordable Care Act (ACA) also has an impact on divorce. The ACA opens up alternatives beyond COBRA for divorcing couples. Therefore, a divorced spouse will have more health insurance options if she or he finds that COBRA coverage is too costly or will not last for as long as coverage is needed. For example, after passage of the ACA, former spouses may seek health insurance coverage through health insurance exchanges in their home state. This health insurance is generally less expensive than COBRA. In addition, subsidies may be available through the ACA to people who meet income qualifications.

d. Investments in a Spouse's Future Success: Degrees, Earning Capacity, and Goodwill

IN RE MARRIAGE OF ROBERTS
670 N.E.2d 72 (Ind. Ct. App. 1996)

Garrard, Judge. . . .

[Matthew and Leigh Anne Roberts] were married on June 24, 1989. In the fall of 1990, Matthew began attending the Valparaiso University Law School as a full-time student. Before law school, Matthew had been employed at Society Bank in

South Bend, Indiana and had been earning a salary of $30,000.00 per year at the time he left employment. Matthew and Leigh Anne agreed that Matthew should quit working and attend school full-time while Leigh Anne continued to work to support them. Leigh Anne also assumed primary responsibility for running the household so that Matthew could devote all of his time to his studies.

Two months before Matthew's graduation, Leigh Anne learned that she was pregnant, and thereafter the couple separated. Matthew finished third in his graduating class and also served as editor-in-chief of the Valparaiso Law Review. After graduation, he took an associate position with a large law firm in Chicago, Illinois. He filed his petition for dissolution of marriage on August 4, 1993.

The major asset of the parties was the marital home, valued at $70,000.00 with a mortgage of $63,245.00. The parties also owned certain personal property and each had 401(k) accounts and IRA accounts. The court determined that Matthew's law degree could not be considered a marital asset subject to distribution. However, the court did include Matthew's student loans, totaling $22,500.00, in valuing the marital estate, and the court found repayment to be the sole responsibility of Matthew. The court determined that, based upon the student loans, the disproportionate earnings history and the earning potential of the parties, the presumption of equal distribution had been rebutted. The court [allocated to Matthew $22,084.96 total assets and $24,500 total debts, resulting in a net debt of $2,415.04; it allocated to Leigh Anne $90,779.98 total assets and $65,245.00 total debts, amounting to net assets of $25,534.98].

Leigh Anne first argues that the trial court should have included Matthew's law degree as a marital asset subject to distribution. . . .

The specific issue of whether a degree obtained during a marriage by one party may be considered marital property upon divorce was addressed in Prenatt v. Stevens, 598 N.E.2d 616 (Ind. Ct. App. 1992). In *Prenatt*, the trial court found that the wife's doctoral degree in English, which was obtained during the marriage, was a marital asset. This determination was reversed on appeal, with the court relying upon Wilcox v. Wilcox [365 N.E.2d 792 (Ind. Ct. App. 1977)] and In re Marriage of McManama [399 N.E.2d 371 (Ind. 1980)]. In *Wilcox*, the court first noted that any award over and above the assets of the marriage must represent some form of support or maintenance. The court then held that the husband's future earnings could not be considered a marital asset as there was no vested present interest in such income. In *McManama*, the trial court had awarded the wife a lump sum in the amount she had contributed to help her husband obtain his advanced degree on the theory that there had been a dissipation of marital property. Our supreme court reversed, finding that the award was in actuality an award to be paid from the husband's future income. Such an award of future income could only be proper as either support or maintenance, and there was no evidence of any incapacity to support such an award.

Based upon this precedent, *Prenatt* concluded that, despite the legislature's intent for "property" to be interpreted as broadly inclusive, a degree simply does not possess the common characteristics of property:

> A degree is an intangible which is personal to the holder. It is a piece of paper and has no real value except for what the holder chooses to pursue with it. Potential worth is dependent upon choice and availability of work, whether the holder is good at what she does, or a myriad of other potentialities.

Valuation of a degree is fraught with uncertainty because of the personal factors described above. Even if valuation could be made certain, such valuation, whether based on future earning capacity or upon cost of acquisition, would ultimately result in an award beyond the actual physical assets of the marriage. As noted in *Wilcox* and *McManama*, such award is improper.

Prenatt, 598 N.E.2d at 620.

The only statutory exception is I.C. §31-1-11.5-11(d), which states:

When the court finds there is little or no marital property, it may award either spouse a money judgment not limited to the property existing at the time of final separation. However, this award may be made only for the financial contribution of one (1) spouse toward tuition, books, and laboratory fees for the higher education of the other spouse.

Thus, a spouse may be reimbursed, even above the assets of the marital estate, but reimbursement is strictly limited.

We agree with the finding in *Prenatt* that a degree does not constitute marital property. [W]hile Indiana does not permit a degree to be included as marital property, and further will not allow an award of future earnings unless the spouse qualifies for maintenance, nevertheless the earning ability of the degree-earning spouse may be considered in determining the distribution of the marital estate. . . .

Leigh Anne also argues that the trial court should have made an award to compensate her for the dissipation of the marital estate by Matthew as a result of the income which the family was deprived of while Matthew attended law school and the contributions Leigh Anne made toward Matthew's education and the household living expenses. [I]n employing the term "dissipation," our legislature intended that it carry its common meaning denoting "foolishly" or "aimlessly." Thus, under the circumstances of this case it cannot be said that the money expended in order to secure Matthew's law degree was dissipated, even though Leigh Anne did not receive the benefits she expected therefrom. . . .

We affirm the judgment. . . .

Joan Williams, Is Coverture Dead? Beyond a New Theory of Alimony

82 Geo. L.J. 2227, 2267-2272, 2274-2275 (1994)

[In this article, Professor Joan Williams criticizes the application in license/degree cases of both property rhetoric as well as human capital theory (positing that workers can become more productive by emphasizing an investment in education to acquire skills and training).]

The typical degree case involves a wife who supported her husband through professional school and who claims "property in his degree" when he divorces her shortly after graduation. Courts, with few exceptions, have rejected wives' claims that the degrees are marital property, often using broad language to the effect that human capital does not have the attributes traditionally associated with property. To justify this rejection, courts rely on the traditional Blackstonian image of property rights as the absolute dominion of people over things. This imagery, however, was never an accurate description of property law, and was formally abandoned in the First Restatement of Property in 1936. The 1936 Restatement adopted instead Wesley Hohfeld's view that property rights defined the relationships among people with respect to some valuable interest. The image is not of "absolute" ownership but of an evolving set of claims, in which courts attach the name "property" as a signal they have accepted someone's claim. . . .

[In most degree cases, the] court starts out with a predefined notion of what "property" entails. It then inquires whether a degree "fits" that image. Upon deciding that it does not, it concludes that no property right exists in the wife. . . . In contrast to the Hohfeldian view's message that "property" is a word courts use to signal their legal conclusion that someone has an entitlement, the [court's] language sends the message that judges play no active role in determining entitlements. But they do. Conclusions about property are legal conclusions, made in a context where the court has to allocate the asset to someone. . . .

Many modern property rights . . . clash with a model of absolute, alienable, inheritable, and exchangeable entitlements. Examples are pensions and goodwill which are widely recognized as property despite their lack of heritability and their status as income streams provided by "many years of . . . hard work." . . . Courts' refusal to recognize "new property" rights in the context of the family stems not from the logic of property, but from unstated assumptions about who is entitled to what. . . .

If the courts' projected image of property rights is so inaccurate and their property theory half a century out of date, why have the degree cases proved so convincing? . . . Family court judges, almost by definition, are successful lawyers. Most are men who have conformed to an ideal worker pattern in a profession notorious for long hours. This workaholic culture tends to marginalize the ideal workers' wives, as they assume more and more family responsibilities to allow for their husbands' "success." It is also the (upper-middle) class context in which the ideology of gender equality is strongest. In short, the judges in degree cases are heavily invested in the polite fiction—observed in most intact marriages—that the husband's career success and the wife's marginalization both result not from a system that privileges ideal workers who can command a flow of domestic services from women, but from the idiosyncrasies of two individuals residing in the republic of choice.

The degree cases also reflect judges' sense that they worked long and hard for their degrees. Their reaction is colored by their struggles in law school and their sense that they have earned everything they have achieved through their own hard work. That degree holders worked long and hard is not the issue. So did their wives, both in the home and (often) at boring, dead-end jobs, passing up opportunities for better positions. The issue is not who worked hard, but whose hard work gives rise to entitlements. . . .

Notes and Questions

1. Majority rule. *Roberts* follows the majority approach that refuses to treat advanced degrees and professional licenses, as well as the enhanced earning capacity therefrom, as marital property. Hence, the supporting spouse's contribution does not make them divisible assets upon divorce. Is Professor Williams's explanation for this rule persuasive?

2. Limited remedy. Although applying the majority rule, *Roberts* considers Matthew's enhanced earning capacity as a *factor* in the distribution of property. The court, in turn, approves a disproportionate division favoring Leigh Anne and assigns debts for Matthew's student loans exclusively to him. Is this approach fair? Suppose that the couple spent everything on the husband's degree, without accumulating any assets. Does the Indiana statute quoted in *Roberts* (now Ind. Code Ann. §31-15-7-6) solve the problem? Does this limited remedy result in unjust enrichment for Matthew? Alternatively, does the supporting spouse (Leigh Anne) deserve compensation not just for her financial contributions, but also for the loss of a return on her investment in his career?

3. Maintenance as a remedy? If the couple has no assets to divide, should a court recognize the supporting spouse's contribution by awarding maintenance? Does Leigh Anne *need* support? In contrast to *Roberts*, other authorities look to maintenance to provide a remedy. See, e.g., Tenn. Code §36-5-121(i)(10); In re Marriage of Andersen, 310 P.3d 1171 (Or. Ct. App. 2013). Which approach is preferable?

4. A fair result by any means. Some courts have used a flexible approach, stating that achieving a fair result is more important than whether a traditional "property" or "alimony" label fits. For example, in Washburn v. Washburn, 677 P.2d 152 (Wash. 1984) (en banc), the court declined to identify the husband's veterinary degree as property but went on to say:

> . . . A professional degree confers high earning potential upon the holder. The student spouse should not walk away with this valuable advantage without compensating the person who helped him or her obtain it.
>
> [T]he supporting spouse may be compensated through a division of property and liabilities. In many cases, however, the wealth of the marriage will have been spent toward the cost of the professional degree, leaving few or no assets to divide. Where the assets of the parties are insufficient to permit compensation to be effected entirely through property division, a supplemental award of maintenance is appropriate.
>
> [W]e recognize that the spouse who is capable of supporting someone through school will in most cases also be capable of supporting him or herself after the marriage is dissolved. However, under the extremely flexible provisions of [the statute], a demonstrated capacity of self-support does not automatically preclude an award of maintenance. . . . Id. at 158, 161.

Under the flexible approach above, how does a judge compute a fair result?

5. New York's property treatment. New York was a longstanding outlier in terms of its liberal treatment of degrees and professional licenses as marital property subject to equitable distribution. See O'Brien v. O'Brien, 489 N.E.2d 712 (N.Y. 1985) (requiring the court to award a certain percentage of the lifetime value of a license or degree to the supporting spouse for the contributions that the latter made toward the titled spouse's attainment of that license or degree). In 2016, the New York legislature reversed the *O'Brien* rule. Under the new law, professional degrees or licenses constitute only *one* factor in the determination of post-divorce maintenance and equitable distribution. See N.Y. Dom. Rel. Law (DRL) §236(B)(6)(d)(7).

6. ALI approach. The ALI Principles follow the majority rule in rejecting the treatment of earning capacity as divisible property. Instead, they provide for "compensatory spousal payments" to reimburse the supporting spouse for the financial contributions made to the other spouse's education or training. ALI Principles §§4.07, 5.12. For compensation under §5.12, the education must have been completed in less than a specified number of years (set out in a rule of statewide application) before the filing of the dissolution petition. Why?

7. Goodwill. In many states, "goodwill" is recognized as "property" that is subject to equitable distribution at divorce. Goodwill is an intangible asset arising as the result of name, reputation, customer loyalty, location, and products, among other factors. The majority approach distinguishes personal goodwill (*not* divisible property) and corporate goodwill (divisible property). See, e.g., Lamm v. Preston, 522 P.3d 1246 (Idaho Sup. Ct. 2023). The ALI Principles (§4.07) follow the majority approach.

8. Awards for lost future earnings. A common question is whether a personal injury award is subject to division at the time of the divorce. Personal injury awards are designed to compensate the injured party and, for that reason, are treated differently than other marital assets. The non-injured spouse is entitled to receive that portion of the settlement that relates to compensation for lost wages and payment for medical expenses. However, most of the injury settlement is allocated to the injured spouse. See, e.g., Benoit v. Benoit, 341 So. 3d 719 (La. Ct. App. 2022).

Problem

Upon dissolution of the 17-year marriage of New York opera singer Frederica von Stade Elkus, her husband argues that her career and celebrity status constitute marital property subject to equitable distribution. At the time of their marriage in 1973, von Stade had just begun her career and was performing minor roles with the Metropolitan Opera Company. During the marriage, she became a highly successful concert and television performer and international recording artist. Although in the first year of the marriage she earned $2,250, by 1989 she earned $621,878. During the marriage, von Stade's husband served as her voice coach and photographer, traveling with her, critiquing her performance, and photographing her for albums and magazine articles. He claims that he sacrificed his own career as an opera teacher and singer to devote himself to her career and to their two children. As a result of his efforts, Elkus contends that he is entitled to equitable distribution of the appreciation of the value of her career and her celebrity status as marital property.

According to New York Domestic Relations Law, marital property is defined as property acquired during the marriage "regardless of the form in which title is held." In enacting the Equitable Distribution Law, the legislature broadly defined the term "marital property" to give effect to the "economic partnership" concept of marriage.

What result and why? See Elkus v. Elkus, 572 N.Y.S.2d 901 (App. Div. 1991). Is celebrity status distinguishable from reputation, which courts in professional goodwill cases have held is not divisible? How should a court rule in a state without New York's expansive definition of property? See, e.g., Ketterle v. Ketterle, 814 N.E.2d 385, 387 (Mass. App. Ct. 2004) (characterizing Nobel Prize–winning husband's status as "superstar in the scientific and academic universe").

e. Taxation

The Internal Revenue Code specifies tax consequences for alimony and child support. This section summarizes important changes in federal tax reform legislation. (Note that state tax laws may differ from federal tax treatment.) Consider how the rules changed under the recent federal reform legislation. Consider also whom the old and new rules benefit—and disadvantage.

1. Tax Cuts and Jobs Act (TCJA) eliminates the tax deduction for alimony payments and no longer requires the recipient to report alimony as income. For the past 75 years, alimony payments received special treatment in federal tax law. Alimony payments were deductible by the payor spouse (IRC §215(a)) and were taxable as income to the recipient spouse (I.R.C. §61(a)(8)). These rules changed when Congress enacted the Tax Cuts and Jobs Act of 2017 (TCJA), Pub. L. No. 115-97, in December 2017. TCJA made several notable reforms regarding payment of alimony upon divorce.

The new law eliminates the deduction for payor-spouses for alimony payments that are required under divorce or separation instruments that are executed after December 31, 2018. TCJA §11051(b)(1)(c). Conversely, the recipients of alimony payments no longer have to report them as taxable income. TCJA §11051(a). For payor-spouses, this reform will be costly because the tax savings enjoyed by these spouses from being able to deduct their alimony payments was substantial.

2. Timing is vital. After the enactment of the TCJA, the timing of when a divorce is finalized or when a separation agreement is modified becomes vital. TCJA is effective for divorce or separation agreements (including divorce decrees, separate maintenance decrees, and written separation agreements) executed after December 31, 2018. The TCJA also applies to any divorce or separation instrument that was executed on or before December 31, 2018, *and* was modified after that date, if the modification expressly provides that the new tax laws apply to such modification. This new TCJA provision does not sunset, as some other provisions in the TCJA do.

3. No change occurs in the federal income tax treatment of divorce-related payments that are required by divorce agreements that were executed before December 31, 2018. Pre-TCJA rules continue to apply to already-existing divorces and separations, as well as divorces and separations that were executed before December 31, 2018. For these payments to qualify as deductible alimony, payor-spouses must have satisfied specific requirements. These requirements include the following: The payments had to be made pursuant to a written divorce or separation instrument; payment had to be made to or on behalf of a spouse or former spouse (not to third parties); payment had to be made in cash or a cash equivalent; the parties had to live separately and apart; the parties could no longer file a joint tax return; and the payor's obligation to make payments had to terminate after the death of the recipient. In other words, the language of the divorce decree and the parties' intent are not dispositive regarding federal income tax treatment.

4. Child support treatment is unchanged. Alimony does not include child support payments. Child support payments are generally not deductible by the payor-spouse and not included in the recipient-spouse's gross income. This rule remains unchanged.

E. Child Support

1. From Discretion to Guidelines

A child support award typically requires payment from the noncustodial parent to the custodial parent for the benefit of the child. Once, courts determined child support in the same way that they set alimony—using open-ended standards to reach unpredictable results. Now, however, the regime of judicial discretion has given way to a new approach prompted by federal legislation—the use by states of mathematical formulas called "guidelines." In the following materials, consider what objectives a child support award should seek to achieve and whether the current approach achieves these goals. Note that all material on child support applies equally to marital and nonmarital children.

TURNER v. TURNER
684 S.E.2d 596 (Ga. 2009)

THOMPSON, Justice.

Raymond and Jessica Turner were married in 1999 and had two children. Raymond filed for divorce in January 2008. The parties reached a partial settlement agreement which provided, inter alia, that husband and wife would share joint legal and physical custody of their two minor children, the custody arrangement being structured so husband is to have physical custody of the children from Friday A.M. until Tuesday A.M., and wife is to have physical custody from Tuesday

A.M. through Friday A.M., with exceptions for holidays and other special occasions. [S]ubmitted to the trial court for determination were issues of child support and the division of extracurricular expenses. [The court] entered a final judgment and divorce decree which incorporated the partial settlement agreement, ordered husband to pay $552.09 in monthly child support, and apportioned the expenses for the children's extracurricular activities two-thirds to husband and one-third to wife. [Husband appeals.]

The trial court's order includes a finding that husband earned gross monthly income of $5,483.56, approximately 65 percent of the parties' combined income. After determining a basic child support obligation of $1,582 for the parties' two minor children, the court calculated husband's pro rata share of the basic child support obligation to be $986.75. As evidenced in Schedule E attached to the court's order, however, the court applied a parenting time deviation of $434.66, reducing husband's monthly child support obligation to $552.09. [See Ga. Code Ann. (OCGA) §19-6-15(i)(2)(K).] Husband does not on appeal challenge the court's decision to deviate from the presumptive child support obligation. Instead, he contends the trial court erred by failing to explain how the court calculated the deviation and failing to include express findings that the deviation was in the best interests of the children and would not seriously impair his ability to provide for the children. We agree. . . .

[The applicable] guidelines permit the factfinder to deviate

> from the presumptive amount of child support when special circumstances make the presumptive amount of child support excessive or inadequate due to extended parenting time as set forth in the order of visitation or when the child resides with both parents equally.

OCGA §19-6-15(i)(2)(K)(i). Where a deviation is determined to apply and the factfinder deviates from the presumptive amount of child support, the order must explain the reasons for the deviation, provide the amount of child support that would have been required if no deviation had been applied, and state how application of the presumptive amount of child support would be unjust or inappropriate and how the best interest of the children for whom support is being determined will be served by the deviation. In addition, the order must include a finding that states how the court's or jury's application of the child support guidelines would be unjust or inappropriate considering the relative ability of each parent to provide support. Because the court in this case applied a discretionary parenting time deviation from the presumptive amount of child support but failed to make all of the findings required under [the statute], we reverse the trial court's final judgment and remand this case to the trial court for further proceedings consistent with this opinion.

[We also] address husband's challenge to the trial court's apportionment of the expenses of the children's extracurricular activities because that issue is likely to recur on remand. The trial court's order requires husband to pay two-thirds of the children's extracurricular activities. Husband contends he is paying twice for the cost of extracurricular activities because such costs are included in the presumptive amount of child support.

The language of OCGA §19-6-15(i)(2)(J)(ii) makes clear that a portion of the basic child support obligation is intended to cover average amounts of special expenses for raising children, including the cost of extracurricular activities. If a factfinder determines that the full amount of special expenses described in that division exceeds seven percent of the basic child support obligation, the "additional amount of special expenses shall be considered as a deviation to cover the full amount of the special expenses." Such a deviation must then be included in Schedule E of the Child Support Worksheet and, as with other deviations from the presumptive amount of child support, the factfinder must make the required written findings.

The trial court here made no provision in its Schedule E for a deviation for special expenses. Instead, the court included a provision in the final judgment apportioning among the parties the entire cost of the children's extracurricular expenses using essentially the same ratio as applied to the basic child support obligation. . . . Under the [applicable] guidelines, a court may only deviate from the presumptive child support amount based on special expenses incurred for child-rearing, including extracurricular expenses, by complying with OCGA §19-6-15(i)(2)(J)(ii) (defining "special expenses" as certain child-rearing expenses exceeding seven percent of basic child support obligation) and OCGA §19-6-15(i)(1)(B) (requiring written findings for all deviations). Thus, [the court] was without authority to make a separate child support award, one outside the parameters of the Child Support Worksheet, based on the cost of such activities. [Reversed and remanded.]

Notes and Questions

1. **Historical background.** Traditionally, American divorce law provided only vague guidance on setting postdissolution child support (e.g., awards that were "just," "reasonable," or "necessary"). Later, legislatures enacted statutes to guide judicial discretion. The result frequently was inadequate, inconsistent, and unpredictable awards that engendered disrespect for support orders and discouraged settlement. A few states responded by enacting *optional* guidelines. The fiscal burdens of providing subsidies to needy children also prompted federal concern. In 1984, Congress mandated that states use child support guidelines as rebuttable presumptions in "Title IV-D cases" (in which the state seeks to recover payments from an absent parent to support a needy child). In 1988, Congress extended the guidelines requirement to *all* cases as a condition for the receipt of federal welfare funds. 42 U.S.C. §667(a)-(b). The guidelines apply equally to marital and non-marital children.

2. **Objectives.** The unpredictability of judicial discretion was exacerbated by the absence of any clear theory or objective for child support awards. What purposes should an award seek to achieve? Fairness to the noncustodial parent? Prevention of child poverty? Support of children to the full extent possible? Continuation of the marital standard of living? Equalization of the standard of living in the custodial and noncustodial households? In such cases, how should child support relate to alimony? In other words, does ensuring a standard of living for the child guarantee the same for the custodial parent?

What objectives for child support does *Turner* suggest? The federal Advisory Panel on Child Support Guidelines recommends adherence to the following principles in developing guidelines: Both parents share responsibility for child support; parental subsistence needs should be considered; child support should cover a child's basic needs while allowing enjoyment of a parent's higher standard of living; each child has an equal right to share in a parent's income, subject to factors such as age, income, and the existence of other dependents; child support amounts should not depend on gender or the marital status of parents; guidelines should not create economic disincentives for remarriage or work; and guidelines should encourage the involvement of both parents in the child's life.[17] See also ALI Principles §3.04.

3. State responses. Jurisdictions complied with the federal mandate for guidelines in three ways.[18] All the models are designed to achieve uniformity and predictability, as *Turner* illustrates, by identifying a precise amount that the court presumptively orders. The income-shares model is the most popular approach, used by 41 states. These states rely on a chart that lists the share of combined parental income allocated for child support at different levels; parents divide the obligation in proportion to their incomes. The second model, the percentage-of-income approach, used by six states, allocates a fraction of the noncustodial parent's income for child support. This model sets support as a percentage of only the noncustodial parent's income; the custodial parent's income is not considered. Finally, three states (Delaware, Hawaii, and Montana) use the Melson formula, developed by a Delaware family court judge, which is a more complicated version of the income-shares model and is designed to ensure that each parent's basic needs are met in addition to the children's needs.

4. Similarities and differences. The above models have certain aspects in common: (1) they incorporate a reserve for the obligor's support; (2) they have a provision relating to imputed income for a parent who is voluntarily unemployed or underemployed to avoid having to make child support payments (a concept that is explored later in this chapter); (3) they take into consideration (by federal regulation) health care expenses for the children (see 42 U.S.C. §652(f); 45 C.F.R. §302.56); and (4) for the most part, they incorporate (into the presumptive child support formula) special additions for childcare expenses; special formulas for shared custody, split custody, and extraordinary visitation; and special deductions for the support of previous and subsequent children.

At the same time, important differences exist. The percentage-of-income model, although the most simple, has been criticized because the obligor pays the same dollar amount regardless of whether the custodial parent earns no income or an amount equal to that of the obligor (based on the implicit assumption that the custodial parent shares his or her income directly with the children). The income-shares model is perceived as the most fair by requiring both parents to make a monetary contribution and adopting a flexible approach in allowing for

[17]. See Laura W. Morgan, Child Support Guidelines: Interpretation and Application §1.04 (2d ed. 2012 & Supp. 2014).

[18]. See Nat'l Conf. of State Legislatures, Child Support Guidelines Model (July 10, 2020), https://www.ncsl.org/human-services/child-support-guideline-models.

the apportionment between the parents of additional basic expenses (such as work-related childcare and extraordinary medical expenses) and a variety of custody arrangements. However, this model reduces the custodial parent's incentive to increase his or her work effort because any increased income serves to lower his or her child support payments, and it fails to acknowledge the nonmonetary contribution of the custodial parent in directly caring for the children.

The Melson formula is the most complex, given the number of additional calculations that take place in determining the child support amount. This model takes into account not only the basic living requirements of each child but also includes those of each parent and is also more reflective of actual costs. However, at low incomes, it often results in minimum orders, while at very high incomes, order amounts tend to flatten out.

5. Applying the guidelines and deviations. Determining child support awards under the guidelines requires several decisions, starting with what counts as parental income and who must pay whom. Given that child support guidelines create a rebuttable presumption of the appropriate award, what findings justify deviating from the presumptive amount? (Deviations, sometimes referred to as "special circumstances," are an increase or decrease in the presumptive amount of child support.) For example, does a parent's failure to exercise visitation constitute a downward deviation factor? See Mize v. Mize, 355 So. 3d 16 (La. Ct. App. 2022). Should a child's travel costs to visit a parent who lives in a foreign country constitute an upward deviation factor? See Hiatt v. Mathieu, 350 So. 3d 387 (Fla. Dist. Ct. App. 2022). How does the statute applicable in *Turner* answer this question? Federal law requires that the deviation criteria "must take into consideration the best interests of the child." 45 C.F.R. §302.56(g).

6. High- and low-income parents. Courts struggle with how to apply the guidelines in cases of high-income parents whose numbers exceed those on the charts. Some jurisdictions reject extrapolations from the guidelines (i.e., determining the presumptive amount based on what the chart would have shown). Other courts determine that application of the guidelines in such cases would be inequitable for failure to recognize the marital standard of living. See Anastasi v. Anastasi, 170 N.Y.S.3d 794 (N.Y. Sup. Ct. App. Div. 2022). Without the guidelines, what criteria govern? "Reasonable needs"? See, e.g., Hanrahan v. Bakker, 186 A.3d 958 (Pa. 2018). Continuation of the predivorce lifestyle? A "three pony rule," to the effect that, regardless of parental wealth, no child needs more than three ponies? See Schieffer v. Schieffer, 826 N.W.2d 627, 646 n.15 (S.D. 2013) (Konekamp, J., concurring in part and dissenting in part).

Almost all approaches provide low-income adjustments for poor nonresidential parents. These adjustments vary widely from state to state. Nonetheless, the adjusted amounts are generally inadequate to meet the needs of poor custodial parents. Low-income parents (both custodial and noncustodial parents) have a difficult time supporting themselves, let alone their children. Even with vigorous efforts to establish and enforce child support obligations, 16 percent of children (amounting to 11.6 million) live in families below the poverty line.[19] The poverty

[19]. U.S. Census Bureau, Income and Poverty in the United States: 2020 (Sept. 14, 2021), https://www.census.gov/library/publications/2021/demo/p60-273.

rate for families with a noncustodial parent remains higher than that for other families, and custodial mothers are more likely to be poor than custodial fathers.[20]

7. Shared custody. Can mathematical formulas adequately address the complexities of modern allocations of parental responsibility? Increasingly, courts must consider how to apply guidelines to joint custody and other shared parenting arrangements, such as the one in *Turner*. Do such arrangements justify a special formula? A deviation from the guidelines? An offset? Should each joint custodian be treated as a support obligor for the time that the child spends with the other parent? Virtually every state treats shared parenting as a deviation factor or as an offset.

8. Beyond today's guidelines. Given the federal goals for child support guidelines, why has Congress not adopted a *national* guideline? Does the formulaic approach to child support work sufficiently well that it should be implemented for allocations of marital property and determinations of spousal support, as suggested by the ALI Principles, which used child support guidelines as a model, and as represented by the Massachusetts Alimony Reform Act (both discussed earlier in the chapter)?

Problem

Denise appeals a trial court order requiring her former husband, Kevin, to pay $816 monthly child support (instead of the presumptive amount of $1,121 required by the guidelines based on Kevin's net disposable income). At the time of the order, Kevin was spending only one hour per week with the couple's two young daughters, subject to an order of supervised visitation stemming from allegations of sexual abuse. In deviating from the guideline, the trial judge explained:

> Presumably the Legislature did not intend to create certain shortfalls in a payor's standard of living solely for the purpose of providing absolute windfalls to the payee parent's and children's standard of living. A child support order of $816 per month will allow Kevin to meet his monthly needs while yet providing Denise and the children with a surplus of $833 over her and the children's stated needs. Such a child support order is in the children's best interest, because to order a guidelines amount providing them with an even larger surplus while leaving Kevin unable to meet his own monthly cost of living would teach them disrespect for the fairness of the legislative and judicial branches of government.

What result when Denise appeals, seeking an award of $1,121 monthly? Was the deviation from the guideline justified? To what extent is the parents' division of time with the children (1 percent for Kevin and 99 percent for Denise) relevant? See In re Marriage of Denise & Kevin C., 67 Cal. Rptr. 2d 508 (Ct. App. 1997). Cf. Perkinson v. Perkinson, 989 N.E.2d 758 (Ind. 2013); In re Marriage of Krieger & Walker, 199 P.3d 450, 457 (Wash. Ct. App. 2008).

---

[20]. Poverty rates for custodial-parent families have remained higher than the poverty rates of other families, with the poverty rate for custodial mothers' families in 2015 (29.2 percent) significantly higher than that for custodial fathers' families (16.7 percent). U.S. Census Bureau, Income and Poverty in the United States, supra note [19].

2. Postmajority Support

McLEOD v. STARNES
723 S.E.2d 198 (S.C. 2012)

Justice HEARN:

Less than two years ago, this Court decided Webb v. Sowell, 692 S.E.2d 543 [(S.C. 2010)], which held that ordering a non-custodial parent to pay college expenses violates equal protection. . . . Today, we hold that Webb was wrongly decided and remand this matter for reconsideration in light of the law as it existed prior to Webb. . . .

Kristi McLeod (Mother) and Robert Starnes (Father) divorced in 1993 following five years of marriage. Mother received custody of their two minor children, and Father was required to pay child support in the amount of $212 per week, which was later reduced to $175 per week by agreement, in addition to thirty-five percent of his annual bonus. At the time, Father earned approximately $29,000 per year plus a $2,500 bonus. However, his salary steadily increased to over $120,000 per year and his bonus to nearly $30,000 by 2007. In 2008, his salary was almost $250,000. During the same time period, Mother's income increased and fluctuated from less than $12,000 per year to a peak of approximately $40,000 per year. Despite the rather sizable increases in Father's income, Mother never sought modification of his child support obligation because, as Father admitted, she had no way of knowing about them.

In August 2006, the parties' older child, Collin, reached the age of majority and enrolled as a student at Newberry College.[1] To help take advantage of this opportunity, he sought all scholarships, loans, and grants that he could. Father wholly supported Collin's decision to attend Newberry [and agreed to pay]. However, Father did not uphold his end of the bargain, nor did he regularly pay the percentage of his bonus as required. [Mother sought an award of college expenses, but the court dismissed her claim on equal protection grounds. Mother appeals.]

In Webb, we were asked to determine whether requiring a non-custodial parent to pay college expenses was a violation of equal protection. [Webb held that it was a violation of equal protection, thereby overruling prior case law, Risinger v. Risinger, 253 S.E.2d 652 (S.C. 1979), in which the court had ruled that a court could order a noncustodial parent to pay college expenses, as an incident of child support, in appropriate and limited circumstances. The majority in Webb viewed the classification created by Risinger for equal protection purposes as those parents who were subject to a child support order at the time the child is emancipated rather than the classification raised by the parties: divorced and non-divorced parents.]

Without any elaboration, the [Webb] majority concluded that there is no rational basis for treating parents subject to such an order differently than those not subject to one with respect to the payment of college expenses. Upon further reflection, we now believe that [our decision in] Webb therefore rests on unsound

---

1. Their younger son, Jamie, has autism; although he attained the age of majority in 2008, he is not expected to graduate from high school until he is twenty-one.

constitutional principles, and stare decisis does not preclude our reconsideration of the issue addressed in that case.

As with any equal protection challenge, we begin by addressing the class *Risinger* created under section 63-3-530(A)(17). [We use] the same lens used by the family court: whether [*Risinger*] improperly treats divorced parents differently than non-divorced parents.

This State has a strong interest in the outcome of disputes where the welfare of our young citizens is at stake. As can hardly be contested, the State also has a strong interest in ensuring that our youth are educated such that they can become more productive members of our society. It is entirely possible "that most parents who remain married to each other support their children through college years. On the other hand, even well-intentioned parents, when deprived of the custody of their children, sometimes react by refusing to support them as they would if the family unit had been preserved." Therefore, it may very well be that *Risinger* sought to alleviate this harm by "minimiz[ing] any economic and educational disadvantages to children of divorced parents." Kujawinski v. Kujawinski, 376 N.E.2d 1382, 1390 (Ill. 1978); see also LeClair v. LeClair, 624 A.2d 1350, 1357 (N.H. 1993), *superseded by statute on other grounds* ("The legitimate State interest served by these statutes is to ensure that children of divorced families are not deprived of educational opportunities solely because their families are no longer intact."). There is no absolute right to a college education, and section 63-3-530(A)(17), as interpreted by *Risinger* and its progeny, does not impose a moral obligation on all divorced parents with children. Instead, the factors identified by *Risinger* and expounded upon in later cases seek to identify those children whose parents would *otherwise* have paid for their college education, but for the divorce, and provide them with that benefit.

We accordingly hold that requiring a parent to pay, as an incident of child support, for postsecondary education under the appropriate and limited circumstances outlined by *Risinger* is rationally related to the State's interest. . . . Indeed, Father's refusal to contribute towards Collin's college expenses under the facts of this case proves the very ill which *Risinger* attempted to alleviate, for Father articulated no defensible reason for his refusal other than the shield erected by *Webb*. What other reason could there be for a father with more than adequate means and a son who truly desires to attend college to skirt the obligation the father almost certainly would have assumed had he not divorced the child's mother? . . . Thus, this case amply demonstrates what we failed to recognize in *Webb*: sometimes the acrimony of marital litigation impacts a parent's normal sense of obligation towards his or her children. While this is a harsh and unfortunate reality, it is a reality nonetheless that *Risinger* sought to address. . . . We now hold *Risinger* does not violate the Equal Protection Clause because there is a rational basis to support any disparate treatment *Risinger* and its progeny created. . . .[8]

---

8. The family court also dismissed Mother's claim because Collin chose to attend a private college. While we agree that the cost of a child's education is a relevant consideration in light of the factors identified in *Risinger* and subsequent cases, attendance at a private school does not foreclose an award of expenses. Instead, the tuition amount is to be factored in with the child's attainment of scholarships, grants, and loans as well as the parents' ability to pay when determining whether to make such an award and in what amount.

Notes and Questions

1. Historical background. The problem of parental responsibility for postmajority education arose because of the national trend to lower the age of majority in the wake of the Vietnam War. The trend resulted from widespread public sentiment that youth who could enter combat should be able to drink, vote, and exercise other rights. In response, most states lowered the age of majority from 21 to 18. This change, however, jeopardized the ability of many children of divorce (formerly the recipients of child support payments) to pursue higher education because child support generally terminates at the age of majority.

2. Different approaches. Most states do not have statutes or case law requiring divorced parents to provide college expenses absent parental agreement.[21] In a few states, like South Carolina in *McLeod*, case law provides for court-ordered college support. In a few other states, statutes provide for such support.[22] In all states, parents can agree to include college support in their child support agreement.

3. Constitutional issues. Webb v. Sowell (overruled by *McLeod*) determined that some parents would suffer unconstitutional discrimination if a court could continue their court-ordered support obligations past majority, given that parents not subject to such orders have no legal obligation to provide such support. Thus, the *Webb* court focused on the rights of parents. By contrast, a different court that similarly invalidated a state postmajority support statute as a violation of equal protection focused on the disadvantage suffered by children in intact families (who have no right to postmajority support), compared to children of divorce. Curtis v. Kline, 666 A.2d 265 (Pa. 1995). What classification does *McLeod* scrutinize? An omitted dissent in *McLeod* describes the classes as "separated, divorced, or unmarried parents and their children versus the parents and children of intact families." To what extent does such framing dictate the result? How does the majority's analysis in *McLeod* address the equal protection concerns?

Do support obligations for higher education interfere with the constitutionally protected autonomy of obligor parents to direct their children's upbringing? (See Meyer v. Nebraska and Pierce v. Society of Sisters, Chapter I.) Suppose a parent believes, as a matter of childrearing philosophy, that the student should be responsible for such expenses.

4. Applications. In states allowing postmajority support for higher education, "reasonable expenses" (not guidelines) determine the amount. What expenses should be included in addition to basic education-related costs? Food? Clothing? Cell phone service? Transportation? What events, if any, should result in the termination of a parent's postmajority educational support? The child receiving poor or failing grades? The child's desire to live with a romantic partner rather than in the dorm? The child's desire to attend a private rather than a public institution? How does *McLeod* address this last issue? Often, the student must achieve a

---

[21]. Charts (A Review of the Year in Family Law), supra note [2], at 660-661 (listing only 12 states that provide for college support).

[22]. Nat'l Conf. of State Legislatures (NCSL), Termination of Support—College Support Beyond the Age of Majority, Apr. 29, 2020, https://www.ncsl.org/human-services/termination-of-child-support.

defined level of academic success and provide the obligor parent with documentation. See, e.g., Cossitt v. Cossitt, 975 So. 2d 274 (Miss. Ct. App. 2008). Do such requirements, imposed by statute or court order, unfairly burden the students to whom they apply? Do they violate their educational privacy rights? See 20 U.S.C. §1232g(d) (requiring consent of students over 18 under federal family and educational privacy rights legislation). What type of postsecondary education should be covered by postmajority educational support? Vocational instruction? Graduate or professional school education? See Allen v. Allen, 54 N.E.3d 344 (Ind. 2016).

5. Children with disabilities. What postmajority obligations do parents have for children with disabilities, like Jamie in *McLeod* (see footnote 1 of the opinion)? Some states impose statutory duties for parents to support such children, regardless of age. See, e.g., Cal. Fam. Code §3910. In other states, courts lack jurisdiction to require a parent to support children with disabilities who have attained their majority. See, e.g., Hays v. Alexander, 114 So. 3d 704 (Miss. 2013).

Problem

Patrick, the son of Cherry and John, was 12 at the time of their divorce. When Patrick turns 18, Cherry (who has custody) files a petition to increase John's child support payments to include $30,000 in combined tuition and expenses at Trinity College, a private college where Patrick has gained admission. Cherry shows that John's net worth exceeds $1 million. Assuming that the court has the authority to order postmajority support for education, what result on Cherry's petition, and why? What additional evidence, if any, might be relevant for the court to decide?

Should the court consider the quality of the relationship between the noncustodial parent and child? See Koontz v. Scott, 60 N.E.3d 1080 (Ind. Ct. App. 2016). The selection of the school without the parent's approval? See Dyke v. Scopetti, 121 A.3d 684 (Vt. 2015). What should be the extent of the noncustodial parent's obligation? What facts must support the determination? Parents' educational background? Academic talent? Wealth of the noncustodial parent? See, e.g., Ex parte Bayliss, 550 So. 2d 986 (Ala. 1989), *appeal after remand*, 575 So. 2d 1117 (Ala. Civ. App. 1990), *overruled*, Ex parte Christopher, 145 So. 3d 60 (Ala. 2013). Cf. In re Marriage of Vaughan, 812 N.W.2d 688 (Iowa 2012).

3. Modification of Child Support

a. Subsequent Families

POHLMANN v. POHLMANN
703 So. 2d 1121 (Fla. Dist. Ct. App. 1997)

PETERSON, J. . . .

[The former husband unsuccessfully petitioned to reduce his child support obligation, alleging that this modification was justified by changed circumstances, including a permanent decrease in his income, his remarriage and his three children from this marriage, and his former wife's remarriage. He appeals.]

We first address the former husband's argument that subsection 61.30(12) is unconstitutional. The subsection provides:

> 61.30 Child Support Guidelines.— . . .
> (12) A parent with a support obligation may have other children living with him or her who were born or adopted after the support obligation arose. The existence of such subsequent children should not as a general rule be considered by the court as a basis for disregarding the amount provided in the guidelines. The parent with a support obligation for subsequent children may raise the existence of such subsequent children as a justification for deviation from the guidelines. However, if the existence of such subsequent children is raised, the income of the other parent of the subsequent children shall be considered by the court in determining whether or not there is a basis for deviation from the guideline amount. *The issue of subsequent children may only be raised in a proceeding for an upward modification of an existing award and may not be applied to justify a decrease in an existing award.*

(Emphasis added.) [W]e apply the rational basis standard of review because neither a suspect classification nor a fundamental right is involved. See Feltman v. Feltman, 434 N.W.2d 590 (S.D. 1989). . . . [W]e find that subsection 61.30(12) furthers a legitimate state interest and affirm the trial court's finding of constitutionality. The statute assures that noncustodial parents will continue to contribute to the support of their children from their first marriage notwithstanding their obligation to support children born during a subsequent marriage. Granting priority of child support to children of an earlier first marriage, the *Feltman* court determined that the South Dakota statute provided a fair and logical prioritization of claims against a noncustodial parent's income. "Without prioritization, the children from the first family might find their standard of living substantially decreased by the voluntary acts of a noncustodial parent. A noncustodial parent who elects to become responsible for supporting the children of a second marriage does so with the knowledge of a continuing responsibility to the children of the first marriage." [434 N.W.2d at 592.]

We also affirm the trial court's finding that the former husband failed to show a substantial change of circumstances. . . . In an attempt to manufacture a substantial change in circumstances, the former husband and his current wife produced the latter's petition for separate maintenance [and child support] which tellingly was filed only two weeks before trial. The current wife testified that while she filed such petition in order to assure that her three children would be provided for, nothing in their marital relationship has changed. The trial court did not abuse its discretion in finding that the former husband failed to meet his burden of proving a permanent, involuntary, and substantial change in circumstances. . . .

HARRIS, J., dissenting.

The issue in this case, quite simply, is whether it is a "legitimate government interest" for the State, through its legislative process, to prefer certain children over others. . . . It is not appropriate for the state to punish the children of a second marriage because their parent was involved in a previous divorce.

Although the state should not involve itself with the divorced parent's decision regarding remarriage, our statute is designed to discourage a parent from having a second family unless he or she is willing to support the second family at

judgment by operation of law when it becomes due and unpaid, and is entitled to full faith and credit to be enforced as any other court judgment.

b. Employment Changes

OLMSTEAD v. ZIEGLER

42 P.3d 1102 (Alaska 2002)

FABE, Chief Justice. . . .

William Olmstead and Elizabeth Ziegler married in August 1989. Their only child, Lauren, was born in January 1990. They divorced in December 1994. [Their settlement agreement, which was incorporated into the divorce decree,] provided for joint legal and physical custody of their daughter and specified that neither party would pay child support to the other. However, Olmstead did agree to pay for their daughter's daycare and education expenses. Their daughter no longer requires constant daycare, and she now attends public schools. Olmstead estimates that he spends approximately $80 per month on child care.

At the time of the divorce, the parties [both attorneys] submitted a child support affidavit, as required by Alaska Civil Rule 90.3(3). Olmstead's estimated 1994 annual gross income was $53,000 and Ziegler's was $25,000. Ziegler's estimate proved to be high, as she actually earned $16,753 in 1994. Ziegler was subsequently hired as an attorney with the firm of Baxter, Bruce & Brand in Juneau, where her annual income increased significantly. In 1998, she earned $53,761.

In August 1996 Olmstead's law partner of several years, Patrick Conheady, left the partnership. Conheady claimed that Olmstead was unproductive and frequently played card games on his computer instead of working on his cases. Olmstead became a solo practitioner. While he sought other positions and applied for several state jobs, he was apparently unsuccessful in obtaining other employment. Olmstead's income decreased significantly during this period. In 1996 his income dropped to $10,157. In 1998 he earned $13,075.

In March 1999 Olmstead informed his friends and colleagues in Juneau that he would be leaving the practice of law, as he had decided to go back to school to become a teacher. In order to make ends meet in the meantime, he offered his legal research and writing services to other attorneys. Olmstead has since remarried. Ziegler remains single.

On June 3, 1999, Olmstead filed a motion for an order modifying child support. . . . The trial court found that, although their financial situations may have changed, the parties still possessed equal earning capacities. The trial court also reasoned that, although Olmstead was free to change careers, he was not entitled to a modification of child support: "[Olmstead] has elected to learn new things for a while, and perhaps take on a new career. He is free to do so, but under our case law [Ziegler] and the child are not expected to finance these choices." Olmstead appeals. . . .

Olmstead claims that the court erred in finding that he was voluntarily underemployed and contends that the court improperly relied upon his decision to change careers in making that finding. Olmstead points out that he did not ask for a modification of child support based upon his income as a student or teacher. Rather, he requested a modification based entirely upon his earnings while he was a practicing attorney. He thus claims that it was improper for the trial court to rely on his career change when he did not make it a basis for his motion. Olmstead adds that he made a mistake by choosing law as a profession, and that he lacks the personality traits necessary for success in the field. . . . Ziegler counters that Olmstead's lack of success in law and subsequent move to teaching are the results of his voluntary actions. . . .

Voluntarily reducing one's income may not justify a modification of child support. Determining whether or not a parent is voluntarily and unreasonably underemployed is essentially a question of fact. . . . A trial court may find that underemployment is voluntary even if the obligor acted in good faith.

We conclude that the trial court did not err in finding that Olmstead was voluntarily and unreasonably underemployed. The evidence before the trial court established that Olmstead took many steps, including closing his office and failing to keep regular business hours, that demonstrated his intent to downsize his practice. He also significantly reduced his workload hoping to obtain a job with the Department of Transportation. In addition, the record contains an affidavit from Olmstead's former partner, Conheady, recounting his difficulties with Olmstead's lack of productivity: Conheady states that he left the partnership because Olmstead was not producing enough billable hours. While Olmstead has repeatedly stated that he was simply a failure at law and was not capable of earning the average lawyer's salary, he has provided scant support for his assertions. In addition, Olmstead's claims that he was unable to make a living practicing law are undermined by the fact that at one time he made over $53,000 a year.

[I]t was permissible for the trial court to consider Olmstead's career change in determining the issue of voluntary and unreasonable underemployment. . . . Moreover, . . . Civil Rule 90.3 recognizes that "[w]hen a parent makes a career change, this consideration should include the extent to which the children will ultimately benefit from the change." . . . Since Olmstead has failed to prove any benefit to the child from his decision to downsize his practice and change careers, the trial court did not err in finding that a modification is not warranted. . . .

[T]he record supports the trial court's view that Olmstead was not working at his full capacity. . . . The trial court based its view of Olmstead's earning capacity on his actual past earnings as well as on other factors discussed above. The trial court had before it ample evidence of Olmstead's work history, qualifications, and job opportunities. . . . The record also contains evidence that Olmstead at one time made over $50,000 per year while practicing law. Implicit in the trial court's evaluation of Olmstead's earning capacity is its rejection of his claims that he is simply not a successful solo practitioner. Also included in the record are Alaska Department of Labor statistics stating that the average income for male attorneys in Alaska is $65,811. In sum, the trial court's determination that Olmstead had the capacity to earn as much as Ziegler is not clearly erroneous. [Affirmed.]

Notes and Questions

1. Decreased income: applicable test. Parental income provides the starting point for computing child support under the guidelines. How should courts respond when a parent who decides to switch careers or pursue additional education cites decreased income in seeking a reduction in child support? What test does *Olmstead* apply? Is the voluntary nature of the change controlling, or must the court deem the change unreasonable too? How should courts assess voluntariness? What criteria determine unreasonableness? Suppose that the obligor must take a lower-paying job because he was fired from his prior job for misconduct. Is that a voluntary or involuntary change? See Busche v. Busche, 272 P.3d 748 (Utah Ct. App. 2012). Is imprisonment a voluntary or involuntary change of circumstances? Currently, 36 states treat incarceration as involuntary unemployment, meaning that the obligor can request a modification.[25]

2. Alternative approaches. An alternative approach to *Olmstead* articulates a motive-based test, disallowing modification only when the change in employment reflects bad faith (i.e., a desire to evade financial responsibility for supporting the children or to otherwise jeopardize their interests). Compare Garcia v. Garcia, 288 P.3d 931 (Okla. 2012), with Iliff v. Iliff, 339 S.W.3d 74 (Tex. 2011). Other approaches include a "best interests" standard and a "balancing test." What are the advantages and disadvantages of these alternative approaches? Are any of these standards preferable to the test used in *Olmstead*?

3. Imputing income. By refusing to reduce Olmstead's child support obligation, the court is imputing his former income to him—that is, calculating his obligation as if he were earning at his capacity. Other courts perform a more searching inquiry before imputing income, looking beyond earning capacity and requiring proof of the availability of employment opportunities at the higher level. See Cash v. Cash, 880 S.E.2d 718 (N.C. Ct. App. 2022). To what extent do dissolution and its financial obligations limit parental freedom to change careers and jobs?

Parents might also be "underemployed" if they choose to care for their children at home. Should the law impute income in such cases, or should the law recognize a "nurturing parent" exception for child support purposes? See Reese v. Reese, 139 N.E.3d 1288 (Ohio Ct. App. 2019). Should the answer turn on whether the parent in question has always stayed home (or had only part-time employment) or whether she or he left a full-time position in order to care for new children in a subsequent marriage?

---

[25]. Lynne Haney & Marie-Dumesle Mercier, U.S. Dept. of Justice, Nat'l Inst. of Justice, Child Support and Reentry 18 (Sept. 2021), https://www.ojp.gov/pdffiles1/nij/300780.pdf.

Problem

Thomas and Elizabeth divorce in 2022 following 20 years of marriage. During the marriage, Elizabeth was the primary caregiver for the couple's three children. Prior to the divorce, the husband was a highly successful director of a private school, earning $450,000 annually. At the divorce, the family court judge assesses Thomas's child support obligation based on his annual salary. However, shortly after the divorce, Thomas resigns from his job, citing "personal reasons," after notifying his supervisor that he had engaged in an extramarital affair with a teacher at the school. Thomas ultimately locates another job at a smaller private school but at a significantly lower salary of $135,000. He files a petition for modification seeking a reduction in his child support obligation. Elizabeth contends that he is not entitled to modification, and it is appropriate to attribute income to him consistent with his prior salary. What result? Is Thomas's decision to resign and the resulting reduction in his income "voluntary"? Emery v. Sturtevant, 76 N.E.3d 1039 (Mass. App. Ct. 2017).

F. Enforcement

Traditionally, enforcement of the financial consequences of family dissolution, such as child support, was largely a matter of private responsibility. Over the years, however, states and the federal government assumed a significant role in child support enforcement. Today, child support enforcement intersects with the state social welfare system through the assignment of child support payments to the state when parents receive public assistance. Enforcement also intersects with the state criminal justice system when noncustodial parents who are delinquent in their support obligations are found in contempt of court and incarcerated. The federal government oversees child support enforcement programs administered in each state.

    This section examines enforcement mechanisms, including traditional state-created private remedies and modern measures triggered by the federalization of this part of family law, with an emphasis on the collection of child support awards. Consider first how the law should allocate enforcement responsibilities among individual obligees, the states, and the federal government. Further, consider how enforcement efforts might harm those whom the law seeks to help. Finally, consider whether the need for effective enforcement should trump even fundamental privacy rights and liberty interests, an issue posed by the following case.

1. Criminal Nonsupport

STATE v. OAKLEY

629 N.W.2d 200 (Wis.), *reconsideration denied & opinion clarified,*
635 N.W.2d 760 (Wis. 2001), *cert. denied,* 537 U.S. 813 (2002)

JON P. WILCOX, J. . . .
    David Oakley (Oakley), the petitioner, was initially charged with intentionally refusing to pay child support for his nine children he has fathered with four

different women. The State subsequently charged Oakley with seven counts of intentionally refusing to provide child support as a repeat offender. [D]uring the relevant time period, Oakley had paid no child support and . . . there were arrears in excess of $25,000. [T]he State argued that Oakley should be sentenced to six years in prison. . . .

After taking into account Oakley's ability to work and his consistent disregard of the law and his obligations to his children, Judge Hazlewood observed that . . . "if Mr. Oakley goes to prison, he's not going to be in a position to pay any meaningful support for these children." [The judge imposed a term of probation and] then imposed the condition at issue here: while on probation, Oakley cannot have any more children unless he demonstrates that he had the ability to support them and that he is supporting the children he already had. After sentencing, Oakley filed for postconviction relief contesting this condition. . . .

Refusal to pay child support by so-called "deadbeat parents" has fostered a crisis with devastating implications for our children. [Census data show that, of] those single parent households with established child support awards or orders, approximately one-third did not receive any payment while another one-third received only partial payment. For example, in 1997, out of $26,400,000,000 awarded by a court order to custodial mothers, only $15,800,000,000 was actually paid, amounting to a deficit of $10,600,000,000. These figures represent only a portion of the child support obligations that could be collected if every custodial parent had a support order established. Single mothers disproportionately bear the burden of nonpayment as the custodial parent. On top of the stress of being a single parent, the nonpayment of child support frequently presses single mothers below the poverty line. In fact, 32.1% of custodial mothers were below the poverty line in 1997, in comparison to only 10.7% of custodial fathers. Indeed, the payment of child support is widely regarded as an indispensable step in assisting single mothers to scale out of poverty, especially when their welfare benefits have been terminated due to new time limits.

. . . In addition to engendering long-term consequences such as poor health, behavioral problems, delinquency and low educational attainment, inadequate child support is a direct contributor to childhood poverty. . . . Child support—when paid—on average amounts to over one-quarter of a poor child's family income. There is little doubt that the payment of child support benefits poverty-stricken children the most. Enforcing child support orders thus has surfaced as a major policy directive in our society.

In view of the suffering children must endure when their noncustodial parent intentionally refuses to pay child support, it is not surprising that the legislature has attached severe sanctions to this crime. Wis. Stat. §948.22(2). This statute makes it a Class E felony for any person "who intentionally fails for 120 or more consecutive days to provide spousal, grandchild or child support which the person knows or reasonably should know the person is legally obligated to provide. . . ."[19] A Class E felony is punishable with "a fine not to exceed $10,000 or imprisonment not to exceed 2 years, or both." The legislature has amended this statute so that

---

19. In Wisconsin, a circuit court typically orders support payments as a percentage of a parent's income, not as an invariable dollar amount. This means that it is within any parent's ability—regardless of his or her actual income or number of children he or she has—to comply with a child support order.

intentionally refusing to pay child support is now punishable by up to five years in prison.

But Wisconsin law is not so rigid as to mandate the severe sanction of incarceration as the only means of addressing a violation of §948.22(2). In sentencing, a Wisconsin judge can take into account a broad array of factors, including the gravity of the offense and need for protection of the public and potential victims. . . . After considering all these factors, a judge may decide to forgo the severe punitive sanction of incarceration and address the violation with the less restrictive alternative of probation coupled with specific conditions. . . . As we have previously observed, "the theory of the probation statute is to rehabilitate the defendant and protect society without placing the defendant in prison." . . .

But Oakley argues that the condition imposed by Judge Hazlewood violates his constitutional right to procreate. This court, in accord with the United States Supreme Court, has previously recognized the fundamental liberty interest of a citizen to choose whether or not to procreate. [Citations omitted.] Accordingly, Oakley argues that the condition here warrants strict scrutiny. That is, it must be narrowly tailored to serve a compelling state interest. Although Oakley concedes, as he must, that the State's interest in requiring parents to support their children is compelling, he argues that the means employed here is not narrowly tailored to serve that compelling interest because Oakley's "right to procreate is not restricted but in fact eliminated." According to Oakley, his right to procreate is eliminated because he "probably never will have the ability to support" his children. Therefore, if he exercises his fundamental right to procreate while on probation, his probation will be revoked and he will face the stayed term of eight years in prison.

. . . We emphatically reject the novel idea that Oakley, who was convicted of intentionally failing to pay child support, has an absolute right to refuse to support his current nine children and any future children that he procreates, thereby adding more child victims to the list. In an analogous case, Oregon upheld a similar probation condition to protect child victims from their father's abusive behavior in State v. Kline, 963 P.2d 697, 699 (Or. Ct. App. 1998). Furthermore, Oakley fails to note that incarceration, by its very nature, deprives a convicted individual of the fundamental right to be free from physical restraint, which in turn encompasses and restricts other fundamental rights, such as the right to procreate. . . .

[The condition of probation is not overly broad. Oakley can satisfy it] by making efforts to support his children as required by law. Judge Hazlewood placed no limit on the number of children Oakley could have. Instead, the requirement is that Oakley acknowledge the requirements of the law and support his present and any future children. If Oakley decides to continue his present course of conduct—intentionally refusing to pay child support—he will face eight years in prison regardless of how many children he has. Furthermore, this condition will expire at the end of his term of probation. He may then decide to have more children, but of course, if he continues to intentionally refuse to support his children, the State could charge him again. . . .

[T]he condition essentially bans Oakley from violating the law again. . . . Accordingly, this condition is reasonably related to his rehabilitation because it will assist Oakley in conforming his conduct to the law. . . .

ANN WALSH BRADLEY, J. [joined by Shirley S. Abrahamson, C.J., and Diane S. Sykes, J.] (dissenting). . . .

. . . Today's decision makes this court the only court in the country to declare constitutional a condition that limits a probationer's right to procreate based on his financial ability to support his children. . . . While on its face the order leaves room for the slight possibility that Oakley may establish the financial means to support his children, the order is essentially a prohibition on the right to have children. Oakley readily admits that unless he wins the lottery, he will likely never be able to establish that ability. . . . In a similar context, the United States Supreme Court has explained that a statutory prohibition on the right to marry, a right closely aligned with the [fundamental] right at issue, was not a justifiable means of advancing the state's interest in providing support for children. Zablocki v. Redhail, 434 U.S. 374, 388-90 (1978). . . . The narrowly drawn means described by the Supreme Court in *Zablocki* still exist today and are appropriate means of advancing the state's interest in a manner that does not impair the fundamental right to procreate. See, e.g., Wis. Stat. §767.265 (garnishment/wage assignment); §767.30 (lien on personal property); §785.03 (civil contempt). These means, as well as other conditions of probation or criminal penalties, are available in the present case. . . .

[U]pholding a term of probation that prohibits a probationer from fathering a child without first establishing the financial wherewithal to support his children [also] carries unacceptable collateral consequences and practical problems. First, prohibiting a person from having children as a condition of probation has been described as "coercive of abortion." . . . Because the condition is triggered only upon the birth of a child [not upon intercourse], the risk of imprisonment creates a strong incentive for a man in Oakley's position to demand from the woman the termination of her pregnancy. It places the woman in an untenable position: have an abortion or be responsible for Oakley going to prison for eight years. . . .

Second, by allowing the right to procreate to be subjected to financial qualifications, the majority imbues a fundamental liberty interest with a sliding scale of wealth. . . . Third, the condition of probation is unworkable. . . . The condition of probation will not be violated until the woman with whom he has sexual relations carries her pregnancy to term. Then, Oakley will be imprisoned, and another child will go unsupported. . . .

I, too, am troubled by the societal problem caused by "deadbeat" parents. . . . Let there be no question that I agree with the majority that David Oakley's conduct cannot be condoned. It is irresponsible and criminal. However, we must keep in mind what is really at stake in this case. The fundamental right to have children, shared by us all, is damaged by today's decision. . . .

NOTE: WHO IS DAVID OAKLEY?

David Ray Papke, State v. Oakley, Deadbeat Dads, and American Poverty

26 W. New Eng. L. Rev. 9, 10-15 (2004)

[David Oakley] was born in 1966 in the Taycheedah Correctional Institution, a women's prison in Fond du Lac, Wisconsin. [He was removed from his mother's custody in the prison after his birth, spent a period in state foster care, and then was raised by his maternal grandparents.] Run-ins with law enforcement officials marked his youth, and while in his teens, Oakley was sent to Lincoln Hills School, a home for delinquent boys. [Thereafter, Oakley lived in Rust-Belt towns with significant unemployment and poverty.]

With a limited formal education and virtually no skills, Oakley was unable to find or hold meaningful jobs. . . . As with many of the poor, Oakley's ability to find and get to work was limited by his lack of a motor vehicle. [W]ithout genuine and meaningful work opportunities, [he might well have ceased] to assume work is a regular and regulating factor in [his daily life]. Oakley's lengthy criminal record [for disorderly conduct, receipt of stolen property, illegal firearm possession, and witness intimidation] also without doubt made him less than an ideal hire in the minds of some employers.

The [four] mothers of Oakley's [nine] children, themselves among Manitowoc County's poor, do not unanimously condemn Oakley. . . . Cheri Pasdo, who gave birth to one of Oakley's sons but never married Oakley, considers him dangerously bewitching. . . . Jill Cochrane, mother of four of Oakley's children, thinks he never understood the seriousness of parenthood. "He likes having the kids but once they're there to him that's a punishment. He doesn't like them once he's got them," Cochrane said. On the other side, Lucretia Thompson-Smith and Rachel Ward remain sympathetic to Oakley. Thompson-Smith, mother of Oakley's fourteen-year-old daughter, does not see much difference between Oakley and the two other fathers of her children when it comes to paying child support faithfully. Even if Oakley had a minimum-wage job, his child support would eat it up. "How could he live?" she asked. . . . The four women and their children survived on an unpredictable combination of welfare payments, earnings from various jobs, and occasional support from Oakley. . . . For what it's worth, Oakley claimed that he paid over seventy percent of his child support to the mothers of his children, and courtroom records confirm that he did at least pay some child support. . . .

Although the specifics of David Oakley's life and the Constitutional issues considered in [*Oakley*] are unique, the ultimate decision in the case and attitudes which buoyed that decision are part of a larger trend. Since at least the mid-1980's, men like Oakley have been demonized [as] "deadbeat dads." . . . The policing and punishing of David Oakley sanctioned by the Wisconsin [courts] had much the same animus as the national legislative and popular campaigns against "deadbeat dads."

"Enough is enough," the judges and legislators [and the community] want to shout. But has anything really been accomplished for Oakley, his children, and the mothers of those children? Does the national campaign have the capacity to affect significantly the conduct of transient, uneducated, and impoverished men or to reduce the poverty of their children and their children's mothers?

Notes and Questions

1. Background. Parents have a legal obligation to provide support for their children. William Blackstone described the duty of parents to support their children as "a principle of natural law."[26] Failure to do so is considered a crime against the state (known as "criminal nonsupport"). Criminal nonsupport statutes exist in all states, with punishment ranging from small fines and short jail sentences (misdemeanor liability) to large fines and lengthy prison terms (felony liability). What was the significance of Turner being charged as a "repeat offender"?

Nonpayment of child support is a significant problem affecting the welfare of millions of children. Less than half of custodial parents receive the full amount of child support due. Approximately two-thirds of custodial parents who are due child support receive only *some* payment from noncustodial parents. Child support debt exceeded $117 billion in October 2020.[27] About a quarter of this debt is owed to the state to reimburse welfare payments; the remaining 75 percent is owed to custodial parents.

2. Reconciling *Zablocki*.   Both *Oakley* and *Zablocki* (reprinted in Chapter II) address methods of child support enforcement. What does *Oakley* hold? Does the majority successfully distinguish this case from *Zablocki* and other constitutional authorities? Does the immediate availability of a prison sentence distinguish these facts from *Zablocki*'s? How should a court apply *Zablocki*'s "narrow tailoring" requirement to a particular obligor after less onerous means of support enforcement have failed?

3. Post-*Dobbs* analysis.   What light does *Dobbs* shed on *Oakley*'s approach to child support enforcement? At the time that *Oakley* was decided, the defendant might have attempted to persuade his intimate partner to have an abortion (to comply with the judicial condition that he refrain from having any more children unless he could demonstrate an ability to support them). How do/should post-*Dobbs* abortion restrictions impact the no-procreation approach?

4. Probation conditions and collateral consequences.   The majority emphasizes that the defendant could have been incarcerated for criminal nonsupport. Hence, probation with conditions, however demanding, constitutes a less intrusive alternative. Is the approach of Judge Hazlewood, the trial court judge in *Oakley*, a welcome innovation designed to address a difficult social problem? Or does it exemplify excessive judicial discretion to fashion probation conditions? What are some of the collateral consequences from imposing conditions, restrictions, and burdens beyond the term of incarceration?

5. Reasons for nonsupport.   Commentators have long noted the pattern of nonresident fathers' parental disengagement from children (by both divorced fathers and nonmarital fathers).[28] For divorced fathers, remarriage often plays

---

[26]. 1 William Blackstone, Commentaries *447-448.

[27]. Office of Child Support Enforcement, Certified Child Support Arrears Shows Sharp Decline (May 11, 2021) (revealing a sharp decline during 2020 and speculating that the decline was attributable to COVID-19 pandemic-era financial challenges in making child care payments), https://www.acf.hhs.gov/css/ocsedatablog/2021/05/certified-child-support-arrears-shows-sharp-decline.

[28]. See, e.g., David L. Chambers, Making Fathers Pay: The Enforcement of Child Support 71-75 (1979) (identifying the anger, confusion, and depression of fathers after divorce; their resentment about payments; their association of money with marital failure; and their weak attachment to their children); Frank F. Furstenberg, Jr., & Andrew J. Cherlin, Divided Families: What Happens to Children When Parents Part 59-60 (1991); Judith S. Wallerstein & Julia M. Lewis, Divorced Fathers and Their Adult Offspring: Report from a Twenty-Five-Year Longitudinal Study, 42 Fam. L.Q. 695 (2009).

a role for "fathers who enter into new partnerships and have more children are subsequently less likely to marshal their time and money in service of older children."[29]

For low-income nonmarital fathers, however, policy-makers point out that noncustodial fathers are more often "deadbroke" rather than "deadbeat."[30] Court-ordered support is initially set unrealistically high, escalates rapidly upon nonpayment, and fails to take into account the factors contributing to high rates of unemployment. What insights does Oakley's personal story provide? To what extent do enforcement efforts help low-income fathers or exacerbate their problems?

6. Reform proposals. Given Oakley's story, evaluate the following proposals for reform: (a) statutorily authorize courts to issue temporary no-procreation orders to delinquent obligors; (b) increase the involvement of poor fathers in children's lives by redefining child support to include nonfinancial and informal contributions; (c) allow jailed fathers temporarily to suspend their child support obligations; and (d) cease enforcement of child support arrearages owed to the state that the Department of Child Support Services has determined to be uncollectible (Calif. Assemb. Bill 25 (2021-2022 Reg. Sess.)).

2. Civil Contempt and the Transformation of Enforcement

TURNER v. ROGERS

564 U.S. 431 (2011)

Justice BREYER delivered the opinion of the Court. . . .

In June 2003 a South Carolina family court entered an order [that] required petitioner, Michael Turner, to pay $51.73 per week to respondent, Rebecca Rogers, to help support their child. . . . Over the next three years, Turner repeatedly failed to pay the amount due and was held in contempt on five occasions [sometimes paying and sometimes serving time in custody. He remained in arrears. After the clerk issued a new "show cause" order, a civil contempt hearing took place]. Turner and Rogers were present, each without representation by counsel.

The hearing was brief. The court clerk said that Turner was $5,728.76 behind in his payments. The judge asked Turner if there was "anything you want to say." Turner [apologized, cited his substance abuse, and said]: "I mean, I know I done

[29]. Kathryn Edin & Timothy J. Nelson, Doing the Best I Can: Fatherhood in the Inner City 192 (2013).

[30]. Stacy Brustin & Lisa Vollendorf Martin, Paved with Good Intentions: Unintended Consequences of Federal Proposals, 48 Ind. L. Rev. 803, 807 (2019). See generally Margaret F. Brinig, Racial and Gender Justice in the Child Welfare and Child Support Systems, 35 Law & Ineq. 199 (2017).

wrong, and I should have been paying and helping her, and I'm sorry. I mean, dope had a hold to me."

[The court found Turner in willful contempt and imposed a 12-month sentence, while allowing him to purge himself of the contempt and avoid the sentence by achieving a zero balance on or before release. The court placed a lien on his Social Security and other benefits. The court made no inquiry or finding about Turner's ability to pay. While serving his sentence, Turner appealed through his pro bono attorney, claiming a federal constitutional right to counsel.]

We must decide whether the Due Process Clause grants an indigent defendant, such as Turner, a right to state-appointed counsel at a civil contempt proceeding, which may lead to his incarceration. [The Sixth Amendment's right to counsel in criminal cases, including criminal contempt,] does not govern civil cases. Civil contempt differs from criminal contempt in that it seeks only to "coerc[e] the defendant to do" what a court had previously ordered him to do. A court may not impose punishment "in a civil contempt proceeding when it is clearly established that the alleged contemnor is unable to comply with the terms of the order." Hicks v. Feiock, 485 U.S. 624, 638, n.9 (1988). And once a civil contemnor complies with the underlying order, he is purged of the contempt and is free. [Id. at 633] (he "carr[ies] the keys of [his] prison in [his] own pockets").

Consequently, the Court has made clear (in a case not involving the right to counsel) that, where civil contempt is at issue, the Fourteenth Amendment's Due Process Clause allows a State to provide fewer procedural protections than in a criminal case. This Court has decided only a handful of cases that more directly concern a right to counsel in civil matters. And the application of those decisions to the present case is not clear. On the one hand, the Court has held that the Fourteenth Amendment requires the State to pay for representation by counsel in a *civil* "juvenile delinquency" proceeding (which could lead to incarceration). In re Gault, 387 U.S. 1, 35-42 (1967). . . . [I]n Lassiter v. Department of Social Servs. of Durham Cty., 452 U.S. 18 (1981), a case that focused upon civil proceedings leading to loss of parental rights, the Court [generalized that the right to counsel exists only when the litigant may lose his physical liberty]. We believe those statements are best read as pointing out that the Court previously had found a right to counsel "*only*" in cases involving incarceration, not that a right to counsel exists in *all* such cases. . . .

Civil contempt proceedings in child support cases constitute one part of a highly complex system designed to assure a noncustodial parent's regular payment of funds typically necessary for the support of his children. Often the family receives welfare support from a state-administered federal program, and the State then seeks reimbursement from the noncustodial parent. See 42 U.S.C. §§608(a)(3), 656(a)(1); S.C. Code Ann. §§43-5-65(a)(1), (2). Other times the custodial parent (often the mother, but sometimes the father, a grandparent, or another person with custody) does not receive government benefits and is entitled to receive the support payments herself.

The Federal Government has created an elaborate procedural mechanism designed to help both the government and custodial parents to secure the payments to which they are entitled. These systems often rely upon wage withholding, expedited procedures for modifying and enforcing child support orders, and automated data processing. But sometimes States will use contempt orders to ensure that the custodial parent receives support payments or the government receives

reimbursement. Although some experts have criticized this last-mentioned procedure, and the Federal Government believes that "the routine use of contempt
for non-payment of child support is likely to be an ineffective strategy," the
Government also tells us that "coercive enforcement remedies, such as contempt,
have a role to play." South Carolina, which relies heavily on contempt proceedings, agrees that they are an important tool.

[We] determine the "specific dictates of due process" by examining the "distinct factors" that this Court has previously found useful in deciding what specific safeguards the Constitution's Due Process Clause requires in order to make
a civil proceeding fundamentally fair. [T]hose factors include (1) the nature of
"the private interest that will be affected," (2) the comparative "risk" of an "erroneous deprivation" of that interest with and without "additional or substitute
procedural safeguards," and (3) the nature and magnitude of any countervailing
interest in not providing "additional or substitute procedural requirement[s]."
[Mathews v. Eldridge, 424 U.S. 319, 335 (1976).]

The "private interest that will be affected" . . . consists of an indigent defendant's loss of personal liberty through imprisonment. . . . Given the importance of
the interest at stake, it is obviously important to assure accurate decisionmaking
in respect to the key "ability to pay" question. Moreover, the fact that ability to
comply marks a dividing line between civil and criminal contempt, Hicks, 485
U.S., at 635, n.7, reinforces the need for accuracy. . . . And since 70% of child support arrears nationwide are owed by parents with either no reported income or
income of $10,000 per year or less, the issue of ability to pay may arise fairly often.

On the other hand, the Due Process Clause does not always require the provision of counsel in civil proceedings where incarceration is threatened. And in
determining whether the Clause requires a right to counsel here, we must take
account of opposing interests, as well as consider the probable value of "additional
or substitute procedural safeguards." Doing so, we find three related considerations that, when taken together, argue strongly against the Due Process Clause
requiring the State to provide indigents with counsel in every proceeding of the
kind before us.

First, the critical question likely at issue in these cases concerns, as we have
said, the defendant's ability to pay. That question is often closely related to the
question of the defendant's indigence. But when the right procedures are in place,
indigence can be a question that in many—but not all—cases is sufficiently
straightforward to warrant determination prior to providing a defendant with
counsel, even in a criminal case. Federal law, for example, requires a criminal
defendant to provide information showing that he is indigent, and therefore entitled to state-funded counsel, before he can receive that assistance. See 18 U.S.C.
§3006A(b).

Second, sometimes, as here, the person opposing the defendant at the hearing
is not the government represented by counsel but the custodial parent unrepresented by counsel. The custodial parent, perhaps a woman with custody of one or
more children, may be relatively poor, unemployed, and unable to afford counsel.
Yet she may have encouraged the court to enforce its order through contempt.
And the proceeding is ultimately for her benefit.

A requirement that the State provide counsel to the noncustodial parent in these cases . . . could mean a degree of formality or delay that would unduly slow payment to those immediately in need. And, perhaps more important for present purposes, [the asymmetry] could make the proceedings *less* fair overall, increasing the risk of a decision that would erroneously deprive a family of the support it is entitled to receive. . . .

Third, as the Solicitor General points out, there is available a set of "substitute procedural safeguards," which, if employed together, can significantly reduce the risk of an erroneous deprivation of liberty . . . without incurring some of the drawbacks inherent in recognizing an automatic right to counsel. Those safeguards include (1) notice to the defendant that his "ability to pay" is a critical issue in the contempt proceeding; (2) the use of a form (or the equivalent) to elicit relevant financial information; (3) an opportunity at the hearing for the defendant to respond to statements and questions about his financial status (*e.g.*, those triggered by his responses on the form); and (4) an express finding by the court that the defendant has the ability to pay. . . .

[W]e ultimately believe that the three considerations we have just discussed must carry the day. . . . We consequently hold that the Due Process Clause does not *automatically* require the provision of counsel at civil contempt proceedings to an indigent individual who is subject to a child support order, even if that individual faces incarceration (for up to a year). In particular, that Clause does not require the provision of counsel where the opposing parent or other custodian (to whom support funds are owed) is not represented by counsel and the State provides alternative procedural safeguards equivalent to those we have mentioned (adequate notice of the importance of ability to pay, fair opportunity to present, and to dispute, relevant information, and court findings).

We do not address civil contempt proceedings where the underlying child support payment is owed to the State, for example, for reimbursement of welfare funds paid to the parent with custody. Those proceedings more closely resemble debt-collection proceedings. The government is likely to have counsel or some other competent representative. . . . Neither do we address what due process requires in an unusually complex case where a defendant "can fairly be represented only by a trained advocate." . . .

[The Supreme Court then determined that Turner did not receive procedural safeguards that were equivalent to those aforementioned safeguards and held that therefore, his incarceration violated the Due Process Clause.] The record indicates that Turner received neither counsel nor the benefit of alternative procedures like those we have described. He did not receive clear notice that his ability to pay would constitute the critical question in his civil contempt proceeding. No one provided him with a form (or the equivalent) designed to elicit information about his financial circumstances. The court did not find that Turner was able to pay his arrearage, but instead left the relevant "finding" section of the contempt order blank. The court nonetheless found Turner in contempt and ordered him incarcerated. Under these circumstances, Turner's incarceration violated the Due Process Clause. . . .

Notes and Questions

1. Background: Contempt. Parents risk incarceration through contempt proceedings for failure to comply with a court order to make child support payments. *Turner* rests on the distinction between civil and criminal contempt. While criminal contempt punishes the contemnor for past misconduct, civil contempt seeks to coerce compliance with the court order. The purpose of each proceeding (punitive or remedial) determines the nature of the offense and the applicable procedural safeguards. Only criminal contempt proceedings afford defendants due process protections. Why? Which type of proceeding occurred in *Turner*? In *Oakley*, supra? What procedural safeguards were at issue in *Turner*? What was Turner's constitutional argument? What considerations weighed against his argument, according to the Court?

2. Extent of incarceration. The use of incarceration for nonpayment of child support is common. Two years before *Turner*, one out of every eight inmates in South Carolina (the setting of *Turner*) was incarcerated for failure to pay child support.[31] Although South Carolina may represent an extreme case, high incarceration rates are pervasive.

3. *Turner*'s holding. *Turner* held that there is no constitutional right to counsel for some noncustodial parents in contempt proceedings. Which? *Turner* thus represents a blow to the civil *Gideon* movement. Gideon v. Wainwright, 372 U.S. 335 (1963) (landmark criminal right-to-counsel decision). Although delinquent obligor-parents face the risk of incarceration in civil contempt proceedings, the Supreme Court reasoned in *Turner* that "substitute procedural safeguards" adequately reduce the risk of wrongful incarceration. What procedural safeguards? Do you agree that such safeguards serve as an adequate substitute for due process? What are the implications of *Turner* for self-represented litigants in other family law contexts generally?

4. Inability to pay. A finding of contempt requires a showing that violation of a court order was willful—that is, the individual knew of the order and was able to comply but nonetheless failed to do so. The present inability to pay precludes the use of civil contempt to coerce compliance. What must a delinquent obligor, like Turner, do to show inability to pay? Is this determination "relatively straightforward," as the Court suggests? What possible sources of funds count? Loans from relatives? Does the definition of "carrying the keys in his own pocket" mean that the contemnor should *personally* be able to control his fate without reliance on others to bail him out? Does the term "ability to pay" mean ability to pay at the time of the hearing or at the time that the balance first became due? Does *Turner* shed light on these questions?

5. *Turner*'s limits. *Turner* left unanswered questions about the right to counsel in those child support proceedings initiated by the state and unusually complex cases. Who initiated the contempt proceeding in *Turner*? What complexities might

---

[31]. Ashley Robertson, Note, Revisiting Turner v. Rogers, 69 Stan. L. Rev. 1541, 1544 (2017) (empirical study of state responses to *Turner*).

invoke the right to counsel? Why might counsel be advisable in such cases? The Court was concerned, in part, that a requirement of appointed counsel would create an "asymmetry of representation." What does that mean? What is the effect of that asymmetry? If Turner obtains an appointed attorney, would fairness compel appointed counsel for Rogers, too?

In the wake of *Turner*, two state supreme courts addressed the issue of representation in state child support proceedings. Both cases held that there is no constitutional right to counsel in civil contempt proceedings, even when the state brings the case. See Miller v. Deal, 761 S.E.2d 274 (Ga. 2014); Dept. of Family Servs. v. Currier, 295 P.3d 837 (Wyo. 2013).

Currently, 14 states guarantee the right to counsel in civil contempt proceedings based on statute, state constitution, or practice. Before *Turner*, 16 states had case law that required counsel in civil contempt cases based on the U.S. Constitution. After *Turner*, eight of these states continue to require counsel.[32] Why might some states consider the right to counsel so important that they mandate it despite *Turner*'s holding?

6. Criticisms. The threat of jail has long been considered an incentive for delinquent obligors. Yet critics charge that punitive policies trap poor men in an unending cycle of debt, unemployment, and imprisonment.[33] The problem begins with child support orders that exceed parents' ability to pay. When parents become delinquent, the state escalates collection efforts, often leading to jail time. Incarceration leads to job loss, mounting back payments (arrearages), and increased difficulties in finding new jobs. One such case captured national attention in 2015 after a police officer in South Carolina fatally shot Walter Scott, a Black man who was fleeing from police, in the back. Scott's previous incarceration for nonsupport resulted in the loss of his job and reportedly prompted his decision to run following a traffic stop for a broken taillight. His death focused renewed attention on the use of jail to pressure parents to pay child support.

7. Federal reforms. In response to *Turner* and the ensuing public attention, the federal Office of Child Support Enforcement (OCSE) published new regulations ("*Turner* Guidance") in 2016 and revised them in 2020. Many of these requirements addressed the problems faced by low-income obligors based on the idea that compliance is lower when income is imputed and result in unpaid arrears accruing unfairly. The federal rule changes also recognized how unpaid child support in some situations inadvertently creates barriers to parent-child interaction.

The *Turner* Guidance encourages states (1) to implement due process safeguards, particularly regarding the determination of the ability to pay; and (2) to ensure parents' right to have child support orders reviewed (and potentially modified while they are incarcerated). 81 Fed. Reg. 93,492 (Dec. 20, 2016). The *Turner* Guidance led to significant policy changes on the federal and state levels. Child support agencies instituted *administrative prescreening* to improve the determination of the ability to pay and to develop alternative means of compliance before

[32]. Id. at 1553, 1555.
[33]. Frances Robles & Shaila Dewan, Skip Child Support. Go to Jail. Lose Job. Repeat, N.Y. Times, Apr. 19, 2015, https://www.nytimes.com/2015/04/20/us/skip-child-support-go-to-jail-lose-job-repeat.html?searchResultPosition=1.

referring cases for contempt proceedings. Such reforms appear to have had a positive effect on the incarceration rate.[34]

NOTE: FROM PRIVATE REMEDIES TO PUBLIC INTERVENTIONS

Government now plays an increasingly visible role in enforcing child support obligations in nonintact families. Until the mid-1970s, the appropriate role of federal versus state government in child support enforcement was hotly debated. According to the traditional approach, child support enforcement was a private concern best resolved by state family courts. A noncustodial parent's failure to comply with a court order of child support required the other parent to initiate judicial proceedings. But that process was time-consuming, expensive, and often ineffective. The high cost of public support for families on welfare ultimately led to acceptance of the idea that child support enforcement was one that required federal involvement.

Federal legislation was prompted by national attention in the early 1970s to the relationship between high welfare costs and the inadequacy of child support. The divorce rate was increasing rapidly, and the nonmarital birth rate was rising, leading to more children growing up in single-parent households marked by poverty. By 1973, welfare payments for needy families cost taxpayers $7.6 billion annually.[35] A large percentage of those federal funds supported children who were entitled to parental financial support.

Congress responded to the fiscal crisis with the Child Support Enforcement Act of 1974, creating a cooperative state and federal program to improve child support enforcement. Although the program experienced considerable success in its first year, its success was mitigated by the rapidly burgeoning number of women with children who needed that support. Congress soon decided to extend enforcement services to *all* families, not merely those on welfare, via the Child Support Enforcement Amendments of 1984, Pub. L. No. 98-378, 98 Stat. 1305 (codified as amended in scattered sections of 42 U.S.C.). That legislation, you will

---

[34]. Specifically, recent revisions to the *Turner* Guidance provide that states consider other evidence of ability to pay in addition to a parent's earning and income; consider the basic subsistence needs of the low-income obligor; consider the specific circumstances of the low-income obligor; and decline to treat incarceration as voluntary unemployment. 5 C.F.R. §302.56(c)(1)(i)), (ii), (iii), & id. at (c)(3). See also Judicial Council of California, Review of the Statewide Uniform Child Support Guideline 2021 (summarizing new federal guidance), https://www.courts.ca.gov/documents/Review-of-Uniform-Child-Support-Guideline-2021.pdf.

Because of the pandemic, several states obtained extensions to comply with these federal requirements until 2024 or 2025. See also Elizabeth G. Patterson, *Turner* in the Trenches: A Study of How Turner v. Rogers Affected Child Support Contempt Proceedings, 25 Geo. J. on Poverty L. & Pol'y 1, 42-43 (2017) (reporting on the effectiveness of law reform in the wake of *Turner;* in South Carolina, the resulting prescreening process and lengthier judicial hearings almost halved the number of contempt rulings).

[35]. Joseph I. Lieberman, Child Support in America 6 (1986). The Temporary Assistance for Needy Families (TANF) program, enacted in 1996 as part of federal welfare reform legislation, replaced Aid to Families with Dependent Children (AFDC), which was created in 1935 by the Social Security Act (42 U.S.C. §§601-617), to provide cash assistance to needy families. Under TANF, the federal government provides a fixed block grant to states which use these funds to operate their own programs. Federal funding for the TANF block grant has been set at $16.5 billion each year since 1996.

recall, also led to establishment of child support guidelines (initially advisory, but later mandatory).

Throughout the 1980s and 1990s, Congress expanded the authority of state agencies to collect child support. Employers became an integral part of the child support enforcement process. Three notable reforms occurred that significantly improved child support enforcement:

1. *Automatic and universal wage withholding.* Wage withholding by employers greatly simplified the collection of child support. Rather than wait for parents to fall delinquent on their support obligations (and then institute formal collection procedures), federal law made wage withholding automatic for delinquent noncustodial obligors (42 U.S.C. §§653a, 666(b)).

2. *New hires registry.* Employers' role was also expanded with the establishment of a national registry of new hires that enabled state agencies to locate a delinquent noncustodial parent wherever that person was employed (42 U.S.C. §§653a, 666(b)). Employers then garnished the wages of delinquent obligors.

3. *Tax intercepts and other innovative mechanisms.* Federal law also authorized child support agencies to intercept federal and state tax refunds and levy bank accounts ((id. §§664, 666(a)(4), 666(a)(2)); suspend driver licenses, disclose overdue support to consumer reporting agencies, and include delinquencies in consumer credit reports (42 U.S.C. §666(a)(7), 15 U.S.C. §1681s-1)); revoke professional licenses and suspend hunting and fishing licenses (id. §666(a)(16)); and deny or revoke passports (id. §652(k)).

The wage withholding provision goes into effect after a court orders child support. Either the court or the child support agency issues a "Notice to Withhold" that is served on the employer of the paying parent. The court's Income Withholding Order (IWO) lists a specific amount of current child support to be withheld from the paying parent's wages monthly. If there is also support owing from an earlier period, an additional amount will be ordered to be withheld. The notice is mandatory and has the same status as a direct court order on the employer, including severe sanctions if the IWO is ignored. Employers who do not comply will be personally liable for the support and may be subject to contempt.

Under the new hires provision, employers report newly hired employees to the state New Employee Registry. New hire reports then are matched against child support records at the state and national levels to locate parents who are not paying child support to enforce existing orders. The information is also sent to the National Directory of New Hires to find late payments in other states. Often, child support cases involve parents who do not live in the same state as their children.

Many of the above changes, at first part of state experiments, were made mandatory pursuant to federal welfare reform legislation in 1996 (the Personal Responsibility and Work Opportunity Reconciliation Act (PRWORA), Pub. L. No. 104-193, 110 Stat. 2105) (codified in scattered sections of 42 U.S.C. and 8 U.S.C.), as a condition of federal funding.

Automatic governmental enforcement efforts now serve as the primary method for collecting child support. Civil contempt proceedings account for less than one-third of child enforcement procedures. Instead, about 70 percent of all child support payments are collected through income withholding and the other aforementioned automated procedures.[36] Yet, even after decades of federally orchestrated efforts, child support enforcement remains an intractable problem, as *Oakley* and *Turner* demonstrate. Nonpayment of child support remains a major factor contributing to children living in poverty.

3. The Challenge of Multistate Cases

A substantial percentage of all child support cases involve parties located in different jurisdictions. What special responses do such cases warrant?

a. Jurisdictional Limitations on Establishing Awards

KULKO v. SUPERIOR COURT
436 U.S. 84 (1978)

Justice MARSHALL delivered the opinion of the Court. . . .

Appellant Ezra Kulko married appellee Sharon Kulko Horn in 1959, during appellant's three-day stopover in California en route from a military base in Texas to a tour of duty in Korea. At the time of this marriage, both parties were domiciled in and residents of New York State. Immediately following the marriage, Sharon Kulko returned to New York, as did appellant after his tour of duty. [They lived together in New York for 13 years and then separated. Ezra remained in New York with their children, Darwin and Ilsa, and Sharon moved to California. Sharon returned briefly to sign a separation agreement, which provided that the children would live in New York with their father but spend Christmas, Easter, and summer vacations in California with their mother.] Ezra Kulko agreed to pay his wife $3,000 per year in child support for the periods when the children were in her care, custody, and control. Immediately after execution of the separation agreement, Sharon Kulko flew to Haiti and procured a divorce there; the divorce decree incorporated the terms of the agreement. She then returned to California, where she remarried and took the name Horn.

The children resided with appellant during the school year and with their mother on vacations, as provided by the separation agreement, until December 1973. At this time, just before Ilsa was to leave New York to spend Christmas vacation with her mother, she told her father that she wanted to remain in California after her vacation. Appellant bought his daughter a one-way plane ticket, and Ilsa left, taking her clothing with her. Ilsa then commenced living in California with her mother during the school year and spending vacations with her father. In January 1976, appellant's other child, Darwin, called his mother from New York and advised her that he wanted to live with her in California. Unbeknownst to

[36]. Office of Child Support Enforcement (OCSE), Alternatives to Incarceration: Information Memorandum, Dec. 21, 2016 (federal guidance on *Turner* case), https://www.acf.hhs.gov/css/resource/alternatives-to-incarceration.

appellant, appellee Horn sent a plane ticket to her son, which he used to fly to California where he took up residence with his mother and sister.

Less than one month after Darwin's arrival in California, appellee Horn commenced this action against appellant in the California Superior Court. She sought to establish the Haitian divorce decree as a California judgment; to modify the judgment so as to award her full custody of the children; and to increase appellant's child-support obligations. Appellant appeared specially and moved to quash service of the summons on the ground that he was not a resident of California and lacked sufficient "minimum contacts" with the State under International Shoe Co. v. Washington, 326 U.S. 310, 316 (1945), to warrant the State's assertion of personal jurisdiction over him.

[The California Supreme Court upheld the lower courts' denial of appellant's motion to quash. It reasoned that California's long-arm statute was meant to reach all bases of *in personam jurisdiction* consistent with the Constitution, and that jurisdiction over appellant for support of both children was "fair and reasonable" because he purposefully availed himself of the benefits and protections of California law by sending one child, Ilsa, to live there. We reverse.]

The Due Process Clause of the Fourteenth Amendment operates as a limitation on the jurisdiction of state courts to enter judgments affecting rights or interests of nonresident defendants. [T]he constitutional standard for determining whether the State may enter a binding judgment against appellant here is that set forth in this Court's opinion in International Shoe Co. v. Washington, supra: that a defendant "have certain minimum contacts with [the forum State] such that the maintenance of the suit does not offend 'traditional notions of fair play and substantial justice.'" 326 U.S., at 316. [A]n essential criterion in all cases is whether the "quality and nature" of the defendant's activity is such that it is "reasonable" and "fair" to require him to conduct his defense in that State. International Shoe Co. v. Washington, [326 U.S.] at 316-317, 319. . . .

In reaching its result, the California Supreme Court did not rely on appellant's glancing presence in the State some 13 years before the events that led to this controversy, nor could it have. Appellant has been in California on only two occasions, once in 1959 for a three-day military stopover on his way to Korea and again in 1960 for a 24-hour stopover on his return from Korean service. To hold such temporary visits to a State a basis for the assertion of in personam jurisdiction over unrelated actions arising in the future would make a mockery of the limitations on state jurisdiction imposed by the Fourteenth Amendment. Nor did the California court rely on the fact that appellant was actually married in California on one of his two brief visits. We agree that where two New York domiciliaries, for reasons of convenience, marry in the State of California and thereafter spend their entire married life in New York, the fact of their California marriage by itself cannot support a California court's exercise of jurisdiction over a spouse who remains a New York resident in an action relating to child support.

Finally, in holding that personal jurisdiction existed, the court below carefully disclaimed reliance on the fact that appellant had agreed at the time of separation to allow his children to live with their mother three months a year and that he had sent them to California each year pursuant to this agreement. [T]o find personal jurisdiction in a State on this basis, merely because the mother was residing there, would discourage parents from entering into reasonable visitation agreements. Moreover, it could arbitrarily subject one parent to suit in any State of the Union where the other parent chose to spend time while having custody of their offspring pursuant to a separation agreement. As we have emphasized: "The unilateral activity of those who claim some relationship with a nonresident defendant cannot satisfy the requirement of contact with the forum State. [I]t is essential in each case that there be some act by which the defendant purposefully avails him[self] of the privilege of conducting activities within the forum State. . . ." Hanson v. Denckla, [357 U.S. 235, 253 (1958)].

The "purposeful act" that the California Supreme Court believed did warrant the exercise of personal jurisdiction over appellant in California was his "actively and fully consent[ing] to Ilsa living in California for the school year . . . and . . . send[ing] her to California for that purpose." [564 P.2d 353, 358 (Cal. 1977).] [Yet, a] father who agrees, in the interests of family harmony and his children's preferences, to allow them to spend more time in California than was required under a separation agreement can hardly be said to have "purposefully availed himself" of the "benefits and protections" of California's laws.[7] . . .

The circumstances in this case clearly render "unreasonable" California's assertion of personal jurisdiction. . . . The cause of action herein asserted arises, not from the defendant's commercial transactions in interstate commerce, but rather from his personal, domestic relations. . . . Furthermore, the controversy between the parties arises from a separation that occurred in the State of New York; appellee Horn seeks modification of a contract that was negotiated in New York and that she flew to New York to sign. [T]he instant action involves an agreement that was entered into with virtually no connection with the forum State.

Finally, basic considerations of fairness point decisively in favor of appellant's State of domicile as the proper forum for adjudication of this case, whatever the merits of appellee's underlying claim. It is appellant who has remained in the State of the marital domicile, whereas it is appellee who has moved across the continent. Appellant has at all times resided in New York State, and, until the separation and appellee's move to California, his entire family resided there as well. As noted above, appellant did no more than acquiesce in the stated preference of one of his children to live with her mother in California. This single act is surely not one that a reasonable parent would expect to result in the substantial financial burden and personal strain of litigating a child-support suit in a forum 3,000 miles away, and we therefore see no basis on which it can be said that appellant could reasonably have anticipated being "haled before a [California] court," Shaffer v. Heitner, 433 U.S. [186, 216 (1977)]. To make jurisdiction in a case such as this turn on whether appellant bought his daughter her ticket or instead unsuccessfully sought to prevent her departure would impose an unreasonable burden on family relations, and one wholly unjustified by the "quality and nature" of appellant's activities in or relating to the State of California. International Shoe Co. v. Washington, 326 U.S., at 319.

In seeking to justify the burden that would be imposed on appellant were the exercise of in personam jurisdiction in California sustained, appellee argues that

---

7. The court below stated that the presence in California of appellant's daughter gave appellant the benefit of California's "police and fire protection, its school system, its hospital services, its recreational facilities, its libraries and museums. . . ." 564 P.2d, at 356. But, in the circumstances presented here, these services provided by the State were essentially benefits to the child, not the father, and in any event were not benefits that appellant purposefully sought for himself.

California has substantial interests in protecting the welfare of its minor residents and in promoting to the fullest extent possible a healthy and supportive family environment in which the children of the State are to be raised. These interests are unquestionably important. But while the presence of the children and one parent in California arguably might favor application of California law in a lawsuit in New York, the fact that California may be the "'center of gravity'" for choice-of-law purposes does not mean that California has personal jurisdiction over the defendant. . . .

Notes and Questions

1. Divisible divorce. Under the doctrine of divisible divorce, due process requires personal jurisdiction over both spouses *to resolve the financial incidents of dissolution,* although one spouse can get an ex parte dissolution of marriage entitled to full faith and credit even without personal jurisdiction over the defendant spouse. Applying this doctrine, *Kulko* finds the father's connections with California insufficient to satisfy due process. Accordingly, the father may remain immune from child support litigation in California, but only until he visits his children there and risks personal service of process. Recall Burnham v. Superior Court, 495 U.S. 604 (1990) (noted in Chapter VI, p. 511). What impact does this rule have on visitation? Why do benefits provided by California to the children not count as benefits to their father? What alternative jurisdictional rules might avoid these practical and policy-based difficulties?

2. Long-arm statutes. With the expansion of personal jurisdiction signaled by International Shoe Co. v. Washington, 326 U.S. 310 (1945), states enacted long-arm statutes designed to reach absent defendants. Some courts construed "single-act statutes" to apply in child support cases, reasoning that failure to pay support constitutes a "tortious act" in the obligee's domicile. Under this approach, did Ezra Kulko commit a tortious act in California for purposes of justifying jurisdiction? Any assertion of jurisdiction under single-act statutes must satisfy the Due Process Clause's minimum contacts requirement, explained in *Kulko*. Accordingly, some states followed a second approach, illustrated by California's statute in *Kulko*: long-arm legislation that allows courts to assert jurisdiction whenever due process permits, thus encompassing all the single acts usually listed and any additional jurisdictional bases permitted by the Constitution.

3. Family law long-arm statutes. More recently, states have enacted long-arm statutes explicitly addressing family law cases. For example, Washington's long-arm statute lists several single acts, including "[l]iving in a marital relationship within this state notwithstanding subsequent departure from this state, [as to all proceedings under dissolution of marriage statutes,] so long as the petitioning party has continued to reside in this state or has continued to be a member of the armed forces stationed in this state." Wash. Rev. Code Ann. §4.28.185(1)(f). How should a court construe the marital relationship language of the Washington statute? Will a long absence from a state so weaken the contacts with the defendant's previous home that long-arm jurisdiction becomes improper? See, e.g., Nelson v. Nelson, 891 So. 2d 317 (Ala. Civ. App. 2004). Some states also allow personal jurisdiction if the activities giving rise to divorce or a related economic claim took place in the state. See, e.g., C.L. v. W.S., 968 A.2d 211 (N.J. Super. Ct. App. Div. 2009) (conception in state suffices for personal jurisdiction in paternity and child support suits). Under any of these approaches, should marrying in the state alone suffice? Recall that the Court rejects as a "mockery" this basis for California's jurisdiction over Ezra Kulko.

4. **Evolution of UIFSA.** Situations like the one in *Kulko* prompted efforts to design multistate solutions, most prominently the Uniform Reciprocal Enforcement of Support Act (URESA), promulgated in 1950 by the National Conference of Commissioners on Uniform State Laws (now called the Uniform Law Commission or ULC) and substantially revised in 1968. URESA required a two-state proceeding, including the filing of a petition in the obligee's state and its transmittal to a court elsewhere with personal jurisdiction over the obligor. The lack of uniformity among the states and the possibility of multiple support orders impaired URESA's success.

The Uniform Interstate Family Support Act (UIFSA) replaced URESA and has been adopted by all states. UIFSA contains new procedures for establishing, enforcing, and modifying support orders. To ensure acceptance by the states, Congress made enactment of UIFSA a condition for federal funding for child support enforcement in its welfare reform legislation of 1996. 42 U.S.C. §666(f). Like its predecessors, UIFSA covers both spousal and child support, but not property distribution, and spells out procedures for establishing support orders and enforcing them. UIFSA responds to several perceived weaknesses in earlier laws, examined below.

5. **Expanding jurisdiction.** Critics claim that traditional jurisdictional rules thwart effective support enforcement. In response, a federal commission initially proposed challenging *Kulko* to allow jurisdiction in most support cases in the state of the child's residence. This approach, called "child-state jurisdiction," parallels jurisdiction in the child's home state in custody adjudications under the Uniform Child Custody Jurisdiction and Enforcement Act (UCCJEA) and the Parental Kidnapping Prevention Act (PKPA) (examined in Chapter VIII).

UIFSA's drafters rejected the broader "child-state" approach in favor of long-arm statutes. UIFSA's eight bases for jurisdiction over absent obligors (set out in §201) include when the individual resided with the child in the state, the child resides in the state "as the result of acts or directives of the individual," the individual engaged in intercourse in the state and the child may have been conceived therefrom, and there is any other basis consistent with the Constitution for the exercise of personal jurisdiction. This expanded long-arm jurisdiction facilitates a one-state proceeding, in place of the two-state approach under URESA.

Would UIFSA change the result in *Kulko*? Would the "acts or directives" provision apply? Would its application satisfy due process? Why did UIFSA's drafters fail to adopt the more expansive "child-state" approach? Is it time to rethink *Kulko*'s limitations on jurisdiction? Compare McCaffrey v. Green, 931 P.2d 407 (Alaska 1997), with Ex parte W.C.R., 98 So. 3d 1144 (Ala. Civ. App. 2012).

6. Choice of law. What state law should govern in multistate support cases? Note that *Kulko* concedes that California law might govern, even though California lacks jurisdiction. Is it fair to subject Ezra Kulko to California law? UIFSA principally applies the forum's procedural and substantive law (§303).

Problems

1. In *Kulko*, assume that Ezra frequently telephones his children in California, writes to them, provides health insurance for them, pays for their orthodontics, and furnishes them airline tickets so they can visit him in New York. Suppose that Sharon then files a petition to establish a child support award in California (which, if granted, would be the first child support award for this family). Would California have personal jurisdiction over Ezra to order him to pay child support? Why? See In re Marriage of Crew, 549 N.W.2d 527 (Iowa 1996). See also Bergaust v. Flaherty, 703 S.E.2d 248 (Va. Ct. App. 2011).

2. Susan and Reginald became common law spouses in Texas. Throughout the marriage, Reginald, a gang member, abused Susan both mentally and physically. When she attempted to leave him, he had a friend stand on her head while he (Reginald) kicked her in the face. He also abused her daughter from a previous relationship and threatened to kill Susan if she reported him. Susan, pregnant, then left and moved to a friend's trailer. When Reginald continued to threaten and harass her, she fled to her father's home in Colorado. Now, after giving birth, she sues Reginald in Colorado for dissolution of marriage and child support. Reginald, who has never visited Colorado, challenges the court's jurisdiction to order child support. What result in Reginald's jurisdictional challenge, and why? Does it matter, in applying *Kulko*'s purposeful availment test, whether Reginald knew where Susan was going when she left Texas? See In re Marriage of Malwitz, 99 P.3d 56 (Colo. 2004); Powers v. District Court, 227 P.3d 1060 (Okla. 2009).

Suppose that Susan seeks a restraining order against Reginald in Colorado. See Caplan v. Donovan, 879 N.E.2d 117 (Mass. 2008). Suppose that she attempts to sue him there for intentional infliction of emotional distress (IIED). See Gordon v. Gordon, 887 N.E.2d 35 (Ill. App. Ct. 2008).

b. Modification and Enforcement

MATTER OF HENSON
464 P.3d 963 (Kan. Ct. App. 2020)

GARDNER, J.:

In this post-divorce case, Christopher Robert Henson ["Chris"] appeals the district court's decisions about child support arrearages, [arguing] that because the district court's decisions were based on a judgment ordered by a California court without subject matter jurisdiction, they must be found void. . . .

FACTUAL AND PROCEDURAL BACKGROUND

Chris and Gina divorced in 1991. They have three children together. Their youngest child turned 18 years old in 2009. At the time of their divorce, Chris, Gina, and their children lived in Kansas.

Kansas issues original child support orders

In a 1991 divorce decree, the district court awarded Gina primary residential custody of all three children. The district court also ordered Chris to pay child support in the amount of $226 per month through September 1991 and $300 per month after that. Chris was also ordered to pay 50% of the children's prescriptions, medications, and medical bills. Sometime in 1993 or 1994, Chris moved to California and found a job as a legal assistant. Gina remained in Kansas. But Chris failed to notify the district court or Gina of his move or change in income. He did, however, continue to make some child support payments.

California enforces the Kansas orders in 1994

In August 1994, Gina moved to enforce Chris' support obligations, so an action commenced under the Uniform Reciprocal Enforcement of Support Act (URESA), K.S.A. 23-451 et seq. By the time Gina filed her motion, however, Chris had an arrearage in past due child support. The district court trustee began an action to enforce the Kansas child support order and to obtain medical reimbursement under URESA. Once opened, the case was forwarded to the Child Support Office of the District Attorney in San Francisco. The Kansas support order was registered there in December 1994. Chris then began paying $300 per month in child support pursuant to an income withholding order issued in the California action. . . .

Chris moves to Colorado

[The California court, at Gina's request, later modified the Kansas order by increasing Chris's child support obligation from $300 to $948 per month.] Chris made semi-regular child support payments until 2005. By 2002, Chris had moved from California to Denver, Colorado. Again, Chris failed to notify the district court or Gina of his move. Gina remained in Kansas. Because Chris had moved to Colorado, California stopped collecting support and closed its case. At that time, its records showed Chris' child support arrearage was $71,687.87. [The Kansas court later found Chris in default and based the amount of arrearage on the California modification for the sum of $73,276.76 and $10,374.82 in unpaid medical expenses.]

Colorado enforces the Kansas default judgment

In July 2006, the trustee registered the Kansas support order and the Kansas arrearage judgment of $75,419.59 in Colorado for collection by an income withholding order. . . . In May 2010, another withholding order began collecting $800 in past due child support from Chris' wages. That continued until January 2014 when Chris moved to set aside the 2005 default judgment. . . .

This appeal centers on the district court's 2005 default judgment, which accepted Gina's child support arrearage numbers that were calculated, at least in part, using the California court's modified support order. Chris first argues that the California modification was void because the California court lacked subject matter jurisdiction under FFCCSOA and UIFSA to modify the Kansas order. Chris then argues that the Kansas district court could not enter a default judgment against him in Kansas for child support arrearages based on the void California modification order, so those Kansas decisions are also void. . . .

FFCCSOA preempts URESA

We thus consider the merits of Chris' argument [that] that the FFCCSOA preempted URESA so the California court lacked jurisdiction under FFCCSOA to modify the Kansas support order. [The district court made] some factual and legal findings about preemption and jurisdiction. It held that California had jurisdiction to modify the support order under URESA—the only law in effect in California in December 1996. The district court then upheld its previous default judgment entered against Chris, using sums based on California's modified support order. For reasons detailed below, we find that California lacked jurisdiction to modify the Kansas support order, although it could have enforced the Kansas order. . . .

When Gina and Chris first divorced in 1991, child support modification and enforcement decisions in Kansas were controlled by URESA. But URESA caused its own problems:

> "Under URESA, a state had jurisdiction to establish, vacate, or modify an obligor's support obligation even when that obligation had been created in another jurisdiction. The result was often multiple, inconsistent obligations existing for the same obligor and injustice in that obligors could avoid their responsibility by moving to another jurisdiction and having their support obligations modified or even vacated. [Citations omitted.]"

[T]he Kansas Legislature repealed URESA effective July 1, 1995, and replaced it with UIFSA. UIFSA incorporated the idea that only one state at a time could issue orders for child support. UIFSA prevented the possibility of multiple support orders being enforced at one time by using a "continuing, exclusive jurisdiction" provision. But California did not replace URESA with UIFSA until January 1, 1998. So when the California court modified Chris' Kansas support order on December 26, 1996, URESA was effective in California, but not in Kansas.

Effective October 20, 1994, however, Congress enacted the FFCCSOA. 28 U.S.C. §1738B (1996 Supp.). The purpose of this Act was:

> "(1) to facilitate the enforcement of child support orders among the States;
> "(2) to discourage continuing interstate controversies over child support in the interest of greater financial stability and secure family relationships for the child; and
> "(3) to avoid jurisdictional competition and conflict among State courts in the establishment of child support orders." Pub. L. No. 103-383, §2.

The FFCCSOA required each state to recognize ongoing child support obligations from other states and to modify those obligations only under certain circumstances defined in the statute. "The FFCCSOA's 'bottom line' established that support obligors would no longer be permitted to 'avoid financial responsibilities to their children by moving to another jurisdiction and availing themselves of preexisting legal loopholes caused by disparate state laws.'"

"Courts have found that the FFCCSOA is intended to be consistent with UIFSA. LeTellier v. LeTellier, 40 S.W.3d 490, 498-99 (Tenn. 2001) (reviewing the legislative history of FFCCSOA and finding that Congress did not intend to preempt UIFSA)."

Yet courts have consistently found that the FFCCSOA preempts state law with respect to the modification of child support orders in a URESA enforcement action. . . . The district court here held that because California had not yet adopted UIFSA, URESA controlled. But the district court failed to recognize that California's URESA had been preempted by FFCCSOA. . . .

California lacked jurisdiction to modify the Kansas support order

FFCCSOA incorporated the same concept of continuing, exclusive jurisdiction as does UIFSA. See 28 U.S.C. §1738B. FFCCSOA establishes a general rule requiring a state to enforce the child support order of another state. See 28 U.S.C. §1738B(a)(1). It further prohibits a state from modifying another state's child support order if the issuing state has "continuing, exclusive jurisdiction" over the matter. See 28 U.S.C. §1738B (a)(2), (d), and (e). Once a state issues an initial child support order, that state's substantive law governs the order, and the State maintains continuing, exclusive jurisdiction to modify a child support order that it lawfully issued, even if parties filed pleadings in another state. . . .

FFCCSOA [below] defines the circumstances under which a court of a state may modify a child support order issued by another state:

"A court of a State that has made a child support order consistently with this section has continuing, exclusive jurisdiction over the order if the State is the child's State or the residence of any individual contestant or the parties have consented in a record or open court that the tribunal of the State may continue to exercise jurisdiction to modify its order, unless the court of another State, acting in accordance with subsections (e) and (f), has made a modification of the order.

"(e) Authority to modify orders.—A court of a State may modify a child support order issued by a court of another State if —

(1) the court has jurisdiction to make such a child support order pursuant to subsection (i); and

(2) (A) the court of the other State no longer has continuing, exclusive jurisdiction of the child support order because that State no longer is the child's State or the residence of any individual contestant and the parties have not consented in a record or open court that the tribunal of the other State may continue to exercise jurisdiction to modify its order; or

(B) each individual contestant has filed written consent with the State of continuing, exclusive jurisdiction for a court of another State to modify the order and assume continuing, exclusive jurisdiction over the order."

. . .

Under FFCCSOA, "modifications are prohibited unless the exceptions are . . . satisfied." [See 28 U.S.C. §1738B (e)(2)(A), above.] Neither exception is satisfied here. When California purported to modify the Kansas child support order in 1996, Gina and her children remained in Kansas—the issuing state—as they did throughout the underlying proceeding. And no one argues that all the parties filed any written consent in Kansas for California to modify the Kansas orders.

Because Gina is still a resident of Kansas and the parties have not provided written consents for a California tribunal to exercise jurisdiction over the matter, Kansas has had exclusive, continuing jurisdiction over the child support orders since they were issued in 1991. Thus, the Kansas child support orders may be enforced in another state, but they cannot be modified by another state.

"The term 'continuing, exclusive jurisdiction' is used in [UIFSA] to indicate that only one tribunal has jurisdiction to modify a child support order at a time." Under the applicable provisions of the FFCCSOA and UIFSA—28 U.S.C. §1738B and K.S.A. 2019 Supp. 23-36,207(b)(1)—only Kansas had and maintained continuing, exclusive jurisdiction over the support order. For that reason, the district court erred in finding that the California court had jurisdiction to modify the support order. . . .

Notes and Questions

1. Interwoven federal and state law. Both federal and state law ensure enforcement of out-of-state child support orders—an outcome that is especially important when a parent who is subject to a child support order moves to a new state. The Full Faith and Credit for Child Support Orders Act (FFCCSOA) is a federal statute that establishes jurisdictional requirements for state courts to recognize, enforce, and modify orders of sister states. It requires a state to give "full faith and credit" to the child support orders, judgments, and decrees issued in another state.

The second applicable law, UIFSA, has two primary purposes, including (1) the elimination of conflicting support orders (by its requirement that states defer to support orders entered by courts of the child's "home state"), and (2) limitations on modification (by its provision that the issuing state maintains "continuing exclusive jurisdiction" unless that tribunal loses jurisdiction). The FFCCSOA mirrors UIFSA by providing that to properly modify another state's child support order, the rendering state must have continuing, exclusive jurisdiction. UIFSA replaced an earlier uniform law—the Uniform Reciprocal Enforcement of Support Act (URESA). In contrast to URESA's requirement of a two-state procedure with the possibility of multiple and conflicting support orders, UIFSA has a "One-Order, One-Time" rule limiting modification, as illustrated by *Henson*.

What did the Kansas court rule on the father's argument that the California court lacked subject matter jurisdiction to modify and enforce the Kansas child support order? Ultimately, where would jurisdiction to modify lie? Why?

2. UIFSA's rules. UIFSA has special jurisdictional rules for modification jurisdiction. What are those rules? What does the term "continuing, exclusive jurisdiction" to modify mean? Explain the rationale underlying the limitations on modification. Suppose that both parents had moved out of Kansas to a new and different state. Which state law applies to modification proceedings in a jurisdiction other than the original forum under UIFSA? Should the law of the state where the child now lives control? See, e.g., In re Edelman and Preston, 38 N.E.3d 50 (Ill. App. Ct. 2015).

3. Enforcement versus modification. Why does the *Henson* court find that "California lacked jurisdiction to modify the Kansas support order, although it could have enforced the Kansas order"?

4. Conflict between UIFSA and FFCCSOA.

a. Background. Together, UIFSA and FFCCSOA create a national regime to ensure interstate consistency regarding the establishment, enforcement, and modification of child support orders. UIFSA was initially promulgated in 1992. Congress enacted FFCCSOA in 1994 because Congress was dissatisfied with the slow pace of state adoptions of UIFSA. Congress wanted to establish interstate conformity more rapidly and to facilitate interstate collection of child support. FFCCSOA required states to give full faith and credit to each other's child support orders regarding ongoing support as well as past due support reduced to a judgment. In 1996, Congress amended FFCCSOA in order to make it consistent with UIFSA and required all states to enact UIFSA. All states have enacted the 2008 version of UIFSA.

b. Preemption argument. Generally, when federal and state statutory provisions conflict, the federal statute governs under the Supremacy Clause (Article VI, §2). However, FFCCSOA failed to include an express preemption provision. As a result, courts had to decide whether federal preemption should apply to state child support decisions. To determine the answer, courts had to decide whether application of the state UIFSA provision would frustrate Congress's purpose in enacting the federal law. How does *Henson* respond regarding whether FFCCSOA preempts state law with respect to the modification of child support orders? Why does that answer matter in *Henson*?

5. Federal parent locator service. Both *Kulko* and *Henson* concern obligors with known whereabouts. Congress responded to the problem of those obligors with unknown whereabouts by creation of the "parent locator service" (PLS) for the establishment, modification, and enforcement of child support orders. 42 U.S.C. §653. PLS relies on social security numbers to track absent parents and incorporates the National Directory of New Hires and the Federal Case Registry of child support orders (different national databases).

6. Federal crime. The Child Support Recovery Act (CSRA), 18 U.S.C. §228, criminalizes the willful failure to pay a past-due support obligation for a child who resides in another state. "Past-due support obligation" means any amount determined by a court order or administrative process to be due for the support and maintenance of a child, or a child and the parent with whom the child is living, if the amount has remained unpaid for more than a year or exceeds $5,000. The CSRA does not create a private right of action. Congress amended the CSRA by enacting harsher penalties in the Deadbeat Parents Punishment Act of 1998, 18 U.S.C. §228(a)(3), which makes willful failure to pay a support obligation for a child in another state a felony if the obligation remains unpaid for more than two years or exceeds $10,000.

7. International support enforcement. Spouses who move to another country are still supposed to pay child support. However, it can be difficult to obtain their compliance with child support orders because few countries have laws or agreements that help obtain payments. Does UIFSA apply to cases involving other countries? That question was answered in one of UIFSA's revisions. The 2008 version of UIFSA modifies the previous version to comport UIFSA's international provisions with the obligations of U.S. law under the 2007 Hague Convention on the International Recovery of Child Support and Other Forms of Family Maintenance. The Hague Child Support Convention is a multilateral treaty governing the enforcement of judicial decisions regarding child support extraterritorially. The convention applies in 40 countries.

G. Separation Agreements

Most divorcing parties themselves settle the financial issues incident to dissolution. They then present their agreement to the court for approval.[37] The rules governing property division and spousal and child support thus establish the framework within which such private ordering takes place.[38] This section presents the legal principles applicable to separation agreements (also known as "property settlement agreements" or "marital settlement agreements").

MILES v. MILES
711 S.E.2d 880 (S.C. 2011)

Justice HEARN . . . .

In March 2000, Theodora Miles ("Wife") petitioned for a divorce from James Richard Miles ("Husband") on the ground of adultery and sought custody of the couple['s] two minor children, child support, equitable division of the marital assets, alimony, and attorney's fees. [T]he parties reached an agreement as to many of the issues. . . . The family court approved the agreement, . . . granted Wife a divorce and incorporated the parties' agreement [in its order]. The following language [based on the agreement] is contained in the order:

> 5. [Husband] is hereby ordered to cover [Wife] through his place of employment with health and dental insurance until such time a[s Wife] remarries or obtains employment which provides such coverage to [Wife] as a fringe benefit.
> 6. Alimony is denied to each party.

The agreement contained no language limiting or otherwise restricting modification of its terms.

Six years later, Husband filed this action seeking to modify various aspects of the final order [including] termination of the requirement that he maintain

---

[37]. See ALI Principles §7.09 cmt. b, Reporter's Note ("Studies consistently find that approximately 90 percent of divorces are uncontested.").

[38]. Robert H. Mnookin & Lewis Kornhauser, Bargaining in the Shadow of the Law, 88 Yale L.J. 950, 950-952 (1979).

health and dental insurance on Wife due to a substantial change in circumstances. . . . At the time of the proposed modification, Wife did not have insurance coverage through her employer and had not re-married, both of which would terminate Husband's obligation by the terms of the agreement and the court's order. Therefore, the issue before the court was whether the agreement to provide health insurance was a modifiable support obligation or a non-modifiable agreement similar to a property division. . . .

Husband argues the court of appeals erred in affirming the determination [that] his obligation to provide insurance benefits to Wife was unambiguously not a form of support. We agree.

We encourage litigants in family court to reach extrajudicial agreements on marital issues. The interpretation of such agreements is a matter of contract law. . . .

Initially, we note that because the agreement is silent as to the family court's power to modify it, it remained modifiable by the court. *See* Moseley v. Mosier, 306 S.E.2d 624, 627 [(S.C. 1983)] ("[U]nless the agreement unambiguously denies the court jurisdiction, the terms will be modifiable by the court. . . ."). As to whether Husband's obligation is an incident of support, the maintenance of health insurance has the hallmark of spousal support: it provides the receiving spouse a benefit which is normally incident to the marital relationship. Additionally, our courts have previously awarded health insurance as a form of support. Awards of spousal support do not become property divisions, and therefore non-modifiable, absent something more.

Here, the agreement simply states Husband will provide health and dental insurance for Wife. It does not indicate Wife surrendered property rights in exchange for it, nor does the agreement provide any indication that Husband's obligation is anything *other* than support. Additionally, this requirement terminates automatically upon Wife's remarriage or her obtaining employment that provides similar coverage, both instances in which she would be able to obtain this benefit through means other than Husband. The language creating Husband's obligation in the agreement even appears in the same paragraph as the language pertaining to alimony. [A]lthough we agree with the family court and the court of appeals that the agreement is unambiguous, we hold that it unambiguously creates a support obligation.

Wife argues that her decision to waive alimony unambiguously demonstrates the insurance obligation is not an incident of support. However, alimony is not the only form of support available in a divorce. Wife and the family court have placed too much emphasis on the language that the parties "waive[d] alimony." Such semantic distinctions have been abolished in family law. As we said in *Moseley*,

> [t]he parties' intent is rarely revealed from the agreement's words of art. Generally, those terms are used without intending or implying any particular legal consequences. Later, courts impose the consequences upon the unsuspecting parties. Today, we overrule those cases which hold that words of art make a major distinction in the operation of divorce law.

[306 S.E.2d at 627.] The mere fact the parties waived alimony—i.e., permanent and periodic, lump sum, rehabilitative, and reimbursement alimony—does not lead to the inescapable conclusion they accordingly waived all other forms of support [under the common sense approach of *Moseley*]. . . .

Next, it must be determined whether Husband has presented a substantial change in circumstances that would entitle him to a modification of his support obligation. . . . Prior case law has indicated that a party faces a heightened burden when seeking to prove a substantial change in circumstances from a court order approving an agreement. This principle has had the effect of chilling the litigants' desire to resolve their disputes by agreement, which is contrary to this Court's longstanding preference in favor of settlement. Accordingly, we take this opportunity to expressly disavow the line of cases that articulate an even higher burden on the party seeking modification when an agreement is involved. Today, we clarify that . . . the same burden applies whether the family court order in question emanated from an order following a contested hearing or a hearing to approve an agreement.

[Since the 2000 decree, Husband] underwent a triple bypass, tore his rotator cuff, and was diagnosed with colon cancer, all of which required seven operations; as a result of his medical conditions, he is no longer employed and is totally disabled; the income he receives on disability ($1,830 gross per month) is less than half of his former earnings as a police officer; and the insurance premiums he pays pursuant to his child support obligations have increased. Wife does not allege any of these events could have been anticipated at the time of their agreement. Husband further testified the insurance premiums he pays for Wife are approximately $370 per month. As for Wife during this time period, her income has increased from $28,000 per year at the time of the divorce to $45,000 per year.

[W]e find that Husband has demonstrated a substantial change in circumstances that merits a modification in his support obligation to provide health and dental insurance coverage for Wife. However, the record is not complete enough for us to determine the precise extent and mechanics of the modification and [so] a remand is in order. . . .

UNIFORM MARRIAGE AND DIVORCE ACT

§306. [SEPARATION AGREEMENT]

(a) To promote amicable settlement of disputes between parties to a marriage attendant upon their separation or the dissolution of their marriage, the parties may enter into a written separation agreement containing provisions for disposition of any property owned by either of them, maintenance of either of them, and support, custody, and visitation of their children.

(b) In a proceeding for dissolution of marriage or for legal separation, the terms of the separation agreement, except those providing for the support, custody and visitation of children, are binding upon the court unless it finds, after considering the economic circumstances of the parties and any other relevant evidence produced by the parties, on their own motion or on request of the court, that the separation agreement is unconscionable.

(c) If the court finds the separation agreement unconscionable, it may request the parties to submit a revised separation agreement or may make orders for the disposition of property, maintenance, and support.

(d) If the court finds that the separation agreement is not unconscionable as to disposition of property or maintenance, and not unsatisfactory as to support:

(1) unless the separation agreement provides to the contrary, its terms shall be set forth in the decree of dissolution or legal separation and the parties shall be ordered to perform them, or

(2) if the separation agreement provides that its terms shall not be set forth in the decree, the decree shall identify the separation agreement and state that the court has found the terms not unconscionable.

(e) Terms of the agreement set forth in the decree are enforceable by all remedies available for enforcement of a judgment, including contempt, and are enforceable as contract terms.

(f) Except for terms concerning the support, custody, or visitation of children, the decree may expressly preclude or limit modification of terms set forth in the decree if the separation agreement so provides. Otherwise, terms of a separation agreement set forth in the decree are automatically modified by modification of the decree.

Notes and Questions

1. **Public policy.** At one time, separation agreements were held to violate public policy because they facilitated divorce by removing uncertainty about how a court would resolve the financial incidents. In contrast, UMDA makes the parties' "amicable settlement of disputes" an explicit policy objective. Why does UMDA reject the traditional approach? Does the transition from fault to no-fault divorce explain the change? What are the advantages of private ordering over judicial resolution? The disadvantages? See Robert H. Mnookin, Divorce Bargaining: The Limits on Private Ordering, 18 U. Mich. J.L. Reform 1015, 1017-1019 (1985).

2. **Unconscionability.** How does a court determine whether a marital settlement agreement is "unconscionable" under UMDA? Does the absence of judicial oversight disproportionately disadvantage women?[39] The ALI Principles make presumptively unenforceable agreements that would substantially change the property rights or compensatory spousal payments otherwise due, when enforcement would substantially impair the economic well-being of either a party with custody of the children or a party with substantially fewer economic resources than the other party. ALI Principles §7.09(2). What advantages does this standard have over the "unconscionability" test? What disadvantages?

3. **Bargaining process.** The conventional wisdom depicts the parties bargaining toward a separation agreement in the "shadow of the law" (the term coined by Professors Mnookin and Kornhauser). Under this theory, the outcome that the judge would order if the spouses did not settle significantly influences the settlement that they will reach. In predicting the outcome that adjudication would yield, however, attorneys necessarily consider the high proportion of cases

---

[39]. See generally Tess Wilkinson-Ryan & Deborah Small, Negotiating Divorce: Gender and the Behavioral Economics of Divorce Bargaining, 26 Law & Ineq. 109 (2008).

that do settle. Further, empirical studies show that judicial review operates primarily as a rubber stamp of the parties' agreements, and settlements often reflect "'the best I can get' solution," in turn reflecting a system of "adjudication in the shadow of bargaining."[40]

4. Incorporation and merger. Separation agreements may be "contractual" or "decretal," a distinction with important consequences. Without its incorporation (sometimes called "merger") into a judicial decree, a separation agreement is simply a contract. UMDA §306 creates a presumption of incorporation that parties seeking to avoid must dispel by a clear statement to the contrary. What is the rationale underlying this presumption?

Enforcement tools depend on the status of the agreement. Contempt of court and possible imprisonment provide remedies for noncompliance with a judicial decree. Such remedies are not available for breach of contract. Similarly, courts can modify some provisions of a judicial decree if circumstances change (i.e., support provisions but not property distribution provisions), as illustrated in *Miles*. However, courts generally cannot rewrite the terms of a contract, no matter how unfair or inadequate they become.

5. Integrated bargain. In reaching agreement, the parties resolve several incidents of divorce. The bargaining process may entail purely financial trade-offs, for example, decreased alimony for a greater share of the marital property. Alternatively, it may entail negotiation of financial and nonfinancial interests. Some jurisdictions have special rules for "integrated bargains"; that is, agreements in which the consideration exchanged between the parties includes both property rights and support payments. For example, support payments in an integrated bargain incorporated into the divorce decree are not modifiable despite changed circumstances because modification would necessarily alter the property division and upset the parties' carefully crafted quid pro quo. Further, some agreements use terms or payment structures that leave unclear whether an obligation represents a division of assets, spousal support, or some of both, as in *Miles*. Was the agreement in *Miles* an integrated bargain? Evaluate the court's analysis and result.

6. Vacating the decree. Orders dividing property are final in the sense that a court cannot modify them upon changed circumstances, although they can be reopened if they form part of an agreement to divide property that was procured by fraud or other improper means.

Should the same standard of unconscionability apply when a party attempts to set aside an agreement after its entry as when the court considers whether to adopt the agreement initially? What would this approach mean for private ordering? Would it invite "judges to patronizingly and paternalistically meddle in the proposed stipulations of presumptively competent divorcing adults"? Crawford v. Crawford, 524 N.W.2d 833, 837 (N.D. 1994) (Neumann, J., dissenting).

The ALI Principles afford the parties a short opportunity to challenge the terms of an agreement to divide property after execution of the agreement when

---

[40]. Mnookin & Kornhauser, supra note [38], at 951; Marygold S. Melli et al., The Process of Negotiation: An Exploratory Investigation in the Context of No-Fault Divorce, 40 Rutgers L. Rev. 1133, 1147, 1159 (1988).

a court finds both that the agreement is "tainted" by noncompliance with the procedural or substantive requirements of §7.09 and that "the challenged terms of the decree were substantially less favorable to the moving party than they would have been without the agreement." ALI Principles §7.11.

7. Bargaining with child support. UMDA §306 treats child support, custody, and visitation specially, making the parties' agreement on these issues not binding on the court and preserving the possibility of future modification, despite agreement to contrary. See ALI Principles §§7.06, 7.07, and 7.09. What explains the special treatment of provisions concerning children?

Problem

In the property settlement agreement judicially ratified, affirmed, and incorporated by reference in the divorce decree, David agrees to relinquish all his equity in the jointly owned family home (the couple's only asset) in exchange for Marilyn's promise never to request child support. Their agreement explicitly states that Marilyn "has accepted all of David's equity in lieu of requesting child support" and that "should a court ever grant a child support award against David, Marilyn covenants and agrees to pay directly to David any amount of support that he is directed to pay to any party." Pursuant to the agreement, David conveys to Marilyn his equity in the family home, valued at $40,000, where she and the children continue to live. Marilyn alone supports the children.

Six years later, David petitions for definite periods of visitation with the children. Marilyn then petitions for David to pay child support. He counters by moving the court to order Marilyn to reimburse him for any amount of child support the court orders. What result? See Kelley v. Kelley, 449 S.E.2d 55 (Va. 1994). See also Esser v. Esser, 586 S.E.2d 627 (Ga. 2003); Guidash v. Tome, 66 A.3d 122 (Md. Ct. Spec. App. 2013); ALI Principles §3.13.

Child Custody

Child custody disputes often arise after dissolution of intimate relationships. Custody law performs a dual function of private dispute resolution and child protection. The resolution of custody disputes thereby reflects the fundamental tension between respect for family autonomy versus the need for state intervention.

When the parents agree on child custody (which occurs in most cases), the state generally defers to family autonomy. However, in some cases, including 10 to 25 percent of divorce cases, the parents cannot agree.[1] This chapter explores how courts resolve these disputes, both substantively and procedurally. What substantive standards should govern custody disputes? What factors may courts consider? What factors should be *precluded* from consideration? How should requests for custody or visitation brought by third parties against parents be assessed? Procedurally, what role should attorneys, experts, and the child or children play in these disputes? By what process should custody disputes be resolved?

A. Parental Disputes Concerning Child Custody

1. Approaches to Allocating Custody: What Should Be the Standard?

a. Presumptions?

DEVINE v. DEVINE
398 So. 2d 686 (Ala. 1981)

Maddox, Justice.

[A]ppellant Christopher P. Devine [and] Appellee, Alice Beth Clark Devine were legally and lawfully married on December 17, 1966, . . . and separated in

---

[1]. Eleanor E. Maccoby & Robert H. Mnookin, Dividing the Child: Social and Legal Dilemmas of Custody 134 (1992). See also Daniel Krauss & Bruce Sales, Legal Standards, Expertise, and Experts in the Resolution of Contested Child Custody Cases, 6 Psychol. Pub. Pol'y & L. 843, 843 (2000) (reporting estimates of 6 to 20 percent); Andrew I. Schepard, Children, Courts, and Custody: Interdisciplinary Models for Divorcing Families 31-32 (2004) (reporting estimates of 5 to 25 percent).

Calhoun County, Alabama, on March 29, 1979. [They have two sons, Matthew, born in 1972, and Timothy, born in 1975.] Since [college] graduation in 1962, Mrs. Devine has taught high school. [I]n 1975, [she] commenced employment with the U.S. Army at Fort McClellan, Alabama, where she was employed continuously through the [trial] as an Educational Specialist. [She] was 38 years of age at the time of [trial]. The Appellant/natural father, Christopher P. Devine [age 41] was a member of the faculty and head of the Guidance and Counseling Department at Jacksonville State University, Jacksonville, Alabama. At the time of the trial, the older son had just completed the first grade at the said University's Elementary Laboratory School and the younger son was enrolled in the said University's Nursery Laboratory School. [The trial court awarded custody of both boys to the mother based on the tender years presumption.]

[T]here exists in Alabama law a presumption that when dealing with children of tender years, the natural mother is presumed, in absence of evidence to the contrary, to be the proper person to be vested with custody of such children. This presumption, while perhaps weaker now than in the past, remains quite viable today. . . .

The sole issue presented for review is whether the trial court's reliance on the tender years presumption deprived the father of his constitutional entitlement to the equal protection of the law. . . .

At common law, it was the father rather than the mother who held a virtual absolute right to the custody of their minor children. This rule of law was fostered, in part, by feudalistic notions concerning the "natural" responsibilities of the husband at common law. The husband was considered the head or master of his family, and, as such, responsible for the care, maintenance, education and religious training of his children. By virtue of these responsibilities, the husband was given a corresponding entitlement to the benefits of his children, i.e., their services and association. It is interesting to note that in many instances these rights and privileges were considered dependent upon the recognized laws of nature and in accordance with the *presumption* that the father could best provide for the necessities of his children. . . .

By contrast, the wife was without any rights to the care and custody of her minor children. By marriage, husband and wife became one person with the legal identity of the woman being totally merged with that of her husband. As a result, her rights were often subordinated to those of her husband and she was laden with numerous marital disabilities. As far as any custodial rights were concerned, Blackstone stated the law to be that the mother was "entitled to no power [over her children], but only to reverence and respect." 1 W. Blackstone, Commentaries on the Law of England 453 (Tucker ed. 1803).

By the middle of the 19th Century, the courts of England began to question and qualify the paternal preference rule. This was due, in part, to the "hardships, not to say cruelty, inflicted upon unoffending mothers by a state of law which took little account of their claims or feelings." W. Forsyth, A Treatise on the Law Relating to the Custody of Infants in Cases of Difference Between Parents or Guardians 66 (1850). Courts reacted by taking a more moderate stance concerning child custody, a stance which conditioned a father's absolute custodial rights upon his fitness as a parent. Ultimately, by a series of statutes culminating with Justice

Talfourd's Act, 2 and 3 Vict. c. 54 (1839), Parliament affirmatively extended the rights of mothers, especially as concerned the custody of young children. Justice Talfourd's Act expressly provided that the chancery courts, in cases of divorce and separation, could award the custody of minor children to the mother if the children were less than seven years old. This statute marks the origin of the tender years presumption in England.

In the United States the origin of the tender years presumption is attributed to the 1830 Maryland decision of Helms v. Franciscus, 2 Bl. Ch. (Md.) 544 (1830). In *Helms*, the court, while recognizing the general rights of the father, stated that it would violate the laws of nature to "snatch" an infant from the care of its mother:

> The father is the rightful and legal guardian of all his infant children; and in general, no court can take from him the custody and control of them, thrown upon him by the law, not for his gratification, but on account of his duties, and place them against his will in the hands even of his wife. . . . Yet even a court of common law will not go so far as to hold nature in contempt, and snatch helpless, pulling infancy from the bosom of an affectionate mother, and place it in the coarse hands of the father. The mother is the softest and safest nurse of infancy, and with her it will be left in opposition to this general right of the father.

Thus began a "process of evolution, perhaps reflecting a change in social attitudes, [whereby] the mother came to be the preferred custodian of young children and daughters. . . ." Foster, Life with Father, 11 Fam. L.Q. 327 (1978). . . .

At the present time, the tender years presumption is recognized in Alabama as a rebuttable factual presumption based upon the inherent suitability of the mother to care for and nurture young children. All things being equal, the mother is presumed to be best fitted to guide and care for children of tender years. To rebut this presumption the father must present clear and convincing evidence of the mother's positive unfitness. Thus, the tender years presumption affects the resolution of child custody disputes on both a substantive and procedural level. Substantively, it requires the court to award custody of young children to the mother when the parties, as in the present case, are equally fit parents. Procedurally, it imposes an evidentiary burden on the father to prove the positive unfitness of the mother.

In recent years, the tender years doctrine has been severely criticized by legal commentators as an outmoded means of resolving child custody disputes. . . . In twenty states the doctrine has been expressly abolished by statute or court decision, and in four other states its existence is extremely questionable. . . . In Orr v. Orr, 440 U.S. 268 (1979), the United States Supreme Court held that any statutory scheme which imposes obligations on husbands, but not on wives, establishes a classification based upon sex which is subject to scrutiny under the Fourteenth Amendment. The same must also be true for a legal presumption which imposes evidentiary burdens on fathers, but not on mothers.

[W]e conclude that the tender years presumption represents an unconstitutional gender-based classification which discriminates between fathers and mothers in child custody proceedings solely on the basis of sex.

Notes and Questions

1. Background. Beginning in the mid- to late-nineteenth century, the tender years presumption applied to custody determinations with regard to children. The presumption (sometimes called the "maternal preference") provided that the mother of a young child was entitled to custody unless she was found unfit. In the 1970s and 1980s, many states (like Alabama in *Devine*) declared that the presumption violated either the Equal Protection Clause or state constitutional provisions.

The tender years presumption was introduced, as *Devine* suggests, in an influential nineteenth-century American case that carved out an exception to the paternal preference for infants. Widespread acceptance of the doctrine stemmed from social conditions (industrialization, urbanization, a growing middle class, increasing privatization of the family, the glorification of motherhood, and an intense concern with childrearing).[2]

2. Presumptions generally. Consider the advantages and disadvantages of presumptions in custody decisionmaking. Like all presumptions, the tender years doctrine offers relative certainty and thereby reduces the likelihood of litigation, which can mitigate the stress and other negative impacts associated with litigation. However, the presumption clearly puts fathers at a disadvantage and is rooted in sex-based stereotypes about parents and their fitness. But might a gender-*neutral* rule disadvantage mothers? Fathers? The child/children?

3. Other presumptions.

a. Primary caretaker. The primary caretaker presumption briefly replaced the tender years presumption in a few states. See Pikula v. Pikula, 374 N.W.2d 705 (Minn. 1985); Garska v. McCoy, 278 S.E.2d 357 (W. Va. 1981). According to this presumption, the best interests of the child are served by placing the child with the parent who has taken primary responsibility for the child's care. This doctrine is gender-neutral and offers continuity of care. Critics, however, contend that it overemphasizes caretaking tasks and devalues the father's role. Others, including some feminists, argue that it minimizes women's less visible contributions to childcare, such as breastfeeding and emotional caretaking.[3] (In many states today, the fact that a parent previously acted as the child's primary caretaker often is *one* factor that the court can consider in the determination of the child's best interests. See, e.g., Vt. Stat. Ann. tit. 15, §665(b)(6).)

b. Parenting plans. When West Virginia rejected the primary caretaker presumption, legislators replaced it with the recommendation included in the American

[2]. See generally Michael Grossberg, Governing the Hearth: Law and the Family in Nineteenth-Century America 234-285 (1985).
[3]. For critical commentary, see Mary E. Becker, Maternal Feelings: Myth, Taboo, and Child Custody, 1 S. Cal. Rev. L. & Women's Stud. 133 (1992); David L. Chambers, Rethinking the Substantive Rules for Custody Disputes in Divorce, 83 Mich. L. Rev. 477 (1984); Martha L. Fineman & Anne Opie, The Uses of Social Science Data in Legal Policymaking: Custody Determinations at Divorce, 1987 Wis. L. Rev. 107.

Law Institute's Principles of the Law of Family Dissolution (ALI Principles), which requires the parties to submit a "parenting plan" (a written agreement specifying authority for caretaking, decisionmaking, and the manner of resolution of future disputes). Many states now authorize such parenting plans. According to the ALI Principles, if the parents agree, the court should enforce their agreement unless the agreement is not voluntary or is harmful to the child (§2.06(1)(a), (b)). If the parents are unable to agree, the ALI Principles provide that the court should award custody based on the allocation of caretaking responsibility prior to the separation (§2.08(1)) (the "approximation standard"). The objective is to replicate the division of responsibility in the former intact family in order to promote stability for the child. The ALI rule may be rebutted by relevant factors (e.g., prior parental agreement, child's preference, harm, etc.) (§2.08(1)(a) to (g)).

c. Other presumptions. Some courts rely on other presumptions, such as that separation of siblings is not in their best interests. See, e.g., Moeller v. Moeller, 714 S.E.2d 898, 903 (S.C. Ct. App. 2011). Still other rules—explored later in this chapter—create presumptions against the granting of physical and/or legal custody to perpetrators of domestic violence.

4. Definitions.

a. Physical vs. legal custody. Historically, an award of custody to a parent meant not only that that person was the person with whom the child lived, but also that they were the person who had the right to make decisions about the child. Today, states distinguish between "physical custody" and "legal custody." Physical custody determines the child's residence and confers responsibility for day-to-day decisions regarding physical care. Legal custody confers responsibility for major decisionmaking (that is, the child's upbringing, health, welfare, and education). (Compare the ALI Principles' preferred terms of "custodial responsibility" for physical custody and "decisionmaking responsibility" for legal custody.)

In the past, courts normally awarded one parent (usually the mother) physical custody and legal control, and the other parent (usually the father) visitation (sometimes referred to as "parenting time"). Today, even if one parent is awarded more custodial time than the other, it is common for the court to award the parents *joint legal custody*, meaning that both parents share responsibility for major childrearing decisions.

b. Restrictions. In addition to making decisions about which parent should be awarded physical custody, legal custody, and/or visitation, a court may impose restrictions on a parent's conduct during their time with the child. In the past, courts in some cases issued orders preventing a parent from exercising custodial time in the presence of a same-sex or nonmarital partner. Such restrictions are less common today.

5. Best interests standard.
The tender years presumption has been replaced in all states by the purportedly gender-neutral "best interests of the child" standard. This highly discretionary standard is based on a list of factors (usually enumerated in statutory text) regarding the child's needs.

b. Best Interests of the Child?

(i) Introduction

The following excerpt explores the nature of the prevailing "best interests of the child" standard and its criticisms. Given the shortcomings of the best interests standard, why has it persisted so long?

Robert H. Mnookin, Child-Custody Adjudication: Judicial Functions in the Face of Indeterminacy

39 Law & Contemp. Probs. 226, 233-237, 255-256, 261-264 (1975)

The history of the legal standards governing custody disputes between a child's parents reveals a dramatic movement from rules to a highly discretionary principle. . . . Divorce custody standards now show the overwhelming dominance of the best-interests principle. [My purpose here] is to expose the inherent indeterminacy of the best-interests standard.

. . . An inquiry about what is best for a child often yields indeterminate results because of the problems of having adequate information, making the necessary predictions, and finding an integrated set of values by which to choose. But some custody cases may still be comparatively easy to decide. While there is no consensus about what is best for a child, there is much consensus about what is very bad (e.g., physical abuse); some short-term predictions about human behavior can be reliably made (e.g., chronic alcoholism or psychosis is difficult quickly to modify). Asking which alternative is in the best interests of a child may have a rather clear-cut answer in situations where one claimant exposes the child to substantial risks of immediate harm and the other claimant already has a substantial personal relationship with the child and poses no such risk. [However, most] custody disputes pose difficult choices. [I]n many private disputes, the court must often choose between parties who each offer advantages and disadvantages, knowing that to deprive the child completely of either relationship will be disruptive.

. . . What are some of the implications of the use of indeterminate standards in custody disputes? Would more precise standards that ask an answerable question be better? [T]he use of an indeterminate standard makes the outcome of litigation difficult to predict. This may encourage more litigation than would a standard that made the outcome of more cases predictable. Because each divorcing parent can often make plausible arguments why a child would be better off with him or her, a best-interests standard probably creates a greater incentive to litigate than would a rule that children should go to the parent of the same sex. . . .

Indeterminate standards also pose an obviously greater risk of violating the fundamental precept that like cases should be decided alike. [W]ith an indeterminate standard, the same case presented to different judges may easily result in different decisions. The use of an indeterminate standard means that state officials may decide on the basis of unarticulated (perhaps even unconscious) predictions and preferences that could be questioned if expressed.

. . . While judges may be ill-equipped to develop and evaluate information about the child, having some other state official decide or making various procedural adjustments (such as giving counsel to the child, providing better staff to courts, or making the proceedings more or less formal) will not cure the root problem. The indeterminacy flows from our inability to predict accurately human behavior and from a lack of social consensus about the values that should inform the decision.

[A]djudication by a more determinate rule would confront the fundamental problems posed by an indeterminate principle. But the choice between indeterminate standards and more precise rules poses a profound dilemma. The absence of rules removes the special burdens of justification and formulation of standards characteristic of adjudication. Unfairness and adverse consequences can result. And yet, rules that relate past events or conduct to legal consequences may themselves create substantial difficulties in the custody area. Our inadequate knowledge about human behavior and our inability to generalize confidently about the relationship between past events or conduct and future behavior make the formulation of rules especially problematic. Moreover, the very lack of consensus about values that makes the best-interests standard indeterminate may also make the formulation of rules inappropriate. . . .

UNIFORM MARRIAGE AND DIVORCE ACT (UMDA)

§402. BEST INTEREST OF CHILD

The court shall determine custody in accordance with the best interest of the child. The court shall consider all relevant factors, including:

(1) the wishes of the child's parent or parents as to his custody;

(2) the wishes of the child as to his custodian;

(3) the interaction and interrelationship of the child with his parent or parents, his siblings, and any other person who may significantly affect the child's best interest;

(4) the child's adjustment to his home, school, and community; and

(5) the mental and physical health of all individuals involved.

The court shall not consider conduct of a proposed custodian that does not affect his relationship to the child.

(ii) Permissible, Impermissible, and Required Considerations

The best interests standard invites courts to consider many factors when deciding how to allocate custody. The materials that follow consider whether there some factors that should *not* be determinative or even relevant, and whether there are some considerations that must be taken into account.

(1) Race

PALMORE v. SIDOTI
466 U.S. 429 (1984)

Chief Justice Burger delivered the opinion of the Court.

We granted certiorari to review a judgment of a state court divesting a natural mother of the custody of her infant child because of her remarriage to a person of a different race.

When petitioner Linda Sidoti Palmore and respondent Anthony J. Sidoti, both Caucasians, were divorced in May 1980 in Florida, the mother was awarded custody of their three-year-old daughter. In September 1981 the father sought custody of the child by filing a petition to modify the prior judgment because of changed conditions. The change was that the child's mother was then cohabiting with a Negro, Clarence Palmore, Jr., whom she married two months later. Additionally, the father made several allegations of instances in which the mother had not properly cared for the child.

After hearing testimony from both parties and considering a court counselor's investigative report, the court noted that the father had made allegations about the child's care, but the court . . . made a finding that "there is no issue as to either party's devotion to the child, adequacy of housing facilities, or respect[a]bility of the new spouse of either parent."

The court then addressed the recommendations of the court counselor, who had made an earlier report "in [another] case coming out of this circuit also involving the social consequences of an interracial marriage. Niles v. Niles, 299 So. 2d 162." From this vague reference to that earlier case, the court turned to the present case and noted the counselor's recommendation for a change in custody because "[t]he wife [petitioner] has chosen for herself and for her child, a life-style unacceptable to her father *and to society.* . . . The child . . . is, or at school age will be, subject to environmental pressures not of choice."

The court then concluded that the best interests of the child would be served by awarding custody to the father. The court's rationale is contained in the following:

> The father's evident resentment of the mother's choice of a black partner is not sufficient to wrest custody from the mother. It is of some significance, however, that the mother did see fit to bring a man into her home and carry on a sexual relationship with him without being married to him. Such action tended to place gratification of her own desires ahead of her concern for the child's future welfare. *This Court feels that despite the strides that have been made in bettering relations between the races in this country, it is inevitable that Melanie will, if allowed to remain in her present situation and attains school age and thus more vulnerable to peer pressures, suffer from the social stigmatization that is sure to come.*

(Emphasis added.)

The Second District Court of Appeal affirmed without opinion, thus denying the Florida Supreme Court jurisdiction to review the case. We granted certiorari, and we reverse.

The judgment of a state court determining or reviewing a child custody decision is not ordinarily a likely candidate for review by this Court. However, the court's opinion, after stating that the "father's evident resentment of the mother's choice of a black partner is not sufficient" to deprive her of custody, then turns to what it regarded as the damaging impact on the child from remaining in a racially-mixed household. This raises important federal concerns arising from the Constitution's commitment to eradicating discrimination based on race.

The Florida court did not focus directly on the parental qualifications of the natural mother or her present husband, or indeed on the father's qualifications to have custody of the child. The court found that "there is no issue as to either party's devotion to the child, adequacy of housing facilities, or respect[a]bility of the new spouse of either parent." This, taken with the absence of any negative finding as to the quality of the care provided by the mother, constitutes a rejection of any claim of petitioner's unfitness to continue the custody of her child.

The court correctly stated that the child's welfare was the controlling factor. But that court was entirely candid and made no effort to place its holding on any ground other than race. Taking the court's findings and rationale at face value, it is clear that the outcome would have been different had petitioner married a Caucasian male of similar respectability.

A core purpose of the Fourteenth Amendment was to do away with all governmentally imposed discrimination based on race. Classifying persons according to their race is more likely to reflect racial prejudice than legitimate public concerns; the race, not the person, dictates the category. [T]o pass constitutional muster, [racial classifications] must be justified by a compelling governmental interest. . . .

The State, of course, has a duty of the highest order to protect the interests of minor children, particularly those of tender years. In common with most states, Florida law mandates that custody determinations be made in the best interests of the children involved. Fla. Stat. §61.13(2)(b)(1) (1983). The goal of granting custody based on the best interests of the child is indisputably a substantial governmental interest for purposes of the Equal Protection Clause.

It would ignore reality to suggest that racial and ethnic prejudices do not exist or that all manifestations of those prejudices have been eliminated. There is a risk that a child living with a step-parent of a different race may be subject to a variety of pressures and stresses not present if the child were living with parents of the same racial or ethnic origin.

The question, however, is whether the reality of private biases and the possible injury they might inflict are permissible considerations for removal of an infant child from the custody of its natural mother. We have little difficulty concluding that they are not. The Constitution cannot control such prejudices but neither can it tolerate them. Private biases may be outside the reach of the law, but the law cannot, directly or indirectly, give them effect. . . .

. . . The effects of racial prejudice, however real, cannot justify a racial classification removing an infant child from the custody of its natural mother found to be an appropriate person to have such custody. The judgment of the District Court of Appeal is reversed.

Notes and Questions

1. Epilogue. Following the U.S. Supreme Court's decision in *Palmore*, the mother filed a petition in Texas (where the father and child had moved) for a writ of habeas corpus to recover the child and, in Florida, a motion to compel the return of the child (which was opposed there by the father). The Florida court declined jurisdiction in favor of the Texas court. When the mother appealed, the Florida Court of Appeals affirmed, stating:

> The Supreme Court's decision [in *Palmore*] was that the modification of custody could not be predicated upon the mother's association with a black man. Its opinion did not direct a reinstatement of the original custody decree and the immediate return of the child. The Supreme Court did not say that a Florida court could not defer to a Texas court. 472 So. 2d 843, 846 (Fla. Dist. Ct. App. 1985).

The court then determined that it would be in the child's best interests to remain in her father's custody given the passage of time and the "substantial upheavals" in the child's life. Id. at 847.

2. Different approaches. Prior to *Palmore*, courts adopted different approaches to the role of race in custody law: (1) race was not relevant to custody, (2) race could be considered as one factor in determining a child's best interests, and (3) race could not be used as the determinative factor. Which view does *Palmore* support? See also ALI Principles §2.12(1)(a) (prohibiting consideration of race or ethnicity of child, parent, or other household members in determining custody arrangements).

3. Applying *Palmore*. It has been four decades since *Palmore* was decided. In many jurisdictions, that case has been interpreted as allowing race to be considered as a factor under the "best interests of the child" standard, so long as it is not the sole factor.[4] In other contexts, the Supreme Court has held that the government (including courts) cannot take race into account until its use is narrowly tailored to fulfill a compelling state interest.[5] What standard of constitutional scrutiny does the court apply in *Palmore*?

4. Pretextual reasoning. Pretextual reasoning sometimes plays a role in custody cases, including those involving race. In several cases involving white mothers who lost custody after beginning intimate relationships with Black men, the court used pretextual rationales for the custody modification (e.g., the mother lied about the relationship; she displayed poor judgment), according to Professor Katharine Bartlett. Bartlett argues that the best interests test does not lend itself to transparency. She adds that the open-endedness of the test facilitates use of

---

[4]. In re Marriage of Gambla and Woodson, 853 N.E.2d 847 (Ill. App. Ct. 2006). See also David D. Meyer, *Palmore* Comes of Age: The Place of Race in the Placement of Children, 18 U. Fla. J.L. & Pub. Pol'y 183, 185-186 (2007).

[5]. See, e.g., Katie Eyer, Constitutional Colorblindness and the Family, 162 U. Pa. L. Rev. 537, 538-540 (2014).

"subjective views of judges about what is good for children, including views about race and sex."[6]

How can an appellate court identify race as the rationale of a trial court ruling when the trial court does not expressly rely on race? Some scholars, including Professor Solangel Maldonado, suggest that it often will be hard to do so:

> Implicit biases are especially difficult to detect because individuals unconsciously attempt to reconcile their explicit and implicit beliefs. Judges, like all human beings, are likely to search for and process information that is consistent with their preferences. Thus, a judge or custody evaluator assessing two parents may find nondiscriminatory reasons to justify a preference for one parent even though his/her evaluation was influenced by race, ethnicity, culture, or one of their proxies. The amorphous best interests standard further increases the risk that the implicit biases that influence custody disputes will go unnoticed.[7]

5. Promoting racial tolerance. While the ALI Principles take the position that a parent's race is an impermissible consideration, parents' attitudes of racial tolerance or their willingness to promote their child's racial identity *may* be taken into account. ALI Principles §2.12(1)(a) & (2) (providing that in making a custodial allocation, "the court should not consider . . . the race or ethnicity of the child, a parent, or other member of the household," but that "[n]othing in this section should preclude the court's consideration of a parent's ability to care for the child, including meeting the child's needs for a positive self-image"). See also, e.g., Tipton v. Aaron, 185 S.W.3d 142 (Ark. Ct. App. 2004) (reversing an award of custody to father in favor of mother, whose childrearing philosophy was more likely to promote racial tolerance).

How much weight *should* courts attach to a parent's willingness and ability to promote a child's cultural or racial heritage? How can a court determine which parent is better able and more willing to expose the child to the child's heritage?

Problem

Teri and Richard, a Caucasian couple, have been married for five years. They have a one-year-old son, Dylan. After Teri files for divorce, both parents seek custody of Dylan. At trial, Richard argues that the court should award him custody because Teri, a nurse, is in a new relationship with a Black doctor for whom she works. A family nurse practitioner testifies, when asked if it would be harmful for Dylan to be raised in this environment, that it would be harmful. She adds that interracial relationships are more acceptable in large cities, but that it may be harmful for a child to be raised in such an environment in a small town such as theirs.

---

[6]. Katherine T. Bartlett, Comparing Race and Sex Discrimination in Custody Cases, 28 Hofstra L. Rev. 877, 883-884 & n.35 (2000). See also Shani King, The Family Law Canon in a (Post?) Racial Era, 72 Ohio St. L.J. 575, 631 (2011) (contending that the best interests standard "immunizes racism and perpetuates racial inequality").

[7]. Solangel Maldonado, Bias in the Family: Race, Ethnicity, and Culture in Custody Disputes, 55 Fam. Ct. Rev. 213, 214 (2017).

The trial court finds both parents fit but awards custody to Richard, stating that extramarital affairs interfere with the well-being of the child. It orders no contact between the child and the doctor (an order that Richard did not even request). Teri appeals. What result? See Parker v. Parker, 986 S.W.2d 557 (Tenn. 1999).

(2) Sex

ROWE v. FRANKLIN

663 N.E.2d 955 (Ohio Ct. App. 1995)

GORMAN, Judge:

Appellant, Kimberly Rowe ("mother"), appeals the trial court's decision designating appellee, Donald J. Franklin ("father"), the residential parent and legal guardian of their then five-year-old son.

[When the parents divorced after four years of marriage, each parent asked for sole custody of the couple's son. While the divorce was pending, the mother moved to Versailles, Kentucky, for her job as a part-time army pilot. In Kentucky, she applied to law school. She had previously earned a degree in international affairs and business. The father, an ironworker, was unemployed. As part of the divorce proceeding, the trial court ordered that neither parent should remove the child from the state without a court order or parental agreement.]

On September 10, 1993, the mother filed a motion to modify the court's order to allow her to remove the child to Versailles, Kentucky, and to establish his residence there. She had applied to take classes through the University of Kentucky Law School in July and had become pregnant sometime in May by a man whom she had begun seeing in March, and who was married but separated from his wife. In August she enrolled her son in a private school for the times she would attend law school classes. In response to her motion, the father filed an emergency motion for contempt and for return of the child to Ohio. The trial court denied the motion, held the father's contempt motion in abeyance, and allowed the child to remain with the mother until the completion of a previously ordered custody investigation. [After further proceedings, the trial court awarded custody to the father, and the mother appealed.]

In determining which parent should have custody of a minor child in a divorce proceeding, the trial court is bound to consider the best interests of the child. . . . Concern for a child's well-being or best interests does not, however, provide the court carte blanche to judge the rights and lifestyles of parents by nonstatutory codes of morals or social values. . . .

We first note that the trial court, using the factors enumerated in R.C. §3109.04(F)(1), concluded that both parents had taken a proper parental interest in the child, that the child was very much attached to both parents, that the child interacted appropriately with both parents, that both parents loved and nurtured the child, and that interference with either relationship could hurt the child. The trial court also determined that the child had bonded with his step-brother, had a good relationship with the mother's male companion, and was doing well in the Kentucky school. Even so, the trial court determined that the child should be removed from the mother and custody granted to the father.

The error in the analysis by which the trial court reached its conclusion, however, is apparent from its comparison of the mother's living situation with the father's. The trial court stated that for the first three years of the child's life,

> [u]ntil Dec. 1991, the child lived in the marital residence which is presently occupied by [father]. He is most familiar with the surroundings, the neighborhood, the people in the neighborhood, etc. [The child] has roots in his home in Cincinnati and but for his mother's move to Kentucky, it appears that his home would be one of stability. He has family here both maternal and paternal. He has friends here. He has friends of both parents who care for him here. The only adjustment necessary for [the child] here is that his mother would not be here.

By contrast, the trial court concluded that the mother and the child did not have substantial roots in the Kentucky community, stating it has not been provided with much information regarding that community. The record, however, belies this contention. Uncontested information was available that: the mother had been working in Kentucky for several years, that she had many friends there that she had met at work, that her son was friendly with and associated with her friends' children, that her son had adapted to the school he attended and had friends there, that the child had friends in the neighborhood with whom he played, and that he attended soccer and karate classes in Kentucky. . . .

The record does not support the trial court's finding that the home, the mother's work or her school schedule has required "tremendous" adjustment by the child.

[The trial court] found the father to be stable. . . . In contrast it found that the mother made decisions that caused the court to question her stability. Included in these "questionable" decisions were the many moves she made prior to her current situation, the move to Kentucky, and the sudden and complete relationship with her new male companion and the resulting pregnancy. The trial court deemed that these were not decisions in the best interest of the child and concluded that appellant placed her needs before the child's needs.

The trial court failed to recognize that the moves were precipitated by the father refusing, upon advice of counsel, to move from the marital residence, thus forcing the mother to leave the marital residence with the child, if she desired to terminate the marriage, and to live with the child in a variety of makeshift homes for a short transitional period. It entirely discounted how the father's decision subjected the child to changes in the environment. . . .

In examining the parties' commitment to the child . . . the trial court concluded that

> [p]ersonal accomplishments and career goals are obviously worthwhile undertakings. To accomplish what Ms. Rowe has as far as academics is concerned is very commendable. However this court perceives that this child has paid a price. The evidence has shown that Ms. Rowe returned to a full-time law school curriculum when the child was three (3) weeks old. Ms. Rowe returned to her job with the Kentucky National Guard when the child was six (6) weeks old. Ms. Rowe's time to nurture the child has been limited tremendously as she pursues other matters. The Court is cognizant of the child [the child] has spent with babysitters and at child care. In summation, this Court questions the priorities of Ms. Rowe. The *number of poor choices made by Ms. Rowe as to the best interests of [the child] coupled with her*

personal agenda indicates to this court that she may not be as committed to [the child's] best interests as she should be.

(Emphasis added.)

The transcript of the mother's law school classes contained in the record indicates that she did not start law school until the fall of 1990 when the child was over two years old. It was at that time that the child received day-care supervision. She had returned to school earlier to continue the coursework necessary to obtain her undergraduate degree during the spring semester of 1998 and began taking graduate courses primarily in the evening the following fall. The child was attended to by the parents, family or friends during this period of time. The record shows that the mother did not retun to flying until the child was approximately eight months old.

Although pursuing his career and designated as the primary financial support for the family, the father was deemed by the trial court to be dedicated to the well-being of his child and to have a "willingness to be a *good and proper parent.*" (Emphasis added.)

The trial court also considered the mother's relationship with her male companion. [T]he trial court did not like that the mother become sexually involved with a man so soon after the breakup of both of their marriages. . . . There is a total absence of evidence in the record to suggest that the mother's relationship had any unfavorable effect on the child. . . . Although the trial court explicitly stated that the best interest of the child was its primary consideration, the plain meaning of its reasons in reality constitute use of a "reproval of the mother" test. Therefore, we conclude that the trial court abused its discretion by its reliance on an erroneous standard to justify the designation of the residential parent.

Notes and Questions

1. Historic approaches to considerations of sex.

a. Common law rule: paternal custody. As noted above, historically, courts expressly considered sex in making custody allocations. Under the common law rule, husbands were the masters of any children in the family. Accordingly, if a divorce was granted (which was rare), custody generally would be given to the father.

b. Tender years presumption. In the mid- to late-nineteenth century, this rule gave way to the tender years presumption, which was another gender-based rule, although one that instead favored mothers of small children.[8] As the *Devine* case illustrates, most states had abandoned the tender-years presumption by the late twentieth century.

c. Modern prohibition. Today, some states expressly prohibit consideration of a parent's sex when making a custody determination. See, e.g., Cal. Fam. Code

---

[8]. See, e.g., Mary Ann Mason, From Father's Property to Children's Rights: The History of Child Custody in the United States (1994); Anne C. Dailey & Laura A. Rosenbury, The New Parental Rights, 71 Duke L.J. 75, 89-90 (2021).

§ 3011(b) ("[T]he court shall not consider the sex . . . of a parent . . . in determining the best interests of the child."). See also ALI Principles §2:12(1)(b) ("In issuing [custody] orders . . . the court should not consider . . . the sex of a parent or the child . . ."). *Should* a parent's sex be relevant in custody decisionmaking? Should there be a preference in favor of placing a child with a parent of the same sex?

2. Sex-based stereotypes. While courts rarely *expressly* rely on a parent's sex when making a custody determination, sex-based stereotypes continue to shape court's decisions in this area. Professor Katharine Bartlett, for example, explains that some courts appear to have attached different significance to mothers' employment outside the home compared to fathers':

> In these [latter] cases, courts seem to expect fathers to work outside the home, and respect them for their employment success. In contrast, mothers, although they also usually work outside the home, are expected to make compromises in their careers for their children, and are penalized when they do not. . . . Similarly, caretaking by mothers sometimes is taken for granted by courts in custody cases, whereas when fathers "help out," their contributions tend to be highly exaggerated.[9]

What are the different role expectations for working mothers versus working fathers? What gender stereotypes does a parent's reliance on day care evoke? Other scholars argue that sex-based stereotypes affect courts' evaluation of other parental conduct, including parental sexual conduct and mothers' claims of child abuse.[10] What sex-based stereotypes arguably impacted the trial court's determination in *Rowe*?

(3) Religion

SAGAR v. SAGAR

781 N.E.2d 54 (Mass. App. Ct. 2003)

Grasso, J.

. . . Sejal Sagar (wife) and Mahendra Sagar (husband) were married in Baroda, India, in 1990 in a traditional religious ceremony. They had known each other for less than a month; the marriage had been arranged by their respective parents. After marriage, the couple moved to the United States, where their only child, a daughter, was born on June 17, 1998. They separated in November, 1998. [In the divorce proceedings, the trial court awarded joint legal custody and granted physical custody to the wife with liberal visitation to the husband.]

---

[9]. Bartlett, supra note [6], at 881-883. See also Deborah Dinner, The Divorce Bargain: The Fathers' Rights Movement and Family Inequalities, 102 Va. L. Rev. 79, 114-115 (2016) (describing how "fathers' rights activists argued that sex-based custody laws discriminated against men").

[10]. See, e.g., Suzanne A. Kim, The Neutered Parent, 24 Yale J.L. & Feminism 1 (2012); Joan S. Meier, Denial of Family Violence in Court: An Empirical Analysis and Path Forward for Family Law, 110 Geo. L.J. 835, 851 (2022). See also generally Deborah Tuerkheimer, Credible: Why We Doubt Accusers and Protect Abusers (2021); Deborah Tuerkheimer, Incredible Women: Sexual Violence and the Credibility Discount, 166 U. Penn. L. Rev. 1 (2017).

During and after marriage, the parties followed substantially the tenets of the Hindu faith. During the wife's pregnancy and after their daughter's birth, the parties engaged in Hindu ceremonies prescribed to mark various transitions in an infant's life, including a religious baby shower, a homecoming ceremony, a naming ceremony, a first visit to the temple, a ceremony for the child's first solid food, and an ear piercing ceremony. The parties attended temple weekly and even had a temple in their home at which they worshiped on a daily basis.

Their relationship was volatile and marred by numerous instances of the husband's physical and mental abuse of the wife. At various times, the husband threw things at the wife, hit her with a rolling pin, pulled her hair, chased her from their house, and burned her with a cigarette. . . . The husband was very controlling. He would allow his wife to telephone her relatives only on birthdays and anniversaries; and the contents of the kitchen cabinets had to be arranged as he specified. He threatened to stop paying tuition for the wife's education should she fail to get straight A's. The husband made questionable transfers of marital assets and refused to comply with a court order to hold certain funds in escrow.

[The parties disagree about the performance of a Hindu religious ritual, Chudakarana, upon their young daughter. The ceremony involves shaving of the child's head, placing an auspicious mark on the head, and conferring blessings.] Apart from disagreement over whether the Hindu sacrament of Chudakarana should be performed, the parties are in substantial agreement over the rearing of their daughter, including her religious upbringing. At trial, the husband presented evidence to support his position that a Hindu may not forgo the ritual of Chudakarana. The ceremony, which is believed to contribute to the child's longevity and ward off illness, should be performed before the child is three years old and is a necessary prerequisite to Hindu marriage. If the ceremony is not performed, an elder (here the father) may atone, allowing the ceremony to be performed at a later date. The wife's position was that Chudakarana is not integral to the Hindu faith. Neither she nor her extended family believe in the efficacy or necessity of the ceremony. . . .

The father claims that the right to insist upon performance of Chudakarana upon his child is protected under both State and Federal Constitutional provisions respecting free exercise of religion. The [trial] judge's decision appears to conclude that the husband's free exercise claim fails because it is not grounded in a sincerely held religious belief. An essential prerequisite to a free exercise claim is a sincerely held religious belief. A court may not examine the truth behind a person's religious beliefs. However, inquiry into the sincerity of a professed belief is constitutionally appropriate under both the First Amendment; and article 2 of the Massachusetts Constitution.

The judge did not question the husband's general devotion to Hinduism. At the same time, he found that "the husband's reasons for his insistence on having the Chudakarana are not purely religious[,] [but] an issue of control." The record supports this determination. We credit, as we must, the judge's finding, based upon his credibility assessment. However, the determination that the husband's motivation is not "purely religious" is different altogether from whether his belief is "sincerely held." We need not, and should not, predicate a decision implicating a parent's free exercise right and his fundamental liberty interest in child rearing upon the tenuous ground that the parents' underlying religious belief is not "sincerely held" because the motivation is not "purely religious."[3]

Although the husband conceptualizes the probate judge's action as a State-imposed limitation on his own free exercise of religion, whether Chudakarana is performed upon the child implicates not only the husband's but also the wife's fundamental rights. These include the right to direct their daughter's upbringing and religious formation.

The due process clause protects certain fundamental rights and liberty interests, including the right of a parent to direct a child's education and upbringing. For the court to issue an order upholding the husband's fundamental right to direct that the ceremony of Chudakarana be performed upon the child would repudiate permanently the wife's corresponding right to direct that the ceremony not be performed. Conversely, to order that the ceremony not be performed, as the wife would have it, would repudiate the husband's fundamental rights.

A court is justifiably loath to order a restriction on either parent's fundamental rights to free exercise of religion and to determine the child's religious upbringing and is constitutionally limited in doing so unless there is a compelling State interest such as preventing demonstrable physical or psychological harm to the child. . . . Here, the husband failed to demonstrate a compelling State interest for performing the ceremony on the child. Evidence was lacking that failure to perform the ceremony would "cause the child significant harm by adversely affecting the child's health, safety, or welfare." [Conversely, the wife] did not establish that performing the ceremony would subject the child to physical or psychological harm, a compelling State interest that would support an order restricting the husband's fundamental rights. [A]bsent proof either way, the order [of the trial court order delaying the ceremony until the child can make that determination, absent the parents' written agreement] is a narrowly tailored accommodation that "intrudes least on the religious inclinations of either parent and . . . is compatible with the health of the child." . . .

Notes and Questions

1. Different approaches. In custody proceedings involving disputes about a child's religion (identity or practice), courts generally follow one of three approaches: (1) religion may be one, but not the sole, factor in allocating custody; (2) religion may be considered only to the extent that it affects the child's secular well-being; or (3) religion may be considered only for children with ascertainable religious preferences or for whom religion has become an important part of their identity.

---

3. We also cannot delve into differences between the parties over whether strict adherence to Hindu religious belief requires that Chudakarana be performed. Resolution of that matter clearly would involve assessment of the religion's doctrine. The First Amendment protects sincerely held religious beliefs even when these differ from the established dogma of a religion or are not accepted as dogma by any religion.

The ALI Principles prohibit a court from considering the "religious practices" of either the parent or child except in cases of "severe and almost certain harm" to the child or to protect the child's ability to practice a religion "that has been a significant part of the child's life." ALI Principles §2.12(1)(c). How does a court determine if the religion has become a "significant part" of the child's life?

2. Constitutional limitations. The U.S. Constitution constrains judicial consideration of religion.

a. Establishment and Free Exercise Clauses. Under the Establishment Clause (requiring separation between church and state and forbidding excessive government entanglement with religion), a court may not weigh the relative merits of parents' religions or favor an observant parent over a nonreligious parent. The First Amendment's Free Exercise Clause limits the government—including courts—from interfering with a parent's right to practice their religion (or not to practice any religion) without a sufficient reason. Thus, even if a parent is not granted primary physical or legal custody, that parent generally has a right to practice their religion in the presence of the child. See, e.g., Moore v. Moore, 2016 WL 4487697, at *3 (Ky. Ct. App. 2016) (holding that because the father had a "constitutional right to express his religion," this expression could not be limited unless the exposure was "substantially likely to result in physical or emotional harm to the child").

b. Criticisms. Critics charge that in practice—both in the context of custody allocation and with regard to the imposition of restrictions—courts often disregard First Amendment rights.[11] How can judges adjudicate these types of parental disputes without violating constitutional guarantees? Should courts follow a policy of noninterference? What compelling interest might justify interference? May a court, consistent with constitutional concerns, require a parent to *support* the other parent's religion? See Gerson v. Gerson, 868 N.Y.S.2d 551 (App. Div. 2009).

3. Adverse effect. As noted above, even when a parent is not awarded primary physical or legal custody of a child, they generally are permitted to practice their religion in the presence of the child. Most courts permit orders restricting a parent's religious beliefs or practices only when there is evidence of harm to the child. However, courts adhere to different thresholds of harm: (1) actual or substantial harm, or (2) risk of harm.

What test does *Sagar* follow? Will the Sagars' child be harmed if the ceremony is performed? If it is not? Should courts make custody determinations based on the possibility of *future* harm? Does a child's *confusion* resulting from exposure to different religious beliefs constitute harm? Compare In re Marriage of Minix, 801 N.E.2d 1201 (Ill. Ct. App. 2003), with Holder v. Holder, 872 N.E.2d 1239 (Ohio Ct. App. 2007). Should courts assume that religious disputes always harm children? See Felton v. Felton, 418 N.E.2d 606, 607-608 (Mass. 1981).

---

[11]. Eugene Volokh, Parent-Child Speech and Child Custody Speech Restrictions, 81 N.Y.U. L. Rev. 631 (2006); Jennifer Ann Drobac, Note, For the Sake of the Children: Court Consideration of Religion in Child Custody Cases, 50 Stan. L. Rev. 1609, 1611 (1998).

4. Premarital agreements. What is the appropriate balance between the parent's constitutional rights and respect for private ordering, for example, when the parents have a premarital agreement that addresses religious upbringing? Cf. Zummo v. Zummo, 574 A.2d 1130 (Pa. Super. Ct. 1990) (noncustodial divorced father wants children to attend Catholic services, contrary to premarital agreement providing that the children will be raised as Jewish). Does enforcement of such an agreement constrain a parent's free exercise of religion? If a parent violates the term of a marital agreement about the child's religion, can the parent be held in contempt? See Greene v. Greene, 701 S.E.2d 911 (Ga. Ct. App. 2010).

5. Child's religious preference. What role should the child's own religious preference play in the adjudication of parental disputes? Did *Sagar* appropriately take into consideration the child's preference? How should a court evaluate whether the child's preference is genuine or the product of parental pressure?

6. Legal custody, religion, and decisionmaking. Legal custody is the right to make important decisions about the child, including, for example, the child's religious upbringing. When the parents disagree about the child's religious upbringing, the court may authorize only one parent to have the right to make decisions with respect to the child's religious upbringing. Does such an award violate the Free Exercise rights of the other parent? Why or why not?

Problems

1. When Jeffrey (who is Christian) marries Barbara (who is Jewish), they agree to raise their children in the Jewish tradition. After the birth of their second child, Jeffrey becomes a member of a fundamentalist Christian faith whose adherents believe that nonmembers are damned to hell. As a result, Jeffrey makes serious efforts to persuade his children to accept his church's teachings. Barbara has recently adopted Orthodox Judaism, and the couple becomes enmeshed in "opposite doctrinal extremes." After the parents file for divorce, both seek custody. Barbara seeks to limit the children's exposure to Jeffrey's religion. The court awards joint legal custody but forbids Jeffrey from exposing the children to religious content that will cause them to feel upset or to worry about themselves or their mother. Barbara appeals the joint custody award, asserting that it is inappropriate because the parents cannot come to any agreement on the children's moral and religious development. What result?

Based on the standard adopted in this jurisdiction, would exposure to the father's religion cause "substantial physical or emotional injury" to the children and have a "similar harmful tendency for the future"? What evidence would suffice to establish substantial harm? Is limiting the children's exposure to Jeffrey's religion appropriate? Is it constitutional? Does the limitation constitute an invasion of privacy? See Kendall v. Kendall, 687 N.E.2d 1228 (Mass. 1997). See also Koch v. Koch, 207 So. 3d 914 (Fla. Dist. Ct. App. 2016); Pankratz v. Pankratz, 2017 WL 4842400 (Tenn. Ct. App. 2017).

2. Shannon and Mathew, the divorced parents of five-year-old Thomas, execute a parenting plan that requires both parents' consent concerning issues of health and education. Shannon is a chiropractor and a proponent of holistic medicine. According to her religious beliefs, "God has provided the human body with an innate immunity system that enables the body to heal itself, and anything introduced into the body to prevent or treat disease violates God's will." For that reason, she opposes vaccinations. Mathew, who is Jewish, prefers their son to receive traditional medical health care, including vaccinations. Thomas is ready to start kindergarten, but his neighborhood public school refuses to admit him unless he is vaccinated. Because Shannon opposes vaccination, she wants to enroll Thomas in a private school that will accommodate her religious beliefs. What result? How should the court assess the element of harm? See Winters v. Brown, 51 So. 3d 656 (Fla. Dist. Ct. App. 2011). See also Brown v. Smith, 235 Cal. Rptr. 3d 218 (Ct. App. 2018) (upholding constitutionality, under state constitution, of mandatory immunization requirement for school children, without exemption for personal beliefs); Miller v. Dicherry, 251 So. 3d 428 (La. Ct. App. 2018) (upholding award of joint custody but awarding father right to make medical decisions, including vaccination).

The parents also disagree about circumcision. Thomas was not circumcised at birth, but Mathew continues to advocate doing so. Mathew argues that he has a constitutionally protected right to circumcise his son and contends that circumcision is medically advisable, independent of the religious reasons for it. He also argues that Thomas himself wants to be circumcised. How should the court rule in this religious dispute? See In re Marriage of Boldt, 176 P.3d 388 (Or. 2008). How should the court assess the element of harm to the child? Suppose that Mathew has Thomas vaccinated or circumcised without Shannon's knowledge or consent. Can the court find him in contempt? See Miller v. Miller, 2013 WL 2382595 (Tenn. Ct. App. 2013). These kinds of disputes sometimes arise for nonreligious reasons. During the early years of the COVID-19 pandemic, for example, some parents disagreed about whether to permit their children to receive the COVID vaccination for non-religious reasons, and courts were called upon to resolve those disputes. Should the fact that the parents' reasons are not religiously grounded affect the way that the disputes are resolved? See, e.g., Nina Feldman, She Wanted to Vaccinate Their Kids Against COVID. He Didn't. A Judge Had to Decide, NPR, May 1, 2022, https://www.npr.org/sections/health-shots/2022/05/01/1091495933/divorced-parents-vaccination.

(4) Parental Sexual Orientation and Gender Identity

IN RE MARRIAGE OF BLACK
392 P.3d 1041 (Wash. 2017)

FAIRHURST, C.J.

. . . Rachelle and Charles Black married in July 1994. [W]hen Rachelle and Charles had their first child in 1999, they agreed Rachelle would stop working and be a stay-at-home parent while Charles continued to work. Rachelle and Charles have three sons together, ages 17, 14, and 9. [F]or most of their marriage, Rachelle was the primary caretaker. . .

Rachelle, Charles, and the children attended a "conservative Christian" church [and the children attended private Christian schools]. Kelly Theriot Leblanc, the guardian ad litem (GAL) assigned to this case, testified that the "family attends a church where the teachings are that homosexuality is a sin." . . . Jennifer Knight, the children's therapist, described their upbringing as "a very dogmatic fundamentalist situation, both at school and at home."

In December 2011, Rachelle told Charles that she believed she might be "gay." . . . Rachelle's recognition of her sexual orientation altered the status quo at the Black household, and trying to maintain the status quo for the sake of the children became increasingly difficult. Although Rachelle and Charles continued to live in the same house, Rachelle began sleeping in a basement room after Charles allegedly sexually assaulted her, which he denies, and after he told friends, family, and church members about her sexual orientation without her permission. Rachelle stopped attending the family church, while Charles and the children continued to attend. Around the same time, Rachelle began a romantic relationship with a woman and began spending more time away from home. . . .

Rachelle Black (middle, top row), with her sons Caleb (top left), Ethan (top right), Jonah (front), and her partner, Angela (second from right, front row)

[Rachelle filed for dissolution in May 2013.] Because Rachelle and Charles had not disclosed Rachelle's sexual orientation to their children, [the children's therapist, Jennifer Knight] was the first person to tell them that their mother is gay. Knight testified that the 15 year old at the time, was "flat" upon hearing the news, and Knight thought he "was still processing it"; that the 12 year old "snuggled up to his mom kind of indicating, you know, I'm going to love you no matter what"; and that the 7 year old was too young to understand. Knight believed "the children are starting to get more used to the idea that their mother, you know, is in a relationship with a female."

Knight's primary concern was [that] Rachelle and Charles' separation "is a major change considering the background of these children," and Knight believed the best outcome for the children would be a stable environment that "minimize[s] . . . future changes." Knight recommended Rachelle's partner have no contact with the children for the time being.

Knight testified that she believed Charles was the more stable parent. Knight noted that Rachelle was unemployed, did not have a plan for future housing, and relied on her partner for support. . . . On the other hand, Knight stated that Charles "has a history of employment and being a good provider, so obviously he is a stable parent." She testified that the children "have reported that over the last couple of years they've seen [Rachelle] a lot less and that they have spent more time with their father." Despite "some concern about him not being as active in the past with the children because he was the main provider," the children reported that Charles "has been more part of their daily life" in recent years.

Leblanc, the GAL, shared many of Knight's concerns. [B]ut Leblanc's recommendation was also based on Rachelle's sexual orientation, at least insofar as she believed it conflicted with the children's religious beliefs. In a preliminary report, Leblanc wrote that Rachelle's "lifestyle choice" might cause controversy given the children's background:

> While it is not my intent to cast judgment on [Rachelle's] lifestyle choice, the fact remains that it is a choice that can result in significant controversy. In this instance, the issue has disrupted the marriage and also resulted in difficulty with extended family. Given the family's faith and historical belief system, it is my opinion that the children should be immediately enrolled in counseling. . . .

Leblanc also suggested the children might experience "bullying" as a result of Rachelle's decision to leave the marriage and begin a relationship with her partner. . . .

Ultimately, Leblanc's final report demonstrates a belief that the children's religious upbringing would hinder their acceptance of Rachelle's new life. . . . Consistent with this belief, Leblanc recommended that Charles serve as the primary residential parent. She also recommended that Knight have the discretion to determine when the children may have contact with Rachelle's partner. Leblanc further recommended broad prohibitions on Rachelle's ability to discuss religion and sexual orientation with her children:

> I recommend that [Rachelle] be ordered to refrain from having further conversations with the children regarding religion, homosexuality, or other alternative lifestyle concepts and further, that she be prohibited from exposing the children to literature or electronic media; taking them to movies or events; providing them with symbolic clothing or jewelry; or otherwise engaging in conduct that could reasonably be interpreted as being related to those topics unless the discussion, conduct, or activity is specifically authorized and approved by Ms. Knight.

Some of these restrictions were recommended in response to Rachelle's parental efforts to explain the circumstances to her children. For example, Rachelle showed her oldest son a video documentary addressing different Christian attitudes toward same-sex relationships after he asked a question about the issue. On another occasion, the second oldest son asked if he could wear a rainbow bracelet Rachelle had with the words "love and pride." [The trial court largely adopted Leblanc's recommendations in designating Charles as the primary residential parent.]

ANALYSIS

When a trial court fashions a permanent parenting plan, it considers a set of statutory factors aimed at evaluating each parent's abilities, the relationship of each parent to the children, and the children's best interests in light of their needs. Although there are few limits on this analysis, a trial court may not consider a parent's sexual orientation as a factor for custody decisions absent an express showing of harm to the children. . . . Custody and visitation rights "must be determined with reference to the needs of the child rather than the sexual preferences of the parent." . . .

Charles concedes that custody decisions cannot be based on a parent's sexual orientation absent a showing of harm. . . . [He] correctly notes that the Court of Appeals upheld a parenting plan under similar circumstances in [In re Marriage of Wicklund, 932 P.2d 652 (Wash. Ct. App. 1996)]. But since *Wicklund* was decided, courts have recognized that members of the LGBT community are vulnerable to discrimination [citing Obergefell v. Hodges, 135 S. Ct. 2584 (2015)]. To guard against discriminatory impulses in custody proceedings, many jurisdictions prohibit consideration of a parent's sexual orientation unless there is an express showing of harm to the children. Even if a parent's sexual orientation is contrary to the children's religious values, a trial court may not consider it in a custody determination unless the evidence shows "direct harm to the children." This approach promotes fairness by fostering an attitude of neutrality. [C]ourts must remain neutral toward a parent's sexual orientation in order to ensure that custody decisions are based on the "needs of the child rather than the sexual preferences of the parent." This neutrality requirement fulfills an underlying purpose of the dissolution statutes by protecting families who are otherwise vulnerable to the "arbitrary imposition of the court's preferences.". . . When the record suggests the trial court failed to maintain a neutral attitude, absent an express showing of direct harm, we cannot be confident that the trial court's allocation of residential time serves the best interests of the children rather than "penaliz[ing] . . . parents for their conduct."

The record here shows the trial court did not remain neutral when it considered Rachelle's sexual orientation as a factor for determining provisions in the parenting plan. [E]ven though the trial court here did not explicitly suggest that Rachelle's sexual orientation made her an unfit parent, its reasoning is nevertheless clear: the children are allegedly uncomfortable with homosexuality due to their religious upbringing, Charles—a heterosexual who shares those same beliefs—is better suited to maintain that religious upbringing, therefore, he is the more stable parent. [S]uch reasoning unfairly punishes a parent in a custody proceeding on the basis of her sexual orientation.

The trial court also adopted a restriction on Rachelle's conduct that prohibited her from discussing "alternative lifestyles" with her children. . . . The prohibitions assume that a parent's discussion of sexual orientation or her own life and beliefs would have a negative impact on the children. The trial court's unnecessary references to "homosexuality" and "alternative lifestyle concepts" cast doubt on its ruling. This is particularly true given the trial court's written ruling emphasizes that both parents have strong relationships with the children and that they both have "good potential for future performance of parenting functions."

[T]he record indicates that improper bias influenced the trial court's decision. For example, Leblanc made several problematic statements suggesting she was biased against Rachelle. First, Leblanc repeatedly referred to Rachelle's sexual orientation as a "lifestyle choice." This is contrary to our current understanding of sexual orientation. See *Obergefell*, 135 S. Ct. at 2596 ("Only in more recent years have psychiatrists and others recognized that sexual orientation is both a normal expression of human sexuality and immutable.").

Second, Leblanc suggested that the controversy surrounding Rachelle's sexual orientation could harm the children by inviting bullying. Other courts have expressly rejected this reasoning in custody disputes [citing] Palmore v. Sidoti,

466 U.S. 429, 433 (1984) ("Private biases may be outside the reach of the law, but the law cannot, directly or indirectly, give them effect."). Third, Leblanc recommended an unconstitutional restriction of Rachelle's conduct that prohibited her from discussing religion, homosexuality, and "other alternative lifestyle concepts" with her children. . . . Finally, Leblanc's opinion that Charles is the more stable parent seems to stem from a belief that Rachelle caused the separation. . . . But "custody and visitation privileges are not to be used to penalize or reward parents for their conduct." . . .

We have acknowledged the presence of biases in other contexts. See State v. Saintcalle, 309 P.3d 326 (2013) (plurality opinion) ("[W]e all live our lives with stereotypes that are ingrained and often unconscious, implicit biases that endure despite our best efforts to eliminate them."). Similarly, one purpose of the dissolution statutes is to prevent "arbitrary imposition of the court's preferences" and thereby protect families who are otherwise "vulnerable to a trial court's biases." The record shows that Leblanc's bias "found its way into the final judgment." The trial court's written ruling and the final parenting plan indicate it failed to remain neutral regarding Rachelle's sexual orientation. The trial court therefore abused its discretion when it designated Charles as the primary residential parent.

[T]he trial court [also] abused its discretion when it favored Charles' religious beliefs. . . . Although a trial court may consider the parents' and the children's religious beliefs when fashioning a parenting plan, it may not favor either parent's religious beliefs without a clear showing of harm to the children. . . . Given the facts of this case, the trial court's improper consideration of Rachelle's sexual orientation was intertwined with an implicit preference for Charles' religious beliefs. Charles has continued to participate in a religion that condemns same-sex relationships, while Rachelle has modified her religious views. Because the children were taught certain religious beliefs, the trial court concluded Charles was better suited to maintain those beliefs and therefore was the more stable parent. In so concluding, the trial court made no express findings of actual or potential harm to the children due to Rachelle's modified religious views. . . .

Bias against Rachelle permeated the proceedings here. [W]e therefore reverse and remand. . . . Given the nature of our conclusion, we agree with Rachelle that the case on remand should be reassigned to a different judge. . . .

NOTE: WHO IS RACHELLE BLACK?

David Ward, Postscript: In re Marriage of Black[*]
Personal communication, Aug. 2, 2019

From the moment Rachelle Black received the trial court's decision severely restricting her residential schedule with her children, she was determined to

[*]. David Ward, former Staff Attorney at Legal Voice in Seattle, WA, was lead counsel for Rachelle Black.

reverse the decision on appeal—not just for herself and her children, but for other LGBTQ+ parents who have faced longstanding discrimination in family courts. She was referred to Legal Voice, a women's rights organization based in Seattle with a long history of advocating for LGBTQ+ people in the Northwest. The Seattle law firm, Perkins Coie, agreed to assist as pro bono cooperating counsel.

Ultimately, the Court of Appeals struck down the restriction that Rachelle couldn't speak with her children about her sexual orientation or changing religious views but refused to change the residential restriction (four days every other week). We petitioned the Washington State Supreme Court for review. Family law cases are rarely accepted for review, but the Supreme Court agreed to take this one.

During oral argument, we had a strong sense that the Justices understood why we were there shortly after our opposing counsel began to speak. The opposing counsel started by arguing that trial courts should be able to consider a parent's sexual orientation in child custody cases, depending on the "emotional place" of the child. Justice Mary Yu (the first openly LGBTQ+ member of the Court), interjected: "As you continue, I just want you to substitute 'sexual orientation' and use 'race' and ask . . . is the analysis the same?" That question set the tone for the rest of the oral argument. It signaled to us that the Court understood that child custody decisions cannot rely on biased stereotypes or speculation that children raised in a conservative religious environment would be unable to adjust to having an LGBTQ+ parent—just as courts had previously rejected similar arguments in cases involving parents who entered interracial relationships after a divorce. Instead, what was most important was Rachelle's connection with her children, which was strong and loving.

The Washington Supreme Court unanimously reversed the trial court's decision and remanded for a new trial. The parents resolved the matter shortly thereafter, agreeing to 50/50 residential time. At that point, it had been two and a half years since the first trial, and the oldest child had already turned 18. Although Rachelle will never get back the time that she lost with her children, she is proud that her case is helping other LGBTQ+ parents and their children. Today, she is still with her partner, Angela, and her youngest child refers to them sometimes as "Mom One" and "Mom Two."

Notes and Questions

1. Parental sexual orientation: Approaches. In the past, courts adopted one of the following approaches in custody cases in which one of the parents had come out as lesbian, gay, bisexual, transgender, and queer/questioning (LGBTQ): (1) an LGBTQ parent was considered per se unfit simply because they were LGBTQ (the "per se" rule); (2) the parent's sexual orientation could be considered as a negative factor in the best interest of the child analysis; or (3) the parent's sexual orientation could not be taken into account unless there was evidence that it had caused an adverse impact or harm on the child (the nexus test). The last approach, the nexus test, is the majority rule today. Which approach does *Black* follow? See also

ALI Principles §2.12(1)(d), (e) (prohibiting a court from considering the sexual orientation of a parent except upon a showing of harm).

2. Adverse impact. Under the nexus text, what showing of adverse impact should suffice? Teasing? Bullying? Even if the child is experiencing teasing or bullying, would denying the LGBTQ parent primary custody likely bring an end to that teasing and bullying? How does *Black* respond to this concern? Suppose that the "adverse impact" consists of children's confusion about a parent's "coming out" or adjustment difficulties in response to parents' separation? See *Wicklund* (cited in *Black*). Is a court more likely to find harm if a parent is "out," or conversely, "in the closet"? See, e.g., Ex parte J.M.F., 730 So. 2d 1190 (Ala. 1998). Can *potential* harm suffice? Compare Pulliam v. Smith, 501 S.E.2d 898, 904 (N.C. 1998), with Taylor v. Taylor, 110 S.W.3d 731 (Ark. 2003).

3. Constitutional issues. Does consideration of a parent's sexual orientation in a custody dispute raise constitutional concerns? Do *Obergefell* and/or *Lawrence* mandate holding that a parent's sexual orientation must be *irrelevant* to the best interests analysis? How does *Black* respond? Returning to the teasing and bullying issue, is it constitutional to deny a parent custody because other people are expressing negative comments to the children about that parent's sexual orientation? Is *Palmore* relevant to this analysis?

4. Pretextual reasoning. *Black* is a rare and remarkable opinion for its candid recognition and rejection of the role of bias (both explicit and implicit) in LGBTQ custody decisionmaking. Bias often takes the form of pretextual reasoning. What pretextual reasoning in the lower court ruling does the court identify in *Black*?

5. Social science research. The per se rule was premised, implicitly at least, on the view that children were necessarily harmed by being raised by a lesbian, gay, or bisexual (LGB) parent. Empirical research fails to support this view. Rather, the overwhelming majority of research that compares heterosexual parents to LGB parents finds that LGB parents "are as fit and capable as heterosexual parents, and that their children are as psychologically healthy and well adjusted."[12] Accordingly, many professional organizations, such as the American Psychological Association, oppose discrimination against LGB parents.[13]

6. First Amendment concerns. The Washington Supreme Court in *Black* found that the trial court abused its discretion by prohibiting Rachelle from discussing "alternative lifestyles" with her children. When may a court limit a parent's First Amendment right to express communications about religion to a child? See, e.g., In re E.L.M.C., 100 P.3d 546 (Colo. Ct. App. 2004) (reversing trial court order

---

[12]. Amicus Brief of American Psychological Association, et al., in Support of Petitioners, Obergefell v. Hodges, 2015 WL 1004713, 22-30 (U.S., 2015).

[13]. The American Psychological Association Council of Representatives position statement (July 28, 2004), https://www.apa.org/news/press/response/gay-parents. Policy statements from other professional organizations can be found at https://www.hrc.org/resources/professional-organizations-on-lgbt-parenting.

enjoining one parent—who had been in a same-sex relationship with the other parent, but who later identified as heterosexual—from exposing the child to "religious upbringing or teaching . . . that can be considered homophobic").[14]

7. Other intimate relationships. In the past, courts sometimes denied custody based on the fact that the parent was in a nonmarital relationship. Under the modern nexus approach (influenced by the UMDA), a parent's intimate relationship(s), including a nonmarital one, should not be considered absent evidence it has caused an adverse impact. See UMDA §402. How does a court separate the effect on the child of a parent's sexual conduct from the effects of the dissolution itself? See, e.g., Gustaves v. Gustaves, 57 P.3d 775 (Idaho 2002) (mother's adultery caused child's regressive behavior).

8. Transgender parents. In the past, LGB parents frequently lost custody simply because they were lesbian, gay, or bisexual. Today, that result is much less likely to occur. The situation, by contrast, is markedly different for transgender parents, who remain extremely vulnerable to losing custody. Indeed, some transgender parents have had their parental rights terminated simply because they identified as transgender or because they transitioned. See, e.g., Daly v. Daly, 715 P.2d 56 (Nev. 1986); M.B. v. D.W., 236 S.W.3d 31 (Ky. Ct. App. 2007).[15]

9. Same-sex dissolution. *Black* involved a custody dispute between an LGBTQ parent and a non-LGBTQ parent. Today, some custody disputes are between two people who both are LGBTQ. In these cases, a parent's sexual orientation is unlikely to be invoked. The usual best interests of the child standard applies in such cases.

Rachel H. Farr & Abbie E. Goldberg, Same-Sex Relationship Dissolution and Divorce: How Will Children Be Affected?

in LGBTQ Divorce and Relationship Dissolution 151, 158-159
(Abbie E. Goldberg & Adam P. Romero eds., 2019)

Little research has examined children's response or adjustment to their same-sex parents' relationship dissolution, but available evidence indicates similarities to children who experience their heterosexual parents' divorce. [However, some differences emerge.]

Some post-separation issues that children face in the wake of their same-sex parents' dissolution are unique to having sexual minority parents. In one study, young adults who had experienced their same-sex parents' relationship

---

[14]. See also Eugene Volokh, Speech as Conduct: Generally Applicable Laws, Illegal Courses on Conduct, "Situation-Altering Utterances," and the Unchartered Zones, 90 Cornell L. Rev. 1277, 1299-1300 (2005) ("Courts may not diminish custody rights of a divorced parent because of the supposed harmfulness of the religious doctrine that he is teaching his children unless the religious teaching is not just against the child's 'best interests' but is actually likely to cause the child significant secular harm.").

[15]. See also Sonia Katyal & Ilona Turner, Transparenthood, 117 Mich. L. Rev. 1593 (2019) (discussing cases).

dissolution noted that the pain they felt about the break-up was accentuated by the lack of legal relationship recognition. In essence, they felt that their parents' relationship dissolution was minimized—and, in turn, they felt that outsiders often did not understand or empathize with their profound sadness surrounding their parents' break-up.

In other research, children of lesbian mothers noted difficulties in disclosing to others about their parents' separation, in light of heteronormative assumptions about having a mother and father rather than two mothers. Children also expressed guilt if they had lied to others about their family structure, yet these children also felt protective of and loyal toward their mothers, expressing strong, positive sentiments about their family. . . .

Problem

Robbie and Tracy married in 1985. They had two children during their marriage, Brian (born in 1991) and Meridith (born in 1998). Robbie is an attorney; Tracy is a doctor. After almost twenty years of marriage, Robbie announced that she was transgender and "would be transitioning from male to female." Prior to her transition, Robbie quit her job. Robbie and Tracy separated in 2004, and thereafter Tracy filed a divorce petition.

After trial, the trial court made a number of findings, including the following: "Both parents are good and loving parents. . . . The children's relationship with each parent is approximately equal. Each has performed equal but very different roles with the children. . . . Historically, the parties were a dual professional family, relying on the assistance of nannies." The trial court also found that both parents had engaged in conduct that adversely affected the children. Tracy, the trial court found, had "denigrated Robbie in front of the child." In one instance, Robbie pushed Tracy's mother and grabbed their daughter. In addition, the trial court found that "[Robbie] has indicated she will be undergoing sexual reassignment surgery sometime in the very near future. [Robbie's] surgery may be everything [she] has hoped for, or it may be disastrous. No one knows what is ahead[,] and the impact of gender reassignment surgery on the children is unknown." The court also noted that Tracy had consistent employment, while Robbie had quit her job. At trial, the guardian ad litem testified that Robbie had been the children's primary parent, that Tracy "had always been the secondary parent," and that "Robbie was the more nurturing and engaged parent." Based on these findings, the guardian ad litem recommended that the court designate Robbie as the primary residential parent.

The trial court granted primary residential placement with Tracy. Robbie appeals on the ground that the trial court improperly relied on her transgender status when allocating custody. What result? See Magnuson v. Magnuson, 170 P.3d 65, 66 (Wash. Ct. App. 2007).

(5) Children's Gender Identity

SMITH v. SMITH

2007 WL 901599 (Ohio Ct. App. 2007)

WAITE, J.

Appellant Victoria Smith is appealing the judgment . . . transferring custody of her children to their father in post-dissolution proceedings. The case revolves around the parties' older son, now twelve years old, who has exhibited signs from a very early age that he wanted to be treated as a girl.

[In their initial divorce proceeding, the court designated the mother, Victoria, to be the residential parent for the parties' two children. Three years later, the father, Kevin, filed a motion seeking a modification based on allegations that the mother had enrolled their older child in a new school as a girl under the name of Christine; that she was taking the child to a transgender support group; and that she was seeking transgender health care for the child. The trial court issued a modification order reallocating parental rights and responsibilities from the mother, Appellant, to the father, Appellee. Appellant appealed.]

Appellant and Appellee separated in January of 2000, when the boy was five. After the marriage was dissolved in 2001, Appellee had very little contact with his children. Appellant was the residential parent of both children and the primary adult influence in their lives.

The [trial] court found that in the spring of 2003, Appellant told Appellee that their older son had GID [gender identity disorder]. Appellee did not accept this conclusion, and produced photos and videos that showed the boy enjoying stereotypical male activities and wearing male clothing. [One year later,] Appellant's older son sent a videotape to Appellee. The videotape recorded the child sitting in a chair and talking about his gender, trying to explain the situation to his father. The boy stated numerous times on the tape that he is a girl, wants to be a girl, and that he would like to live a normal life as a girl. He stated that he looked forward to the time when he could wear girl's clothes all the time. He stated that he is a girl even if he does not have all the body parts of a girl. He expressed a desire to either go to school as a girl or be home-schooled. He also stated a number of times that he hoped his father would understand the situation, but that no matter what, he intended to become a girl. The child was also upset by the fact that his father sent a "spy" to Geauga Lake to get a picture of the boy in a bikini.

Appellee was very upset by this tape. Prior to receiving the tape, Appellee had not had any discussions with his older son about gender or related issues, even though he had known about some of the boy's feelings and gender behavior since before the dissolution . . . .

The trial court's judgment entry concluded that Appellant disobeyed prior court orders concerning her older son. The court noted that Appellant . . . allowed him to wear a bikini . . . Appellant also referred to her son as "Christine" when introducing him . . . . At some point, Appellant began calling her son by the name "Christmas," which the trial judge concluded was a violation of his order not to refer to him by a female name. The judge also noted that, during the very hearing on the motion to reallocate parental rights, Appellant repeatedly referred to the boy as "she" and then corrected herself. Based on these four findings, the court concluded that Appellant could not be counted on to follow any court order that she might disagree with.

[In the trial court proceedings,] each party called two expert witnesses to testify about GID. [Appellee's experts both concluded that the child did not have GID. Appellant's experts both concluded that the child met the criteria for GID. The court] conducted its own interview of the boy. During the interview, the child expressed a desire to wear girl's clothes and to have "girl stuff," although he did not specify what "girl stuff" meant. The court found that the boy enjoyed stereotypical male activities such as wrestling with this brother, shooting his BB gun, and playing video games. The boy did not talk about participating in any stereotypical female activities except for wearing girl's clothes. The court also found that the child's friends were all boys, and that he appeared to be attracted to one particular girl who was not attracted to him. The boy did not report being attracted to any boys except as general friends. He was not able to name any female heroes or idols. The court did not notice the boy exhibit any female mannerisms during the in camera interview.

The trial judge also viewed the . . . videotape in which the boy tried to explain his feelings to his father. The judge was not convinced that the boy was sincere in this videotape and did not believe he was exhibiting any female characteristics in this tape.

The judge filed a judgment entry [that] gave Appellee custody of the children from Tuesday to Sunday, and gave Appellant custody from Sunday to Tuesday. . . . The court ordered the parties to keep both children enrolled in Toronto City Schools. . . . The boy was not to be encouraged or permitted to wear girl's clothes. He was not permitted to go by a girl's name or be referred to as "she" or "her." Appellant was specifically ordered not to refer to the boy by the name "Christmas." The child was not permitted to attend transgender support groups and was to become "disassociated with that lifestyle," absent agreement of both parties or further order of the court. Both Appellant and Appellee were ordered to obtain psychological evaluations of themselves and of their son. The purpose of the evaluations was to "aid the Court to determine, among other things, whether Mother is pushing [the child] toward a feminine identity or if Father simply fails to see that which is plainly there to be seen."

[T]he court designated Mark King, Ph.D. as the doctor to perform the psychological evaluations. . . . Dr. King stated . . . that the child was a very feminized male, and that "five years down the road it might go the other way." He recommended that Appellant's older son be raised as a biological boy. Dr. King noted that the boy was depressed, and he mentioned suicide as a worst case scenario possibility. Dr. King stated that, although he disagreed with some of the actions that Appellant took regarding her older son, "her motivations were honest." He believed that Appellant always acted in the child's best interests. He concluded that Appellant would follow court orders in the future, even if she were designated as the sole residential parent.

On August 19, 2005, the court issued its final order in this case. [The court found that there had been a substantial change of circumstances since the original custody order.] The court found that Appellant was not likely to comply with future court orders, and that her prior failure to obey the court's orders undermined what the court was trying to accomplish in the current proceedings. The court then modified the 2001 custody order and designated Appellee as the sole residential parent. . . . The trial court determined that Appellant's older son needed to be in an environment where he could be treated like a boy and allowed to develop as a boy, so that he could make a more informed decision about his gender at a later point in life. . . . The court decided that by making Appellee the residential parent, the child would be permitted to find out if he was only acting like a girl to please his mother, or if he really was a transgender child.

[On appeal, the appellate court concluded that the facts supported the trial court's conclusion and its modification of custody to the father.]

Notes and Questions

1. Modification of custody. The *Smith* case involves a request to "modify" or change an original judicial allocation of custody. Most states require a showing of substantial change of circumstances in addition to a best interests determination. The purpose of this additional burden is to discourage future litigation and to promote stability/security for the child.

2. Custody litigation regarding transgender children. Parental disputes involving children with non-conforming expressions of gender have proliferated in recent years. One parent may allow the child to express their gender identity, while the other parent may not. The differing parental approaches can create and exacerbate conflict between the parents and harm the child. Such harm may take the form of the child's suicidal ideation.[16] Parental support and the provision of transgender health care may reduce this risk.[17]

Recent empirical research reports the frequency of custody awards to the nonaffirming parent.[18] How should a court allocate custody in such cases? What

---

[16]. Ashley Austin et al., Suicidality among Transgender Youth: Elucidating the Role of Interpersonal Risk Factors, 37 J. of Interpersonal Violence 5 (2022) (noting that, according to one survey, "82% of transgender individuals have considered killing themselves and 40% have attempted suicide").

[17]. Yale School of Medicine, Biased Science: The Texas and Alabama Measures Criminalizing Medical Treatment for Transgender Children and Adolescents Rely on Inaccurate and Misleading Scientific Claims, Apr. 28, 2022 (noting that "in a study of youth receiving transition-related care, parent support of youths' transgender identities was associated with lower rates of depression and higher quality of life scores"), https://medicine.yale.edu/lgbtqi/research/gender-affirming-care/report%20on%20the%20science%20of%20gender-affirming%20care%20final%20april%2028%202022_442952_55174_v1.pdf.

[18]. See Katherina A. Kuvalanka et al., An Exploratory Study of Custody Challenges Experienced by Affirming Mothers of Transgender and Gender-Nonconforming Children, 57 Fam. Ct. Rev. 54, 55 (2019) (noting that "[i]n only one of the five cases summarized in law review articles was an affirming parent awarded custody over a nonaffirming parent"). See also Marie-Amélie George, Exploring Identity, 55 Fam. L.Q. 1, 26 (2021) (concluding that "[c]ases involving a pre-adolescent gender expansive children . . . have produced disjointed results").

factors are relevant? When is joint legal custody—that is, joint decisionmaking power over things like medical care—appropriate, and when is it inappropriate?

3. Children's transgender status and sex discrimination. As revealed by the trial court judge in the principal case, some judges order parents not to dress their children in clothing typically associated with one gender, or to refer to their children by a name typically associated with one gender. Do such orders impermissibly discriminate on the basis of sex, in violation of the Equal Protection Clause?

4. Legislative responses. These cases have prompted a flurry of legislative activity. Recently, Texas Governor Greg Abbott and Texas Attorney General Ken Paxton issued orders directing that certain forms of transgender health care to children can be considered child abuse, as the following excerpt explains.[19] Such determinations may result in custody removals and even termination of parental rights (discussed in Chapter IX).

J. David Goodman, How Medical Care for Transgender Youth Became "Child Abuse" in Texas

N.Y. Times, Mar. 11, 2022
https://www.nytimes.com/2022/03/11/us/texas-transgender-youth-medical-care-abuse.html

Jeffrey Younger, a parent involved in a long-running custody dispute involving the gender identity of one of his children

Jeffrey Younger fought for years with his ex-wife, a pediatrician, over the gender identity of one of their twins. While she followed the advice of their children's doctor to affirm the child's desire to dress as a girl, grow long hair and be known as Luna, Mr. Younger steadfastly objected. He resisted the new name, insisting instead on boys' clothes, short haircuts and the name the couple had chosen at birth.

What began in a single household in a small community outside Dallas became a very public custody battle between Mr. Younger and Dr. Anne Georgulas, transforming him into a folk hero among conservatives and amplifying a growing effort to roll back transgender protections in state houses across America.

It paved the way, too, for an order late last month by Gov. Greg Abbott of Texas to investigate parents for child abuse if they provide certain medical

[19]. See, e.g., Doe v. Abbott, Original Petition, https://www.aclutx.org/sites/default/files/field_documents/petition_-_doe_v._abbott_-_final_redacted.pdf.

treatments to their transgender children. . . . The fight over transgender issues, waged on several fronts in recent years, has increasingly focused on medical treatments for children. [Major medical groups and transgender advocates who support the provision of medically appropriate transgender health care have been pitted against large conservative organizations, such as the Heritage Foundation, the Family Policy Alliance, the Alliance Defending Freedom, and the American Principles Project. Those who support access to transgender health care cite evidence that the approach can improve children's mental health and reduce suicidality. Opponents argue that children are too young to make such a consequential decision and must be shielded from potentially life-altering treatments. Mr. Younger waged an effective battle as an outspoken opponent of access to gender-affirming care.]

In court transcripts, Dr. Georgulas [the mother] said she had followed the lead of her transgender child, who is now 9, and the determinations of doctors. . . .

A court in August gave Dr. Georgulas custody of the children, including control of all medical decisions and the sole right "to make decisions concerning the children's haircuts." But it barred her from providing any puberty-blocking drugs, hormones or surgery without a court order.

The case's growing public profile coincided with broadening medical acceptance of gender-affirming care—and a backlash. The American Academy of Pediatrics in 2018 issued its first policy statement on the approach, which urges parents to support the identity expressed by their child and provides guidance for treatment, including medications that delay puberty.

[Conversely, a range of organizations including the Heritage Foundation, along with the Family Policy Alliance, have hosted discussions suggesting that children are harmed by the provision of transgender health care. Their efforts to enact new laws prohibiting such medical care have made significant headway. As of July 2023, 20 states have enacted laws restricting access to transgender health care for young people. The first such law was enacted in 2021. Litigation challenging Governor Abbott's order remains ongoing.]

NOTE: PARENTS WITH DISABILITIES

The health of the parents is another relevant factor in the best interests determination. All states either mandate or permit consideration of a parent's physical and mental health. See, e.g., UMDA §402(5) (mandating consideration).

Formerly, many trial courts assumed that parents with severe physical disabilities were per se unfit. This presumption depended on the specific disability. "[D]eaf parents are thought to be incapable of effectively stimulating language skills, blind parents cannot provide adequate attention or discipline; and parents with spinal cord injuries cannot adequately supervise their children."[20] Courts were especially concerned when the children themselves did not have disabilities.

---

[20]. Michael Ashley Stein, Mommy Has a Blue Wheelchair: Recognizing the Parental Rights of Individuals with Disabilities, 60 Brook. L. Rev. 1069, 1083 (1994).

In the late 1970s, two cases changed the presumption of unfitness to an emphasis on the *effects* of the parent's disability on the child. See Warnick v. Couey, 359 So. 2d 801 (Ala. Civ. App. 1978); In re Marriage of Carney, 598 P.2d 36, 44 (Cal. 1979). In *Carney*, the California Supreme Court refused to change a custody award to a father after he became a quadriplegic as a result of a Jeep accident while serving in the military reserve. The court reasoned that the "essence of parenting":

> lies in the ethical, emotional, and intellectual guidance the parent gives to the child throughout his formative years, and often beyond. The source of this guidance is the adult's own experience of life; its motive power is parental love and concern for the child's well-being; and its teachings deal with such fundamental matters as the child's feelings about himself, his relationships with others, his system of values, his standards of conduct, and his goals and priorities in life. Even if it were true, as the court herein asserted, that William cannot do "anything" for his sons except "talk to them and teach them, be a tutor," that would not only be "enough"—contrary to the court's conclusion—it would be the most valuable service a parent can render. Yet his capacity to do so is entirely unrelated to his physical prowess: however limited his bodily strength may be, a handicapped parent is a whole person to the child who needs his affection, sympathy, and wisdom to deal with the problems of growing up. Indeed, in such matters his handicap may well be an asset: few can pass through the crucible of a severe physical disability without learning enduring lessons in patience and tolerance.

Today, parents with disabilities still confront substantial bias in legal decisionmaking about their children. Commentators document high removal rates of children from parents with disabilities due to bias, ignorance about disability and adaptive equipment/services, and the lack of appropriate services.[21] See also Wills v. Gregory, 92 N.E.3d 1133, 1142-1144 (Ind. Ct. App. 2018) (dissent criticizes bias).

(6) Domestic Violence

PETERS-RIEMERS v. RIEMERS

644 N.W.2d 197 (N.D. 2002)

NEUMANN, Justice.

. . . Roland met Jenese, a non-U.S. citizen, in Belize in 1995 while vacationing there. . . . In early 1996, at Roland's invitation, Jenese left Belize and moved to North Dakota [to live with Roland]. . . . Jenese became pregnant by Roland, and on June 24, 1997 their son, Johnathan, was born. [O]n March 6, 1999 Roland and Jenese were married. . . . After incurring several instances of physical abuse by Roland, Jenese filed a complaint on March 7, 2000 seeking dissolution of the marriage.

---

[21]. Ella Callow et al., Parents with Disabilities in the United States: Prevalence, Perspectives, and a Proposal for Legislative Change to Protect the Right to Family in the Disability Community, 17 Tex. J. C.L. & C.R. 9, 15 (2011). See also Robyn M. Powell, Family Law, Parents with Disabilities, and the Americans with Disabilities Act, 57 Fam. Ct. Rev. 37 (2019) (criticizing that the American with Disabilities Act (ADA) has "done little to shield parents with disabilities and their families from discrimination, especially in termination of parental rights cases").

[T]he court granted Jenese a decree of divorce from Roland on the grounds of adultery, extreme cruelty, and irreconcilable differences. Upon finding Roland had committed domestic violence, the court awarded physical custody of Johnathan to Jenese and provided Roland "closely supervised" visitation. . . . Roland, acting pro se, has appealed [contending that] the trial court failed to make specific findings in concluding that Roland had perpetrated domestic violence. We disagree.

The trial court made the following specific findings regarding Roland committing domestic violence against Jenese, all of which are supported by the evidence:

In the fall of 1996, Jenese became pregnant with the parties' son. A few months later, in February of 1997, Jenese learned of Roland's physical relationship with [another woman]. A physical argument erupted. During the course of such incident, Roland slapped and punched Jenese. He also kicked her in the stomach. Consequently, Jenese suffered vaginal bleeding and obtained medical treatment. . . .

In October of 1999, Jenese heard Johnathan crying outside. She walked out to discover that Johnathan had fallen down the stairs and had hurt himself. Roland was standing a few yards away from Johnathan, talking on his phone instead of tending to his son. Jenese made an angry comment to Roland about his priorities then went back inside. Roland than came into the kitchen and slapped Jenese in the face.

During the marriage, Roland kept pornographic magazines and videos in the marital residence, sometimes in places where Johnathan would encounter them. In January of 2000, Jenese destroyed one of Roland's pornographic videos. When Roland discovered his destroyed tape, he came up behind Jenese as she was making a bed and kicked her in the back.

On March 4, 2000, after a verbal argument, Jenese attempted to leave the marital residence with the parties' son, Johnathan. Roland refused to allow her to leave with Johnathan, but attempted to force her out of her home alone. He pinned her left arm behind her back as she held Johnathan tight in her other arm. Jenese escaped long enough to call 911, but Roland hung up the phone. He then punched her in the face, knocking her to the ground. He broke a finger in the process. Jenese was later diagnosed with a fractured bone in her face. [Jenese obtained a restraining order against him. Simultaneously, he was charged with felony assault. He pled guilty to a reduced charge of misdemeanor assault.]

Roland's argument that the court did not make specific findings about Roland's abuse of Jenese is without merit. Roland [also] asserts the trial court erred in finding [that] Roland committed domestic violence but Jenese did not. The trial court made the following specific finding:

> Roland committed at least one act of domestic violence which resulted in serious bodily injury to Jenese. During their relationship, there was a pattern of Roland inflicting domestic violence upon Jenese. On occasion, Jenese may have struck, hit, or scratched Roland. However, her actions were largely in self-defense and were of a far less serious nature and degree than Roland's domestic violence.

Under N.D.C.C. §14-09-06.2(j) evidence of domestic violence is a specifically enumerated factor for the court to consider in awarding child custody:

> j. *Evidence of domestic violence.* In awarding custody or granting rights of visitation, the court shall consider evidence of domestic violence. If the court finds credible evidence that domestic violence has occurred, and there exists one incident of domestic violence which resulted in serious bodily injury or involved the use of a dangerous weapon or there exists a pattern of domestic violence within a

reasonable time proximate to the proceeding, this combination creates a rebuttable presumption that a parent who has perpetrated domestic violence may not be awarded sole or joint custody of a child. This presumption may be overcome only by clear and convincing evidence that the best interests of the child require that parent's participation as a custodial parent. The court shall cite specific findings of fact to show that the custody or visitation arrangement best protects the child and the parent or other family or household member who is the victim of domestic violence. . . . The fact that the abused parent suffers from the effects of the abuse may not be grounds for denying that parent custody. . . .

Under this statutory provision, a single incident of domestic violence which results in serious bodily injury or a pattern of domestic violence creates a presumption that the perpetrator may not be awarded custody. With regard to the domestic violence factor, the trial court made clear and specific findings. The court found Roland had a pattern of inflicting domestic violence upon Jenese and that in at least one instance that violence resulted in serious bodily injury to her. The court found that although Jenese may have at times acted violently toward Roland, her actions were "largely in self-defense." Acts of domestic violence are mitigated when committed in self-defense. The trial court did not find Jenese's conduct toward Roland rose to a level of violence triggering the presumption against her receiving child custody. We conclude the trial court's findings are supported by the evidence and are not clearly erroneous.

Roland asserts the trial court's finding that Roland inflicted extreme cruelty on Jenese is clearly erroneous. Extreme cruelty is defined under N.D.C.C. §14-05-05 as "the infliction by one party to the marriage of grievous bodily injury or grievous mental suffering upon the other." The trial court awarded Jenese a divorce on the grounds of adultery, extreme cruelty, and irreconcilable differences. Considering the physical violence perpetrated against Jenese by Roland, and his illicit extramarital affairs, there is substantial evidence to support the trial court's conclusion that extreme cruelty, consisting of both grievous bodily injury and grievous mental suffering, was inflicted by Roland upon Jenese during their marriage. The trial court's underlying findings of extramarital conduct and physical abuse are supported by the evidence and are not clearly erroneous. . . .

Notes and Questions

1. State approaches. Virtually all states now require courts to consider domestic violence in custody decisions. Some states include domestic violence as a factor in the best interests analysis. The trend, however, is to provide that evidence of domestic violence creates a rebuttable presumption against awarding custody to the abusive parent.[22]

---

[22]. See Leslie Joan Harris, Failure to Protect from Exposure to Domestic Violence in Private Custody Contests, 44 Fam. L.Q. 169 (2010) (noting that 28 states consider domestic violence as a factor, whereas 22 states have presumptions against custody awards to an abusive parent). See also Charts 2021: Family Law in the Fifty States, D.C., and Puerto Rico, 55 Fam. L.Q. 513 (2022).

When a court finds that the domestic violence presumption is triggered (and not rebutted), what custodial arrangement should a court order? Should application of the presumption preclude sole custody? Joint custody? Joint physical as well as legal custody? What does the statute in *Peters-Riemers* dictate?

What evidence can a parent introduce to rebut the presumption? In *Peters-Riemers*, what does the statute require? Some states require evidence that persons who are convicted of crimes of domestic violence have undergone treatment programs. Should completion of such programs serve to rebut the presumption?

2. State variations: Problems of proof. Statutes vary in terms of the nature of evidence that triggers the presumption. Some statutes require an incident that results in bodily injury or fear of imminent bodily injury. (Or. Rev. Stat. Ann. §107.705(1)). Others require a pattern of abuse (e.g., Ark. Code Ann. §9-13-101(c)(2)); or a criminal conviction (e.g., Fla. Stat. Ann. §61.13). Which approach is preferable? Why? What does the statute in *Peters-Riemers* require? Did the plaintiff satisfy the requirement? What additional evidence should trigger the custodial presumption? For example, what should be the relevance of the fact that an abuser is subject to a restraining order?

Statutes also differ regarding the relevance of *past* acts of domestic violence. In *Peters-Riemers*, what was the length of time between the last identified act of domestic violence and the proceedings? Some states require that the violence occur within a reasonable time of any judicial proceeding. See Tulintseff v. Jacobsen, 615 N.W.2d 129 (N.D. 2000). What is the basis for this requirement? How might such a temporal requirement pose problems for victims?

3. Mutual acts of domestic violence. How should courts deal with *mutual* acts of domestic violence? How does *Peters-Riemers* address this issue?

Most states lessen the likelihood of mutual arrests by laws requiring arrest of only the "primary aggressor" (discussed in Chapter IV). See also ALI Principles §2.11 cmt. c. Courts sometimes respond to mutual acts of domestic violence by issuing mutual restraining orders. Critics charge, however, that mutual restraining orders (1) are based on insufficient evidence that the parties are equally responsible for the violence and neither acted in self-defense, (2) create enforcement problems because they do not indicate the more serious aggressor, and (3) reflect gender bias on the part of judges.[23] See, e.g., K.L v. R.H., 285 Cal. Rptr. 3d 563 (Ct. App. 2021) (reversing issuance of mutual orders and finding that mother did not engage in intimate partner violence). In response, most states discourage or prohibit mutual protection orders. Federal law disfavors the issuance of mutual restraining orders by providing that they are not entitled to full faith and credit except under very limited circumstances. Violence Against Women Act (VAWA), 18 U.S.C. §2265(c).

4. Gender bias? Gender bias complicates legal responses to domestic violence in custody decisionmaking. For example, some scholars claim that family law professionals, including judges and guardians ad litem, are not taking

---

[23]. Thomas L. Hafemeister, If All You Have Is a Hammer: Society's Ineffective Response to Intimate Partner Violence, 60 Cath. U. L. Rev. 919, 990 (2011); Joan Zorza, What Is Wrong with Mutual Orders of Protection?, 1 Fam. & Intimate Partner Violence Q. 127 (2008).

domestic violence into account properly in custody disputes. Among other things, researchers have found that judges often do not believe a mother's claims of child abuse.[24] The likelihood that the court disbelieves the mother's abuse allegations increases when the father cross-alleges that the mother is alienating the child from him, according to an empirical study by Professor Joan Meier.[25]

Given the increased public attention to the problem of domestic violence, what factors explain the continued judicial skepticism about women's credibility?

5. Friendly parent provisions. Some states have "friendly parent provisions" mandating custody awards to the parent who is most likely to maintain the child's relationship with the other parent. How do such provisions pose risks for victims of domestic violence? Should an exception exist to such provisions in the domestic violence context? See, e.g., Alaska Stat. §25.24.150(c)(6) (providing that a best interest factor includes "the willingness and ability of each parent to facilitate and encourage a close and continuing relationship between the other parent and the child, except that the court may not consider this willingness and ability if one parent shows that the other parent has sexually assaulted or engaged in domestic violence against the parent or a child, and that a continuing relationship with the other parent will endanger the health or safety of either the parent or the child").

6. Failure to protect. Should the fact that a parent has *not* left an abusive relationship weigh against a custody award to that parent? Should state statutes preclude consideration of any effects of domestic violence on the adult *victim* in the determination of the child's best interests? What does the statute in *Peters-Riemers* require?

7. Custody awards to abusers. How often do courts grant custody to perpetrators of domestic violence? Trial courts do so with "disturbing" frequency, according to Professor Joan Meier (author of a multiyear study of appellate opinions). She notes that in a significant number of cases, abusers obtain sole or joint custody even in states with rebuttable presumptions.[26] What might explain this fact?

8. ALI Principles. UMDA does not address the role of domestic violence in custody decisionmaking. However, the ALI Principles recommend that parents disclose battering in the parenting plan that they submit to the court, and that the court have a process to identify abuse. ALI Principles §§2.06, 2.11. Batterers may

---

[24]. Meier, Denial of Family Violence, supra note [10], at 848.
[25]. Id. See also Debra Pogrund Stark et al., Properly Accounting for Domestic Violence in Child Custody Cases: An Evidence-Based Analysis and Reform, 26 Mich. J. Gender & L. 1, 4-5 (2019).
[26]. Joan S. Meier, Domestic Violence, Child Custody, and Child Protection: Understanding Judicial Resistance and Imagining the Solutions, 11 Am. U. J. Gender Soc. Pol'y & L. 657, 662 (2003). See also Meier, Denial of Family Violence, supra note [10]; Joan S. Meier & Sean A. Dickson, Mapping Gender: Shedding Empirical Light on Family Courts' Treatment of Cases Involving Abuse and Alienation, 35 Law & Ineq. 311 (2017).

not receive custodial responsibility unless the court orders appropriate measures (e.g., completion of a treatment program) to ensure protection of family members. Id. at §2.11(2)(i). The Principles suggest that courts be aware that abusers might use custody or visitation rights as harassment. Id. at §2.11 cmt. c. Finally, the Principles assert that acts of self-defense do not constitute abuse. Id. Do these provisions provide sufficient protection to victims of domestic violence?

9. Bifurcating domestic violence and custody decisionmaking. Traditionally, courts considered domestic violence in custody determinations only if the violence has been directed at the child. See, e.g., Baker v. Baker, 494 N.W.2d 282 (Minn. 1992). Does this approach make sense? In fact, research reveals the high correlation between domestic violence and child abuse.[27] Even if the child is not physically abused, how harmful is the mere act of *witnessing* domestic violence (discussed in Chapter IV)?

Problems

1. Shauna Prewitt's daughter was six months old when Shauna found out that the rapist who had fathered her child was petitioning for joint custody. According to state custody law, a court may consider rape as a factor in the best interests of a child. Parental custody rights can be awarded, nonetheless, if the rapist-father is not considered a danger to the child. During her two-year custody battle, Shauna decides to seek passage of a law that would terminate rapist-fathers' custody rights while still requiring them to pay child support. Should the proposed law also cover restrictions on visitation rights? What should be the burden of proof? Should a conviction be a prerequisite? Discuss the pros and cons of such a law. See, e.g., Pa. Cons. Stat. tit. 23, §§4321, 5329.

Federal law also addresses parental rights of perpetrators of sexual assault with the Rape Survivor Child Custody Act, enacted as part of the Justice for Victims of Trafficking Act, 42 U.S.C. §14044b. The law incentivizes states (through eligibility for VAWA grant funds) to enact laws that allow women to petition for termination of parental rights if their child was conceived through rape. Evaluate the federal law in terms of its benefits, shortcomings, and likely effectiveness. See also Nat'l Conf. of State Legislators, Parental Rights and Sexual Assault (Mar. 9, 2020) (surveying state laws), http://www.ncsl.org/research/human-services/paren tal-rights-and-sexual-assault.aspx.

2. The legislature in the State of Blackacre is considering the following bill on child custody. You are a legislative intern who has been asked to draft a memo evaluating the proposed bill (below). How does it alter the traditional best interests standard? Discuss the advantages and shortcomings of the proposed legislation.

---

[27]. Lundy Bancroft et al., The Batterer as Parent: Addressing the Impact of Domestic Violence on Family Dynamics 54-60 (2d ed. 2012).

BLACKACRE FAMILY CODE: BEST INTERESTS OF THE CHILD

(1) The court shall determine the allocation of parental responsibilities, including parenting time and decisionmaking responsibilities, in accordance with the best interests of the child giving paramount consideration to the child's safety and the physical, mental, and emotional conditions and needs of the child as follows:

(a) *Determination of parenting time.* The court may make provisions for parenting time that the court finds are in the child's best interests unless the court finds, after a hearing, that parenting time by the party would endanger the child's physical health or significantly impair the child's emotional development. In addition, in any order imposing or continuing a parenting time restriction, the court shall enumerate the specific factual findings supporting the restriction and may enumerate the conditions that the restricted party could fulfill in order to seek modification in the parenting plan.

(b) *Allocation of decisionmaking responsibility.* The court shall allocate the decisionmaking responsibilities between the parties based upon the best interests of the child. When a claim of child abuse or neglect or domestic violence has been made to the court, prior to allocating decisionmaking responsibility, the court shall follow the provision below:

(2) If the court finds that one of the parties has committed child abuse or neglect or domestic violence or has engaged in a pattern of domestic violence or has a history of domestic violence, which factor must be supported by a preponderance of the evidence, then it shall not be in the best interests of the child to allocate mutual decisionmaking with respect to any issue over the objection of the other party, unless the court finds that there is credible evidence of the ability of the parties to make decisions cooperatively in the best interest of the child in a manner that is safe for the abused party and the child. . . .

The above bill was modeled on Colo. Rev. Stat. Ann. §14-10-124. See also Allen M. Bailey, Prioritizing Child Safety as the Prime Best-Interest Factor, 47 Fam. L.Q. 35 (2013).

———————————

In thinking about the best-interests-of-the-child determination in custody cases involving domestic violence, consider the following excerpt.

Joan S. Meier, Domestic Violence, Child Custody, and Child Protection: Understanding Judicial Resistance and Imagining the Solutions
11 Am. U. J. Gender Soc. Pol'y & L. 657, 705-707 (2003)

[M]any batterers seek custody, not out of a genuine desire to take care of the children, but to retaliate against or further their control of their partner. The persona of many—though not all—batterers, is inconsistent with the qualities needed to make a good parent. People who need to control and abuse their intimate partners are unlikely to be capable of the loving, nurturing, and self-disciplined behavior that good parenting requires. By definition, a father who abuses the mother has indicated that he cannot put the children's interests first, since their mother's abuse, by undermining her well-being, is inherently harmful to the children. Many batterers expect children to meet their needs, rather than vice versa; this can lead him to expect children to give up their other interests to spend time with him; to demand quiet to an inappropriate degree; to demand physical affection regardless of their feelings; and to become blaming, tearful, or yelling when they fail to meet his needs.

Batterers are often patriarchal, believing in strict gender roles and subordination of females, and can be controlling or authoritarian toward children of both sexes. Batterers "tend to be rigid, authoritarian parents." They tend to expect their will to be obeyed unquestioningly, or to be inflexible in their arrangements, extremely angry at any sign of non-compliance or disrespect, spank more often, and be angry more often than other fathers. In short, they tend to use "power parenting." They are unlikely to possess the empathy that allows parents to treat their children with respect and to validate their feelings, two qualities considered important to raising emotionally healthy, conscientious, caring children.

Many, if not most, batterers both consciously and unconsciously undermine the children's mother and relationships with their mother. Many tell the children that it is their mother's fault that the parents are separated, that they cannot see their father more, that they cannot have certain things, or any other source of sadness in the child's life. Many of my clients' batterers would demean the mother to the children, telling them their mother is a "whore" or "slut," and in at least one case, demanding that the children come out of their rooms to watch him beat her up as punishment for some purported wrong.

Finally, batterers are often manipulative to children as well as partners, denying their own conduct and its effects, blaming the mother, and seeking to persuade the children that they are the "nicer" or "better" parent. Often batterers use the children to further their control over the mother, explicitly or implicitly enlisting the children in his vendetta. . . . In short, it is simply fallacious to assume that past domestic violence is in the past, that it is not directly relevant to future custody, or that it can ever really not impact the children.

NOTE: CHILDREN'S PREFERENCES

States have adopted different approaches regarding when and how a child's own preferences should be taken into account in a custody action.[28] Modeled on the UMDA, the law in some states *requires* consideration of a child's wishes. Other states have statutes that require consideration of the child's preference after a preliminary finding of maturity. Still other states require consideration of the wishes of children of a specified age (generally ages 12 to 14). See, e.g., Tenn. Code Ann. §36-6-106 (requiring consideration of preference of children age 12 or older). See

---

[28]. Linda Elrod, Child's Preference, Child Custody Prac. & Proc. §4:11 (surveying state approaches). See also Barbara A. Atwood, The Child's Voice in Custody Litigation: An Empirical Survey and Suggestions for Reform, 45 Ariz. L. Rev. 629, 634-635 (2003).

also ALI Principles §2.08 cmt. f (recommending ages 11 to 14). Finally, the law in some states gives judges discretion on the matter. Where both parents are equally qualified caretakers, the child's preference may serve as a tiebreaker. Conversely, children's preferences may be overridden if the court finds that primary placement with that parent would be contrary to the child's best interests. See, e.g., J.D.V. v. R.M.T., 2004 WL 3245784 (Del. Fam. Ct. 2004) (father's criminal record for sexual abuse).

Consider whether the *reasons* for a child's preference should influence the court analysis. One difficult situation, for example, concerns the weight to be given to children's preferences in cases of substance abuse or domestic violence. See In re Marriage of Sisson, 665 N.W.2d 441 (Iowa Ct. App. 2003). Relocation presents another troubling circumstance (i.e., the custodial parent is relocating and the child wants to remain with the noncustodial parent). See Goodhand v. Kildoo, 560 S.E.2d 463 (Va. Ct. App. 2002). Courts may also be faced with questions such as how much weight to accord to a child's preference where the child wishes to live with the more permissive parent, or with the parent with a higher income, in part because that parent's house is "nicer" than that of the other parent. See Meehan-Greer v. Greer, 415 P.3d 274 (Wyo. 2018).

There are also *procedural questions* that can arise with regard to the child's preference, such as *who* should obtain the evidence regarding the child's references: should it be the judge, the child's representative, a parent's attorney, or a mental health professional? In addition, there are questions about the procedure by which the child's preference is determined. Possibilities include testimony in open court or an in camera meeting with the judge. If the court uses an in camera procedure, there may be disputes about whether someone else should be present during that meeting, and if so, who that should be; whether a parent can object to the meeting altogether (see KES v. CAT, 107 P.3d 779 (Wyo. 2005); Addison v. Addison, 463 S.W.3d 755 (Ky. 2015) (involving disagreement among the parents)); and about whether the meeting should be recorded. See also UMDA §404(a) (providing for in camera interviews with counsel present and recording). One study of state court judges reveals judges' reluctance to conduct in camera interviews of children.[29]

In 2023, the Uniform Law Commission (ULC) approved the creation of a Drafting Committee to draft a uniform law to address judicial interview procedures for children in custody, visitation, parentage, and related proceedings. This project was based on a conclusion that there was substantial variation, not only between states but even between judges, with regard to when children should be interviewed and what the interview should look like, and that this variation can lead to "opposing outcomes and inconsistency for children and families."[30]

[29]. Atwood, supra note [28], at 636.
[30]. Melissa Ann Kucinski, The U.S. Experience in Drafting Guidelines for Judicial Interviews of Children and Its Translation to Hague Abduction Convention Return Proceedings Globally, 12 Laws 54 (2023).

c. Joint Custody: Presumption, Preference, or Option?

BELL v. BELL
794 P.2d 97 (Alaska 1990)

MATTHEWS, Chief Justice.

Greg and Debra Bell were married in January 1986. They separated sixteen months later in July 1987. Greg filed for divorce on September 14, 1987. [Here] Greg challenges . . . the trial court's award of legal and physical custody of Scott, the parties' child, to Debra. . . .

Gregory "Scott" Bell was born on August 19, 1986. While married, Greg and Debra shared most child rearing tasks on an equal basis. Since both parents were employed, Sharon Nollman babysat Scott. . . .

When Greg and Debra separated, they agreed to share custody of Scott, alternating physical custody every week or so. Both used Nollman to babysit. They accommodated each other's employment, social, and vacation schedules and shared babysitting expenses. A two-day interim custody hearing was held before Master Andrew Brown on October 15-16, 1987. Based upon the recommendations of an Alaska Court Custody Investigator, Master Brown issued a report recommending that Scott remain in the babysitting care of Nollman and that the parties continue their weekly alternating schedule of shared physical custody of Scott. The court approved the Master's report.

Greg and Debra cooperated in the weekly custody exchanges for another ten and one-half months until trial on August 26 and 29, 1988. However, in early 1988, Debra unilaterally began placing Scott at the Saakaaya Daycare Center during the weeks that she had physical custody. Greg continued to use Nollman during the weeks that he had physical custody of Scott. . . .

Greg and Debra continued to accommodate each other's schedules and to share physical custody of Scott on an alternating basis. They also cooperated in making major decisions about Scott's medical care. . . .

At trial, Ardis Cry, Custody Investigator, Alaska Court System, recommended that shared legal custody continue. [S]he further recommended that Scott have a primary home and that Debra be the primary physical custodian. The trial court awarded legal and physical custody of Scott to Debra. The court also allowed Greg visitation with Scott (1) on alternate weekends from Friday afternoon through Monday morning and on Wednesday evening through Thursday mornings and (2) during four one-week periods spread throughout the year until Scott reaches school age.

Greg contends that the trial court erred by not awarding joint custody to both parents pursuant to AS §25.20.060. AS §25.20.060 states, in part: "The court may award shared custody to both parents if shared custody is determined to be in the best interests of the child." . . .

In reviewing the propriety of the trial court's denial of joint custody, we find it necessary to distinguish between two interrelated aspects of a joint custody arrangement. First, an award of joint custody gives both parents "legal custody" of the child. This means that they "share responsibility in the making of major decisions affecting the child's welfare." Second, an award of joint custody gives both parents "physical custody" of the child. This means that "each is entitled to the companionship of the child over periodic intervals of time." In an act amending AS §25.20.060, the legislature drew this distinction and expressed a policy favoring the award of joint legal custody, regardless of the physical custody arrangement: The legislature finds that . . . it is in the public interest to encourage parents to share the rights and responsibilities of child rearing. While actual physical custody may not be practical or appropriate in all cases, it is the intent of the legislature that both parents have the opportunity to guide and nurture their child and to meet the needs of the child on an equal footing beyond the considerations of support or actual custody. In light of this expression of legislative intent, and because the controlling factual finding underlying the trial court's ruling is clearly erroneous, we reverse the award of sole legal custody to Debra.

The trial court's award was apparently based on its finding that Greg and Debra "are incapable of meaningful communication and/or negotiation regarding the matters that relate to the best interests of [Scott]." . . . Based on our review of the record, however, we hold that this finding is clearly erroneous.

The trial court record and Debra's arguments on appeal indicate only one area of irreconcilable conflict between Greg and Debra—throughout the proceedings below they could not agree on what form of day care would be best for Scott. Greg wanted Scott in Nollman's home, and Debra wanted Scott in Saakaaya Daycare Center.

Given the abundance of contrary evidence indicative of their ability to cooperate in Scott's best interest, however, we think that this one conflict does not warrant the trial court's finding of an "inability" to cooperate. . . . Throughout the 14 months [of their shared custody], they accommodated each other's employment, social, and vacation schedules, and cooperated in making major decisions about Scott's medical care.

Furthermore, after interviewing Greg and Debra, the custody investigator recommended "joint legal custody" because she found that they had the "ability . . . to deal with each other in a civil and mutual manner" and thought that they demonstrated "potential to facilitate cooperation and compromise." Both Greg and Debra also testified to their ability to work cooperatively in Scott's best interest. Moreover, Debra generally agreed with the investigator's recommendations and was willing to settle the custody issue under the terms the investigator recommended. Thus, at trial, both parties agreed that joint legal custody was appropriate.

In light of such evidence, we are left with a firm conviction that the trial court's finding of an inability to cooperate was erroneous. We realize that the disagreement over daycare relates to a fundamental child care issue. But resolution of this issue did not require denial of that which the Alaska legislature recognizes as the favored course; i.e., joint legal custody. We therefore reverse the trial court's denial of joint legal custody and remand with instructions to enter an award of joint legal custody. . . .

Notes and Questions

1. Historical evolution.

a. Early view: One omnipotent parent. In the 1970s, three famous child development experts (Professors Joseph Goldstein, Anna Freud, and Alfred Solnit) propounded the novel view that stability and minimization of conflict should guide child placement. They said that healthy emotional development requires an "omnipotent" parent, on whom the child can rely for all important decisions. They advocated that custody be awarded to only one parent, who should have the power to decide the extent of the other parent's contact with the child (or even prohibiting it).[31]

b. Modern view: Frequent contact with both parents. More recently, there has been a shift from the omnipotent parent approach in favor of an approach that starts from the premise that children generally benefit from frequent contact with both parents. This view recognizes that fathers, as well as mothers, play important roles in childrearing.

c. Joint custody movement. Starting in the 1970s, a nascent fathers' rights movement spearheaded the introduction, and often passage, of legislation permitting (and, in some cases, providing for) a presumption in favor of joint custody. The movement stems from robust lobbying by fathers' rights advocates, who argued that they felt alienated from their children and burdened by child support obligations.[32] Critics of these legislative reforms, including some women's rights groups and legal associations, contended that such presumptions can endanger women who experience intimate partner violence, unwisely abrogate judicial discretion, are unnecessary because parents (at least parents who are able to get along well) generally prefer shared custody, and lead to the elimination or reduction of child support.[33]

2. Approaches.

Virtually all states now permit some form of joint custody, and some states create a presumption of joint custody. Other states, like Alaska in *Bell*, have a preference for joint custody. Third, and most common, joint custody is an option in the best interests determination. California was the first state to provide for statutory recognition of joint custody in 1980. Cal. Fam. Code §3080 (formerly Cal. Civ. Code §4600.5(a)).

In most states, the presumption in favor of joint custody applies only if the parents agree. Is joint custody to unwilling parents likely to succeed? What light does Bell v. Bell shed? How do you weigh the benefits and disadvantages of joint custody presumptions?

---

[31]. See Joseph Goldstein et al., Beyond the Best Interests of the Child 38 (1973).

[32]. For background on the role of the fathers' rights movement in custody law, see Dinner, supra note [9].

[33]. Michael Alison Chandler, Shared-Parenting Bills Could Reshape Custody Battles, Wash. Post, Dec. 31, 2017, https://www.uticaod.com/news/20171231/shared-parenting-bills-could-reshape-custody-battles.

3. Constitutional considerations? Does a parent have a constitutional right to joint custody?[34] Does a *child* have a constitutional right to have a court award joint custody to the parents? See In re A.R.B., 433 S.E.2d 411 (Ga. Ct. App. 1993).

4. Special considerations. When is an award of joint custody inappropriate? What considerations should influence awards of joint custody? How should time sharing be appropriated, and based on what factors? Equal time? If courts require equal time, should it be six months with each parent, or nine months with one parent subject to summer vacations with the other, or switching homes every week? Or should courts order the children to remain in the family home, with the parents alternating periods there (i.e., "the bird's nest" model)? Should courts consider the effect on each parent of a *loss* of custody?

How well does joint custody serve the interests of infants and young children? What specific dilemmas does joint custody pose for these children?[35] Should overnights be delayed until children reach, perhaps, the third year of life?

A controversial issue is the use of joint custody in cases of domestic violence. In fact, a congressional resolution discourages awards of joint custody in domestic violence cases based on the rationale that such awards perpetuate the abuser's access to and control over the victim through the children. H.R. Cong. Res. 172, 101st Cong. 2d Sess. (1990). When (if ever) is joint custody appropriate in this context?[36] What insights does the excerpt below provide?

5. Parenting plans, parenting coordinators, and parental education. Many states currently provide that parents seeking custody must file a parenting plan (i.e., a written agreement specifying caretaking and decisionmaking authority as well as the manner for resolution of future disputes). What issues should be included in such agreements?

The majority of states currently authorize the appointment of a parenting coordinator to investigate issues and help parents resolve disputes. The parental coordinator can then make recommendations to the court regarding custody and parenting time decisions. The Association of Family and Conciliation Courts (AFCC) promulgated guidelines in 2006 for parenting coordination. Does a requirement that the parents first seek the help of a neutral third party before petitioning the court in the event of future disagreements violate parents' rights to due process in terms of access to the courts? See In re Martin, 8 A.3d 60 (N.H. 2010).

6. Pets. Family lawyers have witnessed a marked increase in disputes about pets at dissolution, and courts are deciding these cases more frequently in recent

[34]. See generally David D. Meyer, The Constitutional Rights of Non-Custodial Parents, 34 Hofstra L. Rev. 1461, 1465-1466 (2006).

[35]. See, e.g., Michael Lamb, Critical Analysis of Research on Parenting Plans and Children's Well-Being, in Parenting Plan Evaluations: Applied Research for the Family Court 214 (Kathryn Kuehnle & Leslie Drozd eds., 2012); Carol George et al., Divorce in the Nursery: On Infants and Overnight Care, 49 Fam. Ct. Rev. 521 (2011); Linda Nielsen, Shared Physical Custody: Does It Benefit Most Children?, 28 J. Am. Acad. Matrim. Law. 79 (2015).

[36]. See Margaret F. Brinig et al., Perspectives on Joint Custody Presumptions as Applied to Domestic Violence Cases, 52 Fam. Ct. Rev. 271 (2014); Zoe Garvin, Note, The Unintended Consequences of Rebuttable Presumptions to Determine Child Custody in Domestic Violence Cases, 50 Fam. L.Q. 173, 174 (2016).

years. In the past, courts generally applied property rules to such cases. Recently, however, several states (including Alaska, California, and Illinois) enacted "pet custody" laws, which typically direct courts to consider either the pet's "well-being" or "care" needs (depending on the jurisdiction) before granting custody or control. What are the pros and cons of these new laws? What is the significance of the term "well-being" or "care"? In states without statutory language, how does a court traditionally determine ownership of a companion animal? To what extent should pet custody be analogized to child custody, or property division?

Judith G. Greenberg, Domestic Violence and the Danger of Joint Custody Presumptions

25 N. Ill. U. L. Rev. 403, 407-413 (2005)

. . . One of the most appealing arguments for joint custody, both legal and physical, is that it is in the best interests of the child. . . . [C]ommentators have argued that custodial arrangements that mimic the two-parent family are the most desirable because they produce stability over time in providing continuing contact with both parents. There have been numerous studies of joint custody arrangements and their effects on children. One concludes bluntly that "children in joint custody are better adjusted, across multiple types of measures, than children in sole . . . custody" [citing Robert Bauserman, Child Adjustment in Joint-Custody Versus Sole-Custody Arrangements, 16 J. Fam. Psychol. 91, 97 (2002)].

Nevertheless, there is reason to wonder whether joint custody is really as good for children as this assessment implies. The studies' results are sometimes difficult to interpret. . . . [M]any samples include families that have opted on their own for joint custody in one form or another. The effects of joint custody on children in such families may be radically different from the effects on children whose parents did not agree to the joint custody, but for whom joint custody was ordered by a court. . . .

Proponents of a presumption in favor of joint custody also argue that it will equalize the positions of men and women and help to undermine traditional gender roles. Sanford Braver argues that awarding sole custody to a mother with visitation to the father leaves men feeling disenfranchised in terms of their children's lives. . . . The argument is that fathers with joint custody, even if only joint legal custody, are able to participate in the lives of their children more equally with their ex-wives. This furthers sexual equality and would be beneficial to everyone. Once again, however, the data on whether joint custody achieves these goals is contradictory. Sanford Braver, in his study of interviews with divorced fathers and mothers, reports that joint legal custody results in higher rates of father-child visitation. . . . However, other studies have had very different findings as to the effect of joint legal custody on role equalization. One large-scale review of studies of the impact of fathers' visitation found that fathers' involvement affected the children in varying ways depending on the type of involvement, the mother's acceptance of the father's involvement and the degree of conflict between the parents. This hardly indicates that fathers who have joint custody automatically are perceived as taking on a nurturing

role. Furthermore, there is evidence that even if the initial custody order provides for joint physical custody, over time the children are likely to end up
living in their mothers' custody. . . .

. . . Most commentators recognize that where there has been domestic violence, joint custody is inappropriate. . . . Unfortunately, cases that get to litigation (or even to judicial intervention short of litigation) are exactly those most
likely to involve domestic violence. Recent research shows that approximately
seventy-five percent of the contested custody cases that require judicial intervention are cases in which there is a history of domestic violence. This means
that in situations in which the court sends a case to mediation, orders an evaluation or holds a trial, it is significantly more likely than not that there has been
domestic violence. Presumptions in favor of shared custody then do not make
sense given that so many of the cases in which the parties cannot resolve the
children's custody without judicial intervention are cases involving domestic
violence.

Batterers often use any contact afforded them by the court as a means of
continuing the abusive relationship with their former partners. Abusive relationships usually involve the batterer establishing control over his victim
through a combination of physical, emotional, and financial methods. This
is not likely to end with divorce. Indeed, for many targets, the abuse becomes
worse at separation. Batterers use any opportunity or contact to perpetuate the
abuse in an effort to maintain their control. Some use the continuing connection that comes from joint custody or visitation rights to harass or verbally
abuse their victims. Others use it as an opportunity to pressure the victim to
return to the batterer. Still others continue their physical abuse during these
times. . . .

2. Standards Governing the Noncustodial Parent: Visitation

a. Traditional Rule

Before the rise of joint custody, a court usually granted one parent custody of the
child. A presumption applied that the other parent should be awarded reasonable
visitation. However, this presumption could be overcome by evidence that the
noncustodial parent was unfit or that visitation was detrimental to the child's welfare. That presumption continues to apply today, where the court awards physical
custody to only one parent.

Courts have broad discretion to specify the time, place, and circumstances
of visitation, including the imposition of conditions on visitation by the noncustodial parent. Procedurally, if one parent requests the court to order restrictions on visitation, that parent bears the burden of proof on the need for that
restriction.

The model statute below illustrates the traditional rule and its limitations.

UNIFORM MARRIAGE AND DIVORCE ACT (UMDA)

§407. VISITATION

(a) A parent not granted custody of the child is entitled to reasonable visitation rights unless the court finds, after a hearing, that visitation would endanger seriously the child's physical, mental, moral, or emotional health.

(b) The court may modify an order granting or denying visitation rights whenever modification would serve the best interest of the child; but the court shall not restrict a parent's visitation rights unless it finds that the visitation would endanger seriously the child's physical, mental, moral, or emotional health.

b. Restrictions on Visitation

HANKE v. HANKE

615 A.2d 1205 (Md. Ct. Spec. App. 1992)

BELL, Judge.

Appellant, Mary Elizabeth Hanke, brings this appeal, asking us to review an order granting her ex-husband, Dan Wolf Hanke, appellee, overnight visitation with the parties' four-year-old daughter. Ms. Hanke's concern for this child stems, in part, from an incident of sexual abuse by Mr. Hanke of one of Ms. Hanke's daughters (stepchild) from a previous marriage. . . .

On August 1, 1990, Mr. and Ms. Hanke were divorced by a judgment of the Circuit Court for Harford County. Ms. Hanke was granted custody of the parties' child and the issue of Mr. Hanke's visitation privileges was reserved for a later hearing. On March 15, 1991, hearings began to consider visitation. On March 18, 1991, the court ordered unsupervised four-hour visitations on alternate Sunday afternoons from noon until 4:00 P.M. On March 20, 1991, the court ordered Mr. Hanke to submit to a mental health examination by Lawrence Raifman, PhD, J.D. . . . The order of the Harford County judge, who transferred custody to Mr. Hanke, has not been enforced, pending the outcome of the investigation by the Kentucky DSS. [The mother had moved to Kentucky, where her family lived, because she was unable to find employment.]

Mr. Hanke has admitted sexually abusing his 11-year-old stepchild in 1986. This particular instance of sexual abuse was one event, but there is overwhelming evidence that other instances of excessive punishment with sexual overtones had occurred prior to this incident. . . . During a therapy session, Mr. Hanke stated that he was drunk when he sexually molested his stepchild. . . . Mr. Hanke feels that he does not "need any therapy for alcoholism." He did, however, secure therapy for the sexual abuse incident.

At the time of the separation, Ms. Hanke was pregnant with the parties' child who is the subject of this case. The parties separated as soon as Ms. Hanke learned from the 11-year-old child that she had been sexually molested by Mr. Hanke. Criminal charges of sexual molestation were brought against Mr. Hanke for the incident involving his stepchild. As part of the plea bargain entered into by Mr. Hanke for a suspended sentence in the criminal case, he agreed to, among other things, supervised visitation with the parties' child. . . .

The trial judge granted Mr. Hanke unsupervised four-hour weekly visitation periods with the child, beginning in March of 1991. After one of these visits, the parties' child reported to a teenage friend of her stepsister that Mr. Hanke "was touching her where he was not supposed to." Ms. Hanke examined the child and found scarring in the genital area. She immediately reported the matter to the Harford County Department of Social Services (DSS). Based on Ms. Hanke's complaint, DSS had the child examined at Mercy Hospital. The examination was conducted on May 23, 1991, by Dr. Reichel at the Mercy Hospital outpatient clinic. His report states ". . . Prior abuse cannot be excluded." Annetta Bloxham, the DSS caseworker investigating the complaint . . . also testified that she had verified the child's report of sexual molestation . . . by the parents of the teenager, to whom the child had reported the molestation, that the child did indeed report the molestation. This family refused, however, to permit the teenager to testify. . . .

Dr. Raifman, who evaluated Mr. Hanke pursuant to a court order, [concluded] that Mr. Hanke stated that he abused his stepchild to "get at her mother"; that the stepchild had been physically abused by Mr. Hanke for a long time before the incident of sexual abuse; that Mr. Hanke should not be placed in a situation where he is alone with his child; that Mr. Hanke should not continue to use alcohol because he was drunk at the time he sexually abused his stepchild; that Mr. Hanke had not come to terms with his abuse of alcohol as a factor in his abuse of his stepchild. [U]ntil these issues are resolved therapeutically, he is at risk and, therefore, his child is at risk.

Ms. Hanke's attorney, the attorney representing the Harford County DSS, and the attorney representing the child were unanimous in their call for supervised visitation. There was, however, also a small amount of contradictory evidence presented, which the judge seemed to favor, that Ms. Hanke was overreacting to the situation and Mr. Hanke was not a potential danger to their child. On March 18, 1991, the court ordered unsupervised visitation and on August 16, 1991, the court ordered visitation overnight, specifying one of four persons who were close to Mr. Hanke to "be present during visitation periods." The judge refused to protect the child further, and he found that overnight visitation was appropriate.

We have reviewed the findings and holdings in this case, bearing in mind that the ultimate test for custody and visitation is the best interests of the child. In most instances, the decision of the trial judge is accorded great deference, unless it is arbitrary or clearly wrong. We hold that, given the circumstances presented in this case, the decision of the trial judge was clearly wrong.

It is obvious that the trial judge was annoyed because Ms. Hanke moved to Kentucky with the child and was unwilling to allow visitation. Even if the judge were correct that Ms. Hanke was not acting in compliance with the judge's orders, his primary responsibility was to protect this minor child, and not to punish Ms. Hanke by ordering overnight visitation. Then, when he could not enforce the overnight visitation order, the judge next removed the child from her custody with no provisions to protect the child. Where the evidence is such that a parent is justified in believing that the other parent is sexually abusing the child, it is inconceivable that that parent will surrender the child to the abusing parent without stringent safeguards. The fact that the judge does not agree with that parent's fear is immaterial. This is not a case in which there is no basis for the mother's belief. Past behavior is the best predictor of future behavior, and Ms. Hanke, while perhaps incorrect, is not unjustified in her belief that there may be some unresolved problems.

Assuming without deciding that the trial judge was correct in ruling that the child was at no or minimal risk in the overnight visitation, he abused his discretion in failing to provide a specific place for the supervised visitation designed to protect the child fully, with supervisors satisfactory to all parties. He could do no less. . . .

Notes and Questions

1. **Traditional approach.** Courts restrict or even deny visitation (sometimes called "parenting time") if the judge believes that visitation might endanger the child's well-being. Common reasons for restrictions include physical and sexual abuse. In such cases, the judge may order supervised visitation to protect the child; that is, the alleged abusive parent must spend time with the child in the presence of a third party who supervises the visitation. Does the abusive parent have a constitutionally protected right to visitation?

2. **Supervised visitation programs.** Many states provide programs that furnish supervision services in custody disputes involving abuse and neglect. Services range from close supervision by a constant observer to minimal supervision. Supervision may occur only for transfers of the child. Supervised visits might take place at a program center or another public or private location. What are the advantages and disadvantages of supervision by center staff compared to supervision by a friend or family member?

The determination of whether visitation should be supervised is left to the trial court's discretion. How does a judge decide when supervised visitation should give way to unsupervised visitation? Suppose that the parent contends that supervised visitation is interfering with the establishment of a good relationship with the child. Should the judge take that factor into account? See Grant v. Grant, 1995 WL 136775 (Ohio Ct. App. 1995).

3. **Rebuttable presumption.** Some states create a rebuttable presumption against unsupervised visitation if credible evidence exists of physical or sexual abuse. See, e.g., Tex. Fam. Code §153.004. Some courts may even terminate visitation in such cases.

4. **Considerations.** Supervised visitation gives rise to difficulties in framing the order. For example, how frequent should visitation be? Should it include overnights? Who should supervise the visitation? Professionals? Relatives? If the supervisor is a relative, should it be a relative of the abuser? Should the relative be required to complete any training? See Fla. Stat. Ann. §39.0139(5) (requiring

training in child sexual abuse). Should the supervisor be someone the child knows? Should the child's feelings be considered in choosing a supervisor? See Matter of Brown v. Erbstoesser, 928 N.Y.S.2d 92 (N.Y. 2011). The supervisor may be someone agreed upon by the parents or someone appointed by the court. What are the pros and cons of either approach to choosing the supervisor? What role, if any, should the cost of supervision play? If payment for the supervisor is required, who should pay? See Leslie Kaufman, In Custody Rights, a Hurdle for the Poor, N.Y. Times, Apr. 8, 2007, https://www.nytimes.com/2007/04/08/nyregion/08visit.html.

5. Treatment conditions. What types of restrictions are enforceable in cases of physical or sexual abuse? Can a court order an abuser to undergo psychological treatment (e.g., for substance abuse, physical abuse, or sexual abuse)? See, e.g., Catley v. Sampson, 66 A.3d 834 (R.I. 2013) (suspending visitation until completion of domestic violence counseling and substance abuse treatment). Can a court deny visitation until a therapist recommends otherwise? See Linda R. v. Ari Z., 895 N.Y.S.2d 412 (N.Y. 2010).

Should supervised or unsupervised visitation commence only after a parent *seeks* treatment? *Completes* treatment? See, e.g., La. Rev. Stat. Ann. §9:364(C) (requiring completion of treatment). Only after a parent is successfully "rehabilitated"? See, e.g., Mo. Ann. Stat. §452.400 (requiring proof of rehabilitation before unsupervised visitation). If so, who makes such determinations? Can a court order a parent to comply with a treatment program's requirement of admission of guilt? See Wirsching v. Colorado, 360 F.3d 1191, 1205 (10th Cir. 2004).

6. Empirical research. A majority of children who are subject to supervised visitation are victims of parental abuse and neglect, substance abuse, and mental illness.[37] What are the policy implications of this finding?

7. Other contexts. Restrictions on visitation also arise in the following contexts:

a. Religious practices. Because visitation often involves weekends, disputes about church attendance occur. Can a court order a parent to take children to a religious institution during visits? Can a court preclude a parent from attending religious worship services with their child during their custodial time? For more discussion of restrictions on a parent's religious practice, see supra p. 635.

b. Sexual conduct. In the past, courts routinely prohibited parents from exercising visitation rights in the presence of a parent's intimate partner if the parties were unmarried. See, e.g., McGriff v. McGriff, 99 P.3d 111 (Idaho 2004); Carter v. Escevedo, 175 So. 3d 583 (Miss. Ct. App. 2015). Are such restrictions constitutional after Lawrence v. Texas?

---

[37]. Janet R. Johnston & Robert B. Straus, Traumatized Children in Supervised Visitation: What Do They Need?, 37 Fam. & Conciliation Cts. Rev. 135, 135 (1999); Jessica Pearson et al., A New Look at an Old Issue: An Evaluation of the State Access and Visitation Grant Program, 43 Fam. Ct. Rev. 371, 376 (2005).

c. Substance abuse. Courts also impose conditions on parents who are substance abusers. What are appropriate restrictions in this context? Random drug screens? See Gonzalez v. Ross, 33 N.Y.S.3d 394 (App. Div. 2016).

d. Firearms possession. May a court restrict a parent's access to firearms or order safe storage of firearms/ammunition during visitation? Would such a restriction be constitutional?[38]

e. Criminal convictions. Parents may be subject to conditions on visitation if they have been convicted of certain crimes (e.g., child abuse, homicide), or if they are required to register as sex offenders.[39]

f. Smoking. Should a parent's smoking lead to conditions on that parent's visitation?

8. Refusal to visit. Can a court require a custodial parent to force a child to visit with the noncustodial parent against the child's wishes? Courts sometimes respond to the child's refusal to visit by holding the custodial parent in contempt. See, e.g., Woodward v. Woodward, 776 N.W.2d 567 (N.D. 2009). Is this sound policy?

9. Penalty. What should be the penalty if a parent *violates* a condition on visitation? Temporary suspension of visitation? See Epstiner v. Spears, 796 S.E.2d 919 (Ga. Ct. App. 2017). Denial of visitation? Contempt? Modification of custody?

Problems

1. When Julie and Randy divorce, the court declares Julie to be the sole custodial parent of their two preschool daughters. The trial court orders Randy to have overnight visitation that is supervised by his parents because of Randy's "penchant for pornography." The court orders the restriction because Julie presented evidence that Randy liked to view Internet sites exhibiting sexual material and had placed a personal advertisement on an Internet site to attract sexual partners. Randy counters that he views Internet material only late at night, after the children are asleep, and that he placed the advertisement out of curiosity. Randy contends that the trial court's restriction on his visitation was an abuse of discretion. What result? See Petty v. Petty, 2005 WL 1183149 (Tenn. Ct. App. 2005).

Suppose that Randy likes to relax by smoking marijuana while he views sexually explicit Internet content. Can the court restrict his recreational marijuana use through conditions on visitation? Would it make a difference if his state has legalized the use of marijuana? See, e.g., In re Marriage of Parr & Lyman, 240 P.3d 509 (Colo. Ct. App. 2010).

[38]. Cf. United States v. Rahimi, 61 F.4th 443 (5th Cir. 2023) (holding unconstitutional federal statute prohibiting possession of firearms by persons subject to domestic violence restraining order). The Supreme Court granted certiorari. See also New York State Rifle & Pistol Ass'n, Inc. v. Bruen, 142 S. Ct. 2111 (2022) (holding unconstitutional state law regulating the carrying of concealed firearms).

[39]. See generally Dana Harrington Conner, Do No Harm: An Analysis of the Legal and Social Consequences of Child Visitation Determinations for Incarcerated Perpetrators of Extreme Acts of Violence Against Women, 17 Colum. J. Gender & L. 163 (2008).

2. Roxie and Jeffrey separate after two years of marriage. Roxie and the couple's baby move in with Roxie's parents. Because Jeffrey performed limited childcare during the marriage and also because of Jeffrey's "unstable lifestyle" (details unspecified), Roxie requests that Jeffrey's contact be limited to supervised visitation at Roxie's home. Jeffrey does not contest the need for supervised visitation. When Jeffrey moves out of state, to New Jersey, he requests a different visitation schedule and proposes as "supervisor" his 21-year-old brother and a friend who lives nearby. At the subsequent divorce proceeding, Roxie is awarded custody. The court awards visitation to Jeffrey on "alternative holidays and during the summer vacation provided he gives twenty-four hours' notice of his intent to visit [and] that one of the individuals [whom he has suggested] be present during said visitation."

Roxie appeals the visitation order, claiming that it is vague and gives no consideration to the qualifications of the visitation supervisors. What result? Would your reasoning change based on the reason for the supervision? Substance abuse? Sexual abuse? Immaturity? If the court does elaborate further, how should it structure the visitation order (based on each of these possibilities)? See Weber v. Weber, 457 S.E.2d 488 (W. Va. 1995).

c. Denial of Visitation

TURNER v. TURNER

919 S.W.2d 340 (Tenn. Ct. App. 1995)

KOCH, J.

This appeal involves an acrimonious postdivorce dispute over child support and visitation. . . . This appeal involves the denial of the father's latest petition for modification and the summary suspension of his visitation for not paying child support. . . .

Rebecca Diane Turner (now Turpin) and Charles Daniel Turner were married in September 1984. They had two children before separating in May 1987. After an unsuccessful attempt at reconciliation, Ms. Turner filed for divorce in June 1989. On August 15, 1990, the trial court entered a final order granting Ms. Turner the divorce and awarding her custody of the parties' children. The trial court also granted Mr. Turner visitation rights and ordered him to pay $704.13 per month in child support and to pay for the children's medical insurance. The trial court later denied Mr. Turner's posttrial motion to alter or amend the child support award but granted him additional visitation.

In early November 1990, Ms. Turner sought to have Mr. Turner held in contempt for being $2,166.52 in arrears in his child support. Mr. Turner responded with a petition admitting that he was delinquent in his child support payments and requesting a reduction in his child support because he was financially unable to comply with the August 1990 order. Thereafter, Mr. Turner paid all the child support due through November 30, 1990, and agreed to pay an additional $475 for the children's medical expenses. Following a hearing in January 1991, the trial court entered an order on February 1, 1991, finding Mr. Turner in contempt for failing to pay child support and to obtain medical insurance for his children. The trial court decided not to act on Mr. Turner's petition to modify his child support because "he comes to the Court with unclean hands." In addition, the trial court directed Mr. Turner to begin paying an additional $177 per month to reimburse Ms. Turner for obtaining medical insurance for the children through her group insurance plan at work.

Ms. Turner filed a second petition in May 1991 seeking to hold Mr. Turner in contempt for inappropriate conduct while he was returning her son from visitation. In December 1993, she filed her third contempt petition complaining that Mr. Turner had harassed and abused her and the children and that he was seriously delinquent in his child support obligations. Following an ex parte hearing, the trial court ordered Mr. Turner's arrest and suspended his visitation rights. Mr. Turner responded, as he had in the past, that he was financially unable to meet his child support obligations and again requested the trial court to reduce his child support.

Following a January 1994 hearing, the trial court filed an order on February 14, 1994, finding Mr. Turner in criminal contempt for violating the orders prohibiting him from harassing and abusing Ms. Turner and the children and also finding him in civil contempt for failing to make his child support payments. The trial court sentenced Mr. Turner to ten days for the criminal contempt to be served consecutively with a six-month sentence for civil contempt but determined that Mr. Turner could purge himself of the civil contempt by paying $40,908.86. The trial court also ordered that Mr. Turner's visitation would be summarily suspended if he did not make prompt and timely support payments.

The trial court summarily suspended Mr. Turner's visitation before he was released from jail because he failed to pay his child support. Mr. Turner filed another petition in July 1994 requesting modification of his child support and reinstatement of his visitation. On December 20, 1994, the trial court filed an order denying Mr. Turner's petition. . . .

Mr. Turner . . . takes issue with the trial court's refusal to permit him to visit his children because he is delinquent in paying his child support. While we are not prepared to say that this sanction is never appropriate, we find that the present facts do not warrant suspending Mr. Turner's visitation rights.

Child custody and visitation decisions should be guided by the best interests of the child. They are not intended to be punitive. Pizzillo v. Pizzillo, 884 S.W.2d 749, 757 (Tenn. Ct. App. 1994); Barnhill v. Barnhill, 826 S.W.2d 443, 453 (Tenn. Ct. App. 1991). As a general rule, the most preferable custody arrangement is one which promotes the children's relationships with both the custodial and noncustodial parent.

Ms. Turner argues in her brief that the children are adversely affected by Mr. Turner's failure to support them, and thus their best interests will be served by cutting off their visitation with their father unless he begins supporting them. This assertion would have some merit if the record contained proof to substantiate it. We find no such proof. The record, however, contains some support for concluding that the children are not going without basic necessities because Ms. Turner is presently able to provide for their needs.

The courts may deny or condition continuing visitation on the grounds of parental neglect. See Mimms v. Mimms, 780 S.W.2d 739, 745 (Tenn. Ct. App. 1989) (parental neglect may be considered in relation to the children's best interests). The denial of visitation is warranted, however, only when the noncustodial parent is financially able to support his or her children but refuses to do so. Since the trial court has not conclusively determined that Mr. Turner is at present willfully refusing to support his children even though he is financially able to do so, we have determined that the order curtailing Mr. Turner's visitation rights should likewise be vacated and that this issue should likewise be addressed and definitively decided on remand. Pending the remand hearing, the trial court should enter an interim order permitting Mr. Turner visitation on whatever terms the trial court determines are just and appropriate. . . .

Notes and Questions

1. **Factors.** Because the Constitution protects the parent-child relationship, courts deny visitation reluctantly. Does the failure to pay child support justify denial of visitation, according to *Turner*? What other situations justify denial of visitation? Physical or sexual abuse? See, e.g., Grossman v. Grossman, 772 N.Y.S.2d 559 (App. Div. 2004). Domestic violence? See, e.g., Beverly v. Bredice, 751 N.Y.S.2d 79 (App. Div. 2002). The risk of child abduction? See, e.g., Damiani v. Damiani, 835 So. 2d 1168 (Fla. Dist. Ct. App. 2002). What purpose does denial of visitation serve? Protection? Coercion? Punishment? How does *Turner* respond? Is it ever in the child's best interests to deny all contact with a parent?

If a parent's rights are terminated, does the parent still have an obligation to pay child support? Some states provide, by case law or statute, that the common law duty to support a child continues after termination of parental rights in limited circumstances. See Marian F. Dobbs, Determining Child and Spousal Support §4:6 (2016). What should those circumstances be? See, e.g., Ex parte M.D.C., 39 So. 3d 1117 (Ala. 2009); In re Ryan B., 686 S.E.2d 601 (W. Va. 2009).

2. **Rule and exception.** As *Turner* illustrates, visitation normally will *not* be conditioned upon payment of child support. Nor may support be withheld because an ex-spouse interferes with visitation. Some courts, however, like *Turner*, make an exception for willful and intentional failure to pay support that is detrimental to the child. What explains the traditional reluctance to link the two issues?

3. **Defenses.** Should certain actions that deprive a parent of visitation (e.g., concealment of the child) provide a defense to that parent's failure to pay child support? Should it matter if the child is a minor or an adult at the time that the claim for payment of support arrearages is brought?

4. **Policy.** What are the advantages and disadvantages of untethering child support and visitation? Of tethering them? Professor Karen Czapanskiy argues that both approaches limit the custodial parent's need for personal autonomy and reflect gender-based parental roles. She adds that connecting child support and

visitation invites retaliatory withholding of support payments and limitations on the opportunity to spend time with a child.[40]

Should the usual rule of independence of support and visitation be abrogated when a parent conceals the child from the other parent? If so, should this rule be subject to exceptions? What justification(s) would be sufficient?

5. Remedies. If interference with visitation is not a defense to nonpayment of support, should interference be grounds for custody modification? Compare Vernon v. Vernon, 800 N.E.2d 1085 (N.Y. 2003) (modifying custody), with Bittick v. Bittick, 987 So. 2d 1058 (Miss. Ct. App. 2008) (contra). Should courts invoke other remedies in cases of a parent's interference with visitation such as the following: (a) compensatory parenting time (e.g., Mich. Comp. Laws §552.642); (b) payment of attorneys' fees to enforce visitation (e.g., Kolbet v. Kolbet, 760 N.E.2d 1146 (Ind. Ct. App. 2002)); (c) attendance at parenting classes or performance of community service?

6. Coercion. Can (should) a parent be compelled to exercise visitation rights? If the noncustodial parent fails to pick up the child at the scheduled time, what remedies (if any) should be available to the custodial parent? See Lederle v. Spivey, 965 A.2d 621 (Conn. Ct. App. 2009).

Does empirical research support the rule that the right to visit and duty to support should not depend on each other? Consider the excerpt below.

Jessica Pearson & Nancy Thoennes, The Denial of Visitation Rights: A Preliminary Look at Its Incidence, Correlates, Antecedents, and Consequences
10 Law & Pol'y 363, 375-379 (1988)

This paper explores the nature and incidence of the denial of visitation rights and the non-payment of child support. [V]isitation denial is a problem with approximately 22 percent of sample mothers reputedly failing to comply with the visitation terms of their divorce decree. . . . [T]hese levels fall far below the reported levels of non-compliance with child support. Only about half of all custodial parents owed child support receives the full amount of support owed to them in any given year. Even fewer custodians receive all the payments on time.

[In many cases, noncustodial parents lose contact with their children.] Hetherington, et al. (1978) report that two years following the divorce, 30 percent of the children saw their fathers about once a month or less. . . . Clearly, it is inaccurate to assume that all of these are cases in which custodians encourage sporadic visitation or deny the non-custodian regular access to the children. Indeed in her study, Luepnitz notes that:

---

[40]. Karen Czapanskiy, Child Support and Visitation: Rethinking the Connections, 20 Rutgers L.J. 619, 619-620 (1989).

In half of the cases when the non-custodial father visits rarely or never, it is because the children dislike him and have decided not to see him. But in many other cases, custodial mothers report that their ex had split the scene "in order to evade child support payments."

[Deborah A. Luepnitz, Child Custody 34 (1982).]

Further investigation of visitation non-compliance reveals that it rarely stands alone as a postdivorce problem and that such allegations are accompanied by a host of other visitation-related complaints. Moreover, for most parents visitation difficulties appear to become established fairly early on and fail to deviate over time.

Couples with visitation problems are decidedly more embittered than their compliant counterparts and their lack of cooperation, conflict and anger are apparent at the earliest interview, well before the promulgation of a divorce decree and are corroborated by independent interviewer ratings. Although non-payment of child support cases do not always involve a visitation problem, the two phenomena are related and cases with visitation problems are substantially more likely to involve child support non-payment or disputes over support. Both phenomena appear to stem from conflict patterns between the parents, although we were unable to assess causal order in cases that involved both types of non-compliance. . . .

These findings inspire several policy recommendations. Minimally, there is a need for reliable record keeping of both child support and visitation arrears. Without reliable record keeping, violations are difficult to prove, make-up policies are impossible to establish or supervise. . . .

Secondly, these findings underscore the importance of interventions with divorcing couples aimed at enhancing their communication skills and reducing levels of anger and hostility. [A] preliminary assessment of relationships between the non-custodial parent and his children reveals that conflict between divorced parents is a good prediction of both child support payment, visitation and other types of involvement. . . .

A third conclusion of this research is the need to consider child support and visitation issues concurrently. While there is no evidence to suggest that the two issues should be made contingent upon one another so that the denial of one should be a remedy for the withholding of the other, policy should reflect the fact that they co-occur and that grievances in both areas should be jointly aired. This conclusion runs counter to current practice. To date, most court-based mediation services deal with the issues of contested child custody and/or visitation only. . . .

A fourth implication of our research is the need to create and evaluate mechanisms for the enforcement of both child support and visitation orders. [Some states authorize] a make-up visitation policy, including compensatory visitation. Other states have explored the use of fines, tort remedies, etc. Improved visitation enforcement is warranted by the observed incidence of interference, the co-occurrence of visitation and child support problems and equity considerations.

3. Standards Governing Parent Versus Third Party Disputes

TROXEL v. GRANVILLE
530 U.S. 57 (2000)

Justice O'CONNOR announced the judgment of the Court and delivered an opinion, in which CHIEF JUSTICE REHNQUIST, Justice GINSBURG, and Justice BREYER join. . . .

Tommie Granville and Brad Troxel shared a relationship that ended in June 1991. The two never married, but they had two daughters, Isabelle and Natalie. Jenifer and Gary Troxel are Brad's parents, and thus the paternal grandparents of Isabelle and Natalie. After Tommie and Brad separated in 1991, Brad lived with his parents and regularly brought his daughters to his parents' home for weekend visitation. Brad committed suicide in May 1993. Although the Troxels at first continued to see Isabelle and Natalie on a regular basis after their son's death, Tommie Granville informed the Troxels in October 1993 that she wished to limit their visitation with her daughters to one short visit per month.

[Two months later, the Troxels filed this petition for visitation.] At trial, the Troxels requested two weekends of overnight visitation per month and two weeks of visitation each summer. Granville did not oppose visitation altogether, but instead asked the court to order one day of visitation per month with no overnight stay. [T]he Superior Court [ordered] visitation one weekend per month, one week during the summer, and four hours on both of the petitioning grandparents' birthdays.

[The Court of Appeals reversed the visitation order based on their statutory interpretation that nonparents lack standing unless a custody action is pending. The state supreme court held that the state statute granting visitation rights to "any parent" at "any time" (Wash. Rev. Code §26.10.160 (3) (1994)) infringed on parents' fundamental right to rear their children. While the appeal was pending, the mother remarried, and her husband adopted the children.]

The demographic changes of the past century make it difficult to speak of an average American family. The composition of families varies greatly from household to household. While many children may have two married parents and grandparents who visit regularly, many other children are raised in single-parent households. In 1996, children living with only one parent accounted for 28 percent of all children under age 18 in the United

Gary and Jenifer Troxel (plaintiffs in Troxel v. Granville) outside the U.S. Supreme Court

States. Understandably, in these single-parent households, persons outside the nuclear family are called upon with increasing frequency to assist in the everyday tasks of child rearing. In many cases, grandparents play an important role. For example, in 1998, approximately 4 million children—or 5.6 percent of all children under age 18—lived in the household of their grandparents.

The nationwide enactment of nonparental visitation statutes is assuredly due, in some part, to the States' recognition of these changing realities of the American family. Because grandparents and other relatives undertake duties of a parental nature in many households, States have sought to ensure the welfare of the children therein by protecting the relationships those children form with such third parties. The States' nonparental visitation statutes are further supported by a recognition, which varies from State to State, that children should have the opportunity to benefit from relationships with statutorily specified persons—for example, their grandparents. The extension of statutory rights in this area to persons other than a child's parents, however, comes with an obvious cost. For example, the State's recognition of an independent third-party interest in a child can place a substantial burden on the traditional parent-child relationship. . . .

The liberty interest at issue in this case—the interest of parents in the care, custody, and control of their children—is perhaps the oldest of the fundamental liberty interests recognized by this Court [citing Meyer v. Nebraska, and Pierce v. Soc'y of Sisters]. In light of this extensive precedent, it cannot now be doubted that the Due Process Clause of the Fourteenth Amendment protects the fundamental right of parents to make decisions concerning the care, custody, and control of their children.

Section 26.10.160(3), as applied to Granville and her family in this case, unconstitutionally infringes on that fundamental parental right. The Washington nonparental visitation statute is breathtakingly broad. According to the statute's text, "[a]ny person may petition the court for visitation rights at any time," and the court may grant such visitation rights whenever "visitation may serve the best interest of the child." §26.10.160(3) (emphases added). That language effectively permits any third party seeking visitation to subject any decision by a parent concerning visitation of the parent's children to state-court review. Once the visitation petition has been filed in court and the matter is placed before a judge, a parent's decision that visitation would not be in the child's best interest is accorded no deference. Section 26.10.160(3) contains no requirement that a court accord the parent's decision any presumption of validity or any weight whatsoever. Instead, the Washington statute places the best-interest determination solely in the hands of the judge. Should the judge disagree with the parent's estimation of the child's best interests, the judge's view necessarily prevails. Thus, in practical effect, in the State of Washington a court can disregard and overturn any decision by a fit custodial parent concerning visitation whenever a third party affected by the decision files a visitation petition, based solely on the judge's determination of the child's best interests. . . .

Turning to the facts of this case, the record reveals that the Superior Court's order was based on precisely the type of mere disagreement we have just described and nothing more. The Superior Court's order was not founded on any special factors that might justify the State's interference with Granville's fundamental right to make decisions concerning the rearing of her two daughters. [T]he combination of several factors here compels our conclusion that §26.10.160(3), as applied, exceeded the bounds of the Due Process Clause.

First, the Troxels did not allege, and no court has found, that Granville was an unfit parent. That aspect of the case is important, for there is a presumption that fit parents act in the best interests of their children. [S]o long as a parent adequately cares for his or her children (i.e., is fit), there will normally be no reason for the State to inject itself into the private realm of the family to further question the ability of that parent to make the best decisions concerning the rearing of that parent's children.

The problem here is not that the Washington Superior Court intervened, but that when it did so, it gave no special weight at all to Granville's determination of her daughters' best interests. More importantly, it appears that the Superior Court [adopted "a commonsensical approach [that] it is normally in the best interest of the children to spend quality time with the grandparent" and placed] on Granville, the fit custodial parent, the burden of *disproving* that visitation would be in the best interest of her daughters. . . .

The decisional framework employed by the Superior Court directly contravened the traditional presumption that a fit parent will act in the best interest of his or her child. In that respect, the court's presumption failed to provide any protection for Granville's fundamental constitutional right to make decisions concerning the rearing of her own daughters. In an ideal world, parents might always seek to cultivate the bonds between grandparents and their grandchildren. Needless to say, however, our world is far from perfect, and in it the decision whether such an intergenerational relationship would be beneficial in any specific case is for the parent to make in the first instance. And, if a fit parent's decision of the kind at issue here becomes subject to judicial review, the court must accord at least some special weight to the parent's own determination.

Finally, we note that there is no allegation that Granville ever sought to cut off visitation entirely. Rather, the present dispute originated when Granville informed the Troxels that she would prefer to restrict their visitation with Isabelle and Natalie to one short visit per month and special holidays. . . . The Superior Court gave no weight to Granville's having assented to visitation even before the filing of any visitation petition or subsequent court intervention. . . . Significantly, many other States expressly provide by statute that courts may not award visitation unless a parent has denied (or unreasonably denied) visitation to the concerned third party.

Considered together with the Superior Court's reasons for awarding visitation to the Troxels, the combination of these factors demonstrates that the visitation order in this case was an unconstitutional infringement on Granville's fundamental right to make decisions concerning the care, custody, and control of her two daughters. The Washington Superior Court failed to accord the determination of Granville, a fit custodial parent, any material weight. In fact, the Superior Court made only two formal findings in support of its visitation order. First, the Troxels "are part of a large, central, loving family, all located in this area, and the [Troxels] can provide opportunities for the children in the areas of cousins and music." Second, "[t]he children would be benefitted from spending quality time with the [Troxels], provided that that time is balanced with time with the childrens' [sic] nuclear family." These slender findings, in combination with the court's announced presumption in favor of grandparent visitation and its failure to accord significant weight to Granville's already having offered meaningful visitation to the Troxels, show that this case involves nothing more than a simple disagreement between the Washington Superior Court and Granville concerning her children's best interests. The Superior Court's announced reason for ordering one week of visitation in the summer demonstrates our conclusion well: "I look back on some personal experiences. . . . We always spen[t] as kids a week with one set of grandparents and another set of grandparents, [and] it happened to work out in our family that [it] turned out to be an enjoyable experience. Maybe that can, in this family, if that is how it works out." [T]he Due Process Clause does not permit a State to infringe on the fundamental right of parents to make childrearing decisions simply because a state judge believes a "better" decision could be made. [W]e hold that §26.10.160(3), as applied in this case, is unconstitutional. . . .

Because we rest our decision on the sweeping breadth of §26.10.160(3) and the application of that broad, unlimited power in this case, we do not consider the primary constitutional question passed on by the Washington Supreme Court—whether the Due Process Clause requires all nonparental visitation statutes to include a showing of harm or potential harm to the child as a condition precedent to granting visitation. We do not, and need not, define today the precise scope of the parental due process right in the visitation context. [T]he constitutionality of any standard for awarding visitation turns on the specific manner in which that standard is applied. . . . Because much state-court adjudication in this context occurs on a case-by-case basis, we would be hesitant to hold that specific nonparental visitation statutes violate the Due Process Clause as a *per se* matter. . . .

[In separate, omitted, concurring opinions, Justice Souter upheld the state court's determination of the statute's facial unconstitutionality, and Justice Thomas noted that strict scrutiny ought to apply. In an omitted dissenting opinion, Justice Scalia declined to recognize "unenumerated constitutional rights."]

Justice STEVENS, dissenting.

. . . While, as the Court recognizes, the Federal Constitution certainly protects the parent-child relationship from arbitrary impairment by the State, we have never held that the parent's liberty interest in this relationship is so inflexible as to establish a rigid constitutional shield, protecting every arbitrary parental decision from any challenge absent a threshold finding of harm. The presumption that parental decisions generally serve the best interests of their children is sound, and clearly in the normal case the parent's interest is paramount. But even a fit parent is capable of treating a child like a mere possession.

Cases like this do not present a bipolar struggle between the parents and the State over who has final authority to determine what is in a child's best interests. There is at a minimum a third individual, whose interests are implicated in every case to which the statute applies—the child. . . .

[Justice Stevens discusses *Lehr* and *Michael H.* to support his argument that limitations to parental liberty interests exist.] A parent's rights with respect to her child have thus never been regarded as absolute, but rather are limited by the existence of an actual, developed relationship with a child, and are tied to the presence or absence of some embodiment of family. These limitations have arisen, not simply out of the definition of parenthood itself, but because of this Court's assumption that a parent's interests in a child must be balanced against the State's long-recognized interests as parens patriae, and, critically, the child's own complementary interest in preserving relationships that serve her welfare and protection.

While this Court has not yet had occasion to elucidate the nature of a child's liberty interests in preserving established familial or family-like bonds, it seems to me extremely likely that, to the extent parents and families have fundamental liberty interests in preserving such intimate relationships, so, too, do children have these interests, and so, too, must their interests be balanced in the equation. At a minimum, our prior cases recognizing that children are, generally speaking, constitutionally protected actors require that this Court reject any suggestion that when it comes to parental rights, children are so much chattel. The constitutional protection against arbitrary state interference with parental rights should not be extended to prevent the States from protecting children against the arbitrary exercise of parental authority that is not in fact motivated by an interest in the welfare of the child.

This is not, of course, to suggest that a child's liberty interest in maintaining contact with a particular individual is to be treated invariably as on a par with that child's parents' contrary interests. Because our substantive due process case law includes a strong presumption that a parent will act in the best interest of her child, it would be necessary, were the state appellate courts actually to confront a challenge to the statute as applied, to consider whether the trial court's assessment of the "best interest of the child" incorporated that presumption. . . . But presumptions notwithstanding, we should recognize that there may be circumstances in which a child has a stronger interest at stake than mere protection from serious harm caused by the termination of visitation by a "person" other than a parent. The almost infinite variety of family relationships that pervade our ever-changing society strongly counsel against the creation by this Court of a constitutional rule that treats a biological parent's liberty interest in the care and supervision of her child as an isolated right that may be exercised arbitrarily. It is indisputably the business of the States, rather than a federal court employing a national standard, to assess in the first instance the relative importance of the conflicting interests that give rise to disputes such as this. . . .

Justice KENNEDY, dissenting.

[T]he custodial parent has a constitutional right to determine, without undue interference by the state, how best to raise, nurture, and educate the child. The parental right stems from the liberty protected by the Due Process Clause of the Fourteenth Amendment [citing Meyer v. Nebraska, Pierce v. Soc'y of Sisters, Stanley v. Illinois, among others]. The [Washington] State Supreme Court sought to give content to the parent's right by announcing a categorical rule that third parties who seek visitation must always prove the denial of visitation would harm the child. . . . [T]he law of domestic relations, as it has evolved to this point, treats as distinct the two standards, one harm to the child and the other the best interests of the child. The judgment of the Supreme Court of Washington rests on that assumption, and I, too, shall assume that there are real and consequential differences between the two standards.

On the question whether one standard must always take precedence over the other in order to protect the right of the parent or parents, "[o]ur Nation's history, legal traditions, and practices" do not give us clear or definitive practices. . . . To say that third parties have had no historical right to petition for visitation does not necessarily imply, as the Supreme Court of Washington concluded, that a parent has a constitutional right to prevent visitation in all cases not involving harm. True, this Court has acknowledged that States have the authority to intervene to prevent harm to children, but that is not the same as saying that a heightened harm to the child standard must be satisfied in every case in which a third party seeks a visitation order. . . .

My principal concern is that the [state supreme court's] holding seems to proceed from the assumption that the parent or parents who resist visitation have always been the child's primary caregivers and that the third parties who seek visitation have no legitimate and established relationship with the child. That idea, in turn, appears influenced by the concept that the conventional nuclear family ought to establish the visitation standard for every domestic relations case. As we all know, this is simply not the structure or prevailing condition in many households. For many boys and girls, a traditional family with two or even one permanent and caring parent is simply not the reality of their childhood. . . .

[S]ince 1965 all 50 States have enacted a third-party visitation statute of some sort. Each of these statutes, save one, permits a court order to issue in certain cases if visitation is found to be in the best interests of the child. . . . In my view, it would be more appropriate to conclude that the constitutionality of the application of the best interests standard depends on more specific factors. In short, a fit parent's right vis-a-vis a complete stranger is one thing; her right vis-a-vis another parent or a de facto parent may be another. . .

Notes and Questions on *Troxel*

1. Common law presumption. Custody disputes sometimes arise between parents and others who have a close but non-parental relationship with the child. Many such disputes involve disagreements between parents and grandparents, but they can also include disputes between parents and stepparents. Traditionally, courts resolved these disputes by application of a rebuttable presumption that custody should be awarded to the parent absent evidence of parental unfitness.

2. Background. At common law, grandparents had no right to visitation in the face of parental objection. However, all states now have third-party visitation statutes that permit grandparents (and sometimes other persons, as revealed in the statute at issue in *Troxel*) to petition for visitation and, in some states, custody. These statutes recognize that a third party may have an interest in maintaining a relationship with a child with whom they have formed an important connection.

What societal factors explain the expanding legal recognition of grandparents' rights? Professors Andrew Cherlin and Frank Furstenberg identify several factors:

> All of these trends taken together—changes in mortality, fertility, transportation, communications, the work day, retirement, Social Security, and standards of living—have transformed grandparenthood from its pre-World War II state. More people are living longer to become grandparents and to enjoy a lengthy period of life as grandparents. They can keep in touch more easily with their grandchildren; they have more time to devote to them; they have more money to spend on them; and they are less likely still to be raising their own children.[41]

Today, an increasing number of grandparents (and other relatives) are caring for children in cases of parents' opioid addiction when parents have died, are incarcerated, are in treatment, or are otherwise unable to take care of their children. These caregivers face a range of social, financial, physical, and mental health challenges. For example, approximately one in five caregiving grandparents lives below the poverty line, and about one in four has a disability.[42]

3. Constitutional issues. Third-party visitation statutes, such as the statute in *Troxel*, can raise constitutional concerns. Some parties have argued that statutes allowing third parties to seek custody or visitation over the objection of a legal parent unconstitutionally intrude upon the fundamental right of a parent to control the upbringing of the child (based on Meyer v. Nebraska and Pierce v. Society of Sisters, reprinted in Chapter I).

In *Troxel*, the plurality held that the Washington statute, as applied to Tommie Granville, violated the mother's due process rights. In what way was the statute constitutionally defective? By holding the statute unconstitutional as applied, the Supreme Court avoided ruling that the statute was facially unconstitutional. Why does the Court adopt this approach?

4. Standard of review. *Troxel* declined to identify the appropriate standard of review for evaluating the permissibility of third-party visitation statutes. What standard of review should apply? Should courts apply strict scrutiny? Rational basis review? Why? Which standard is more protective of parental interests? Which standard is less protective?

5. Substantial harm. *Troxel* also left unanswered the question of whether a showing of harm to the child is necessary as a condition precedent to granting visitation to a third party. Which standard do you think is preferable—the best interests standard, the harm standard, some other standard? How does Justice Kennedy address this question in his dissent in *Troxel*?

Parties in such custody disputes often rely on expert testimony to prove or disprove that a ban on contact will create serious harm to the child. In the wake of *Troxel*, many states revised their third-party visitation statutes to impose a harm standard, although the extent of the requisite harm differs. The Restatement on

---

[41]. Andrew J. Cherlin & Frank Furstenberg, Jr., The Modernization of Grandparenthood, in The Intimate Environment 131 (Arlene S. Skolnick ed., 6th ed. 1989).

[42]. Pew Research Ctr., Grandparents Living with or Serving as Primary Caregivers for their Grandchildren, Sept. 4, 2013.

Children and the Law adopts the following harm standard: "a court may not override the parent's decision about a third party's contact with a child unless the third party demonstrates that the parent's decision poses a substantial risk of serious harm to the child's health or well-being."[43] This standard requires proof of a significant deleterious effect on the child and not merely proof that contact would be beneficial or cause the child to feel sadness at the loss of the relationship. The Restatement explains that this standard protects families from intrusive third-party proceedings except when necessary for the child's health or well-being, while at the same time furthering the child's best interests in most cases.

6. Other third parties: Stepparents. According to U.S. Census data, 7 percent of children are living with a stepparent.[44] Traditionally, if a stepparent sought custody over parental objection at divorce, the stepparent had to overcome the legal parent presumption. Today, a minority of states have statutory provisions providing for stepparent visitation.[45] (Note that if stepparents adopt stepchildren, they are then legal parents and have the same rights and responsibilities as any other legal parents.)

7. Child's interests? To what extent does the Constitution protect the child's right to retain a relationship with a nonparent? Is *Troxel* concerned with the child's interests? In his dissent in *Troxel*, how does Justice Stevens urge consideration of the child's interests?

8. "De facto" parents. In the majority of states, actions brought by third parties typically are distinguished from cases brought by people who have functioned as a parent to a child but who may not be considered the child's legal parent under the state's parentage rules. Different states use different terms to describe the latter; commonly used terms include "de facto parent," "psychological parent," or "person standing in loco parentis." In many states, such persons have the right to seek custody or visitation under a best interests of the child standard.[46] In some circumstances, a grandparent who has been raising their grandchild may be able to seek custody or visitation under one of these doctrines. This issue is discussed in more detail in Chapter IX.

9. Law reform: Uniform Nonparent Custody and Visitation Act. The Uniform Nonparent Custody and Visitation Act (UNCVA, below) addresses the legal rights of nonparents by providing a right to seek custody or visitation for certain categories of nonparents. Which nonparents have this right pursuant to the act? What are the differences in the act's treatment of relatives and nonrelatives? What factors guide the court's discretion in determining the best interests of the child? Would the UNCVA apply to the Troxels? Why or why not?

[43]. Rest. of Children and the Law, § 1.80 (Child's Contact with a Third Party) cmts. g & j (reporting that in many states, third parties must show "harm or substantial risk of harm").
[44]. U.S. Census, Living Arrangements of Children: 2019 (Feb. 2022), https://www.census.gov/content/dam/Census/library/publications/2022/demo/p70-174.pdf.
[45]. Compiled from ABA, Chart 6: Third-Party Visitation, 46 Fam. L.Q. 537 (2013).
[46]. See, e.g., Courtney G. Joslin & Douglas NeJaime, How Parenthood Functions, 123 Colum. L. Rev. 319, 340 (2023) (describing and cataloguing doctrines).

UNIFORM NONPARENT CUSTODY AND VISITATION ACT

§2. DEFINITIONS.

In this [act]:

(1) "Child" means an unemancipated individual who is less than [18] years of age.

(2) "Compensation" means wages or other remuneration paid in exchange for care of a child. The term does not include reimbursement of expenses for care of the child, including payment for food, clothing, and medical expenses.

(3) "Consistent caretaker" means a nonparent who meets the requirements of Section 4(b). . . .

(5) "Harm to a child" means significant adverse effect on a child's physical, emotional, or psychological well-being. . . .

(7) "Nonparent" means an individual other than a parent of the child. The term includes a grandparent, sibling, or stepparent of the child.

(8) "Parent" means an individual recognized as a parent under law of this state other than this [act]. . . .

(13) "Substantial relationship with the child" means a relationship between a nonparent and child which meets the requirements of Section 4(c).

§4. REQUIREMENTS FOR ORDER OF CUSTODY OR VISITATION

(a) A court may order custody or visitation to a nonparent if the nonparent proves that:

(1) the nonparent:

(A) is a consistent caretaker; or

(B) has a substantial relationship with the child and the denial of custody or visitation would result in harm to the child; and

(2) an order of custody or visitation to the nonparent is in the best interest of the child.

(b) A nonparent is a consistent caretaker if the nonparent without expectation of compensation:

(1) lived with the child for not less than 12 months, unless the court finds good cause to accept a shorter period;

(2) regularly exercised care of the child;

(3) made day-to-day decisions regarding the child solely or in cooperation with an individual having physical custody of the child; and

(4) established a bonded and dependent relationship with the child with the express or implied consent of a parent of the child, or without the consent of a parent if no parent has been able or willing to perform parenting functions.

(c) A nonparent has a substantial relationship with the child if:

(1) the nonparent:

(A) is an individual with a familial relationship with the child by blood or law; or

(B) formed a relationship with the child without expectation of compensation; and

(2) a significant emotional bond exists between the nonparent and the child.

§5. PRESUMPTION FOR PARENTAL DECISION

(a) In an initial proceeding under this [act], a decision by a parent regarding a request for custody or visitation by a nonparent is presumed to be in the best interest of the child.

(b) Subject to Section 15, a nonparent has the burden to rebut the presumption under subsection (a) by clear-and-convincing evidence of the facts required by Section 4(a). Proof of unfitness of a parent is not required to rebut the presumption under subsection (a).

§12. BEST INTEREST OF CHILD

In determining whether an order of custody or visitation to a nonparent is in the best interest of a child, the court shall consider:

(1) the nature and extent of the relationship between the child and the parent;

(2) the nature and extent of the relationship between the child and the nonparent;

(3) the views of the child, taking into account the age and maturity of the child;

(4) past or present conduct by a party, or individual living with a party, which poses a risk to the physical, emotional, or psychological well-being of the child;

(5) the likely impact of the requested order on the relationship between the child and the parent;

(6) the applicable factors in [cite to this state's law other than this [act] pertaining to factors considered in custody or visitation disputes between parents]; and

(7) any other factor affecting the best interest of the child.

[Section 13 includes a rebuttable presumption against custody in cases in which the nonparent, or individual living with a nonparent, has committed child abuse, child neglect, domestic violence, sexual assault, or stalking. Section 14 authorizes awards of both sole or joint custody and visitation to a nonparent. Section 15 allows modification of custody and visitation based on a substantial change in circumstances combined with the best interests standard.]

4. The Role of Special Participants

a. Representation for the Child

HOSKINS v. HOSKINS

2015 WL 222177 (Ky. Ct. App. 2015)

Thompson, Judge:

Cory David Hoskins appeals from an order of the Morgan Circuit Court modifying timesharing with his son. He contends the trial court erroneously considered the report of a guardian *ad litem* (GAL). . . . Based on our Supreme Court's recent clarification of the role of GAL's in domestic child custody and visitation matters, we reverse and remand.

Cory and Melissa Hoskins were divorced on June 26, 2008. [Based on their separation agreement], Cory and Melissa shared joint custody of their son. . . . Melissa was awarded timesharing with the child every Sunday from 6:00 P.M. through the following Wednesday at 6:00 P.M. and Cory was awarded timesharing every Wednesday from 6:00 P.M. until the following Friday at 6:00 P.M. The parties were awarded alternating weekends [and] timesharing on the various traditional holidays.

On March 4, 2013, Melissa filed a motion to modify custody and the parties' parenting schedule, asserting [as the basis that] Cory received a speeding ticket, had remarried and divorced, and moved three times since the parties' divorce. [At the conclusion of the hearing on July 3, 2013, the trial court appointed an attorney as GAL to represent the child's interest and ordered the GAL to file a report with the court.] The GAL reported that the child conveyed that his parents were very active in his life and love him. The GAL also reported [that] the child stated Cory becomes upset when [the parents fight about the custody arrangements]. The GAL recommended [that] the parties refrain from speaking directly to the child or in front of him regarding their personal and legal disputes [and] making derogatory remarks in front of the child. . . .

The trial court entered an order continuing joint custody with the child but ordered that the child reside primarily with Melissa. Cory was awarded timesharing in accordance with the local visitation schedule. Cory appealed.

During the pendency of this appeal, our Supreme Court issued its opinion in Morgan v. Getter, 441 S.W.3d 94 (Ky. 2014) [in which the issue was]: "What is the role of a . . . GAL in a custody, shared parenting, visitation, or support proceeding?" . . . Artfully written, the Court's opinion explains how a hybrid [friend of the court (FOC)/guardian ad litem] has emerged in the realm of family law. However, it pointed out that the two are distinct and disavowed the practice of appointing an attorney as counsel for the child and as an investigator and advisor to the court.

The FOC is a creature of statute. The FOC may or may not be an attorney and is appointed as an officer of the court to "investigate the child's and the parents' situations, to file a report summarizing his or her findings, and to make recommendations as to the outcome of the proceeding." . . . [M]ore common in the present-day courts is the appointment of a GAL in vehemently contested domestic custody and visitation matters. However, the GAL is not a replacement for the FOC and has decidedly different roles. The GAL, who is always an attorney, is appointed to "participate actively as legal counsel for the child, to make opening and closing statements, to call and to cross-examine witnesses, to make evidentiary objections and other motions, and to further the child's interest in expeditious, non-acrimonious proceedings."

Despite the distinctions between a FOC and GAL, the Court noted the trial courts have often expected the GAL-appointee to "blur" these roles and "to investigate for the court and to litigate for the child." The Court found it problematic for a GAL appointed to represent the child to also examine records, interview family members and file a report with the court. Its concerns were both ethical and constitutional.

The Court agreed with those commentators and courts that have noted the ethical problems for the attorney and the potential deprivation of due process to a parent when the roles of a FOC and GAL are interchanged. The GAL is subject to the Rules of the Supreme Court (SCR) governing attorneys' conduct including duties of loyalty and confidentiality to his or her client. Additionally, the Court pointed out that SCR 3.130–3.7 prohibits an attorney from being an advocate at a proceeding in which he or she is likely to be a necessary witness. Yet, when ordered by the Court, the GAL is required to submit a report in the very action that he or she is acting as the child's counsel.

These same rules that bind attorneys present constitutional implications for the parent. By definition, a GAL represents the child in the custody or visitation proceeding and, therefore, cannot be a witness. Because the parent cannot cross-examine a GAL as to the basis for any facts or recommendations contained in the GAL's report, there is no opportunity to confront adverse evidence as required by due process. Emphasizing a parent has a protected liberty interest in the care and custody of his or her child, the Court agreed with "the many courts that have held that in these circumstances the party's constitutional due process right trumps the [ethical] rule."

Noting the potential ethical and constitutional implications of the appoint-ment of a hybrid FOC/GAL and the need of our trial courts to have the authority to appoint not only an investigator and advisor to the court but also to appoint an advocate for the child's best interest, the Court asked the rhetorical question: "What is a Court to do?" The Court [in the *Morgan* case] responded to its own question with exceptional clarity [explaining that the court could appoint a FOC to investigate the circumstances on the court's behalf, file a report, and make custodial recommenda-tions. Or, the trial court could appoint a GAL to represent the child's best interests.] The [*Morgan*] Court cautioned that the GAL should not be confused with the FOC.

> The FOC "investigates, reports, and makes custodial recommendations on behalf of the court, and is subject to cross-examination[.]" The GAL "is a lawyer for the child, counseling the child and representing him or her in the course of proceed-ings by, among other things, engaging in discovery, in motion practice, and in presentation of the case at the final hearing." Important to the outcome of this case, the GAL "*neither testifies (by filing a report or otherwise) nor is subject to cross-examination.*" (emphasis added).

Here, the circuit court admittedly was without the benefit of the *Morgan* opinion. Nevertheless, it erroneously appointed the GAL to represent the child *and* to conduct an investigation and file a report and, by judicial fiat, created a hybrid FOC/GAL disapproved of in *Morgan*.

[T]he question remains whether the error was harmless. Melissa contends the error was harmless because the trial court relied on other evidence produced at the hearing when modifying timesharing. [But] the only facts recited in the trial court's modification order to support its decision pertain to those stated in the GAL's report. Although the trial court stated its decision was also based on evidence produced at the hearing, its order does not recite what evidence supports its decision to modify timesharing. It is impossible for this Court to determine what admissible evidence supported the trial court's decision. Based on the forgoing, the order of the Morgan Circuit Court is reversed and the case remanded for further proceedings.

Notes and Questions

1. Background. The debate over mandatory representation for children in custody disputes began in the 1960s, prompted by the rising divorce rate, concern about the effects of divorce on children, and recognition of the child's right to counsel in the delinquency context (In re Gault, 387 U.S. 1 (1967)). Should counsel for the child in custody disputes be mandatory? What problems are posed by the mandatory appointment of counsel in custody disputes?[47]

2. Current situation. Only a small number of jurisdictions mandate the appointment of a a guardian ad litem (GAL) in custody litigation. In most other states, the court is permitted but not required to appoint a GAL or an attorney for the child at the court's discretion.[48] In these states, what factors should influence judicial discretion to appoint a representative?

3. Models of representation. As *Hoskins* reveals, considerable debate exists about the appropriate role of the child's representative. Most jurisdictions authorize a GAL who operates as a best interests attorney; a few jurisdictions appoint a child's attorney. The remaining jurisdictions appoint either a hybrid (best interests attorney and child's attorney) or a combination of representatives depending on the circumstances.[49]

What roles are most invasive of family privacy? Least invasive? If the representative serves as an advocate, should he or she argue for the child's wishes (regardless of what the attorney believes) or the child's best interests? If the representative ascertains the child's best interests, does this role usurp the authority of the judge? Does the investigator-neutral fact finder's role conflict with the duty to represent a client zealously (ABA Model Rules of Professional Conduct, Rule 1.3)? What difficulties does each role evoke? Should the representative's role depend on the type of proceeding (e.g., abuse, delinquency, custody)? Depend on the child's age? The child's abilities?

4. Role overlap and confusion. The GAL's role often overlaps with the functions performed by other professionals in the custody dispute resolution process. In addition, considerable role confusion exists. Sometimes attorneys characterize their role as either advocate or fact finder but then act inconsistently. Factors that might influence an attorney's perception of roles include (a) the state law description of the role; (b) instructions given by, or exceptions of, the judge; (c) training that the guardian ad litem received; (d) age of the child and the guardian's understanding of child development, attachment, and permanency planning. What risks are posed by role confusion?[50]

---

[47]. Schepard, Children, Courts, and Custody, supra note [1], at 146-147 (reporting estimates of 5 to 25 percent).

[48]. Linda Elrod, Child Custody Prac. & Proc., Representation—Child, §2:10 (2022).

[49]. See, e.g., id. (describing various approaches and controversy regarding these approaches).

[50]. See, e.g., Kimbrell v. Kimbrell, 331 P.3d 915 (N.M. 2014) (finding that a GAL acting as a "best interests" attorney is shielded by quasi-judicial immunity from tort suits). See generally Dana E. Prescott, Inconvenient Truths: Facts and Frictions in Defense of Guardians Ad Litem for Children, 67 Me. L. Rev. 43 (2014).

5. Law reform. Beginning in 2001, several states recommended sweeping changes in the role of GALs in custody cases. For example, an Ohio task force recommended statewide standards regarding qualifications, fees, training, and responsibilities. A Minnesota task force proposed changes in role definition, training, caseload size, supervision, and accountability. Criticisms focused on the following problems: that GALs occupy roles that are not subject to consistent definitions, undermine fact finding by usurping the judicial role, deprive parents of due process, undermine parental authority and privacy, entail significant costs, are ineffectual in cases of domestic violence, and lack accountability for their decisions.[51]

6. ABA Standards of Practice. In response to such criticisms, the ABA formulated Standards of Practice for Lawyers Representing Children in Custody Cases. The ABA Standards abolish the name "guardian ad litem" and provide instead for two types of lawyers, each of whom makes evidence-based legal arguments: the child's attorney, who provides independent legal representation in a traditional attorney-client relationship, and the best interests attorney, who independently investigates, assesses, and advocates the child's best interests *as a lawyer*. See Standard II(B) ("Definitions" and cmt.).

Lawyers appointed in either capacity should not "play any other role in the case, and should not testify, file a report, or make recommendations." See Standard III(B) ("Lawyer's Roles"). The Standards also provide that a lawyer should accept an appointment only with a full understanding of the functions to be performed. Otherwise, the lawyer should either decline appointment or alternatively, request clarification and/or change of the order. See Standards III(A) ("Accepting the Appointment").

7. Uniform Act. In response to the adoption by the ABA of two different sets of standards (Standards for Representation of Children in Abuse, Neglect, and Dependency Cases, adopted in 1995; and Standards of Practice of Lawyers Representing Children in Custody Cases, adopted in 2003), the ULC promulgated the Uniform Representation of Children in Abuse, Neglect, and Custody Proceedings Act in 2007. The purpose of the act is to define the roles and responsibilities of representatives, as well as to address the ethical dimensions of the lawyer-client relationship, access to the child and information relating to the child, and the child's right of action for damages against the representative. Commentators criticize the Uniform Act, as well as the ABA Custody Standards, for the extent of judicial discretion that they vest in the best interests lawyer.[52] To date, no state has enacted the Uniform Law on the representation of children.

---

[51]. Richard Ducote, Guardians Ad Litem in Private Custody Litigation: The Case for Abolition, 3 Loy. J. Pub. Int. L. 106, 116 (2002).

[52]. See Katherine Hunt Federle, Righting Wrongs: A Reply to the Uniform Commission on Law's Uniform Representation of Children in Abuse, Neglect and Custody Proceedings Act, 42 Fam. L.Q. 103 (2008). But see Barbara Atwood, The Uniform Representation of Children in Abuse, Neglect and Custody Proceedings Act: Bridging the Gap Between Pragmatism and Idealism, 42 Fam. L.Q. 63 (2008).

b. Role of Experts

IN RE REBECCA B.

611 N.Y.S.2d 831 (App. Div. 1994)

MEMORANDUM DECISION

[In 1986, after Renee B. and Michael B. had been married for five years, Renee filed for divorce and sole custody of their daughter, Rebecca. The Family Court granted both motions. In 1992, upon discovering that Michael was sleeping in the same bed as Rebecca, Renee petitioned to eliminate Michael's overnight visitation and to require supervised visitation. Michael cross-petitioned for sole custody. The Family Court denied Michael's cross-petition and affirmed the award of sole custody to the mother. The father appealed.]

[The Family Court] Order, dated May 8, 1992, which, inter alia, denied the motion of appellant father for a transfer of the sole legal custody of his daughter from her mother, to him, [is] unanimously modified on the law and the facts, and in the exercise of discretion, to the extent of granting the transfer of the sole legal custody to appellant, with liberal visitation rights to respondent mother, and otherwise, insofar as consistent with such transfer of sole legal custody to appellant, in all respects [is] otherwise affirmed, without costs or disbursements. It is ordered that any further proceedings in the matter in the Family Court be held before another judge.

The Clinical Director of the Family Court's Mental Health Service was qualified to testify as an expert in clinical psychology. He had met with the child on three occasions for a total of three hours and with her and each parent for about forty minutes. He also had met with each parent separately for about seven hours. He concluded that the child's best interests required the transfer of custody to appellant with liberal visitation for the mother noting that appellant was a much less detrimental influence on the child than was the mother, that he was less likely to cause long-term harm to her than was the mother, that the child perceived him as more loving than her mother, and that she had a more profound bond with him. The child made it clear repeatedly to the Clinical Director that she would prefer to live with her father; the mother's spanking, slapping, and locking of the child in her room was difficult for the child to comprehend.

Another psychiatrist also recommended a change in custody, for the "main reason" that the mother tried so to exclude appellant from the child's life; he believed that appellant as the custodial parent would give better access to the noncustodial parent. From age seven to eight the child had slept with her father on overnight visits, but there had been no suggestion of any improper action by appellant and the practice had ceased. The psychiatrist had found nothing "intrinsically detrimental" in the arrangement. A supervising social worker employed by the Legal Aid Society also recommended that custody be transferred to appellant.

A psychiatrist retained by the mother testified that custody should be continued with the mother. However, he had spoken only with the mother and with people to whom he was referred by the mother and not to the child or appellant.

The law guardian, believing that appellant was more likely to foster the non-custodial parent's relationship, concluded that the transfer of custody to him was in the best interest of the child.

The trial court denied appellant's motion to transfer custody to him, terming the testimony of the Clinical Director, the first mentioned psychiatrist and the Social Worker not credible. They were, however, the only experts making a recommendation as to custody who had spoken to all three family members, but the trial court repeatedly described their testimony as "flawed." By discounting the testimony of these three witnesses, the trial court essentially left itself without expert testimony on the child's preferences and the quality of her relationships with her parents. Since the mother's psychiatrist had not interviewed the child or appellant, moreover, little weight should be accorded to his recommendation that custody be awarded to the mother. . . .

A determination had been made by Family Court in 1987 that the mother should have custody. The burden was thus on appellant to demonstrate a substantial change of circumstances to justify a change in custody. He did so in 1991 by showing the preference of the child—then seven years of age—to live with him, by showing the bond which had grown between them, by showing petitioner's rather punitive disciplining of the child, which would over time have a deleterious effect on the child, and especially by his showing of petitioner's efforts to exclude him from the child's life.

We must respect the advantage of the trial judge in observing the witnesses, but the authority of this court in matters of custody is as broad as that of the trial court. It always comes down, however, to the best interests of the child and the ability of the parents "to provide for the child's emotional and intellectual development, the quality of the home environment, and the parental guidance provided." The psychiatrist, testifying on behalf of petitioner, said of her: "She is a somewhat temperamental lady who has a temper, and it would be better if she kept her mouth shut more and didn't get into fights with her former husband and her child, but that's normal within the context of this kind of situation." This is not a severe indictment of a person, but it does support other testimony that petitioner tends to be short-tempered and punitive with her daughter and the inference therefrom that the child is being harmed. There has been no showing, on the other hand, that appellant, despite his social isolation, tends to be other than helpful, patient, and constructive in his relationship with his daughter.

It has been shown that petitioner attempts to exclude appellant from the child's life. The Clinical Director and the psychiatrist who met with all concerned believe that, if awarded custody, she will continue to do so. Such acts are "so inconsistent with the best interests of the children as to, per se, raise a strong probability that the mother is unfit to act as custodial parent" (Entwistle v. Entwistle, 402 N.Y.S.2d 213 (1978), *appeal dismissed*, 44 N.Y.2d 851 (1978)).

This court finds the testimony of those experts favoring custody of the child to appellant convincing. . . . The trial court's custody award lacked a sound and substantial basis in the record and should not be allowed to stand.

Notes and Questions

1. Different roles. Mental health experts play different roles in custody deter-mination: (a) conduct evaluations to assess parenting and children's functioning; (b) gather data (e.g., from schools, medical personnel, social service agencies, etc.); (c) conduct observations of, and interviews with, the parties; and (d) serve as expert witnesses on issues of child development. Most custody evaluators are psy-chologists, psychiatrists, or social workers. How might their different backgrounds and training influence their work? Should courts limit the number of experts? Can you identify the various roles of the mental health experts in *Rebecca B.*?

2. Ethical standards. Professionals in custody determinations must observe professional codes of ethics and standards of practice. Stemming from concerns that custody evaluators should be subject to more strict standards, the Association of Family and Conciliation Courts (AFCC) drafted Model Standards for Custody Evaluators in 2006.[53] The AFCC Standards aim to promote good practices, provide information to those who utilize the services of custody evaluators, and increase public confidence in the services of custody evaluators.

3. Trial court findings. The appellate court in *Rebecca B.* reversed two prior rulings in favor of the mother (and an eight-year-long custody arrangement) on the basis that the trial judge erred by rejecting much of the expert testimony. In a lengthy opinion (Renee B. v. Michael B., No. V5272186 (N.Y. Fam. Ct. May 8, 1992)), the trial judge, George L. Jurow (who has a PhD in clinical psychology), explained his reasons for finding certain testimony "not credible" and "flawed":

- The father's expert's objectivity was compromised by his employment as the father's psychiatrist for four years; the expert engaged in "collusive interac-tions" by interviewing the daughter without the mother's knowledge or con-sent; the expert's conclusion that the mother was alienating the daughter and was responsible for communication difficulties was "factually incorrect and contradicted by other credible evidence" (because the father's confron-tations with school officials led them to ban him from the premises, and the father taped all conversations with the wife and daughter); the expert applied a gender-biased standard in recommending paternal custody based on the mother's demanding career as a corporate lawyer.
- The supervising social worker (who recommended custody transfer to the father) adopted "uncritically and without reflection" the opinion of the father's expert without conducting a thorough evaluation.
- The court-appointed expert's evaluation (1) had "important inquiry lapses" (regarding the father's lack of work history and plan to withdraw the daughter from school); (2) conflicted with that expert's own observations that the father was an "individual who is socially isolated, has no friends,

---

[53]. Ass'n of Fam. & Conciliation Cts. (AFCC), Model Standards for Custody Evaluators (2006), https://www.afccnet.org/Portals/0/ModelStdsChildCustodyEvalSept2006.pdf.

is prone to continued confrontations with people, [and] is 'interpersonally retarded'"; and (3) failed to recognize that the daughter's desire to live with her father was the "product of paternal pressure or an excessive degree of overbearing influence."

Do you agree with the appellate court that the trial court award "lacked a sound and substantial basis" in the record?

4. Parental alienation syndrome. The father's expert based his opinion, in part, on evidence of "parental alienation syndrome," a term that he coined to signify a parent's conscious or subconscious attempts to alienate a child from the other parent.[54] Although the theory is admissible in court, it has been the subject of longstanding, severe criticisms by professionals who claim that it lacks empirical basis; relies on speculations about mothers' purported unconscious desires and their effects on children; and minimizes abuse and its effects on mothers and children.

Claims of parental alienation continue to gain substantial traction in court. In a recent comprehensive study of family court decisions involving parental alienation, abuse, and child custody, Professor Joan Meier's findings confirm considerable judicial skepticism of mothers' claims of child abuse perpetrated by fathers. Moreover, fathers' cross-claims of allegations of parental alienation by mothers increases (indeed, virtually doubles) courts' rejection of mothers' claims, as well as mothers' losses of custody to the suspected abusive fathers. When guardians ad litem or custody evaluators are appointed in these cases, case outcomes show enhanced judicial skepticism of mothers' (but not fathers') claims, as well as an increase in custody removals from mothers (but not from fathers).[55]

5. Criticisms. Some mental health experts make custody recommendations to the court. What problems are posed by this practice? Are mental health professionals capable of determining custodial arrangements in the best interests of children? Critics charge that the practice allows professionals to play a dispositive role, gives a false aura of reliability, and results in the application of subjective biases and lifestyle preferences.[56] Critics also note that mental health professionals reflect a bias toward joint custody, even in cases (such as domestic violence) when it might be contraindicated. Specifically, many custody evaluators recommend awards to abusers based on the evaluators' denial or minimization of mothers' reports of intimate partner violence (IPV).[57] What reforms might address these criticisms?

---

[54]. Richard A. Gardner, The Parental Alienation Syndrome: A Guide for Mental Health and Legal Professionals (1992). For classic, trenchant critiques, see Carol S. Bruch, Parental Alienation Syndrome and Parental Alienation: Getting It Wrong in Child Custody Cases, 35 Fam. L.Q. 527 (2001); Joan S. Meier, Parental Alienation Syndrome and Parental Alienation: A Research Review (Sept. 2013), www.vawnet.org/assoc_files_vawnet/ar_pasupdate.pdf.

[55]. Meier, Denial of Family Violence, supra note [10].

[56]. For an analysis of the risks posed by custody evaluators who make recommendations to the court, compare Timothy M. Tippins & Jeffrey P. Wittmann, Empirical and Ethical Problems with Custody Recommendations: A Call for Clinical Humility and Judicial Vigilance, 43 Fam. Ct. Rev. 193 (2005), with Philip M. Stahl, The Benefits and Risks of Child Custody Evaluators Making Recommendations to the Court: A Response to Tippins and Wittmann, 43 Fam. Ct. Rev. 260 (2005).

[57]. See Ruth Leah Perrin, Overcoming Biased Views of Gender and Victimhood in Custody Evaluations When Domestic Violence Is Alleged, 25 Am. U. J. Gender & Soc. Pol'y & L., 155 (2017); Daniel G. Saunders et al., Nat'l Inst. of Justice, U.S. Dept. of Justice, Child Custody Evaluators' Beliefs About Domestic Abuse Allegations: Their Relationship to Evaluator Demographics, Background,

See, e.g., Cal. Fam. Code §3111(a) (child custody evaluation "may be considered by the court only if it is conducted in accordance with [certain] requirements" regarding training and protocols for conducting evaluations).

6. Epilogue. The custody suit cost Renee B. $340,000; the stress resulted in the loss of her job. Her subsequent appeal was denied. 645 N.E.2d 1217 (N.Y. 1994). Her ex-husband then sought to hold her in contempt for failure to pay child support. He arranged for the process server to accompany Rebecca on her visitation with her mother. Rebecca, then 12 years old, read the legal papers and became distraught at the threat of imprisonment of her mother. On her own initiative, Rebecca contacted her court-appointed guardian and refused to return to her father. She subsequently described her life with her father as verging on abusive: He prohibited her from calling her mother or sending her letters. The guardian ad litem petitioned for a change of custody. The trial court appointed a new expert, awarded the mother temporary custody, and granted the father supervised visitation. On appeal, the court upheld the custody award to the mother. The father subsequently moved away. By his choice, he had no further contact with the daughter, not even telephone calls on her birthday.[58]

Reflections on the Legacy of In re Rebecca B.

by Judge George L. Jurow
Personal communication, May 12, 2015

In almost 30 years as a trial judge on the New York State Family Court bench in Manhattan, *Rebecca B.* was and remains the most notorious custody case I ever tried. The case was the "perfect [bad] storm" of clinical experts. Three of them aligned with the father for very flawed reasons:

The court-appointed "impartial" psychologist severely misdiagnosed the mother, a corporate attorney, as having serious psychiatric pathology, including being "delusional" in her complaints about the father. In a devastating cross-examination, the mother's concerns were all determined to have a solid basis in fact. The psychologist even admitted that the

Attorney Bernard E. Clair, who represented Renee B.

Domestic Violence Knowledge and Custody-Visitation Recommendations 129 (2011); Stephen J. Yanni, Note, Experts as Final Arbiters: State Law and Problematic Expert Testimony on Domestic Violence in Child Custody Cases, 116 Colum. L. Rev. 533 (2016).

[58]. Telephone interview with Bernard H. Clair, attorney for Renee B. (Clair Greifer LLP, 555 Madison Avenue, 9th Floor, New York City), Aug. 19, 1997, and June 10, 2006.

mother had better skills to be the custodial parent, as she had been for the prior eight years. The real, but shadowy, reason for the psychologist's misdiagnosis of the mother was that he, with a very stoic and humorless demeanor, could not relate to the mother, whose temperament was extroverted and sometimes flippant. In my experience, a disconnect in personality styles between an evaluator and a parent, a form of "interview bias," is a common cause of defective forensic reports.

In very biased testimony, Dr. Richard Gardner promoted his controversial theory of Parental Alienation (watering the label down to maternal "exclusionary" behavior). His conflict of interest was substantial, as the father secretly brought the child to see Gardner and cultivated his input. This was "hired gun" testimony at its worst. The third aligned expert's testimony, by a clinical social worker, added nothing because it was her first child custody case so she chose to rely on the reports of the former two experts.

The shining star apart from this trio of dysfunctional experts was Dr. Allen Frances, a renowned psychiatrist and diagnostic expert who later chaired the Duke University Department of Psychiatry. He was brought in to refute the psychologist's diagnosis of the mother. He did so, evaluating the mother as having no psychiatric diagnosis or pathology, concluding that she simply was the custodian in a difficult custody dispute that would upset any such similarly situated parent. He also "peer reviewed" the reports by the psychologist and Dr. Gardner, calling them facially "ludicrous." In dismissing Dr. Frances's testimony because he did not interview the father and child, the appellate court misunderstood that his role was to address the mother's misdiagnosis, which did not require him to see the entire family. Nor did Dr. Frances make a custody recommendation as the appellate court misstated.

The erroneous appellate court reversal—no doubt primarily caused by the misleading anomalous line-up of the flawed experts—was met by a critical reaction by the New York matrimonial bar, who publicly objected that too much power was being given to forensic experts. The uproar was heard by the appellate courts who later "clarified" that they did not intend to usurp the role of trial judges in favor of clinicians.

In recent years, New York appellate courts have done a 180-degree turn by expressing major skepticism about the merits of forensic custody experts. In particular, court-appointed experts who were previously blessed with the imprimatur of neutrality are now more scrutinized because of increased attention paid to bias and methodology problems, as foreshadowed by *Rebecca B.*

5. Modification

a. Standard

The paramount concern with child welfare gives courts continuing power to modify custody orders. The standard for modification is higher than for initial awards in order to ensure stability for the child. The emphasis on stability in child placement decisionmaking is a central tenet of the work by Professors Goldstein, Freud, and Solnit, who strongly oppose alteration in child placement based on the child's need for continuity of care. See Joseph Goldstein et al., Beyond the Best Interests of the Child 37 (1973).

According to the prevailing standard, the plaintiff has the burden of showing by a preponderance of the evidence that conditions since the dissolution decree have so materially and substantially changed that the children's best interests require a change of custody. A few states have a more liberal requirement that modification serve the best interests of the child (regardless of any change in circumstances). Some states adopt an even lower standard when the change pertains to custodial time allocation or a modification of sole to joint custody. See, e.g., Alaska Stat. §25.20.110; Mont. Code Ann. §40-4-219. Several states have more stringent rules, influenced by UMDA §409(b) requiring endangerment for non-consensual changes. Absent serious endangerment, UMDA §409(a) provides for a two-year waiting period following the initial decree.

The American Law Institute's Principles of the Law of Family Dissolution (ALI Principles), similarly, includes a harm requirement. The ALI Principles allow for modification upon a showing of (1) a substantial change in the circumstances (relating to the child or one or both parents) on which the parenting plan was based that makes modification necessary for the child's welfare; or (2) harm to the child. ALI Principles §2.15(1) & (2). Note that the requirement that the modification is "necessary to the child's welfare" is stricter than that in many states. Modification based on a more liberal standard is available for consensual changes, minor parenting plan modifications, or the child's preference when the child attains a specified age.

Problem

When Roderic and Melinda divorce, they agree to share joint legal custody of their daughter, Geena, who is a preschooler. Melinda has primary physical custody and Roderic has liberal visitation. Four years later, after both Roderic and Melinda have remarried, Roderic files a motion to modify custody. He argues that the circumstances warrant a change to joint physical custody because, in the last four months, Geena's school performance has seriously declined. At the hearing, Geena's elementary schoolteacher, Barbara, testifies that Geena, an exceptionally bright student, performed very well during the first two quarters of the school year, but recently she has failed to complete assignments, forgotten to turn in homework, started talking in class, and earned failing grades. Barbara also testifies that she often discusses Geena's academic performance with Roderic and communicates with him by e-mail because he regularly inquires about Geena's progress. By contrast, Barbara has little contact with Melinda.

Roderic testifies regarding his frequent contacts with Geena's teacher. He also explains that he and his new wife value education and therefore can best assist Geena in her studies. Melinda testifies that she and her new husband also frequently assist Geena with her homework. Melinda attributes the decline in Geena's school performance to the increased conflict from her parents' constant custody disputes. Joann Lippert, a psychologist who conducted a family evaluation report, testifies about Geena's strong attachment to both parents and her desire to maintain a relationship with each. Dr. Lippert recommends that both parents should share physical custody because Geena's best interests would be served if both of her parents were actively involved in their daughter's education. Has there been a substantial change in circumstances affecting Geena's welfare that would warrant modification of custody? In addition, is modification in the child's best interests? What result? Ellis v. Carucci, 161 P.3d 239 (Nev. 2007).

b. Relocation

BISBING v. BISBING
166 A.3d 1155 (N.J. 2017)

Justice PATTERSON delivered the opinion of the Court.

Plaintiff Jaime Taormina Bisbing and defendant Glenn R. Bisbing divorced when their twin daughters were seven years old. Their judgment of divorce incorporated their settlement agreement that plaintiff would be the parent of primary residence and defendant would be the parent of alternate residence. [The settlement agreement] provided that neither party would permanently relocate out of state with the children without the prior written consent of the other. . . .

[I]n the months that followed their divorce, plaintiff and defendant lived near one another and cooperated in the care of their children. . . . Plaintiff took primary responsibility for the girls' school and extracurricular activities. Defendant was also extensively involved in his daughters' lives. He served as their soccer coach, assisted with their ski team, and oversaw their activities at church. Because plaintiff departed for her job in New York City early in the morning, defendant went to her home several mornings each week to assist the children as they prepared for school.

[Several months after the parties' divorce, plaintiff advised defendant that she intended to marry the man whom she had been dating, a resident of Utah] and asked defendant to consent to the permanent relocation of the children to Utah. Defendant replied that plaintiff was free to move to Utah, but that the children must remain in New Jersey with him. . . .

Plaintiff filed a motion pursuant to N.J.S.A. 9:2-2 [seeking] an order permitting her to permanently relocate the children to Utah [explaining] that she planned to marry Jake Fackrell and that his business interests precluded him from moving to New Jersey. She told the trial court that the children disliked their school in New Jersey and would have better educational opportunities in Utah. Plaintiff assured the court [that] defendant would still be afforded regular visitation with the children in New Jersey and Utah, as well as the opportunity to communicate with them on a daily basis by telephone and various forms of electronic communication. She argued that . . . the relocation would not be "inimical to the children's interests" because it would enable her to stay home with the children instead of returning to work and it would benefit the children to have a stay-at-home parent.

Defendant contended that plaintiff had negotiated the parties' Settlement Agreement in bad faith [arguing] that plaintiff secured his consent to her designation as parent of primary residence without informing him that she contemplated relocating to Utah in order to gain an advantage under the [applicable standard of Baures v. Lewis, 770 A.2d 214 (N.J. 2001) favoring the custodial parent's right to move]. He asserted that the relocation would make it impossible for him to maintain a full and continuous relationship with his daughters and that electronic communications would not serve as a substitute for the time that he would spend with them were they to remain in New Jersey.

[The trial court granted plaintiff's request, applying the *Baures* standard, under which a parent with primary custody seeking to relocate children out of state, over the objection of the other parent, must demonstrate only that there is a good faith reason for an interstate move and that the relocation "will not be inimical to the child's interests." Defendant appealed. The appellate court reversed, holding that if plaintiff had negotiated the parties' custody agreement in bad faith, the trial court on remand should instead determine whether relocation would be in the best interests of the child. The panel thus imposed on a plaintiff who has negotiated a custody arrangement in bad faith a higher burden of proof on the question of "cause" under N.J.S.A. 9:2-2 than the burden imposed under *Baures*.]

The provision of the custody statute at the center of this appeal is N.J.S.A. 9:2-2. It requires a showing of "cause" before a court will authorize the permanent removal of a child to another state without the consent of both parents or, if the child is of "suitable age" to decide, the consent of the child. . . . The Legislature required a showing of "cause" for an out-of-state relocation under N.J.S.A. 9:2-2 in order "to preserve the rights of the noncustodial parent and the child to maintain and develop their familial relationship."

As this Court has observed, a court making the sensitive determination of "cause" must weigh "the custodial parent's interest in freedom of movement as qualified by his or her custodial obligation, the State's interest in protecting the best interests of the child, and the competing interests of the noncustodial parent." When a parent of alternate residence objects to a proposal by the parent of primary residence to relocate children out of state, "there is a clash between the custodial parent's interest in self-determination and the noncustodial parent's interest in the companionship of the child." . . .

In *Baures*, the Court substantially eased the burden imposed on a custodial parent to demonstrate "cause" for a relocation under N.J.S.A. 9:2-2. Under the standard prescribed in that case, a trial court's threshold determination is whether . . . the parent seeking removal is the custodial parent. [If so,] that parent would establish "cause" under N.J.S.A. 9:2-2 if he or she proved "good faith and that the move will not be inimical to the child's interest." . . .

The Court identified two developments in support of its [adoption of the *Baures* custodial parent preference]. First, the Court concluded that when a relocation benefits a "custodial parent," it will, as a general rule, similarly benefit the child. The Court commented that "social science research links a positive outcome for children of divorce with the welfare of the primary custodian and the stability and happiness within that newly formed post-divorce household," and that such research "has uniformly confirmed the simple principle that, in general, what is good for the custodial parent is good for the child." For that conclusion, the Court relied on two studies [co-authored by the psychologist Judith Wallerstein].

Second, the Court invoked "the growing trend in the law easing restrictions on the custodial parent's right to relocate with the children and recognizing the identity of interest of the custodial parent and child." In support of the custodial parent's "presumptive right" to move, the Court relied primarily on the California Supreme Court's decision in [In re Marriage of Burgess, 913 P.2d 473 (Cal. 1996); but that case was later overturned by In re Marriage of LaMusga, 88 P.3d 81 (Cal. 2004)].

[With that background in mind], we consider whether to retain the *Baures* standard as the benchmark for contested relocation determinations decided pursuant to N.J.S.A. 9:2-2. [W]e do not lightly alter one of our rulings because consistent jurisprudence "provides stability and certainty to the law.". . . We find [however] justification for a departure from precedent in this case. In deciding *Baures*, the Court did not intend to diverge from the best interests of the child standard at the core of our custody statute, or to circumvent the legislative policy that parents have equal rights [in custody decisionmaking]. Instead, confronting a dispute that defies simple solutions, the Court sought guidance in social science research as to the best interests of the child, which at that time tethered the best interests of the child to the custodial parent's well-being. The Court also discerned a trend in the law "significantly eas[ing] the burden on custodial parents in removal cases." On those grounds, the Court replaced the best interests of the child test in relocation applications brought by parents with primary custody in favor of its two-pronged "good faith" and "not . . . inimical to the child" test.

[Since that time], social scientists who have studied the impact of relocation on children following divorce have not reached a consensus. Instead, the vigorous scholarly debate reveals that relocation may affect children in many different ways. . . . Moreover, the progression in the law toward recognition of a parent of primary residence's presumptive right to relocate with children, anticipated by this Court in *Baures*, has not materialized. . . . Today, the majority of states, either by statute or by case law, impose a best interests test when considering a relocation application filed by a parent with primary custody or custody for the majority of the child's time. . . .

Accordingly, we do not consider the [*Baures* custodial parent preference] to be compelled by social science or grounded in legal authority today, as the Court anticipated that it would be when it decided that case. We recognize a "special justification" in this case to abandon that standard. In place of the *Baures* standard, courts should conduct a best interests analysis to determine "cause" under N.J.S.A. 9:2-2 in all contested relocation disputes in which the parents share legal custody—whether the custody arrangement designates a parent of primary residence and a parent of alternate residence, or provides for equally shared custody. That standard comports with our custody statute, in which the Legislature unequivocally declared that the rights of parents are to be equally respected in custody determinations and stated that custody arrangements must serve the best interests of the child. . . .

We briefly address plaintiff's contention [that the] application of N.J.S.A. 9:2-2 infringes on her due process right to travel out of state. We do not [agree]. The statute places no constraint on plaintiff's right to travel. It does, however, place a limitation on her claimed right to permanently relocate her children from our State without the court's approval when another parent's rights and the child's best interests are at stake. [A] court that has determined "custody on the assumption of residence within New Jersey so as to protect, among other things, the visitation rights of the noncustodial parent and the interest of the child in maintaining a close relationship with that parent" has the authority to constrain a parent from altering custody without violating that parent's due process right to travel. . . .

Our holding compels a remand of this matter. [P]laintiff must demonstrate that there is "cause" for an order authorizing such relocation. In that inquiry, "cause" should be determined by a best interests analysis in which the court will consider all relevant factors set forth in N.J.S.A. 9:2-4(c), supplemented by other factors as appropriate. . . . Because the best interests standard applies to the determination of "cause" under N.J.S.A. 9:2-2 notwithstanding plaintiff's designation as the parent of primary residence, the question whether plaintiff anticipated a relocation when she negotiated for that designation does not determine the governing standard. In the remand hearing, the court need not decide whether plaintiff negotiated the parties' Agreement in bad faith. . . .

Notes and Questions

1. Frequency of relocation. Geographic mobility is a fact of life. Within four years after separation or divorce, 75 percent of custodial mothers relocate at least once, and half of these will relocate again.[59] Custodial parents generally relocate for reasons of remarriage, employment, educational opportunities, or support from relatives.

Disputes arise because a decree, statute, marital settlement agreement, or parenting plan requires a parent to seek permission to relocate with the child. What prompted the need for judicial resolution in *Bisbing*? If parents (like the Bisbings) execute a written agreement that governs relocation disputes, should their written agreement preclude judicial resolution of their dispute?

2. Good faith and motive. Many courts consider good faith as a threshold requirement in relocation disputes. Should good faith be required? What role does good faith play in *Bisbing*? How does a court determine its existence? Many courts also require that the custodial parent have a legitimate motive. What is the difference between good faith and motive?

What motives should be considered "legitimate"? The desire to be closer to petitioner's parents? See, e.g., Bruce H. v. Jennifer L., 407 P.3d 432 (Alaska 2017); Levitin v. Levitin, 89 N.Y.S.3d 256 (App. Civ. 2018). Remarriage? See Raffa v. Raffa, 945 N.Y.S.2d 766 (App. Div. 2012). Better employment? Compare Odell v. Odell, 139 So. 3d 1275 (La. Ct. App. 2014) (hope of employment opportunity was insufficient), with Newman v. Duffy, 3 N.Y.S.3d 847 (App. Div. 2015) (allowing relocation due to stepfather's transfer). What was plaintiff's motive in *Bisbing*? Was it legitimate?

3. ALI standard. The ALI Principles permit a primary parent to relocate with the child if that parent has been exercising "the clear majority" of custodial responsibility, shows a valid purpose and good faith for the move, and the destination is "reasonable in light of the purpose." ALI Principles §2.17(4)(a).

4. Burden of proof. What should the burden of proof be in relocation disputes, and who should bear it? Some courts place the burden on the relocating

---

[59]. Sarah L. Gottfried, Note, Virtual Visitation: The New Wave of Communication Between Children and Non-Custodial Parents in Relocation Cases, 9 Cardozo Women's L.J. 567, 568 (2003) (citing data).

parent to prove that the move is in the child's best interests. Other states place the burden on the parent opposing the move to demonstrate the adverse impact of the relocation. Courts also differ on the nature of the burden of proof. According to *Bisbing*, what is the burden of proof, and who should bear it?

Should courts require that the move is "necessary"? Should courts require that "a compelling reason" or "exceptional circumstances" justify the move? The relocation will provide a real advantage to the child and/or the new family unit? Does a direct benefit in the custodial parent's quality of life translate into a direct benefit to the child? See J.M.R. v. J.M., 1 A.3d 902 (Pa. Super. Ct. 2010). Should a custodial parent have to prove that relocation serves a "reasonable purpose"? If so, what purpose is "reasonable"? For example, does a relocation to obtain better career opportunities constitute a "reasonable purpose" if the custodial parent has not explored whether better career opportunities exist in the present location? See Aragon v. Aragon, 513 S.W.3d 447 (Tenn. 2017).

Conversely, should the noncustodial parent be required to show that the move will result in detriment to the child? What constitutes detriment? Does any interference with visitation suffice? Should the court consider also the possible detriment from disrupting the child's relationship with the custodial parent? See In re Marriage of LaMusga, 88 P.3d 81, 100 (Cal. 2004) (Justice Kennard, dissenting). How would *Bisbing* be decided based on the above considerations?

5. Modification. Does (should) relocation automatically constitute a substantial change in circumstances that warrants modification? See Fowler v. Sowers, 151 S.W.3d 357 (Ky. 2003); Arnott v. Arnott, 293 P.3d 440 (Wyo. 2012). In modification disputes about relocation, should courts consider the legal label regarding each parent's custodial status contained in the marital settlement agreement or court degree? If so, should the court consider a parent's *actual* involvement with a child? How does *Bisbing* address these issues?

6. Trend: Fact-specific best interests. Until recently, the trend favored the custodial parent's presumptive right to move. California initiated the trend in 1996, influenced by the work of the psychologist Judith Wallerstein on the effects of divorce on children. See In re Marriage of Burgess, 913 P.2d 473 (Cal. 1996) (initiating trend). Some jurisdictions continue to adhere to this presumption but preclude its application if parents share residential time equally. See, e.g., Bergerson v. Zurbano, 432 P.3d 850 (Wash. Ct. App. 2018).

Most courts today adopt a fact-specific, best interests approach (as illustrated by *Bisbing*). Why does *Bisbing* reject the custodial parent preference? What facts are particularly relevant in the best interests analysis in relocation disputes? How relevant should the following factors be: past parental involvement, age of the child, gender of the child, distance of the proposed move, cost of travel, parents' financial situation, a move away from extended family or stepsiblings, the child's loss of extracurricular activities/sports, or the child's school situation? How would you apply the best interests test, on remand, in *Bisbing*?

In *Bisbing*, the mother argued that the father would still have visitation, as well as the chance to communicate daily with the children by phone and "various forms of communication." What does the father respond? Whose argument is more persuasive? What role should the availability of electronic communications play in resolution of relocation disputes?

7. Right to travel. How does *Bisbing* accommodate the parents' constitutional rights in relocation disputes? Do relocation restrictions infringe on a parent's right to travel or only on a parent's right to travel with the child? How does *Bisbing* respond? Do the best interests of the child serve as a compelling state interest to overcome the custodial parent's right to travel? Should courts consider the *non-custodial* parent's ability and/or plans to relocate as well? See Quainoo v. Morelon-Quainoo, 87 So. 3d 364 (La. Ct. App. 2012). By inhibiting custodial parents, but not noncustodial parents, from moving, do relocation restrictions constitute gender bias because most custodial parents are women? Do the restrictions violate equal protection? See, e.g., Fredman v. Fredman, 960 So. 2d 52 (Fla. Dist. Ct. App. 2007).

Should the same rules govern interstate and intercountry moves? See, e.g., Ainsworth v. Ainsworth, 186 A.3d 1074 (R.I. 2018) (denying mother's request to move to Australia). May a parent restrict the other parent's right to travel with the children to *certain* countries, particularly where a state's jurisdiction over child custody may not be enforced? Several states require courts to consider certain abduction factors, such as whether the other country is a signatory to the Hague Convention on the Civil Aspects of International Child Abduction.

8. Children's interests. Do courts pay enough attention to children's interests in relocation disputes? The Bisbings' twins were seven years old at the time of the divorce. Does the *Bisbing* court consider their preferences? See, e.g., Townsend v. Mims, 90 N.Y.S.3d 799 (App. Div. 2018) (considering teenagers' wish to relocate with their father). If not, should it?

9. Effect of relocation on children. In accommodating the parties' interests, should courts consider research on the effects of relocation on children? How does *Bisbing* address the role of social science data?

Considerable controversy exists on the effects of relocation on children. Wallerstein argues that allowing the custodial parent to relocate with the children promotes the latter's best interests because children's postdivorce adjustment is closely entwined with the well-being of the custodial parent.[60] Another psychologist, Richard Warshak, counters that these findings rest on studies of few cases and derive from an earlier era, when divorced fathers played a less important role in childrearing.[61] Another study confirms the negative effects of relocation for children who move at least one hour's drive from the noncustodial parent.[62] In rebuttal, the sociologist Norval Glenn points out that the effects are not significant regarding the most important areas of psychological well-being (i.e., friendships, dating behavior, substance abuse, and general life satisfaction).[63]

Should judges in relocation disputes consider research that documents the gradual *decrease* in divorced fathers' visitation patterns? Sociologists Frank

---

[60]. Judith S. Wallerstein & Tony J. Tanke, To Move or Not to Move: Psychological and Legal Considerations in the Relocation of Children Following Divorce, 30 Fam. L.Q. 305, 318 (1996).

[61]. Richard A. Warshak, Social Science and Children's Best Interests in Relocation Cases: *Burgess* Revisited, 34 Fam. L.Q. 83 (2000).

[62]. Sanford L. Braver et al., Relocation of Children After Divorce and Children's Best Interests: New Evidence and Legal Considerations, J. Fam. Psychol., June 2003, at 206.

[63]. Norval Glenn & David Blankenhorn, Does Moving After Divorce Damage Kids? (2003). For another critique, see Carol S. Bruch, Sound Research or Wishful Thinking in Child Custody Cases? Lessons from Relocation Law, 40 Fam. L.Q. 281 (2006).

Furstenberg and Andrew Cherlin challenge the importance of children's main-tenance of ties with their noncustodial parents. They conclude that although strengthening such ties is important, "public policy should place lower priority on this objective" than on principles that emphasize promoting the effective func-tioning of custodial parents in order to improve their children's adjustment and to decrease children's exposure to parental conflict.[64] Do you find their views persuasive?

10. Domestic violence. Relocation controversies pose special risks for vic-tims of domestic violence. Why? Can such risks be alleviated? How should courts address requests that are motivated by a parent's desire to move away from an abuser? See, e.g., Matter of Eddington v. McCabe, 949 N.Y.S.2d 734 (App. Div. 2012); Francis-Miller v. Miller, 975 N.Y.S.2d 74 (App. Div. 2013).

Some state laws provide that if a parent relocates because of domestic violence, the relocation may not be a factor that weighs against the parent in determining custody or visitation. See, e.g., Haw. Rev. Stat. §571-46(a). Do such statutory provi-sions help resolve relocation disputes in cases of domestic violence?

Problem

Mother and Father divorce in Vermont when their daughter is two years old. The divorce order, based on the parties' stipulation, provides that Mother will have sole legal custody. For the next few years until the daughter starts school, the par-ents share her time roughly equally. Father's contact is reduced to one-third when the daughter starts school. Soon thereafter, Mother notifies Father that she and her fiancé intend to move to Maryland for his employment. Mother, who had lost her teaching job because of budget cuts, plans to look for a teaching position in Maryland. Mother files a motion to modify the parent-child contact schedule that was established in final divorce orders, and Father opposes her motion and seeks sole custody. What result? See Hawkes v. Spence, 878 A.2d 273 (Vt. 2005) (adopting ALI relocation standard). See also Hayes v. Gallacher, 972 P.2d 1138 (Nev. 1999).

6. Jurisdiction and Enforcement

Prior to the late 1960s, a state could assert jurisdiction over child custody if it had a "substantial interest" in the case. This interest might signify the state of the mar-ital domicile or the current residence of either parent or the child. Such a vague standard often led to concurrent assertions of jurisdiction. In addition, because of judicial willingness to reopen custody decisions at the behest of a state resident, decrees were freely modifiable in other states. Supreme Court decisions left unclear

[64]. Frank F. Furstenberg, Jr. & Andrew J. Cherlin, Divided Families: What Happens to Children When Parents Part? 107 (1991). See also William G. Austin et al., Relocation Issues in Child Custody Evaluations: A Survey of Professionals, 54 Fam. Ct. Rev. 477 (2016); Patrick Parkinson & Judy Cashmore, Reforming Relocation Law: An Evidence-Based Approach, 53 Fam. Ct. Rev. 23 (2015).

whether custody decisions were entitled to the protection of the Full Faith and Credit Clause. The ease with which parents could reopen child custody cases in other states has been described as "a rule of seize-and-run." May v. Anderson, 345 U.S. 528, 542 (1953) (Jackson, J., dissenting). Law reform addressed this problem by uniform legislation, as well as federal legislation.

1. UCCJA. The Uniform Child Custody Jurisdiction Act (UCCJA) was drafted in 1968 to reduce jurisdictional competition and confusion, as well as to deter parents from forum shopping to relitigate custody. A version of the UCCJA, which applied to initial custody decisions as well as modifications, was adopted in all states by 1981. The UCCJA identified four alternative bases of jurisdiction; sought to locate jurisdiction in the forum with access to the most evidence relevant to the custody decision; attempted to ensure that proceedings would occur in only one state at a time; and mandated recognition, enforcement, and nonmodification of a decree from another state with jurisdiction under the UCCJA. The four alternative bases for jurisdiction included: the child's home state, a significant connection between the state and the parties, emergency jurisdiction when the child is present and the child's welfare is threatened, and the fact that no other state has jurisdiction. "Home state" was defined as the state in which the child lived (immediately preceding the time involved) with a parent or parents for at least six consecutive months.

2. PKPA. In 1980 Congress enacted the Parental Kidnapping Prevention Act (PKPA), 28 U.S.C. §1738A. The purpose of the PKPA was to ensure that custody decrees receive recognition and enforcement in other states through full faith and credit. Despite its title, the PKPA is relevant to child custody jurisdiction. The PKPA was drafted in light of the fact that the UCCJA had not obtained the anticipated uniformity: States were slow to adopt it and state modifications of its provisions were common. The PKPA made two improvements to the UCCJA. First, the PKPA prioritizes the UCCJA's bases of jurisdiction, giving priority to the child's home state. Second, the PKPA addresses a problem under the UCCJA in which multiple states assert jurisdiction to modify. The PKPA provides that once a state has exercised jurisdiction, the initial decree-granting state has "exclusive continuing jurisdiction," so long as it remains the residence of the child or any contestant.

3. UCCJEA. Every state except for Massachusetts has adopted the Uniform Child Custody Jurisdiction and Enforcement Act (UCCJEA), promulgated in 1997 to harmonize differences between the UCCJA and PKPA. The UCCJEA differs from its predecessor the UCCJA in several ways. Whereas the UCCJA did not prioritize among the four bases of jurisdiction, the UCCJEA follows the PKPA in giving priority to home state jurisdiction. The UCCJEA remedies shortcomings of the PKPA by eliminating the "best interests" language from the second basis of jurisdiction (the vague "significant connection" basis) and, in addition, severely restricts the use of emergency jurisdiction to the issuance of temporary orders. Like the PKPA, the UCCJEA provides for "exclusive continuing jurisdiction" for modification. The UCCJEA encompasses all custody and visitation decrees (temporary, permanent, initial, and modifications) and covers those proceedings related to divorce, separation, neglect, abuse, dependency, guardianship, paternity, termination of parental rights, and protection from domestic violence (but not adoptions).

Another important UCCJEA reform concerns the law's response in cases of domestic violence. Under the UCCJA and the PKPA, temporary emergency jurisdiction arises in extraordinary circumstances where a child is present in a state and subjected to, or threatened with, mistreatment or abuse. However, the UCCJEA §204(a) permits a court to exercise emergency jurisdiction to protect the child, its siblings, or its parents (not only the child in question).

The UCCJEA provisions regarding initial jurisdiction, exclusive continuing jurisdiction, and modification are set forth below.

UNIFORM CHILD CUSTODY JURISDICTION AND ENFORCEMENT ACT

§102. DEFINITIONS.

In this [Act] . . .

(7) "Home State" means the State in which a child lived with a parent or a person acting as a parent for at least six consecutive months immediately before the commencement of a child-custody proceeding. In the case of a child less than six months of age, the term means the State in which the child lived from birth with any of the persons mentioned. A period of temporary absence of any of the mentioned persons is part of the period.

§201. INITIAL CHILD-CUSTODY JURISDICTION

(a) Except as otherwise provided in Section 204 [dealing with emergency jurisdiction over abandoned or abused/neglected children] (below), a court of this State has jurisdiction to make an initial child-custody determination only if:

(1) this State is the home state of the child on the date of the commencement of the proceeding, or was the home State of the child within six months before the commencement of the proceeding and the child is absent from this State but a parent or person acting as a parent continues to live in this State;

(2) a court of another State does not have jurisdiction under paragraph (1), or a court of the home State of the child has declined to exercise jurisdiction on the ground that this State is the more appropriate forum . . . and:

(A) the child and the child's parents, or the child and at least one parent or a person acting as a parent, have a significant connection with this State other than mere physical presence; and

(B) substantial evidence is available in this State concerning the child's care, protection, training, and personal relationships;

(3) all courts having jurisdiction under paragraph (1) or (2) have declined to exercise jurisdiction on the ground that a court of this State is the more appropriate forum to determine the custody of the child . . . or

(4) no court of any other State would have jurisdiction under the criteria specified in paragraph (1), (2), or (3).

(b) Subsection (a) is the exclusive jurisdictional basis for making a child-custody determination by a court of this State.

(c) Physical presence of, or personal jurisdiction over, a party or a child is not necessary or sufficient to make a child-custody determination.

§202. EXCLUSIVE, CONTINUING JURISDICTION

(a) Except as otherwise provided in Section 204 [emergency jurisdiction] (below), a court of this State which has made a child-custody determination consistent with Section 201 or 203 has exclusive, continuing jurisdiction over the determination until:

(1) a court of this State determines that neither the child, the child's parents, and any person acting as a parent do not have a significant connection with this State and that substantial evidence is no longer available in this State concerning the child's care, protection, training, and personal relationships; or

(2) a court of this State or a court of another State determines that the child, the child's parents, and any person acting as a parent do not presently reside in this State.

(b) A court of this State which has made a child-custody determination and does not have exclusive, continuing jurisdiction under this section may modify that determination only if it has jurisdiction to make an initial determination under Section 201.

§203. JURISDICTION TO MODIFY DETERMINATION

(a) Except as otherwise provided in Section 204 [emergency jurisdiction] (below), a court of this State may not modify a child-custody determination made by a court of another State unless a court of this State has jurisdiction to make an initial determination under Section 201(a)(1) or (2) and:

(1) the court of the other State determines it no longer has exclusive, continuing jurisdiction under Section 202 or that a court of this State would be a more convenient forum . . .; or

(2) a court of this State or a court of the other State determines that the child, the child's parents, and any person acting as a parent do not presently reside in the other State.

§204. TEMPORARY EMERGENCY JURISDICTION

(a) A court of this State has temporary emergency jurisdiction if the child is present in this State and the child has been abandoned or it is necessary in an emergency to protect the child because the child, or a sibling or parent of the child, is subjected to or threatened with mistreatment or abuse. . . .

Additional remedies to enforce custody determinations include contempt proceedings and the writ of habeas corpus. Some states also recognize civil or criminal liability for custodial interference in cases of abduction or concealment of a child. See, e.g., Khalifa v. Shannon, 945 A.2d 1244 (Md. 2008); State v. Froland, 936 A.2d

947 (N.J. 2007). See also Restatement (Second) of Torts §700 (1977) (recognizing the tort of custodial interference). Some states provide exceptions to custodial interference laws for victims of domestic violence who flee with a child. See, e.g., Fla. Stat. §787.03(2), (4)(b).

Note that federal court jurisdiction is not available to parents who are awarded conflicting custody decrees by different states. See Thompson v. Thompson, 484 U.S. 174 (1988) (holding that the PKPA did *not* create an implied cause of action in federal court to determine which of two conflicting state custody decrees is valid, based on the statutory language and legislative history).

NOTE: INTERNATIONAL CHILD ABDUCTION

International parental abductions pose a vexing legal problem. More than 1,000 children are abducted either to or from the United States annually.[65] The rise in international abductions stems from the ease of international transportation as well as the increasing number of binational marriages. The return of these children to the United States depends on the application of the Hague Convention on the Civil Aspects of International Child Abduction. As of 2022, there are 103 nation-parties to the Convention, including the United States. The United States implemented the Convention by enabling legislation, the International Child Abduction Remedies Act (ICARA), 42 U.S.C. §§9001-9011.

The goal of the Hague Convention is to secure the return of children who are wrongfully removed from or retained in a signatory state and to return them to the country of their "habitual residence" (which must be another contracting nation), where the merits of the custody dispute can be adjudicated. In 2018, 232 children were returned to the United States under the Hague Convention, according to the U.S. State Department.[66]

Article 13 of the Convention specifies three affirmative defenses to defeat the child's return: (1) if the taking parent establishes that the child's caretaker was not actually exercising custody rights at the time of removal or retention or had consented to removal or retention; (2) if the taking parent establishes a grave risk that the return would entail physical or psychological harm to the child; and (3) if the court in the forum of the taking parent finds that the child, who has attained an appropriate age and maturity (based on the court's discretion), objects to the return.

The Hague Convention was based on the idea that the likely abductor was a noncustodial father. However, most international abductions are carried out by custodial mothers, many of whom are fleeing domestic violence. As a government report explains, "the intended beneficiaries of the Convention have become its primary targets."[67] An effort is currently underway by the Hague Domestic Violence

---

[65]. U.S. Senate Comm. on Foreign Relations, Chairman Menendez Opening Remarks at Hearing on International Parental Child Abduction (2014), http://www.foreign.senate.gov/press/chair/release/chairman-menendez-opening-remarks-at-hearing-on-international-parental-child-abduction.

[66]. U.S. Dept. of State, Annual Report on International Child Abduction i (2019), https://travel.state.gov/content/dam/NEWIPCAAssets/pdfs/2019%20Report.pdf.

[67]. Nat'l Inst. of Justice, U.S. Dept. of Justice, Multiple Perspectives on Battered Mothers and Their Children Fleeing to the United States for Safety: A Study of Hague Convention Cases 304-305 (2010).

Project, based at the American Bar Association (ABA) Commission on Domestic and Sexual Violence, to establish children's exposure to domestic violence as an explicit exception to the automatic return of the child to the country of habitual residence.

In the past two decades, the Supreme Court has heard several important Hague Convention cases. In 2010, the Court held in Abbott v. Abbott, 557 U.S. 933 (2010), that a common clause in custody decrees that restricts a custodial parent from removing the child from the jurisdiction ("ne exeat order") constitutes a "right of custody" for purposes of the Convention, thereby permitting a father who only had visitation rights to invoke the remedy of return. Later, in Chafin v. Chafin, 568 U.S. 165 (2013), the Court found that a child's return to her home country did not moot the father's appeal. And, in Lozano v. Montoya Alvarez, 572 U.S. 1 (2014), the Court recognized that concealment of a child's location could be a factor when determining if a child is well settled in the new country.

The most recent Hague Convention case, Golan v. Saada, 142 S. Ct. 1880 (2022), involved a couple (Isacco Saada and Narkis Golan) who married in Italy and had a son. From the start of their relationship, Saada was violent toward Golan, including in front of their son (although allegedly not toward the son himself). When the child was three years old, Golan and the child traveled to the United States and remained there. The father petitioned for the child's return under the Hague Convention. The Second Circuit Court of Appeals affirmed the district court's finding that (1) Italy was the child's "country of habitual residence"; (2) return of the child to Italy would subject him to a grave risk of psychological harm based on IPV; and (3) certain "ameliorative measures" would mitigate the risk of harm (i.e., ordering Saada to stay away from Golan, requiring him to visit the son only with Golan's consent, and paying her financial support). (Ameliorative measures, also known as "undertakings," are not specified in the Convention but are judicially created measures.) Golan urged the Supreme Court to reverse, contending that the ameliorative measures were inadequate for the child's safety, unenforceable, and otherwise improper. (Golan argued that Saada's previous conduct suggested that he would not comply with any court orders.)

The Supreme Court unanimously held that a court may deny a Hague Convention petition for return of a child based on grave risk of harm without the need to consider all possible ameliorative measures. The Court found that the Convention permits, but does not mandate, consideration of ameliorative measures, and further recognized that ameliorative measures may be inappropriate or ineffective to mitigate the risk to the child.

Following the conclusion of the Supreme Court decision, Golan, 41 years old, was found dead in her New York City apartment on October 18, 2022. Her sudden death raised the question of the fate of her then 6-year-old son, who had severe autism. That is, would he be returned to his father in Italy or remain in the United States with Golan's relatives? The decision is pending in a lower court in the Eastern District of New York.

Note that both federal law and a uniform law address international child abduction. The International Parental Kidnapping Act (IPKA), 18 U.S.C. §1204, imposes criminal sanctions (unlike the Hague Convention), making it a federal felony for a parent to wrongfully remove or retain a child outside the United States. IPKA has an explicit defense for parents fleeing from domestic violence. The Uniform Child Abduction Prevention Act (UCAPA) attempts to prevent parental abduction by identifying risk factors and establishing various remedies. The act authorizes courts to impose "abduction prevention measures" either *sua sponte* or upon the motion of a parent or child welfare agency. The act has been adopted by 14 states and the District of Columbia.

B. What Process Should Govern Custody Disputes?

1. The Adversary System Versus the Mediation Process

Elizabeth S. Scott & Robert Emery, Child Custody Dispute Resolution: The Adversarial System and Divorce Mediation

in Psychology and Child Custody Determinations: Knowledge, Roles and Expertise 23-27, 39-42, 45-51 (Lois A. Weithorn ed., 1987)

The adversary system has been well established in Anglo-American law for hundreds of years. There are two basic characteristics of this dispute resolution model: the decision maker is a neutral party not involved in the dispute (the judge), and the evidence about the dispute that the judge considers is controlled and developed by the disputing parties themselves. These characteristics have several implications for the process. Each litigant, through an attorney, attempts to present all the evidence favorable to his or her side of the case and unfavorable to the opponent's. . . . Adjudication through this process is designed to produce a "winner" and "a loser." . . .

Few other legal confrontations involve the emotional intensity of a custody dispute. In most litigation the adversaries are strangers, business associates, or acquaintances. The divorcing couple's prior intimate relationship exaggerates from the outset the potential for hostility. Because of the prior relationship, each parent may know particularly hurtful and damaging facts about the other. Further, the subject of the dispute, the custody of their child, may be crucially important to each parent. . . . The nature of the inquiry in custody disputes further heightens the tendency to promote hostility. [C]ustody adjudication focuses on the personal qualities of the parent. Each parent's efforts to persuade the judge that he or she is the better custodian may involve presenting evidence about the character, habits, lifestyle, and moral fitness of the former spouse. While in theory only evidence relating to an individual's capacity as a parent is relevant, any character deficiency or behavior that the judge is likely to view negatively often will be exposed. . . .

DIVORCE MEDIATION

Because of the dissatisfaction with the adversary system, there has been an increased interest in developing alternative methods of resolving child custody disputes. In the past several years, divorce mediation has grown dramatically as the major alternative to either litigation or out-of-court negotiation between attorneys. . . .

In divorce mediation the divorcing parties meet with an impartial third party (or parties) to identify, discuss, and one hopes, settle the disputes that result from marital dissolution. While it shares features with some types of marital and family therapy, mediation can be distinguished from many forms of psychotherapy in that it is short term and problem-focused. The process also requires that the mediator be knowledgeable in the legal and economic as well as the social and psychological consequences of divorce. Further, mediation differs from therapy in its objectives, and the exploration of emotional issues is circumscribed by the goal of negotiating a fair and acceptable agreement. Finally, unlike marital therapy, the goal of mediation is *not* reconciliation.

Divorce mediation embraces a model of dispute resolution considerably different from that characterizing the adversary process. Whereas in mediation the parties give up some procedural control in that the mediator directs much of the process, decisional control is not handed over to a third party as it is in adjudication. That the parents retain decisional control also distinguishes mediation from arbitration. Arbitration, like mediation, may encompass less formal procedures than does litigation, but unlike the mediator, the arbitrator is expected to make a decision for the parties if they do not do so themselves. . . .

Some divorce mediators attempt to settle all four of the major issues that must be decided in a divorce: property division, spousal support, custody and visitation, and child support. Almost all mediators, however, [who] work in public court settings [limit] their practice to the issues of custody and visitation. . . . The process by which decisions are reached and the impact it has on the parents' relationship is critical to the integrative decisions regarding child rearing, since both parents are likely to maintain at least some contact with their children after a divorce. . . .

Proponents have argued that mediation will have benefits in areas that have been termed the "four C's." That is, mediation is said to reduce *conflict*, increase *cooperation*, give people more *control* over important decisions in their lives, and achieve these goals at a reduced public or private *cost*. . . .

[A] number of questions remain about the mediation alternative. . . . These questions encompass debates on whether attorneys or mental health professionals are better trained to conduct mediation, whether mediation should be conducted by teams including one member of each profession, or whether a new, distinct profession must be created. . . .

Another set of questions about mediation concerns who should be included or excluded: whether referrals to court-based mediation programs should be mandatory; whether participation in mediation should be completely voluntary; and whether parents should be referred to mediation at individual judges' discretion. These three options now are variously used in jurisdictions throughout the United States. It has also been asked whether certain cases should automatically be excluded from mediation: for example, cases where there are apparently great discrepancies in the parties' relative bargaining power, as where spouse abuse has occurred, or where independent legal findings on matters such as child abuse or neglect must be made.

A third set of questions pertains to the process of mediation itself. Should children be included in mediation sessions? Should grandparents, stepparents, or other interested relatives have a role? What part should mediators play in deciding the content of the negotiated agreement? Should mediators, for example, work toward negotiating joint custody settlements? Moreover, should mediators refuse to be party to agreements they object to on ethical or psychological grounds? . . .

Finally, a set of questions has been raised about what is to happen once mediation ends. What role should attorneys play in regard to a mediated settlement? Can a single attorney review the agreement, should it be reviewed by two attorneys who hold an adversarial perspective, or need it be reviewed by an attorney at all? Perhaps the most controversial debate about the termination of mediation, however, concerns the mediator's role in any subsequent court hearing. Some have argued that when a court hearing is held after mediation fails to produce an agreement, the mediator *should* make a recommendation to the court.

Proponents of this perspective point to the fact that the mediator is already familiar with the family and that such a recommendation will avoid the duplication of efforts inherent in beginning a new custody investigation. Others argue that strict confidentiality is essential to the mediation process. . . . Practice and judicial policy remain unresolved in regard to the important issue of confidentiality. . . .

The following case wrestles with "the most controversial debate" (according to the above excerpt) concerning the mediator's role in making a recommendation to the court.

McLAUGHLIN v. SUPERIOR COURT

189 Cal. Rptr. 479 (Ct. App. 1983)

RATTIGAN, Associate Justice.

Civil Code section 4607 requires prehearing mediation of child custody and visitation disputes in marital dissolution proceedings conducted pursuant to the Family Law Act. The statute also provides that, if the parties fail to agree in the mediation proceedings, the mediator "may, consistent with local court rules, render a recommendation to the court as to the custody or visitation of the child or children" involved. Pursuant to this provision, respondent superior court has adopted a "local court rule," or policy, which (1) requires the mediator to make a recommendation to the court if the parties fail to agree in the mediation proceedings, but (2) prohibits cross-examination of the mediator by the parties. We hold in this original proceeding that the policy is constitutionally invalid in significant respects. . . .

Petitioner Thomas J. McLaughlin and real party in interest Linda Lee McLaughlin were married in 1969. They have three children, whose ages range between 6 and 13 years. [In May 1982, the husband petitioned for dissolution and custody. In response, the wife requested joint legal custody, as well as physical custody. Husband then applied for temporary custody with visitation to the wife. The court issued an order to show cause in which the questions of temporary custody and visitation were set for hearing on June 30. The wife filed a declaration in which she requested temporary custody with visitation to the father.

At the hearing on the order to show cause,] petitioner's counsel recited his understanding that the pending issues of temporary custody and visitation were to be "referred for mediation." Counsel also stated his view that "the mediation procedure[,] insofar as it allows the mediator to make a recommendation for the Court, and bars the introduction of any testimony from the mediator about what the parties tell him or her[,] is unconstitutional as a denial of the right to cross-examine." On that ground, counsel in effect moved for a "protective order" which would permit mediation proceedings, but which would provide that if they did not result in agreement by the parties, on the issues of temporary custody and visitation, the mediator would be prohibited from making a recommendation to the court unless petitioner were guaranteed the right to cross-examine the mediator. [T]he court denied the motion on the ground that the "protective order" requested would violate a policy the court had adopted pursuant to Civil Code section 4607, subdivision (e).

[An exchange with counsel] included the only available description of respondent court's policy, which has apparently not been memorialized in a written rule. For these reasons, we quote pertinent passages of the exchange in the margin.[3]

[After the court denied petitioner's motion and request for a stay, he appealed to the California Supreme Court. The Supreme Court stayed the hearing and returned the case to the court of appeals for a hearing on the issue of the constitutionality of the practice of mediator recommendations.]

Civil Code section 4607, subdivision (a), clearly requires prehearing mediation of child custody and visitation disputes in marital dissolution proceedings. Subdivision (e) of the statute is also clear to the effect that the mediator "may, consistent with local court rules," make a recommendation to the court on either issue, or both, if the parties fail to reach agreement in the mediation proceedings. Subdivision (e) does not require or authorize disclosure to the parties of a recommendation made by the mediator to the court, nor of the mediator's reasons; it neither requires nor authorizes cross-examination of the mediator by the parties,

---

3. "The Court [addressing Mr. Brunwasser, petitioner's counsel]: Some counties, as you probably know, do not permit or require a recommendation from the mediator in the event the parties are unable to agree. Some do. This county [i.e., respondent court] does, and therefore, I'm not prepared to give you the protective order you wish. The court feels that in the event the mediator were free to testify as to any of the matters mediated, that is[,] the substance of the matter as gleaned from the mediation session, . . . certainly you would have the right to cross-examine the mediator." However, our instructions as a matter of court policy to the mediators are that they are not to state the basis for their . . . recommendation. . . . In short, the recommendation of the mediator is simply . . . a recommendation to the court without any statement of underlying basis. . . . That's the way we do business here. . . ."

Mr. Brunwasser: . . . I have no objection to mediation. What I have an objection to is a procedure which allows the mediator . . . to communicate with the court and not be subject to defend [sic] his or her opinion by cross-examination.

"The Court: I understand that. I hope you equally understand that it is our policy to require a recommendation if the mediation is unsuccessful. It's a starting point which enables the court . . . [,] in the absence of other evidence, to make an interim order based upon the opinion of the trained counselor, and it's a procedure we opted for when this law was enacted. We're satisfied that the law permits that, and so your motion for a protective order is denied."

which would necessarily require or bring about disclosure of the recommendation and the reasons for it; and the statute's express deference to "local court rules" has the effect of making disclosure and cross-examination matters of local option.

As we have seen, respondent court has exercised this option by adopting a policy which requires that the mediator make a recommendation to the court if the parties have failed to agree on child custody or visitation in the mediation proceedings; requires that the mediator not state his or her reasons for the recommendation; and denies the parties the right to cross-examine the mediator on the ground that the reasons have not been disclosed to the court. Amicus curiae has shown us that one large metropolitan superior court follows an entirely different procedure, and that another has adopted a policy which is essentially similar to respondent court's.[7]

The feature of respondent court's policy which prohibits cross-examination of the mediator is consistent with the provision in subdivision (c) of the statute that the mediation proceedings "shall be confidential." The requirement that the mediator not state to the court his or her reasons for the recommendation is consistent with the provision in subdivision (c) which protects the confidentiality of the parties' "communications" to the mediator by making them "official information within the meaning of Section 1040 of the Evidence Code." The facts remain that the policy permits the court to receive a significant recommendation on contested issues but denies the parties the right to cross-examine its source. This combination cannot constitutionally be enforced. . . .

Respondent court contends that the enforcement of its policy prohibiting cross-examination of a mediator who makes a recommendation to it is constitutionally permissible because only "temporary" child custody and visitation are involved and "due process is not required at every stage of a proceeding." . . . However, the word "temporary" does not appear in Civil Code section 4607. We are not at liberty to interpolate it, by construction. . . . The constitutional infirmities in respondent court's policy are such that it may not be enforced on the theory that only "temporary" custody or visitation are [sic] involved. . . .

. . . Our conclusions are consistent with our duty to harmonize the provisions of subdivisions (a) and (e) of the statute without doing violence to its salutary purposes. In addition, it has been shown in the present proceeding that disparities among "local court rules" adopted pursuant to subdivision (e) have had the effect of guaranteeing due process in some superior courts but not in others. Our conclusions will terminate this effect, which the Legislature obviously did not intend.

---

7. Amicus curiae describes the practice of the Los Angeles County Superior Court . . .: Where prehearing mediation proceedings have been conducted . . ., the court (1) neither receives nor permits a recommendation by the mediator and (2) proceeds to hear and determine the contested issue or issues without referring to the unsuccessful mediation process in any way.

Amicus curiae has filed declarations showing the related practice followed in the Superior Court for the City and County of San Francisco. . . . When the initial hearing is called on the same day [as the mediation session], the parties' attorneys communicate the mediator's recommendation to the court. . . . This (appellate) court interprets the [above declaration] to mean that the mediator's reasons for his or her recommendation are not disclosed to the parties, the attorneys, or the court when the recommendation is made in the first instance. This declaration fairly shows that the court makes the initial order on temporary custody or visitation without permitting cross-examination of the mediator. The declaration does not show whether cross-examination of the mediator is permitted at any later hearing.

[The court concluded that the husband was entitled to a writ of mandate that] directs that the court not receive a recommendation from the mediator, as to any contested issue on which agreement is not reached, unless (1) the court has first made a protective order which guarantees the parties the rights to have the mediator testify and to cross-examine him or her concerning the recommendation or (2) the rights have been waived. . . .

Notes and Questions

1. Benefits. In the adversarial system, the judiciary asserts authority over the financial aspects of dissolution and child custody. Mediation, however, confers broad latitude on the divorcing couple to resolve such matters for themselves. In this way, one might see mediation is a form of alternative dispute resolution that respects the parties' autonomy in decisionmaking. Why do Scott and Emery, in the excerpt supra, suggest that mediation is better suited to the resolution of custody disputes? What are the benefits and costs of the adversary system? Of the mediation process? How does mediation differ from other forms of alternative dispute resolution (such as arbitration) and from psychotherapy in terms of objectives, process, and the ultimate decisionmaker? Mental health professionals and lawyers constitute the largest percentage of mediators. How might these different orientations affect the role of the mediator and the practice of mediation?

2. Historical background. Mediation has longstanding roots in ancient China, Japan, and Africa. In the United States, mediation flourished in the late 1970s, fueled by acceptance of no-fault divorce and dissatisfaction with traditional dispute resolution. In 1981, California became the first state to require mediation (Cal. Fam. Code §3170) (requiring mediation in all cases of contested custody or visitation disputes before the parties can proceed to a hearing).

Many states now provide for mediation, either by encouraging the parties to mediate, providing for discretionary referrals by the court (most common), or mandating mediation. Most statutes provide for court-connected mediation of custody disputes only (rather than those involving spousal support and property issues). What are the advantages and disadvantages of mandatory, as opposed to voluntary, mediation? Does mandatory mediation infringe on the constitutional right of access to the judicial system? See Fuchs v. Martin, 845 N.E.2d 1038 (Ind. 2006).

3. Mediation and domestic violence. Research reveals high rates of domestic violence among couples in divorce mediation.[68] Commentators note that mediation poses special dangers for victims of intimate partner violence (IPV).[69] Such

---

[68]. Robin H. Ballard et al., Detecting Intimate Partner Violence in Family and Divorce Mediation: A Randomized Trial of Intimate Partner Violence Screening, 17 Psychol. Pub. Pol'y & L. 241, 243 (2011) (citing rates from 50 to 85 percent).

[69]. See Jane Murphy & Robert Rubinson, Domestic Violence and Mediation: Responding to the Challenges of Crafting Effective Screens, 39 Fam. L.Q. 53 (2005); Linda C. Neilson, At Cliff's Edge: Judicial Dispute Resolution in Domestic Violence Cases, 52 Fam. Ct. Rev. 529 (2014).

dangers include the risk to victims before and after mediation sessions; agreements that provide additional opportunities for abuse; and mediators who are not trained to recognize abusive relationships or to counteract the power imbalance that characterizes the parties' relationship.

Different schools of thought exist about the practice of mediation in domestic violence cases. Some commentators believe that mediation should never be used; others contend that it can be used with adequate safeguards; still others believe that the choice should be left to the victim; and some believe that mediation can always be used even in cases of domestic violence.[70] Which view do you find most persuasive?

Many states have state or local rules that apply to mediation in cases of domestic violence. See, e.g., Mont. Code Ann. §40-4-301-2 (prohibiting court from authorizing or continuing mediation if a party has been physically, sexually, or emotionally abused); Lucas County (Ohio) Court of Common Pleas, Rule 18: Mediation ("in any case where there has been a finding of domestic violence, the Court will determine whether mediation is appropriate, and if so, under what terms and conditions"). Some professional organizations require domestic violence training of and screening by mediators, as well as imposition of safeguards for victims.

4. Ethical concerns. Ethical concerns were raised when mediation first became popular. Early questions focused on the proper role of the attorney-mediator. That is, did a lawyer-mediator violate the prohibition on representation of conflicting or potentially differing interests or the prohibition of dual representation (of both spouses)? State bar ethics committees ruled that a lawyer-mediator could mediate a dispute for both spouses, so long as the parties were informed that the mediator represents neither spouse and will refrain from representing either party if mediation proves unsuccessful, and advised to seek independent legal counsel to review the agreement.[71]

Whether a lawyer-mediator can wear two hats (as a mediator as well as the draftsperson of the parties' written agreement) poses a recurring ethical dilemma. When a lawyer-mediator drafts a settlement agreement for divorcing spouses, the mediator is acting as an attorney who is representing opposing litigants. Such representation may violate the ethical ban on representing adverse parties in litigation. (Moreover, many jurisdictions specifically prohibit dual representation in divorce cases.) The Utah State Bar's Board of Bar Commissioners issued an opinion prohibiting a lawyer-mediator from representing both spouses in this manner. Utah State Bar Ethics Advisory Op. Comm., Op. 05-03 (2005).

5. Role of attorneys. Attorneys fill a variety of roles in the mediation process. Some serve as mediators and/or as reviewers of mediated agreements. The ABA drafted Model Standards of Conduct for Mediators in 1994 and revised them in 2005. The standards address such issues as impartiality, conflicts of interest,

---

[70]. Susan Landrum, The Ongoing Debate About Mediation in the Context of Domestic Violence: A Call for Empirical Studies of Mediation Effectiveness, 12 Cardozo J. Conflict Resol. 425-426 (2011).

[71]. Linda J. Silberman, Professional Responsibility Problems of Divorce Mediation, 16 Fam. L.Q. 107, 110-119 (1982).

competence, confidentiality, and fees, among others. See ABA Model Standards of Conduct for Mediators, https://www.americanbar.org/content/dam/aba/adminis trative/dispute_resolution/dispute_resolution/model_standards_conduct_april2 007.pdf. Model standards also exist for arbitration of family law disputes.

6. Limitations. What limitations should exist on private ordering? Should a mediator draft an agreement that the mediator does not believe is "fair" to one or both parties? Should the mediator defer to the parties' sense of fairness? Mediators have different views about the extent to which they should intervene in dispute resolution.

7. Children's role. Should children play a role in mediation? What might be the advantages and disadvantages? If children play a role, what should that role consist of? Active participants? Consultants? What factors should influence the nature and extent of children's participation? One study concludes that when children are consulted, relitigation rates decrease.[72]

8. Confidentiality. Confidentiality is central to the mediation process. As *McLaughlin* explains, some jurisdictions permit the mediator to make a recommendation to the court if mediation proves unsuccessful. This is true, for example, in some counties in California. What is the practical effect of this policy? Consider the following:

> California's mandatory mediation statute circumvents the basic principles of confidentiality and neutrality by allowing mediators to take the disclosures of the parties to the judge. In essence, the statute eliminates the protection of confidential information and transforms the mediator's neutral role from neutral to partisan.[73]

Also consider that once a mediator makes a recommendation and is subject to cross-examination, the mediator may have to divulge confidential communications that were elicited during mediation. Might warning the parties of this possibility interfere with the creation of trust?

McLaughlin also has implications for victims of IPV. The policy of permitting mediators to make recommendations (even if the mediators are subject to cross-examination) permits the disclosure of private information that the victim has chosen to reveal in the mediation. Many states permit exemptions from mediator confidentiality requirements for the reporting of child abuse and threats of injury/harm to an intended victim or the victim's property.

9. Collaborative law. Collaborative law is a form of alternative dispute resolution in which the parties and their attorneys agree to use cooperative techniques without resorting to judicial intervention except for court approval of the agreement. If the parties fail to reach an agreement, their attorneys must withdraw from representation. The Uniform Collaborative Law Act (UCLA), promulgated

---

[72]. Jennifer E. McIntosh et al., Child-Focused and Child-Inclusive Divorce Mediation: Comparative Outcomes from a Prospective Study of Postseparation Adjustment, 46 Fam. Ct. Rev. 105 (2008). See generally Pauline Muto, A Family Affair: Acknowledging Children's Voices in Custody Mediation, 71 Disp. Resol. J. 171 (2016).

[73]. Sofya Perelshteyn, Comment, Mediator or Judge?: California's Mandatory Mediation Statute in Child Custody Disputes, 17 Pepp. Disp. Resol. L.J. 1, 8 (2017).

in 2010, clarifies issues of informed consent, disqualification, party disclosure of information, and evidentiary privileges.

Critics argue that collaborative law is incompatible with the duty to represent clients zealously; fails to meet the standards of full disclosure and informed consent regarding limited scope representation; creates problems regarding attorney-client confidentiality and conflicts of interest; and is not appropriate in many cases (e.g., domestic violence, substance abuse, and mental illness). Advocates point to the benefits from the saving of cost and time, as well as the diminution in the emotional toll of family law disputes.[74]

The most controversial aspect of collaborative law is the disqualification agreement (requiring a lawyer to withdraw if the parties fail to reach an agreement). In 2007, the Colorado Bar Association Ethics Committee declared that collaborative law was per se unethical, reasoning that the disqualification agreement creates an insurmountable conflict of interest impairing the lawyer's independent judgment about the need for litigation. See Colo. Bar Assn., Ethics Op. 115, Ethical Considerations in the Collaborative and Cooperative Law Contexts (Feb. 24, 2007). In contrast, the ABA's ethics committee asserts that collaborative law is consistent with professional conduct rules. ABA Standing Comm. on Ethics and Prof'l Responsibility, Formal Op. 07-447 (2007). Which view do you find most persuasive?

Postscript. In 2021, the Colorado legislature enacted the Uniform Collaborative Law Act. Colo. Leg., S.B. 21-143 (2021 Sess.). As of August 2023, 23 states, including Colorado, had adopted the Act.

Problem

Diane and Michael have been married for nine years. They have four children. Diane was the primary caregiver of the children during most of the marriage. She files for divorce after she begins a relationship with another man, Sam, who is a previously convicted sex offender. The court-appointed GAL recommends that Michael be given sole legal and physical custody because he is "the more stable parent," "more cooperative to work with," and the children are "calmer and more stable" when they are with him. In contrast, according to the GAL, Diane's home is more "chaotic and disorganized."

After the parties are unable to reach an agreement, the judge awards sole legal and physical custody of the oldest child to Michael, with custody of the remaining children to Diane. The court restricts the mother's custody by requiring that her contact with the children may occur only in the absence of Sam. Further, the parties' settlement agreement is merged and incorporated into their divorce decree. Their agreement contains the following provision (required by the judge): "If the parties are unable to reach an agreement about parenting, the parties shall engage the services of a mediator before either may file an action in court. The costs associated with mediation shall be shared equally by the parties, unless otherwise reallocated by the mediator." Michael appeals the court order to mediate at the

---

[74]. Compare Diana M. Comes, Note, Meet Me in the Middle: The Time Is Ripe for Tennessee to Adopt the Uniform Collaborative Law Act, 41 U. Mem. L. Rev. 551, 562-569 (2011), with Marsha B. Freeman, Collaborative Law: Recognizing the Need for a New Default Method of Family Law Resolution, 17 Barry L. Rev. 15, 27 (2011).

parties' expense, claiming that the judge's order violates his state constitutional right of free access to the courts. What result? See *Ventrice v. Ventrice*, 26 N.E.3d 1128 (Mass. App. Ct. 2015).

2. Coin Flipping

Robert H. Mnookin, Child-Custody Adjudication: Judicial Functions in the Face of Indeterminacy
39 Law & Contemp. Probs. 226, 289-291 (1975)

[Would] a random process of decision be fairer and more efficient than adjudication under a best-interests principle? Individualized adjudication means that the result will often turn on a largely intuitive evaluation based on unspoken values and unproven predictions. We would more frankly acknowledge both our ignorance and the presumed equality of the natural parents were we to flip a coin. Whether one had a separate flip for each child or one flip for all the children, the process would certainly be cheaper and quicker. It would avoid the pain associated with an adversary proceeding that requires an open exploration of the intimate aspects of family life and an ultimate judgment that one parent is preferable to the other. And it might have beneficial effects on private negotiations.

Resolving a custody dispute by state-administered coin-flip would probably be viewed as unacceptable by most in our society. Perhaps this reaction reflects an abiding faith, despite the absence of an empirical basis for it, that letting a judge choose produces better results for the child. Alternatively, flipping a coin might be unacceptable for some because it represents an abdication of the search for wisdom. . . .

[A] coin-flip would be a government affirmation of the equality of the parents. In a custody case, however, a coin-flip also symbolically abdicates government responsibility for the child and symbolically denies the importance of human differences and distinctiveness. Moreover, flipping a coin would deprive the parents of a process and a forum where their anger and aspirations might be expressed. In all, these symbolic and participatory values of adjudication would be lost by a random process. . . .

IX

Parentage: Establishment and Disestablishment

Historically, most children were born to married women. The law reflected and shaped this reality. Legal parents were identified based only on childbirth and the marriage of the child's birth parent. Under the common law, children born to unmarried women were considered *filius nullius*, "heirs of no one."

Family structures today are much more varied. Close to half of all children in the United States are born to unmarried women. Same-sex couples are having children together. And many families—including marital, nonmarital, same-sex, different-sex, and single-parent—are having children through assisted reproduction. New ways of forming families have led courts and state legislatures to expand the routes for establishing parentage. Collectively, these social and legal changes challenge assumptions about parentage, including its gendered nature and the numerical norm of two. In addition to exploring the rules for *establishing* parentage, the chapter considers the *disestablishment* of this relationship, including through the termination of parental rights (TPR).

A. Establishing Parentage

1. Marriage

Douglas NeJaime, The Nature of Parenthood
126 Yale L.J. 2260, 2272-2273 (2017)

The Anglo-American legal system initially understood parentage as a relationship defined through marriage. The marital presumption, or presumption of legitimacy, recognized the mother's husband as the child's legal father. At English common law, overcoming the presumption required showing that "the husband be out of the kingdom of England . . . for above nine months, so that no access to his wife can be presumed." As this factual showing suggests, the presumption purported to reflect biological parenthood.

Nonetheless, the law assumed, but did not in fact require, blood ties. Instead, the marital presumption both facilitated parental recognition that departed from biological facts and cut off claims to parental recognition based on biological facts. If the child was conceived through an extramarital relationship with another man, the marital presumption allowed the husband to pretend he was the biological and thus legal father. Indeed, traditionally neither the husband nor wife were permitted to testify to the husband's "nonaccess," meaning that the couple themselves could not penetrate the presumption with inconsistent biological facts. A jury "could not legally find against . . . legitimacy, except on facts which prove, beyond all reasonable doubt, that the husband could not have been the father." . . .

By allowing the marital presumption to hide situations in which the husband was not in fact the biological father, the law ensured the child's "legitimacy." At common law, a child born outside a marital relationship was deemed the child and heir of no one (*filius nullius*). Traditionally, the "illegitimate" child, as historian Michael Grossberg explains, "had no recognized legal relations with his or her parents, particularly not those of inheritance, maintenance, and custody."

McLAUGHLIN v. JONES

401 P.3d 492 (Ariz. 2017)

Chief Justice BALES, opinion of the Court.

Under [Arizona law], a man is presumed to be a legal parent if his wife gives birth to a child during the marriage. We here consider whether this presumption applies to similarly situated women in same-sex marriages. [T]he facts are not in dispute. In October 2008, Kimberly and Suzan, a same-sex couple, legally married in California. After the couple decided to have a child through artificial insemination, Suzan unsuccessfully attempted to conceive using an anonymous sperm donor. In 2010, Kimberly underwent the same process and became pregnant.

During the pregnancy, Kimberly and Suzan moved to Arizona. In February 2011, they entered a joint parenting agreement declaring Suzan a "co-parent" of the child. The agreement specifically states that "Kimberly McLaughlin intends for Suzan McLaughlin to be a second parent to her child, with the same rights, responsibilities, and obligations that a biological parent would have to her child" and that "[s]hould the relationship between [them] end . . . it is the parties [sic] intention that the parenting relationship between Suzan McLaughlin and the child shall continue with shared custody, regular visitation, and child support proportional to custody time and income." . . .

In June 2011, Kimberly gave birth to a baby boy, E. While Kimberly worked as a physician, Suzan stayed at home to care for E. When E. was almost two years old, Kimberly and Suzan's relationship deteriorated to the point that Kimberly moved out of their home, taking E. and cutting off Suzan's contact with him. Consequently, in 2013, Suzan filed petitions for dissolution and for legal decision-making and parenting time in loco parentis. [During the litigation, the U.S.

Supreme Court decided Obergefell v. Hodges (2015).] We granted review because the application of §25-814(A)(1) to same-sex marriages after *Obergefell* is a recurring issue of statewide importance. . . .

Under Arizona law, "[a] man is presumed to be the father of the child if . . . [h]e and the mother of the child were married at any time in the ten months immediately preceding the birth or the child is born within ten months after the marriage is terminated. . . ." A.R.S. §25-814(A)(1). The "paternity" presumed by this statute, as explained further below, refers to a father's legal parental rights and responsibilities rather than biological paternity. Because Arizona does not have any statutes addressing parental rights . . . in cases of artificial insemination, a husband in an opposite-sex marriage whose wife is artificially inseminated by an anonymous sperm donor can establish his parental rights through §25-814(A)(1). Kimberly argues the trial court erred when it applied this marital paternity presumption to Suzan, because the statute by its terms only applies to males and *Obergefell* does not mandate extending the presumption to females.

As Kimberly correctly notes, the text of §25-814(A)(1) clearly indicates that the legislature intended the marital paternity presumption to apply only to males. [B]y its terms, the statute applies to a "man" who is married to the "mother" within ten months of the child's birth [and] therefore, applies to husbands in opposite-sex marriages. As written, §25-814(A)(1) does not apply to Suzan.

However, in the wake of *Obergefell*, excluding Suzan from the marital paternity presumption violates the Fourteenth Amendment. In *Obergefell*, the United States Supreme Court reiterated that marriage is a fundamental right, long protected by the Due Process Clause. Describing marriage as "a keystone of our social order," the Court noted that states have "made marriage the basis for an expanding list of governmental rights, benefits, and responsibilities," such as "child custody, support, and visitation rules," further contributing to its fundamental character. Denying same-sex couples "the same legal treatment" in marriage, and "all the benefits" afforded opposite-sex couples, "works a grave and continuing harm" on gays and lesbians in various ways—demeaning them, humiliating and stigmatizing their children and family units, and teaching society that they are inferior in important respects. . . .

Despite *Obergefell*'s holding requiring states to provide same-sex couples "the same terms and conditions" of marriage, Kimberly urges this Court to interpret *Obergefell* narrowly. She contends that *Obergefell* only established two points of law: that marriage is a fundamental right the states cannot deny to same-sex couples and that all states must give full faith and credit to same-sex marriages performed in other states. Under this reading, *Obergefell* does not require extending statutory benefits linked to marriage to include same-sex couples; rather, it only invalidates laws prohibiting same-sex marriage.

Such a constricted reading, however, is precluded by *Obergefell* itself and the Supreme Court's recent decision in Pavan v. Smith, 137 S. Ct. 2075 (2017) (per curiam). . . . In *Pavan*, an Arkansas law generally required that when a married woman gives birth, the name of the mother's male spouse appear on the birth certificate, regardless of the male spouse's biological relationship to the child. The Arkansas Supreme Court concluded that *Obergefell* did not require the state to similarly list the name of the mother's female spouse on the child's birth certificate, in part because the state law did not involve the right to same-sex marriage or its recognition by other states. The United States Supreme Court summarily reversed, stating that such differential treatment of same-sex couples infringed *"Obergefell's* commitment to provide same-sex couples 'the constellation of benefits that the States have linked to marriage.'" *Pavan*, 137 S. Ct. at 2077 (quoting *Obergefell*, 135 S. Ct. at 2601).

Consistent with *Obergefell* and *Pavan*, we must determine whether §25-814(A)(1) affords a benefit linked to marriage and authorizes disparate treatment of same-sex and opposite-sex marriages. Clearly, §25-814(A)(1) is an evidentiary benefit flowing from marriage. If a child is born during an opposite-sex marriage, the husband is presumed to be the child's legal parent. Legal parent status is, undoubtedly, a benefit of marriage. . . .

On its face, §25-814(A)(1) authorizes differential treatment of similarly situated same-sex couples. For instance, if a woman in an opposite-sex marriage conceives a child through an anonymous sperm donor, her husband will be presumed the father under §25-814(A)(1) even though he is not biologically related to the child. However, when a woman in a same-sex marriage conceives a child in a similar fashion, her female spouse will not be a presumptive parent under §25-814(A)(1) simply because the presumption only applies to males. Consequently, a female spouse in a same-sex marriage is only afforded one route to becoming the legal parent of a child born to her marital partner—namely, adoption—whereas a male spouse in an opposite-sex marriage can either adopt or rely on the marital paternity presumption to establish his legal parentage. Thus, applying §25-814(A)(1) as written excludes same-sex couples from civil marriage on the same terms and conditions as opposite-sex couples.

Kimberly counters that §25-814(A)(1) is constitutional despite its disparate treatment of same-sex couples because it simply concerns identifying biological parentage. However, as the previous example illustrates, the marital paternity presumption encompasses more than just rights and responsibilities attendant to biologically related fathers. When the wife in an opposite-sex couple conceives a child, her husband is presumed to be the father even when he is not biologically related to the child. . . . Because the marital paternity presumption does more than just identify biological fathers, Arizona cannot deny same-sex spouses the benefit the presumption affords.

In sum, the presumption of paternity under §25-814(A)(1) cannot, consistent with the Fourteenth Amendment's Equal Protection and Due Process Clauses, be restricted to only opposite-sex couples. The marital paternity presumption is a benefit of marriage, and following *Pavan* and *Obergefell*, the state cannot deny same-sex spouses the same benefits afforded opposite-sex spouses. . . .

Extending the marital paternity presumption to same-sex spouses . . . promotes strong family units. In *Obergefell*, the Supreme Court concluded that the right to marry is fundamental in part because "it safeguards children and families." By denying same-sex couples "the recognition, stability, and predictability marriage offers," the Court found that children of same-sex couples "suffer the stigma of knowing their families are somehow lesser" and "suffer the significant material costs of being raised by unmarried parents, relegated to a more difficult and uncertain family life." Extending the marital paternity presumption mitigates these harms. Children born to same-sex spouses will know that they will have meaningful parenting time with both parents even in the event of a dissolution of marriage. . . .

For these reasons, we extend §25-814(A)(1) to same-sex spouses such as Suzan. By extending §25-814(A)(1) to same-sex spouses, we ensure all children, and not just children born to opposite-sex spouses, have financial and emotional support from two parents and strong family units. . . .

[The court next considers Kimberly's argument that Suzan's presumption of parentage is rebutted by evidence that she is not a genetic parent. The court rejects this argument, on the ground that Kimberly is equitably estopped from rebutting Suzan's presumptive parentage.] Equitable estoppel "precludes a party from asserting a right inconsistent with a position previously taken to the prejudice of another acting in reliance thereon." . . . Here, Kimberly and Suzan agree that they intended for Kimberly to be artificially inseminated with an anonymous sperm donor and that Kimberly gave birth to E. during the marriage. During the pregnancy, they signed a joint parenting agreement declaring Suzan a "co-parent" of the child and their intent that the parenting relationship between Suzan McLaughlin and the child would continue if Suzan and Kimberly's relationship ended. After E.'s birth, Suzan stayed home to care for him during the first two years of his life. Thus, the undisputed facts unequivocally demonstrate that Kimberly intended for Suzan to be E.'s parent, that Kimberly conceived and gave birth to E. while married to Suzan, and that Suzan relied on this agreement when she formed a mother-son bond with E. and parented him from birth. [Based on these facts,] Kimberly is equitably estopped from rebutting Suzan's presumptive parentage of E. . . .

Notes and Questions

1. **Marital presumption.** The marital presumption, derived from English common law, creates a legal presumption that a child born during a marriage is the legal child of the mother's husband. Thus, parentage is based on the *marital relationship* of the child's parents, rather than the *biological relationship* between the child and the father. What was the rationale for this presumption at common law? Are those rationales still applicable? Today, all 50 states have a marital presumption. In most states, the presumption is codified.

2. **The marital presumption and same-sex couples.** Like the Arizona statute at issue in the principal case, the marital presumption is commonly written in gendered terms, referring to a woman or wife and a husband or man married to the woman. Why did the Arizona Supreme Court conclude that this rule must be applied equally to a female spouse? What is the relevance of *Obergefell* (reprinted in Chapter II)? Does *Pavan* (reprinted in Chapter III) strengthen or weaken the impact of *Obergefell*? Why did Kimberly argue that *Obergefell* did not apply? Why did the Arizona Supreme Court disagree?

Most courts have reached the same result. But cf. Turner v. Steiner, 398 P.3d 110, 113 (Ariz. Ct. App. 2017), abrogated by *McLaughlin*, 401 P.3d 492 (Ariz. 2017) ("[The nonbirth same-sex spouse] argues that *Obergefell* nevertheless requires that the presumption statute be read gender-neutrally. . . . But the purpose of the presumption statute is to assist in determining whether a man is a child's biological father . . . not to broadly establish a term or condition associated with marriage.").

3. Rebuttal. The marital presumption is just that—a presumption. As noted in the NeJaime excerpt, the presumption was very difficult to rebut in the past. Today, it is generally easier to rebut, although some states place limits on such challenges. Some limits are temporal. See, e.g., Conn. Gen. Stat. Ann. §46b-489(b) (providing that the marital presumption generally cannot be rebutted or "overcome" after the child's second birthday). Why place time limits on challenges to the marital presumption?

In some states, courts are directed to consider equitable factors or doctrines in deciding whether the presumption should be rebutted. Equitable estoppel is one such doctrine, preventing one party from taking unfair advantage of the other when the former induced the latter to act and, as a result, the latter has been injured. What specific facts triggered the application of equitable estoppel in *McLaughlin*?

4. Law reform. In the wake of *Obergefell*, some states updated their marital presumption to make it gender neutral. See, e.g., 15 R.I. Gen. Laws Ann. §15-8.1-401(a)(1) ("*[A]n individual* is presumed to be a parent of a child if: The individual and the individual who gave birth to the child are married to each other and the child is born during the marriage.") (emphasis added); see also the Uniform Parentage Act (UPA (2017)), §204(a)(1) (reprinted below).

2. Biology

STANLEY v. ILLINOIS
405 U.S. 645 (1972)

Justice WHITE delivered the opinion of the Court.

Joan Stanley lived with Peter Stanley intermittently for 18 years during which time they had three children. When Joan Stanley died, Peter Stanley lost not only her but also his children. Under Illinois law the children of unwed fathers become wards of the State upon the death of the mother. Accordingly, upon Joan Stanley's death, in a dependency proceeding instituted by the State of Illinois, Stanley's children were declared wards of the State and placed with court-appointed guardians. Stanley appealed, claiming that he had never been shown to be an unfit parent and that since married fathers and unwed mothers could not be deprived of their children without such a showing, he had been deprived of the equal protection of the laws guaranteed him by the Fourteenth Amendment. . . .

Stanley presses his equal protection claim here. The State continues to respond that unwed fathers are presumed unfit to raise their children. . . . We granted certiorari to determine whether this method of procedure by presumption could be allowed to stand in light of the fact that Illinois allows married fathers — whether divorced, widowed, or separated — and mothers — even if unwed — the benefit of the presumption that they are fit to raise their children.

We must [examine the following question]: Is a presumption that distinguishes and burdens all unwed fathers constitutionally repugnant? We conclude that, as a matter of due process of law, Stanley was entitled to a hearing on his fitness as a parent before his children were taken from him and that by denying him a hearing and extending it to all other parents whose custody of their children is challenged, the State denied Stanley the equal protection of the laws guaranteed by the Fourteenth Amendment.

Illinois has two principal methods of removing nondelinquent children from the homes of their parents. In a dependency proceeding, it may demonstrate that the children are wards of the State because they have no surviving parent or guardian. In a neglect proceeding, it may show that children should be wards of the State because the present parent(s) or guardian does not provide suitable care.

The State's right — indeed duty — to protect minor children through a judicial determination of their interests in a neglect proceeding is not challenged here. Rather, we are faced with a dependency statute that empowers state officials to circumvent neglect proceedings on the theory that an unwed father is not a "parent" whose existing relationship with his children must be considered. "Parents," says the State, "means the father and mother of a legitimate child, or the survivor of them, or the natural mother of an illegitimate child, and includes any adoptive parent" (Ill. Rev. Stat., c. 37, §701-14), but the term does not include unwed fathers.

Under Illinois law, therefore, while the children of all parents can be taken from them in neglect proceedings, that is only after notice, hearing, and proof of such unfitness as a parent as amounts to neglect, an unwed father is uniquely subject to the more simplistic dependency proceeding. By use of this proceeding, the State, on showing that the father was not married to the mother, need not prove unfitness in fact, because it is presumed at law. . . .

In considering this procedure under the Due Process Clause, we recognize, as we have in other cases, that due process of law does not require a hearing "in every conceivable case of government impairment of private interest." [The rule is] firmly established that "what procedures due process may require under any given set of circumstances must begin with a determination of the precise nature of the government function involved as well as of the private interest that has been affected by governmental action." . . . The private interest here, that of a man in the children he has sired and raised, undeniably warrants deference and, absent a powerful countervailing interest, protection. . . . The Court has frequently emphasized the importance of the family. The rights to conceive and to raise one's children have been deemed "essential," [citing Meyer v. Nebraska, among other cases]. . . .

Nor has the law refused to recognize those family relationships unlegitimized by a marriage ceremony. The Court has declared unconstitutional a state statute denying natural, but illegitimate, children a wrongful-death action for the death of their mother, emphasizing that such children cannot be denied the right of other children because familial bonds in such cases were often as warm, enduring, and important as those arising within a more formally organized family unit. Levy v. Louisiana, 391 U.S. 68, 71-72 (1968). "To say that the test of equal protection should be the 'legal' rather than the biological relationship is to avoid the issue. For the Equal Protection Clause necessarily limits the authority of a State to draw such 'legal' lines as it chooses." Glona v. American Guarantee Co., 391 U.S. 73, 75-76 (1968). These authorities make it clear that, at the least, Stanley's interest in retaining custody of his children is cognizable and substantial.

For its part, the State has made its interest quite plain: Illinois has declared that the aim of the Juvenile Court Act is to protect "the moral, emotional, mental, and physical welfare of the minor and the best interests of the community" and to "strengthen the minor's family ties whenever possible, removing him from the custody of his parents only when his welfare or safety or the protection of the public cannot be adequately safeguarded without removal. . . ." Ill. Rev. Stat., c. 37, §701-2. These are legitimate interests well within the power of the State to implement. We do not question the assertion that neglectful parents may be separated from their children.

But we are here not asked to evaluate the legitimacy of the state ends, rather, to determine whether the means used to achieve these ends are constitutionally defensible. What is the state interest in separating children from fathers without a hearing designed to determine whether the father is unfit in a particular disputed case? We observe that the State registers no gain towards its declared goals when it separates children from the custody of fit parents. Indeed, if Stanley is a fit father, the State spites its own articulated goals when it needlessly separates him from his family. . . .

It may be, as the State insists, that most unmarried fathers are unsuitable and neglectful parents. It may also be that Stanley is such a parent and that his children should be placed in other hands. But all unmarried fathers are not in this category; some are wholly suited to have custody of their children. This much the State readily concedes, and nothing in this record indicates that Stanley is or has been a neglectful father who has not cared for his children. Given the opportunity to make his case, Stanley may have been seen to be deserving of custody of his offspring. Had this been so, the State's statutory policy would have been furthered by leaving custody in him. . . .

It may be argued that unmarried fathers are so seldom fit that Illinois need not undergo the administrative inconvenience of inquiry in any case, including Stanley's. The establishment of prompt efficacious procedures to achieve legitimate state ends is a proper state interest worthy of cognizance in constitutional adjudication. But the Constitution recognizes higher values than speed and efficiency. . . . Procedure by presumption is always cheaper and easier than individualized determination. But when, as here, the procedure forecloses the determinative issues of competence and care, when it explicitly disdains present realities in deference to past formalities, it needlessly risks running roughshod over the important interests of both parent and child. It therefore cannot stand.

. . . The State's interest in caring for Stanley's children is de minimis if Stanley is shown to be a fit father. It insists on presuming rather than proving Stanley's unfitness solely because it is more convenient to presume than to prove. Under the Due Process Clause that advantage is insufficient to justify refusing a father a hearing when the issue at stake is the dismemberment of his family.

The State of Illinois assumes custody of the children of married parents, divorced parents, and unmarried mothers only after a hearing and proof of neglect. The children of unmarried fathers, however, are declared dependent children without a hearing on parental fitness and without proof of neglect. Stanley's claim in the state courts and here is that failure to afford him a hearing on his parental qualifications while extending it to other parents denied him equal protection of the laws. We have concluded that all Illinois parents are constitutionally entitled to a hearing on their fitness before their children are removed from their custody. It follows that denying such a hearing to Stanley and those like him while granting it to other Illinois parents is inescapably contrary to the Equal Protection Clause. . . .

Notes and Questions

1. Common law rule. Under the common law, a nonmarital child was regarded as *filius nullius*—literally, the heir of no one. Such children were referred to as "illegitimate." While child support could be ordered for such children under "bastardy laws," an "illegitimate" child was not considered "the kin" of either parent for purposes of inheritance. By the late nineteenth century, states generally recognized nonmarital mothers as parents of their children, including, for example, for purposes of custody and intestate succession.[1] The law was slower, however, to recognize a parent-child relationship between a nonmarital child and the biological father.

In *Stanley*, the Supreme Court declared Illinois' refusal to recognize a nonmarital father's relationship with his child for purposes of exercising rights to custody unconstitutional. In Gomez v. Perez, 409 U.S. 535 (1973), decided one year later, the Supreme Court grappled with the legal obligations of nonmarital fathers. There, the Court held that a state cannot grant marital children a statutory right to support from their marital fathers while denying this right to children of nonmarital fathers.

2. Statutory developments. In the wake of *Stanley*, *Gomez*, and other Supreme Court decisions regarding the rights and obligations of nonmarital fathers, states updated their statutes to provide methods for establishing the parentage of nonmarital fathers.

The original version of the Uniform Parentage Act (UPA) was promulgated in 1973 to provide a model for states. It was heavily influenced by the work of Professor Harry Krause.[2] In his classic law review article, Krause refuted common justifications for discrimination against nonmarital children: the uncertainty surrounding the paternity of nonmarital children, the desire to discourage promiscuity, the need to protect the family unit, the belief that nonmarital children lack a close relationship with their father, and the need to respect the father's choice whether to recognize the children. Shaped by Krause's work, the original UPA (1973) transformed this policy by providing for equal treatment of all children, without regard to the marital status of their parents.

In 1973, there was no way to determine with certainty whether a man was a child's genetic parent. Thus, to identify the father of a nonmarital child, the UPA (1973) includes two conduct-based presumptions applicable to nonmarital children. The "holding out" presumption creates a presumption of parentage based on a man having "receive[d] the child into his home and openly [held] out the child as his natural child." UPA (1973), §4(a)(4). This presumption is discussed in more detail below. The second presumption—based on the man having "acknowledged his paternity . . . in a writing filed with" the Vital Records Department, UPA (1973), §4(a)(5)—is a precursor to the Voluntary Acknowledgment of Paternity or Parentage process, which now exists in all 50 states. (See Note 6 below.)

---

[1]. Martha F. Davis, Male Coverture: Law and the Illegitimate Family, 56 Rutgers L. Rev. 73, 81 (2003). See also Douglas NeJaime, The Nature of Parenthood, 126 Yale L.J. 2260 (2017).

[2]. For his classic law review article, see Harry D. Krause, Bringing the Bastard into the Great Society — A Proposed Uniform Act on Legitimacy, 44 Tex. L. Rev. 829 (1966).

3. Blood/genetic testing. Today, genetic parents can be identified with a high degree of certainty, and the testing is fairly cheap and accessible. The law has evolved to reflect this technological development. Consistent with federal law, all states now allow a nonmarital father to establish parentage through proof of a genetic parent-child relationship. See, e.g., UPA (2017), §607. See also 42 U.S.C. §666(a)(5)(G). The Supreme Court has held that states must provide payment for the cost of blood/genetic testing for indigent parties in parentage actions. Little v. Streater, 452 U.S. 1 (1981).

However, state law often permits a court to deny a request for genetic testing in some circumstances. For example, the most recent version of the UPA—UPA (2017)—permits courts to deny motions for genetic testing based on the child's best interest after consideration of certain factors (i.e., child's age, nature of parent-child relationship, and harm to the child from nonrecognition of the relationship). UPA (2017), §§503 & 613(a). A court might deny a request for genetic testing from the alleged genetic father if, for example, the child was born to a married woman and her husband has been acting as the child's parent.

4. Statutes of limitations. Even after states enacted laws authorizing nonmarital fathers to establish their parentage, many states initially imposed strict statutes of limitations governing these actions, arguably to prevent the filing of stale claims and to discourage fraud. Gradually, states lengthened their statutory periods in response to Supreme Court decisions. Now, federal law requires states (as a condition for receipt of federal funds) to permit parentage establishment until the child is 18, if the child's parentage has not already been established. 42 U.S.C. §666(a)(5)(A)(i).

5. Petitioners. Traditionally, actions to establish a nonmarital father's parentage were brought by the mother, most commonly for the purpose of establishing his obligation to provide child support. Gradually, states expanded the classes of people who can bring such an action to include the putative father, the child, the child's representative, and state child support officials. Moreover, unlike the common law rules, parentage proceedings today are generally civil proceedings held without a jury.

6. Administrative process. A nonmarital father's parentage can be established through a court proceeding, adjudicated under the relevant state's parentage rules. Alternatively, a man who alleges himself to be the genetic parent of a nonmarital child can also establish his parentage through a simple, streamlined administrative process. These latter procedures are often referred to as voluntary acknowledgments of paternity or parentage (VAPs). Beginning in 1992, a few states adopted voluntary programs that targeted mothers at birth facilities, providing that in-hospital affidavits established a rebuttable presumption of paternity. These programs were so successful that the U.S. Congress included a requirement in the Omnibus Budget Reconciliation Act of 1993, 42 U.S.C. §666(a)(5)(C)(ii), for all states to adopt voluntary paternity establishment programs. Federal legislation provides that a valid, nonrescinded, and unchallenged acknowledgment of parentage is equivalent to a judicial determination and is entitled to full faith and credit. 42 U.S.C. §666(a)(5). To be valid, the acknowledgment must be signed by both the birth parent and the person seeking to establish their parentage. The acknowledgment process is an important development because it allows a child's parentage to be established quickly, often immediately after the child's birth, without having to go to court and without the need for an attorney. Today, this is the most common means for establishing the parentage of a nonmarital father.[3]

Recently, some states have expanded their VAP procedures to allow women to establish their parentage through this process.[4]

7. Intestacy rights of nonmarital children. Historically, nonmarital children were denied a range of important benefits, including the right of intestate succession. Over time, states permitted nonmarital children to inherit via intestate succession from their mothers. States were slower to allow intestate succession from a nonmarital father. Indeed, even as the Supreme Court held that the U.S. Constitution protected nonmarital children from discrimination, it nonetheless upheld intestate succession laws requiring higher levels of proof for nonmarital children to inherit from their genetic fathers. See, e.g., Lalli v. Lalli, 439 U.S. 259 (1978).[5]

8. Nonmarital children and sex discrimination. Historically, the laws treated children differently based on the marital status of their parents. Parentage rules applicable to nonmarital children also differed depending on the sex of the parent. This was true of the Illinois laws at issue in *Stanley*. A nonmarital mother was considered a parent; a nonmarital father was not. Similarly, as discussed in Note 7, states were much quicker to recognize the child's right to intestate succession from a nonmarital mother than from a nonmarital father. Why did these rules differ? Should states be permitted to have different parentage rules for mothers and fathers?

9. Citizenship rights of nonmarital children. Another area of law in which nonmarital children continue to face differential treatment is citizenship. The rules governing the citizenship of children born abroad to a U.S. citizen parent (so-called derivative citizenship) differ on the basis of both marital status and the parent's sex.

Initially, the Supreme Court upheld citizenship rules that treated nonmarital mothers and fathers differently. See, e.g., Nguyen v. INS, 533 U.S. 53 (2001); Fiallo v. Bell, 430 U.S. 787 (1977). In Sessions v. Morales-Santana, 582 U.S. 47 (2017), however, the Supreme Court held unconstitutional a federal derivative citizenship law that imposed a longer residency requirement on nonmarital fathers than on nonmarital mothers. According to the Court, the rule was based on a "familiar stereotype" that nonmarital fathers "would care little about, and have scant contact with, their nonmarital children," and, therefore that they are "invariably less qualified and entitled than mothers" to take responsibility for nonmarital children." Ultimately, the Court held that because the rule was based on a sex-based

---

[3]. Leslie Joan Harris, The Basis for Legal Parentage and the Clash Between Custody and Child Support, 42 Ind. L. Rev. 611, 620 (2009).

[4]. See, e.g., Courtney G. Joslin, Nurturing Parenthood Through the UPA (2017), 127 Yale L.J. F. 589, 604 (2018).

[5]. See Solangel Maldonado, Illegitimate Harm: Law, Stigma, and Discrimination Against Nonmarital Children, 63 Fla. L. Rev. 345 (2011).

stereotype, it classified on the basis of sex and had to be subjected to intermediate scrutiny, a standard that the law did not pass.

PP v. DD

2017 ONCA [Ontario Court of Appeal] 180 (Can.)

ROULEAU, J.A.

. . . PP is a medical doctor and DD also works in the health care field. In the spring of 2014, they began dating at the suggestion of a mutual friend. Their first date was on May 14, 2014. Three days later, on May 17, 2014, they went on a second date. On that occasion, they had dinner and retired to DD's apartment where they engaged in consensual sexual activity. During the course of that activity, PP asked DD whether she had any condoms. When she replied that she did not, he asked if she was "on the pill." She told him that she was. After accepting this assurance from DD, PP consented to sexual intercourse that included intravaginal ejaculation. PP and DD went on four more dates in the following three weeks. On each occasion, they again engaged in consensual sexual intercourse and DD did not say or do anything to suggest that her prior representations of fact with respect to being "on the pill" were not, or were no longer, true.

On June 10, 2014, they repeated the pattern of sexual activity that began on the second date, this time at PP's condominium. Prior to having sexual intercourse on that day, they discussed their practice of not using a condom. PP advised DD that he would happily wear one and that he did not want her to feel uncomfortable. DD stated that she preferred to have intercourse with him without a condom. Again, DD did not say or do anything to suggest that her prior representations of fact were not, or were no longer, true. They engaged in consensual sexual intercourse and intravaginal ejaculation. There were two more dates in June 2014, during both of which the same pattern of sexual activity was repeated.

In July 2014, the pair decided to end their sexual relationship and agreed to remain friends. During the following weeks, they contacted one another several times by text message with respect to inconsequential matters.

In the early evening of August 10, 2014, PP received a text message from DD that shocked him, in which DD informed him that she was 10 weeks pregnant with his child. PP stated that he would call DD on his way to work. During that telephone conversation, DD told PP that she intended to deliver and keep the baby. PP stated that he thought she was "on the pill," to which DD simply responded, "yah." PP told DD he did not intend to have a child at that point in his life and, in shock, he suggested that DD have an abortion. She insisted that she would not do so, to which PP responded in anger: "I don't want to have a baby with some random girl. I waited my whole life to decide who I have a baby with."

After ending the telephone conversation, they exchanged several text messages in which DD expressed confidence that she could raise the child on her own and stated that she did not want to force PP's involvement in the child's upbringing. She told PP that "this random girl is fine doing it on her own." . . . On September 18, DD contacted PP to advise him that he was the father and that she had decided to keep the child. PP expressed his disagreement and the pair did not communicate directly with one another after that time.

On March 28, 2015, DD delivered a healthy child. [About four months later], PP commenced his action for damages against DD. . . . PP sought to avoid child support obligations under the Family Law Act, R.S.O. 1990 c. F.3. [He brought a civil action for fraud, deceit, and fraudulent misrepresentation against DD, claiming as damages that the deception deprived him of the benefit of choosing when and with whom he would assume the responsibility of fatherhood. In his words, "he wanted to meet a woman, fall in love, get married, enjoy his life as husband with his wife and then, when he and his wife thought the time was 'right,' to have a baby." He pleaded that he consented to sexual intercourse with DD on the understanding that she was using effective contraception. In his view, this was an express or implied misrepresentation and his consent was vitiated, having been obtained through deception and dishonesty. The trial judge granted the defendant's motion to dismiss. Plaintiff appeals.]

[This appeal can be resolved, in part, by answering the following question. C]an the appellant . . . recover damages from the respondent, the mother, for involuntary parenthood? [T]he appellant has not made out a viable claim for recoverable damages. As I will explain, I regard it as plain and obvious that those damages are not and, as a matter of legal policy, ought not to be recoverable by way of a fraudulent misrepresentation action. . . .

Although it was not presented in this way, the claim can be viewed as a tort claim for involuntary parenthood made by one parent against the other. . . . In essence, the damages consist of the appellant's emotional upset, broken dreams, possible disruption to his lifestyle and career, and a potential reduction in future earnings, all of which are said to flow from the birth of a child he did not want. Although the claim is not for the direct costs associated with raising the child, all of the damages claimed by the appellant are the result of consequences flowing from the unwanted birth of a child, albeit unwanted only by the father.

There have been numerous cases dealing with involuntary parenthood both in Canada and abroad. [T]o award damages in this case would be contrary to the spirit and purpose of Ontario's statutory family law regime. [T]his is not a claim being advanced by unwilling parents as against a third party. Rather, it is a claim being advanced by the unwilling father against the mother, who does not claim to be an involuntary parent and who has willingly taken on the responsibility of raising the child. In effect, the father is claiming that, to the extent that he views the birth as a disadvantage to himself—emotionally, professionally and/or financially—the mother, who has agreed to raise the child, must compensate him. . . . To allow the appellant to recover damages as against the respondent for the unwanted birth in the circumstances of this case would, in my view, run against the clear trend in the law moving away from fault-based claims in the family law context.

Since the 1970s, Canadian jurisdictions have moved away from a fault-based divorce and child support regime. . . . When a couple's dispute involves costs related to their child, the imposition of civil liability raises similar concerns. It is well established that child support is the right of the child. There is a corresponding obligation "placed equally upon both parents" to financially support the child. . . . The legislative scheme for child support is broad and does not take blame into account in relation to the manner of conception. The statutory remedies available to ensure support for the child flow from the simple fact of being a parent as defined by statute. It would be contrary to the spirit, purpose and policy reflected in Ontario's no-fault child support regime to view parents as equally responsible for maintaining a child but, at the same time, to allow recovery by the appellant against the mother for the loss purportedly suffered by him as a result of that responsibility, which loss would presumably increase as he devotes more of his time and resources to the child's upbringing.

The appellant asserts that he accepts and has complied with his statutory duty to pay child support. Nevertheless, the appellant seeks to recover in excess of $4 million in damages from the child's mother in compensation for losses flowing from the child's birth and his responsibilities toward that child. In the circumstances of this case, to allow the appellant's claim would, in effect, be to allow the appellant to circumvent the equal obligations to the child imposed on parents by law—obligations that are imposed without regard to fault or intention.

[A]ppellate courts in the United States have decided a number of cases highly analogous in their facts to the present one. In Barbara A. v. John G. (1983), 145 Cal. App. 3d 369, the California Court of Appeal . . . emphasized its concern that to allow one parent to sue the other over the wrongful birth of their child, and thereby to use the child as the damage element in a tortious claim of one parent against the other, would effectively erase much or all of the former parent's financial [child] support obligation. In that court's view, this type of action would seldom, if ever, result in a benefit to the child or be consistent with that state's family law legislation. . . . For these reasons, as a matter of legal policy the alleged damages should not be recoverable in tort. . . .

I turn now to the appellant's [argument that] the misrepresentation of the respondent vitiated the appellant's consent to sexual intercourse [and resulted in the tort of "sexual battery"]. To prove a battery, the plaintiff must also demonstrate that the interference with his or her body was "harmful" or "offensive," but this element is implied (assuming a lack of consent) in the context of a sexual battery. [In the present case], appellant's alleged damage is principally emotional harm or, in other words, hurt feelings and lost aspirations and/or career opportunities flowing from the birth of his child. . . . The appellant was not exposed to any serious transmissible disease or other significant risk of serious bodily harm flowing from the intercourse. Moreover, it is noteworthy that the appellant was willing to assume some risk, albeit small, that pregnancy would result from the several instances of sexual intercourse, a risk present even where the woman is taking contraceptive pills. . . .

There was therefore no violation of the appellant's right to physical or sexual autonomy that would give rise to a claim in battery. This is not to minimize the significance of fathering a child and the legal and moral responsibilities that ensue therefrom, nor to condone the alleged conduct of the respondent. The issue is only whether the alleged misrepresentation is actionable and whether, if proven, it would constitute the tort of battery. In my view, it would not. . . .

Notes and Questions

1. **Challenging the legal parentage of a biological parent.** Proof of genetic parentage is one means of establishing a legal parent-child relationship. Are there any circumstances under which a genetic parent of a child conceived through sexual

intercourse can challenge or dispute their parentage? In PP v. DD, the woman did not use birth control but asserted that she did. Should a person like PP be found to be a legal parent under such circumstances? How does the court respond? Does the result change if, as in PP v. DD, the man offers to pay for an abortion and the woman refuses? Suppose the woman was on birth control pills, was properly taking them, but became pregnant anyway? Or that the woman was on birth control pills but had taken her pills late and did not disclose that to the man? (Oral birth control pills are to be taken at the same time every day.) Does any man who engages in sexual intercourse "assume the risk" with all attendant duties?

PP v. DD illustrates the general rule in Canada and in the United States: the court will not alter a person's parental status or child support obligations under such circumstances. See Wallis v. Smith, 22 P.3d 682, 684 (N.M. Ct. App. 2001) ("To our knowledge, no jurisdiction recognizes contraceptive fraud or breach of promise to practice birth control as a ground for adjusting a natural parent's obligation to pay child support."). What explains the judicial reluctance to do so?

2. "Purloined sperm."[6] Suppose the woman gets pregnant without the man's knowledge, where, for example, he was unconscious (see, e.g., S.F. v. State ex rel. T.M., 695 So. 2d 1186 (Ala. Civ. App. 1996))? Or without his legal consent, such as in cases involving a teenage male victim of statutory rape (see, e.g., In re Paternity of K.B., 104 P.3d 1132 (Okla. Civ. App. 2004))? Under those circumstances, should the man be relieved of his obligation of child support?

3. Preconception agreements for support. Suppose that DD knew that PP wanted to conceive a child, but the two entered into a written preconception agreement relieving him of support. Is the agreement enforceable? Does it relieve the man of legal parenthood? Financial responsibility for the child? Should it matter whether the woman would otherwise require public assistance to support the child? See Kristine M. v. David P., 37 Cal. Rptr. 3d 748 (Ct. App. 2006). Preconception intent might be relevant in the context of assisted reproduction. Does it make sense to apply different parentage rules depending on the method of conception?

4. Tort liability. If people like PP are legal parents, should they be able to recover monetary damages for the cost of any child support that they are required to pay? Should a man in PP's position be permitted to maintain a tort action for fraud or infliction of emotional distress? How much is the emotional harm of "unwanted fatherhood" worth? PP also alleged a tort claim for sexual battery. Did DD commit the tort of sexual battery?

Here, this case involves deceit by a woman. Men also sometimes engage in deceit, such as agreeing to wear a condom but later sabotaging the condom or removing it without consent (stealthing). Stealthing is a form of reproductive coercion. According to the National Domestic Violence Hotline, stealthing behavior "is rooted in one partner's desire for control and wanting the power to determine

[6]. See Donald C. Hubin, Daddy Dilemmas: Untangling the Puzzles of Paternity, 13 Cornell J.L. & Pub. Pol'y 29 (2003) (coining the term "purloined sperm"). See also Dara E. Purvis, The Origin of Parental Rights: Labor, Intent, and Fathers, 41 Fla. St. U. L. Rev. 645, 665 (2014) (discussing cases).

if their partner potentially gets pregnant or not."[7] Do (and should) men incur tort liability for such conduct? In January 2022, California became the first state to expressly permit civil penalties for stealthing. Cal. Civ. Code §1708.5(a)(5) (defining "sexual battery" to include "caus[ing] contact between an intimate part of the person and a sexual organ of another from which the person removed a condom without verbal consent").

5. Constitutional claims. Does PP have any constitutional claims? Does a man have a constitutional right to avoid fatherhood? Is the Fourteenth Amendment violated if the woman has the right to reject parenthood after conception via abortion or adoption but the man has no corresponding right? See Dubay v. Wells, 506 F.3d 422 (6th Cir. 2007).

3. Function

Another possible basis for establishing parentage is proof that the person functioned or acted as a parent. Suppose that someone engages in this conduct but is not the child's genetic parent? Should the person nonetheless be entitled to a presumption of parentage? If so, should the presumption necessarily be rebutted by evidence of lack of genetic parentage?

IN RE NICHOLAS H.

46 P.3d 932 (Cal. 2002), *as modified on denial of rehearing* (2002)

Brown, Justice.

A man who receives a child into his home and openly holds the child out as his natural child is presumed to be the natural father of the child. [Cal. Fam. Code §7611(d).] The presumption that he is the natural father "is a rebuttable presumption affecting the burden of proof and may be rebutted in an appropriate action only by clear and convincing evidence." [Cal. Fam. Code §7612(a).] The question presented by this case is whether a presumption arising under section 7611(d) is, under section 7612(a), necessarily rebutted when the presumed father seeks parental rights but admits that he is not the biological father of the child.

The answer to this question is of the gravest concern to the six-year-old boy involved in this case. While his presumed father is providing a loving home for him, his mother has not done so, and his biological father, whose identity has never been judicially determined, has shown no interest in doing so. Therefore, if, as the Court of Appeal concluded, the juvenile court had no discretion under section 7612(a) but to find that the presumption arising under section 7611(d) was rebutted by the presumed father's admission that he is not the biological father, this child will be rendered fatherless and homeless.

This harsh result, we conclude, is not required by section 7612(a). [T]he section provides that "a presumption under Section 7611 is a rebuttable presumption

[7]. Nat'l Domestic Violence Hotline, Stealthing, https://www.thehotline.org/resources/stealthing/.

affecting the burden of proof and *may* be rebutted *in an appropriate action* only by clear and convincing evidence." (§7612(a), italics added.) The juvenile court acted well within its discretion in concluding that this case, in which no one else was a candidate for the privilege and responsibility of fathering this little boy, was not *an appropriate action* in which to find that the section 7611(d) presumption of fatherhood had been rebutted.

[T]he evidence, viewed in the light most favorable to the findings and orders of the juvenile court, may be summarized as follows. When Kimberly was pregnant with Nicholas, she moved in with Thomas. Thomas is not Nicholas's biological father, as he admits, but both Kimberly and Thomas wanted Thomas to act as a father to Nicholas, so Thomas participated in Nicholas's birth, was listed on Nicholas's birth certificate as his father, and provided a home for Kimberly and Nicholas for several years.

Thomas has been the constant in Nicholas's life. . . . Thomas has lived with Nicholas for long periods of time, he has provided Nicholas with significant financial support over the years, and he has consistently referred to and treated Nicholas as his son. "In addition, there is undisputed evidence that Nicholas has a strong emotional bond with Thomas and that Thomas is the only father Nicholas has ever know[n]."

Kimberly, on the other hand, has been a frail reed for Nicholas to lean upon. . . . The juvenile court's finding that Nicholas had to be removed from her custody was based on the following grounds: "One, [Kimberly] continues to lead an unstable lifestyle, without housing or means of support of her own.. . . Number two, Nicholas has continually stated he does not wish to reside with his mother because she is mean to him; she hits and slaps him; and she smokes weed. Three, and most importantly to me as I have observed [Kimberly's] demeanor throughout this case, particularly during her testimony, I have grown increasingly concerned about [her] mental and emotional health.. . ." . . .

The Court of Appeal concluded that Thomas qualified as Nicholas's presumed father under section 7611(d), but that, under section 7612(a), his admission that he is not Nicholas's biological father necessarily rebutted that presumption. [E]ven though its decision would have the effect of rendering Nicholas fatherless, the Court of Appeal felt it was "not free to ignore the statute, which [it said] expressly states that the section 7611(d) presumption *is* rebutted by clear and convincing evidence that the presumed father is not the child's natural father." (Italics added.)

[The Court of Appeal, however, "misread" §7612(a). Section 7612(a) does not say that the presumption "is" rebutted by clear and convincing evidence. Instead, it provides that, "a presumption under Section 7611(d) is a rebuttable presumption affecting the burden of proof and *may* be rebutted *in an appropriate action* only by clear and convincing evidence." (Italics added.) . . . Our conclusion—that a man does not lose his status as a presumed father by admitting he is not the biological father—is also supported by subdivision (b) of section 7612. Subdivision (b) provides: "If two or more presumptions arise under section 7611 which conflict with each other, the presumption which on the facts is founded on the weightier considerations of policy and logic controls." As a matter of statutory construction, if the Legislature had intended that a man who is not a biological father cannot be a presumed father under section 7611, it would not have provided for such weighing, for among two competing claims for presumed father status under section 7611, there can be only one biological father.

[This conclusion is consistent with several Court of Appeal decisions. For example, i]n *Steven W. v. Matthew S.* [33 Cal. App. 4th 1108 (1995)], two men qualified as presumed fathers of Michael. Matthew qualified under [what is now Cal. Fam. Code §7611(a)(1)] because he was married to Michael's mother, Julie, when Michael was born. Matthew also qualified under [what is now Cal. Fam. Code §7555] on the basis of blood test evidence. Steven qualified under [what is now Cal. Fam. Code §7611(d)] because he had received Michael into his home and held him out as his child. The trial court found Steven's presumption of paternity controlling on the ground he had the "'more prolonged, intensive and continuing relationship'" with Michael.

The Court of Appeal affirmed. "[Cal. Fam. Code §7612(b)] provide[s] that when presumptions conflict, 'the presumption which on the facts is founded on the weightier consideration of policy and logic controls.' The paternity presumptions are driven by state interest in preserving the integrity of the family and legitimate concern for the welfare of the child. The state has an '"interest in preserving and protecting the developed parent-child . . . relationships which give young children social and emotional strength and stability."' The courts have repeatedly held, in applying paternity presumptions, that the extant father-child relationship is to be preserved at the cost of biological ties. . . . '"[I]n the case of an older child [over two years of age] the familial relationship between the child and the man purporting to be the child's father is considerably more palpable than the biological relationship of actual paternity. A man who has lived with a child, treating it as his son or daughter, has developed a relationship with the child that should not be lightly dissolved . . . . This social relationship is much more important, to the child at least, than a biological relationship of actual paternity . . . ."'"

To review: Section 7612(a) provides that "a presumption under Section 7611 [that a man is the natural father of a child] is a rebuttable presumption affecting the burden of proof *and may be rebutted in an appropriate action* only by clear and convincing evidence." (Italics added.) When it used the limiting phrase *an appropriate action,* the Legislature is unlikely to have had in mind an action like this—an action in which no other man claims parental rights to the child, an action in which rebuttal of the section 7611(d) presumption will render the child fatherless. Rather, we believe the Legislature had in mind an action in which another candidate is vying for parental rights and seeks to rebut a section 7611(d) presumption in order to perfect his claim, or in which a court decides that the legal rights and obligations of parenthood should devolve upon an unwilling candidate. . . . The judgment of the Court of Appeal is reversed and the matter remanded for further proceedings consistent with this opinion.

Notes and Questions

1. **Non-biological functional parents.** The Court of Appeal and the California Supreme Court both agreed that Thomas was entitled to a presumption of parentage based on having lived with and held Nicholas out as his child. The two courts disagreed, however, on whether his lack of genetic parentage *necessarily* rebutted that presumption. The California Supreme Court here answered that question in the negative. On what basis did the court reach that conclusion?

2. Other states. The holding out presumption at issue in *Nicholas H.* was based on the original UPA (1973). A number of other states have similar provisions in place today. See, e.g., Haw. Rev. Stat. Ann. §584-4(a)(4); Minn. Stat. Ann. §257.55, subd. 1(d).

3. Law reform developments. The most recent version of the UPA continues to include the holding out presumption. However, a time requirement has been added: an individual is presumed to a child's parent if, "for the first two years of the [child's] life," the individual resided with and held out the child as their child. UPA (2017), §204(a)(2). Why did the drafters add this time requirement?

4. Rebuttal. This holding out rule creates a presumption that the person is a parent, but this presumption can be rebutted. Under the UPA (1973), if the person is the only candidate for the second parent slot, the presumption "may" be rebutted "in an appropriate case." The California Supreme Court held that this text meant that the presumption was not necessarily rebutted by proof that the person was not a genetic parent. What would be "an appropriate case" in which to find the presumption rebutted?

Where there is another person with a competing presumption—say, a spouse of the birth parent—the UPA (1973) directs the court to determine which presumption is founded on "weightier considerations of policy and logic." What does that mean? How should a court decide such cases?

The most recent version of the UPA—UPA (2017)—seeks to provide additional guidance to courts in cases involving "competing presumptions." In such cases, courts are directed to adjudicate parentage "in the best interest of the child," taking into account a number of factors, including the age of the child, "the length of time during which each individual assumed the role of parent to the child," and "the harm to the child if the relationship between the child and each individual is not recognized." UPA (2017), §613(a). Which version of the UPA provides clearer direction for courts?

The holding out provision of the original UPA (1973) creates a presumption that a "man" is a child's parent if "he" engaged in the required conduct. A number of states still have parentage laws based on this provision. See, e.g., Minn. Stat. Ann. §257.55, subd. 1(d). Should such a rule apply equally to a woman? Would it be constitutional to refuse to apply it equally to a woman? The next case addresses these issues.

CHATTERJEE v. KING
280 P.3d 283 (N.M. 2012)

Chávez, Justice.

Bani Chatterjee and Taya King are two women who were in a committed, long-term domestic relationship when they agreed to bring a child into their relationship. [W]ith Chatterjee's active participation, King adopted a child from Russia. Chatterjee supported King and Child financially, lived in the family home, and co-parented Child for a number of years before their commitment to each other foundered and they dissolved their relationship. Chatterjee never adopted Child. After they ended their relationship, King moved to Colorado and sought to prevent Chatterjee from having any contact with Child.

Chatterjee filed a petition to establish parentage and determine custody and timesharing. Chatterjee alleged that she was a presumed natural parent under the former codification of the New Mexico Uniform Parentage Act. [W]e must now determine whether Chatterjee, as a woman, can establish a presumed natural parent and child relationship under [N.M. Stat. Ann. §40-11-5(A)(4)].

Chatterjee argues that the Court of Appeals erred in holding that none of the UPA provisions relating to the father and child relationship may be applied to women. . . . We find support for Chatterjee's argument not only in the plain language of the statute itself, but also in the purpose of the UPA, the application of paternity provisions to women in jurisdictions with similar UPA provisions, and in public policy that encourages the love and support of children from able and willing parents. . . .

We begin our analysis with Section 40-11-2 of the UPA, which states that a "'parent and child relationship' means the legal relationship existing between a child and his natural or adoptive parents incident to which the law confers or imposes rights, privileges, duties, and obligations. It includes the mother and child relationship and the father and child relationship." For a mother, Section 40-11-4(A) provides that "the natural mother may be established by proof of her having given birth to the child, or *as provided by Section* [40-11-21 NMSA 1978]." ([E]mphasis added.) Section 40-11-21 states that "[a]ny interested party may bring an action to determine the existence or nonexistence of a mother and child relationship. Insofar as practicable, the provisions of the Uniform Parentage Act applicable to the father and child relationship apply."

[The court first held that Chatterjee had standing as an "interested party" because the term applied to any person who is able to establish presumed natural parenthood under Section 40-11-5(A)(4). The court then addressed the conclusion of the Court of Appeals that reading Section 40-11-21 to allow Chatterjee to establish parentage through Section 40-11-5(A)(4) was "impracticable," and that the legislature, in enacting Section 40-11-4(A), created separate sections for how a woman, as opposed to a man, can prove natural parenthood, implying that it intended each sex to have different means available for proving parenthood.] The Court therefore concluded that applying the means for proving paternity to proving maternity would contravene the legislature's intent. We disagree.

It is practicable to apply Section 40-11-5 to determine maternity in certain circumstances [because] Section 40-11-5(A)(4), which establishes a parental presumption is reasonably capable of being accomplished by either a man or a woman. [That section] provides, in relevant part, that "[a] man is presumed to be the natural father of a child if . . . while the child is under the age of majority, he openly holds out the child as his natural child and has established a personal, financial or custodial relationship with the child." Because the presumption is based on a person's conduct, not a biological connection, a woman is capable of holding out a child as her natural child and establishing a personal, financial, or custodial relationship with that child. This is particularly true when, as is alleged in this case, the relationship between the child and both the presumptive and the adoptive parent occurred simultaneously.

In addition, by limiting proof of natural motherhood to biology under Section 40-11-4(A), the Court of Appeals renders meaningless the clear instruction in Section 40-11-4(A) that a "natural mother may [also] be established . . . . as provided by Section 21 [40-11-21 NMSA 1978]." A straightforward reading of Section 40-11-4(A) is that motherhood may be established by giving birth, by adoption, and in any other way in which a father and child relationship may be established when it is practicable to do so. Because it is practicable for a woman to hold a child out as her own, the plain language instructs us to recognize that Section 40-11-5(A)(4) relating to the father and child relationship also applies to the mother and child relationship. . . .

Moreover, we seek to avoid an interpretation of a statute that would raise constitutional concerns. In this case, the Court of Appeals' reading would yield different results for a man than for a woman in precisely the same situation. If this Court interpreted Section 40-11-5(A)(4) as applying only to males, then a man in a same-sex relationship claiming to be a natural parent because he held out a child as his own would have standing simply by virtue of his gender, while a woman in the same position would not. . . . We avoid this disparate treatment, giving effect to the Legislature's intent, with a plain and simple application of Section 40-11-5(A)(4) to both men and women under Section 40-11-21.

The authors of the Uniform Parentage Act of 1973 (the original UPA), anticipating situations such as this case, provided in a comment that masculine terminology was used for the sake of simplicity and not to limit application of its provisions to males. . . . There is no indication that our Legislature intended a different reading of this statute in New Mexico when it adopted the original UPA.

[The court next points out that other jurisdictions with virtually identical statutes have applied provisions relating to the father-child relationship to the mother-child relationship. Further, the court explains, public policy supports applying the state version of the UPA to women. The] state has a strong interest in ensuring that a child will be cared for, financially and otherwise, by two parents. If that care is lacking, the state will ultimately assume the responsibility of caring for the child. This is one of the primary reasons that the original UPA was created, and it makes little sense to read the statute without keeping this overarching legislative goal in mind. The original UPA was also written to address the interest that children have in their own support. The rationale underlying the original UPA is that every child should be treated equally, regardless of the marital status of the child's parents. In deciding illegitimacy cases, the United States Supreme Court recognized that it is "illogical and unjust" for a state to deny a child's essential right to be supported by two parents simply because the child's parents are not married. Gomez v. Perez, 409 U.S. 535, 538 (1973). . . . With this in mind, we see no reason for children to be penalized because of the decisions that their parents make, legal or otherwise.

Consistent with the underlying policy-based rationale of the New Mexico UPA that equality in child welfare requires laws that achieve equality in parentage, Child's need for love and support is no less critical simply because her second parent also happens to be a woman. Experts in child psychology recognize that sometimes the law is too limiting when it comes to actually addressing what is in the child's best interests. The attachment bonds that form between a child and a parent are formed regardless of a biological or legal connection. See Joseph

Goldstein et al., Beyond the Best Interests of the Child 27 (rev. ed. 1979). These bonds are formed as a result of "provision of physical and emotional care, continuity or consistency in the child's life, and emotional investment in the child." The law needs to address traditional expectations in light of current realities to keep up with the changing demographic of American families and to protect the children born into them. . . .

It is inappropriate to deny Chatterjee the opportunity to establish parentage, when denying Chatterjee this opportunity would only serve to harm both Child and the state. In our view, it is against public policy to deny parental rights and responsibilities based solely on the sex of either or both of the parents. The better view is to recognize that the child's best interests are served when intending parents physically, emotionally, and financially support the child from the time the child comes into their lives. This is especially true when both parents are able and willing to care for the child. Therefore, we hold that the Legislature intended that Section 40-11-5(A)(4) be applied to a woman who is seeking to establish a natural parent and child relationship with a child whom she has held out as her natural child from the moment the child came into the lives of both the adoptive mother and the presumptive mother. . . .

The fact that Chatterjee did not adopt Child does not impact our decision. Section 40-11-5 of the New Mexico UPA delineates the ways in which parentage can be presumed. Thus, our Legislature has recognized that there will be many situations in which someone is caring for a child but has not taken any steps to legalize that relationship. While taking legal action is the best way to ensure that both the alleged parent and the child have rights arising from that relationship, both our Legislature and this Court have indicated a willingness to confer rights to relationships that have not been legally established. This is so because parental rights are not automatically conferred when there is a biological relationship, but rather when an alleged parent has taken the responsibility of caring for a child. Considering the specific facts of this case, we hold that Chatterjee has alleged sufficient facts to attempt to establish that she is an interested party, and therefore she has standing to establish parentage under Section 40-11-21 of the New Mexico UPA. . . .

Notes and Questions

1. Holding and rationale. What was the nature of the dispute in *Chatterjee*? What are the different views of the appellate and state supreme courts? Why did Chatterjee's former partner (Taya King) argue that Chatterjee had to make a showing of King's unfitness? What did the respective courts respond?

2. Benefit. Who benefits from the ruling in *Chatterjee*? Lesbian partners? Gay male partners who are parents? Birth mothers? The children? The state? Does *Chatterjee* address the application of the relevant doctrines and statutes to gay male couples?

3. UPA. Which provisions of the original UPA does the court apply? What is the basis of the court's reasoning that the UPA's paternity provisions should apply to women? Is the court's reasoning persuasive? As *Chatterjee* explains, the trend is to apply gendered UPA provisions in a gender-neutral manner. As the *Chatterjee* court explains, the UPA itself provides that "[i]nsofar as practicable, the provisions of this Act applicable to the father and child relationship apply" to "an action to determine the existence of nonexistence of a mother and child relationship." UPA (1973), §21. Do you agree with the *Chatterjee* court that it is "practicable" to apply the holding out presumption to a woman? The UPA (2017) addresses this question directly by including a "holding out" presumption that applies to any "individual." UPA (2017), §204(a)(2).

The UPA (2017) also incorporates a new route for recognizing functional parents—the de facto parent provision. UPA (2017), §609 provides that a person claiming to be a de facto parent can petition to be recognized as a legal parent provided that the person proves by clear and convincing evidence that they resided with the child as a regular member of the child's household for a significant period, engaged in the consistent caretaking of the child, took on full and permanent responsibilities for the child without the expectation of financial compensation, presented the child as their child, established a bonded and dependent parent-child relationship with at least one legal parent's approval, and that continuing the relationship is in the child's best interest. If this provision was applied to Chatterjee, would she qualify?

4. Child support. Generally, when a person is adjudicated to be a parent, they are a legal parent for all purposes, including for purposes of child support. See, e.g., UPA (2017), §203 ("Unless parental rights are terminated, a parent-child relationship established under this [act] applies for all purposes . . . .").

5. Alternative theories. Some states, like New Mexico in *Chatterjee* and California in *Nicholas H.*, recognize people who have functioned as parents as legal parents under a statutory "holding out" provision. See, e.g., Guardianship of Madelyn B., 98 A.3d 494 (N.H. 2014).

As an alternative argument, the plaintiff in *Chatterjee* claimed that she was entitled to protection under common law or equitable functional parent doctrines, although the court did not reach either issue. Under one of the most widely recognized common law functional parent doctrines, the criteria that must be established to qualify are:

(1) that the biological or adoptive parent consented to, and fostered, the petitioner's formation and establishment of a parent-like relationship with the child;
(2) that the petitioner and the child lived together in the same household;
(3) that the petitioner assumed obligations of parenthood by taking significant responsibility for the child's care, education, and development, including contributing towards the child's support, without expectation of financial compensation; and
(4) that the petitioner has been in a parental role for a length of time sufficient to have established with the child a bonded, dependent relationship parental in nature.

Conover v. Conover, 146 A.3d 433, 446-447 (Md. 2016). Individuals who meet the requirements typically are entitled to seek custody of the child under the "best interest of the child" standard; often, however, in some states they are not considered legal parents for other purposes.

6. Scholarly commentary. While most states have one or more functional parent doctrines—either statutory, judge-made, or both—and while these doctrines have been recognized for decades in many states, scholarly debate about their wisdom continues. Some scholars, including Professor Katharine Baker, worry that these doctrines result in "invasive, ineffective, and often damaging interference in family relationships."[8] Others fear that functional parent doctrines will be used by abusive former partners as a means of continuing to harass the child's mother.

To evaluate these claims, Professors Courtney Joslin and Douglas NeJaime conducted an empirical study of all electronically reported judicial decisions in every U.S. jurisdiction with a functional parent doctrine over a 40-year period. Based on this study, they conclude the following:

> While commentators worry about unleashing meritless and abusive claims, we find that in the overwhelming majority of cases, the functional parent appears to have been the child's primary caregiver. While commentators fear that recognition of functional parents will introduce instability in children's lives, we find that courts routinely apply the doctrines to protect children's relationships with the person who is parenting them. In addition to undermining purportedly empirically-based objections to functional parent doctrines, our findings lend support to normative arguments in favor of functional parent doctrines. We find that courts commonly apply the doctrines in ways that make children's lives more stable and secure by protecting their relationships with their primary caregivers, preserving their home placements, and shielding their families from further state intervention.[9]

4. Competing Claims to Parentage

In some cases, there are two people, in addition to the birth parent, who claim parentage of a child. For example, suppose that the genetic father in *Nicholas H.* also sought to establish his parentage? Whom should the court recognize, Thomas or the child's genetic father? Or suppose that a married woman gives birth to a child who is not the genetic child of her husband? Should the court recognize the husband or the child's genetic parent as the child's parent? The next case explores this issue.

---

[8]. Katharine K. Baker, Equality and Family Autonomy, 24 U. Pa. J. Const. L. 412, 415 (2022).
[9]. Courtney G. Joslin & Douglas NeJaime, How Functional Parent Doctrines Function: Findings from an Empirical Study, 35 J. Amer. Acad. of Matrim. Law. 589 (2023); see also Courtney Joslin & Douglas NeJaime, How Parenthood Functions, 123 Colum. L. Rev. 319 (2023).

MICHAEL H. v. GERALD D.
491 U.S. 110 (1989)

Justice SCALIA announced the judgment of the Court and delivered an opinion, in which THE CHIEF JUSTICE joins, and in all but note 6 of which Justice O'CONNOR and Justice KENNEDY join.

Under California law, a child born to a married woman living with her husband is presumed to be a child of the marriage. Cal. Evid. Code Ann. §621 (West Supp. 1989). The presumption of legitimacy may be rebutted only by the husband or wife, and then only in limited circumstances. The instant appeal presents the claim that this presumption infringes upon the due process rights of a man who wishes to establish his paternity of a child born to the wife of another man, and the claim that it infringes upon the constitutional right of the child to maintain a relationship with her natural father.

The facts of this case are, we must hope, extraordinary. On May 9, 1976, in Las Vegas, Nevada, Carole D., an international model, and Gerald D., a top executive in a French oil company, were married. The couple established a home in Playa del Rey, California, in which they resided as husband and wife when one or the other was not out of the country on business. In the summer of 1978, Carole became involved in an adulterous affair with a neighbor, Michael H. In September 1980, she conceived a child, Victoria D., who was born on May 11, 1981. Gerald was listed as father on the birth certificate and has always held Victoria out to the world as his daughter. Soon after delivery of the child, however, Carole informed Michael that she believed he might be the father.

In the first three years of her life, Victoria remained always with Carole, but found herself within a variety of quasi-family units. In October 1981, Gerald moved to New York City to pursue his business interests, but Carole chose to remain in California. At the end of that month, Carole and Michael had blood tests of themselves and Victoria, which showed a 98.07% probability that Michael was Victoria's father. In January 1982, Carole visited Michael in St. Thomas, where his primary business interests were based. There, Michael held Victoria out as his child. In March, however, Carole left Michael and returned to California, where she took up residence with yet another man, Scott K. Later that spring, and again in the summer, Carole and Victoria spent time with Gerald in New York City, as well as on vacation in Europe. In the fall, they returned to Scott in California.

In November 1982, rebuffed in his attempts to visit Victoria, Michael filed a filiation action in California Superior Court to establish his paternity and right to visitation. In March 1983, the court appointed an attorney and guardian ad litem to represent Victoria's interests. Victoria then filed a cross-complaint asserting that if she had more than one psychological or de facto father, she was entitled to maintain her filial relationship, with all of the attendant rights, duties, and obligations, with both. In May 1983, Carole filed a motion for summary judgment. During this period, from March through July 1983, Carole was again living with Gerald in New York. In August, however, she returned to California, became involved once again with Michael, and instructed her attorneys to remove the summary judgment motion from the calendar.

For the ensuing eight months, when Michael was not in St. Thomas, he lived with Carole and Victoria in Carole's apartment in Los Angeles and held Victoria out as his daughter. In April 1984, Carole and Michael signed a stipulation that Michael was Victoria's natural father. Carole left Michael the next month, however, and instructed her attorneys not to file the stipulation. In June 1984, Carole reconciled with Gerald and joined him in New York, where they now live with Victoria and two other children since born into the marriage.

In May 1984, Michael and Victoria, through her guardian ad litem, sought visitation rights for Michael *pendente lite*. To assist in determining whether visitation would be in Victoria's best interests, the Superior Court appointed a psychologist to evaluate Victoria, Gerald, Michael, and Carole. The psychologist recommended that Carole retain sole custody, but that Michael be allowed continued contact with Victoria pursuant to a restricted visitation schedule. The court concurred and ordered that Michael be provided with limited visitation privileges *pendente lite*.

On October 19, 1984, Gerald, who had intervened in the action, moved for summary judgment on the ground that under Cal. Evid. Code §621 there were no triable issues of fact as to Victoria's paternity. This law provides that "the issue of a wife cohabiting with her husband, who is not impotent or sterile, is conclusively presumed to be a child of the marriage." The presumption may be rebutted by blood tests, but only if a motion for such tests is made, within two years from the date of the child's birth, either by the husband or, if the natural father has filed an affidavit acknowledging paternity, by the wife. [The trial court granted Gerald's motion for summary judgment. Michael and Victoria appeal.]

We address first the [due process] claims of Michael. At the outset, it is necessary to clarify what he sought and what he was denied. California law, like nature itself, makes no provision for dual fatherhood. Michael was seeking to be declared the father of Victoria. The immediate benefit he evidently sought to obtain from that status was visitation rights. But if Michael were successful in being declared the father, other rights would follow — most importantly, the right to be considered as the parent who should have custody. . . . All parental rights, including visitation, were automatically denied by denying Michael status as the father. . . .

Michael contends as a matter of substantive due process that, because he has established a parental relationship with Victoria, protection of Gerald's and Carole's marital union is an insufficient state interest to support termination of that relationship. This argument is, of course, predicated on the assertion that Michael has a constitutionally protected liberty interest in his relationship with Victoria. . . .

In an attempt to limit and guide interpretation of the [Due Process] Clause, we have insisted not merely that the interest denominated as a "liberty" be "fundamental" (a concept that, in isolation, is hard to objectify), but also that it be an interest traditionally protected by our society. . . . This insistence that the asserted liberty interest be rooted in history and tradition is evident, as elsewhere, in our cases according constitutional protection to certain parental rights. Michael reads the landmark case of Stanley v. Illinois, 405 U.S. 645 (1972), and the subsequent cases of Quilloin v. Walcott, 434 U.S. 246 (1978), Caban v. Mohammed, 441 U.S. 380 (1979), and Lehr v. Robertson, 463 U.S. 248 (1983), as establishing that a liberty interest is created by biological fatherhood plus an established parental relationship — factors that exist in the present case as well. We think that distorts the rationale of those cases. As we view them, they rest not upon such isolated factors but upon the historic respect — indeed, sanctity would not be too strong a term — traditionally accorded to the relationships that develop within the unitary family.[3] . . .

Thus, the legal issue in the present case reduces to whether the relationship between persons in the situation of Michael and Victoria has been treated as a protected family unit under the historic practices of our society, or whether on any other basis it has been accorded special protection. We think it impossible to find that it has. In fact, quite to the contrary, our traditions have protected the marital family (Gerald, Carole, and the child they acknowledge to be theirs) against the sort of claim Michael asserts.[4]

The presumption of legitimacy was a fundamental principle of the common law. Traditionally, that presumption could be rebutted only by proof that a husband was incapable of procreation or had had no access to his wife during the relevant period. As explained by Blackstone, nonaccess could only be proved "if the husband be out of the kingdom of England (or, as the law somewhat loosely phrases it, *extra quatuor maria* [beyond the four seas]) for above nine months. . . ." 1 Blackstone's Commentaries 456 (J. Chitty ed., 1826). And, under the common law both in England and here [neither parent could testify to bastardize the child]. The primary policy rationale underlying the common law's severe restrictions on rebuttal of the presumption appears to have been an aversion to declaring children illegitimate, thereby depriving them of rights of inheritance and succession, and likely making them wards of the state. A secondary policy concern was the interest in promoting the "peace and tranquillity of States and families," a goal that is obviously impaired by facilitating suits against husband and wife asserting that their children are illegitimate. . . .

We have found nothing in the older sources, nor in the older cases, addressing specifically the power of the natural father to assert parental rights over a child born into a woman's existing marriage with another man. Since it is Michael's burden to establish that such a power (at least where the natural father has established a relationship with the child) is so deeply embedded within our traditions as to be a fundamental right, the lack of evidence alone might defeat his case. But the evidence shows that even in modern times — when, as we have noted, the rigid protection

---

3. Justice Brennan asserts that only "a pinched conception of 'the family'" would exclude Michael, Carole, and Victoria from protection. We disagree. The family unit accorded traditional respect in our society, which we have referred to as the "unitary family," is typified, of course, by the marital family, but also includes the household of unmarried parents and their children. Perhaps the concept can be expanded even beyond this, but it will bear no resemblance to traditionally respected relationships — and will thus cease to have any constitutional significance — if it is stretched so far as to include the relationship established between a married woman, her lover, and their child, during a 3-month sojourn in St. Thomas, or during a subsequent 8-month period when, if he happened to be in Los Angeles, he stayed with her and the child.

4. Justice Brennan insists that in determining whether a liberty interest exists we must look at Michael's relationship with Victoria in isolation, without reference to the circumstance that Victoria's mother was married to someone else when the child was conceived, and that that woman and her husband wish to raise the child as their own. We cannot imagine what compels this strange procedure of looking at the act which is assertedly the subject of a liberty interest in isolation from its effect upon other people — rather like inquiring whether there is a liberty interest in firing a gun where the case at hand happens to involve its discharge into another person's body. The logic of Justice Brennan's position leads to the conclusion that if Michael had begotten Victoria by rape, that fact would in no way affect his possession of a liberty interest in his relationship with her.

of the marital family has in other respects been relaxed — the ability of a person in Michael's position to claim paternity has not been generally acknowledged. . . .

Moreover, even if it were clear that one in Michael's position generally possesses, and has generally always possessed, standing to challenge the marital child's legitimacy, that would still not establish Michael's case. As noted earlier, what is at issue here is not entitlement to a state pronouncement that Victoria was begotten by Michael. It is no conceivable denial of constitutional right for a State to decline to declare facts unless some legal consequence hinges upon the requested declaration. What Michael asserts here is a right to have himself declared the natural father and *thereby to obtain parental prerogatives.* What he must establish, therefore, is not that our society has traditionally allowed a natural father in his circumstances to establish paternity, but that it has traditionally accorded such a father parental rights, or at least has not traditionally denied them. . . . What counts is whether the States in fact award substantive parental rights to the natural father of a child conceived within, and born into, an extant marital union that wishes to embrace the child. We are not aware of a single case, old or new, that has done so. This is not the stuff of which fundamental rights qualifying as liberty interests are made.[6] . . .

We have never had occasion to decide whether a child has a liberty interest, symmetrical with that of her parent, in maintaining her filial relationship. We need not do so here because, even assuming that such a right exists, Victoria's claim must fail. Victoria's due process challenge is, if anything, weaker than Michael's. Her basic claim is not that California has erred in preventing her from establishing that Michael, not Gerald, should stand as her legal father. Rather, she claims a due process right to maintain filial relationships with both Michael and Gerald. This assertion merits little discussion, for, whatever the merits of the guardian ad litem's belief that such an arrangement can be of great psychological benefit to a child, the claim that a State must recognize multiple fatherhood has no support in the history or traditions of this country. . . .

Victoria claims in addition that her equal protection rights have been violated because, unlike her mother and presumed father, she had no opportunity to rebut the presumption of her legitimacy. We find this argument wholly without merit. We reject, at the outset, Victoria's suggestion that her equal protection challenge must be assessed under a standard of strict scrutiny because, in denying her the right to maintain a filial relationship with Michael, the State is discriminating against her on the basis of her illegitimacy. See Gomez v. Perez, 409 U.S. 535, 538 (1973). Illegitimacy is a legal construct, not a natural trait. Under California law,

_____

6. Justice Brennan criticizes our methodology in using historical traditions specifically relating to the rights of an adulterous natural father, rather than inquiring more generally "whether parenthood is an interest that historically has received our attention and protection." . . .

We do not understand why, having rejected our focus upon the societal tradition regarding the natural father's rights vis-à-vis a child whose mother is married to another man, Justice Brennan would choose to focus instead upon "parenthood." Why should the relevant category not be even more general — perhaps "family relationships"; or "personal relationships"; or even "emotional attachments in general"? Though the dissent has no basis for the level of generality it would select, we do: We refer to the most specific level at which a relevant tradition protecting, or denying protection to, the asserted right can be identified. If, for example, there were no societal tradition, either way, regarding the rights of the natural father of a child adulterously conceived, we would have to consult, and (if possible) reason from, the traditions regarding natural fathers in general. But there is such a more specific tradition, and it unqualifiedly denies protection to such a parent. . . .

Victoria is not illegitimate, and she is treated in the same manner as all other legitimate children: she is entitled to maintain a filial relationship with her legal parents. . . . Since it pursues a legitimate end [protecting the integrity of the marital family] by rational means, California's decision to treat Victoria differently from her parents is not a denial of equal protection. . . .

Justice BRENNAN, with whom Justice MARSHALL and Justice BLACKMUN join, dissenting. . . .

Today's plurality . . . does not ask whether parenthood is an interest that historically has received our attention and protection; the answer to that question is too clear for dispute. Instead, the plurality asks whether the specific variety of parenthood under consideration — a natural father's relationship with a child whose mother is married to another man — has enjoyed such protection. . . .

If we had looked to tradition with such specificity in past cases, many a decision would have reached a different result. Surely the use of contraceptives by unmarried couples, or even by married couples; the freedom from corporal punishment in schools; . . . and even the right to raise one's natural but illegitimate children, were not "interest[s] traditionally protected by our society" at the time of their consideration by this Court. . . .

In construing the Fourteenth Amendment to offer shelter only to those interests specifically protected by historical practice, moreover, the plurality ignores the kind of society in which our Constitution exists. We are not an assimilative, homogeneous society, but a facilitative, pluralistic one, in which we must be willing to abide someone else's unfamiliar or even repellant practice because the same tolerant impulse protects our own idiosyncracies. Even if we can agree, therefore, that "family" and "parenthood" are part of the good life, it is absurd to assume that we can agree on the content of those terms and destructive to pretend that we do. In a community such as ours, "liberty" must include the freedom not to conform. The plurality today squashes this freedom by requiring specific approval from history before protecting anything in the name of liberty. . . .

. . . This is not a case in which we face a "new" kind of interest, one that requires us to consider for the first time whether the Constitution protects it. On the contrary, we confront an interest — that of a parent and child in their relationship with each other — that was among the first that this Court acknowledged in its cases defining the "liberty" protected by the Constitution [citing Meyer v. Nebraska, Skinner v. Oklahoma, Prince v. Massachusetts].

The evidence is undisputed that Michael, Victoria, and Carole did live together as a family; that is, they shared the same household, Victoria called Michael "Daddy," Michael contributed to Victoria's support, and he is eager to continue his relationship with her. Yet they are not, in the plurality's view, a "unitary family," whereas Gerald, Carole, and Victoria do compose such a family. The only difference between these two sets of relationships, however, is the fact of marriage. . . . However, the very premise of *Stanley* and the cases following it is that marriage is not decisive in answering the question whether the Constitution protects the parental relationship under consideration. . . .

The plurality's exclusive rather than inclusive definition of the "unitary family" is out of step with other decisions as well. This pinched conception of "the family," crucial as it is in rejecting Michael's and Victoria's claims of a liberty interest, is jarring in light of our many cases preventing the States from denying important interests or statuses to those whose situations do not fit the government's narrow view of the family. From Loving v. Virginia, 388 U.S. 1 (1967), to Levy v. Louisiana, 391 U.S. 68 (1968), and from Gomez v. Perez, 409 U.S. 535 (1973), to Moore v. East Cleveland, 431 U.S. 494 (1977), we have declined to respect a State's notion, as manifested in its allocation of privileges and burdens, of what the family should be. Today's rhapsody on the "unitary family" is out of tune with such decisions. . . .

NOTE: CONSTITUTIONAL PROTECTION FOR NONMARITAL FATHERS

The constitutional rights of nonmarital, biological fathers were addressed by the Supreme Court in three cases decided after *Stanley* but before *Michael H.*

In Quilloin v. Walcott, 434 U.S. 246 (1978), the Court upheld a Georgia adoption statute that required only the consent of the mother absent the father's acknowledgment, marriage to the child's mother, or court order of parentage. The mother, shortly after her child's birth, married another man who petitioned for adoption after the child had lived with him for nine years. The biological father, who had been given notice, requested that the court deny the adoption, declare him the father, and grant him visitation. Although he had never lived with or "legitimated" the child, he had paid some support and visited occasionally. Rejecting the father's due process argument, the Court distinguished the case from *Stanley* because this biological father failed to have or seek child custody and rejected his equal protection claim because, unlike a married father, this man had not borne legal childrearing responsibility.

In Caban v. Mohammed, 441 U.S. 380 (1979), an unmarried father brought a successful challenge to a New York law that permitted adoption of his children, without his consent, by the husband of the children's mother. Caban had fathered two children with Mohammed during their five years together. When the couple separated, the mother married another man. Caban continued to see his children frequently, contributed to their support, and at one point had custody. After the new husband petitioned for adoption, Caban and his new wife cross-petitioned. The Supreme Court found that Caban had participated in the children's care and support, and also that the state's interest in promoting adoption was not advanced in the case. The Court elaborated:

> [I]n cases such as this, where the father has established a substantial relationship with the child and has admitted his paternity, a State should have no difficulty in identifying the father even of children born out of wedlock. Thus, no showing has been made that the different treatment afforded unmarried fathers and unmarried mothers under [the statute] bears a substantial relationship to the proclaimed interest of the State in promoting the adoption of illegitimate children.[10]

---

[10]. *Caban,* 441 U.S. at 392-393.

Finally, in Lehr v. Robertson, 463 U.S. 248 (1983), the Court upheld another adoption statute that dispensed with notice of an adoption proceeding to some nonmarital fathers. This biological father, Jonathan Lehr, never contributed to his daughter's support and saw her infrequently. When the child was two, the mother and her new husband (whom she married eight months after the birth) filed an adoption petition. Lehr claimed that the Due Process and Equal Protection Clauses, as interpreted in *Stanley*, gave him a right to notice and an opportunity to be heard. New York law required notice for fathers who had registered with a "putative father registry," as well as those who were adjudicated to be the father, identified on the birth certificate, lived openly with the child and the child's mother, or were married to the mother before the child was six months old. Lehr fit none of these categories. The Supreme Court concluded in *Lehr* that due process does not require notice if the biological father had not assumed any responsibility for the care of his child:

> The significance of the biological connection is that it offers the natural father an opportunity that no other male possesses to develop a relationship with his offspring. If he grasps that opportunity and accepts some measure of responsibility for the child's future, he may enjoy the blessings of the parent-child relationship and make uniquely valuable contributions to the child's development. If he fails to do so, the Federal Constitution will not automatically compel a state to listen to his opinion of where the child's best interests lie.[11]

Although not mentioned by the majority, the dissent in *Lehr* explained that while the biological father had had limited contact with the child, that was not for lack of trying. Lehr claimed his efforts to establish a parent-child relationship were thwarted by the mother, who concealed her whereabouts after the birth.

The *Quilloin-Caban-Lehr* trilogy stands for the principle that a nonmarital father does not have a constitutional interest in his relationship with the child based on biological connection alone. Instead, as stated in *Lehr*, he has a constitutionally protected interest only if "he grasps" the opportunity to develop a relationship with the child and "accepts some measure of responsibility for the child's future" (the "biology plus test").

Notes and Questions on *Michael H.*

1. Factual epilogue. Victoria D. became a freelance fashion photographer in Santa Monica, California. Her parents, Gerald and Carole, residents of New York, are both deceased. Michael H., a resident of California and the Virgin Islands, passed away in 2013, in Marina Del Rey, California, at the age of 70.

2. Legal epilogue. California subsequently amended its parentage statutes. Today, a nonmarital, genetic father in California can seek to establish his parentage of a child born to a married woman if (1) he received the child into his home and held the child out as his own (that is, he is a "presumed parent"), *and*

[11]. *Lehr*, 463 U.S. at 262.

(2) he files and serves his action no later than the child's second birthday. Cal. Fam. Code §7541(b).

Today, state law varies on whether and under what circumstances a nonmarital, genetic father can seek to establish his parentage of a marital child. In some states, the nonmarital, genetic father may not be permitted to challenge the marital presumption (as was true in California at the time of the *Michael H.* litigation). In other states, such a challenge may be permitted so long as it is initiated within a designated period of time.

3. Reconciling *Michael H.* Can you reconcile *Michael H.* with *Stanley*? To what extent is *Michael H.* consistent with these earlier precedents? To what extent is *Michael H.* inconsistent with these precedents? With the other cases described in the above Note? Is footnote 3 in the plurality opinion persuasive? What is the rule governing the constitutional rights of nonmarital fathers after *Michael H.*?

According to Professor Janet Dolgin, familial relationships are the determinative variables in these cases. She explains the factors that give rise to a nonmarital father's constitutionally protected parent-child relationship are the man's biological relationship to the child, his social relationship with the child, and his relationship with the child's mother. She continues:

> In this regard, *Michael H.* clarifies the earlier cases. A biological father does protect his paternity by developing a social relationship with his child, but this step demands the creation of a family, a step itself depending upon an appropriate relationship between the man and his child's mother.[12]

4. Marital presumption redux. According to Justice Scalia, what is the purpose of the marital presumption? *Michael H.* suggests that the marital presumption was designed to preserve marital harmony and establish the marital family as the norm. What other purposes does it serve?

5. Must a state choose the husband? The question in *Michael H.* was whether California's rule—one that precluded a nonmarital, genetic parent from establishing his parentage of a marital child—was constitutional. The Supreme Court said that it was. The Court did not decide whether such a rule was constitutionally *required*. Thus, the decision does not *mandate* a rule that recognizes a husband over a claim by a biological parent. Is that result constitutionally required?

6. Competing presumptions. The parentage laws in many states would not dictate a clear result in a case like *Michael H.* Consider the original UPA. Under UPA (1973), both Gerald (the husband) and Michael (the genetic father) would be entitled to parentage presumptions: Gerald, because he was married to the child's mother and the child was born during their marriage, UPA (1973), §4(a)(1), and Michael because "he receive[d] the child into his home and held the child out

---

[12]. Janet L. Dolgin, Just a Gene: Judicial Assumptions About Parenthood, 40 UCLA L. Rev. 637, 671 (1993).

as his natural child." UPA (1973), §4(a)(4). In such cases, the UPA (1973) directs the court to determine which presumption "is founded on the weightier considerations of policy and logic." UPA (1973), §4(b). Under that rule, who should be recognized as Victoria's legal parent? Does this open-ended standard—"weightier considerations of policy and logic"—provide sufficient guidance to courts? To litigants?

The most recent version of the UPA—UPA (2017)—enumerates factors a court must consider in such cases, including the "length of time during which each individual assumed the role of parent of the child," "the nature of the relationship between the child and each individual," and "the harm to the child if the relationship between the child and each individual is not recognized." UPA (2017), §613(a). Under that standard, which of the two candidates—Gerald or Michael—should be recognized as Victoria's legal parent? Why? Which approach is better?

7. Weighing of factors. When assessing competing claims of parentage, how much weight should be given to the fact that a person is a child's genetic parent? To the fact that a person is married to the child's birth parent? How does UPA (2017) address these questions?

8. Parentage *disestablishment*. Some jurisdictions permit, by case law or statute, the *disestablishment* of parentage (for someone previously held to be a legal parent) based on evidence that the person is *not* a child's genetic parent. A man might seek disestablishment to evade child support obligations. If the man had already been determined to be a parent, and he had had an opportunity to obtain genetic testing in that previous judicial proceeding, is allowing subsequent disestablishment on this basis sound policy? Should it matter if the man has been assuming the role of parent to the child? After disestablishment, who becomes responsible for child support? Are there any circumstances that should cause a court to deny a disestablishment request based on genetic testing?

9. Multiple fathers. *Michael H.* is based on the assumption that a child may have, at most, a total of two parents, and, more specifically, only one father. Recall Justice Scalia's comment: "California law, like nature itself, makes no provision for dual fatherhood." What is the basis for this belief? Given the high divorce and separation rate, the remarriage rate, and increased use of assisted reproduction, does this assumption make sense?

Today, some states (including California) now expressly allow a court to find that a child has more than two legal parents. (The issue of multiparentage is discussed in more detail below.) This possibility is also provided for in UPA (2017). Under UPA (2017), §613, Alternative B, a court can find that a child has more than two parents "if failure to recognize more than two parents would be detrimental to the child." If *Michael H.* arose today under California law (which has adopted UPA (2017)), how should the case be decided?

UNIFORM PARENTAGE ACT (2017)

ARTICLE 2: PARENT-CHILD RELATIONSHIP

§201. ESTABLISHMENT OF PARENT-CHILD RELATIONSHIP

A parent-child relationship is established between an individual and a child if:

(1) the individual gives birth to the child [except as otherwise provided in Article 8];

(2) there is a presumption under Section 204 of the individual's parentage of the child, unless the presumption is overcome in a judicial proceeding or a valid denial of parentage is made under [Article 3];

(3) the individual is adjudicated a parent of the child under [Article 6];

(4) the individual adopts the child;

(5) the individual acknowledges parentage of the child under [Article 3], unless the acknowledgment is rescinded under Section 308 or successfully challenged under [Articles 3 or 6]; [or]

(6) the individual's parentage of the child is established under [Article 7]; or

(7) the individual's parentage of the child is established under [Article 8].

§204. PRESUMPTION OF PARENTAGE

(a) An individual is presumed to be a parent of a child if:

(1) except as otherwise provided under [Article 8 or] law of this state other than this [act]:

(A) the individual and the woman who gave birth to the child are married to each other and the child is born during the marriage, whether the marriage is or could be declared invalid;

(B) the individual and the woman who gave birth to the child were married to each other and the child is born not later than 300 days after the marriage is terminated by death, [divorce, dissolution, annulment, or declaration of invalidity, or after a decree of separation or separate maintenance], whether the marriage is or could be declared invalid; or

(C) the individual and the woman who gave birth to the child married each other after the birth of the child, whether the marriage is or could be declared invalid, the individual at any time asserted parentage of the child, and:

(i) the assertion is in a record filed with the [state agency maintaining birth records]; or

(ii) the individual agreed to be and is named as a parent of the child on the birth certificate of the child; or

(2) the individual resided in the same household with the child for the first two years of the life of the child, including any period of temporary absence, and openly held out the child as the individual's child.

(b) A presumption of parentage under this section may be overcome, and competing claims to parentage may be resolved, only by an adjudication under [Article] 6 or a valid denial of parentage under [Article] 3.

§607. ADJUDICATING PARENTAGE OF A CHILD WITH ALLEGED GENETIC PARENT

. . .

(b) [I]f the woman who gave birth to the child is the only other individual with a claim to parentage of the child[, t]he court shall adjudicate an alleged parent to be a parent of the child if the alleged genetic parent [has been identified as the genetic parent or the court determines the alleged genetic parent to be a parent of the child];

(c) [I]f in a proceeding involving an alleged genetic parent, at least one other individual in addition to the woman who gave birth to the child has a claim to parentage of the child, the court shall adjudicate parentage under Section 613.

§608. ADJUDICATING PARENTAGE OF CHILD WITH PRESUMED PARENT

. . .

(b) A presumption of parentage under section 204 cannot be overcome after the child attains two years of age unless the court determines:

(1) the presumed parent is not a genetic parent, never resided with the child, and never held out the child as the presumed parent's child; or

(2) the child has more than one presumed parent.

[Subsections (c) and (d) then provide that if the presumed parent is not the child's genetic parent, the court shall adjudicate the parentage of the presumed parent based on the best interest of the child under Section 613.]

§609. ADJUDICATING COMPETING CLAIMS OF PARENTAGE

. . .

(d) In a proceeding to adjudicate parentage of an individual who claims to be a de facto parent of the child, if there is only one other individual who is a parent or has a claim to parentage of the child, the court shall adjudicate the individual who claims to be a de facto parent to be a parent of the child if the individual demonstrates by clear-and-convincing evidence that:

(1) the individual resided with the child as a regular member of the child's household for a significant period;

(2) the individual engaged in consistent caretaking of the child;

(3) the individual undertook full and permanent responsibilities of a parent of the child without expectation of financial compensation;

(4) the individual held out the child as the individual's child'

(5) the individual established a bonded and dependent relationship with the child which is parental in nature;

(6) another parent of the child fostered or supported the bonded and dependent relationship required under paragraph (5); and

(7) continuing the relationship between the individual and the child is in the best interest of the child.

(e) [I]f in a proceeding to adjudicate parentage of an individual who claims to be a de facto parent of the child, there is more than one other individual who is a parent or has a claim to parentage of the child and the court determines that the requirements of subsection (d) are satisfied, the court shall adjudicate parentage under Section 613.

§613. ADJUDICATING COMPETING CLAIMS OF PARENTAGE

(a) [I]n a proceeding to adjudicate competing claims of [parentage between individuals who are presumed parents, individuals who meet the de facto parent requirements, and/or individuals who have been identified as genetic parents], . . ., the court shall adjudicate parentage in the best interest of the child, based on:

(1) the age of the child;

(2) the length of time during which each individual assumed the role of parent of the child;

(3) the nature of the relationship between the child and each individual;

(4) the harm to the child if the relationship between the child and each individual is not recognized;

(5) the basis for each individual's claim to parentage of the child; and

(6) other equitable factors arising from the disruption of the relationship between the child and each individual or the likelihood of other harm to the child.

(b) If an individual challenges parentage based on the results of genetic testing, in addition to the factors listed in subsection (a), the court shall consider:

(1) the facts surrounding the discovery the individual might not be a genetic parent of the child; and

(2) the length of time between the time that the individual was placed on notice that the individual might not be a genetic parent and the commencement of the proceeding.

Alternative A

(c) The court may not adjudicate a child to have more than two parents under this [act].

Alternative B

(c) The court may adjudicate a child to have more than two parents under this [act] if the court finds that failure to recognize more than two parents would be detrimental to the child. A finding of detriment to the child does not require a finding of unfitness of any parent or individual seeking an adjudication of parentage. In determining detriment to the child, the court shall consider all relevant factors, including the harm if the child is removed from a stable placement with an individual who has fulfilled the child's physical needs and psychological needs for care and affection and has assumed the role for a substantial period.

Problems

1. When Stephanie marries Jeffrey, she is not motivated by love, but by a desire to obtain military benefits and to share rent. Thereafter, Stephanie begins an intimate relationship with Paul and eventually gives birth to Paul's biological child. Before the birth, Stephanie and Paul move in together. During the two years that they live together, Paul holds the child out as his son. Subsequently, Stephanie and Paul break up. At that time, Stephanie lies to Paul, telling him that he might not be the father. Paul files suit to establish parentage. Stephanie opposes his lawsuit, alleging that Jeffrey is the child's father based on the marital presumption. What result under the UPA (2017) if the court can only recognize one of the men as a legal parent? See *Comino v. Kelley*, 30 Cal. Rptr. 2d 728 (Ct. App. 1994).

2. Sally married Martin and had a son. Four years later, Sally and Martin separated for almost 18 months. During the estrangement, Sally began dating Walter. Sarah soon became pregnant with Walter's child and gave birth to a daughter (Debra). However, by the time of Debra's birth, Sally had reconciled with Martin. Sally told Walter that he was not Debra's father. Instead, she let Martin believe that Debra was his child. After Debra's birth, Martin helped with all of Debra's childcare — changing her, feeding her, washing her laundry, rocking her to sleep, playing with her, and taking her to medical appointments.

When Debra was several months old, a DNA test confirmed that Walter was her biological father. Sally told Walter but kept that fact from Martin, who continued to co-parent Debra. During the first few years of Debra's life, Sally brought Debra to visit Walter about once or twice a week for brief visits (one to two hours). Debra stayed overnight at Walter's apartment only three or four times during her few years. When Debra went to visit Walter, Sally remarked (based on the fact that Walter hid the child's toys) that Walter did not disclose the fact that Debra was his daughter to most of his friends and relatives.

When Debra was five years old, Sally decided to tell Martin about Debra's parentage. Martin was very upset and initiated divorce proceedings, but he and Sally later reconciled. After learning about Sally's second reconciliation with Martin, Walter filed a petition requesting joint legal and physical custody as well as visitation rights, contending that he was Debra's biological father. Martin countered that Debra had been born during Sally's marriage to him while the couple was living together. How should the case be decided under the different versions of the UPA? See *W.S. v. S.T.*, 228 Cal. Rptr. 3d 756 (Ct. App. 2018).

5. Assisted Reproduction

a. Intended Parents

John LaRose, 6 Things to Know About the U.S. Fertility Clinics Industry

Market Research Blog, Dec. 10, 2018
https://blog.marketresearch.com/top-6-things-to-know-about-the-u.s.-fertility-clinics-industry

[T]he fertility clinics industry in the United States is booming, thanks to growing demand from American couples that have delayed childbearing, more widespread acceptance of fertility treatment and usage by gay couples, improved success rates, a strong economy, and significant demand from medical tourists coming from Europe and China. The industry is fragmented, largely untapped, and is ripe for consolidation.

The number of Assisted Reproductive Technology (ART) cycles performed by U.S. fertility clinics has risen strongly since 2014 and is estimated to total a record 333,600 IVF procedures this year, with demand still growing from the ranks of 7+ million infertile American women.

However, the high price of IVF cycles ($12,400 each cycle, sometimes requiring multiple cycles), plus fertility drugs, exams and diagnostic tests, deters many. The total price tag can top $50,000 or more. And fertility clinics tend to be located in large metro areas, so accessibility is an issue for rural patients. Only 15 states mandate insurance coverage, so most pay out-of-pocket.

6 Key Facts About the Fertility Clinics Industry:

- Marketdata estimates that the U.S. infertility services market will reach $5.87 billion this year, up 21% from 2016. Marketdata forecasts 7.0% average annual growth in revenues through 2023, to $7.93 billion.
- The market is comprised of about 500 fertility clinics, 100+ sperm donor banks, the egg donor market, fertility drugs, and 1,700 reproductive endocrinologists—all competing for the business. ART/IVF procedures performed by fertility clinics are worth $4.1 billion of the total.
- This market is largely untapped, as 75% of potential clients are not using infertility services. Only 15% of U.S. women have used fertility drugs, only 5.5% have tried artificial insemination, and just 1% have used IVF.
- The global market for fertility drugs is worth $976 million. The U.S. market is worth $600-700 million, and is a mature market segment growing 6% annually. As IVF procedures' success rates improve, less of these medications are needed.
- Only one "chain" of fertility clinics, IntegraMed, exists, as most programs are small regional operations or are part of a hospital or University. Most are privately owned. IntegraMed operates some of the industry's top fertility clinics—capturing 7.6% of market revenues.
- The egg donor/frozen eggs market is growing strongly, estimated to be worth $182 million this year, propped up by high demand from non-U.S. patients in Europe and the Middle East.

ADOPTION OF ANONYMOUS
74 Misc. 2d 99 (N.Y. Surr. Ct. 1973)

SOBEL, Surrogate. . . .

The issue in this proceeding is one of first impression in this or any other jurisdiction. The problem however has been with the courts since the first utilization by the medical profession of artificial insemination.

As a preliminary, there are two types of artificial insemination. Homologous insemination is the process by which the wife is artificially impregnated with the semen of her husband. This procedure is referred to as AIH (Artificial Insemination Husband) and creates no legal problems since the child is considered the natural child of the husband and wife. Heterologous insemination is the artificial insemination of the wife by the semen of a third party donor. This procedure is referred to as AID (Artificial Insemination Donor). AID may be "consensual" i.e. with the consent of the husband or "nonconsensual" i.e. without his consent. . . . As yet the legislatures and the courts have been unresponsive in declaring the status and rights of AID children.

The facts in this proceeding are briefly stated. During the marriage the child was born of consensual AID. The husband was listed as the father on the birth certificate. Later the couple separated and the separation was followed by a divorce. Both the separation agreement and the divorce decree declare the child to be the "daughter" and "child" of the couple. The wife was granted support and the husband visitation rights. He has faithfully visited and performed all the support conditions of the decree. The wife later remarried and her new husband is petitioning to adopt the child. The first husband has refused his consent. Confronted with that legal impediment, the petitioner has suggested that the first husband's consent is not required since he is not the "parent" of the child.

The [adoption] statute . . . requires the consent of both "parents" of a child born in wedlock. There are circumstances in which consent may be dispensed with (abandonment, insanity, divorce for adultery, etc.) but none are present here. If the husband is the 'parent' of a child born of consensual AID, in the absence of his consent to the adoption, the petition must be dismissed.

[V]ery few states have enacted statutes governing the status and rights of AID children. [The] only reported decision by an appellate court [is People v. Sorensen[, 437 P.2d 495 (Cal. 1968)]. Sorensen was a criminal prosecution on complaint of the welfare authorities against the husband for failure to support a minor child born during the marriage of consensual AID. The California Supreme Court without dissent held: the defendant is the lawful father of a dependent child born of consensual AID; that the term "father" as used in the penal statute is not limited to a biologic[al] or natural father; the determinative factor is whether the *legal* relationship of father and child exists. The Court reasoned that a child conceived through AID does not have a "natural" father; that the anonymous donor is not the "natural" father; that he does have a "lawful" father and the intent of the legislature was to include a lawful father in the penal sanctions; further that

> In light of these principles of statutory construction, a reasonable man who, because of his inability to procreate, actively participates and consents to his wife's artificial insemination in the hope that a child will be produced whom they will treat as their own, knows that such behavior carries with it the legal responsibilities of fatherhood and criminal responsibility for nonsupport. One who consents to the production of a child cannot create a temporary relation to be assumed and disclaimed at will, but the arrangement must be of such character as to impose an obligation of supporting those for whose existence he is directly responsible.

This is the principle of equitable estoppel found in several other cases. [The court next rejected the idea that the use of AID constitutes adultery.] As respects the legitimacy of the child:

> Nor are we persuaded that the concept of legitimacy demands that the child be the actual offspring of the husband of the mother and if semen of some other male is utilized[,] the resulting child is illegitimate.

The leading case in New York and the only one which discusses the issue, is Gursky v. Gursky [242 N.Y.S.2d 406 (1963)]. The husband sued the wife for separation and despite the birth of a child to them by consensual AID, he alleged that there were no issue of the marriage. The wife counterclaimed for annulment [and sought child support].

[There, the court found that the child was] not the legitimate issue of the husband. This conclusion was premised on (a) "The concept which historically is deeply imbedded in the law is that a child who is begotten through a father who is not the mother's husband is deemed to be illegitimate"; (b) on the statutory definition of a "child born out of wedlock" as a child who is "begotten and born out of lawful matrimony"; (c) on the failure of the legislature to enact statutes legalizing the status of AID children. . . .

At the outset, it is observed that *Gursky* is not persuasive. . . . It has been criticized. The "historical concept" and the statutory definition of "a child born out of wedlock" upon which it relies were developed and enacted long before the advent of the practice of artificial insemination. The birth of AID children was not then contemplated. An AID child is not "begotten" by a father who is not the husband; the donor is anonymous; the wife does not have sexual intercourse or commit adultery with him; if there is any "begetting" it is by the doctor who in this specialty is often a woman. The suggestion that the husband might not regard the child as his own has been dispelled by our gratifying experience with adoptive parents. Since there is consent by the husband, there is no marital infidelity. The child is not born "out of wedlock" but in and during wedlock. . . .

The two cases discussed represent all the decisional law on the subject. This is not much in the way of precedent since the issues in both cases were limited by the nature of each proceeding. Basically the problem of the status of AID children vis-a-vis the "father" is one of policy. Policy is best made by our appellate courts. . . .

New York has a strong policy in favor of legitimacy. [Under a recently enacted New York statute,] a child born of a void or voidable marriage, even if the marriage is deliberately and knowingly bigamous, incestuous or adulterous, is legitimate and entitled to all the rights (inheritance, support, etc.) of a child born during a perfectly valid marriage. In the face of the liberal policy expressed by such a statute, it would seem absurd to hold illegitimate a child born during a valid marriage, of parents desiring but unable to conceive a child, and both consenting and agreeing to the impregnation of the mother by a carefully and medically selected anonymous donor.

It must be recognized that there exist moral and religious objections to artificial insemination. But . . . our liberal policy is for the protection of the child, not the parents. It serves no purpose whatsoever to stigmatize the AID child; or to compel the parents formally to adopt in order to confer upon the AID child the status and rights of a naturally conceived child.

It is determined that a child born of consensual AID during a valid marriage is a legitimate child entitled to the rights and privileges of a naturally conceived child of the same marriage. The father of such child is therefore the 'parent' whose consent is required to the adoption of such child by another. . . .

Notes and Questions

1. Holding and rationale. What is the holding in this case? Who are the parents? What is the court's rationale for reaching that conclusion?

2. Reasons for using assisted reproduction. Assisted reproduction may be used when couples experience either medical or social infertility. "Medical infertility" refers to medical conditions that inhibit a couple's ability to achieve pregnancy without assistance. Medical infertility affects 10 to 15 percent of different-sex couples.[13] The rates are even higher for Black women. "Social infertility" refers to situations where a person lacks a partner who can provide the needed gamete. Same-sex couples and single people may experience social infertility.

3. Insurance coverage. Fertility care can be costly. Even when insurance coverage is available, it often covers only people who are medically infertile. See, e.g., Tex. Ins. Code Ann. §1366.005 (requiring insurance coverage only if the in vitro fertilization (IVF) procedure is used to fertilize "the patient's oocytes . . . with the sperm of the patient's spouse"). But cf. Cal. Health & Safety Code §1374.55; Cal. Ins. Code §10119.6 (requiring insurers to offer coverage for infertility treatment without discrimination based on sexual orientation and gender identity). Is that fair? In August 2023, two lawsuits, one in New York on behalf of the National Organization for Women - New York City and one in Massachusetts on behalf of a class of veterans, were filed against the Department of Veterans Affairs challenging the department's policy regarding infertility coverage, which is limited to married different-sex couples.

4. Early statutory developments. In 1973, the time of the principal case, few states governed the parentage of children conceived through assisted reproduction. Today, most states have some statutes. Often, however, the statutes only address children born to married couples and are written in gendered terms.[14] See, e.g., Minn. Stat. Ann. §257.56(a) ("If, under the supervision of a licensed physician and with the consent of her husband, a wife is inseminated artificially with semen donated by a man not her husband, the husband is treated in law as if he were the biological father of a child thereby conceived. The husband's consent must be in writing and signed by him and his wife.") (based on UPA (1973)).

5. Assisted reproduction and unmarried couples. In states with marriage-only assisted reproduction statutes, most courts have held they do not apply to children born to unmarried couples. See, e.g., Herman v. Lennon, 3 Misc. 3d 873 (N.Y. Sup. 2004); Doe v. Doe, 395 P.3d 1287, 1291 (Idaho 2017) ("The plain language of

---

[13]. Am. Soc'y for Reprod. Med., Fact Sheet, Defining Infertility, https://www.reproductivefacts.org/news-and-publications/patient-fact-sheets-and-booklets/documents/fact-sheets-and-info-booklets/defining-infertility/. See also Ctrs. for Disease Control & Prevention (CDC), FastStats — Infertility (July 15, 2016) (reporting that about 12 percent of women of reproductive age have used infertility services), https://www.cdc.gov/nchs/fastats/infertility.htm.

[14]. See, e.g., NeJaime, supra note [1].

the statute simply does not address a situation like at issue here where a child is conceived through artificial insemination by an unmarried couple."). Often, that means the partner is not a legal parent. As a nonlegal parent, the partner may have no right to seek custody, or, conversely, no obligation to provide support. What reasons justify limiting assisted reproduction statutes to married couples?

6. Law reform. Some assisted reproduction statutes cover all children born through assisted reproduction, regardless of the marital status or sex of the intended parents. See, e.g., Conn. Gen. Stat. Ann. §46b-511 ("*A person* who consents . . . to assisted reproduction by another person with the intent to be a parent of a child conceived by the assisted reproduction is a parent of the child.") (emphasis added). In addition to removing the marriage-based limitation, the Connecticut scheme (enacted in 2021) eliminates the requirements included in the UPA (1973) that the insemination be supervised by a physician and the requirement of written consent. Why did the UPA (1973) include these requirements? Why eliminate them?

UNIFORM PARENTAGE ACT (1973)

§5. ARTIFICIAL INSEMINATION

(a) If, under the supervision of a licensed physician and with the consent of her husband, a wife is inseminated artificially with semen donated by a man not her husband, the husband is treated in law as if he were the natural father of a child thereby conceived. The husband's consent must be in writing and signed by him and his wife. . . .

(b) The donor of semen provided to a licensed physician for use in artificial insemination of a married woman other than the donor's wife is treated in law as if he were not the natural father of a child thereby conceived.

UNIFORM PARENTAGE ACT (2017)

ARTICLE 7. ASSISTED REPRODUCTION

§703. PARENTAGE OF CHILD OF ASSISTED REPRODUCTION.

An individual who consents under Section 704 to assisted reproduction by a woman with the intent to be a parent of a child conceived by the assisted reproduction is a parent of the child.

§704. CONSENT TO ASSISTED REPRODUCTION.

(a) Except as otherwise provided in subsection (b), the consent described in Section 703 must be in a record signed by a woman giving birth to a child conceived by assisted reproduction and an individual who intends to be a parent of the child.

(b) (1) Failure to consent in a record as required by subsection (a), before, on, or after birth of the child does not preclude the court from finding consent to parentage if the woman or the individual proves by clear-and-convincing evidence the existence of an express agreement entered into before conception that the individual and the woman intended they both would be parents of the child[.]

Problems

1. Angie and Kami are a married, same-sex couple who decide to have a child through assisted reproduction using sperm from an unknown donor. With Angie's knowledge and consent, Kami becomes pregnant through assisted reproduction performed at the University of Utah School of Medicine. Prior to the procedure, both women sign a document entitled "Donor Semen Storage Agreement," which acknowledged the use of donor sperm; the document identified Angie as Kami's wife. After Kami gave birth, the two signed another document "memorializing, ratifying, and reaffirming Angie's consent for Kami to conceive with the assistance of donor semen." After the birth of the child, Utah refuses to recognize Angie as a legal parent of the child or to identify her as one of the child's parents on the child's birth certificate. Angie files a lawsuit seeking a determination that she is a legal parent. Assume that the state's law is based on UPA (1973). What result, and why? See Roe v. Patton, 2015 WL 4476734 (D. Utah 2015). But see In re A.E., 2017 WL 1535101 (Tex. Ct. App. 2017).

2. At the time Alexis and "Jim Richardson" begin dating, Jim tells Alexis that he was divorced. During their 10-year nonmarital relationship, the parties discuss marriage and having children. After discovering that they are unable to conceive through sexual intercourse, Jim suggests assisted reproduction. He pays for the procedure and helps choose a sperm donor, but he never signs a written consent form. Alexis becomes pregnant and gives birth to twin boys. Jim helps choose their names; he holds the child out as his own; he provides monthly support payments; and pays for food, clothing, and toys. The four go on family vacations together, and Jim pays for the children's medical, travel, and entertainment expenses. When the children are 10, Alexis ends their relationship after discovering that Jim is actually named "Raymond" and that he is married to another woman. Alexis files an action seeking a determination that Jim/Raymond is a parent and ordering him to provide child support. Jim/Raymond opposes the action, arguing that the statute, which is based on UPA (1973), applies only to married, intended parents and requires written consent. What result, and why? In re Parentage of M.J., 787 N.E.2d 144 (Ill. 2003). Should Jim/Raymond be recognized as a parent? Should he be obligated to support the children?

NOTE: POSTHUMOUS CONCEPTION

There have always been some children who were born after the death of a parent (posthumous birth). Assisted reproductive technology makes it possible for a child to be *conceived* after the death of the parent (posthumous conception). This could happen, for example, if a couple created embryos using their own gametes and the woman uses the embryos after the death of the male partner. When this happens, there may be a question of whether the deceased male partner should be treated as the child's legal parent. The issue may be relevant for purposes of intestate succession or access to government benefits, such as children's Social Security survivor benefits.

The law in many states does not address this issue. Where state law exists, it typically provides that the man is not a legal parent unless he agreed in writing to be a parent if his gametes were used after his death. See, e.g., La. Rev. Stat. Ann. §9:391.1(A) (providing that the husband must have "specifically authorized in writing his surviving spouse to use his gametes"); Tex. Fam. Code Ann. §160.707 (deceased must consent "in a record kept by a licensed physician that if assisted reproduction were to occur after death the deceased spouse would be a parent of the child"). See also UPA (2017), §708(b)(1) (providing that the person is not a parent unless, prior to their death, they "consented in a record that if assisted reproduction were to occur after the death of the individual, the individual would be a parent," or where "the individual's intent to be a parent of a child conceived by assisted reproduction after the individual's death is established by clear-and-convincing evidence."). Relevant laws also generally place a time limit on the length of time between the death and the child's birth. See, e.g., La. Rev. Stat. Ann. §9:391.1(A) (3 years); Iowa Code Ann. §633.220A (2 years).

Questions may also arise about a surviving spouse or partner's right to use a deceased person's gametes after their death. Here too, few state statutes exist. In the absence of statutory direction, some courts have considered whether a court should grant a request to retrieve gametes from the body of a deceased person for purposes of future use in assisted reproduction. See Matter of Zhu, 103 N.Y.S.3d 775 (App. Div. 2019) (request filed by parents after the death of their son in a skiing accident). Some courts have also considered whether a deceased person has a testamentary right of disposition over his or her genetic material. See, e.g., Hecht v. Superior Court, 20 Cal. Rptr. 2d 275 (Ct. App. 1993) (holding that decedent's interest in his cryogenically preserved sperm was "property" over which probate court had jurisdiction).

b. Gamete Providers

IN RE M.F.
938 N.E.2d 1256 (Ind. Ct. App. 2010)

FRIEDLANDER, Judge. . . .

[Mother was in a long-term relationship with another woman, referred to here as Life Partner. The women wanted to have a child. A male friend, referred to here as Father, agreed to provide sperm for assisted reproduction. Mother got pregnant and gave birth to a child, M. F. A few weeks before M. F.'s birth,] the parties signed an agreement (the Donor Agreement) prepared by counsel for Mother [that] contained the following provisions:

6. Waiver and Release by Mother. Mother hereby waives all rights to child support and financial assistance from Donor. . . .
7. Waiver and Release by Donor. Donor hereby waives all rights to custody of or visitation with such child. . . .
8. Mutual Covenant Not to Sue. Mother and Donor mutually agree to forever refrain from initiating, pressing, or in any way aiding or proceeding upon

an action to establish legal paternity of the child due to be born on or about September 19, 1996.

[Mother later asked Father to provide sperm for a second child. He agreed, and C. F. was born seven years later.] Mother and Life Partner's relationship ended sometime around 2008, when the [two] children were approximately twelve and five years old, respectively. [When Mother sought public assistance, the county prosecutor filed, on her behalf, a petition to establish Father's paternity for purposes of obtaining child support. Father cited the Donor Agreement as his defense. Although DNA evidence established Father's paternity, the trial court denied Mother's petition (by the county welfare agency) to establish his paternity, based on contract grounds. This appeal followed.

The court points out that other states have resolved child support issues in the context of artificial insemination by resort to state versions of the Uniform Parentage Act — particularly the UPA provision (reprinted below) specifying that a donor who provides sperm "to a licensed physician for use in artificial fertilization" is not the child's natural parent.]

[B]oth Mother and Father appear to concede that the viability of the Donor Agreement in the instant case depends upon the manner in which insemination occurred. [According to our prior case law], if insemination occurred via intercourse, the Donor Agreement would be unenforceable as against public policy (citing Straub v. B.M.T., 645 N.E.2d 597 (Ind. 1994)). . . . Thus, an apparently complicated issue can be boiled down to simple legal question — who bore the burden of proof [on the method of conception]?

In this case, the parties entered into a facially valid contract whereby Mother agreed that she would not seek to establish paternity of M.F. in Father. Mother seeks to invalidate that Donor Agreement on the ground that the manner of insemination renders the Donor Agreement void as against public policy. As such, she seeks to avoid the contract. We conclude that this case is governed by the rule providing that a party that seeks to avoid a contract bears the burden of proof on matters of avoidance. . . . Thus, Mother bore the burden of proving that [conception occurred by intercourse, not artificial insemination, in turn rendering] the Donor Agreement unenforceable. [We] can find no indication of the manner in which Mother was inseminated with respect to the first pregnancy. . . . Therefore, Mother failed to prove that insemination [occurred] in such a way as to render the Donor Agreement unenforceable and void as against public policy. [Hence,] the trial court did not err in denying her petition to establish paternity with respect to M.F.

We pause at this point to make several observations about [an] area of concern expressed by the dissent, i.e., the formalities of the contract itself. Specifically, we address our colleague's concern that our holding today might enable parties to easily escape the responsibility of supporting one's biological child [by] concocting an informal, spur-of-the-moment written instrument whereby the biological mother and father agree that the father is absolved of any responsibility in connection with the child. [W]e do not mean to sanction the view that a writing consisting of a few lines scribbled on the back of a scrap of paper found lying about will suffice in this kind of case. To the contrary, the instrument in question must reflect the parties' careful consideration of the implications of such an agreement and a thorough understanding of its meaning and import. The Donor Agreement in the instant case easily meets these requirements. . . .

The Donor Agreement itself is a six-page, twenty-four-paragraph document [prepared by counsel] that covers in detail matters such as acknowledgment of rights and obligations, waiver, mutual consent not to sue, a consent to adopt, a hold-harmless clause, mediation and arbitration, penalties for failure to comply, amending the agreement, severability, a four-corners clause, and a choice-of-laws provision. [P]arties who execute a contract less formal and thorough than this one do so at their own peril.

Although we have affirmed the trial court's order with respect to M.F., we address sua sponte an issue not separately presented by the parties, i.e., the correctness of the order denying the petition to establish paternity with respect to the second child, C.F. In its order, the trial court found: "Shortly before the birth of the first child, the mother and Respondent entered into a written agreement stating that the Respondent would not be responsible for the child and any further children which might result from the Respondent's donated sperm." The highlighted language reflects the trial court's determination that the Donor Agreement applied to C.F. as well as M.F. We conclude this construction of the Donor Agreement is erroneous.

The Donor Agreement provided as follows . . .

2. Donor has provided his semen to Mother for the purpose of inseminating Mother, and as a result, Mother has become pregnant and is expected to give birth on or about September 19, 1996. . . .

Throughout the remainder of the Donor Agreement, the product of insemination, i.e., the subject of the Donor Agreement, is referred to as either "the child" or "such child." [Because of the specificity of the reference, this contract] cannot be construed to apply to future children conceived as a result of artificial insemination involving Mother and Father. Therefore, the trial court erred in holding that a valid, enforceable contract existed that would prohibit an action to establish paternity of C.F. in Father. In view of the fact that DNA testing established, and Father concedes, that he is the biological father of C.F., this cause is remanded with instructions to grant Mother's petition to establish paternity with respect to C.F. . . .

CRONE, Judge, concurring in part and dissenting in part:
. . . I agree with the majority [that] assisted conception contracts might be enforceable in Indiana in certain circumstances. I would hold that those circumstances must be extremely limited. . . . At the very least, an assisted conception contract should provide that a donor's semen must be given to a licensed physician and that the artificial insemination must be performed by (or at least under the supervision of) the physician. Such a provision would both impress upon the parties the seriousness of their endeavor and safeguard the health of everyone involved. [Physician involvement can also create a formal, documented structure for the donor-recipient relationship, preventing misunderstandings between the parties.] I believe that such prerequisites to finding a valid exception to the general obligation to support would be consistent with [our precedents]. . . .

UNIFORM PARENTAGE ACT (1973)

§5. ARTIFICIAL INSEMINATION

. . .

(b) The donor of semen provided to a licensed physician for use in artificial insemination of a married woman other than the donor's wife is treated in law as if he were not the natural father of a child thereby conceived.

UNIFORM PARENTAGE ACT (2017)

ARTICLE 1. GENERAL PROVISIONS

§102. DEFINITIONS

. . .

(9) "Donor" means an individual who provides gametes intended for use in assisted reproduction, whether or not for consideration. . . .

(10) "Gamete" means sperm, egg, or any part of a sperm or egg. . . .

ARTICLE 7. ASSISTED REPRODUCTION

§702. PARENTAL STATUS OF DONOR

A donor is not a parent of a child conceived by assisted reproduction.

Notes and Questions

1. Background. "Mother" in the principal case asked a male friend to provide sperm for her use. Why might she have preferred this option over using an unknown donor through a sperm bank? What are the advantages and disadvantages of using a known donor? (A vial of sperm from a sperm bank typically costs more than $1,000 today.)

2. Holding and rationale. In *M.F.*, the state had no statutes regarding the legal status of sperm donors. What rule did the court develop? What was the result under that rule? Does that result seem correct? Fair? Why did the prior written agreement in *M.F.* prevent establishment of the man's parentage regarding one child, but not the other? What are the implications of this finding?

3. Statutory developments. Many states have statutes governing the legal status of gamete providers in at least some circumstances. Some statutes are based on UPA (1973), excerpted above. What result if that provision had been applied in *M.F.*? What result in *M.F.* under UPA (2017)? Which rule is better? Although the donor non-parentage provision of the original UPA (cited in *M.F.*) required physician participation, the revised version abandons this requirement. UPA (2017), §702.

4. Means of conception and intent. Under UPA (2017) and the law of some states, the legal status of the gamete provider turns on intent: if the parties did not intend the gamete donor to be a parent, the donor is not a parent. See UPA (2017), §702. In contrast, if a child is conceived through sexual intercourse, the man who supplied the sperm will likely be considered a parent and accorded parental rights and responsibilities, even if the parties agreed to the contrary. Should the means of conception matter in determining legal parentage?[15]

5. Single women and donor insemination. Under some state statutes, a single woman can be the only legal parent of a child born through assisted reproduction. Some courts have also reached this conclusion in states without relevant statutes. Ferguson v. McKiernan, 940 A.2d 1236 (Pa. 2007). What interests and policies explain this result? While protecting donors and facilitating choices by prospective parents, do such results undermine the interests of children? Some scholars think so. See, e.g., Marsha Garrison, Law Making for Baby Making: An Interpretive Approach to the Determination of Legal Parentage, 113 Harv. L. Rev. 835 (2000).

6. Legal regulation of sperm banks. Federal law mandates only minimal regulation of sperm banks (i.e., requiring information about success rates and requiring screening/testing donors for certain diseases, such as HIV, hepatitis B and C, and other sexually transmitted diseases (STDs)). Fertility Clinic Success Rate and Certification Act (FCSRCA) of 1992, 42 U.S.C. §§263a-1 to 8.

a. Discrimination. In the past, some health care providers refused to provide fertility care to lesbian, gay, bisexual, transgender, and queer/questioning (LGBTQ) people. Some lawsuits challenged these practices. See, e.g., North Coast Women's Care Med. Grp. v. Superior Court, 189 P.3d 959 (Cal. 2008); Benitez v. North Coast Women's Care Med. Grp., 131 Cal. Rptr. 2d 364 (Ct. App. 2003).

b. Litigation. The lack of governmental regulation has led to lawsuits alleging inadequate screening of donors (Zelt v. Xytex, 766 Fed. Appx. 735 (11th Cir. 2019)); the use of gametes without informed consent (Rousseau v. Coates, 2019 WL 3220327 (D. Vt. 2019)); and switching donors' genetic material.[16] How should these lawsuits be decided? What is the nature of the "injury" in each of the preceding cases?

c. Law reform. Legislatures in a few states have passed laws to provide criminal and/or civil penalties for various types of fraud in the fertility care process. One specific type of alleged fraud is where the treating doctor used his own sperm without the patient's knowledge or consent. See, e.g., Utah Code Ann. §76-7-402 (third-degree felony for fertility care provider to knowingly use his own semen without the patient's consent).[17]

---

[15]. See, e.g., Courtney Megan Cahill, Reproduction Reconceived, 101 Minn. L. Rev. 617, 619 (2016) (challenging "reproductive binarism, the belief that sexual and alternative reproduction are essentially different in fact and therefore deserve different treatment in law").

[16]. See, e.g., Dov Fox, Reproductive Negligence, 117 Colum. L. Rev. 149 (2017).

[17]. Alyssa Lukpat, Fertility Doctor Accused of Using His Own Sperm Is Ordered to Pay Millions, N.Y. Times, Apr. 28, 2022, https://www.nytimes.com/2022/04/28/us/paul-jones-fertility-settlement-colorado.html.

d. Comparative perspective. Some countries impose more oversight on fertility service providers. For example, in the United Kingdom, a national agency oversees fertility clinics. The Human Fertilization and Embryology Authority, created in 1990, conducts regular inspections of fertility centers, imposes corrective measures, and publicizes all regulatory actions. Should the United States adopt a similar regulatory regime?

7. Disclosure of information regarding gamete donors. In the past, gamete providers were often assured anonymity. The advent of consumer genetic testing has challenged this practice. People conceived using donated gametes and their families have utilized genetic testing and other means to identify their gamete providers, as well as other children conceived using gametes from the same provider.[18] Recently, some advocates have pushed for laws regulating the disclosure of information about gamete providers.

Article 9 of the UPA (2017) addresses this by requiring the collection and retention of both medical and identifying information regarding gamete providers. UPA (2017), §903 (collection); §906 (recordkeeping). Article 9 requires sperm banks and fertility centers to provide all non-identifying medical information about the gamete provider to recipient parents upon request at any time. UPA (2017), §905(b). Article 9 also requires the disclosure of the gamete providers' identifying information upon request by the child once they are 18 if the gamete provider agreed to the disclosure of this information. UPA (2017), §905(a). Evaluate the benefits and shortcomings of these provisions.

c. Surrogacy

P.M. v. T.B.
907 N.W.2d 522 (Iowa 2018)

WATERMAN, Justice.

[W]e must decide a question of first impression: whether gestational surrogacy contracts are enforceable under Iowa law. . . . The plaintiffs, the intended parents, are a married couple unable to conceive their own child. . . . P.M. and C.M. were high school sweethearts but parted ways when P.M. joined the Navy upon graduation. After marrying and divorcing other spouses, they reconnected and married each other in 2013. . . . The Ms were nearing age fifty and wanted to have a child together. C.M. was no longer able to conceive, so the Ms placed an advertisement on Craigslist in 2015 seeking a woman willing to act as a surrogate mother.

[Ultimately, they signed a contract on January 5, 2016, with T. B. and her husband, D. B. The wife, T. B., has four children from a prior marriage but her husband, D. B., has no children and had never been married. They wanted the

---

[18]. See, e.g., Eli Baden-Lasar, I'm 20. I Have 32 Half Siblings. This Is My Family Portrait, N.Y. Times Mag., June 26, 2019, https://www.nytimes.com/interactive/2019/06/26/magazine/sperm -donor-siblings.html.

money for their own fertility services because, although T. B. could carry a child, she could not conceive one with her husband D. B. and their insurance would not cover infertility treatment or IVF.]

[The] Ms selected Midwest Fertility Clinic (Midwest) in Downers Grove, Illinois, to perform the IVF and embryo transfers. Midwest required a written contract between the parties, so the Ms hired a lawyer to draft the agreement. . . . In exchange for the gestational service, the Ms agreed to pay up to $13,000 for an IVF procedure for T.B. to enable her and D.B. to conceive their own child. This payment was conditioned upon T.B. surrendering custody of a live child upon birth. . . . The contract also provided that the Ms would pay T.B.'s pregnancy-related medical expenses [and partial payment in the event of miscarriage or a stillbirth.] . . . The Surrogacy Agreement provided [that:] T.B. and D.B. "agree[d] to surrender custody of the child to the Intended Parents immediately upon birth" and "agree[d] that the Intended Parents are the parents to be identified on the birth certificate for this child." . . .

The Surrogacy Agreement also stated that [each party had the opportunity to consult with an attorney of his or her own choice about the terms of the agreement and its effect on the interests of the parties.] T.B. and D.B. did not exercise their right to consult a lawyer before the Surrogacy Agreement was signed by all four parties. But each person acknowledged in writing [that he or she "carefully read and understood every word in this agreement and its legal effect, and each party is signing this agreement freely and voluntarily"].

On March 27, Midwest implanted two embryos into T.B.'s uterus. The embryos were the ova of an anonymous donor fertilized with P.M.'s sperm. On April 4, blood testing confirmed T.B.'s pregnancy. The parties' relationship soon began to break down over their disagreement as to payment of medical expenses. All four attended the first ultrasound, which D.B. videotaped. The Ms later objected to his videotaping and to T.B. posting information about the baby on social media.

Their relationship worsened after the women exchanged text messages on April 13. They were discussing whether T.B. could attend a doctor's appointment scheduled by the IVF coordinator when C.M. wrote, "Well, we have to go next Thursday [because the coordinator] made the [appointment] and this is our journey not anyone else's. She said you have to end with [a doctor's] exam in Chicago and [a] couple more ultrasounds. . . ." T.B. replied, "I'm not going through this with you today. She just called me." C.M. replied, "We are in charge, we hired you so just let us be parents and enjoy this ok!"

A second ultrasound confirmed that T.B. was carrying viable twins. T.B. shared that news with the Ms, but the relationship remained rocky. In late April, C.M. texted this to T.B.:

> Every time we question you or try to make a decision (as we should be able to) we are paying you, we hired you, and we are in charge, you get mad and upset and blow up. A carrier shouldn't act like that as the doctors told me they should be saying yes ma'am, Whatever you guys want to do. But you can't stand not being in charge and you have some mental disorder for sure but yet you blame everything on us. . . . So if you wanna say u have it bad, try feeling how we feel. This is our baby not yours and imagine how U would feel. I know u don't care but just for a moment stop blaming us and look what U have done to us only cuz we have ask[ed] u to do something. Compare the two and u will see we have NEVER did u wrong. This is a nightmare.

When T.B. replied, "You're crazy," C.M. wrote back, "Oh really that's what everyone says about u[.]" T.B. then stated that "everything can be handled through attorneys from here[.]" The Bs retained an attorney to speak for them and cut off direct communication with the Ms, who nevertheless persisted in trying to reach them for updates on the pregnancy.

In a May 20 letter from her attorney, T.B. sought more money from the Ms beyond the $13,000 agreed to in their contract so she could use a costlier clinic for her own IVF . . . .

On August 19, P.M. sent Facebook messages to D.B.'s sister, using racial slurs and profanity to insult D.B. D.B.'s sister shared the communication with T.B. On August 24, C.M. sent an email to T.B. and T.B.'s attorney, triggering a lengthy exchange, during which C.M. called T.B. the "N" word. That statement, along with the comments P.M. sent to D.B.'s sister, convinced T.B. that the Ms were racist. T.B. then called the Ms' attorney. When T.B. expressed concern that the Ms would not pay her, the Ms' attorney assured T.B. that the money for the Bs had already been set aside. The Ms' attorney attempted to make payment arrangements with T.B. and arrange P.M.'s listing on the birth certificate, but those matters remained unresolved. Later that day, T.B. decided that she would not turn over the babies to the Ms.

Twin babies were born thirteen weeks prematurely on August 31. T.B. did not tell the Ms about the birth. The babies were placed in the neonatal intensive care unit. One died eight days after birth. T.B. did not inform the Ms about the baby's illness or death. The Bs unilaterally arranged for the deceased baby's cremation.

On October 31, the Ms filed a motion for an emergency ex parte injunction, alleging their belief that the babies had been born. The same day, the district court entered an order granting a temporary injunction that ordered T.B. and D.B. to surrender custody of "Baby H" to the Ms. . . . The Bs responded by filing an answer and counterclaim [seeking] a declaration that T.B. is the biological and legal mother of the babies and that D.B. is the legal father of the babies. The Bs also sought a declaration that P.M. has no legal right to a relationship with the surviving baby and that the Surrogacy Agreement is unenforceable. . . .

We begin with an overview of the law governing gestational surrogacy arrangements. . . . A majority of states lack statutes addressing surrogacy. . . . In the minority of states with statutes specifically addressing surrogacy . . . most of the statutes can be grouped into three categories. First, some states have legislatively prohibited all surrogacy contracts, declaring their terms unenforceable and, in some instances, imposing criminal penalties for those who attempt to enter into or assist in creating such a contract. A second category of states prohibit only certain types of surrogacy contracts—typically those involving a traditional surrogacy. Finally, states in the third category authorize both traditional and gestational surrogacy contracts, subject to regulation and specified limitations.

There are two commonly cited model acts dealing with surrogacy agreements: the American Bar Association Model Act Governing Assisted Reproductive Technology (2008) and article 8 of the Uniform Parentage Act (2002). [Both acts allow for traditional and gestational surrogacy contracts subject to extensive regulation that includes judicial pre-approval, limits on compensation, and provisions concerning the revocation rights of the parties to the agreement.] The 2017 Uniform Parentage Act (UPA)[, while continuing to permit both types of surrogacy,] imposes greater restrictions on traditional surrogacy agreements. . . .

Against this backdrop, we turn to the issue of whether the Surrogacy Agreement at issue is enforceable under Iowa law. T.B. argues the Surrogacy Agreement is unenforceable under Iowa law as inconsistent with statutory provisions and public policy. We first examine whether this contract between consenting adults is "prohibited by statute, condemned by judicial decision, [or] contrary to the public morals." We find no such statutory or judicial prohibition in our state. To the contrary, the Iowa legislature tacitly approved of surrogacy arrangements by exempting them from potential criminal liability for selling children [in Iowa Code §710.11]. This provision was enacted in 1989, one year after extensive national publicity over the [Baby M.] decision of the New Jersey Supreme Court. . . .

We conclude, based on the timing of the enactment of Iowa Code section 710.11, the very next legislative session, that our state's general assembly chose in 1989 to allow surrogacy arrangements, not prohibit them. Section 710.11 specifically mentions artificial insemination of the birth mother . . ., but we decline to infer the legislature intended to allow only traditional surrogacy . . . and yet criminalize gestational surrogacy arrangements. IVF . . . was then in its infancy and had not been the subject of a court decision of national prominence. As other courts have noted, a gestational surrogacy in which the birth mother lacks a genetic connection to the child raises fewer concerns than the traditional surrogacy expressly mentioned in section 710.11. The legislature's decision to allow traditional surrogacy arrangements can be taken as a signal that it would also allow gestational surrogacy arrangements. We conclude that neither traditional nor gestational surrogacy contracts are prohibited under section 710.11.

Our conclusion is reinforced by the regulations adopted by the DPH that specifically contemplate IVF gestational surrogacy agreements. The regulations are entitled "Establishment of new certificate of live birth following a birth by gestational surrogate arrangement." See Iowa Admin. Code r. 641-99.15. . . . The DPH regulations provide for establishment of a new certificate of live birth following a birth by gestational surrogate arrangement [and providing] for court orders disestablishing the surrogate mother and her legal spouse as the legal parents and establishing the intended father and mother as the legal parents. . . .

Another reason the Surrogacy Agreement does not violate Iowa Code section 710.11 is because the Ms' payment was for T.B.'s gestational services rather than for her sale of a baby. The Surrogacy Agreement states,

> The consideration of this agreement is compensation for services and expenses as limited by law and in no way is to be construed as a fee for termination of parental rights or a payment in exchange for consent to surrender the child for adoption.

The California Supreme Court held under equivalent circumstances that the contractual payment is for gestational services, not for the sale of a baby [citing Johnson v. Calvert, 851 P.2d 776, 784 (Cal. 1993)] (explaining that the payments to the surrogate mother "were meant to compensate her for her services in gestating the fetus and undergoing labor"). We reach the same conclusion.

T.B. [also] relies on Iowa Code section 600A.4, which requires parents to wait seventy-two hours after a child's birth before signing a release of custody for an adoption. T.B. claims that the safeguards established in [Iowa Code §600A.4(2)(g)] are violated by the Surrogacy Agreement. We disagree because T.B. is not the genetic mother of Baby H, and section 600A.4 is therefore inapplicable. . . . This is not a situation in which T.B. is choosing to give up her own genetically related child in order to avoid the consequences of an unwanted pregnancy or the burdens of childrearing. . . . But for the acted-on intention of the Ms, Baby H would not exist. . . . We hold that the adoption statute is inapplicable and the Surrogacy Agreement is not inconsistent with Iowa statutes on termination of parental rights.

T.B. also claims enforcement of the Surrogacy Agreement violates Iowa's public policy. We disagree based on the freedom of contract enjoyed by consenting adults. We start with the presumption that under Iowa law a "contractual agreement is binding on the parties." . . . The party claiming the contract is contrary to public policy bears the burden of proof. [That burden has not been met.]. . .

T.B. argues a surrogacy agreement violates public policy against the exploitation of women, and contends:

> Surrogacy agreements, if enforced embody deviant societal pressures, the object of which is to use the woman, and destroy her interests as a mother to satisfy the desires of third parties. Surrogacy exploits women by treating the mother as if she is not a whole woman. It assumes she can be used much like a breeding animal and act as though she is not, in fact, a mother [citing a Declaration in the Appellate Brief of sociologist Barbara Katz Rothman, who has written on the ethics of reproductive technologies].

Yet T.B. entered into the Surrogacy Agreement voluntarily. She had given birth to four children of her own before signing the Surrogacy Agreement and was no stranger to the effects of pregnancy. T.B. does not allege she signed the Surrogacy Agreement under economic duress or that its terms are unconscionable. . . .

T.B. alternatively argues the Surrogacy Agreement violates the state's public policy favoring families. . . . T.B. characterizes surrogacy agreements as deliberately destroying the surrogate mother–child relationship (a relationship, we note, that would not exist but for the Ms' contribution of their embryos in reliance on T.B.'s willingness to serve as a gestational carrier). We conclude that gestational surrogacy agreements *promote* families by enabling infertile couples to raise their own children and help bring new life into this world through willing surrogate mothers. . . . T.B. has failed to show the Surrogacy Agreement violates the public policy of our state. . . .

T.B. claims that as the birth mother she is the legal and biological mother of Baby H and that she therefore is entitled to custody of Baby H unless and until she is proven unfit by clear and convincing evidence. . . . Iowa Code chapter 232 defines "parent" as ". . . a *biological or adoptive mother or father* of a child. . . ." (emphasis added). [W]e hold the statutory definition of "biological parent" . . . does not include a surrogate birth mother who is not the genetic parent. . . .

We next address T.B.'s constitutional claims. . . . T.B. claims that she has a fundamental liberty interest in the parent–child relationship. That liberty interest belongs to P.M., the only party in this case who is a biological parent of Baby H. By contrast, T.B.'s constitutional claims rest on an incorrect premise—that she has parental rights in Baby H without being the child's genetic mother. Any constitutionally protected interest she may have as the surrogate birth mother is overcome by P.M.'s undisputed status as the biological and intended father of Baby H. . . .

T.B. was provided sufficient procedural due process. She cannot claim lack of notice. [She also] claims that enforcement of the Surrogacy Agreement would violate the substantive due process and equal protection rights of Baby H. . . . We assume without deciding that T.B., as Baby H's birth mother, would have had standing to raise constitutional claims of Baby H. But as noted above, T.B. waived her rights to assert claims on behalf of Baby H in the Surrogacy Agreement.

For these reasons, we affirm the rulings of the district court [holding that the surrogacy contract was enforceable, terminating the presumptive parental rights of the surrogate mother and her husband, establishing paternity in the biological father, and awarding him permanent legal and physical custody].

NOTE: THE *BABY M* CASE

Elizabeth and William Stern arrive to testify in the *Baby M* case.

Surrogacy first commanded national attention in the landmark case of In re Baby M., 537 A.2d 1227 (N.J. 1988) (cited in the principal case). In 1986, a married woman, Mary Beth Whitehead, gave birth to a baby girl who was conceived with Whitehead's ovum and the sperm of the intended parent, William Stern. Stern wanted a genetically related child because he was the only child of parents who were Holocaust survivors. However, he and his wife, who had multiple sclerosis, were worried about the potential health implications of a pregnancy for her.

After locating Whitehead through an advertisement, the parties entered into a surrogacy contract in which Mr. Stern agreed to pay her $10,000. After the baby's birth, Whitehead refused to relinquish the child as agreed. The ensuing legal battle captured the attention of the nation. Ultimately, in the first state supreme court decision on the matter, the New Jersey Supreme Court held that the surrogacy was unlawful and unenforceable. The agreement, the court said, conflicted with a number of state laws, including laws prohibiting payment in connection with adoption, laws regulating the termination of parental rights, and laws making consent to adoption revocable. The court also held that the agreement violated state public policy: "The surrogacy contract guarantees permanent separation of the child from one of its natural parents. Our policy, however, has long been that to the extent possible, children should remain with and be brought up by both of their natural parents." Id. at 1246-1247.

The court continued:

> The long-term effects of surrogacy contracts are not known, but feared—the impact on the child who learns her life was bought, that she is the offspring of someone who gave birth to her only to obtain money; the impact on the natural mother as the full weight of her isolation is felt along with the full reality of the sale of her body and her child; the impact on the natural father and adoptive mother once they realize the consequences of their conduct.

After finding the agreement unenforceable, the court held that the child's parents were Whitehead and Stern.[19]

Baby M sparked enormous controversy. The next state high court to weigh in was the California Supreme Court in Johnson v. Calvert, in a dispute involving the parentage of a child born through gestational surrogacy. 851 P.2d 776, 781 (Cal. 1993). In *Johnson*, the California Supreme Court recognized the intended genetic parents as the legal parents. Both the surrogate and the intended genetic mother had bases for claiming parentage under the state's statutes: the person acting as a surrogate, by virtue of having given birth; and the intended mother, by virtue of being genetically related to the child. In such cases, the court declared, "she who intended to procreate the child—that is, she who intended to bring about the birth of a child that she intended to raise as her own—is the natural mother under California law." Id. at 782.

Mary Beth Whitehead testifies at a hearing about whether to outlaw surrogacy.

In reaching this conclusion, the *Johnson* court rejected the argument that adoption statutes are applicable to surrogacy arrangements, at least gestational ones. Gestational surrogacy, the court said, differs in important ways from adoption: "[In gestational surrogacy arrangements, t]he parties voluntarily agreed to participate in in vitro fertilization and related medical procedures before the child was conceived; at the time when Anna entered into the contract, therefore, she was not vulnerable to financial inducements to part with her own expected offspring." Id. at 783. The California Supreme Court rejected speculative concerns regarding potential exploitation of people acting as surrogates:

> The argument that a woman cannot knowingly and intelligently agree to gestate and deliver a baby for intending parents carries overtones of the reasoning that for centuries prevented women from attaining equal economic rights and professional status under the law. To resurrect this view is both to foreclose a personal and economic choice on the part of the surrogate mother, and to deny intending parents what may be their only means of procreating a child of their own genetic stock. Certainly in the present case it cannot seriously be argued that Anna, a licensed vocational nurse who had done well in school and who had previously borne a child, lacked the intellectual wherewithal or life experience necessary to make an informed decision to enter into the surrogacy contract. Id. at 785.

---

[19]. When "Baby M" turned 18, she initiated proceedings to terminate Mary Beth Whitehead's parental rights, and Elizabeth Stern then adopted her. See Mike Kelly, 25 Years After Baby M, Surrogacy Questions Remain Unanswered, NorthJersey.com, Mar. 30, 2012, https://northjersey.newspapers.com/search/#query=Baby+M&dr_year=2012-2012. "Baby M," reared as Melissa Stern, later married and had a daughter. She lives and works in London. Clyde Haberman, Baby M and the Question of Surrogate Motherhood, N.Y. Times, Mar. 23, 2014.

Notes and Questions

1. Surrogacy: Background. In the early years of compensated surrogacy, it was utilized primarily by married different-sex couples. Today, surrogacy is also used by single people, unmarried couples, and same-sex couples. The traditional or genetic surrogacy arrangements exemplified in *Baby M*, in which the surrogate provides the ova, have largely given way to gestational surrogacy arrangements, the type of surrogacy at issue in *Johnson*, in which the ova come either from an intended parent or a third-party donor. What type of surrogacy arrangement was used in P.M. v. T.B.? How might this fact have affected the outcome?

2. Eligibility. Health care providers sometimes limit access to infertility services based on various criteria, including age. The UPA makes no reference to the outer age of the parties. Would an age restriction be legally permissible? Ethical? What state interests are advanced by such regulation? What is the harm of older parenthood to children, parents, society?

Should health care providers have the right to refuse to provide fertility care based on religious objections? State conscience clauses shield physicians from liability for refusals to perform abortions that violate their religious or moral beliefs. Do these conscience clauses extend to the provision of ART? Does *303 Creative* (excerpted in Chapter II) have any bearing on this question?

3. Baby-selling statutes. Many states prohibit "baby selling" (i.e., compensation in connection with an adoption or TPR). Initially, some courts, including the *Baby M.* court, characterized compensated surrogacy as baby selling. How is surrogacy like baby selling? How is it different? Which view is more persuasive? Do these objections apply to all forms of surrogacy (gestational, genetic, and arrangements that do not involve compensation)?

4. Breach by the parties. What happens when disputes arise — either on the part of the person acting as a surrogate or the intended parents? In P.M. v. T.B. the person acting as a surrogate refused to relinquish the child. How does the Iowa Supreme Court resolve the dispute? On what rationale(s)?

Other possibilities also exist for breach by the surrogate. For example, suppose that she wants an abortion. Or suppose that the surrogate is pregnant with multiple fetuses and the intended parents want her to undergo "selective reduction" to reduce the number of fetuses she is carrying against her wishes. What remedy, if any, should be available in such cases? Are money damages adequate? Could a court order specific performance? If the court allows a surrogate to keep the child, must she reimburse the intended parent(s) for fees and expenses? Disputes also arise in case of breach by the intended parents. For example, suppose that they refuse to accept an infant born with a disability. How does UPA (2017) (see below) handle issues of breach by the respective parties?

5. Policy concerns. Initially, feminists were divided about surrogacy. Some urged laws banning the practice altogether. These advocates often raised fears that surrogacy commodified and exploited women and children, reduced women to "baby machines," subjected them to the (largely) patriarchal control of the medical profession, and resembled slavery and prostitution.[20] In particular, some feared that gestational surrogacy would produce a "breeder class" of poor women of color (here and abroad) for wealthy white intended parents.[21] In contrast, other feminists argued that surrogacy restrictions constituted an unwarranted intrusion into reproductive autonomy, reflecting gender stereotypes and paternalism.[22] Which arguments are most compelling?

6. Legislation. In the cases discussed above, there were no statutes governing surrogacy. The courts had to draw from statutes and public policies developed to address other contexts.

a. Domestic. Initially, state legislative responses to surrogacy were mixed. Today, the strong trend is in favor of laws that permit and regulate surrogacy. A small number of states, including Indiana and Michigan, retain earlier enacted bans on surrogacy.[23]

With respect to intended parents, state surrogacy law increasingly covers and protects all intended parents, regardless of sex, sexual orientation, or marital status. More variation exists with regard to surrogates. California law, for example, includes few requirements or safeguards. The main requirements are that the parties must be represented by independent counsel; and the agreement must disclose the manner of payment of medical expenses. Cal. Fam. Code §7962. New York law, by contrast, imposes more requirements, including that the agreement must allow the surrogate to make all health and welfare decisions about themself and the pregnancy and must require the intended parents to pay for the surrogate's health insurance. N.Y. Fam. Ct. Act §581-401 et seq.

b. International. Some countries (e.g. Finland, France, Germany, Iceland, Italy, Portugal, Spain, and Switzerland) ban surrogacy. Other countries (e.g. Australia, Belgium, Canada, Denmark, Netherlands, New Zealand, and the United Kingdom) allow only uncompensated surrogacy arrangements. Still other countries (e.g. Georgia, Israel, Mexico, Russia, and Ukraine) allow both compensated

---

[20]. On these and other feminist criticisms, see Anita L. Allen, Privacy, Surrogacy, and the *Baby M* Case, 76 Geo. L.J. 1759, 1783, 1791 (1988) (exploitation); Anita L. Allen, Surrogacy, Slavery and the Ownership of Life, 13 Harv. J.L. & Pub. Pol'y 132, 140 (1990) (slavery analogy); Gena Corea, Junk Liberty, in Reconstructing Babylon: Essays on Women and Technology 142, 153-156 (H. Patricia Hynes ed., 1991) (baby machines); Gena Corea, The Mother Machine: Reproductive Technologies from Artificial Insemination to Artificial Wombs (1985) (patriarchal control of medical profession); Carole Pateman, The Sexual Contract 209-218 (1988) (prostitution analogy); Margaret Jane Radin, Contested Commodities 131-153 (1996) (prostitution analogy); Cass R. Sunstein, Neutrality in Constitutional Law (with Special Reference to Pornography, Abortion, and Surrogacy), 92 Colum. L. Rev. 1, 47 (1992) (exploitation). For criticisms of the market analogy, see Dorothy E. Roberts, Why Baby Markets Aren't Free, 7 UC Irvine L. Rev. 611 (2017); David M. Smolin, The One Hundred Thousand Dollar Baby: The Ideological Roots of an American Export, 49 Cumb. L. Rev. 1 (2018-2019).

[21]. See, e.g., Khiara M. Bridges, *Windsor*, Surrogacy, and Race, 89 Wash. L. Rev. 1125 (2014).

[22]. See, e.g., Lori B. Andrews, Surrogate Motherhood: The Challenge for Feminists, 16 L. Med. & Health Care 72, 72 (1998); Debra Satz, Markets in Women's Reproductive Labor, 21 Phil. & Pub. Aff. 107, 117 (1992); Carmel Shalev, Birth Power 9-10 (1989).

[23]. See Courtney G. Joslin, (Not) Just Surrogacy, 109 Cal. L. Rev. 401, 412-413 (2021). For an exploration of the practice of surrogacy on the ground, see, e.g., Rachel Rebouché, Contracting Pregnancy, 105 Iowa L. Rev. 1591 (2020).

and uncompensated surrogacy. Finally, some countries impose other restrictions, like restricting surrogacy to different-sex couples. Several countries that formerly allowed surrogacy arrangements involving foreign intended parents (e.g., India, Nepal, and Thailand) changed their policy in response to reports of exploitation.[24]

c. Reproductive tourism. In a practice known as "reproductive tourism," some U.S. citizens travel abroad to have children born through surrogacy, drawn by favorable laws and lower costs. And, more common today, intended parents from other countries come to the United States for the same purpose. What are the benefits and risks of this practice? What legal issues ensue? For example, if the children are born abroad and are considered the children of the intended parents under the law of that country, do the children acquire derivative citizenship through their intended parents in the parents' home country? The European Union is currently grappling with how to address this highly contested issue.[25] The Hague Convention has established a Parentage/Surrogacy Project to explore the need for an international treaty on surrogacy.

7. Constitutional claims. What are the constitutional claims of the respective parties in P.M. v. T.B.? How does the court resolve these claims? A Utah Supreme Court case explored the constitutionality of a requirement of "medical evidence [that] the intended mother is unable to bear a child or is unable to do so without unreasonable risk to her physical or mental health or to the unborn child." Taking this provision literally, the trial judge held that the gay male plaintiffs failed to fulfill this requirement (and indeed never could). Reversing, the Utah Supreme Court unanimously held that the statutory requirement was unconstitutional as a violation of equal protection and due process. The court explained that the requirement "squarely violates *Obergefell* in that it deprives married same-sex male couples of the ability to obtain a valid gestational agreement — a marital benefit freely provided to opposite-sex couples." In re Gestational Agreement, 449 P.3d 69, 80 (Utah 2019). The Utah legislature has since abrogated this requirement. 2020 Utah Laws Ch. 101 (H.B. 234). What light does Pavan v. Smith (Chapter III) shed on this case?

8. Adoption. When should the law make adoption necessary for children conceived through assisted reproduction, including surrogacy? Note that in P.M. v. T.B., the state supreme court held that the intended/genetic father was a legal parent without the need for an adoption. Does his wife have to adopt the child to establish her parentage? Do such rules constitute impermissible sex-based discrimination. See, e.g., Douglas NeJaime, The Nature of Parenthood, 126 Yale L.J. 2260 (2017) (so arguing). In some states, an intended mother of a child born through *genetic surrogacy* must adopt the child, while an intended mother of a child born through *gestational surrogacy* need not. Should the legal status of an intended mother differ depending on the type of surrogacy use? Why?

---

[24]. Chelsea E. Caldwell, Note, Baby Got Back? Enforcing Guardianship in International Surrogacy Agreements When Tragedy Strikes, 49 U. Mem. L. Rev. 847, 858-863 (2019).

[25]. See, e.g., Cross-Border Legal Recognition of Parenthood in the EU (Apr. 2023), https://www.europarl.europa.eu/RegData/etudes/STUD/2023/746632/IPOL_STU(2023)746632_EN.pdf. See also Alice Margaria, Parenthood and Cross-Border Surrogacy: What Is "New"? The ECtHR's First Advisory Opinion, 28 Med. Law Rev. 412 (2020).

9. Statutory approaches. The surrogacy laws in some states are based on the UPA, which has included provisions permitting and regulating surrogacy arrangements since 2000. UPA (2017) updates the surrogacy provisions in several ways. First, UPA (2017) removes gendered terms and recognizes intended parents without regard to sex or sexual orientation, facilitating surrogacy arrangements involving same-sex couples. Second, UPA (2017) sets forth new requirements intended to safeguard the interests of all parties, including the person acting as a surrogate. See UPA (2017), §802 (included below). What are these requirements? What is the rationale for these requirements? Third, UPA (2017) liberalizes the enforcement process for gestational agreements by, for example, eliminating required court appearances and home studies. Where the agreement complies with the requirements and safeguards that are set forth in the statutes, the intended parents are treated as legal parents as a matter of law.

UNIFORM PARENTAGE ACT (2017)

ARTICLE 8. SURROGACY AGREEMENT

§802. ELIGIBILITY TO ENTER GESTATIONAL OR GENETIC SURROGACY AGREEMENT

(a) To execute an agreement to act as a gestational or genetic surrogate, a woman must:

(1) have attained 21 years of age;

(2) previously have given birth to at least one child;

(3) complete a medical evaluation related to the surrogacy arrangement by a licensed medical doctor;

(4) complete a mental-health consultation by a licensed mental-health professional; and

(5) have independent legal representation of her choice throughout the surrogacy arrangement regarding the terms of the surrogacy agreement and the potential legal consequences of the agreement.

(b) To execute a surrogacy agreement, each intended parent, whether or not genetically related to the child, must:

(1) have attained 21 years of age;

(2) complete a medical evaluation related to the surrogacy arrangement by a licensed medical doctor;

(3) complete a mental-health consultation by a licensed mental health professional; and

(4) have independent legal representation of the intended parent's choice throughout the surrogacy arrangement regarding the terms of the surrogacy agreement and the potential legal consequences of the agreement.

§804. REQUIREMENTS OF GESTATIONAL OR GENETIC SURROGACY AGREEMENT: CONTENT

(a) A surrogacy agreement must comply with the following requirements:

(1) A surrogate agrees to attempt to become pregnant by means of assisted reproduction.

(2) Except as otherwise provided . . ., the surrogate and the surrogate's spouse or former spouse, if any, have no claim to parentage of a child conceived by assisted reproduction under the agreement.

(3) The surrogate's spouse, if any, must acknowledge and agree to comply with the obligations imposed on the surrogate by the agreement.

(4) Except as otherwise provided . . ., the intended parent or, if there are two intended parents, each one jointly and severally, immediately on birth will be the exclusive parent or parents of the child, regardless of number of children born or gender or mental or physical condition of each child. . . .

(6) The agreement must include information disclosing how each intended parent will cover the surrogacy-related expenses of the surrogate and the medical expenses of the child. . . .

(7) The agreement must permit the surrogate to make all health and welfare decisions regarding herself and her pregnancy. This [act] does not enlarge or diminish the surrogate's right to terminate her pregnancy.

(8) The agreement must include information about each party's right under this [article] to terminate the surrogacy agreement.

(b) A surrogacy agreement may provide for:

(1) payment of consideration and reasonable expenses; and

(2) reimbursement of specific expenses if the agreement is terminated under this [article]. . . .

§809. PARENTAGE UNDER GESTATIONAL SURROGACY AGREEMENT

(a) [O]n the birth of a child conceived by assisted reproduction under a gestational surrogacy agreement, each intended parent is, by operation of law, a parent of the child.

(b) Except as otherwise provided in subsection (c) or Section 812, neither a gestational surrogate nor the surrogate's spouse or former spouse, if any, is a parent of the child.

(c) . . . If the child is a genetic child of the woman who agreed to be a gestational surrogate, parentage must be determined [under other law].

(d) Except as otherwise provided in subsection (c) or Section 810(b) or 812, if, due to a clinical or laboratory error, a child conceived by assisted reproduction under a gestational surrogacy agreement is not genetically related to an intended parent or a donor who donated to the intended parent or parents, each intended parent, and not the gestational surrogate and the surrogate's spouse or former spouse, if any, is a parent of the child, subject to any other claim of parentage.

. . .

§812. EFFECT OF GESTATIONAL SURROGACY AGREEMENT

(a) A gestational surrogacy agreement that complies with Sections 802, 803, and 804 is enforceable.

(b) If a child was conceived by assisted reproduction under a gestational surrogacy agreement that does not comply with Sections 802, 803, and 804, the court shall determine the rights and duties of the parties to the agreement consistent with the intent of the parties at the time of execution of the agreement.

Each party to the agreement and any individual who at the time of the execution of the agreement was a spouse of a party to the agreement has standing to maintain a proceeding to adjudicate an issue related to the enforcement of the agreement.

(c) Except as expressly provided in a gestational surrogacy agreement or subsection (d) or (e), if the agreement is breached by the gestational surrogate or one or more intended parents, the non-breaching party is entitled to the remedies available at law or in equity.

(d) Specific performance is not a remedy available for breach by a gestational surrogate of a provision in the agreement that the gestational surrogate be impregnated, terminate or not terminate a pregnancy, or submit to medical procedures.

(e) Except as otherwise provided in subsection (d), if an intended parent is determined to be a parent of the child, specific performance is a remedy available for:

(1) breach of the agreement by a gestational surrogate which prevents the intended parent from exercising immediately on birth of the child the full rights of parentage; or

(2) breach by the intended parent which prevents the intended parent's acceptance, immediately on birth of the child conceived by assisted reproduction under the agreement, of the duties of parentage. . . .

Problems

1. Robert and his wife, Denise, arranged to have Denise become pregnant using embryos created for them with Robert's sperm and eggs from an anonymous donor. Clinic doctors transferred some of these embryos not only to Denise, but also *mistakenly* to Susan, an unmarried woman who had intended to become pregnant using an embryo created with gametes from anonymous donors. Denise gave birth to a girl and Susan a boy; the children were conceived using gametes from the same people. After the clinic disclosed that they had transferred the wrong embryo to Susan, Robert and Denise file an action seeking a determination that they are the boy's legal parents; in response, Susan asserts that she is his sole legal parent. Whom should the court recognize? Why? Can intent-based parentage rules resolve this dispute? Should the court recognize all three as legal parents of the child? See Robert B. v. Susan B., 135 Cal. Rptr. 2d 785 (Ct. App. 2003). See also Marjorie M. Shultz, Taking Account of ARTs in Determining Parenthood: A Troubling Dispute in California, 19 Wash. U. J.L. & Pol'y 77 (2005).

If the mix-up had resulted in one woman giving birth to twin boys, one of whom was genetically hers and her husband's and the other was the genetic child of a second married couple, would your answers change? Suppose that the error were disclosed before the twins' birth. Suppose that the second couple's own efforts to have a child had failed — so the twin in question was their only chance for genetic offspring. Suppose that the first couple and their genetic son are Caucasian and the second couple and the second twin are African-American. See Perry-Rogers v. Fasano, 715 N.Y.S.2d 19 (App. Div. 2000); Leslie Bender, Genes, Parents, and Assisted Reproductive Technologies: ARTs, Mistakes, Sex, Race, & Law, 12 Colum. J. Gender & L. 1 (2003).

2. You are an aide to a state legislator. Currently, the state has a law banning all forms of surrogacy. The legislator asks you to draft a memo discussing whether she should introduce a bill that would repeal the existing ban and replace it with a statutory scheme permitting and regulating surrogacy. She also asks you to address a number of key issues with regard to a permissive scheme (assuming that she decides to propose one), including, but not limited to, (1) whether the legislative proposal should permit both gestational and genetic surrogacy; (2) whether the rules governing gestational and genetic surrogacy agreements should be the same; (3) what eligibility requirements must be met by the parties; and (4) what provisions must be included in the agreement for the agreement to be considered enforceable.

6. Multi-Parenthood

RAYMOND T. v. SAMANTHA G.
74 N.Y.S.3d 730 (N.Y. Fam. Ct. 2018)

GOLDSTEIN, Judge.

In the instant case, three parties—the biological mother, the biological father and the father's husband—agreed to conceive and raise a child together in a tri-parent arrangement. The question before the court is whether the father's husband has standing to seek custody and visitation with the subject child . . . even though the child already has two legal parents. . . .

The parties in the instant case, a married same-sex male couple, petitioners David S. and Raymond T., and a single woman, respondent Samantha G., were all friends. Over brunch in May 2016, the three friends discussed how each wished to be a parent and devised a plan whereby a child would be conceived and raised by the three parties in a tri-parent arrangement. While the parties agreed that the mother would continue to live in New York City and the men would continue to reside together in Jersey City, the parties agreed that they would consider themselves to be a "family." The parties then proceeded to execute their plan. For an eight-day period, Misters S. and T. alternated the daily delivery of sperm to Ms. G. for artificial insemination. On or about Labor Day weekend, 2016, Ms. G. announced that she was pregnant. The three parties publicized the impending birth on social media with a picture of all three parties dressed in T-shirts. Misters S. and T.'s shirt each said, "This guy is going to be a daddy" and Ms. G.'s shirt said, "This girl is going to be a mama."

[The parties jointly chose and paid for the midwife, attended prebirth medical appointments together, were all present when the child was born, and selected a name for the child (Matthew Z. S.-G.) that recognized all three parties. Mr. T. arranged to take a 16-week paternity leave after the child was born. After a private genetic marker test determined that Mr. S. was the child's biological father, Mr. S. signed a New Jersey acknowledgment of paternity when the child was five days old. After the child's birth, Ms. G., Matthew and Ms. G.'s mother all spent a week at the home of Misters S. and T.]

At the week's conclusion, Matthew went to live with Ms. G. in New York County, where he continues to live. Misters S. and T. have regular daytime parenting time. . . . When speaking to Matthew, all parties refer to Ms. G. as "Momma," Mr. S. as "Daddy" and Mr. T. as "Papai," which is Portuguese for father. . . .

Issues arose between the two men and Ms. G. with respect to the parenting of Matthew as well as to the extent of parental access by Misters S. and T. The relationship among the parties became strained, and on November 12, 2017, Misters S. and T. filed a joint petition against Ms. G. seeking "legal custody and shared parenting time" with Matthew. [The two men contended that not only should Mr. T. be declared to have standing to seek custody and visitation as a "parent," but he should also be declared the third legal parent of Matthew.]

On December 6, 2017, Ms. G. filed a cross-petition against Misters S. and T. seeking sole custody of Matthew with Misters S. and T. being granted reasonable visitation. [S]he conceded that because all three parties agreed to conceive and raise a child together, Mr. T. should have standing to seek custody and visitation under DRL §70 (a). However, she argued strenuously that the right to seek custody and visitation as a "parent" under the Domestic Relations Law does not automatically bestow parentage on the non-biological party and asked that this court not declare Mr. T. to be a third legal parent.

The landmark Court of Appeals case *Brooke S.B.* changed the legal landscape regarding the rights of a partner who is not a legal parent to seek custody and visitation. [Brooke S.B. v. Elizabeth A.C.C., 61 N.E.3d 488 (N.Y. 2016), conferred standing, under N.Y. DRL §70, on a non-biologically related same-sex former partner to seek visitation and custody, as a parent, where a partner shows by clear and convincing evidence that the parties agreed to conceive and raise the child together.]

Domestic Relations Law §70 (a) provides:

[T]he court may award the custody of a child to either parent for such time, under such regulations and restrictions as the case may require. [T]here shall be no prima facie right to the custody of the child in either parent, but *the court shall determine solely what is for the best interest of the child, and what will best promote its welfare and happiness, and make award accordingly* (emphasis added).

Significantly, *Brooke S.B.* overruled the Court's ruling in Allison D. v. Virginia M., 572 N.E.2d 27 (NY 1991), which denied a partner who lacked a biological or adoptive relationship with a child the right to seek visitation under DRL §70, despite having an established "parental" type relationship with the child. In determining to break with precedent, the *Brooke S.B.* court gave primary consideration to the well-being of children being raised in nontraditional families and to how the *Allison D.* decision had negatively impacted those children. In making its ruling, the *Brooke S.B.* court also recognized the fundamental right of parents to control the upbringing of their children and required that the relationship between the child and the partner came into being with the consent of the legal parent.

In reaching its decision, the *Brooke S.B.* court relied heavily on the dissent of Judge Kaye in *Allison D.* Judge Kaye foresaw that the *Allison D.* ruling would " 'fall[] hardest' on the millions of children raised in nontraditional families—including families headed by same-sex couples, unmarried opposite-sex couples, and step-parents." "The dissent [in *Brooke S.B.*] asserted that, because DRL §70 does not define 'parent'—and because the statute made express reference to 'the best interests of the child,' the court was free to draft a definition that accommodated the welfare of the child." [T]he *Brooke S.B.* court also noted that legal commentators have "taken issue with *Allison D.* for its negative impact on children" and that "[a] growing body of social science reveals the trauma children suffer as a result of separation from a primary attachment figure—such as a de facto parent—regardless of the figure's biological or adoptive ties to the children."

Against this backdrop, this court is now called upon to determine if the ruling in *Brooke S.B.* would be applicable to the situation at hand, where three—not just two—parties agreed to a preconception plan to raise a child together. . . . The court finds that under the above circumstances where the three parties entered and followed through with a preconception plan to raise a child together in a tri-parent arrangement, the biological father's spouse has standing to seek custody and visitation as a parent pursuant to *Brooke S.B.* In making this decision, this court is specifically taking into consideration that the relationship between Mr. T. and Matthew came into being with the consent and blessing of the two biological parents and that both biological parents agree that Mr. T. should have standing to seek custody and visitation.

The court further finds that its ruling that Mr. T. has standing to seek custody and visitation despite the existence of two legal parents, to be consistent with the fundamental principle of *Brooke S.B.*—that DRL §70 must be read to effectuate the welfare and best interests of children, particularly those who are being raised in a non-traditional family structure. The parent-child relationships fostered by children like Matthew, who are being raised in a tri-parent arrangement, should be entitled to no less protection than children raised by two parties.

It is worth noting that the situation before the court—where three parties are involved in raising a child—is likely to recur. Realistically, where same-sex couples seek to conceive and rear a child who is the biological child of one member of the couple, there is always a third party who provides either the egg or the sperm. While in many cases, an anonymous donor is used or all persons involved agree that the donor will *not* be a parent, this is not the situation in the instant case and in many other cases where the parties agree that the provider of the egg or sperm *will* be a parent. . . .

The situation in the instant case [is] very different from the situation where a same-sex married couple enters into an agreement with a third party to donate an egg or sperm with the understanding that the donor will not be a parent to the child who is conceived. Under such circumstances, the presumption of legitimacy—that a child born during a marriage is the legitimate child of the marriage—is of critical importance. If the presumption of legitimacy is not rebutted, the court may deem the child to be the legal child of both same-sex spouses and deny the sperm or egg donor parental status. . . .

In the instant case, although two of the parties, Misters S. and T. are married, the presumption of legitimacy is not relevant to the court's analysis. This is because the presumption that Matthew is the legitimate child of the married couple, Misters S. and T., would indisputably be rebutted by evidence that all three parties agreed that Matthew would be raised in a tri-parent arrangement and that Ms. G., the biological mother, would be a parent to Matthew.

In sum, for the reasons explained above, the court is granting Mr. T. standing to seek custody and visitation with Matthew. The court will set this matter down for a trial to determine what orders of custody and visitation are in Matthew's best interest. . . . The court is not, however, granting Mr. T. an order of parentage. That issue is not properly before the court since no petition was filed for paternity or parentage. Moreover, there is no need for the issue of parentage to be addressed since pursuant to *Brooke S.B.*, Mr. T. may seek custody and visitation as a "parent" under DRL §70(a) without a determination that he is a legal parent. If, in the future, a proper application for a declaration of parentage is made and there is a need for a determination of parentage, for instance, to rule on a request for child support, the court may address this issue. This court, however, notes that there is not currently any New York statute which grants legal parentage to three parties, nor is there any New York case law precedent for such a determination.

Notes and Questions

1. Traditional assumption. In the past, courts often assumed that the law permitted a total of two parents for a child — one parent of each gender. Recall Justice Scalia's refusal (in *Michael H.*, reprinted above) to recognize "dual fatherhood." 491 U.S. 110, 118 (1989) ("California law, like nature itself, makes no provision for dual fatherhood"). What is the rationale for this view? Today, a range of family forms challenge that assumption, including blended families, multi-generational and skipped generational families, and families formed through assisted reproduction.

2. Holding. In *Raymond T.*, the New York family court granted standing to Raymond to seek custody and visitation. On what basis did the court determine that Raymond had standing? Despite conferring standing, however, the court did not grant Raymond an order of parentage. Why? What parental rights and responsibilities are dictated by this holding? Which are not?

3. Evolving nature of parenthood. The law has often regarded parentage as exclusive and complete, so the parental relationship cannot be bifurcated. According to Professor Katherine Bartlett, parents' rights and duties are generally considered "exclusive and indivisible. . . . They are exclusive in that only a child's legal parents will have rights and duties ordinarily considered parental; nonparents cannot acquire them. They are indivisible in that each parent, with respect to his or her own child, will have every right and duty generally available to parents."[26] How does *Raymond T.* change that conceptualization?

4. Common law doctrines. In *Raymond T.*, the court recognized a third person — Raymond — as having the right to seek visitation or custody under a judge-made doctrine. Specifically, under the rule developed in *Brooke S.B.* (cited in the principal case), Raymond established by clear and convincing evidence

---

[26]. See Katharine T. Bartlett, Rethinking Parenthood as an Exclusive Status: The Need for Legal Alternatives When the Premise of the Nuclear Family Has Failed, 70 Va. L. Rev. 879, 883 (1984).

that the parties agreed to conceive and raise the child together. The court then held that this rule (recognizing that such a person has standing to seek custody or visitation under a best interests of the child standard) applies equally where "three—not just two—parties agreed to a preconception plan to raise a child together." Should courts apply common law or equitable rules that allow a person to seek custody or visitation even when the child already has two legal parents? Most courts have said yes.[27]

5. Best interests and multi-parenthood. How should the court on remand determine what custody and visitation orders are in Matthew's best interest? Here, two of the three parents live together. How should that fact be taken into account when allocating custody? A 50/50 split between the households? Or one-third custody among all three parents? Should custody decisionmaking be allocated so that unanimity (or, instead, majority vote) is required for decisions regarding the child's medical treatment, education, religious activities, and other important decisions? In the future, if a court orders Raymond to pay child support, should the amount be divided among all the legal parents? What other practical problems might arise? Suppose, for example, that Raymond travels with Matthew to another state. What problems might that pose?

6. Legislative developments. Many courts have recognized multi-parent families under common law or equitable doctrines. More recently, some states enacted statutes that allow courts to recognize that a child has *more than two legal parents*.[28] See, e.g., Cal. Fam. Code §7612(c). Some of these laws are based on UPA (2017), §613, Alternative B (below), which permits a court to conclude that a child has more than two legal parents in some circumstances. What are those circumstances? If the New York legislature had enacted this provision before *Raymond T.*, how would the case have been decided?

7. Public policy. Should states enact legislation allowing a court to find that a child has more than two legal parents? Should the law place a ceiling on the maximum number of parents? Should recognition be limited to people who are already engaging in caretaking responsibilities? Are there any categories of people who should be excluded from recognition under the statute? Stepparents? Grandparents? Foster parents?

UNIFORM PARENTAGE ACT (2017)

§613. ADJUDICATING COMPETING CLAIMS OF PARENTAGE

(a) [I]n a proceeding to adjudicate competing claims of, or challenges [to] parentage of a child by two or more individuals, the court shall adjudicate parentage in the best interest of the child, based on:

(1) the age of the child;

---

[27]. See Courtney G. Joslin & Douglas NeJaime, Multiparenthood (manuscript on file with authors).

[28]. See Naomi Cahn & June Carbone, Custody and Visitation with Three (or More) Parents, 56 Fam. Ct. Rev. 399 (2018).

(2) the length of time during which each individual assumed the role of parent of the child;

(3) the nature of the relationship between the child and each individual;

(4) the harm to the child if the relationship between the child and each individual is not recognized;

(5) the basis for each individual's claim to parentage of the child; and

(6) other equitable factors arising from the disruption of the relationship between the child and each individual or the likelihood of other harm to the child.

(b) If an individual challenges parentage based on the results of genetic testing, in addition to the factors listed in subsection (a), the court shall consider:

(1) the facts surrounding the discovery the individual might not be a genetic parent of the child; and

(2) the length of time between the time that the individual was placed on notice that the individual might not be a genetic parent and the commencement of the proceeding.

ALTERNATIVE A

(c) The court may not adjudicate a child to have more than two parents under this [act].

ALTERNATIVE B

(c) The court may adjudicate a child to have more than two parents under this [act] if the court finds that failure to recognize more than two parents would be detrimental to the child. A finding of detriment to the child does not require a finding of unfitness of any parent or individual seeking an adjudication of parentage. In determining detriment to the child, the court shall consider all relevant factors, including the harm if the child is removed from a stable placement with an individual who has fulfilled the child's physical needs and psychological needs for care and affection and has assumed the role for a substantial period.

Problem

Erica and Yessini are a same-sex couple. They register as domestic partners with the state of California. (At the time, same-sex couples could not marry in California; registered domestic partners were entitled to all state-conferred rights extended to married spouses, including parentage rights.) Erica and Yessini decide to have a child together. They ask a friend, Sam, to be their sperm donor. The parties find a sample donor contract on the Internet. All three parties sign the agreement, and Erica and Yessini pay Sam $300 for his semen samples. Unbeknownst to Yessini, at the time that Erica is trying to get pregnant through assisted reproduction using Sam's sperm, Erica is also having sex with Sam. Erica becomes pregnant; she does not know whether the pregnancy resulted from the assisted reproduction or from sexual intercourse. At the time, Sam does not intend to be a parent.

When the child is born, Yessini is present at the birth and immediately holds the child out to the world as her child. Yessini provides health insurance for the child through her employer-provided health insurance and names the child as her beneficiary for life insurance and other benefits. At the time of her birth, both Erica and Yessini intend that the child will be raised in a family unit consisting of the three of them. The child's surname is a hyphenated version of Erica and Yessini's surnames. Yessini and Erica separate about eight months after the child's birth. Yessini begins paying child support voluntarily after the couple separates. When the child is about one year old, Erica moves in with Sam, and Sam thereafter begins holding the child out as his own.

Just after the child's first birthday, Yessini initiates an action to dissolve the domestic partnership. In the petition, she alleges that she is a parent and seeks an order of joint legal and physical custody. About six months later, Sam moves to intervene in the action, seeking a determination that he is a parent of the child. At the time, Erica and Sam are still living together and are expecting another child. Assume that UPA (2017) applies. What result? Should the court recognize all three adults as parents to the child? If not, who should the court find are the child's two parents, and why? See S.M. v. E.C., 2014 WL 2921905 (Cal. Ct. App. 2014).

7. Embryo Disputes

IN RE MARRIAGE OF ROOKS
429 P.3d 579 (Colo. 2018)

Justice MARQUEZ delivered the opinion of the court.

In vitro fertilization ("IVF") has given individuals and couples who are unable to conceive conventionally the opportunity to have genetic children. [H]owever, when married couples turn to this technology and later divorce, IVF can present a host of legal dilemmas, including how to resolve disagreements over the disposition of cryogenically preserved pre-embryos that remain at the time of dissolution. [The court uses the technical term "pre-embryos" to refer to ova that have been fertilized via IVF but are not yet transferred to the uterus.]

Petitioner Ms. Mandy Rooks and Respondent Mr. Drake Rooks married in 2002. They separated in August 2014, and Mr. Rooks filed a petition for dissolution of marriage the following month. . . . Mr. and Ms. Rooks used IVF to have their three children. [They previously entered into agreements that recorded the couple's decisions regarding the disposition of their frozen pre-embryos under certain scenarios. They agreed that, in the event of the husband's death, the pre-embryos would be transferred to the wife. In the event of her death, or if both parties died, the pre-embryos would be discarded. The agreements failed to specify how any remaining pre-embryos should be allocated in the event of divorce. The agreements merely provided that "the disposition of our embryos will be part of the divorce/dissolution decree paperwork." At the time of the divorce, there were six remaining cryogenically preserved pre-embryos.] Ms. Rooks wished to preserve the pre-embryos for future implantation. . . . Mr. Rooks wished to . . . discard the pre-embryos; he testified that he did not wish to have more children from his relationship with Ms. Rooks. . . .

Although this case concerns the equitable division of marital property in a divorce proceeding, we recognize that the parties' competing interests in the disputed pre-embryos derive from constitutional rights in the realm of reproductive choice. We therefore briefly discuss the governing case law in this area.

The U.S. Supreme Court has recognized the importance of individual autonomy over decisions involving reproduction. Over seventy-five years ago, the Court recognized that procreation is "one of the basic civil rights" and that marriage and procreation are fundamental to human existence and survival [citing Skinner v. Oklahoma, 316 U.S. 535 (1942)]. As the Court considered new questions involving reproductive rights . . . , it began to articulate those rights as part of a cluster of privacy rights grounded in several fundamental constitutional guarantees [citing *Griswold, Eisenstadt,* and Roe v. Wade]. "Reading [the abortion] cases in conjunction with *Skinner* leads to the conclusion that an individual has the fundamental right not only to bear children, but to decide not to be the source of another life as well."

[C]ourts [in other jurisdictions] have adhered to or combined aspects of three main approaches: (1) interpreting the parties' contract or agreement regarding disposition of the pre-embryos; (2) balancing the parties' respective interests in receiving the pre-embryos; or (3) requiring the parties' mutual contemporaneous consent regarding disposition of the pre-embryos.

Many jurisdictions begin by looking for a preexisting agreement between the parties regarding disposition of remaining pre-embryos, as evidenced by consent or storage agreements between the IVF facility and the parties. See, e.g., Kass v. Kass, 696 N.E.2d 174, 180 (N.Y. 1998) ("Agreements between progenitors, or gamete donors, regarding disposition of their pre-zygotes should generally be presumed valid and binding, and enforced in any dispute between them."). . . . In *Kass,* the New York Court of Appeals determined that the IVF program consent forms signed by the couple during their marriage manifested their mutual intent that, in the event of divorce, the pre-embryos should be donated for research to the IVF program. The court thus ordered that the agreement be enforced. . . .

In cases where no enforceable agreement exists [or where an existing agreement does not address who should receive the remaining pre-embryos], many courts have conducted what has been termed a "balancing of interests" test to decide how to award or dispose of the pre-embryos. The Supreme Court of Tennessee employed such an approach in [Davis v. Davis, 842 S.W.2d 588 (Tenn. 1992)]. There, the court acknowledged that the conflicting interests at stake were of "equal significance—the right to procreate and the right to avoid procreation." Given the absence of an enforceable agreement, the court resolved the dispute by considering "the positions of the parties, the significance of their interests, and the relative burdens that will be imposed by differing resolutions." In balancing these interests, the court considered several factors, including (1) the burden of unwanted parenthood on the ex-husband who wished to discard the pre-embryos, particularly in light of his own childhood experience of being separated from his parents; (2) the ex-wife's interest in donating the pre-embryos to another couple to avoid the emotional burden of knowing that the IVF procedures were futile; and (3) the ex-wife's ability to become a parent by other reasonable means in the future. Ultimately, the *Davis* court concluded that the balance of interests weighed in favor of the ex-husband's desire to discard the pre-embryos. . . .

Finally, a small minority of courts have adopted a "mutual contemporaneous consent" approach, under which the court will not award the pre-embryos over the objection of either party. Instead, "no transfer, release, disposition, or use of the [pre-]embryos can occur without the signed authorization of both donors." This approach recognizes that disputed pre-embryos are "not easily susceptible to a just division because conflicting constitutional rights are at issue." [McQueen v. Gadberry, 507 S.W.3d 127, 157 (Mo. Ct. App. 2016).] In theory, the mutual contemporaneous consent approach purportedly "subjects neither party to any unwarranted governmental intrusion but rather leaves the intimate decision of whether to potentially have more children to the parties alone."

However, the mutual contemporaneous consent approach has been criticized by other courts as being "totally unrealistic" because if the parties were capable of reaching an agreement, then they would not be in court. [Reber v. Reber, 42 A.3d 1131, 1135 n.5 (Pa. Super. Ct. 2012).] As both the trial court and court of appeals recognized in this case, the mutual contemporaneous consent approach gives one party a de facto veto over the other party by avoiding any resolution until the issue is eventually mooted by the passage of time. And as at least one scholar has pointed out, this de facto veto creates incentives for one party to leverage his or her power unfairly. See Mark P. Strasser, You Take the Embryos but I Get the House (and the Business): Recent Trends in Awards Involving Embryos Upon Divorce, 57 Buff. L. Rev. 1159, 1210 (2009) . . . . Because the mutual contemporaneous consent approach allows one party to "change his or her mind about disposition up to the point of use or destruction of any stored [pre-]embryo," regardless of any preexisting agreement, it injects legal uncertainty into the process. Thus, this approach potentially increases litigation in already emotionally charged and fundamentally private matters.

Although these three approaches have been characterized and discussed as three different "rules" or "methods" for resolving disputes over frozen pre-embryos, we note that the approaches share conceptual underpinnings and reflect common goals. Both the contract approach and the mutual contemporaneous consent approach prioritize the parties' mutual consent and agreement. The contract approach simply encourages the parties to arrive at agreement regarding the disposition of the pre-embryos in advance of divorce. By contrast, the mutual contemporaneous consent approach requires the parties' mutual consent whenever a disposition occurs—regardless of any preexisting agreements. (Indeed, the mutual contemporaneous consent approach eliminates any incentive for parties to agree up front about what should happen with the pre-embryos in the event of divorce and thereby avoid litigation.) . . .

[W]e now address how courts in Colorado should resolve disagreements over a couple's cryogenically preserved pre-embryos when that couple divorces. [C]onsidering the nature and equivalency of the underlying liberty and privacy interests at stake, we conclude that a court presiding over dissolution proceedings should strive, where possible, to honor both parties' interests in procreational autonomy when resolving these disputes. Thus, we hold that a court should look first to any existing agreement expressing the spouses' intent regarding disposition of the couple's remaining pre-embryos in the event of divorce. [B]inding agreements "minimize misunderstandings and maximize procreative liberty by reserving to the progenitors [gamete donors] the authority to make what is in the first instance a quintessentially personal, private decision." We agree that, "[t]o the extent possible, it should be the progenitors—not the State and not the courts—who by their prior directive make this deeply personal life choice." . . .

However, in the absence of an enforceable agreement regarding disposition of the pre-embryos, and where the parties have turned to the courts to resolve their dispute, the dissolution court should balance the parties' respective interests and award the pre-embryos accordingly. Recognizing a couple's cryogenically preserved pre-embryos as marital property of a special character, the underlying principle that informs our balancing test is autonomy over decisions involving reproduction. . . .

We first discuss a non-exhaustive list of considerations that a court should weigh in disposing of the marital pre-embryos. . . . To begin with, courts should consider the intended use of the party seeking to preserve the disputed pre-embryos. A party who seeks to become a genetic parent through implantation of the pre-embryos, for example, has a weightier interest than one who seeks to donate the pre-embryos to another couple.

A court should also consider the demonstrated physical ability (or, conversely, inability) of the party seeking to implant the disputed pre-embryos to have biological children through other means. Compare [J.B. v. M.B., 783 A.2d 707, 717 (N.J. 2001)] (observing that ex-husband's opportunity to have additional genetic children did not depend on the pre-embryos), with [Reber v. Reiss, 42 A.3d 1131, 1137 (Pa. Super. Ct. 2012)] (considering that ex-wife had "no ability to procreate biologically without the use of the disputed pre-embryos").

Relatedly, the court should consider the parties' original reasons for pursuing IVF, which may favor preservation over disposition. For example, the couple may have turned to IVF to preserve a spouse's future ability to have biological children in the face of fertility-implicating medical treatment, such as chemotherapy.

The court's analysis should also include consideration of hardship for the person seeking to avoid becoming a genetic parent, including emotional, financial, or logistical considerations. [See Davis v. Davis, 842 S.W.2d 588, 603-04 (Tenn. 1992)] (considering ex-husband's opposition to fathering a child who would not live with both parents because of his own childhood experiences involving separation from his parents). In addition, a court should consider either spouse's demonstrated bad faith or attempt to use the pre-embryos as unfair leverage in the divorce proceedings.

Factors other than the ones described above may be relevant on a case-by-case basis. That said, we hold that the following are *improper* considerations in a dissolution court's allocation of a couple's cryogenically preserved pre-embryos. First, we decline to adopt a test that would allow courts to limit the size of a family based on financial and economic distinctions. Thus, a dissolution court should not assess whether the party seeking to become a genetic parent using the pre-embryos can afford another child. Nor shall the sheer number of a party's existing children, standing alone, be a reason to preclude preservation or use of the pre-embryos. Finally, we note that some courts have mentioned adoption as an alternative to biological or genetic parenthood through conventional or assisted reproduction. However, because we conclude the relevant interest at stake is the interest in achieving or avoiding genetic parenthood, courts should not consider whether a spouse seeking to use the pre-embryos to become a genetic parent could instead adopt a child or otherwise parent non-biological children.

The framework that we adopt today recognizes that both spouses have equally valid, constitutionally based interests in procreational autonomy. It encourages couples to record their mutual consent regarding the disposition of remaining pre-embryos in the event of divorce by an express agreement. [However,] where the parties' consent to disposition of the pre-embryos in the event of divorce is not memorialized in an enforceable agreement, and the parties therefore must turn to a court to resolve their dispute, [the balancing of interests approach that we adopt] is consistent with Colorado law directing dissolution courts to divide marital property based on a consideration of relevant factors, while taking into account that pre-embryos are marital property of a special character.

Here, Mr. and Ms. Rooks reached agreement regarding the disposition of pre-embryos in the event of certain contingencies (such as the death of one or both of the spouses). However, they failed to agree in advance how the remaining cryogenically preserved pre-embryos should be allocated in the event of divorce. [Instead], their written agreement left it to the dissolution court to determine how to allocate the pre-embryos. Thus, awarding the pre-embryos in accordance with law governing the distribution of marital property also satisfies the expectations of the parties, who specified that in the event of divorce, the dissolution decree would address the disposition of any remaining cryogenically preserved pre-embryos. Because we announce a new framework for resolving disputes regarding the disposition of pre-embryos frozen during marriage in the event of divorce, [we reverse] and remand the case with instructions to return the matter to the trial court to balance the parties' interests under the approach we adopt today. . . .

Notes and Questions

1. Background: Excess embryos. When people undergo infertility treatment, they usually produce excess embryos. Cryopreservation (freezing) allows embryos that were created earlier to be used later. It is estimated that there are more than 1.5 million cryopreserved embryos in the United States.[29] The existence of these excess cryopreserved embryos gives rise to disputes like that faced by the couple in *Rooks*.

2. Parties' agreement and intent. Fertility clinics commonly require couples undergoing IVF to sign a cryopreservation consent agreement before starting treatment. The agreement typically addresses the disposition of the embryos in a variety of circumstances, such as death, dissolution, and abandonment. Disputes commonly arise when one party no longer wants to abide by the agreement or, alternatively, when the agreement fails to resolve the situation at hand. How did the dispute arise in *Rooks*? What did the Rooks' agreement provide about their wishes regarding disposition of any remaining embryos in the event of divorce?

The court in *Rooks* identifies three prevailing state approaches to embryo disposition. In the first approach, a court applies the parties' disposition agreement. See, e.g., Finkelstein v. Finkelstein, 79 N.Y.S.3d 17, 21 (N.Y. App. Div. 2018). What

---

[29]. Gerard Letterie, M.D., In re: The Disposition of Frozen Embryos: 2022, 117 Fertility & Sterility 477 (Mar. 2022), https://www.sciencedirect.com/science/article/pii/S0015028222000012.

are the advantages of this approach, according to the court? What are the disadvantages? What weight should be given to agreements that are memorialized in boilerplate clinic consent forms? Do these agreements accurately reflect the parties' intentions? Should they be regarded as binding, or modifiable based on changed circumstances? The remaining approaches are discussed below.

3. Balancing interests. In the second prevailing approach, courts balance the parties' interests. What are the advantages and disadvantages of this approach?

Most courts applying this approach have ruled in favor of the party who wants to *avoid* procreation. See, e.g., J.B. v. M.B., 783 A.2d 707 (N.J. 2001). This outcome reflects a reluctance to force "parenthood" on an unwilling party. What does "forced parenthood" mean in this context? Legal parenthood? Simply the knowledge that a child who is genetically related to the person exists? To what extent did Roe v. Wade (Chapter I) address the burdens of forced genetic parenthood, apart from the burdens of forced pregnancy? Recall too Judith Jarvis Thomson's classic essay (Chapter I).

4. Contemporaneous mutual consent. In the third prevailing approach, a small minority of states require contemporaneous mutual consent.[30] See, e.g., McQueen v. Gadberry, 507 S.W.3d 127, 133 (Mo. Ct. App. 2016). According to this approach, the parties must agree (at the subsequent time) to the use of the embryos regardless of any preexisting agreement. The court will not allow a party to use the pre-embryos over the objection of the other party. What are the advantages and disadvantages of this approach? Consider the implication of requiring contemporaneous mutual consent for posthumous reproduction.

5. Marital property of a special character. Are frozen embryos property? Something else? If so, what? Early embryo disputes wrestled with this question. Compare York v. Jones, 717 F. Supp. 421 (E.D. Va. 1989) (property), with *Davis*, 842 S.W.2d at 594-597 (intermediate category between "persons" and "property"). Does *Rooks* resolve this issue? If courts treat embryos as marital property, how should the embryos be divided? Should they be awarded to the couple jointly? See McQueen v. Gadberry, 507 S.W.3d 127 (E.D. Mo. 2016). If so, does that mean they should be divided equally? Or, does it mean that the couple must both agree to their disposition?

The *Rooks* court adopts a special framework for distribution of the embryos. What is that framework? What considerations, according to *Rooks*, should a court evaluate? What are improper considerations? How relevant is the consideration of whether use of the embryos constitutes a party's "last procreative chance"? Does this factor apply differently to men and women, given that women have a limited number of gametes, while men do not?

The pregnancy success rate for IVF using cryopreserved embryos is fairly high. At least in the past, however, the success rate for IVF was lower when frozen, unfertilized ova were used. However, recent advances in "egg vitrification" technology

---

[30]. See, e.g., Dara E. Purvis, Frozen Embryos, Male Consent, and Masculinities, 97 Ind. L.J. 611 (2022) (exploring approaches).

have improved success rates.[31] How might this technological development affect embryo disputes at divorce?

6. Legal status of embryos: Personhood statutes. Do state laws on abortion play a role in resolution of embryo disputes? Several states have laws, prompted by anti-abortion activists, that define a "juridical person" to include fertilized human ova. See, e.g., La. Rev. Stat. Ann. §§9:121-9:126. What is the likely effect of these laws on the creation, storage, distribution, and disposal of embryos?

7. Destruction. What legal rules should govern the storage of the growing number of unused cryopreserved pre-embryos? Under the ABA Model Act Governing Assisted Reproductive Technologies, approved by the ABA in 2008 and revised in 2019, embryos are deemed abandoned (absent a contrary agreement) after five years and an unsuccessful search to find the interested participants. Disposal of abandoned embryos must follow the most recent recorded agreement between the participants and the storage facility, with a court order for disposition required in the absence of such agreement. ABA Model Act Governing Assisted Reproduction §504(1), (2) (2019). Evaluate the benefits and shortcomings of these provisions.

8. Constitutional issues. If a court allows one party to use the embryo(s) to procreate, does that violate the other person's right "not to procreate"?[32] What if the law clearly provides that the person who opposes this use will not be considered a legal parent? How does the court resolve these competing interests in *Rooks*? Does the "mutual contemporaneous consent" approach better protect the constitutional rights of the parties, as the judge in an omitted dissent in *Rooks* asserts? Why or why not? Does *Dobbs* change the analysis of embryo disputes?

9. High-profile case. In a well-publicized series of cases, the actress Sofia Vergara and her ex-fiancé, Nick Loeb, engaged in a lengthy and multi-state battle over the disposition of two embryos that they created while they were engaged. Loeb wanted to use the embryos. Vergara, who later married someone else, wanted them to remain frozen. During the litigation, an anti-abortion group sued Vergara, claiming that the embryos have a constitutional "right to live."[33] How would you resolve this dispute?

10. ABA Model Act Governing Assisted Reproduction. The ABA Model Act, referenced above, requires intended parents to enter into a written agreement prior to

---

[31]. Fertility Partnership Blog Post, Cold Cases: The Major Advances in the Freezing of Eggs and Embryos, Jan. 2, 2019, https://www.bostonplace.co.uk/blog/cold-cases-the-major-advances-of-freezing-eggs-and-embryos/.

[32]. See, e.g., I. Glenn Cohen, The Constitution and the Rights Not to Procreate, 60 Stan. L. Rev. 1135 (2008) (arguing that the "right not to procreate" is "best conceived as a bundle of rights containing three possible sticks: the right not to be a genetic parent, the right not to be a legal parent, and the right not to be a gestational parent").

[33]. See Laura Martin, Modern Family's Sofia Vergara's Embryo Lawsuit with Her Ex Is Causing Stress in Her New Marriage, UK Mirror, Oct. 29, 2018, https://www.mirror.co.uk/3am/celebrity-news/modern-familys-sofia-vergaras-embryo-13500940. In 2022, a California appellate court affirmed an order permanently enjoining Loeb from using the pre-embryos. Vergara v. Loeb, 2022 WL 4393915, at *4 (Cal. Ct. App. 2022), *review denied* (Jan. 11, 2023).

the IVF process addressing their intended use of the embryos, as well as their embryo disposition decision in the event of the dissolution of the parties' relationship or the death of one or both parties. ABA Model Act, §501(1). The act also clarifies that if a party withdraws consent prior to the assisted reproduction procedure, that person is not a parent. ABA Model Act, §606. Evaluate the benefits and shortcomings of this approach. How would these provisions apply to the dispute in *Rooks*?

Problem

Arizona became the first state in 2018 to pass a law governing the disposition of frozen embryos after divorce. The statute, promoted by anti-abortion advocates, directs courts at divorce to "award the in vitro human embryos to the spouse who intends to allow the in vitro human embryos to develop to birth." Even if the spouses have a preexisting disposition agreement, the court must award the embryos as prescribed. The statute also provides that the spouse who is not awarded the embryos "has no parental responsibilities and no right, obligation or interest with respect to any [ensuing] child," unless the spouse provided gametes and consents in writing to be a parent. This statute applies only to married couples. See Ariz. Rev. Stat. Ann. §25-318.03.

Evaluate the benefits and shortcomings of the law. The Arizona law was spurred in part by the lower court decision in Terrell v. Torres, 438 P.3d 681 (Ariz. Ct. App. 2019) (reversing a trial court order requiring the embryos to be donated to a third party, and instead holding that the wife is permitted to use the embryos to attempt to become pregnant).

B. Adoption

1. Overview and Background

Some children are brought into families through adoption. Adoption, unknown at common law, is a purely statutory creation. Generally, with the exception of step-parent adoptions and "second parent adoptions," adoption is a legal procedure that "cuts off" the child's legal connections to their family of origin (if those relationships have not already been severed) and creates new parent-child relationships between the child and the adopting parent or parents. The termination of the parental rights of the parents of origin occurs either involuntarily, based on a showing that the parent is "unfit"; or voluntarily, based on the parent's relinquishment.

Approximately 2 percent of children under the age of 18 in the United States are adopted.[34] In 2019, just over 120,000 children were adopted in the United

[34]. Rose M. Kreider & Daphne A. Lofquist, U.S. Census Bureau, Adopted Children and Stepchildren: 2010, at 4 (Apr. 2014), https://www.census.gov/library/publications/2014/demo/p20-572.html.

States.[35] Most of these are "unrelated adoptions" (i.e., adoptions by unrelated adults). The remainder consists of adoptions by relatives. About half of all adoptions are handled by public agencies. In many of the latter adoptions, the children were removed involuntarily from their families of origin through the child welfare or family regulation system. In addition to public agencies, some licensed adoption agencies are private (either nonprofit or for-profit). A smaller number of adoptions are "independent adoptions," in which the birth parents choose who will adopt their child.

Stephen B. Presser, *The Historical Background of the American Law of Adoption*
11 J. Fam. L. 443, 446-489 (1971)

We can document the practice of adoption among the ancient Babylonians, Egyptians, and Hebrews, as well as the Greeks, but the most advanced early law on adoption which we have is from the Romans. In contrast with current adoption law, which has as its purpose the "best interests" of the child, it appears that ancient adoption law, and particularly the Roman example, was clearly designed to benefit the *adopter*, and any benefits to the adoptee were secondary. There were two broad purposes that Roman adoption law served: (1) to avoid extinction of the family, and (2) to perpetuate rites of family religious worship.

[Adoption was not known at common law.] The usual explanation for the absence of a legal recognition of adoption in the English common law is the inordinately high regard for blood lineage of the English. . . .

The purpose of the American adoption statutes passed in the middle of the nineteenth century was to provide for the welfare of dependent children, a purpose quite different from that of the old Roman laws. . . . The first comprehensive adoption statute was passed in 1851 in Massachusetts. Among its key provisions were requirements 1) that written consent be given by the natural parents . . . ; 2) that the child himself must consent if he is fourteen years of age or older; 3) that the adopter's [spouse] must join in the petition for adoption; 4) that the probate judge . . . must be satisfied that the petitioner(s) were "of sufficient ability to bring up the child . . . and that it is fit and proper that such adoption should take effect" . . . ; 5) that once the adoption was approved by the probate court, the adopted child would become "to all intents and purposes" the legal child of the petitioner(s); [and] 6) that the natural parents would be deprived by the decree of adoption of all legal rights and obligations respecting the adopted child. . . .

[The widespread passage of state adoption laws in the nineteenth century] came about as a result of the economic changes which made the stop-gap institutions of apprenticeship, service, and indenture quite unable to cope with the great numbers of children who had been neglected by their families and [the state]. In order to understand better the motives that lay behind the passage of

---

[35]. Child Welfare Information Gateway, Trends in U.S. Adoptions: 2010–2019 (2022), https://www.childwelfare.gov/pubPDFs/adopted2010_19.pdf.

the adoption statutes, it is important to understand some of these other developments in child welfare work. . . .

[P]hilanthropic motives [of private agencies for the care of neglected children were] most probably inspired by the continuing plight of dependent children in the hands of public authorities. . . . Around 1850, however, private agencies began to be founded with the avowed purpose of placing younger children in a suitable family atmosphere. The work of some of the "infant's hospitals," "foundling asylums," and "maternity hospitals" in New York and Boston stands out in this regard, as does the work of the Children's Aid Societies started in those cities in 1853 and 1865, respectively. . . . The Children's Aid Societies made efforts to place children in suitable homes, usually homes far from the city, in the expanding states and territories of the West. [T]he Children's Aid Society of New York [placed] over twenty thousand children in homes out of New York City in the twenty years after it was founded.

[Many of] the children placed by such agencies [found] themselves in situations which not only resembled "adoption" as we know it today but which was called by the same name. As the phenomenon of children in adopted homes became more common, there was increased pressure not only to pass laws regulating and ensuring the legal relations between adopted children and their natural and adoptive parents, but to guarantee that some benefits of heirship were conferred on the adopted child. . . .

2. Involuntary Termination of Parental Rights

SANTOSKY v. KRAMER
455 U.S. 745 (1982)

Justice BLACKMUN delivered the opinion of the Court. . . .

Under New York law, the State may terminate, over parental objection, the rights of parents in their natural child upon a finding that the child is "permanently neglected." The New York Family Court Act §622 requires that only a "fair preponderance of the evidence" support that finding. Thus, in New York, the factual certainty required to extinguish the parent-child relationship is no greater than that necessary to award money damages in an ordinary civil action. . . . The question here is whether New York's "fair preponderance of the evidence" standard is constitutionally sufficient.

Petitioners John Santosky II and Annie Santosky are the natural parents of Tina and John III. In November 1973, after incidents reflecting parental neglect, respondent Kramer, Commissioner of the Ulster County Department of Social Services, initiated a neglect proceeding under Fam. Ct. Act §1022 and removed Tina from her natural home. About 10 months later, he removed John III and placed him with foster parents. On the day John was taken, Annie Santosky gave birth to a third child, Jed. When Jed was only three days old, respondent transferred him to a foster home on the ground that immediate removal was necessary to avoid imminent danger to his life or health.

In October 1978, respondent petitioned the Ulster County Family Court to terminate petitioners' parental rights in the three children. [The family court weighed the evidence under the "preponderance of the evidence" standard. When petitioners objected, the judge rejected their constitutional challenge. The court concluded that the agency made "diligent efforts" to strengthen the parental relationship but the parents were incapable of planning for their children's future even with public assistance. The court then held a dispositional hearing and ruled that the best interests of the three children required permanent termination of the Santoskys' custody. Petitioners appealed.]

[There are] two central questions here — whether process is constitutionally due a natural parent at a State's parental rights termination proceeding, and, if so, what process is due. . . .

The fundamental liberty interest of natural parents in the care, custody, and management of their child does not evaporate simply because they have not been model parents or have lost temporary custody of their child to the State. Even when blood relationships are strained, parents retain a vital interest in preventing the irretrievable destruction of their family life. If anything, persons faced with forced dissolution of their parental rights have a more critical need for procedural protections than do those resisting state intervention into ongoing family affairs. When the State moves to destroy weakened familial bonds, it must provide the parents with fundamentally fair procedures.

[The Court then applies a three-part balancing test, based on Mathews v. Eldridge, 424 U.S. 319, 335 (1976), to determine whether the Santosky parents received due process during the TPR hearing. According to that test, courts must consider the private interests affected by the proceeding; the risk of error created by the State's chosen procedure; and the countervailing governmental interest supporting use of the challenged procedure.]

"The extent to which procedural due process must be afforded the recipient is influenced by the extent to which he may be 'condemned to suffer grievous loss.'" [It is plain] that a natural parent's "desire for and right to 'the companionship, care, custody, and management of his or her children'" is an interest far more precious than any property right. When the State initiates a parental rights termination proceeding, it seeks not merely to infringe that fundamental liberty interest, but to end it. . . . Thus, the first *Eldridge* factor — the private interest affected — weighs heavily against use of the preponderance standard at a state-initiated permanent neglect proceeding. . . .

[W]e next must consider both the risk of erroneous deprivation of private interests resulting from use of a "fair preponderance" standard and the likelihood that a higher evidentiary standard would reduce that risk. [T]he factfinding stage of a state-initiated permanent neglect proceeding bears many of the indicia of a criminal trial. [T]he judge then determines whether the State has proved the statutory elements of permanent neglect by a fair preponderance of the evidence.

At such a proceeding, numerous factors combine to magnify the risk of erroneous factfinding. Permanent neglect proceedings employ imprecise substantive standards that leave determinations unusually open to the subjective values of the judge. [T]he court possesses unusual discretion to underweigh probative facts that might favor the parent. Because parents subject to termination proceedings are often poor, uneducated, or members of minority groups, such proceedings are often vulnerable to judgments based on cultural or class bias.

The State's ability to assemble its case almost inevitably dwarfs the parents' ability to mount a defense. . . . The State's attorney usually will be expert on the issues contested and the procedures employed at the factfinding hearing and enjoys full access to all public records concerning the family. [T]he primary witnesses at the hearing will be the agency's own professional caseworkers whom the State has empowered both to investigate the family situation and to testify against the parents. . . .

The disparity between the adversaries' litigation resources is matched by a striking asymmetry in their litigation options. Unlike criminal defendants, natural parents have no "double jeopardy" defense against repeated state termination efforts. . . . Coupled with a "fair preponderance of the evidence" standard, these factors create a significant prospect of erroneous termination. . . .

The Appellate Division approved New York's preponderance standard on the ground that it properly "balanced rights possessed by the child [with] those of the natural parents. . . ." 427 N.Y.S.2d, at 320. By so saying, the court suggested that a preponderance standard properly allocates the risk of error between the parents and the child. That view is fundamentally mistaken.

The [appellate] court's theory assumes that termination of the natural parents' rights invariably will benefit the child.[15] Yet we have noted above that the parents and the child share an interest in avoiding erroneous termination. Even accepting the court's assumption, we cannot agree with its conclusion that a preponderance standard fairly distributes the risk of error between parent and child. Use of that standard reflects the judgment that society is nearly neutral between erroneous termination of parental rights and erroneous failure to terminate those rights. For the child, the likely consequence of an erroneous failure to terminate is preservation of an uneasy status quo. For the natural parents, however, the consequence of an erroneous termination is the unnecessary destruction of their natural family. A standard that allocates the risk of error nearly equally between those two outcomes does not reflect properly their relative severity.

Two state interests are at stake in parental rights termination proceedings — a parens patriae interest in preserving and promoting the welfare of the child and a fiscal and administrative interest in reducing the cost and burden of such proceedings. A standard of proof more strict than preponderance of the evidence is consistent with both interests.

. . . As parens patriae, the State's goal is to provide the child with a permanent home. Yet while there is still reason to believe that positive, nurturing parent-child relationships exist, the parens patriae interest favors preservation, not severance, of natural familial bonds. . . . We cannot believe that it would burden the State unduly to require that its factfinders have the same factual certainty when

---

15. This is a hazardous assumption at best. Even when a child's natural home is imperfect, permanent removal from that home will not necessarily improve his welfare. See, e.g., Wald, State Intervention on Behalf of "Neglected" Children: A Search for Realistic Standards, 27 Stan. L. Rev. 985, 993 (1975) ("In fact, under current practice, coercive intervention frequently results in placing a child in a more detrimental situation than he would be in without intervention").

Nor does termination of parental rights necessarily ensure adoption. Even when a child eventually finds an adoptive family, he may spend years moving between state institutions and "temporary" foster placements after his ties to his natural parents have been severed.

terminating the parent-child relationship as they must have to suspend a driver's license. [Without deciding the outcome under a constitutionally proper standard], we vacate the judgment of the Appellate Division and remand the case for further proceedings. . . .

NOTE: THE CHILD WELFARE OR FAMILY REGULATION SYSTEM

Some children who are ultimately adopted are children who have been involuntarily removed from their families of origin based on allegations of parental neglect or abuse. The system that regulates this process is often referred to as the "child welfare system." Increasingly, however, scholars are instead using the phrase "family policing" or "family regulation system." The use of the term "child welfare" to describe the system, some argue, is misleading, given that children are often harmed by the process. Professor Lisa Washington prefers the term "family regulation." This term, she argues, "better highlights the punitive nature of a system that mirrors and intersects with the criminal legal system."[36] However denominated, the system refers to the network of organizations that interact with families when parents are alleged to be unable to adequately care for their children.

In the vast majority of cases, child welfare involvement is triggered by allegations of neglect; child abuse cases are much less common.[37] Neglect allegations often are based on facts that are hard to separate from the consequences of poverty. As Professor Sara Greene writes:

> [In one study of parent neglect cases handled by child protection services], more than eighty percent involve unmarried mothers living in poverty. . . . This disproportionate involvement of poor families is due in part to a system that penalizes poverty conditions—children may be removed from their homes (and their parent(s) charged with neglect) for poverty alone. [In another study,] almost ten percent of children were removed because of 'environmental neglect,' which was defined as a lack of adequate food, shelter, or clothing, rather than any kind of deliberate action on the part of the parent involved.[38]

Families of color—particularly Black, Native American, and Native Alaskan families—are disproportionately likely to experience child welfare involvement.[39]

---

[36]. S. Lisa Washington, Survived & Coerced: Epistemic Injustice in the Family Regulation System, 122 Colum. L. Rev. 1097, 1103 (2022). See also Nancy D. Polikoff & Jane M. Spinak, Foreword: Strengthened Bonds: Abolishing the Child Welfare System and Re-Envisioning Child Well-Being, 11 Colum. J. Race & L. 427, 431 (2021) (rejecting the terms "child welfare" and "child protection" because the system "does not protect nor support child well-being, and too often perpetrates harm on children, families, and communities").

[37]. U.S. Dept. of Health & Hum. Servs., Admin. Children & Families, Children's Bureau, How the Child Welfare System Works 5 (2020) ("Nearly three-quarters of all child maltreatment cases are related to some form of neglect[.]").

[38]. Sara S. Greene, A Theory of Poverty: Legal Immobility, 96 Wash. U. L. Rev. 753, 778-779 (2019). See also Josh Gupta-Kagan, Distinguishing Family Poverty from Child Neglect, __ Iowa L. Rev. __ (forthcoming).

[39]. Child Welfare Info. Gateway, Racial Disproportionality and Disparity in Child Welfare 3-5 (2016). Children with parents with disabilities and with LGBTQ parents are also disproportionately represented in the system. See, e.g., Robyn M. Powell, Achieving Justice for Disabled Parents

Several factors contribute to these disparities, including the correlation between race and poverty, limited access to services, geographic restrictions, and the personal biases of child welfare professionals that (knowingly or unknowingly) affect their actions or decisions.[40]

Children of color, particularly Black and Native American children, also have worse outcomes once they are removed from their homes. They are "more likely to experience multiple placements, less likely to be reunited with their birth families, more likely to experience group care, less likely to establish a permanent placement and more likely to experience poor social, behavioral and educational outcomes."[41]

An asserted goal of the system is to achieve permanency for the children who are swept up into it. For many, however, this goal is never achieved. Instead, many children—particularly children of color—spend many years in foster care, often in multiple placements. The removal of a child from the family of origin, even for short periods of time, can inflict harm on the child. According to two commentators:

> When a child is removed from his home, it upsets all aspects of that child's life. Removal strips the child of his connection to his birth parents, his siblings, his extended family, his friends, and often, his school. It abruptly disrupts his attachment to his primary caregiver and it thrusts the child into a foreign system: foster care. In foster care, children often are placed in unfamiliar placements, with unfamiliar caretakers. The experience of removal and placement in foster care traumatizes children in complex ways.[42]

Some scholars and advocates, including Professor Dorothy Roberts, argue that radical transformation is necessary. In her groundbreaking book Shattered Bonds: The Color of Child Welfare (2001), she draws attention to the effects of the disproportionate representation of Black families in the child welfare system. This system, she argues, "disrupts, restructures, and polices Black families."[43] More recently, Roberts repeated her call for the abolition of this system: "[Child Protective Services or] CPS affirmatively harms children and their families while failing to address the structural causes for their hardships."[44]

Others warn against making large structural changes to the existing system. For example, Professor Elizabeth Bartholet argues: "[Some] may think it is useful to

and Their Children: An Abolitionist Approach, 33 Yale J.L. & Feminism 37 (2022); L. Frunel & Sarah H. Lorr, Lived Experience and Disability Justice in the Family Regulation System, 12 Colum. J. Race & L. 1 (2022); Courtney G. Joslin & Catherine Sakimura, Fractured Families: LGBTQ People and the Family Regulation System, 13 Cal. L. Rev. Online 78 (2022).

[40]. See, e.g., S. Lisa Washington, Pathology Logics, 117 Nw. U. L. Rev. 1523, 1531 (2023).

[41]. Racial Disproportionality, supra note [39]. See also, e.g., Clare Huntington & Elizabeth S. Scott, Conceptualizing Legal Childhood in the Twenty-First Century, 118 Mich. L. Rev. 1371, 1389 (2020).

[42]. Vivek S. Sankaran & Christopher Church, Easy Come, Easy Go: The Plight of Children Who Spend Less than Thirty Days in Foster Care, 19 U. Pa. J.L. & Soc. Change 207, 211 (2016). See also, e.g., Shanta Trivedi & Matthew Fraidin, A Role for Communities in Reasonable Efforts to Prevent Removal, 12 Colum. J. Race & L. 1, 2 (2022).

[43]. Dorothy Roberts, Shattered Bonds: The Color of Child Welfare viii (2001).

[44]. Dorothy Roberts, Abolishing Policing Also Means Abolishing Family Regulation, The Imprint, June 16, 2020, https://imprintnews.org/child-welfare-2/abolishing-policing-also-means-abolishing-family-regulation/44480.

identify the disproportionate breakup of black families as a form of racism. They may think that by promoting preservation of black families they will force a stingy society to commit more resources for supportive family services." She continues:

> But if this is the strategy, it is wrong, both because it puts black children at unfair risk, and because it seems far too limited in its goals for the black community. Leaving black children with their parents to suffer ongoing maltreatment hurts those children, and sends them on to adult lives characterized by poverty, substance abuse, unemployment, and a high likelihood that they will in turn victimize the next generation through maltreatment of their children. The increased family support services that might result from an expansion of family preservation programs will be limited, and will do little to protect children from ongoing maltreatment, or to make any dent on the problems suffered by the black community.[45]

Professor Bartholet concludes that claims of racism regarding child welfare workers focus attention inappropriately on a "non-problem," while ignoring the structural challenges that Black families face.

Notes and Questions

1. Constitutional framework: Harm principle. *Meyer* and *Pierce* (reprinted in Chapter I) establish the foundation for the right to privacy by interpreting the "liberty" protected by the Due Process Clause to encompass parental autonomy, i.e., the right to rear a child as the parent sees fit. In a subsequent case, the U.S. Supreme Court explored the limitations on parents' right to control the upbringing of their children. In Prince v. Massachusetts, 321 U.S. 158 (1944), the Supreme Court upheld the conviction of a Jehovah's Witness (Sarah Prince) who was convicted of violating state child labor law after she took her nine-year-old niece with her to sell religious literature, ruling that the state may limit parental rights in the interest of child welfare. The unique role of the state vis-à-vis children (parens patriae) provided the rationale.

Prince thereby established the principle that the state interest in protecting children from harm circumscribes parental autonomy. Based on this principle, the state may intervene in the family to protect children, such as by removing the child from the home in cases of abuse and neglect. And if the court determines that the parents are unfit, their rights can be terminated in TPR proceedings.

2. Forms of state intervention. In *Santosky*, the family court terminated the Santoskys' parental rights after determining that the children were permanently neglected. State intervention in cases of child abuse and neglect typically takes two initial forms: summary seizure and the assertion of temporary custody. Jurisdiction in these cases is sometimes called "dependency jurisdiction" because the child becomes a dependent of the state.

Summary seizure occurs when a court determines that an emergency exists and orders the child's removal from the home in an ex parte hearing. The court

---

[45]. Elizabeth Bartholet, The Racial Disproportionality Movement in Child Welfare: False Facts and Dangerous Directions, 51 Ariz. L. Rev. 871, 878 (2009).

then holds a jurisdictional (adversarial) proceeding to determine temporary custody in which the court determines whether the child falls within the statutory definition of an abused or neglected child. The court next conducts a dispositional hearing to select among various dispositions, including foster care and termination of parental rights. (*Santosky* refers somewhat differently to these stages of a child neglect proceeding, pursuant to New York statute, as "the fact-finding (jurisdictional) hearing" and the "dispositional hearing," at which the court determines which placement serves the child's best interests.) These stages sometimes occur in a single hearing. As the majority mentions in *Santosky*, these decisions take place against a backdrop of "imprecise subjective standards" that invite value judgments about proper parenting that often reflects bias based on race, culture, and class.

3. Standard of proof. What are the different choices for the constitutionally permissible standard of proof in TPR hearings? Why did the Supreme Court choose the higher standard? How did the Court balance the competing interests of the participants? Does the clear-and-convincing-evidence standard, required in *Santosky*, adequately protect family integrity and parental autonomy? Adequately protect the interests of children?

Justice Rehnquist, dissenting in *Santosky*, argued that the lower standard of proof reflected a constitutionally permissible balance of interests. He emphasized the state's efforts to aid the Santosky parents in regaining custody of their children and the numerous procedural protections afforded them. He asserted that the higher standard of proof constituted a worrisome intrusion into an area of law traditionally entrusted to the states. Which standard of proof do you think provides a better balance of the competing interests?

States have adopted different responses to the standard of proof required by *Santosky*. Most states follow *Santosky* and require clear and convincing evidence. However, some states hold that *Santosky* applies only to the initial determination of parental unfitness in a TPR hearing, but not to the dispositional stage (sometimes called the "best interests" stage). These states apply a preponderance-of-the-evidence standard in the latter stage.

4. Abuse or neglect. In a TPR proceeding, the government has the burden of proving (usually by clear and convincing evidence) that the parent has engaged in either "child abuse" or "child neglect." The definitions of these terms vary state to state. Until recently, a federal law—the Child Abuse Prevention and Treatment Act (CAPTA)—provided that, at a minimum, child abuse and neglect included "any recent act or failure to act on the part of a parent or caretaker, which results in death, serious physical or emotional harm, sexual abuse or exploitation, or an act or failure to act which presents an imminent risk of serious harm." How easy would this language be for a court to apply? For state child welfare officials? This language was struck from 42 U.S.C. §5106(g) in 2022.

Suppose that the risks stem from the parent's poverty. Should the risks nonetheless provide a basis for removal of the child and TPR? Some states expressly exclude poverty-associated risks from the definition of abuse or neglect. For example, New York defines "neglect" to include the failure to provide children "with adequate food, clothing, shelter, or education," but only when the parent is "financially able to do so or offered financial or other reasonable means to do so." N.Y. Fam. Ct. Act §1012(f)(i)(A). Even when the state does exempt poverty-related cases from the definition of abuse and neglect, it can be difficult to distinguish poverty from neglect.[46]

5. ASFA. Every state has statutory provisions authorizing the permanent removal of children from the home. Before termination of parental rights, however, federal law requires that states must provide services to families of origin, including reunification efforts. See Adoption Assistance and Child Welfare Act (AACWA), 42 U.S.C. §§620 et seq., 670 et seq. (requiring states to make "reasonable efforts" to prevent placement of a child in foster care and to reunify the child with the parents).

In response to criticisms that children often languish in foster care, Congress in 1997 enacted the Adoption and Safe Families Act (ASFA), Pub. L. No. 105-89, 111 Stat. 2115. ASFA eliminates the requirement that the state must undertake reasonable efforts to reunify the family in certain severe cases (i.e., torture, sexual abuse, a parent's murder of another child, or a parent's loss of parental rights to a sibling). 42 U.S.C. §671(a)(15)(D). In addition, ASFA shortens the period triggering permanency hearings to no later than 12 months after the child's entry into foster care and requires states, with some exceptions, to seek TPRs for children who have been in foster care for 15 of the last 22 months (id. §675(5)(E)).

Critics claim that these reforms undervalue minority families, discount the harm to children of removing them from their families of origin, and ultimately encourage the permanent destruction of Black families.[47]

6. Right to counsel. One year before *Santosky*, the Supreme Court determined that an indigent parent has no due process right to counsel in TPR proceedings. In Lassiter v. Department of Social Services, 452 U.S. 18 (1981), the Court held that appointment of counsel for parents in TPR hearings should be based on a case-by-case balancing test. Is *Santosky* consistent with *Lassiter*? Which procedural protection — the right to counsel or a heightened standard of proof — is more valuable to parents fighting terminations? Which better protects children's interests? Which imposes greater costs on the state? Despite *Lassiter*, the vast majority of states guarantee indigent parents the right to counsel in TPR proceedings.[48]

7. Modern trend: Restoration of parental rights. As of 2020, nearly half the states passed laws authorizing the reinstatement or restoration of parental rights following termination.[49] Parental rights restoration and reinstatement is an important alternative for the small subset of youth who have spent a lengthy period in foster care and whose parents have been able to remedy the issues that prompted

---

[46]. Gupta-Kagan, supra note [38], at *16.

[47]. See Roberts, Shattered Bonds, supra note [43], at 165-172 (2002); Ashley Albert & Amy Mulzer, Adoption Cannot Be Reformed, 12 Colum. J. Race & L. 1 (2022); Cynthia Godsoe, Parsing Parenthood, 17 Lewis & Clark L. Rev. 113 (2013).

[48]. In 45 states, parents have a statutory right to counsel in state-initiated TPR hearings. In some states, the right is constitutional as well as statutory. Vivek Sankaran & John Pollock, A National Survey on a Parent's Right to Counsel in State-Initiated Dependency and Termination of Parental Rights Cases, Oct. 27, 2016, http://civilrighttocounsel.org/uploaded_files/219/Table_of _parents__RTC_in_dependency_and_TPR_cases_FINAL.pdf.

[49]. Nat'l Conf. of State Legs., Reinstatement of Parents Rights State Statute Summary, https://www.ncsl.org/human-services/reinstatement-of-parental-rights-state-statute-summary.

TPR. California pioneered this trend in 2005 in response to a 14-year-old foster child's unsuccessful plea to undo the order terminating his parents' rights after a planned stepparent adoption failed. See Cal. Welf. & Inst. Code §366.26(i)(2). Judicial restoration of parental rights generally requires the parent to demonstrate substantial progress in correcting the conditions that led to the termination of parental rights; that they are both willing and able to provide a safe permanent home; that the restoration is in the best interests of the child; and that both the parent and the child agree.

Problem

T. C. is the biological mother of A. T. M. When A. T. M. was approximately 6 months old, the Division of Child Protection and Permanency ("the Division") conducted an emergency removal of the child on the ground that the mother had been admitted to the hospital and that A. T. M. was found in the care of J. K., who was using an open oven and an electric fan to heat the apartment. The child was found sitting in a car seat on the sofa. The child was dressed in dirty clothes. J. K. told the division that he, T. C., and the child slept together in a bed because they did not have a baby bassinette or crib. When asked about the child's food, J. K. showed the Division worker a half-full can of baby formula.

After a hearing, the court determined that the child should remain in the custody of the Division because T. C. did not have appropriate housing due to the lack of heat in the apartment and T. C.'s mental health issues. At a subsequent hearing, the Division presented the court with T. C.'s psychiatric evaluation, which recommended medication and individual therapy. The Division had previously referred T. C. to mental health services, but the evidence indicated that T. C. was not following the recommendations. The evidence also showed that T. C. was receiving $741 per month in Social Security benefits; this represented her total monthly income. The trial court concluded that T. C. had abused or neglected the child by placing the child at substantial risk of harm and approved the Division's permanent plan, which called for the termination of T. C.'s parental rights.

Assume that the state law defines child neglect to include the failure to provide children "with adequate food, clothing, shelter, or education," but only when the parent is "financially able to do so or offered financial or other reasonable means to do so." T. C. appeals. What result? See New Jersey Div. of Child Prot. & Permanency v. T.C., 2017 WL 2375693, at *5 (N.J. Super. Ct. App. Div. 2017).

3. Voluntary Relinquishment or Surrender

Sometimes the adoption process is the result of involuntary termination of the birth family through the child welfare or family regulation system based on allegations of child abuse or neglect. Alternatively, the adoption process can begin when the birth parent voluntarily relinquishes (or "surrenders") the child to a state-licensed or state-operated agency. The agency takes legal custody of the child and selects a placement following an evaluation of the prospective adoptive parents, often called a "home study" or a "preplacement investigation." After a residential period under the agency's supervision, a court issues an adoption decree. In the past, neither the birth parents nor the adopters learned the others' identities. In this type of adoption, if the placement fails during the trial period, the child is returned to the agency's custody, not to the birth parents, whose rights are terminated by the relinquishment. By contrast, in independent adoptions, the birth parents typically select the adopters, often with assistance from an intermediary. Today, public agencies process far more adoptions than do private agencies, with independent adoptions accounting for a smaller number.

Between World War II and the *Roe* decision in 1973, unmarried mothers faced enormous social and legal pressure to surrender children upon birth. The stories of some of these birth mothers reflect coercion, shame, and lifelong emotional scars, despite the contentions of some experts that surrender would help these women reconstitute their lives in a healthy way. Such information prompted the historian Rickie Solinger to conclude that "adoption is rarely about mothers' choices; it is, instead, about the abject choicelessness of some resourceless women."[50] In the years following *Roe*, the percent of unmarried women who relinquished their children for adoption declined. Some commentators predict, however, that this trend might reverse in the wake of *Dobbs* because many people will lack access to abortion care. Others, including Professor Diana Greene Foster, dispute this claim. Foster, who was the lead researcher on The Turnaway Study (see Chapter I), found that 91 percent of women who were forced to carry an unwanted pregnancy to term opted to keep their babies.[51]

In addition to the formal relinquishment process, all 50 states now have "safe haven" laws (also known as "Baby Moses" or "safe surrender" laws). Enacted in response to publicized cases of infanticide and abandonment, these laws allow the mothers of young infants to anonymously relinquish their babies at designated centers. Provisions vary depending on the jurisdiction.

Justice Amy Coney Barrett famously referred to these safe haven laws in her questioning during the *Dobbs* oral argument, implying that the negative impact of abortion bans on the lives of women experiencing unwanted pregnancies would be "take[n] care of" by such laws. Others contend that this position diminishes the harms imposed by forced pregnancy and is based on an incorrect assumption that most women who experience unwanted pregnancies will relinquish the child upon birth. As noted above, the vast majority of women who are forced to carry unwanted pregnancies keep the child. With regard to safe haven laws in particular, even though such laws exist in all 50 states, they are rarely utilized.[52]

---

[50]. Rickie Solinger, Beggars and Choosers: How the Politics of Choice Shapes Adoption, Abortion, and Welfare in the United States 67, 69-70 (2001). See also Ann Fessler, The Girls Who Went Away: The Hidden History of Women Who Surrendered Children for Adoption in the Decades Before Roe v. Wade (2006).

[51]. Abortion Decision Making Among Women Seeking Abortions, Advancing New Standards in Reproductive Health (ANSIRH), https://www.ansirh.org/research/publication/adopt ion-decision-making-among-women-seeking-abortion.

[52]. See, e.g., Sara Luterman, What Are Safe Haven Laws, and Why Did They Come Up in a Supreme Court Case on Abortion?, The 19th, Dec. 8, 2021 (noting that there "are typically only a handful of cases per year"), https://19thnews.org/2021/12/what-are-safe-haven-laws -supreme-court-case-abortion/. See also Carol Sanger, Infant Safe Haven Laws: Legislating in the Culture of Life, 106 Colum. L. Rev. 753 (2006).

Some parents who relinquish their children for adoption change their minds. Different states have different rules governing relinquishment or the withdrawal of consent. In some jurisdictions, a parent's consent is effective immediately. Other jurisdictions designate a time period (e.g., 72 hours) after the child's birth for revocation of consent. 750 Ill. Comp. Stat. Ann. 50/9; id. 50/11. Another approach allows withdrawal of consent any time before the final decree of termination of parental rights or adoption. See, e.g., 25 U.S.C. §1913(c) (Indian Child Welfare Act). Sometimes the parent alleges that consent was procured by fraud or coercion; courts tend to read such terms narrowly in adoption cases. See, e.g., In re S.K.L.H., 204 P.3d 320, 327 (Alaska 2009) (confusion, mistake, and change of heart do not suffice).

NOTE: ADOPTION AND NONMARITAL FATHERS

Traditionally, most states required only the birth mother's consent before adoption of a nonmarital child. The Supreme Court's 1972 decision in Stanley v. Illinois (reprinted above) prompted reconsideration of this practice to protect adoptive placements from subsequent collateral challenge by fathers excluded from the process. *Stanley* established that some nonmarital biological fathers have a constitutionally protected parent-child relationship. *Stanley* and the decisions that followed it made clear, however, that biology alone does not give rise to constitutional protection; something more was required. This emphasis on the "something more" left unclear when a nonmarital biological father had a constitutionally protected parent-child relationship in situations in which they had not yet had time to develop a social relationship with the child, as might be the case with a recently born infant. There were also questions about whether a biological father should be recognized as having a constitutionally protected parent-child interest where he sought to see the child, but these efforts were allegedly thwarted or prevented by the birth mother, as was the case in Lehr v. Robertson, 463 U.S. 248 (1983).

The Supreme Court precedents including *Stanley*, *Quilloin*, *Caban*, and *Lehr* (also discussed above), invite different readings. According to Dean David Meyer, under the "child-centered" view, only an actual parent-child relationship matters, not the efforts of a biological father whom the mother successfully thwarts. Under a second reading, the Court is concerned not simply with the existence of the relationship, but also with "the strength of the father's moral claim [that is,] whether the claimant has acted in a way deserving of protection."[53] Consider how a father would show that he is "deserving," including in cases in which he did not know about the conception or birth. See, e.g., In re Adoption of Anderson, 624 S.E.2d 626 (N.C. 2006); In re Marquette S., 734 N.W.2d 81 (Wis. 2007). Consider whether the mother's conduct, including her false claim of miscarriage or promising not to place the child for adoption, should be relevant. Compare In re Adoption of Baby Girl P., 242 P.3d 1168 (Kan. 2010), with In re Adoption of B.Y., 356 P.3d 1215 (Utah 2015).

In the wake of such questions, states have developed several approaches for addressing the rights of unmarried birth fathers in the adoption process. About

---

[53]. David D. Meyer, Family Ties: Solving the Constitutional Dilemma of the Faultless Father, 41 Ariz. L. Rev. 753, 764 (1999).

half of the states have statutes establishing "putative father registries" for men who believe that they are (or may be) a child's father. By registering, the unmarried father acquires certain rights, such as the right to receive notice of court proceedings (if registration occurs within a designated timeline), petitions for adoption, and actions to terminate parental rights; registering, however, does not establish their parental rights. These registries place the burden on a nonmarital, biological father to register if he wishes to receive notice of an adoption. In states with registries, failure to register generally eliminates the need to notify him or secure his consent. The Supreme Court approved reliance on this registry system in *Lehr*. See also UPA (2017), §402 (requiring registration no later than 30 days after birth or commencement of parentage proceedings before termination of parental rights).

The effectiveness of putative father registries is limited by the fact that many nonmarital fathers are unaware that such registries exist. Lack of knowledge, however, generally does not excuse noncompliance with the law. In addition, registry laws leave several issues unaddressed including whether sexual intercourse puts the man on notice that he should register; see, e.g., Utah Code Ann. §78B-6-110(1)(a) (putting putative fathers on constructive notice of their legal obligations arising from engaging in intercourse); and in which state the man should register if he is uncertain about the woman's location. (There is no national paternity registry.)

Other states have rules that require notice of an adoption to a nonmarital father who demonstrates that he sought to take responsibility for the child, but was prevented from doing so by the child's mother. In California, these men are called "*Kelsey S.* fathers," named after a state supreme court case that developed the doctrine. See Adoption of Kelsey S., 823 P.2d 1216 (Cal. 1992); V.S. v. M.L., 166 Cal. Rptr. 3d 376 (Ct. App. 2014). (The problem below seeks to apply this doctrine.)

Problem

After a short acquaintance, Mark (then 20) asks Stephanie (then 15) to marry. She declines. A few months later, they learn that Stephanie is pregnant. They decide on adoption. Stephanie then leaves Arizona to visit California. While in California, Stephanie meets a prospective adoptive couple, John and Margaret, and she chooses them to adopt the baby. On her return to Arizona, Stephanie's relationship with Mark deteriorates. Stephanie excludes him from birthing classes. Following two violent outbursts, Mark attempts suicide and enters drug rehabilitation therapy. He then informs Stephanie he no longer favors adoption.

Stephanie returns to California, gives birth, places the child with John and Margaret, and consents to their adoption. Mark, when he learns of the birth a week later, immediately consults an attorney, sends out birth announcements, and purchases baby supplies. Thereafter, he consistently expresses his desire to take full parental responsibilities.

John and Margaret seek to terminate Mark's parental rights in California. They claim that California law (Adoption of Kelsey S., 823 P.2d 1216 (Cal. 1992)) gives Mark no veto over the adoption because he failed to demonstrate a full commitment to parental responsibilities throughout the pregnancy. Mark also invokes *Kelsey S.*, counterarguing that he attempted to maintain a relationship with Stephanie during the pregnancy and that, since birth, he has done everything possible to assume full parental responsibility. He also claims that John and Margaret's interpretation of *Kelsey S.* discriminates by allowing mothers to decide after birth to withhold consent for adoption, while requiring fathers to decide early in the pregnancy. What result, and why? What policy issues does each reading of *Kelsey S.* raise? See Adoption of Michael H., 898 P.2d 891 (Cal. 1995).

4. Contemporary Controversies in Adoption

INDIAN CHILD WELFARE ACT (ICWA): HISTORICAL CONTEXT[54]

[The Indian Child Welfare Act (ICWA) is a federal statute governing the removal and out-of-home placement of Indian children. ICWA] came as a direct response to the mass removal of Indian children from their families during the 1950s, 1960s, and 1970s by state officials and private parties. That practice, in turn, was only the latest iteration of a much older policy of removing Indian children from their families—one initially spearheaded by federal officials . . . nearly 150 years ago. In all its many forms, the dissolution of the Indian family has had devastating effects on children and parents alike. It has also presented an existential threat to the continued vitality of Tribes—something many federal and state officials over the years saw as a feature, not as a flaw.

When Native American Tribes were forced onto reservations, they understood that life would never again be as it was. [Initially,] Indian education typically came in the form of day schools [where] the children lived at home with their families [and were able to] practice "their languages, beliefs, and traditional knowledge." . . .

[But t]he federal government had darker designs. By the late 1870s, its goals turned toward destroying tribal identity and assimilating Indians into broader society. Achieving those goals, officials reasoned, required the "complete isolation of the Indian child from his savage antecedents." And because "the warm reciprocal affection existing between parents and children" was "among the strongest characteristics of the Indian nature," officials set out to eliminate it by dissolving Indian families.

Thus began Indian boarding schools [with the following mission:] "[A]ll the Indian there is in the race should be dead. Kill the Indian in him, and save the man." [If Indian families resisted and refused to send their children, Congress] authorized the Secretary of the Interior to "prevent the issuing of rations or the furnishing of subsistence" to Indian families who would not surrender their children. When economic coercion failed, officials sometimes resorted to abduction. . . .

---

[54]. The following excerpt from Justice Gorsuch's concurring opinion in Haaland v. Brackeen, 143 S. Ct. 1609 (2023) (excerpted below), provides background about the historic treatment of Native American children by the federal government and the states that prompted the passage of ICWA in 1978, as well as a basic description of how ICWA works. For more information about the historic treatment of Native American children, see, e.g., Matthew L. M. Fletcher, Federal Indian Law (2016).

[T]he boarding schools would often seek to strip [the children] of nearly every aspect of their identity. The schools would take away their Indian names and give them English ones. The schools would cut their hair—a point of shame in many native communities [and] confiscate their traditional clothes. [T]he schools frequently prohibited children from speaking their native language or engaging in customary cultural or religious practices. Nor could children freely associate with members of their own Tribe. . . . Resistance could invite punishments that included "withholding food" and "whipping." [Students also faced] "[r]ampant physical, sexual, and emotional abuse; disease; malnourishment; overcrowding; and lack of health care." To lower costs further and promote assimilation, some schools [sent] Indian children to live "with white families" and perform "household and farm chores" for them, thereby taking] many Indian children "even further from their homes, families, and cultures." . . .

[A Brookings Institute report in 1928 found that the provisions for the care of the Indian children were grossly inadequate and recommended that the government move toward day schools or public schools.] That transition would be slow to materialize, though. As late as 1971, federal boarding schools continued to house "more than 17 per cent of the Indian school-age population." As federal boarding schools closed their doors and Indian children returned to the reservations, States with significant Native American populations found themselves facing significant new educational and welfare responsibilities. [Around this time, states recognized they could save money] by "promoting the *adoption* of Indian children by private families."

This restarted a now-familiar nightmare for Indian families. The same assimilationist rhetoric previously invoked by the federal government persisted, "voiced this time by state and county officials" [who advocated allowing] "'civilized people'" to raise the children . . . . Through the 1960s and 1970s, Indian-child removal reached new heights. . . . Surveys conducted in 1969 and 1974 showed that "approximately 25–35 per cent of all Indian children [were] separated from their families." Often, these removals whisked children not only out of their families but out of their communities. Some estimate that "more than 90 percent of non-related adoptions of Indian children [were] made by non-Indian couples." These family separations frequently lacked justification. . . . These determinations [to remove the children from their families], came mainly from non-Indian social workers, many of whom were "ignorant of Indian cultural values and social norms." They routinely penalized Indian parents for conditions of "[p]overty, poor housing, lack of modern plumbing, and overcrowding." . . . Aggravating matters, these separations were frequently "carried out without due process of law." Children and their parents rarely had counsel [and few cases saw the inside of a courtroom].

Like the boarding school system that preceded it, this new program of removal had often-disastrous consequences. . . . For many children, separation from their families caused "severe distress" that "interfere[d] with their physical, mental, and social growth and development." [and] translated into long-lasting adverse health and emotional effects. . . .

Eventually, Congress could ignore the problem no longer. In 1978, it responded with the Indian Child Welfare Act [in the recognition that] "[A]n alarmingly high percentage of Indian families," [were] being "broken up by the removal, often unwarranted, of their children from them by nontribal [state] public and private agencies." 25 U.S.C. §1901(4). And "an alarmingly high percentage of such children" were "placed in non-Indian foster and adoptive homes and institutions." *Ibid.* Removal at that scale threatened the "continued existence and integrity of Indian [T]ribes." §1901(3).

[ICWA governs both voluntary removal and involuntary removal.] It installs substantive and procedural guardrails against the unjustified termination of parental rights and removal of Indian children from tribal life [as described below].

ICWA is not a panacea. . . . Still, the statute "has achieved considerable success in stemming unwarranted removals by state officials of Indian children from their families and communities." And considerable research "[s]ubsequent to Congress's enactment of ICWA" has "borne out the statute's basic premise"—that "[i]t is generally in the best interests of Indian children to be raised in Indian homes." . . .

HAALAND v. BRACKEEN
143 S. Ct. 1609 (2023)

Justice BARRETT delivered the opinion of the Court, joined by Chief Justice ROBERTS, and Justices SOTOMAYOR, KAGAN, GORSUCH, KAVANAUGH, and JACKSON.

This case is about children who are among the most vulnerable: those in the child welfare system. In the usual course, state courts apply state law when placing children in foster or adoptive homes. But when the child is an Indian, a federal statute—the Indian Child Welfare Act—governs. Among other things, this law requires a state court to place an Indian child with an Indian caretaker, if one is available. That is so even if the child is already living with a non-Indian family and the state court thinks it in the child's best interest to stay there.

Before us, a birth mother, foster and adoptive parents, and the State of Texas challenge the Act on multiple constitutional grounds. They argue that it exceeds federal authority, infringes state sovereignty, and discriminates on the basis of race. The United States, joined by several Indian Tribes, defends the law. [W]e reject all of petitioners' challenges to the statute, some on the merits and others for lack of standing.

. . . In 1978, Congress enacted the Indian Child Welfare Act (ICWA) out of concern that "an alarmingly high percentage of Indian families are broken up by the removal, often unwarranted, of their children from them by nontribal public and private agencies." Congress found that many of these children were being "placed in non-Indian foster and adoptive homes and institutions," and that the States had contributed to the problem by "fail[ing] to recognize the essential tribal relations of Indian people and the cultural and social standards prevailing in Indian communities and families." §§1901(4), (5). This harmed not only Indian parents and children, but also Indian tribes. As Congress put it, "there is no resource that is more vital to the continued existence and integrity of Indian tribes than their children." §1901(3). . . . The Act thus aims to keep Indian children connected to Indian families. . . .

Any party who initiates an "involuntary proceeding" in state court to place an Indian child in foster care or terminate parental rights must "notify the parent or Indian custodian and the Indian child's tribe." §1912(a). The parent or custodian and tribe have the right to intervene in the proceedings; the right to request extra time to prepare for the proceedings; the right to "examine all reports or other documents filed with the court"; and, for indigent parents or custodians, the right to court-appointed counsel. §§1912(a), (b), (c). The party attempting to terminate parental rights or remove an Indian child from an unsafe environment must first "satisfy the court that active efforts have been made to provide remedial services and rehabilitative programs designed to prevent the breakup of the Indian family and that these efforts have proved unsuccessful." §1912(d). Even then, the court cannot order a foster care placement unless it finds "by clear and convincing evidence . . . that the continued custody of the child by the parent or Indian custodian is likely to result in serious emotional or physical damage to the child." §1912(e). . . . The Act applies to voluntary proceedings too. . . . The child's tribe has "a right to intervene. . . . §§1911(c), 1914. As a result, the tribe can sometimes enforce ICWA's placement preferences against the wishes of one or both biological parents, even after the child is living with a new family. [For purposes of adoption placements, ICWA provides that] "a preference shall be given" to placements with "(1) a member of the child's extended family; (2) other members of the Indian child's tribe; or (3) other Indian families. §1915(a). . . . Courts must adhere to the placement preferences absent "good cause" to depart from them. §§1915(a), (b). . . .

This case arises from three separate child custody proceedings governed by ICWA. [Two of the three families, the Brackeens and the Librettis, completed adoptions of children falling within the scope of ICWA. Both families, however, claim that they might want to adopt other Indian children in the future. A third family, the Cliffords, sought but was denied an adoption of a child falling within the scope of ICWA.] The Brackeens, the Librettis, Hernandez [a biological parent of one of the children], and the Cliffords (whom we will refer to collectively as the "individual petitioners") filed this suit in federal court [against various federal agencies and individuals (including Deborah Haaland, Secretary of the Interior), challenging ICWA as unconstitutional on multiple grounds]. The individual petitioners were joined by the States of Texas, Indiana, and Louisiana—although only Texas continues to challenge ICWA before this Court. Several Indian Tribes intervened to defend the law alongside the federal parties.

[The Fifth Circuit Court of Appeals en banc concluded that ICWA does not exceed Congress's legislative power but affirmed the district court ruling that some ICWA's placement preferences prioritizing Indian families were unconstitutional.] We granted certiorari.

. . . We begin with petitioners' claim that ICWA exceeds Congress's power under Article I. In a long line of cases, we have characterized Congress's power to legislate with respect to the Indian tribes as "'plenary and exclusive.'" [Precedent traces that power to multiple sources, including the Indian Commerce Clause, which we have held reaches not only trade but also Indian affairs; the Treaty Clause, which authorizes the President to make treaties with the advice and consent of the Senate; the principles inherent in the Constitution's structure that empower Congress to act in the "field of Indian affairs"; and finally the "trust relationship between the United States and the Indian people."] In sum, Congress's power to legislate with respect to Indians is well established and broad. . . .

Petitioners contend that ICWA exceeds Congress's power. Their principal theory [is] that ICWA treads on the States' authority over family law. Domestic relations have traditionally been governed by state law; thus, federal power over Indians stops where state power over the family begins. Or so the argument goes. It is true [that] responsibility for regulating marriage and child custody remains primarily with the States, ... But the Constitution does not erect a firewall around family law. On the contrary, when Congress validly legislates pursuant to its Article I powers, we "ha[ve] not hesitated" to find conflicting state family law preempted. . . . Petitioners are trying to turn a general observation (that Congress's Article I powers rarely touch state family law) into a constitutional carveout (that family law is wholly exempt from federal regulation). . . .

Petitioners come at the problem from the opposite direction too: Even if there is no family law carveout to the Indian affairs power, they contend that Congress's authority does not stretch far enough to justify ICWA. Ticking through the various sources of power, petitioners assert that the Constitution does not authorize Congress to regulate custody proceedings for Indian children. Their arguments fail to grapple with our precedent. . . .

Take the Indian Commerce Clause. . . . According to petitioners, the Clause authorizes Congress to legislate only with respect to Indian tribes as government entities, not Indians as individuals. . . . But we held more than a century ago that "commerce with the Indian tribes, means commerce with the individuals composing those tribes." . . . So that argument is a dead end. Petitioners also assert that ICWA takes the "commerce" out of the Indian Commerce Clause. Their consistent refrain is that "children are not commodities that can be traded." . . . Rhetorically, it is a powerful point—*of course* children are not commercial products. Legally, though, it is beside the point. As we already explained, our precedent states that Congress's power under the Indian Commerce Clause encompasses not only trade but also "Indian affairs." . . . Next, petitioners argue that ICWA cannot be authorized by principles inherent in the Constitution's structure because those principles "extend, at most, to matters of war and peace." . . . But that is not what our cases say. We have referred generally to the powers "necessarily inherent in any Federal Government[.]" . . . Finally, petitioners observe that ICWA does not implement a federal treaty. . . . This does not get them very far either, since Congress did not purport to enact ICWA pursuant to the Treaty Clause power. . . .

We therefore decline to disturb the Fifth Circuit's conclusion that ICWA is consistent with Article I.

We now turn to petitioners' host of anticommandeering arguments . . . .. First, petitioners challenge certain requirements [including the requirement to demonstrate "active efforts" to provide remedial services and rehabilitative programs, prior to termination of parental right, that are designed to prevent the breakup of the Indian family and that these efforts have proved unsuccessful]; serve notice of the proceeding on the parent or Indian custodian and tribe; and demonstrate, by a heightened burden of proof and expert testimony, that the child is likely to suffer "serious emotional or physical damage" if the parent or Indian custodian retains custody. Second, petitioners challenge ICWA's placement preferences. . . . Third, they insist that Congress cannot force state courts to maintain or transmit to the Federal Government records of custody proceedings involving Indian children.

. . . It is well established that the Tenth Amendment bars Congress from "command[ing] the States' officers, or those of their political subdivisions, to administer or enforce a federal regulatory program." . . . The "active efforts" provision, petitioners say, does just that. Petitioners' argument has a fundamental flaw: To succeed, they must show that [the challenged provisions] harness[] a State's legislative or executive authority. But the provision applies to "any party" who initiates an involuntary proceeding, thus sweeping in private individuals . . . as well as government entities. A demand that either public or private actors can satisfy is unlikely to require the use of sovereign power. . . . When a federal statute applies on its face to both private and state actors, a commandeering argument is a heavy lift—and petitioners have not pulled it off. . . .

Petitioners also raise a Tenth Amendment challenge to §1915, which dictates placement preferences for Indian children. [T]his argument fails . . . too: Section 1915 does not require *anyone*, much less the States, to search for alternative placements. . . . Instead, the burden is on the tribe or other objecting party to produce a higher-ranked placement. . . . So, . . . petitioners assert an anticommandeering challenge to a provision that does not command state agencies to do anything.

State courts are a different matter. ICWA indisputably requires them to apply the placement preferences in making custody determinations. §§1915(a), (b). Petitioners argue that this too violates the anticommandeering doctrine. . . . This argument runs headlong into the [Supremacy Clause of the Constitution]. Thus, when Congress enacts a valid statute . . . "state law is naturally preempted to the extent of any conflict with a federal statute." . . . End of story. . . .

[The Court then turned to petitioners' argument that ICWA's recordkeeping provisions requiring state courts to maintain and make available upon request certain records impermissibly conscripted states into federal service. The Court rejected this argument, confirming that Congress may impose ancillary record-keeping requirements related to state court proceedings without violating the Tenth Amendment.] Such requirements [are] a logical consequence of our system of "dual sovereignty" in which state courts are required to apply federal law. . . .

[The Court failed to reach the merits, for lack of standing, on petitioners' equal protection challenge to ICWA's placement preferences and a nondelegation challenge to the provision allowing tribes to alter the placement preferences.] For these reasons, we affirm the judgment of the Court of Appeals regarding Congress's constitutional authority to enact ICWA. On the anticommandeering claims, we reverse. On the equal protection and nondelegation claims, we vacate the judgment of the Court of Appeals and remand with instructions to dismiss for lack of jurisdiction.

NOTE: WHO IS DEB HAALAND?

We know who the Brackeens are (one of the sets of adoptive/prospective adoptive parents), but who is the "Haaland" in Haaland v. Brackeen? Deb Haaland is the Secretary of the Interior, the federal department that oversees a fifth of the land in the United States, including the national parks, national monuments, and other public lands. In the past, the Secretary of the Interior was charged with removing Native people from their homelands. Haaland is an enrolled member of the Pueblo of Laguna, and she is the first Native person to serve as a U.S. Cabinet Secretary.[55]

---

[55]. Secretary Deb Haaland, U.S. Dept. of the Interior, https://www.doi.gov/secretary-deb-haaland.

Having a Native person in this role has been meaningful to many people. For example, Holly Cook Macarro, a political consultant and strategic advisor to the Advance Native Political Leadership, explains: "Every day, she's fully representing our community in ways that have never been visible in America. You see the earrings she wears and what that represents to Native women in Indian Country. Every time I see her, it hits me. And America is seeing her fill that space."[56]

Deb Haaland, Secretary of the U.S. Department of the Interior

Among the many projects that Haaland has worked on during her tenure as Secretary of the Interior is the "Road to Healing," which seeks to "address the residual damage" of the "history of Indian boarding schools" in the United States. As the materials above explain, for more than 150 years, tens of thousands of Indian children were removed from their families of origin and placed in boarding schools whose "primary objectives were to assimilate and 'civilize' Native children, to rob them of their language and culture."[57] Indeed, Haaland's own maternal grandparents were sent to one of these Indian boarding schools. Of her grandparents, Haaland said, "It's hard for me not to think about . . . how things would have been different for them had our country had an awakening much earlier."[58] Haaland's father was a Marine who was awarded the Silver Star, and her mother is a Navy veteran who also worked for 25 years at the Bureau of Indian Affairs, an agency that Haaland now oversees in her role as Secretary of the Interior.[59]

Haaland has a long history of political activism and involvement. In 2014, she ran unsuccessfully for New Mexico Lieutenant Governor. She then became the head of the New Mexico Democratic Party; she was the first Native woman to serve in that role in any state. In 2019, she was elected to the U.S. House of Representatives, one of the few Native women to do so. While in Congress, she worked on a range of issues, including environmental justice and climate change issues, raising awareness about and addressing missing and murdered indigenous women, and advocating for policies to help families. Her work has been shaped

---

[56]. Quoted in Karen Heller, Interior Secretary Deb Haaland's Charged Mission of Healing, Wash. Post, July 17, 2023, https://www.washingtonpost.com/lifestyle/2023/07/17/deb-haaland-road-to-healing/.

[57]. Id.

[58]. Id.

[59]. The remaining information in this Note is drawn from the official biography of Secretary Haaland. See supra note [55].

by her own experience, including as a single mother, at times living paycheck to paycheck and relying on food stamps.

Notes and Questions

1. *Brackeen*: Holding. A majority of the Court held that Congress had the authority to enact ICWA and that the challenged provisions did not impermissibly commandeer state officials in violation of the Tenth Amendment. The Court declined, however, to reach the merits of two asserted claims on standing grounds: (1) ICWA violates the Equal Protection Clause by impermissibly discriminating on the basis of race; and (2) ICWA violates the nondelegation doctrine, which places limits on Congress's authority to delegate rule-making authority to federal executive agencies.

2. Federalism. In his dissent, Justice Alito argued that ICWA is unconstitutional because it regulates a topic—the "very nature" of family law or domestic relations—within the States' reserved powers:

> While we have never comprehensively enumerated the States' reserved powers, we have long recognized that governance of family relations—including marriage relationships and child custody—is among them. . . . This does not mean that federal law may never touch on family matters. . . . But we have never held that Congress under any of its enumerated powers may regulate the very nature of those relations or dictate their creation, dissolution, or modification. . . . ICWA's mandates do not simply touch on family matters. They override States' authority to determine—and implement through their courts—the child custody and welfare policies they deem most appropriate for their citizens. . . . Congress's Indian affairs power, broad as it is, does not extend that far.

Does Justice Alito offer guidance about how to determine when federal laws related to family relations would impermissibly intrude in what he describes as "the States' reserved powers"? Is it advisable, from a policy perspective, to keep the federal government completely out of family relations?

3. ICWA and equal protection. The majority declined to reach the question whether the classification "Indian child" is a racial or a political classification for equal protection purposes. For racial classifications, strict scrutiny applies. For political, rational basis review applies. A majority of the en banc panel of the Fifth Circuit, like many prior decisions, concluded that it is a political, not a racial classification:

> Though inevitably tied in part to ancestry, tribal recognition and tribal sovereignty center on a group's status as a continuation of a historical political entity. . . . Tribal eligibility does not inherently turn on race, but rather on the criteria set by the tribes, which are present-day political entities. . . . That tribes may use ancestry as part of their criteria for determining membership eligibility does not change that ICWA does not classify in this way; instead, ICWA's Indian child designation classifies on the basis of a child's connection to a political entity . . . .[60]

---

[60]. Brackeen v. Haaland, 994 F.3d 249 (5th Cir. 2021) (en banc).

The majority from the en banc panel also noted that because "[l]iterally every piece of legislation dealing with Indian tribes and reservations . . . single[s] out for special treatment a constituency of tribal Indians living on or near reservations," any contrary conclusion could have an enormous ripple effect. But cf. In re Santos Y., 92 Cal. App. 4th 1274, 1321 (Ct. App. 2001) (holding that application of ICWA was unconstitutional "based solely, or at least predominantly, upon race," as applied to a foster child who had become attached to his foster parents). Which court is right? Does it depend on the facts of the case?

4. Race and adoption. ICWA *requires* consideration of the child's Native American status. ICWA also prioritizes placement with a member of the child's extended family, other members of the child's Tribe, or members of another Tribe. In contrast, current federal law strictly limits considerations of race by adoption placement agencies. This issue—consideration of race in the context of foster care and adoption—has long been controversial.

The position of the federal government has fluctuated. The current federal statute, the Multi-Ethnic Placement Act (MEPA), enacted in 1994, provides that "adoption or foster care placements" may not be "delay[ed] or den[ied]" on the basis of the race, color, or national origin of the adoptive or foster parent, or the child. 42 U.S.C. §1996b(1)(B). According to Congress, the purpose of the current law was to mitigate existing equities for Black children.

Some commentators, however, question whether the current version of MEPA effectively mitigates these inequalities in achieving permanency for Black children awaiting adoption and, therefore, recommend allowing greater consideration of race and ethnicity in adoption placements and permanency planning.[61] Professor Elizabeth Bartholet disagrees, arguing: "Recreating race as a reason to disqualify prospective parents, and deter them from even applying, is not the way to find more homes for the waiting children."[62] What explains the federal government's different approaches regarding considerations of race and Native American status in adoption? Do you agree with these positions?

5. Adoptive placement: matching. Adoption matching is based on the theory that it is important for children to be raised by parents who look like them.

a. Background. The issue of race-matching in adoption has evoked considerable controversy for decades. Historically, adoption was meant to "imitate nature" (to make the adopted child's experience the same as if he or she had been born to the adopting parents). As a result, a longstanding policy favored race-matching. However, this policy began to change during the civil rights movement, leading to more supportive attitudes toward "transracial adoption," as it was then called. But a tremendous backlash soon emerged. In 1972, the National Association of Black

---

[61]. Evan B. Donaldson Adoption Inst., Finding Families for African American Children: The Role of Race & Law in Adoption from Foster Care, at 5 (2008), https://sociologyinfocus.com/files/old/publications/mepapaper20080527.pdf. See also Twila L. Perry, The Transracial Adoption Controversy: An Analysis of Discourse and Subordination, 21 N.Y.U. Rev. L. & Soc. Change 33, 34 (1994).

[62]. Elizabeth Bartholet, Response to Donaldson Institute Call for Amendment of the Multiethnic Placement Act (MEPA) to Reinstate Use of Race as a Placement Factor, CCAI Briefing, June 10, 2008, http://cap.law.harvard.edu/wp-content/uploads/2016/04/Bartholetdonaldsonresponse.pdf. To hear an audio of this debate, see https://www.npr.org/transcripts/90858428.

Social Workers (NABSW) condemned transracial adoption as a form of genocide and contended that white parents could not teach their Black children to deal with social prejudice. The Child Welfare League of America, the nation's oldest and largest child welfare organization, joined NABSW in advocating for race-matching.

Race-matching came under renewed attack because of the decreased availability of white infants due to the decriminalization of abortion and the decreased stigma of nonmarital parenthood. In addition, federal legislation on child abuse and neglect (Child Abuse Prevention and Treatment Act (CAPTA), 42 U.S.C.A. §5106g) increased the number of children in foster care. Congress responded to the rise in interest in adoption by enacting a policy in 1996 prohibiting efforts to keep children within same-race families. Federal legislation in 1996 (Removal of Barriers to Interethnic Adoption) prohibited the use of race, color, and national origin, either categorically or presumptively, to delay or deny adoptive or foster care placements by state entities. 42 U.S.C. §1996b (amending the earlier, less restrictive, federal Multi-Ethnic Placement Act or MEPA).

b. ICWA. Congress enacted ICWA in 1978 after congressional hearings revealed the high rate of removals of children from Native American parents by child welfare authorities. ICWA does *not* ban non-Native parents from adopting Native children. Rather, ICWA accords preferences to the tribe and the right to intervene in such adoptions.

What is the rationale for these preferences? How do ICWA's preferences differ from race-matching measures? How can you reconcile Congress's disapproval of race-matching in adoption with ICWA's placement preferences? Note that in independent adoptions (when birth parents and adoptive parents make an agreement, without state agency involvement, for an adoption), birth parents typically select placements according to their preferences. What constraints, if any, should limit their choices?

6. Adoptive placement: Screening. The adoption process includes a home study (i.e., an investigation of the home and lives of prospective adoptive parents prior to an adoption). See Uniform Adoption Act (UAA) §§3-601 to 3-603 (requiring individualized evaluation before adoption becomes final). Do you agree with the criticism that such regulation of adoption, in comparison to the "privacy" that shields sexual reproduction, reflects a preference for biological relationships and signals distrust of those who would raise a "child born to another" or who seek to parent "someone else's child"?[63]

7. Open adoption. Historically, considerable secrecy accompanied adoption. Original birth records were sealed. Adoptive parents were often advised not to tell their children they were adopted. Today, this approach is criticized by many who instead urge greater sharing of information. Moreover, "open adoptions" are increasingly popular. In open adoptions, the biological parents and adoptive parents know each other's identity; the biological parents may exercise significant control over the selection of adoptive parents; and the parties have an agreement concerning the biological parents' postadoption relationship to the child.

---

[63]. Elizabeth Bartholet, Family Bonds: Adoption, Infertility, and the New World of Child Production 69 (rev. ed. 1999). See id. at 34, 93.

Biological parents may continue to stay in touch with the adoptee by mail, the Internet, or face-to-face visits (the degree and frequency of contact is negotiable).

8. Adoptions by LGBTQ people. In the past, a small number of states banned adoption and/or foster care by gay and lesbian parents. Today, these laws have now all been struck down or repealed. While no state today expressly bans LGBTQ individuals from adopting, discrimination by individuals involved in the process (including social workers and other agency workers) persists. Moreover, some states now have laws that permit adoption service providers to decline to provide services if the provision of those services would violate the religious or moral beliefs of the provider. See, e.g., Ala. Code §38-7C-5(a) (prohibiting the state from taking adverse actions against child placing agencies that decline placements that conflict with the agency's sincerely-held religious beliefs).

Should states permit exemptions from antidiscrimination laws for religiously-based adoption agencies?[64] After *303 Creative* (Chapter II), *must* states provide such exemptions? See also Fulton v. City of Philadelphia, 141 S. Ct. 1868 (2021) (holding that the city of Philadelphia violated the Free Exercise Clause when it refused to grant exemptions from a nondiscrimination requirement to religious adoption service organizations when the city's contract allowed for exemptions).

9. Stepparent and second-parent adoption. State adoption laws have long included provisions for stepparent adoptions, in which one parent's spouse adopts the other parent's child. Stepparent adoption provides a streamlined legal procedure, often dispensing with some formalities (such as the home study). (If there is another legal parent, however, that parent's consent is required.)

Prior to *Obergefell*, same-sex partners could not petition for stepparent adoptions because the procedure was restricted to spouses. Beginning in the 1990s, however, courts in some states began permitting nonmarital partners, including same-sex nonmarital partners, to use a similar process that does not terminate the original parents' rights. These adoptions are often referred to as "second-parent adoptions." Does marriage equality compel states to apply stepparent adoption laws equally to same-sex couples? Do married LGBTQ parents still need to secure adoption decrees after *Obergefell*? Why do many legal advocates continue to recommend that LGBTQ parents, including married parents, obtain adoptions or other judgments establishing parentage?

10. Full faith and credit to adoption decrees. Adoptions are court judgments. As such, they must be recognized and respected in other jurisdictions, even if the adoption could not have been obtained in the first instance in the forum. See V.L. v. E.L., 577 U.S. 404 (2016) (involving the question of recognition of second-parent adoption by a same-sex nonmarital partner).

---

[64]. Compare Douglas NeJaime, Marriage Inequality: Same-Sex Relationships, Religious Exemptions, and the Production of Sexual Orientation Discrimination, 100 Cal. L. Rev. 1169 (2012) (criticizing such exemptions, as part of the larger movement for conscience protection in the face of gay rights), with Robin Fretwell Wilson, A Matter of Conviction: Moral Clashes over Same-Sex Adoption, 22 BYU J. Pub. L. 475 (2008) (recommending conscience clauses to resolve moral clashes over same-sex adoption).

11. Access to information about birth parents. Secrecy traditionally shrouded the adoption process. Reasons included the stigma surrounding nonmarital births, the fear that birth parents would invade the privacy of adoptive families, and the belief that adoptive families should imitate biological families. To maintain this secrecy, statutes provide for the issuance of a new birth certificate upon adoption and a change in the surname of the adoptee to that of the adoptive parents. (The original birth certificate is then sealed.)

Courts traditionally rejected adult adoptees' attempts to get information about their birth parents. See, e.g., In re Roger B., 418 N.E.2d 751 (Ill. 1981). An adoption reform movement in the 1970s sought to open adoption records and to allow the exchange of information between the adopted child and the biological parents. In response, states adopted different approaches. Some states provide limited information, whereas other states grant adult adoptees unlimited access to their adoption records or original birth certificates. Other states have "mutual consent" registries, which allow the release of identifying information if both parties register their consent. The Internet has also facilitated disclosure, as previously mentioned.

NOTE: INTERCOUNTRY ADOPTION

Some parents in the United States seek to adopt children born in other countries. Intercountry adoption remains controversial. Supporters contend that such adoptions represent humanitarian and empathetic responses to the plight of children living in institutions or on the streets in other countries — indeed, a compelling matter of international human rights. Critics, however, point out the underlying colonialism reflected by the practice, while others emphasize the similarity to baby selling, given the predominance of market behavior.[65]

Since 2005, the number of intercountry adoptions in the United States has continued to decline.[66] Primary reasons for the decline include foreign governments' dislike of lax practices by U.S. adoption service providers (e.g., careless home studies, poor supervision, and nonexistent or fraudulent postplacement reporting) and inadequate federal and state regulation. Some foreign governments (e.g., South Korea) have strengthened their own child welfare programs and thereby limited the number of children available for international adoption. Officials in some countries (i.e., Cambodia, Ethiopia, Guatemala, and Nepal) have

---

[65]. For supporters, see, e.g., Elizabeth Bartholet, International Adoption: A Way Forward, 55 N.Y.L. Sch. L. Rev. 687 (2010/2011); James G. Dwyer, Inter-Country Adoption and the Special Rights Fallacy, 35 U. Pa. J. Int'l L. 189 (2013). For critics, see, e.g., Shani King, Challenging MonoHumanism: An Argument for Changing the Way We Think About Intercountry Adoption, 30 Mich. J. Int'l L. 413 (2009); Twila L. Perry, Transracial and International Adoption: Mothers, Hierarchy, Race, and Feminist Legal Theory, 10 Yale J.L. & Feminism 101, 130-137 (1998); David M. Smolin, Child Laundering as Exploitation: Applying Anti-Trafficking Norms to Intercountry Adoption Under the Coming Hague Regime, 32 Vt. L. Rev. 1 (2007).

[66]. Child Welfare Info. Gateway, Trends in U.S. Adoptions: 2010–2019 (2022), https://www.childwelfare.gov/pubPDFs/adopted2010_19.pdf. See also Adoptive Families, News Brief: Domestic Adoptions Rise Slightly, Despite Overall Decrease in Adoption (2017), https://www.adoptivefamilies.com/resources/adoption-news/domestic-adoptions-statistics-slight-increase-in-2014/.

closed their intercountry adoption programs due to concerns about child trafficking, "rehoming" (adoptive parents transferring custody of a child to another individual or group without the involvement of relevant authorities), and questionable practices by U.S. adoption service providers.[67] Travel restrictions imposed in the early months and years of the COVID pandemic affected international adoption. Politics also plays a role: Russia banned U.S. citizens from adopting Russian children in 2012, purportedly in retaliation for a U.S. law known as the Magnitsky Act, which sanctioned Russian officials and nationals for human rights abuses.

Various laws apply to international adoptions: federal immigration laws, state adoption standards, and foreign countries' relinquishment requirements. Two adoptions might be routinely required — the first in the country of origin, to enable the child to travel to the United States, and the second in the adoptive parents' home state, given that the exacting requirement of full faith and credit does not apply to decrees from foreign countries.

The Hague Convention on Protection of Children and Cooperation in Respect of Intercountry Adoption ushered in notable reforms in 1993. This is an international agreement that establishes international standards of practices for intercountry adoptions. It applies only when both countries (sending and receiving country) are signatories; the United States recognizes more than 100 countries as Hague Convention countries. It was designed to protect against the risks of illegal, irregular, premature, or ill-prepared adoptions abroad. To achieve those ends, the Convention requires a finding that the child is adoptable, requires a determination that the adoption would serve the child's best interests, establishes supervisory central authorities to impose minimum norms and procedures, and mandates recognition of such adoptions in other signatory countries.

5. Adoption Disruption and Dissolution

IN RE ADOPTION OF M.S.
103 Cal. Rptr. 3d 715 (Ct. App. 2010)

SIMS, J.

This is a tragic case in which there can be no good ending for anyone. Appellants Eleanor P. and Martin S. appeal from an order denying their petition to set aside their Ukrainian adoption of a Ukrainian girl, M.S. The petition was opposed by the State Department of Social Services (the Department or DSS). Appellants contend the trial court erred in construing Family Code section 9100, which authorizes the court to vacate adoptions [in cases where the child "shows evidence of a developmental disability or mental illness" existing before the adoption that render the

[67]. Susan Jenkins & Maureen Flatley, The Truth About Intercountry Adoption's Decline, Apr. 23, 2019, https://chronicleofsocialchange.org/adoption/the-truth-about-intercountry- adoptions -decline/34658.

child to be considered "unadoptable"], as inapplicable to an "intercountry adoption" completed in Ukraine.

In early 2003, appellants began the process to adopt a foreign-born child. Appellants engaged a California lawyer and a private California adoption agency, Heartsent Adoptions, Inc., which was licensed by the Department to provide noncustodial intercountry adoption services. [Appellants traveled to Ukraine, where they adopted three-year-old M.S. pursuant to a Ukrainian court decree that stated in part:] "It was found out from the case documents that the child's [biological] mother is mentally sick. She left the child at the hospital and never visited her. The place of father's residence was not identified. Since February 2002 the child has been made the ward of the government. The medical history of the girl says that she is almost healthy though psychologically delayed." A hospital record says the mother has epilepsy. [Appellants claimed they were not aware of this information.] Appellants brought M.S. to live in their Davis home. They did not "readopt" M.S. in California, as authorized by [California law].

In California, various evaluations were performed due to M.S.'s low level of functioning. Health care professionals diagnosed her with spastic cerebral palsy, reactive attachment disorder, oppositional defiance disorder, moderate mental retardation, global developmental delay, ataxia, fetal alcohol syndrome or effect, microcephaly, and posttraumatic stress disorder. Appellants assert M.S. cannot live in a normal home environment, is unadoptable, and has been living in intensive foster care placement in Arizona since 2005. . . .

Appellants cite no legal authority for undoing the Ukraine adoption except section 9100 [which] authorizes the superior court to vacate an adoption of a child "adopted pursuant to the law of this state." . . . However, the language of section 9100 itself, plus the language of a companion statute — section 9101 — clearly show that section 9100 is limited to undoing adoptions that were granted by California state courts. [T]he California Legislature surely did not intend to legislate court filings in a Ukrainian court. We therefore infer [that] "the court that granted the adoption petition" in section 9100 must be a California state court.

. . . In the event an adoption is vacated under section 9100, section 9101 places responsibility for the support of the now unadopted child on "[t]he county in which the proceeding for adoption was had." In this case, there is no such county in California, and the California Legislature obviously has no power to order a Ukrainian county (if such even exists) to support the child. . . .

Appellants offer two main arguments against our conclusion [that they cannot vacate the adoption here]. First, they say that where section 9100 provides that a petition "may be filed . . . with the court that granted the adoption petition," the word "may" is permissive, not mandatory. . . . In this sentence, the word "may" is used in the permissive sense of giving a parent or parents discretion whether to file a petition under section 9100. This is in stark contrast to section 8919, which *requires* a readoption of a child adopted in a foreign country "if it is required by the Department of Homeland Security." . . .

[O]nce the decision is made to file a petition, the petition must be filed "with the court that granted the adoption petition." This is the only construction that makes sense. No other court is designated as the proper place for the filing of a petition. If the petition could be filed in *any* court, then reference to "the court that granted the adoption petition" would be unnecessary. Moreover, since the petition seeks to unadopt a child, it is only reasonable to require the petition to be filed in the court that has the records of the original adoption. Thus, if a petition under section 9100 is filed, it *must* be filed "with the court that granted the adoption petition." [In this case, that forum is in Ukraine.

The California court also rejects Appellants' second argument, urging a liberal construction of section 9100. W]e conclude that section 9100 applies only to adoptions granted by a California state court. . . .

Sarah Kershaw, In Some Adoptions, Love Doesn't Conquer All
N.Y. Times, Apr. 18, 2010, at ST1

At times, Kelly Lytle Baehr wondered how they would all get through it. Two years ago, she and her husband adopted three boys from Ukraine — two of them 8, the other 16 — and brought them back to their home in Omaha. She knew assimilation into a family life would not be easy; all had come from troubled backgrounds, including one who had spent the first five years of his life in a prison orphanage back in Ukraine, and had a mother who drank while she was pregnant.

Justin Hansen returned alone to Russia, sent by his American adoptive mother.

She was often tested by the strains of raising these three new sons. The youngest of them, Ian (born Igor) had rummaged in garbage dumps in Ukraine for toys, with [hubcaps] and discarded car parts his only possessions. At the Baehrs's home in Nebraska, he soon became a wild, uncontrollable kleptomaniac, she said. The other 8-year-old, Erik, struggled to attach to her — kicking, screaming, biting and yelling, "I hate you." Only the oldest son, Viktor, seemed to welcome his new life quickly, blending easily into the family and eventually making the honor roll at his high school.

When Ms. Lytle Baehr, who is going through a divorce and has custody of her children, heard the news break two weeks ago about Torry Ann Hansen shipping her 7-year-old adopted son [Justin] back to Russia on a plane, unaccompanied, with just a note to the authorities, she felt something approaching sympathy. "When it boils down to it, I'm really similar to the woman in Tennessee," Ms. Lytle Baehr said in a telephone interview this week. "We've all been there." . . .

"Most of these parents are grossly, grossly ill-prepared," said Ronald S. Federici, a developmental neuropsychologist. "Agencies say they do all this training and support — that's a bunch of junk. Some do, most don't. A lot of families are uneducated at huge levels about the psychological trauma of being deprived and neglected, of under-socialized children who have had profound developmental failures."

Russia is the third largest source of adoptions to the United States, after China and Ethiopia, with about 1,600 adoptions in 2009, according to State Department figures. About 3,500 Russian children and 3,000 American families were in some stage of the adoption process when the country reportedly halted adoptions. Russia has been a popular choice because the process can be much faster than in countries like China, and because there are often more boys available. . . .

The majority of both international and domestic adoptions turn out well, but the Hansen case has shined a spotlight on those that are problematic and the need for more postadoption services for struggling families, adoption experts say. Some agencies, including the one Ms. Hansen used, offer extensive training and preparation and continuing support services, training parents on issues like fetal alcohol syndrome and the psychological and neurological effects of institutionalization on children. Studies show, for example, that for every month in an orphanage a child's I.Q. drops one point. . . .

[Ellen McDaniels] took her daughter, whom she adopted from Russia in 2001 at the age of 8, to therapists for years. The child spent her first five years in an orphanage and was later adopted by two families who ended the adoptions before Ms. McDaniels, who lives in western Massachusetts, and her husband adopted her. Ms. McDaniels, 52, said she later discovered [that] the child had a history of being sexually abused and was sent to the orphanage when she was 18 months old, after her mother, an alcoholic, died of tuberculosis. A psychiatrist diagnosed severe reactive attachment disorder and posttraumatic stress disorder, and an inability to understand or have remorse for her actions. . . .

[T]wo months ago, after what Ms. McDaniels described as nine years of frightening, exhausting and heartbreaking efforts to cope with her daughter's behavioral problems — including, she said, her sexually abusing and threatening other children, threatening to burn down the house, hiding knives in her trundle bed, refusing to take medication and running away — she terminated her parental rights. . . .

The decision to end the adoption, even after so many awful years, was heartbreaking, Ms. McDaniels said, and she was wracked with shame and guilt. "I felt that I was a failure and that I condemned her to a life of hopelessness," she said. "I knew I couldn't help her, but I knew I didn't want to throw her away. But sometimes as a parent you feel like you have a lot more power than you do. You say to yourself, 'Can I make a difference in this child's life?' And if the answer is no, you need to walk away."

"I don't agree with what Torry Hansen did," she said. "But I almost think there's a certain little part of me that says, 'You just saved yourselves nine years of torment.' Knowing what I know now, I would have given up sooner. . . ." . . .

Notes and Questions

1. Adoption failure. Adoption failure occurs either when the child is removed from the home before the adoption is final ("disruption") or when a final adoption is abrogated or annulled ("dissolution"). In either case, the child usually enters (or returns to) foster care or placement with new adoptive parents. Although dissolutions are difficult to track, studies place the rate of disruptions at between 10 and 25 percent.[68] Adoption failure attracted considerable public attention through news stories of parents who, frustrated by the difficulties experienced by some adopted children, sent the children to live with others without state scrutiny. This practice, known as "rehoming," may jeopardize the child's safety. In one prominent case, an Arkansas legislator sent his adopted daughters to live with a man who sexually abused one of them.[69]

2. Standards. What criteria must be met to set aside an adoption? Should adoptive parents who seek to end their relationship to a child be limited to the same avenues available to other legal parents — voluntary or involuntary termination of parental rights, with consideration of best interests? Should cases be decided by courts based on equitable discretion or legislative criteria? Consider the criteria in the California statute (footnote 1 in *M.S.*, supra). Who may petition? What time limits, if any, should control? See, e.g., Mich. Comp. Laws Ann. §710.64(1) (21 days). Does dissolution infringe the adoptee's constitutional rights? See In re Adoption of Kay C., 278 Cal. Rptr. 907 (Ct. App. 1991).

In *M.S.*, the appellate court held that the statute authorizing setting aside an adoption applies only to adoptions granted by California state courts, and therefore the lower court lacked the authority to set aside the Ukrainian adoption. Is the court's conclusion convincing? Why might the appellants have failed to readopt the child in California? Why did the court reject a liberal construction of the statute? Who benefits from the strict approach? What additional insights does the *New York Times* story offer? As a matter of policy, should courts be more (or less) willing to permit the voluntary severance of legal ties when parentage is based on adoption, rather than procreation? Why?

3. Wrongful adoption. Some states recognize the remedy of "wrongful adoption." This remedy responds to the dual problems of misrepresentation by adoption agencies and judicial reluctance to nullify adoption decrees. In this alternative to dissolving an adoption, some parents have successfully sued adoption agencies for fraud or misrepresentation based on the defendant's intentional or negligent concealment of the child's medical condition. See, e.g., Jackson v. State, 956 P.2d 35 (Mont. 1998); Mallette v. Children's Friend & Serv., 661 A.2d 67 (R.I. 1995). What public policy issues do such negligence suits raise? Compare Richard P. v. Vista Del Mar Child Care Serv., 165 Cal. Rptr. 370, 374 (Ct. App. 1980), with M.H. v. Caritas Family Servs., 488 N.W.2d 282, 288 (Minn. 1992).

This remedy raises a host of questions. Must plaintiffs prove that they would not have adopted but for the misrepresentation? Can plaintiffs recover punitive damages? Can they recover for emotional distress? Compare Price v. State, 57 P.3d 639 (Wash. 2002) (permitting recovery), with Rowey v. Children's Friend & Servs., 2003 WL 23196347 (R.I. Super. Ct. 2003) (only when supported by medical

---

[68]. Children's Bureau, Child Welfare Information Gateway, Adoption Disruption/Dissolution 6 (2021), https://www.childwelfare.gov/topics/adoption/adopt-parenting/disruption/.

[69]. See Abby Phillip, The Story of an Arkansas Politician Who Gave Away His Adopted Child, and the Tragedy That Followed, Wash. Post, Mar. 13, 2015, https://www.washingtonpost.com/news/morning-mix/wp/2015/03/13/the-story-of-an-arkansas-politician-who-gave-away-his-adopted-child-and-the-tragedy-that-followed/.

evidence). Does the adopted child have a claim? Compare *Dresser v. Cradle of Hope Adoption Ctr., Inc.*, 358 F. Supp. 2d 620, 640-642 (E.D. Mich. 2005) (agency owes duty to child to provide medical information so adopters can obtain proper treatment), with *Rowey*.

4. Disclosure laws. Statutes in some states require disclosure to prospective adoptive parents of the child's medical history (e.g., Ariz. Rev. Stat. Ann. §8-129(A); Cal. Fam. Code §8706). Do biological parents have a duty of full disclosure when relinquishing their children? To the extent that such laws impose disclosure duties on birth parents upon relinquishment, should these duties include updating the information in the event of subsequent familial health problems?

5. Adoption in the Internet era. The Internet dramatically changed the face of the adoption process and has major implications for adoption practices.[70] In particular, social media websites significant broaden the market for adoptable children by means of unregulated websites that compete with traditional adoption service providers. Social media also enable adoptees to locate birth relatives with relative ease (hastening the demise of the principle of the closed anonymous adoption).

At the same time, the Internet has facilitated the growth of the "unregulated custody transfer (UCT)" or "rehoming." Rehoming enables child placements to adults who are not subject to background checks; placements that are unknown and unsupervised by social welfare agencies or the courts; and placements to caretakers who have no legal responsibility for children placed in their home. Many of these cases involve children adopted from other countries.

The practice has been the focus of congressional regulatory efforts. At the state level, there is now a relevant Uniform Law—the Unregulated Child Custody Transfer Act (UCCTA), promulgated in 2021. The UCCTA prohibits a parent or guardian with whom a child is placed for adoption from transferring custody to another person with the intent to abandon the rights and responsibilities concerning the child. Some persons are exempt as transferees (including another parent, a stepparent, an adult relative, or an adult who has a close relationship with the child or parent). The UCCTA has been enacted in three states (Colorado, Utah, and Washington).

---

[70]. See generally Jeanne A. Howard, Untangling the Web: The Internet's Transformative Impact on Adoption (Dec. 2012) (research report), https://www.npr.org/assets/news/2012/12/untangling.pdf; Megan Twohey, Americans Use the Internet to Abandon Children Adopted from Overseas, Sept. 9, 2013, https://www.reuters.com/investigates/adoption/#article/part1.

■ TABLE OF CASES

■ INDEX